3-2-1 Code It!

Michelle A. Green, MPS, RHIA, FAHIMA, CPC

SIXTH EDITION

3-2-1 Code It!

Michelle A. Green, MPS, RHIA, FAHIMA, CPC

SIXTH EDITION

3-2-1 Code It! Sixth Edition
Michelle A. Green

SVP, Product & Market Strategy, GPM:
  Jonathan Lau

Senior Director, Development | Global Product
  Management, Skills: Marah Bellegarde

Product Team Manager: Stephen G. Smith

Product Development Manager: Juliet Steiner

Senior Content Developer: Elisabeth F. Williams

Product Assistant: Mark Turner

Vice President, Marketing Services:
  Jennifer Ann Baker

Marketing Coordinator: Andrew Ouimet

Senior Production Director: Wendy Troeger

Production Director: Andrew Crouth

Senior Content Project Manager:
  Kara A. DiCaterino

Managing Art Director: Jack Pendleton

Cover image(s):
  © jijomathaidesigners/Shutterstock.com

For product information and technology assistance, contact us at
Cengage Learning Customer & Sales Support, 1-800-354-9706

For permission to use material from this text or product,
submit all requests online at **www.cengage.com/permissions**.
Further permissions questions can be e-mailed to
permissionrequest@cengage.com

Library of Congress Control Number: 2016942638

ISBN: 978-1-305-97023-6

Cengage Learning
20 Channel Center Street
Boston, MA 02210
USA

Cengage Learning is a leading provider of customized learning solutions with employees residing in nearly 40 different countries and sales in more than 125 countries around the world. Find your local representative at **www.cengage.com.**

Cengage Learning products are represented in Canada by Nelson Education, Ltd.

To learn more about Cengage Learning, visit **www.cengage.com**

Purchase any of our products at your local college store or at our preferred online store **www.cengagebrain.com**

The 2017 versions of CPT, HCPCS Level II, ICD-10-CM, and ICD-10-PCS were used in preparation of this product.

CPT copyright 2016 American Medical Association. All rights reserved. CPT is a registered trademark of the American Medical Association. Applicable FARS/DFARS Restrictions Apply to Government Use. Fee schedules, relative value units, conversion factors and/or related components are not assigned by the AMA, are not part of CPT, and the AMA is not recommending their use. The AMA does not directly or indirectly practice medicine or dispense medical services. The AMA assumes no liability for data contained or not contained herein.

Notice to the Reader
Publisher does not warrant or guarantee any of the products described herein or perform any independent analysis in connection with any of the product information contained herein. Publisher does not assume, and expressly disclaims, any obligation to obtain and include information other than that provided to it by the manufacturer. The reader is expressly warned to consider and adopt all safety precautions that might be indicated by the activities described herein and to avoid all potential hazards. By following the instructions contained herein, the reader willingly assumes all risks in connection with such instructions. The publisher makes no representations or warranties of any kind, including but not limited to, the warranties of fitness for particular purpose or merchantability, nor are any such representations implied with respect to the material set forth herein, and the publisher takes no responsibility with respect to such material. The publisher shall not be liable for any special, consequential, or exemplary damages resulting, in whole or part, from the readers' use of, or reliance upon, this material.

Printed in the United States of America
Print Number: 02   Print Year: 2017

Table of Contents

List of Tables

Preface

Introduction

Accurate coding is crucial to the successful operation of any health care facility or provider's office because reported codes determine the amount of reimbursement received. The annual (and sometimes more frequent) revision of coding guidelines and payer requirements serve to challenge coders. Those responsible for assigning and reporting codes in any health care setting require thorough instruction in the use of the ICD-10-CM, ICD-10-PCS, CPT, and HCPCS level II coding systems. Students who are completing formal coursework as part of an academic program and experienced coders who are already employed in the health care field will find that *3-2-1 Code It!* provides the required information in a clear and comprehensive manner.

Due to the comprehensive nature of the *3-2-1 Code It!* textbook, instructors may choose to cover its content in more than one course.

- Chapters 1 through 6 could be taught in an ICD-10-CM and ICD-10-PCS coding course.

- Chapters 7 through 18 could be taught in a CPT and HCPCS level II coding course.

- Chapter 19 could be included as required reading in an insurance and reimbursement course, either as an introductory or summary chapter.

Instructors for medical assistant (MA) and medical office administration (MOA) programs may choose to cover the following chapters only in their coding course(s):

- Chapters 2 through 4, and 7 in an ICD-10-CM, and HCPCS level II coding course (ICD-10-PCS is not used for outpatient or physician office coding.)

- Chapters 8 through 9, selected sections of 11 through 15, and 16 through 18 in a CPT coding course

 Note:

> Your academic program's community of interest (e.g., employers of graduates) will determine which sections of Chapters 11 through 15 (CPT Surgery) should be covered in your CPT coding course. Likewise, if your graduates obtain employment assigning and submitting CPT Anesthesia codes, your course should include Chapter 10. If your graduates do not assign radiology or pathology/laboratory codes during their employment, Chapters 16 and 17 can be excluded from your CPT coding course.

Instructors can refer to the Instructor's Manual for sample course syllabi that organize textbook content into one or two courses. For example, the syllabus for a one-semester course includes content from *3-2-1 Code It!* appropriate for an introductory course.

The *3-2-1 Code It!* text requires users to have access to paper-based coding manuals (ICD-10-CM, ICD-10-PCS, HCPCS level II, and CPT) because they are used as references when coding rules are explained and for completing exercises and reviews in each chapter.

 Note:

> HCPCS level II previously included dental codes (D codes), which are copyrighted by the American Dental Association. Purchase of a separate Current Dental Terminology (CDT) coding manual is required to assign dental codes.

The intended use of *3-2-1 Code It!* is for

- Academic programs in coding and reimbursement, health information management, medical assisting, medical office administration, and so on

- In-service education programs in health care facilities (e.g., physicians' offices, hospitals, nursing facilities, home health agencies, hospices, and so on), health insurance companies, quality improvement organizations, and so on

- Individuals who want to use it for self-instruction to learn how to code or to update their coding skills

- Health care professionals who need a comprehensive coding reference to assist them in accurately assigning codes

It is recommended that students complete the following course work before they begin and/or during the same time they are learning concepts presented in *3-2-1 Code It!*:

- Essentials of health information management

- Medical terminology

- Anatomy and physiology

- Essentials of pharmacology

- Human diseases/pathophysiology

Organization of This Textbook

This textbook is organized into 19 chapters and 2 appendices.

- Chapter 1 includes an overview of coding systems used to report inpatient and outpatient diagnoses and procedures and services to health plans. It also focuses on coding career opportunities in health care, the importance of joining professional organizations and obtaining coding credentials, the impact of networking with other coding professionals, and the development of opportunities for career advancement.

> **Note:**
>
> Content about long-term care, home health care, and hospice coding is located at the textbook's Student Companion Web Site at www.cengagebrain.com.

- Chapters 2 and 3 cover general ICD-10-CM/PCS coding concepts and provide coding practice. Chapter 3 covers ICD-10-CM official coding guidelines.

- Chapter 5 is specific to inpatient coding concepts (and not typically covered by academic programs that focus on outpatient and physician coding), and Chapter 6 is specific to outpatient coding concepts. Inpatient coding concepts apply to acute care hospitals, and the chapters include ICD-10-CM and ICD-10-PCS official coding guidelines. Outpatient coding concepts covered include the physicians' office, and hospital emergency and outpatient departments. ICD-10-CM/PCS chapters are sequenced before HCPCS level II and CPT chapters in this textbook because diagnosis codes are reported to justify the medical necessity of procedures and/or services provided.

- Chapter 7 covers the HCPCS level II national coding system, which was developed by the Centers for Medicare & Medicaid Services.

- Chapters 8 through 18 cover CPT coding concepts. Each CPT section has its own chapter, except for the Surgery section, which requires five separate chapters.

- Chapter 19 contains a detailed discussion of insurance and reimbursement concepts. (For comprehensive coverage of third-party payers and reimbursement methodologies, refer to

Cengage Learning's *Understanding Health Insurance: A Guide to Billing and Reimbursement*, by Michelle A. Green.)

- Appendix I contains the E/M CodeBuilder, which can also be downloaded from the Student Companion Web Site site at **www.cengagebrain.com** and printed for use with Chapter 9 cases to select evaluation and management (E/M) service codes.

Features of the Textbook

Each textbook chapter contains the following elements:

- List of topics
- Key terms
- Chapter objectives
- Introduction
- Exercises
- Internet links
- Summary
- Study checklist
- Review

Textbook features include:

- Key terms and learning objectives located at the beginning of each chapter to help organize the material
- Boldfaced terms throughout each chapter to assist students in learning the technical vocabulary associated with coding systems
- Coding tips and notes that highlight important concepts presented in each chapter
- Exercises after each chapter section that reinforce content presented
- Multiple choice and coding practice reviews that allow for mastery of coding concepts

New to Edition

- The textbook and its ancillaries have been updated to include the latest ICD-10-CM, ICD-10-PCS, CPT, and HCPCS level II code sets, conventions, and guidelines.
- Textbook and workbook coding assignments, examples, exercises, and reviews have been updated to include the most recent ICD-10-CM, ICD-10-PCS, CPT, and HCPCS level II codes. Case studies in textbook reviews have been renumbered to match the numbering in MindTap™.
- Answer keys have been updated in the *Instructor's Manual to Accompany 3-2-1 Code It!*, which is located at the Instructor Companion Web Site (**www.cengagebrain.com**).
- Chapter 1 includes new content about other classification systems and databases, including ABC codes, CCC, CDT, DSM-V, HIPPS, ICD-O-3, ICF, LOINC, NDC, RxNorm, SNOMED, and UMLS.
- Chapter 2 was revised to remove ICD-9-CM content and update ICD-10-CM and ICD-10-PCS content. Content about ICD-9-CM as a legacy classification system content was also updated.

- Chapter 3 includes updated content about coding conventions in ICD-10-CM and ICD-10-PCS, and examples allow educators and students to compare the use of conventions in the classification systems. Examples, exercises, and the chapter review have also been updated.

- Chapter 4 includes updated content about the ICD-10-CM *Official Guidelines for Coding and Reporting*. Examples, exercises, and the chapter review have also been updated.

- Chapter 5 includes updated content about inpatient ICD-10-CM diagnosis coding guidelines and inpatient ICD-10-PCS procedure coding guidelines. New content includes instructions (from the *ICD-10-CM Official Coding and Reporting Guidelines*) about how to select the principal procedure and the relation to the principal diagnosis when more than one procedure is performed. Examples, exercises, and the chapter review were also updated.

- Chapter 6 contains updated content about outpatient ICD-10-CM diagnosis coding guidelines. New content about DEEDS and OASIS data sets was added. Examples, exercises, and the chapter review have also been updated.

- Chapter 7 contains updated content about HCPCS level II coding. New content about four new HCPCS modifiers that define specific subsets of the -59 modifier was added.

- Chapter 8 contains updated introductory content about CPT coding. New content about CPT's blue reference arrow was added.

- Chapter 9 contains updated content about CPT's evaluation and management (E/M) section.

- Chapter 10 contains updated content about CPT's Anesthesia section.

- Chapters 11 through 15 contain updated content about CPT's Surgery section. New content about the CPT Surgery imaging guidance guideline was added along with clarification about skin replacement surgery and surgical preparation for such surgery.

- Chapter 16 contains updated content about CPT's Radiology section.

- Chapter 17 contains updated content about CPT's Pathology and Laboratory section.

- Chapter 18 contains updated content about CPT's Medicine section.

- Chapter 19 contains updated content about insurance and reimbursement, including new content about *intensity of services and severity of illness (ISSI)* as well as *value-based purchasing (VBP)*.

- Appendix I contains an E/M CodeBuilder (also available on the Student Companion Web Site), which can be used with Chapter 9 to assign evaluation and management codes.

Supplements

The following supplements accompany this text:

- Instructor Companion Web Site
- Student Workbook

- Student Companion Web Site at **www.cengagebrain.com**
- MindTap at **www.cengagebrain.com**

Instructor Companion Web Site

Spend less time planning and more time teaching with Cengage Learning's Instructor Companion Web Site to Accompany the Sixth Edition of *3-2-1 Code It!* As an instructor, you will have access to all of your resources online, anywhere and at any time. All instructor resources can be accessed by going to **www.cengagebrain.com** to create a unique user login. Contact your sales representative for more information. Online instructor resources at the Instructor Companion Web Site are password-protected and include the following:

- The Instructor's Manual consists of seven sections:
  - Section I—Instructor's Resources
  - Section II—Answer Keys to Textbook Chapter Exercises and Reviews
  - Section III—Answer Keys to Workbook Assignments and Reviews
  - Section IV—Answer Keys to Coding Patient Records (Workbook Appendices A–D)
  - Section V—Answer Key to Mock Certified Professional Coder (CPC) Certification Examination (Workbook Appendix E)
  - Section VI—Answer Key to Mock Certified Coding Specialist—Physician (CCS-P) Certification Examination (Workbook Appendix F)
  - Section VII—Answer Key to Mock Certified Coding Specialist (CCS) Certification Examination (Workbook Appendix G)
- *Cengage Learning Testing Powered by Cognero*, a flexible, online system that allows you to author, edit, and manage test bank content from multiple Cengage Learning solutions; you can also create multiple test versions in an instant, and deliver tests from your learning management system (LMS), classroom, or elsewhere.
- Customizable instructor support slide presentations in PowerPoint® format focus on key points for each chapter.
- *Insurance Billing & Coding Curriculum Guide* helps you plan your course using *3-2-1 Code It!* and other coding resources, and also maps content to certification exams.
- Conversion grids, map the 6th edition to the 5th edition and to competing texts to make adapting your course to *3-2-1 Code It!* a snap.
- Access to all free student supplements, including additional textbook content.

Student Workbook

(ISBN: 978-1-305-97025-0)

The workbook follows the chapter organization of the text and contains application-based assignments, including numerous diagnosis/procedure statements and case studies so that students can practice coding. Each assignment contains a list of objectives, an overview of content relating to the assignment, and instructions for completing the assignment. The last assignment in each workbook chapter contains review questions in multiple-choice format to emulate credentialing exam questions. The workbook also contains actual patient records and mock CPC, CCS-P, and CCS certification examinations.

Student Companion Web Site

Additional textbook resources for students and instructors can be found online by following the instructions that follow.

All resources located on the Student Companion Web Site to accompany *3-2-1 Code It!* are free to textbook users. Student resources include:

- Revisions to textbook and workbook due to coding changes as they become available
- E/M Codebuilder (also found in Appendix I of the textbook)
- Presentations in PowerPoint®
- Electronic patient records (also found in Appendices A–D of the workbook)
- Extra content about related coding topics, including long-term care, home health care, and hospice coding

MindTap

(ISBNs: 978-1-305-97041-0 [electronic access code]/
978-1-305-97042-7 [printed access card])

New: Green's *3-2-1 Code It!* 6th Edition on MindTap is the first
of its kind in an entirely new category: the Personal Learning
Experience (PLE). This personalized program of digital products
and services uses interactivity and customization to engage students, while offering instructors a wide range
of choice in content, platforms, devices, and learning tools. MindTap is device agnostic, meaning that it will
work with any platform or learning management system and will be accessible anytime, anywhere: on desktops,
laptops, tablets, mobile phones, and other Internet-enabled devices.

This MindTap includes:

- An interactive eBook with highlighting, note-taking (integrated with Evernote), and more

- Flashcards for practicing chapter terms

- Computer-graded activities and exercises

  ○ Self-check and application activities, integrated with the eBook

  ○ Case studies with videos

- Easy submission tools for instructor-graded exercises

- Brand-new Medical Coding Trainer software for a real-world interactive coding experience

Optum360™ EncoderPro.com

Go to **www.EncoderPro.com** to register for a 30-day free trial of *EncoderPro.com Expert*, which automates the
ICD-10-CM, ICD-10-PCS, CPT, and HCPCS level II coding manuals. (ICD-10-CM and ICD-10-PCS crosswalks for
ICD-9-CM codes are also included.)

Students should not register for the 30-day free trial until instructed to do so by faculty. Students should use paper-
based coding manuals to learn how to assign codes. Then, **www.EncoderPro.com** software can be used to assign
codes for exercises as assigned by the instructor.

Note:

The numbering of textbook
review case studies now matches
MindTap™ numbering.

About the Author

Michelle A. Green, MPS, RHIA, FAHIMA, CPC, has been a college professor since 1984. She taught traditional classroom-based courses until 2000 at Alfred State College, when she transitioned all of the health information management and coding courses to an Internet-based format. In 2016, she began teaching for the health information management program at Mount Wachusett Community College, Gardner, Massachusetts. In 2017, she also began teaching for the health information technology program at Mohawk Valley Community College, Utica, New York. Prior to 1984, she worked as a director of health information management at two acute care hospitals in Florida's Tampa Bay area. Both positions required her to assign codes to inpatient cases. Upon becoming employed as a college professor, she routinely spent the semester breaks coding for a number of health care facilities so that she could further develop her inpatient and outpatient coding skills.

A Note About CPT Coding Manual Editions

Every attempt is made to make the material within this textbook and its ancillary products (e.g., Workbook, Instructor's Manual) as current as possible by updating to CPT 2017 just prior to publication.

Reviewers

Content Reviewers

Acknowledgments

In memory of my son, Eric, who always kept me "on task" by asking, "How much did you get finished in the chapter today, Mom?" Thank you for truly understanding my need to pursue my passion for teaching and writing. You always proudly introduced me as your mom, the teacher and writer. You remain forever in my heart, Eric. A special thank you to my brother, Dave Bartholomew, for his encouragement and help. You are my rock!

To my students, located throughout the world! You always ask me the toughest coding questions, and you also make me want to find the answers. You are truly critical thinkers!

To my technical reviewer, Jessica Rosati, thank you for your incredible attention to detail!

To my content developer, Beth Williams, for her invaluable support, patience, and guidance.

To Jadin Kavanaugh, Product Manager, for listening so carefully to everything I have to say about a new edition and for making the revision process fun!

To my mom, Alice B. Bartholomew, for her unending support and assistance. Between writing real-life case studies for my textbooks and having originally helped me select a health care career, your guidance is appreciated beyond words.

Special appreciation is expressed to Optum360 Publishing Group for granting permission to reprint selected images, tables, and pages from:

- *Coder's Desk Reference for Diagnoses*
- *Coders Desk Reference for Procedures*
- *Coding & Payment Guide for Anesthesia Services*
- *EncoderPro.com*
- *HCPCS Level II Professional*
- *ICD-10-CM Professional*
- *ICD-10-PCS Professional*

Michelle A. Green, MPS, RHIA, FAHIMA, CPC

Feedback

Contact the author at **michelle.ann.green@gmail.com** with questions, suggestions, or comments about the text or its supplements. Please realize that the publisher (**www.cengage.com**) authorizes the release of the Instructor's Manual (with coding answers) to educators only. The publisher also posts AAPC CEU exams on the Student Companion Web Site.

How to Use This Text

Chapter Outline and Key Terms

The **Chapter Outline** organizes the chapter material at a glance. The **Key Terms** list represents new vocabulary in each chapter. Each term is highlighted in color in the chapter, where it is also defined and used in context. A complete definition of each term appears in the Glossary at the end of the textbook.

Objectives

The **Objectives** list the outcomes expected of the learner after a careful study of the chapter. Read the objectives before reading the chapter content. When you complete the chapter, read the objectives again to see if you can say for each one, "Yes, I know that." If you cannot say this about an objective, go back to the appropriate content and reread. These outcomes are critical to a successful career as an insurance specialist.

Introduction

The **Introduction** provides a brief overview about major topics covered in the chapter. The introduction (and the objectives) provides a framework for your study of the content.

Notes

Notes appear throughout the text and serve to bring important points to your attention. The notes clarify content, refer you to reference material, provide more background for selected topics, or emphasize exceptions to rules.

HIPAA Alerts

The **HIPAA Alert** feature highlights issues related to the privacy and security of personal health information.

Chapter Outline

- Radiology Terminology
- Overview of Radiology Section
- Radiology Section Guidelines
- Radiology Subsections
- Diagnostic Radiology (Diagnostic Imaging)
- Diagnostic Ultrasound
- Radiologic Guidance
- Breast, Mammography
- Bone/Joint Studies
- Radiation Oncology
- Nuclear Medicine

Chapter Objectives

At the conclusion of this chapter, the student should be able to:

- Define key terms.
- Explain the organization, format, and content of the CPT Radiology section.
- Interpret CPT radiology coding guidelines and notes.
- Assign CPT radiology codes.
- Add CPT and/or HCPCS level II modifiers to codes, as appropriate.

Key Terms

A-mode
amplitude modulation
angiography
anteroposterior projection
aortography
arthrography
axial plane
biometric A-scan
biomicroscopy
block
bone density study
brightness mode
B-scan
cardiac blood pool imaging
compensator
component coding
computed axial tomography (CT) (CAT)
computed tomography angiography (CTA)
contrast material
contrast medium injection device
corneal pachymetry
coronal plane
cystography
cytoreduction surgery
debulking
diagnostic mammography
Doppler ultrasonography
dual energy x-ray absorptiometry
echo
epidurography
equivalent dose
external radiation
fluoroscopy
fraction (in radiation treatment management)
frontal plane

Introduction

This chapter provides an overview of coding systems used to report inpatient and outpatient diagnoses and procedures and services to health plans. It also focuses on coding career opportunities in health care, the importance of joining professional associations and obtaining coding credentials, the impact of networking with other coding professionals, and the development of opportunities for career advancement.

 Note:

This chapter does *not* require the use of ICD-10-CM, ICD-10-PCS, CPT, or HCPCS level II coding manuals. However, later chapters in this textbook do require them (because learning how to code is easier when you use paper-based coding manuals). A 59-day trial of www.EncoderPro.com software is included with this textbook. Therefore, do *not* install the software until directed to do so by your instructor.

⚠ **HIPAA Alert!**

HIPAA regulations for electronic transactions require providers and payers (including MACs) to adhere to the *Official Guidelines for Coding and Reporting*. Thus, a violation of the coding guidelines is a HIPAA violation. Unfortunately, some payers do not appear to be aware of or understand this HIPAA provision. Payers should be informed of the provision in the HIPAA regulation that references the use of coding guidelines. If payers deny claims because certain codes are reported as principal diagnosis, contact your regional CMS office or the HIPAA enforcement office (at CMS) to alert them about the HIPAA violation.

Coding Tip:

Construct valid ICD-10-PCS codes using a *build-a-code* approach to assign values to each of the seven unique hierarchies (positions).

Coding Tips

The **Coding Tips** feature provides recommendations and hints for selecting codes and for the correct use of the coding manuals.

Examples

EXAMPLE: A 51-year-old male patient presented to the ED, complaining of ringing in his ears, dizziness, blurred vision, confusion, and difficulty walking. Upon evaluation by the ED physician, the patient stated that these symptoms started suddenly just two hours ago. Past history revealed that the patient takes medication for hypercholesterolemia and hypertension. The patient used to smoke two packs of cigarettes daily until 5 years ago, when he quit. Physical examination revealed blood pressure of 175/110. When asked, the patient stated that he had been taking his hypertension medication as prescribed.

Examples appear throughout the text to promote understanding of presented concepts.

Exercise 1.1 – Career as a Coder

Instructions: Match the description with its career. Answers may be assigned more than once.

_____ 1. Answers telephones, greets patients, and updates and files patient medical records

_____ 2. Communicates with providers about documentation and compliance issues related to code assignment

_____ 3. Reviews claims for third-party payers to determine whether costs are reasonable and medically necessary

_____ 4. Schedules hospital admission and laboratory services

_____ 5. Verifies claims against third-party payer guidelines to authorize appropriate payments

a. Coder
b. Health insurance specialist
c. Medical assistant

Exercises

Exercises reinforce chapter content.

Summary

The **Summary** at the end of each chapter recaps the key points of the chapter. The summary also serves as a review aid when preparing for tests.

Summary

A coder is expected to master the use of coding systems, coding principles and rules, government regulations, and third-party payer requirements to ensure that all diagnoses, services, and procedures documented in patient records are accurately coded for reimbursement, research, and statistical purposes. To prepare for entry into the profession, students are encouraged to join a professional association. They usually pay a reduced membership fee and receive most of the same benefits as active members. The benefits of joining a professional association include eligibility for scholarships and grants, opportunity to network with members, free publications, reduced certification exam fees, and website access for members only.

Internet Links

JustCoding.com: Go to *www.justcoding.com*, and sign up for the free e-newsletter by clicking on the "eNewsletter Signup" link.

Medicare PFS look-up: Go to *www.cms.gov*, and click on the Medicare link. Scroll down to the Medicare Fee-for-Service Payment heading, and click on the Physician Fee Schedule Look-Up Tool link.

MedlinePlus: *www.medlineplus.gov*

National Correct Coding Initiative (NCCI) Edits: Go to *www.cms.gov*, and click on the Medicare link. Scroll down to the Coding heading, and click on the National Correct Coding Initiative Edits link.

RiteCode.com: Go to *www.ritecode.com*, hover over the FREE STUFF link, and then click on the Free Coding Quizzes link.

Internet Links

Internet Links are provided to encourage you to expand your knowledge at various state and federal government agency, commercial, and organization sites.

Study Checklist

Study Checklist

☐ Read this chapter and highlight key concepts.

☐ Create an index card for each key term.

☐ Access the chapter Internet links to learn more about concepts.

☐ Complete the chapter exercises and review, verifying answers with your instructor.

☐ Complete Workbook chapter, verifying answers with your instructor.

☐ Go to *www.cengagebrain.com* to access the Student Companion Web Site Login instructions are located in the Preface.

☐ Form a study group with classmates to discuss chapter concepts in preparation for an exam.

The **Study Checklist** appears toward the end of each chapter and directs you to other learning and application aids. Completing each of the items in the checklist will help you to gain confidence in your understanding of the key concepts and in your ability to apply them correctly.

Review

Review

Multiple Choice

Instructions: Circle the most appropriate response.

1. Which mandated that CPT codes be reported for outpatient hospital surgical procedures?
   a. Health Insurance, Portability, and Accountability Act of 1996 (HIPAA)
   b. Healthcare Common Procedure Coding System (HCPCS)
   c. Medicare Prescription Drug, Improvement, and Modernization Act (MMA)
   d. Omnibus Budget Reconciliation Act (OBRA) of 1986

Each chapter **Review** includes multiple-choice questions and coding practice cases that will test your understanding of chapter content and critical thinking ability.

Notes

PART I

Coding Overview

Overview of Coding

Chapter Outline

Career as a Coder

Professional Associations and Discussion
   Boards

Coding Overview

Documentation as Basis for Coding

Health Data Collection

Chapter Objectives

At the conclusion of this chapter, the student should be able to:

- Define key terms.
- Explain coding career opportunities and the coding credentialing process.
- Identify professional associations and describe the benefits of membership.
- Clarify student responsibilities during a coding internship.
- Identify coding systems used for reimbursement, and indicate the relationship between patient record documentation and accurate coding.

Key Terms

application service
   provider (ASP)

Assessment (A)

assumption coding

automated case
   abstracting software

automated record

Centers for Medicare
   & Medicaid Services
   (CMS)

claims examiner

classification system

clearinghouse

CMS-1450

CMS-1500

code

coder

coding

coding system

computer-assisted
   coding (CAC)

concurrent coding

continuity of care

*Current Procedural
   Terminology* (CPT)

database

demographic data

*Diagnostic and Statistical
   Manual of Mental
   Disorders* (DSM)

diagnostic/management
   plan

discharge note

documentation

document imaging

downcoding

electronic health record
   (EHR)

electronic medical
   record (EMR)

encoding

evidence-based coding

HCPCS level II

HCPCS national codes

health care
   clearinghouse

Healthcare Common
   Procedure Coding
   System (HCPCS)

health care provider

health data collection

Health Insurance
   Portability and
   Accountability Act
   of 1996 (HIPAA)

health insurance specialist

health plan

hospitalist

hybrid record

indexed

initial plan

integrated record

International Classification of Diseases, Ninth Revision, Clinical Modification (ICD-9-CM)

International Classification of Diseases, Tenth Revision, Clinical Modification (ICD-10-CM)

International Classification of Diseases, Tenth Revision, Clinical Modification/Procedure

Coding System (ICD-10-CM/PCS)

International Classification of Diseases, Tenth Revision, Procedure Coding System (ICD-10-PCS)

International Classification of Diseases for Oncology, Third Edition (ICD-O-3)

International Classification of Functioning, Disability and Health (ICF)

internship

internship supervisor

jamming

jukebox

listserv

Logical Observation Identifiers Names and Codes (LOINC)

manual record

medical assistant

medical coding process

medical management software

medical necessity

medical nomenclature

medical record

National Drug Codes (NDC)

Objective (O)

online discussion board

optical disk imaging

overcoding

patient education plan

patient record

physician query process

Plan (P)

problem list

problem-oriented record (POR)

progress notes

provider

resident physician

RxNorm

scanner

sectionalized record

SNOMED CT

source-oriented record (SOR)

specialty coders

Subjective (S)

teaching hospital

teaching physician

therapeutic plan

third-party administrator (TPA)

third-party payer

transfer note

UB-04

unbundling

Unified Medical Language System (UMLS)

upcoding

Introduction

This chapter provides an overview of coding systems used to report inpatient and outpatient diagnoses and procedures and services to health plans. It also focuses on coding career opportunities in health care, the importance of joining professional associations and obtaining coding credentials, the impact of networking with other coding professionals, and the development of opportunities for career advancement.

Note:

This chapter does *not* require the use of ICD-10-CM, ICD-10-PCS, CPT, or HCPCS level II coding manuals. However, later chapters in this textbook do require them (because learning how to code is easier when you use paper-based coding manuals).

Note:

The following additional content is located on the Student Companion Web Site at www.cengagebrain.com:

- *Documentation Requirements for Teaching Physicians 2012*
- History of Medical Classification and Coding Systems
- Alternate Health Care Coding Systems

Career as a Coder

A **coder** acquires a working knowledge of coding systems (e.g., CPT, HCPCS level II, ICD-10-CM, ICD-10-PCS), coding conventions and guidelines, government regulations, and third-party payer requirements to ensure that all diagnoses (conditions), services (e.g., office visits), and procedures (e.g., surgery, x-rays) documented in patient records are coded accurately for reimbursement, research, and statistical purposes. Excellent interpersonal skills are required of coders because they communicate with providers about documentation and compliance issues related to the appropriate assignment of diagnosis and procedure/service codes.

 Note:

Although graduates of medical assistant and medical office administration programs typically do not become employed as full-time coders, they often are responsible for the coding function in a physician's office or medical clinic. This chapter provides the following resources for students pursuing any health-related academic program that includes coding as a job function:

- Professional associations that offer coding and other certification exams
- Internet-based discussion boards that cover coding and other topics
- Impact of HIPAA federal legislation on coding and reimbursement
- Coding references and other resources that facilitate accurate coding
- Physician query process as a way to prevent assumption coding
- Manual and automated patient record formats and health data collection

Training

Training methods for those interested in pursuing a coding career include college-based programs that contain coursework in medical terminology, anatomy and physiology, health information management, pathophysiology, pharmacology, ICD-10-CM, ICD-10-PCS, HCPCS level II, and CPT coding, and reimbursement methodologies. Many college programs also require students to complete a nonpaid internship (e.g., 240 hours) at a health care facility. Professional associations (e.g., the American Health Information Management Association) offer noncredit-based coding training, usually as distance learning (e.g., Internet-based), and some health care facilities develop internal programs to retrain health professionals (e.g., nurses) who are interested in a career change.

Note:

Refer to the *Documentation Requirements for Teaching Physicians 2012* document, which is located on the Student Companion Web Site at www.cengagebrain.com.

 Note:

Pharmacology plays a significant role in accurate and complete coding. Coders review the medication administration record (MAR) to locate medications administered that impact diagnosis coding. For example, upon review of the MAR the coder notices that the patient received a course of Librium (chlordiazepoxide) during inpatient hospitalization. Librium is classified as an antianxiety medication, but it can be also used to counteract alcohol withdrawal symptoms. If the latter is the reason that the patient received the Librium (based on physician documentation), the coder can assign an appropriate alcohol dependence diagnosis code as well as alcohol detoxification procedure codes.

Coding Internship

The coding **internship** benefits the student and the facility that accepts the student for placement. Students receive on-the-job experience prior to graduation, and the internship assists them in obtaining permanent employment. Facilities benefit from the opportunity to participate in and improve the formal education process. Quite often, students who complete professional practice experiences (or internships) are later employed by the facility at which they completed the internship.

The **internship supervisor** is the person to whom the student reports at the site. Students are often required to submit a professional résumé to the internship supervisor and to schedule an interview prior to being accepted for placement. While this experience can be intimidating, it is excellent practice for the interview process that the student will undergo prior to obtaining permanent employment. Students should research the résumé writing and interview technique services available from the college's career services office. This office will review résumés and will provide interview tips. (Some even videotape mock interviews for students.)

The internship is on-the-job training even though it is nonpaid, and students should expect to provide proof of immunizations (available from a physician) and possibly undergo a preemployment physical examination and participate in facility-wide and department-specific orientations. In addition, because of the focus on privacy and security of patient information, the facility will likely require students to sign a nondisclosure agreement (to protect patient confidentiality), which is kept on file at the college and by the professional practice site.

During the internship, students are expected to report to work on time. Students who cannot attend the internship on a particular day (or who arrive late) should contact their internship supervisor and program faculty. Students are also required to make up any lost time. Because the internship is a simulated job experience, students are to be well groomed and should dress professionally. Students should show interest in all aspects of the experience, develop good working relationships with coworkers, and react appropriately to criticism and direction. If any concerns arise during the internship, students should discuss them with their internship supervisor and/or program faculty.

> **Note:**
>
> Breach of patient confidentiality can result in termination from the internship site, failure of the internship course, and even possible suspension and/or expulsion from your academic program. Make sure you check out your academic program's requirements regarding this issue.

Credentials

The American Health Information Management Association (AHIMA) and the American Academy of Professional Coders (AAPC) offer certification in coding. Credentials available from AHIMA include the following:

- Certified Coding Associate (CCA)
- Certified Coding Specialist (CCS)
- Certified Coding Specialist—Physician-based (CCS-P)

The AAPC offers the following core coding certification exams:

- Certified Professional Coder (CPC)
- Certified Inpatient Coder (CIC)
- Certified Outpatient Coder (COC)

- Certified Risk Adjustment Coder (CRC)
- Certified Professional Coder—Payer (CPC-P)

The AAPC also offers specialty certifications in response to a demand for **specialty coders** who have obtained advanced training in medical specialties and who are skilled in compliance and reimbursement areas, such as the Certified Ambulatory Surgical Center Coder (CASCC) credential.

 Note:

> The AAPC continues to investigate further expansion of its body of certifications to prepare coders for proficiency in medical and surgical specialty coding. Technological advancements and changes in outpatient and inpatient prospective payment system regulations, such as Medicare severity diagnosis-related groups (MS-DRGs), create a compliance risk that has to be carefully monitored. Specialty coders have the expertise to monitor such areas, impacting the facility's coding and reimbursement process. Specialty coders typically perform the following tasks:
>
> - Analyze provider documentation for accuracy, completeness, and timeliness
> - Maintain and update chargemasters and/or encounter forms
> - Meet with coding staff members to educate them about revised rules and regulations
> - Review patient charges to ensure accuracy in reported codes and modifiers, and enter billing edits
> - Write letters of appeals to address third-party payer reimbursement denials

The American Medical Billing Association (AMBA) offers the Certified Medical Reimbursement Specialist (CMRS) exam, which recognizes the competency of members who have met high standards of proficiency. According to AMBA, Certified Medical Reimbursement Specialists (CMRS) are skilled in facilitating the claims reimbursement process from the time a service is rendered by a health care provider until the balance is paid. The CMRS is knowledgeable in ICD, CPT, and HCPCS level II coding; medical terminology; insurance claims and billing; appeals and denials; fraud and abuse; Health Insurance Portability and Accountability Act (HIPAA) regulations; Office of Inspector General (OIG) compliance; information and Internet technology; and reimbursement methodologies.

The type of setting in which you seek employment will indicate which credential(s) you should pursue. Inpatient and/or outpatient coders obtain CCS and/or CIC certification, and physician office coders choose the CCS-P and/or CPC credential. Outpatient coders also have the option of selecting the COC credential. Insurance specialists who work for health care facilities and third-party payers obtain the CCS-P. Those who have not met requirements for field experience as a coder can seek apprentice-level certification as a CCA. (Once certified, professional associations require maintenance of the credential through continuing education [CE] recertification per two-year cycle.)

Employment Opportunities

Coders can obtain employment in a variety of settings, including clinics, consulting firms, government agencies, hospitals, insurance companies, nursing facilities, home health agencies, hospice organizations, and physicians' offices. Coders also have the opportunity to work at home for employers who partner with an Internet-based **application service provider (ASP)**, which is a third-party entity that manages and distributes software-based services and solutions to customers across a *wide area network (WAN)* (computers that are far apart and are connected via the Internet) from a central data center.

Other Professions Related to the Coder

One profession that is closely related to a coder is that of a **health insurance specialist** (or **claims examiner**). When employed by third-party payers, these specialists review health-related claims to determine whether the costs are reasonable and medically necessary based on the patient's diagnosis. This process involves verification of the claim against third-party payer guidelines to authorize appropriate payment or to refer the claim to an investigator for a more thorough review.

Another profession that is closely related to a coder is the **medical assistant**. When employed by a provider, this person performs administrative and clinical tasks to keep the office and clinic running smoothly. Medical assistants who specialize in administrative aspects of the profession answer telephones, greet patients, update and file patient medical records, complete insurance claims, process correspondence, schedule appointments, arrange for hospital admission and laboratory services, and manage billing and bookkeeping.

When employed by a physician's office, health insurance specialists and medical assistants perform medical billing, coding, record keeping, and other medical office administrative duties. Health insurance specialists (or claims examiners) and medical assistants receive formal training in college-based programs or at vocational schools. They also receive on-the-job training.

- Health insurance specialists (or claims examiners) and medical assistants often become certified as a CCS or a CCS-P (through the AHIMA) or as a CPC-P (through the AAPC).

- The health insurance specialist also has the option of becoming credentialed by the:

  ○ Medical Association of Billers (MAB) as a Certified Medical Billing Specialist (CMBS)

  ○ National Electronic Billers Alliance (NEBA) as a Certified Healthcare Reimbursement Specialist (CHRS)

- Health insurance specialists can participate in the International Claim Association (ICA) program of education. The ICA offers Associate, Life and Health Claims (ALHC) and Fellow, Life and Health Claims (FLHC) examinations to claims examiners in the life and health insurance industries.

- Medical assistants often become credentialed as a Certified Medical Assistant (CMA) through the American Association of Medical Assistants (AAMA) or as a Registered Medical Assistant (RMA) through the American Medical Technologists (AMT).

Health insurance specialists (or claims examiners) and medical assistants obtain employment in clinics, health care clearinghouses, health care facility billing departments, insurance companies, and physicians' offices and with third-party administrators (TPAs). When employed by clearinghouses, insurance companies, or TPAs, they often have the opportunity to work at home, where they process and verify health care claims using an Internet-based application service provider (ASP).

Exercise 1.1 – Career as a Coder

Instructions: Match the description with its career. Answers may be assigned more than once.

_____   **1.** Answers telephones, greets patients, and updates and files patient medical records

_____   **2.** Communicates with providers about documentation and compliance issues related to code assignment

_____   **3.** Reviews claims for third-party payers to determine whether costs are reasonable and medically necessary

_____   **4.** Schedules hospital admission and laboratory services

_____   **5.** Verifies claims against third-party payer guidelines to authorize appropriate payments

a. Coder

b. Health insurance specialist

c. Medical assistant

Professional Associations and Discussion Boards

Students are often able to join a professional association (Table 1-1) for a reduced membership fee and receive most of the same benefits as active members (who pay much more!). Benefits of joining a professional association include the following:

- Eligibility for scholarships and grants
- Opportunity to network with members (internship and job placement)
- Free publications (e.g., professional journals)
- Reduced certification exam fees
- Website access for members only

Attending professional association conferences and meetings provides opportunities to network with professionals. Another way to network is to join an **online discussion board** (or **listserv**) (Table 1-2), which is an Internet-based or email discussion forum that covers a variety of topics and issues.

Table 1-1 Professional Associations

Career	Professional Association
Coder	American Academy of Professional Coders (AAPC)
	American Health Information Management Association (AHIMA)
Health Insurance Specialist	International Claim Association (ICA)
	Alliance of Claims Assistance Professionals (ACAP)
	American Medical Billing Association (AMBA)
	Medical Association of Billers (MAB)
Medical Assistant	American Association of Medical Assistants (AAMA)
	American Medical Technologists (AMT)

Table 1-2 Internet-Based Discussion Boards (Listservs)

Discussion Board	Website
AHIMA Engage communities	AHIMA members can log in at www.ahima.org.
Billing-Coding forum	Go to www.billing-coding.com and select Online Forums from the Other Resources drop-down menu.
Medicare Part B	Go to www.partbnews.com, scroll over the Community link, and click on the ListServ link to join.

Exercise 1.2 – Professional Associations and Discussion Boards

Instructions: Match the professional association with the type of professional. Answers may be assigned more than once.

_____ **1.** AAMA   **a.** Coder

_____ **2.** AAPC   **b.** Health insurance specialist

_____ **3.** ACAP   **c.** Medical assistant

_____ **4.** AHIMA

_____ **5.** AMT

Coding Overview

Coding systems and medical nomenclatures are used by health care facilities, health care providers, and third-party payers to collect, store, and process data for a variety of purposes (e.g., health care reimbursement). A **coding system** (or **classification system**) organizes a medical nomenclature according to similar conditions, diseases, procedures, and services, and it contains codes for each (e.g., ICD-10-CM arranges these elements into appropriate chapters and sections). A **medical nomenclature** is a vocabulary of clinical and medical terms (e.g., arthritis, gastritis, pneumonia) used by health care providers to document patient care. A **code** includes numeric and alphanumeric characters that are reported to health plans for health care reimbursement, to external agencies (e.g., state departments of health) for data collection, and internally (acute care hospital) for education and research. **Coding** is the assignment of codes to diagnoses, services, and procedures based on patient record documentation.

 Note:

You are already familiar with a well-known coding system called the United States Postal Service ZIP Code system, which classifies addresses as numbers (e.g., 12345-9876).

Coding Systems

- The *International Classification of Diseases, Ninth Revision, Clinical Modification (ICD-9-CM)* was adopted in 1979 to classify diagnoses (Volumes 1 and 2) and procedures (Volume 3). The *International Classification of Diseases, Tenth Revision, Clinical Modification (ICD-10-CM)* (and ICD-10-PCS) replaced ICD-9-CM on October 1, 2015 to classify all diagnoses.

- The *International Classification of Diseases, Tenth Revision, Procedure Coding System (ICD-10-PCS)* was developed by the National Center for Health Statistics (NCHS) to classify inpatient procedures and services, and it was implemented on October 1, 2015 (replacing Volume 3 of ICD-9-CM).

 Note:

International Classification of Diseases, Tenth Revision, Clinical Modification/Procedure Coding System (ICD-10-CM/PCS) is the shortened name the Centers for Medicare & Medicaid Services uses to identify both classification systems.

- The *Current Procedural Terminology (CPT)* was originally published by the American Medical Association (AMA) in 1966. Subsequent editions were published about every five years until the late 1980s, when the AMA began publishing annual revisions. CPT classifies procedures and services, and it is used by physicians and outpatient health care settings (e.g., the hospital ambulatory surgery department) to assign CPT codes for reporting procedures and services on health insurance claims. CPT is considered level I of the Healthcare Common Procedure Coding System (HCPCS).

- The **Healthcare Common Procedure Coding System (HCPCS)** also includes level II (national) codes, called **HCPCS level II** (or **HCPCS national codes**), which are managed by the **Centers for Medicare & Medicaid Services (CMS)**, an administrative agency in the federal Department of Health & Human Services (DHHS). HCPCS level II classifies medical equipment, injectable drugs, transportation services, and other services not classified in CPT. Physicians and ambulatory care settings use HCPCS level II to report procedures and services.

> **Note:**
>
> HCPCS level III local codes were discontinued in 2004. They had been managed by Medicare carriers and fiscal intermediaries (FIs). You might come across their legendary use in health care facility or insurance company databases. Some payers still use them.

Medical Nomenclatures

- The *Systematized Nomenclature of Medicine* (SNOMED) was originally developed by the College of American Pathologists (CAP) in 1974 and cross-referenced to the *International Classification of Diseases, Ninth Revision, Clinical Modification* (ICD-9-CM). SNOMED was considered a classification system because it contained codes for activities within the patient record (e.g., medical diagnoses, procedures, nursing diagnoses, nursing procedures, patient signs and symptoms, occupational history, and causes and etiologies of diseases).

- The current revision, created in 2002, is called **SNOMED Clinical Terms** (or **SNOMED CT**); it includes comprehensive coverage of diseases, clinical findings, therapies, procedures, and outcomes. It combines the content and structure of a previous revision of SNOMED with medical nomenclatures titled the United Kingdom's *National Health Service's Clinical Terms Version 3* (formerly called *Read Codes*, developed in the early 1980s by Dr. James Read to record and retrieve primary care data in a computer) and the *Logical Observation Identifier Names and Codes (LOINC®)* database that provides a universal code system for reporting laboratory and other clinical observations. SNOMED CT supports the development of comprehensive high-quality clinical content in patient records; it provides a standardized way to represent clinical phrases documented by clinicians, facilitating automatic interpretation (e.g., computer-assisted coding).

The **Health Insurance Portability and Accountability Act of 1996 (HIPAA)** is federal legislation that amended the Internal Revenue Code of 1986 to:

- improve portability and continuity of health insurance coverage in the group and individual markets;

- combat waste, fraud, and abuse in health insurance and health care delivery;

- promote the use of medical savings accounts;

- improve access to long-term care services and coverage;

- simplify the administration of health insurance by creating unique identifiers for providers, health plans, employers, and individuals;

- create standards for electronic health information transactions; and

- create privacy and security standards for health information.

To facilitate the creation of standards for electronic health information transactions, HIPAA requires two types of code sets to be adopted for the purpose of encoding data elements (e.g., procedure and service codes). **Encoding** is the process of standardizing data by assigning alphanumeric values (codes or numbers) to text or other information (e.g., diagnosis and gender).

Large code sets encode:

- diseases, injuries, impairments, other health-related problems, and their manifestations;

- causes of injury, disease, impairment, or other health-related problems;

- actions taken to prevent, diagnose, treat, or manage diseases, injuries, and impairments; and

- substances, equipment, supplies, or other items used to perform these actions.

EXAMPLE: The diagnosis of *essential hypertension* is assigned ICD-10-CM code I10.

Small code sets encode:

- race/ethnicity;
- type of facility; and
- type of unit.

EXAMPLE: A patient's gender is assigned a 1 if male, a 2 if female, or a 3 if undetermined.

HIPAA also requires specific code sets to be adopted for use by clearinghouses, health plans, and providers.

- *International Classification of Diseases, Tenth Revision, Clinical Modification* and *Procedure Coding System* (ICD-10-CM/PCS)
- *Current Procedural Terminology* (CPT)
- HCPCS level II (national codes)
- *Current Dental Terminology* (CDT)
- *National Drug Codes* (NDC)

A **clearinghouse** (or **health care clearinghouse**) is a public or private entity (e.g., billing service) that processes or facilitates the processing of health information and claims from a nonstandard to a standard format. A **health plan** (or **third-party payer**) (e.g., Blue Cross/Blue Shield, a commercial insurance company) is an insurance company that establishes a contract to reimburse health care facilities and patients for procedures and services provided. A **provider** (or **health care provider**) is a physician or another health care professional (e.g., a nurse practitioner or physician assistant) who performs procedures or provides services to patients. Adopting HIPAA's standard code sets has improved data quality and simplified claims submission for health care providers who routinely deal with multiple third-party payers. The code sets have also simplified claims processing for health plans. Health plans that do not accept standard code sets are required to modify their systems to accept all valid codes or to contract with a health care clearinghouse that does accept standard code sets.

Coding References

Professional organizations that are recognized as national authorities on CPT, HCPCS level II, ICD-10-CM, and ICD-10-PCS coding publish references and resources that are invaluable to coders. To ensure the development of excellent coding skills, make sure you become familiar with and use the following references and resources:

- *AHA Coding Clinic for ICD-10-CM and ICD-10-PCS,* and *AHA Coding Clinic for HCPCS*, quarterly newsletters published by the American Hospital Association and recognized by the CMS as official coding resources
- *Conditions of Participation* (CoP) and *Conditions for Coverage* (CfC), Medicare regulations published by CMS

 Note:

A health care clearinghouse is not a **third-party administrator (TPA)**, which is an entity that processes health care claims and performs related business functions for a health plan. The TPA might contract with a health care clearinghouse to standardize data for claims processing.

Note:

- Official coding policy is published in the AHA *Coding Clinic for ICD-10-CM and ICD-10-PCS,* AHA *Coding Clinic for HCPCS,* and AMA *CPT Assistant,* and as National Correct Coding Initiative (NCCI) edits.

- The AAPC and AHIMA publish coding newsletters, journals, and so on, but such publications do not contain official coding policy.

- *CPT Assistant* and *HCPCS Assistant*, monthly newsletters published by the AMA and recognized by CMS as official coding resources

- *National Correct Coding Initiatives* (NCCI), code edit pairs that cannot be used in the same claim (developed by CMS and published by the federal government's National Technical Information Service [NTIS])

- Compliance program guidance documents, guidelines published by the DHHS OIG

- *ICD-10-CM Official Guidelines for Coding and Reporting*, guidelines provided by CMS and NCHS to be used as a companion document to the official version of the ICD-10-CM

- *ICD-10-PCS Official Guidelines for Coding and Reporting*, guidelines provided by CMS and NCHS to be used as a companion document to the official version of ICD-10-PCS

- *Outpatient Code Editor with Ambulatory Payment Classification* (OCE/APC), software developed by CMS, distributed by NTIS, and used by hospitals to edit outpatient claims to help identify possible CPT/HCPCS level II coding errors and assign Ambulatory Payment Classifications (APCs) that are used to generate reimbursement

Incorporating the use of the above references and resources assists coders in avoiding the following abusive and fraudulent (dishonest and illegal) coding practices, depending on intent. (Abuse involves mistakenly submitting incorrect codes, and fraud involves intentionally submitting incorrect codes to increase reimbursement.)

- **Unbundling**: Reporting multiple codes to increase reimbursement when a single combination code should be reported.

- **Upcoding**: Reporting codes that are not supported by documentation in the patient record for the purpose of increasing reimbursement.

- **Overcoding**: Reporting codes for signs and symptoms in addition to the established diagnosis code.

- **Jamming**: Routinely assigning an unspecified ICD-10-CM disease code instead of reviewing the coding manual to select the appropriate code.

- **Downcoding**: Routinely assigning lower-level CPT codes as a convenience instead of reviewing patient record documentation and the coding manual to determine the proper code to be reported.

Medical Coding Process

The **medical coding process** requires the review of patient record documentation to identify diagnoses, procedures, and services for the purpose of assigning ICD-10-CM, ICD-10-PCS, HCPCS level II, and/or CPT codes. Each health care covered entity (e.g., hospital, medical clinic, physician office) implements a unique medical coding process, which requires adherence to the following:

- Code of ethics
- Steps to accurate coding
- Avoid assumption coding
- Physician query process
- Coding compliance program

Code of Ethics

Professional associations establish a *code of ethics* to help members understand how to differentiate between "right" and "wrong" and apply that understanding to decision making. The AAPC publishes a code of ethics, and AHIMA publishes standards of ethical coding; both serve as guidelines for ethical coding conduct, and they demonstrate a commitment to coding integrity.

Steps to Accurate Coding

Regardless of health care setting, the *steps to accurate coding* begin with a review of the entire patient record (manual or electronic) before selecting diagnoses, procedures, and services to which codes are assigned. Depending on the setting, coders perform retrospective coding, concurrent coding, or a combination of both.

Retrospective coding is the review of records to assign codes after the patient is discharged from the health care facility (e.g., hospital inpatient) or released from same-day outpatient care (e.g., hospital outpatient surgery unit). It is most commonly associated with inpatient hospital stays because accurate coding requires verification of diagnoses and procedures by reviewing completed face sheets, discharge summaries, operative reports, pathology reports, and progress notes in the patient records.

Concurrent coding is the review of records and/or use of encounter forms and chargemasters to assign codes during an inpatient stay (e.g., hospital) or an outpatient encounter (e.g., hospital outpatient visit for laboratory testing or x-rays, physician office visit). It is typically performed for outpatient encounters because encounter forms (e.g., physician office) and chargemasters (e.g., hospital emergency department visit, hospital outpatient visit for laboratory testing, etc.) are completed in "real time" by health care providers as part of the charge-capture process.

- *Encounter forms* are used to record data about office procedures and services provided to patients.

- *Chargemasters* contain a computer-generated list of procedures, services, and supplies and corresponding revenue codes along with charges for each.

> **Note:**
>
> Information about encounter forms and chargemasters is located in Chapter 19 of this textbook, along with samples of each.

Coding Quality

According to the American Hospital Association, "The importance of understanding and following the basic ICD-10-CM, and ICD-10-PCS coding principles cannot be overemphasized in the training of coders and in quality control activities undertaken to improve the accuracy of data reported for internal and external hospital use. The measures for coding accuracy include (a) adherence to ICD-10-CM and ICD-10-PCS coding principles and instructions, (b) attention to specificity in code selection where indicated by physician documentation in the medical record [patient record], (c) grasp of medical terminology, and (d) absence of clerical-type errors, such as those due to carelessness in reading or in transposing [letters and] numbers. Auditing of coded diagnostic and procedural information for accuracy should not be confused with the review for relevancy in sequencing of the codes at hand. They are separate tasks linked together in the data reporting process."

EHR Results in Greater Implementation of Concurrent Coding

Concurrent coding was introduced for inpatient coding just after the inpatient prospective payment system (using diagnosis-related groups) was implemented on October 1, 1983. Coders from the health information department worked part of the day on nursing units, accessing paper-based manual medical records to begin the process of assigning codes to diagnoses and procedures. On discharge of the patient from the hospital, the coders performed a final review of the patient record to ensure accuracy of reported codes.

Because the paper-based manual patient record can be handled by just one individual at a time, coders "competed" with nurses, physicians, and other health care providers for access to the record. As a result, concurrent coding as a process was discontinued in some facilities because it was inefficient.

Today, implementation of the electronic health record (EHR) has resulted in a resurgence of concurrent coding practices because coders (still located in the health information department) access

(continues)

> ## EHR Results in Greater Implementation of Concurrent Coding (*continued*)
>
> patient records in an electronic format. They no longer "compete" with other health care providers for access to the record and, as a result, efficiency associated with the concurrent coding concept has been realized. In practice, coders remain at their work stations in the health information department (and *remote coders* use their at-home work stations) to access patient EHRs to begin the discharge coding process. Rising health care costs created an impetus for concurrent coding processes because it is a much faster method for coders to review and verify the accuracy of codes on discharge of inpatients based on concurrent coding work performed (according to an established schedule) up until the date of discharge. For tertiary-care facilities that provide complex health care (e.g., transplant surgery) and quaternary-care facilities that provide highly specialized care (e.g., experimental medicine), both of which are also characterized as providing high-cost care (e.g., $500,000 transplant surgery), having the ability to submit codes for reimbursement purposes within hours (instead of days) of inpatient discharge significantly and positively impacts their accounts receivables (and their "bottom line"). In addition, community-based hospitals that submit claims averaging $50,000 or higher also realize the benefits of concurrent coding.

The statement located in (b) of the aforementioned quote is significant because it means that coders are expected to review the *entire* record when assigning codes to diagnoses and procedures documented on the face sheet and in the discharge summary. Thus, coders should review the face sheet, discharge summary, and other documentation (e.g., progress notes, operative reports, pathology reports, laboratory data, and so on) to assign the most specific codes possible.

Remember! Coders must avoid assumption coding, and when a problem with documentation quality is noted (e.g., conflicting diagnostic statements on the discharge summary, face sheet, and elsewhere in the record) the physician query process is initiated (discussed below).

EXAMPLE 1: The provider documented *congestive heart failure* on the face sheet of the patient record. On review of progress notes that document the patient's response to treatment, the coder finds documentation of *acute and chronic diastolic and systolic congestive heart failure* in the discharge progress note. Instead of reporting a code for *congestive heart failure*, report the more specific code for *acute and chronic diastolic and systolic congestive heart failure*.

EXAMPLE 2: The provider documented *malnutrition* on the discharge summary in the patient record. On review of progress notes, the coder finds documentation of *moderate malnutrition*. Instead of reporting the nonspecific code for *malnutrition*, report the more specific code for *moderate malnutrition*.

Avoid Assumption Coding

Coders are prohibited from performing **assumption coding**, which is the assignment of codes based on assuming, from a review of clinical evidence in the patient's record, that the patient has certain diagnoses or received certain procedures/services even though the provider did not specifically document those diagnoses or procedures/services. According to the *Compliance Program Guidance for Third-Party Medical Billing Companies*, published by the Department of Health & Human Services' Office of the Inspector General, assumption coding creates risk for fraud and abuse because the coder assumes certain facts about a patient's condition or procedures/services, although the physician has not specifically documented the level of detail to which the coder assigns codes. (Coders can avoid fraudulent assumption coding by implementing the physician query process discussed in the following section.)

EXAMPLE: An elderly patient is admitted to the hospital for treatment of a fractured femur. Upon examination, the physician documents that the skin around the fractured femur site has split open. X-ray of the left femur reveals a displaced fracture of the shaft. The patient underwent fracture reduction and full-leg casting. The physician documents *open Type I fracture of shaft, left femur* as the final diagnosis.

The coder assigns code S72.302B for the *open Type I fracture of shaft, left femur*, which is correct. The coder assigns code 0QS90ZZ for the *fracture reduction and full leg casting procedure*, which is incorrect because its code description is *open reduction (reposition) of fracture without internal fixation (no device), femur (shaft)*. Although the patient has an open fracture, the physician did *not* perform an open reduction procedure. (An open reduction involves making a surgical incision to align displaced bones, and it may require external fixation to heal properly.) In this case, the coder incorrectly "assumed" that an open reduction was performed because the patient's open fracture was treated. The code that should be assigned for this procedure is 0QS9XZZ because its code description is *closed reduction of fracture without internal fixation, femur*. (A closed reduction involves casting the affected limb to stabilize the fracture for healing, and it might also require the physician to pull back two ends of bone that are touching each other and/or to correct any wide angles.)

Physician Query Process

When coders have questions about documented diagnoses and procedures or services, they use a **physician query process** to contact the responsible physician to request clarification about documentation and the code(s) to be assigned. The electronic health record (EHR) allows for development of an *automated* physician query process, which is used by utilization managers (or case managers), clinical documentation improvement specialists, and coders to obtain clarification about patient record documentation. Integrating the automated physician query process with the EHR allows physicians to more easily receive and reply to queries, which results in better and timely responses from physicians.

 Note:

> The query should not lead the physician to a desired outcome.
>
> - A leading query would be phrased as, "Is the patient's anemia due to blood loss?" and leads the physician to add due to blood loss to the anemia diagnosis for more specific code assignment and possible increased reimbursement.
>
> - A nonleading query would be phrased as, "Can the cause of the patient's anemia be specified? The history documents symptoms of fatigue, headaches, inflamed tongue, and lightheadedness. The CBC reveals low hemoglobin levels." This query allows the physician to determine whether the anemia can be qualified according to type.

The following guidelines should be followed when activating the physician query process:

- Establish a policy to indicate when a coder should generate a physician query, such as when documentation in the patient's record fails to meet one of the following five criteria (according to AHIMA's practice brief, entitled *Managing an Effective Query Process*):

   o *Legibility* (e.g., illegible handwritten patient record entries)

   o *Completeness* (e.g., abnormal test results but clinical significance of results is not documented)

   o *Clarity* (e.g., signs and symptoms are present in the patient record, but a definitive diagnosis is not documented)

   o *Consistency* (e.g., discrepancy among two or more treating providers regarding a diagnosis, such as a patient who presents with shortness of breath and the consulting physician documents pneumonia as the cause while the attending physician documents congestive heart failure as the cause)

   o *Precision* (e.g., clinical documentation indicates a more specific diagnosis than is documented, such as a sputum culture that indicates bacterial pneumonia and the diagnosis does not indicate the cause of the pneumonia)

- Query the physician when the following are noted by the coder and when provider documentation in the patient record is not present (according to AHIMA's practice brief, entitled *Managing an Effective Query Process*):

  - Clinical indicators of a diagnosis (e.g., lab, x-ray) but the diagnosis is not documented

  - Clinical evidence for a higher degree of specificity or severity (e.g., progress notes) but specificity or severity is not documented in the diagnosis

  - Cause-and-effect relationship between two conditions or an organism but the relationship is not documented in the diagnosis (e.g., due to, with)

  - An underlying cause when a patient is admitted with symptoms (e.g., shortness of breath is documented instead of diagnosed pneumonia)

  - Treatment is documented without a corresponding diagnosis for medical necessity (e.g., antibiotics for a secondary diagnosis of UTI, which is not documented as a diagnosis)

  - Lack of present on admission (POA) indicator status (e.g., history did not indicate diagnoses that were present on admission, such as chronic asthma) (The POA indicator status is discussed in textbook Chapter 19.)

- Determine whether the query will be generated concurrently (during inpatient hospitalization) or retrospectively (after patient discharge).

- Designate an individual who will serve as the physician's contact during the physician query process (e.g., coding supervisor, utilization manager). Remember that the coder's role is to assign codes based on documentation and that asking for clarification is appropriate, but making an assumption about codes to be assigned is considered fraud. That means that coders should ask physicians open-ended questions to avoid leading the physicians by indicating a preference for a particular response. Coders do not make clinical assumptions—that is the sole responsibility of the physician.

 Note:

Utilization managers (or case managers) are responsible for coordinating inpatient care to ensure the appropriate utilization of resources, delivery of health care services, and timely discharge or transfer. They usually have a bachelor's degree (e.g., nursing), professional licensure (e.g., RN), and clinical practice experience.

Utilization managers work closely with physicians on a daily basis, and they are a logical choice to facilitate the physician query process. In this role, they serve as the liaison for coders (and physicians) by helping coders write appropriate queries and clarifying queries for physicians so that responses are timely and complete.

Use a query form (Figure 1-1), not scrap paper, to document the coder's query and the physician's response. If the completed query form is filed in the patient's record, determine whether it is considered an official part of the record and subject to disclosure by those requesting copies of records or whether it is an administrative form that is not subject to disclosure. The query form could also be stored in an administrative file in the coding supervisor's office and the information resulting from the query documented kept in the patient record by the physician (e.g., an addendum to the discharge summary). The length of time that the completed query form is retained is determined by each health care organization.

EXAMPLE: A patient is admitted with severe dyspnea (shortness of breath), chest pain, and fever. Upon physical examination, the physician documents rhonchi (gurgling sound in the lungs), wheezing, and rales (clicking, bubbling, or rattling sounds in the lungs). Laboratory data during the hospitalization include a culture and sensitivity report of sputum that documents the presence of gram-negative bacteria. A review of the physician orders reveals documentation of appropriate medications to treat *pneumonia due to gram-negative bacteria*. The medication administration record (MAR) documents administration of the medications, and the physician progress notes document the patient's positive response to medications (and resolution of the pneumonia). The physician documents *viral pneumonia* as the final diagnosis.

PHYSICIAN QUERY FORM

Patient Name: _____   Date: _____
Admission Date: _____   Coder: _____
Patient Number: _____   Email Address: _____
                                      Office Number: _____

Dear Dr. _____,

The diagnosis or procedure of _____ requires more specific information in order to assign the most accurate and complete code. The following information is documented in the _____.

_____
_____
_____
_____

I have the following question(s) about this record:

_____
_____
_____
_____

Please respond to this question in the space below, and also document an amendment in the patient record (if appropriate):

_____
_____
_____
_____
_____

Figure 1-1 Sample physician query form

Depending on the health care facility's coding policy and procedure, the coder has two options.

1. If the coding policy and procedure allow coders to use the entire patient record as the basis of assigning codes to final diagnoses and procedures, because documentation in the record supports a final diagnosis of *pneumonia due to gram-negative bacteria* (instead of viral pneumonia), the coder would assign the code for that condition.

2. If the coding policy and procedure require coders to generate a *physician query* when the final diagnosis (on the face sheet or in the discharge summary) differs from documentation found in the patient record, the coder would submit the following query to the physician, which allows the physician an opportunity to correct the documented final diagnosis if warranted. In this case, the physician changed *viral pneumonia* to *pneumonia due to gram-negative bacteria* (using the proper procedure for amending the patient record).

EXAMPLE OF PHYSICIAN QUERY:

```
To: Dr. Smith

From: Michelle G.

The final diagnosis documented on this case is viral pneumonia. A review
of laboratory results indicates gram-negative bacteria.

Would you reply to (1) confirm the original final diagnosis of viral
pneumonia or to (2) indicate that you have documented a different final
diagnosis in the patient record?

Thank you for your attention to this query. —Michelle G
```

The assignment of a code to pneumonia due to *gram-negative bacteria* results in reimbursement of about $3,500, and the assignment of a code to *viral pneumonia* results in reimbursement of about $2,500. Not querying the physician would have resulted in a loss of $1,000 to the facility.

This case also includes documentation of signs and symptoms, which are due to the pneumonia. Thus, the coder would *not* assign codes to symptoms of dyspnea, chest pain, fever or signs of rhonchi, wheezing, and rales.

Clinical Documentation Improvement Program

The purpose of a *clinical documentation improvement (CDI) program* is to help health care facilities comply with government programs (e.g., RAC audits, ARRA/HITECH) and other initiatives (Joint Commission accreditation) with the goal of improving health care quality. As part of a CDI program, the CDI specialist initiates concurrent and retrospective reviews of inpatient records to identify conflicting, incomplete, or nonspecific provider documentation. Concurrent reviews are performed on patient care units (to access paper-based patient records) or remotely (to access EHRs). The CDI program helps ensure that patient diagnoses and procedures are supported by ICD-10-CM and ICD-10-PCS codes, and CDI specialists use a physician query form to communicate with physicians (and other health care providers) with the intended result of improving documentation, coding, reimbursement, and severity of illness (SOI) and risk of mortality (ROM) classifications. CDI programs are usually associated with acute health care facilities; however, they are also implemented in alternate health care settings (e.g., acute rehabilitation facility, skilled nursing facility). A *clinical documentation improvement (CDI) specialist* is responsible for performing inpatient record reviews for the purpose of:

- implementing documentation clarification and specificity processes (as part of the physician query process);
- using and interpreting clinical documentation improvement statistics;
- conducting research and providing education to improve clinical documentation; and
- ensuring compliance with initiatives that serve to improve the quality of health care, which include:
  - ○ complying with fraud and abuse regulations;
  - ○ enforcing privacy and security of patient information; and
  - ○ monitoring a *health information exchange (HIE)*.

Coding Compliance Program

A *coding compliance program* ensures that the assignment of codes to diagnoses, procedures, and services follows established coding guidelines, such as those published by the Centers for Medicare & Medicaid Services (CMS). Health care organizations write *policies* (guiding principles that indicate "what to do") and *procedures* (processes that indicate "how to do it") to assist in implementing the coding compliance stages of detection, correction, prevention, verification, and comparison.

- *Detection* is the process of identifying potential coding compliance problems. For example, a coder notices that some patient records contain insufficient or incomplete documentation, which adversely impacts coding specificity. The coder brings these records to the attention of the coding compliance officer (e.g., coding supervisor), who implements the next stage of the coding compliance program.
- *Correction* is based on the review of patient records that contain potential coding compliance problems, during which specific compliance issues are identified and problem-solving methods are used to implement necessary improvements (corrections). For example, the coding compliance officer conducts a careful review of the patient records that contain insufficient or incomplete documentation.

She determines that all of them are the responsibility of a physician new to the practice, and she prepares educational material specific to documentation issues noted during her review of the patient records.

- *Prevention* involves educating coders and providers so as to prevent coding compliance problems from recurring. For example, the coding compliance officer schedules a meeting with the physician responsible for insufficient or incomplete documentation, and educates the physician about the specific areas of insufficient or incomplete documentation that adversely impact medical coding. This meeting is conducted in a nonconfrontational manner, with education and correction as its goals.

- *Verification* provides an "audit trail" that the detection, correction, and prevention functions of the coding compliance program are being actively performed. For example, the coding compliance officer maintains a file that contains the following:

  - Original codes assigned based on insufficient and incomplete documentation

  - Educational materials prepared specific to the documentation issues

  - Minutes of the educational meeting with the responsible physician

  - Final codes assigned based on sufficient and complete documentation

  - Remittance advice from third-party payer, which contains adjudication (decision about reimbursement, including possible claims denial)

- *Comparison* requires the analysis of internal coding patterns over specified periods of time (e.g., quarterly) as well as the analysis of external coding patterns by using external benchmarks (trends). For example, the coding compliance officer reviews reports of quarterly medical audits to determine whether the new physician's documentation has improved. Such reports contain the results of claims submission, which indicate the number of claims denials based on nonspecific codes submitted as a result of insufficient and incomplete documentation. In addition, the coding compliance officer obtains benchmark data (reports) from third-party payers and compares the coding practices in her facility with those of similar providers; if reimbursement to similar providers is significantly higher (or lower) than that paid to her provider, she initiates the *detection* process in an attempt to identify related coding compliance problems.

An effective coding compliance program monitors coding processes for completeness, reliability, validity, and timeliness.

- *Completeness* ensures that codes are assigned to all *reportable* diagnoses, procedures, and services documented in the patient record. For example, coders review the entire patient record to assign the most specific codes possible.

- *Reliability* allows for the same results to be consistently achieved. For example, when the same patient record is coded by different coding professionals, they assign identical diagnosis and procedure/service codes.

- *Validity* confirms that assigned codes accurately reflect the patient's diagnoses, procedures, and services. For example, coders do *not* assign codes to diagnoses that were not medically managed or treated during an encounter.

- *Timeliness* means that patient records are coded in accordance with established policies and procedures to ensure timely reimbursement.

Computer-Assisted Coding

Computer-assisted coding (CAC) uses software to automatically generate medical codes by "reading" transcribed clinical documentation provided by health care practitioners (Figure 1-2). CAC uses "natural language

Computer-assisted coding (CAC) software obtains and displays a patient's electronic health record (EHR)

CₒDE
Computer-Assisted Coding

Key terms associated with diagnoses and procedures are highlighted, and CAC software displays ICD, CPT, and HCPCS level II codes

Coder clicks on highlighted EHR key terms to manually review and validate accuracy of displayed codes, using references (e.g., official coding guidelines) to edit codes

Codes are delivered to financial management system and included on UB-04 bill or CMS-1500 claim

Codes are delivered to clinical management system, and data are used to improve quality of care provided

Figure 1-2 Computer-assisted coding (CAC)

processing" theories to generate codes that are reviewed and validated by coders for reporting on third-party payer claims. Similar to the medical editor's role in ensuring the accuracy of reports produced from speech recognition technology, the coder's role changes from that of data entry to validation or audit. The coder reviews and approves the CAC-assigned codes, improving efficiency and offering expanded career opportunities for enthusiastic coders.

Coding auditors performed **evidence-based coding**, which involves clicking on codes that CAC software generates (Figure 1-3) to review electronic health record documentation (evidence) used to generate the code. When it is determined that documentation supports the CAC-generated code, the coding auditor clicks to accept the code. When documentation does not support the CAC-generated code, the coding auditor replaces it with an accurate code. For example, when the CAC-generated ICD-10-CM code does not indicate laterality or does not include a manifestation code, the coding auditor edits codes to ensure accurate reporting.

Figure 1-3 Sample screen from Optum360 Enterprise computer-assisted coding (CAC) software

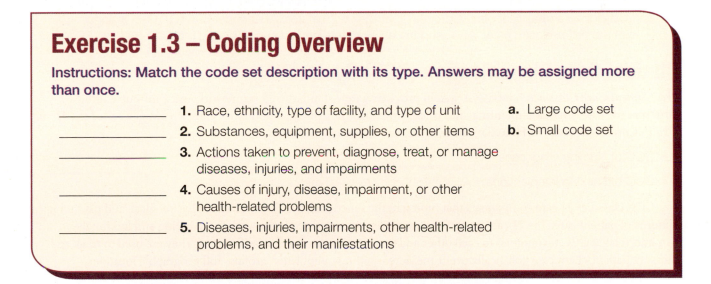

Exercise 1.3 – Coding Overview

Instructions: Match the code set description with its type. Answers may be assigned more than once.

_____ **1.** Race, ethnicity, type of facility, and type of unit

_____ **2.** Substances, equipment, supplies, or other items

_____ **3.** Actions taken to prevent, diagnose, treat, or manage diseases, injuries, and impairments

_____ **4.** Causes of injury, disease, impairment, or other health-related problems

_____ **5.** Diseases, injuries, impairments, other health-related problems, and their manifestations

a. Large code set

b. Small code set

Other Classification Systems and Databases

In addition to the ICD-10-CM, ICD-10-PCS, HCPCS level II national, and CPT coding systems, health care providers use the following classifications, clinical vocabularies, nomenclatures, taxonomies, and terminologies:

- *Alternative Billing Codes* (ABC codes)
- *Clinical Care Classification* (CCC) *System*
- *Current Dental Terminology* (CDT)
- *Diagnostic and Statistical Manual of Mental Disorders* (DSM)

- *Health Insurance Prospective Payment System* (HIPPS) Rate Codes
- *International Classification of Diseases for Oncology, Third Edition* (ICD-O-3)
- *International Classification of Functioning, Disability and Health* (ICF)
- Logical Observation Identifiers Names and Codes (LOINC)
- *National Drug Codes* (NDC)
- RxNorm
- Unified Medical Language System (UMLS)

Alternative Billing Codes (ABC Codes)

The *Alternative Billing Codes* (ABC codes) classify services not included in the CPT manual to describe the service, supply, or therapy provided; they may also be assigned to report nursing services and alternative medicine procedures. Codes are five characters in length, consisting of letters, and are supplemented by two-digit code modifiers to identify the practitioner performing the service.

HIPAA authorized the Secretary of DHHS to permit exceptions from HIPAA transaction and code set standards to commercialize and evaluate proposed modifications to those standards. The ABC code set was granted that exception in 2003, and the codes were being commercialized and evaluated through 2005. The intent was for ABC codes to be adopted as part of the electronic code set (as HCPCS level I and level II were in 2000); however, in 2006, ABC codes could no longer be used in electronic claims processing.

> **EXAMPLE:** During an office visit, an acupuncture physician assessed the health status of a new client and developed a treatment plan, a process that took 45 minutes. ABC code ACAAC-1C is assigned. (The office visit is closed as ACAAC, and the acupuncture physician is assigned modifier 1C.)

Clinical Care Classification (CCC) System

The *Clinical Care Classification* (CCC) *System* provides a new standardized framework and a unique coding structure for assessing, documenting, and classifying home health and ambulatory care. Previously called the *Home Health Care Classification* (HHCC) *System*, CCC consists of two interrelated taxonomies:

- CCC of Nursing Diagnoses
- CCC of Nursing Interventions

CCC classifies 21 care components that represent the functional, health, behavioral, physiological, and psychological patterns of patient care. The 21 care components serve as a standardized framework for mapping and linking the two interrelated CCC taxonomies to each other and to other health-related classifications. They are used to track and measure patient/client care holistically over time, across settings, population groups, and geographic locations.

> **EXAMPLE:** A 73-year-old female patient was discharged from the hospital after treatment for acute myocardial infarction. Patient presents today for the first of 18 scheduled outpatient cardiac rehabilitation sessions. CCC code C08.1 (cardiac rehabilitation) is assigned.

Current Dental Terminology (CDT)

The *Current Dental Terminology* (CDT) is published by the American Dental Association (ADA) as an annual revision. It classifies dental procedures and services. Dental providers and ambulatory care settings use the CDT to report procedures and services. CDT codes are also included in HCPCS level II, beginning with the first digit of D. The CDT also includes the Code on Dental Procedures and Nomenclature (Code), instructions for use of the Code, questions and answers, ADA dental claim form completion instructions, and tooth numbering systems.

> **EXAMPLE:** Patient underwent incision and drainage of intraoral soft tissue abscess. CDT code D7510 is assigned.

Diagnostic and Statistical Manual of Mental Disorders (DSM)

The ***Diagnostic and Statistical Manual of Mental Disorders* (DSM)** is published by the American Psychiatric Association as a standard classification of mental disorders used by mental health professionals in the United States. The first edition was published in 1952, and subsequent revisions have been published as:

- DSM-II (1968)
- DSM-III (1980)
- DSM-III-R (1987)
- DSM-IV (1994)
- DSM-IV-TR (2000) (This includes a *text revision* to correct DSM-IV errors, the updating of codes according to ICD-9-CM or ICD-10-CM annual revisions, and so on.)
- DSM-5 (2014)

  DSM-5 is designed for use in a variety of health care settings and consists of three major components:

- Diagnostic classification
- Diagnostic criteria sets
- Descriptive text

  DSM-5 is a multiaxial classification that allows for the collection and classification of information as:

- Axis I: Mental disorders or illnesses, such as substance abuse
- Axis II: Personality disorders or traits, such as mental retardation
- Axis III: General medical illnesses, such as hypertension
- Axis IV: Life events or problems, such as divorce
- Axis V: Global assessment of functioning, or GAF, such as occupational

  EXAMPLE: A patient is admitted to the hospital with the diagnosis to agoraphobia with panic attacks. The 38-year-old female also has the diagnosis of hypertension and diabetes mellitus. The patient has an avoidant personality disorder as well, as a result of the agoraphobia. After extensive therapy, the clinician has decided that the patient may be discharged. The clinician believed that the patient's condition could have been attributed to her recent divorce and the death of a close relative. He thinks that her anticipated level of functioning will be quite poor, as in the past year she has had trouble in social and occupational functioning. DSM-5 codes are assigned as follows:

  Axis I: Agoraphobia with panic attacks; F40.01

  Axis II: Avoidant personality disorder; F60.6

  Axis III: Hypertension; I10, and diabetes mellitus; E11.9

  Axis IV: Recent divorce and death of close relative

  Axis V: Poor

Health Insurance Prospective Payment System (HIPPS) Rate Codes

The *Health Insurance Prospective Payment System* (HIPPS) rate codes are alphanumeric codes consisting of five digits. Each HIPPS code contains intelligence, with certain positions of the code indicating the case-mix group itself and other positions providing additional information (e.g., information about the clinical assessment used to arrive at the code). HIPPS was created as part of the prospective payment system for skilled nursing facilities in 1998. Additional HIPPS codes were created for other prospective payment systems, including a system for home health agencies in October 2000, and one for inpatient rehabilitation facilities in January 2002. The HIPPS represents specific sets of patient characteristics (or case-mix groups) on which payment determinations are made under several prospective payment systems. HIPPS codes are not assigned from a coding manual; they are created when information for a data set is entered into software.

> **EXAMPLE:** The home health prospective payment system (HHPPS) requires entry of the Outcome and Assessment Information Set (OASIS) data set into grouper software, which generates the five-digit alphanumeric HIPPS code that is entered on the UB-04 claim. For example, HIPPS code HAEJ1 is entered on the UB-04 claim.

International Classification of Diseases for Oncology, Third Edition (ICD-O-3)

The *International Classification of Diseases for Oncology, Third Edition* (ICD-O-3) was implemented in 2001 as a classification of neoplasms used by cancer registries throughout the world to record incidence of malignancy and survival rates. The data produced are used to inform cancer control, research activity, treatment planning, and health economics. (The first edition of ICD-O was published in 1976, and a revision of topography codes was published in 1990.) ICD-O-3 codes classify a tumor in the following way:

- Primary site (four-character topography code)
- Morphology (six-character code)
  - Four-digit histology (cell type) code
  - One-digit behavior code (such as malignant, benign, and so on)
  - One-digit aggression code (differentiation or grade)

> **EXAMPLE:** Fibrosarcoma of the left knee. ICD-O-3 codes C49.2 (Knee, NOS) and M8810/39 (Fibroscarcoma, NOS) are assigned.

ICD-O Morphology Codes

ICD-O morphology codes indicate the type of cell that has become neoplastic and its biologic activity; in other words, the kind of tumor that developed and how it behaves. There are three parts to a complete morphology code:

- M as the first character of each morphology code
- 4-digit cell type (histology) (e.g., 8010)
- 1-digit behavior (e.g., /o)
- 1-digit grade, differentiation, or phenotype (e.g., /x1)

A common root codes the cell type of a tumor, an additional digit codes the behavior, and yet an additional digit codes the grade, differentiation, or phenotype to provide supplementary information about the tumor.

Cancer and Carcinoma

The words *cancer* and *carcinoma* are often (incorrectly) used interchangeably. For example, squamous cell cancer is often used for squamous cell carcinoma. Both conditions happen to have the same ICD-10-CM code. However, a condition such as "spindle cell cancer" could refer to "spindle cell sarcoma" or "spindle cell carcinoma." Each condition has an entirely different ICD-10-CM code assigned to it.

Behavior

The behavior of a tumor is the way it acts within the body. Pathologists use a variety of observations to characterize the behavior of a tumor. A tumor can grow in place without the potential for spread (/0, benign); it can be malignant but still growing in place (/2, noninvasive or in situ); it can invade surrounding tissues (/3, malignant, primary site); or it can disseminate from its point of origin and begin to grow at another site (/6, metastatic).

Fifth-Digit Behavior Codes for Neoplasms

Code	Behavior of Neoplasm
/0	Benign
/1	Uncertain whether benign or malignant
	Borderline malignancy
	Low malignant potential
	Uncertain malignant potential
/2	Carcinoma in situ
	Intraepithelial
	Noninfiltrating
	Noninvasive
/3	Malignant, primary site
/6	Malignant, metastatic site
	Malignant, secondary site
/9	Malignant, uncertain whether primary or metastatic site

 Note:

Cancer registries collect data on malignant and in situ neoplasms, or /2 and /3 behavior codes. They do not collect data about behavior codes /6, malignant, metastatic site, or /9, malignant, uncertain whether primary or metastatic site. For example, carcinoma that has spread to the lung and for which the site of origin is unknown is assigned ICD-10-CM code C80.1 (unknown primary site) and ICD-O code M-8010/3 (carcinoma). (The /3 signifies the existence of a malignant neoplasm of a primary site.)

Use of Behavior Code in Pathology Laboratories

Pathologists are usually interested in "specimen coding" (whereas a cancer registry identifies just the primary tumor). A pathologist receives the following tissue specimens on the same patient:

- Biopsy of supraclavicular lymph node
- Resection of fundus of stomach
- Resection of upper lobe bronchus

The pathologist has to track each of these specimens (while the cancer registry tracks only the primary cancer.) Each pathological specimen is coded with the appropriate topography and morphology; however, in (b) the behavior would be /6 (metastatic), indicating that the associated topography code is not the site of origin. On the other hand, the cancer registrar would report only (b) the primary site and morphology with a behavior code/3.

Tissue Specimen	Pathological Diagnosis	Codes
Supraclavicular lymph node (biopsy)	Metastatic signet ring cell adenocarcinoma, most likely from stomach (metastatic site	C77.0 M8490/6
Fundus of stomach (resection)	Signet ring cell adenocarcinoma (primary site)	C16.1 M8490/3
Upper lobe bronchus (resection)	Metastaic signet ring cell adenocarcinoma (metastaic site)	C34.10 M8490/6

Code for Histologic Grading and Differentiation

The highest grade code is assigned according to the description documented in the diagnostic statement. The sixth digit of the morphology code is a single-digit code number that designates the grade of malignant neoplasms. Only malignant tumors are graded. The practice of assigning codes for Histologic grading varies greatly among pathologists throughout the world, and many malignant tumors are not routinely graded.

Sixth Digit Code for Histologic Grading and Differentiation

Code	Grade	Differentiation
1	I	Well differentiated Differentiated, NOS
2	II	Moderately differentiated Moderately well differentiated Intermediate differentiation
3	III	Poorly differentiated
4	IV	Undifferentiated Anaplastic
9		Grade or differentiation not determined, not stated or not applicable

Differentiation describes how much or how little a tumor resembles the normal tissue from which it arose. There is great variability in pathologists' use of differentiation descriptors. In general, adverbs such as *well, moderately, and poorly* indicate degrees of differentiation, which map to grades I, II, and III. Adjectives such as *undifferentiated* and *anaplastic* usually map to grade IV. Grading codes are assigned to all malignant neoplasms listed in ICD-O *if the diagnosis documents the grade and/or differentiation.*

> **EXAMPLE:** The diagnosis *squamous cell carcinoma, grade* II, which is described as *moderately well differentiated squamous cell carcinoma*, is assigned morphology code M-8070/32.

When a diagnosis indicates two different degrees of grading or differentiation, the higher number is assigned as the grading code.

> **EXAMPLE:** *Moderately differentiated squamous cell carcinoma with poorly differentiated areas* is assigned grading code 3, and the morphology code is M-8070/33.

This same sixth-digit column is also used to indicate cell lineage for leukemias and lymphomas, which provides useful ICD-O-3 comparison data (with ICD-O-2). Cell lineage is implicit in the four-digit histology code, and an additional grade of differentiation (sixth digit) code is not required. However, some registries assign the sixth digit to identify cases in which the diagnosis is supported by immunophenotypic data. In such instances, the immunophenotype code takes precedence over other diagnostic terms for grade or differentiation (e.g., well differentiated, grade III).

Sixth Digit for Immunophenotype Designation for Lymphomas and Leukemias

Code	Designation
5	T-cell
6	B-cell
	Pre-B
	B-precursor
7	Null cell
	Non T-non B
8	NK cell
	Natural killer cell
9	Cell type not determined, not stated, or not applicable

International Classification of Functioning, Disability and Health (ICF)

The *International Classification of Functioning, Disability and Health* (ICF) classifies health and health-related domains that describe body functions and structures, activities, and participation. (The ICF was originally published as the *International Classification of Injuries, Disabilities, and Handicaps (ICIDH)* in 1980.) The ICF complements ICD-10, looking beyond mortality and disease.

> **EXAMPLE:** A trauma patient is evaluated two years after the initial injury, and the physician determines that the patient has a severe impairment in mental function as well as a severe impairment of the upper extremity. The patient experiences moderate difficulty in bathing without the use of assistive devices. Products for education are a moderate barrier for this patient. The following ICF codes are assigned:
>
> - b175.3 (severe impairment in mental function)
> - s730.3 (severe impairment of the upper extremity)
> - a5101.2 (moderate difficulty bathing without use of assistive devices)
> - e145.2 (products for education are a moderate barrier)

Logical Observation Identifiers Names and Codes (LOINC)

Logical Observation Identifiers Names and Codes (LOINC) is an electronic database and universal standard that is used to identify medical laboratory observations and for the purpose of clinical care and management. Developed in 1994, it is currently maintained by the Regenstrief Institute, a US non-profit medical research organization. Health care providers use LOINC codes when reportable disease results are sent to state and federal public health laboratories.

The Centers for Disease Control and Prevention (CDC) has developed a LOINC panel specifically for public health case reporting called the Reportable Condition Mapping Tool (RCMT). This panel should be of considerable assistance to health care providers in identifying the correct LOINC code for their reports. Laboratories are also required to archive LOINC codes for test results they receive from other laboratories to which they have referred specimens and, similarly, referral laboratories should provide their clients with LOINC codes when sending results.

> **EXAMPLE:** The complete blood count (CBC) laboratory test of blood (without differential) is assigned LOINC code 24317-0.

National Drug Codes (NDC)

The *National Drug Codes* (NDC) is published by a variety of vendors, and the coding system is in the public domain. It is managed by the Food and Drug Administration (FDA) and was originally established as part of an out-of-hospital drug reimbursement program under Medicare Services as a universal product identifier for human drugs. The current edition is limited to prescription drugs and a few selected over-the-counter (OTC) products. Pharmacies use NDC to report transactions, and some health care professionals also report NDC on claims.

> **EXAMPLE:** Aspirin tablets, 800 milligrams, is assigned NDC code 64125-*106-01. (There are many different NDC codes for aspirin, depending on dosage, manufacturer, and so on.)

RxNorm

RxNorm provides normalized names for clinical drugs and links its names to many of the drug vocabularies commonly used in pharmacy management and drug interaction software, including those of First Databank, Micromedex, MediSpan, Gold Standard Drug Database, and Multum. By providing links among these vocabularies, RxNorm can mediate messages among systems that do not use the same software and vocabulary.

RxNorm is a normalized naming system for generic and branded drugs, and it is a tool for supporting semantic interoperation among drug terminologies and pharmacy knowledge base systems. The National Library of Medicine (NLM) produces RxNorm. The NLM receives drug names from many data sources, analyzes and processes the data, and outputs the data into RxNorm files in a standard format.

Purpose of RxNorm

RxNorm is a terminology built on and derived from other terminologies. RxNorm reflects and preserves the meanings, drug names, attributes, and relationships from its sources. Hospitals, pharmacies, and other organizations use computer systems to record and process drug information. Because these systems use many different sets of drug names, it can be difficult for one system to communicate with another. To address this challenge, RxNorm provides normalized names and unique identifiers for medicines and drugs. The goal of RxNorm is to allow computer systems to communicate drug-related information efficiently and unambiguously.

Scope of RxNorm

RxNorm contains the names of prescription and many over-the-counter drugs available in the United States.

RxNorm includes generic and branded:

- Clinical drugs (pharmaceutical products given to or taken by a patient with therapeutic or diagnostic intent)

- Drug packs (packs that contain multiple drugs, or drugs designed to be administered in a specified sequence)

- Radiopharmaceuticals, bulk powders, contrast media, food, dietary supplements, and medical devices, such as bandages and crutches, which are out of scope for RxNorm

 Note:

RxNorm also includes the National Drug File—Reference Terminology (NDF-RT), created for the Veterans Health Administration. NDF-RT is a terminology used to code clinical drug properties, including mechanism of action, physiologic effect, and therapeutic category.

EXAMPLE: When Synthroid is entered in the RxNorm database, results display levothyroxine as the ingredient and Levothyroxine Sodium as the precise ingredient. In addition, all possible dosages of the ingredient and brand name are listed under the clinical drug component, branded drug component, clinical drug or pack, and branded drug or pack. Oral product or pill is listed below the dose form group, with expanded information listed below the clinical dose form group and branded dose form group.

Unified Medical Language System (UMLS)

The **Unified Medical Language System (UMLS)** is a set of files and software that allows many health and biomedical vocabularies and standards to enable interoperability among computer systems. UMLS can be used to enhance or develop applications, including electronic health records, classification tools, dictionaries and language translators. The UMLS is used to link health information, medical terms, drug names, and billing codes across different computer systems.

EXAMPLE 1: UMLS is used to link billing codes, drug names, medical terms, and health information across different computer systems, such as among a patient's health care provider, pharmacy, and third-party payer or patient care coordination among several departments within a hospital.

EXAMPLE 2: UMLS uses include search engine retrieval, data mining, public health statistics reporting, and medical terminology research.

The UMLS contains three tools, called Knowledge Sources, and include the following:

- Metathesaurus (terms and codes from many vocabularies, including CPT, ICD-10-CM, LOINC, MeSH®, RxNorm, and SNOMED CT) (MeSH is the National Library of Medicine's controlled vocabulary thesaurus.)

- Semantic network (broad categories, which are semantic types, and their relationships, which are semantic relations)

- SPECIALIST lexicon and lexical tools (natural language processing tools)

Exercise 1.4 – Other Classification Systems and Databases

Instructions: Match the classification or database description with its name.

_____ **1.** Classifies dental procedures and services

_____ **2.** Classifies health and health-related domains that describe body functions and structures, activities, and participation

_____ **3.** Classifies services not included in the CPT manual to describe the alternative medical service, supply, or therapy provided

_____ **4.** Electronic database and universal standard used to identify medical laboratory observations and for clinical care and management

_____ **5.** Implemented in 2001 to classify neoplasms

_____ **6.** Links health information, medical terms, drug names, and billing codes across different computer systems

_____ **7.** Provides new standardized framework and unique coding structure for assessing, documenting, and classifying home health and ambulatory care

_____ **8.** Represents specific sets of patient characteristics (or case-mix groups) on which payment determinations are made under several prospective payment systems

_____ **9.** Standard classification of mental disorders used by mental health professionals in the United States

_____ **10.** Allows computer systems to communicate drug-related information efficiently and unambiguously

a. ABC codes
b. CCC
c. CDT
d. DSM
e. HIPPS
f. ICD-O-3
g. ICF
h. LOINC
i. RxNorm
j. UMLS

Documentation as Basis for Coding

Health care providers are responsible for documenting and authenticating legible, complete, and timely patient records in accordance with federal regulations (e.g., Medicare CoP) and accrediting agency standards (e.g., The Joint Commission). The provider is also responsible for correcting or altering errors in patient record documentation.

A **patient record** (or **medical record**) is the business record for a patient encounter (inpatient or out-patient) that documents health care services provided to a patient. It stores patient demographic data and documentation that supports diagnoses, and justifies treatment. It also contains the results of treatment provided. (**Demographic data** are patient identification information that is collected according to facility policy and includes information such as the patient's name, date of birth, and mother's maiden name.) The primary purpose of the record is to provide for **continuity of care**, which involves documenting patient care services so that others who treat the patient have a source of information on which to base additional care and treatment. The record also serves as a communication tool for physicians and other patient care professionals. It assists in planning individual patient care and documenting a patient's illness and treatment. Secondary purposes of the record do not relate directly to patient care and include:

- Evaluating the quality of patient care
- Providing data for use in clinical research, epidemiology studies, education, public policy making, facilities planning, and health care statistics

- Providing information to third-party payers for reimbursement

- Serving the medicolegal interests of the patient, facility, and providers of care

Documentation includes dictated and transcribed, keyboarded or handwritten, and computer-generated notes and reports recorded in the patient's records by a health care professional. Documentation must be dated and authenticated (with a legible signature or electronic authentication).

In a teaching hospital, documentation must identify what service was furnished, how the teaching physician participated in providing the service, and whether the teaching physician was physically present when care was provided. A **teaching hospital** is engaged in an approved graduate medical education (GME) residency program in medicine, osteopathy, dentistry, or podiatry. A **teaching physician** is a physician (other than another resident physician) who supervises residents during patient care. A **resident physician** is an individual who participates in an approved GME program. A **hospitalist** is a physician who provides care for hospital inpatients. They are often internists (e.g., internal medicine specialists) who handle a patient's entire admission process, including examining the patient, reviewing patient history and medications, writing admission orders, counseling the patient, and performing other tasks that would have required the primary care physician to travel to the hospital to coordinate the inpatient admission. Similar to the concept of emergency physicians practicing in the hospital's emergency department, hospitalists are based in the hospital and provide inpatient care. Thus, their practice is location-based instead of organ-centered (e.g., neurology) or age-centered (e.g., gerontology).

Medical Necessity

Documentation in the patient record serves as the basis for coding. The information in the record must support codes submitted on claims for third-party payer reimbursement processing. The patient's diagnosis must also justify diagnostic and therapeutic procedures or services provided. This is called **medical necessity** and requires providers to document services or supplies that are proper and needed for the diagnosis or treatment of a medical condition; provided for the diagnosis, direct care, and treatment of a medical condition; consistent with standards of good medical practice in the local area; and not mainly for the convenience of the physician or health care facility.

It is important to remember the familiar phrase, "If it wasn't documented, it wasn't done." The patient record serves as a medicolegal document and a business record. If a provider performs a service but does not document it, the patient (or third-party payer) can refuse to pay for that service, resulting in lost revenue for the provider. In addition, because the patient record serves as an excellent defense of the quality of care administered to a patient, missing documentation can result in problems if the record has to be admitted as evidence in a court of law.

EXAMPLE OF MISSING PATIENT RECORD DOCUMENTATION: A representative from XYZ Insurance Company reviewed 100 outpatient claims submitted by the Medical Center to ensure that all services billed were documented in the patient records. Upon reconciliation of claims with patient record documentation, the representative denied payment for 13 services (totaling $14,000) because reports of the services billed were not found in the patient records. The facility must pay back the $14,000 it received from the payer as reimbursement for the claims submitted.

EXAMPLE OF MEDICAL NECESSITY: The patient underwent an x-ray of his right knee, and the provider documented "severe right shoulder pain" in the record. The coder assigned a CPT code to the "right knee x-ray" and an ICD code to the "right shoulder pain." In this example, the third-party payer will deny reimbursement for the submitted claim because the *reason* for the x-ray (shoulder pain) does not match the *type* of x-ray performed. For medical necessity, the provider should have documented a diagnosis such as "right knee pain."

Patient Record Formats

Health care facilities and physicians' offices usually maintain either manual or automated records, and sometimes maintain a hybrid record. A **manual record** is paper-based, while an **automated record** uses computer technology. A **hybrid record** consists of both paper-based and computer-generated documents, which means the facility or office creates and stores some patient reports as paper-based records (e.g., handwritten progress notes, physician orders, and graphic charts) and some documents using a computer (e.g., transcribed reports and automated laboratory results). A variety of formats are used to maintain manual records, which include the source-oriented record (SOR), problem-oriented record (POR), and integrated record. Automated record formats include the electronic health record (EHR) (or computer-based patient record, CPR), electronic medical record (EMR), and optical disk imaging. Hybrid records use a combination format, such as the POR for paper-based reports and EMR for computer-stored reports.

 Note:

True EHRs are generated by multiple providers using specialized software, and results are stored electronically in a format that is easily retrievable and viewable by users.

Manual Record Formats

Source-oriented record (SOR) (or **sectionalized record**) reports are organized according to documentation (or data) source (e.g., ancillary, medical, and nursing). Each documentation (or data) source is located in a labeled section.

The **problem-oriented record (POR)** systematic method of documentation consists of four components:

- Database
- Problem list
- Initial plan
- Progress notes

The POR **database** contains patient information collected on each patient, including the following:

- Chief complaint
- Present conditions and diagnoses
- Social data
- Past, personal, medical, and social history
- Review of systems
- Physical examination
- Baseline laboratory data

The POR **problem list** serves as a table of contents for the patient record because it is filed at the beginning of the record and contains a numbered list of the patient's problems, which helps to index documentation throughout the record. The POR **initial plan** contains the strategy for managing patient care and any actions taken to investigate the patient's condition and to treat and educate the patient. The initial plan consists of three categories:

- **Diagnostic/management plans**: Plans to learn more about the patient's condition and the management of the conditions.
- **Therapeutic plans**: Specific medications, goals, procedures, therapies, and treatments used to treat the patient.
- **Patient education plans**: Plans to educate the patient about conditions for which the patient is being treated.

The POR **progress notes** are documented for each problem assigned to the patient, using the SOAP structure:

- **Subjective (S)**: Patient's statement about how he or she feels, including symptomatic information (e.g., "I have a headache.").
- **Objective (O)**: Observations about the patient, such as physical findings, or lab or x-ray results (e.g., chest x-ray negative).
- **Assessment (A)**: Judgment, opinion, or evaluation made by the health care provider (e.g., acute headache).
- **Plan (P)**: Diagnostic, therapeutic, and education plans to resolve the problems (e.g., patient to take Tylenol as needed for pain).

A **discharge note** is documented in the progress notes section of the POR to summarize the patient's care, treatment, response to care, and condition on discharge—documentation of all problems is included. A **transfer note** is documented when a patient is being transferred to another facility. It summarizes the reason for admission, current diagnoses and medical information, and reason for transfer.

Integrated record reports are arranged in strict chronological date order (or in reverse date order), which allows for observation of how the patient is progressing (e.g., responds to treatment) based on test results. Many facilities integrate only physician and ancillary services (e.g., physical therapy) progress notes, which require entries to be identified by appropriate authentication (e.g., complete signature of the professional documenting the note as Mary Smith, RRT, registered respiratory therapist).

Automated Record Formats

The **electronic health record (EHR)** is a collection of patient information documented by a number of providers at different facilities regarding one patient. It is a multidisciplinary (many specialties) and multienterprise (many facilities) approach to record keeping. The EHR provides access to complete and accurate health problems, status, and treatment data; it contains alerts (e.g., of drug interaction) and reminders (e.g., prescription renewal notice) for health care providers. According to the *Journal of Contemporary Dental Practice*, February 15, 2002, some professionals prefer to "use *electronic* instead of the earlier term *computer-based* because *electronic* better describes the medium in which the patient record is managed."

The **electronic medical record (EMR)** is created on a computer, using a keyboard, a mouse, an optical pen device, a voice-recognition system, a scanner, or a touch screen. Records are created using vendor software, which also assists in provider decision making (e.g., alerts, reminders, clinical decision support systems, and links to medical knowledge). Numerous vendors offer EMR software, mostly to physician office practices that require practice management solutions (e.g., appointment scheduling, claims processing, clinical notes, patient registration).

Optical disk imaging (or **document imaging**) provides an alternative to traditional microfilm or remote (off-site) storage systems because patient records are converted to an electronic image and saved on storage media (e.g., optical disks). Optical disk imaging uses laser technology to create the image, and a **scanner** is used to capture paper record images onto the storage media (e.g., optical disk). It allows for rapid automated retrieval of records. Although labor-intensive, optical disk imaging serves as an interim measure for facilities that want to move away from paper-based medical records toward development of an EHR. For optical disk imaging, the paper record must be prepared for scanning (e.g., removal of staples and separation of pages) so documents can pass through the scanner properly. The paper record is inserted into a document feeder (similar to that on a copy machine) that is attached to the scanner, and each report is pulled through the scanner so the image is saved to optical disk. Each scanned page is **indexed**, which means it is identified according to a unique identification number (e.g., patient record number). A unique feature is that documents for the same patient do *not* have to be scanned at the same time. Because each scanned page is indexed, the complete patient record can be retrieved even when a patient's reports are scanned at a later time. A **jukebox** stores large numbers of optical disks, resulting in huge storage capabilities (e.g., gigabytes of data). Optical disk imaging systems can also be networked, or connected, to other computer equipment in the facility, such as transcription systems and diagnostic imaging systems, which allows other data and documents to be added to the optical disk imaging system, thus creating a complete patient record.

Documentation Cloning Is an EMR/EHR Concern

Office of Inspector General Work Plan, Fiscal Year 2012. (Permission to reuse in accordance with http://oig.hhs .gov content reuse and linking policy.)

Medicare administrative contractors have noted an increased frequency of electronic medical records (EMRs) and electronic health records (EHRs) that contain identical documentation across services. This may be the result of *documentation cloning*, which involves using the EMR/EHR to bring information from previous patient encounters forward to the current encounter without updating that information. As a result, questions about the validity of services have been raised and they are supported by Office of Inspector General (OIG) statistics that indicate Medicare paid $25 billion (or 19 percent of all Medicare Part B payments) for evaluation and management services in 2009. The OIG work plan includes the review of multiple E/M services for the same providers and Medicare beneficiaries to identify EMR/EHR documentation practices associated with potentially improper payments.

Exercise 1.5 – Documentation as Basis for Coding

Instructions: If the statement in the first column indicates a primary purpose of the patient record, enter *a*. If the statement indicates a secondary purpose of the patient record, enter *b*.

_____ **1.** Continuity of patient care

_____ **2.** Evaluating quality of patient care

_____ **3.** Providing data for use in clinical research

_____ **4.** Serving medicolegal interests of patient, facility, and providers

_____ **5.** Submitting information to payers for reimbursement

a. Primary purpose

b. Secondary purpose

Health Data Collection

Health data collection is performed by health care facilities and providers for the purpose of administrative planning, submitting statistics to state and federal government agencies (and other organizations), and reporting health claims data to third-party payers.

Reporting Hospital Data

Hospitals and other health care facilities use **automated case abstracting software** to collect and report inpatient and outpatient data for statistical analysis and reimbursement purposes. Data are entered in an abstracting software program (Figure 1-4), and the facility's billing department imports it to the **UB-04** (or **CMS-1450**) claim (Figure 1-5) for submission to third-party payers. The facility's information technology department generates reports (e.g., procedure index) (Figure 1-6), which are used for statistical analysis. The UB-04 (or CMS-1450) is a standard claim (uniform bill) submitted by health care institutions to payers for inpatient and outpatient services.

Figure 1-4 Sample data entry screen with ICD-10-CM and ICD-10-PCS codes and descriptions

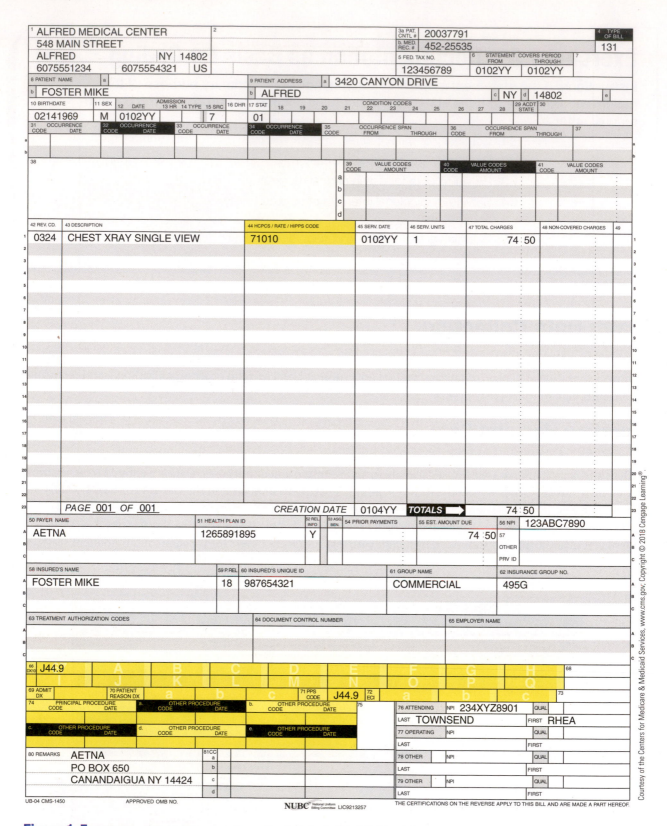

Figure 1-5 UB-04 claim with sample patient data in highlighted form locators that also contain ICD-10-CM and CPT codes

```
                    Alfred State Medical Center

                         Procedure Index

Reporting Period      0301YYYY-0301YYYY           Date Prepared   03-02-YYYY

                                                          Page    1 of 5


  Principal       Secondary        Attending      Age    Gender    Payer    Patient
  Procedure       Procedures       Physician                                Number

CLOSED BIOPSY OF BRAIN
00B03ZX                              248          42      F         01       562359

CRANIOTOMY
0N800ZZ                             235          56      F         03       231587

0N800ZZ                             326          27      M         02       239854

0N800ZZ                             236          08      F         05       562198

0N800ZZ                             236          88      M         05       615789

DEBRIDEMENT OF SKULL
0NB00ZZ                             326          43      M         03       653218
```

Figure 1-6 Sample procedure index containing ICD-10-PCS codes

(The UB-04 is based on the UB-92, which was developed in 1992 and discontinued in 2007. There was also a UB-82, which was developed in 1982 and discontinued when the UB-92 was implemented.)

EXAMPLE: Procedure indexes, profit and loss statements, and patient satisfaction surveys are used by health care planning and forecasting committees to determine the types of procedures performed at their facilities and the costs associated with providing such services. As a result of report analysis, procedures that contribute to a facility's profits and losses can be determined; in addition, some services may be expanded while others are eliminated.

Reporting Physician Office Data

Computerized physicians' offices use medical management software to enter claims data and either electronically submit CMS-1500 claims data to third-party payers or print paper-based CMS-1500 claims that are mailed or faxed to clearinghouses or payers for processing. The **CMS-1500** is a standard claim submitted by physicians' offices to third-party payers. **Medical management software** (e.g., MediSoft, The Medical Manager) is a combination of practice management and medical billing software that automates the daily workflow and procedures of a physician's office or clinic. The software automates the following functions:

- Appointment scheduling (e.g., initial and follow-up appointments) (Figure 1-7)
- Claims processing (e.g., CMS-1500 claims processing) (Figure 1-8)
- Patient invoicing (e.g., automated billing) (Figure 1-9)
- Patient management (e.g., patient registration) (Figure 1-10)
- Report generation (e.g., accounts receivable aging report) (Figure 1-11)

Medical assistants and insurance specialists use medical management software to collect data for reimbursement purposes by locating patient information, inputting ICD-10-CM, ICD-10-PCS, CPT, and HCPCS level II codes for

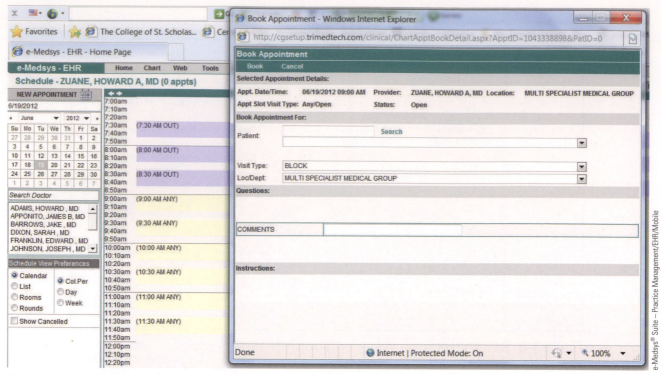

Figure 1-7 Appointment schedule screens in e-Medsys®

Figure 1-8 Claims processing screen

diagnoses and procedures/services, and generating and processing CMS-1500 claims. Medical management software generates claims for a variety of medical specialties, and claims can be printed and mailed to clearinghouses, TPAs, or third-party payers for processing. The software also allows for submission of HIPAA-compliant electronic claims to clearinghouses, TPAs, or third-party payers.

Figure 1-9 Billing screen

Figure 1-10 Patient registration screen in e-Medsys®

When records are reviewed to select ICD-10-CM, ICD-10-PCS, CPT, and HCPCS level II codes for reporting to third-party payers, documentation in the patient record serves as the basis for coding. Coders are responsible for reviewing patient records to select the appropriate diagnoses and procedures/services to which codes are assigned. Information in the record must support the codes submitted on claims for third-party payer reimbursement

Payer 03/19/YYYY						Dates of Service: 03/01/YYYY to 03/10/YYYY		
	Claim ID	Last Bill	Current	31 to 60	61 to 90	91 to 120		>120
AETNA								
Adams, Cynthia 800123456	243567	03/05/YYYY	160.00	0.00	0.00	0.00		0.00
AETNA			160.00	0.00	0.00	0.00		0.00
BLUE CROSS BLUE SHIELD								
Bennett, John 800234567	345678	03/01/YYYY	160.00	0.00	0.00	0.00		0.00
Bennett, John 800234567	345678	03/01/YYYY	240.00	0.00	0.00	0.00		0.00
Bennett, John 800234567	345678	03/10/YYYY	80.00	0.00	0.00	0.00		0.00
Bennett, John 800234567	345678	03/04/YYYY	113.00	0.00	0.00	0.00		0.00
BLUE CROSS BLUE SHIELD			593.00	0.00	0.00	0.00		0.00
MEDICAID								
Clark, Matthew 800345678	456789	03/03/YYYY	1,580.00	0.00	0.00	0.00		0.00
MEDICAID			1,580.00	0.00	0.00	0.00		0.00

Current	31 to 60	61 to 90	91 to 120	>120	Grand Total
2,393.000	0.00	0.00	0.00	0.00	2,393.00
100.00%	0.00%	0.00%	0.00%	0.00%	

Figure 1-11 Accounts receivable aging report

processing. The patient's diagnosis must justify diagnostic or therapeutic procedures or services provided (medical necessity), and the provider must document services or supplies that:

- are proper and needed for the diagnosis or treatment of a medical condition;
- are provided for the diagnosis, direct care, and treatment of a medical condition;
- meet the standards of good medical practice in the local area; and
- are not mainly for the convenience of the physician or health care facility.

Claims can be denied if the medical necessity of procedures or services is not established. Each procedure or service reported on the CMS-1500 claim must be linked to a condition that justifies the necessity for performing that procedure or providing that service. If the procedures or services delivered are determined to be unreasonable and unnecessary, the claim is denied. On the UB-04 claim, procedures/services are not linked; however, payers often request copies of patient records to review documentation to verify diagnoses, procedures, and services reported on the claim.

Exercise 1.6 – Health Data Collection

Instructions: Complete each statement.

1. Appointment scheduling and claims processing are processes associated with medical _____ software.
2. Hospital coders and abstractors use automated case _____ software to collect and report inpatient and outpatient data for statistical analysis and reimbursement purposes.
3. Physicians' offices submit data to third-party payers on the _____ claim.
4. Hospitals submit data to third-party payers on the _____ claim.
5. Claims are denied if _____ necessity of procedures or services is not established.

Summary

A coder is expected to master the use of coding systems, coding principles and rules, government regulations, and third-party payer requirements to ensure that all diagnoses, services, and procedures documented in patient records are accurately coded for reimbursement, research, and statistical purposes. To prepare for entry into the profession, students are encouraged to join a professional association. They usually pay a reduced membership fee and receive most of the same benefits as active members. The benefits of joining a professional association include eligibility for scholarships and grants, opportunity to network with members, free publications, reduced certification exam fees, and website access for members only.

Coding systems and medical nomenclatures are used by health care facilities, health care providers, and third-party payers to collect, store, and process data for a variety of purposes. A coding system organizes a medical nomenclature according to similar conditions, diseases, procedures, and services; it contains codes for each. A medical nomenclature is a vocabulary of clinical and medical terms used by health care providers to document patient care. Codes include numeric and alphanumeric characters that are reported to health plans for health care reimbursement and to external agencies for data collection and internally for education and research. Coding is the assignment of codes to diagnoses, services, and procedures based on patient record documentation.

Health care providers are responsible for documenting and authenticating legible, complete, and timely patient records in accordance with federal regulations and accrediting agency standards. The provider is also responsible for correcting or altering errors in patient record documentation. Health data collection is performed by health care facilities to do administrative planning, to submit statistics to state and federal government agencies, and to report health claims data to third-party payers for reimbursement purposes.

Internet Links

Alternate Billing Codes (ABC codes) Go to: *www.abccodes.com*, click on the Why ABC Codes link.

AHA Central Office Go to: *www.ahacentraloffice.org* to review resources available at the AHA Central Office website. The American Hospital Association's (AHA) Central Office serves as the official U.S. clearinghouse for proper use of ICD-10-CM, ICD-10-PCS, and HCPCS level II codes for hospitals, physicians, and other health professionals.

American Academy of Professional Coders (AAPC): *www.aapc.com*

American Association of Medical Assistants (AAMA): *www.aama-ntl.org*

American Health Information Management Association (AHIMA): *www.ahima.org*

American Institute for Chartered Property Casualty Underwriter and Insurance Institute of America (AICPCU/IIA): *www.aicpcu.org*

American Medical Billing Association (AMBA): Go to *www.ambanet.net* and click on the American Medical Billing Association Main Website link.

American Medical Technologists (AMT): *www.americanmedtech.org*

Clinical Care Classification (CCC): *www.sabacare.com*

Current Dental Terminology (CDT): Go to *www.ada.org*, click on the Publications link, and then click on the CDT: Code on Dental Procedures and Nomenclature link.

Diagnostic and Statistical Manual of Mental Disorders (DSM): Go to *www.dsm5.org*.

Health Insurance Prospective Payment System (HIPPS) Rate Codes: Go to *www.cms.gov*, click on the Medicare link, locate the Medicare Fee-for-Service Payment heading, click on the Prospective Payment Systems - General Information link, and click on the HIPPS Codes link.

International Classification of Diseases for Oncology (ICD-O-3): Go to *www.who.int*, click on the Programmes link, click on the Classifications link, click on the International Classifications of Diseases (ICD) link, and scroll down and click on the International Classification of Diseases for Oncology, 3rd Edition (ICD-O-3) link, which is located below the Derived Classifications heading.

International Classification of Functioning, Disability and Health (ICF): Go to *www.who.int*, click on the Programmes link, and scroll down and click on the International Classification of Functioning, Disability and Health (ICF) link.

Medical Association of Billers (MAB): *www.physicianswebsites.com*

National Drug Codes (NDC): Go to *www.fda.gov*, click on the Drugs tab, and click on National Drug Code Directory link (located in the Spotlight box).

National Cancer Institute's Surveillance, Epidemiology and End Result (SEER) Program: Go to *training.seer.cancer.gov*, and click on the Archived Modules link to locate the free ICD-O-3 module.

PlatoCode: Go to *www.platocode.com* to learn more about computer assisted coding (CAC).

RxNorm: Go to *www.nlm.nih.gov*, and enter RxNorm in the Search box.

UMLS: Go to *www.nlm.nih.gov*, and enter UMLS in the Search box.

Study Checklist

- ❏ Read this textbook chapter and highlight key concepts.
- ❏ Create an index card for each key term.
- ❏ Access the chapter Internet links to learn more about concepts.
- ❏ Complete the chapter exercises and review, verifying answers with your instructor.
- ❏ Complete Workbook chapter, verifying answers with your instructor.
- ❏ Go to *www.cengagebrain.com* to access the Student Companion Web Site. Login instructions are located in this textbook's Preface.
- ❏ Form a study group with classmates to discuss chapter concepts in preparation for an exam.

Review

Multiple Choice

Instructions: Circle the most appropriate response.

1. The Health Insurance Portability and Accountability Act of 1996 (HIPAA) requires _____ types of code sets to be adopted for the purpose of encoding data elements.
   - a. two
   - b. three
   - c. four
   - d. five

2. Which is considered to be a small code set according to HIPAA?
   - a. Actions taken to prevent, diagnose, treat, and manage diseases and injuries
   - b. Causes of injury, disease, impairment, or other health-related problems
   - c. Diseases, injuries, impairments, and other health-related problems
   - d. Race, ethnicity, type of facility, and type of unit

3. Which is a code set adopted by HIPAA for use by clearinghouses, health plans, and providers?
   - a. ABC codes
   - b. CMIT
   - c. NDC
   - d. SNOMED

4. The purpose of adopting standard code sets was to:
   a. establish a medical nomenclature to standardize HIPAA data submissions.
   b. improve data quality and simplify claims submission for providers.
   c. increase costs associated with processing health insurance claims.
   d. regulate health care clearinghouses and third-party administrators.

5. According to HIPAA, health plans that do not accept standard code sets are required to modify their systems to accept all valid codes or to contract with a(n):
   a. electronic data interchange.
   b. health care clearinghouse.
   c. insurance company.
   d. third-party administrator.

6. Which is a vocabulary of clinical terms used by health care providers to document patient care?
   a. Classification system
   b. Demographic data
   c. Medical nomenclature
   d. *Nosologia Methodica*

7. The requirement that the patient's diagnoses justify diagnostic and/or therapeutic procedures or services provided is called:
   a. continuity of care.
   b. facilities planning.
   c. medical necessity.
   d. policy making.

8. Which is the business record for a patient encounter (inpatient or outpatient) that documents health care services provided to a patient?
   a. Demographic data
   b. Financial record
   c. Jukebox
   d. Medical record

9. The primary purpose of the record is _____, which involves documenting patient care services so that others who treat the patient have a source of information on which to base additional care and treatment.
   a. continuity of care
   b. medical necessity
   c. medicolegal
   d. quality of care

10. Which is a secondary purpose of the medical record that does not relate directly to patient care?
    a. Clinical research
    b. Continuity of care
    c. Discharge note
    d. Hybrid record

11. Which type of medical record format stores documentation in labeled sections?
    a. Integrated record
    b. Problem-oriented record
    c. Source-oriented record
    d. SOAP notes

12. A progress note contains diagnoses of muscle strain and weakness. This statement would be located in the _____ portion of the POR progress note.
    a. Assessment   b. Objective   c. Plan   d. Subjective

13. A progress note contains documentation that the patient is to be followed up with in the physician's office two weeks after discharge from the hospital. This statement would be located in the _____ portion of the POR progress note.
    a. Assessment   b. Objective   c. Plan   d. Subjective

14. A progress note contains documentation that the EKG showed elevated T-wave changes. This statement would be located in the _____ portion of the POR progress note.
    a. Assessment   b. Objective   c. Plan   d. Subjective

15. Which is documented in the progress note section of the POR to summarize the patient's care, treatment, response to care, and condition on discharge?
    a. Demographic data
    b. Discharge note
    c. Medical necessity
    d. Transfer note

16. Which is used to capture paper record images onto the storage media?
    a. EHR
    b. EMR
    c. Jukebox
    d. Scanner

17. To provide the maximum benefit to students, internships are typically _____ work experiences that are arranged by academic program faculty.
    a. elective
    b. nonpaid
    c. optional
    d. voluntary

18. To whom does the student report at the professional practice experience (or internship) site?
    a. Supervisor
    b. Patient
    c. Physician
    d. Program faculty

19. Which is a benefit of joining a professional association?
    a. Free certification examination fees
    b. Opportunities to network with other members
    c. Reduced benefits as compared with nonmembers
    d. Website-only access to professional journals

20. Which processes health care claims and performs related business functions for a health plan?
    a. Health care clearinghouse
    b. Health care provider
    c. Third-party administrator
    d. Third-party payer

PART II

ICD-10-CM and ICD-10-PCS Coding Systems

Part II of *3-2-1 Code It!* contains the following individual chapters that cover ICD-10-CM and ICD-10-PCS coding.

Introduction to ICD-10-CM and ICD-10-PCS Coding

Chapter Outline

Overview of ICD-10-CM and ICD-10-PCS

ICD-10-CM Tabular List of Diseases and Injuries

ICD-10-CM Index to Diseases and Injuries

ICD-10-PCS Index and Tables

Official ICD-10-CM and ICD-10-PCS Guidelines for Coding and Reporting

ICD-9-CM Legacy Coding System

Chapter Objectives

At the conclusion of this chapter, the student should be able to:

- Define key terms.
- Explain the organization of the ICD-10-CM Tabular List of Diseases and Injuries and Index to Diseases and Injuries.
- Explain the organization of the ICD-10-PCS Index and Tables.
- List and describe the official guidelines for coding and reporting ICD-10-CM and ICD-10-PCS codes.
- Interpret ICD-10-CM and ICD-10-PCS guidelines for coding and reporting.
- Apply guidelines for coding and reporting when assigning ICD-10-CM and ICD-10-PCS codes.
- Describe ICD-9-CM as a legacy coding system, including the use of general equivalence mappings (GEMs).

Key Terms

category

cooperating parties for the ICD-10-CM/PCS

encoder

encounter

essential modifier

etiology

general equivalence mapping (GEM)

ICD-10 Coordination and Maintenance Committee

Index to Diseases and Injuries

International Classification of Diseases (ICD)

legacy classification system

legacy coding system

main term

Medicare Prescription Drug, Improvement, and Modernization Act (MMA)

morbidity

mortality

nonessential modifier

Official ICD-10-CM Guidelines for Coding and Reporting

Official ICD-10-PCS Guidelines for Coding and Reporting

placeholder

subcategory

subterm

Tabular List of Diseases and Injuries

Introduction

There are two related classifications of diseases with similar titles. The ***International Classification of Diseases (ICD)*** is published by the World Health Organization (WHO) and is used to classify **mortality** (death) data from death certificates. WHO published the tenth revision of ICD in 1994 with a new name, *International Statistical Classification of Diseases and Related Health Problems*, and reorganized its 3-digit categories. (Although the name of the publication was changed, the familiar abbreviation ICD was kept.)

The *International Classification of Diseases, Tenth Revision, Clinical Modification* (ICD-10-CM) was developed in the United States and is used to code and classify **morbidity** (disease) data from inpatient and outpatient records, including physician office records. ICD-10-CM is a closed classification system that is used in the United States to classify diagnoses, which means that ICD-10-CM provides just one place to classify each condition.

All health care settings use ICD-10-CM to report diagnoses. The *International Classification of Diseases, Tenth Revision, Procedure Classification System* (ICD-10-PCS) is used to code and classify procedure data from hospital inpatient records only. (ICD-10-CM and ICD-10-PCS are abbreviated as ICD-10-CM/PCS.)

> **Note:**
>
> Provider offices and health care facilities (e.g., hospitals) use ICD-10-CM to code diagnoses. Hospitals use ICD-10-PCS to code inpatient procedures. (Provider offices and outpatient health care settings use CPT and HCPCS level II to code procedures and services.) ICD-10-CM and ICD-10-PCS are abbreviated as ICD-10-CM/PCS.

Overview of ICD-10-CM and ICD-10-PCS

ICD-10-CM is a clinical modification of WHO's *International Classification of Diseases, Tenth Revision* (ICD-10). The term *clinical* is used to emphasize the modification's intent. This means that the coding system serves as a useful tool in the classification of morbidity data for indexing of patient records, reviewing quality of care, and compiling basic health statistics. Used to describe the clinical picture of the patient, ICD-10-CM and ICD-10-PCS codes are more precise than those needed for statistical groupings and trends analysis.

ICD-10-CM is divided into two main parts:

- Index to Diseases and Injuries, which is an alphabetical list of terms and corresponding codes, and includes a Neoplasm Table, Table of Drugs and Chemicals, and an Index to External Causes
- Tabular List of Diseases and Injuries, which is a sequential, alphanumeric list of codes divided into chapters based on body system or condition

ICD-10-PCS is divided into two main parts:

- Index, which is an alphabetic list of procedures according to general type of procedure (e.g., resection), or a more commonly used term (e.g., appendectomy), and includes the first three or four values of the code (or directs the user to see another term)
- Tables, which are organized according to sections that contain rows that specify valid combinations of code values

ICD-10-CM and ICD-10-PCS (ICD-10-CM/PCS)

The *International Classification of Diseases, Tenth Revision, Clinical Modification* (ICD-10-CM) and the *International Classification of Diseases, Tenth Revision, Procedure Coding System* (ICD-10-PCS) are abbreviated as ICD-10-CM/PCS. This classification system includes many more codes and applies to more users than its predecessor, ICD-9-CM, because it is designed to collect data on every type of health care encounter (e.g., inpatient, outpatient, hospice, home health care, and long-term care). ICD-10-CM/PCS also enhances accurate payment for services rendered

> **Note:**
>
> The Centers for Medicare & Medicaid Services (CMS) shortens the name of the classification systems to *International Classification of Diseases, 10th Edition, Clinical Modification/Procedure Coding System*, abbreviating it as ICD-10-CM/PCS.

and facilitates evaluation of medical processes and outcomes. The term *clinical* emphasizes the modification's intent, which is to:

- Describe the clinical picture of the patient, which means the codes must be more precise than those needed only for statistical groupings and trend analysis.

- Serve as a useful tool in the area of classification of morbidity data for indexing of medical records, medical care review, and ambulatory and other medical care programs, as well as for basic health statistics.

ICD-10-CM is the diagnosis classification system developed by the Centers for Disease Control and Prevention (CDC) for use in *all* U.S. health care treatment settings. ICD-10-CM codes require up to 7 characters, are entirely alphanumeric, and have new coding conventions (e.g., Excludes1 and Excludes2 notes).

ICD-10-CM and ICD-10-PCS (or ICD-10-CM/PCS) incorporate much greater specificity and clinical information, resulting in:

- Decreased need to include supporting documentation with claims

- Enhanced ability to conduct public health surveillance

- Improved ability to measure health care services

- Increased sensitivity when refining grouping and reimbursement methodologies

ICD-10-CM/PCS also includes updated medical terminology and classification of diseases, provides codes to allow comparison of mortality and morbidity data, and provides better data for:

- Conducting research

- Designing payment systems

- Identifying fraud and abuse

- Making clinical decisions

- Measuring care furnished to patients

- Processing claims

- Tracking public health

To prepare for implementation of ICD-10-CM/PCS, health care professionals should assess their coding staff to determine whether they require education and training to:

- Apply anatomy and physiology, medical terminology, pathophysiology, and pharmacology concepts.

- Apply official coding guidelines to assign ICD-10-CM/PCS codes to diagnoses and procedures.

- Effectively communicate with members of the medical staff (e.g., physician query).

- Interpret patient record documentation (e.g., identify conditions associated with medications administered).

- Interpret patient record documentation requirements (e.g., authentication, use of abbreviations).

 ICD-10-PCS is an entirely new procedure classification system developed by the CMS for use in the United States for inpatient hospital settings *only*. ICD-10-PCS uses a multiaxial 7-character alphanumeric code structure (e.g., 047K04Z) that provides a unique

 Note:

The *International Classification of Diseases, Ninth Edition, Clinical Modification (ICD-9-CM)* did not provide the necessary detail about patients' medical conditions or procedures performed on hospitalized inpatients. It could not accurately describe diagnoses or inpatient procedures of care delivered in the 21st century.

Note:

In ICD-10-PCS, *multiaxial* means the codes contain independent characters, with each axis retaining its meaning across broad ranges of codes (to the extent possible). There is no decimal used in ICD-10-PCS codes. The letters I and O are *never* used in ICD-10-PCS because they are too easily confused with the numbers 1 and 0.

code for all substantially different procedures. It also allows new procedures to be easily incorporated as new codes. ICD-10-PCS contains more than 87,000 7-character alphanumeric procedure codes.

ICD-10-CM was expanded to (1) include health-related conditions, (2) provide much greater specificity at the sixth character level, and (3) add a seventh character extension (for some codes). Assigning the sixth and seventh characters when available for ICD-10-CM codes is mandatory because they report information documented in the patient record.

EXAMPLE 1: The diagnosis is stage III pressure ulcer of the right lower back. In ICD-10-CM, combination code L89.133 is reported to classify the condition along with its depth, location, and laterality (e.g., right side).

ICD-10-CM Tabular List of Diseases and Injuries
L89.133 Pressure ulcer of right lower back, stage III
Healing pressure ulcer of right lower back, stage III
Pressure ulcer with full thickness skin loss involving damage or necrosis of subcutaneous tissue, right lower back

EXAMPLE 2: The diagnosis is mechanical breakdown of right femoral arterial graft. In ICD-10-CM, combination code T82.312A is reported, and the right side is classified.

ICD-10-CM Tabular List of Diseases and Injuries		
The appropriate 7th character is to be added to each code from category T82.		
A	initial encounter	
D	subsequent encounter	
S	sequela	
T82.3	Mechanical complication of other vascular grafts	
	T82.31	Breakdown (mechanical) of other vascular grafts
		T82.310 Breakdown (mechanical) of aortic (bifurcation) graft (replacement)
		T82.311 Breakdown (mechanical) of carotid arterial graft (bypass)
		T82.312 Breakdown (mechanical) of femoral arterial graft (bypass)
		T82.318 Breakdown (mechanical) of other vascular grafts
		T82.319 Breakdown (mechanical) of unspecified vascular grafts

Coding Manuals

Many publishers produce their own versions of ICD-10-CM and ICD-10-PCS coding manuals. Companies also publish **encoders**, which automate the coding process. Computerized or web-based software is used instead of coding books, and the coder uses the software's Search feature to locate and verify codes.

Updating ICD-10-CM and ICD-10-PCS **Note:**

The National Center for Health Statistics (NCHS) and the Centers for Medicare & Medicaid Services (CMS) are the U.S. Department of Health & Human Services (DHHS) agencies that comprise the **ICD-10 Coordination and Maintenance Committee**, which is responsible for overseeing all changes and modifications to ICD-10-CM and ICD-10-PCS. The NCHS works with the WHO to coordinate official disease classification activities for ICD-10-CM. Activities include the use, interpretation, and periodic revision of the classification system. CMS is responsible

ICD-10-CM is published as a single-volume coding manual, with the Index to Diseases and Injuries located in front of the Tabular List of Diseases and Injuries. ICD-10-PCS is published as a separate single-volume coding manual, with the Index to Procedures located in front of the Tables.

for annually updating the ICD-10-PCS procedure classification. The Committee also updates the ICD-9-CM and ICD-10-CM/PCS general equivalency mappings (GEMs) for a minimum of three years after the 2014 implementation date for ICD-10-CM and ICD-10-PCS.

The **Medicare Prescription Drug, Improvement, and Modernization Act (MMA)** requires all code sets (e.g., ICD-10-CM, ICD-10-PCS) to be valid at the time services are provided. This means that midyear (April 1) and end-of-year (October 1) coding updates must be implemented immediately so accurate codes are reported on claims. (HIPAA legislation also requires the reporting of codes on health insurance claims.)

It is crucial that updated coding manuals be purchased and billing systems be updated with coding changes so that billing delays (e.g., due to waiting for new coding manuals to arrive) and claims rejections are avoided. If outdated codes are submitted on claims, providers and health care facilities will incur administrative costs associated with resubmitting corrected claims and delayed reimbursement for services provided.

- Coders should consider using updateable coding manuals, which publishers offer as a subscription service. These coding manuals are usually stored in a three-ring binder so that coders can remove outdated pages and add newly printed pages provided by the publisher.

- Another option is to purchase encoder software, which publishers also offer as a subscription service. Coders routinely download the most up-to-date encoder software, which contains edits for new, revised, and discontinued codes. An *encoder* automates the coding process using computerized or web-based software; instead of manually looking up conditions (or procedures) in the coding manual index, the coder uses the software's search feature to locate and verify diagnosis and procedure codes.

- Automating the medical coding process is the goal of *computer-assisted coding (CAC)*, which uses a natural language processing engine to "read" patient records and generate ICD-10-CM, ICD-10-PCS, HCPCS level II, and CPT codes. Because of this process, coders become coding auditors (or coding editors), responsible for ensuring the accuracy of codes reported to payers. (CAC can be compared to speech recognition technology that has transitioned the role of medical transcriptionists in certain fields, such as radiology, to that of medical editors.)

History of the International Classification of Diseases (ICD)

The WHO's original intent for ICD was that it would serve as a statistical tool for the international collection and exchange of mortality (death) data. A subsequent revision was expanded to accommodate data collection for morbidity (disease) statistics. The seventh revision (ICD-7), published by WHO in 1955, was clinically modified for use in the United States after a joint study was conducted to evaluate the efficiency of indexing hospital diseases (cataloging diseases and procedures by code). The study participants included the American Hospital Association (AHA) and the American Association of Medical Record Librarians (AAMRL) (now called the American Health Information Management Association, or AHIMA). Results of that study led to the 1959 publication of the International Classification of Diseases, Adapted for Indexing Hospital Records (ICDA), by the federal Public Health Service. The ICDA uniformly modified ICD-7, and it gave the United States a way to classify patient operations and treatments.

An eighth edition of ICD (ICD-8), published by WHO in 1965, lacked the depth of clinical data required for America's emerging health care delivery system. In 1968, two widely accepted modifications were published in the United States: the Eighth Revision of the International Classification of Diseases, Adapted for Use in the United States (ICDA-8), and the Hospital Adaptation of ICDA (H-ICDA).

History of the International Classification of Diseases (ICD) (*continued*)

Hospitals used either of these two systems until 1979, when ICD-9-CM was implemented. The ninth revision of the ICD (ICD-9), published by WHO in 1975, once again prompted the development of a clinical modification. This time the incentive resulted from a process initiated in 1977 by the National Center for Health Statistics (NCHS) for hospital indexing and the retrieval of case data for clinical studies. After more than 30 years since its adoption in the United States, ICD has proven to be indispensable to anyone interested in payment schedules for the delivery of health care services to patients.

The WHO published ICD-10 in 1994 with a new name (*International Statistical Classification of Diseases and Related Health Problems*) and reorganized its 3-digit categories. Although the title was amended to clarify content and purpose and to reflect development of codes and descriptions beyond diseases and injuries, the familiar abbreviation "ICD" was kept.

ICD-10 contains clinical detail, expands information about previously classified diseases, and classifies diseases discovered since the last revision. ICD-10 also incorporates organizational changes and new features, but its format and conventions remain largely unchanged. ICD-10 chapter titles, organization, and includes notes are similar to ICD-9. The greatest difference is that the new ICD-10 codes are alphanumeric, new excludes1 and excludes2 notes were added, and there is more detail in ICD-10-CM than in ICD-9-CM.

A number of other countries have already adopted ICD-10, including the United Kingdom (1995), France (1997), Australia (1998), Germany (2000), and Canada (2001). ICD-10-CM and ICD-10-PCS provides significant improvements through greater detailed information and the ability to expand in order to capture additional advancements in clinical medicine. The change from ICD-9-CM to the NCHS-developed ICD-10-CM and the CMS-developed ICD-10-PCS (Procedure Coding System) took effect October 1, 2015.

Mandatory Reporting of ICD-10-CM Codes

The Medicare Catastrophic Coverage Act of 1988 mandated the reporting of diagnosis codes on Medicare claims; in subsequent years, private third-party payers adopted similar requirements for claims submission.

Reporting ICD-10-CM codes on submitted claims (Figure 2-1) ensures the medical necessity of procedures and services provided to patients during an encounter. An **encounter** is a face-to-face contact between a patient and

Courtesy of the Centers for Medicare & Medicaid Services, www.cms.gov; Copyright © 2018 Cengage Learning®

Figure 2-1 CMS-1500 claim Blocks 21 (ICD-10-CM codes) and 24F, which illustrate medical necessity of procedures and services a health care provider (e.g., physician, nurse practitioner) who assesses and treats the patient's condition. Medicare defines medical necessity as "the determination that a service or procedure rendered is reasonable and necessary for the diagnosis or treatment of an illness or injury."

Note:

The Administrative Simplification subtitle of the Health Insurance Portability and Accountability Act of 1996 (HIPAA) mandated the adoption of code set standards in the Transactions and Code Sets final rule published in the *Federal Register*. The final rule modifies the standard medical data code sets for coding diagnoses and inpatient hospital procedures by concurrently adopting the *International Classification of Diseases, 10th Revision, Clinical Modification* (ICD-10-CM) for diagnosis coding (including the *Official ICD-10-CM Guidelines for Coding and Reporting*, as maintained and distributed by the U.S. Department of Health and Human Services) and the *International Classification of Diseases, 10th Revision, Procedure Coding System* (ICD-10-PCS) for inpatient hospital procedure coding (including the *Official ICD-10-PCS Guidelines for Coding and Reporting*, as maintained and distributed by the HHS).

Medical Necessity

Today's concept of medical necessity determines the extent to which individuals with health conditions receive health care services. (The concept was introduced in the 1970s when health insurance contracts intended to exclude care, such as voluntary hospitalizations prescribed primarily for the convenience of the provider or patient.) *Medical necessity* is the measure of whether a health care procedure or service is appropriate for the diagnosis and treatment of a condition. This decision-making process is based on the payer's contractual language and the treating provider's documentation. Generally, the following criteria are used to determine medical necessity:

- *Purpose:* The procedure or service is performed to treat a medical condition.

- *Scope:* The most appropriate level of service is provided, taking into consideration potential benefit and harm to the patient.

- *Evidence:* The treatment is known to be effective in improving health outcomes.

- *Value:* The treatment is cost-effective for this condition when compared to alternative treatments, including no treatment.

Note:

Cost-effective does not necessarily mean least expensive.

EXAMPLE: A 70-year-old male patient with type 1 diabetes mellitus is treated at the physician's office for severe wrist pain resulting from a fall. When the physician asks the patient whether he has been regularly taking his insulin and checking his blood glucose levels, the patient says that most of the time he takes his insulin and sometimes he forgets to check his blood glucose levels. The physician orders a blood glucose test to be done in the office, which reveals elevated blood glucose levels. The physician provides counseling and education to the patient about the importance of taking his daily insulin and checking his blood glucose levels. The physician also orders an x-ray of the wrist, which proves to be negative for a fracture. The physician provides the patient with a wrist brace and instructs the patient to follow up in the office within four weeks.

The insurance specialist reports ICD-10-CM codes for type 1 diabetes mellitus and sprained wrist along with CPT and/or HCPCS level II codes for an office visit, blood glucose lab test, and the wrist brace. If the only diagnosis reported on the claim (Figure 2-1) was a sprained wrist, the blood glucose lab test would be rejected for payment by the insurance company as an unnecessary medical procedure.

Exercise 2.1 – Overview of ICD-10-CM and ICD-10-PCS

Instructions: Complete each statement.

1. ICD-10-CM and ICD-10-PCS were adopted in the year _____ to replace ICD-9-CM.

2. The ICD-10 Coordination and _____ Committee is responsible for overseeing all changes to ICD-10-CM and ICD-10-PCS.

3. The U.S. Department of Health & Human Services agencies responsible for overseeing all changes and modifications to ICD-10-CM is _____.

4. The Medicare Prescription Drug, Improvement, and_____ Act (MMA) requires all code sets to be valid at the time services are provided, which means that midyear (April 1) and end-of-year (October 1) coding updates must be implemented immediately so accurate codes are reported on claims.

5. Updateable coding manuals, which publishers offer as an annual _____ service, are popular because coders can remove outdated pages and insert updated pages into the binders.

6. The coding process is automated when computerized or web-based _____ software is used instead of coding books to locate codes manually; the coder uses the software's search feature to locate and verify codes.

7. The reporting of _____ codes on Medicare claims was originally mandated by the Medicare Catastrophic Coverage Act of 1988 while reporting of ICD-10-CM/PCS codes was mandated by HIPAA and the MMA.

8. Reporting ICD-10-CM codes on submitted claims ensures the medical_____ of procedures and services provided to patients during an encounter, which is defined as "the determination that a service or procedure rendered is reasonable and necessary for the diagnosis or treatment of an illness or injury."

9. A patient is seen in the office for the following conditions: chest pain, chronic hypertension, and controlled diabetes mellitus. The provider orders a blood glucose level, chest x-ray, and EKG. For medical necessity, the chest x-ray would be linked to the _____.

10. A patient is seen in the hospital emergency department for treatment of multiple lacerations; the patient also complains of dizziness and a severe headache that is unrelieved by pain medications. The emergency department physician orders a brain scan and performs extensive suturing. For medical necessity, the suturing would be linked to the _____.

ICD-10-CM Tabular List of Diseases and Injuries

The ICD-10-CM **Tabular List of Diseases and Injuries** (Table 2-1) contains 21 chapters. Chapters in ICD-10-CM classify diseases and injuries according to specific body systems as well as **etiology** (cause of disease).

Format and Structure of ICD-10-CM

ICD-10-CM is divided into two main parts:

- Index to Diseases and Injuries, which is an alphabetical list of terms and their corresponding codes (and includes a Neoplasm Table, Table of Drugs and Chemicals, and an Index to External Causes)

Note:

ICD-10, which was created by the WHO, has 22 chapters. ICD-10-CM excludes the ICD-10 chapter entitled *Codes for Special Purposes, U00–U99*.

Note:

ICD-10-PCS Tables are organized into sections (e.g., medical and surgical, obstetrics, imaging), each of which contains a code table. Refer to the *ICD-10-PCS Index and Tables* heading later in this chapter for more information about the organization and structure of the ICD-10-PCS coding system.

Table 2-1 ICD-10-CM Tabular List of Diseases and Injuries

Chapter Number	Range of Codes	Chapter Title
Chapter 1	A00–B99	Certain Infectious and Parasitic Diseases
Chapter 2	C00–D49	Neoplasms
Chapter 3	D50–D89	Diseases of the Blood and Blood-forming Organs and Certain Disorders Involving the Immune Mechanism
Chapter 4	E00–E89	Endocrine, Nutritional, and Metabolic Diseases
Chapter 5	F01–F99	Mental, Behavioral, and Neurodevelopmental Disorders
Chapter 6	G00–G99	Diseases of the Nervous System
Chapter 7	H00–H59	Diseases of the Eye and Adnexa
Chapter 8	H60–H95	Diseases of the Ear and Mastoid Process
Chapter 9	I00–I99	Diseases of the Circulatory System
Chapter 10	J00–J99	Diseases of the Respiratory System
Chapter 11	K00–K95	Diseases of the Digestive System
Chapter 12	L00–L99	Diseases of the Skin and Subcutaneous Tissue
Chapter 13	M00–M99	Diseases of the Musculoskeletal System and Connective Tissue
Chapter 14	N00–N99	Diseases of the Genitourinary System
Chapter 15	O00–O9A	Pregnancy, Childbirth, and the Puerperium
Chapter 16	P00–P96	Certain Conditions Originating in the Perinatal Period
Chapter 17	Q00–Q99	Congenital Malformations, Deformations, and Chromosomal Abnormalities
Chapter 18	R00–R99	Symptoms, Signs, and Abnormal Clinical and Laboratory Findings, Not Elsewhere Classified
Chapter 19	S00–T88	Injury, Poisoning, and Certain Other Consequences of External Causes
Chapter 20	V00–Y99	External Causes of Morbidity
Chapter 21	Z00–Z99	Factors Influencing Health Status and Contact with Health Services

- Tabular List of Diseases and Injuries, which is a sequential, alphanumeric list of codes organized according to chapters based on body system or condition

ICD-10-CM disease and injury codes consist of 3 characters, and most are followed by a decimal point and between 1 and 4 additional characters. (ICD-10-PCS procedure codes contain 7 characters, and there is no decimal point.) The ICD-10-CM Tabular List of Diseases and Injuries is a sequential list of alphanumeric codes contained within chapters that are organized according to body system or condition. The ICD-10-CM Tabular List of Diseases and Injuries (Figure 2-2) uses an indented format for ease of reference and contains category codes, subcategory codes, and codes. Organization of the tabular list includes:

- Major topic headings, which are printed in bold uppercase letters and followed by groups of ICD-10-CM 3-character disease categories within a chapter (e.g., Intestinal Infectious Diseases, A00–A09). *The first character of an ICD-10-CM code is always a letter.*

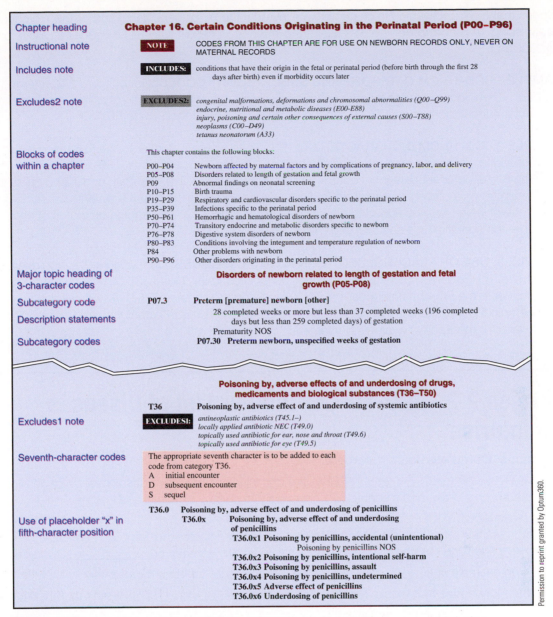

Figure 2-2 Sample page from ICD-10-CM Tabular List of Diseases and Injuries

- Categories, subcategories, and codes, which contain a combination of letters and numbers.

  - A **category** contains 3 characters.

  - A 3-character category code that has no further subdivision is a valid code. For example, code I10 (hypertension) has no further subdivisions and is a valid code.

  - A **subcategory** contains 4, 5, or 6 characters. Subcategory codes that require additional characters are invalid if the 5th, 6th, and/or 7th character(s) are absent.

  - Codes may contain 4, 5, 6, or 7 characters.

    - The final level of subdivision is a code.

    - All codes in the ICD-10-CM tabular list are boldfaced.

  - Codes that have an applicable 7th character are referred to as codes (not subcategories).

○ Codes that have applicable 7th characters are invalid if the "x" placeholder(s) and/or the 7th character are missing. (A **placeholder** involves use of the letter "x" in certain ICD-10-CM codes to allow for future expansion.)

EXAMPLE 1: ICD-10-CM CATEGORY AND SUBCATEGORY CODES: Go to Figure 2-2, refer to the *Disorders of newborn related to length of gestation and fetal growth (P05–P08)* section, and locate the 4-character subcategory code (P07.3) and the 5-character subcategory code P07.30.

EXAMPLE 2: ICD-10-CM 6-CHARACTER CODES: Go to Figure 2-2, refer to the *Poisoning by, adverse effects of and underdosing of drugs, medicaments and biological substances (T36–T50)* section, and locate the 6-character subcategory codes (T36.0x1, T36.0x2, T36.0x3, T36.0x4, and T36.0x5), which also contain "x" as a placeholder to allow for future expansion. Then, locate the seventh characters (A, D, and S), one of which is to be added to each code from category T36 (depending on status of encounter or whether the condition is a sequela) (e.g., T36.0x1A).

EXAMPLE 3: USE OF PLACEHOLDER "X" IN ICD-10-CM CODES: Go to Figure 2-2, and refer to code *T36.0x1 Poisoning by penicillins, accidental (unintentional)*. Code T36.0x1A requires "x" as a placeholder in the 5th-character position. Thus, reporting the code as T36.01A (without the "x" placeholder in the 5th-character position) is an invalid code, which is incorrect if reported and results in a denied claim for third-party payer reimbursement.

Exercise 2.2 – ICD-10-CM Tabular List of Diseases and Injuries

Instructions: Complete each statement.

1. The ICD-10-CM _____ of Diseases and Injuries arranges codes and descriptions in alphanumerical order, and it contains 21 chapters that classify diseases and injuries.

2. The last chapter of ICD-10-CM tabular list codes that are reported for patient encounters when a circumstance other than disease or injury is documented (located in Table 2-1) are called Factors Influencing Health Status and Contact with Health Services or _____ codes.

3. I10 is an example of a _____ code, which has no further subdivisions.

4. Subcategory codes that require additional characters are _____ if the 4th, 5th, 6th, and/or 7th character(s) are absent.

5. The 5th and 6th characters of "x" in code O40.1xx0 are called _____.

ICD-10-CM Index to Diseases and Injuries

The ICD-10-CM **Index to Diseases and Injuries** (Figure 2-3) is an alphabetical list of main terms and their corresponding codes. Main terms are printed in boldfaced type, and subterms and qualifiers are indented below main terms. The ICD-10-CM index is subdivided into two parts (Table 2-2):

- Index to Diseases and Injuries, which includes a Table of Neoplasms and a Table of Drugs and Chemicals
- Index to External Causes of Injuries

Main terms in the Index to Diseases and Injuries are listed in alphabetical order, which means hyphens within main terms are ignored, but a single space within a main term is not ignored. A code listed next to a main term in the index is referred to as a *default code*. The *default code* represents the code for the condition most commonly

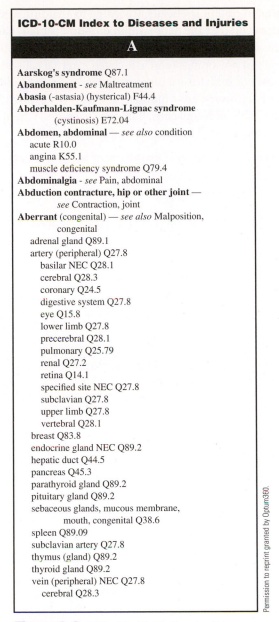

ICD-10-CM Index to Diseases and Injuries

A

Aarskog's syndrome Q87.1
Abandonment - *see* Maltreatment
Abasia (-astasia) (hysterical) F44.4
Abderhalden-Kaufmann-Lignac syndrome
    (cystinosis) E72.04
Abdomen, abdominal — *see also* condition
  acute R10.0
  angina K55.1
  muscle deficiency syndrome Q79.4
Abdominalgia - *see* Pain, abdominal
Abduction contracture, hip or other joint —
    see Contraction, joint
Aberrant (congenital) — *see also* Malposition,
    congenital
  adrenal gland Q89.1
  artery (peripheral) Q27.8
    basilar NEC Q28.1
    cerebral Q28.3
    coronary Q24.5
    digestive system Q27.8
    eye Q15.8
    lower limb Q27.8
    precerebral Q28.1
    pulmonary Q25.79
    renal Q27.2
    retina Q14.1
    specified site NEC Q27.8
    subclavian Q27.8
    upper limb Q27.8
    vertebral Q28.1
  breast Q83.8
  endocrine gland NEC Q89.2
  hepatic duct Q44.5
  pancreas Q45.3
  parathyroid gland Q89.2
  pituitary gland Q89.2
  sebaceous glands, mucous membrane,
    mouth, congenital Q38.6
  spleen Q89.09
  subclavian artery Q27.8
  thymus (gland) Q89.2
  thyroid gland Q89.2
  vein (peripheral) NEC Q27.8
    cerebral Q28.3

Permission to reprint granted by Optum360.

Figure 2-3 ICD-10-CM Index to Diseases
and Injuries (partial)

associated with the main term, or it may represent an unspecified code for the condition. (The Tabular List of Diseases and Injuries must always be referenced so that the most accurate and complete code is assigned.) If a condition is documented in a medical record (for example, appendicitis) without any additional information, such as acute or chronic, the default code should be assigned (after reviewing the Tabular List of Diseases and Injuries).

Table 2-2 ICD-10-CM Index to Diseases and Injuries

Index to Diseases and Injuries (contains two tables)
Table of Neoplasms
Table of Drugs and Chemicals
Index to External Causes of Injuries

The Table of Neoplasms is organized alphabetically according to anatomical site. For each site, there are six possible code numbers according to whether the neoplasm in question is malignant, benign, in situ, of uncertain behavior, or of unspecified nature. The Table of Drugs and Chemicals is an alphabetic index of medicinal, chemical, and biological substances that result in poisonings (and associated external causes) and external causes of adverse effects. The Index to External Causes of Injuries is a separate index (from the Index to Diseases and Injuries) that contains main terms for external causes of morbidities (diseases) (e.g., burns) and injuries (e.g., motorcycle accident) in alphabetic order. (The Table of Neoplasms, Table of Drugs and Chemicals, and Index to External Causes of Injuries are described in more detail in Chapter 3 of this textbook.)

EXAMPLE 1: ICD-10-CM Index to Disease and Injuries main terms are listed in alphabetical order, such as:

```
Catatonic

Cat-scratch
```

The hyphen in "Cat-scratch" is ignored, resulting in sequencing of that main term after "Catatonic".

Bee sting (with allergic or anaphylactic shock)—see Toxicity, venom, arthropod, bee

Beer-drinkers' heart (disease) I42.6

Begbie's disease (exophthalmic goiter)—see Hyperthyroidism, with, goiter

The space between "bee" and "sting" is considered, resulting in that main term being sequenced above "Beer-drinkers' heart (disease)".

EXAMPLE 2: ICD-10-CM Index to Diseases and Injuries numbered cranial nerves are listed in alphabetical order below the main term "Disorder", subterm "nerve", and second qualifier "cranial".

```
Disorder
  nerve G58.9
      cranial G52.9
          eighth — see subcategory H93.3
          eleventh G52.8
          fifth G50.9
          first G52.0
          fourth NEC — see Strabismus, paralytic, fourth nerve
          multiple G52.7
          ninth G52.1
          second NEC — see Disorder, nerve, optic
          seventh NEC G51.8
          sixth NEC — see Strabismus, paralytic, sixth nerve
          specified NEC G52.8
          tenth G52.2
          third NEC — see Strabismus, paralytic, third nerve
          twelfth G52.3
```

Main Terms, Subterms, and Qualifiers

ICD-10-CM and ICD-10-PCS index **main terms** (e.g., conditions) are printed in boldfaced type and are followed by the code. Main terms may or may not be followed by a listing of parenthetical terms, which serve as nonessential modifiers of the main term. **Nonessential modifiers** are qualifying words contained in parentheses after the main term that do not have to be included in the documented diagnostic or procedural statement for the code listed after the parentheses to be assigned.

Subterms (or **essential modifiers**) qualify the main term by listing alternative sites, etiology, or clinical status. A subterm is indented two spaces under the main term. Second qualifiers are indented two spaces under a subterm, and third qualifiers are indented two spaces under a second qualifier (Figure 2-4).

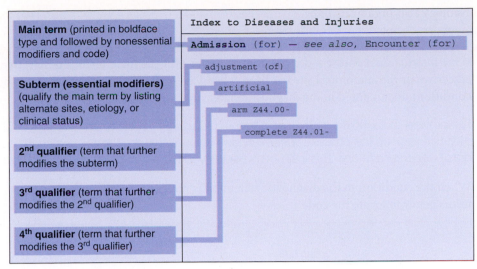

Figure 2-4 Display of main terms, subterms (nonessential modifiers), and qualifiers in the ICD-10-CM Index to Diseases and Injuries

Care must be taken when moving from the bottom of one column to the top of the next column or when turning to the next page of the index. The main term will be repeated and followed by —*continued*. When moving from one column to another, watch carefully to determine whether the subterm has changed or new second or third qualifiers appear.

EXAMPLE 1: CONTINUATION OF TERMS IN ICD-10-CM INDEX TO DISEASES AND INJURIES:
ICD-10-CM Index to Diseases and Injuries entries are organized according to main terms, subterms, second qualifiers, and third qualifiers. Refer to the index entry for "stricture, anus (sphincter) K62.4" and note the indented subterm and qualifiers. Notice that when the main term continues at the top of a column (or on the next page of the Index to Diseases and Injuries), the word —*continued* appears after the main term. The subterms and qualifiers are indented below the main term.

Start of Main Term in Index to Diseases and Injuries		Continuation of Main Term (Next Page)	
Main term:	Stricture *(see also*	Main Term:	Stricture — *continued*
Continuation line:	Stenosis)	Subterm:	urethra (organic) (spasmodic) N35.9
Subterm:	anus (sphincter) K62.4	Second qualifier:	postprocedural
Second qualifier:	congenital Q42.3	Third qualifier:	female N99.12
Third qualifier:	with fistula Q42.2		

Basic Steps for Using the ICD-10-CM Index to Diseases and Injuries

It is important to remember that you should never code directly from the Index to Diseases and Injuries. After locating a code in the index, go to that code in the Tabular List of Diseases and Injuries to find important instructions (e.g., includes notes) and to verify the code selected. Instructions may require the assignment of additional codes or indicate conditions that are classified elsewhere.

STEP 1   Locate the main term in the ICD-10-CM Index to Diseases and Injuries.

Begin the coding process in the Index to Diseases and Injuries by locating the condition's boldfaced main term and then reviewing subterms and qualifiers listed below the main term to locate the proper disease or injury.

EXAMPLE: The underlined terms in the following conditions are main terms:

Allergens <u>investigation</u>

Auditory <u>agnosia</u> secondary to organic lesion

<u>Intussusception</u>, ileocolic

<u>Status</u> (post) angioplasty

STEP 2   If the instructional phrase —*see condition* is found after the main term, a descriptive term (an adjective) or the anatomical site has been referenced instead of the disorder or the disease (the condition) documented in the diagnostic statement.

EXAMPLE: The provider's diagnostic statement is "upper respiratory infection." In the ICD-10-CM Index to Diseases and Injuries, look up the phrase *upper respiratory*. Notice that the term —*see condition* appears next to the phrase *upper respiratory*. This instruction directs you to the condition, which is "infection."

STEP 3   When the condition in the diagnostic statement is not easily found in the index, use the main terms below to locate the code.

Abnormal	Findings	Neoplasm
Anomaly	Foreign body	Obstruction
Complication	Infection	Pregnancy
Delivery	Injury	Sequelae
Disease	Late effect(s)	Syndrome
Disorder	Lesion	Wound

STEP 4   Select and verify the code in the ICD-10-CM Tabular List of Diseases and Injuries.

 Note:

To locate a code that describes an external cause of injury, refer to the separate Index to External Causes, which is located after the Table of Drugs and Chemicals at the back of the ICD-10-CM Index to Diseases and Injuries.

Exercise 2.3 – ICD-10-CM Index to Diseases and Injuries

Instructions: Complete each statement.

1. The alphabetical listing of main terms or conditions printed in boldfaced type that may be expressed as nouns, adjectives, or eponyms is called the ICD-10-CM _____ to Diseases and Injuries.

2. Adverse effects and poisonings associated with medicinal, chemical, and biological substances are located in the ICD-10-CM Table of _____ and Chemicals.

3. Main terms in the ICD-10-CM Index to Diseases and Injuries are listed in _____ order, which means hyphens within main terms are ignored, but a single space within a main term is not ignored.

4. When numerical characters and words appear under a main term or subterm, they are listed in _____ order.

5. Main terms are printed in _____ type and are followed by the code.

6. Qualifying words that are contained in parentheses after the main term, which do not have to be included in the diagnostic statement for the code listed after the parentheses to be assigned, are called _____ modifiers.

Exercise 2.3 (*continued*)

7. Subterms are considered _____ modifiers, and they qualify the main term by listing alternative sites, etiology, or clinical status.

8. The provider documents "congenital asplenia." The main term in the ICD-10-CM index is _____.

9. The provider documents "history of affective psychosis." The main term in the ICD-10-CM index is _____.

10. When the instructional phrase —*see condition* is found after the main term in the index, a descriptive term (an adjective) or the anatomic site has been referenced instead of the disorder or the _____ (the condition) documented in the diagnostic statement.

ICD-10-PCS Index and Tables

The *International Classification of Diseases, 10th Revision, Procedure Coding System (ICD-10-PCS)* is an entirely new procedure classification system developed by the Centers for Medicare & Medicaid Services (CMS) for use in the United States for inpatient hospital settings *only*. ICD-10-PCS uses a multiaxial 7-character alphanumeric code structure (e.g., 047K04Z) that provides a unique code for all substantially different procedures. It also allows new procedures to be easily incorporated as new codes. ICD-10-PCS contains more than 87,000 7-character alphanumeric procedure codes.

 Note:

The letters I and O are *never* used in ICD-10-PCS because they are too easily confused with the numbers 1 and 0. Decimals are also *never* used in ICD-10-PCS codes.

Development of ICD-10-PCS

The development of ICD-10-PCS incorporates four major attributes:

- *Completeness*. There are unique codes for all substantially different procedures.

- *Expandability*. As new procedures are developed, the structure of ICD-10-PCS allows them to be easily incorporated as unique codes.

- *Multiaxial*. ICD-10-PCS codes consist of independent characters, with each individual axis retaining its meaning across broad ranges of codes to the extent possible.

  EXAMPLE: The Medical and Surgical Section axes include:

  1. Section (medical and surgical)

  2. Body system (e.g., heart and great vessels)

  3. Root operation (e.g., dilation)

  4. Body part (e.g., skin)

  5. Approach (e.g., open)

  6. Device (e.g., drainage device)

  7. Qualifier (e.g., anterior)

 Note:

ICD-10-PCS uses a "build-a-code" approach to classify procedures, which means one character is assigned to each of seven axes (multiaxial) (e.g., code 02700ZZ is assigned for open dilation of one coronary artery).

 Note:

ICD-10-PCS requires detailed knowledge of medical terminology and anatomy and physiology, and its unique vocabulary also requires mastery.

However, the Imaging Section axes include:

1. Section (imaging)

2. Body system (e.g., respiratory system)

3. Root type (e.g., fluoroscopy)

4. Body part (e.g., lungs, right)

5. Contrast (e.g., low osmolar)

6. Qualifier (e.g., laser)

7. Qualifier (e.g., intraoperative)

- *Standardized terminology*. ICD-10-PCS includes definitions of the terminology used, and while the meaning of specific words varies in common usage, each term is assigned a specific meaning.

Development of ICD-10-PCS followed the below-listed general principles:

- *Diagnostic information is not included in procedure code descriptions*. Instead, ICD-10-CM diagnosis codes classify diseases, disorders, injuries, signs, symptoms, external causes, and so on.

- *"Not otherwise specified" (NOS) options are not provided*. A minimal level of specificity is required for each component of the procedure.

- *Use of "not elsewhere classified" (NEC) is limited*. ICD-10-PCS specifies all significant components of a procedure, generally eliminating the need for an NEC code option. Some NEC options are included in ICD-10-PCS where necessary (e.g., "other device" because new devices are frequently developed).

- *Level of specificity is enhanced*. All procedures currently performed can be assigned a specific code in ICD-10-PCS. The frequency (or infrequency) with which a procedure is performed is *not* a consideration. Thus, a unique code is classified for each variation of a procedure performed.

Structure of ICD-10-PCS Codes

ICD-10-PCS has a 7-character alphanumeric code structure, and the code assigned is the result of a build-a-code process instead of verifying codes in a tabular list of codes (after locating the procedure name in an index).

- Each character contains up to 34 possible values (because characters in positions 2–7 can have different meanings in different sections).

  EXAMPLE: In the Medical and Surgical Section of ICD-10-PCS, the character in position 1 is the number 0 (for Medical and Surgical Section). The character in position 2 refers to body system (e.g., central nervous system, peripheral nervous system, and so on).

  In the Physical Rehabilitation and Diagnostic Audiology Section, the character in position 1 is the letter F (for Physical Rehabilitation and Diagnostic Audiology Section). The character in position 2 refers to "section qualifier" (e.g., rehabilitation or diagnostic audiology).

- Each value represents a specific option for the general character definition.

 Note:

In ICD-10-PCS, the term "procedure" refers to the complete specification of the 7 characters that comprise a complete code. The first character of the 7-character procedure code always specifies the section. Then, depending on the ICD-10-PCS section in which a procedure is classified, the values of characters 2–7 may vary. However, the values of characters 2–7 within a particular section remain the same.

EXAMPLE: In the Administration Section of ICD-10-PCS, the character in position 2 refers to body system, and it contains just three values:

○ Circulatory system, assigned number 0.

○ Indwelling device, assigned letter C.

○ Physiological systems and anatomical regions, assigned letter E.

- The 10 digits 0–9 and the 24 letters A–H, J–N, and P–Z may be used in each of the 7 characters, depending on the documented procedure. *The letters O and I are not used so as to avoid confusion with the digits 0 and 1.*

- A code is built by selecting a specific value for each of the 7 characters (Table 2-3). Thus, a step-by-step "build-a-code" approach is used when assigning ICD-10-PCS procedure codes. As such, a number or a letter is assigned to *each* of the 7 characters of an ICD-10-PCS code based on documentation of the procedure performed.

ICD-10-PCS procedures are first divided into sections (Table 2-3, column 1), which identify the general type of procedure (e.g., medical and surgical, obstetrics, imaging, and so on). *The first character of the 7-character procedure code always specifies the section.* While the characters 2–7 have the same meaning within a section, they may have different meanings in different sections (Table 2-3, columns 2–7). Within all sections, the third character specifies either the root operation, root type (of procedure performed), or modality. Characters 4–7 provide additional information (e.g., body part, approach, and so on) that formulate the procedure code.

Then, depending on the ICD-10-PCS section in which a procedure is classified, the values of characters 2–7 may vary (Table 2-3, columns 2–7). However, the values of characters 2–7 *within a particular section* remain the same.

Format of ICD-10-PCS Coding Manual

The ICD-10-PCS coding manual contains two separate parts:

- Index

- Tables

Some publishers include appendices to assist in accurate ICD-10-PCS coding. For example, Optum360 includes the following appendices in its coding manual:

- Appendix A (Root Operations Definitions)

- Appendix B (Comparison of Medical and Surgical Root Operations)

- Appendix C (Body Part Key)

- Appendix D (Type and Type Qualifier Definitions for Sections B–H)

- Appendix E (Components of the Medical and Surgical Approach Definitions)

- Appendix F (Character Meanings)

Build-a-Code Using ICD-10-PCS

The ICD-10-PCS index allows the first 3–5 values, and sometimes all 7 characters, of a 7-character procedure code to be located alphabetically according to general type of procedure (e.g., excision), commonly used medical terms (e.g., appendectomy), or body part (e.g., adductor brevis muscle).

The first 3–5 values of a 7-character procedure code as listed in the index entry direct the coder to a specific location in the ICD-10-PCS tables, which must be used to construct a complete and valid

 Note:

Some ICD-10-PCS tables are extensive, and coders must continue on to the next page of the coding manual to build an accurate code. (Coders say "a table bleeds onto the next page" to describe this.)

Table 2-3 Value Assigned to Each Character in a 7-Character ICD-10-PCS Code

Character 1	Character 2	Character 3	Character 4	Character 5	Character 6	Character 7
Medical and Surgical Section	Body system	Root operation	Body part	Approach	Device	Qualifier
Obstetrics Section	Body system	Root operation	Body part	Approach	Device	Qualifier
Placement Section	Anatomical region	Root operation	Body region/ orifice	Approach	Device	Qualifier
Administration Section	Body system	Physiological system and anatomical region	Body system/ Region	Approach	Substance	Qualifier
Measurement and Monitoring Section	Physiological system	Root operation	Body system	Approach	Function/ Device	Qualifier
Extracorporeal Assistance and Performance Section	Physiological system	Root operation	Body system	Duration	Function	Qualifier
Extracorporeal Therapies Section	Physiological system	Root operation	Body system	Duration	Qualifier	Qualifier
Osteopathic Section	Anatomical region	Root operation	Body region	Approach	Method	Qualifier
Other Procedures Section	Body system	Root operation	Body region	Approach	Method	Qualifier
Chiropractic Section	Anatomical region	Root operation	Body region	Approach	Method	Qualifier
Imaging Section	Body system	Root type	Body part	Contrast	Qualifier	Qualifier
Nuclear Medicine Section	Body system	Root type	Body part	Radionuclide	Qualifier	Qualifier
Radiation Therapy Section	Body system	Modality	Treatment site	Modality qualifier	Isotope	Qualifier
Physical Rehabilitation and Diagnostic Audiology Section	Section qualifier	Root type	Body system & region	Type qualifier	Equipment	Qualifier
Mental Health Section	Body system	Root type	Type qualifier	Qualifier	Qualifier	Qualifier
Substance Abuse Treatment Section	Body system	Root type	Type qualifier	Qualifier	Qualifier	Qualifier
New Technology	Body System	Root Operation	Body Part	Approach	Device/ Substance/ Technology	Qualifier

7-character code. When the sixth character of an ICD-10-PCS code indicates a device, a device character is assigned only when a device is inserted (e.g., pacemaker, drain). In many cases, ICD-10-PCS tables include just one option for a device, the letter Z (no device). (Sometimes the coder is directed to a different main term by the instructional note *see*, which is located next to a main term.) It is important to realize that the letters I and O are *never* used in ICD-10-PCS because they are too easily confused with the numbers 1 and 0. Decimals are also *never* used in ICD-10-PCS codes.

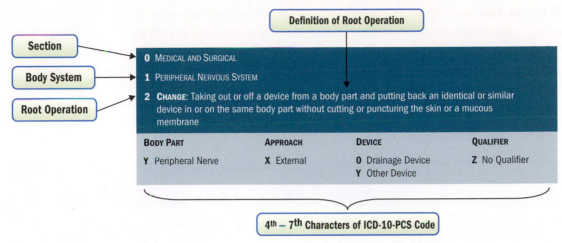

Figure 2-5 ICD-10-PCS table 012 with rows that specify valid combination of code values

Each ICD-10-PCS table identifies the first three values of the 7-character code (e.g., 027). Thus, locating the first 3 values of the 7-character code in the index allows the corresponding table to be located. Tables are organized beginning with numbers (0-9) as the first character, then letters (A-Z, except letters I and O). This means that a table 001 (in the Medical and Surgical Section) precedes table B00 (in the Imaging Section). The table is then used to determine the complete code by assigning the last 4 values, which is based on documentation of the procedure performed. ICD-10-PCS tables contain rows that specify the valid combinations of code values. Within a *body system* (or *section qualifier*, for the Physical Rehabilitation and Diagnostic Section Audiology Section), the three rows of text above each table specify values for characters 1–3 of an ICD-10-PCS code. The fifth row labels characters 4–7 of a possible code. Subsequent rows in the table specify valid combinations of values for characters 4–7 (Figure 2-5).

EXAMPLE: The patient underwent an *open procedure of the spinal canal to insert a subarachnoid-peritoneal shunt using synthetic substitute for the purpose of decreasing cerebrospinal fluid levels via bypass (using the shunt) to the peritoneal cavity*, which is assigned ICD-10-PCS code 001U0J6. Refer to each step and the yellow-highlighted items below to *build-a-code*.

STEP 1   After identifying the name of the procedure performed in the operative report, locate the main term in the ICD-10-PCS Index.

Index
Shortening
—*see* Excision
—*see* Repair
—*see* Reposition
Shunt creation—*see* Bypass

STEP 2   After following any instructional notes (e.g., *see*) present after a main term, locate the appropriate main term, subterm, and qualifier to identify the first 3 (or 4–5) values of a 7-character code.

Index
Bypass
Spinal Canal 001U
Stomach 0D16
Trachea 0B11

STEP 3   Locate the ICD-10-PCS table that corresponds to the first 3 values of a 7-character code, and review the procedure performed to assign a character to each position in the complete 7-character code.

ICD-10-PCS code 001U0J6 is assigned because 001 represents the table, 4th character U represents the spinal canal where the shunt was inserted, 0 represents an open approach (documented in the example), J represents use of a synthetic substitute (documented in the example), and 6 represents the peritoneal cavity. Thus, the shunt was inserted so fluid could move (be bypassed) from the spinal canal to the peritoneal cavity.

0 Medical and Surgical

0 Central Nervous System

1 Bypass: Altering the route of passage of the contents of a tubular body part

Body Part Character 4	Approach Character 5	Device Character 6	Qualifier Character 7
6 Cerebral Ventricle	0 Open 3 Percutaneous	7 Autologous Tissue Substitute J Synthetic Substitute K Nonautologous Tissue Substitute	0 Nasopharynx 1 Mastoid Sinus 2 Atrium 3 Blood Vessel 4 Pleural Cavity 5 Intestine 6 Peritoneal Cavity 7 Urinary Tract 8 Bone Marrow B Cerebral Cisterns
U Spinal Canal	0 Open 3 Percutaneous	7 Autologous Tissue Substitute J Synthetic Substitute K Nonautologous Tissue Substitute	4 Pleural Cavity 6 Peritoneal Cavity 7 Urinary Tract 9 Fallopian Tube

Exercise 2.4 – ICD-10-PCS Index and Tables

Instructions: Complete each statement.

1. The *International Classification of Diseases, 10th Revision, Procedure Coding System* is abbreviated as _____.

2. ICD-10-PCS is an entirely new procedure classification system developed by CMS for use in the United States for hospital_____ settings only.

3. ICD-10-PCS uses a multiaxial alphanumeric code structure that contains _____ characters and provides a unique code for all substantially different procedures.

4. The letters I and _____ are never used in ICD-10-PCS codes.

5. Refer to steps 1 through 3 on the previous pages, and use the build-a-code method to assign an ICD-10-PCS code for an *open procedure of the spinal canal to insert a subarachnoid-pleural shunt using autologous tissue substitute for the purpose of decreasing cerebrospinal fluid levels via bypass (using the shunt) to the peritoneal cavity*: _____.

Official ICD-10-CM and ICD-10-PCS Guidelines for Coding and Reporting

The CMS and the NCHS are two agencies in the DHHS that prepare guidelines for coding and reporting using the ICD-10-CM and ICD-10-PCS. These guidelines, which have been approved by the four organizations that comprise the **cooperating parties for the ICD-10-CM/PCS**, should be used as a companion document when coding from ICD-10-CM and ICD-10-PCS. The organizations include the American Hospital Association (AHA), American Health Information Management Association (AHIMA), CMS, and NCHS.

> ### Note:
> Official coding advice (e.g., interpretation of ICD-10-CM and ICD-10-PCS coding principles) is developed by the four cooperating parties for ICD-10-CM/PCS and is published in the Coding Clinic for ICD-10-CM/PCS by the central office of the AHA.

The ***Official ICD-10-CM Guidelines for Coding and Reporting*** and the ***Official ICD-10-PCS Guidelines for Coding and Reporting*** are rules that were developed to accompany and complement the official conventions and instructions provided in the classification system. They are based on coding and sequencing instructions in the classification system, but provide additional instruction. Adherence to these guidelines when assigning diagnosis and procedure codes is required under HIPAA. ICD-10-CM diagnosis codes were adopted for all health care settings. ICD-10-PCS procedure codes were adopted for inpatient procedures reported by hospitals. A joint effort between the health care provider and the coder is essential to achieve complete and accurate documentation, code assignment, and reporting of diagnoses and procedures. The importance of consistent, complete documentation in the patient record cannot be overemphasized because without such documentation, accurate coding cannot be achieved. Make sure you review the entire patient record to determine the specific reason for the encounter and the conditions treated.

The guidelines use the term *encounter* to indicate all health care settings, including inpatient hospital admissions. The term *provider* is used throughout the guidelines to refer to physicians or any qualified health care practitioners who are legally accountable for establishing the patient's diagnosis. The guidelines are organized as follows:

- Structure and coding conventions (refer to Chapter 3)
- Chapter-specific ICD-10-CM coding guidelines (refer to Chapter 4)
- Selection of principal and additional diagnoses and procedures, including ICD-10-PCS procedure coding, for inpatient settings (refer to Chapter 5)
- Outpatient coding and reporting (refer to Chapter 6)

Exercise 2.5 – Official Guidelines for Coding and Reporting

Instructions: Complete each statement.

1. The guidelines for coding and reporting using ICD-10-CM and ICD-10-PCS have been approved by the four organizations that comprise the _____ parties for ICD-10-CM and ICD-10-PCS.

2. The abbreviations for the four organizations that develop and approve the coding guidelines are AHA, AHIMA, CMS, and _____.

(continues)

Exercise 2.5 (*continued*)

3. Adherence to the coding guidelines when assigning ICD-10-CM and ICD-10-PCS diagnosis and procedure codes is required by _____ legislation.

4. The guidelines use the term _____ to indicate all health care settings, including inpatient hospital admissions.

5. The term _____ is used throughout the guidelines to refer to physicians or any qualified health care practitioners who are legally accountable for establishing the patient's diagnosis.

ICD-9-CM Legacy Coding System

As a result of implementing the ICD-10-CM and ICD-10-PCS coding systems, the *International Classification of Diseases, Ninth Revision, Clinical Modification* (ICD-9-CM) became a **legacy coding system** (or **legacy classification system**), which means it is used to archive data but is no longer supported or updated by the ICD-9-CM Coordination and Maintenance Committee. However, because ICD-9-CM was used since 1979 in the United States to classify inpatient and outpatient/physician office diagnoses (Volumes 1 and 2) and inpatient procedures (Volume 3), *general equivalence mappings (GEMs)* (discussed below) will be annually published by the National Center for Health Statistics (NCHS) and Centers for Medicare & Medicaid Services (CMS).

ICD-9-CM was over 30 years old, had outdated and obsolete terminology, used outdated codes that produced inaccurate and limited data, and was inconsistent with current medical practice. It did not accurately describe diagnoses or inpatient procedures of care delivered in the 21st century. ICD-9-CM did not provide the necessary detail about patients' medical conditions or procedures performed on hospitalized inpatients; thus, effective October 1, 2015, provider offices and health care facilities (e.g., hospitals) adopted ICD-10-CM to code diagnoses. (Hospitals use ICD-10-PCS to code inpatient procedures. Provider offices and outpatient health care settings use CPT and HCPCS level II to code procedures and services.)

General Equivalence Mappings (GEMs)

NCHS and CMS annually publish **general equivalence mappings (GEMs)**, which are translation dictionaries or crosswalks of codes that can be used to roughly identify ICD-10-CM codes for their ICD-9-CM equivalent codes (and vice versa). (GEMs published by the NCHS and CMS do not contain code descriptions; however, other publishers include code descriptions to facilitate code translation.) GEMs facilitate the location of corresponding diagnosis codes between two code sets. In some areas of the classification, the correlation between codes is close, and since the two code sets share the conventions of organization and formatting common to both revisions of ICD, translating between them is straightforward.

EXAMPLE 1: There is straightforward correspondence between the two code sets for the conditions, *Salmonella meningitis*.

ICD-9-CM to ICD-10-CM General Equivalence Mapping	
ICD-9-CM DIAGNOSIS CODE AND DESCRIPTION	ICD-10-CM DIAGNOSIS CODE AND DESCRIPTION
003.21 Salmonella meningitis	A02.21 Salmonella meningitis

EXAMPLE 2: In other areas of the two code sets, such as obstetrics, entire chapters are organized according to a different axis of classification, and translating between them offers a series of possible codes that must be verified in the appropriate tabular list (ICD-9-CM or ICD-10-CM) or table of codes (ICD-10-PCS) to identify the correct code. (Think about translating the English language into Chinese or any other foreign language, and you will see the problems inherent in such translation.)

ICD-9-CM to ICD-10-CM General Equivalence Mapping	
ICD-9-CM DIAGNOSIS CODE AND DESCRIPTION	**ICD-10-CM DIAGNOSIS CODE AND DESCRIPTION**
649.51 Spotting complicating pregnancy, delivered, with or without mention of antepartum complication	O26.851 Spotting complicating pregnancy, first trimester
	O26.852 Spotting complicating pregnancy, second trimester
	O26.853 Spotting complicating pregnancy, third trimester

EXAMPLE 3: Procedures located in ICD-9-CM Volume 3 that correspond to ICD-10-PCS codes are contained within its general equivalent mapping.

ICD-9-CM to ICD-10-PCS General Equivalence Mapping	
ICD-9-CM PROCEDURE CODE AND DESCRIPTION	**ICD-10-CM PROCEDURE CODE AND DESCRIPTION**
47.11 Laparoscopic incidental appendectomy	0DTJ4ZZ Laparoscopic appendectomy

Exercise 2.6 – ICD-9-CM Legacy Coding System

Instructions: Use the diagnosis GEM depicted in the table below to complete each statement.

ICD-9-CM to ICD-10-CM General Equivalence Mapping	
ICD-9-CM Diagnosis Code and Description	ICD-10-CM Diagnosis Code and Description
078.81 Epidemic vertigo	A88.1 Epidemic vertigo
078.82 Epidemic vomiting syndrome	R11.11 Vomiting without nausea
078.88 Other specified diseases due to *Chlamydiae*	A74.89 Other chlamydial diseases
078.89 Other specified diseases due to viruses	A96.2 Lassa fever
	A98.3 Marburg virus disease
	A98.4 Ebola virus disease
	B33.8 Other specified viral diseases

1. ICD-9-CM code 078.82 maps to ICD-10-CM code _____.
2. ICD-9-CM code 078.81 maps to ICD-10-CM code _____.
3. ICD-9-CM code 078.88 maps to ICD-10-CM code _____.
4. ICD-10-CM code A74.89 maps to ICD-9-CM code _____.
5. ICD-10-CM code B33.8 maps to ICD-9-CM code _____.

Summary

The *International Classification of Diseases, 10th Revision, Clinical Modification* (ICD-10-CM) and the *International Classification of Diseases, 10th Revision, Procedure Coding System* (ICD-10-PCS), abbreviated as ICD-10-CM/PCS, replaced ICD-9-CM. ICD-10-CM is a clinical modification of the World Health Organization's *International Classification of Diseases, Ninth Revision* (ICD-9). ICD-10-CM/PCS includes many more codes and applies to more users than ICD-9-CM because it is designed to collect data on every type of health care encounter (e.g., inpatient, outpatient, hospice, home health care, and long-term care). The ICD-10-CM Tabular List of Diseases and Injuries contains 21 chapters. The ICD-10-CM Tabular List of Diseases and Injuries is a sequential list of codes contained within chapters based on body system or condition, and codes are then organized within major topic headings, categories, subcategories, and codes. ICD-10-CM disease and injury codes consist of three characters, but most are followed by a decimal point and between one and four additional characters. ICD-10-CM Index to Diseases and Injuries entries are organized according to main terms, subterms, second qualifiers, and third qualifiers.

The *International Classification of Diseases, 10th Revision, Procedure Coding System* (ICD-10-PCS) is a procedure classification system developed by the Centers for Medicare & Medicaid Services (CMS) for use in the United States for inpatient hospital settings *only*. ICD-10-PCS uses a multiaxial 7-character alphanumeric code structure (e.g., 047K04Z) that provides a unique code for all substantially different procedures. It also allows new procedures to be easily incorporated as new codes. ICD-10-PCS contains more than 87,000 seven-character alphanumeric procedure codes.

Medical necessity is the measure of whether a health care procedure or service is appropriate for the diagnosis or treatment of a condition. This decision-making process is based on the payer's contractual language and the treating provider's documentation. Generally, the following criteria are used to determine medical necessity: purpose, scope, evidence, and value.

The DHHS agencies CMS and NCHS prepare guidelines for coding and reporting using ICD-10-CM and ICD-10-PCS. The guidelines are approved by the four organizations that comprise the cooperating parties for the ICD-10-CM/PCS. The organizations include the AHA, AHIMA, CMS, and NCHS. The guidelines should be used as a companion document when coding from ICD-10-CM and ICD-10-PCS. The guidelines are rules that were developed to accompany and complement the official conventions and instructions provided in ICD-10-CM and ICD-10-PCS. They are based on coding and sequencing instructions in ICD-10-CM and ICD-10-PCS, but provide additional instruction. Adherence to these guidelines when assigning ICD-10-CM and ICD-10-PCS diagnosis and procedure codes is required under the MMA.

ICD-9-CM diagnosis codes (Volumes 1 and 2) were originally adopted under HIPAA for all health care settings, and ICD-9-CM Volume 3 procedure codes were adopted for inpatient procedures reported by hospitals. A joint effort between the health care provider and the coder is essential to achieving complete and accurate documentation, code assignment, and reporting of diagnoses and procedures. Consistent, complete documentation in the patient record is crucial because without such documentation, accurate codes cannot be assigned. In addition, the entire patient record must be reviewed to determine the specific reason for the encounter and the conditions treated so that appropriate codes are assigned.

Upon implementation of ICD-10-CM and ICD-10-PCS, ICD-9-CM became a *legacy coding system (or legacy classification system)*, which means it is used as archive data but is no longer supported or updated. *General equivalence mappings (GEMs)*, which are translation dictionaries or crosswalks of codes that can be used to roughly identify ICD-10-CM codes for their ICD-9-CM equivalent codes (and vice versa), are annually published by NCHS and CMS.

Internet Links

AHA Central Office: *www.ahacentraloffice.org*

Federal Register Listserv: At *listserv.access.gpo.gov*, click on the "Online mailing list archives" link, click on the FEDREGTOC-L link, and click on the Subscribe or Unsubscribe link to register to receive the daily *Federal Register* table of contents via e-mail. The document contains the Centers for Medicare & Medicaid Services final rule about implementation of ICD-10-CM and ICD-10-PCS.

ICD-10-CM and ICD-10-PCS encoders (subscription-based): *www.encoderpro.com* (free trial available)

ICD-10-CM/PCS updates: Go to *www.cdc.gov*, click on the Data & Statistics link under More CDC Topics, click on the Classification of Diseases, Functioning, and Disability link under Tools & Resources, and click on any of the ICD links.

GEMs for ICD-10-CM/PCS: Go to *www.cms.gov*, click on Medicare, click on ICD-10 under Coding, and click on links in the first column to locate coding manual PDF files, general equivalence mappings (GEMs), and more.

Study Checklist

❑ Read this textbook chapter and highlight key concepts.

❑ Create an index card for each key term.

❑ Access the chapter Internet links to learn more about concepts.

❑ Complete the chapter exercises and review, verifying answers with your instructor.

❑ Complete Workbook chapter, verifying answers with your instructor.

❑ Go to *www.cengagebrain.com* to access the Student Companion Web Site. Login instructions are located in this textbook's Preface.

❑ Form a study group with classmates to discuss chapter concepts in preparation for an exam.

Review

Multiple Choice

Instructions: Circle the most appropriate response.

1. ICD-10-CM was developed to code and classify _____ data from inpatient and outpatient records, including physician office records.
    a. morbidity
    b. mortality
    c. procedure
    d. service

2. Which entities work together to coordinate official ICD-10-CM disease classification activities?
    a. National Center for Health Statistics (NCHS) and the Centers for Medicare & Medicaid Services (CMS)
    b. National Center for Health Statistics (NCHS) with the World Health Organization (WHO)
    c. U.S. Department of Health & Human Services (DHHS)
    d. World Health Organization (WHO)

3. General equivalence mappings are translation dictionaries or _____ of codes.
    a. appendices
    b. crosswalks
    c. indexes
    d. tabular lists

4. Outcome of delivery, follow-up, history, and vaccination are examples of ICD-10-CM:
    a. external causes of morbidity.
    b. factors influencing health status.
    c. conditions originating in the perinatal period.
    d. symptoms, signs, and abnormal findings.

5. The Table of Neoplasms is located in the _____.
   a. ICD-10-CM Index to Diseases and Injuries
   b. ICD-10-CM Tabular List of Disease and Injuries
   c. ICD-10-PCS Index
   d. ICD-10-PCS Tables

6. Review the ICD-10-CM Index to Diseases and Injuries entry for main term *Contusion*, and locate sub-term "arm" below it. Which ICD-10-CM code appears next to the subterm?
   a. S40   b. S40.0   c. S40.02   d. S40.02-

7. The ICD-10-PCS Index and Tables are used to classify _____ procedures and services.
   a. emergency department
   b. hospital inpatient
   c. outpatient
   d. physician office

8. The *Current Procedural Terminology* (CPT) is published by the:
   a. American Medical Association (AMA).
   b. Centers for Medicare & Medicaid Services (CMS).
   c. National Center for Health Statistics (NCHS).
   d. World Health Organization (WHO).

9. ICD-10-CM _____ codes are reported by all health care settings.
   a. disease
   b. medical equipment
   c. procedure
   d. service

10. Adhering to official coding guidelines is:
   a. at the discretion of a health care facility's operating procedures.
   b. mandated by the cooperating parties.
   c. not necessary if the facility has a 90 percent or higher coding accuracy rate.
   d. required by the Health Insurance Portability and Accountability Act.

Matching

Instructions: Match the format in Column 2 with each line of the ICD-10-CM Tabular List of Diseases and Injuries entry in Column 1.

Tabular List of Diseases and Injuries Entry

_____ 1.   DISEASES OF THE NERVOUS SYSTEM
              (G00-G99)

_____ 2.   EPISODIC AND PAROXYSMAL DISORDERS
              (G40-G47)

_____ 3.   G43 Migraine

_____ 4.   G43.C Periodic headache syndromes
                       in child or adult

_____ 5.   G43.C0 Periodic headache syndromes
                          in child or adult, not
                          intractable

Format
a. Category
b. Chapter title
c. Section title
d. Subcategory
e. Code

Coding Practice – ICD-10-CM

Instructions: Underline the main term and assign the appropriate ICD-10-CM code.

_____	1. Abdominal hernia
_____	2. Abnormal nonfasting glucose tolerance test
_____	3. Acute otitis media
_____	4. Hyperplasia of endometrium
_____	5. Traumatic fracture (closed), right humerus (initial encounter)
_____	6. Congenital fibrocystic disease of the lung
_____	7. Degenerative arthritis
_____	8. Fibrocystic disease of right and left breasts
_____	9. Hereditary epistaxis
_____	10. Personal history of cancer

Coding Practice – ICD-10-PCS

Instructions: Underline the main term and assign the appropriate ICD-10-PCS code.

_____	1. Open biopsy, left axillary lymph node
_____	2. Open cholecystectomy, total
_____	3. Cystoscopy
_____	4. Exploratory laparotomy, open
_____	5. Intravenous right pyelogram (using fluoroscopy)
_____	6. Incidental appendectomy (open)
_____	7. Open biopsy of left frontal nasal sinus
_____	8. Percutaneous biopsy of prostate
_____	9. Right frontal craniotomy (open approach)
_____	10. Transurethral biopsy of bladder

ICD-10-CM and ICD-10-PCS Coding Conventions

Chapter Outline

Format and Typeface

Eponyms

Abbreviations

Punctuation

Boxed Notes

Tables

Includes Notes

Excludes1 and Excludes2 Notes

Inclusion Terms

Other, Other Specified, and Unspecified Codes

Etiology and Manifestation Rules

And

Due To

In

With

Cross-References

Chapter Objectives

At the conclusion of this chapter, the student should be able to:

- Define key terms.
- List ICD-10-CM and ICD-10-PCS coding conventions.
- Explain ICD-10-CM and ICD-10-PCS coding conventions.
- Interpret ICD-10-CM and ICD-10-PCS coding conventions to assign codes accurately.

Key Terms

coding conventions

  abbreviations

    NEC (not elsewhere classifiable)

    NOS (not otherwise specified)

  and

  boxed note

  code also

  cross-references

    see

    see also

    see category

see condition

default code

due to

eponym

etiology and manifestation rules

  code first underlying disease

  code, if applicable, any causal condition first

  in diseases classified elsewhere

use additional code

excludes1 note

excludes2 note

format

in

includes note

inclusion term

manifestation

modifier

other

other specified

punctuation

  brackets

  colon

  parentheses

syndrome

tables

trust the index

typeface

unspecified code

use

with

Introduction ✏

The ICD-10-CM and ICD-10-PCS coding conventions (rules) can usually be found at the beginning of any ICD-10-CM or ICD-10-PCS coding manual. Coders are required to reference this material when reviewing case scenarios (and patient records) to assign ICD-10-CM and ICD-10-PCS codes. It is also helpful to coders when health care providers become familiar with coding conventions (and guidelines). When a coder initiates a physician query, an understanding of coding conventions and guidelines helps ensure the assignment of accurate codes for certain conditions and diagnoses.

Note:

When reviewing examples and completing exercises and review questions in this chapter, use your ICD-10-CM and ICD-10-PCS to locate disease and procedure index entries and verify codes in the tabular lists and tables.

Coding conventions for ICD-10-CM and ICD-10-PCS are general rules used in the classification, and they are independent of the coding guidelines (covered in Chapters 2, 4, 5, and 6 of this textbook). The conventions are incorporated into ICD-10-CM and ICD-10-PCS as instructional notes. General ICD-10-CM coding conventions include the following:

- *Default codes*: In ICD-10-CM, a code listed next to a main term in the ICD-10-CM indexes is referred to as a **default code**. The default code represents that condition that is most commonly associated with the main term, or is the unspecified code for the condition. If a condition is documented in a patient record (e.g., appendicitis) without any additional information, such as acute or chronic, the default code should be assigned.

- *Syndromes*: In ICD-10-CM, coders should follow the alphabetic index guidance when assigning codes to **syndromes**, which is an association of clinically recognizable features such as signs (observed by others), symptoms (reported by the patient), and/or characteristics that often occur together, so that the presence of one or more features alerts the health care provider as to the possible presence of the others. Coders should follow ICD-10-CM index guidance when assigning codes to a syndrome, and in the absence of index guidance, assign codes for the documented manifestations of the syndrome.

Specific ICD-10-CM and/or ICD-10-PCS coding conventions include the following:

- Format and typeface
- Eponyms
- Abbreviations
- Punctuation
- Boxed notes
- Tables

- Excludes1 and Excludes2 Notes
- Includes notes
- Inclusion terms
- Other, other specified, and unspecified codes
- Etiology and manifestation rules
- And

- Due to
- In
- With
- Cross-references, including, *see, see also, see* category, *see* condition, and *use*
- Code assignment and clinical criteria

Format and Typeface

Each ICD-10-CM and ICD-10-PCS index uses an indented **format** for ease in reference (Figure 3-1). All ICD-10-CM Index to Diseases and Injuries subterms associated with an index entry's main term are indented two spaces, with any 2nd and 3rd qualifiers associated with the main term further indented by two and four spaces, respectively. In addition, if an index entry requires more than one line, the additional text is printed on the next line and indented five spaces.

ICD-10-CM and ICD-10-PCS also makes use of the boldface and italic **typeface** for ease in reference. Boldface type is used for main term entries in the ICD-10-CM and ICD-10-PCS alphabetical indexes, all codes and descriptions in the ICD-10-CM tabular list, and sections and characters in ICD-10-PCS tables. Italicized type is used for all ICD-10-CM tabular list excludes1 and excludes2 notes and to identify manifestation codes, which are codes that should not be reported as the first-listed or principal diagnoses.

Additional terms are indented below the term to which they are linked in the ICD-10-CM tabular list; if a definition or disease requires more than one line, that text is printed on the next line and indented five spaces.

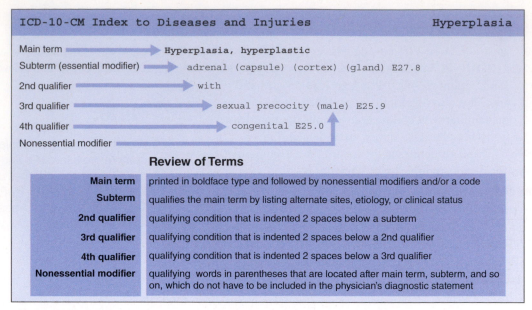

Figure 3-1 Display of main terms, subterms, qualifiers, nonessential modifiers in ICD-10-CM Index to Diseases and Injuries

EXAMPLE 1: ICD-10-CM INDEX TO DISEASES AND INJURIES—INDENTED FORMAT AND BOLDFACE: Locate main term *ulcer* in the ICD-10-CM Index to Diseases and Injuries, and notice that it is boldfaced. Also, notice that subterm *aphthous (oral) (recurrent) K12.0* is indented two spaces below the "U" of main term *ulcer*. Then, notice that second qualifier *genital organ(s)* is further indented two spaces.

EXAMPLE 2: ICD-10-CM TABULAR LIST OF DISEASES AND INJURIES—INDENTED FORMAT AND BOLDFACE: Locate code *K12.0 Recurrent Oral Aphthae* in the ICD-10-CM Tabular List of Diseases and Injuries, and notice that it is in boldface and its synonyms (e.g., Bednar's aphthae) are indented.

EXAMPLE 3: ICD-10-PCS INDEX—INDENTED FORMAT: Locate main term *Laparotomy* in the ICD-10-PCS index, and notice that it is boldfaced and subterm *Drainage* is indented two spaces below the "L" of *Laparotomy*.

 Note:

The indented format is *not* used in the ICD-10-PCS tables.

EXAMPLE 4: ICD-10-PCS TABLES—BOLDFACE: Locate 001 in the ICD-10-PCS tables, and notice that section heading *Central Nervous System 001–00X* and the first three characters and descriptions are boldfaced. Then, notice that additional characters used to build an ICD-10-PCS code are also boldfaced. (Indenting is *not* used in ICD-10-PCS tables.)

Exercise 3.1 – Format and Typeface

Exercise 3.1A – ICD-10-CM

Instructions: Assign an ICD-10-CM code to each statement. Make sure you appropriately interpret the use of indented format and typeface in the ICD-10-CM disease index.

_____ **1.** Acariasis infestation

_____ **2.** Pityriasis rubra pilaris

Exercise 3.1 (*continued*)

_____ **3.** Admission for adjustment of artificial leg

_____ **4.** Adjustment disorder with anxiety

_____ **5.** Anorexia nervosa

Exercise 3.1B – ICD-10-PCS

Instructions: Assign an ICD-10-PCS code to each statement. Make sure you appropriately interpret the use of indented format and typeface in the ICD-10-PCS index.

_____ **1.** High forceps delivery

_____ **2.** Magnetic resonance imaging (MRI), left breast

_____ **3.** Termination of pregnancy (by) dilation and curettage

_____ **4.** Heart transplantation, allogenic

_____ **5.** Ultrasonography, abdomen

Eponyms

Eponyms are diseases or syndromes that are named for people. They are listed in appropriate alphabetical sequence as main terms in the ICD-10-CM Index to Diseases and Injuries. They are also listed as subterms below main terms *Disease* and *Syndrome* in the index. A description of the disease, syndrome, or procedure is usually included in parentheses following the eponym.

> **Note:**
>
> There are no eponyms (e.g., Billroth procedure) or common procedure terms (e.g., appendectomy) in ICD-10-PCS.

> **EXAMPLE: ICD-10-CM INDEX TO DISEASES AND INJURIES—EPONYM:** The Index to Diseases and Injuries entry for *Barlow's syndrome* can be located in alphabetical order. However, it can be located under main term *Disease*. (Although the Tabular List of Diseases and Injuries entry for code E54 does not list Barlow's syndrome, other eponyms are routinely listed in the tabular list.)

Exercise 3.2 – Eponyms

Instructions: Assign an ICD-10-CM code to each statement. Make sure that you appropriately interpret the use of eponyms in the ICD-10-CM disease index.

_____ **1.** Costen's complex

_____ **2.** Madelung's deformity

_____ **3.** Coats' disease

_____ **4.** Kaschin-Beck disease

_____ **5.** Meniere's disease, right ear

Abbreviations

The ICD-10-CM indexes and tabular list contain **abbreviations** to save space. The abbreviation **NEC (not elsewhere classifiable)** means "other" or "other specified" and identifies codes that are to be assigned when information needed to assign a more specific code cannot be located in the code book. When a specific code is not available in the disease index for a condition, the coder is directed to the "other specified" code in the tabular list.

> **Note:**
>
> The NEC abbreviation does not appear in the ICD-10-PCS index or tables.

EXAMPLE 1: ICD-10-CM INDEX TO DISEASES AND INJURIES—NEC ABBREVIATION: The Index to Diseases and Injuries entry for *aberrant, artery, basilar* contains the NEC abbreviation in front of code Q28.1, which means a more specific code cannot be assigned in the code book. When verifying code Q28.1 in the Tabular List of Diseases and Injuries, notice that the code description is *Other malformations of precerebral vessels* and that the NEC abbreviation does not appear in the code description. Code Q28.1 is assigned to *aberrant basilar artery* because the index's NEC abbreviation directs the coder to that code.

EXAMPLE 2: ICD-10-CM TABULAR LIST OF DISEASES AND INJURIES—NEC ABBREVIATION: Locate code Q28.8 in the tabular list, and notice that the NEC abbreviation is included next to *Congenital aneurysm, specified site NEC* below the code description.

The ICD-10-CM disease index and tabular list contain the abbreviation **NOS (not otherwise specified)**, which is the equivalent of "unspecified." It identifies codes that are to be assigned when information needed to assign a more specific code cannot be obtained from the provider. Because selecting a code from the disease index based on limited documentation results in the coder being directed to an "unspecified" code in the tabular list, the coder should contact the physician to request that additional documentation be provided so that a more specific diagnosis or procedure code can be assigned. A review of the patient record to assign a more specific code is also an important part of the coding process (e.g., laboratory data, radiology reports, operative report, pathology report).

> **Note:**
>
> It is appropriate to ask the physician for clarification about a diagnosis if the patient's record contains documentation (e.g., laboratory data) to support the assignment of a more specific code.

EXAMPLE 1: ICD-10-CM INDEX TO DISEASES AND INJURIES—NOS ABBREVIATION: The index entry for *Bronchomycosis NOS B49 [J99]* directs the coder to B49, which is an *unspecified* code.

> **Note:**
>
> The NOS abbreviation does not appear in the ICD-10-PCS index or tables.

EXAMPLE 2: ICD-10-CM TABULAR LIST OF DISEASES AND INJURIES—NOS ABBREVIATION: Locate code A03.9 in the tabular list, and notice the NOS abbreviation appears after *dysentery*.

Exercise 3.3 – Abbreviations

Instructions: Assign an ICD-10-CM code to each statement. Make sure that you appropriately interpret the use of abbreviations in the ICD-10-CM disease index and tabular list.

_____ **1.** Purpura

_____ **2.** Femoral hernia

Exercise 3.3 *(continued)*

_____   **3.** ST elevation myocardial infarction, anterior wall

_____   **4.** Hyperinsulinism

_____   **5.** Laceration, right eyeball (initial encounter)

Punctuation

ICD-10-CM includes the following **punctuation**:

- Brackets
- Parentheses
- Colons

Brackets are used to identify manifestation codes in the ICD-10-CM Index to Diseases and Injuries. A **manifestation** is a condition that occurs as the result of another condition, and manifestation codes are always reported as secondary codes. The code and description may or may not appear in italics in the tabular list. When code descriptions are not italicized in the tabular list, make sure you sequence the codes according to the sequence in the index entry.

 Note:

When reporting manifestation codes, do not enclose them in brackets.

CORRECT: E85.4

                  I43

INCORRECT: E85.4

                  [I43]

EXAMPLE: ICD-10-CM INDEX TO DISEASES AND INJURIES—BRACKETS: The index entry for *Amyloid heart (disease) E85.4 [I43]* indicates that two codes should be reported: E85.4 and I43. Because code I43 appears in brackets, it is reported as a secondary code. When verifying code I43 in the tabular list, notice that its description is italicized and includes a *Code first underlying disease*, such as: instruction is provided, prompting you to report code I43 as the second code.

Brackets are used in the ICD-10-CM indexes and tabular list to enclose abbreviations, synonyms, alternative wording, or explanatory phrases.

EXAMPLE 1: ICD-10-CM INDEX TO DISEASES AND INJURIES—SQUARE BRACKETS: The index entry for *Abnormal, electrocardiogram [ECG] [EKG] R94.31* encloses abbreviations in square brackets.

EXAMPLE 2: ICD-10-CM TABULAR LIST OF DISEASES AND INJURIES—SQUARE BRACKETS: Code I45.89 uses square brackets to enclose the abbreviation for *atrioventricular* as *[AV]*.

Parentheses are used in both the ICD-10-CM indexes and tabular list and ICD-10-PCS index to enclose nonessential modifiers, which are supplementary words that may be present in or absent from the physician's statement of a disease or procedure without affecting the code to which it is assigned. The nonessential modifiers in the indexes apply to subterms that are located below a main term; *however, when a nonessential modifier and a subterm are mutually exclusive, the subterm takes precedence.*

EXAMPLE 1: ICD-10-CM INDEX TO DISEASES AND INJURIES—PARENTHESES (supplementary terms): Index entry *abasia (-astasia) (hysterical) F44.4* contains two nonessential modifiers in parentheses, which means that the terms may be present or absent from the provider's diagnostic statement.

EXAMPLE 2: ICD-10-CM INDEX TO DISEASES AND INJURIES—PARENTHESES (mutually exclusive modifiers): Index entry *Enteritis* contains nonessential modifier *acute* in parentheses and essential modifier *chronic* as a subterm; in this case, nonessential modifier *acute* does *not* apply to subterm *chronic*.

EXAMPLE 3: ICD-10-CM TABULAR LIST OF DISEASES AND INJURIES—PARENTHESES: Code I47.9 contains a nonessential modifier, (-*Hoffman*), in parentheses, which means that the term may be present or absent from the provider's diagnostic statement.

EXAMPLE 4: ICD-10-PCS INDEX—PARENTHESES: Index entry *acromion (process)* contains a nonessential modifier in parentheses, which means the term may be present or absent from the provider's procedural statement.

A **colon** is used after an incomplete term or phrase in the ICD-10-CM disease index and tabular list when one or more of the **modifiers** (additional terms) following the colon is needed to make the condition assignable to a given category.

EXAMPLE 1: ICD-10-CM INDEX TO DISEASES AND INJURIES—COLON: The 2nd qualifier *with retinal:* (located after index main term *Detachment* and subterm *retina*) requires the type of detachment (e.g., giant break) to be documented in the patient record so that a specific code can be selected.

EXAMPLE 2: ICD-10-CM TABULAR LIST OF DISEASES AND INJURIES—COLON: Underneath category *A40 Streptococcal sepsis*, a colon is used in the *Code first*: instruction to indicate conditions (e.g., postprocedural streptococcal sepsis, T81.4) that are to be reported first when documented in the patient record.

Exercise 3.4 – Punctuation

Instructions: Assign an ICD-10-CM code to each statement. Make sure that you appropriately interpret the use of punctuation in the ICD-10-CM disease index and tabular list.

_____ **1.** Acquired acanthosis

_____ **2.** Malaria fever

_____ **3.** Dimorphous leprosy

_____ **4.** Acute pyogenic thyroiditis

_____ **5.** Neuritis due to beriberi

Boxed Notes

Certain main terms in the ICD-10-CM disease index, including the Table of Neoplasms, are followed by **boxed notes**, which define terms and provide coding instruction.

EXAMPLE: ICD-10-CM INDEX TO DISEASES AND INJURIES—BOXED NOTE:

- The Index to Diseases and Injuries main term *Epilepsy* contains a boxed note that includes terms that are to be considered equivalent to intractable, such as *pharmacoresistant*.

- The Table of Neoplasms contains a boxed note that clarifies how to use the columns and rows in the table.

Exercise 3.5 – Boxed Notes

Instructions: Assign an ICD-10-CM code to each statement. Make sure that you interpret the content of boxed notes in the ICD-10-CM disease index, which includes the Table of Neoplasms.

_____ **1.** Pharmacoresistant epilepsy

_____ **2.** Treatment-resistant epilepsy

_____ **3.** Refractory epilepsy with status epilepticus

_____ **4.** Poorly controlled epilepsy with status epilepticus

_____ **5.** Malignant mesonephroma, right ovary (primary malignancy)

_____ **6.** Malignant embryoma, right kidney (primary malignancy)

_____ **7.** Bowen's disease

Tables

The ICD-10-CM disease index includes **tables**, which organize subterms, 2nd qualifiers, and 3rd qualifiers and their codes in columns and rows to make it easier to select the proper code. ICD-10-PCS also uses tables, but not in its index; instead of a tabular list of codes, ICD-10-PCS uses tables that are used to assign procedure codes (Figure 3-2).

ICD-10-CM organizes the following main terms in tables, which are located at the end of the Index to Diseases and Injuries (before the Index to External Causes of Injuries):

- Table of Neoplasms
- Table of Drugs and Chemicals

SECTION	0	Medical and Surgical		
BODY SYSTEM	J	Subcutaneous Tissue and Fascia		
OPERATION	H	*Insertion*: putting in a nonbiological appliance that monitors, assists, performs, or prevents a physiological function but does not physically take the place of a body part		

Body Part	Approach	Device	Qualifier
S Subcutaneous Tissue and Fascia, Head and Neck	0 Open	1 Radioactive Element	Z No Qualifier
V Subcutaneous Tissue and Fascia, Upper Extremity	3 Percutaneous	3 Infusion Device	
W Subcutaneous Tissue and Fascia, Lower Extremity			
T Subcutaneous Tissue and Fascia, Trunk	0 Open	1 Radioactive Element	Z No Qualifier
	3 Percutaneous	3 Infusion Device	
		V Infusion Pump	

Figure 3-2 Sample ICD-10-PCS table

Courtesy of the Centers for Medicare & Medicaid Services, www.cms.gov.

	Malignant Primary	Malignant Secondary	Ca *in situ*	Benign	Uncertain Behavior	Unspecified Nature
Notes— The list below gives the code numbers for neoplasms by anatomical site. For each site there are six possible code numbers according to whether the neoplasm in question is malignant, benign, *in situ*, of uncertain behavior, or of unspecified nature. The description of the neoplasm will often indicate which of the six columns is appropriate; e.g., malignant melanoma of skin, benign fibroadenoma of breast, carcinoma *in situ* of cervix uteri. Where such descriptors are not present, the remainder of the Index should be consulted where guidance is given to the appropriate column for each morphologic (histological) variety listed; e.g., Mesonephroma —*see* Neoplasm, malignant; Embryoma —*see also* Neoplasm, uncertain behavior; Disease, Bowen's —*see* Neoplasm, skin, *in situ*. However, the guidance in the Index can be overridden if one of the descriptors mentioned above is present; e.g., malignant adenoma of colon is coded to C18.9 and not to D12.6 as the adjective "malignant" overrides the Index entry "Adenoma —*see also* Neoplasm, benign." Codes listed with a dash -, following the code have a required additional character for laterality. The tabular must be reviewed for the complete code.						
Neoplasm, neoplastic	C80.1	C79.9	D09.9	D36.9	D48.9	D49.9
abdomen, abdominal	C76.2	C79.9	D09.8	D36.7	D48.7	D49.9
cavity	C76.2	C79.8-	D09.8	D36.7	D48.7	D49.89
organ	C76.2	C79.8-	D09.8	D36.7	D48.7	D49.89
viscera	C76.2	C79.8-	D09.8	D36.7	D48.7	D49.89
wall —*see also* Neoplasm, abdomen,						
wall, skin	C44.509	C79.2	D04.5	D23.5	D48.5	D49.2
connective tissue	C49.4	C79.8-	—	D21.4	D48.1	D49.2
skin	C44.509	—	—	—	—	—
basal cell carcinoma	C44.519	—	—	—	—	—
specified type NEC	C44.599	—	—	—	—	—
squamous cell carcinoma	C44.529	—	—	—	—	—

Courtesy of the Centers for Medicare & Medicaid Services, www.cms.gov.

Figure 3-3 ICD-10-CM Table of Neoplasms (partial)

The Table of Neoplasms is an alphabetic index of anatomical sites for which there are six possible codes according to whether the neoplasm in question is malignant, benign, *in situ*, of uncertain behavior, or of unspecified nature. The description of the neoplasm will often indicate which of the six columns is appropriate (e.g., malignant melanoma of skin, benign fibroadenoma of breast, carcinoma *in situ* of cervix uteri) (Figure 3-3).

The Table of Drugs and Chemicals in ICD-10-CM is an alphabetic index of medicinal, chemical, and biological substances that result in poisonings and adverse effects as well as underdosings. The first column of the table lists generic names of drugs and chemicals (although some publishers have added brand names) with six columns for *Poisoning: Accidental (Unintentional)* (poisoning that results from an inadvertent overdose, wrong substance administered/taken, or intoxication that includes combining prescription drugs with nonprescription drugs or alcohol); *Poisoning: Intentional Self-harm* (poisoning that results from a deliberate overdose, such as a suicide attempt, of substance[s] administered/taken or intoxication that includes purposely combining prescription drugs with nonprescription drugs or alcohol); *Poisoning: Assault* (poisoning inflicted by another person who intended to kill or injure the patient); *Poisoning: Undetermined* (subcategory used if the patient record does not document whether the poisoning was intentional or accidental); *Adverse Effect* (development of a pathological condition that results from a drug or chemical substance that was properly administered or taken); and *Underdosing* (taking less of a medication than is prescribed by a provider or a manufacturer's instruction) (Figure 3-4).

Note:

Tables appear in the ICD-10-CM Index to Diseases and Injuries, and their use is further discussed in Chapters 4–6 of this textbook. ICD-10-PCS also uses tables to facilitate the assignment of procedure codes, but the tables do not appear in the ICD-10-PCS index.

Substance	Poisoning, Accidental (unintentional)	Poisoning, Intentional Self-harm	Poisoning, Assault	Poisoning, Undetermined	Adverse Effect	Underdosing
1-Propanol	T51.3x1	T51.3x2	T51.3x3	T51.3x4	—	—
2-Propanol	T51.2x1	T51.2x2	T51.2x3	T51.2x4	—	—
2, 4-D (dichlorophen-oxyacetic acid)	T60.3x1	T60.3x2	T60.3x3	T60.3x4	—	—
2, 4-toluene diisocyanate	T65.0x1	T65.0x2	T65.0x3	T65.0x4	—	—
2, 4, 5-T (trichloro-phenoxyacetic acid)	T60.1x1	T60.1x2	T60.1x3	T60.1x4	—	—
14-hydroxydihydro-morphinone	T40.2x1	T40.2x2	T40.2x3	T40.2x4	T40.2x5	T40.2x6
ABOB	T37.5x1	T37.5x2	T37.5x3	T37.5x4	T37.5x5	T37.5x6
Abrine	T62.2x1	T62.2x2	T62.2x3	T62.2x4	—	—
Abrus (seed)	T62.2x1	T62.2x2	T62.2x3	T62.2x4	—	—
Absinthe	T51.0x1	T51.0x2	T51.0x3	T51.0x4	—	—
beverage	T51.0x1	T51.0x2	T51.0x3	T51.0x4	—	—
Acaricide	T60.8x1	T60.8x2	T60.8x3	T60.8x4	—	—
Acebutolol	T44.7x1	T44.7x2	T44.7x3	T44.7x4	T44.7x5	T44.7x6
Acecarbromal	T42.6x1	T42.6x2	T42.6x3	T42.6x4	T42.6x5	T42.6x6
Aceclidine	T44.1x1	T44.1x2	T44.1x3	T44.1x4	T44.1x5	T44.1x6
Acedapsone	T37.0x1	T37.0x2	T37.0x3	T37.0x4	T37.0x5	T37.0x6
Acefylline piperazine	T48.6x1	T48.6x2	T48.6x3	T48.6x4	T48.6x5	T48.6x6

Courtesy of the Centers for Medicare & Medicaid Services, www.cms.gov.

Figure 3-4 ICD-10-CM Table of Drugs and Chemicals (partial)

Exercise 3.6 – Tables

Instructions: Assign an ICD-10-CM code to each statement. Make sure that you appropriately interpret the use of tables in the ICD-10-CM disease index.

_____ **1.** Ethmoid sinus tumor

_____ **2.** Basal cell carcinoma, skin of external cheek

_____ **3.** Carcinoma of liver

_____ **4.** Prostate cancer

_____ **5.** Poisoning due to inhalation of paint fumes (initial encounter)

_____ **6.** Circulatory collapse due to therapeutic use of magnesium sulfate (oral) (initial encounter)

_____ **7.** Accidental overdose of antidepressants (initial encounter)

Includes Notes

An **includes note** appears in the ICD-10-CM tabular list below certain categories to further define, clarify, or give examples about the content below a code category.

EXAMPLE: ICD-10-CM TABULAR LIST OF DISEASES AND INJURIES—INCLUDES NOTE:
The includes note located below category code _H80 Otosclerosis_ in the Tabular List of Diseases and Injuries indicates that _otospongiosis_ is classified to that same category. This means that the provider could document _otosclerosis_ or _otospongiosis_, and a code from category H80 would be assigned.

Exercise 3.7 – Includes Notes

Instructions: Assign an ICD-10-CM code to each statement. Make sure that you appropriately interpret the use of includes notes in the ICD-10-CM tabular list.

1. Meningoencephalitis
_____

2. Nephrosclerosis
_____

3. Anastomotic ulcer
_____

4. Hypertensive vascular degeneration
_____

5. Acute pharyngitis
_____

Excludes1 and Excludes2 Notes

The ICD-10-CM Tabular List of Diseases and Injuries contains two types of excludes notes. Each note has a different definition for use. However, they are similar in that they both indicate that codes excluded from each other are independent of each other.

An **excludes1 note** is a pure excludes. It means "not coded here" and indicates mutually exclusive codes, in other words—two or more conditions that cannot be reported together.

 Note:

ICD-10-PCS does not use excludes notes.

⚠ **EXAMPLE 1: ICD-10-CM EXCLUDES1 NOTE:**
Locate ICD-10-CM code **Q03 Congenital hydrocephalus**, and find the Excludes1 note for *acquired hydrocephalus (G91.-)*. Hydrocephalus diagnosed in a newborn is assigned a code from Q03.0–Q03.9. For hydrocephalus that develops later in life, a code from G91.0–G91.9 is assigned. A congenital form of a disease is not reported with an

⚠ **Coding Tip:**

An excludes1 note instructs you to assign one code or the other *except when documentation supports existence of both conditions.*

acquired form of the same condition. Thus, the excluded code is never reported with the code located above the Excludes1 note.

EXAMPLE 2: ICD-10-CM EXCLUDES1 NOTE: Locate ICD-10-CM code **E10 type 1 diabetes mellitus**, and find the Excludes1 note for *type 2 diabetes mellitus (E11.-)*. Type 1 diabetes mellitus is classified to a code from E10.1x–E10.9. Thus, a code for type 2 diabetes mellitus (E11.0x–E11.9) would never be assigned with a code for type 1 diabetes mellitus.

An exception to the excludes1 definition is the circumstance when the two conditions are unrelated to each other. If it is not clear whether the two conditions involving an excludes1 note are related or not, query the provider.

EXAMPLE 1: The Excludes1 note for code range R40-R46 states that symptoms and signs constituting part of a pattern of mental disorder (F01-F99) cannot be assigned with the R40-R46 codes. However, if dizziness (R42) is not a component of the mental health condition (e.g., dizziness is unrelated to bipolar disorder), then separate codes may be assigned for both dizziness and bipolar disorder.

EXAMPLE 2: Code range I60-I69 (Cerebrovascular Diseases) has an Excludes1 note for traumatic intracranial hemorrhage (S06.-). Codes in I60-I69 should not be used for a diagnosis of traumatic intracranial hemorrhage. However, if the patient has both a current traumatic intracranial hemorrhage and sequelae from a previous stroke, it would be appropriate to assign both a code from S06.- and I69.-.

An **excludes2 note** means not included here and indicates that although the excluded condition is not classified as part of the condition it is excluded from, a patient may be diagnosed with all conditions at the same time. Therefore, when an excludes2 note appears under a code, it may be acceptable to assign both the code and the excluded code(s) together if supported by the medical documentation.

Coding Tip:

> An excludes2 note instructs you to assign more than one code when medical documentation supports all conditions.

EXAMPLE: ICD-10-CM EXCLUDES2 NOTE: Locate ICD-10-CM code **M19.14 Post-traumatic osteoarthritis, right hand**, and find the Excludes2 note for post-traumatic osteoarthritis of first carpometacarpal joint (M18.2-, M18.3-). The Excludes2 note means that because a patient can be diagnosed with both "post-traumatic osteoarthritis of the hand" and "post-traumatic osteoarthritis of the first carpometacarpal joint," it is acceptable to assign codes to both conditions if supported by medical documentation.

Exercise 3.8 – Excludes1 and Excludes2 Notes

Instructions: Assign an ICD-10-CM code to each statement. Make sure that you appropriately interpret the use of excludes1 and excludes2 notes in the ICD-10-CM tabular list.

_____ 1. Cardiovascular disease of native coronary artery

_____ 2. Arteritis

_____ 3. Absence of menstruation

_____ 4. Herpetiformis dermatosis

_____ 5. Dextrocardia

_____ 6. Meningeal tuberculoma. Tuberculoma of brain and spinal cord.

_____ 7. Malignant neoplasm of dorsal surface of base of tongue

_____ 8. Sucrase-isomaltase deficiency. Congenital lactase deficiency.

_____ 9. Psychotic disorder with hallucinations. Paranoid schizophrenia.

_____ 10. Hemorrhage from the throat. Hemoptysis.

Inclusion Terms

Lists of inclusion terms are included below certain codes in the ICD-10-CM tabular list. The **inclusion terms** indicate some of the conditions for which that code may be assigned. They may be synonyms with the code title, or, in the case of "other specified" codes, the terms may also provide a list of various conditions included within a code. The list of inclusion terms in the tabular list is not exhaustive. The index may provide additional terms that may also be assigned to a given code.

The ICD-10-CM disease index is an important supplement to the tabular list because it contains many diagnostic terms that do not appear in the tabular list. The inclusion terms listed below codes in the tabular list are not meant to be exhaustive, and additional terms found only in the disease index may also be assigned to a tabular list code. This concept is called **trust the index**, because when you find a term in the disease index that is not repeated in the

 Note:

> Although inclusion terms are _not_ technically associated with the ICD-10-CM index, it contains many more terms that do not appear in the tabular list.

 ICD-10 Alert!

> ICD-10-PCS does not contain inclusion terms.

tabular list (below a category or subcategory), the code can still be assigned. The tabular list would be too cumbersome to use if all disease index terms were included below categories and subcategories.

> ### EXAMPLE 1: ICD-10-CM TABULAR LIST OF DISEASES AND INJURIES—INCLUSION TERMS:
> The following inclusion terms are located in the Tabular List of Diseases and Injuries for diagnosis code M54.5, Low back pain:
>
> - Loin pain
>
> - Lumbago NOS
>
> ### EXAMPLE 2: ICD-10-CM TABULAR LIST OF DISEASES AND INJURIES—INCLUSION TERMS
> **(conditions classified to "other specified" subcategory codes):** If the provider documents *polyalgia* as the patient's condition, assign code M79.89 even though the code description indicates it is an *other specified* code.
>
> ### EXAMPLE 3: ICD-10-CM INDEX TO DISEASES AND INJURIES AND TABULAR LIST OF DISEASES AND
> **INJURIES—*TRUST THE INDEX:*** Locate the index entry for *infection, fish tapeworm, larval B70.1.* Then, go to the tabular list to verify code B70.1, where you will notice that *infection due to fish tapeworm, larval* is not listed as an inclusion term. The coder has to *trust the index* and assign code B70.1 for the documented condition.

Exercise 3.9 – Inclusion Terms

Instructions: Assign an ICD-10-CM code to each statement. Make sure that you appropriately interpret the use of inclusion terms in the ICD-10-CM tabular list.

_____   **1.** Acute amebic dysentery

_____   **2.** Disseminated blastomycosis

_____   **3.** Megakaryocytic (thrombocytic) leukemia, acute

_____   **4.** GM2 gangliosidosis, juvenile

_____   **5.** Congenital toxoplasmosis

Other, Other Specified, and Unspecified Codes

When **other** or **other specified** appears in a code description, the code is assigned when patient record documentation provides detail for which a specific code does not exist in ICD-10-CM. The ICD-10-CM tabular list "other and other specified codes" often contains a fourth and/or fifth character of 8 or 9. ICD-10-CM index entries that contain the abbreviation NEC are classified to "other" codes in the tabular lists. These index entries represent specific disease entities for which no specific code exists in the tabular list, so the term is included within an "other" code.

ICD-10 Alert!

The *other, other specified,* and *unspecified* coding convention does not appear in ICD-10-PCS.

Unspecified codes are assigned because patient record documentation is insufficient to assign a more specific code. ICD-10-CM tabular list codes designated as "unspecified" often contain a fourth character of 8 or 9 or a fifth character of 9. (Before assigning an unspecified code, ask the provider to document additional information so that a more specific code can be reported.) When an ICD-10-CM tabular list category does not contain an unspecified code, the "other specified" code may represent both "other and unspecified." In ICD-10-CM, "other and unspecified" category and subcategory codes require assignment of extra character(s) to classify the condition.

When the ICD-10-CM index directs the coder to an "other, other specified, or unspecified code" in the tabular list, it is important to review the record carefully (or ask the physician for clarification of documentation) to determine if a more specific code can be assigned. This is referred to as "moving up the ladder of specificity" of codes in the tabular list.

EXAMPLE: ICD-10-CM TABULAR LIST OF DISEASES AND INJURIES—OTHER, OTHER SPECIFIED, AND UNSPECIFIED CODES:

- D64.89 is an *other specified* code.

- D64.9 is an *unspecified* code.

- I70.9 is an *other and unspecified* code.

Exercise 3.10 – Other, Other Specified, and Unspecified Codes

Instructions: Assign an ICD-10-CM code to each statement. Make sure that you appropriately interpret the use of other, other specified, and unspecified codes in the ICD-10-CM tabular list.

_____   **1.** Intussusception of appendix

_____   **2.** Ectopic pregnancy, week 6

_____   **3.** Hepatorenal syndrome (postpartum condition)

_____   **4.** Arterial atheroembolism

_____   **5.** Glaucoma

Etiology and Manifestation Rules

Etiology and manifestation rules include the following notes in the ICD-10-CM Tabular List of Diseases and Injuries:

- Code first underlying disease

- Code, if applicable, any causal condition first

- Use additional code

- In diseases classified elsewhere

To classify certain conditions completely, codes must be assigned to the underlying *etiology* (cause or origin of disease) and multiple body system manifestations (resulting symptoms or conditions) due to the underlying etiology. For such conditions, the underlying condition is sequenced first, if applicable, followed by the manifestation. Wherever an etiology and manifestation combination of codes exists, the tabular list etiology code contains a **use additional code** note and the manifestation code contains a **code first underlying disease** note. These instructional notes assist coders in the proper sequencing of the codes: etiology code followed by manifestation code. In most cases, the manifestation code will have in its title an **in diseases classified elsewhere** note, which indicates that the manifestation codes are a component of the etiology/manifestation coding convention. A manifestation code that does not contain *in diseases classified elsewhere* in its title will contain a "use additional code" note. (Make sure you sequence the manifestation code after the etiology code.)

The instruction to **code, if applicable, any causal condition first** requires the causal condition to be sequenced first if present. A *causal condition* is a disease (e.g., diabetes mellitus) that manifests (or results in) another condition (e.g., diabetic cataracts). If no causal condition is documented, the code that contains the instruction (*code, if applicable, any causal condition first*) may be reported without the causal condition code.

 Note:

Manifestation codes that include the instruction code *first underlying condition* are never reported first on health insurance claims. They must be reported in conjunction with an underlying condition (etiology) code, and they must be listed after the underlying condition code.

(This differs from the instruction to *code first underlying condition*, which does not allow for the code that contains the instruction to be reported without first sequencing the underlying condition.)

Etiology/manifestation conditions are listed together in the ICD-10-CM Index to Diseases and Injuries; the etiology code is listed first, followed by the manifestation codes in brackets. (The manifestation code listed in brackets is always sequenced second.)

☞ **EXAMPLE 1: ICD-10-CM INDEX TO DISEASES AND INJURIES AND TABULAR LIST OF DISEASES AND INJURIES—ETIOLOGY/MANIFESTATION CODES:**
Diagnostic statement *idiopathic pulmonary hemosiderosis* includes two codes in the ICD-10-CM index: E83.1 [J84.03]. Code J84.03 is listed in brackets in the index, which indicates it is the manifestation code and is reported second. The ICD-10-CM tabular list entry for J84.03 is in italics, and it contains a *code first underlying disease* note.

Note:

A **code also** note alerts the coder that more than one code may be required to fully describe the condition. Code sequencing is discretionary.

EXAMPLE 2: ICD-10-CM TABULAR LIST OF DISEASES AND INJURIES—USE ADDITIONAL CODE:
The patient is diagnosed with *benign hypertrophy of the prostate with urge and stress incontinence*. Locate subcategory code N40.1 in the ICD-10-CM tabular list, and notice that the *use additional code …* note instructs you to report an additional code. Therefore, assign codes N40.1 and N39.46. Next, notice that category code N39.4 in the tabular list includes a *code also any associated overactive bladder (N32.81)* note. Because the diagnostic statement (above) does not include *overactive bladder*, do not assign code N32.81.

EXAMPLE 3: ICD-10-CM TABULAR LIST OF DISEASES AND INJURIES—CODE, IF APPLICABLE, ANY CAUSAL CONDITION FIRST: A patient with an alcohol addiction (F10.20) was seen in the office, complaining of urinary incontinence. The physician determined that the condition was nonorganic in origin and most likely the result of the patient being too inebriated to realize he had urinated while unconscious. Code F98.0 is assigned to urinary incontinence that is of nonorganic origin. Code R32 is assigned to urinary incontinence that is organic in nature (e.g., due to urethritis, N34.2).

Exercise 3.11 – Etiology and Manifestation Rules

Instructions: Assign an ICD-10-CM code to each statement. Make sure that you appropriately interpret etiology and manifestation rules in the ICD-10-CM disease index and tabular list.

_____ **1.** Tetanic cataract in hypoparathyroidism

_____ **2.** Cardiac sarcoidosis

_____ **3.** Uremic pericarditis

_____ **4.** Congenital syphilitic peritonitis

_____ **5.** Typhoid osteomyelitis

And

When the word **and** appears in category titles and code descriptions in the ICD-10-CM Tabular List of Diseases and Injuries, ICD-10-PCS Index, and ICD-10-PCS Tables, it is interpreted as meaning *and/or*.

EXAMPLE 1: ICD-10-CM TABULAR LIST OF DISEASES—AND: The word *and* in category code J04 (Acute laryngitis and tracheitis) means that codes are reported for conditions of the larynx, trachea, or larynx and trachea.

EXAMPLE 2: ICD-10-PCS INDEX—AND: The word *and* in subterm *use* Bursa and Ligament, Shoulder, Left (located below main term Acromioclavicular ligament) means that the body part character (located in an ICD-10-PCS table) is reported for procedures performed on the bursa, ligament, or bursa and ligament.

EXAMPLE 3: ICD-10-PCS TABLES—AND: The word *and* in the table for section 0 (Medical and Surgical), value N (Head and Facial Bones) means that the body part character is assigned for procedures performed on head bones, facial bones, or head and facial bones.

Exercise 3.12 – And

Exercise 3.12A – ICD-10-CM

Instructions: Assign an ICD-10-CM code to each statement. Make sure that you appropriately interpret the use of the subterm *and* in the ICD-10-CM tabular list.

_____   **1.** Venereal disease of the rectum due to chlamydia

_____   **2.** Malignant neoplasm of costal cartilage

_____   **3.** Acromegaly

_____   **4.** Parietoalveolar pneumopathy

_____   **5.** Carcinoma *in situ* of scalp

Exercise 3.12B – ICD-10-PCS

Instructions: Assign an ICD-10-PCS code to each statement. Make sure you appropriately interpret the use of the subterm *and* in the ICD-10-PCS index and tables.

_____   **1.** Ultrasonography of head

_____   **2.** Insertion of oropharyngeal (mouth and throat) airway

_____   **3.** Open division of muscle, left upper arm

_____   **4.** Repair of skin, right hand

_____   **5.** Open biopsy, tonsils

Due To

The subterm **due to** is located in the ICD-10-CM Index to Diseases and Injuries in alphabetical order to indicate the presence of a cause-and-effect (or causal) relationship between two conditions. When the disease index includes *due to* as a subterm, the code is assigned only if the physician documented the causal relationship between two conditions, such as meningitis due to adenovirus. It is possible that a patient could have meningitis along with an unrelated adenovirus at the same time. (The *due to* phrase is included in tabular list code descriptions, but it is not a coding instruction.)

ICD-10-CM occasionally presumes a causal relationship between two conditions. This means that the physician is not required to document *due to* in the diagnostic statement, such as when the patient has hypertension and renal failure. This condition is coded as hypertensive renal failure, which is interpreted as hypertension due to renal failure. (Chapter 4 of this textbook contains further discussion about causal relationships that are presumed by ICD-10-CM.)

ICD-10 Alert!

The *due to* instruction does not appear in the ICD-10-PCS Index.

 Note:

The ICD-10-CM disease index also includes subterm *in* (*due to*) to indicate the presence of a cause-and-effect (or causal) relationship between two conditions.

EXAMPLE 1: ICD-10-CM INDEX TO DISEASES AND INJURIES—DUE TO: When the physician documents *pneumonitis due to inhalation of regurgitated food*, a causal relationship exists and code J69.0 is assigned.

EXAMPLE 2: ICD-10-CM INDEX TO DISEASES AND INJURIES—IN (DUE TO): When the physician documents *anemia in moderate chronic kidney disease*, a causal relationship exists, and codes N18.3 and D63.1 are assigned.

Exercise 3.13 – Due To

Instructions: Assign an ICD-10-CM code to each statement. Make sure that you appropriately interpret the use of subterm *due to* in the ICD-10-CM disease index.

_____ **1.** Cirrhosis due to Wilson's disease

_____ **2.** Bubo due to *Haemophilus ducreyi*

_____ **3.** Carnitine deficiency due to hemodialysis

_____ **4.** Hypothyroidism due to irradiation therapy

_____ **5.** Airway obstruction due to laryngospasm

In

When the word **in** appears in the ICD-10-CM disease index, it is located in alphabetical order below the main term. To assign a code from the list of qualifiers below the word *in*, the physician must document both conditions in the patient's record. ICD-10-CM classifies certain conditions as if there were a cause-and-effect relationship present because they occur together much of the time (e.g., pneumonia in Q fever).

ICD-10 Alert!

The *in* instruction does not appear in ICD-10-PCS.

EXAMPLE: ICD-10-CM INDEX TO DISEASES AND INJURIES—IN: Locate main term *pneumonia* in the index, and notice that the word *in* appears in alphabetical order above a list of second qualifiers. To assign a code from the list, the physician must document a relationship between both conditions, such as *pneumonia in measles* (or *postpneumonia measles*) to which combination code B05.2 is assigned. (Other conditions that occur together may require the assignment of multiple codes, one for the etiology and another for the manifestation.)

Exercise 3.14 – In

Instructions: Assign an ICD-10-CM code to each statement. Make sure that you appropriately interpret the use of subterm *in* when reviewing the ICD-10-CM disease index.

_____ **1.** Bicornis uterus in pregnancy, week 12

_____ **2.** Adenocarcinoma in adenomatous polyposis coli

_____ **3.** Uterine fibroid tumor in pregnancy (antepartum, second trimester, week 14)

_____ **4.** Keratoconjunctivitis in exanthema

_____ **5.** Nephrosis in epidemic hemorrhagic fever

With

When the word **with** appears in the ICD-10-CM Index to Diseases and Injuries, it is located immediately below the main term, not in alphabetical order. To assign a code from the list of qualifiers below the word *with*, the physician must document the presence of both conditions (or procedures) in the patient's record.

ICD-10-CM presumes a causal relationship between the two conditions linked by the term "with" in the index or tabular list. Such conditions should be coded as related even in the absence of provider documentation explicitly linking them, *unless the documentation clearly states the conditions are unrelated.* For conditions not specifically linked by these relational terms in the classification, provider documentation must link the conditions in order to code them as related.

> **! ICD-10 Alert!**
>
> Subterm *with* occasionally appears in the ICD-10-PCS Index.

EXAMPLE 1: ICD-10-CM INDEX TO DISEASES AND INJURIES—WITH: Locate main term *measles* in the index, and notice that the word *with* appears above a list of second qualifiers. To assign a code from the list, the physician must document both conditions, such as *measles with keratitis* (B05.81). The physician could also document:

- Measles keratitis
- Measles associated with keratitis
- Measles and keratitis

EXAMPLE 2: ICD-10-PCS INDEX—WITH: Locate main term *phacoemulsification* in the index, and notice the terms *with* (and *without*) appear as subterms. The subterm entries refer coders to ICD-10-PCS tables 08R or 08D, depending on the procedure performed.

EXAMPLE 3: ICD-10-PCS INDEX—WITH: Locate main term *Fixation, bone* in the index, and subterm *External, with fracture reduction* see *Reposition*. Notice that the word *with* appears in the phrase *with fracture reduction*. To assign a character for "bone fixation, external, with fracture reduction" from the appropriate Reposition table, the physician must document both the "bone fixation" and "fracture reduction" procedures.

Exercise 3.15 – With

Exercise 3.15A – ICD-10-CM

Instructions: Assign an ICD-10-CM code to each statement. Make sure you appropriately interpret the use of subterm *with* in the ICD-10-CM index.

_____   **1.** Appendicitis with perforation

_____   **2.** Thyrotoxicosis with uninodular adenomatous goiter

_____   **3.** Traumatic hemothorax with pneumothorax (initial encounter)

_____   **4.** Adjustment disorder with anxiety

_____   **5.** Skull agenesis with anencephalus (or anencephaly)

Exercise 3.15B – ICD-10-PCS

Instructions: Assign an ICD-10-PCS code to each statement. Make sure you appropriately interpret the use of subterm *with* in the ICD-10-PCS index. For ICD-10-PCS answers, enter the code found in the index entry; it may be less than seven characters in length.

_____   **1.** Computer-assisted procedure of the lower extremity with computerized tomography

(continues)

Exercise 3.15 (*continued*)

_____ **2.** Herniorrhaphy with synthetic substitute

_____ **3.** Interrogation, cardiac rhythm related device, with cardiac function testing

_____ **4.** Phacoemulsification of right lens, with intraocular lens implant

_____ **5.** Vasotomy with ligation

Cross-References

The ICD-10-CM and ICD-10-PCS indexes include **cross-references**, which instruct the coder to refer to another entry in the index (e.g., *see*, *see also*, *see* condition) or to the tabular list (e.g., *see* category) to assign the correct code.

- The ***see*** instruction after a main term directs the coder to refer to another term in the ICD-10-CM and ICD-10-PCS indexes to locate the code. The coder must go to the referenced main term to locate the correct code.

- The ***see also*** instruction is located after a main term or subterm in the ICD-10-CM indexes and directs the coder to another main term (or subterm) that may provide additional useful index entries. The *see also* instruction does not have to be followed if the original main term (or subterm) provides the correct code.

- The ***see category*** instruction directs the coder to the ICD-10-CM tabular list, where a code can be selected from the options provided there.

- The ***see condition*** instruction directs the coder to the main term for a condition, found in the ICD-10-CM disease index.

- The ***use*** instruction directs the coder to a body part or a device in the ICD-10-PCS index. The coder must go to the appropriate ICD-10-PCS table to assign a character for the body part or device referenced in the index.

EXAMPLE 1: ICD-10-CM INDEX TO DISEASES AND INJURIES—*SEE*: Locate main term *Laceration* and subterm *blood vessel* in the ICD-10-CM index. Notice that a cross-reference directs you to "See Injury, blood vessel," which is at a different location in the index where the code can be found.

EXAMPLE 2: ICD-10-CM INDEX TO DISEASES AND INJURIES—*SEE ALSO*: The *see also* instruction is optional if the correct code can be located below the main term (e.g., laceration of lower back, S31.010). If the correct code cannot be located, the *see also* cross-reference directs the coder to a different location in the index where the code can be found.

EXAMPLE 3: ICD-10-CM INDEX TO DISEASES AND INJURIES—*SEE* CATEGORY: Locate main term *pyelitis*, subterm *with*, and second qualifier *calculus* in the ICD-10-CM index. Notice that a cross-reference directs you to *see* category N20. To assign the correct code, review category N20 in the tabular list to select the appropriate fourth character.

EXAMPLE 4: ICD-10-CM INDEX TO DISEASES AND INJURIES—*SEE* CONDITION: Locate main term *Accidental* in the ICD-10-CM index, and notice that a cross-reference directs you to *see* condition, which means the patient record needs to be reviewed to determine the condition (e.g., fracture).

EXAMPLE 5: ICD-10-PCS INDEX—*SEE*: Locate main term *Abdominohysterectomy* in the ICD-10-PCS index, and notice that a cross-reference directs you to *see* Excision, Uterus 0UB9, which is at a different location in the index. (The four characters 0UB9 direct the coder to the 0UB Excision table in ICD-10-PCS.)

EXAMPLE 6: ICD-10-PCS INDEX—*USE*: Locate main term *Abdominal esophagus* in the ICD-10-PCS index. Notice that a cross-reference directs you to *use* Esophagus, Lower, which is a body part that is assigned a character from an ICD-10-PCS table (e.g., Bypass table). Go to main term *Bypass*, and locate subterms *esophagus* and *lower* to identify an ICD-10-PCS table (from which the code is built, and for which a character is selected for body part *lower esophagus*).

Exercise 3.16 – Cross-References

Exercise 3.16A – ICD-10-CM

Instructions: Enter the ICD-10-CM index cross-reference instruction for each ICD-10-CM main term. For example, an ICD-10-CM cross-reference instruction is *see Laceration*.

_____ **1.** Abnormal, abnormality, abnormalities

_____ **2.** Toxicosis

_____ **3.** Strangulation, strangulated

_____ **4.** Undescended testis

_____ **5.** Proteinuria complicating pregnancy

Exercise 3.16B – ICD-10-PCS

Instructions: Enter the ICD-10-PCS index cross-reference instruction for each ICD-10-PCS main term. For example, an ICD-10-PCS cross-reference instruction is *use Esophagus, Lower*.

_____ **1.** Ablation

_____ **2.** Achillorrhaphy

_____ **3.** Canthorrhaphy

_____ **4.** Accessory obturator nerve

_____ **5.** Cardiac event recorder

Code Assignment and Clinical Criteria

The assignment of a diagnosis code is based on the physician's diagnostic statement that the condition exists. The physician's statement that the patient has a particular condition is sufficient. Code assignment is *not* based on clinical criteria used by the physician to establish the diagnosis.

> **EXAMPLE:** The patient is admitted to the hospital for "severe confusion" (R41.0). The physician documented "Alzheimer's disease with dementia and behavioral disturbances" (G30.9, F02.81) as the discharge diagnoses. Clinical criteria (e.g., brain imaging study) are not documented in the hospital record. Codes G30.9 and F02.81 are reported instead of code R41.0 because code assignment is based on the physician's diagnostic statement that the condition exists, not clinical criteria. In this case, the physician used *pattern recognition* to establish the discharge diagnoses. This involves the physician using experience to recognize a "pattern" of clinical characteristics; it is based on certain signs and/or symptoms typically associated with a disease process.

EXERCISE 3.17 – Code Assignment and Clinical Criteria

Instructions: Assign an ICD-10-CM code to each statement. Make sure that you appropriately interpret the intent of the *code assignment and clinical criteria* coding convention.

_____ **1.** Patient admitted for difficulty breathing and fever. Physician's discharge diagnosis is pneumonia.

_____ **2.** Patient admitted with malaise. Physician's discharge diagnosis is depression.

(continues)

Exercise 3.17 *(continued)*

_____ **3.** Patient admitted with severe headache. Physician's discharge diagnosis is intractable migraine.

_____ **4.** Patient admitted with abdominal pain and fever. Physician's discharge diagnosis is acute appendicitis.

_____ **5.** Patient admitted with pain and swelling, left ankle. Physician's discharge diagnosis is sprain, left ankle.

Summary

Coding conventions are general rules used in the ICD-10-CM and ICD-10-PCS classifications, independent of official coding guidelines. An indented format is used for ease in reference in the ICD-10-CM and ICD-10-PCS indexes.

Eponyms are diseases or syndromes that are named for people, and they appear in ICD-10-CM. Abbreviations include NEC and NOS, and they appear in ICD-10-CM. Punctuation includes parentheses, brackets, square brackets, and colons. Certain main terms in the ICD-10-CM disease index, including the Table of Neoplasms, are followed by boxed notes, which contain special instructions. The ICD-10-CM disease index contains a Table of Neoplasms and a Table of Drugs and Chemicals. The ICD-10-PCS index does not contain tables; however, instead of a tabular list of codes, ICD-10-PCS contains tables (discussed in Chapter 5).

The ICD-10-CM tabular list contains includes notes, excludes1 and excludes2 notes, and inclusion terms.

"Other" and "other specified" codes are assigned when patient record documentation provides detail for which a specific code does not exist in ICD-10-CM. "Unspecified" codes are assigned because patient record documentation is insufficient for the assignment of a more specific code. Etiology and manifestation codes contain the following notes in the ICD-10-CM tabular list: code first underlying disease; code, if applicable, any causal condition first; use additional code; and in diseases classified elsewhere. When the word *and* appears in category titles and code descriptions in the ICD-10-CM indexes and tabular list, it is interpreted as meaning "and/or." The instruction *due to* is located in ICD-10-CM as a subterm (in alphabetical order) to indicate the presence of a cause-and-effect relationship between two conditions. The word *in* as it appears in the ICD-10-CM disease index is located in alphabetical order below the main term. The word *with* appears in the ICD-10-CM and ICD-10-PCS indexes immediately below the main term, and it is not in alphabetical order. A causal relationship is presumed between two conditions linked by terms *with* and *due to* in the index and tabular list; such conditions are coded as related even when physician documentation explicitly linking them is absent (unless the documentation clearly states the conditions are unrelated). For conditions not specifically linked by the terms *with* and *due to* in the ICD-10-CM index, physician documentation must link the conditions to code them as related. Cross-reference terms in the ICD-10-CM and ICD-10-PCS indexes instruct the coder to refer to another entry in the index or to go directly to the tabular list or table, respectively, to assign or build the correct code.

The code assignment and clinical criteria coding convention bases the assignment of a diagnosis code on the physician's diagnostic statement that the condition exists, not clinical criteria used to establish the diagnosis.

Internet Links

ICD-10-CM/PCS updates: Go to **www.cms.gov**, click on the Medicare link, click on the ICD-10 link under Coding, and scroll down to click on this year's ICD-10-CM or ICD-10-PCS link.

JustCoding News free e-newsletter: Go to **www.justcoding.com**, and click on the eNewsletter Signup link at the top of the page.

Optum360 Coding Central Articles: Go to *www.optum360coding.com*, hover over the Coding Central link, and click on the Inside Track to ICD-10 link or the Coding Articles link.

Study Checklist

☐ Read this chapter and highlight key concepts.

☐ Create an index card for each key term.

☐ Access the chapter Internet links to learn more about concepts.

☐ Complete the chapter exercises and review, verifying answers with your instructor.

☐ Complete Workbook chapter, verifying answers with your instructor.

☐ Go to *www.cengagebrain.com* to access the Student Companion Web Site. Login instructions are located in the Preface.

☐ Form a study group with classmates to discuss chapter concepts in preparation for an exam.

Review

Matching – ICD-10-CM

Instructions: Match the format in Column 2 with each line of the ICD-10-CM Index to Diseases and Injuries entries in Column 1.

ICD-10-CM Index to Diseases and Injuries

_____ 1. `Abnormal, abnormality, abnormalities (see`

_____ 2. `also Anomaly)`

_____ 3. `chromosome, chromosomal Q99.9`

_____ 4. `sex Q99.8`

_____ 5. `female phenotype Q97.9`

Format

a. 2nd qualifier

b. 3rd qualifier

c. Continuation line

d. Main term

e. Subterm

Multiple Choice – ICD-10-CM

Instructions: Circle the most appropriate response.

1. If an index entry is too long to fit on one line, additional text is:
   a. edited so that the content fits onto just one line.
   b. located on the next line, flush with the preceding line.
   c. moved to the second line and indented two spaces.
   d. printed on the next line and indented five spaces.

2. A coder locates a code in the ICD-10-CM disease index, which contains the abbreviation NEC. Upon verification of the code in the tabular list, the coder assigns that code. Which coding convention explains this code assignment?
   a. Information needed to assign a more specific code has not been obtained from the provider.
   b. The coder is directed to an "other specified" code by the index when a specific code is not available in the tabular list.
   c. Use of a more general code is indicated when the coder is unsure about information contained in documentation.
   d. Whenever a specific code is not available in the index for a condition, the coder is directed to the "other specified" code in the tabular list.

3. When the ICD-10-CM tabular list contains the abbreviation NOS, which coding convention explains the code assignment?
   a. If the coder is not sure about the information contained in the documentation, use of a more general code is indicated.
   b. Information needed to assign a more specific code has not been obtained from the provider.
   c. The coder is directed to an "other specified" code by the index when a specific code is not available in the tabular list.
   d. Whenever a specific code is not available in the index for a condition, the coder is directed to the "other specified" code in the tabular list.

4. The use of a colon in the ICD-10-CM tabular list:
   a. identifies the use of manifestation codes, which are to be sequenced second.
   b. indicates that one or more additional terms are to be included in the diagnostic statement to classify a condition or procedure.
   c. means that the words following the colon may be present in or absent from the provider's diagnostic statement.
   d. suggests the use of synonyms, alternative wording, or explanatory phrases.

5. *Includes* notes appear:
   a. below an ICD-10-CM category in the tabular list.
   b. after main terms in the ICD-10-CM index.
   c. above an ICD-10-CM code in the tabular list.
   d. underneath essential modifiers in the ICD-10-CM index.

6. *Excludes1* and *Excludes2* notes appear in the:
   a. ICD-10-CM and ICD-10-PCS indexes.
   b. ICD-10-CM index and tabular list.
   c. ICD-10-CM tabular list only.
   d. ICD-10-CM index only.

7. *Trust the index* is an ICD-10-CM concept that is used when:
   a. a subterm located in the index is not listed in the tabular list.
   b. additional information was not obtained from the provider.
   c. insufficient documentation prevents the assignment of a more specific code.
   d. the coder is directed to the "other specified" code in the tabular list.

8. Unspecified codes:
   a. are classified as "other" codes in the ICD-10-CM tabular list.
   b. contain the NEC abbreviation in the ICD-10-CM index.
   c. result when a code is not found in the ICD-10-CM index for a specified condition.
   d. often contain a fourth or fifth character of 8 or 9.

9. Etiology codes:
   a. are designated in the ICD-10-CM index by brackets.
   b. classify a condition that occurs as the result of another condition.
   c. contain a *use additional code* instruction in the ICD-10-CM tabular list.
   d. must be sequenced second as the underlying condition code.

10. The *see also* instruction in the ICD-10-CM index follows a subterm and refers the coder to another main term that:
    a. allows for assignment of a secondary code.
    b. contains the code that is to be assigned.
    c. may provide additional useful index entries.
    d. must be followed to assign the correct code.

11. Two weeks ago, the patient was riding her bicycle when she fell and scraped her right knee on the gravel road. She had her mother look at it, and after washing it with warm soap and water and pouring some hydrogen peroxide on the abrasion, the patient returned to riding her bicycle. Today the patient is seen due to complaints of tenderness and pain of her right knee. Upon examination, it was determined that small pebbles are embedded below the skin's surface. The pebbles were successfully removed, the wound was wrapped, and the patient was discharged home. The discharge diagnosis is retained stones, skin of right knee.

ICD-10-CM INDEX TO DISEASES AND INJURIES

`Retained` —*see* `Retention`

`Retention, retained`

    `foreign body` —*see* also `Foreign body,`

        `retained`

      `current trauma` —`code as Foreign body,`

        `by site or type`

Upon review of the ICD-10-CM Index to Diseases and Injuries entry above, the coder locates main term *Retained* and notes the "*see* Retention" instruction, which means the coder should:

    a. generate a physician query to ask the physician to document a more specific diagnosis.

    b. go to main term *Retention* in the ICD-10-CM index to begin locating the code.

    c. locate the main term in the ICD-9-CM disease index, and use the GEM to assign the ICD-10-CM code.

    d. review the ICD-10-CM Tabular List of Diseases and Injuries to locate the code.

12. A patient was installing a new roof on his house using a nail gun when he got distracted by someone calling his name from the sidewalk. He proceeded to nail the fleshy skin between his left thumb and forefinger to the roof. He was able to pull the flesh free, but the nail remained embedded in his skin. The nail was removed, the wound irrigated and bandaged, and the patient discharged home with a diagnosis of puncture wound with nail (from nail gun) located in the skin and soft tissue between left thumb and forefinger.

ICD-10-CM INDEX TO DISEASES AND INJURIES

`Foreign body`

  `in`

    `puncture wound` —*see* `Puncture, by site,`

      `with foreign body`

    `soft tissue (residual) M79.5`

`Puncture`

  `hand S61.439`

    `with`

      `foreign body S61.449`

    `finger` —*see* `Puncture, finger`

(continues)

ICD-10-CM INDEX TO DISEASES AND INJURIES (*continued*)

```
Puncture (continued)
    left S61.432
      with
        foreign body S61.442
    right S61.431
      with
        foreign body S61.441
```

Upon review of the ICD-10-CM entry above and main term *Foreign body*, the coder follows the instructional note to "*see* Puncture, by site"; the coder follows the instruction by locating "Puncture, hand S61.439" and reviews index entries to identify the code. Next, the coder should:

    a. assign code M79.5 after verifying it in the tabular list.

    b. follow the cross-reference *see* Puncture, finger.

    c. look up code S61.439 in the diseases tabular list.

    d. verify code S61.442 in the tabular list, and assign it.

13. Three months ago, the 17-year-old patient broke up with his girlfriend, and she stuck him in the right eye with a plastic straw. Luckily, she missed the eyeball and embedded the straw in the soft tissue of the outer right eye. The patient presents today with pain and swelling of the right eye, and upon examination a tiny piece of plastic is found to have embedded in the soft tissue. The foreign body was removed, the wound irrigated, and the patient discharged home with a prescription for an antibiotic.

ICD-10-CM TABULAR LIST OF DISEASES AND INJURIES

```
H05.5 Retained (old) foreign body following penetrating
        wound of orbit
            Retrobulbar foreign body
      Use additional code to identify the type of retained
      foreign body (Z18.-)
                EXCLUDES1      current penetrating wound of orbit (S05.4-)
                EXCLUDES2      retained foreign body of eyelid (H02.81-)
                               retained intraocular foreign body
                                  (H44.6-, H44.7-)
      H05.50    Retained (old) foreign body following
                penetrating wound of unspecified orbit
      H05.51    Retained (old) foreign body following
                penetrating wound of right orbit
      H05.52    Retained (old) foreign body following
                penetrating wound of left orbit
      H05.53    Retained (old) foreign body following
                penetrating wound of bilateral orbits
```

Upon review of the ICD-10-CM tabular list entry above, in addition to external causes of injuries codes W45.8xxA and Y07.04 and factors influencing health status and contact with health services code Z18.2, select the appropriate disease and injury code.

    a. H02.81–

    b. H05.50

    c. H05.51

    d. S05.4–

Multiple Choice – ICD-10-PCS

Instructions: Circle the most appropriate response.

1. The patient underwent an angiotripsy procedure of the right brachial artery. Review the following ICD-10-PCS Index entry, and select the appropriate cross-reference.

ICD-10-PCS INDEX

Angiotripsy

   –*See* Occlusion, Upper Arteries 03L

   –*See* Occlusion, Upper Veins 05L

---

    a. *See* Occlusion, Upper Arteries 03L

    b. *See* Occlusion, Upper Veins 05L

2. The patient underwent replacement of a spinal canal drainage device. Review the following ICD-10-PCS Table entry, and using the build-a-code approach, which ICD-10-PCS code would be assigned?

ICD-10-PCS TABLE

Central Nervous System 001–00X

0	Medical and Surgical
0	Central Nervous System
2	Change:	Taking out or off a device from a body part and putting back an identical or similar device in or on the same body part without cutting or puncturing the skin or a mucous membrane

Body Part Character 4	Approach Character 5	Device Character 6	Qualifier Character 7
0 Brain	X External	0 Drainage Device	Z No Qualifier
E Cranial Nerve		Y Other Device	
U Spinal Canal			

---

    a. 0020X0Z

    b. 002EX0Z

    c. 002UX0Z

    d. 002UXYZ

ICD-10-CM Coding Guidelines

Chapter Outline

ICD-10-CM Official Guidelines for Coding
and Reporting
General ICD-10-CM Diagnosis Coding
Guidelines
ICD-10-CM Chapter-Specific Diagnosis
Coding Guidelines

 Note:

The ICD-10-PCS procedure
coding guidelines are located in
Chapter 5 because they impact
inpatient hospital coding only.

Chapter Objectives

At the conclusion of this chapter, the student should be able to:

- Define key terms.
- Explain HIPAA's impact on the adherence to *ICD-10-CM Official Guidelines for Coding and Reporting*.
- Describe the content of each section of the *ICD-10-CM Official Guidelines for Coding and Reporting*.
- Apply general ICD-10-CM coding guidelines when assigning codes to diagnoses.
- Apply chapter-specific ICD-10-CM coding guidelines when assigning codes to diagnoses.

Key Terms

benign	laterality	open fracture	sequela
carcinoma (Ca) *in situ*	malignant	opportunistic infection	simple fracture
closed fracture	malunion	overlapping sites	type 1 diabetes mellitus
combination code	metastatic cancer	perinatal period	type 2 diabetes mellitus
compound fracture	multiple codes	primary malignancy	uncertain behavior
contiguous sites	neoplasm	residual effect	unspecified nature
fracture	nonunion	secondary malignancy	

Introduction

This chapter includes an interpretation of the following coding guidelines, which are published in the *ICD-10-CM Official Guidelines for Coding and Reporting*:

- General ICD-10-CM diagnosis coding guidelines

- ICD-10-CM chapter-specific diagnosis coding guidelines

The coding guidelines are to be used as a companion to the official version of the ICD-10-CM coding manual, which contains coding conventions to ensure accurate coding.

ICD-10-CM disease and injury codes describe causes of illness or clinical symptoms exhibited by the patient, and codes assigned must be supported by documentation in the patient's record. Third-party payers require that claims submitted for reimbursement demonstrate medical necessity for treatment, which means that a diagnosis code must be reported for each procedure or service code included on the claim. (ICD-10-PCS procedure codes describe procedures performed for the inpatient hospital treatment of illness and injury. HCPCS level II and CPT codes are reported on outpatient claims, and these coding systems are discussed in Chapters 7–18.)

> **Note:**
>
> When reviewing examples and completing exercises and review questions in this chapter, use your ICD-10-CM coding manual to locate disease and injury index entries and to verify them in the tabular list.

> **Note:**
>
> ICD-10-PCS procedure coding guidelines apply to inpatient hospitalizations only, and the guidelines are discussed in Chapter 5.

 Note:

> The following additional content is located on the Student Companion Web Site at www.cengagebrain.com.
>
> - *Alternate Health Care Facilities and Coding Guidelines*
> - *HIV-Related Conditions and Opportunistic Infections*

ICD-10-CM Official Guidelines for Coding and Reporting

The Centers for Medicare & Medicaid Services (CMS) and the National Center for Health Statistics (NCHS) are the agencies in the U.S. Department of Health & Human Services (DHHS) that develop official guidelines for coding and reporting using ICD-10-CM. The *Official Guidelines for Coding and Reporting* are approved by the four organizations that make up the Cooperating Parties for the ICD-10-CM. They include the American Hospital Association (AHA), American Health Information Management Association (AHIMA), CMS, and NCHS. The guidelines are a set of rules developed to accompany and complement the official conventions and instructions provided within ICD-10-CM. They are based on the coding and sequencing instructions in ICD-10-CM and provide additional instruction. The health care provider is responsible for complete and accurate patient record documentation, and the coder is responsible for providing complete and accurate code assignment and reporting diagnoses and procedures. The guidelines were developed to assist both health care providers and coders in identifying diagnoses and procedures that are to be reported. Coders should review the entire patient record to determine the reason for an encounter and the conditions treated. This means that if the provider documents a disease (or procedure) on the face sheet or in the discharge summary, the coder should review other patient record reports (e.g., progress notes, laboratory data, operative report, pathology report) to assign appropriate codes, including level of specificity. Quite often the provider will document additional information about a disease (or procedure) elsewhere in the patient record that will contribute to the assignment of a specific code (e.g., laterality, acute or chronic nature).

Note:

The structure and conventions of ICD-10-CM and ICD-10-PCS are discussed in Chapter 3. ICD-10-CM general coding guidelines and ICD-10-CM chapter-specific coding guidelines are discussed later in this chapter.

The ICD-10-CM *Official Guidelines for Coding and Reporting* are organized into four sections and one appendix.

- Section I includes the structure and conventions of the classification and general guidelines that apply to the entire classification and chapter-specific guidelines that correspond to the chapters as they are arranged in the classification.

- Section II includes guidelines for selection of the principal diagnosis for nonoutpatient settings. (Nonoutpatient settings include acute care hospitals, long-term care facilities, home health care agencies, nursing homes, and so on.)

- Section III includes guidelines for reporting additional diagnoses (e.g., coexisting conditions, complications) in nonoutpatient settings.

- Section IV includes guidelines for outpatient diagnosis coding and reporting.

- Appendix I includes present on admission (POA) reporting guidelines. (POA reporting is discussed in Chapter 19.)

Note:

Selection of principal diagnosis (and principal procedure) is discussed in Chapter 5.

Note:

Reporting additional diagnoses (e.g., comorbidities and complications) (and secondary procedures) for inpatient care is discussed in Chapter 5.

Note:

Outpatient diagnosis coding and reporting guidelines, which include selection of the first-listed diagnosis (formerly called the primary diagnosis) and secondary diagnoses, are discussed in Chapter 6.

Note:

Present on admission (POA) reporting guidelines are discussed in Chapter 19.

The *Official Guidelines for Coding and Reporting* contain rules that accompany and complement the official conventions and instructions provided within ICD-10-CM; they are based on coding and sequencing instructions in the coding manual. A joint effort between the health care provider and the coder is essential to achieving complete and accurate documentation, code assignment, and reporting of diagnoses and procedures. The coding guidelines were developed to assist both the health care provider and the coder in identifying diagnoses and procedures that are to be reported. The importance of consistent, complete documentation in the medical record is crucial because without such documentation, accurate coding cannot be achieved. In addition, the entire record must be reviewed to determine the specific reason for the encounter and the conditions treated. (The term *encounter* is used in the coding guidelines for all health care settings, including inpatient hospital admissions. The term *provider* is used in the coding guidelines to mean physician or any qualified health care practitioner who is legally accountable for establishing the patient's diagnosis.)

Note:

The ICD-10-PCS procedure coding guidelines are located in Chapter 5.

HIPAA Alert!

The HIPAA regulations for electronic transactions require providers and third-party payers, including Medicare administrative contractors (MACs), to adhere to the *Official Guidelines for Coding and Reporting*. Thus, a violation of the coding guidelines is technically a HIPAA violation. Because some third-party payers and MACs do not appear to be aware of (or understand) this HIPAA provision, to obtain appropriate reimbursement for submitted ICD-10-CM (and ICD-10-PCS) codes, you may need to point out specific provisions in the regulation that reference the coding guidelines. For example, the Z51 codes in ICD-10-CM can be reported as a first-listed code for outpatient care. However, some third-party payers and MACs deny claims that report Z51 codes. In that case, you will need to contact your regional CMS office or the HIPAA enforcement office (which is located at CMS) for resolution. Third-party payers and MACs should not be allowed to violate the *Official Guidelines for Coding and Reporting* because that means they are violating HIPAA provisions!

Exercise 4.1 – ICD-10-CM Official Guidelines for Coding and Reporting

Instructions: Complete each statement.

1. The *Official Guidelines for Coding and Reporting* are approved by the _____ for ICD-10-CM to accompany and complement the official conventions and instructions provided within ICD-10-CM.

2. Coding guidelines use the term _____ for all health care settings, including inpatient hospital admissions.

3. Coding guidelines use the term _____ to mean physician or any qualified health care practitioner who is legally accountable for establishing the patient's diagnosis.

4. The _____ regulations for electronic transactions require providers and third-party payers, including Medicare administrative contractors (MACs), to adhere to the *Official Guidelines for Coding and Reporting*.

5. Section I of the *Official Guidelines for Coding and Reporting* includes the _____ of the classification and general guidelines that apply to the entire classification and chapter-specific guidelines that correspond to the chapters as they are arranged in the classification.

6. Section II of the *Official Guidelines for Coding and Reporting* includes guidelines for selection of the _____ for nonoutpatient settings.

7. Section III of the *Official Guidelines for Coding and Reporting* includes guidelines for reporting _____ in nonoutpatient settings.

8. Inpatient care requires the reporting of additional diagnoses, which are called _____.

9. Section IV of the *Official Guidelines for Coding and Reporting* covers _____ coding and reporting.

10. Appendix I of the *ICD-10-CM Official Guidelines for Coding and Reporting* covers _____ reporting guidelines.

General ICD-10-CM Diagnosis Coding Guidelines

The *International Classification of Diseases (ICD)* was originally created to track diseases for statistical reporting purposes. Its origin is based on the Bertillon *International Statistical Classification of Causes of Death*, which was revised by the American Public Health Association (APHA) every 10 years. In 1948, the World Health Organization (WHO) assumed responsibility for revisions and the official name of the classification system was changed to the *International Classification of Diseases*. The NCHS created the clinical modification (CM) of ICD-9, and ICD-9-CM was implemented in 1979. Although ICD-9-CM contained additional clinical information, its three-digit codes and their sequence correlate to the ICD-9 system developed by the WHO. *ICD-10-CM and ICD-10-PCS replaced ICD-9-CM on October 1, 2015* (Figure 4-1). ICD-10-CM contains additional clinical information, as compared with ICD-9-CM Volumes I and II, but its three-character codes and their sequence correlate to the ICD-10 system developed by the WHO. ICD-10-PCS is a classification system developed to report inpatient procedure codes; its content is included in Chapter 5.

The general coding guidelines are followed when assigning ICD-10-CM diagnosis codes for inpatient, outpatient, and physician office settings.

Courtesy of Amphion Medical

Figure 4-1 History of coding

Locating a Code in ICD-10-CM— Use of Both Index and Tabular List

Use both the index and the tabular list when locating and assigning codes because relying on just the index or tabular list results in coding errors and less specificity when selecting codes.

Locate Each Term in the Alphabetic Index

Locate each term in the ICD-10-CM disease index first, and verify the code selected in the tabular list. Make sure you read and are guided by coding conventions (e.g., instructional notations such as NOS and NEC) that appear in either the index or the tabular list.

> **Note:**
>
> Before assigning codes, review the explanation and examples of ICD-10-CM coding conventions in Chapter 3.

 Note:

> Use *both* the ICD-10-CM index and tabular list because the ICD-10-CM index does not always provide the complete code. Selection of the complete code, including laterality (e.g., bilateral, right side, left side) and any applicable seventh character is done using the tabular list. A dash (-) at the end of a code in the index indicates that additional character(s) are required. Even if a dash is *not* included at the index entry, refer to the tabular list to verify whether additional character(s) are required.

EXAMPLE: The ICD-10-CM Index to Diseases and Injuries entry for *diabetes mellitus* lists code E11.9, as verified in the tabular list.

Level of Detail in Coding

Pay attention to the level of detail when assigning codes because diagnosis codes are to be reported using the highest number of digits or characters available.

 Note:

> ICD-10-CM codes contain three, four, five, six, or seven characters. Codes with three characters are called categories, and they may be further subdivided by assigning up to four additional characters to provide greater detail.
>
> Codes with four, five, or six characters that require additional character(s) are subcategories. Codes that do *not* require additional character(s) are simply called *codes*. (It might be helpful to think of such *codes* as *complete codes* or *valid codes*.) A three-character code is reported only if it is not further subdivided. Where fourth through seventh characters are provided, they *must* be assigned. A code is invalid if the complete number of characters required for that code have not been assigned.

EXAMPLE: ICD-10-CM category M1a (chronic gout) requires the assignment of a fourth, fifth, sixth, and seventh character to complete the code. It is incorrect to report a category M1a code without the fourth through seventh characters. Thus, you would assign code M1a.0110 to a patient diagnosed with idiopathic chronic gout of the right shoulder, without tophus.

Codes from A00.0 Through T88.9, Z00–Z99.8

Appropriate codes from ICD-10-CM (A00.0 through T88.9, Z00–Z99.8) are reported to identify diagnoses, symptoms, conditions, problems, complaints, or other reason(s) for the encounter.

The selection of ICD-10-CM codes A00.0 through T88.9 frequently will be used to describe the reason for the encounter (instead of an ICD-10-CM Z code). Make sure you verify these codes in the disease tabular list.

 Note:

Codes V00 through Y99 are reported for external causes of morbidity.

Signs and Symptoms

Codes that describe symptoms and signs are reported when a related definitive diagnosis has not been established (or confirmed) by the provider.

 Note:

ICD-10-CM Chapter 18 (Symptoms, Signs, and Abnormal Clinical and Laboratory Findings, Not Elsewhere Classified) contains many, but not all, codes for signs and symptoms. Some codes are found in other ICD-10-CM chapters (e.g., acute neoplasm-related pain, G89.3).

EXAMPLE: The patient is seen at a physician's office for an initial visit, complaining of pain and limited range of motion of her right little finger knuckle. The physician examines the joint and notices a solid mass. He orders an x-ray to rule out ganglion. Upon the follow-up visit, the x-ray results reveal no arthritis or stalklike growth. The diagnosis is ganglion cyst (Figure 4-2), little finger knuckle joint, right. The patient is scheduled for outpatient surgery to remove the ganglion.

For the initial visit, assign ICD-10-CM codes for pain (M79.644), stiffness (M25.641), and mass of the little finger knuckle joint (R22.31).

For the follow-up visit, assign ICD-10-CM code M67.441 to the ganglion cyst, little finger knuckle joint, right. Code M67.441 is reported as a definitive diagnosis, which means signs and symptoms codes for pain, limited range of motion, or mass of the little finger knuckle joint are *not* reported on the claim for the follow-up visit.

Figure 4-2 Ganglion cyst

Conditions That Are an Integral Part of a Disease Process

Signs and symptoms that are associated with a disease process should *not* be assigned as additional codes (unless otherwise instructed by ICD-10-CM) because they are included in the disease process.

EXAMPLE: The patient is seen at the hospital's emergency department (ED) with a complaint of shortness of breath. A chest x-ray reveals pneumonia (Figure 4-3), and the ED physician prescribes an antibiotic.

Assign ICD-10-CM code J18.9 to the pneumonia, and do not assign a code for the shortness of breath because it is a symptom of pneumonia.

Figure 4-3 Pneumonia: alveoli filling with fluid

Conditions That Are *Not* an Integral Part of a Disease Process

Conditions that are not considered an integral part of a disease process, such as additional signs and symptoms that may not be associated routinely with a disease process, should be coded when present (e.g., severe headache for which treatment or medical management is provided is coded when the patient is diagnosed with pneumonia).

> **EXAMPLE:** The patient is seen at the physician's office for follow-up care of her controlled hypertension. During the visit, she tells the physician that she has been experiencing some insomnia. The physician discussed possible reasons for the insomnia with the patient, who admitted to being under extreme stress recently. The patient was reluctant to take over-the-counter or prescription medications for the insomnia, and the physician suggested alternative solutions. The physician also instructed the patient to return in two weeks for follow-up of the insomnia.
>
> Assign ICD-10-CM code I10 to the hypertension. In addition, assign ICD-10-CM code G47.00 to the insomnia because it is not a symptom of hypertension and it was medically managed during the visit.

Multiple Coding for a Single Condition

The etiology/manifestation coding convention requires that two codes be reported to completely describe a single condition that affects multiple body systems.

> **EXAMPLE:** The diagnosis amyloid neuritis requires ICD-10-CM codes E85.1 and G63 be reported in that order. (Remember: italicized codes in the tabular list are never sequenced first.)

In addition, other single conditions require more than one code to be reported, such as those associated with "use additional code" notes found in the tabular list. These codes are not part of an etiology/manifestation pair where a secondary code is useful to describe a condition fully. The sequencing rule for "use additional code" is the same as the etiology/manifestation pair in that a secondary code should be reported. A "use additional code" note will usually be found at the infectious disease code, indicating the need to report the organism code as a secondary code.

> **Note:**
>
> Multiple codes also may need to be reported for ICD-10-CM *sequelae*, complications, and obstetrical cases to describe more fully the patient's conditions. (Refer to specific guidelines below for further instruction.) (Historically, ICD-9-CM used the term *late effect* to refer to the sequela of a disease or injury.)

EXAMPLE: For a diagnosis of urinary tract infection due to *Escherichia coli*, report ICD-10-CM codes N39.0 and B96.20, in that order.

"Code first" notes are also located below certain ICD-10-CM codes in the tabular lists that are not specifically manifestation codes but may be due to an underlying cause. When a "code first" note is present *and* an underlying condition is documented in the patient record, the underlying condition is reported first.

> **EXAMPLE:** The physician documents rheumatic pneumonia in the patient's record. Upon review of the index and tabular list, assign ICD-10-CM codes I00 and J17 for the condition, in that order.

Note:

For bacterial infections not included in ICD-10-CM Chapter 2, a secondary code from category B96 (Other bacterial agents as the cause of diseases classified elsewhere) may be required to identify the bacterial organism causing the infection.

"Code, if applicable, any causal condition first" notes in the ICD-10-CM tabular list indicates that this code may be assigned as a first-listed or principal diagnosis when the causal condition is unknown or not applicable. If a causal condition is known, the code for that condition should be reported as the first-listed or principal diagnosis.

> **EXAMPLE:** The patient is diagnosed with urinary incontinence and congenital ureterocele. Assign ICD-10-CM codes Q62.31 and R32 (although generating a physician query could result in a more specific urinary incontinence code), in that order.

Acute and Chronic Conditions

If the same condition is described as both acute (or subacute) and chronic and separate subentries exist in the ICD-10-CM index at the same indentation level, code both and sequence the acute (or subacute) code first.

> **EXAMPLE:** The diagnoses acute gastritis and chronic gastritis are assigned ICD-10-CM codes K29.00 and K29.50, in that order.

Combination Code

Assign combination codes when available and multiple codes as needed. A **combination code** is a single code that is used to classify two diagnoses (or procedures), a diagnosis with an associated secondary process (manifestation), or a diagnosis with an associated complication. Combination codes are located by referring to subterm entries in the ICD-10-CM index and by following "includes" and "excludes" notes in the ICD-10-CM tabular list. Assign two or more **multiple codes** to completely classify the elements of a complex diagnosis statement, which contain words or phrases such as *due to, incidental to, secondary to*, and *with*. Make sure you carefully review tabular list entries, which provide guidance regarding the assignment of multiple codes.

Make sure you assign only the combination code when that code fully identifies the diagnostic conditions involved or when the index so directs. Do not report multiple codes when ICD-10-CM provides a combination code that clearly identifies all of the elements documented in the diagnosis. When a combination code lacks necessary specificity in describing the manifestation or a complication, an additional code should be reported as a secondary code.

> **EXAMPLE 1: COMBINATION CODE:** Assign ICD-10-CM combination code K80.00 to the diagnosis acute cholecystitis and cholelithiasis because the code description includes both conditions. (The fifth-character 0 is assigned to this code because there is no mention of obstruction in the diagnostic statement.)

> **EXAMPLE 2: MULTIPLE CODES:** The diagnosis trigonitis due to *Escherichia coli* is assigned ICD-10-CM codes N30.30 and B96.20, in that order.

Sequelae (Late Effects)

A **sequela** is the **residual effect** (condition produced) after the acute phase of an illness or injury has terminated. *There is no time limit on when a sequela code can be used.* The residual may be apparent early (e.g., hemiparesis in cerebral infarction), or it may occur months or years later (e.g., scarring due to a previous burn).

Coding of a sequela generally requires two codes sequenced in the following order:

- Residual condition or nature of the sequela is sequenced first.

- Sequela code is sequenced second.

An exception to the above guidelines are those instances where the code for the sequela is followed by a manifestation code identified in the ICD-10-CM tabular list, or the sequela code has been expanded (at the fourth-, fifth-, or sixth-character levels) to include the manifestation(s). *The code for the acute phase of an illness or injury that led to the sequela is never used with a code for the late effect.*

In the ICD-10-CM Index to Diseases and Injuries, the main term is *Sequela (of)* and it includes a "*—see also* condition" instruction because in the tabular list. Seventh-character "S" is added to condition codes for which sequelae (residual conditions) are treated. (Historically, ICD-9-CM referred to a sequela as a *late effect* of an illness or injury.)

 Note:

- The code for the acute phase of an illness or injury that led to the sequela is never reported with a code for the sequela (because treatment for the acute phase has ended).

- Do not confuse sequelae with complications that are associated with current acute illness or injuries and usually develop from problems that occur during the course of medical or surgical care (e.g., postoperative wound infection).

- Multiple codes are assigned to classify a sequela when no combination code exists, such as "headaches due to intracranial injury without loss of consciousness that occurred several years ago" for which ICD-10-CM codes G44.309 and S06.9x0S are both assigned. (In ICD-10-CM, the sequelae of injuries are classified by assigning an S as the seventh character of the injury code.)

- A combination code is assigned to classify a sequela when it exists, such as "nondominant left-sided paralysis due to previous CVA" for which ICD-10-CM I69.864 only is assigned.

EXAMPLE: The patient was in an automobile accident last year and sustained fractures of the left femur and right tibia, which healed without incident. The patient presents today with stiffness of the left hip and numbness of the left leg. Assign codes to the stiffness of the left hip (M25.652); numbness of the left leg (R20.0); and sequela of fracture, femur (S72.92xS).

Impending or Threatened Condition

Code any condition described at the time of encounter/visit as "impending" or "threatened" as follows:

- If the condition did occur, code as confirmed diagnosis.

- If the condition did not occur, reference the disease index to determine if the condition has a subentry term for *impending* or *threatened* and also reference main term entries for *impending* and *threatened*.

- If subterms for *impending* or *threatened* are listed, assign the listed code.

- If subterms for *impending* or *threatened* are not listed, code the existing underlying condition(s), and *not* the condition described as *impending* or *threatened*.

Note:

Coding impending or threatened conditions applies to inpatient cases only.

EXAMPLE: The patient is treated for impending myocardial infarction (MI) and is assigned ICD-10-CM code I20.0 because the MI diagnosis has not been confirmed.

Reporting Same Diagnosis Code More Than Once

Each unique ICD-10-CM diagnosis code is reported only once for an encounter. This applies to bilateral conditions *when there are no distinct ICD-10-CM codes identifying laterality* or two different conditions that are classified to the same ICD-10-CM diagnosis code.

> **EXAMPLE:** On March 14, the patient was diagnosed with bilateral lung abscesses. Even though both lungs contain abscesses, assign ICD-10-CM code J85.2 only once.

Laterality

ICD-10-CM codes that indicate **laterality** specifically classify conditions that occur on the left, right, or bilaterally. If a bilateral ICD-10-CM code is not provided *and the condition is bilateral*, assign separate codes for both the left and right side. If the side is not identified in the patient record, assign a code for unspecified side.

When a patient has a bilateral condition and each side is treated during separate encounters, assign the bilateral code (because the condition still exists on both sides) for the first encounter. After one side has been successfully treated, assign the unilateral code for the second encounter (because the condition now exists on just one side). However, if treatment on the first side did not resolve the condition, assign the bilateral code for the second and subsequent encounters until that side is successfully treated.

> **EXAMPLE:** *Bilateral contusion of fallopian tubes, initial encounter* is assigned ICD-10-CM code S37.522A.

When a patient has a bilateral condition *and each side is treated during separate encounters*, assign the "bilateral" code for the encounter during which the first side is treated (because the condition still exists on both sides). For the second encounter during which the other side is treated (and after the other side has been successfully treated and because the condition no longer exists on that side), assign the appropriate unilateral code for the side where the condition still exists. The bilateral code is not assigned for the subsequent encounter because the patient no longer has the condition at the previously-treated site. However, if treatment for the first side did not completely resolve the condition, reporting the bilateral code would still be appropriate.

> **EXAMPLE:** The patient was diagnosed with bilateral cataracts. On May 5, the patient successfully underwent cataract surgery of the left eye. The ICD-10-CM code for *cataracts, bilateral eyes*, is reported for this encounter. On July 5, the patient successfully underwent cataract surgery of the right eye. The ICD-10-CM code for *cataract, left eye*, is reported for this encounter.

Documentation for Body Mass Index (BMI), Depth of Non-pressure Ulcers, Pressure Ulcer Stages, Coma Scale, and NIH Stroke Scale

The assignment of body mass index (BMI), depth of nonpressure chronic ulcers, pressure ulcer stage, coma scale, and NIH stroke scale (NIHSS) codes may be based on documentation from clinicians who are not the patient's provider (e.g., physician, other qualified health care practitioner legally accountable for establishing the patient's diagnosis) *because such information is typically documented by other clinicians involved in the care of the patient* (e.g., dietitians document BMI, nurses document pressure ulcer stages, emergency medical technician documents coma scale). However, associated diagnosis (e.g., overweight, obesity, acute stroke, pressure ulcer) must be documented by the patient's provider. If conflicting documentation is evident in the patient record, either from the same clinician or different clinicians, query the patient's attending provider for clarification.

BMI, coma scale, and National Institutes of Health stroke scale (NIHSS) codes are reported only as secondary diagnoses. As with all other secondary diagnosis codes, BMI and pressure ulcer stage codes are assigned only when they meet the definition of a reportable additional diagnosis.

> **EXAMPLE:** Patient's BMI of 39.4 was documented by the dietician, and patient has an established diagnosis of morbid obesity. Report ICD-10-CM codes E66.01 and Z68.39, in that order.

Syndromes

Follow the alphabetic index guidance when coding syndromes. In the absence of index guidance, assign codes for the documented manifestations of the syndrome. Additional codes for manifestations that are *not an integral part of the disease process* may also be assigned when the condition does not have a unique code.

Documentation of Complications of Care

Complications of care codes are based upon documentation of a relationship between a condition and the procedure unless otherwise instructed by ICD-10-CM. Not all conditions that occur during or following medical care or surgery are classified as complications. There must be a cause-and-effect relationship between the condition and procedure or service provided along with documentation that the condition is a complication. If a complication is not clearly documented, query the provider for clarification.

Borderline Diagnosis

If the provider documents a *borderline diagnosis* at the time of discharge, code the diagnosis as confirmed unless ICD-10-CM provides a specific entry (e.g., borderline diabetes). If a borderline condition has a specific index entry in ICD-10-CM, it should be coded as such. Since borderline conditions are not uncertain diagnoses, no distinction is made between the care setting (inpatient versus outpatient). Whenever the documentation is unclear regarding a borderline condition, coders are encouraged to query for clarification.

Use of Sign/Symptom/Unspecified Codes

Assigning codes to signs, symptoms, and unspecified conditions is acceptable, and it is sometimes even necessary. Specific diagnosis codes should be reported when supported by available patient record documentation and clinical knowledge of the patient's health condition. However, there are instances when signs, symptoms, or unspecified codes are the best choices for accurately reflecting the encounter. Each encounter should be coded to the level of certainty known. When a definitive diagnosis is *not* established during an encounter, report codes for signs and/or symptoms instead.

When a specific code cannot be assigned because sufficient clinical information about a particular health condition is unknown or unavailable, report the appropriate unspecified code instead. Unspecified codes are reported when they most accurately reflect what is known about the patient's condition at the end of an encounter. It is inappropriate to assign a more specific code that is *not* supported by the patient record documentation. It is also inappropriate for a provider to order diagnostic testing that is medically *un*necessary to determine a more specific code.

> **EXAMPLE:** The patient is diagnosed with pneumonia, and the specific type was not able to be determined by the end of an encounter. Report code J18.9 (Pneumonia, unspecified organism).

Exercise 4.2 – General ICD-10-CM Diagnosis Coding Guidelines

Instructions: Indicate whether the statement is true (T) or false (F).

_____   1. If the provider documents a *borderline diagnosis* at the time of discharge, code the diagnosis as confirmed even when the ICD-10-CM Index to Diseases and Injuries provides a specific entry that includes the word "borderline."

_____   2. When reviewing ICD-10-CM Index to Disease and Injuries entries, if the code listed contains a fifth, sixth, or seventh character, it is unnecessary to verify the code in the ICD-10-CM Tabular List of Diseases and Injuries.

_____   3. Upon verification of codes in the ICD-10-CM Tabular List of Diseases and Injuries, when seventh characters are provided, they must be assigned.

_____   4. Certain Z codes can be reported as a first-listed code for outpatient care.

_____   5. Codes that describe symptoms and signs are always reported with established diagnoses.

(continues)

Exercise 4.2 (*continued*)

_____ 6. Some symptoms, signs, and ill-defined condition codes are found in ICD-10-CM chapters other than Chapter 18, Symptoms, Signs, and Abnormal Clinical and Laboratory Findings, Not Elsewhere Classified (R00-R99).

_____ 7. Signs and symptoms that are integral to the disease process should be assigned as additional codes because they are included in the disease process.

_____ 8. Conditions that are not considered an integral part of a disease process, such as additional signs and symptoms that may not be associated routinely with a disease process, should be coded when present.

_____ 9. Etiology/manifestation conditions often require that two codes be reported to completely describe a single condition that affects multiple body systems.

_____ 10. If the same condition is described as acute (or subacute) *and* chronic, always assign a combination code.

_____ 11. One multiple code can be assigned as a single code to classify two entirely different conditions.

_____ 12. Combination codes are located by referring to subterm entries in the disease index and by reading "includes" and "excludes" notes in the tabular list.

_____ 13. A late effect is the condition produced after the acute phase of an illness or injury has ended.

_____ 14. Residual conditions are coded as such only if they occur at least one year after the previous condition has resolved.

_____ 15. Conditions described at the time of visit as *impending* or *threatened* are always coded as if the condition is confirmed, regardless of the type of patient encounter.

ICD-10-CM Chapter-Specific Diagnosis Coding Guidelines

In addition to coding conventions and general coding guidelines, the *Official Guidelines for Coding and Reporting* contain chapter-specific coding guidelines that clarify the assignment of disease codes. Unless otherwise indicated in an individual chapter-specific guideline, the chapter-specific guidelines apply to all health care settings. Some of the guidelines include the following terms, which apply to the reporting of inpatient and outpatient diagnoses (covered in this chapter and Chapters 5 and 6). The terms are briefly defined below to clarify their use in the chapter-specific guidelines.

- *Principal diagnosis*: Reported for inpatient care, it is "that condition established after study to be chiefly responsible for occasioning the admission of the patient to the hospital for care."

- *Secondary diagnoses*: Additional conditions that affect patient care in terms of requiring clinical evaluation, therapeutic treatment, diagnostic procedures, extended length of hospital stay, or increased nursing care and/or monitoring.

- *First-listed diagnosis*: Reported for outpatient care instead of the principal diagnosis, it is the diagnosis, condition, problem, or other reason for an encounter or visit documented in the medical record to be chiefly responsible for the services provided. (The first-listed diagnosis was previously called the *primary diagnosis*.)

ICD-10-CM Chapter-Specific Coding Guidelines

To locate the ICD-10-CM chapter-specific coding guidelines online, go to **www.cdc.gov**, click on the letter **I** link, and click on the ICD-10-CM link. Scroll down and click on the ICD-10-CM Guidelines link, which will open as an Adobe PDF file.

The *ICD-10-CM Official Guidelines for Coding and Reporting* publication includes a table of contents that organizes the chapter-specific guidelines according to the chapters in the ICD-10-CM classification system (Table 4-1).

Although the chapter-specific guidelines have not been created for every ICD-10-CM chapter, the title of each ICD-10-CM chapter is included in the table of contents with the statement "Reserved for future guideline expansion." Refer to the chapter-specific guidelines when assigning ICD-10-CM diagnosis codes. (This section of the textbook defines terminology associated with each ICD-10-CM chapter, interprets official chapter-specific coding guidelines, and includes exercises for coding practice.)

Table 4-1 Portion of Chapter-Specific Coding Guidelines Table of Contents from *ICD-10-CM Official Guidelines for Coding and Reporting*

Courtesy of the Centers for Medicare & Medicaid Services, www.cms.gov

 Note:

Go to Chapter 5 to locate content about ICD-10-PCS coding.

ICD-10-CM Chapter 1: Certain Infectious and Parasitic Diseases (A00–B99)

This ICD-10-CM chapter classifies the following infectious and parasitic diseases (Table 4-2):

- Intestinal infectious diseases
- Tuberculosis
- Certain zoonotic bacterial diseases
- Other bacterial diseases

Table 4-2 Organisms

Organism	Definition
Bacteria	• Single-celled organisms that in certain conditions cause illnesses such as strep throat, most ear infections, and bacterial pneumonia • Some bacteria are considered helpful (e.g., intestinal *Escherichia coli*)
Chlamydia	• Infection caused by a parasitic bacteria called *Chlamydia trachomatis* • Affects male and female genitals
Fungi	• Opportunistic pathogens such as aspergillus, candida, and cryptococcus that cause infections in immunocompromised people such as cancer patients, transplant recipients, and people with AIDS • Pathogens such as endemic mycoses, histoplasmosis, coccidioidomycosis, and superficial mycoses that cause infections in healthy people
Helminths	• Parasitic worms that usually lodge in the intestines • Include roundworm, pinworm, *Trichnella spiralis* (causes thrichinosis), tapeworm, and fluke
Mycoplasmas	• Surface parasites of the human respiratory and urogenital tracts • Mainly affect children aged 5 to 9 years • Spread by close personal contact • Have a long incubation period

Protozoans	• Single-celled organisms (e.g., ameba) that cause parasitic diseases in people with AIDS
	   o Toxoplasmosis
	   o Cryptosporidiosis
	• *Pneumocystis carinii* pneumonia (PCP) is caused by a fungus called *Pneumocystis jiroveci*.

Rickettsias	• Intracellular parasites that grow and reproduce only in living cells of their host • Named for U.S. pathologist Howard T. Ricketts, who died of typhus in 1910 while investigating the spread of the disease • Typhus fever is caused by *Rickettsia prowazekii* when transmitted to humans by lice • Rocky Mountain spotted fever is a rickettsial disease transmitted to humans by ticks
Viruses	• Submicroscopic parasites that cause disease • Contain DNA or RNA, are surrounded by protein, and use host cells to replicate • Include varicella (chickenpox virus), cold viruses, hepatitis viruses, herpesviruses, and human immunodeficiency virus (HIV)

• Infections with a predominantly sexual mode of transmission

• Other spirochetal diseases

• Other diseases caused by chlamydiae

• Rickettsioses

• Viral infections of the central nervous system

• Arthropod-borne viral fevers and viral hemorrhagic fevers

• Viral infections characterized by skin and mucous membrane lesions

• Other human herpesviruses

• Viral hepatitis

• Human immunodeficiency virus (HIV) disease

- Other viral diseases

- Mycoses

- Protozoal diseases

- Helminthiases

- Pediculosis, acariasis, and other infestations

- Sequelae of infectious and parasitic diseases

- Bacterial and viral infectious agents

- Other infectious diseases

⚠ Refer to tabular list code descriptions to locate ICD-10-CM fourth, fifth, sixth, and seventh characters that further classify infectious and parasitic diseases according to anatomical site.

Human Immunodeficiency Virus (HIV)

HIV is a virus that attacks the body's immune system, which provides protection against infections and disease; however, people's immune systems have no clear way to protect them from HIV. Individuals infected with HIV are unable to ward off microorganisms that do not usually make a healthy person sick. Although those infected with HIV may exhibit no symptoms for 10 or more years, because the HIV-positive patient's immune system has been weakened by the virus, these microorganisms ultimately cause life-threatening infections and cancers. To determine whether a patient is considered HIV-positive, review the patient record to locate the following phrases: ☞

- Has HIV disease
- Has HIV infection
- HIV infected
- HIV-positive

Note:

HIV is not spread through saliva (spit), nor is it spread by casual contact (e.g., coughing, eating or drinking from common utensils, hugging, shaking hands, sneezing, or using restrooms and drinking fountains).

When the above phrases are included in the patient's record, the person has HIV in his or her body and can spread the virus to other people. HIV spreads when infected blood, breast milk, semen, or vaginal fluid enters the bloodstream of another person through

- Break in the skin (e.g., abrasion, laceration, or other open wound)

- Direct entry into a blood vessel

- Mucous linings (e.g., eyes, mouth, nose, penis, rectum, or vagina) ☞

Note:

A list of HIV-related conditions and opportunistic infections and definitions can be found on the Student Companion Web Site for *3-2-1 Code It!* at www.cengagebrain.com.

Acquired immune deficiency syndrome (AIDS) is a late stage of HIV disease, and it is considered the most severe manifestation of HIV. The Centers for Disease Control and Prevention (CDC) includes a list of opportunistic infections and cancers that, in an HIV-positive patient, establishes the diagnosis of AIDS. Although medications help HIV-positive and AIDS patients live longer, healthier lives, there is no cure. (An **opportunistic infection** takes advantage of the body's weakened defenses.)

When a patient is treated for an HIV-related condition, report ICD-10-CM code B20 first on the health insurance claim and assign (and report) additional diagnosis codes for all documented HIV-related conditions and opportunistic infections, such as candidiasis or Kaposi's sarcoma (Figure 4-4).

Coding Tip:

Infections are also classified in other ICD-10-CM chapters, such as Chapter 10, Diseases of the Respiratory System.

Figure 4-4　Kaposi's sarcoma

ICD-10-CM Chapter-Specific Coding Guidelines

Chapter 1: Certain Infectious and Parasitic Diseases (A00–B99)

a. Human Immunodeficiency Virus (HIV) infections

1) Code only confirmed cases

Code only confirmed cases of HIV infection/illness. This is an exception to the hospital inpatient guideline Section II, H (Uncertain Diagnosis). In this context, "confirmation" does not require documentation of positive serology or culture for HIV; the provider's diagnostic statement that the patient is HIV positive, or has an HIV-related illness is sufficient.

EXAMPLE: A 38-year-old symptomatic HIV-positive female patient was seen in follow-up at the office. The patient was discharged from the hospital last week after inpatient treatment of *Pneumocystis carinii* pneumonia (PCP). Lab tests today reveal CBC hemoglobin of 9.0, hematocrit 27, and normal WBC differential and platelets. Hepatitis A, B, and C tests negative. Cytomegalovirus (CMV) test negative. Rapid plasma reagin test negative. Decreased reticulocytes of 0.3 noted. Normal peripheral smear. Parvovirus B19 antibody test negative. Comprehensive metabolic panel was normal. CD4 test revealed somewhat depressed T helper cell level of 460. Viral load is 22,000. Erythropoietin level elevated at 120 milliunits per milliliter. Patient was started on medications of nevirapine plus Combivir.

In this example, the provider's statement of a "symptomatic HIV-positive female patient" is sufficient to assign ICD-10-CM code B20 for HIV infection. Because the PCP is resolved, a code to that HIV-related condition is not assigned.

2) Selection and sequencing of HIV codes

(a) Patient admitted for HIV-related condition

If a patient is admitted for an HIV-related condition, the principal diagnosis should be B20, Human immunodeficiency virus [HIV] disease, followed by additional diagnosis codes for all reported HIV-related conditions.

EXAMPLE: A 42-year-old HIV-positive male underwent treatment for septic arthritis of the left shoulder. Culture and sensitivity lab test revealed *Klebsiella pneumoniae* as the bacterial agent. Because septic arthritis is considered an opportunistic infection in an HIV-positive patient, sequence the HIV code (B20) first and then the opportunistic infection codes (M00.812 and B96.1).

(b) Patient with HIV disease admitted for unrelated condition

If a patient with HIV disease is admitted for an unrelated condition (such as a traumatic injury), the code for the unrelated condition (e.g., the nature of injury code) should be the principal diagnosis. Other diagnoses would be B20 followed by additional diagnosis codes for all reported HIV-related conditions.

EXAMPLE: A 53-year-old female patient with symptomatic HIV disease undergoes treatment for a closed left wrist fracture. In this example, a fracture is not considered an opportunistic infection or disease in an HIV-positive patient and it is considered a condition unrelated to HIV status. Therefore, sequence the closed left wrist fracture code (S62.102A) and then the HIV code (B20).

(c) Whether the patient is newly diagnosed

Whether the patient is newly diagnosed or has had previous admissions/encounters for HIV conditions is irrelevant to the sequencing decision.

(d) Asymptomatic human immunodeficiency virus

Z21, Asymptomatic human immunodeficiency virus [HIV] infection, is to be applied when the patient without any documentation of symptoms is listed as being "HIV positive," "known HIV," "HIV test positive," or similar terminology. Do not use this code if the term *AIDS* is used or if the patient is treated for any HIV-related illness or is described as having any condition(s) resulting from her HIV-positive status; use B20 in these cases.

EXAMPLE: A 42-year-old female HIV-positive asymptomatic patient undergoes routine CD4 testing to determine current levels. In this example, even though the patient is HIV-positive, she is also asymptomatic, which means that there are no documented symptoms. Therefore, assign code Z21 for asymptomatic HIV status. *Do not assign code B20, which is assigned to patients diagnosed as HIV positive who are treated for HIV-related illness(es) or to patients described as having AIDS.*

(e) Patients with inconclusive HIV serology

Patients with inconclusive HIV serology, but no definitive diagnosis or manifestations of the illness, may be assigned code R75, Inconclusive laboratory evidence of human immunodeficiency virus [HIV].

EXAMPLE: A 52-year-old asymptomatic male patient was seen in the office after having undergone HIV testing, the results of which proved inconclusive. Patient is scheduled for repeat HIV test. In this example, assign code R75 for an inconclusive laboratory evidence of HIV and code Z11.4 for "screening for HIV status" because the patient is being seen to determine his HIV status. If HIV counseling was provided during the encounter, code Z71.7 would also be assigned. If the patient was determined to be in a high-risk group for HIV, such as *high risk bisexual behavior*, code Z72.53 would also be assigned.

(f) Previously diagnosed HIV-related illness

Patients with any known prior diagnosis of an HIV-related illness should be coded to B20. Once a patient has developed an HIV-related illness, the patient should always be assigned code B20 on every subsequent admission/encounter. Patients previously diagnosed with any HIV illness (B20) should never be assigned to R75 (inconclusive laboratory evidence of human immunodeficiency virus [HIV]) or Z21 (asymptomatic human immunodeficiency virus [HIV] infection status).

EXAMPLE: A 29-year-old female HIV-positive patient was seen in the office to undergo routine CD4 testing. She has a past history of having been treated for HIV wasting syndrome and Hodgkin's disease. The patient is currently asymptomatic. In this example, because the patient has known prior diagnoses of HIV-related illnesses, assign code B20 for HIV disease. *Although the patient is currently asymptomatic, according to official coding guidelines, it is incorrect to assign code R75 for inconclusive HIV test or code Z21 for asymptomatic HIV status.*

(continues)

ICD-10-CM Chapter-Specific Coding Guidelines (*continued*)

(g) HIV infection in pregnancy, childbirth, and the puerperium

During pregnancy, childbirth or the puerperium, a patient admitted (or presenting for a health care encounter) because of an HIV-related illness should receive a principal diagnosis code of O98.7-, Human immunodeficiency [HIV] disease complicating pregnancy, childbirth and the puerperium, followed by B20 and the code(s) for the HIV-related illness(es). Codes from Chapter 15 (of ICD-10-CM) always take sequencing priority. Patients with asymptomatic HIV infection status admitted (or presenting for a health care encounter) during pregnancy, childbirth, or the puerperium should be assigned codes O98.7- and Z21.

EXAMPLE: A 33-year-old HIV-positive patient in her second trimester received inpatient treatment for cytomegalovirus (CMV) disease. The patient was discharged to follow up with Dr. Jones regarding the CMV, and she will continue to receive prenatal care from Dr. Miller. When a pregnant patient is admitted for an HIV-related illness, assign code O98.512 for "other maternal viral disease complicating pregnancy, childbirth, or the puerperium." Then, assign code B20 for HIV disease and code B25.9 for the HIV-related condition of CMV.

When this patient is admitted for delivery, even if she has an asymptomatic HIV infection status upon admission, assign codes O98.72 and B20 (because she was admitted during her antepartum period for treatment of an HIV-related condition). (The case of an HIV-positive patient who delivers and who has not been treated for an HIV-related condition in the past is assigned codes O98.72 and Z21.) (An outcome of delivery code is also assigned.)

(h) Encounters for testing for HIV

If a patient is being seen to determine his/her HIV status, use code Z11.4, Encounter for screening for human immunodeficiency virus [HIV]. Use additional codes for any associated high risk behavior. If a patient with signs or symptoms is being seen for HIV testing, code the signs and symptoms. An additional counseling code Z71.7, Human immunodeficiency virus [HIV] counseling, may be used if counseling is provided during the encounter for the test.

When a patient returns to be informed of his/her HIV test results and the test result is negative, use code Z71.7, Human immunodeficiency virus [HIV] counseling. If the results are positive see previous guidelines and assign codes as appropriate.

b. Infectious agents as the cause of diseases classified to other chapters

Certain infections are classified in chapters other than Chapter 1 and no organism is identified as part of the infection code. In these instances, it is necessary to use an additional code from ICD-10-CM Chapter 1 to identify the organism. A code from category B95, *Streptococcus*, *Staphylococcus*, and *Enterococcus* as the cause of diseases classified to other chapters, B96, Other bacterial agents as the cause of diseases classified to other chapters, or B97, Viral agents as the cause of diseases classified to other chapters, is to be used as an additional code to identify the organism. An instructional note will be found at the infection code advising that an additional organism code is required.

c. Infections resistant to antibiotics

Many bacterial infections are resistant to current antibiotics. It is necessary to identify all infections documented as antibiotic resistant. Assign a code from category Z16, Resistance to antimicrobial drugs.

d. Sepsis, Severe Sepsis, and Septic Shock

1) Coding of Sepsis and Severe Sepsis

(a) Sepsis

For a diagnosis of sepsis, assign the appropriate code for the underlying systemic infection. If the type of infection or causal organism is not further specified, assign code A41.9, Sepsis, unspecified organism. A code from subcategory R65.2, Severe sepsis, should not be assigned unless severe sepsis or an associated acute organ dysfunction is documented.

(i) Negative or inconclusive blood cultures and sepsis

Negative or inconclusive blood cultures do *not* preclude a diagnosis of sepsis in patients with clinical evidence of the condition; however, the provider should be queried.

(ii) Urosepsis

The term *urosepsis* is a nonspecific term. It is not to be considered synonymous with sepsis. It has no default code in the ICD-10-CM Index to Diseases and Injuries. Should a provider use this term, he/she must be queried for clarification.

(iii) Sepsis with organ dysfunction

If a patient has sepsis and associated acute organ dysfunction or multiple organ dysfunction (MOD), follow the instructions for coding severe sepsis.

(iv) Acute organ dysfunction that is not clearly associated with the sepsis

If a patient has sepsis and an acute organ dysfunction, but the patient record documentation indicates that the acute organ dysfunction is related to a medical condition other than the sepsis, do not assign a code from subcategory R65.2, Severe sepsis. An acute organ dysfunction must be associated with the sepsis in order to assign the severe sepsis code. If the documentation is not clear as to whether an acute organ dysfunction is related to the sepsis or another medical condition, query the provider.

(b) Severe sepsis

The coding of severe sepsis requires a minimum of two codes: a code for the underlying systemic infection, followed by a code from subcategory R65.2, Severe sepsis. If the causal organism is not documented, assign code A41.9, Sepsis, unspecified organism, for the infection. Additional code(s) for the associated acute organ dysfunction are also required. Due to the complex nature of severe sepsis, some cases may require querying the provider prior to assignment of the codes.

2) Septic shock

(a) Septic shock generally refers to circulatory failure associated with severe sepsis, and therefore, it represents a type of acute organ dysfunction.

For cases of septic shock, the code for the systemic infection should be sequenced first, followed by code R65.21, Severe sepsis with septic shock or code T81.12, Postprocedural septic shock. Any additional codes for the other acute organ dysfunctions should also be assigned. As noted in the sequencing instructions in the ICD-10-CM tabular list, the code for septic shock *cannot* be assigned as a principal diagnosis.

3) Sequencing of severe sepsis

If severe sepsis is present on admission, and meets the definition of principal diagnosis, the underlying systemic infection should be assigned as principal diagnosis followed by the appropriate code from subcategory R65.2 as required by the sequencing rules in the ICD-10-CM tabular list. A code from subcategory R65.2 can never be assigned as a principal diagnosis.

When severe sepsis develops during an encounter (it was not present on admission) the underlying systemic infection and the appropriate code from subcategory R65.2 should be assigned as secondary diagnoses.

Severe sepsis may be present on admission but the diagnosis may not be confirmed until sometime after admission. If the documentation is not clear whether severe sepsis was present on admission, the provider should be queried.

4) Sepsis and severe sepsis with a localized infection

If the reason for admission is both sepsis or severe sepsis and a localized infection, such as pneumonia or cellulitis, a code(s) for the underlying systemic infection should be assigned first and the code for the localized infection should be assigned as a secondary diagnosis. If the patient has severe sepsis, a code from subcategory R65.2 should also be assigned as a secondary diagnosis. If the patient is admitted with a localized infection, such as pneumonia, and sepsis/severe sepsis doesn't develop until after admission, the localized infection should be assigned first, followed by the appropriate sepsis/severe sepsis codes.

1) Sepsis due to a postprocedural infection

(a) Documentation of causal relationship

As with all postprocedural complications, code assignment is based on the provider's documentation of the relationship between the infection and the procedure.

(b) Sepsis due to a postprocedural infection

For such cases, the postprocedural infection code, such as, T80.2, Infections following infusion, transfusion, and therapeutic injection, T81.4, Infection following a procedure, T88.0, Infection following

(continues)

ICD-10-CM Chapter-Specific Coding Guidelines (*continued*)

immunization, or O86.0, Infection of obstetric surgical wound, should be coded first, followed by the code for the specific infection. If the patient has severe sepsis the appropriate code from subcategory R65.2 should also be assigned with the additional code(s) for any acute organ dysfunction.

(c) **Postprocedural infection and postprocedural septic shock**

In cases where a postprocedural infection has occurred and has resulted in severe sepsis and postprocedural septic shock, the code for the precipitating complication such as code T81.4, Infection following a procedure, or O86.0, Infection of obstetrical surgical wound should be coded first followed by code R65.20, Severe sepsis without septic shock. A code for the systemic infection should also be assigned.

If a postprocedural infection has resulted in postprocedural septic shock, the code for the precipitating complication such as code T81.4, Infection following a procedure, or O86.0, Infection of obstetrical surgical wound should be coded first followed by code T81.12-, Postprocedural septic shock. A code for the systemic infection should also be assigned.

6) **Sepsis and severe sepsis associated with a noninfectious process (condition)**

In some cases a noninfectious process (condition), such as trauma, may lead to an infection which can result in sepsis or severe sepsis. If sepsis or severe sepsis is documented as associated with a noninfectious condition, such as a burn or serious injury, and this condition meets the definition for principal diagnosis, the code for the noninfectious condition should be sequenced first, followed by the code for the resulting infection. If severe sepsis is present a code from subcategory R65.2 should also be assigned with any associated organ dysfunction(s) codes. It is not necessary to assign a code from subcategory R65.1, Systemic inflammatory response syndrome (SIRS) of non-infectious origin, for these cases.

If the infection meets the definition of principal diagnosis it should be sequenced before the non-infectious condition. When both the associated non-infectious condition and the infection meet the definition of principal diagnosis either may be assigned as principal diagnosis.

Only one code from category R65, Symptoms and signs specifically associated with systemic inflammation and infection, should be assigned. Therefore, when a non-infectious condition leads to an infection resulting in severe sepsis, assign the appropriate code from subcategory R65.2, Severe sepsis. Do not additionally assign a code from subcategory R65.1, Systemic inflammatory response syndrome (SIRS) of non-infectious origin.

7) **Sepsis and septic shock complicating abortion, pregnancy, childbirth, and the puerperium**

See Section I.C.15. Sepsis and septic shock complicating abortion, pregnancy, childbirth and the puerperium.

8) **Newborn sepsis**

See Section I.C.16. f. Bacterial sepsis of Newborn.

e. **Methicillin-Resistant *Staphylococcus aureus* (MRSA) conditions**

1) **Selection and sequencing of MRSA codes**

(a) **Combination codes for MRSA infection**

When a patient is diagnosed with an infection that is due to methicillin-resistant *Staphylococcus aureus* (MRSA), and that infection has a combination code that includes the causal organism (e.g., septicemia, pneumonia) assign the appropriate code for the condition (e.g., code A41.02, Sepsis due to Methicillin-resistant *Staphylococcus aureus*, or code J15.212, Pneumonia due to Methicillin-resistant *Staphylococcus aureus*). Do not assign code B96.52, Methicillin-resistant *Staphylococcus aureus*, as an additional code because the code includes the type of infection and the MRSA organism. Do not assign a code from subcategory Z16.11, Resistance to penicillins, as an additional diagnosis.

See Section C.1. for instructions on coding and sequencing of sepsis and severe sepsis.

(b) **Other codes for MRSA infection**

When there is documentation of a current infection (e.g., wound infection, stitch abscess, urinary tract infection) due to MRSA, and that infection does not have a combination code that includes the causal organism, assign the appropriate code to identify the condition along with code B95.62, Methicillin-resistant *Staphylococcus aureus* infection as the cause of diseases classified elsewhere, for the MRSA infection. Do not assign a code from subcategory Z16.11, Resistance to penicillins.

(c) **Methicillin-susceptible *Staphylococcus aureus* (MSSA) and MRSA colonization**

The condition or state of being colonized or carrying MSSA or MRSA is called colonization or carriage, while an individual person is described as being colonized or being a carrier.

Colonization means that MSSA or MSRA is present on or in the body without necessarily causing illness. A positive MRSA colonization test might be documented by the provider as "MRSA screen positive" or "MRSA nasal swab positive."

Assign code Z22.322, Carrier or suspected carrier of Methicillin-resistant *Staphylococcus aureus*, for patients documented as having MRSA colonization. Assign code Z22.321, Carrier or suspected carrier of Methicillin-susceptible *Staphylococcus aureus*, for patient documented as having MSSA colonization. Colonization is not necessarily indicative of a disease process or as the cause of a specific condition the patient may have unless documented as such by the provider.

(d) **MRSA colonization and infection**

If a patient is documented as having both MRSA colonization and infection during a hospital admission, code Z22.322, Carrier or suspected carrier of Methicillin-resistant *Staphylococcus aureus*, and a code for the MRSA infection may both be assigned.

f. **Zika virus infections**

1) **Code only confirmed cases**

Code only a confirmed diagnosis of Zika virus (A92.5, Zika virus disease) as documented by the provider. (This is an exception to the hospital "uncertain diagnosis" inpatient guideline. In that context, "confirmation" does not require documentation of the type of test performed; the physician's diagnostic statement that the condition is confirmed is sufficient.) The Zika virus code should be assigned regardless of the stated mode of transmission. If the provider documents "suspected", "possible" or "probable" Zika, do *not* assign code A92.5. Instead, assign code(s) explaining the reason for encounter (e.g., fever, rash, joint pain) or code Z20.828, Contact with and (suspected) exposure to other viral communicable diseases.

Exercise 4.3 – Certain Infectious and Parasitic Diseases

Instructions: Underline the main term in each diagnosis statement and assign the appropriate ICD-10-CM code(s).

_____   **1.** AIDS

_____   **2.** Botulism

_____   **3.** Lyme disease

_____   **4.** Postmeasles pneumonia

_____   **5.** Rabies

ICD-10-CM Chapter 2: Neoplasms (C00–D49)

This ICD-10-CM chapter classifies malignant, *in situ*, and benign neoplasms according to anatomical site (e.g., breast) and body system (e.g., urinary tract). Neoplasms are also classified according to primary, secondary, and unspecified sites as well as uncertain and unspecified behavior.

Neoplasms are new growths or tumors in which cell reproduction is out of control, and they are classified according to appearance and growth pattern (Figure 4-5). For coding purposes, the provider should specify whether the tumor is benign (noncancerous, nonmalignant, or noninvasive) or **malignant** (cancerous, invasive, or capable of spreading to other parts of the body). It is highly advisable that neoplasms be coded directly from the pathology report (generated by a hospital's or stand-alone laboratory's pathology department and mailed to the provider's office); however, until the diagnostic statement specifies whether the neoplasm is benign or malignant, coders should code the patient's sign (e.g., breast lump) or report a subcategory code from the Unspecified Nature column of the documented site using the Table of Neoplasms in the Index to Diseases and Injuries.

> **Note:**
>
> Functionally active malignant neoplasms behave like their surrounding tissue, such as a thyroid tumor that secretes thyroxine and causes hyperthyroidism.

Another term associated with neoplasms is *lesion*, which is defined as "any discontinuity of tissue (e.g., skin or organ) that may or may not be malignant." Index entries for *lesion* contain subterms according to anatomical site (e.g., organs or tissue), and the term *lesion* should be referenced if the diagnostic statement does not confirm a malignancy. In addition, the following conditions are examples of benign lesions and are listed as separate Index to Disease entries:

- Adenosis
- Cys
- Dysplasia
- Mass (unless the word *neoplasm* is included in the diagnostic statement)
- Polyp

Do not reference the neoplasm table to assign codes for the above conditions. Instead, first locate the specific term in the disease index; then locate the subterm for the specific organ or body area. When the specific organ or body area is not listed as subterm, follow the instructions provided (e.g., *see, see also*, or *see* category).

EXAMPLE: The provider documents "liver mass" as the final diagnosis because the pathology report of examined tissue is not yet available. A "mass" is not a "neoplasm." In the ICD-10-CM index, locate main term *Mass* and subterm *liver* to assign R16.0 (after verifying it in the tabular list). (When pathology reports are available, assign a more appropriate code.)

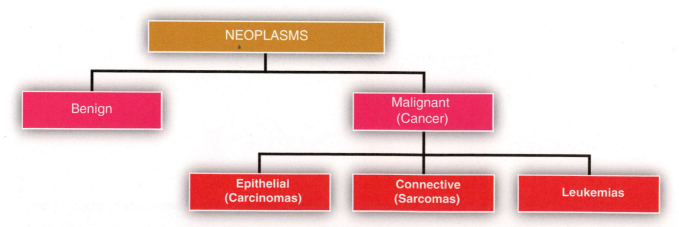

Figure 4-5 Classification of neoplasms

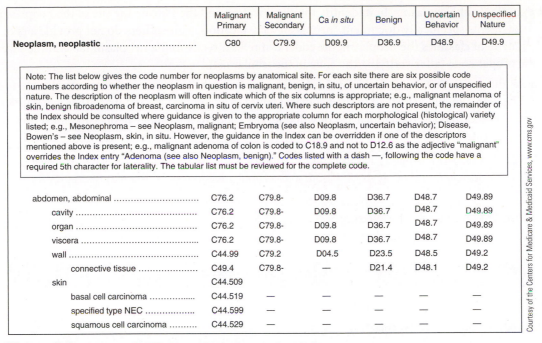

Neoplasm, neoplastic	Malignant Primary	Malignant Secondary	Ca *in situ*	Benign	Uncertain Behavior	Unspecified Nature
Neoplasm, neoplastic	C80	C79.9	D09.9	D36.9	D48.9	D49.9

Note: The list below gives the code number for neoplasms by anatomical site. For each site there are six possible code numbers according to whether the neoplasm in question is malignant, benign, in situ, of uncertain behavior, or of unspecified nature. The description of the neoplasm will often indicate which of the six columns is appropriate; e.g., malignant melanoma of skin, benign fibroadenoma of breast, carcinoma in situ of cervix uteri. Where such descriptors are not present, the remainder of the Index should be consulted where guidance is given to the appropriate column for each morphological (histological) variety listed; e.g., Mesonephroma – see Neoplasm, malignant; Embryoma (see also Neoplasm, uncertain behavior); Disease, Bowen's – see Neoplasm, skin, in situ. However, the guidance in the Index can be overridden if one of the descriptors mentioned above is present; e.g., malignant adenoma of colon is coded to C18.9 and not to D12.6 as the adjective "malignant" overrides the Index entry "Adenoma (see also Neoplasm, benign)." Codes listed with a dash —, following the code have a required 5th character for laterality. The tabular list must be reviewed for the complete code.

	Malignant Primary	Malignant Secondary	Ca *in situ*	Benign	Uncertain Behavior	Unspecified Nature
abdomen, abdominal	C76.2	C79.8-	D09.8	D36.7	D48.7	D49.89
cavity	C76.2	C79.8-	D09.8	D36.7	D48.7	D49.89
organ	C76.2	C79.8-	D09.8	D36.7	D48.7	D49.89
viscera	C76.2	C79.8-	D09.8	D36.7	D48.7	D49.89
wall	C44.99	C79.2	D04.5	D23.5	D48.5	D49.2
connective tissue	C49.4	C79.8-	—	D21.4	D48.1	D49.2
skin	C44.509					
basal cell carcinoma	C44.519	—	—	—	—	—
specified type NEC	C44.599	—	—	—	—	—
squamous cell carcinoma	C44.529	—	—	—	—	—

Figure 4-6 ICD-10-CM Table of Neoplasms (partial)

The ICD-10-CM Table of Neoplasms (Figure 4-6) is indexed by anatomical site and contains four cellular classifications: malignant, benign, uncertain behavior, and unspecified nature. The malignant classification is subdivided into three divisions: primary, secondary, and carcinoma *in situ*. The six neoplasm classifications are defined as follows:

- **Primary malignancy**: Original tumor site.
- **Secondary malignancy** (or **metastatic cancer**): Tumor that has metastasized, or spread, to a secondary site either adjacent to the primary site or to a remote region of the body.
- **Carcinoma (Ca)** *in situ*: Malignant tumor that is localized, circumscribed, encapsulated, and noninvasive, but has not spread to deeper or adjacent tissues or organs.
- **Benign**: Noninvasive, nonspreading, nonmalignant tumor.
- **Uncertain behavior**: Subsequent morphology or behavior that cannot be predicted based on the submitted specimen; the tissue appears to be in transition, and the pathologist cannot establish a definitive diagnosis.

 Note:

Malignant tumors are considered primary unless otherwise documented as metastatic or secondary.

Coding Tip:

To assign a code from the Uncertain Behavior column, the pathology report must specifically indicate the "uncertain behavior" of the neoplasm.

- **Unspecified nature**: A neoplasm is identified, but the results of pathology examination are not available; thus, there is no indication as to histology or nature of the tumor.

 Coding Tip:

Assign a code from the Unspecified Nature column when the neoplasm was destroyed or removed and a tissue biopsy was performed and results are pending.

To use the Table of Neoplasms, first identify the classification and then locate the site of the neoplasm. Some diagnostic statements specifically document "neoplasm" classification, while others do not provide a clue. If the diagnostic statement classifies the neoplasm, the coder can refer directly to the neoplasm table in the disease index to assign the proper code (after verifying the code in the tabular list).

When the diagnostic statement does not classify the neoplasm, the coder must refer to the disease index entry for the condition documented (instead of the neoplasm table) (e.g., lipoma). That entry either will contain a code number that can be verified in the tabular list or will refer the coder to the proper neoplasm table entry under which the code can be located.

EXAMPLE 1: For non-Hodgkin's lymphoma, go to main term *Lymphoma* in the ICD-10-CM index, subterm *non-Hodgkin*, and verify code C85.9 in the tabular list to assign the fifth character for the anatomical site.

EXAMPLE 2: For adrenal gland adenolymphoma, go to main term *Adenolymphoma* in the ICD-10-CM index, and follow the instruction to *see Neoplasm, benign*, and verify code D35.00 in the tabular list.

ICD-10-CM Index Entries
Lymphoma
non-Hodgkin (*see also* Lymphoma, by type) C85.9
Adenolymphoma
specified site—*see* Neoplasm, benign, by site
unspecified site D11.9

Coding Tip:

Assigning codes from the neoplasm table is a two-step process. First, classify the neoplasm by its behavior (e.g., malignant or benign); then classify the neoplasm by its anatomical site (e.g., acoustic nerve). To classify the neoplasm's behavior, review the provider's diagnostic statement (e.g., carcinoma of the throat) and locate the term *carcinoma* in the disease index. The entry will classify the behavior, directing you to the proper column in the Table of Neoplasms. (If the neoplasm is malignant, you still need to determine primary, secondary, or *in situ* based on documentation in the patient's record.)

Primary and Secondary Malignancies

A malignancy is coded as a primary site if the diagnostic statement documents

- Metastatic *from* a site
- Spread *from* a site
- *Primary neoplasm* of a site
- A malignancy for which no specific classification is documents
- A *recurrent* tumor

EXAMPLE 1: For "carcinoma of cervical lymph nodes, metastatic from the breast," the primary site is female breast and the secondary site is cervical lymph nodes.

EXAMPLE 2: For "oat cell carcinoma of the lung with spread to the brain," the primary site is lung and the secondary site is brain.

Coding Tip:

> The sequencing of neoplasm codes depends on the reason for the encounter. Review the patient's record to determine whether the primary or secondary cancer site is being treated or medically managed.
>
> - If the primary site is being treated or medically managed during the encounter, report that code first, followed by code(s) for secondary site(s) if present.
> - If the secondary site is being treated or medically managed, report that code first, followed by a code for the primary site.

Secondary malignancies are metastatic and indicate that a primary cancer has spread (metastasized) to another part of the body. Cancer described as *metastatic from* a site is *primary of* that site. Assign one code to the primary neoplasm and a second code to the secondary neoplasm of the specified site (if secondary site is known) or unspecified site (if secondary site is unknown). (Remember that sequencing of codes depends on which site is being treated.)

EXAMPLE 1: For "metastatic carcinoma from left female breast to lung," assign two codes.

- Primary malignant neoplasm of female breast (C50.912)
- Secondary neoplasm of lung (C78.00)

EXAMPLE 2: For "metastatic carcinoma from left female breast," assign two codes.

- Primary malignant neoplasm of female breast (C50.912)
- Secondary neoplasm of unspecified site (C79.9)

Cancer described as *metastatic to* a site is considered *secondary of* that site. Assign one code to the secondary site and a second code to the specified primary site (if primary site is known) or unspecified site (if primary site is unknown).

EXAMPLE 1: For "metastatic carcinoma from liver to right lung," assign two codes.

- Primary malignant neoplasm of liver (C22.0)
- Secondary neoplasm of right lung (C78.01)

EXAMPLE 2: For "metastatic carcinoma to right lung," assign two codes.

- Primary malignant neoplasm of unspecified site (C80.1)
- Secondary neoplasm of right lung (C78.01)

When anatomical sites are documented as *metastatic*, assign *secondary* neoplasm code(s) to those sites and assign an *unspecified site* code to the primary malignant neoplasm.

EXAMPLE 1: For "metastatic renal carcinoma, right kidney, of right lung," assign two codes.

- Primary renal carcinoma, right kidney (C64.1)
- Secondary neoplasm of right lung (C78.01)

EXAMPLE 2: For "metastatic osteosarcoma of brain," assign two codes.

- Primary malignant neoplasm of bone (C41.9)
- Secondary neoplasm of brain (C79.31)

EXAMPLE 3: For "metastatic melanoma of right lung and liver," assign three codes.

- Primary malignant melanoma of unspecified site (C43.9)
- Secondary neoplasm of right lung (C78.01)
- Secondary neoplasm of liver (C78.7)

EXAMPLE 4: For "metastatic adenocarcinoma of prostate and vertebra," assign three codes.

- Primary adenocarcinoma of unspecified site (C80.1)

- Secondary neoplasm of prostate (C79.82)

- Secondary neoplasm of vertebra (C79.51)

📝 If the diagnostic statement does not specify whether the neoplasm site is primary or secondary, code the site as *primary*, except for the following sites, which are considered *secondary* sites (unless the physician specifies that they are primary):

- Bone
- Brain
- Diaphragm
- Heart
- Liver
- Lymph nodes
- Mediastinum

- Meninges
- Peritoneum
- Pleura
- Retroperitoneum
- Spinal cord
- Neoplasms classifiable to ICD-10-CM category C76

 Note:

Lung is not included in the list of secondary sites. Therefore, lung cancer is coded as a primary site (unless the physician specifies that it is a secondary site).

EXAMPLE 1: For "breast cancer," assign one code.

- Primary malignant neoplasm of left female breast (C50.912)

EXAMPLE 2: For "brain cancer," assign two codes.

- Primary malignant neoplasm of unspecified site (C80.1)

- Secondary neoplasm of brain (C79.31)

EXAMPLE 3: For "metastatic cancer of hip," assign two codes.

- Primary malignant neoplasm of unspecified site (C80.1)

- Secondary neoplasm of left hip (C79.51)

Anatomical Site Is Not Documented

If the cancer diagnosis does not contain documentation of the anatomical site but the term *metastatic* is documented, assign codes for "unspecified site" for both the primary and secondary sites.

EXAMPLE: For "metastatic chromophobe adenocarcinoma," assign two codes.

- Secondary neoplasm of unspecified site (C79.9)

- Primary chromophobe adenocarcinoma of unspecified site (C75.1)

Primary Malignant Site Is No Longer Present

If the primary site of malignancy is no longer present and no further treatment is directed to the site, do not assign the code for primary of unspecified site. Instead, classify the previous primary site by assigning the appropriate code from category V10, "Personal history of malignant neoplasm."

EXAMPLE: For "metastatic carcinoma to right lung from right female breast (left radical mastectomy performed last year)," assign two codes.

- Secondary neoplasm of right lung (C78.01)

- Personal history of malignant neoplasm of right female breast (Z85.3)

- Acquired absence of right breast and nipple (status post right mastectomy) (Z90.11)

Inoperable Primary Site with Metastasis

When the primary neoplasm site is considered inoperable and is not treated, assign a code for the metastatic site first.

> **EXAMPLE:** For "carcinoma of fundus of stomach (inoperable) with metastasis to liver," assign two codes.
>
> - Secondary malignant neoplasm of liver (C78.7)
> - Malignant neoplasm of fundus of stomach (C16.1)

Contiguous or Overlapping Sites

Contiguous sites (or **overlapping sites**) occur when the origin of the tumor (primary site) involves two adjacent sites. Neoplasms with overlapping site boundaries are classified to the fourth-digit subcategory .8, "Other."

> **EXAMPLE:** For "cancer of the jejunum and ileum," in the ICD-10-CM neoplasm table, locate "intestine, small, overlapping lesion" and verify code C17.8 in the tabular list.

Reexcision of Tumors

A reexcision of a tumor occurs when the pathology report recommends that the surgeon perform a second excision to widen the margins of the original tumor site. The reexcision is performed to ensure that all tumor cells have been removed and that a clear border (margin) of normal tissue surrounds the excised specimen. Use the diagnostic statement found in the report of the original excision to code the reason for the reexcision. The pathology report for the reexcision may not specify a malignancy at that time, but the patient is still under treatment for the original neoplasm.

 Coding Tip:

1. Read all notes in the neoplasm table that apply to the condition you are coding.
2. Never assign a code directly from the neoplasm table or index.
3. Report only those codes that represent the current status of the neoplasm.
4. Assign a neoplasm code if the tumor has been excised and the patient is still undergoing radiation or chemotherapy treatment.
5. Assign an ICD-10-CM Z code if the tumor is no longer present or if the patient is not receiving treatment but is returning for follow-up care (e.g., personal history of a malignancy).
6. The classification documented on a pathology report overrides the morphology classification entry in the Index to Diseases.

 Coding Tip:

Morphology of Neoplasms

The World Health Organization (WHO) has published an adaptation of the International Classification of Diseases for Oncology (ICD-O) that contains a coded nomenclature for the morphology of neoplasms. (Refer to the Student Companion Web Site at **www.cengagebrain.com** for the morphology of neoplasms codes document.) The morphology codes consist of five characters, and these codes are reported to state cancer registries and other entities for cancer research purposes. The first four characters identify the histological type of the neoplasm, and the fifth character indicates behavior of the neoplasm (e.g., M8000/0). The one-character behavior codes include:

/0 Benign
/1 Uncertain whether benign or malignant
    Borderline malignancy

(continues)

Coding Tip (*continued*)

/2 Carcinoma *in situ*

    Intraepithelial

    Noninfiltrating

    Noninvasive

/3 Malignant, primary site

/6 Malignant, metastatic site

    Secondary site

/9 Malignant, uncertain whether primary or metastatic site

EXAMPLE 1: Malignant chordoma is assigned morphology code M9370/3. However, benign chordoma is assigned morphology code M9370/0.

EXAMPLE 2: Superficial spreading adenocarcinoma is assigned morphology code M8143/3. However, noninvasive adenocarcinoma is assigned morphology code M8143/2.

EXAMPLE 3: Melanoma is assigned morphology code M8720/3. However, secondary melanoma is assigned morphology code M8720/6.

When a morphological diagnosis contains two qualifying adjectives that result in more than one morphology code, the higher morphology code is assigned.

EXAMPLE: Transitional cell epidermoid carcinoma is assigned morphology code M8120/3 (Transitional cell carcinoma NOS), while epidermoid carcinoma is assigned morphology code M8070/3 (Epidermoid carcinoma NOS). In this situation, the higher morphology code (M8120/3) is used because it is usually more specific.

ICD-10-CM Chapter-Specific Coding Guidelines

Chapter 2: Neoplasms (C00-D49)

General guidelines

Chapter 2 of the ICD-10-CM contains the codes for most benign and all malignant neoplasms. Certain benign neoplasms, such as prostatic adenomas, may be found in the specific body system chapters. To properly code a neoplasm, it is necessary to determine from the record if the neoplasm is benign, *in situ*, malignant, or of uncertain histologic behavior. If malignant, any secondary (metastatic) sites should also be determined.

Primary malignant neoplasms overlapping site boundaries

A primary malignant neoplasm that overlaps two or more contiguous (next to each other) sites should be classified to the subcategory/code .8 ('overlapping lesion'), unless the combination is specifically indexed elsewhere. For multiple neoplasms of the same site that are not contiguous, such as tumors in different quadrants of the same breast, codes for each site should be assigned.

Malignant neoplasm of ectopic tissue

Malignant neoplasms of ectopic tissue are to be coded to the site of origin mentioned; e.g., ectopic pancreatic malignant neoplasms involving the stomach are coded to pancreas, unspecified (C25.9).

The neoplasm table in the ICD-10-CM Alphabetic Index should be referenced first. However, if the histological term is documented, that term should be referenced first, rather than going immediately to the neoplasm table, in order to determine which column in the neoplasm table is appropriate. For example, if the documentation indicates "adenoma," refer to the term in the ICD-10-CM Alphabetic Index to review the entries under this term and the instructional note to "see also neoplasm, by site, benign." The table provides the proper code based on the type of neoplasm and the site. It is important to select the proper column in the table that corresponds to the type of neoplasm. The ICD-10-CM tabular list should then be referenced to verify that the correct code has been selected from the table and that a more specific site code does not exist.

See Section I.C.21. Factors influencing health status and contact with health services, Status, for information regarding Z15.0, codes for genetic susceptibility to cancer.

a. Treatment directed at the malignancy

If the treatment is directed at the malignancy, designate the malignancy as the principal diagnosis.

The only exception to this guideline is if a patient admission/encounter is solely for the administration of chemotherapy, immunotherapy, or radiation therapy, assign the appropriate Z51.-- code as the first-listed or principal diagnosis, and the diagnosis or problem for which the service is being performed as a secondary diagnosis.

b. Treatment of secondary site

When a patient is admitted because of a primary neoplasm with metastasis and treatment is directed toward the secondary site only, the secondary neoplasm is designated as the principal diagnosis even though the primary malignancy is still present.

c. Coding and sequencing of complications

Coding and sequencing of complications associated with the malignancies or with the therapy thereof are subject to the following guidelines:

1) Anemia associated with malignancy

When admission/encounter is for management of an anemia associated with the malignancy, and the treatment is only for anemia, the appropriate code for the malignancy is sequenced as the principal or first-listed diagnosis followed by the appropriate code for the anemia (such as code D63.0, Anemia in neoplastic disease).

2) Anemia associated with chemotherapy, immunotherapy, and radiation therapy

When the admission/encounter is for management of an anemia associated with an adverse effect of the administration of chemotherapy or immunotherapy and the only treatment is for the anemia, the anemia code is sequenced first followed by the appropriate codes for the neoplasm and the adverse effect (T45.1X5, Adverse effect of antineoplastic and immunosuppressive drugs).

When the admission/encounter is for management of an anemia associated with an adverse effect of radiotherapy, the anemia code should be sequenced first, followed by the appropriate neoplasm code and code Y84.2, Radiological procedure and radiotherapy as the cause of abnormal reaction of the patient, or of later complication, without mention of misadventure at the time of the procedure.

3) Management of dehydration due to the malignancy

When the admission/encounter is for management of dehydration due to the malignancy and only the dehydration is being treated (e.g., intravenous rehydration), the dehydration is sequenced first, followed by the code(s) for the malignancy.

4) Treatment of a complication resulting from a surgical procedure

When the admission/encounter is for treatment of a complication resulting from a surgical procedure, designate the complication as the principal or first-listed diagnosis if treatment is directed at resolving the complication.

(continues)

ICD-10-CM Chapter-Specific Coding Guidelines (*continued*)

d. Primary malignancy previously excised

When a primary malignancy has been previously excised or eradicated from its site and there is no further treatment directed to that site and there is no evidence of any existing primary malignancy, a code from category Z85, Personal history of malignant neoplasm, should be used to indicate the former site of the malignancy. Any mention of extension, invasion, or metastasis to another site is coded as a secondary malignant neoplasm to that site. The secondary site may be the principal or first-listed, with the Z85 code used as a secondary code.

e. Admissions/Encounters involving chemotherapy, immunotherapy, and radiation therapy

1) Episode of care involves surgical removal of neoplasm

When an episode of care involves the surgical removal of a neoplasm, primary or secondary site, followed by adjunct chemotherapy or radiation treatment during the same episode of care, the code for the neoplasm should be assigned as principal or first-listed diagnosis.

2) Patient admission/encounter solely for administration of chemotherapy, immunotherapy, and radiation therapy

If a patient admission/encounter is solely for the administration of chemotherapy, immunotherapy, or radiation therapy, assign code Z51.0, Encounter for antineoplastic radiation therapy, or Z51.11, Encounter for antineoplastic chemotherapy, or Z51.12, Encounter for antineoplastic immunotherapy as the first-listed or principal diagnosis. If a patient receives more than one of these therapies during the same admission, more than one of these codes may be assigned, in any sequence.

The malignancy for which the therapy is being administered should be assigned as a secondary diagnosis.

3) Patient admitted for radiation therapy, chemotherapy or immunotherapy and develops complications

When a patient is admitted for the purpose of radiotherapy, immunotherapy, or chemotherapy and develops complications such as uncontrolled nausea and vomiting or dehydration, the principal or first-listed diagnosis is Z51.0, Encounter for antineoplastic radiation therapy, or Z51.11, Encounter for antineoplastic chemotherapy, or Z51.12, Encounter for antineoplastic immunotherapy, followed by any codes for the complications.

f. Admission/encounter to determine extent of malignancy

When the reason for admission/encounter is to determine the extent of the malignancy, or for a procedure such as paracentesis or thoracentesis, the primary malignancy or appropriate metastatic site is designated as the principal or first-listed diagnosis, even though chemotherapy or radiotherapy is administered.

g. Symptoms, signs, and ill-defined conditions listed in ICD-10-CM Chapter 18 associated with neoplasms

Symptoms, signs, and ill-defined conditions listed in ICD-10-CM Chapter 18 characteristic of, or associated with, an existing primary or secondary site malignancy cannot be used to replace the malignancy as principal or first-listed diagnosis, regardless of the number of admissions or encounters for treatment and care of the neoplasm.

See section I.C.21. Factors influencing health status and contact with health services, Encounter for prophylactic organ removal.

h. Admission/encounter for pain control/management

See Section I.C.6. for information on coding admission/encounter for pain control/management.

i. Malignancy in two or more noncontiguous sites

A patient may have more than one malignant tumor in the same organ. These tumors may represent different primaries or metastatic disease, depending on the site. Should the documentation be unclear, the provider should be queried as to the status of each tumor so that the correct codes can be assigned.

j. **Disseminated malignant neoplasm, unspecified**

Code C80.0, Disseminated malignant neoplasm, unspecified, is for use only in those cases where the patient has advanced metastatic disease and no known primary or secondary sites are specified. It should not be used in place of assigning codes for the primary site and all known secondary sites.

k. **Malignant neoplasm without specification of site**

Code C80.1, Malignant (primary) neoplasm, unspecified, equates to Cancer, unspecified. This code should only be used when no determination can be made as to the primary site of a malignancy. This code should rarely be used in the inpatient setting.

l. **Sequencing of neoplasm codes**

1) **Encounter for treatment of primary malignancy**

If the reason for the encounter is for treatment of a primary malignancy, assign the malignancy as the principal/first-listed diagnosis. The primary site is to be sequenced first, followed by any metastatic sites.

2) **Encounter for treatment of secondary malignancy**

When an encounter is for a primary malignancy with metastasis and treatment is directed toward the metastatic (secondary) site(s) only, the metastatic site(s) is designated as the principal/first-listed diagnosis. The primary malignancy is coded as an additional code.

3) **Malignant neoplasm in a pregnant patient**

When a pregnant woman has a malignant neoplasm, a code from subcategory O9A.1-, Malignant neoplasm complicating pregnancy, childbirth, and the puerperium, should be sequenced first, followed by the appropriate code from Chapter 2 to indicate the type of neoplasm.

4) **Encounter for complication associated with a neoplasm**

When an encounter is for management of a complication associated with a neoplasm, such as dehydration, and the treatment is only for the complication, the complication is coded first, followed by the appropriate code(s) for the neoplasm.

The exception to this guideline is anemia. When the admission/encounter is for management of an anemia associated with the malignancy, and the treatment is only for anemia, the appropriate code for the malignancy is sequenced as the principal or first-listed diagnosis followed by code D63.0, Anemia in neoplastic disease.

5) **Complication from surgical procedure for treatment of a neoplasm**

When an encounter is for treatment of a complication resulting from a surgical procedure performed for the treatment of the neoplasm, designate the complication as the principal/first-listed diagnosis. See guideline regarding the coding of a current malignancy versus personal history to determine if the code for the neoplasm should also be assigned.

6) **Pathologic fracture due to a neoplasm**

When an encounter is for a pathological fracture due to a neoplasm, and the focus of treatment is the fracture, a code from subcategory M84.5, Pathological fracture in neoplastic disease, should be sequenced first, followed by the code for the neoplasm.

If the focus of treatment is the neoplasm with an associated pathological fracture, the neoplasm code should be sequenced first, followed by a code from M84.5 for the pathological fracture.

m. **Current malignancy versus personal history of malignancy**

When a primary malignancy has been excised but further treatment, such as an additional surgery for the malignancy, radiation therapy or chemotherapy is directed to that site, the primary malignancy code should be used until treatment is completed.

(continues)

ICD-10-CM Chapter-Specific Coding Guidelines (*continued*)

When a primary malignancy has been previously excised or eradicated from its site, there is no further treatment (of the malignancy) directed to that site, and there is no evidence of any existing primary malignancy, a code from category Z85, Personal history of malignant neoplasm, should be used to indicate the former site of the malignancy.

See Section I.C.21. Factors influencing health status and contact with health services, History (of)

n. **Leukemia, multiple myeloma, and malignant plasma cell neoplasms in remission versus personal history**

The categories for leukemia, and category C90, Multiple myeloma and malignant plasma cell neoplasms, have codes indicating whether or not the leukemia has achieved remission. There are also codes Z85.6, Personal history of leukemia, and Z85.79, Personal history of other malignant neoplasms of lymphoid, hematopoietic and related tissues. If the documentation is unclear, as to whether the leukemia has achieved remission, the provider should be queried.

See Section I.C.21. Factors influencing health status and contact with health services, History (of)

o. **Aftercare following surgery for neoplasm**

See Section I.C.21. Factors influencing health status and contact with health services, Aftercare

p. **Follow-up care for completed treatment of a malignancy**

See Section I.C.21. Factors influencing health status and contact with health services, Follow-up

q. **Prophylactic organ removal for prevention of malignancy**

See Section I.C. 21. Factors influencing health status and contact with health services, Prophylactic organ removal

r. **Malignant neoplasm associated with transplanted organ**

A malignant neoplasm of a transplanted organ should be coded as a transplant complication. Assign first the appropriate code from category T86.-, Complications of transplanted organs and tissue, followed by code C80.2, Malignant neoplasm associated with transplanted organ. Use an additional code for the specific malignancy.

Exercise 4.4 – Neoplasms

Instructions: Underline the main term in each diagnosis statement and assign the appropriate ICD-10-CM code(s).

_____ **1.** Carcinoma *in situ*, cervix uteri (neoplasm)

_____ **2.** Choriocarcinoma (female patient)

_____ **3.** Hemangioma

_____ **4.** Kaposi's sarcoma

_____ **5.** Lipoma, skin of abdomen

ICD-10-CM Chapter 3: Diseases of the Blood and Blood-Forming Organs and Certain Disorders Involving the Immune Mechanism (D50–D89)

This ICD-10-CM chapter classifies the following:

- Nutritional anemias

- Hemolytic anemias

- Aplastic and other anemias and other bone marrow failure syndromes

- Coagulation defects, purpura, and other hemorrhagic conditions

- Other disorders of blood and blood-forming organs

- Intraoperative and postprocedural complications of the spleen

- Certain disorders involving the immune mechanism

Bone marrow is the principal site for hemopoietic cell proliferation and differentiation. One of the largest organs in the human body, hemopoietic tissue is responsible for producing erythrocytes (red blood cells), neutrophils, eosinophils, basophils, monocytes, platelets, and lymphocytes.

Anemia refers to a lower-than-normal erythrocyte count or level of hemoglobin in the circulating blood. A clinical sign rather than a diagnostic entity, anemia can be classified by three morphological variations of the erythrocyte: size (volume), hemoglobin content, and shape. These variations give clinicians clues to the specific type of anemia. In laboratory blood tests, erythrocyte size is gauged by estimating the volume of red cells in the circulating blood.

- Red cell volume (or mean corpuscular volume) is estimated by dividing the patient's hematocrit (percentage of red blood cells in whole blood) by the red blood cell count (RBC). Normal values are normocytic, abnormally low values are microcytic, and abnormally high values are macrocytic.

- Hemoglobin content refers to the average amount of hemoglobin in each red blood cell. This value, called the mean cell hemoglobin, is calculated by dividing the patient's hemoglobin by the number of red blood cells. Normal values are normochromic, less-than-normal values are hypochromic, and greater-than-normal values are hyperchromic.

- Shape is determined by microscopy. Normally, red blood cells have a smooth, concave shape. Erythrocytes with irregular shapes are called poikilocytes, a general term meaning "abnormally shaped." Terms referring to specific abnormal cell shapes include *acanthocytes, leptocytes, nucleated erythrocytes, macro-ovalocytes, schistocytes, helmet cells, teardrop cells, sickle cells*, and *target cells*.

Once the cell morphology is determined, the anemia can be further classified based on certain physiological and pathological criteria.

EXAMPLE: Constitutional aplastic anemia (D61.09) is classified physiologically as an anemia of hypoproliferation and pathologically as inborn error of heredity.

The term *coagulation defect* refers to deficiencies or disorders of hemostasis. A complicated process involving substances in the injured tissues, formed elements of blood (platelets and monocytes), and the coagulation proteins, coagulation requires the production of thrombin, a substance that stabilizes the platelet plug and forms the fibrin clot. Together they mechanically block the extravasation of blood from ruptured vessels. The coagulation process can be interrupted by a genetic or disease-caused protein deficiency, by an increase in the catabolism of coagulation proteins, or by antibodies directed against the coagulation proteins. Many proteins are involved in coagulation, many of which are identified by the term *factor* followed by a Roman numeral. The appropriate Roman numeral followed by the suffix *a* indicates the activated form of a coagulation factor.

EXAMPLE: When protein factor II (prothrombin) is activated by the enzyme thrombin, it is designated factor IIa.

The term *purpura* refers to a condition characterized by hemorrhage, or extravasation of blood, into the tissues, producing bruises and small red patches on the skin. Purpura may be associated with thrombocytopenia or can occur in a nonthrombocytopenic form. Thrombocytopenia is a decrease of the number of platelets in the circulating blood and may be primary (hereditary or idiopathic) or secondary to a known cause.

Diseases of white blood cells refer to increases, decreases, or genetic or idiopathic anomalies of white blood cells not associated with malignant disease classified to categories C81–C96, *Malignant neoplasms of lymphoid, hematopoietic and related tissue.*

ICD-10-CM Chapter-Specific Coding Guidelines

Chapter 3: Diseases of the Blood and Blood-Forming Organs and Certain Disorders Involving the Immune Mechanism (D50–D89)
Reserved for future guideline expansion.

Exercise 4.5 – Diseases of the Blood and Blood-Forming Organs and Certain Disorders Involving the Immune Mechanism

Instructions: Underline the main term in each diagnosis statement and assign the appropriate ICD-10-CM code(s).

_____ **1.** Acquired polycythemia

_____ **2.** Acute posthemorrhagic anemia

_____ **3.** Agranulocytosis

_____ **4.** Chronic simple anemia

_____ **5.** Chronic congestive splenomegaly

ICD-10-CM Chapter 4: Endocrine, Nutritional, and Metabolic Diseases (E00–E89)

This ICD-10-CM chapter classifies the following:

- Disorders of thyroid gland
- Diabetes mellitus
- Other disorders of glucose regulation and pancreatic internal secretion
- Disorders of other endocrine glands
- Intraoperative complications of endocrine system
- Malnutrition
- Other nutritional deficiencies
- Overweight, obesity, and other hyperalimentation

- Metabolic disorders

- Postprocedural endocrine and metabolic complications and disorders, not elsewhere classified

The endocrine system includes specialized organs and body tissues that produce, secrete, and store hormones. Hormones regulate the body's development, control the function of various tissues, support reproduction, and regulate metabolism. Hormones from the endocrine system are secreted into the blood, where proteins keep them intact and regulate their release. Other changes in the body also influence hormone secretions.

EXAMPLE 1: NORMAL HORMONE FUNCTION: Parathyroid hormone causes the body to increase the level of calcium in blood. As calcium levels rise, the secretion of parathyroid hormone decreases.

EXAMPLE 2: HORMONE FUNCTION DURING ILLNESS: During illness, the adrenal glands increase the secretions of certain hormones to help the body overcome the stress of illness. The normal regulation of hormone secretion is suspended, allowing for a tolerance of higher levels of hormone in the blood until the illness is resolved.

Nutritional deficiencies in ICD-10-CM Chapter 4 cover deficiencies in vitamins, minerals, and protein-calorie malnutrition. Metabolic diseases in ICD-10-CM Chapter 4 cover a wide range of diseases, including problems with amino acid and carbohydrate transport; lipoid metabolism; plasma protein metabolism; gout; mineral metabolism; and fluid, electrolyte, and acid-base imbalances. Cystic fibrosis, porphyrin, purine and pyrimidine metabolism, and obesity are also classified.

Coding Diabetes Mellitus

ICD-10-CM categories E08–E13 classify diabetes mellitus, such as drug- or chemical-induced diabetes mellitus, diabetes mellitus due to underlying conditions, type 1 diabetes mellitus, type 2 diabetes mellitus, or other diabetes mellitus. Subcategories further classify the existence or absence of complications (e.g., E11.9, Type 2 diabetes mellitus without complications). To assign the code for type 1 diabetes mellitus, the provider must document it in the patient record. With **type 1 diabetes mellitus**, the patient's body is *unable to produce insulin*; with **type 2 diabetes mellitus**, the patient's body is *unable to properly use insulin produced*.

 Coding Tip:

If the patient's record documents the administration of insulin, do not assume that the patient is a type 1 diabetic. The provider must document "type 1" to assign that code.

Review the patient record to identify any disease complications (e.g., ketoacidosis or ophthalmological manifestations). Do not forget to assign a code to documented manifestations (e.g., diabetic cataract), and make sure you sequence the diabetes mellitus code first.

ICD-10-CM Chapter-Specific Coding Guidelines

Chapter 4: Endocrine, Nutritional, and Metabolic Diseases E00–E89

a. Diabetes mellitus

The diabetes mellitus codes are combination codes that include the type of diabetes mellitus, the body system affected, and the complications affecting that body system. As many codes within a particular category as are necessary to describe all of the complications of the disease may be used. They should be sequenced based on the reason for a particular encounter. Assign as many codes from categories E08–E13 as needed to identify all of the associated conditions that the patient has.

1) Type of diabetes

The age of a patient is not the sole determining factor, though most type 1 diabetics develop the condition before reaching puberty. For this reason, type 1 diabetes mellitus is also referred to as juvenile diabetes.

(continues)

ICD-10-CM Chapter-Specific Coding Guidelines (*continued*)

2) Type of diabetes mellitus not documented

If the type of diabetes mellitus is not documented in the patient record, the default is E11.-, Type 2 diabetes mellitus.

3) Diabetes mellitus and the use of insulin and hypoglycemics

If the documentation in a patient record does not indicate the type of diabetes but does indicate that the patient uses insulin, code E11, Type 2 diabetes mellitus, should be assigned. Code Z79.4, Long-term (current) use of insulin, or Z79.84, Long term (current) use of oral hypoglycemic drugs, should also be assigned to indicate that the patient uses insulin or hypoglycemic drugs. Code Z79.4 should not be assigned if insulin is given temporarily to bring a type 2 patient's blood sugar under control during an encounter.

4) Diabetes mellitus in pregnancy and gestational diabetes

See Section I.C.15. Diabetes mellitus in pregnancy.
See Section I.C.15. Gestational (pregnancy induced) diabetes.

5) Complications due to insulin pump malfunction

(a) Underdose of insulin due to insulin pump failure

An underdose of insulin due to an insulin pump failure should be assigned T85.6, Mechanical complication of other specified internal and external prosthetic devices, implants and grafts, that specifies the type of pump malfunction, as the principal or first-listed code, followed by code T38.3x6-, Underdosing of insulin and oral hypoglycemic [antidiabetic] drugs. Additional codes for the type of diabetes mellitus and any associated complications due to the underdosing should also be assigned.

(b) Overdose of insulin due to insulin pump failure

The principal or first-listed code for an encounter due to an insulin pump malfunction resulting in an overdose of insulin should also be T85.6-, Mechanical complication of other specified internal and external prosthetic devices, implants and grafts, followed by code T38.3x1-, Poisoning by insulin and oral hypoglycemic [antidiabetic] drugs, accidental (unintentional).

6) Secondary diabetes mellitus

Codes under category E08, Diabetes mellitus due to underlying condition, E09, Drug or chemical induced diabetes mellitus, and E13, Other specified diabetes mellitus, identify complications/manifestations associated with secondary diabetes mellitus. Secondary diabetes is always caused by another condition or event (e.g., cystic fibrosis, malignant neoplasm of pancreas, pancreatectomy, adverse effect of drug, or poisoning).

(a) Secondary diabetes mellitus and the use of insulin or hypoglycemic drugs

For patients who routinely use insulin or hypoglycemic drugs, code Z79.4, Long-term (current) use of insulin, or Z79.84, Long term (current) use of oral hypoglycemic drugs, should also be assigned. Code Z79.4 should not be assigned if insulin is given temporarily to bring a patient's blood sugar under control during an encounter.

(b) Assigning and sequencing secondary diabetes codes and its causes

The sequencing of the secondary diabetes codes in relationship to codes for the cause of the diabetes is based on the Tabular List instructions for categories E08, E09 and E13.

(i) Secondary diabetes mellitus due to pancreatectomy

For postpancreatectomy diabetes mellitus (lack of insulin due to the surgical removal of all or part of the pancreas), assign code E89.1, Postsurgical hypoinsulinemia. Assign a code from category E13 and a code from subcategory Z90.41-, Acquired absence of pancreas, as additional codes.

(ii) Secondary diabetes due to drugs

Secondary diabetes may be caused by an adverse effect of correctly administered medications, poisoning, or sequela of poisoning.

See Section I.C.19.e. for coding of adverse effects and poisoning, and section I.C.20. for external code reporting.

Exercise 4.6 – Endocrine, Nutritional, and Metabolic Diseases

Instructions: Underline the main term in each diagnosis statement and assign the appropriate ICD-10-CM code(s).

_____ **1.** Diabetes mellitus, type 1, with hyperglycemia

_____ **2.** Diabetes mellitus, type 2

_____ **3.** Hyperprolactinemia

_____ **4.** Morbid obesity due to excess calories

_____ **5.** Polycystic ovaries

ICD-10-CM Chapter 5: Mental, Behavioral, and Neurodevelopmental Disorders (F01–F99)

This ICD-10-CM chapter classifies the following:

- Mental disorders due to known physiological conditions
- Mental and behavioral disorders due to psychoactive substance use
- Schizophrenia, schizotypal and delusional, and other non-mood psychotic disorders
- Mood [affective] disorders
- Anxiety, dissociative, stress-related, somatoform, and other nonpsychotic mental disorders
- Behavioral syndromes associated with physiological disturbances and physical factors
- Disorders of adult personality and behavior
- Mental retardation
- Pervasive and specific developmental disorders
- Behavioral and emotional disorders with onset usually occurring in childhood and adolescence
- Unspecified mental disorders

ICD-10-CM Chapter-Specific Coding Guidelines

Chapter 5: Mental, Behavioral, and Neurodevelopmental Disorders (F01–F99)

a. Pain disorders related to psychological factors

Assign code F45.41, for pain that is exclusively related to psychological disorders. As indicated by the Excludes1 note under the category G89, a code from category G89 should not be assigned with code F45.41. Code F45.4, Pain disorders related to psychological factors, should be used with a code from category G89, Pain, not elsewhere classified, if there is documentation of a psychological component for a patient with acute or chronic pain.

See Section I.C.6. Pain.

(continues)

ICD-10-CM Chapter-Specific Coding Guidelines (*continued*)

b. **Mental and behavioral disorders due to psychoactive substance use**

1) **In remission**

Selection of codes for "in remission" for categories F10-F19, Mental and behavioral disorders due to psychoactive substance use (categories F10-F19 with -.21) requires the provider's clinical judgment. The appropriate codes for "in remission" are assigned only on the basis of provider documentation (as defined in the Official Guidelines for Coding and Reporting).

2) **Psychoactive substance use, abuse and dependence**

When the provider documentation refers to use, abuse and dependence of the same substance (e.g. alcohol, opioid, cannabis, etc.), only one code should be assigned to identify the pattern of use based on the following hierarchy:

- If both use and abuse are documented, assign only the code for abuse.

- If both abuse and dependence are documented, assign only the code for dependence.

- If use, abuse and dependence are all documented, assign only the code for dependence.

- If both use and dependence are documented, assign only the code for dependence.

3) **Psychoactive substance use**

As with all other diagnoses, the codes for psychoactive substance use (F10.9-, F11.9-, F12.9-, F13.9-, F14.9-, F15.9-, F16.9-) should only be assigned based on provider documentation and when they meet the definition of a reportable diagnosis (*see Section III, Reporting Additional Diagnoses*). The codes are to be used only when the psychoactive substance use is associated with a mental or behavioral disorder, and such a relationship is documented by the provider.

Exercise 4.7 – Mental, Behavioral, and Neurodevelopmental Disorders

Instructions: Underline the main term in each diagnosis statement and assign the appropriate ICD-10-CM code(s).

_____ **1.** Alzheimer's disease

_____ **2.** Paranoid schizophrenia

_____ **3.** Alcoholic delirium tremens

_____ **4.** Episodic cocaine abuse

_____ **5.** Major depressive disorder, recurrent episode

ICD-10-CM Chapter 6: Diseases of the Nervous System (G00–G99)

This ICD-10-CM chapter classifies the following:

- Inflammatory diseases of the central nervous system

- Systemic atrophies primarily affecting the central nervous system

- Extrapyramidal and movement disorders

- Other degenerative diseases of the nervous system

- Demyelinating diseases of the central nervous system

- Episodic and paroxysmal disorders

- Nerve, nerve root, and plexus disorders

- Polyneuropathies and other disorders of the peripheral nervous system

- Diseases of myoneural junction and muscle

- Cerebral palsy and other paralytic syndromes

- Other disorders of the nervous system

ICD-10-CM Chapter-Specific Coding Guidelines

Chapter 6: Diseases of the Nervous System (G00-G99)

a. Dominant/nondominant side

Codes from category G81, *Hemiplegia and hemiparesis*, and subcategories, G83.1, *Monoplegia of lower limb*, G83.2, *Monoplegia of upper limb*, and G83.3, *Monoplegia, unspecified*, identify whether the dominant or nondominant side is affected. Should the affected side be documented, but not specified as dominant or nondominant, and the classification system does not indicate a default, code selection is as follows:

- For ambidextrous patients, the default should be dominant.

- If the left side is affected, the default is non-dominant.

- If the right side is affected, the default is dominant.

b. Pain – Category G89

1) General coding information

Codes in category G89, Pain, not elsewhere classified, may be used in conjunction with codes from other categories and chapters to provide more detail about acute or chronic pain and neoplasm-related pain, unless otherwise indicated below.

If the pain is not specified as acute or chronic, post-thoracotomy, postprocedural, or neoplasm-related, do not assign codes from category G89.

A code from category G89 should not be assigned if the underlying (definitive) diagnosis is known, unless the reason for the encounter is pain control/management and *not* management of the underlying condition.

(a) Category G89 codes as principal or first-listed diagnosis

Category G89 codes are acceptable as principal diagnosis or the first-listed code:

- When pain control or pain management is the reason for the admission/encounter (e.g., a patient with displaced intervertebral disc, nerve impingement, and severe back pain presents for injection of steroid into the spinal canal). The underlying cause of the pain should be reported as an additional diagnosis, if known.

- When a patient is admitted for the insertion of a neurostimulator for pain control, assign the appropriate pain code as the principal or first-listed diagnosis. When an admission or encounter is for a procedure aimed at treating the underlying condition and a neurostimulator is inserted

(continues)

ICD-10-CM Chapter-Specific Coding Guidelines (*continued*)

for pain control during the same admission/encounter, a code for the underlying condition should be assigned as the principal diagnosis and the appropriate pain code should be assigned as a secondary diagnosis.

(b) **Use of category G89 codes in conjunction with site-specific pain codes**

    (i) **Assigning category G89 codes and site-specific pain codes**

        Codes from category G89 may be used in conjunction with codes that identify the site of pain (including codes from Chapter 18) if the category G89 code provides additional information. For example, if the code describes the site of the pain but does not fully describe whether the pain is acute or chronic, both codes should be assigned.

    (ii) **Sequencing of category G89 codes with site-specific pain codes**

        The sequencing of category G89 codes with site-specific pain codes (including Chapter 18 codes), is dependent on the circumstances of the encounter/admission as follows:

- If the encounter is for pain control or pain management, assign the code from category G89 followed by the code identifying the specific site of pain (e.g., encounter for pain management for acute neck pain from trauma is assigned code G89.11, Acute pain due to trauma, followed by code M54.2, Cervicalgia, to identify the site of pain).

- If the encounter is for any other reason except pain control or pain management, and a related definitive diagnosis has not been established (confirmed) by the provider, assign the code for the specific site of pain first, followed by the appropriate code from category G89.

2) **Pain due to devices, implants, and grafts**
   See Section I.C.19. Pain due to medical devices.

3) **Postoperative pain**
   The provider's documentation should be used to guide the coding of postoperative pain, as well as *Section III. Reporting Additional Diagnoses* and *Section IV. Diagnostic Coding and Reporting in the Outpatient Setting.* The default for post-thoracotomy and other postoperative pain not specified as acute or chronic is the code for the acute form.
   Routine or expected postoperative pain immediately after surgery should not be coded.

   (a) **Postoperative pain not associated with specific postoperative complication**
       Postoperative pain not associated with a specific postoperative complication is assigned to the appropriate postoperative pain code in category G89.

   (b) **Postoperative pain associated with specific postoperative complication**
       Postoperative pain associated with a specific postoperative complication (such as painful wire sutures) is assigned to the appropriate code(s) found in Chapter 19, Injury, Poisoning, and Certain Other Consequences of External Causes. If appropriate, use additional code(s) from category G89 to identify acute or chronic pain (G89.18 or G89.28).

4) **Chronic pain**
   Chronic pain is classified to subcategory G89.2. There is no time frame defining when pain becomes chronic pain. The provider's documentation should be used to guide the use of these codes.

5) **Neoplasm-related pain**
   Code G89.3 is assigned to pain documented as being related, associated with or due to cancer, primary or secondary malignancy, or tumor. This code is assigned regardless of whether the pain is acute or chronic.
   This code may be assigned as the principal or first-listed code when the stated reason for the admission/encounter is documented as pain control/pain management. The underlying neoplasm should be reported as an additional diagnosis.

When the reason for the admission/encounter is management of the neoplasm and the pain associated with the neoplasm is also documented, code G89.3 may be assigned as an additional diagnosis. It is not necessary to assign an additional code for the site of the pain.

See Section I.C.2. for instructions on the sequencing of neoplasms for all other stated reasons for the admission/encounter (except pain control/pain management).

6) **Chronic pain syndrome**

Central pain syndrome (G89.0) and chronic pain syndrome (G89.4) are different than the term "chronic pain," and therefore codes should only be used when the provider has specifically documented this condition.

See Section I.C.5. Pain disorders related to psychological factors.

Exercise 4.8 – Diseases of the Nervous System

Instructions: Underline the main term in each diagnosis statement and assign the appropriate ICD-10-CM code(s).

_____ **1.** Central pain syndrome

_____ **2.** Bell's palsy

_____ **3.** Acute pain due to trauma; cervicalgia

_____ **4.** Congenital quadriplegia

_____ **5.** Intraspinal abscess

ICD-10-CM Chapter 7: Diseases of the Eye and Adnexa (H00–H59)

This ICD-10-CM chapter classifies the following:

- Disorders of eyelid, lacrimal system, and orbit
- Disorders of conjunctiva
- Disorders of sclera, cornea, iris, and ciliary body
- Disorders of lens
- Disorders of choroid and retina
- Glaucoma
- Disorders of vitreous body and globe
- Disorders of optic nerve and visual pathways
- Disorders of ocular muscles, binocular movement, accommodation, and refraction
- Visual disturbances and blindness
- Other disorders of eye and adnexa
- Intraoperative and postprocedural complications and disorders of eye and adnexa

ICD-10-CM Chapter-Specific Coding Guidelines

Chapter 7: Diseases of the Eye and Adnexa (H00–H59)

a. Glaucoma

1) **Assigning glaucoma codes**

Assign as many codes from category H40, Glaucoma, as needed to identify the type of glaucoma, the affected eye, and the glaucoma stage.

2) **Bilateral glaucoma with same type and stage**

When a patient has bilateral glaucoma and both eyes are documented as being the same type and stage, and there is a code for bilateral glaucoma, report only the code for the type of glaucoma, bilateral, with the seventh character for the stage. When a patient has bilateral glaucoma and both eyes are documented as being the same type and stage, and the classification does not provide a code for bilateral glaucoma (e.g., subcategories H40.10, H40.11, and H40.20) report only one code for the type of glaucoma with the appropriate seventh character for the stage.

3) **Bilateral glaucoma stage with different types or stages**

When a patient has bilateral glaucoma and each eye is documented as having a different type or stage, and the classification distinguishes laterality, assign the appropriate code for each eye rather than the code for bilateral glaucoma. When a patient has bilateral glaucoma and each eye is documented as having a different type, and the classification does not distinguish laterality (i.e., subcategories H40.10, H40.11, and H40.20), assign one code for each type of glaucoma with the appropriate seventh character for the stage.

When a patient has bilateral glaucoma and each eye is documented as having the same type, but different stage, and the classification does not distinguish laterality (e.g., subcategories H40.10, H40.11, and H40.20), assign a code for the type of glaucoma for each eye with the seventh character for the specific glaucoma stage documented for each eye.

4) **Patient admitted with glaucoma and stage evolves during the admission**

If a patient is admitted with glaucoma and the stage progresses during the admission, assign the code for highest stage documented.

5) **Indeterminate stage glaucoma**

Assignment of the seventh character "4" for "indeterminate stage" should be based on the clinical documentation. The seventh character "4" is used for glaucomas whose stage cannot be clinically determined. This seventh character should not be confused with the seventh character "0," unspecified, which should be assigned when there is no documentation regarding the stage of the glaucoma.

Exercise 4.9 – Diseases of the Eye and Adnexa

Instructions: Underline the main term in each diagnosis statement and assign the appropriate ICD-10-CM code(s).

_____ **1.** Primary open-angle glaucoma, mild stage

_____ **2.** Vitreous hemorrhage, left eye

_____ **3.** Degenerative myopia, bilateral eyes

_____ **4.** Alternating exotropia

_____ **5.** Cystoid macular degeneration, bilateral eyes

ICD-10-CM Chapter 8: Diseases of the Ear and Mastoid Process (H60–H95)

This ICD-10-CM chapter classifies the following:

- Diseases of external ear
- Diseases of middle ear and mastoid
- Diseases of inner ear
- Other disorders of the ear
- Intraoperative and postprocedural complications and disorders of the ear and mastoid process, not elsewhere classified

ICD-10-CM Chapter-Specific Coding Guidelines

Chapter 8: Diseases of the Ear and Mastoid Process (H60-H95)
Reserved for future guideline expansion.

Exercise 4.10 – Diseases of the Ear and Mastoid Process

Instructions: Underline the main term in each diagnosis statement and assign the appropriate ICD-10-CM code(s).

_____ **1.** Swimmer's ear, right ear
_____ **2.** Acute serous otitis media, left ear
_____ **3.** Central perforation of tympanic membrane, left ear
_____ **4.** Vertigo of central origin, bilateral
_____ **5.** Granulation of postmastoidectomy cavity, left ear

ICD-10-CM Chapter 9: Diseases of the Circulatory System (I00–I99)

This ICD-10-CM chapter classifies the following:

- Acute rheumatic fever
- Chronic rheumatic heart diseases
- Hypertensive diseases
- Ischemic heart diseases
- Pulmonary heart disease and diseases of pulmonary circulation
- Other forms of heart disease

- Cerebrovascular diseases
- Diseases of arteries, arterioles, and capillaries
- Diseases of veins, lymphatic vessels, and lymph nodes, not elsewhere classified
- Other and unspecified disorders of the circulatory system

ICD-10-CM Chapter-Specific Coding Guidelines

Chapter 9: Diseases of the Circulatory System (I00-I99)

a. Hypertension

The classification presumes a causal relationship between hypertension and heart involvement and between hypertension and kidney involvement, as the two conditions are linked by the term "with" in the Alphabetic Index. These conditions should be coded as related even in the absence of provider documentation explicitly linking them, unless the documentation clearly states the conditions are unrelated. For hypertension and conditions not specifically linked by relational terms such as "with," "associated with" or "due to" in the classification, provider documentation must link the conditions in order to code them as related.

1) Hypertension with heart disease

Hypertension with heart conditions classified to I50.- or I51.4-I51.9, are assigned to a code from category I11, Hypertensive heart disease. Use an additional code from category I50, Heart failure, to identify the type of heart failure in those patients with heart failure (Figure 4-7). The same heart conditions (I50.-, I51.4-I51.9) with hypertension are coded separately if the provider has specifically documented a different cause. Sequence according to the circumstances of the admission/encounter.

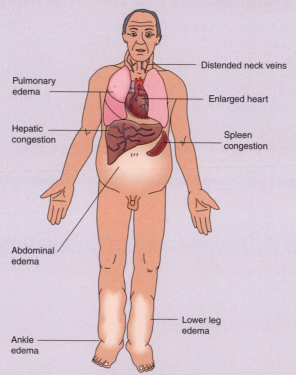

Pulmonary edema

Distended neck veins

Enlarged heart

Hepatic congestion

Spleen congestion

Abdominal edema

Lower leg edema

Ankle edema

Figure 4-7 Signs of congestive heart failure

2) Hypertensive chronic kidney disease

Assign codes from category I12, Hypertensive chronic kidney disease, when both hypertension and a condition classifiable to category N18, Chronic kidney disease (CKD), are present. CKD should not be coded as hypertensive if the physician has specifically documented a different cause.

The appropriate code from category N18 should be used as a secondary code with a code from category I12 to identify the stage of chronic kidney disease.

See Section I.C.14. Chronic kidney disease.

If a patient has hypertensive chronic kidney disease and acute renal failure, an additional code for the acute renal failure is required.

3) Hypertensive heart and chronic kidney disease

Assign codes from combination category I13, Hypertensive heart and chronic kidney disease, when there is hypertension with both heart and kidney involvement. Assume a relationship between the hypertension and the chronic kidney disease, whether or not the condition is so designated. If heart failure is present, assign an additional code from category I50 to identify the type of heart failure.

The appropriate code from category N18, Chronic kidney disease, should be used as a secondary code with a code from category I13 to identify the stage of chronic kidney disease.

See Section I.C.14. Chronic kidney disease.

The codes in category I13, Hypertensive heart and chronic kidney disease, are combination codes that include hypertension, heart disease and chronic kidney disease. The Includes note at I13 specifies that the conditions included at I11 and I12 are included together in I13. If a patient has hypertension, heart disease and chronic kidney disease, then a code from I13 should be used, not individual codes for hypertension, heart disease and chronic kidney disease, or codes from I11 or I12.

For patients with both acute renal failure and chronic kidney disease, an additional code for acute renal failure is required.

4) Hypertensive cerebrovascular disease

For hypertensive cerebrovascular disease, first assign the appropriate code from categories I60-I69, followed by the appropriate hypertension code.

5) Hypertensive retinopathy

Subcategory H35.0, Background retinopathy and retinal vascular changes, should be used with a code from category I10-I15, Hypertensive disease to include the systemic hypertension. The sequencing is based on the reason for the encounter.

6) Hypertension, secondary

Secondary hypertension is due to an underlying condition. Two codes are required: one to identify the underlying etiology and one from category I15 to identify the hypertension. Sequencing of codes is determined by the reason for admission/encounter.

7) Hypertension, transient

Assign code R03.0, Elevated blood pressure reading without diagnosis of hypertension, unless patient has an established diagnosis of hypertension. Assign code O13.-, Gestational [pregnancy-induced] hypertension without significant proteinuria, or O14.-, Pre-eclampsia, for transient hypertension of pregnancy.

8) Hypertension, controlled

This diagnostic statement usually refers to an existing state of hypertension under control by therapy. Assign the appropriate code from categories I10-I15, Hypertensive diseases.

(continues)

ICD-10-CM Chapter-Specific Coding Guidelines (*continued*)

9) Hypertension, uncontrolled

Uncontrolled hypertension may refer to untreated hypertension or hypertension not responding to current therapeutic regimen. In either case, assign the appropriate code from categories I10-I15, Hypertensive diseases.

10) Hypertensive crisis

Assign a code from category I16, Hypertensive crisis, for documented hypertensive urgency, hypertensive emergency or unspecified hypertensive crisis. Code also any identified hypertensive disease (I10-I15). The sequencing is based on the reason for the encounter.

b. Atherosclerotic coronary artery disease and angina

ICD-10-CM has combination codes for atherosclerotic heart disease with angina pectoris. The subcategories for these codes are I25.11, Atherosclerotic heart disease of native coronary artery with angina pectoris and I25.7, Atherosclerosis of coronary artery bypass graft(s) and coronary artery of transplanted heart with angina pectoris.

When using one of these combination codes it is not necessary to use an additional code for angina pectoris. A causal relationship can be assumed in a patient with both atherosclerosis and angina pectoris, unless the documentation indicates the angina is due to something other than the atherosclerosis.

If a patient with coronary artery disease is admitted due to an acute myocardial infarction (AMI), the AMI should be sequenced before the coronary artery disease.

See Section I.C.9. Acute myocardial infarction (AMI)

c. Intraoperative and postprocedural cerebrovascular accident

Medical record documentation should clearly specify the cause-and-effect relationship between the medical intervention and the cerebrovascular accident in order to assign a code for intraoperative or postprocedural cerebrovascular accident.

Proper code assignment depends on whether it was an infarction or hemorrhage and whether it occurred intraoperatively or postoperatively. If it was a cerebral hemorrhage, code assignment depends on the type of procedure performed.

d. Sequelae of cerebrovascular disease

1) Category I69, sequelae of cerebrovascular disease

Category I69 is used to indicate conditions classifiable to categories I60-I67 as the causes of sequela (neurologic deficits), themselves classified elsewhere. These "late effects" include neurologic deficits that persist after initial onset of conditions classifiable to categories I60-I67. The neurologic deficits caused by cerebrovascular disease may be present from the onset or may arise at any time after the onset of the condition classifiable to categories I60-I67.

Codes from category I69, Sequelae of cerebrovascular disease, that specify hemiplegia, hemiparesis and monoplegia identify whether the dominant or nondominant side is affected. Should the affected side be documented, but not specified as dominant or nondominant, and the classification system does not indicate a default, code selection is as follows:

- For ambidextrous patients, the default should be dominant.

- If the left side is affected, the default is non-dominant.

- If the right side is affected, the default is dominant.

2) Codes from category I69 with codes from I60–I67

Codes from category I69 may be assigned on a health care record with codes from I60-I67, if the patient has a current cerebrovascular disease and deficits from an old cerebrovascular disease.

3) **Codes from category I69 and Personal history of transient ischemic attack (TIA) and cerebral infarction (Z86.73)**

Codes from category I69 should not be assigned if the patient does not have neurologic deficits.

See Section I.C.21.4. History (of) for use of personal history codes.

e. **Acute myocardial infarction (AMI)**

1) **ST elevation myocardial infarction (STEMI) and non-ST elevation myocardial infarction (NSTEMI)**

The ICD-10-CM codes for acute myocardial infarction (AMI) identify the site, such as anterolateral wall or true posterior wall. Subcategories I21.0-I21.2 and code I21.3 are used for ST elevation myocardial infarction (STEMI). Code I21.4, Non-ST elevation (NSTEMI) myocardial infarction, is used for non-ST elevation myocardial infarction (NSTEMI) and nontransmural MIs.

If NSTEMI evolves to STEMI, assign the STEMI code. If STEMI converts to NSTEMI due to thrombolytic therapy, it is still coded as STEMI.

For encounters occurring while the myocardial infarction is equal to, or less than, four weeks old, including transfers to another acute setting or a postacute setting, and the myocardial infarction meets the definition for "other diagnoses" (*see Section III, Reporting Additional Diagnoses*), codes from category I21 may continue to be reported. For encounters after the 4 week time frame and the patient is still receiving care related to the myocardial infarction, the appropriate aftercare code should be assigned, rather than a code from category I21. For old or healed myocardial infarctions not requiring further care, code I25.2, Old myocardial infarction, may be assigned.

2) **Acute myocardial infarction, unspecified**

Code I21.3, ST elevation (STEMI) myocardial infarction of unspecified site, is the default for the unspecified term acute myocardial infarction. If only STEMI or transmural MI without the site is documented, query the provider as to the site, or assign code I21.3.

3) **AMI documented as nontransmural or subendocardial but site provided**

If an AMI is documented as nontransmural or subendocardial, but the site is provided, it is still coded as a subendocardial AMI.

See Section I.C.21.3. for information on coding status post administration of tPA in a different facility within the last 24 hrs.

4) **Subsequent acute myocardial infarction**

A code from category I22, Subsequent ST elevation (STEMI) and non-ST elevation (NSTEMI) myocardial infarction, is to be used when a patient who has suffered an AMI has a new AMI within the 4 week time frame of the initial AMI. A code from category I22 must be used in conjunction with a code from category I21. The sequencing of the I22 and I21 codes depends on the circumstances of the encounter.

Exercise 4.11 – Diseases of the Circulatory System

Instructions: Underline the main term in each diagnosis statement and assign the appropriate ICD-10-CM code(s).

_____ **1.** Acute ST elevation myocardial infarction, inferolateral wall, initial episode of care

_____ **2.** Acute rheumatic endocarditis

_____ **3.** Aphasia, late effect of cerebrovascular disease

_____ **4.** Hypertension

_____ **5.** Mitral and aortic valve insufficiency

ICD-10-CM Chapter 10: Diseases of the Respiratory System (J00–J99)

This ICD-10-CM chapter classifies the following:

- Acute upper respiratory infections
- Influenza and pneumonia
- Other acute lower respiratory infections
- Other diseases of upper respiratory tract
- Chronic lower respiratory diseases
- Lung diseases due to external agents
- Other respiratory diseases principally affecting the interstitium
- Suppurative and necrotic conditions of the lower respiratory tract
- Other diseases of the pleura
- Intraoperative and postprocedural complications and disorders of respiratory system, not elsewhere classified
- Other diseases of the respiratory system

The respiratory system is responsible for pulmonary ventilation and the exchange of oxygen and carbon dioxide between the lungs and ambient air. The organs of the respiratory system also perform nonrespiratory functions such as warming and moisturizing the air passing into the lungs, providing airflow for the larynx and vocal cords for speech, and releasing excess body heat in the process of thermoregulation for homeostasis. The lungs also perform important metabolic and embolic filtering functions.

ICD-10-CM Chapter-Specific Coding Guidelines

Chapter 10: Diseases of the Respiratory System (J00-J99)

a. Chronic obstructive pulmonary disease [COPD] and asthma

1) **Acute exacerbation of chronic obstructive bronchitis and asthma**

The codes in categories J44 and J45 distinguish between uncomplicated cases and those in acute exacerbation. An acute exacerbation is a worsening or a decompensation of a chronic condition. An acute exacerbation is not equivalent to an infection superimposed on a chronic condition, though an exacerbation may be triggered by an infection.

b. Acute respiratory failure

1) **Acute respiratory failure as principal diagnosis**

A code from subcategory J96.0, Acute respiratory failure, or subcategory J96.2, Acute and chronic respiratory failure, may be assigned as a principal diagnosis when it is the condition established after study to be chiefly responsible for occasioning the admission to the hospital, and the selection is supported by the Alphabetic Index and Tabular List. However, chapter-specific coding guidelines (such as obstetrics, poisoning, HIV, newborn) that provide sequencing direction take precedence.

2) Acute respiratory failure as secondary diagnosis

Respiratory failure may be listed as a secondary diagnosis if it occurs after admission, or if it is present on admission but does not meet the definition of principal diagnosis.

3) Sequencing of acute respiratory failure and another acute condition

When a patient is admitted with respiratory failure and another acute condition (e.g., myocardial infarction, cerebrovascular accident, aspiration pneumonia), the principal diagnosis will not be the same in every situation. This applies whether the other acute condition is a respiratory or nonrespiratory condition. Selection of the principal diagnosis will be dependent on the circumstances of admission. If both the respiratory failure and the other acute condition are equally responsible for occasioning the admission to the hospital and there are no chapter-specific sequencing rules, the guideline regarding two or more diagnoses that equally meet the definition for principal diagnosis (Section II, C.) may be applied in these situations.

If the documentation is not clear as to whether acute respiratory failure and another condition are equally responsible for occasioning the admission, query the provider for clarification.

c. Influenza due to certain identified influenza viruses

Code only confirmed cases of influenza due to certain identified influenza viruses (category J09), and due to other identified influenza virus (category J10). This is an exception to the hospital inpatient guideline Section II, H. (Uncertain Diagnosis).

In this context, "confirmation" does not require documentation of positive laboratory testing specific for avian or other novel influenza A or other identified influenza virus. However, coding should be based on the provider's diagnostic statement that the patient has avian influenza, or other novel influenza A, for category J09, or has another particular identified strain of influenza, such as H1N1 or H3N2, but not identified as novel or variant, for category J10.

If the provider records "suspected" or "possible" or "probable" avian influenza, or novel influenza, or other identified influenza, then the appropriate influenza code from category J11, Influenza due to unidentified influenza virus, should be assigned. A code from category J09, Influenza due to certain identified influenza viruses, should not be assigned nor should a code from category J10, Influenza due to other identified influenza virus.

d. Ventilator associated pneumonia

1) Documentation of ventilator associated pneumonia

As with all procedural or postprocedural complications, code assignment is based on the provider's documentation of the relationship between the condition and the procedure.

Code J95.851, Ventilator associated pneumonia, should be assigned only when the provider has documented ventilator associated pneumonia (VAP). An additional code to identify the organism (e.g., *Pseudomonas aeruginosa,* code B96.5) should also be assigned. Do not assign an additional code from categories J12-J18 to identify the type of pneumonia.

Code J95.851 should not be assigned for cases where the patient has pneumonia and is on a mechanical ventilator and the provider has not specifically stated that the pneumonia is ventilator-associated pneumonia. If the documentation is unclear as to whether the patient has a pneumonia that is a complication attributable to the mechanical ventilator, query the provider.

2) Ventilator associated pneumonia develops after admission

A patient may be admitted with one type of pneumonia (e.g., code J13, Pneumonia due to Streptococcus pneumonia) and subsequently develop VAP. In this instance, the principal diagnosis would be the appropriate code from categories J12-J18 for the pneumonia diagnosed at the time of admission.

Code J95.851, Ventilator associated pneumonia, would be assigned as an additional diagnosis when the provider has also documented the presence of ventilator associated pneumonia.

Exercise 4.12 – Diseases of the Respiratory System

Instructions: Underline the main term in each diagnosis statement and assign the appropriate ICD-10-CM code(s).

_____   **1.** Acute frontal sinusitis

_____   **2.** Allergic rhinitis due to pollen

_____   **3.** Chronic obstructive pulmonary disease

_____   **4.** Atelectasis

_____   **5.** Croup

ICD-10-CM Chapter 11: Diseases of the Digestive System (K00–K95)

This ICD-10-CM chapter classifies the following:

- Diseases of oral cavity and salivary glands

- Diseases of esophagus, stomach, and duodenum

- Diseases of appendix

- Hernia

- Noninfective enteritis and colitis

- Other diseases of intestines

- Diseases of peritoneum and retroperitoneum

- Diseases of liver

- Disorders of gallbladder, biliary tract, and pancreas

- Other diseases of the digestive system

The alimentary tract (or digestive tract) is the long, muscular tube that begins at the mouth and ends at the anus. Major digestive organs include the pharynx, esophagus, stomach, and intestines. Accessory, or secondary, organs include the salivary and parotid glands; jaw; teeth; and supporting structures of the teeth, tongue, liver, gallbladder and biliary tract, pancreas, and peritoneum. Structures that support the digestive process from outside this continuous tube are also included in this system: gallbladder, pancreas, and liver. (These organs provide secretions that are critical to food absorption and use by the body.)

EXAMPLE: The following are examples of diseases that interfere with the digestive function, and they are classified in ICD-10-CM Chapter 11.

- Dental caries (tooth decay), assigned ICD-10-CM code K02.9, has a direct effect on digestion because the disease process interferes with mastication, the mechanical breakdown of food by chewing.

- Portal hypertension, assigned ICD-10-CM code K76.6, is high blood pressure in the liver's portal circulatory system. Although it does not directly affect digestion, portal hypertension is included because it represents a disease of a digestive system organ. Portal hypertension has no apparent effect on the digestive process until the disease has progressed to the point that the liver can no longer perform its function as a digestive organ. (Portal hypertension can be caused by cirrhosis of the liver and other conditions that cause obstruction to the portal vein, such as cancer.)

ICD-10-CM Chapter-Specific Coding Guidelines

Chapter 11: Diseases of the Digestive System (K00-K95)
Reserved for future guideline expansion.

Exercise 4.13 – Diseases of the Digestive System

Instructions: Underline the main term in each diagnosis statement and assign the appropriate ICD-10-CM code(s).

_____ **1.** Crohn's disease

_____ **2.** Canker sore

_____ **3.** Acute gastrojejunal ulcer, with perforation

_____ **4.** Gastroesophageal reflux

_____ **5.** Inguinal hernia

ICD-10-CM Chapter 12: Diseases of the Skin and Subcutaneous Tissue (L00–L99)

This ICD-10-CM chapter classifies the following:

- Infections of the skin and subcutaneous tissue
- Bullous disorders
- Dermatitis and eczema
- Papulosquamous disorders
- Urticaria and erythema
- Radiation-related disorders of the skin and subcutaneous tissue
- Disorders of skin appendages
- Intraoperative and postprocedural complications of skin and subcutaneous tissue
- Other disorders of the skin and subcutaneous tissue

ICD-10-CM Chapter-Specific Coding Guidelines

Chapter 12: Diseases of the Skin and Subcutaneous Tissue (L00-L99)

a. **Pressure ulcer stage codes**

1) **Pressure ulcer stages**

Codes from category L89, Pressure ulcer, are combination codes that identify the site of the pressure ulcer as well as the stage of the ulcer.

(continues)

ICD-10-CM Chapter-Specific Coding Guidelines (*continued*)

The ICD-10-CM classifies pressure ulcer stages based on severity, which is designated by stages 1–4, unspecified stage and unstageable.

Assign as many codes from category L89 as needed to identify all the pressure ulcers the patient has, if applicable.

2) Unstageable pressure ulcers

Assignment of the code for unstageable pressure ulcer (L89.--0) should be based on the clinical documentation. These codes are used for pressure ulcers whose stage cannot be clinically determined (e.g., the ulcer is covered by eschar or has been treated with a skin or muscle graft) and pressure ulcers that are documented as deep tissue injury but not documented as due to trauma. This code should not be confused with the codes for unspecified stage (L89.--9). When there is no documentation regarding the stage of the pressure ulcer, assign the appropriate code for unspecified stage (L89.--9).

3) Documented pressure ulcer stage

Assignment of the pressure ulcer stage code should be guided by clinical documentation of the stage or documentation of the terms found in the Alphabetic Index. For clinical terms describing the stage that are not found in the Alphabetic Index, and there is no documentation of the stage, the provider should be queried.

4) Patients admitted with pressure ulcers documented as healed

No code is assigned if the documentation states that the pressure ulcer is completely healed.

5) Patients admitted with pressure ulcers documented as healing

Pressure ulcers described as healing should be assigned the appropriate pressure ulcer stage code based on the documentation in the medical record. If the documentation does not provide information about the stage of the healing pressure ulcer, assign the appropriate code for unspecified stage.

If the documentation is unclear as to whether the patient has a current (new) pressure ulcer or if the patient is being treated for a healing pressure ulcer, query the provider.

For ulcers that were present on admission but healed at the time of discharge, assign the code for the site and stage of the pressure ulcer at the time of admission.

6) Patient admitted with pressure ulcer evolving into another stage during the admission

If a patient is admitted with a pressure ulcer at one stage and it progresses to a higher stage, two separate codes should be assigned: one code for the site and stage of the ulcer on admission and a second code for the same ulcer site and the highest stage reported during the stay.

Exercise 4.14 – Diseases of the Skin and Subcutaneous Tissue

Instructions: Underline the main term in each diagnosis statement and assign the appropriate ICD-10-CM code(s).

_____   **1.** Alopecia areata

_____   **2.** Carbuncle, left foot

_____   **3.** Decubitus ulcer

_____   **4.** Impetigo

_____   **5.** Keloid

ICD-10-CM Chapter 13: Diseases of the Musculoskeletal and Connective Tissue (M00–M99)

This ICD-10-CM chapter classifies the following:

- Infectious arthropathies
- Inflammatory polyarthropathies
- Osteoarthritis
- Other joint disorders
- Dentofacial anomalies [including malocclusion] and other disorders of jaw
- Systemic connective tissue disorders
- Deforming dorsopathies
- Spondylopathies
- Other dorsopathies
- Disorders of muscles
- Disorders of synovium and tendon
- Other soft tissue disorders
- Disorders of bone density and structure
- Other osteopathies
- Chondropathies
- Other disorders of the musculoskeletal system and connective tissue
- Intraoperative and postprocedural complications and disorders of musculoskeletal system, not elsewhere classified
- Biomechanical lesions, not elsewhere classified

Localized osteoarthrosis is classified as primary or secondary. Primary osteoarthritis (or polyarticular degenerative arthritis) has an unknown etiology (cause), which means it is idiopathic. It affects apophyseal joints (joints with nodular or bony eminence) of the hips, knees, spine, and small joints of the hands and feet. Secondary osteoarthritis (or monarticular arthritis) is caused by external or internal injuries (acute or chronic trauma) or disease processes and is confined to the joints of one area. Disease processes include endocrine, infectious, metabolic, and neuropathic disease, as well as disease processes that alter the normal structure and function of hyaline cartilage (e.g., chondrocalcinosis, gout, and Paget's disease).

EXAMPLE: A patient is diagnosed with degenerative joint disease, bilateral knees. Assign ICD-10-CM code M17.0 (Bilateral osteoarthritis of knee).

ICD-10-CM Chapter-Specific Coding Guidelines

Chapter 13: Diseases of Musculoskeletal and Connective Tissue (M00-M99)

a. Site and laterality

Most of the codes within Chapter 13 have site and laterality designations. The site represents the bone, joint or the muscle involved. For some conditions where more than one bone, joint or muscle is usually involved,

(continues)

ICD-10-CM Chapter-Specific Coding Guidelines (*continued*)

such as osteoarthritis, there is a "multiple sites" code available. For categories where no multiple site code is provided and more than one bone, joint or muscle is involved, multiple codes should be used to indicate the different sites involved.

1) Bone versus joint

For certain conditions, the bone may be affected at the upper or lower end (e.g., avascular necrosis of bone, M87, Osteoporosis, M80, M81). Though the portion of the bone affected may be at the joint, the site designation will be the bone, not the joint.

b. Acute traumatic versus chronic or recurrent musculoskeletal conditions

Many musculoskeletal conditions are a result of previous injury or trauma to a site, or are recurrent conditions. Bone, joint or muscle conditions that are the result of a healed injury are usually found in chapter 13. Recurrent bone, joint or muscle conditions are also usually found in chapter 13. Any current, acute injury should be coded to the appropriate injury code from chapter 19. Chronic or recurrent conditions should generally be coded with a code from chapter 13. If it is difficult to determine from the documentation in the record which code is best to describe a condition, query the provider.

c. Coding of Pathologic Fractures

7th character A is for use as long as the patient is receiving active treatment for the fracture. While the patient may be seen by a new or different provider over the course of treatment for a pathological fracture, assignment of the 7th character is based on whether the patient is undergoing active treatment and not whether the provider is seeing the patient for the first time.

7th character, D is to be used for encounters after the patient has completed active treatment. The other 7th characters, listed under each subcategory in the Tabular List, are to be used for subsequent encounters for routine care of fractures during the healing and recovery phase as well as treatment of problems associated with the healing, such as malunions, nonunions, and sequelae.

Care for complications of surgical treatment for fracture repairs during the healing or recovery phase should be coded with the appropriate complication codes.

See Section I.C.19. Coding of traumatic fractures.

d. Osteoporosis

Osteoporosis is a systemic condition, meaning that all bones of the musculoskeletal system are affected. Therefore, site is not a component of the codes under category M81, Osteoporosis without current pathological fracture. The site codes under category M80, Osteoporosis with current pathological fracture, identify the site of the fracture, not the osteoporosis.

1) Osteoporosis without pathological fracture

Category M81, Osteoporosis without current pathological fracture, is for use for patients with osteoporosis who do not currently have a pathologic fracture due to the osteoporosis, even if they have had a fracture in the past. For patients with a history of osteoporosis fractures, status code Z87.310, Personal history of (healed) osteoporosis fracture, should follow the code from M81.

2) Osteoporosis with current pathological fracture

Category M80, Osteoporosis with current pathological fracture, is for patients who have a current pathologic fracture at the time of an encounter. The codes under M80 identify the site of the fracture. A code from category M80, not a traumatic fracture code, should be used for any patient with known osteoporosis who suffers a fracture, even if the patient had a minor fall or trauma, if that fall or trauma would not usually break a normal, healthy bone.

Exercise 4.15 – Diseases of the Musculoskeletal and Connective Tissue

Instructions: Underline the main term in each diagnosis statement and assign the appropriate ICD-10-CM code(s).

_____ **1.** Arthralgia, left hand, left lower leg, and left ankle

_____ **2.** Claw foot, left (acquired)

_____ **3.** Contracture of joint, left hip

_____ **4.** Kissing spine

_____ **5.** Muscle spasm, back

ICD-10-CM Chapter 14: Diseases of the Genitourinary System (N00–N99)

This ICD-10-CM chapter classifies the following:

- Glomerular diseases
- Renal tubulo-interstitial diseases
- Acute kidney failure and chronic kidney disease
- Urolithiasis
- Other disorders of kidney and ureter
- Other diseases of the urinary system
- Diseases of male genital organs
- Disorders of breast
- Inflammatory diseases of female pelvic organs
- Noninflammatory disorders of female genital tract
- Intraoperative and postprocedural complications and disorders of genitourinary system, not elsewhere classified

ICD-10-CM Chapter-Specific Coding Guidelines

Chapter 14: Diseases of the Genitourinary System (N00-N99)

a. Chronic kidney disease

1) Stages of chronic kidney disease (CKD)

The ICD-10-CM classifies CKD based on severity. The severity of CKD is designated by stages 1-5. Stage 2, code N18.2, equates to mild CKD; stage 3, code N18.3, equates to moderate CKD; and stage 4, code N18.4, equates to severe CKD. Code N18.6, End stage renal disease (ESRD), is assigned when the provider has documented end-stage-renal disease (ESRD).

If both a stage of CKD and ESRD are documented, assign code N18.6 only.

(continues)

ICD-10-CM Chapter-Specific Coding Guidelines (*continued*)

2) **Chronic kidney disease and kidney transplant status**

Patients who have undergone kidney transplant may still have some form of CKD because the kidney transplant may not fully restore kidney function. Therefore, the presence of CKD alone does not constitute a transplant complication. Assign the appropriate N18 code for the patient's stage of CKD and code Z94.0, Kidney transplant status. If a transplant complication such as failure or rejection is documented, see Section I.C.19.g. for information on coding complications of a kidney transplant. If the documentation is unclear as to whether the patient has a complication of the transplant, query the provider.

3) **Chronic kidney disease (CKD) with other conditions**

Patients with CKD may also suffer from other serious conditions, most commonly diabetes mellitus and hypertension. The sequencing of the CKD code in relationship to codes for other contributing conditions is based on the conventions in the Tabular List.

See I.C.9. Hypertensive chronic kidney disease.
See I.C.19. Chronic kidney disease and kidney transplant complications.

Exercise 4.16 – Diseases of the Genitourinary System

Instructions: Underline the main term in each diagnosis statement and assign the appropriate ICD-10-CM code(s).

_____ **1.** Abscess of epididymis

_____ **2.** Chronic cystic mastitis, right breast

_____ **3.** Chronic prostatitis

_____ **4.** Diverticulitis of bladder

_____ **5.** Excessive menstruation with regular cycle

ICD-10-CM Chapter 15: Pregnancy, Childbirth, and the Puerperium (O00–O9A)

This ICD-10-CM chapter classifies the following, which occur during pregnancy, childbirth, and the six weeks immediately following childbirth:

- Pregnancy with abortive outcome
- Supervision of high-risk pregnancy
- Edema, proteinuria, and hypertensive disorders in pregnancy, childbirth, and the puerperium
- Other maternal disorders predominantly related to pregnancy
- Maternal care related to the fetus and amniotic cavity and possible delivery problems
- Complications of labor and delivery

- Encounter for delivery

- Complications predominantly related to the puerperium

- Other obstetric conditions, not elsewhere classified

All obstetrical discharges require a code from ICD-10-CM Chapter 15, and these codes are never reported on the baby's record.

- When the physician's documentation indicates that the pregnancy is incidental to the encounter, assign code Z33.1, Pregnant state, incidental.

- When an obstetrical patient's encounter is related to her pregnancy, sequence codes O00–O9A first, followed by codes for secondary conditions.

- When the obstetrical patient delivers, assign an outcome of delivery codes Z37.1–Z37.9 as a secondary code.

Pregnancy with Abortive Outcome

When an ectopic pregnancy occurs during a pregnancy admission, assign a code from category O00–O02. However, when complications of ectopic pregnancies occur, assigned a code from category O08 (Complications following ectopic and molar pregnancy).

EXAMPLE 1: Tubal pregnancy with pelvic sepsis, without intrauterine pregnancy. ICD-10-CM codes O00.10 and O08.0 are assigned.

EXAMPLE 2: Pelvic infection following ectopic pregnancy. ICD-10-CM code O08.0 is assigned.

When fetal complications are documented as a causal factor in an abortion, two codes are assigned.

- One code for the abortion (ICD-10-CM codes O03–O08)

- A second code for the fetal complication (ICD-10-CM codes O35–O36)

An abortion that results in a live birth is assigned a code from ICD-10-CM subcategory O60.1. If the abortion was induced, a procedure code for "termination of pregnancy" is assigned along with a code from ICD-10-CM code Z33.2, Encounter for elective termination of pregnancy.

Complications of Labor and Delivery

When a patient experiences a delivery and an antepartum or a postpartum condition during the same encounter, assign two separate codes.

EXAMPLE: Patient is discharged from the hospital with the diagnoses of "ablatio placenta, pregnancy at term, third trimester, delivered" and "delayed postpartum bleed." Codes O45.93 and O72.2 are assigned. (Also report the appropriate code from category Z37.)

Normal Delivery

ICD-10-CM code O80 is assigned for a normal delivery, which required minimal or no assistance. An episiotomy is permitted, but fetal manipulation (e.g., use of forceps) is not permitted. In addition, code O80 is *never* reported with any other code in range O00–O99.

EXAMPLE: Patient admitted to the hospital and delivered a liveborn male infant. ICD-10-CM codes O80 and Z37.0 are assigned.

ICD-10-CM Chapter-Specific Coding Guidelines

Chapter 15: Pregnancy, Childbirth, and the Puerperium (O00-O9A)

a. General rules for obstetric cases

1) **Codes from Chapter 15 and sequencing priority**

   Obstetric cases require codes from Chapter 15, codes in the range O00-O9A, Pregnancy, Childbirth, and the Puerperium. Additional codes from other chapters may be used in conjunction with Chapter 15 codes to further specify conditions. Should the provider document that the pregnancy is incidental to the encounter, code Z33.1, Pregnant state, incidental, should be used in place of any chapter 15 codes. It is the provider's responsibility to state that the condition being treated is not affecting the pregnancy.

2) **Chapter 15 codes used only on the maternal record**

   Chapter 15 codes are to be used only on the maternal record, never on the record of the newborn.

3) **Final character for trimester**

   The majority of codes in Chapter 15 have a final character indicating the trimester of pregnancy. The time frames the trimesters are indicated at the beginning of the chapter. If trimester is not a component of a code it is because the condition always occurs in a specific trimester, or the concept of trimester of pregnancy is not applicable. Certain codes have characters for only certain trimesters because the condition does not occur in all trimesters, but it may occur in more than just one.

   Assignment of the final character for trimester should be based on the provider's documentation of the trimester (or number of weeks) for the current admission/encounter. This applies to the assignment of trimester for pre-existing conditions as well as those that develop during or are due to the pregnancy. The provider's documentation of the number of weeks may be used to assign the appropriate code identifying the trimester.

   Whenever delivery occurs during the current admission, and there is an "in childbirth" option for the obstetric complication being coded, the "in childbirth" code should be assigned.

4) **Selection of trimester for inpatient admissions that encompass more than one trimester**

   In instances when a patient is admitted to a hospital for complications of pregnancy during one trimester and remains in the hospital into a subsequent trimester, the trimester character for the antepartum complication code should be assigned on the basis of the trimester when the complication developed, not the trimester of the discharge. If the condition developed prior to the current admission/encounter or represents a pre-existing condition, the trimester character for the trimester at the time of the admission/encounter should be assigned.

5) **Unspecified trimester**

   Each category that includes codes for trimester has a code for "unspecified trimester." The "unspecified trimester" code should rarely be used, such as when the documentation in the record is insufficient to determine the trimester and it is not possible to obtain clarification.

6) **7th character for fetus identification**

   Where applicable, a 7th character is to be assigned for certain categories (O31, O32, O33.3-O33.6, O35, O36, O40, O41, O60.1, O60.2, O64, and O69) to identify the fetus for which the complication code applies. Assign 7th character "0":

   - For single gestations

   - When the documentation in the record is insufficient to determine the fetus affected and it is not possible to obtain clarification.

   - When it is not possible to clinically determine which fetus is affected.

b. Selection of OB principal or first-listed diagnosis

1) **Routine outpatient prenatal visits**

For routine outpatient prenatal visits when no complications are present, a code from category Z34, Encounter for supervision of normal pregnancy, should be used as the first-listed diagnosis. These codes should not be used in conjunction with chapter 15 codes.

2) **Supervision of high-risk pregnancy**

Codes from category O09, Supervision of high-risk pregnancy, are intended for use only during the prenatal period. For complications during the labor or delivery episode as a result of a high-risk pregnancy, assign the applicable complication codes from Chapter 15. If there are no complications during the labor or delivery episode, assign code O80, Encounter for full-term uncomplicated delivery.

For prenatal outpatient visits for patients with high-risk pregnancies, a code from category O09, Supervision of high-risk pregnancy, should be used as the first-listed diagnosis.

Secondary chapter 15 codes may be used in conjunction with these codes if appropriate.

3) **Episodes when no delivery occurs**

In episodes when no delivery occurs, the principal diagnosis should correspond to the principal complication of the pregnancy, which necessitated the encounter. Should more than one complication exist, all of which are treated or monitored, any of the complications codes may be sequenced first.

4) **When a delivery occurs**

When an obstetric patient is admitted and delivers during that admission, the condition that prompted the admission should be sequenced as the principal diagnosis. If multiple conditions prompted the admission, sequence the one most related to the delivery as the principal diagnosis. A code for any complication of the delivery should be assigned as an additional diagnosis. In cases of cesarean delivery, if the patient was admitted with a condition that resulted in the performance of a cesarean procedure, that condition should be selected as the principal diagnosis. If the reason for the admission was unrelated to the condition resulting in the cesarean delivery, the condition related to the reason for the admission should be selected as the principal diagnosis.

5) **Outcome of delivery**

A code from category Z37, Outcome of delivery, should be included on every maternal record when a delivery has occurred. These codes are not to be used on subsequent records or on the newborn record.

c. **Pre-existing conditions versus conditions due to the pregnancy**

Certain categories in Chapter 15 distinguish between conditions of the mother that existed prior to pregnancy (pre-existing) and those that are a direct result of pregnancy. When assigning codes from Chapter 15, it is important to assess if a condition was pre-existing prior to pregnancy or developed during or due to the pregnancy in order to assign the correct code.

Categories that do not distinguish between pre-existing and pregnancy-related conditions may be used for either. It is acceptable to use codes specifically for the puerperium with codes complicating pregnancy and childbirth if a condition arises postpartum during the delivery encounter.

d. **Pre-existing hypertension in pregnancy**

Category O10, Pre-existing hypertension complicating pregnancy, childbirth and the puerperium, includes codes for hypertensive heart and hypertensive chronic kidney disease. When assigning one of the O10 codes that includes hypertensive heart disease or hypertensive chronic kidney disease, it is necessary to add a secondary code from the appropriate hypertension category to specify the type of heart failure or chronic kidney disease.

See Section I.C.9. Hypertension.

e. **Fetal conditions affecting the management of the mother**

1) **Codes from category O35 and O36**

Codes from categories O35, Maternal care for known or suspected fetal abnormality and damage, and O36, Maternal care for other fetal problems, are assigned only when the fetal condition is actually responsible

(continues)

ICD-10-CM Chapter-Specific Coding Guidelines (*continued*)

for modifying the management of the mother (i.e., by requiring diagnostic studies, additional observation, special care, or termination of pregnancy). The fact that the fetal condition exists does not justify assigning a code from this series to the mother's record.

2) *In utero surgery*

In cases when surgery is performed on the fetus, a diagnosis code from category O35, Maternal care for known or suspected fetal abnormality and damage, should be assigned identifying the fetal condition. Assign the appropriate procedure code for the procedure performed.

No code from Chapter 16, the perinatal codes, should be used on the mother's record to identify fetal conditions. Surgery performed *in utero* on a fetus is still to be coded as an obstetric encounter.

f. HIV infection in pregnancy, childbirth, and the puerperium

During pregnancy, childbirth, or the puerperium, a patient admitted because of an HIV-related illness should receive a principal diagnosis from subcategory O98.7-, Human immunodeficiency [HIV] disease complicating pregnancy, childbirth and the puerperium, followed by the code(s) for the HIV-related illness(es).

Patients with asymptomatic HIV-infection status admitted during pregnancy, childbirth, or the puerperium should receive codes of O98.7- and Z21, Asymptomatic human immunodeficiency virus [HIV] infection status.

g. Diabetes mellitus in pregnancy

Diabetes mellitus is a significant complicating factor in pregnancy. Pregnant women who are diabetic should be assigned a code from category O24, Diabetes mellitus in pregnancy, childbirth, and the puerperium, first, followed by the appropriate diabetes code(s) (E08-E13) from Chapter 4.

h. Long term use of insulin and oral hypoglycemics

Code Z79.4, Long-term (current) use of insulin, or code Z79.84, Long term (current) use of oral hypoglycemic drugs, should also be assigned if the diabetes mellitus is being treated with insulin or oral medications. If the patient is treated with both oral medications and insulin, only the code for insulin-controlled should be assigned.

i. Gestational (pregnancy-induced) diabetes

Gestational (pregnancy-induced) diabetes can occur during the second and third trimesters of pregnancy in women who were not diabetic prior to pregnancy. Gestational diabetes can cause complications in the pregnancy similar to those of pre-existing diabetes mellitus. It also puts the woman at greater risk of developing diabetes after the pregnancy. Codes for gestational diabetes are in subcategory O24.4, Gestational diabetes mellitus. No other code from category O24, Diabetes mellitus in pregnancy, childbirth, and the puerperium, should be used with a code from O24.4.

The codes under subcategory O24.4 include diet controlled, insulin controlled, and controlled by oral hypoglycemic drugs. If a patient with gestational diabetes is treated with both diet and insulin, only the code for insulin-controlled is required. If a patient with gestational diabetes is treated with both diet and oral hypoglycemic medications, only the code for "controlled by oral hypoglycemic drugs" is required.

Code Z79.4, Long-term (current) use of insulin, or code Z79.84, Long-term (current) use of oral hypoglycemic drugs, should not be assigned with codes from subcategory O24.4.

An abnormal glucose tolerance in pregnancy is assigned a code from subcategory O99.81, Abnormal glucose complicating pregnancy, childbirth, and the puerperium.

j. Sepsis and septic shock complicating abortion, pregnancy, childbirth and the puerperium

When assigning a chapter 15 code for sepsis complicating abortion, pregnancy, childbirth, and the puerperium, a code for the specific type of infection should be assigned as an additional diagnosis. If severe sepsis is present, a code from subcategory R65.2, Severe sepsis, and code(s) for associated organ dysfunction(s) should also be assigned as additional diagnoses.

k. **Puerperal sepsis**

   Code O85, Puerperal sepsis, should be assigned with a secondary code to identify the causal organism (e.g., for a bacterial infection, assign a code from category B95-B96, Bacterial infections in conditions classified elsewhere). A code from category A40, Streptococcal sepsis, or A41, Other sepsis, should not be used for puerperal sepsis. If applicable, use additional codes to identify severe sepsis (R65.2-) and any associated acute organ dysfunction.

l. **Alcohol and tobacco use during pregnancy, childbirth and the puerperium**

   1) **Alcohol use during pregnancy, childbirth and the puerperium**

      Codes under subcategory O99.31, Alcohol use complicating pregnancy, childbirth, and the puerperium, should be assigned for any pregnancy case when a mother uses alcohol during the pregnancy or postpartum. A secondary code from category F10, Alcohol related disorders, should also be assigned to identify manifestations of the alcohol use.

   2) **Tobacco use during pregnancy, childbirth and the puerperium**

      Codes under subcategory O99.33, Smoking (tobacco) complicating pregnancy, childbirth, and the puerperium, should be assigned for any pregnancy case when a mother uses any type of tobacco product during the pregnancy or postpartum. A secondary code from category F17, Nicotine dependence, should also be assigned to identify the type of nicotine dependence.

m. **Poisoning, toxic effects, adverse effects and underdosing in a pregnant patient**

   A code from subcategory O9A.2, Injury, poisoning and certain other consequences of external causes complicating pregnancy, childbirth, and the puerperium, should be sequenced first, followed by the appropriate injury, poisoning, toxic effect, adverse effect or underdosing code, and then the additional code(s) that specifies the condition caused by the poisoning, toxic effect, adverse effect or underdosing.

   See Section I.C.19. Adverse effects, poisoning, underdosing and toxic effects.

n. **Normal delivery, code O80**

   1) **Encounter for full term uncomplicated delivery**

      Code O80 should be assigned when a woman is admitted for a full-term normal delivery and delivers a single, healthy infant without any complications antepartum, during the delivery, or postpartum during the delivery episode. Code O80 is always a principal diagnosis. It is not to be used if any other code from chapter 15 is needed to describe a current complication of the antenatal, delivery, or perinatal period. Additional codes from other chapters may be used with code O80 if they are not related to or are in any way complicating the pregnancy.

   2) **Uncomplicated delivery with resolved antepartum complication**

      Code O80 may be used if the patient had a complication at some point during the pregnancy, but the complication is not present at the time of the admission for delivery.

   3) **Outcome of delivery for O80**

      Z37.0, Single live birth, is the only outcome of delivery code appropriate for use with O80.

o. **The peripartum and postpartum periods**

   1) **Peripartum and postpartum periods**

      The postpartum period begins immediately after delivery and continues for six weeks following delivery. The peripartum period is defined as the last month of pregnancy to five months postpartum.

   2) **Peripartum and postpartum complication**

      A postpartum complication is any complication occurring within the six-week period.

   3) **Pregnancy-related complications after 6-week period**

      Chapter 15 codes may also be used to describe pregnancy-related complications after peripartum or postpartum period if the provider documents that a condition is pregnancy related.

(continues)

ICD-10-CM Chapter-Specific Coding Guidelines (*continued*)

4) Admission for routine postpartum care following delivery outside hospital
When the mother delivers outside the hospital prior to admission and is admitted for routine postpartum care and no complications are noted, code Z39.0, Encounter for care and examination of mother immediately after delivery, should be assigned as the principal diagnosis.

5) Pregnancy associated cardiomyopathy
Pregnancy associated cardiomyopathy, code O90.3, is unique in that it may be diagnosed in the third trimester of pregnancy but may continue to progress months after delivery. For this reason, it is referred to as peripartum cardiomyopathy. Code O90.3 is only for use when the cardiomyopathy develops as a result of pregnancy in a woman who did not have pre-existing heart disease.

p. Code O94, Sequelae of complication of pregnancy, childbirth, and the puerperium

1) Code O94
Code O94, Sequelae of complication of pregnancy, childbirth, and the puerperium, is for use in those cases when an initial complication of a pregnancy develops a sequelae requiring care or treatment at a future date.

2) After the initial postpartum period
This code may be used at any time after the initial postpartum period.

3) Sequencing of code O94
This code, like all late effect codes, is to be sequenced following the code describing the sequelae of the complication.

q. Termination of pregnancy and spontaneous abortions

1) Abortion with liveborn fetus
When an attempted termination of pregnancy results in a liveborn fetus, assign code Z33.2, Encounter for elective termination of pregnancy and a code from category Z37, Outcome of Delivery.

2) Retained products of conception following an abortion
Subsequent encounters for retained products of conception following a spontaneous abortion or elective termination of pregnancy are assigned the appropriate code from category O03, Spontaneous abortion, or codes O07.4, Failed attempted termination of pregnancy without complication and Z33.2, Encounter for elective termination of pregnancy. This advice is appropriate even when the patient was discharged previously with a discharge diagnosis of complete abortion.

3) Complications leading to abortion
Codes from Chapter 15 may be used as additional codes to identify any documented complications of the pregnancy in conjunction with codes in categories in O07 and O08.

r. Abuse in a pregnant patient
For suspected or confirmed cases of abuse of a pregnant patient, a code(s) from subcategories O9A.3, Physical abuse complicating pregnancy, childbirth, and the puerperium, O9A.4, Sexual abuse complicating pregnancy, childbirth, and the puerperium, and O9A.5, Psychological abuse complicating pregnancy, childbirth, and the puerperium, should be sequenced first, followed by the appropriate codes (if applicable) to identify any associated current injury due to physical abuse, sexual abuse, and the perpetrator of abuse.

See Section I.C.19.f. Adult and child abuse, neglect and other maltreatment.

Exercise 4.17 – Pregnancy, Childbirth, and the Puerperium

Instructions: Underline the main term in each diagnosis statement and assign the appropriate ICD-10-CM code(s).

_____ **1.** Amnionitis

_____ **2.** Engorgement of female breasts (postpartum)

_____ **3.** Gestational hypertension, third trimester

_____ **4.** Incoordinate uterine contractions

_____ **5.** Laceration of cervix (obstetric)

ICD-10-CM Chapter 16: Certain Conditions Originating in the Perinatal Period (P00–P96)

This ICD-10-CM chapter classifies the following:

- Newborn affected by maternal factors and by complications of pregnancy, labor, and delivery
- Disorders of newborn related to length of gestation and fetal growth
- Abnormal findings on neonatal screening
- Birth trauma
- Respiratory and cardiovascular disorders specific to the perinatal period
- Infections specific to the perinatal period
- Hemorrhagic and hematological disorders of newborn
- Transitory endocrine and metabolic disorders specific to newborn
- Digestive system disorders of newborn
- Conditions involving the integument and temperature regulation of newborn
- Other problems with newborn
- Other disorders originating in the perinatal period

This chapter classifies conditions that begin during the perinatal period even if death or morbidity occurs later. The **perinatal period** is the interval of time occurring before, during, and up to 28 days following birth. These codes classify causes of morbidity and mortality in the fetus or newborn. Additional codes can be assigned from other ICD-10-CM chapters to further specify the newborn's condition.

 Coding Tip:

Codes from ICD-10-CM Chapter 16 are never reported for the mother's episode of care.

ICD-10-CM Chapter-Specific Coding Guidelines

Chapter 16: Certain Conditions Originating in the Perinatal Period (P00-P96)

For coding and reporting purposes, the perinatal period is defined as "before birth through the 28th day following birth." The following guidelines are provided for reporting purposes.

a. General perinatal rules

1) Use of Chapter 16 codes

They are *never* for use on the maternal record. Codes from Chapter 15, the obstetrics chapter, are never permitted on the newborn record. Chapter 16 codes may be used throughout the life of the patient if the condition is still present.

2) Principal diagnosis for birth record

When coding the birth episode in a newborn record, assign a code from category Z38, Liveborn infants according to place of birth and type of delivery, as the principal diagnosis. A code from category Z38 is assigned only once, to a newborn at the time of birth. If a newborn is transferred to another institution, a code from category Z38 should not be used at the receiving hospital.

A code from category Z38 is used only on the newborn record, not on the mother's record.

3) Use of codes from other chapters with codes from Chapter 16

Codes from other chapters may be used with codes from chapter 16 if the codes from the other chapters provide more specific detail. Codes for signs and symptoms may be assigned when a definitive diagnosis has not been established. If the reason for the encounter is a perinatal condition, the code from chapter 16 should be sequenced first.

4) Use of Chapter 16 codes after the perinatal period

Should a condition originate in the perinatal period, and continue throughout the life of the patient, the perinatal code should continue to be used regardless of the patient's age.

5) Birth process or community-acquired conditions

If a newborn has a condition that may be either due to the birth process or community-acquired and the documentation does not indicate which it is, the default is "due to the birth process" and the code from Chapter 16 should be used. If the condition is "community-acquired," a code from Chapter 16 should not be assigned.

6) Code all clinically significant conditions

All clinically significant conditions noted on routine newborn examination should be coded. A condition is clinically significant if it requires or has:

- Clinical evaluation
- Therapeutic treatment
- Diagnostic procedures

- Extended length of hospital stay
- Increased nursing care and/or monitoring
- Implications for future health care needs

Note: The perinatal guidelines listed above are the same as the general coding guidelines for "additional diagnoses" except for the final point regarding implications for future health care needs. Codes should be assigned for conditions that have been specified by the provider as having implications for future health care needs.

b. Observation and evaluation of newborns for suspected conditions not found

1) Assign a code from category Z05, Observation and evaluation of newborns and infants for suspected conditions ruled out, to identify those instances when a healthy newborn is evaluated for a suspected condition that is determined after study not to be present. Do not use a code from category Z05 when the patient has identified signs or symptoms of a suspected problem; in such cases code the sign or symptom.

2) A code from category Z05 may also be assigned as a principal or first-listed code for readmissions or encounters when the code from category Z38 code no longer applies. Codes from category Z05 are for use only for healthy newborns and infants for which no condition after study is found to be present.

3) Z05 on a birth record

A code from category Z05 is to be used as a secondary code after the code from category Z38, Liveborn infants according to place of birth and type of delivery.

c. Coding additional perinatal diagnoses

1) **Assigning codes for conditions that require treatment**
Assign codes for conditions that require treatment or further investigation, prolong the length of stay, or require resource utilization.

2) **Codes for conditions specified as having implications for future health care needs**
Assign codes for conditions that have been specified by the provider as having implications for future health care needs.
Note: This guideline should not be used for adult patients.

d. **Prematurity and fetal growth retardation**
Providers utilize different criteria in determining prematurity. A code for prematurity should not be assigned unless it is documented. Assignment of codes in categories P05, Disorders of newborn related to slow fetal growth and fetal malnutrition, and P07, Disorders of newborn related to short gestation and low birth weight, not elsewhere classified, should be based on the recorded birth weight and estimated gestational age.
Codes from category P05 should not be assigned with codes from category P07.
When both birth weight and gestational age are available, two codes from category P07 should be assigned, with the code for birth weight sequenced before the code for gestational age.

e. **Low birth weight and immaturity status**
Codes from category P07, Disorders of newborn related to short gestation and low birth weight, not elsewhere classified, are for use for a child or adult who was premature or had a low birth weight as a newborn and this is affecting the patient's current health status.
See Section I.C.21. Factors influencing health status and contact with health services, Status.

f. **Bacterial sepsis of newborn**
Category P36, Bacterial sepsis of newborn, includes congenital sepsis. If a perinate is documented as having sepsis without documentation of congenital or community acquired, the default is congenital and a code from category P36 should be assigned. If the P36 code includes the causal organism, an additional code from category B95, Streptococcus, Staphylococcus, and Enterococcus as the cause of diseases classified elsewhere, or B96, Other bacterial agents as the cause of diseases classified elsewhere, should not be assigned. If the P36 code does not include the causal organism, assign an additional code from category B96. If applicable, use additional codes to identify severe sepsis (R65.2-) and any associated acute organ dysfunction.

g. **Stillbirth**
Code P95, Stillbirth, is only for use in institutions that maintain separate records for stillbirths. No other code should be used with P95. Code P95 should not be used on the mother's record.

Exercise 4.18 – Certain Conditions Originating in the Perinatal Period

Instructions: Underline the main term in each diagnosis statement and assign the appropriate ICD-10-CM code(s).

_____ 1. Cyanotic attacks of newborn

_____ 2. Exceptionally large baby

_____ 3. Facial palsy, newborn

_____ 4. Feeding problems in newborn

_____ 5. Fetal blood loss

ICD-10-CM Chapter 17: Congenital Malformations, Deformations, and Chromosomal Abnormalities (Q00–Q99)

This ICD-10-CM chapter classifies the following congenital malformations (and deformations) according to body system (e.g., nervous system), along with cleft lip and cleft palate, and chromosomal abnormalities. Congenital malformations may be the result of genetic factors (chromosomes), teratogens (agents causing physical defects in the embryo), or both. The malformations may be apparent at birth or hidden and identified sometime after birth. Regardless of origin, dysmorphology (clinical structural abnormality) is generally the primary indication of a congenital anomaly; in many cases, a syndrome may be classified according to a single anatomical anomaly rather than a complex of symptoms.

> **EXAMPLE:** Apert's syndrome (or acrocephalosyndactyly) is a group of congenital syndromes that include peaking at the head due to premature closure of skull sutures and fusion or webbing of digits. Apert's syndrome is a single anatomical anomaly of a multicomplex syndrome, which can include fusion in the hands *and* facial anomalies. ICD-10-CM Q87.0 is assigned.

ICD-10-CM does not differentiate between intrinsic abnormalities (defects related to the fetus) or extrinsic abnormalities (defects that are the result of intrauterine problems). ICD-10-CM also does make a distinction in the classification of an anomaly as compared to a deformity. An anomaly is a malformation caused by abnormal fetal development (e.g., transposition of great vessels, or spina bifida). A deformity is an alteration in structure caused by an extrinsic force, such as intrauterine compression. The force may cause a disruption in a normal fetal structure, including congenital amputations from amniotic bands. In some cases, assigning two codes is necessary to describe the condition.

> **EXAMPLE:** Thalidomide phocomelia results from influence of the drug thalidomide on the developing fetus during the perinatal period. It is a congenital birth defect in which the hands and feet are attached to abbreviated arms and legs, respectively. To classify this condition, multiple codes are assigned.
>
> - Q71.13 Congenital absence of upper arm and forearm with hand present, bilateral
>
> - Q72.13 Congenital absence of thigh and lower leg with foot present, bilateral
>
> - P04.1 Newborn (suspected to be) affected by other maternal medication
>
> Codes Q71.13 and Q72.13 classify the limb deformities. Code P04.1 classifies the transmission of the drug across the placenta, which resulted in the limb deformities.

ICD-10-CM Chapter-Specific Coding Guidelines

Chapter 17: Congenital Malformations, Deformations, and Chromosomal Abnormalities (Q00-Q99)

Assign an appropriate code(s) from categories Q00-Q99, Congenital malformations, deformations, and chromosomal abnormalities, when a malformation/deformation or chromosomal abnormality is documented. A malformation/deformation/or chromosomal abnormality may be the principal/first-listed diagnosis on a record or a secondary diagnosis.

When a malformation/deformation or chromosomal abnormality does not have a unique code assignment, assign additional code(s) for any manifestations that may be present.

When the code assignment specifically identifies the malformation/deformation or chromosomal abnormality, manifestations that are an inherent component of the anomaly should not be coded separately. Additional codes should be assigned for manifestations that are not an inherent component.

Codes from Chapter 17 may be used throughout the life of the patient. If a congenital malformation or deformity has been corrected, a personal history code should be used to identify the history of the malformation or deformity. Although present at birth, malformation/deformation/or chromosomal abnormality may not be identified until later in life.

Whenever the condition is diagnosed by the physician, it is appropriate to assign a code from codes Q00–Q99.

For the birth admission, the appropriate code from category Z38, Liveborn infants, according to place of birth and type of delivery, should be sequenced as the principal diagnosis, followed by any congenital anomaly codes, Q00–Q99.

When a malformation/deformation/or chromosomal abnormality does not have a unique code assignment, assign additional code(s) for any manifestations that may be present. When the code assignment specifically identifies the malformation/deformation/or chromosomal abnormality, manifestations that are an inherent component of the anomaly should not be coded separately. Additional codes should be assigned for manifestations that are not an inherent component.

Codes from ICD-10-CM Chapter 17 may be used throughout the life of the patient. If a congenital malformation or deformation has been corrected, a personal history code should be used to identify the history of the malformation or deformity. Although present at birth, a malformation/deformation/or chromosomal abnormality, may not be identified until later in life. Whenever the condition is diagnosed by the physician, it is appropriate to assign a code from codes Q00–Q99.

Exercise 4.19 – Congenital Malformations, Deformations, and Chromosomal Abnormalities

Instructions: Underline the main term in each diagnosis statement and assign the appropriate ICD-10-CM code(s).

_____ **1.** Anomalies of aortic arch (tortuous)

_____ **2.** Congenital heart block

_____ **3.** Congenital hydrocephalus

_____ **4.** Cystic eyeball, congenital

_____ **5.** Fissure of tongue, congenital

ICD-10-CM Chapter 18: Symptoms, Signs, and Abnormal Clinical and Laboratory Findings, Not Elsewhere Classified (R00–R99)

This chapter includes symptoms, signs, and abnormal clinical and laboratory findings, abnormal tumor markers, and ill-defined and unknown causes of mortality. In general, codes from this chapter are used to report symptoms, signs, and ill-defined conditions that point with equal suspicion to two or more diagnoses or represent important problems in medical care that may affect management of the patient. In addition, this chapter classifies abnormal findings that are reported without a corresponding definitive diagnosis. Codes for such findings can be located in the alphabetic index under the following terms:

- Abnormal, abnormality, abnormalities
- Decrease, decreased
- Elevation
- Findings, abnormal, without diagnosis

Codes from this chapter also are used to report symptoms and signs that existed on initial encounter but proved to be transient and without a specified cause. Also included are provisional diagnoses for patients who fail to return for further investigation, cases referred elsewhere for further investigation before being diagnosed, and cases in which a more definitive diagnosis was not available for other reasons. Do not assign a code from ICD-10-CM categories R00–R99 when the symptoms, signs, and abnormal findings pertain to a definitive diagnosis.

> **EXAMPLE:** Do not assign code R10.9 for abdominal pain or code R19.30 for abdominal rigidity when a patient is diagnosed with acute appendicitis. Such signs and symptoms are associated with acute appendicitis, and they add no value to the patient's coding profile when assigned as other (additional) diagnosis codes.

Coders may assign codes from ICD-10-CM Chapter 18 to report symptoms, signs, and abnormal findings that pertain to a particular clinical diagnosis if the findings represent important problems in medical care. Such problems are useful to record because they may affect length of stay or level of nursing care and/or monitoring. Such problems also may require additional diagnostic or clinical evaluation or may affect treatment plans. In these cases, list the definitive condition as the principal diagnosis, and the symptoms secondarily. List as a secondary diagnosis any symptoms, signs, and abnormal findings that are not integral to the principal diagnosis but provide important clinical information.

> **EXAMPLE:** For a patient admitted with uncontrolled type 1 diabetes mellitus and acute urinary retention, report both codes E10.65 and R33.9. Acute urinary retention is not integral to uncontrolled type 1 diabetes mellitus, and it is an indication for catheterization or surgery. (In ICD-10-CM, *uncontrolled* is reported as *with hyperglycemia.*) Acute urinary retention can also be viewed as an "important medical problem" when patient record documentation indicates the need for clinical evaluation or diagnostic procedures to rule out pathology other than benign prostatic hypertrophy as the etiology. Therapeutic treatment (e.g., catheterization prior to surgery) includes increased nursing care and/or monitoring, such as catheter care or extended length of hospital stay.

Report as the principal diagnosis any symptoms, signs, and abnormal findings that, after study, *cannot be attributed to a definitive diagnosis classifiable to another ICD-10-CM chapter.*

> **EXAMPLE:** Patient was admitted with right lower quadrant abdominal pain. Pelvic ultrasound was negative. Assign code R10.31 because the provider did not document a definitive diagnosis.

Also report as the principal diagnosis any symptom, sign, or abnormal finding that is associated with contrasting or comparative diagnoses (e.g., sign or symptom associated with two or more suspected or possible diagnoses). Report the contrasting or comparative diagnoses as other (additional) diagnosis codes.

> **EXAMPLE:** Patient was admitted for treatment of severe chest pain. Provider documented severe chest pain due to acute myocardial infarction (AMI) versus hiatal hernia. Assign code R07.9 (chest pain) as the principal diagnosis. Assign code I21.3 (acute MI) as other (additional) diagnosis code.

ICD-10-CM Chapter-Specific Coding Guidelines

Chapter 18: Symptoms, Signs, and Abnormal Clinical and Laboratory Findings, Not Elsewhere Classified (R00-R99)

Chapter 18 includes symptoms, signs, abnormal results of clinical or other investigative procedures, and ill-defined conditions regarding which no diagnosis classifiable elsewhere is recorded. Signs and symptoms that point to a specific diagnosis have been assigned to a category in other chapters of the classification.

a. Use of symptom codes

Codes that describe symptoms and signs are acceptable for reporting purposes when a related definitive diagnosis has not been established (confirmed) by the provider.

b. Use of a symptom code with a definitive diagnosis code

Codes for signs and symptoms may be reported in addition to a related definitive diagnosis when the sign or symptom is not routinely associated with that diagnosis, such as the various signs and symptoms associated with complex syndromes. The definitive diagnosis code should be sequenced before the symptom code.

Signs or symptoms that are associated routinely with a disease process should not be assigned as additional codes, unless otherwise instructed by the classification.

c. **Combination codes that include symptoms**

ICD-10-CM contains a number of combination codes that identify both the definitive diagnosis and common symptoms of that diagnosis. When using one of these combination codes, an additional code should not be assigned for the symptom.

d. **Repeated falls**

Code R29.6, Repeated falls, is for use for encounters when a patient has recently fallen and the reason for the fall is being investigated. Code Z91.81, History of falling, is for use when a patient has fallen in the past and is at risk for future falls. When appropriate, both codes R29.6 and Z91.81 may be assigned together.

e. **Coma scale**

The coma scale codes (R40.2-) can be used in conjunction with traumatic brain injury codes, acute cerebrovascular disease or sequelae of cerebrovascular disease codes. These codes are primarily for use by trauma registries, but they may be used in any setting where this information is collected. The coma scale may also be used to assess the status of the central nervous system for other non-trauma conditions, such as monitoring patients in the intensive care unit. The coma scale codes should be sequenced after the diagnosis code(s).

These codes, one from each subcategory, are needed to complete the scale. The 7th character indicates when the scale was recorded.

The 7th character should match for all three codes.

At a minimum, report the initial score documented on presentation at your facility. This may be a score from the emergency medicine technician (EMT) or in the emergency department. If desired, a facility may choose to capture multiple Glasgow coma scale scores.

Assign a code from subcategory R40.24, Glasgow coma scale, total score, when only the total score is documented in the medical record and not the individual score(s).

f. **Functional quadriplegia**

Functional quadriplegia (code R53.2) is the lack of ability to use one's limbs or to ambulate due to extreme debility. It is not associated with neurologic deficit or injury, and code R53.2 should not be used for cases of neurologic quadriplegia. It should only be assigned if functional quadriplegia is specifically documented in the medical record.

g. **SIRS due to non-infectious process**

The systemic inflammatory response syndrome (SIRS) can develop as a result of certain non-infectious disease processes, such as trauma, malignant neoplasm, or pancreatitis. When SIRS is documented with a noninfectious condition, and no subsequent infection is documented, the code for the underlying condition, such as an injury, should be assigned, followed by code R65.10, Systemic inflammatory response syndrome (SIRS) of non-infectious origin without acute organ dysfunction, or code R65.11, Systemic inflammatory response syndrome (SIRS) of non-infectious origin with acute organ dysfunction. If an associated acute organ dysfunction is documented, the appropriate code(s) for the specific type of organ dysfunction(s) should be assigned in addition to code R65.11. If acute organ dysfunction is documented, but it cannot be determined if the acute organ dysfunction is associated with SIRS or due to another condition (e.g., directly due to the trauma), the provider should be queried.

h. **Death NOS**

Code R99, Ill-defined and unknown cause of mortality, is only for use in the very limited circumstance when a patient who has already died is brought into an emergency department or other health care facility and is pronounced dead upon arrival. It does not represent the discharge disposition of death.

i. **NIHSS Stroke Scale**

The NIH stroke scale (NIHSS) codes (R29.7- -) can be used in conjunction with acute stroke codes (I63) to identify the patient's neurological status and the severity of the stroke. The stroke scale codes should be sequenced after the acute stroke diagnosis code(s).

At a minimum, report the initial score documented. If desired, a facility may choose to capture multiple stroke scale scores.

See Section I.B.14. for information concerning the medical record documentation that may be used for assignment of the NIHSS codes.

Exercise 4.20 – Symptoms, Signs, and Abnormal Clinical and Laboratory Findings, Not Elsewhere Classified

Instructions: Underline the main term in each diagnosis statement and assign the appropriate ICD-10-CM code(s).

_____ **1.** Abnormal reflex

_____ **2.** Ataxia

_____ **3.** Elevated prostate specific antigen

_____ **4.** Failure to thrive (child)

_____ **5.** Elevated blood pressure reading

ICD-10-CM Chapter 19: Injury, Poisoning, and Certain Other Consequences of External Causes (S00–T88)

This chapter classifies the following:

- Injuries

- Effects of foreign body entering through natural orifice

- Burns and corrosions

- Frostbite

- Poisonings by, adverse effects of, and underdosing of drugs, medicaments, and biological substances

- Toxic effects of substances chiefly nonmedicinal as to source

- Other and unspecified effects of external causes

- Certain early complications of trauma

- Complications of surgical and medical care, not elsewhere classified

Coding Tip:

Injury and poisoning codes are not assigned for normal, healing surgical wounds or to identify complications of surgical wounds. (To classify complications of surgical wounds, refer to main term *Complication* in the ICD-10-CM Index to Diseases and Injuries.)

Separate codes are assigned for each injury except when a combination code is provided in ICD-10-CM. When multiple codes are assigned, the code for the most serious injury is sequenced first (as determined by the provider and based on treatment provided).

Fractures

A **fracture** is a break in a bone resulting from two possible causes.

- Direct or indirect application of undue force against the bone (injury)

- Pathological changes resulting in spontaneous fractures (disease process)

The provider always determines whether a fracture is open or closed, which is one of the first determinations made. A **closed fracture** (or **simple fracture**) is contained beneath the skin and has intact ligaments and skin, while an **open fracture** (or **compound fracture**) indicates an associated open wound.

 Coding Tip:

ICD-10-CM Chapter 19 does not contain codes for the **malunion** (or **nonunion**) of fractured bones, which is the failure of the ends of a fractured bone to heal (unite). Such codes are located in Chapter 13. In ICD-10-CM, malunion and nonunion of fractured bones are classified in Chapter 19 by adding a seventh character (e.g., S72.001k, S72.001p).

The following terms typically describe closed fractures: ⚠

- *Comminuted fracture:* A splintering of the fractured bone
- *Depressed fracture:* Portion of the skull broken and driven inward from a forceful blow
- *Fissured fracture:* Fracture that does not split the bone
- *Greenstick fracture:* Occurs in children; the bone is somewhat bent and partially broken
- *Impacted fracture:* One fractured bone end wedged into another
- *Linear fracture:* Fracture that is in a straight line
- *Slipped epiphysis:* Separation of the growth plate, which is the growing end of the bone, or epiphysis, from the shaft of the bone; occurs in children and young adults who still have active epiphyses
- *Spiral fracture:* Fracture resembles a helix or has a corkscrew shape

 Coding Tip:

If there is no documentation in the patient record as to whether a fracture is open or closed, the fracture is coded as closed.

An open fracture is classified as a compound fracture because it contains a wound that leads to the fracture or has broken bone ends protruding through the skin. There is a very high risk of infection with open fractures because the tissues are exposed to contaminants (toxins). There may be foreign bodies (or missiles) embedded in the tissues that must be removed during surgery, and puncture wounds may also be present.

Open and closed fractures may both be described as "complicated," which means a bone fragment has injured an internal organ.

EXAMPLE: The ribs may injure the lungs, liver, and spleen, depending on the nature and direction of the force causing the fracture.

Burns

Burns (ICD-10-CM categories T20–T32) are classified according to the following:

- Depth
  - First-degree (erythema)
  - Second-degree (blistering)
  - Third-degree (full-thickness involvement)
  - Extent (percentage of body surface involved) (Figure 4-8)
  - Agent (e.g., chemicals, fire, sun) (assigned an external cause code)

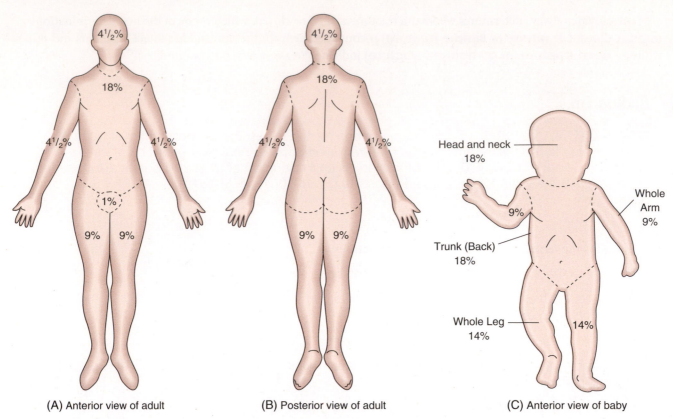

Figure 4-8 The rule of nines is used to calculate the percentage of body surface affected by burns (ICD-10-CM category T32). (Percentage assignments are modified to accommodate infants and children who have proportionately larger heads than adults or for patients who have large buttocks, thighs, or abdomen.)

Adverse Effects, Poisonings, Underdosings, and Toxic Effects

Certain drugs, medicinal substances, and biological substances (or combinations of them) may cause toxic reactions. Such drug toxicity is classified in ICD-10-CM as

- *Adverse effects* (or adverse reaction): Appearance of a pathological condition caused by ingestion or exposure to a chemical substance properly administered or taken

- *Poisonings:* Occur as the result of an overdose, wrong substance administered or taken; or intoxication, which involves combining prescribed drugs with nonprescribed drugs or (ethyl) alcohol

- *Underdosings:* Taking less of a medication than is prescribed by a provider or a manufacturer's instruction

- *Toxic effects:* When a harmful substance is ingested or comes in contact with a person

 Coding Tip:

To locate the code for an adverse effect, go to main term *Effect, adverse* in the ICD-10-CM Index to Diseases and Injuries, and locate the appropriate subterm (e.g., drugs and medicinals). Or, go to main term *Reaction*, and locate the appropriate subterm(s) (e.g., *drug NEC*). Then, assign the appropriate external cause code from the Table of Drugs and Chemicals, Therapeutic Use column.

Coding Tip:

To locate the code for a poisoning or toxic effect, go to the Table of Drugs and Chemicals, determine the circumstances for the poisoning (e.g., accidental, intentional self-harm, assault, undetermined), and assign the code from the appropriate Poisoning column. If more than one substance is documented as causing the poisoning, assign codes from the Table of Drugs and Chemicals for *each* substance. Verify each code in the ICD-10-CM Tabular List of Diseases and Injuries.

 Coding Tip:

- The term *intoxication* often indicates that ethyl alcohol (e.g., beer, wine) was involved (e.g., alcohol intoxication) or that an accumulation effect of a medication in the patient's bloodstream occurred (e.g., Coumadin intoxication). When this occurs, assign a code from the appropriate Poisoning column of the ICD-10-CM Table of Drugs and Chemicals along with the appropriate external cause code. In this situation, intoxication means "poisoning."

- When an accumulation effect of a medication occurs, assign the manifestation code first (e.g., dizziness) and an external cause code from the ICD-10-CM Adverse Effect column in the Table of Drugs and Chemicals.

- When less of a medication than is prescribed by a provider or a manufacturer's instruction is taken, first code the medical condition for which the (*underdosing*) drug was prescribed by referring to the appropriate entry in the ICD-10-CM Index to Diseases and Injuries. Then, code the medication by referring to the Underdosing column in the Table of Drugs and Chemicals (highlighted in yellow in Figure 4-9).

Refer to the Table of Drugs and Chemicals in the ICD-10-CM index (Figure 4-9) when assigning codes for adverse effects, poisonings, and toxic effects.

Substance	Poisoning, Accidental (unintentional)	Poisoning, Intentional Self-harm	Poisoning, Assault	Poisoning, Undetermined	Adverse Effect	Under-dosing
1-propanol	T51.3x1	T51.3x2	T51.3x3	T51.3x4	—	—
2-propanol	T51.2x1	T51.2x2	T51.2x3	T51.2x4	—	—
2, 4-D (dichloro-phenoxyacetic acid)	T60.3x1	T60.3x2	T60.3x3	T60.3x4	—	—
2, 4-toluene diisocyanate	T65.0x1	T65.0x2	T65.0x3	T65.0x4	—	—
2, 4, 5-T (trichloro-phenoxyacetic acid)	T60.1x1	T60.1x2	T60.1x3	T60.1x4	—	—
14-hydroxydihydromorphinone	T40.2x1	T40.2x2	T40.2x3	T40.2x4	T40.2x5	T40.2x6
ABOB	T37.5x1	T37.5x2	T37.5x3	T37.5x4	T37.5x5	T37.5x6
Abrine	T62.2x1	T62.2x2	T62.2x3	T62.2x4	—	—
Abrus (seed)	T62.2x1	T62.2x2	T62.2x3	T62.2x4	—	—
Absinthe	T51.0x1	T51.0x2	T51.0x3	T51.0x4	—	—
beverage	T51.0x1	T51.0x2	T51.0x3	T51.0x4	—	—
Acaricide	T60.8x1	T60.8x2	T60.8x3	T60.8x4	—	—
Acebutolol	T44.7x1	T44.7x2	T44.7x3	T44.7x4	T44.7x5	T44.7x6
Acecarbromal	T42.6x1	T42.6x2	T42.6x3	T42.6x4	T42.6x5	T42.6x6
Aceclidine	T44.1x1	T44.1x2	T44.1x3	T44.1x4	T44.1x5	T44.1x6
Acedapsone	T37.0x1	T37.0x2	T37.0x3	T37.0x4	T37.0x5	T37.0x6
Acefylline piperazine	T48.6x1	T48.6x2	T48.6x3	T48.6x4	T48.6x5	T48.6x6

Courtesy of the Centers for Medicare & Medicaid Services, www.cms.gov

Figure 4-9 ICD-10-CM Table of Drugs and Chemicals (partial)

Coding Tip:

> The ICD-10-CM Table of Drugs and Chemicals contains a listing of the generic names of the drugs or chemicals. (Some publishers are now adding brand names to the list of drugs and chemicals.)

For adverse effects, first code the nature of the adverse effect (e.g., rash), followed by the chemical substance by referring to the Therapeutic Use column of the Table of Drugs and Chemicals. If more than one substance is documented as causing the adverse effect, assign codes from the Table of Drugs and Chemicals for *each* substance.

EXAMPLE: Gastritis due to prescribed tetracycline. In this statement, gastritis is the adverse effect (or manifestation) of the properly administered drug tetracycline. ICD-10-CM codes are reported as K29.70 (gastritis) and T36.4x5A (adverse effect of tetracycline), in that order.

For poisonings and toxic effects in ICD-10-CM, go to the appropriate Poisoning column of the Table of Drugs and Chemicals to assign the code. If more than one substance is documented as causing the poisoning or toxic effect, assign codes from the Table of Drugs and Chemicals for *each* substance. Next code the result or manifestation of the poisoning or toxic effect (e.g., coma).

EXAMPLE: Accidental (unintentional) overdose of tetracycline resulting in severe vomiting. ICD-10-CM codes are reported as T36.4x1A (unintentional accidental poisoning by tetracycline) and R11.2 (vomiting), in that order.

ICD-10-CM Chapter-Specific Coding Guidelines

Chapter 19: Injury, Poisoning, and Certain Other Consequences of External Causes (S00-T88)

a. **Application of 7th Characters in Chapter 19**

   Most categories in chapter 19 have a 7th character requirement for each applicable code. Most categories in this chapter have three 7th character values (with the exception of fractures): A, initial encounter, D, subsequent encounter and S, sequela. Categories for traumatic fractures have additional 7th character values. While the patient may be seen by a new or different provider over the course of treatment for an injury, assignment of the 7th character is based on whether the patient is undergoing active treatment and not whether the provider is seeing the patient for the first time.

   For complication codes, active treatment refers to treatment for the condition described by the code, even though it may be related to an earlier precipitating problem. For example, code T84.50XA, Infection and inflammatory reaction due to unspecified internal joint prosthesis, initial encounter, is used when active treatment is provided for the infection, even though the condition relates to the prosthetic device, implant, or graft that was placed at a previous encounter.

   7th character "A", initial encounter is used for each encounter where the patient is receiving active treatment for the condition. Examples of active treatment are: surgical treatment, emergency department encounter, and continuing treatment by the same or a different physician.

   7th character "D" subsequent encounter is used for encounters after the patient has completed active treatment of the condition and is receiving routine care for the condition during the healing or recovery phase. Examples of subsequent care are: cast change or removal, an x-ray to check healing status of fracture, removal of external or internal fixation device, medication adjustment, other aftercare and follow up visits following treatment of the injury or condition.

   The aftercare Z codes should not be used for aftercare for conditions such as injuries or poisonings, where 7th characters are provided to identify subsequent care. For example, for aftercare of an injury, assign the acute injury code with the 7th character "D" (subsequent encounter).

   7th character "S", sequela, is for use for complications or conditions that arise as a direct result of a condition, such as scar formation after a burn. The scars are sequelae of the burn. When using 7th character "S", it is necessary to use both the injury code that precipitated the sequela and the code for the sequela itself. The "S" is added only to the injury code, not the sequela code. The 7th character "S" identifies the injury responsible for the sequela. The specific type of sequela (e.g. scar) is sequenced first, followed by the injury code.

   See Section I.B.10 Sequelae, (Late Effects).

b. **Coding of injuries**

When coding injuries, assign separate codes for each injury unless a combination code is provided, in which case the combination code is assigned. Code T07, Unspecified multiple injuries should not be assigned in the inpatient setting unless information for a more specific code is not available. Traumatic injury codes (S00-T14.9) are not to be used for normal, healing surgical wounds or to identify complications of surgical wounds.

The code for the most serious injury, as determined by the provider and the focus of treatment, is sequenced first.

1) **Superficial injuries**

Superficial injuries such as abrasions or contusions are not coded when associated with more severe injuries of the same site.

2) **Primary injury with damage to nerves/blood vessels**

When a primary injury results in minor damage to peripheral nerves or blood vessels, the primary injury is sequenced first with additional code(s) for injuries to nerves and spinal cord (such as category S04), and/or injury to blood vessels (such as category S15). When the primary injury is to the blood vessels or nerves, that injury should be sequenced first.

c. **Coding of traumatic fractures**

The principles of multiple coding of injuries should be followed in coding fractures. Fractures of specified sites are coded individually by site in accordance with both the provisions within categories S02, S12, S22, S32, S42, S49, S52, S59, S62, S72, S79, S82, S89, S92 and the level of detail furnished by medical record content. A fracture not indicated as open or closed should be coded to closed. A fracture not indicated whether displaced or not displaced should be coded to displaced.

More specific guidelines are as follows:

1) **Initial vs. subsequent encounter for fractures**

Traumatic fractures are coded using the appropriate 7th character extension for initial encounter (A, B, C) for each encounter where the patient is receiving active treatment for the fracture. Examples of active treatment are: surgical treatment, emergency department encounter, and evaluation and continuing (ongoing) treatment by the same or different physician. The appropriate 7th character for initial encounter should also be assigned for a patient who delayed seeking treatment for the fracture or nonunion.

Fractures are coded using the appropriate 7th character extension for subsequent care for encounters after the patient has completed active treatment of the fracture and is receiving routine care for the fracture during the healing or recovery phase.

Care for complications of surgical treatment for fracture repairs during the healing or recovery phase should be coded with the appropriate complication codes.

Care of complications of fractures, such as malunion and nonunion, should be reported with the appropriate 7th character extensions for subsequent care with nonunion (K, M, N) or subsequent care with malunion (P, Q, R).

Malunion/nonunion: The appropriate 7th character for initial encounter should also be assigned for a patient who delayed seeking treatment for the fracture or nonunion.

The open fracture designations in the assignment of the 7th character for fractures of the forearm, femur and lower leg, including ankle are based on the Gustilo open fracture classification. When the Gustilo classification type is not specified for an open fracture, the 7th character for open fracture type I or II should be assigned (B, E, H, M, Q).

A code from category M80, not a traumatic fracture code, should be used for any patient with known osteoporosis who suffers a fracture, even if the patient had a minor fall or trauma, if that fall or trauma would not usually break a normal, healthy bone.

See Section I.C.13. Osteoporosis.

The aftercare Z codes should not be used for aftercare for traumatic fractures. For aftercare of a traumatic fracture, assign the acute fracture code with the appropriate 7th character.

2) **Multiple fractures sequencing**

Multiple fractures are sequenced in accordance with the severity of the fracture.

(continues)

ICD-10-CM Chapter-Specific Coding Guidelines (*continued*)

d. Coding of burns and corrosions

The ICD-10-CM makes a distinction between burns and corrosions. The burn codes are for thermal burns, except sunburns, that come from a heat source, such as a fire or hot appliance. The burn codes are also for burns resulting from electricity and radiation. Corrosions are burns due to chemicals. The guidelines are the same for burns and corrosions.

Current burns (T20-T25) are classified by depth, extent and by agent (X code). Burns are classified by depth as first degree (erythema), second degree (blistering), and third degree (full-thickness involvement). Burns of the eye and internal organs (T26-T28) are classified by site, but not by degree.

1) Sequencing of burn and related condition codes

Sequence first the code that reflects the highest degree of burn when more than one burn is present.

(a) When the reason for the admission or encounter is for treatment of external multiple burns, sequence first the code that reflects the burn of the highest degree.

(b) When a patient has both internal and external burns, the circumstances of admission govern the selection of the principal diagnosis or first-listed diagnosis.

(c) When a patient is admitted for burn injuries and other related conditions such as smoke inhalation and/or respiratory failure, the circumstances of admission govern the selection of the principal or first-listed diagnosis.

2) Burns of the same local site

Classify burns of the same local site (three-digit category level, T20-T28) but of different degrees to the subcategory identifying the highest degree recorded in the diagnosis.

3) Nonhealing burns

Nonhealing burns are coded as acute burns.
Necrosis of burned skin should be coded as a nonhealed burn.

4) Infected burn

For any documented infected burn site, use an additional code for the infection.

5) Assign separate codes for each burn site

When coding burns, assign separate codes for each burn site. Category T30, Burn and corrosion, body region, unspecified, is extremely vague and should rarely be used.

6) Burns and corrosions classified according to extent of body surface involved

Assign codes from category T31, Burns classified according to extent of body surface involved, or T32, Corrosions classified according to extent of body surface involved, when the site of the burn is not specified or when there is a need for additional data. It is advisable to use category T31 as additional coding when needed to provide data for evaluating burn mortality, such as that needed by burn units. It is also advisable to use category T31 as an additional code for reporting purposes when there is mention of a third-degree burn involving 20 percent or more of the body surface.

Categories T31 and T32 are based on the classic "rule of nines" in estimating body surface involved: head and neck are assigned nine percent, each arm nine percent, each leg 18 percent, the anterior trunk 18 percent, posterior trunk 18 percent, and genitalia one percent. Providers may change these percentage assignments where necessary to accommodate infants and children who have proportionately larger heads than adults, and patients who have large buttocks, thighs, or abdomen that involve burns.

7) Encounters for treatment of sequela of burns

Encounters for the treatment of the late effects (sequelae) of burns or corrosions (i.e., scars or joint contractures) should be coded with a burn or corrosion code with the 7th character "S" for sequela.

8) **Sequelae with a late effect code and current burn**

When appropriate, both a code for a current burn or corrosion with 7th character "A" or "D" and a burn or corrosion code with 7th character "S" may be assigned on the same record (when both a current burn and sequelae of an old burn exist). Burns and corrosions do not heal at the same rate and a current healing wound may still exist with sequela of a healed burn or corrosion.

9) **Use of an external cause code with burns and corrosions**

An external cause code should be used with burns and corrosions to identify the source and intent of the burn, as well as the place where it occurred.

e. **Adverse effects, poisoning, underdosing, and toxic effects**

Codes in categories T36-T65 are combination codes that include the substance that was taken as well as the intent. No additional external cause code is required for poisonings, toxic effects, adverse effects and underdosing codes.

1) **Do not code directly from the Table of Drugs and Chemicals**

Do not code directly from the Table of Drugs and Chemicals. Always refer back to the Tabular List.

2) **Use as many codes as necessary to describe**

Use as many codes as necessary to describe completely all drugs, medicinal or biological substances.

3) **If the same code would describe the causative agent**

If the same code would describe the causative agent for more than one adverse reaction, poisoning, toxic effect or underdosing, assign the code only once.

4) **If two or more drugs, medicinal or biological substances**

If two or more drugs, medicinal or biological substances are reported, code each individually unless a combination code is listed in the Table of Drugs and Chemicals.

5) **The occurrence of drug toxicity is classified in ICD-10-CM as follows:**

(a) **Adverse effect**

When coding an adverse effect of a drug that has been correctly prescribed and properly administered, assign the appropriate code for the nature of the adverse effect followed by the appropriate code for the adverse effect of the drug (T36-T50). The code for the drug should have a 5th or 6th character "5" (for example T36.0X5-). Examples of the nature of an adverse effect are tachycardia, delirium, gastrointestinal hemorrhaging, vomiting, hypokalemia, hepatitis, renal failure, or respiratory failure.

(b) **Poisoning**

When coding a poisoning or reaction to the improper use of a medication (e.g., overdose, wrong substance given or taken in error, wrong route of administration), first assign the appropriate code from categories T36-T50. The poisoning codes have an associated intent as their 5th or 6th character (accidental, intentional self-harm, assault and undetermined). If the intent of the poisoning is unknown or unspecified, code the intent as accidental intent. The undetermined intent is only for use if the documentation in the record specifies that the intent cannot be determined. Use additional code(s) for all manifestations of poisonings.

If there is also a diagnosis of abuse or dependence of the substance, the abuse or dependence is assigned as an additional code.

Examples of poisoning include:

(i) **Error was made in drug prescription**

Errors made in drug prescription or in the administration of the drug by provider, nurse, patient, or other person.

(ii) **Overdose of a drug intentionally taken**

If an overdose of a drug was intentionally taken or administered and resulted in drug toxicity, it would be coded as a poisoning.

(continues)

ICD-10-CM Chapter-Specific Coding Guidelines (*continued*)

    (iii) Nonprescribed drug taken with correctly prescribed and properly administered drug

        If a nonprescribed drug or medicinal agent was taken in combination with a correctly prescribed and properly administered drug, any drug toxicity or other reaction resulting from the interaction of the two drugs would be classified as a poisoning.

    (iv) Interaction of drug(s) and alcohol

        When a reaction results from the interaction of a drug(s) and alcohol, this would be classified as poisoning.

        See Section I.C.4. if poisoning is the result of insulin pump malfunctions.

(c) Underdosing

Underdosing refers to taking less of a medication than is prescribed by a provider or a manufacturer's instruction.

For underdosing, assign the code from categories T36-T50 (fifth or sixth character "6").

Codes for underdosing should never be assigned as principal or first-listed codes. If a patient has a relapse or exacerbation of the medical condition for which the drug is prescribed because of the reduction in dose, then the medical condition itself should be coded.

Noncompliance (Z91.12-, Z91.13-) or complication of care (Y63.6-Y63.9) codes are to be used with an underdosing code to indicate intent, if known.

(d) Toxic effects

When a harmful substance is ingested or comes in contact with a person, this is classified as a toxic effect. The toxic effect codes are in categories T51-T65.

Toxic effect codes have an associated intent: accidental, intentional self-harm, assault and undetermined.

f. Adult and child abuse, neglect and other maltreatment

Sequence first the appropriate code from categories T74.- (Adult and child abuse, neglect and other maltreatment, confirmed) or T76.- (Adult and child abuse, neglect and other maltreatment, suspected) for abuse, neglect and other maltreatment, followed by any accompanying mental health or injury code(s).

If the documentation in the medical record states abuse or neglect it is coded as confirmed (T74.-). It is coded as suspected if it is documented as suspected (T76.-).

For cases of confirmed abuse or neglect an external cause code from the assault section (X92-Y09) should be added to identify the cause of any physical injuries. A perpetrator code (Y07) should be added when the perpetrator of the abuse is known. For suspected cases of abuse or neglect, do not report external cause or perpetrator code.

If a suspected case of abuse, neglect or mistreatment is ruled out during an encounter code Z04.71, Encounter for examination and observation following alleged physical adult abuse, ruled out, or code Z04.72, Encounter for examination and observation following alleged child physical abuse, ruled out, should be used, not a code from T76.

If a suspected case of alleged rape or sexual abuse is ruled out during an encounter, code Z04.41, Encounter for examination and observation following alleged adult rape, or code Z04.42, Encounter for examination and observation following alleged child rape, should be used, not a code from T76.

See Section I.C.15. Abuse in a pregnant patient.

g. Complications of care

1) General guidelines for complications of care

(a) Documentation of complications of care

See Section I.B.16. for information on documentation of complications of care.

2) Pain due to medical devices

Pain associated with devices, implants or grafts left in a surgical site (for example painful hip prosthesis) is assigned to the appropriate code(s) found in Chapter 19, Injury, poisoning, and certain other consequences of external causes. Specific codes for pain due to medical devices are found in the T code section of the ICD-10-CM.

Use additional code(s) from category G89 to identify acute or chronic pain due to presence of the device, implant or graft (G89.18 or G89.28).

3) **Transplant complications**

(a) **Transplant complications other than kidney**

Codes under category T86, Complications of transplanted organs and tissues, are for use for both complications and rejection of transplanted organs. A transplant complication code is only assigned if the complication affects the function of the transplanted organ. Two codes are required to fully describe a transplant complication: the appropriate code from category T86 and a secondary code that identifies the complication.

Pre-existing conditions or conditions that develop after the transplant are not coded as complications unless they affect the function of the transplanted organs.

See Section I.C.21. for transplant organ removal status.

See Section I.C.2. for malignant neoplasm associated with transplanted organ.

(b) **Kidney transplant complications**

Patients who have undergone kidney transplant may still have some form of chronic kidney disease (CKD) because the kidney transplant may not fully restore kidney function. Code T86.1- should be assigned for documented complications of a kidney transplant, such as transplant failure or rejection or other transplant complication. Code T86.1- should not be assigned for post kidney transplant patients who have chronic kidney disease (CKD) unless a transplant complication such as transplant failure or rejection is documented. If the documentation is unclear as to whether the patient has a complication of the transplant, query the provider.

Conditions that affect the function of the transplanted kidney, other than CKD, should be assigned from subcategory T86.1, Complications of transplanted organ, Kidney, and a secondary code that identifies the complication.

For patients with CKD following a kidney transplant, but who do not have a complication such as failure or rejection, *see Section I.C.14. Chronic kidney disease and kidney transplant status.*

4) **Complication codes that include the external cause**

As with certain other T codes, some of the complications of care codes have the external cause included in the code. The code includes the nature of the complication as well as the type of procedure that caused the complication. No external cause code indicating the type of procedure is necessary for these codes.

5) **Complications of care codes within the body system chapters**

Intraoperative and postprocedural complication codes are found within the body system chapters with codes specific to the organs and structures of that body system. These codes should be sequenced first, followed by a code(s) for the specific complication, if applicable.

Exercise 4.21 – Injury, Poisoning, and Certain Other Consequences of External Causes

Instructions: Underline the main term in each diagnosis statement and assign the appropriate ICD-10-CM code(s). (Do *not* enter codes for external cause of diseases and injuries.)

_____ **1.** Closed fracture mandible, subcondylar, right (initial encounter)

_____ **2.** Closed dislocation of clavicle (initial encounter)

(continues)

Exercise 4.21 *(continued)*

_____ 3. Concussion with brief loss of consciousness (30 minutes) (initial encounter)

_____ 4. Foot burn, left, blisters, epidermal loss (second-degree) (initial encounter)

_____ 5. Heart laceration without penetration of heart chambers (initial encounter)

_____ 6. Hives resulting from penicillin taken as prescribed (initial encounter)

_____ 7. Coma due to overdose of barbiturates during an attempted suicide (initial encounter)

_____ 8. Adverse reaction to pertussis vaccine (initial encounter)

_____ 9. Cardiac arrhythmia due to interaction of prescribed ephedrine and ethyl alcohol intoxication (accident) (initial encounter)

_____ 10. Stupor due to overdose of Nytol (accident) (initial encounter)

Chapter 20: External Causes of Morbidity (V00–Y99)

This ICD-10-CM chapter classifies the following:

- Pedestrian injured in transport accident
- Pedal cycle rider injured in transport accident
- Motorcycle rider injured in transport accident
- Occupant of three-wheeled motor vehicle injured in transport accident
- Car occupant injured in transport accident
- Occupant of pick-up truck or van injured in transport accident
- Occupant of heavy transport vehicle injured in transport accident
- Bus occupant injured in transport accident
- Other land transport accidents
- Water transport accidents
- Air and space transport accidents
- Other and unspecified transport accidents
- Other external causes of accidental injury
- Slipping, tripping, stumbling, and falls
- Exposure to inanimate mechanical forces
- Exposure to animate mechanical forces
- Accidental non-transport drowning and submersion
- Exposure to electric current, radiation, and extreme ambient air temperature and pressure
- Exposure to smoke, fire, and flames
- Contact with heat and hot substances
- Exposure to forces of nature
- Accidental exposure to other specified factors
- Intentional self-harm

Coding Tip:

ICD-10-CM Chapter 20 classifies the reporting of *external causes of morbidity* codes. The external cause code(s) are reported as secondary codes for use in any health care setting.

- Assault
- Event of undetermined intent
- Legal intervention, operations of war, military operations, and terrorism
- Complications of medical and surgical care
- Misadventures to patients during surgical and medical care
- Medical devices associated with adverse incidents in diagnostic and therapeutic use
- Surgical and other medical procedures as the cause of abnormal reaction of the patient, or of later complication, without mention of misadventure at the time of the procedure
- Supplementary factors related to causes of morbidity classified elsewhere

EXAMPLE: A patient fell off the toilet in the downstairs bathroom of her single-family house during an attempt to coax her cat to come down from the top of a cabinet. It apparently worked because the cat jumped off the cabinet and landed on the patient. However, the patient was so surprised that she screamed and fell off the toilet onto the floor. The patient landed on her left arm due to the fall and experienced extremely sharp pain. She was evaluated in the emergency department where she was diagnosed with a closed nondisplaced comminuted fracture of the shaft of the humerus, left. She received treatment and was discharged home to follow-up with her primary care physician in the office.

For ICD-10-CM, report the injury (fracture) (S42.355A), cause of injury (fall) (W18.11xA), and place of injury (bathroom of patient's home) (Y92.012). ICD-10-CM's level of specificity results in different codes for other locations in the patient's home (e.g., bathroom). For ICD-10-CM code W18.11xA (fall from toilet), the 7th character (A) indicates she received initial treatment.

The ICD-10-CM place of injury codes for this case indicate that the patient's health insurance policy should be billed, not a liability or workers' compensation policy. If the place of injury had been at a grocery store or other place of business, the business's liability insurance would be billed instead of the patient's health insurance.

Transport Accidents (V00–V99)

The transport accident section of ICD-10-CM is structured in 12 groups, and codes relating to land transport accidents (V01–V89) reflect the victim's mode of transport and are subdivided to identify the victim's counterpart or the type of event. The vehicle of which the injured person is an occupant is identified using the first two characters of the code (because it is the most important factor in identifying prevention purposes). A *transport accident* is one in which the vehicle involved must be moving or running or in use for transport purposes at the time of the accident.

- V00–V09 Pedestrian injured in transport accident
- V10–V19 Pedal cycle rider injured in transport accident
- V20–V29 Motorcycle rider injured in transport accident
- V30–V39 Occupant of three-wheeled motor vehicle injured in transport accident
- V40–V49 Car occupant injured in transport accident
- V50–V59 Occupant of pick-up truck or van injured in transport accident
- V60–V69 Occupant of heavy transport vehicle injured in transport accident
- V70–V79 Bus occupant injured in transport accident
- V80–V89 Other land transport accidents
- V90–V94 Water transport accidents
- V95–V97 Air and space transport accidents
- V98–V99 Other and unspecified transport accidents

ICD-10-CM Chapter-Specific Coding Guidelines

Chapter 20: External Causes of Morbidity (V00-Y99)

The external causes of morbidity codes should never be sequenced as the first-listed or principal diagnosis.

External cause codes are intended to provide data for injury research and evaluation of injury prevention strategies. These codes capture how the injury or health condition happened (cause), the intent (unintentional or accidental; or intentional, such as suicide or assault), the place where the event occurred, the activity of the patient at the time of the event, and the person's status (e.g., civilian, military).

There is no national requirement for mandatory ICD-10-CM external cause code reporting. Unless a provider is subject to a state-based external cause code reporting mandate or these codes are required by a particular payer, reporting of ICD-10-CM codes in Chapter 20, External Causes of Morbidity, is not required. In the absence of a mandatory reporting requirement, providers are encouraged to voluntarily report external cause codes, as they provide valuable data for injury research and evaluation of injury prevention strategies.

a. General external cause coding guidelines

1) Used with any code in the range of A00.0-T88.9, Z00-Z99

An external cause code may be used with any code in the range of A00.0-T88.9, Z00-Z99, classification that is a health condition due to an external cause. Though they are most applicable to injuries, they are also valid for use with such things as infections or diseases due to an external source, and other health conditions, such as a heart attack that occurs during strenuous physical activity.

2) External cause code used for length of treatment

Assign the external cause code, with the appropriate 7th character (initial encounter, subsequent encounter, or sequela) for each encounter for which the injury or condition is being treated.

Most categories in Chapter 20 have a 7th character requirement for each applicable code. Most categories in this chapter have three 7th character values: A, initial encounter, D, subsequent encounter, and S, sequela. While the patient may be seen by a new or different provider over the course of treatment for an injury or condition, assignment of the 7th character for external cause should match the 7th character of the code assigned for the associated injury or condition for the encounter.

3) Use the full range of external cause codes

Use the full range of external cause codes to completely describe the cause, the intent, the place of occurrence, and if applicable, the activity of the patient at the time of the event, and the patient's status, for all injuries, and other health conditions due to an external cause.

4) Assign as many external cause codes as necessary

Assign as many external cause codes as necessary to fully explain each cause. If only one external code can be recorded, assign the code most related to the principal diagnosis.

5) The selection of the appropriate external cause code

The selection of the appropriate external cause code is guided by the Alphabetic Index of External Causes and by Inclusion and Exclusion notes in the Tabular List.

6) External cause code can never be a principal diagnosis

An external cause code can never be a principal (first-listed) diagnosis.

7) Combination external cause codes

Certain of the external cause codes are combination codes that identify sequential events that result in an injury, such as a fall which results in striking against an object. The injury may be due to either event or both. The combination external cause code used should correspond to the sequence of events regardless of which caused the most serious injury.

8) No external cause code needed in certain circumstances

No external cause code from Chapter 20 is needed if the external cause and intent are included in a code from another chapter (e.g., T36.0x1-Poisoning by penicillins, accidental (unintentional)).

b. **Place of occurrence guideline**

   Codes from category Y92, Place of occurrence of the external cause, are secondary codes for use after other external cause codes to identify the location of the patient at the time of injury or other condition. Generally, a place of occurrence code is assigned only once, at the initial encounter for treatment. However, in the rare instance that a new injury occurs during hospitalization, an additional place of occurrence code may be assigned. No 7th characters are used for Y92. Only one code from Y92 should be recorded on a medical record. A place of occurrence code should be used in conjunction with an activity code, Y93.

   Do not use place of occurrence code Y92.9 if the place is not stated or is not applicable.

c. **Activity code**

   Assign a code from category Y93, Activity code, to describe the activity of the patient at the time the injury or other health condition occurred.

   An activity code is used only once, at the initial encounter for treatment. Only one code from Y93 should be recorded on a medical record.

   The activity codes are not applicable to poisonings, adverse effects, misadventures, or sequelae.

   Do not assign Y93.9, Unspecified activity, if the activity is not stated.

   A code from category Y93 is appropriate for use with external cause and intent codes if identifying the activity provides additional information about the event.

d. **Place of occurrence, activity, and status codes used with other external cause code**

   When applicable, place of occurrence, activity, and external cause status codes are sequenced after the main external cause code(s).

   Regardless of the number of external cause codes assigned, there should be only one place of occurrence code, one activity code, and one external cause status code assigned to an encounter.

e. **If the reporting format limits the number of external cause codes**

   If the reporting format limits the number of external cause codes that can be used in reporting clinical data, report the code for the cause/intent most related to the principal diagnosis. If the format permits capture of additional external cause codes, the cause/intent, including medical misadventures, of the additional events should be reported rather than the codes for place, activity, or external status.

f. **Multiple external cause coding guidelines**

   More than one external cause code is required to fully describe the external cause of an illness or injury. The assignment of external cause codes should be sequenced in the following priority:

   If two or more events cause separate injuries, an external cause code should be assigned for each cause. The first-listed external cause code will be selected in the following order:

   External codes for child and adult abuse take priority over all other external cause codes.

   See Section I.C.19., Child and Adult abuse guidelines.

   External cause codes for terrorism events take priority over all other external cause codes except child and adult abuse.

   External cause codes for cataclysmic events take priority over all other external cause codes except child and adult abuse and terrorism.

   External cause codes for transport accidents take priority over all other external cause codes except cataclysmic events, child and adult abuse, and terrorism.

   Activity and external cause status codes are assigned following all causal (intent) external cause codes.

   The first-listed external cause code should correspond to the cause of the most serious diagnosis due to an assault, accident, or self-harm, following the order of hierarchy listed above.

g. **Child and adult abuse guideline**

   Adult and child abuse, neglect and maltreatment are classified as assault. Any of the assault codes may be used to indicate the external cause of any injury resulting from the confirmed abuse.

(continues)

ICD-10-CM Chapter-Specific Coding Guidelines (*continued*)

For confirmed cases of abuse, neglect and maltreatment, when the perpetrator is known, a code from Y07, Perpetrator of maltreatment and neglect, should accompany any other assault codes.
See Section I.C.19. Adult and child abuse, neglect and other maltreatment.

h. Unknown or undetermined intent guideline

If the intent (accident, self-harm, assault) of the cause of an injury or other condition is unknown or unspecified, code the intent as accidental intent. All transport accident categories assume accidental intent.

1) Use of undetermined intent

External cause codes for events of undetermined intent are only for use if the documentation in the record specifies that the intent cannot be determined.

i. Sequelae (Late Effects) of external cause guidelines

1) Sequelae external cause codes

Sequelae are reported using the external cause code with the 7th character extension "S" for sequela. These codes should be used with any report of a late effect or sequela resulting from a previous injury.
See Section I.B.10 Sequela (Late Effects).

2) Sequela external cause code with a related current injury

A sequela external cause code should never be used with a related current nature of injury code.

3) Use of sequela external cause codes for subsequent visits

Use a late effect external cause code for subsequent visits when a late effect of the initial injury is being treated. Do not use a late effect external cause code for subsequent visits for follow-up care (e.g., to assess healing, to receive rehabilitative therapy) of the injury when no late effect of the injury has been documented.

j. Terrorism guidelines

1) Cause of injury identified by the Federal Government (FBI) as terrorism

When the cause of an injury is identified by the Federal Government (FBI) as terrorism, the first-listed external cause code should be a code from category Y38, Terrorism. The definition of terrorism employed by the FBI is found at the inclusion note at the beginning of category Y38. Use additional code for place of occurrence (Y92.-). More than one Y38 code may be assigned if the injury is the result of more than one mechanism of terrorism.

2) Cause of an injury is suspected to be the result of terrorism

When the cause of an injury is suspected to be the result of terrorism, a code from category Y38 should not be assigned.

Suspected cases should be classified as assault.

3) Code Y38.9, terrorism, secondary effects

Assign code Y38.9, Terrorism, secondary effects, for conditions occurring subsequent to the terrorist event. This code should not be assigned for conditions that are due to the initial terrorist act.

It is acceptable to assign code Y38.9 with another code from Y38 if there is an injury due to the initial terrorist event and an injury that is a subsequent result of the terrorist event.

k. External cause status

A code from category Y99, External cause status, should be assigned whenever any other external cause code is assigned for an encounter, including an Activity code, except for the events noted below. Assign a code from category Y99, External cause status, to indicate the work status of the person at the time the event occurred. The status code indicates whether the event occurred during military activity, whether a non-military person was at work or whether an individual, including a student or volunteer, was involved in a non-work activity at the time of the causal event.

A code from Y99, External cause status, should be assigned, when applicable, with other external cause codes, such as transport accidents and falls. The external cause status codes are not applicable to poisonings, adverse effects, misadventures or late effects.

Do not assign a code from category Y99 if no other external cause codes (cause, activity) are applicable for the encounter.

An external cause status code is used only once, at the initial encounter for treatment. Only one code from Y99 should be recorded on a medical record.

Do not assign code Y99.9, Unspecified external cause status, if the status is not stated.

Exercise 4.22 – External Causes of Morbidity

Instructions: Underline the main term in each diagnosis statement and assign the appropriate ICD-10-CM external cause V through Y code(s).

_____   1. Fall from skateboard at public park (initial encounter)

_____   2. Burning bedclothes resulting from cooking in kitchen of mobile home (initial encounter)

_____   3. Explosion in watercraft (initial encounter)

_____   4. Fall from ladder (initial encounter)

_____   5. Left foot injury taking place on baseball field (accident) (initial encounter)

Chapter 21: Factors Influencing Health Status and Contact with Health Services (Z00–Z99)

This ICD-10-CM chapter classifies circumstances other than a disease, injury or external cause classifiable to categories A00-Y89, which are recorded as "diagnoses" or "problems." The chapter classifies the following:

- Persons encountering health services for examinations

- Genetic carrier and genetic susceptibility to disease

- Resistance to antimicrobial drugs

- Estrogen receptor status

- Retained foreign body fragments

- Persons with potential health hazards related to communicable diseases

- Persons encountering health services in circumstances related to reproduction

- Encounters for other specific health care

- Persons with potential health hazards related to socioeconomic and psychosocial circumstances

- Do not resuscitate status

Coding Tip:

Certain Z codes in ICD-10-CM can be reported as a first-listed or additional diagnosis for outpatient care.

- Blood type

- Body mass index (BMI)

- Persons encountering health services in other circumstances

- Persons with potential health hazards related to family and personal history and certain conditions influencing health status ⚠

  Such circumstances can arise when

- A person who may or may not be sick encounters the health services for some specific purpose.

  o Limited care or service for a current condition

  o Donation of an organ or tissue

  o Prophylactic vaccination (immunization)

  o Discussion of a problem which is in itself not a disease or injury

- A situation or problem is present that influences the person's health status but is not in itself a current illness or injury.

- A person with a known disease or injury, whether it is current or resolving, encounters the health care system for a specific treatment of that disease or injury (e.g., dialysis for renal disease, chemotherapy for malignancy, or a cast change).

- Some circumstance or problem is present that influences the person's health status but is not in itself a current illness or injury. Such factors may be elicited during population surveys, when the person may or may not be currently sick, or may be recorded as an additional factor to be borne in mind when the person is receiving care for some current illness or injury classifiable to ICD-10-CM categories A00–Y99.

  In this situation, the ICD-10-CM Z code should be assigned as an other (additional) code and is not selected as the principal diagnosis for inpatient cases or the first-listed diagnosis for outpatient cases. For example, such circumstances include personal history of certain diseases or a person with an artificial heart valve *in situ*.

> **⚠ Coding Tip:**
>
> Verify history of codes in the tabular list before reporting. Also do not confuse personal history of with family history of codes.

Coding Tip:

Refer to ICD-10-CM index main terms to begin the process of assigning an ICD-10-CM Z code. Common main terms include:

Admission	Donor	Outcome of delivery
Aftercare	Encounter for	Pregnancy
Attention to	Examination	Procedure (surgical) not done
Carrier (suspected) of	Exposure	Prophylactic
Checking	Fitting	Removal
Checkup	Follow-up	Resistance, resistant
Closure	History, family	Routine postpartum follow-up
Contact	History (personal) of	Screening
Contraception, contraceptive	Maladjustment	Status
Counseling	Newborn	Test(s)
Dialysis	Observation	Vaccination

EXAMPLE 1: Patient is diagnosed with breast cancer, undergoes mastectomy, and is admitted for chemotherapy. Report code Z51.11 as the first-listed diagnosis and the appropriate breast cancer code as the secondary diagnosis.

EXAMPLE 2: A 5-year-old male patient was seen for an annual well-child visit, during which the provider planned to administer the Menactra meningococcal vaccine. The mother refused to allow the vaccine to be administered to her child because she had read an article about an alert being issued by government agencies that five cases of Guillain-Barré syndrome (GBS) had been diagnosed following administration of the Menactra meningococcal vaccine. Assign code from ICD-10-CM subcategory Z00.129 (Routine infant or child health check) and a code from ICD-10-CM subcategory Z28.2 (Vaccination not carried out because of caregiver refusal). (The provider should document the vaccine refusal and reason in the patient's record.)

EXAMPLE 3: Patient pretends to be in pain so a narcotic will be prescribed, and the provider is alerted to the pretense by another provider. Assign code Z76.5.

EXAMPLE 4: Patient is admitted to the hospital for palliative care during a terminal phase of an illness. Report code Z51.5 as the secondary code. Report the underlying disease process (e.g., cancer, end-stage renal disease) as the first-listed or principal diagnosis code.

EXAMPLE 5: Patient with a history of colon cancer, removed two years ago, is seen for follow-up examination to determine whether there is recurrence. Report codes Z08 and Z85.038.

EXAMPLE 6: Patient undergoes outpatient chest x-ray as part of routine physical examination. The patient has no signs or symptoms. Report code Z01.89 as the first-listed diagnosis.

EXAMPLE 7: Patient has extensive family history of ovarian cancer (e.g., mother, aunts, and sisters) (Z80.41) and elects to undergo screening as a preventive measure (Z12.73).

ICD-10-CM Chapter-Specific Coding Guidelines

Chapter 21: Factors Influencing Health Status and Contact with Health Services (Z00-Z99)

   NOTE: The chapter-specific guidelines provide additional information about the use of Z codes for specified encounters.

a. **Use of Z codes in any healthcare setting**
      Z codes are for use in any healthcare setting. Z codes may be used as either a first-listed (principal diagnosis code in the inpatient setting) or secondary code, depending on the circumstances of the encounter. Certain Z codes may only be used as first-listed or principal diagnosis.

b. **Z Codes indicate a reason for an encounter**
      Z codes are not procedure codes. A corresponding procedure code must accompany a Z code to describe any procedure performed.

c. **Categories of Z codes**
   1) **Contact/Exposure**
         Category Z20 indicates contact with or exposure to communicable diseases. These codes are for patients who do not show any sign or symptom of a disease but have been exposed to it by close personal contact with an infected individual or are in an area where a disease is epidemic.
         Category Z77, Other contact with and (suspected) exposures hazardous to health, indicates contact with and suspected exposures hazardous to health.

(continues)

ICD-10-CM Chapter-Specific Coding Guidelines (*continued*)

Contact/exposure codes may be used as a first-listed code to explain an encounter for testing, or, more commonly, as a secondary code to identify a potential risk.

2) Inoculations and vaccinations

Code Z23 is for encounters for inoculations and vaccinations. It indicates that a patient is being seen to receive a prophylactic inoculation against a disease. Procedure codes are required to identify the actual administration of the injection and the type(s) of immunizations given. Code Z23 may be used as a secondary code if the inoculation is given as a routine part of preventive health care, such as a well-baby visit.

3) Status

Status codes indicate that a patient is either a carrier of a disease or has the sequela or residual of a past disease or condition. This includes things such as the presence of prosthetic or mechanical devices resulting from past treatment. A status code is informative because the status may affect the course of treatment and its outcome. A status code is distinct from a history code. The history code indicates that the patient no longer has the condition.

A status code should not be used with a diagnosis code from one of the body system chapters *if the diagnosis code includes the information provided by the status code*. For example, code Z94.1, Heart transplant status, should not be used with code T86.2, Complications of transplanted heart. The complication code indicates that the patient is a heart transplant patient.

For encounters for weaning from a mechanical ventilator, assign a code from subcategory J96.1, Chronic respiratory failure, followed by code Z99.11, Dependence on respirator [ventilator] status.

The status Z codes/categories are:

Z14   Genetic carrier

Genetic carrier status indicates that a person carries a gene, associated with a particular disease, which may be passed to offspring who may develop that disease. The person does not have the disease and is not at risk of developing the disease.

Z15   Genetic susceptibility to disease

Genetic susceptibility indicates that a person has a gene that increases the risk of that person developing the disease.

Codes from category Z15 should not be used as principal or first-listed codes. If the patient has the condition to which he/she is susceptible, and that condition is the reason for the encounter, the code for the current condition should be sequenced first. If the patient is being seen for follow-up after completed treatment for this condition, and the condition no longer exists, a follow-up code should be sequenced first, followed by the appropriate personal history and genetic susceptibility codes. If the purpose of the encounter is genetic counseling associated with procreative management, code Z31.5, Encounter for genetic counseling, should be assigned as the first-listed code, followed by a code from category Z15.

Additional codes should be assigned for any applicable family or personal history.

Z16   Resistance to antimicrobial drugs

This code indicates that a patient has a condition that is resistant to antimicrobial drug treatment. Sequence the infection code first.

Z17   Estrogen receptor status

Z18   Retained foreign body fragments

Z19   Hormone sensitivity malignancy status

Z21   Asymptomatic HIV infection status

This code indicates that a patient has tested positive for HIV but has manifested no signs or symptoms of the disease.

Z22   Carrier of infectious disease

Carrier status indicates that a person harbors the specific organisms of a disease without manifest symptoms and is capable of transmitting the infection.

Z28.3   Underimmunization status

Z33.1   Pregnant state, incidental

This code is a secondary code only for use when the pregnancy is in no way complicating the reason for visit.

Otherwise, a code from the obstetrics chapter is required.

Z66   Do not resuscitate

This code may be used when it is documented by the provider that a patient is on do not resuscitate status at any time during the stay.

Z67   Blood type

Z68   Body mass index (BMI)

As with all other secondary diagnosis codes, the BMI codes should only be assigned when they meet the definition of a reportable diagnosis (*see Section III, Reporting Additional Diagnoses*).

Z74.01   Bed confinement status

Z76.82   Awaiting organ transplant status

Z78   Other specified health status

Code Z78.1, Physical restraint status, may be used when it is documented by the provider that a patient has been put in restraints during the current encounter.

Please note that this code should not be reported when it is documented by the provider that a patient is temporarily restrained during a procedure.

Z79   Long-term (current) drug therapy

Codes from this category indicate a patient's continuous use of a prescribed drug (including such things as aspirin therapy) for the long-term treatment of a condition or for prophylactic use. It is not for use for patients who have addictions to drugs. This subcategory is not for use of medications for detoxification or maintenance programs to prevent withdrawal symptoms in patients with drug dependence (e.g., methadone maintenance for opiate dependence). Assign the appropriate code for the drug dependence instead.

Assign a code from Z79 if the patient is receiving a medication for an extended period as a prophylactic measure (such as for the prevention of deep vein thrombosis) or as treatment of a chronic condition (such as arthritis) or a disease requiring a lengthy course of treatment (such as cancer). Do not assign a code from category Z79 for medication being administered for a brief period of time to treat an acute illness or injury (such as a course of antibiotics to treat acute bronchitis).

Z88   Allergy status to drugs, medicaments and biological substances

Except: Z88.9, Allergy status to unspecified drugs, medicaments and biological substances status

(continues)

ICD-10-CM Chapter-Specific Coding Guidelines (*continued*)

Z89   Acquired absence of limb

Z90   Acquired absence of organs, not elsewhere classified

Z91.0-   Allergy status, other than to drugs and biological substances

Z92.82   Status post administration of tissue plasminogen activator (tPA) (recombinant [rtPA]) in a different facility within the last 24 hours prior to admission to a current facility.

Assign code Z92.82, Status post administration of tPA (rtPA) in a different facility within the last 24 hours prior to admission to current facility, as a secondary diagnosis when a patient is received by transfer into a facility and documentation indicates they were administered tPA within the last 24 hours prior to admission to the current facility.

This guideline applies even if the patient is still receiving the tPA at the time they are received into the current facility.

The appropriate code for the condition for which the tPA was administered (such as cerebrovascular disease or myocardial infarction) should be assigned first.

Code Z92.82 is only applicable to the receiving facility record and not to the transferring facility record.

Z93   Artificial opening status

Z94   Transplanted organ and tissue status

Z95   Presence of cardiac and vascular implants and grafts

Z96   Presence of other functional implants

Z97   Presence of other devices

Z98   Other postprocedural states

Assign code Z98.85, Transplanted organ removal status, to indicate that a transplanted organ has been previously removed. This code should not be assigned for the encounter in which the transplanted organ is removed. The complication necessitating removal of the transplant organ should be assigned for that encounter.

See section I.C.19. for information on the coding of organ transplant complications.

Z99   Dependence on enabling machines and devices, not elsewhere classified

Note: Categories Z89-Z90 and Z93-Z99 are for use only if there are no complications or malfunctions of the organ or tissue replaced, the amputation site or the equipment on which the patient is dependent.

4) **History (of)**

There are two types of history Z codes, personal and family. Personal history codes explain a patient's past medical condition that no longer exists and is not receiving any treatment but that has the potential for recurrence and, therefore, may require continued monitoring.

Family history codes are for use when a patient has a family member(s) who has had a particular disease that causes the patient to be at higher risk of also contracting the disease.

Personal history codes may be used in conjunction with follow-up codes, and family history codes may be used in conjunction with screening codes to explain the need for a test or procedure. History codes are also acceptable on any medical record regardless of the reason for visit. A history of an illness, even if no longer present, is important information that may alter the type of treatment ordered.

The history Z code categories are:

Z80	Family history of primary malignant neoplasm
Z81	Family history of mental and behavioral disorders
Z82	Family history of certain disabilities and chronic diseases (leading to disablement)
Z83	Family history of other specific disorders
Z84	Family history of other conditions
Z85	Personal history of malignant neoplasm
Z86	Personal history of certain other diseases
Z87	Personal history of other diseases and conditions
Z91.4-	Personal history of psychological trauma, not elsewhere classified
Z91.5	Personal history of self-harm
Z91.8-	Other specified personal risk factors, not elsewhere classified

> Exception: Z91.83, Wandering in diseases classified elsewhere

Z92	Personal history of medical treatment

> Except: Z92.0, Personal history of contraception

> Except: Z92.82, Status post administration of tPA (rtPA) in a different facility within the last 24 hours prior to admission to a current facility

5) Screening

Screening is the testing for disease or disease precursors in seemingly well individuals so that early detection and treatment can be provided for those who test positive for the disease (e.g., screening mammogram).

The testing of a person to rule out or confirm a suspected diagnosis because the patient has some sign or symptom is a diagnostic examination, not a screening. In these cases, the sign or symptom is used to explain the reason for the test.

A screening code may be a first-listed code if the reason for the visit is specifically the screening exam. It may also be used as an additional code if the screening is done during an office visit for other health problems. A screening code is not necessary if the screening is inherent to a routine examination, such as a Pap smear done during a routine pelvic examination.

Should a condition be discovered during the screening, then the code for the condition may be assigned as an additional diagnosis.

The Z code indicates that a screening exam is planned. A procedure code is required to confirm that the screening was performed.

The screening Z code categories are:

Z11	Encounter for screening for infectious and parasitic diseases
Z12	Encounter for screening for malignant neoplasms
Z13	Encounter for screening for other diseases and disorders

> Except: Z13.9, Encounter for screening, unspecified

Z36	Encounter for antenatal screening for mother

6) Observation

There are three observation Z code categories. They are for use in very limited circumstances when a person is being observed for a suspected condition that is ruled out. The observation codes are not for use if

(continues)

ICD-10-CM Chapter-Specific Coding Guidelines (*continued*)

an injury or illness or any signs or symptoms related to the suspected condition are present. In such cases, the diagnosis/symptom code is used with the corresponding external cause code.

The observation codes are to be used as principal diagnosis only. The only exception to this is when the principal diagnosis is required to be a code from category Z38, Liveborn infants according to place of birth and type of delivery. Then a code from category Z05, Encounter for observation and evaluation of newborn for suspected diseases and conditions ruled out, is sequenced after the Z38 code. Additional codes may be used in addition to the observation code but only if they are unrelated to the suspected condition being observed.

Codes from subcategory Z03.7, Encounter for suspected maternal and fetal conditions ruled out, may be used either as a first listed or as an additional code assignment depending on the case. They are for use in very limited circumstances on a maternal record when an encounter is for a suspected maternal or fetal condition that is ruled out during that encounter (for example, a maternal or fetal condition may be suspected due to an abnormal test result). These codes should not be used when the condition is confirmed. In those cases, the confirmed condition should be coded. In addition, these codes are not for use if an illness or any signs or symptoms related to the suspected condition or problem are present. In such cases, the diagnosis/symptom code is used.

Additional codes may be used in addition to the code from subcategory Z03.7, but only if they are unrelated to the suspected condition being evaluated.

Codes from subcategory Z03.7 may not be used for encounters for antenatal screening of mother. *See Section I.C.21.c.5. Screening.*

For encounters for suspected fetal condition that are inconclusive following testing and evaluation, assign the appropriate code from category O35, O36, O40, or O41.

The observation Z code categories are:

Z03   Encounter for medical observation for suspected diseases and conditions ruled out

Z04   Encounter for examination and observation for other reasons

     Except: Z04.9, Encounter for examination and observation for unspecified reason

Z05   Encounter for observation and evaluation of newborn for suspected diseases and conditions ruled out

7) Aftercare

Aftercare visit codes cover situations when the initial treatment of a disease or an injury has been performed and the patient requires continued care during the healing or recovery phase, or for the long-term consequences of the disease. The aftercare Z code should not be used if treatment is directed at a current, acute disease or injury. The diagnosis code is to be used in these cases. Exceptions to this rule are codes Z51.0, Encounter for antineoplastic radiation therapy, and codes from subcategory Z51.1, Encounter for antineoplastic chemotherapy and immunotherapy. These codes are to be first-listed, followed by the diagnosis code when a patient's encounter is solely to receive radiation therapy, chemotherapy or immunotherapy for the treatment of a neoplasm. If the reason for the encounter is more than one type of antineoplastic therapy, code Z51.0 and a code from subcategory Z51.1 may be assigned together, in which case one of these codes would be reported as a secondary diagnosis.

The aftercare Z codes should also not be used for aftercare for injuries. For aftercare of an injury, assign the acute injury code with the appropriate 7th character (for subsequent encounter).

The aftercare codes are generally first-listed to explain the specific reason for the encounter. An aftercare code may be used as an additional code when some type of aftercare is provided in addition to the reason for admission and no diagnosis code is applicable. An example of this would be the closure of a colostomy during an encounter for treatment of another condition.

Aftercare codes should be used in conjunction with other aftercare codes or diagnosis codes to provide better detail on the specifics of an aftercare encounter visit, unless otherwise directed by the classification. Should a patient receive multiple types of antineoplastic therapy during the same encounter, code Z51.0,

Encounter for antineoplastic radiation therapy, and codes from subcategory Z51.1, Encounter for antineoplastic chemotherapy and immunotherapy, may be used together on a record. The sequencing of multiple aftercare codes depends on the circumstances of the encounter.

Certain aftercare Z code categories need a secondary diagnosis code to describe the resolving condition or sequela. For others, the condition is included in the code title.

Additional Z code aftercare category terms include fitting and adjustment, and attention to artificial openings.

Status Z codes may be used with aftercare Z codes to indicate the nature of the aftercare. For example, code Z95.1, Presence of aortocoronary bypass graft, may be used with code Z48.812, Encounter for surgical aftercare following surgery on the circulatory system, to indicate the surgery for which the aftercare is being performed. A status code should not be used when the aftercare code indicates the type of status, such as using Z43.0, Encounter for attention to tracheostomy, with Z93.0, Tracheostomy status.

The aftercare Z category/codes are:

Z42	Encounter for plastic and reconstructive surgery following medical procedure or healed injury
Z43	Encounter for attention to artificial openings
Z44	Encounter for fitting and adjustment of external prosthetic device
Z45	Encounter for adjustment and management of implanted device
Z46	Encounter for fitting and adjustment of other devices
Z47	Orthopedic aftercare
Z48	Encounter for other postprocedural aftercare
Z49	Encounter for care involving renal dialysis
Z51	Encounter for other aftercare and medical care

8) Follow-up

The follow-up codes are used to explain continuing surveillance following completed treatment of a disease, condition, or injury. They imply that the condition has been fully treated and no longer exists. They should not be confused with aftercare codes, or injury codes with a seventh character for subsequent encounter, that explain current treatment for a healing condition or its sequela. Follow-up codes may be used in conjunction with history codes to provide the full picture of the healed condition and its treatment. The follow-up code is sequenced first, followed by the history code.

A follow-up code may be used to explain multiple visits. Should a condition be found to have recurred on the follow-up visit, then the diagnosis code for the condition should be assigned in place of the follow-up code.

The follow-up Z code categories are:

Z08	Encounter for follow-up examination after completed treatment for malignant neoplasm
Z09	Encounter for follow-up examination after completed treatment for conditions other than malignant neoplasm
Z39	Encounter for maternal postpartum care and examination

9) Donor

Codes in category Z52, Donors of organs and tissues, are used for living individuals who are donating blood or other body tissue. These codes are only for individuals donating for others, not for self-donations. They are not used to identify cadaveric donations.

10) Counseling

Counseling Z codes are used when a patient or family member receives assistance in the aftermath of an illness or injury, or when support is required in coping with family or social problems. They are not used in conjunction with a diagnosis code when the counseling component of care is considered integral to standard treatment.

(continues)

ICD-10-CM Chapter-Specific Coding Guidelines (*continued*)

The counseling Z codes/categories are:

Z30.0-   Encounter for general counseling and advice on contraception

Z31.5   Encounter for genetic counseling

Z31.6-   Encounter for general counseling and advice on procreation

Z32.2   Encounter for childbirth instruction

Z32.3   Encounter for childcare instruction

Z69   Encounter for mental health services for victim and perpetrator of abuse

Z70   Counseling related to sexual attitude, behavior and orientation

Z71   Persons encountering health services for other counseling and medical advice, not elsewhere classified

Z76.81   Expectant mother prebirth pediatrician visit

11) Encounters for obstetrical and reproductive services

See Section I.C.15. Pregnancy, Childbirth, and the Puerperium, for further instruction on the use of these codes.

Z codes for pregnancy are for use in those circumstances when none of the problems or complications included in the codes from the Obstetrics chapter exist (a routine prenatal visit or postpartum care). Codes in category Z34, Encounter for supervision of normal pregnancy, are always first-listed and are not to be used with any other code from the OB chapter. Codes in category Z3A, Weeks of gestation, may be assigned to provide additional information about the pregnancy.

The outcome of delivery, category Z37, should be included on all maternal delivery records. It is always a secondary code. Codes in category Z37 should not be used on the newborn record.

Codes in category Z3A, Weeks of gestation, may be assigned to provide additional information about the pregnancy. Category Z3A codes should not be assigned for pregnancies with abortive outcomes (categories O00-O08), elective termination of pregnancy (code Z33.32), nor for postpartum conditions, as category Z3A is not applicable to these conditions. The date of the admission should be used to determine weeks of gestation for inpatient admissions that encompass more than one gestational week.

Z codes for family planning (contraceptive) or procreative management and counseling should be included on an obstetrical record either during the pregnancy or the postpartum stage, if applicable.

Z codes/categories for obstetrical and reproductive services are:

Z30   Encounter for contraceptive management

Z31   Encounter for procreative management

Z32.2   Encounter for childbirth instruction

Z32.3   Encounter for childcare instruction

Z33   Pregnant state

Z34   Encounter for supervision of normal pregnancy

Z36   Encounter for antenatal screening of mother

Z3A   Weeks of gestation

Z37   Outcome of delivery

Z39   Encounter for maternal postpartum care and examination

Z76.81   Expectant mother prebirth pediatrician visit

12) Newborns and infants

See Section I.C.16. Newborn (Perinatal) Guidelines, for further instruction on the use of these codes. Newborn Z codes/categories are:

Z76.1   Encounter for health supervision and care of foundling

Z00.1-   Encounter for routine child health examination

Z38   Liveborn infants according to place of birth and type of delivery

13) Routine and administrative examinations

The Z codes allow for the description of encounters for routine examinations, such as a general check-up, or examinations for administrative purposes, such as a preemployment physical. The codes are not to be used if the examination is for diagnosis of a suspected condition or for treatment purposes. In such cases, the diagnosis code is used. During a routine exam, should a diagnosis or condition be discovered, it should be coded as an additional code. Preexisting and chronic conditions and history codes may also be included as additional codes as long as the examination is for administrative purposes and not focused on any particular condition.

Some of the codes for routine health examinations distinguish between "with" and "without" abnormal findings. Code assignment depends on the information that is known at the time the encounter is being coded. For example, if no abnormal findings were found during the examination, but the encounter is being coded before test results are back, it is acceptable to assign the code for "without abnormal findings." When assigning a code for "with abnormal findings," additional code(s) should be assigned to identify the specific abnormal finding(s).

Preoperative examination and preprocedural laboratory examination Z codes are for use only in those situations when a patient is being cleared for a procedure or surgery and no treatment is given.

The Z codes/categories for routine and administrative examinations are:

Z00   Encounter for general examination without complaint, suspected or reported diagnosis

Z01   Encounter for other special examination without complaint, suspected or reported diagnosis

Z02   Encounter for administrative examination

         Except: Z02.9, Encounter for administrative examinations, unspecified

Z32.0-   Encounter for pregnancy test

14) Miscellaneous Z codes

The miscellaneous Z codes capture a number of other health care encounters that do not fall into one of the other categories. Certain of these codes identify the reason for the encounter, others are for use as additional codes that provide useful information on circumstances that may affect a patient's care and treatment.

Prophylactic organ removal

For encounters specifically for prophylactic removal of an organ (such as prophylactic removal of breasts due to a genetic susceptibility to cancer or a family history of cancer), the principal or first-listed code should be a code from category Z40, Encounter for prophylactic surgery, followed by the appropriate codes to identify the associated risk factor (such as genetic susceptibility or family history).

(continues)

ICD-10-CM Chapter-Specific Coding Guidelines (*continued*)

If the patient has a malignancy of one site and is having prophylactic removal at another site to prevent either a new primary malignancy or metastatic disease, a code for the malignancy should also be assigned in addition to a code from subcategory Z40.0, Encounter for prophylactic surgery for risk factors related to malignant neoplasms. A Z40.0 code should not be assigned if the patient is having organ removal for treatment of a malignancy, such as the removal of the testes for the treatment of prostate cancer.

Miscellaneous Z codes/categories are:

Z28   Immunization not carried out

       Except: Z28.3, Underimmunization status

Z29   Encounter for other prophylactic measures

Z40   Encounter for prophylactic surgery

Z41   Encounter for procedures for purposes other than remedying health state

       Except: Z41.9, Encounter for procedure for purposes other than remedying health state, unspecified

Z53   Persons encountering health services for specific procedures and treatment, not carried out

Z55   Problems related to education and literacy

Z56   Problems related to employment and unemployment

Z57   Occupational exposure to risk factors

Z58   Problems related to physical environment

Z59   Problems related to housing and economic circumstances

Z60   Problems related to social environment

Z62   Problems related to upbringing

Z63   Other problems related to primary support group, including family circumstances

Z64   Problems related to certain psychosocial circumstances

Z65   Problems related to other psychosocial circumstances

Z72   Problems related to lifestyle

       Note: These codes should be assigned only when the documentation specifies that the patient has an associated problem.

Z73   Problems related to life management difficulty

Z74   Problems related to care provider dependency

       Except: Z74.01, Bed confinement status

Z75   Problems related to medical facilities and other health care

Z76.0   Encounter for issue of repeat prescription

Z76.3   Healthy person accompanying sick person

Z76.4   Other boarder to healthcare facility

Z76.5   Malingerer [conscious simulation]

Z91.1- Patient's noncompliance with medical treatment and regimen

Z91.83 Wandering in diseases classified elsewhere

Z91.89 Other specified personal risk factors, not elsewhere classified

15) Nonspecific Z codes

Certain Z codes are so nonspecific, or potentially redundant with other codes in the classification, that there can be little justification for their use in the inpatient setting. Their use in the outpatient setting should be limited to those instances when there is no further documentation to permit more precise coding. Otherwise, any sign or symptom or any other reason for visit that is captured in another code should be used.

Nonspecific Z codes/categories are:

Z02.9	Encounter for administrative examinations, unspecified
Z04.9	Encounter for examination and observation for unspecified reason
Z13.9	Encounter for screening, unspecified
Z41.9	Encounter for procedure for purposes other than remedying health state, unspecified
Z52.9	Donor of unspecified organ or tissue
Z86.59	Personal history of other mental and behavioral disorders
Z88.9	Allergy status to unspecified drugs, medicaments and biological substances status
Z92.0	Personal history of contraception

16) Z codes that may only be principal/first-listed diagnosis

The following Z codes/categories may only be reported as the principal/first-listed diagnosis, except when there are multiple encounters on the same day and the medical records for the encounters are combined:

Z00	Encounter for general examination without complaint, suspected or reported diagnosis 　　Except: Z00.6
Z01	Encounter for other special examination without complaint, suspected or reported diagnosis
Z02	Encounter for administrative examination
Z03	Encounter for medical observation for suspected diseases and conditions ruled out
Z04	Encounter for examination and observation for other reasons
Z31.81	Encounter for male factor infertility in female patient
Z31.82	Encounter for Rh incompatibility status
Z31.83	Encounter for assisted reproductive fertility procedure cycle
Z31.84	Encounter for fertility preservation procedure
Z33.2	Encounter for elective termination of pregnancy
Z34	Encounter for supervision of normal pregnancy
Z38	Liveborn infants according to place of birth and type of delivery
Z39	Encounter for maternal postpartum care and examination
Z42	Encounter for plastic and reconstructive surgery following medical procedure or healed injury
Z51.0	Encounter for antineoplastic radiation therapy
Z51.1-	Encounter for antineoplastic chemotherapy and immunotherapy
Z52	Donors of organs and tissues 　　Except: Z52.9, Donor of unspecified organ or tissue
Z76.1	Encounter for health supervision and care of foundling
Z76.2	Encounter for health supervision and care of other healthy infant and child
Z99.12	Encounter for respirator [ventilator] dependence during power failure

Exercise 4.23 – Factors Influencing Health Status and Contact with Health Services

Instructions: Underline the main term in each diagnosis statement and assign the appropriate ICD-10-CM code(s).

_____ **1.** Bone marrow donor

_____ **2.** Chemotherapy encounter

_____ **3.** Examination for summer camp

_____ **4.** Exposure to smallpox (laboratory)

_____ **5.** Family history of stroke

Summary

The National Center for Health Statistics (NCHS) created the clinical modification (CM) of ICD-10, and ICD-10-CM, which was implemented on October 1, 2015. Although ICD-10-CM contains additional clinical information, its three-character codes and their sequence correlate to the ICD-10 system developed by the World Health Organization (WHO). (ICD-10-PCS was created by the Centers for Medicare & Medicaid Services (CMS), and its codes are reported for hospital inpatient procedures only; ICD-10-PCS is included in Chapter 5 of this textbook.)

The CMS and the NCHS are the agencies in the U.S. Department of Health and Human Services (DHHS) that provide official guidelines for coding and reporting using the _International Classification of Diseases, Tenth Revision, Clinical Modification_ (ICD-10-CM). The _ICD-10-CM Official Guidelines for Coding and Reporting_, as approved by the four organizations that make up the cooperating parties (the AHA, AHIMA, CMS, and NCHS), are used as a companion document to the official version of the ICD-10-CM. The guidelines are a set of rules developed to accompany and complement the official conventions and instructions provided within ICD-10-CM. They are based on the coding and sequencing instructions in ICD-10-CM and provide additional instruction.

In addition to coding conventions and general coding guidelines, the _Official Guidelines for Coding and Reporting_ contains chapter-specific coding guidelines that clarify the assignment of ICD-10-CM disease codes. Unless otherwise indicated in an individual chapter-specific guideline, the ICD-10-CM chapter-specific guidelines apply to all health care settings.

Internet Links

ICD-10-CM/PCS updates: Go to **www.cdc.gov**. Click on Diseases & Conditions, click on the Data & Statistics link, scroll to the Tools & Resources heading, click on the Classification of Diseases, Functioning, and Disability link, and click on any of the ICD links.

ICD-10-CM Official Guidelines for Coding and Reporting: Go to **www.cdc.gov**. Click on the CDC A-Z Index link, and click on the letter _I_. Then click on the _ICD-10-CM (International Classification of Diseases, 10th Revision, Clinical Modification)_ link. Scroll down and click on the ICD-10-CM Guidelines link.

MedLine Plus Interactive Tutorials (for diseases and procedures): Go to **www.nlm.nih.gov**. Click on the Medline Plus link below Databases, and click on Videos & Tools; then click to select any activity.

Study Checklist

❑ Read this chapter and highlight key concepts.

❑ Create an index card for each key term.

❑ Access the chapter Internet links to learn more about concepts.

❑ Complete the chapter exercises and review, verifying answers with your instructor.

❑ Complete Workbook chapter, verifying answers with your instructor.

❑ Go to *www.cengagebrain.com* to access the Student Companion Web Site. Login instructions are located in the Preface.

❑ Form a study group with classmates to discuss chapter concepts in preparation for an exam.

Review

Multiple Choice

Instructions: Circle the most appropriate response after locating the code(s) using ICD-10-CM.

1. Gram-negative septicemia due to *E. coli*.
    - a. A41.4
    - b. A41.50
    - c. A41.51
    - d. A41.9

2. Metastatic carcinoma from the lung.
    - a. C34.90, C79.9
    - b. C79.9, D49.1
    - c. D49.9, C34.90
    - d. D49.9, C80

3. Type 2 diabetes mellitus with iritis.
    - a. E08.39
    - b. E09.39
    - c. E10.39
    - d. E11.39

4. Anemia, neutropenia, and thrombocytopenia.
    - a. D61.09
    - b. D61.9
    - c. D64.9, D70.9, D69.6
    - d. P61.4, D70.4, D69.3

5. Alcohol-induced delirium tremens.
    - a. F10.121, F10.20
    - b. F10.231
    - c. F10.96, F10.26
    - d. G25.1, F10.20

6. Hemiparesis due to old spinal cord injury, lumbar region.
    - a. G81.90, S34.01xS
    - b. G81.90, S30.91xS
    - c. G81.90, S34.109S
    - d. G81.90, S34.119S

7. Cerebral thrombosis.
    - a. I66.09
    - b. I66.19
    - c. I66.29
    - d. I66.9

8. Male patient admitted for ligation of vas deferens sterilization procedure.
    - a. Z30.2
    - b. Z31.0
    - c. Z31.42
    - d. Z31.89

9. Diverticulitis of the colon with hemorrhage.
    - a. K57.20
    - b. K57.21
    - c. K57.32
    - d. K57.33

10. Acute prostatitis due to streptococci.
    - a. N41.0, B95.5
    - b. N41.1, B95.5
    - c. N41.8, B95.5
    - d. N41.9, B95.5

11. Spontaneous delivery of full-term pregnancy (single liveborn).
    - a. O80, Z37.0
    - b. O82, Z37.0
    - c. Z34.00, Z37.0
    - d. Z34.90, Z38.00

12. Hard corn of right little toe.
    - a. L84
    - b. M20.5x1
    - c. M20.61
    - d. M21.271

13. Herniated cervical intervertebral disc. No evidence of myelopathy.
    - a. M50.00
    - b. M50.10
    - c. M50.20
    - d. M50.30

14. Congenital partial dislocation of the hip.
    - a. Q65.1
    - b. Q65.2
    - c. Q65.4
    - d. Q65.5

15. Liveborn infant, born in taxi cab, and then admitted for evaluation. Discharged in excellent condition.
    - a. Z38.00
    - b. Z38.01
    - c. Z38.1
    - d. Z38.2

16. Abnormal mammogram.
    - a. R92.0
    - b. R92.1
    - c. R92.2
    - d. R92.8

17. First- and second-degree burns of right forearm, initial encounter.
    - a. T22.019A
    - b. T22.011A
    - c. T22.111A, T22.211A
    - d. T22.211A

18. Stage 4 chronic kidney disease (CKD) patient undergoes outpatient renal dialysis.
    - a. N18.4
    - b. N18.6, Z49.31
    - c. N18.9, Z91.15
    - d. N19, Z99.2

19. Acute nasopharyngitis.
    - a. J00
    - b. J02.9
    - c. J31.1
    - d. J31.2

20. Family history of sudden cardiac death (SCD).
    - a. Z82.41
    - b. Z82.49
    - c. Z86.74
    - b. Z87.898

Coding Practice—Diseases

Instructions: Underline the main term in each diagnosis statement and assign the appropriate ICD-10-CM code(s).

_____ 1. Classical hemophilia

_____ 2. Fitting of cardiac pacemaker

_____ 3. Gray syndrome from chloramphenicol administration in newborn as prescribed (initial encounter)

_____ 4. Injury by shotgun, undetermined whether accidental or intentional (shooting) (initial encounter)

_____ 5. Irritable bowel syndrome

_____ 6. Malignant neoplasm, right breast (female)

_____ 7. Medial dislocation of tibia, proximal end, open (initial encounter)

_____ 8. Motor vehicle traffic accident involving a collision with a pedestrian (initial encounter)

_____ 9. Multiple personality

_____   10.   Nausea with vomiting

_____   11.   Personal history of penicillin allergy

_____   12.   Pneumonia due to streptococcus, group B

_____   13.   Polyarticular juvenile rheumatoid arthritis, acute

_____   14.   Polycystic kidney, autosomal recessive

_____   15.   Postsurgical hypothyroidism

_____   16.   Pulmonary arteriosclerosis

_____   17.   Sand flea infestation

_____   18.   Spontaneous abortion, complicated by excessive hemorrhage, complete

_____   19.   Preterm labor with preterm delivery of liveborn twins, third trimester

_____   20.   Uterine prolapse, first degree

ICD-10-CM and ICD-10-PCS Hospital Inpatient Coding

Chapter Outline

Acute Care Facilities (Hospitals)

Inpatient Diagnosis Coding Guidelines

Inpatient Procedure Coding Guidelines

ICD-10-PCS Procedure Coding

Chapter Objectives

At the conclusion of this chapter, the student should be able to:

- Define key terms.
- List and explain differences among acute care inpatient settings.
- Interpret inpatient diagnosis and procedure coding and reporting guidelines.
- Assign ICD-10-CM diagnosis and ICD-10-PCS procedure codes for acute care inpatient cases.

Key Terms

acute care facility (ACF)

acute care hospital

admitting diagnosis

ancillary service

axis of classification (ICD-10-PCS)

bed count

bed size

behavioral health care hospital

comorbidity

complication

critical access hospital (CAH)

general hospital

Index (ICD-10-PCS)

inpatient

long-term acute care hospital (LTACH)

long-term hospital

maximizing reimbursement

multiaxial structure (ICD-10-PCS)

multihospital system

newborn patient

optimizing reimbursement

other (additional) diagnoses

other significant procedure

principal diagnosis

principal procedure

rehabilitation hospital

secondary procedure

short-term hospital

single hospital

specialty hospital

subacute care patient

swing bed

tables (ICD-10-PCS)

Uniform Hospital Discharge Data Set (UHDDS)

value (ICD-10-PCS)

Introduction

This chapter defines inpatient acute care settings and includes an interpretation of the guidelines for sequencing diagnosis (and procedures, as required by some third-party payers) published in the *CMS ICD-10-CM Official Guidelines for Coding and Reporting* and *ICD-10-PCS Coding Guidelines*.

Coding guidelines discussed in this chapter are to be used as a companion to the official version of the ICD-10-CM and ICD-10-PCS, which contain coding conventions to ensure accurate coding. ICD-10-CM and ICD-10-PCS (abbreviated as ICD-10-CM/PCS) codes are assigned to inpatient cases to collect statistical data for education and research, determine third-party payer reimbursement, and facilitate health care financial planning. Once codes are assigned to an inpatient case, patient-demographic data and codes are entered directly into an automatedcase abstracting software, using a data entry screen (Figure 5-1).

Once entered into the facility's database, the codes are transmitted to the facility's billing department, which generates the inpatient UB-04 claim for submission to third-party payers (to obtain reimbursement). (Inpatient reimbursement systems are discussed in Chapter 19). As a result of data entry, the facility's IT department has the capability of producing disease, procedure and service, and physician indexes from abstracted data. Indexes are used to retrieve patient records for quality management purposes, and the IT department can generate summary data from the computer system for education, research, and statistical purposes. Statistical data allow the facility to conduct financial planning to determine which facility services to expand or deactivate.

When assigning codes, coders carefully review patient records to locate conditions, diseases, procedures, and services to which codes are assigned. Coders are prohibited from assigning codes when the provider does not specifically document those diagnoses or procedures/services. This is called *assumption coding*, and it is considered

> **Note:**
>
> The following additional content is located on the Student Companion Web Site at www.cengagebrain.com.
>
> - *ICD-10-PCS Root Operations, Definitions, and Examples*
> - *Inpatient Coding Tutorial*

> **Note:**
>
> Students enrolled in medical assistant and medical office administration academic programs may notice that their instructor skips this chapter.

Figure 5-1 Inpatient data entry abstracting screen

Permission to reprint granted by QuadraMed.

fraud because the coder assumes certain facts about a patient's condition or procedures/services although the physician has not specifically documented the level of detail to which the coder assigns codes.

- When patient record documentation appears to support the assignment of a specific code but the provider has not completely documented the diagnosis or procedure on the record's face sheet or discharge summary, the coder should query the physician to determine whether the more specific code should be assigned. (Refer to Chapter 1 for more information about the physician query process.)

- *Reviewing the patient record to assign a more specific code to a documented diagnosis is appropriate.* For example, when a physician documents "fracture of femur," the coder reviews the x-ray report to assign a specific code for the fracture site (e.g., shaft of femur). In addition, codes may be assigned if they are based on other physician (e.g., consultant, resident, or anesthesiologist) documentation as long as there is no conflicting documentation from the attending physician.

- It is appropriate to base the assignment of codes on patient record documentation by any physician involved in the care and treatment of a patient. A physician query is unnecessary if a physician involved in the care and treatment of the patient documents a diagnosis and no conflicting documentation by another physician exists. However, if documentation by two or more physicians conflicts, query the attending physician.

⬛ Hospital inpatient cases usually have multiple diagnoses and procedures documented; once codes are assigned, the coder sequences diagnoses according to principal diagnosis and other (additional) diagnoses as defined by the UHDDS. The following instructions (from the ICD-10-CM Official Coding and Reporting Guidelines) should be applied in the selection of principal procedure and clarification on the importance of the relation to the principal diagnosis when more than one procedure is performed:

1. Procedure performed for definitive treatment of both principal diagnosis and secondary diagnosis.
   a. Sequence procedure performed for definitive treatment most related to principal diagnosis as principal procedure.

2. Procedure performed for definitive treatment and diagnostic procedures performed for both principal diagnosis and secondary diagnosis.
   a. Sequence procedure performed for definitive treatment most related to principal diagnosis as principal procedure.

3. A diagnostic procedure was performed for the principal diagnosis and a procedure is performed for definitive treatment of a secondary diagnosis.
   a. Sequence diagnostic procedure as principal procedure, since the procedure most related to the principal diagnosis takes precedence.

4. No procedures performed that are related to principal diagnosis; procedures performed for definitive treatment and diagnostic procedures were performed for secondary diagnosis.
   a. Sequence procedure performed for definitive treatment of secondary diagnosis as principal procedure, since there are no procedures (definitive or nondefinitive treatment) related to principal diagnosis.

> ✎ **Note:**
>
> Nursing facilities (NFs) are required to report the Minimum Data Set (MDS) for all residents regardless of age, diagnosis, LOS, or payment category. *The Minimum Data Set (MDS)* includes screening elements (e.g., demographic data, ICD-10-CM codes, cognitive patterns, and communicating/hearing patterns) used for the comprehensive assessment of NF residents. NFs use the Resident Assessment Validation and Entry (RAVEN) data entry system to report MDS data, which standardize communication about resident problems and conditions and facilitates quality monitoring and improvement. (More information about skilled nursing coding can be found on the Student Companion Web Site at www.cengagebrain.com.)

The **Uniform Hospital Discharge Data Set (UHDDS)** was established by the federal government to define data collected for inpatient hospitalizations (e.g., age, gender, race, patient's residence, length of stay [LOS], diagnoses and procedures, physicians, patient disposition, and payment sources). UHDDS definitions also apply to all non-outpatient settings (e.g., acute care, short term, long term care and psychiatric hospitals; home health agencies; hospice services, rehab facilities; nursing homes, and so on.

Acute Care Facilities (Hospitals)

An **acute care facility (ACF)** is a hospital that provides health care services to patients who have serious, sudden, or acute illnesses or injuries and/or who need certain surgeries. ACFs provide a full range of health care services including ancillary services, emergency and critical care, surgery, and obstetrics (labor and delivery). **Ancillary services** are diagnostic and therapeutic services provided to inpatients and outpatients (e.g., laboratory, physical therapy). Most hospital inpatient stays are short (fewer than 30 days), although some patients may stay for a longer time if medically necessary. Because each inpatient day is expensive, a utilization or case manager closely monitors patient care to determine whether acute health care services are required.

Hospitals have an organized medical and professional staff, and inpatient beds are available 24 hours per day. The primary function of hospitals is to provide inpatient medical, nursing, and other health-related services to patients for surgical and nonsurgical conditions; hospitals usually provide some outpatient services as well. Hospitals are categorized as (1) **single hospitals** (hospitals are self-contained and not part of larger organizations) and (2) **multihospital systems** (where two or more hospitals are owned, managed, or leased by a single organization; these may include acute, long-term, pediatric, rehabilitation, or psychiatric care facilities).

Another consideration when discussing hospital organization is to identify the *population served by a health care facility*, which means that health care is provided to specific groups of people in that some hospitals specialize in the treatment of children (e.g., pediatric hospitals), while others have special units (e.g., burn unit). The hospital **bed size** (or **bed count**) is the total number of inpatient beds for which the facility is licensed by the state; the hospital must be equipped and staffed to care for these patient admissions. The hospital's average length of stay (LOS) determines classification as a

- **Short-term hospital** (or **acute care hospital**): Average LOS of 4–5 days and a total LOS of fewer than 25 days.

- **Long-term hospital** (or long-term acute care hospital or LTACH): Average LOS is more than 25 days.

EXAMPLE: Patient was admitted 4/5/YYYY and discharged on 4/10/YYYY. To calculate the LOS, count the day of admission but not the day of discharge. This patient's LOS is 5 days.

Hospitals are also categorized by type.

- **Critical access hospitals (CAHs)** are located more than 35 miles from any hospital or another CAH, or they are state-certified as being a necessary provider of health care to area residents. (The requirement is reduced to 15 miles in areas where only secondary roads are available or in mountainous terrains.) CAHs must provide emergency services 24 hours per day and maintain no more than 15 inpatient beds (except swing-bed facilities, which can have up to 25 inpatient beds if no more than 15 are used at any one time for acute care). Inpatients are restricted to 96-hour stays unless a longer period is required due to inclement weather or the development of another emergency condition. (A **swing bed** allows a rural hospital to admit a nonacute care patient.)

- **General hospitals** provide emergency care, perform general surgery, and admit patients for a range of problems from fractures to heart disease based on licensing by the state.

 Note:

Inpatient health care settings include:

- Acute care hospitals
- Critical access hospitals (CAHs)
- Behavioral health care facilities
- Hospice inpatient care
- Long-term acute care facilities

Note:

Content about other than acute care inpatient settings (e.g., hospice) is located on the Student Companion Web Site at www.cengagebrain.com.

- **Long-term acute care hospitals (LTACH)** provide care designed specifically for patients who need functional restoration or rehabilitation and medical management for an average of 3 to 6 weeks.

- **Specialty hospitals** concentrate on a particular population of patients (e.g., children) or diseases (e.g., cancer).

- **Rehabilitation hospitals** admit patients who are diagnosed with trauma (e.g., car accident) or disease (e.g., stroke) and need to learn how to function.

- **Behavioral health care hospitals** specialize in treating individuals with mental health diagnoses.

 Note:

Do not confuse LTACHs with long-term care facilities (LTCFs) (e.g., nursing facilities) that provide a range of services including custodial, intermediate, rehabilitative, and skilled nursing care.

Hospital patients who receive care while residing in the facility are categorized as inpatients, newborn patients, and subacute care patients.

- **Inpatients** stay overnight in the facility for 24 or more hours and are provided with room and board and nursing services.

- **Newborn patients** receive infant care upon birth, and, if necessary, they receive neonatal intensive care (either within the hospital or as the result of transfer to another hospital).

- **Subacute care patients** receive specialized long-term acute care such as chemotherapy, injury rehabilitation, ventilator (breathing machine) support, wound care, and other types of health care services provided to seriously ill patients. Subacute care facilities look like *mini-intensive care units*, and they usually do not offer the full range of health care services

 Note:

Hospital outpatients, ambulatory surgery patients, emergency care patients, and observation care patients are discussed in Chapter 6.

available in acute care facilities (e.g., emergency departments [EDs], obstetrics, and surgery). Subacute care costs less than acute care, and patients are often transferred directly from an intensive care unit. Medicare will reimburse subacute care facilities if care provided is appropriate and medically necessary.

Medicare Part A Hospital Inpatient Order and Physician Certification

Coverage and reimbursement of Medicare Part A hospital inpatient services requires physician certification of *medical necessity* that such services be provided on an inpatient basis. A critical element of physician certification is the *practitioner order*, which is an inpatient admission order that must be documented by the provider in the patient record. In 2014, CMS issued a final rule (CMS-1599-F) called the *2-Midnight Rule*, which modified and clarified the policy about Medicare Administrative Contractor (MAC) review of inpatient hospital and critical access hospital (CAH) admissions for payment purposes. Under the final rule, surgical procedures, diagnostic tests, and other treatments (in addition to services designated as inpatient-only) are generally appropriate for inpatient hospital admission and payment under Medicare Part A *when the physician expects the beneficiary to require a stay that crosses at least two midnights and admits the beneficiary to the hospital based upon that expectation.* The rule was published as a response to facilities' and beneficiaries' concerns about increasingly long stays as outpatients (e.g., observation care) due to hospital uncertainties about payment.

Physician certification requires physician authentication of the practitioner order, documentation of a reason for inpatient services, estimated or actual length of time the beneficiary requires as an inpatient in the hospital, and plans for posthospital care.

For inpatient CAH services only, the physician must certify that the beneficiary may reasonably be expected to be discharged or transferred to a hospital within 96 hours after admission to the CAH. For inpatient rehabilitation facilities (IRF) services only, the documentation that IRFs are already required to complete to meet the IRF coverage requirements (e.g., preadmission screening physician review and concurrence, the post-admission physician evaluation, and the required admission orders) may be used to satisfy the certification and recertification statement requirements.

Exercise 5.1 – Acute Care Facilities (Hospitals)

Instructions: Complete each statement.

1. The type of hospital that provides health care services to patients who have serious, sudden, or acute illnesses or injuries and/or who need certain surgeries is called a(n) _____ care facility.

2. Diagnostic and therapeutic services provided to inpatients and outpatients (e.g., laboratory, physical therapy) are called _____ services.

3. Hospitals that are self-contained and not part of larger organizations are called _____; while two or more hospitals owned, managed, or leased by a single organization are called multihospital systems.

4. The total number of inpatient beds for which a facility is licensed by the state is called the hospital _____ size or count.

5-6. A hospital's average length of stay (LOS) determines whether the hospital is classified as

(5.) _____ or acute (average LOS of 4–5 days and a total LOS of fewer than

25 days) or (6.) _____ (average LOS is more than 25 days).

7. A patient was admitted on May 30 and discharged on June 3 of the same year. The LOS is calculated as _____ days.

8. A swing bed allows a rural hospital to admit a(n) _____ care patient.

9. Patients who are diagnosed with trauma or disease and who need to learn how to function are usually admitted to _____ hospitals.

10. A health care facility that concentrates on a particular population of patients (e.g., children) or disease (e.g., cancer) is called a(n) _____ hospital.

Inpatient Diagnosis Coding Guidelines

The circumstances of inpatient admission govern the sequencing of diagnoses. UHDDS definitions have always been used by acute care hospitals to report inpatient data elements in a standardized manner. Since the creation of the UHDDS in 1985, the application of the UHDDS definitions has been expanded to include all nonoutpatient settings (e.g., acute care, short-term, long-term, and psychiatric hospitals; home health agencies; rehabilitation facilities; and skilled nursing facilities and nursing homes).

Circumstances associated with an inpatient admission govern the sequencing of the following diagnoses:

- Admitting diagnosis
- Principal diagnosis
- Other (additional) diagnoses (or secondary diagnoses, which include comorbidities and complications)

 Coding Tip:

> Inpatient and outpatient health care settings require different diagnosis definitions (e.g., principal diagnosis versus first-listed diagnosis) because of the time frame available for patient care and treatment. The first-listed diagnosis, reported as an ICD-10-CM code for outpatient and physician office care, is defined in Chapter 6.

The attending physician does not document final diagnoses until an inpatient is discharged from the hospital; by that time, a definitive diagnosis has usually been established. Because inpatient coding guidelines prohibit the coding of signs and symptoms when a definitive diagnosis has been established, signs and symptoms are seldom documented as the principal diagnosis on inpatient charts. In addition, qualified (uncertain) diagnoses can be coded as principal and other diagnoses for hospital inpatients because physicians use hospital resources to treat the patient for these types of conditions and because hospital reimbursement is based on the utilization and consumption of resources. (In the outpatient setting, the physician usually does not have time to establish a definitive diagnosis during one encounter. Thus, signs and symptoms are often reported as the first-listed diagnosis for third-party payer reimbursement purposes.)

 Note:

> The attending physician is responsible for documenting the list of final diagnoses in the patient record (e.g., face sheet, discharge summary, or final progress note).

Admitting Diagnosis

The **admitting diagnosis** is the provisional or tentative diagnosis upon which initial patient care is based. It is obtained from the patient's attending physician by the admissions office staff, who enter it in a field on the inpatient face sheet. The admitting diagnosis is often a sign (e.g., fever, cough, rash) or symptom (chest pain, sore throat, numbness). One admitting diagnosis ICD-10-CM code is reported on the UB-04.

Principal Diagnosis

The **principal diagnosis** is defined in the UHDDS as "that condition established after study to be chiefly responsible for occasioning the admission of the patient to the hospital for care." The most important part of the definition is the phrase *after study*, which directs the coder to review all patient record documentation associated with an inpatient hospitalization to determine the clinical reason for the admission. The circumstances of admission that impact selection of the principal diagnosis include the chief complaint and the patient's signs and symptoms on admission, which are documented on the history and physical examination. In addition, the entire patient record is reviewed to determine which condition was *established after study*; this means that the coder reviews ancillary test results (e.g., laboratory, x-ray) and other reports (e.g., operative report, pathology report) to select the principal diagnosis. If selection of the principal diagnosis is unclear, the physician should be queried and the outcome of the query corroborated with supporting documentation in the patient record. One principal diagnosis code is reported on the UB-04.

Note:

> When determining the principal diagnosis, ICD-10-CM coding conventions take precedence over official coding guidelines.

HIPAA Alert!

HIPAA regulations for electronic transactions require providers and payers (including MACs) to adhere to the *Official Guidelines for Coding and Reporting*. Thus, a violation of the coding guidelines is a HIPAA violation. Unfortunately, some payers do not appear to be aware of or understand this HIPAA provision. Payers should be informed of the provision in the HIPAA regulation that references the use of coding guidelines. If payers deny claims because certain codes are reported as principal diagnosis, contact your regional CMS office or the HIPAA enforcement office (at CMS) to alert them about the HIPAA violation.

EXAMPLE: A 51-year-old male patient presented to the ED, complaining of ringing in his ears, dizziness, blurred vision, confusion, and difficulty walking. Upon evaluation by the ED physician, the patient stated that these symptoms started suddenly just two hours ago. Past history revealed that the patient takes medication for hypercholesterolemia and hypertension. The patient used to smoke two packs of cigarettes daily until 5 years ago, when he quit. Physical examination revealed blood pressure of 175/110. When asked, the patient stated that he had been taking his hypertension medication as prescribed.

Patient underwent carotid ultrasound to evaluate the blood flow of the carotid arteries, and results indicated the need for carotid angiogram to measure blockage of the carotid arteries. The ED physician transferred the case to a cardiologist, who performed a bilateral carotid angiogram that revealed 90% blockage of the right carotid artery and 20% blockage of the left carotid artery. The patient was admitted to the hospital and scheduled for carotid angioplasty with insertion of carotid stent in the morning, which was performed uneventfully. Final diagnoses were documented as carotid artery occlusion, hypertension, and hypercholesterolemia. Procedures performed included carotid ultrasound, carotid angiogram, and carotid angioplasty.

In this example, the principal diagnosis is the carotid artery occlusion (I65.29). Other diagnoses (or secondary diagnoses) include hypertension (I10), and hypercholesterolemia (E78.00). Do not assign codes to the symptoms of ringing in his ears, dizziness, blurred vision, confusion, and difficulty walking because they are associated with the carotid artery occlusion. Signs and symptoms are often documented in the patient's record, but they are not coded if they are considered part of an established diagnosis.

Codes for Symptoms, Signs, and Ill-Defined Conditions

Codes for symptoms, signs, and ill-defined conditions from ICD-10-CM Chapter 18 are *not* to be reported as the principal diagnosis when a related definitive diagnosis has been established.

EXAMPLE: The patient is admitted as a hospital inpatient after having been treated in the ED for chest pain and a positive electrocardiogram (EKG), which revealed anterolateral MI. The patient underwent cardiac catheterization (Figure 5-2) during hospitalization and subsequent quadruple coronary artery bypass graft surgery. The principal diagnosis for this case is acute anterolateral MI, first episode. The chest pain is not assigned a code because it is a symptom of the MI.

Two or More Interrelated Conditions, Each Potentially Meeting the Definition for Principal Diagnosis

When two or more interrelated *inpatient* conditions (e.g., diseases located in the same ICD-10-CM chapter, manifestations associated with a certain disease) potentially meet the definition of principal diagnosis, either condition may be sequenced first unless the circumstances of the admission, the therapy provided, or the ICD-10-CM index or tabular list indicates otherwise.

Figure 5-2 Cardiac catheterization

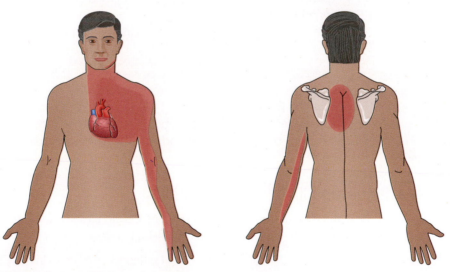

Figure 5-3 Patterns of angina

EXAMPLE: A patient is admitted as a hospital inpatient with chest pain, fever, and shortness of breath. Chest x-ray reveals exacerbated congestive heart failure (CHF). Physical examination reveals acute bronchitis. The patient's prior history and current EKG findings are consistent with unstable angina (Figure 5-3). All three conditions of CHF, acute bronchitis, and unstable angina were treated with medications, and all three diagnoses equally meet the criteria for the definition of principal diagnosis. The coder can code and sequence any one of the three diagnoses as the principal diagnosis.

As an alternative scenario, this patient underwent coronary arteriography that revealed coronary artery disease and 95% blockage of two prominent arterial branches. Subsequently, the patient was taken to the operating room for percutaneous transluminal coronary angioplasty (PTCA). In this scenario, the coronary arteriography diagnostic workup and PTCA treatment criteria clearly distinguish coronary artery disease, identified as the etiology (cause) of the patient's unstable angina, as the principal diagnosis.

Two or More Diagnoses That Equally Meet the Definition for Principal Diagnosis

In the unusual instance when two or more *inpatient* diagnoses *equally* meet the criteria for principal diagnosis, *as determined by one or more of the following*, any one of the diagnoses may be reported as the principal diagnosis:

- Circumstances of admission
- Diagnostic workup and/or therapy provided
- ICD-10-CM index, tabular list, or other coding guidelines do not provide sequencing direction

Determining which of several diagnoses to report as the principal diagnosis when multiple diagnoses equally meet the criteria for selection as the principal diagnosis is called **optimizing reimbursement**, and it is permitted under the inpatient prospective payment system (IPPS), which uses diagnosis-related groups (DRGs). (Trauma cases often result in several diagnoses, any one of which could be selected and reported as the principal diagnosis.) **Maximizing reimbursement** is *not* permitted because it involves (1) selecting and reporting as principal diagnosis the code that results in the highest level of reimbursement for the facility, whether that diagnosis meets the criteria for selection or not, or (2) assigning a higher-paying code (upcoding) to a diagnosis (or ICD-10-PCS, CPT, or HCPCS level II code to a procedure) even if patient record documentation does not support that code selection. (Under the IPPS, upcoding and maximizing reimbursement is called DRG creep.)

EXAMPLE 1: OPTIMIZING REIMBURSEMENT: The patient was admitted to the hospital after an automobile accident, initial evaluation was performed in the ED, and the patient was diagnosed with fractured left femur and fractured right humerus. Inpatient treatment included an open reduction internal fixation of the fractured left femur and open reduction internal fixation of the fractured right humerus. In this case, either the fractured left femur or the fractured right humerus could be reported as the principal diagnosis. The best practice would be to assign codes to each diagnosis and procedure, enter them into the diagnosis-related grouper, determine which would result in optimal reimbursement for the hospital, and report that code as the principal diagnosis.

EXAMPLE 2: MAXIMIZING REIMBURSEMENT AND UPCODING: The patient was admitted as a hospital inpatient for treatment of urosepsis, which is a urinary tract infection (UTI). (A secondary code is assigned to indicate the cause of the infection, such as *E. coli*.) The DRG reimbursement rate is approximately $2,300. Using encoder and MS-DRG grouper software, the coder may notice that the code for sepsis results in the higher MS-DRG rate of approximately $6,400. If the code for sepsis is reported as principal diagnosis, this case would most likely be reviewed by the Medicare administrative contractor (MAC) and/or the quality improvement organization (QIO) to verify accuracy of the reported code. Upon review, the error would be discovered and the hospital could be subject to sanctions (e.g., loss of Medicare participating provider status) and fines.

Two or More Comparative or Contrasting Conditions

In those rare instances when two or more *inpatient* contrasting or comparative diagnoses are documented as *either/or* (or similar terminology), they are coded as if the diagnoses were confirmed. The diagnoses are sequenced according to the circumstances of the admission. If no further determination can be made as to which diagnosis should be principal, either diagnosis may be sequenced first.

EXAMPLE: An elderly patient was treated for complaints of chest pain and shortness of breath, and the physician documented "acute asthma or acute pneumonia" on the patient's record. The patient died before diagnostic workup could be initiated, and the family declined to have the patient undergo an autopsy. Assign an ICD-10-CM code to both conditions, and either diagnosis may be sequenced as the principal diagnosis to optimize reimbursement.

Original Treatment Plan Not Carried Out

Even though treatment may not have been carried out during an inpatient stay due to unforeseen circumstances, the condition which, after study, occasioned the admission to the hospital is sequenced as the principal diagnosis.

> **EXAMPLE:** The patient was scheduled for surgery due to severe ureteritis. After administration of anesthesia, the patient was prepped for an endoscopic biopsy of the right ureter. The endoscope passed easily into the urinary bladder but was unable to advance to the right ureter due to ureteral blockage. The surgeon removed the endoscope, and the patient was taken to the recovery room.
>
> In this example, the surgery was halted because after the cystourethroscope was advanced through the urinary bladder, it could not be advanced into the ureter. The principal diagnosis is ureteritis, and the significant other diagnosis is ureteral blockage.

Complications of Surgery and Other Medical Care

When an inpatient admission is for treatment of a complication resulting from surgery or other medical care, the complication code is sequenced as the principal diagnosis. If the complication is classified to the ICD-10-CM T80–T88 series and the code lacks the necessary specificity in describing the complication, an additional code for the specific complication should be assigned.

> **EXAMPLE:** A 54-year-old male patient was admitted to the hospital for severe stomach pain, nausea, vomiting, and fever of 102 degrees. The abdomen was rigid and distended. Past history revealed that two months ago, the patient had undergone open cholecystectomy for cholecystitis with cholelithiasis. Laboratory tests revealed elevated white blood cell count. Patient was scheduled for exploratory laparotomy, which revealed the presence of abscessed stitches. Cultures taken were positive for *Staphylococcus aureus*.
>
> In this example, the principal diagnosis is abscessed stitches, which is a complication of the open cholecystectomy. The significant other diagnoses include staphylococcal infection and postoperative status. The principal procedure is exploratory laparotomy, and the significant other procedure is reopening of recent laparotomy site.

Uncertain Diagnosis (or Qualified Diagnosis)

If the principal diagnosis documented at the time of discharge is uncertain or qualified with words such as *probable*, *suspected*, *likely*, *questionable*, *possible*, or *still to be ruled out*, code the diagnosis as if it existed or was established. The basis for this guideline is the diagnostic workup, arrangements for further workup or observation, and initial therapeutic approach that correspond most closely with the established diagnosis.

 Note:

> The *uncertain diagnosis* guideline applies only to diagnoses reported for inpatient admissions to acute short-term, acute long-term, and psychiatric *hospitals*. Other nonoutpatient health care settings (e.g., home health care, rehabilitation hospitals, skilled nursing facilities, nursing homes) and all outpatient health care settings do not assign codes to uncertain diagnoses. They assign codes to signs and symptoms when a provider has not documented a definitive diagnosis.

> **EXAMPLE:** A 24-year-old female was admitted due to fever of 102 degrees for a period of two days, as well as chills. The patient has a past history of having undergone a recent laparoscopic appendectomy, for which she was prescribed postoperative antibiotics. She had completed the prescription when she spiked a fever and started experiencing chills. Review of systems reveals complaints of painful urination for two days. The patient states that she has frequent UTIs. Although the urine culture was negative, it is likely that this patient has a UTI, which has to be treated aggressively given her postoperative status.

Patient received intravenous ciprofloxacin and aminoglycoside for a period of 72 hours, after which she improved and was discharged for follow-up in the office. She was prescribed an oral antibiotic to be continued 10 days after discharge. Final diagnosis is possible UTI. In this example, although the final diagnosis of possible UTI is uncertain (or qualified), it is the principal diagnosis. The other significant diagnosis is postoperative surgical status.

Admission from Observation Unit

Admission Following Medical Observation. When a patient is admitted to an observation unit for a medical condition that either worsens or does not improve *and* is subsequently admitted as an inpatient to the same hospital for this same medical condition, the principal diagnosis would be the medical condition that led to the hospital inpatient admission.

Admission Following Postoperative Observation. When a patient is admitted to an observation unit to monitor a condition (or complication) that develops following outpatient surgery and is subsequently admitted as an inpatient of the same hospital, hospitals should apply the Uniform Hospital Discharge Data Set (UHDDS) definition of principal diagnosis as "that condition established after study to be chiefly responsible for occasioning the admission of the patient to the hospital for care."

Admission from Outpatient Surgery

When a patient undergoes surgery in the hospital's outpatient surgery department and is subsequently admitted for continuing inpatient care at the same hospital, the following guidelines should be followed in selecting the principal diagnosis for the inpatient admission:

- If the reason for the inpatient admission is a complication, assign the complication as the principal diagnosis.

- If no complication, or other condition, is documented as the reason for the inpatient admission, assign the reason for the outpatient surgery as the principal diagnosis.

- If the reason for the inpatient admission is another condition unrelated to the surgery, assign the unrelated condition as the principal diagnosis.

Admissions/Encounters for Rehabilitation

When the purpose for the admission or encounter is rehabilitation, sequence first the code for the condition for which the service is being performed. However, if the condition for which the rehabilitation service is performed is no longer present, report the appropriate aftercare code as the first-listed or principal diagnosis.

EXAMPLE 1: The patient is admitted for rehabilitation services for right-sided dominant hemiplegia following a cerebrovascular infarction. Report code I69.351 as the first-listed or principal diagnosis.

EXAMPLE 2: The patient is admitted for rehabilitation services due to severe degenerative osteoarthritis of the hip. The patient previously underwent hip replacement surgery. Report aftercare code Z47.1 as the first-listed or principal diagnosis.

Other (Additional) Diagnoses with Documentation That Supports Reporting

For reporting purposes, the definition for *other (additional) diagnoses* is interpreted as additional conditions that affect patient care by requiring one or more of the following:

- Clinical evaluation
- Therapeutic treatment
- Diagnostic procedures

- Extended length of hospital stay
- Increased nursing care and/or monitoring

The UHDDS defines **other (additional) diagnoses** as "all conditions that coexist at the time of admission, that develop subsequently, or that affect the treatment received and/or the length of stay." Diagnoses related to an earlier episode that have no bearing on the current hospital stay are not coded. Up to 17 secondary diagnoses are reported on a UB-04 claim. The UB-04 claim contains separate fields for entry of three external cause of morbidity ICD-10-CM codes (in addition to the 17 secondary diagnosis codes).

The Centers for Medicare & Medicaid Services (CMS) has developed a standard list of other (additional) diagnoses that are recognized as comorbidities and/or complications (CCs) or major comorbidities and/or complications (MCCs) for MS-DRGs. When a CC or MCC is present as a secondary diagnosis, it can affect MS-DRG assignment. A **comorbidity** is a condition that coexists at the time of admission (e.g., diabetes mellitus, hypertension, asthma), and a **complication** is a condition that occurs during the course of the inpatient hospital episode (e.g., fractured hip resulting from fall while gait training, postoperative infection, hospital-acquired staphylococcal infection).

MS-DRGs with CC or MCC require a substantial increase in utilization of hospital resources, and the reimbursement for these DRGs reflects an increase in payment. While just one CC or MCC can change a *MS-DRG without CC or MCC* to a *MS-DRG with CC or MCC*, there are a number of stand-alone MS-DRGs that are not affected by the presence or absence of CCs. For stand-alone MS-DRGs, the MS-DRG (and reimbursement amount) will change (and increase) only if the principal diagnosis is changed or a significant surgical procedure is reported.

> **EXAMPLE:** An 86-year-old female was admitted to the hospital with complaints of severe shortness of breath, dyspnea, and chest pain. Upon evaluation, the attending physician determined that the patient has a history of intrinsic asthma and is currently experiencing acute exacerbation of that condition. The patient also has a past history of hypertension, for which she takes medication. Last year the patient was treated in the hospital's pain clinic on an outpatient basis for cluster headaches, which have not recurred. Patient received respiratory therapy and drug therapy for the asthma. The physician also ordered medications and patient education for the hypertension and blood pressure monitoring three times per nursing shift. The final diagnoses documented upon discharge include acute exacerbation of intrinsic asthma and hypertension.
>
> In this example, the principal diagnosis is acute exacerbation of intrinsic asthma and the comorbidity (coexisting condition or other significant diagnosis) is hypertension. The hypertension increased nursing care and monitoring because medications were administered, patient teaching was performed, and the patient's blood pressure was taken three times per shift.

 Coding Tip:

> When other diagnoses are documented and no supporting documentation can be found in the patient record, make sure you query the physician to determine whether the diagnosis is to be coded and reported. For example, when a patient is admitted for treatment of an acute condition (e.g., trauma, illness) and the physician notes positive findings on the physical examination (e.g., tendonitis) that are not treated during the hospitalization, do not code the positive findings because they do not impact the episode of care.

Previous Conditions Stated as a Diagnosis

If the provider has documented a diagnosis in the list of diagnoses on the discharge summary or the face sheet in the patient record, it should ordinarily be coded. However, some providers document diagnoses for resolved conditions or chronic diagnoses and status-post procedures from previous admissions that have no bearing on the current inpatient stay. Such conditions are not coded and reported for reimbursement purposes. However, family and personal history codes are reported as secondary codes *if* the historical condition or family history impacts current care or influences the patient's treatment.

> **EXAMPLE:** A 92-year-old female patient was admitted as a hospital inpatient for acute MI of the anterolateral wall. The patient's history is negative for cardiovascular or respiratory complaints, and she

states that she has not had an MI in the past. The patient does have a past history of localized uterine adenocarcinoma 20 years ago, for which she underwent vaginal hysterectomy. The final diagnosis is acute anterolateral wall MI, initial episode of care.

In this example, the principal diagnosis is acute anterolateral wall MI, initial episode of care. The localized uterine adenocarcinoma is not assigned a neoplasm code from ICD-10-CM Chapter 2. Instead, it is appropriate to assign a code for history of uterine cancer.

Abnormal Findings

Abnormal findings (e.g., ancillary tests such as laboratory, x-ray, pathologic, and other diagnostic results) are not coded and reported unless the provider documents their clinical significance. If the ancillary test findings are outside the normal range and the attending provider has ordered other tests to evaluate the condition or prescribed treatment, it is appropriate to ask the provider whether the abnormal finding should be added.

 Note:

In the outpatient setting, the provider interprets diagnostic test results, and codes are assigned for such encounters.

Exercise 5.2 – Inpatient Diagnosis Coding Guidelines

Instructions: Match the case scenario with the sequencing guideline.

_____ 1. Patient undergoes appendectomy and develops postoperative wound infection.

_____ 2. Patient admitted with acute asthma and acute CHF, both of which were treated.

_____ 3. The patient is admitted for rehabilitation services for left-sided dominant hemiplegia following a stroke.

_____ 4. Patient admitted and treated for acute gastroenteritis has extremely low potassium level. (Physician query initiated.)

_____ 5. Patient admitted with acute gastroenteritis versus acute gastric ulcer; patient treated symptomatically.

_____ 6. Elderly patient admitted with recent history of severe abdominal pain for which testing was performed. Final diagnoses are peritonitis and acute ulcerative colitis.

_____ 7. Patient admitted for treatment of acute MI and receives medication and patient education for previously diagnosed insulin-dependent diabetes mellitus.

_____ 8. Patient admitted with right lower quadrant pain and elevated fever. Possible ectopic pregnancy. Possible acute appendicitis.

_____ 9. Patient admitted for treatment of fractured hip; has a past history of cholecystitis with cholecystectomy one year ago.

_____ 10. Patient with a diagnosis of multiparity, admitted for elective sterilization, was found to have elevated temperature, and surgery was canceled.

a. Abnormal findings

b. Complications of surgery and other medical care

c. Original treatment plan not carried out

d. Other (additional) diagnoses reported

e. Previous conditions stated as diagnoses

f. Rehabilitation admission/ encounter

g. Two or more comparative or contrasting conditions coded as if the diagnosis is confirmed

h. Two or more diagnoses equally meeting definition for principal diagnosis

i. Two or more interrelated conditions equally meeting definition of principal diagnosis

j. Uncertain, or qualified, diagnosis

EXAMPLE: A 49-year-old male patient was admitted as a hospital inpatient for acute pneumonia due to *Staphylococcus aureus*, which was evaluated and successfully treated. During hospitalization, the patient underwent an EKG that was interpreted by the cardiologist as being normal. The EKG report did document abnormal T-wave changes.

In this example, the principal diagnosis is acute pneumonia due to *Staphylococcus aureus*. The coder should query the physician to determine if a code should be assigned to "abnormal T-wave changes" as documented on the EKG. It is likely that the coder will be told by the physician that such changes are commonly associated with EKGs performed on anxious patients and that this male patient was quite ill, which could cause anxiety.

Uncertain Diagnosis (as Other/Additional Diagnosis)

If the diagnosis documented at the time of discharge is qualified as "probable," "suspected," "likely," "questionable," "possible," or "still to be ruled out" or other similar terms indicating uncertainty, code the condition as if it existed or was established. The basis for these guidelines are the diagnostic workup, arrangements for further workup or observation, and initial therapeutic approach that correspond most closely with the established diagnosis.

> **Note:**
>
> The "uncertain diagnosis" is applicable only to inpatient admissions to short-term, acute, long-term care, and psychiatric hospitals. ("Uncertain diagnosis" is also called "qualified diagnosis.")

Inpatient Procedure Coding Guidelines

Depending on state reporting requirements, when the circumstances of inpatient admission govern the sequencing of procedure codes, UHDDS definitions are used to report inpatient data elements in a standardized manner. Circumstances associated with an inpatient admission govern the sequencing of

- Principal procedure

- Significant other procedures (or secondary procedures)

EXAMPLE: New York State's (NYS) *Statewide Planning and Research Cooperative System (SPARCS)* is a comprehensive data reporting system that was established in 1979 in cooperation with the health care industry and state government. Initially created to collect information on discharges from hospitals, SPARCS now collects patient-level detail on patient characteristics, diagnoses and treatments, services, and charges for every NYS hospital discharge, ambulatory surgery patient, and emergency department admission. SPARCS created *output data dictionaries*, which include definitions, codes and values, and edit applications for inpatient and outpatient *output data elements*. For electronic claims purposes, SPARCS requires reporting of the principal procedure and significant other procedures. The SPARCS outpatient data dictionary's definition of these terms is based on the federal government's UHDDS definition. ▲

> ⚠️ **Coding Tip:**
>
> Inpatient procedures are classified using ICD-10-PCS. Outpatient and physician office settings report CPT and HCPCS level II codes for procedures/ services (discussed in Chapters 7–18.)

> **Note:**
>
> All operating room procedures performed that are surgical in nature, carry a procedural risk, carry an anesthetic risk, or require specialized training are assigned ICD-10-PCS codes and reported.

Principal Procedure and Other Significant Procedures

When required for reimbursement purposes, the principal procedure is sequenced first, followed by other significant procedure(s) (when more than one procedure is reported on an inpatient claim). The following instructions should be applied in the selection of **principal procedure**, and they provide clarification regarding the importance of the relation to the principal diagnosis when more than one procedure is performed:

1. When the procedure is performed for definitive treatment of both the principal diagnosis and secondary diagnosis, sequence the procedure performed for definitive treatment most related to principal diagnosis as the principal procedure.

2. When the procedure is performed for definitive treatment and diagnostic procedures are performed for both the principal diagnosis and secondary diagnosis, sequence the procedure performed for definitive treatment most related to principal diagnosis as the principal procedure.

3. When a diagnostic procedure was performed for the principal diagnosis, and a procedure is performed for definitive treatment of a secondary diagnosis, sequence the diagnostic procedure as the principal procedure because the procedure most related to the principal diagnosis takes precedence.

4. When no procedures performed were related to the principal diagnosis, but procedures were performed for definitive treatment or diagnostic procedures were performed for the secondary diagnosis, sequence the procedure performed for definitive treatment of the secondary diagnosis as the principal procedure.

Other significant procedures (or **secondary procedures**)

- Are surgical in nature (e.g., incision, excision, amputation)
- Carry a procedural (or operative) risk
- Carry an anesthetic risk
- Require highly trained personnel
- Require special facilities or equipment

One principal procedure is reported on a paper-based UB-04 claim, and up to five significant procedures can be reported on the same paper-based UB-04 claim. Similarly, one principal procedure is reported on an electronic claim, but up to 14 significant procedures can be reported on the same electronic claim.

 Note:

> DRG grouper software allows for the entry of one ICD-10-PCS principal procedure code and up to 24 other (additional) ICD-10-PCS procedure codes.

EXAMPLE: A 64-year-old male patient presented to the ED complaining of ringing in his ears, dizziness, blurred vision, confusion, and difficulty walking. Upon evaluation by the ED physician, the patient stated that these symptoms started about 24 hours ago. Past history revealed that the patient takes medication for hypercholesterolemia and hypertension. Physical examination revealed blood pressure of 180/115. When asked, the patient stated that he had been taking his hypertension medication as prescribed. Patient underwent carotid ultrasound to evaluate the blood flow of the carotid arteries, and results indicated the need for carotid angiogram to measure blockage of the carotid arteries.

The ED physician transferred the case to a cardiologist, who admitted the patient to the hospital and performed a bilateral carotid angiogram. Angiogram revealed 92% blockage of the right carotid artery and 24% blockage of the left carotid artery. The patient was admitted to the hospital and scheduled for carotid angioplasty with insertion of carotid stent in the morning, which was performed uneventfully. Final diagnoses were documented as carotid artery occlusion, hypertension, and hypercholesterolemia. Procedures performed included carotid ultrasound, carotid angiogram, and carotid angioplasty.

In this example, the principal procedure is carotid angioplasty, Other significant procedures include insertion of carotid stent and carotid angiogram. (The carotid ultrasound is not categorized as an operating room procedure and is not reported.)

Exercise 5.3 – Inpatient Procedure Coding Guidelines

Instructions: Complete each statement.

1. Depending on state reporting requirements, when the circumstances of inpatient admission govern the sequencing of procedure codes, _____ are used to report inpatient data elements in a standardized manner.

2. Inpatient procedures are classified using _____.

3. Outpatient and physician office settings report _____ and HCPCS level II codes for procedures and services.

4. When CMS implemented _____, they discontinued the practice of sequencing procedure codes for reimbursement purposes.

5. When required for reimbursement purposes, the principal procedure is sequenced _____.

6. The principal procedure is defined as being performed for _____ treatment rather than for diagnostic or exploratory purposes, necessary to treat a complication, or most closely related to the principal diagnosis.

7. Other significant procedures (or secondary procedures) are defined as _____, carrying a procedural (or operative) risk, carrying an anesthetic risk, requiring highly trained personnel, and/or requiring special facilities or equipment.

8. A paper-based UB-04 claim allows for the reporting of one principal procedure and _____ significant procedure(s).

9. An electronic inpatient claim allows for reporting of one principal procedure and up to _____ significant procedures.

10. The number of other (secondary) significant procedure codes that can be reported in DRG grouper software is _____.

ICD-10-PCS Procedure Coding

The *International Classification of Diseases, 10th Revision, Procedure Classification System* (ICD-10-PCS) is used by hospitals to code and classify procedure data from inpatient records only. ICD-10-PCS codes use a **multiaxial structure** for its seven-character alphanumeric codes, which means a value from each of seven hierarchies (positions) is assigned to construct a code. As a result, unique codes are constructed for all substantially different procedures, and the multiaxial structure allows new procedures to be easily incorporated as new codes.

The ICD-10-PCS coding manual contains the following:

- Index
- Tables

ICD-10-PCS Index

The ICD-10-PCS **Index** (Figure 5-4) organizes main terms in alphabetical order, providing the first three or four characters (and sometimes all seven characters) of a code as well as direction to a specific location in the tables. The Index is used to access the tables, and it mirrors the structure of the tables so it follows a consistent

ICD-10-PCS Index

A

Abdominal aortic plexus *use* Nerve, Abdominal Sympathetic
Abdominal esophagus *use* Esophagus, Lower
Abdominohysterectomy
     see Resection, Uterus 0UT9
     see Resection, Cervix 0UTC
Abdominoplasty
     see Alteration, Wall, Abdominal 0W0F
     see Repair, Wall, Abdominal 0WQF
     see Supplement, Abdominal Wall 0WUF
Abductor hallucis muscle
     use, Foot Muscle, Right
     use, Foot Muscle, Left
AbioCor® Total Replacement Heart *use* Synthetic Substitute
Ablation *see* Destruction
Abortion
     Abortifacient 10A07ZX
     Laminaria 10A07ZW
     Products of Conception 10A0
     Vacuum 10A07Z6
Abrasion *see* Extraction
Absolute Pro Vascular (OTW) Self-Expanding Stent System
     use Intraluminal Device
Accessory cephalic vein
     use Cephalic Vein, Right
     use Cephalic Vein, Left
Accessory obturator nerve *use* Lumbar Plexus Nerve
Accessory phrenic nerve *use* Phrenic Nerve
Accessory spleen *use* Spleen

Courtesy of the Centers for Medicare & Medicaid Services, www.cms.gov

Figure 5-4 ICD-10-PCS Index (partial)

pattern of organization and use of hierarchies. The Index is organized as an alphabetical lookup, and the two types of main terms used are

- Based on the value of the third character, which is the *root operation* (e.g., bypass, excision, incision)

- Common procedure terms (e.g., appendectomy, cholecystectomy), which usually provide direction to a root operation main term

Purpose of ICD-10-PCS Index

The purpose of the ICD-10-PCS Index is to locate the appropriate table that contains all information necessary to construct a procedure code. The ICD-10-PCS tables must always be consulted to construct the most appropriate valid code. It is not possible to construct a procedure code by using just the alphabetic index.

Main Terms

The ICD-10-PCS Index reflects the structure of the tables and is organized as an alphabetical listing. The Index is based on the value of the third character, contains common procedure terms, lists anatomical sites, and uses device terms. The main terms in the alphabetic index are root operations, root procedure types, or common procedure names. In addition, anatomical sites from the body part key (Appendix C of ICD-10-PCS) and the device key and aggregation table (Appendix D of ICD-10-PCS) were added for ease of use. Examples of main terms in the ICD-10-PCS Index include:

- **Resection** (root operation)

- **Fluoroscopy** (root type)

- **Prostatectomy** (common procedure name)
- **Brachial artery** (body part)
- **Bard® Dulex™ mesh** (device)

The ICD-10-PCS Index provides at least the first three or four values of the code, and some entries may provide complete valid codes. However, the user should always consult the appropriate ICD-10-PCS table to verify that the most appropriate valid code has been selected.

Root Operation and Procedure Type Main Terms

For the *Medical and Surgical* and related sections, the root operation values are used as main terms in the Index. The subterms under the root operation main terms are body parts. For the *Ancillary* section of the tables, the main terms in the Index are the general type of procedure performed. Examples of root operations and procedure type as main terms in the ICD-10-PCS Index include:

- **Destruction** (root operation)

  Acetabulum

    Left 0Q55

    Right 0Q54

  Adenoids 0C5Q

  Ampulla of Vater 0F5C

- **Biofeedback** GZC9ZZZ (procedure type)

ICD-10-PCS Index Coding Conventions

See The ICD-10-PCS Index includes common procedure names, such as *appendectomy* or *fundoplication*. These common terms are listed as main terms with a *see* reference directing coders to ICD-10-PCS root operations as possible valid code tables based on the objective of the procedure. Examples of common procedure names as main terms in the ICD-10-PCS Index include:

- **Tendonectomy**

  see Excision, Tendons 0LB

  see Resection, Tendons 0LT

Use The ICD-10-PCS Index includes anatomical sites from the Body Part Key (Appendix C of the ICD-10-PCS coding manual) and device terms from the Device Key (Appendix D of the ICD-10-PCS coding manual). When these terms appear as main terms in the ICD-10-PCS Index, they contain a *use* reference as an additional reference when constructing a procedure code using the ICD-10-PCS tables. The *use* reference does *not* direct coders to another main term in the Index, but it provides guidance regarding the selection of character values within an ICD-10-PCS table. Examples of common body part and device main terms in the ICD-10-PCS Index include:

- **Epitrochlear lymph node**

  use Lymphatic, Right Upper Extremity

  use Lymphatic, Left Upper Extremity

- **CoAxia NeuroFlo catheter**

  use Intraluminal Device

- **SynCardia Total Artificial Heart**

  use Synthetic Substitute

Note:

- The ICD-10-PCS index contains a hierarchical alphabetical lookup for locating a table that includes supplemental procedure terms (e.g., appendectomy) that correspond to root operation options.

- It is *not* possible to construct an ICD-10-PCS procedure code from the index. The purpose of the index is to locate the appropriate table that contains all information necessary to construct a procedure code.

- Coders are *not* required to consult the index before proceeding to the tables to construct an ICD-10-PCS code. A valid code can be constructed directly from the tables (by locating the appropriate section, body system, and root operation table).

ICD-10-PCS Tables

ICD-10-PCS **tables** (Figure 5-5) are used to construct a complete and valid code (using a build-a-code approach). Tables include terms (and definitions) and rows, which contain **values** that are characters (individual letters and numbers) assigned to each of seven unique hierarchies (positions) needed to construct a valid ICD-10-PCS code. The first three rows of each table list values and descriptions of the first three characters of codes in that table; subsequent rows list values (and descriptions) for the fourth through seventh characters of the ICD-10-PCS code.

> **EXAMPLE:** Refer to Figure 5-5, and notice that the first three characters in the upper portion of the table are 001. This indicates that codes will be constructed for procedures in the Medical and Surgical *section*, Central Nervous System *body system*, and Bypass *root operation* (defined in the table). Use the table in Figure 5-5 to construct an ICD-10-PCS code for the procedural statement (below) by assigning the fourth through seventh character values for each element of the procedure.

0	**Medical and Surgical**		
0	**Central Nervous System**		
1	**Bypass:** Altering the route of passage of the contents of a tubular body part		

Body Part Character 4	Approach Character 5	Device Character 6	Qualifier Character 7
6 Cerebral Ventricle	0 Open 3 Percutaneous	7 Autologous Tissue Substitute J Synthetic Substitute K Nonautologous Tissue Substitute	0 Nasopharynx 1 Mastoid sinus 2 Atrium 3 Blood Vessel 4 Pleural Cavity 5 Intestine 6 Peritoneal Cavity 7 Urinary Tract 8 Bone Marrow B Cerebral Cisterns
U Spinal Canal	0 Open 3 Percutaneous	7 Autologous Tissue Substitute J Synthetic Substitute K Nonautologous Tissue Substitute	4 Pleural Cavity 6 Peritoneal Cavity 7 Urinary Tract 9 Fallopian Tube

Figure 5-5 ICD-10-PCS table (sample)

ICD-10-PCS SECTIONS	
0	Medical and Surgical
1	Obstetrics
2	Placement
3	Administration
4	Measurement and Monitoring
5	Extracorporeal Assistance and Performance
6	Extracorporeal Therapies
7	Osteopathic
8	Other Procedures
9	Chiropractic
B	Imaging
C	Nuclear Medicine
D	Radiation Therapy
F	Physical Rehabilitation and Diagnostic Audiology
G	Mental Health
H	Substance Abuse Treatment
X	New Technology

Courtesy of the Centers for Medicare & Medicaid Services, www.cms.gov

Figure 5-6 ICD-10-PCS sections

After *open incision into the cerebral ventricle, a synthetic shunt was inserted to allow excess cerebrospinal fluid (CSF) to flow* (bypass) *into the peritoneal cavity* (to decrease CSF pressure). ICD-10-PCS code 00160J6 is constructed by assigning a character for each value of the seven-character code:

Section	Body System	Root Operation	Body Part	Approach	Device	Qualifier
Medical and Surgical	Central Nervous System	Bypass	Cerebral Ventricle	Open	Synthetic Substitute	Peritoneal Cavity
0	0	1	6	0	J	6

ICD-10-PCS tables are organized in sections (Figure 5-6) that identify the general type of procedure, and each of the seven characters in a table has a specific meaning (Figure 5-7). Within a section, all character meanings remain constant. (The first character of the ICD-10-PCS procedure code *always* specifies the section.) Within an ICD-10-PCS table, valid values include all combinations of choices for the fourth through seventh characters that are contained in the same row of a table. ⚠

- The columns in ICD-10-PCS tables contain values for the fourth through seventh characters.

- The rows in ICD-10-PCS tables delineate valid combinations of values.

- Any combination of values not contained in a single row of the tables is invalid.

EXAMPLE: Refer to the portion of a Medical and Surgical section table below, and notice that 0JHT3VZ is a valid code, but 0JHW3VZ is not a valid code. The "V" in code 0JHW3VZ is not a valid value for sixth character device because it is associated with the subcutaneous tissue and fascia, trunk body part.

Coding Tip:

Construct valid ICD-10-PCS codes using a *build-a-code* approach to assign values to each of the seven unique hierarchies (positions).

			Meaning of Each Character Within a Section			
Section	**1st**	**2nd**	**3rd**	**4th**	**5th**	**6th**	**7th**
Medical and Surgical	Section	Body system	Root operation	Body part	Approach	Device	Qualifier
Obstetrics	Section	Body system	Root operation	Body part	Approach	Device	Qualifier
Placement	Section	Anatomical region	Root operation	Body region/ orifice	Approach	Device	Qualifier
Administration	Section	Physiological system and anatomical region	Root operation	Body system/ Region	Approach	Substance	Qualifier
Measurement and Monitoring	Section	Physiological device/system	Root operation	Body system	Approach	Function/ Device	Qualifier
Extracorporeal Assistance and Performance	Section	Physiological system	Root operation	Body system	Duration	Function	Qualifier
Extracorporeal Therapies	Section	Physiological system	Root operation	Body system	Duration	Qualifier	Qualifier
Osteopathic	Section	Anatomical region	Root operation	Body region	Approach	Method	Qualifier
Other Procedures	Section	Body system	Root operation	Body region	Approach	Method	Qualifier
Chiropractic	Section	Anatomical region	Root operation	Body region	Approach	Method	Qualifier
Imaging	Section	Body system	Root type	Body part	Contrast	Qualifier	Qualifier
Nuclear Medicine	Section	Body system	Root type	Body part	Radionuclide	Qualifier	Qualifier
Radiation Therapy	Section	Body system	Modality	Treatment site	Modality qualifier	Isotope	Qualifier
Physical Rehabilitation and Diagnostic Audiology	Section	Section qualifier	Root type	Body system/ Region	Type qualifier	Equipment	Qualifier
Mental Health	Section	Body system	Root type	Qualifier	Qualifier	Qualifier	Qualifier
Substance Abuse Treatment	Section	Body system	Root type	Qualifier	Qualifier	Qualifier	Qualifier
New Technology	Section	Body system	Operation	Body Part	Approach	Device/ Substance/ Technology	Qualifier

Figure 5-7 Meaning of first through seventh characters within each ICD-10-PCS section

Courtesy of the Centers for Medicare & Medicaid Services, www.cms.gov

Section: 0   **Medical and Surgical**

Body System: J   Subcutaneous Tissue and Fascia

Operation: H   Insertion: Putting in a nonbiological appliance that monitors, assists, performs, or prevents a physiological function but does not physically take the place of a body part

Body Part Character 4		Approach Character 5		Device Character 6		Qualifier Character 7	
S	Subcutaneous Tissue and Fascia, Head and Neck	0	Open	1	Radioactive Element	Z	No Qualifier
V	Subcutaneous Tissue and Fascia, Upper Extremity	3	Percutaneous	3	Infusion Device		
W	Subcutaneous Tissue and Fascia, Lower Extremity						
T	Subcutaneous Tissue and Fascia, Trunk	0	Open	1	Radioactive Element	Z	No Qualifier
		3	Percutaneous	3	Infusion Device		
				V	Infusion Pump		

All seven characters *must* contain valid values (selected from the appropriate table) to construct a valid ICD-10-PCS procedure code. If documentation is incomplete for coding purposes, query the physician for the necessary information. However, according to ICD-10-PCS coding guidelines, the coder is *not* required to query the physician when the correlation between documentation and defined ICD-10-PCS terms is clear (e.g., surgeon documents "partial resection" and coder determines that "partial resection" is root operation "excision").

- Columns in the ICD-10-PCS tables contain values for characters 4 through 7.

- Rows in the ICD-10-PCS tables delineate valid combinations of values.

- Any combination of values *not* contained in a single row of the ICD-10-PCS tables is invalid (and results in construction of an invalid code if used).

ICD-10-PCS inpatient coding guidelines are organized as follows:

- Structure
- Values
- Index

- Tables
- Medical and surgical section guidelines
- Obstetrics section guidelines

Structure of ICD-10-PCS Codes

ICD-10-PCS codes contain seven characters. Each character is associated with an **axis of classification** (e.g., section, body part, root operation, and so on), which specifies information about the procedure performed. Within a defined code range, a character specifies the same type of information for that axis of classification.

All seven characters must be specified to construct a valid code. If documentation is incomplete for coding purposes, query the physician for the necessary information to construct a valid code.

> **EXAMPLE:** The fifth *axis of classification* specifies the approach in the Medical and Surgical section.

ICD-10-PCS Values

One of 34 possible *values* may be assigned to each axis of classification in the seven-character code. The values include numbers 0 through 9 and the alphabet (except for letters I and O because they are easily confused with numbers 1 and 0, respectively). The number of unique values used in an axis of classification differs as needed.

> **EXAMPLE:** Where the fifth axis of classification specifies the approach, seven different approach values are currently used to specify the approach.

Valid values for an axis of classification can be added (by the Centers for Medicare & Medicaid Services [CMS]) as needed. This means that when a significantly distinct type of device is used during performance of a new procedure, a new device value can be added to the system.

> **EXAMPLE:** There are currently no device values listed in the *Medical and Surgical* section, *Skin and Breast* body system, and *Repair* root operation. In the future, perhaps CMS will add *surgical glue* as a device. That means instead of selecting value Z for the device, the coder would select the appropriate value for surgical glue (or some other new device).

The meaning of any single value is based on its axis of classification *and* any preceding values on which it may be dependent.

> **EXAMPLE:** A body part value in the *Medical and Surgical* section is *always* dependent on the body system value. Thus, body part value 0 in the *Central Nervous System* body system always classifies Brain, while body part value 0 in the *Peripheral Nervous System* body system always classifies Cervical Plexus.

As ICD-10-PCS expands to become increasingly more detailed, more values will depend on preceding values for their meaning.

EXAMPLE: In the *Medical and Surgical* section, *Lower Joints* body system, *Insertion* root operation, device value 3 refers to *Infusion Device*. In the *Medical and Surgical* section, *Lower Joints* body system, *Fusion* root operation, device value 3 refers to *Interbody Internal Fixation Device*.

ICD-10-PCS Coding Conventions

ICD-10-PCS codes are composed of seven characters. Each character is an axis of classification that specifies information about the procedure performed. Within a defined code range, a character specifies the same type of information in that axis of classification.

EXAMPLE: The fifth axis of classification specifies the approach in sections 0 through 4 and 7 through 9 of ICD-10-PCS.

One of 34 possible values can be assigned to each axis of classification in the seven-character code. The values include numbers 0 through 9 and the alphabet (except I and O because they are easily confused with the numbers 1 and 0). The number of unique values used in an axis of classification differs as needed.

EXAMPLE: Where the fifth axis of classification specifies the approach, seven different approach values are currently used to specify the approach.

The valid values for an axis of classification can be added to as needed.

EXAMPLE: If a significantly distinct type of device is used in a new procedure, a new device value can be added to the system.

As with words in their context, the meaning of any single value is a combination of its axis of classification and any preceding values on which it may be dependent.

EXAMPLE: The meaning of a body part value in the Medical and Surgical section is always dependent on the body system value. The body part value 0 in the Central Nervous body system specifies Brain, while the body part value 0 in the Peripheral Nervous body system specifies Cervical Plexus.

As the system is expanded to become increasingly detailed, over time more values will depend on preceding values for their meaning.

EXAMPLE: In the Lower Joints body system, device value 3 in the root operation Insertion specifies Infusion Device, while device value 3 in the root operation Replacement specifies Ceramic Synthetic Substitute.

The purpose of the alphabetic index is to locate the appropriate table that contains all information necessary to construct a procedure code. The PCS tables should always be consulted to find the most appropriate valid code.

It is not required to consult the index first before proceeding to the tables to complete the code. A valid code may be chosen directly from the tables.

All seven characters must be specified to be a valid code. If the documentation is incomplete for coding purposes, the physician should be queried for the necessary information.

Within a PCS table, valid codes include all combinations of choices in characters 4 through 7 contained in the same row of the table.

EXAMPLE: For Table 0JH, code 0JHT3VZ is valid; however, 0JHW3VZ is not a valid code.

"And," when used in a code description, means "and/or."

EXAMPLE: Lower Arm and Wrist Muscle means lower arm and/or wrist muscle.

Many of the terms used to construct PCS codes are defined within the system. It is the coder's responsibility to determine what the documentation in the medical record equates to in the PCS definitions. The physician is not expected to use the terms used in PCS code descriptions, nor is the coder required to query the physician when the correlation between the documentation and the defined PCS terms is clear.

EXAMPLE: When the physician documents "partial resection," the coder can independently correlate "partial resection" to root operation Excision without querying the physician for clarification.

Medical and Surgical Section Coding Guidelines

Coding guidelines associated with the *Medical and Surgical* section of ICD-10-PCS include:

- Body system
- Root operation
- Body part
- Approach
- Device

Body System—General Coding Guidelines

Procedure codes in the *General Anatomical Regions* body system are used *only when*

- The procedure is performed on an anatomical region rather than a specific body part.

- Insufficient information is available to support the assignment of a value to a specific body part.

  EXAMPLE: *Control of postoperative hemorrhage of the gastrointestinal tract, open approach*, procedure is performed. Index main term *Control postprocedural bleeding in*, and subterm *Gastrointestinal Tract* list values 0W3P. Go to ICD-10-PCS Table 0W3 to construct code 0W3P3ZZ.

Body systems designated as upper or lower contain body parts that are located above or below the diaphragm, respectively.

  EXAMPLE: The jugular veins are located above the diaphragm (in the neck), and they are assigned values from the *Medical and Surgical* section and *Upper Veins* body system. The saphenous veins are located below the diaphragm (in the legs), and they are assigned values from the *Medical and Surgical* section and *Lower Veins* body system.

Root Operation—General Coding Guidelines

To determine the appropriate root operation, apply the *complete* definition and explanation of the root operation (located in the ICD-10-PCS tables). The root operation is specified in the third character, and in the *Medical and Surgical* section of ICD-10-PCS, there are 31 different root operations. The root operation identifies the objective of the procedure, and each root operation has a precise definition (Table 5-1), which was created specifically for ICD-10-PCS and may differ from those found in medical dictionaries and other resources.

- Components of a procedure that are included in the root operation's definition and explanation are *not* coded separately.

  EXAMPLE: During an *open left knee joint replacement procedure using a synthetic substitute*, the original knee joint was resected. Index main term *Replacement*, subterm *Joint*, second qualifier *Knee*, third qualifier *Left* list values 0SRD. Go to ICD-10-PCS Table 0SR to construct code 0SRD0JZ for the joint replacement procedure *only*. (The resection of the original joint is *not* assigned a separate code.)

- Procedural steps necessary to reach the operative site *and* to close the operative site are *not* coded separately.

  EXAMPLE: A laparotomy is performed to reach the site where an open liver biopsy (diagnostic) is carried out. Index main term *Biopsy* and its subterm provide a cross reference to *—see Excision, Diagnostic*. Index main term *Excision* and subterm *Liver* list values 0FB0. Go to ICD-10-PCS Table 0FB to construct code 0FB00ZX for the open liver biopsy *only*.

  - The Index cross reference for main term *Biopsy* included the term *Diagnostic*, which means seventh qualifier value X is assigned instead of Z.

  - The laparotomy is *not* coded separately.

Table 5-1 Medical and Surgical Section Root Operations and Definitions

Root Operation	Definition
Alteration	Modifying the natural anatomical structure of a body part without affecting the function of the body part
Bypass	Altering the route of passage of the contents of a tubular body part
Change	Taking out or off a device from a body part and putting back an identical or similar device in or on the same body part without cutting or puncturing the skin or a mucous membrane
Control	Stopping, or attempting to stop, postprocedural or other acute bleeding
Creation	Putting in or on biological or synthetic material to form a new body part that to the extent possible replicates the anatomic structure or function of an absent body part
Destruction	Physical eradication of all or a portion of a body part by the direct use of energy, force, or a destructive agent
Detachment	Cutting off all or a portion of the upper or lower extremities
Dilation	Expanding an orifice or the lumen of a tubular body part
Division	Cutting into a body part without draining fluids and gases from the body part in order to separate or transect a body part
Drainage	Taking or letting out fluids and gases from a body part
Excision	Cutting out or off, without replacement, a portion of a body part
Extirpation	Taking or cutting out solid matter from a body part
Extraction	Pulling or stripping out or off all or a portion of a body part by the use of force
Fragmentation	Breaking solid matter in a body part into pieces
Fusion	Joining together portions of an articular body part rendering the articular body part immobile
Insertion	Putting in a nonbiological appliance that monitors, assists, performs, or prevents a physiological function but does not physically take the place of a body part
Inspection	Visually or manually exploring a body part
Map	Locating the route of passage of electrical impulses and locating functional areas in a body part
Occlusion	Completely closing an orifice or lumen of a tubular body part
Reattachment	Putting back in or on all or a portion of a separated body part to its normal location or other suitable location
Release	Freeing a body part from an abnormal physical constraint
Removal	Taking out or off a device from a body part by cutting or by use of force
Repair	Restoring, to the extent possible, a body part to its normal anatomical structure and function
Replacement	Putting in or on biological or synthetic material that physically takes the place and/or function of all or a portion of a body part
Reposition	Moving to its normal location or other suitable location all or a portion of a body part
Resection	Cutting out or off, without replacement, all of a body part
Restriction	Partially closing an orifice or lumen of a tubular body part
Revision	Correcting, to the extent possible, a malfunctioning or displaced device
Supplement	Putting in or on biological or synthetic material that physically reinforces and/or augments the function of a portion of a body part
Transfer	Moving, without taking out, all or a portion of a body part to another location to take over the function of all or a portion of a body part
Transplantation	Putting in or on all or a portion of a living body part taken from another individual or animal to physically take the place and/or function of all or a portion of a similar body part

Root Operation—Multiple Procedures

During the same operative episode, codes are constructed for multiple procedures performed *if* the

- Same root operation (e.g., excision, replacement) is performed on different body parts, as defined by distinct values of the body part axis of classification.

EXAMPLE: Two different ICD-10-PCS codes are constructed for a diagnostic excision (e.g., biopsy) of the liver and of the pancreas.

- Index main term *Biopsy* and its subterm provide a cross reference to —*see Excision, Diagnostic*. Index main term *Excision* and subterm *Liver* list values 0FB0. Go to ICD-10-PCS Table 0FB to construct code 0FB00ZX for the liver biopsy.

- Index main term *Excision* and subterm *Pancreas* list values 0FBG. Return to ICD-10-PCS Table 0FB to construct code 0FBG0ZX for the pancreatic biopsy.

- The Index cross reference for main term *Biopsy* included the term *Diagnostic*, which means seventh qualifier value X is assigned instead of Z.

- Same root operation is repeated at different body sites that are included in the same body part axis of classification.

  EXAMPLE: Two ICD-10-PCS codes are constructed for *biopsy of the right sartorius muscle and right gracilis muscle*, both of which are classified to the *Upper Leg Muscle, Right* body part.

  - Index main term *Biopsy* and its subterm provide a cross reference to —*see Excision, Diagnostic*. Index main term *Excision*, subterm *Muscle*, second qualifier *Upper Leg*, and third qualifier *Right* list values 0KBQ. Go to ICD-10-PCS Table 0KB to construct both codes 0KBQ3ZX (right sartorius muscle) and 0KBQ3ZX (right gracilis muscle).

  - The codes are identical (and both are reported) because the biopsy was performed on two different muscles, which are considered two different body sites within the same *Upper Leg Muscle, Right*, body part axis of classification.

  - The Index cross reference for main term *Biopsy* included the term *Diagnostic*, which means seventh qualifier value X is assigned instead of Z.

 Note:

> Root operations and definitions were created specifically for ICD-10-PCS and may differ from those found in medical dictionaries and other resources.

- Multiple root operations with distinct objectives are performed on the same body part.

  EXAMPLE: Two codes are constructed for *Endoscopic destruction of lesion, sigmoid colon*, and *bypass of sigmoid colon, open*.

  - Index main term *Destruction*, subterm *Colon*, and second qualifier *Sigmoid* list values 0D5N. Go to ICD-10-PCS Table 0D5 to construct code 0D5N8ZZ.

  - Index main term *Bypass*, subterm *Colon*, and second qualifier *Sigmoid* list values 0D1N. Go to ICD-10-PCS Table 0D1 to construct code 0D1N0ZN.

- The intended root operation is attempted using one approach, but it is converted to a different approach.

  EXAMPLE: *Laparoscopic cholecystectomy converted to an open cholecystectomy* is assigned two codes: one for the percutaneous endoscopic *Inspection* root operation and a different code for the open *Resection* root operation.

  - Index main term *Inspection* and subterm *Gallbladder* list values 0FJ4. Go to ICD-10-PCS Table 0FJ to construct code 0FJ44ZZ.

  - Index main term *Resection* and subterm *Gallbladder* list values 0FT4. Go to ICD-10-PCS Tables 0FT to construct code 0FT40ZZ.

Root Operation—Discontinued Procedures

- When the intended procedure is discontinued, code the procedure to the root operation performed.

  EXAMPLE: A planned *total abdominal hysterectomy was discontinued after resecting just the uterus, leaving the ovaries and fallopian tubes intact*, because there was no evidence of dysplasia. Index main term *Hysterectomy* provides a cross reference to —*see Resection, Uterus 0UT9*. Go to ICD-10-PCS Table 0UT to construct code 0UT90ZZ. (If bilateral ovaries and fallopian tubes had also been resected, codes 0UT20ZZ and 0UT70ZZ would also be constructed.)

- When a procedure is discontinued before any other root operation is performed, assign a code to the *Inspection* root operation of the body part or anatomical region inspected.

  EXAMPLE: A planned *aortic valve replacement procedure was discontinued after initial thoracotomy, but before any incision was made into the heart muscle*, due to the patient becoming hemodynamically unstable. Index main term *Inspection* and subterm *Mediastinum* list values 0WJC. Go to ICD-10-PCS Table 0WJ to construct code 0WJC0ZZ.

  - Do not go to Index main term *Thoracotomy* because its cross reference is to —*see Drainage, Anatomical Regions, General 0W9*, which was not the procedure performed.

  - The coding guideline provides direction to locate Index main term *Inspection*, and the subterm is the body part or anatomical region that was inspected.

Root Operation—Biopsy Procedures

Biopsy procedures are coded using the root operations Excision, Extraction, or Drainage and the qualifier Diagnostic.

EXAMPLE 1: Fine needle aspiration biopsy of lung is coded to the root operation Drainage with qualifier Diagnostic.

EXAMPLE 2: Biopsy of bone marrow is coded to the root operation Extraction with qualifier Diagnostic.

EXAMPLE 3: Lymph node sampling for biopsy is coded to the root operation Excision with qualifier Diagnostic.

Root Operation—Biopsy Followed by More Definitive Treatment

If a diagnostic excision, extraction, or drainage procedure (biopsy) is followed by a more definitive procedure (e.g., destruction, excision, resection) *at the same procedure site*, assign separate codes for the biopsy and the more definitive treatment.

EXAMPLE: For *open biopsy of left breast with left partial mastectomy*, assign a code for the biopsy *and* a separate code for the partial mastectomy.

- Index main term *Biopsy* provides a cross reference to —*see Excision, Diagnostic*. Index main term *Excision*, subterm *Breast*, and second qualifier *Left* list values 0HBU. Go to ICD-10-PCS Table 0HB to construct code 0HBU0ZX. (The Index cross reference for main term *Biopsy* included the term *Diagnostic*, which means seventh qualifier value X is assigned instead of Z.)

- Index main term *Mastectomy* provides a cross reference to —*see Resection, Skin and Breast 0HT*. Go to ICD-10-PCS Table 0HT to construct code 0HTU0ZZ.

Root Operation—Overlapping Body Layers

When root operations Excision, Repair, or Inspection are performed on overlapping layers of the musculoskeletal system, the body part specifying the *deepest layer* is coded.

EXAMPLE: For an *open excisional debridement of the skin, subcutaneous tissue, and muscle, left foot*, assign just one code for the procedure performed on the *Muscle* body part (because muscle is the deepest layer). Index main term *Debridement* and subterm *Excisional* include cross reference —*see Excision.* Thus, Index main term *Excision*, subterm *Muscle*, second qualifier *Foot*, and third qualifier *Left* list values 0KBW. Go to ICD-10-PCS Table 0KB to construct code 0KBW0ZZ.

Root Operation—Bypass Procedures

Bypass procedures are coded by identifying the body part bypassed *from* and the body part bypassed *to*.

- The fourth character (body part) specifies the body part bypassed *from.*
- The seventh character qualifier specifies the body part bypassed *to.*

   EXAMPLE: For an *open bypass from stomach to jejunum*, stomach is the body part (fourth character) and jejunum is the qualifier (seventh character). Index main term *Bypass*, subterm *Stomach* list values 0D16. Go to ICD-10-PCS Table 0D1 to construct code 0D160ZA.

Root Operation—Coronary Bypass Procedures

Coronary artery bypass procedures are coded differently than other bypass procedures that are described in the previous guideline. Rather than identifying the body part bypassed from, the *body part identifies the number of coronary arteries bypassed to*, and the *qualifier specifies the vessel bypassed from.*

- The fourth character (body part) value classifies the number of coronary arteries bypassed *to.*
- The seventh character qualifier classifies the vessel bypassed *from.*

 Coding Tip:

> Coronary artery bypass procedures are classified the *opposite* of other bypass procedures (as explained in the above *Root Operation—Bypass Procedures* coding guideline) because the fourth character body part classifies the number of coronary arteries bypassed *to*, and the seventh character qualifier classifies the vessel bypassed *from.*

   EXAMPLE: For an *open aortocoronary artery bypass of left anterior descending coronary artery and obtuse marginal coronary artery, using synthetic substitute for each bypass*, the two coronary arteries are the body part (fourth character) and aorta is the qualifier (seventh character). Index main term *Bypass*, subterm *Artery*, second qualifier *Coronary*, third qualifier *Two Arteries* list values 0211. Go to ICD-10-PCS Table 021 to construct code 02110JW.

When multiple coronary arteries are bypassed, a separate procedure code is assigned for each coronary artery *that uses a different device and/or qualifier.*

   EXAMPLE: For an *open aortocoronary artery bypass and open right internal mammary coronary artery bypass using synthetic substitute for each bypass*, assign two codes because there are different seventh character qualifier values for the aorta and for the right internal mammary artery. Index main term *Bypass*, subterm *Artery*, second qualifier *Coronary*, and third qualifier *One Artery* list values 0210. Go to ICD-10-PCS Table 021 to construct both codes 02100JW and 02100J8. (Index third qualifier *Two Arteries* is *not* used because the seventh character qualifiers differ for each code.)

Root Operation—Control vs. More Definitive Root Operations

Root operation *Control* is defined as *stopping, or attempting to stop, postprocedural or other acute bleeding.* If an attempt to stop postprocedural or other acute bleeding is initially unsuccessful, and the procedure performed to stop the bleeding requires any of the following root operations, the ICD-10-PCS code is constructed using the indicated root operation (instead of the *Control* root operation):

- Bypass
- Detachment
- Excision
- Extraction

- Reposition
- Replacement
- Resection

EXAMPLE: The ICD-10-PCS code for *open splenectomy to stop bleeding* is constructed using the *Medical and Surgical* section, *Lymphatic and Hemic Systems* body system, and *Resection* root operation. Index main term *Splenectomy* contains a subterm cross reference to *—see Resection, Lymphatic and Hemic Systems*, which list values 07T. Go to ICD-10-PCS Table 07T to construct code 07TP0ZZ.

- Although the objective of the procedure was to *stop postprocedural bleeding*, the *Control* root operation is not used because the spleen was resected.

- If surgical cautery or sutures had been performed to stop postprocedural bleeding, the code would have been constructed using the *Control* root operation in the *Anatomical Regions*, *General* body system and *Medical and Surgical* system.

Root Operation—Excision vs. Resection

ICD-10-PCS contains specific body parts for anatomical subdivisions of a body part (e.g., lobes of the lungs or liver, regions of the intestine). The resection of a specific body part is coded whenever all of that body part is cut out or off (instead of coding an excision of a less specific body part).

EXAMPLE: For an *open left upper lung lobectomy*, go to the *Resection* root operation and *Upper Lung Lobe, Left* body part (instead of the *Excision* root operation and *Lung, Left* body part). Index main term *Resection*, subterm *Lung*, second qualifier *Upper Lobe*, and third qualifier *Left* list values 0BTG. Go to ICD-10-PCS Table 0BT to construct code 0BTG0ZZ.

Root Operation—Excision for Graft

When an autograft is obtained from a different body part in order to complete the objective of the procedure, a separate procedure is coded.

EXAMPLE: For an *open aortocoronary bypass with open excision of right greater saphenous vein (for use as aortocoronary bypass graft material)*, the *excision of saphenous vein* is assigned a separate code.

- Index main term *Bypass*, subterm *Artery*, second qualifier *Coronary*, third qualifier *One Site* list values 0210. Go to ICD-10-PCS Table 021 to construct code 021009W.

- Index main term *Excision*, subterm *Vein*, second qualifier *Greater Saphenous*, and third qualifier *Right* list values 06BP. Go to ICD-10-PCS Table 06B to construct code 06BP0ZZ.

Root Operation—Fusion Procedures of the Spine

The body part coded for a *spinal vertebral joint(s) rendered immobile by a spinal fusion procedure* is classified according to the level of the spine (e.g., thoracic). There are distinct body part values for a single vertebral joint and for multiple vertebral joints at each spinal level.

EXAMPLE: Go to ICD-10-PCS Table 0RG, and locate values 1, 2, and 4 for body parts *Cervical Vertebral Joint*, *Cervical Vertebral Joints, 2 or more*, and *Cervicothoracic Vertebral Joint*, respectively.

When multiple vertebral joints are fused, a separate procedure code is assigned for *each vertebral joint that uses a different device and/or qualifier*.

EXAMPLE: *Open fusion of lumbar vertebral joint, posterior approach, anterior column* and *open fusion of lumbar vertebral joint, posterior approach, posterior column* are each assigned separate codes. Index main term *Fusion* and subterm *Lumbar Vertebral* list values 0SG0. Go to ICD-10-PCS Table 0SG to construct codes 0SG00ZJ and 0SG00Z1.

Combinations of devices and materials are often used on a vertebral joint to render the joint immobile. When combinations of devices are used on the *same* vertebral joint, the device value assigned to the procedure code is as follows:

- If an interbody fusion device is used to render the joint immobile (alone or containing other material like bone graft), refer to device value *Interbody Fusion Device*.

EXAMPLE: *Open fusion of two lumbar vertebral joints, posterior approach, posterior column, using a cage style interbody internal fusion device containing morsellized bone graft* is assigned a device value for *Interbody Internal Fusion Device*. Index main term *Fusion*, subterm *Lumbar Vertebral* 0SG0, and second qualifier *2 or more* list values 0SG1. Go to ICD-10-PCS Table 0SG to construct code 0SG10A1.

- If bone graft is the *only* device used to render the joint immobile, refer to device value *Nonautologous Tissue Substitute* or *Autologous Tissue Substitute*.

EXAMPLE: *Open fusion of the right elbow joint using bone graft material from a bone bank* is assigned a device value for *Nonautologous Tissue Substitute*. Index main term *Fusion*, subterm *Elbow*, and second qualifier *Right* list values 0RGL. Go to ICD-10-PCS Table 0RG to construct code 0RGL0KZ.

- If a mixture of autologous and nonautologous bone graft (with or without biological or synthetic extenders or binders) is used to render the joint immobile, refer to device value *Autologous Tissue Substitute*.

EXAMPLE: *Open fusion of the left temporomandibular joint using both autologous bone graft and bone bank bone graft* is assigned a device value for *Autologous Tissue Substitute*. Index main term *Fusion*, subterm *Temporomandibular*, and second qualifier *Left* list values 0RGD. Go to ICD-10-PCS Table 0RG to construct code 0RGD07Z.

Root Operation—Inspection Procedures

Inspection of a body part(s) that is performed to achieve the objective of a procedure is *not* coded separately.

EXAMPLE: For *fiberoptic bronchoscopy with irrigation of bronchus*, code only the *irrigation of bronchus* procedure. Index main term *Irrigation* and subterm *Respiratory Tract, Irrigating Substance* list values 3E1F. Go to ICD-10-PCS Table 3E1 to construct code 3E1F88Z.

- The bronchus is a part of the respiratory tract.

- Do *not* assign code 0BJ08ZZ for the bronchoscopy.

- When *multiple tubular body parts are inspected*, the most distal body part inspected is assigned a body part value.

EXAMPLE: For *cystoureteroscopy with inspection of urethra, urinary bladder and ureters*, code only the inspection of the ureter (ureteroscopy) because it is distal to both the urethra and the urinary bladder. Index main term *Ureteroscopy* lists code 0TJ98ZZ. Go to ICD-10-PCS Table 0TJ to construct code 0TJ98ZZ (to verify its accuracy).

- When *multiple nontubular body parts in a region are inspected*, the body part that specifies the entire area inspected is assigned a body part value.

EXAMPLE: Exploratory laparotomy with percutaneous endoscopic inspection of abdominal contents is assigned the *Peritoneal Cavity* body part value. Index main term *Laparotomy* provides a cross reference for *Exploratory —see Inspection, Peritoneal Cavity* 0WJG. Go to ICD-10-PCS Table 0WJ to construct code 0WJG4ZZ.

- When both an inspection procedure and another procedure are performed on the same body part during the same operative episode, if the inspection procedure is performed using a different approach than the other procedure, the inspection procedure is coded separately.

EXAMPLE: For *percutaneous endoscopic inspection of the duodenum and open biopsy of the duodenum*, two codes are assigned. (The duodenum is part of the lower intestinal tract.)

- Index main term *Inspection*, subterm *Intestinal Tract*, and second qualifier *Lower* list values 0DJD. Go to ICD-10-PCS Table 0DJ to construct code 0DJD4ZZ.

- Index main term *Biopsy* contains a cross reference to *—see Excision, Diagnostic*. Index main term *Excision* and subterm *Duodenum* list values 0DB9. Go to ICD-10-PCS Table 0DB to construct code 0DB90ZX. (The Index cross reference for main term *Biopsy* included the term *Diagnostic*, which means seventh qualifier value X is assigned instead of Z.)

Root Operation—Occlusion vs. Restriction for Vessel Embolization Procedures

- When the objective of an embolization procedure is to completely close a vessel, a value for root operation *Occlusion* is assigned.

    EXAMPLE: *Percutaneous tumor embolization, left axillary artery,* is assigned a value for root operation *Occlusion* because the objective of the procedure is to cut off the blood supply to the vessel. Index main term *Embolization* includes a cross reference to *—see Occlusion*. Index main term *Occlusion*, subterm *Artery*, second qualifier *Axillary,* and third qualifier *Left* list values 03L6. Go to ICD-10-PCS Table 03L to construct code 03L63ZZ.

- When the objective of an embolization procedure is to narrow the lumen of a vessel, a value for root operation *Restriction* is assigned.

    EXAMPLE: *Clipping of right popliteal artery with intraluminal device, open,* is assigned a value for root operation *Restriction* because the objective of the procedure is to narrow the lumen of the vessel at the site of the aneurysm where it is abnormally wide (not to close off the vessel entirely). Index main term *Clipping, Aneurysm* includes a cross reference to *—see Restriction*. Index main term *Restriction*, subterm *Popliteal*, and second qualifier *Right* list values 04VM. Go to ICD-10-PCS Table 04V to construct code 04VM0DZ.

Root Operation—Release Procedures

In root operation *Release*, a value is assigned to the body part being freed, *not* to the tissue being manipulated or cut to free the body part.

    EXAMPLE: *Open lysis of ascending colon adhesions* is assigned a value for the *Ascending Colon* body part. Index main term *Lysis* includes a cross reference to *—see Release*. Index main term *Release*, subterm *Colon*, and second qualifier *Ascending* list values 0DNK. Go to ICD-10-PCS Table 0DN to construct code 0DNK0ZZ.

Root Operation—Release vs. Division

- When the sole objective of the procedure is to free a body part *without cutting into the body part*, a value is assigned to root operation *Release*.

    EXAMPLE: *Freeing of vagus nerve root from surrounding scar tissue via open approach to relieve pain* is coded to root operation *Release*. Index main term *Release*, subterm *Nerve*, and second qualifier *Vagus* list values 00NQ. Go to ICD-10-PCS Table 00N to construct code 00NQ0ZZ.

- When the sole objective of the procedure is to separate or transect a body part, a value is assigned to root operation *Division*.

    EXAMPLE: *Severing a vagus nerve root via open approach* to stop hiccups is coded to the root operation *Division*. Index main term *Division*, subterm *Nerve*, and second qualifier *Vagus* list values 008Q. Go to ICD-10-PCS Table 008 to construct code 008Q0ZZ.

Root Operation—Reposition for Fracture Treatment

The reduction of a displaced fracture is coded to root operation *Reposition*, and the application of a cast or splint in conjunction with the reposition procedure is *not* coded separately. Treatment of a nondisplaced fracture is coded to the procedure performed.

    EXAMPLE 1: *Open insertion of pin as an internal fixation device in a nondisplaced fracture of left fibula* is coded to root operation *Insertion of device in*. Index main term *Insertion of device in*, subterm *Fibula*, second qualifier *Left* list values 0QHK. Go to ICD-10-PCS Table 0QH to construct code 0QHK04Z.

    EXAMPLE 2: *Applying a cast to a nondisplaced right radial fracture* is coded to root operation *Immobilization* in the *Placement* section. Index main term *Casting* includes a cross reference to *—see Immobilization*. Index main term *Immobilization*, subterm *Arm*, second qualifier *Lower,* and third qualifier *Right* list values 2W3CX. Go to ICD-10-PCS Table 2W3 to construct code 2W3CX2Z.

Root Operation—Transplantation vs. Administration

- Inserting a mature and functioning living body part taken from another individual or animal is coded to root operation *Transplantation*.

  EXAMPLE: For *left kidney transplant, allogeneic*, Index main term *Transplantation*, subterm *Kidney*, and second qualifier *Left* list values 0TY10Z. Go to ICD-10-PCS Table 0TY to verify code 0TY10Z0.

- Inserting autologous or nonautologous cells is coded to the *Administration* section (and root operation *Transfusion*).

  EXAMPLE: *Percutaneous autologous bone marrow transplant via central venous line* is coded to the *Administration* section. Index main term *Bone marrow transplant* includes a cross reference to —see *Transfusion*. Index main term *Transfusion*, subterm *Vein*, second qualifier *Central*, and third qualifier *Blood, Whole* list values 3024. Go to ICD-10-PCS Table 302 to construct code 30243G0.

Body Part—General Guidelines

- When a procedure is performed on a portion of a body part that does not have a separate body part value, code the body part value corresponding to the whole body part.

  EXAMPLE: A procedure performed on the alveolar process of the mandible is assigned a value for body part *Mandible*. Index main term *Alveolar process of mandible* includes a cross reference to —use *Mandible, Left* or —use *Mandible, Right*.

- If the prefix *peri* is combined with a body part to identify the site of the procedure, the procedure is coded to the body part named.

  EXAMPLE: A procedure site identified as *perirenal* is assigned a value for the body part *Kidney*.

Body Part—Branches of Body Parts

Where a specific branch of a body part does not have its own body part value in ICD-10-PCS, the body part is typically coded to the closest proximal branch that has a specific body part value. In the cardiovascular body systems, if a general body part is available in the correct root operation table, and coding to a proximal branch would require assigning a code in a different body system, the procedure is coded using the general body part value.

  EXAMPLE: A procedure performed on the *mandibular branch of the trigeminal nerve* is assigned a value for body part *Trigeminal Nerve*.

  EXAMPLE: Occlusion of the bronchial artery is coded to body part value Upper Artery in body system Upper Arteries, *not to body part value Thoracic Aorta, Descending in body system Heart and Great Vessels*.

Body Part—Bilateral Body Part Values

Bilateral body part values are available for a limited number of body parts. If the identical procedure is performed on contralateral body parts, and a bilateral body part value exists for that body part, just one code is assigned using the bilateral body part value. If no bilateral body part value exists, each procedure is assigned a separate code using the appropriate body part value.

  EXAMPLE 1: An identical procedure performed on both fallopian tubes is assigned a value for body part *Fallopian Tube, Bilateral*.

  EXAMPLE 2: An identical procedure performed on both knee joints is assigned two different codes, which means assigning values for body part *Knee Joint, Right* and *Knee Joint, Left* to each code.

Body Part—Coronary Arteries

The coronary arteries are classified as a single body part that is further specified by number of arteries treated. One procedure code specifying multiple arteries is used when the same procedure is performed, including the same device and qualifier values.

  EXAMPLE 1: An angioplasty of two distinct coronary arteries with placement of two stents is assigned a code as *Dilation of Coronary Arteries, Two Arteries, with two Intraluminal Devices*.

EXAMPLE 2: An angioplasty of two distinct coronary arteries, one with stent placement and one without, is assigned two separate codes as *Dilation of Coronary Artery, One Artery with Intraluminal Device*, and *Dilation of Coronary Artery, One Artery with No Device*.

Body Part—Tendons, Ligaments, Bursae, and Fascia Near a Joint

Procedures performed on tendons, ligaments, bursae, and fascia supporting a joint are coded to the body part in the respective body system that is the focus of the procedure. Procedures performed on joint structures themselves are coded to the body part in the joint body systems.

EXAMPLE 1: *Repair of anterior cruciate ligament, left knee* is assigned a value from body part *Knee Bursae and Ligament* in the body system *Bursae and Ligaments*.

EXAMPLE 2: A *knee arthroscopy with shaving of articular cartilage* is assigned a value from body part *Knee Joint* in body system *Lower Joints*.

Body Part—Skin, Subcutaneous Tissue, and Fascia Overlying a Joint

When a procedure is performed on skin, subcutaneous tissue, or fascia overlying a joint, assign a value to body parts as indicated below:

- Shoulder is assigned a value for body part *Upper Arm*.
- Elbow is assigned a value for body part *Lower Arm*.
- Wrist is assigned a value for body part *Lower Arm*.
- Hip is assigned a value for body part *Upper Leg*.
- Knee is assigned a value for body part *Lower Leg*.
- Ankle is assigned a value for body part *Foot*.

Body Part—Fingers and Toes

When a body system does not contain a separate body part value for the fingers, procedures performed on the fingers are assigned value(s) for body part *Hand*. If a body system does not contain a separate body part value for the toes, procedures performed on the toes are assigned value(s) for body part *Foot*.

EXAMPLE: *Excision of finger muscle* is assigned a value for body part *Hand Muscle* in body system *Muscles*.

Body Part—Upper and Lower Intestinal Tract

For gastrointestinal body system, general body part values *Upper Intestinal Tract* and *Lower Intestinal Tract* are provided as an option for the root operations *Change, Inspection, Removal,* and *Revision.* The upper intestinal tract includes the portion of the gastrointestinal tract from the esophagus down to and including the duodenum. The lower intestinal tract includes the portion of the gastrointestinal tract from the jejunum down to and including the rectum and anus.

EXAMPLE: Change of a device in the jejunum is coded as 0D2DXUZ, using body part *lower intestinal tract*.

Approach

The technique used to reach the site of the procedure is called the *approach*, and there are seven different approaches.

- *Open*: Cutting through the skin or mucous membrane and any other body layers necessary to expose the site of the procedure
- *Percutaneous*: Entry, by puncture or minor incision, of instrumentation through the skin or mucous membrane and any other body layers necessary to reach the site of the procedure
- *Percutaneous Endoscopic*: Entry, by puncture or minor incision, of instrumentation through the skin or mucous membrane and any other body layers necessary to reach and visualize the site of the procedure

- *Via Natural or Artificial Opening*: Entry of instrumentation through a natural or artificial external opening to reach the site of the procedure

- *Via Natural or Artificial Opening Endoscopic*: Entry of instrumentation through a natural or artificial external opening to reach and visualize the site of the procedure

- *Via Natural or Artificial Opening Endoscopic with Percutaneous Endoscopic Assistance*: Entry of instrumentation through a natural or artificial external opening to reach and visualize the site of the procedure, and entry, by puncture or minor incision, of instrumentation through the skin or mucous membrane and any other body layers necessary to aid in the performance of the procedure

- *External*: Procedures performed directly on the skin or mucous membrane and procedures performed indirectly by the application of external force through the skin or mucous membrane

An approach also includes the following three components:

- *Access location*: For procedures performed on an internal body part, the access location specifies the external site through which the site of the procedure is reached. There are two general types of access locations.

  - Skin or mucous membranes, which can be cut or punctured to reach the procedure site

  - External openings, which are natural (e.g., mouth) or artificial (e.g., colostomy stoma)

- *Method*: For procedures performed on an internal body part, the method specifies how the external access location is entered, including:

  - Open method, which specifies cutting through skin or mucous membrane and any other intervening body layers necessary to expose the site of the procedure

Note:

Punctures and minor incisions are not considered open approaches because they do not expose the site of the procedure.

  - Instrumentation method, which specifies the entry of instrumentation through an access location (e.g., puncture, minor incision, external opening) to the internal procedure site

- *Type of instrumentation*: For procedures performed on an internal body part, instrumentation refers to specialized equipment used to perform the procedure (e.g., sigmoidoscope)

Approach—Open Approach with Percutaneous Endoscopic Assistance

Procedures performed using the open approach with percutaneous endoscopic assistance are coded to the approach *Open*.

> **EXAMPLE:** *Laparoscopic-assisted sigmoidectomy* is assigned a value for approach *Open*.

Approach—External Approach

- Procedures performed within an orifice on structures that are visible without the aid of any instrumentation are coded to the approach *External*.

  > **EXAMPLE:** *Resection of tonsils* is assigned a value for approach *External*.

- Procedures performed indirectly by the application of external force through the intervening body layers are coded to the approach *External*.

  > **EXAMPLE:** Closed reduction of fracture is assigned a value for approach *External*.

Approach—Percutaneous Procedure via Device

Procedures performed percutaneously via a device placed for the procedure are coded to the approach *Percutaneous*.

> **EXAMPLE:** *Fragmentation of kidney stone performed via percutaneous nephrostomy* is assigned a value for approach *Percutaneous*.

Device

The sixth character device value is assigned for devices that remain after the procedure is completed. There are four general types of devices.

- Biological or synthetic material that takes the place of all or a portion of a body part (e.g., skin grafts and joint prosthesis)

- Biological or synthetic material that assists or prevents a physiological function (e.g., IUD)

- Therapeutic material that is not absorbed by, eliminated by, or incorporated into a body part (e.g., radioactive implant)

- Mechanical or electronic appliances used to assist, monitor, take the place of, or prevent a physiological function (e.g., cardiac pacemaker, orthopedic pins)

Device—General Guidelines

A device value is assigned *only if a device remains after the procedure is completed*. If no device remains, the *No Device* device value is assigned.

Materials such as sutures, ligatures, radiological markers, and temporary postoperative wound drains are considered integral to the performance of a procedure; thus, they are not coded as devices.

Procedures performed on a device only, and not on a body part, are classified to root operations *Change, Irrigation, Removal,* or *Revision*, and they are coded to the procedure performed.

> **EXAMPLE:** *Irrigation of percutaneous nephrostomy tube* is classified to root operation *Irrigation, indwelling device* in the *Administration* section. Index main term *Irrigation*, subterm *Genitourinary Tract, Irrigating Substance* list values 3E1K. Go to ICD-10-PCS Table 3E1 to construct code 3E1K38Z.

Device—Drainage Device

A separate procedure to insert a drainage device is assigned a value for root operation *Drainage* and a value for device *Drainage Device*.

> **EXAMPLE:** *Percutaneous insertion of peritoneal cavity drainage device*. Index main term *Drainage*, subterm *Peritoneal Cavity* list values 0W9G. Go to ICD-10-PCS Table 0W9 to construct code 0W9G30Z.

 Note:

Index main term *Insertion of device in*, subterm *Peritoneal Cavity* list values 0WHG, which directs you to ICD-10-PCS Table 0WH. Table 0WH is not used to construct the code because drainage devices are not classified in the Device column.

Obstetrics Section Coding Guidelines

The Obstetrics section includes two additional root operations.

- *Abortion*: Artificially terminating a pregnancy

- *Delivery*: Assisting the passage of the products of conception from the genital canal

A cesarean section is *not* a separate root operation because the underlying objective is *Extraction* (e.g., pulling out all or a portion of a body part).

Obstetrics Section—Products of Conception

Procedures performed on the products of conception are coded to the *Obstetrics* section. Procedures performed on a pregnant female, other than those performed on the products of conception, are coded to the appropriate root operation in the *Medical and Surgical* section.

> **EXAMPLE 1:** *Amniocentesis* is assigned a value from body part *Products of Conception* in the *Obstetrics* section.

> **EXAMPLE 2:** *Repair of obstetric urethral laceration* is assigned a value from body part *Urethra* in the *Medical and Surgical* section.

Obstetrics Section—Procedures Following Delivery or Abortion

Procedures performed following a delivery or abortion for (1) curettage of the endometrium or (2) evacuation of retained products of conception are coded to the *Obstetrics* section, *Pregnancy* body system, *Extraction* root operation, and *Products of Conception, Retained* body part.

Diagnostic or therapeutic dilation and curettage performed during times *other than* the postpartum or post-abortion period are coded in the *Medical and Surgical* section, *Female Reproductive* body system, *Extraction* root operation, and *Endometrium* body part.

> **EXAMPLE 1:** After delivery of a healthy male term infant, the patient underwent endometrial dilatation and curettage (D & C) to remove retained placenta. D & C code 10D17ZZ is constructed using values from the *Obstetrics* section, *Pregnancy* body system, *Extraction* root operation, and *Products of Conception, Retained* body part.

> **EXAMPLE 2:** A 58-year-old patient underwent diagnostic D & C. Code 0UDB7ZX is constructed using values from the *Medical and Surgical* section, *Female Reproductive* body system, *Extraction* root operation, and *Endometrium* body part.

Placement Section

The Placement section includes seven root operations.

- *Change*: Taking out or off a device from a body part and putting back an identical or similar device in or on the same body part without cutting or puncturing the skin or a mucous membrane

- *Compression*: Putting pressure on a body region

- *Dressing*: Putting material on a body region for protection

- *Immobilization*: Limiting or preventing motion of an external body region

- *Packing*: Putting material in a body region or orifice

- *Removal*: Taking out or off a device from a body part

- *Traction*: Exerting a pulling force on a body region in a distal direction

Administration Section

The Administration section includes three root operations.

- *Introduction*: Putting in or on a therapeutic, diagnostic, nutritional, physiological, or prophylactic substance except blood or blood products

- *Irrigation*: Putting in or on a cleansing substance

- *Transfusion*: Putting in blood or blood products

Measurement and Monitoring Section

The Measurement and Monitoring section includes two root operations.

- *Measurement*: Determining the level of a physiological or physical function at a point in time
- *Monitoring*: Determining the level of a physiological or physical function repetitively over a period of time

Extracorporeal Assistance and Performance Section

The Extracorporeal Assistance and Performance section includes three root operations.

- *Assistance*: Taking over a portion of a physiological function by extracorporeal means
- *Performance*: Completely taking over a physiological function by extracorporeal means
- *Restoration*: Returning, or attempting to return, a physiological function to its natural state by extracorporeal means; this root operation contains a single procedure code that identifies *extracorporeal cardioversion*

Extracorporeal Therapies Section

The Extracorporeal Therapies section includes 11 root operations.

- *Atmospheric Control*: Extracorporeal control of atmospheric pressure and composition
- *Decompression*: Extracorporeal elimination of undissolved gas from body fluids; this root operation involves just one type of procedure, *treatment for decompression sickness* (or *the bends*) in a hyperbaric chamber
- *Electromagnetic Therapy*: Extracorporeal treatment by electromagnetic rays
- *Hyperthermia*: Extracorporeal raising of body temperature; *hyperthermia* describes both a temperature imbalance treatment and an adjunct radiation treatment for cancer. For temperature imbalance treatment, assign a code from the Extracorporeal Therapy section; for adjunct radiation treatment, assign a code from the Radiation Therapy section.
- *Hypothermia*: Extracorporeal lowering of body temperature
- *Perfusion*: extracorporeal treatment by diffusion of therapeutic fluid
- *Pheresis*: Extracorporeal separation of blood products; *pheresis has* two main purposes: the treatment of diseases when too much of a blood component is produced (e.g., leukemia) and the removal of a blood product (e.g., platelets) from a donor for transfusion into another patient.
- *Phototherapy*: Extracorporeal treatment by light rays; *phototherapy* involves using a machine that exposes blood to light rays outside the body, recirculates it, and then returns it to the body.
- *Shock Wave Therapy*: Extracorporeal treatment by shock waves
- *Ultrasound Therapy*: Extracorporeal treatment by ultrasound
- *Ultraviolet Light Therapy*: Extracorporeal treatment by ultraviolet light

Osteopathic Section

The Osteopathic section includes just one root operation, *treatment,* which is the manual treatment to eliminate or alleviate somatic dysfunction and related disorders.

Other Procedures Section

The Other Procedures section has just one root operation, *other procedures,* which are methodologies that attempt to remediate or cure a disorder or disease.

Chiropractic Section

The Chiropractic section has just one root operation, *manipulation*, which is a manual procedure that involves a directed thrust to move a joint past the physiological range of motion, without exceeding the anatomical limit.

Imaging Section

The Imaging section includes five root types.

- *Computerized Tomography (CT Scan)*: Computer-reformatted digital display of multiplanar images developed from the capture of multiple exposures of external ionizing radiation

- *Fluoroscopy*: Single plane or bi-plane real-time display of an image developed from the capture of external ionizing radiation on fluorescent screen. The image may also be stored by either digital or analog means.

- *Magnetic Resonance Imaging (MRI)*: Computer reformatted digital display of multiplanar images developed from the capture of radiofrequency signals emitted by nuclei in a body site excited within a magnetic field

- *Plain Radiography*: Planar display of an image developed from the capture of external ionizing radiation on photographic or photoconductive plate

- *Ultrasonography*: Real-time display of images of anatomy or flow information developed from the capture of reflected and attenuated high-frequency sound waves

Nuclear Medicine Section

The Nuclear Medicine section includes seven root types.

- *Nonimaging Uptake*: Introduction of radioactive materials into the body for measurements of organ function, from the detection of radioactive emissions

- *Nonimaging Nuclear Medicine Probe*: Introduction of radioactive materials into the body for the study of distribution and fate of certain substances by the detection of radioactive emissions; alternatively, measurement of absorption of radioactive emissions from an external source

- *Nonimaging Assay*: Introduction of radioactive materials into the body for the study of body fluids and blood elements, by the detection of radioactive emissions

- *Planar Nuclear Medicine Imaging*: Introduction of radioactive materials into the body for single-plane display of images developed from the capture of radioactive emissions

- *Positron Emission Tomography (PET) Imaging*: Introduction of radioactive materials into the body for three-dimensional display of images developed from the simultaneous capture, 180 degrees apart, of radioactive emissions

- *Systemic Nuclear Medicine Therapy*: Introduction of unsealed radioactive materials into the body for treatment

- *Tomographic (Tomo) Nuclear Medicine Imaging*: Introduction of radioactive materials into the body for three dimensional display of images developed from the capture of radioactive emissions

Radiation Therapy Section

The Radiation Therapy section includes the following modalities: beam radiation, brachytherapy, stereotactic radiosurgery, and other radiation.

Physical Rehabilitation and Diagnostic Audiology Section

The Physical Rehabilitation and Diagnostic Audiology section includes the following root types.

- *Activities of Daily Living Assessment*: measurement of functional level for activities of daily living

- *Activities of Daily Living Treatment*: exercise or activities to facilitate functional competence for activities of daily living

- *Caregiver Training*: Educating caregiver with the skills and knowledge used to interact with and assist the patient

- *Cochlear Implant Treatment*: application of techniques to improve the communication abilities of individuals with cochlear implant

- *Device Fitting*: fitting of a device designed to facilitate or support achievement of a higher level of function

- *Hearing Aid Assessment*: measurement of the appropriateness and/or effectiveness of a hearing device

- *Hearing Assessment*: measurement of hearing and related functions

- *Hearing Treatment*: application of techniques to improve, augment, or compensate for hearing and related functional impairment

- *Motor and/or Nerve Function Assessment*: measurement of motor, nerve, and related functions

- *Motor Treatment*: Exercise or activities to increase or facilitate motor function

- *Speech Assessment*: measurement of speech and related functions

- *Speech Treatment*: application of techniques to improve, augment, or compensate for speech and related functional impairment

- *Treatment*: Use of specific activities or methods to develop, improve, and restore the performance of necessary functions, compensate for dysfunction, and minimize debilitation

- *Vestibular Assessment*: measurement of the vestibular system and related functions

- *Vestibular Treatment*: application of techniques to improve, augment, or compensate for vestibular and related functional impairment

Mental Health Section

The Mental Health section includes the following mental health procedures and services:

- *Biofeedback*: provision of information from the monitoring and regulating of physiological processes in conjunction with cognitive-behavioral techniques to improve patient functioning or well-being

- *Counseling*: application of psychological methods to treat an individual with normal developmental issues and psychological problems in order to increase function, improve well being, alleviate distress, maladjustment or resolve crises

- *Crisis Intervention*: treatment of a traumatized, acutely disturbed or distressed individual for the purpose of short-term stabilization

- *Electroconvulsive Therapy*: application of controlled electrical voltages to treat a mental health disorder

- *Family Psychotherapy*: treatment that includes one or more family members of an individual with a mental health disorder by behavioral, cognitive, psychoanalytic, psychodynamic or psychophysiological means to improve functioning or well-being

- *Group Psychotherapy*: treatment of two or more individuals with a mental health disorder by behavioral, cognitive, psychoanalytic, psychodynamic or psychophysiological means to improve functioning or well-being

- *Hypnosis*: induction of a state of heightened suggestibility by auditory, visual and tactile techniques to elicit an emotional or behavioral response

- *Individual Psychotherapy*: treatment of an individual with a mental health disorder by behavioral, cognitive, psychoanalytic, psychodynamic or psychophysiological means to improve functioning or well-being

- *Light Therapy*: application of specialized light treatments to improve functioning or well-being

- *Medication Management*: monitoring and adjusting the use of medications for the treatment of a mental health disorder

- *Narcosynthesis:* administration of intravenous barbiturates in order to release suppressed or repressed thoughts

- *Psychological Tests:* administration and interpretation of standardized psychological tests and measurement instruments for the assessment of psychological function

Substance Abuse Treatment Section

The Substance Abuse Treatment section includes seven root types.

- *Detoxification Services*: Not a treatment modality but helps the patient stabilize physically and psychologically until the body becomes free of drugs and the effects of alcohol

- *Individual Counseling*: Comprising several techniques, which apply various strategies to address drug addiction

- *Group Counseling*: Provides structured group counseling sessions and healing power through the connection with others

- *Family Counseling*: Provides support and education for family members of addicted individuals. Family member participation is seen as critical to substance abuse treatment.

- *Individual Psychotherapy*: Includes behavior, cognitive/behavioral, cognitive, interactive, interpersonal, psychoanalysis, psychodynamic, psychophysiological, and supportive types

- *Medication Management*: Management of prescription drug dosages through laboratory testing and other evaluation and management services

- *Pharmacotherapy*: Management of mental disorders using pharmacological agents

New Technology

ICD-10-PCS Section X contains stand alone codes to uniquely identify procedures that are requested as a result of the New Technology Application Process or that capture services not routinely captured in ICD-10-PCS. (Codes are created to maintain continuity with the other sections in ICD-10-PCS to the extent possible.)

Section X codes use the same root operation values as their closest counterparts in other sections of ICD-10-PCS. Section X codes classify technologies that are not usually captured by coders or that do not usually have the desired specificity within the current ICD-10-PCS structure required for new technology approval. Root operations include assistance, extirpation, fusion, introduction, monitoring, replacement, and reposition.

(Codes for new technologies that are consistent with current ICD-10-PCS codes may also be created within the current ICD-10-PCS structure.)

The structure of ICD-10-PCS Section X codes includes:

- First character – letter X

- Second character – body system/region value

- Third character – root operation value

- Fourth character – body part value

- Fifth character – approach value

- Sixth character – device/substance/technology value
- Seventh character – information indicating the year created

The structure of ICD-10-PCS Section X codes is consistent with the general architecture of ICD-10-PCS, and each of the seven characters has a consistent definition within the section. The third, fourth, and fifth characters specify the root operation, body part, and approach, respectively, because that is the type of information defined in those characters for the majority of the ICD-10-PCS sections.

As part of the Section X Code transition to ICD-10-PCS, after Section X codes have served their purpose, proposals to delete the codes and create new codes in the existing ICD-10-PCS tables will be addressed at ICD-10 Coordination and Maintenance meetings.

Section X codes are standalone codes, they are not supplemental codes, and they fully represent the specific procedure described in the code title. No additional codes from other sections of ICD-10-PCS are needed. When section X contains a code title that describes a specific new technology procedure, only that X code is reported for the procedure; do not also report a broader, non-specific code from another section of ICD-10-PCS.

EXAMPLE: Ceftazidime-Avibactam anti-infective was administered via a central vein. ICD-10-PCS code XW04321 (Introduction of Ceftazidime Avibactam Anti-infective into Central Vein, Percutaneous Approach, New Technology Group 1) is reported. A separate code from ICD-10-PCS Table 3E0 in the Administration section is *not* coded.

Exercise 5.4 – ICD-10-PCS Procedure Coding

Instructions: Underline the main term in each procedure statement and construct the appropriate ICD-10-PCS procedure code(s).

_____ 1. Bilateral augmentation mammoplasty using synthetic substitute, open approach

_____ 2. Percutaneous biopsy of spleen

_____ 3. Injection of neurolytic agent (nerve block) into peripheral nerve

_____ 4. Laparoscopic oophorectomy, left

_____ 5. Open stripping of varicose veins, left lesser saphenous vein

_____ 6. Open biopsy of prostate

_____ 7. Esophagoscopy

_____ 8. Parathyroidectomy, complete, via open approach

_____ 9. Partial breech extraction with high forceps

_____ 10. Partial left hip joint replacement, synthetic substitute

_____ 11. Percutaneous nephrostomy with fragmentation of stone in right kidney pelvis

_____ 12. Drainage of bilateral ethmoid sinuses for aspiration

_____ 13. Replacement of cardiac resynchronization defibrillator pulse generator device, heart, open approach

_____ 14. Repair of pterygium of conjunctiva, left eye

_____ 15. Left tympanoplasty (via natural opening)

Exercise 5.5 – Coding Inpatient Diagnoses and Procedures

Instructions: Review each case scenario, and assign and properly sequence the ICD-10-CM diagnosis and ICD-10-PCS procedure codes.

Note:

> Do not assign procedure codes to ancillary tests (e.g., laboratory tests, x-rays) because they do not impact DRG assignment or the reimbursement amount for an inpatient case. (Some hospitals do assign codes to ancillary tests even though doing so does not impact the level of reimbursement received; therefore, you should be aware of this practice.)

1. Patient admitted for treatment of AIDS-related conditions and underwent diagnostic fiberoptic bronchoscopy with cell washings for specimen collection. Final diagnoses included AIDS-related *Pneumocystis jiroveci* and oral candidiasis.

   _____

2. Patient admitted with slurred speech and weakness on the right side. Patient is right-handed. CT scan reveals left carotid artery occlusion with cerebral infarction. Patient discharged to inpatient rehabilitation facility for continued treatment of dysphasia and right hemiparesis.

   _____

3. Patient was seen during an initial encounter after having sustained a closed fracture of the distal radius, left, due to a fall from the roof of his single-family house while cleaning gutters. X-ray of the left lower arm revealed nondisplaced fracture of distal radius with fracture fragments in good alignment. The physician determined that reduction was unnecessary, and a plaster splint was applied as a stabilizing device.

   _____

4. Patient admitted for treatment of diabetic toe (skin) ulcer, left, with gangrene of the bone. The underlying cause was type 1 diabetic peripheral neuropathy with long-term insulin use. Patient underwent a complete left foot amputation.

   _____

5. Patient admitted following repeated temporal lobe seizures. History revealed that the patient had had 18 seizures within the past 24 hours. He has had seizures since the age of 16, previously well controlled with long-term use of phenobarbital. Blood levels indicate an acceptable therapeutic level. During hospitalization, patient continued to seize at least hourly. Patient was immediately transferred to the neurology unit of tertiary care hospital due to localization-related intractable epilepsy with complex partial seizures.

   _____

Summary

Inpatient health care settings include acute care facilities (hospitals), behavioral health care facilities, hospice inpatient care, and long-term acute care hospitals (LTACHs). The circumstances of inpatient admission always govern sequencing of diagnoses for DRG purposes. Upon implementation of MS-DRGs, CMS eliminated the requirement to sequence principal and secondary procedures. However, third-party payers might still require this practice. Uniform Hospital Discharge Data Set (UHDDS) definitions have always been used by acute care hospitals to report inpatient data elements in a standardized manner. Since the creation of the UHDDS in 1985, the application of the UHDDS definitions has been expanded to include all nonoutpatient settings (e.g., acute, short-term, long-term, and behavioral health care facilities; home health agencies; rehabilitation facilities; and skilled nursing facilities and nursing homes). (Content about home health, hospice, and skilled nursing facility care can be found on the Student Companion Web Site at *www.cengagebrain.com*.)

CMS publishes official ICD-10-CM and ICD-10-PCS guidelines for coding and reporting, which provide direction about assignment of diagnosis and procedure codes and the sequencing of diagnosis codes for reimbursement purposes. Depending on state reporting requirements, when the circumstances of inpatient admission govern the sequencing of procedure codes, UHDDS definitions are used to report inpatient data elements in a standardized manner. Circumstances associated with an inpatient admission govern the sequencing of principal procedure and significant other procedures (or secondary procedures).

Internet Links

HCPro, Inc.: Go to *www.hcmarketplace.com*, and click on the "Sign up for our FREE e-Newsletters" link. Click on the box located in front of the *JustCoding News: Inpatient* (along with other e-Newsletters that interest you) and fill out your name and contact information to subscribe.

NYS DOH SPARCS: Go to *www.health.ny.gov*, click on the Search link, and enter SPARCS in the search box to locate information about the Statewide Planning and Research Cooperative System (SPARCS).

Virtual Pediatric Hospital: *www.virtualpediatrichospital.org*

Study Checklist

❏ Read this chapter and highlight key concepts.

❏ Create an index card for each key term.

❏ Access the chapter Internet links to learn more about concepts.

❏ Complete the chapter exercises and review, verifying answers with your instructor.

❏ Complete the Workbook chapter, verifying answers with your instructor.

❏ Go to *www.cengagebrain.com* to access the Student Companion Web Site. Login instructions are located in the Preface.

❏ Form a study group with classmates to discuss chapter concepts in preparation for an exam.

Review

Multiple Choice

Instructions: Circle the most appropriate response.

1. Fever of unknown origin. Rule out tuberculosis. (Final diagnosis at time of inpatient hospital discharge.)
   a. A15.0   b. R50.9   c. R50.9, A15.0   d. Z03.89

2. Primary pancreatic cancer.
   a. C25.1   b. C25.9   c. C77.2   d. C79.89

3. Graves disease with thyrotoxic crisis.
   - a. E05.01
   - b. E05.09
   - c. E05.00, E05.91
   - d. E05.00

4. Acute posthemorrhagic anemia.
   - a. D50.0
   - b. D61.9
   - c. D62
   - d. D64.9, R58

5. Anorexia nervosa.
   - a. F50.00
   - b. F50.9
   - c. R63.0
   - d. R63.3

6. Percutaneous myringotomy with placement of tube in right tympanic membrane.
   - a. 099700Z
   - b. 099730Z
   - c. 099740Z
   - d. 099770Z

7. Hypertensive heart disease with CHF. Old anterior wall MI, diagnosed on EKG (currently presenting no symptoms).
   - a. I50.9, I10
   - b. I11.0, I50.9, I25.2
   - c. I10, I11.9, I50.9
   - d. I50.9, I10, I25.2

8. Diagnostic lingula bronchial drainage via endoscopy.
   - a. 0BJ08ZZ
   - b. 0B998ZX
   - c. 3E1L38Z
   - d. 3E1F88Z

9. Repair of direct inguinal hernia, right side, via percutaneous endoscopic approach.
   - a. 0YQ50ZZ
   - b. 0YQ53ZZ
   - c. 0YQ54ZZ
   - d. 0YQ64ZZ

10. Extracorporeal shock wave lithotripsy of the right kidney pelvis (external approach).
    - a. 0TF3XZZ
    - b. 0TF6XZZ
    - c. 0TFDXZZ
    - d. 0WFRXZZ

11. Classical cesarean section by hysterotomy.
    - a. 10207YZ
    - b. 10900ZC
    - c. 10A00ZZ
    - d. 10D00Z0

12. Excision of pilonidal abscess.
    - a. 0H98X0Z
    - b. 0H90X0Z
    - c. 0HB8XZZ
    - d. 0HC0XZZ

13. Open temporomandibular joint (TMJ) repair, right.
    - a. 0RQC0ZZ
    - b. 0MM00ZZ
    - c. 0C00X7Z
    - d. 0KQ00ZZ

14. Congenital hydrocephalus.
    - a. G91.0
    - b. G91.9
    - c. Q03.8
    - d. Q03.9

15. Transurethral cystoscopy for control of postoperative hemorrhage of bladder.
    - a. 0TJB8ZZ
    - b. 0W3R0ZZ
    - c. 0W3R8ZZ
    - d. 0WWR4YZ

16. Respiratory distress syndrome of newborn.
    - a. J80
    - b. P22.0
    - c. P27.8
    - d. P28.81

17. Stab wound (from knife) of thoracic aorta, repaired with synthetic graft.
    - a. S21.109A, X99.9xxA, 02UP0JZ
    - b. S31.000A, X99.9xxA, 02UW0KZ
    - c. S25.00xA, X99.1xxA, 02UW0JZ
    - d. S29.001A, X99.8xxA, 02UJ0JZ

18. Partial splenectomy.
    - a. 009F0ZX
    - b. 075P0ZZ
    - c. 07BP0ZZ
    - d. 07TP0ZZ

19. Needle biopsy of cerebral meninges.
    - a. 00B13ZX
    - b. 00B13ZZ
    - c. 00C13ZZ
    - d. 00D13ZZ

20. Complete substernal thyroidectomy.
    - a. 0GBG0ZX, 0GBH0ZX
    - b. 0GBH0ZZ
    - c. 0GPKX0Z
    - d. 0GTK0ZZ

Coding Practice—Hospital Inpatient Cases

Instructions: Review each case scenario, and assign and properly sequence the ICD-10-CM diagnosis and ICD-10-PCS procedure codes. (Adobe.pdf files of the ICD-10-CM and ICD-10-PCS coding manuals can be found at *www.cms.gov*.)

1. A 70-year-old female presented to the hospital with fever, myalgia, arthralgia, tachycardia, and dehydration and was believed to be septic. This patient has a history of hypertension, CHF, and migraines. Routine medications include Lasix 40 milligrams by mouth each morning, if needed, for significant pedal edema and Isordil 20 milligrams by mouth four times a day.

   A variety of studies were obtained to further delineate the source of her problem. Urine cultures were negative. Blood cultures grew *Escherichia coli*. The blood urea nitrogen level was 22, and a random glucose was 149. An anterior-posterior film of the chest taken at the same time showed acute pulmonary edema.

   The patient received intravenous fluids. The patient's routine medications were continued, and she received intravenous antibiotics. On the fourth day of her hospital stay, it was believed that the patient had reached maximal hospital benefit and was therefore switched to oral antibiotics and was discharged. The patient left the hospital in good condition.

   DISCHARGE DIAGNOSES: Septicemia. Dehydration. Positive blood culture, *Escherichia coli*. Acute pulmonary edema due to CHF. Hypertensive heart disease.

2. A 2-year-old male presented with fever, vomiting, and abdominal pain. The patient was severely dehydrated with a blood urea nitrogen level of 54, indicating acute renal failure. Blood cultures obtained grew *Staphylococcus aureus*. The patient was treated with a 10-day course of intravenous vancomycin. The patient also received intravenous fluids and had improved renal function. Upon admission, the patient was noted to have a rash on his buttocks and was treated with topical ointment. The patient improved and was discharged.

   DISCHARGE DIAGNOSES: Septic shock. Acute renal failure, secondary to *Staphylococcus aureus* septicemia. Diaper rash. Dehydration.

3. A 70-year-old white female with pancreatic head carcinoma, confirmed by previous percutaneous fine-needle aspiration and determined to be unresectable. The patient was also found to have probable metastasis to the lower lobe of the left lung, and she was admitted now for resection of the lower lobe of the left lung. The patient had a history of hypothyroidism and diet-controlled diabetes.

   During hospitalization, the patient was continued on Levoxyl, and a "no-concentrated-sweets diet" was ordered. The patient was taken to the operative suite, where a partial left lower lobe lung resection was performed. Pathology from this procedure revealed adenocarcinoma. The patient had an uneventful postoperative course and was discharged with an appointment to see the oncologist to discuss radiation and chemotherapy options.

   DISCHARGE DIAGNOSES: Pancreatic adenocarcinoma metastatic to left lung. Hypothyroidism. Diet-controlled type 2 diabetes mellitus.

   PROCEDURE: Left lower lung lobe resection (open).

4. A 94-year-old male was admitted to the hospital with a chief complaint of abdominal pain and loss of weight. The patient had a history of coronary artery disease and myocardial infarction. There is no history of coronary bypass surgery. The patient had a nebulizer at home and takes metoprolol.

These medications were continued during the patient's stay. Physical examination revealed abdomen to be tender to palpation in the left mid and lower quadrants with some rebound. Bowel sounds were present, and there was no guarding. Blood pressure was normal. Pulse, respirations, and temperature were normal.

During hospitalization, EKG showed sinus rhythm with myocardial changes of ischemia. Sputum cytology was suggestive of adenocarcinoma, compatible with bronchoalveolar growth. Chest x-ray showed metastatic lesions and chronic obstructive lung disease in both lung fields. Barium enema showed adenocarcinoma of proximal sigmoid colon. Abdominal series showed no evidence of obstruction, but moderate dilation of his transverse colon was evident. Patient was seen in consultation, and it was decided to do as little as possible at this time due to the patient's age and lung conditions. The patient agreed with this approach and requested discharge to home to receive hospice care.

DISCHARGE DIAGNOSES: Carcinoma of sigmoid colon. Probable metastatic bronchogenic carcinoma. End-stage chronic obstructive lung disease. Coronary artery disease. Previous myocardial infarction.

---

5. After outpatient treatment was unsuccessful, a 62-year-old white female was admitted to the hospital for metatarsal amputation due to diabetic gangrene of the left foot. The patient had a 10-year history of type 2 diabetes mellitus, and her blood sugars had been controlled with Actos. Wound culture and sensitivity testing revealed *Pseudomonas aeruginosa* and *Escherichia coli*. The patient was treated with wide-spectrum antibiotics prior to surgery. On the fourth hospital day, the patient was taken to the operative suite and underwent complete amputation of the left great toe. The patient healed slowly and was discharged to home care.

DISCHARGE DIAGNOSIS: Type 2 diabetic peripheral angiopathy with gangrene, left great toe. Bacterial infection was due to *Pseudomonas aeruginosa* and *Escherichia coli*.

PROCEDURE: Complete amputation, metatarsal, left great toe.

---

6. This patient is a 43-year-old female with a long history of joint pain. Lately she had been feeling very tired and weak. She also has had intermittent abdominal pain with nausea and vomiting. Her joint exam showed tenderness of the knees. She denied any problems suggestive of hypothyroidism (myxedema). The patient's hematocrit was 27.6, serum iron was found to be decreased at 27, and thyroid functions were found to be markedly low. Upper GI series showed a 4-millimeter ulcer at the posterior wall of the duodenal bulb. The patient was transfused 2 units of packed red cells. She was started on ferrous sulfate 300 milligrams twice a day. She was also begun on Tagamet for the ulcer. Further questioning revealed that she had indeed been hypothyroid in the past and has been on thyroid medication until stopped by another physician. The patient was restarted on Synthroid 0.2 milligrams per day. She was discharged on the sixth hospital day.

DISCHARGE DIAGNOSES: Anemia due to myxedema. Acute duodenal ulcer.

---

7. This patient is a 14-year-old African American male who was admitted due to sickle cell crisis and acute chest syndrome. His mother has sickle cell anemia, and his father has the sickle cell trait. Because of this, the patient was tested at birth; a blood sample was drawn, and it was sent to the laboratory for hemoglobin electrophoresis to obtain a definitive diagnosis. Unfortunately, the test was positive for sickle cell disease. The patient was given intravenous fluids and was started on Darvocet for pain management. When the Darvocet failed to keep his pain at an acceptable level, he was switched to Vicodin. The patient is to be discharged with follow-up in the pediatrician's office tomorrow.

DISCHARGE DIAGNOSES: Sickle cell disease with crisis and acute chest syndrome.

---

8. This unfortunate 34-year-old woman was diagnosed 6 months ago with breast cancer. At the time of diagnosis, she was also found to have metastases to the bone and the liver. Her oncologist has recommended that she undergo intensive chemotherapy before she has surgery to remove her breast tumor and liver tumor. She is currently undergoing this chemotherapy on an outpatient basis. She presented to the hospital with extreme fatigue. She stated that she feels light-headed and just generally does not feel well. Her blood work revealed her to have a hematocrit of 27.5, and her anemia is apparently due to her neoplastic disease. She received 4 units of packed red blood cells, and her hematocrit improved. At the time of discharge, hematocrit is 32.3; the patient is discharged in improved condition. She is to follow up with her oncologist to determine if she needs to start undergoing Epogen injections.

    DISCHARGE DIAGNOSES: Anemia in neoplastic disease. Carcinoma of the right breast with metastases to bone and liver.

9. A 31-year-old white male presented to the emergency room reportedly having taken 8 to 10 naproxen at home in a suicide attempt. He reported that he had been having trouble with his girlfriend, and he is unemployed. He had apparently become despondent over this and attempted to take his own life with his girlfriend's pills. The patient is admitted to the telemetry unit due to paroxysmal ventricular tachycardia. The patient was started on metaraminol for the tachycardia. Fortunately, the patient seemed to sustain no other ill effects from the naproxen. The mental health service was consulted, and an appointment was made for outpatient services. He was given Prozac to treat his depression. At this time, the patient does not appear to be a threat to himself or to others. He appears remorseful and denies any suicidal ideations. He was discharged in good condition.

    DISCHARGE DIAGNOSES: Suicide attempt with naproxen. Paroxysmal ventricular tachycardia. Depression.

10. A 52-year-old male bus driver is admitted to receive a course of electroconvulsive therapy for his depressive symptomatology. This patient was seen approximately one year ago in consultation; at that time, he was showing early evidence of involutional psychotic reaction. He has had several admissions since that time, and on each occasion, he had been drinking excessively. It appears that he attempts to use alcohol as a tranquilizer. During the first two days of his admission, he continued to show marked depressive symptomatology and he was started on electroconvulsive therapy. After treatment, he showed a mitigation of his depressive symptomatology. He was discharged home on Pertofrane 25 milligrams twice a day and was instructed to call for follow-up care. Condition on discharge was improved.

    DISCHARGE DIAGNOSIS: Moderate involutional psychotic reaction, recurrent.

11. A 71-year-old male presented to the hospital with the chief complaint of increasing confusion. The patient has been wandering away from home and has displayed aggressive behavior to his family members. The patient is a known type 2 diabetic and is on Orinase 0.5 milligrams daily. He also uses an albuterol inhaler, two puffs, twice daily. The patient is thin and emaciated and has diminished breath sounds. During his period of hospitalization, the patient was uncooperative in all aspects. He refused food and medications. He was confused and seemed slightly paranoid. The family was consulted about the patient's worsening dementia, and the decision was made to transfer the patient to the state psychiatric hospital for care. The patient was transferred on the fifth hospital day.

    DISCHARGE DIAGNOSES: Alzheimer's disease with senile dementia and increasing confusion. Emphysema. Type 2 diabetes mellitus, controlled.

12. An 84-year-old female was admitted to the hospital because of severe dizziness and weakness. The patient has had previous brain stem transient ischemic attacks and also has completed radiation for what was assumed to be cancer of the endometrium. The patient is currently receiving short-term chemotherapy for the endometrial carcinoma on an outpatient basis, and she was administered her chemotherapy during this inpatient stay. The patient had 3+ hyperreflexia and rotary nystagmus on admission. The urinalysis showed white blood cells and bacteria. Her urine culture grew *Klebsiella pneumoniae*. The patient was started on Velosef. Over the next several days, the dizziness cleared, but the patient continued to be quite weak. Gait training physical therapy was started, and she was eventually able to walk with her walker without assistance. Her reflexia had come back down to 1+, which is her usual state. The patient had no more nystagmus and was switched from heparin to Persantine. The patient was discharged home and was to be seen as an outpatient in one month.

    DISCHARGE DIAGNOSES: Brain stem transient ischemic attack. Endometrial carcinoma. UTI due to *Klebsiella pneumoniae*.

13. This patient is a practical nurse who presented to the hospital because her blood pressure was 240/140 at home. Her blood pressure at admission was 220/120. This patient has had multiple strokes, and her first stroke was 5 years ago. This patient has a history of hypertension and paroxysmal atrial fibrillation. She was started on intravenous Aldomet, Dyazide, Catapres, and Lanoxin. Her blood pressure lowered to 190/98. On admission, her radial, brachial, popliteal, and femoral pulses were 2–4. The next day, the femoral pulse was decreased to 1–4, and the posterior tibial pulses were not palpable. The leg on the left side was clammy and cold. There was minimal cyanosis over the heel of the left foot. Possible femoral and popliteal artery embolism had to be ruled out, and it was decided to transfer the patient.

    DISCHARGE DIAGNOSES: Hypertensive crisis. Possible bilateral iliofemoral emboli. Multiple previous CVAs resulting in hemiplegia on the nondominant left side and aphasia. Paroxysmal atrial fibrillation.

14. A 47-year-old male corrections officer presented to the emergency room with an acute onset of chest pain. The pain was described as a crushing pain and was accompanied with radiation of the pain into the jaw and diaphoresis. He does not have a history of previous myocardial infarction (MI). His risk factors include morbid obesity, hypertension, and hypercholesterolemia. The patient takes metoprolol and Lipitor. The cardiologist was consulted, and the patient was found to have an acute ST elevation anterior wall MI. The patient was admitted to the intensive care unit and was observed on telemetry. On the second day of hospitalization, the patient was thought to be stable for transfer. The patient was transferred for coronary angiography and possible angioplasty.

    DISCHARGE DIAGNOSES: Acute ST elevation anterior wall MI. Hypertension. Hypercholesterolemia. Morbid obesity.

15. A 16-month-old infant was admitted from the emergency room because of nausea and vomiting and some cough. She was felt to have acute bronchitis due to respiratory syncytial virus (RSV) with possible pneumonia. This child was hospitalized previously with meningitis but has had no other serious illnesses until the present time. She has no prior history of diabetes or tuberculosis. Her parents are alive and well. The physical examination revealed generalized sibilant rales. The patient's chest x-ray was normal. Pneumonia was ruled out. Her urinalysis was normal. Her hematocrit was 34. The low hematocrit was thought to be due to the persistent vomiting and lack of iron intake from her diet. The patient was given penicillin and Phenergan injections. She was also given nebulizer treatments every 6 hours on an as-needed basis. The patient was started on clear liquids, and she progressed to a general diet. After the first few days, the vomiting ceased. She was discharged with prescriptions for ferrous gluconate, ampicillin, and Phenergan.

DISCHARGE DIAGNOSES: Acute bronchitis due to RSV. Nutritional anemia due to inadequate dietary iron intake. Nausea and vomiting.

---

16. The patient is a 77-year-old male admitted to the hospital due to shortness of breath and progressive chest pain. The patient has had evidence of acute bronchitis with discolored sputum for 5 days and, despite antibiotics, was not improving. With this, he developed an increasing need for nitroglycerin. During his hospitalization, the patient was treated with intravenous antibiotics, steroids, theophylline, and hand-held nebulizer with Alupent. The patient improved with the cough clearing nicely. Unfortunately, several days prior to discharge, he developed severe precordial chest pain typical of his angina. This required three nitroglycerin plus morphine to stop the pain. The EKG showed significant ischemic distress, which cleared over the next few hours, and there was no evidence of damage by isoenzyme study. The patient was monitored on telemetry and increased his activity slowly. The patient improved and was discharged to home on Procardia 10 milligrams every other day, nitroglycerin patch 5 milligrams daily, Isordil 10 milligrams every other day, Lasix 40 milligrams daily, Theo-Dur 300 milligrams twice a day, prednisone in a decreasing dose, and Velosef 500 milligrams twice a day and is to be seen in the office in one week.

    DISCHARGE DIAGNOSES: Respiratory distress secondary to chronic obstructive pulmonary disease with acute bronchitis. Arteriosclerotic cardiovascular disease, native coronary artery, with progressive angina. Mitral insufficiency.

---

17. This patient is a 62-year-old woman with a 15-year history of Parkinson's disease on Sinemet. She is otherwise in good health. She was admitted with progressive abdominal distension over the past 5 days. She had had no bowel movement for the week prior to admission. She had vomited several times with intermittent nausea. She was able to keep down liquids. Her physical examination showed a distended abdomen with tympanitic, high-pitched bowel sounds. The patient's rectal exam showed no areas of tenderness and no stool. Her admission EKG was within normal limits. The abdominal films showed gas-filled large and small bowel with air fluid levels in both. There was no evidence of free air. The impression was of distal colonic obstruction versus impaction with an incompetent ileocecal valve. She was admitted and treated conservatively with nasogastric suction and intravenous hydration. Her Parkinson's disease was medically managed. The abdominal distension became slowly but progressively worse. A Gastrografin enema was done, which revealed an intrinsic mass obstructing retrograde flow beyond the mid sigmoid that was consistent in appearance with carcinoma of the mid sigmoid colon. The distension of the colon had increased greatly, and she was taken to the operating room for cutaneous open transverse loop colostomy, sigmoid colon. The patient tolerated the procedure well. Her diet has been slowly advanced. The patient and her daughter are able to manage changing of the colostomy bag. She was discharged with follow-up arranged for sigmoid resection and return of the loop colostomy to the abdomen.

    DISCHARGE DIAGNOSES: Intrinsic mass obstructing the mid sigmoid region of the colon consistent with carcinoma. Parkinson's disease.

    PROCEDURES: Cutaneous loop colostomy, sigmoid colon, via open transverse incision.

---

18. This patient was admitted to the hospital due to severe low back pain and a great amount of indigestion. She has had frequent episodes of abdominal pain in the past, but this is more severe and has failed to respond to therapy as an outpatient. She is known to have chronic ulcer disease, esophageal hiatus hernia, and polyps of the gallbladder in addition to her osteoporosis and stenosis of the lumbar spine, all of which were medically managed during the inpatient stay. The physical examination revealed a 74-year-old white woman who appeared to be acutely and chronically ill. She had epigastric tenderness

with no masses palpable. The patient's EKG was normal. An upper gastrointestinal series showed a small sliding hiatal hernia and a chronic duodenal ulcer with considerable evidence for an active ulcer. The gallbladder showed abnormal filling defects, which were consistent with polyps. The x-rays of the spine showed a great deal of osteoporosis and stenosis of the lumbar spine. The patient was given Demerol and Phenergan for the pain and was started on intravenous Prevacid. She was given Dalmane 30 milligrams at bedtime and a calcium supplement one time daily. She was started on a bland diet. The patient has slowly improved as far as the back pain. She is now up and about and is having less indigestion since therapy for the ulcer was begun. The patient is being discharged to be followed as an outpatient. She will continue on a bland diet and will be discharged on Prevacid, Carafate, a calcium substitute, and Darvocet.

DISCHARGE DIAGNOSES: Acute and chronic duodenal ulcer. Sliding esophageal hiatus hernia. Gallbladder polyps. Osteoporosis. Spinal stenosis of the lumbar region.

---

19. This patient is an 84-year-old female who was admitted to the hospital because of extreme weakness and inability to eat. The patient had been a resident of the nursing home when she suddenly developed progression of her symptoms of weakness. She refused to eat. Several days later she was not responding well. Laboratory studies done at that time revealed the hemoglobin to be 8.4 and her white count to be 14,700. There were significant abnormalities of her blood work that included a blood urea nitrogen level of 181, a sodium level of 149, a potassium level of 5.1, and glucose of 232. The patient was admitted to the hospital and hydrated with intravenous fluids. With that, her hemoglobin dropped to a low of 6. The patient was given a total of 4 units of packed red blood cells, and this brought her blood count up to 14.3. With appropriate hydration, there was a continual decline of her blood urea nitrogen level and improvement of her electrolytes. Despite this, she did not seem to be as strong as expected. We were trying to switch her from intravenous to oral medication. The next day, it became apparent that despite the intravenous fluids and blood transfusions, the patient was not responding. Her blood urea nitrogen level was beginning to rise, and she was becoming less responsive. Her breathing began to slow, and she became completely unresponsive. At 1:10 A.M. of the next morning, she was pronounced dead.

DISCHARGE DIAGNOSES: Acute renal failure and dehydration. Anemia in end-stage renal disease.

---

20. This is a 62-year-old patient seen in the office because of urinary difficulty. The patient noticed that he had to strain when he had to urinate. He has been having this problem off and on during the past year. Also, sometimes he has to move his bowels when he urinates because of the strain. His urinary stream is very slow. He has no history of dysuria or hematuria. His past history reveals that he has high blood pressure, and he is taking medication for that with occasional Valium. He also has been complaining of some pain in the lower back at the area of the coccyx bone. On his physical examination, the abdomen was soft with no tenderness or mass palpable. He has normal external genitalia with a rectally grade III smooth prostate gland. The patient's urological workup was done as an outpatient, and this showed an essentially normal upper urinary tract and enlarged prostate. He is admitted to the hospital for transurethral resection of the prostate. On the day of admission, under general anesthesia, transurethral resection of the prostate (via artificial opening) to trim away excess prostate tissue only was performed. Postoperatively, the patient did well. When his catheter was removed, he was able to void well without any difficulty. The pathology report revealed benign prostatic hyperplasia. Because of a tender coccyx bone, he did have several x-rays, which were negative. The pain was improved by injecting Aristocort and Novocain into this area. The patient's hypertension medication was continued. The patient was discharged and will be seen in the office in 3 weeks.

DISCHARGE DIAGNOSES: Benign hyperplasia of the prostate with urinary obstruction and lower urinary tract symptoms. Coccygodynia. Hypertension.

PROCEDURE: Transurethral resection of the prostate, which involved trimming away excess prostate tissue only.

21.   The patient is a 35-year-old female who had been seen in the emergency room on a couple previous occasions. She also had been seen at the clinic and underwent pelvic examination with cervical culture. She appeared to be ill and was unable to take oral antibiotics. Therefore, she was admitted to the hospital for treatment. At admission, she appeared ill and toxic. Her chest x-ray was normal. A pelvic ultrasound showed a 3-centimeter bulge involving the left posterior uterus, which was thought to be fibroid, and a 2-centimeter cyst in the left ovary. A pregnancy test was negative. Her urine culture and sensitivity showed no growth. A plain urinalysis was normal. She was started on ampicillin 500 milligrams intravenously every six hours, and she required Demerol for pain. It is believed that both the ovarian cyst and uterine fibroid were the cause of her pain. The intravenous therapy was continued until the next day, at which time it was stopped. The patient's condition improved, and she was discharged to be seen in follow-up for possible endometriosis.

DISCHARGE DIAGNOSES: Ovarian cyst. Degenerating fibroid with leiomyomata of the uterus. Possible endometriosis.

22.   The patient is a 23-year-old white female, gravida 2, para 1, who has had no problems with her pregnancy until two days prior to admission. She began with some spotting, which progressed to heavier bleeding with cramping. The cramping became severe on the morning of admission; she began to bleed excessively then, and she presented herself to the emergency room. At that point, it was believed that she had had an incomplete abortion. At the time of admission, she was a well-developed, well-nourished white female in no apparent distress. Her vital signs are stable. She is afebrile. Her pertinent physical findings included a negative abdominal exam and a pelvic exam that revealed blood, clots, and mucus in the external cervical canal and in the vaginal vault. The bimanual exam was deferred until the time of surgery when sterile conditions could be met. She was taken to the operating room after her complete blood count and urinalysis showed nothing unusual. In the operating room, a dilatation and curettage was done without problem. Postoperatively, she has done fine. She has had no unusual vaginal bleeding. She has had no problem with ambulation to the bathroom. Her abdomen is soft and nontender this morning. She feels fine. She is discharged to home in good condition.

DISCHARGE DIAGNOSIS: Incomplete spontaneous abortion with excessive vaginal bleeding.

PROCEDURE: Dilatation and curettage to remove retained products of conception.

23.   The patient is a 25-year-old white female, gravida 1, whose pregnancy has been benign. She had gone into spontaneous labor late in the evening and came to the obstetric unit at about 0230 hours. She was dilated a fingertip. She came to 50% effacement, and labor picked up every few minutes. By 8 o'clock in the morning, she was only 2 to 3 centimeters dilated. This continued until late in the afternoon. She was station minus 2 and had good contractions for several hours with no further progression of labor. Pelvimetry showed borderline cephalopelvic disproportion. It was finally decided to do a cesarean section. She was taken to the operating room and underwent a low transverse cervical incision with delivery of a live female child. She had an essentially uneventful postoperative course. Her incision has been healing well, and her bowels have been moving. The abdomen is soft and nontender. The patient was anxious to go home and was discharged to home to be seen in the office for her 2-week postpartum check.

DISCHARGE DIAGNOSES: Borderline cephalopelvic disproportion with obstructed labor. Failure to progress at labor.

PROCEDURE: Cesarean section, low cervical.

24.   A 35-year-old white male had a mass on his right wrist for quite some time. It had become tender and quite achy. It was, therefore, recommended that this be excised under axillary block anesthesia. Incidentally, he also had a mass of the skin of the nose and requested removal of the mass as well as sterilization by vasectomy to be done at the same time. The patient was admitted to undergo these surgeries under local anesthesia following excision of the ganglion cyst. His orthopedic examination at the

time of admission revealed him to have a 1 × 2–centimeter fluctuant but fairly firm mass of the radial volar aspect of the right wrist, which was just proximal to the flexor crease. This was nonpulsatile. He also had what appeared to be a sebaceous cyst involving the skin on the tip of the nose. The patient's preoperative chest x-ray, complete blood count, and urinalysis were all within normal limits. An x-ray of the right wrist revealed no bony abnormality, but it did reveal a soft tissue mass on the lateral aspect of the wrist. The patient underwent the operative procedures described above, the first under axillary block and the other two under local anesthetic. The patient tolerated the procedures well and left the operating room in good condition. The pathology report revealed a ganglion cyst of the wrist and a sebaceous cyst of the nose. He was discharged the next day with instructions to return to the office for follow-up.

DISCHARGE DIAGNOSES: Ganglion cyst, right wrist. Sterilization. Sebaceous cyst, nose.

PROCEDURES: Excision, ganglion cyst, right wrist. Bilateral vasectomy, open approach. Excision, lesion, skin of nose.

---

25. This patient has had a decubitus gangrenous ulcer on the dorsum of his left heel that had not improved and was, in fact, getting worse. He was given intensive medical treatment as an outpatient, but the entire foot became more swollen and red, and he was brought to the hospital for more intensive therapy. Studies revealed a *Staphylococcus aureus* infection from the wound culture. He was treated for cellulitis with intravenous vancomycin and following surgery was placed on gentamicin and intravenous Vibramycin. These medications were effective in controlling his infection and improving the cellulitis. They were not, however, able to improve the ulcer. Whirlpool treatments and dressing changes also failed to improve the ulcer. It was ultimately decided that an above-the-knee amputation was necessary. After 5 days of intravenous antibiotics, the patient was taken to the operative suite, where it was determined that below-the-knee amputation of the left leg was appropriate, and that procedure was performed. He is now being transferred to a rehabilitation facility for continued care. His leg stump sutures will be removed as able, probably in about 2 weeks.

DISCHARGE DIAGNOSES: Gangrenous decubitus ulcer of the left heel, stage IV. *Staphylococcus aureus* infection.

PROCEDURE: Below-the-knee amputation, left leg.

---

26. A 62-year-old white female had been hospitalized 5 months previously with a subcapital fracture of the right hip. She underwent open reduction with internal fixation of the fracture. The fracture healed, but she continued to have difficulty with pain over the ends of the Gouffon pins. She was admitted for surgical removal of these pins. Postoperatively, her blood pressure dropped in the recovery room. This was treated with and responded to ephedrine. For the rest of her hospitalization, she had no further problems with her blood pressure. Her incision began to drain serous-type drainage. She was dangled on the side of her bed on her first postoperative day and was transferred out of bed and into the chair on her second postoperative day, and subsequently started on physical therapy for gait training with a walker. Serous drainage persisted from the hip, and a culture of the wound from her right hip incision grew *Escherichia coli*. She was treated with cephalothin for this postoperative infection. She was ultimately discharged to home with care by the visiting nurse, who will do twice-a-week dressing changes.

DISCHARGE DIAGNOSES: Painful Gouffon pins of the right hip. Postoperative hypotension. Postoperative wound infection, right hip, with *Escherichia coli*. (Initial encounter.)

PROCEDURE: Open removal of Gouffon pins, right hip.

---

27. A 64-year-old male was admitted to the hospital, complaining of right knee pain. X-rays revealed that he had degenerative arthritis of the right knee. His options were discussed with him. He decided to undergo a right total knee replacement with insertion of a molded polyethylene synthetic knee implant.

He underwent the procedure without incident. Postoperatively, he has done well. He began with physical therapy, ambulating with a walker. He was afebrile, and his wound was clean, dry, and intact upon discharge. He was stable upon discharge. He will have a home health nurse come to his house to remove his staples in 2 weeks' time. He should continue to work on range of motion and strengthening of his right leg. He should ambulate with the assistance of a walker. The patient should call immediately if he notices any redness, pain, or swelling around his incision.

DISCHARGE DIAGNOSIS: Degenerative primary osteoarthritis of right knee.

PROCEDURE: Total knee replacement, right knee.

---

28. This child was delivered vaginally during this admission to a 24-year-old mother, gravida 2, para 2, with blood type A positive. The child was born at term (38 weeks) and had a birth weight of 2425 grams. The mother's pregnancy was uncomplicated, and delivery was by sterile spontaneous vaginal delivery without difficulties. The child was noted to have multiple congenital defects on birth. This child had multiple anomalies, including small for gestation age size, bilateral cleft lip and hard palate, prominent sternum, an accessory finger of the left hand (below the pinky finger), and penile hypospadias; on x-ray, he had 11 ribs with hemivertebra at the T5 to T6 level. He also had dextroversion malrotation of the left kidney but no apparent cardiac anomalies. During the majority of his course, he was maintained on intravenous fluids and nutrition. Because of the child's multiple anomalies, bone marrow chromosomes were done. These were positive, showing trisomy 13 in all of the cells counted. Because of this, he also had consultation with the genetics service, which agreed with the diagnosis. The child also had evaluation by the cardiology service, which believed the child had kidney dextroversion malrotation but no structural heart disease. As mentioned, the child has trisomy 13, which is uniformly poor in terms of prognosis. The parents were informed of this, and they elected to do no heroic treatment or resuscitation for the child. The child stopped breathing and was pronounced dead later that same day. Autopsy was denied by the parents, and disposition has been arranged.

DISCHARGE DIAGNOSES: Trisomy 13. Term male. Small for dates. Cleft lip and hard palate, complete. Accessory finger, left hand. Hypospadias, penile. Eleven ribs. Hemivertebra. Dextroversion malrotation, left kidney.

---

29. This patient is a 17-year-old male who had a syncopal episode at his football practice that lasted approximately 2 minutes. The patient has a completely benign medical history. He is a well-developed, well-nourished teenager who is active in sports. Upon questioning, the patient admits to feeling dizzy during practices, with vague chest pain. He has been tired lately, but he attributes that to daily practices. The patient admits to shortness of breath. There is no family history of heart disease. The patient's EKG in the emergency room was abnormal. The patient was admitted, and a cardiology consult was ordered. Ultrasonography of the heart revealed the patient to have persistent truncus arteriosus. The findings were discussed with the patient's parents, and the decision was made to transfer the patient to the care of a pediatric cardiologist at the nearby Children's Hospital. The patient was transferred in stable condition.

DISCHARGE DIAGNOSES: Persistent truncus arteriosus. Syncope.

---

30. The patient is a premature female infant who was born during this admission to a 20-year-old woman who has a known drug problem. The patient was born by spontaneous vaginal delivery. The infant was born at 32 weeks' gestation and weighed 1760 grams. On the second day of admission, it was apparent that the infant was beginning to experience withdrawal symptoms. She was agitated and cried inconsolably. She required constant attention from the nursing staff. She was rocked almost continuously and bundled tightly in her blanket. The mother tested positive for cocaine, and the matter

was turned over to social services. The infant is being discharged to foster care and will be seen in the office in the morning.

DISCHARGE DIAGNOSES: Premature female infant born by spontaneous vaginal delivery. Withdrawal symptoms due to mother's drug addiction.

---

31. The patient is a male infant who was born during this admission via cesarean section. The day after delivery he appeared jaundiced. His blood was drawn, and he was found to have an elevated bilirubin level. The patient was treated with phototherapy and was discharged the next day with great improvement of his bilirubin level. He is scheduled to see the pediatrician in 2 days for a repeat bilirubin test.

DISCHARGE DIAGNOSES: Term male, born by cesarean section. Hyperbilirubinemia.

PROCEDURE: Phototherapy of a newborn.

---

32. The patient is a 2-year-old male who was admitted to the hospital after a febrile seizure at home. He had been pulling at his ears and crying intermittently for 2 days prior to admission. At home, his temperature was 103.5 degrees. By the time he arrived in the emergency room, his fever had dropped to 102; he was admitted for treatment. On examination, his ears looked red and had serous drainage. He was placed on phenobarbital elixir for seizures and amoxicillin 125 milligrams every 8 hours for acute otitis media. He responded well to this therapy; by the end of the second day of hospitalization, his fever was down. He had a urine culture that did show some *Staphylococcus epidermis*, thought to be due to a contaminant. His throat culture showed normal flora. His hemaglobin was 11.1 with a white blood cell count of 10,800. His chest x-ray was normal. The patient was discharged on the amoxicillin and will be seen in 1 week for follow-up.

DISCHARGE DIAGNOSES: Febrile seizure with acute serous otitis media on the right.

---

33. This patient is an 18-year-old female who presented to the emergency room for severe right lower quadrant abdominal pain. She was given morphine in the emergency room, which did little to help the pain. A surgical consult was requested, and she was admitted to the hospital. Her pelvic and abdominal computed tomography scans were negative. They showed no abnormalities with her liver, spleen, kidneys, gallbladder, or ovaries. Her amylase, complete blood count, white blood cell count, and glucose were all within normal limits. Her urinalysis was completely normal. Despite these findings, the patient's abdominal pain continued. She was continued on morphine. She had no nausea or vomiting. Gynecology was consulted, and an intravaginal ultrasound ordered. This was also negative. By the third day of the patient's hospitalization, her pain began to abate. She was started on a liquid diet and quickly advanced to solid food. She was discharged to be followed up with her physician. A copy of all reports will be sent to his office.

DISCHARGE DIAGNOSIS: Right lower quadrant abdominal pain.

---

34. This patient is a 5-year-old female who presented to the ED one day after experiencing at home a coffee burn injury on her right forearm, right and left legs, and vulva. She presented to this burn center for evaluation. The patient was admitted with a 7% total body surface area burn to her right forearm, vulva, and right and left legs in each thigh area. The wounds were second-degree burns with no evidence of any full-thickness burn. She was taken to the operating room for an irrigation debridement as well as application of a burn dressing. The patient's hospital course was essentially uneventful. She had twice

daily dressing changes, and her wounds were assessed daily. On hospital day four, she was thought ready to be discharged. The mother felt quite comfortable doing the dressing changes. Her pain was well controlled with medications. She remained afebrile. There was no evidence of any infection in any of her wounds. The patient is to continue Silvadene dressing changes twice a day. The mother is to call for any temperature higher than 101 degrees or pain uncontrolled by medication.

DISCHARGE DIAGNOSES: Second-degree burns to right forearm, vulva, and right and left legs in each thigh area (7% total body surface area). (Initial encounter.)

---

35. A 22-year-old white male was involved in a motorcycle-truck accident and was admitted with open comminuted type IIIA fractures of the shaft of the left tibia and fibula; a closed Colles' fracture of the distal radius on the right arm; and a laceration of the tongue, which was approximately 1 inch in length. He was the driver of the motorcycle, and he lost control and hit a parked truck in a parking lot. The remainder of his physical and history was essentially noncontributory. He was started on lactated Ringer's and D5% dextrose and given 1 gram of Kefzol. His tetanus immunization was up-to-date. The laboratory studies included an EKG that was read as abnormal with nonspecific myocardial changes in the inferolateral region, not felt to be significant or warranting further follow-up. His chest x-ray was grossly normal on admission. The cervical spine was normal. He was taken to the operating room, where he underwent an open reduction and internal fixation of the fractured tibia and fibula, casting of the right radial fracture, and suturing of the tongue laceration. The patient was treated for a full 10 days with intravenous Keflex. His wounds looked good. His postreduction x-rays revealed good position of the right wrist and left leg fractures. He was discharged to follow-up in the office in 10 days. At that time, he will have an x-ray of the right wrist and left lower leg. He was given a prescription for Talwin 50 milligrams by mouth every four hours as needed for pain.

DISCHARGE DIAGNOSES: Traumatic open comminuted type IIIA fractures, left tibia shaft and fibula. Traumatic Colles' closed, distal radius, right. Laceration, tongue, approximately 1 inch in length. (Initial encounter.)

PROCEDURES: Open reduction, internal fixation, left tibia and fibula. Suture repair, tongue laceration.

CHAPTER 6

ICD-10-CM Outpatient and Physician Office Coding

Chapter Outline

Outpatient Care

Diagnostic Coding and Reporting Guidelines
   for Outpatient Services

Chapter Objectives

At the conclusion of this chapter, the student should be able to:

- Define key terms.
- List and explain differences among outpatient and physician office health care settings.
- Interpret diagnosis coding and reporting guidelines for outpatient services.
- Assign ICD-10-CM diagnosis codes for outpatient and physician office care.

Key Terms

ambulatory care

ambulatory patient

ambulatory surgery patient

clinic outpatient

Data Elements for Emergency
   Department Systems (DEEDS)

*Diagnostic Coding and Reporting
   Guidelines for Outpatient
   Services*

emergency care patient

first-listed diagnosis

inconclusive diagnosis

observation patient

Outcome and Assessment
   Information Set (OASIS)

outpatient

outpatient care

preadmission testing (PAT)

primary care

primary care provider

qualified diagnosis

referred outpatient

triage

Uniform Ambulatory Care Data
   Set (UACDS)

Introduction

This chapter defines outpatient care settings and interprets the *Diagnostic Coding and Reporting Guidelines for Outpatient Services*, published in the CMS *ICD-10-CM Official Guidelines for Coding and Reporting.*

It is important to remember that coding guidelines are to be used as a companion to the official version of the *International Classification of Diseases, Tenth Revision, Clinical Modification* (ICD-10-CM), which contains coding conventions to ensure accurate coding.

ICD-10-CM codes are assigned to outpatient and physician office diagnoses for health care financial planning, reimbursement, and statistical purposes. (Outpatient reimbursement systems are discussed in Chapter 19 after students have learned how to assign HCPCS level II and CPT codes to procedures and services.) Patient demographic data and codes are reported to third-party payers on the CMS-1500 claim to generate reimbursement.

> **Note:**
>
> Outpatient health care settings, such as home health care and hospice, use the UB-04 claim instead of the CMS-1500 claim.

Coders review patient records to locate conditions and diseases to which ICD-10-CM codes are assigned. Coders also assign HCPCS level II and CPT codes to procedures and services (discussed in Chapters 7–18). Similar to the inpatient coding process, outpatient coders may not assign codes to conditions and diseases when the provider does not specifically document the diagnoses or procedures/services. Such assumption coding is considered fraud, and the coder should query the physician to determine whether the documented diagnosis should be edited so a more specific code can be assigned. (Refer to Chapter 1 for more information about the physician query process.)

 Note:

> The **Uniform Ambulatory Care Data Set (UACDS)** was established by the federal government as a standard data set for ambulatory care facility records. Its goal is to improve data comparison for ambulatory and outpatient care settings.
>
> Home health agencies (HHAs) report data according to the **Outcome and Assessment Information Set (OASIS)**, which is a core set of comprehensive assessments for adult home care patients that is used to
>
> - Measure patient outcomes for Outcome-Based Quality Improvement (OBQI)
>
> - Conduct patient assessment, patient care planning, and internal HHA performance improvements
>
> - Generate agency-level case mix reports that contain aggregate statistics about various patient characteristics such as demographic, health, or functional status at start of care
>
> HHAs use Home Assessment and Validation and Entry (HAVEN) data entry software to report OASIS data. Hospital-based emergency departments report **Data Elements for Emergency Department Systems (DEEDS)** for uniform collection of data to reduce incompatibility in emergency department records.

Outpatient Care

Outpatient care (or **ambulatory care**) includes any health care service provided to a patient who is not admitted as an inpatient to a facility. Such care may be provided in a physician's office, a stand-alone health care facility, a hospital outpatient or emergency department (ED), or the patient's home.

Primary Care Services

Primary care includes both preventive and acute care services, which are often provided as outpatient care and are referred to as the *point of first contact*. Services are usually provided by a general practitioner or another health professional (e.g., nurse practitioner) who has first contact with a patient seeking medical treatment, including general dental, ophthalmic, and pharmaceutical services. These services are usually provided in an office setting where the care is continuous (e.g., quarterly office visits for a chronic condition) and comprehensive (e.g., preventive and medical care). The **primary care provider** manages and coordinates the patient's care, including referring the patient to a medical specialist (Table 6-1) for consultation and a second opinion. Primary care services include the following:

- Annual physical examinations
- Early detection of disease
- Family planning
- Health education

- Immunizations
- Treatment of minor illnesses and injuries
- Vision and hearing screening

Hospital Outpatient Services

Hospital outpatients include ambulatory patients, ambulatory surgery patients, emergency care patients, and observation care patients. The maximum length of stay of an outpatient is 23 hours, 59 minutes, and 59 seconds. **Ambulatory patients** (or **outpatients**) are treated and released the same day and do not stay overnight in the hospital. **Ambulatory surgery patients** undergo certain procedures that can be performed on an outpatient basis, with the patient treated and released the same day. An ambulatory surgery patient who requires a longer stay must be admitted to the facility as an inpatient. **Emergency care patients** are treated for urgent problems (e.g., trauma) and are either released the same day or admitted to the hospital as inpatients. **Observation patients** receive services furnished on a hospital's premises that are ordered by a physician (or another authorized individual), including use of a bed and periodic monitoring by nursing or other staff, and that are reasonable and necessary to evaluate the outpatient's condition or determine the need for possible admission as an inpatient.

Outpatient care allows patients to receive care in one day without the need for inpatient hospitalization. Care is provided in either a freestanding or a hospital-based facility and includes the following (Table 6-2):

- Ambulatory surgical centers (freestanding)
- Hospital-based outpatient department
- Hospital-based ED
- Hospital-based ambulatory surgery program
- Hospital-based partial hospitalization program
- Hospital-owned physician practice
- Hospital-owned satellite clinics
- Industrial health clinic
- Neighborhood health centers
- Physicians' offices
- Public health departments
- Satellite clinics
- Staff model health maintenance organizations (HMOs)
- Urgent care centers

Table 6-1   Medical Specialties

Medical Specialty	Description
Allergy & Immunology	Evaluation and treatment of immune system disorders (e.g., asthma, anaphylaxis, eczema, rhinitis, and adverse reactions to drugs/foods/insect stings)
Anesthesiology	Assessment of patient risks for undergoing surgery, management of pain relief, monitoring of patients during and after surgery (postanesthesia recovery), and resuscitative care of patients with cardiac or respiratory emergencies (assessment of need for artificial ventilation)
Colon & Rectal Surgery	Diagnosis and medical/surgical treatment of diseases in the intestinal tract, colon, rectum, anal canal, perianal region, and related organs and tissues (e.g., liver)
Dermatology	Diagnosis and treatment of skin disorders (e.g., contact dermatitis and benign and malignant lesions, or growths) and cosmetic disorders of the skin (e.g., scars)
Family Practice	Management of an individual's or family's total health care, including geriatrics, gynecology, internal medicine, obstetrics, pediatrics, and psychiatry, with an emphasis on preventive and primary care
General Surgery	Management of conditions for which general surgery is warranted (e.g., appendectomy, tonsillectomy, and hernia repair), including diagnosis and preoperative, intraoperative, and postoperative care to surgical patients
Gynecology	Diagnosis and treatment (includes preventive management) of female reproductive and urinary system disorders
Internal Medicine	Management of common and complex illnesses of patients of all ages (e.g., cancer; infections; and diseases of blood, digestive system, heart, joints, kidneys, and respiratory and vascular systems). Primary care internal medicine includes disease prevention, mental health, substance abuse, and wellness. Subspecialties include the following: • Adolescent medicine • Immunology • Cardiovascular medicine • Infectious disease • Critical care medicine • Nephrology • Electrophysiology • Oncology • Endocrinology • Pulmonary medicine • Gastroenterology • Rheumatology • Geriatrics • Sports medicine • Hematology
Medical Genetics	Diagnosis and treatment of patients with genetically linked diseases
Neurology	Diagnosis and treatment of disorders of the nervous system
Obstetrics	Management of pregnancy, from prenatal to puerperium
Ophthalmology	Diagnosis and treatment of eye disorders
Orthopedics	Diagnosis and treatment of musculoskeletal disease and injury
Otorhinolaryngology	Diagnosis and treatment of ear, nose, and throat diseases
Plastic & Reconstructive Surgery	Surgery for the purpose of reconstructing, repairing, or restoring body structures
Psychiatry	Diagnosis and treatment of behavioral health diseases
Radiology	Diagnosis of diseases and injuries, using radiological methods (e.g., electromagnetic radiation, x-ray, radionuclides, and ultrasound). Treatment of diseases (e.g., cancer), using radiant energy (e.g., radiation oncologist)
Thoracic Surgery	Surgical management of disease within the chest (e.g., coronary artery disease and lung cancer)
Urology	Diagnosis and treatment of disorders of the genitourinary system and the adrenal gland

Table 6-2 Freestanding, Hospital-Based, and Hospital-Owned Ambulatory Facilities

Type of Facility	Characteristics
Freestanding Centers and Facilities	
Ambulatory surgery center	• Surgery is performed on an outpatient basis. • Patients arrive on the day of procedure, undergo surgery in an operating room, and recover under the care of nursing staff.
Cardiovascular center	• Provides ambulatory cardiovascular services to include diagnosis and treatment, disease prevention, research, education, and cardiac rehabilitation. • Diagnostic and treatment services include cardiac catheterization, Coumadin care, echocardiography, enhanced external counterpulsation (EECP), heart scans, pacemaker care, and percutaneous transluminal coronary angioplasty (PTCA).
Clinical laboratory	• Performs diagnostic testing in microbiology, clinical chemistry, and toxicology, which are ordered by physicians on samples of body fluids, tissues, and wastes. • Information obtained from tests helps physicians diagnose illness, monitor treatment, and check general health. Results from tests are reported to physicians, who interpret them and explain them to patients. • Directed by a pathologist; testing is performed by certified professional technologists and technicians.
Imaging center	• Provides radiographic (e.g., x-rays) and other imaging services (e.g., magnetic resonance imaging) to ambulatory patients. • May also provide training and participate in national research projects.
Industrial health clinic	• Located in a business setting (e.g., factory). • Emphasis is on employee health and safety.
Infusion center	• Dispenses and administers prescribed medications by continuous or intermittent infusion to ambulatory patients. • Infusion is supervised by a licensed health care professional (e.g., registered nurse). • Also called ambulatory infusion centers (AICs).
Neighborhood health center	• Health care is provided to economically disadvantaged and treatment is family-centered because illnesses may result indirectly from crowded living conditions, unsanitary facilities, and other socioeconomic factors. • Family care team consisting of a physician, nurse, and social worker provides continuity of care to families.
Pain management center	• Specializes in treatment of acute and chronic pain syndromes, using proven medications and procedures. • Usually uses a multidisciplinary approach involving participating specialists such as physiatrists, psychiatrists, neurologists, neurosurgeons, internists, and physical and occupational therapists.
Physician's office	• Solo physicians' practices do not have physician partners or employment affiliations with other practice organizations. • Single-specialty group physician practices consist of two or more physicians who provide patients with one specific type of care (e.g., primary care). • Multispecialty group physician practices offer various types of medical specialty care in one organization, and they may be located in more than one location.
Primary care center	• Offers adult and family care medicine in internal medicine, pediatrics, and family practice. • Internal medicine physicians specialize in the care of adults. • Pediatricians provide comprehensive services for infants, children, and adolescents. • Family practitioners provide care for the entire family and focus on general medicine, obstetrics, pediatrics, and geriatrics.
Public health department	• Provides preventive medicine services such as well-baby clinics. • Care includes immunizations and routine checkups.

Table 6-2 (*continued*)

Type of Facility	Characteristics

Radiology center	• Provides image-guided procedures, as follows:
	  ○ Computerized tomography (CT scan), in which the source of x-ray beams rotates around the patient, the beams are detected by sensors, and information from sensors is computer-processed and displayed as an image on a video screen.
	  ○ Magnetic resonance imaging (MRI), which uses a large magnet that surrounds the patient, along with radiowaves and a computer, to produce images.
	  ○ Mammography, which is a method for detecting early-stage breast abnormalities.
	  ○ Nuclear medicine, which uses very small amounts of radioactive materials or radiopharmaceuticals to study organ function and structure and to treat disease. (Radiopharmaceuticals are substances that are attracted to specific organs, bones, or tissues.)
	  ○ Positron emission tomography (PET), which measures radioactive tracers (e.g., radioactive glucose) injected into the body.
	  ○ Radiography (x-ray), which detects disease or injury in the body when an image (x-ray film) is produced as the result of passing a small amount of radiation through the body to expose sensitive film on the other side.
	  ○ Ultrasonography, which uses high-frequency sound waves to study parts of the body, including the heart and vessels, to generate an image of the area being studied.
	• Directed by a radiologist and staffed by registered x-ray technicians.

Rehabilitation facility	• Provides occupational, physical, and speech therapy to patients with orthopedic injuries, work-related injuries, sports-related injuries, and various neurologic and neuromuscular conditions. • Occupational therapy provides services to patients who have experienced loss of function resulting from injury or disease. Physical therapy uses physical agents of exercise, massage, and other modalities. Speech/language pathology provides services to evaluate, diagnose, plan, and provide therapy to patients with speech, language, and swallowing difficulties.
Staff model health maintenance organization (HMO)	• Similar to large, multispecialty group practices. • May be partially owned by physician employees, with the physicians typically functioning as employees of either the physician group owning the practice or the insurer. • Most physicians are paid a salary.
Student health center	• Provides health care to full- and part-time students who become ill or injured. • Services usually include allergy injections, contraception and counseling, health education, immunizations, HIV testing, laboratory services, routine medications, primary care and preventive medicine, screening for sexually transmitted diseases (STDs), smoking cessation, and women's health care.
Urgent care center (or emergency care center)	• Immediate care is provided by an on-duty physician (usually salaried). • May be owned by private corporations (e.g., Humana) in states where they are permitted or by nonprofit facilities (e.g., municipal hospital).
Hospital-Based Departments and Programs	
Ambulatory surgery	• Elective surgery is performed on patients who are admitted and discharged the same day (e.g., biopsy); both general and local anesthesia are administered. • Also called short-stay or day surgery. • Patients undergo **preadmission testing (PAT)** to register with Admitting, undergo preoperative nursing assessment, and receive preanesthesia evaluation by an anesthesiologist. As part of PAT, phlebotomists draw blood samples for preoperative testing and electrocardiograms and chest x-rays are performed if ordered. PAT results are documented in the patient's record and are available to the patient care team prior to the patient's surgery.
Emergency department	• Crisis care is provided 24 hours per day by an on-duty physician to patients who have sustained trauma or have urgent problems (e.g., heart attack). • Patients initially undergo **triage**, which is an organized method of identifying and treating patients according to urgency of care required.

(*continues*)

Table 6-2 (*continued*)

Type of Facility	Characteristics
Outpatient department	• **Clinic outpatients** receive scheduled diagnostic and therapeutic care (e.g., chemotherapy, kidney dialysis). • **Referred outpatients** receive diagnostic (e.g., laboratory tests) or therapeutic care (e.g., physical therapy) because such care is unavailable in the primary care provider's office; follow-up is done at the primary care provider's office.
Partial hospitalization program	• Program for hospital patients who regularly use the hospital facilities for a substantial number of daytime or nighttime hours (e.g., behavioral health, geriatric, and rehabilitative care).
Hospital-Owned Facilities	
Hospital-owned physician practice	• Hospital-owned practices are at least partially owned by the hospital. • Physicians participate in a compensation plan provided by the hospital.
Satellite clinics	• Ambulatory care centers that are established remotely from the hospital. • Primary care is provided by an on-duty physician (usually salaried).

Exercise 6.1 – Outpatient Care

Instructions: Complete each statement.

1. Care provided in a physician's office, a stand-alone health care facility, a hospital outpatient or emergency department, or the patient's home is classified as _____ care.

2. Both preventive and acute care are often provided as outpatient care and are referred to as the point of first contact, which is categorized as _____ care.

3. The physician who manages and coordinates the patient's care, including referring the patient to a medical specialist for consultation and a second opinion, is called the _____.

4. Patients who are treated and released the same day and do not stay overnight in the hospital are called _____ patients.

5. Patients who undergo certain procedures that can be performed on an outpatient basis, with the patient treated and released the same day, are called _____ patients.

6. Patients who are treated for urgent problems (e.g., trauma) and are either released the same day or admitted to the hospital as inpatients are called _____ patients.

7. Patients who receive services furnished on a hospital's premises that are ordered by a physician (or another authorized individual), including use of a bed and periodic monitoring by nursing or other staff, and that are reasonable and necessary to evaluate the outpatients' conditions or determine the need for possible admission as inpatients (and who are in the unit no longer than 23 hours, 59 minutes, and 59 seconds), are called _____ patients.

8. An organized method of identifying and treating patients according to urgency of care required is called _____.

9. Patients who receive scheduled diagnostic and therapeutic care are called _____ outpatients.

10. Patients who receive diagnostic or therapeutic care because such care is unavailable in the primary care provider's office are called _____ outpatients.

Diagnostic Coding and Reporting Guidelines for Outpatient Services

The ***Diagnostic Coding and Reporting Guidelines for Outpatient Services*** were developed by the federal government and approved for use by hospitals and providers for coding and reporting hospital-based outpatient services and provider-based office visits. Although the guidelines were originally developed for use in submitting government claims, insurance companies have also adopted them (sometimes with variation).

 Note:

Because variations may contradict the official coding guidelines, make sure you review each insurance company's coding guidelines.

Selection of First-Listed Condition

In the outpatient setting, the **first-listed diagnosis** is reported (instead of the inpatient setting's *principal diagnosis*); it is the diagnosis, condition, problem, or other reason for encounter/visit documented in the patient record to be chiefly responsible for the services provided. It is determined in accordance with ICD-10-CM *coding conventions* (or rules) as well as general and disease-specific coding guidelines. Because diagnoses are often not established at the time of the patient's initial encounter or visit, two or more visits may be required before a diagnosis is confirmed.

Note:

When reviewing the coding guidelines, the terms *encounter* and *visit* are used interchangeably when describing outpatient and physician office services.

Coding guidelines for inconclusive or qualified diagnoses (e.g., probable, suspected, rule out) were developed for inpatient reporting only; they do not apply to outpatients.

An outpatient is a person treated in one of four settings.

- *Ambulatory surgery center*: Patient is released prior to a 24-hour stay and length of stay must be 23 hours, 59 minutes, and 59 seconds or less

- *Health care provider's office* (e.g., physician)

- *Hospital clinic, ED, outpatient department, same-day surgery unit*: Length of stay must be 23 hours, 59 minutes, and 59 seconds or less

Note:

The first-listed diagnosis reflects the reason for the encounter, which often is a sign or symptom.

- *Hospital observation status or hospital observation unit*: Patient's length of stay is 23 hours, 59 minutes, and 59 seconds or less unless documentation for additional observation is medically justified

 Note:

- The *first-listed diagnosis* was previously called the *primary diagnosis*.

- When determining the *first-listed diagnosis*, ICD-10-CM coding conventions and general and disease-specific guidelines take precedence over the outpatient guidelines (e.g., etiology/manifestation coding convention).

- Chapter 5 contains the definition of an inpatient and a discussion of principal diagnosis, comorbidities, complications, principal procedure, and secondary procedures. The term *encounter* also applies to inpatient hospitalizations.

EXAMPLE: A patient received ED care for an injury to the right arm, which upon x-ray revealed closed displaced oblique fracture of the shaft of the right humerus (S42.331A). While receiving treatment for the fracture, the physician also medically managed the patient's chronic obstructive asthma (J44.9).

The first-listed diagnosis code is S42.331A and the secondary diagnosis code is J44.9.

 Note:

- *Outpatient Surgery*: When a patient presents for outpatient surgery, code the reason for the surgery as the first-listed diagnosis (reason for the encounter), even if the surgery is canceled due to a contraindication (e.g., patient's blood pressure increases unexpectedly upon administration of anesthesia).

- *Observation Stay*: When a patient is admitted for observation for a medical condition, assign a code for the medical condition as the first-listed diagnosis.

     When a patient presents for outpatient surgery and develops complications requiring admission to observation, code the reason for the surgery as the first-listed diagnosis (reason for the encounter), followed by codes for the complications (e.g., respiratory distress) as secondary diagnoses.

Codes from A00.0 Through T88.9, Z00–Z99

The appropriate code or codes from the ICD-10-CM Tabular List of Diseases (A00.0 through T88.9, Z00–Z99) must be used to identify diagnoses, symptoms, conditions, problems, complaints, or other reason(s) for the encounter/visit.

Accurate Reporting of ICD-10-CM Diagnosis Codes

For accurate reporting of ICD-10-CM diagnosis codes, the documentation should describe the patient's condition, using terminology that includes specific diagnoses as well as symptoms, problems, or reasons for the encounter. There are ICD-10-CM codes to describe all of these.

Codes That Describe Signs and Symptoms

Codes that describe symptoms and signs, as opposed to definitive diagnoses, are acceptable for reporting purposes when the physician has not documented an established diagnosis or confirmed diagnosis.

In ICD-10-CM, Chapter 18 (Symptoms, Signs, and Abnormal Clinical and Laboratory Findings Not Elsewhere Classified) (R00–R99) contains many, but not all, codes for symptoms.

Some symptom codes are located in other ICD-10-CM chapters, which can be found by properly using the ICD-10-CM Index to Diseases and Injuries.

Encounters for Circumstances Other Than a Disease or Injury

ICD-10-CM provides codes to deal with encounters for circumstances other than a disease or an injury.

Factors Influencing Health Status and Contact with Health Services (Z00–Z99) are provided to deal with occasions when circumstances other than a disease or injury are recorded as diagnosis or problems.

Level of Detail in Coding

ICD-10-CM diagnosis codes contain 3, 4, 5, 6, or 7 characters.

1. *ICD-10-CM codes with 3, 4, 5, 6, or 7 characters*: Disease codes with three characters are included in ICD-10-CM as the heading of a category of codes that may be further subdivided by the use of fourth, fifth, sixth, or seventh characters to provide greater specificity.

2. *Use of full number of characters required for a code*: A three-character code is to be assigned only if it cannot be further subdivided. A code is invalid if it has not been coded to the full number of characters required for that code, including the seventh character extension, if applicable.

ICD-10-CM Code for the Diagnosis, Condition, Problem, or Other Reason for Encounter/Visit

Report first the ICD-10-CM code for the diagnosis, condition, problem, or other reason for encounter documented in the patient record as chiefly responsible for the services provided. Then report additional codes that describe any coexisting conditions that were treated or medically managed or that influenced the treatment of the patient during the encounter. In some cases, the first-listed diagnosis may be a sign or symptom when a diagnosis has not been established (confirmed) by the physician.

Uncertain Diagnoses

Do *not* code diagnoses documented as probable, suspected, questionable, rule out, or working diagnosis, or other similar terms indicating uncertainty, all of which are considered **inconclusive diagnoses** or **qualified diagnoses**. Instead, code condition(s) to the highest degree of certainty for that encounter/visit, such as symptoms, signs, abnormal test results, or other reasons for the visit.

 Note:

> This differs from coding practices used by short-term, acute care, long-term, and psychiatric hospitals, where qualified diagnoses are coded and reported.

EXAMPLE:

For Qualified Diagnosis:	Code the Following Sign or Symptom:
Suspected pneumonia	Shortness of breath, wheezing
Questionable Raynaud's	Numbness of hands
Possible wrist fracture	Wrist pain and swelling
Rule out pneumonia	Chest pain and fever

Qualified or uncertain diagnoses are a necessary part of the hospital and office chart until a specific diagnosis can be determined. Although qualified diagnoses are routinely coded for hospital inpatient admissions and reported on the UB-04 claim, CMS *specifically prohibits the reporting of qualified diagnoses on the CMS-1500 claim submitted for outpatient care.* CMS regulations permit the reporting of patients' signs and/or symptoms instead of the qualified diagnoses.

An additional incentive for not coding qualified diagnoses resulted from the Missouri case of *Stafford v. Neurological Medicine Inc.*, 811 F. 2d 470 (8th Cir., 1987). In this case, the diagnosis stated in the physician's office chart was *rule out brain tumor*. The claim submitted by the office listed the diagnosis code for *rule out brain tumor*, although test results were available that proved a brain tumor did not exist. The physician assured the patient that although she had lung cancer, there was no metastasis to the brain. Some time after the insurance company received the provider's claim, it was inadvertently sent to the patient. When the patient received the claim, she was so devastated by the diagnosis that she committed suicide. Her husband sued and was awarded $200,000 on the basis of *negligent paperwork* because the physician's office had reported a *qualified or uncertain diagnosis*.

Chronic Diseases

Chronic diseases treated on an ongoing basis may be coded and reported as many times as the patient receives treatment and care for the condition(s).

Code All Documented Conditions That Coexist

Code all documented conditions that coexist at the time of the encounter/visit and that require or affect patient care, treatment, or management. Do not code conditions that were previously treated and no longer exist. However, history codes ICD-10-CM categories Z80–Z87 may be reported as secondary codes if the historical condition or family history has an impact on current care or influences treatment.

Patients Receiving Diagnostic Services Only

For patients receiving *diagnostic services only* during an encounter, report first the diagnosis, condition, problem, or other reason for encounter that is documented as being chiefly responsible for the outpatient services provided during the encounter. (This is the *first-listed diagnosis*.) Codes for other diagnoses (e.g., chronic conditions) may be reported as additional diagnoses.

For encounters for routine laboratory/radiology testing in the absence of any signs, symptoms, or associated diagnosis, assign Z01.89 (Encounter for other specified special examinations). If routine testing is performed during the same encounter as a test to evaluate a sign, symptom, or diagnosis, it is appropriate to assign both the Z code and the code describing the reason for the nonroutine test.

For outpatient encounters for diagnostic tests that have been interpreted by a physician and for which the final report is available at the time of coding, code any confirmed or definitive diagnoses documented in the interpretation. *Do not code related signs and symptoms as additional diagnoses.*

Note:

Third-party payers review claims for "family history of" codes to determine reimbursement eligibility. Some plans reimburse for conditions that may not normally be eligible for payment when family history of a related condition is documented in the patient's record and reported on the claim.

Note:

This differs from the coding practice in the hospital inpatient setting regarding abnormal findings on test results, for which the physician may document a qualified diagnosis that is coded and reported.

Patients Receiving Therapeutic Services Only

For patients receiving *therapeutic services only* during an outpatient encounter, sequence first the diagnosis, condition, problem, or other reason for encounter chiefly responsible for the outpatient services provided during the encounter.

Assign codes to other diagnoses (e.g., chronic conditions) that are treated or medically managed or that would affect the patient's receipt of therapeutic services during this encounter.

The only exception to this rule is when the reason for encounter is for chemotherapy, radiation therapy, or rehabilitation. For these services, the appropriate ICD-10-CM Z code for the service is listed first and the diagnosis or problem for which the service is being performed is reported second.

Patients Receiving Preoperative Evaluations Only

For patients receiving *preoperative evaluations only*, assign and report first the appropriate code from ICD-10-CM subcategory Z01.81 (Encounter for preprocedural examinations) to describe the preoperative consultations.

Assign an additional code for the condition that describes the reason for the surgery. Also assign additional code(s) to any findings discovered during the preoperative evaluation.

Ambulatory Surgery (or Outpatient Surgery)

For *ambulatory surgery* (or *outpatient surgery*), assign a code to the diagnosis for which the surgery was performed. If the postoperative diagnosis is different from the preoperative diagnosis when the diagnosis is confirmed, assign a code to the postoperative diagnosis instead (because it is more definitive).

 Note:

> Preadmission testing (PAT) is routinely completed prior to an inpatient admission or outpatient surgery to facilitate the patient's treatment and reduce the length of stay. As an incentive to facilities that perform PAT, some payers provide higher reimbursement for PAT, making it important to assign codes properly.

Routine Outpatient Prenatal Visits

For routine outpatient prenatal visits when no complications are present, report a code from ICD-10-CM category Z34 (Encounter for supervision of normal pregnancy) as the first-listed diagnosis. *Do not report this code in combination with ICD-10-CM Chapter 15 codes.*

For routine prenatal outpatient visits for patients with high-risk pregnancies, report an ICD-10-CM code from category O09 (supervision of high-risk pregnancy) as the first-listed diagnosis. A code from ICD-10-CM Chapter 15 may also be reported as a secondary diagnosis, if appropriate.

Encounters for General Medical Examinations with Abnormal Findings

The subcategories for encounters for general adult medical examinations, Z00.0-, provide codes for with and without abnormal findings. Should a general medical examination result in an abnormal finding, the code for general medical examination with abnormal finding should be assigned as the first-listed diagnosis. An *examination with abnormal findings* refers to a condition or diagnosis that is newly identified or a change in severity of a chronic condition (e.g., uncontrolled hypertension, acute exacerbation of COPD) during a routine physical examination. A secondary code for the abnormal finding should also be assigned.

Encounters for Routine Health Screenings

Screening is the testing for disease or disease precursors in seemingly well individuals so that early detection and treatment can be provided for those who test positive for the disease (e.g., screening mammogram).

The testing of a person to rule out or confirm a suspected diagnosis because the patient has some sign or symptom is a diagnostic examination, not a screening. In these cases, the sign or symptom is used to explain the reason for the test.

A screening code may be a first-listed code if the reason for the visit is specifically the screening exam. It may also be used as an additional code if the screening is done during an office visit for other health problems.

A screening code is not necessary if the screening is inherent to a routine examination, such as a Pap smear done during a routine pelvic examination.

Should a condition be discovered during the screening then the code for the condition may be assigned as an additional diagnosis.

The Z code indicates that a screening exam is planned. A procedure code is required to confirm that the screening was performed.

The screening Z codes/categories include the following:

- Z11 Encounter for screening for infectious and parasitic diseases
- Z12 Encounter for screening for malignant neoplasms
- Z13 Encounter for screening for other diseases and disorders

     Except: Z13.9, Encounter for screening, unspecified

- Z36 Encounter for antenatal screening for mother

Exercise 6.2 – Diagnostic Coding and Reporting Guidelines for Outpatient Services: Hospital-Based and Physician Office

Instructions: Underline the first-listed diagnosis in each statement.

1. The patient underwent office treatment for removal of a skin lesion from her face. She also received a renewed prescription for her chronic asthma.

2. Dr. Smith ordered a chest x-ray to rule out pneumonia; he also documented shortness of breath in the record.

3. Sally Jones fell out of her tree house and sustained a fractured humerus, which was treated in the emergency department (ED). While in the ED, the physician noted severe swelling of the arm.

4. Cindy Frasier was seen in the office, complaining of severe stomach pain and vomiting. The physician diagnosed gastroenteritis.

5. Tom Noble was treated in the outpatient department for urinary frequency. The physician documented probable cystitis in the record.

6. The patient was treated on an outpatient basis for both acute and chronic bronchitis, for which each was assigned an ICD-10-CM diagnosis code.

7. Eric Fischer was treated for back pain in the physician's office. The physician documented that Eric's previously diagnosed influenza had completely resolved.

8. Scott Taylor was seen for complaints of dizziness, shakiness, and fainting spells; his blood was drawn and sent to the lab to have a blood glucose level performed. Lab results revealed blood glucose level of 325, Scott was placed on oral insulin, and the physician documented diabetes mellitus in the record.

9. Tina Day had an encounter for outpatient chemotherapy for treatment of breast cancer.

10. Joe Daly's preoperative diagnosis was cholelithiasis, for which he underwent laparoscopic cholecystectomy. The postoperative diagnosis was acute cholecystitis with cholelithiasis.

Summary

Outpatient care includes any health care service provided to a patient who is not admitted to a facility. Such care may be provided in a physician's office, a stand-alone health care facility, a hospital outpatient or emergency department, or the patient's home. The CMS *Diagnostic Coding and Reporting Guidelines for Outpatient Services: Hospital-Based and Physician Office* were developed by the federal government and have been approved for use by hospitals and providers for coding and reporting hospital-based outpatient services and provider-based office visits. Although the guidelines were originally developed for use in submitting government claims, insurance companies have also adopted them (sometimes with variation). The CMS Coding Guidelines for Outpatient Diagnostic Tests includes instructions and examples that are to be used when assigning ICD-10-CM codes for diagnostic test results. The instructions and examples provide guidance regarding the appropriate assignment of ICD-10-CM diagnosis codes to simplify coding for diagnostic tests, consistent with the CMS *Diagnostic Coding and Reporting Guidelines for Outpatient Services: Hospital-Based and Physician Office.*

Internet Links

AHA Central Office: Go to **www.ahacentraloffice.com** to access coding resources.

Encoder Pro: www.EncoderPro.com

HCPro, Inc.: Go to **www.hcmarketplace.com**, and click on the "Sign up for our FREE e-Newsletters" link. Click on the box located in front of the *JustCoding News: Outpatient* (along with other e-Newsletters that interest you) and fill out your name and contact information to subscribe.

Medical Information Bureau (MIB): www.mib.com

National Practitioner Data Bank (NPDB) and the Healthcare Integrity and Protection Data Bank (HIPDB): www.npdb-hipdb.com

Web-based training courses (free from CMS): Go to **https://learner.mlnlms.com**, and click on the Create Account link.

Study Checklist

- ❏ Read this chapter and highlight key concepts.
- ❏ Create an index card for each key term.
- ❏ Access the chapter Internet links to learn more about concepts.
- ❏ Complete the chapter exercises and review, verifying answers with your instructor.
- ❏ Complete Workbook chapter, verifying answers with your instructor.
- ❏ Go to **www.cengagebrain.com** to access the Student Companion Web Site. Login instructions are located in the Preface.
- ❏ Form a study group with classmates to discuss chapter concepts in preparation for an exam.

Review

Multiple Choice

Instructions: Select the most appropriate response.

1. A patient was seen on an outpatient basis to have lab tests performed. The next day the patient underwent an outpatient procedure. Due to complications, he was admitted to the hospital. One week after

discharge from the hospital, he was seen in the physician's office for a follow-up visit. Coding guidelines classify all of these visits as

    a. admissions.   b. appointments.   c. claims.   d. encounters.

2. A patient's record underwent review because the outpatient diagnosis about multiple injuries was unclear. Who is authorized to clarify the diagnosis?

    a. Health care provider   c. Insurance company

    b. HIM supervisor   d. Outpatient coder

Use the tabular list entries to answer the question that follows.

INDEX TO DISEASES

Osteoarthritis M19.90

TABULAR LIST OF DISEASES

```
M19  Other and unspecified osteoarthritis
          EXCLUDES1
                  polyarthritis (M15.-)
          EXCLUDES2
                  arthrosis of spine (M47.-)
                  hallux rigidus (M20.2)
                  osteoarthritis of spine (M47.-)
M19.9 Osteoarthritis, unspecified site
      M19.90 Unspecified osteoarthritis, unspecified site
                  Arthrosis NOS Osteoarthritis NOS
                  Arthritis NOS
      M19.91 Primary osteoarthritis, unspecified site
                  Primary osteoarthritis NOS
      M19.92 Post-traumatic osteoarthritis, unspecified site
                  Post-traumatic osteoarthritis NOS
      M19.93 Secondary osteoarthritis, unspecified site
                  Secondary osteoarthritis NOS
```

---

3. A patient is diagnosed with osteoarthritis, and the encounter is assigned code M19.90. When referring to the ICD-10-CM index and following tabular list entries, the code assignment of M19.90 was

    a. correct because M19.9 is listed in the index as the code for osteoarthritis.

    b. correct because no further information was available in the patient record to assign a more specific code.

    c. invalid because upon verifying M19.90 in the tabular list, the coder should have assigned a sixth digit.

    d. incorrect because the tabular list's excludes1 note directs the coder to assign a code for polyarthritis (M15.-)

4. In ICD-10-CM, code Z85.020 (personal history of malignant carcinoid tumor of stomach) is reported as a _____.
    - a. complication
    - b. first-listed
    - c. primary
    - d. secondary

5. When a definitive diagnosis has not been established or confirmed by the provider, which should be reported?
    - a. Codes that describe symptoms and signs
    - b. None because code assignment must wait until a diagnosis is confirmed
    - c. Office visit only
    - d. Qualified diagnosis, such as rule out, possible, or suspected

Use the tabular list entries to answer the question that follows.

INDEX TO DISEASES AND INJURIES

`Drunkenness` (without dependence) F10.129

  with dependence F10.229

TABULAR LIST OF DISEASES AND INJURIES

`F10.2 Alcohol dependence`

  `F10.20 Alcohol dependence, uncomplicated`

  `F10.21 Alcohol dependence, in remission`

  `F10.22 Alcohol dependence with intoxication`

    `F10.220 Alcohol dependence with intoxication, uncomplicated`

    `F10.221 Alcohol dependence with intoxication delirium`

    `F10.229 Alcohol dependence with intoxication, unspecified`

---

6. When referring to the ICD-10-CM index and following tabular list entries, drunkenness with dependence (F10.229) is an example of a(n) _____ code.
    - a. combination
    - b. history
    - c. late effect
    - d. multiple

7. When a bacterial organism is documented as the cause of a condition (e.g., UTI), it is
    - a. coded as either a first-listed or a secondary code.
    - b. coded as a first-listed diagnosis only.
    - c. reported as a secondary code, below the code for the condition.
    - d. not coded because bacterial organisms are always classified in the disease code.

8. When determining the first-listed diagnosis, the ICD-10-CM coding conventions and _____ guidelines take precedence over the official outpatient guidelines.
    - a. drugs and adverse effects
    - b. eponyms and procedure/surgical
    - c. external cause of injury and poisoning
    - d. general and disease-specific

9. For accurate reporting of ICD-10-CM diagnosis codes,
    a. a definitive diagnosis must be documented by the physician who provides care to the patient.
    b. all diagnosis and condition codes must contain seven characters.
    c. A00.0 through T88.9 and Z00–Z99.89 are used to classify the encounter.
    d. definitive diagnoses in addition to all signs and symptoms are classified.

10. Which section of ICD-10-CM would be referenced to assign codes that deal with encounters for circumstances other than a disease or an injury?
    a. Classification of Diseases and Injuries
    b. Morphology of Neoplasms
    c. Factors Influencing Health Status and Contact with Health Services
    d. Table of Drugs and Chemicals

11. An encounter is reported with codes for symptoms listed first, followed by an unrelated secondary condition code. Thus, the reason for the visit has
    a. been confirmed, and a coexisting condition was treated or medically managed during the same encounter.
    b. been confirmed, and the patient also exhibited unrelated signs and symptoms during the same encounter.
    c. not been confirmed at the time of coding, and a coexisting condition was treated or medically managed during the same encounter.
    d. not been confirmed at the time of coding, and the patient also exhibited unrelated signs and symptoms during the same encounter.

12. A woman is examined for a routine prenatal visit, with no apparent complications. Which would be the reason for this encounter?
    a. Complications of pregnancy and childbirth
    b. Encounter for pregnancy test, result positive
    c. Personal history of complications of pregnancy
    d. Supervision of normal uncomplicated pregnancy

13. Which is assigned when the provider documents a reason for a patient seeking health care that is not a disorder or disease?
    a. Conditions that are ruled out
    b. Diagnoses that are qualified
    c. External causes of morbidity
    d. Factors influencing health status

14. The "x" character in an ICD-10-CM code is called a(n) _____.
    a. eponym   b. modifier   c. placeholder   d. qualifier

15. Which ICD-10-CM Index to Diseases and Injuries entry (below) identifies the second qualifier?
    Stricture (*see also* Stenosis)
      aqueduct of Sylvius (congenital) Q03.0
        with spina bifida—*see* Spina bifida, by site, with hydrocephalus

    a. Aqueduct of Sylvius
    b. Stenosis
    c. Stricture
    d. With spina bifida

16. The patient is seen in the office because of chronic asthma. Coding guidelines for chronic conditions state that such codes
    a. are not to be reported if the condition is already being medically managed.
    b. may be reported as additional diagnosis only if medically managed.
    c. may be reported as first-listed if medically managed during the encounter.
    d. should never be reported on an outpatient claim.

17. A patient complains of nausea and abdominal pain and undergoes an endoscopy for suspected hiatal hernia. The test results were negative, so the physician instructed the patient to return next week to be tested for gastroesophageal reflux disease. To code this encounter to the highest degree of accuracy and completeness, which would be reported?
    a. Gastroesophageal reflux disease
    b. Hiatal hernia
    c. Nausea and abdominal pain
    d. Nausea and vomiting and gastroesophageal reflux disease

18. Urinary tract infection due to E. coli is coded as _____.
    a. B96.20
    b. B96.20, N39.0
    c. N39.0
    d. N39.0, B96.20

19. Well-child visit is coded as _____.
    a. Z00.129
    b. Z00.2
    c. Z71.89
    d. Z00.00

20. The patient is diagnosed with pneumonia. A sputum specimen is sent to a pathologist and growth of streptococcus, type B, is confirmed and documented in the patient's record. Use your ICD-10-CM coding manual to determine which code is reported for this diagnosis.
    a. J13
    b. J15.3
    c. J17
    d. J18.9

Coding Practice

Instructions: Review each case scenario, and assign and properly sequence the ICD-10-CM diagnosis codes, including ICD-10-CM external cause codes, as appropriate.

Coding Practice — Ambulatory Surgery Center (ASC)

1. SUBJECTIVE: 20-year-old female patient with past medical history significant for asthma underwent total thyroidectomy due to feelings of fatigue and weight gain for the past six months.

   OBJECTIVE: Thyroid function tests revealed that the patient was hypothyroid with a thyroid-stimulating hormone level of 110.2, free thyroxine index of 0.9, and total T3 of 0.41. The patient also has a palpable mass in the left lobe of the thyroid, and thyroid ultrasound revealed diffuse enlargement of the thyroid gland and microcalcifications. Thyroid lobes were biopsied bilaterally; based on those results, the patient underwent total thyroidectomy.

   DIAGNOSES: Hypothyroidism. Enlargment of thyroid gland. History of asthma.

   _____

2. SUBJECTIVE: 42-year-old female with past family history of gastric polyposis underwent upper gastro-intestinal endoscopy, which revealed multiple gastric polyps in the fundus and body.

   OBJECTIVE: Biopsies of the gastric polyps were submitted for pathological examination.

   DIAGNOSES: Multiple gastric (stomach) polyps. Family history of gastric polyposis.

   _____

3. This 35-year-old states that her menstrual periods have been regular, and she had been taking birth control pills until January of this year. Since that time, she has been using other methods of birth control that are unsatisfactory to her. She and her husband also desire tubal ligation for prevention of further pregnancies.

   PHYSICAL EXAMINATION reveals a morbidly obese white female in no obvious distress; heart and lungs normal to auscultation; abdomen flat; on pressure, the cervix protrudes to the opening of the vaginal os;

otherwise, the uterus was average size. Patient was taken to surgery and underwent laparoscopic bilateral tubal ligation. She was discharged in stable condition to be seen by Dr. Baker for follow-up care next week.

DIAGNOSES: Elective sterilization. Morbid obesity.

---

4. A 53-year-old male is admitted with a right inguinal hernia. Laboratory results were within normal limits. Right inguinal herniorrhaphy was performed, and the patient did well; there were no complications. He was discharged to be seen in the office in several days for suture removal. No specific diet or medication was prescribed. The patient was advised to avoid any strenuous activities.

   DIAGNOSIS: Right inguinal hernia.

---

5. This 31-year-old white female is admitted to the ambulatory surgery unit with chief complaint of multiparity. She states that she wants to undergo a sterilization procedure. She underwent laparoscopic tubal fulguration, bilateral. There are no familial diseases such as epilepsy, diabetes, bleeding tendency, tuberculosis, or heart attacks. She smokes a pack of cigarettes a day and takes no alcohol. She is married, but now separated. She has been in good health and has had no other problems. Her menses are every 28 days and last 4 days. No clots or pains. Her last period was January 1. She has two children living and well, ages 11 and 5.

   DIAGNOSES: Encounter for sterilization procedure. Multiparity. History of tobacco use.

Coding Practice — Chiropractic Office

Special Instructions: Also assign external cause codes for any applicable activity performed, external cause status, place of occurrence, and/or type of accident.

1. A 37-year-old civilian contractor was hired by a home owner. While lifting boards from his truck while on the job in the private driveway at a single family residence, he began to experience acute burning pain in his neck from this sudden strenuous movement. His symptoms persisted, and he was seen by his chiropractor who checked the range of motion in his neck and noted restriction in lateral bending and rotation. Neurologic screening revealed decreased sensation at the left thumb and first finger. Reflexes were normal (intact), but there was some muscle weakness in the arm. Patient underwent magnetic resonance imaging (MRI), which was negative, and received chiropractic treatment.

   DIAGNOSIS: Cervical disc syndrome.

---

2. A 15-year-old high school student was playing in a basketball game one evening on the basketball court at his public high school; when he went up for a rebound, he collided with another player. He felt his neck "wrench" backward, and he experienced immediate pain in both sides of his neck. That evening he felt pain and stiffness in his neck, and he had trouble turning his head.

   DIAGNOSIS: Acute cervical sprain. (Initial encounter.)

---

3. A 48-year-old online college professor who sits at a computer, keyboarding all day in her office at the college, has been experiencing neck pain accompanied by soreness and stiffness in her upper back. She became concerned when she began to experience numbness and tingling in her left arm, especially at night. History reveals no weakness in her arms and minor arm pain. All neurologic signs are normal, and the patient has full range of motion in her neck except for some restriction when she bends her

head to the left. Tight and very tender muscles in the upper back and along both side of the neck are palpated. There are also joint restrictions in the middle back. Chiropractic treatment was provided.

DIAGNOSES: Cervical neck strain. Myalgia, upper back.

---

4. A 77-year-old individual experiences neck pain and seeks chiropractic treatment. Upon examination, all neurologic signs are normal. There is restricted joint motion and tight muscles along both sides of the neck and into the upper and midback. Previous x-ray of the neck revealed osteoarthritis. The patient undergoes chiropractic treatment.

   DIAGNOSIS: Osteoarthritis, cervical spine.

---

5. A 25-year-old college student is seen for chiropractic treatment. She complains of neck stiffness, shoulder and back pain, and headaches. Neck x-rays are negative. Chiropractic treatment included adjustment and heat therapy.

   DIAGNOSIS: Neck sprain. (Initial encounter.)

Coding Practice — Hospital Emergency Department

1. SUBJECTIVE: 15-year-old male patient with previous diagnoses of congenital cataracts and retinal detachments had experienced an episode of orbital hemorrhage, which was treated in the past. He arrived in the ED today after developing pain behind his right eye yesterday.

   OBJECTIVE: Physical examination revealed no redness of the eye. The left pupil is deviated medially with a steamy anterior chamber. This is the normal appearance, according to the mother. There was no sight in that eye. Funduscopic examination shows a pigmented retina in the right eye, but no evidence of hemorrhage or optic disc cupping. Schiotz tonometry showed a right orbital pressure of 21 and left orbital pressure of 0. There was no cervical lymphadenopathy. Tympanic membranes were clear. Chest was clear, and heart is regular rate and rhythm. There is full range of motion of the neck. No palpable temporal arteries; no abrasions or swelling. There has been no fever.

   ASSESSMENT: Headache, etiology unknown.

   PLAN: I called his primary care physician, who explained that this has been a problem in the past and that neurologically, the patient has been evaluated for this type of problem but nothing was ever found. He believed that the pressure of 21 was okay and that the patient could be discharged on some sort of analgesic. The patient is scheduled to be seen by him in two weeks.

   DIAGNOSIS: Headache.

---

2. SUBJECTIVE: 25-year-old male was working with a heavy sledgehammer in the garden on his personal property when he noted pain in his right shoulder area. The pain developed suddenly as he was swinging the hammer rather vigorously. The pain has persisted over the past three weeks. At certain times, it was somewhat better, but it became painful once again. The patient has continued working, which involves swinging this sledgehammer.

   OBJECTIVE: Physical examination reveals tenderness over the anterior joint line; there is no swelling or abnormal mass present. The rotator cuff does not seem involved, as the patient can tolerate extreme downward pressure on his elbows without any pain whatsoever. What really causes the patient's pain is bringing the arms apart when they are in the midline in front of his chest. Distal neurovascular status is intact. X-ray of the shoulder was negative.

DIAGNOSIS: Pain, right shoulder. Probable strain, deltoid muscle, and possibly the deeper muscles of the anterior shoulder area.

TREATMENT: The patient was given a prescription for Motrin 600 milligrams three times daily and advised to apply heat to the area once or twice each day. He is also to rest the arm as much as possible; however, he says he must work and will not take time off. He was told that this pain may last for a number of weeks before it resolves completely. He is to return to see Dr. Callus if there are any problems.

---

3. SUBJECTIVE: This 48-year-old man is a patient of mine who complains of midsternal chest pain but no radiation. This has occurred intermittently today since 10 P.M. and did not occur reliably with exertion. He has not been exerting himself too much, as he is a pastor at a Baptist church. He complains of feeling quite warm, but has had no diaphoresis or shortness of breath. He previously had his gallbladder removed. He has been taking Inderal 40 milligrams four times each day, and he took Isordil sublingually with mixed results during the day today. He says that Tylenol will help somewhat with the pain in the midsternal area.

OBJECTIVE: Physical examination reveals a mildly anxious middle-aged male in little distress. The neck is supple; carotids are two plus without bruits. Chest is symmetrical in expansion, and lungs show few abnormal sounds and some rales in the right base. Heart is regular rate and rhythm; S1 and S2 and 2/4; no murmurs, clicks, heaves, gallops, or rubs were appreciated. The abdomen is soft and nontender. There is a right upper quadrant surgical scar; no masses or organomegaly noted. EKG was done and read as normal. Chest x-ray shows slightly increased density at right lower lobe. He was given Mylanta without any change in his pain.

DIAGNOSIS: Bronchitis and early pneumonia on the right.

---

4. SUBJECTIVE: This 22-year-old female twisted her ankle yesterday while playing softball at a local baseball field. She states that she developed pain in the ankle subsequent to this injury and has been on crutches prior to her arrival in the ED this morning. She denies any previous significant injuries to the ankle.

OBJECTIVE: Physical examination reveals a healthy, cooperative 22-year-old female in no acute distress. There is tenderness about the left ankle. There is no ecchymoses or swelling present. There is tenderness beneath both malleoli and anteriorly across the ankle. X-rays of the ankle show no evidence of fracture.

PLAN: The patient was instructed to use crutches for seven days and to avoid any weight-bearing and then begin partial weight-bearing. If she is uncomfortable, she is to return to using crutches for several more days before attempting weight-bearing. She is to elevate the leg and use ice compresses, and she was advised to be reevaluated if she is not able to walk comfortably in 7 to 10 days.

DIAGNOSIS: Sprain, left ankle.

---

5. SUBJECTIVE: This is a 28-year-old female who was handed a knife by her husband, blade first; she accidentally punctured her left ring finger on the blade.

OBJECTIVE: Patient has a superficial puncture wound over the lateral aspect of the left fourth finger. The area has been cleansed well, and a bandage was applied.

ASSESSMENT: Puncture wound, left ring finger. (Initial encounter.)

PLAN: Patient is to watch for any signs of infection and follow up with her primary care physician.

Coding Practice — Hospital Outpatient Department

1. A 39-year-old female patient undergoes a screening electrocardiogram (EKG) as an outpatient. She has a family history of cardiovascular disease. EKG results were negative. The nonspecific T-wave changes illustrated on the EKG were explained to the patient as probably due to anxiety and positional changes.

   _____

2. A 42-year-old male patient diagnosed with systemic lupus erythematosus received a scheduled transfusion of erythrocytes and platelets in the ambulatory transfusion clinic.

   _____

3. A 54-year-old male previously diagnosed with arteriosclerotic heart disease (ASHD) underwent scheduled right and left cardiac catheterization as an outpatient. The patient has no past history of previous coronary artery bypass graft (CABG) surgery. Cardiac catheterization results revealed 40% blockage of the right coronary artery, 70% blockage of the left main coronary artery, and 80% blockage of the left anterior descending coronary artery. Surgical intervention options to treat the blockages were discussed with the patient, and the patient will be admitted in two days to undergo triple CABG.

   _____

4. A 62-year-old patient with known congestive heart failure registered for outpatient services at the heart failure clinic and receives lifestyle modification counseling about his diet and activities. He received instruction from the dietician about following a low-sodium, low-fat diet, and he was also counseled to avoid tobacco and heavy alcohol use. His current medications were reviewed, and his diuretic dosage was adjusted.

   _____

5. A 45-year-old patient registered as an outpatient to undergo scheduled hemodialysis. The patient was born with just one kidney, which failed when she was 30 years old. She previously underwent a kidney transplant, which also failed. Currently, dialysis is her only option as she awaits the availability of another kidney for transplant. The hemodialysis takes three hours and is uneventful.

   _____

Coding Practice — Hospital Same Day Surgery

1. This 5-year-old white male is admitted with the chief complaint of recurrent bouts of tonsillitis and tonsils so large that food gets stuck in them and he chokes on it. He has had a sore throat now for four to five weeks, and this is the second time this year that this has happened. He has consulted Dr. Blair, and she advised that the patient undergo tonsillectomy and adenoidectomy (T&A). The patient has no ear problems, and he has not had strep throat that his father knows of.

   PAST MEDICAL HISTORY: He has had no operations, serious illnesses, or injuries.

   FAMILY HISTORY: He has had no familial diseases such as cancer, tuberculosis, epilepsy, diabetes, bleeding tendency, or heart attacks.

   SOCIAL HISTORY: The patient is in kindergarten. He lives with his parents and has no social problems.

   SYSTEMIC REVIEW: The father states that his son has been in good health and has had no other problems.

   PHYSICAL EXAMINATION: Reveals his tonsils to be huge. There is evidence that he had an anterior lymphadenopathy.

LABORATORY STUDIES: Urinalysis negative. Bleeding time 1 minute 30 seconds. Partial prothrombin time 30 seconds. Hemoglobin 12.3 grams, hematocrit 37 volume percent, white blood count 6500 with 34 polys. Chest x-ray normal. The patient was prepared for surgery and taken to the operating room where, under satisfactory general intratracheal anesthesia, T&A was performed. Following the operation, he had an uncomplicated postoperative recovery. He had no bleeding, he was afebrile, tonsillar fossa are clean, and he has had no anesthetic complications.

DIAGNOSIS: Greatly hypertrophied tonsils and adenoids.

2. This is an 89-year-old white male who was apparently in good health except for pneumonia in 1938 and had never had any serious medical problems since then. For about a month prior to outpatient surgery, he developed urgency and frequency upon urination and marked nocturia every hour, followed finally by the passing of blood in the urine. He was seen in the emergency room (ER) last week due to passing blood in the urine every day for several days and having a great deal of difficulty voiding. ER treatment involved inserting a Foley catheter, from which 400 cc of grossly bloody urine was evacuated.

PHYSICAL EXAMINATION: Reveals a degree of blindness due to cataracts. The testes are atrophic. Prostate is a grade II benign, enlarged gland.

LABORATORY AND X-RAY FINDINGS: BUN 62, blood sugar 155, CO_2 14, creatinine 3.6. Urinalysis reveals many red blood cells per high-power field and WBC 4–6. Urine culture reveals innumerable enterococci. Complete blood count reveals hemoglobin of 11.9 grams, hematocrit of 35. Blood gases reveal pH of 7.38, pCO_2 of 22.9, PO_2 of 91, HCO of 313. WBC of 12,200. EKG was negative. Drip infusion IVP revealed poorly functioning kidneys and one bladder diverticulum with elevation of the bladder floor consistent with a large prostate gland. Chest x-ray showed bilateral basal pulmonary infiltration and calcification of the thoracic aorta. Upper gastrointestinal and gallbladder series and small bowel series revealed small active ulcer crater of the lesser curvature of the pyloric canal. Patient underwent cystoscopy and retropubic prostatectomy.

DIAGNOSES: Benign prostatic hypertrophy. Chronic renal insufficiency secondary to benign prostatic hypertrophy. Urinary tract infection.

3. This 48-year-old male patient has had an anal fissure for several months and is complaining of pain and bleeding. This has not responded to conservative measures, and he is scheduled to undergo outpatient fissurectomy and hemorrhoidectomy.

PHYSICAL EXAMINATION: Reveals no other pertinent positive findings except the presence of obesity, anal fissure, and hemorrhoids. X-ray of the chest was unremarkable. Barium enema studies were unremarkable. EKG showed no abnormality. Lab results revealed blood sugar 92, BUN 14, normal electrolytes, and normal enzymes. CBC and differential were normal. Urinalysis was essentially unremarkable. After adequate workup, the patient was taken to surgery; under endotracheal anesthesia, a fissurectomy, hemorrhoidectomy, and sphincterotomy were performed. Post-op, the patient was voiding and comfortable. The patient was prescribed Tylenol with Codeine, Metamucil, sitz baths, and limited activity. The patient will be followed in my office.

DIAGNOSES: Anal fissure. First-degree bleeding hemorrhoids.

4. This 51-year-old white female has noticed a steady enlargement on the left side of the neck for the past year. A thyroid scan revealed a cold nodule in the right lobe, and carcinoma is to be ruled out. The patient also complains of some difficulty with pain in the neck and on swallowing.

PHYSICAL EXAMINATION: Reveals a large mass in the left lobe of the thyroid and a questionable mass on the right side. The patient was taken to surgery, where at the time of exploration, both lobes of the thyroid were markedly enlarged and revealed multiple nodules. A total thyroidectomy was performed after identifying the parathyroid glands and protecting them. The patient was discharged and instructed to return for follow-up examination within two weeks. She was placed on Synthroid 0.15 daily and no other medication.

DIAGNOSES: Nodular colloid goiter, left and right lobes of thyroid. Degenerating follicular adenoma, right lobe of thyroid.

---

5. Patient was diagnosed as missed abortion at 20 weeks' gestation. The patient was noted to have grown appreciably in the last month of her prenatal care, and it was noted that she had begun bleeding three days before being seen in the office yesterday. At the time of the office visit, she was passing clots. The cervix was dilated, and she was developing a foul-smelling discharge but no morbidity. She was scheduled for outpatient surgery, during which pregnancy was removed with curettage of the uterus. The patient was discharged in satisfactory condition. Her hemoglobin was 13.8 gm, white blood cell count was normal differential. Pathology revealed products of conception and degenerated decidual and placental tissue.

DIAGNOSIS: Missed abortion.

Coding Practice — Physician Office

1. This 38-year-old man was accidentally poked in his left eye by his nine-month-old little girl yesterday when she came to visit him in his office on a college campus, where he teaches. He says that she was very excited about seeing him, and when she reached up to be lifted into his arms, her finger accidentally poked him in the eye and her fingernail scratched his eyeball. He had to teach a class after he saw her, or he would have been in my office earlier. He states, "My eye is killing me!" Since that time, he has pain in his left eye and a lot of watering. He has had no changes in vision, no blurriness noted, and he is otherwise well. Physical examination shows the conjunctiva to be inflamed. Funduscopic examination is normal, and extraocular movements are intact. Stain with fluorescein shows positive corneal abrasion. I administered an ophthalmic topical analgesic to relieve his discomfort and Chloromycetin ointment to the eye to prevent infection. He was fitted with an eye patch, and he is to see me tomorrow for a recheck.

DIAGNOSIS: Corneal laceration.

---

2. This 15-year-old male was struck on the left leg by a stick yesterday, which created a puncture wound in the skin of his leg. The patient presents today with swelling and localized redness around the wound. Physical exam reveals a healthy and cooperative 15-year-old male in no acute distress with a small puncture-type wound approximately 5 millimeters in length on the anterior aspect of the left leg, just proximal to the knee. The wound is noted to have a small amount of induration, approximately 2 centimeters in diameter around the area with localized redness. There is no discomfort to motion of the knee.

DIAGNOSIS: Puncture wound, left knee. (Initial encounter.)

PLAN: The patient was instructed to use warm soaks to that knee several times each day and have it rechecked if it becomes worse. He will return or be seen sooner if the knee does not appear to improve. He was started on Keflex 500 milligrams four times daily.

---

3. This 34-year-old male, who has had a hydrocele in the past and had been seen and treated by Dr. Wise, returns now for continued pain and swelling in the hydrocele, which is causing poor sleep habits. Apparently, the patient has been given some kind of "fluid pill" for the discomfort.

   OBJECTIVE: Patient has a tender, swelling right scrotal region about the size of a grapefruit, which is very tense.

   ASSESSMENT: Right-sided hydrocele.

   PLAN: The patient is to wear tight, supportive underwear; take Tylenol #3 for pain; and see Dr. Wise for evaluation.

---

4. This man cut his left thumbnail and thumb with a powered hand saw today, which flapped back the lateral aspect of the thumb. The thumb was cleansed, numbed, and one stitch put through the nail, fixing the flap in place. He is current on his tetanus immunizations. He will return to the office to have the stitch removed in six to eight days unless he experiences symptoms, in which case he is to call the office to be seen.

   DIAGNOSIS: Laceration, thumbnail and thumb, left.

---

5. This 1-year-old little girl injured her hand while "playing the drum" by banging away at pots and pans on the floor of the kitchen while her mother was nearby preparing last evening's meal. The child slept fitfully last night, and this morning her left hand is somewhat swollen and painful to touch. X-ray was taken and is negative for fracture. I treated her with a sling, ice, and elevation, which will continue at home. She will be rechecked as needed. She left the office in good condition.

Coding Practice — Stand-Alone Radiology Center

1. A 50-year-old male patient underwent ultrasound of neck and ultrasound-guided placement of internal jugular dialysis catheter. Indication for radiographic procedures is chronic renal failure and occluded dialysis access graft. Real-time ultrasound examination was done of the neck and showed patency of both internal jugular veins. Following sterile prep and drape and infiltration with local anesthetic, puncture was done of the lower aspect of the right internal jugular vein using a 21-gauge needle. Using Seldinger technique, the tract was dilated and a 14 French dialysis catheter was introduced and positioned within the right atrium. The catheter was secured with a silk suture and irrigated and the patient sent for dialysis.

---

2. Gallbladder cholecystogram shows moderate concentration of dye in the gallbladder, no evidence of stone, and moderate hypertrophic change of lumbar spine. Small intestinal pattern is normal below the level of the duodenum. Impression is hypertrophic gallbladder with no diagnostic evidence of stones.

---

3. Patient underwent upper gastrointestinal study due to severe stomach pain. Study reveals esophagus and stomach to be normal in appearance, and first portion of duodenum is normal. There is moderate deformity of the medial aspect of the second portion of the duodenum with moderate flattening of the mucosal pattern in this area, but without any definite evidence of ulceration. The duodenal loop is not

significantly widened, but there does appear to be slight extrinsic pressure and probable stiffening of the medial wall of the second portion of the duodenum.

IMPRESSION: Second portion of duodenum is consistent with residues of recurrent pancreatitis with probable exacerbation of the pancreatitis at this time. The possibility of neoplasm arising in the head of the pancreas is not excluded.

---

4. Patient underwent excretory urogram for complaints of urinary incontinence. Urogram revealed that both kidneys appear to concentrate Renografin media in a satisfactory manner. Renal collecting system on the left appears grossly normal. Visualized lateral contour of right kidney appears normal. Renal pelvis and ureters are of normal caliber. Urinary bladder is moderately distended, normal in contour, and shows some indentation on its dome, probably due to the adjacent uterus. There is moderate post voiding residual. Impression is normal right and left calices, small post voiding residual with indentation on dome of urinary bladder, possibly due to an enlarged uterus.

---

5. Patient underwent opaque right knee arthrogram for severe pain and limited mobility. Following shaving and scrubbing of the knee in the usual manner, local anesthetic was infiltrated along the lateral approach to the patellofemoral joint. A needle was directed through the anesthetized tissue and into the joint with subsequent removal of 30 cc of pink-colored joint fluid. Then, 11 cc of Renografin 76 was injected and films taken in various projections. Fissures are demonstrated in the posterior segment of the medial meniscus. Cruciate ligaments and lateral meniscus appear intact. Impression is knee joint effusion and rupture of posterior segment of right medial meniscus. (Initial encounter.)

Coding Practice — Stand-Alone Urgent Care Center

1. SUBJECTIVE: A 45-year-old female was seen complaining of severe pain of the right knee and ankle after having been in a motorcycle accident earlier today. She has difficulty bearing weight on her right leg.

   OBJECTIVE: Multiple abrasions are noted on both forearms. Two lacerations are noted on the left elbow, approximately 2 centimeters in length. She has a sprain of the right knee, lower leg, and ankle. X-rays of the right knee, lower leg, and ankle were negative. Multiple views revealed no bony abnormality. There was slight soft tissue swelling over the lateral malleolus.

   TREATMENT: The lacerations on the left elbow were 1 inch long and 1/2 inch long. They were closed with interrupted 4-0 Prolene sutures after thorough cleansing. The abrasions were cleansed. She was given a tetanus toxoid booster, and a sterile dressing was applied. The patient is to be rechecked by her primary care physician in 48 hours. She left in good condition.

   DIAGNOSES: Multiple abrasions, arms and legs. Laceration, left elbow. Sprain, right knee, lower leg, and ankle.

---

2. The patient is a 41-year-old male seen for treatment of a scratch on the dorsum of his right hand that occurred about a week ago. It did not seem to bother him, and he did not think too much of it. He accidentally stepped on the edge of a piece of 2×4 wood and the opposite end raised up and struck his right hand about two days ago, and it stung a little bit and became a little swollen. It was rather tender today and looking a bit red. He was quite concerned because he has had blood poisoning once before due to an infected hair follicle on his hand. I instructed him to come to the urgent care center for evaluation. The patient does have swelling and induration around the area where he had the

original scratch. It is red and warm, but there is no streaking that I can see in the lymphatic channels. I think he is developing an infection there, or cellulitis.

IMPRESSION: Cellulitis, right hand. (Initial encounter.)

DISPOSITION: Hot soaks three or four times each day. Amoxil 250 milligrams three times each day for a week. If it should progressively worsen and become more swollen, the patient should call and have it checked again to be sure he isn't developing an abscess; otherwise, we'll give him a few days. If it hasn't cleared within five to seven days, he is to let me know.

---

3. This 44-year-old male presents with a chief complaint of back pain. HPI: 44-year-old gentleman states that he went fishing Wednesday. He did not fall or injure himself, but Thursday he was feeling quite bad with right flank pain radiating into the back of his leg and into the testicle. He stated that he had no change in the color of his urine and that the pain actually started to subside. Friday, he had another recurrence of pain, and it gradually worsened and stayed with him. Today, it was much worse, he was unable to work, and he came to the urgent care center for evaluation and treatment. The patient walks leaning to the right where his pain is. He has a significant amount of difficulty in hyperextension and also forward bending. It does not hurt him too much to bend to the right, but it hurts him quite a bit to bend to the left. He has a lot of tenderness in the sacroiliac region and also in the superior rim of the ilium and the sacrum. X-rays of the area appear normal to my eye. The radiology report is not back at this time.

PLAN: We will treat him with Tylenol with Codeine, two tablets every four hours as needed, and Flexeril 10 milligrams three times a day. He should not work tomorrow or Monday, and perhaps he will be able to return to work on Tuesday. He was instructed to call the urgent care center if he gets any worse. He is instructed to schedule a follow-up visit in one week. He left the urgency care center in satisfactory condition.

DIAGNOSIS: Sacroiliac inflammation.

---

4. This 15-year-old male presents to the urgent care center with the complaint of a cyst on his right cheek. Over the past two days, the patient has developed a reddened, tender mass on the right cheek, just lateral to the nose. Physical exam reveals an erythematous, tender mass approximately 7 millimeters in diameter on the right cheek. It is hard and tender, but does not seem to be fluctuant at this time.

DIAGNOSIS: Infected sebaceous cyst, right cheek.

PLAN: The patient was instructed to use warm soaks frequently, and he was given a prescription for tetracycline 250 milligrams four times daily. He was instructed to see Dr. Smith in two days. He is to return sooner if he has further difficulty.

---

5. This young lady was accidentally hit in her nose and mouth two days ago by another resident; she has had intermittent nosebleeds since that time. She resides at the detention center in the village and was brought to the urgent care center and examined. There was moderate swelling in the nose and quite a bit of edema and swelling in the nasal mucosa, but there is no active bleeding noted at the present time. No treatment was given other than Dimetapp one every 12 hours, and the patient was told to avoid taking aspirin. She is to take Tylenol and apply ice to her nose. The detention center staff person who accompanied the patient to the urgent care center was told to call if the patient experienced further problems.

PART III

Health Care Procedure Coding System (HCPCS), Level II National Coding System

HCPCS Level II National Coding System

Chapter Outline

Overview of HCPCS

HCPCS Level II National Codes

Assigning HCPCS Level II Codes

Determining Payer Responsibility

Chapter Objectives

At the conclusion of this chapter, the student should be able to:

- Define key terms.
- List the HCPCS levels and their components.
- Assign HCPCS level II procedure and services codes for outpatient care.
- Identify situations in which both HCPCS levels I and II codes are assigned.
- Assign claims to primary Medicare administrative contractors (MACs) or durable medical equipment MACs according to HCPCS level II code number.

Key Terms

advance beneficiary notice (ABN)

certificate of medical necessity (CMN)

DME MAC medical review policies

durable medical equipment, prosthetics, orthotics, and supplies (DMEPOS)

durable medical equipment, prosthetics, orthotics, and supplies (DMEPOS) dealer

HCPCS level I

HCPCS level II miscellaneous codes

HCPCS level II modifiers

HCPCS level II permanent national codes

HCPCS level II temporary codes

local coverage determinations (LCDs)

Medicare Carriers Manual (MCM)

Medicare National Coverage Determinations Manual

Medicare Pricing, Data Analysis, and Coding (PDAC) contractor

national coverage determinations (NCDs)

orthotics

prosthetics

transitional pass-through payment

Introduction

The HCPCS level II national coding system contains alphanumeric codes that were developed to complement the Current Procedural Terminology (CPT) coding system. HCPCS level II was introduced in 1983 after Medicare found that its payers used more than 100 different coding systems, making it difficult to analyze claims data. HCPCS level II furnishes health care providers and suppliers with a standardized language for reporting professional and nonphysician services, procedures, supplies, and equipment. (Most state Medicaid programs and many commercial payers also use the HCPCS level II coding system.)

Note:

When reviewing examples and completing exercises and review questions in this chapter, use your HCPCS Level II coding manual to locate index entries and to verify them in the tabular list.

Note:

Instruction about the HCPCS level II coding system is sequenced prior to CPT Chapters 8–18 in this textbook to familiarize students with HCPCS level II modifiers that must be added to CPT codes and HCPCS level II codes that must be reported with CPT codes. Examples, exercises, and review questions in Chapters 8–18 of this textbook require students to report HCPCS level II modifiers and codes, where appropriate. (Code ranges included in parentheses after section titles in the textbook and workbook chapters may differ from your HCPCS level II coding manual.)

Overview of HCPCS

Two levels of codes are associated with HCPCS, commonly referred to as HCPCS level I and II codes. Most of the procedures and services are reported using CPT (HCPCS level I) codes. However, CPT does not describe durable medical equipment, prosthetics, orthotics, supplies (DMEPOS), and certain other services. Therefore, the Centers for Medicare & Medicaid Services (CMS) developed HCPCS level II national codes to report DMEPOS and other services. (Medicare carriers previously developed HCPCS level III local codes, which were discontinued December 31, 2003. However, some third-party payers continue to use level III codes.)

HCPCS Level I

HCPCS level I includes the five-digit (and some five-character) CPT codes developed and published by the American Medical Association (AMA). The AMA is responsible for the annual update of this coding system and its two-digit modifiers. (CPT was defined in Chapter 1 of this textbook, and its content is covered is Chapters 8–18.)

HCPCS Level II

HCPCS level II (or HCPCS national codes) was created in the 1980s to describe common medical services and supplies not classified in CPT. HCPCS level II national codes are five characters in length, and they begin with the letters *A–V* followed by four numbers. The codes identify services performed by physician and nonphysician providers (e.g., nurse practitioners and speech therapists), services provided by ambulance companies, and supplies and equipment provided by durable medical equipment (DME) companies, which are called durable medical equipment, prosthetics, orthotics, and supplies (DMEPOS) dealers. *Durable medical equipment (DME)* is defined by Medicare as equipment that

- Can withstand repeated use
- Is primarily used to serve a medical purpose
- Is used in the patient's home
- Would not be used in the absence of illness or injury

Durable medical equipment, prosthetics, orthotics, and supplies (DMEPOS) include artificial limbs, braces, medications, surgical dressings, and wheelchairs. **Durable medical equipment, prosthetics, orthotics, and supplies (DMEPOS) dealers** supply patients with DME (e.g., canes, crutches, walkers, commode chairs, and blood-glucose monitors). DMEPOS claims are submitted to DME Medicare administrative contractors (MACs) (previously called durable medical equipment regional carriers, or DMERCs) that were awarded contracts by CMS. Each DME MAC covers a specific geographic region of the country and is responsible for processing DMEPOS claims for its specific region.

 Note:

When claims are to be submitted to one of the four DME MACs, DMEPOS dealers that have coding questions should check with the **Medicare Pricing, Data Analysis, and Coding (PDAC) contractor** (formerly called the Statistical Analysis Durable Medical Equipment Regional Carrier, or SADMERC), which assists suppliers and manufacturers in determining HCPCS codes to be used. The PDAC has a toll-free help line for this purpose at (877) 735-1326.

When people refer to HCPCS codes, they are most likely referring to HCPCS level II national codes. CMS is responsible for the annual updates to HCPCS level II codes and the two-character alphanumeric modifiers. HCPCS level II national codes are further discussed in this chapter.

HCPCS Level III

Effective December 31, 2003, HCPCS level III local codes were no longer required. They had the same structure as level II codes, but were assigned by the local Medicare carrier (LMC) (now called MAC), which processes Medicare claims. Level III codes began with the letters *W, X, Y,* or *Z*. (Some third-party payers continue to use level III codes.)

Exercise 7.1 – Overview of HCPCS

Instructions: **Complete each statement.**

1. HCPCS level II codes are considered _____ codes.
2. HCPCS level II codes describe procedures, services, and _____.
3. CPT codes are included as HCPCS _____ codes.
4. HCPCS level II national codes are _____ characters in length.
5. HCPCS level II national codes begin with the letters _____.

HCPCS Level II National Codes

The HCPCS level II national coding system classifies similar medical products and services for the purpose of efficient claims processing. Each code contains a description, and the codes are used primarily for billing purposes. The codes describe the following:

- DME devices, accessories, supplies, and repairs; prosthetics; orthotics; and medical and surgical supplies
- Medications
- Provider services

- Temporary Medicare codes (e.g., Q codes)

- Other items and services (e.g., ambulance services)

  EXAMPLE: DMEPOS dealers report HCPCS level II national codes to identify equipment reported on claims submitted to private or public health insurers.

HCPCS is *not* a reimbursement methodology or payment system; it is important to understand that just because codes exist for certain products or services, coverage (e.g., payment) is not guaranteed. The HCPCS level II national coding system

- Ensures uniform reporting of medical products or services on claims

- Has code descriptors that identify similar products or services (instead of specific products or brand/trade names)

- Is not a reimbursement methodology for making coverage or payment determinations (Each payer makes determinations on coverage and payment outside this coding process.)

Responsibility for HCPCS Level II National Codes

HCPCS level II national codes are developed and maintained by the *CMS HCPCS Workgroup,* which is comprised of representatives of the major components of CMS, Medicaid state agencies, and the Pricing, Data Analysis and Coding (PDAC). HCPCS level II codes are revised annually, and the revised codes are implemented each January. (The revision involves adding and deleting codes and revising code descriptors.)

HCPCS level II national codes do not carry the copyright of a private organization; they are in the public domain, which allows many publishers to print annual coding manuals. Each publisher may elect to color-code the print or pages, include supplemental explanatory material, or provide reimbursement information from the *Medicare Carriers Manual (MCM)* for Part B or the *Medicare National Coverage Determinations Manual.* The **Medicare Carriers Manual (MCM)** provides direction about services and procedures to be reimbursed by the MAC. The **Medicare National Coverage Determinations Manual** indicates whether a service is covered or excluded under the Medicare program.

Some publishers include the following HCPCS level II references in their version of the coding manual:

- General instructions or guidelines for each section

- Appendix that summarizes additions, deletions, and terminology revisions in level II codes

- Separate tables of drugs or deleted codes

- Symbols to identify codes excluded from Medicare coverage

- Codes for which payment is left to the discretion of the responsible MAC

- Codes with special coverage instructions

- Current HCPCS level II national modifiers

CMS has stated that it is not responsible for any errors that might occur in or from the use of these private printings of HCPCS level II national codes.

Types of HCPCS Level II Codes

HCPCS level II codes are organized according to type depending on the purpose of the codes and the entity responsible for establishing and maintaining them. The four types are as follows:

- Permanent national codes
- Miscellaneous codes
- Temporary codes
- HCPCS level II modifiers

Note:

HCPCS level II previously included dental codes (D codes), which are copyrighted by the American Dental Association. Effective 2012, purchase of a separate *Current Dental Terminology* (CDT) coding manual is required to assign dental codes.

Permanent National Codes

HCPCS level II permanent national codes are maintained by the CMS HCPCS Workgroup, which unanimously makes decisions about additions, revisions, and deletions. Because HCPCS level II is a national coding system, none of the parties, including CMS, can make unilateral decisions regarding permanent level II national codes, which are intended for use by all private and public health insurers.

Miscellaneous Codes

HCPCS level II miscellaneous codes include *miscellaneous/not otherwise classified* codes that are reported when a DMEPOS dealer submits a claim for a product or service for which there is no existing HCPCS level II code. Miscellaneous codes allow DMEPOS dealers to submit a claim for a product or service as soon as it is approved by the Food and Drug Administration (FDA) even though there is no code that describes the product or service. The use of miscellaneous codes also helps avoid the inefficiency of assigning codes for items or services that are rarely furnished or for which carriers expect to receive few claims.

Claims that contain miscellaneous codes are manually reviewed by the payer, and the following must be provided for use in the review process:

- Complete description of product or service
- Pricing information for product or service
- Documentation to explain why the item or service is needed by the beneficiary

Before reporting a miscellaneous code on a claim, a DMEPOS dealer should check with the payer to determine if a specific code has been identified for use (instead of a miscellaneous code).

Temporary Codes

HCPCS level II temporary codes (Table 7-1) are maintained by the CMS and other members of the CMS HCPCS Workgroup, independent of permanent level II codes. Permanent national codes are updated once a year on January 1, but temporary codes allow payers the flexibility to establish codes that are needed before the next January 1 annual update. Approximately 35 percent of the HCPCS level II codes are temporary codes. Certain sections of the HCPCS level II codes were set aside to allow CMS HCPCS Workgroup members to develop temporary codes, and decisions regarding the number and type of temporary codes and the way they are used are made independently by each CMS HCPCS Workgroup member. Temporary codes serve the purpose of meeting short time frame operational needs of a particular payer.

Although the CMS HCPCS Workgroup may decide to replace temporary codes with permanent codes, if permanent codes are not established, the temporary codes remain "temporary" indefinitely.

 Note:

- Decisions regarding temporary codes are made by an internal CMS HCPCS Workgroup, and other payers may also use these codes.
- Whenever a permanent code is established by the CMS HCPCS Workgroup to replace a temporary code, the temporary code is deleted and cross-referenced to the new permanent code.

Table 7-1 Categories of HCPCS Level II Temporary Codes

Category	Descriptions
C codes	• Reported to Medicare administrative contractors (MACs) for hospital outpatient department procedures and services, including device categories, new technology procedures, and drugs, biologicals, and radiopharmaceuticals that do not have other HCPCS code assignments, which are provided exclusively for Outpatient Prospective Payment System (OPPS) purposes.
G codes	• Identify professional health care procedures and services that do not have codes identified in CPT. • G codes can be reported to all payers.
H codes	• Reported to state Medicaid agencies that are mandated by state law to establish separate codes for identifying mental health services (e.g., alcohol and drug treatment services).
K codes	• Reported to MACs when existing permanent national codes do not include codes needed to implement a medical review coverage policy.
Q codes	• Identify services that would not ordinarily be assigned a CPT code (e.g., drugs, biologicals, and other types of medical equipment or services). • Q codes can be reported to all payers.
S codes	• Used by private payers when no HCPCS level II national codes exist to report drugs, services, and supplies, but codes are needed to implement private payer policies and programs for claims processing. • S codes are reported to BCBS, Medicaid, and private third-party payers.
T codes	• Reported to state Medicaid agencies when no HCPCS level II permanent codes exist, but codes are needed to administer the Medicaid program. • T codes are not reported to Medicare, but they can be reported to private third-party payers.

HCPCS Level II Modifiers

HCPCS level II modifiers are attached to any HCPCS level I (CPT) or II (national) code to provide additional information regarding the product or service reported. Modifiers supplement the information provided by a HCPCS code descriptor to identify specific circumstances that may apply to an item or a service. HCPCS level II modifiers contain alpha or alphanumeric characters (Figure 7-1) (unlike CPT modifiers, which contain numeric characters only, as covered in Chapter 8). (Modifiers are located in an appendix of the HCPCS level II coding manual and the CPT coding manual.)

 Note:

Because modifiers are attached to HCPCS level II codes, chapter content about modifiers precedes content about the assignment of HCPCS level II codes.

 Coding Tip:

• HCPCS level II alpha and alphanumeric modifiers may also be added to CPT codes to further define the procedure or service reported (e.g., 69436-RT, tympanostomy, right ear).

• Refer to the inside cover (or an appendix) of the HCPCS level II and CPT coding manuals for a comprehensive list of modifiers.

• Encoder software often contains guidance regarding selection of modifiers. For example, www.EncoderPro.com contains a clickable ⓜ icon that displays a list of applicable modifiers for a code.

EXAMPLE 1: A clinical psychologist provides 45 minutes of group psychotherapy in a partial hospitalization setting. Report G0410-AH.

EXAMPLE 2: A Medicare patient undergoes tendon surgery on the right palm and left middle finger. Report 26170-RT and 26180-59-F2.

HCPCS Level II Modifiers	
AA	Anesthesia services performed personally by anesthesiologist
AD	Medical supervision by a physician: more than 4 concurrent anesthesia procedures
AE	Registered dietician
AF	Specialty physician
AG	Primary physician
AH	Clinical psychologist

Figure 7-1 Sample listing of HCPCS level II modifiers

General Guidelines for Modifier Use

Not all HCPCS level I and II codes require modifiers. The CMS has clarified the use of modifiers when codes are reported for outpatient hospital services. (These rules also apply to the use of modifiers when reporting codes for physician services. Modifiers for physician services that differ from those used to report outpatient hospital services are clarified here.)

- Do not add a modifier to a code when its description indicates multiple occurrences, such as:
  - Two or more lesions
  - Multiple extremities
  - Different body parts

  EXAMPLE: 11600 Excision malignant lesion, trunks, arms, or legs; excised diameter 0.5 cm or less.

- Modifiers -GN, -GO, and -GP are added to codes reported for an outpatient plan of care.
  - Speech language therapy (-GN)
  - Occupational therapy (-GO)
  - Physical therapy (-GP)

- The following modifiers are added to codes reported for hospital outpatient surgical procedures *from the CPT Surgery section and certain codes from the CPT Medicine section (e.g., cardiac catheterization) only*:
  - Modifier -50 (Bilateral Procedure)
  - Modifier -73 (Discontinued Outpatient Hospital/Ambulatory Surgery Center (ASC) Procedure Prior to the Administration of Anesthesia)
  - Modifier -74 (Discontinued Outpatient Hospital/Ambulatory Surgery Center (ASC) Procedure After Administration of Anesthesia)

 Coding Tip:

- For physician services, the following modifiers are added to codes reported for Surgery and Medicine procedures:
  - -50 (Bilateral Procedure)
  - -52 (Reduced Services)
  - -53 (Discontinued Procedure)

- Modifiers are added to codes reported for procedures and services when they

  o Add more information regarding the anatomical site of the procedure

  EXAMPLE: Cataract surgery on the right or left eye. Add modifier -RT or -LT to the CPT code reported for cataract surgery

  o Help to eliminate the appearance of duplicate billing

  EXAMPLE: Add modifier -76 to the reported code when the same procedure is performed more than once by the same physician

  o Help to eliminate the appearance of unbundling

  EXAMPLE: When codes Q0081 (Infusion therapy, using other than chemotherapeutic drugs, per visit) and 36000 (Introduction of needle or intracatheter, vein) are reported on the same claim, the payer will deny payment for one of the codes because they are duplicate services. Adding modifier -59 to code 36000, *if that procedure was performed for a reason other than as part of the IV infusion*, ensures appropriate processing of the claim and reimbursement for both procedures.

- Report modifiers on the hard copy UB-04 (CMS-1450) in Form Locator 44 (next to Form Locators where HCPCS codes are entered). (There is space for two modifiers on each hard copy UB-04.) For electronic claims, the UB-04 flat file allows entry of modifiers as record type 61, field numbers 6 and 7. (There is space for two modifiers, one in field 6 and one in field 7.)

- Report modifier(s) in Block 24D of the CMS-1500 claim, spacing once after the CPT or HCPCS level II code. (Space once between modifiers when multiple modifiers are added to the same code.)

- Do not report the dash that precedes a modifier.

  EXAMPLE: Modifier -AH is reported as AH in Block 24D of the CMS-1500.

24.	A DATE(S) OF SERVICE						B Place of	C Type of	D PROCEDURES, SERVICES, OR SUPPLIES (Explain Unusual Circumstances)		E DIAGNOSIS		F		G DAYS OR	H EPSDT Family	I	J	K
	From			To			Service	Service	CPT/HCPCS	MODIFIER	POINTER		$ CHARGES		UNITS	Plan	EMG	COB	RESERVED FOR LOCAL USE
	MM	DD	YY	MM	DD	YY													
1									G0410	AH									

Courtesy of the Centers for Medicare & Medicaid Services, www.cms.gov; Copyright © 2018 Cengage Learning®.

- When multiple modifiers are added to a code, the most specific modifier is listed first. For example, the following HCPCS level II modifiers are added (instead of modifier -LT or -RT):

  o -E1 through -E4

  o -FA and -F1 through -F9

  o -LC

  o -LD

  o -RC

  o -TA and -T1 through -T9

Modifiers Added to Surgical Procedures

Add modifier -50 (Bilateral Procedure) to codes for procedures that are performed on both sides during the same operative session (and when the code description does *not* include *bilateral* terminology).

EXAMPLE: Patient underwent correction of hallus valgus (bunion), right and left feet. Since this procedure was performed bilaterally, report 28292-50. (*Do not report 28292-RT and 28292-LT.*)

The following rules clarify the use of modifier -50:

- Do not add modifiers -RT and -LT to a code when modifier -50 is added to that code.

- Add modifier -50 to surgical procedures only (CPT Surgery section codes, 10040–69990).

- Modifier -50 is *not* added to surgical procedure codes when the code description contains the following terminology:
  - Bilateral
  - Unilateral or bilateral

- Modifier -LT or -RT is added to the code that identifies a procedure performed on just one of two paired organs (e.g., ears, eyes, nostrils, kidneys, lungs, or ovaries).

  EXAMPLE: Code 69100 is eligible for modifier -50 if the procedure is performed on both ears. However, if a procedure (e.g., biopsy) is performed on the right or left ear, report code 69100-RT or 69100-LT.

 Coding Tip:

- Do not add modifier -50 to codes reported for Evaluation and Management, Anesthesia, Radiology, Pathology and Laboratory, or Medicine procedures and services. Do not add modifier -50 to HCPCS level II codes.

- Modifier -LT or -RT is added to the code for a procedure that is performed on just one side.

- Modifiers for discontinued procedures for Outpatient Hospital/Ambulatory Surgery Center (ASC) (-73 and -74) are added to diagnostic and surgical procedure codes so hospitals can be reimbursed for expenses incurred during the preparation of a patient for surgery, which includes scheduling a room for performing the procedure.

  - Add modifier -73 when an Outpatient Hospital/Ambulatory Surgery Center (ASC) diagnostic or surgical procedure is terminated after a patient has been prepared for surgery (including sedation when provided) and taken to the room where the procedure is to be performed, but before the induction of anesthesia (e.g., local, regional block, or general anesthesia).

  - Add modifier -74 when an Outpatient Hospital/Ambulatory Surgery Center (ASC) procedure is terminated after the induction of anesthesia (e.g., local, regional block, or general anesthesia) or after the procedure was started (incision made, intubation started, or scope inserted).

  - Do *not* add modifier -73 or -74 to a code for the *elective* cancellation of a procedure.

 Coding Tip:

- Add modifiers -73 and -74 to codes reported from the CPT Surgery section and to certain codes reported from the Medicine (e.g., cardiac catheterization) section. Do not add modifiers -73 and -74 to codes reported for Evaluation and Management, Anesthesia, Radiology, or Pathology and Laboratory procedures and services.

- When services are discontinued in the physician's office, report modifier -52 or -53 (instead of modifier -73 or -74).

- Add modifier -76 to the code for a procedure or service that was repeated during a separate operative session on the same day by the same physician. Add modifier -77 to the code for a procedure or service that was repeated during a separate operative session on the same day by another physician. The following rules apply to adding modifier -76 or -77:

  - Adding modifier -76 or -77 is based on whether the physician performing the procedure is the same or different.

  - The repeated procedure must be the same as the originally performed procedure. (On the claim, the code for the original procedure is entered once. Then it is entered again with the appropriate modifier.)

Modifiers Added to Radiology Services

The following modifiers are added to codes for CPT Radiology services:

- -52 (Reduced Services)
- -59 (Distinct Procedural Service)

> **Coding Tip:**
>
> Do not add modifier -53, -73, or -74 to Radiology codes.

 Note:

Effective January 1, 2015, CMS created four new HCPCS modifiers to define specific subsets of the -59 modifier:

- XE Separate Encounter, A Service That Is Distinct Because It Occurred During A Separate Encounter
- XS Separate Structure, A Service That Is Distinct Because It Was Performed On A Separate Organ/Structure
- XP Separate Practitioner, A Service That Is Distinct Because It Was Performed By A Different Practitioner
- XU Unusual Non-Overlapping Service, The Use of A Service That Is Distinct Because It Does Not Overlap Usual Components of The Main Service

CMS will continue to recognize the -59 modifier; however, CPT instructions state that modifier -59 should not be used when a more descriptive modifier (e.g., -XE) is available.

- -76 (Repeat Procedure by Same Physician or Other Qualified Health Care Professional)
- -77 (Repeat Procedure by Another Physician or Other Qualified Health Care Professional)
- HCPCS level II modifiers

When a radiology procedure is canceled, report a code to describe the extent of the procedure performed. If no code exists for what was done, report the intended code and add modifier -52.

EXAMPLE: The physician orders a chest x-ray, two views, frontal and lateral (code 71020). Just the frontal view is performed because the patient started feeling faint and needed to lie down. Report code 71010 (Radiologic examination, chest: single view, frontal). (Do *not* report code 71020-52.)

Reporting HCPCS Level II Modifiers

HCPCS level II modifiers are added to HCPCS level I (CPT) and level II (national) codes. When more than one level II modifier applies, report the code on more than one line of the UB-04 claim, with the appropriate HCPCS level II modifier.

EXAMPLE: Patient underwent simple drainage of a finger abscess, left-hand thumb and second finger (code 26010). On the UB-04, report the code on two lines as follows:

- 26010 FA
- 26010 F1

Do not add modifiers -LT or -RT to

- Allergy and clinical immunology codes
- Ambulance codes
- Codes that do not specify a limb or paired organ

> **Note:**
>
> On the CMS-1500, report the code and multiple modifiers on just one line of Block 24D, such as 26010 FA F1.

- Drug administration codes (J and Q codes)
- DME (HCPCS level II E codes) that do not specify a limb
- Evaluation and management codes
- Immunization and vaccines/toxoid codes
- Medicine codes that contain *right* or *left* in the code description
- Orthotics/prosthetics codes that do not specify a limb
- Osteopathic and chiropractic manipulation codes
- Pathology and laboratory codes
- Physical medicine and rehabilitation codes
- Supply codes
- Temporary procedure and service codes (G codes) that do not specify a limb

---

Exercise 7.2 – HCPCS Level II National Codes

Instructions: Complete each statement.

1. HCPCS level II codes are developed and maintained by the _____.
2. Services and procedures that are reimbursed by a MAC can be found in the _____.
3. Whether a service is covered or excluded under the Medicare program can be found in the _____.
4. HCPCS level II permanent codes are maintained by the _____.
5. HCPCS level II and CPT codes and multiple modifiers are reported on the same line of Block 24D on the _____ claim, such as 26010 FA F1.
6. HCPCS level II miscellaneous codes are reported when a(n) _____ submits a claim for a product or service for which there is no existing HCPCS level II national code.
7. HCPCS level II temporary codes allow payers the flexibility to establish codes that are needed before the next _____ update.
8. Refer to Figure 7-1, and identify the modifier that is added to a code when a procedure is performed by a registered dietician: _____.
9. Modifier _____ is added to codes for procedures that are performed on both sides during the same operative session.
10. HCPCS level II _____ are added to HCPCS level I (CPT) and level II (national) codes.

Assigning HCPCS Level II Codes

Some services must be reported by assigning both a CPT and an HCPCS level II national code. The most common scenario uses the CPT code for the administration of an infusion or injection and the HCPCS level II code to identify the medication. Most drugs have qualifying terms such as *dosage limits* that could alter the quantity reported (Figure 7-2).

- If a drug is administered in a 70-mg dose and the HCPCS level II code description states "per 50 mg," the quantity billed is 2.
- If just 15 mg of a drug were administered and the HCPCS level II code description stated "up to 20 mg," the quantity billed is 1.

> **Note:**
>
> CMS developed HCPCS level II codes for Medicare, but commercial payers also adopted them.

DRUGS ADMINISTERED OTHER THAN ORAL METHOD
J0475 Injection, baclofen, 10 mg
J0476 Injection, baclofen, 50 mcg for intrathecal trial
J0480 Injection, basiliximab, 20 mg
J0485 Injection, belatacept, 1 mg
J0490 Injection, belimumab, 10 mg
J0500 Injection, dicyclomine HCl, up to 20 mg
J0515 Injection, benztropine mesylate, per 1 mg
J0520 Injection, bethanechol chloride, Mytonachol or Urecholine, up to 5 mg

Permission to reprint granted by Optum360.

Figure 7-2 Sample listing of HCPCS level II J codes

Imagine how much money providers lose by reporting only the CPT code for injections. Unless the payer or insurance plan advises the provider that it does not pay separately for the medication injected, always report this combination of codes. It is possible that a particular service would be assigned a CPT code and a level II HCPCS code. Which one should you report? The answer is found in the instructions from the payer. Most commercial payers require the CPT code. Medicare gives HCPCS level II codes the highest priority if the CPT code is general and the HCPCS national (level II) code is more specific.

Most supplies are included in the charge for the office visit or the procedure. CPT provides code 99070 for all supplies and materials exceeding those usually included in the primary service or procedure performed. However, this CPT code may be too general to ensure correct payment. If the office provides additional supplies when performing a service, the HCPCS level II codes may identify the supplies in sufficient detail to secure proper reimbursement.

Although CMS developed this system, some HCPCS level I and II services are not payable by Medicare. Medicare may also place qualifications or conditions on payment for some services. As an example, an electrocardiogram (ECG) is a covered service for a cardiac problem but is not covered when performed as part of a routine examination. Also, the payment for some services may be left to the discretion of the MAC. Two CMS publications assist MACs in correctly processing claims: the *Medicare National Coverage Determinations Manual* advises the MAC as to whether a service is covered or excluded under Medicare regulations, and the MCM directs the MAC to pay or reject a service, using a specific "remark" or explanation code.

There are more than 4,000 HCPCS level II codes, but you may find that no code exists for the procedure or service you need to report. Unlike CPT, HCPCS level II does not have a consistent method of establishing codes for reporting "unlisted procedure" services. If the MAC does not provide special instructions for reporting these services in HCPCS, report them with the proper "unlisted procedure" code from CPT. Remember to submit documentation explaining the procedure or service when using the "unlisted procedure" codes.

HCPCS Level II Index

Because of the wide variety of services and procedures described in HCPCS level II, the alphabetical index (Figure 7-3) is very helpful in finding the correct code. The various publishers of the reference may include an expanded index

Index
Abdomen
dressing holder/binder, A4461, A4463
pad, low profile, L1270
Abduction
control, each, L2624
rotation bar, foot, L3140-L3170
Ablation
ultrasound, C9734

Permission to reprint granted by Optum360.

Figure 7-3 Sample listing of HCPCS level II index entries

Drug Name	Unit Per	Route	Code
10% LMD	500 mL	IV	J7100
4-FACTOR PROTHROMBIN COMPLEX CONCENTRATE	1 IU	IV	C9132
5% Dextrose and .45% Normal Saline	1000 mL	IV	S5010
5% Dextrose in Lactated Ringers	1000 mL	IV	J7121
5% Dextrose with Potassium Chloride	1000 mL	IV	S5012

Figure 7-4 Sample listing of HCPCS level II table of drugs

that lists "alcohol wipes" and "wipes," as well as "Ancef" and "cefazolin sodium," making the search for codes easier and faster. Some references also include a table of drugs (Figure 7-4) that lists J codes assigned to medications. Some publishers print brand names beneath each generic description, and others provide a special expanded index of the drug codes. It is important never to code directly from the index and always to verify the code in the appropriate code section of the coding manual. You may want to review the HCPCS references from several publishers and select the one that best meets your needs and is easiest for you to use. If you have difficulty locating the service or procedure in the HCPCS level II index, review the table of contents (if available in your coding manual) to locate the code section (Figure 7-5). Or, page through the tabular list to familiarize yourself with the procedures and services classified in the coding manual. Read the code descriptions very carefully before selecting a code.

HCPCS Level II Code Sections

HCPCS level II code sections are identified by an alphabetical first character (e.g., B for *enteral and parenteral therapy* and C for *outpatient PPS*). Some code sections are logical, such as R for *radiology*, whereas others, such as J for *drugs*, appear to be arbitrarily assigned.

Transportation Services Including Ambulance (A0021–A0999)

The Transportation Services Including Ambulance section of HCPCS level II includes codes for ancillary transportation-related fees, ground and air ambulance, and nonemergency transportation (e.g., automobile, bus, taxi, and wheelchair van).

EXAMPLE: A Medicaid patient received emergency transport from her home to the hospital emergency department in an ambulance that contained basic life support (BLS). Report code A0429-RH. (The origin was the patient's residence, and the destination was the hospital; therefore, modifier -RH is added to code A0429.)

Medical and Surgical Supplies (A4206–A9999)

The Medical and Surgical Supplies section of HCPCS level II includes codes for DME-related supplies, accessories, maintenance, and repair (to ensure proper functioning of DME); medical supplies and accessories; and surgical supplies and accessories.

EXAMPLE: A 68-year-old patient who is undergoing treatment for unresected liver cancer was supplied with a refill kit for an implantable infusion pump. Report code A4220.

Coding Tip:

Some supplies are included during the administration of an evaluation and management (E/M) service, and separate HCPCS level II codes are not assigned (e.g., sterile gauze). E/M services are assigned separate CPT codes, which is discussed in Chapter 9.

Contents

Figure 7-5 Sample HCPCS level II coding manual table of contents

Enteral and Parenteral Therapy (B4000–B9999)

The Enteral and Parenteral Therapy section of HCPCS level II includes codes for enteral and parenteral infusion pumps, enteral and parenteral supplies, enteral formulae, and parenteral nutritional solutions.

> **EXAMPLE:** The patient was supplied with a fiber additive for enteral formula. Report code B4104.

Outpatient PPS (C1300–C9899)

The Outpatient PPS section of HCPCS level II includes codes for biologicals, devices, and drugs eligible for transitional pass-through payments for hospitals, as well as items included in the new technology APCs under the OPPS. **Transitional pass-through payments** are temporary additional payments (over and above the OPPS payment) made for certain innovative medical devices, drugs, and biologicals provided to Medicare beneficiaries.

EXAMPLE: Patient underwent insertion of a directional transluminal atherectomy catheter. Report code C1714.

 Coding Tip:

> The OPPS requires hospitals and ambulatory surgery centers to report product-specific HCPCS level II "C codes" to obtain reimbursement for biologicals, devices, drugs, and other items associated with implantable device technologies. Reporting C codes in conjunction with CPT procedure codes greatly improves the quality of claims data Medicare uses to establish future APC payments. Outpatient coding edits (updated on a quarterly basis) identify C codes that should be billed with CPT procedure codes.
>
> Applications are also submitted to CMS for "new" biologicals, devices, and drugs for consideration of "transitional pass-through payment status" and items for consideration of "new-technology APC designation." If certain criteria are met and CMS approves the "new" biologicals, devices, drugs, and items, C codes are assigned and published in program memorandums.

Durable Medical Equipment (E0100–E9999)

The Durable Medical Equipment section of HCPCS level II includes codes for equipment (e.g., artificial kidney machines, oxygen and related respiratory equipment, and pacemakers) and supplies (e.g., bath and toilet aids, commodes, cranes, crutches, hospital beds, and walkers).

EXAMPLE: The patient was supplied with a pair of aluminum underarm crutches. Report code E0114.

Procedures/Professional Services (Temporary) (G0000–G9999)

The Procedures/Professional Services (Temporary) section of HCPCS level II includes codes for professional health care procedures and services that do not have codes identified in the CPT.

EXAMPLE: A patient became a Medicare beneficiary on March 1 and underwent an initial preventive physical examination (IPPE) and in-office electrocardiogram (ECG) on May 30. Report codes G0402 and G0403. (Make sure you report the appropriate ICD-10-CM Z code as the first-listed diagnosis.)

Alcohol and Drug Abuse Treatment Services (H0001–H2037)

The Alcohol and Drug Abuse Treatment Services section of HCPCS level II includes codes used by state Medicaid agencies mandated by state law to establish separate codes for identifying mental health services that include alcohol and drug treatment services.

EXAMPLE: A patient underwent alcohol assessment prior to participating in psychotherapy. Report code H0001.

Drugs Administered Other Than Oral Method (J0120–J8499)

The Drugs Administered Other Than Oral Method section of HCPCS level II includes codes for drugs that ordinarily cannot be self-administered, chemotherapy drugs, immunosuppressive drugs, inhalation solutions, and other miscellaneous drugs and solutions.

EXAMPLE: A female home health patient received an injection of 10 mcg of teriparatide (brand name Forteo) for treatment of osteoporosis. Report code J3110.

Chemotherapy Drugs (J8501–J9999)

The Chemotherapy Drugs section of HCPCS level II includes codes reported for the administration of chemotherapy.

EXAMPLE: The patient was administered 5 milligrams of oral aprepitant. Report code J8501.

Temporary Codes (K0000–K9999)

The Temporary Codes section of HCPCS level II includes codes for DME, as established by DME MACs (formerly DMERCs), when permanent national codes do not include codes needed to implement a DME MAC medical review policy.

> **EXAMPLE:** The patient was supplied with a standard wheelchair. Report code K0001.

Orthotic Procedures and Devices (L0000–L4999)

The Orthotic Procedures section of HCPCS level II includes codes for orthopedic shoes, orthotic devices and procedures, and scoliosis equipment. **Orthotics** is the branch of medicine that deals with the design and fitting of orthopedic (relating to bone disorders) devices (e.g., braces). Several orthotic procedures subsections include "addition" codes, which means they are reported in addition to base codes from the same subsection or a previous subsection.

> **EXAMPLE:** Patient underwent a halo procedure during which the cervical halo was incorporated into a jacket vest. Patient also received a magnetic resonance image compatible system during the same encounter. Report codes L0810 and L0859.
>
> Because the description for code L0859 states "Addition to halo procedure, magnetic resonance image compatible system," it must be reported in addition to another HCPCS code, such as L0810.

Prosthetic Procedures and Devices (L5000–L9999)

The Prosthetic Procedures section of HCPCS level II includes codes for prosthetic devices, implants, and procedures. **Prosthetics** is the branch of medicine that deals with the design, production, and use of artificial body parts (e.g., artificial limbs). Several prosthetic procedures subsections include "addition" codes, meaning that they are reported in addition to base codes from the same subsection or from a previous subsection.

> **EXAMPLE:** The patient received a below-knee PTB type socket, nonalignable system, pylon, no cover, SACH foot, plaster socket, direct-formed. The patient also received a test socket, below knee, during the same encounter. Report codes L5500 and L5620.
>
> Because the description for code L5620 states "Addition to lower extremity, test socket, below knee," it must be reported in addition to another HCPCS code, such as L5500.

Medical Services (M0000–M0301)

The Medical Services section of HCPCS level II includes codes for cellular therapy, fabric wrapping of an abdominal aneurysm, intragastric hypothermia, intravenous (IV) chelation therapy, and prolotherapy.

- *Cellular therapy* involves injecting processed tissue from animal embryos, fetuses, or organs for the purpose of rejuvenating diseased tissue; its therapeutic effect has not been established.

- *Fabric wrapping of an abdominal aneurysm* is performed to reinforce an aneurysm with a fabric-wrapped stent (a small, flexible mesh tube used to "patch" the blood vessel). This procedure has largely been replaced with other more effective treatment methods.

- *Intragastric hypothermia* is a form of gastric freezing for the treatment of chronic peptic ulcer disease; CMS considers this procedure obsolete.

- *IV chelation therapy* is also called chemical endarterectomy, and it is performed to treat arteriosclerosis; it is considered experimental in the United States.

- *Prolotherapy* is a form of nonsurgical ligament reconstruction as a treatment for chronic pain; its therapeutic effect has not yet been established.

> **EXAMPLE:** The patient received cellular therapy services. Report code M0075.

Pathology and Laboratory Services (P0000–P9999)

The Pathology and Laboratory Services section of HCPCS level II includes codes for chemistry, microbiology, and toxicology tests; screening Papanicolaou smears; and miscellaneous blood tests.

> **EXAMPLE:** The patient underwent screening cervical Papanicolaou smear, which was interpreted by the physician. Report code P3001.

Q Codes (Temporary) (Q0035–Q9999)

The Q Codes (Temporary) section of HCPCS level II includes temporary codes for drugs, services, supplies, and tests until permanent codes are available. Effective 2001, casting supplies were removed from the practice expenses for all HCPCS codes, including CPT codes for fracture management, casts, and splints. This means that when CPT codes are reported for services that include the provision of a cast or splint, codes Q4001–Q4051 are also reported to provide reimbursement to providers for the supplies used in creating casts.

> **EXAMPLE:** A Medicare patient received brachytherapy services, which included the administration of radioisotopes. Report code Q3001.
>
> CPT code 79900 was deleted in 2005, and HCPCS level II code Q3001 was created to report the administration of radioisotopes during brachytherapy. Report as the first-listed procedure the appropriate CPT brachytherapy code from 77316–77318 and/or 77750–77799.

Diagnostic Radiology Services (R0000–R5999)

The Diagnostic Radiology Service section of HCPCS level II includes codes that are reported for the transportation of portable x-ray and/or EKG equipment, including testing.

> **EXAMPLE:** The provider transported portable EKG equipment to the nursing facility for the purpose of testing his patients. Report code R0076.
>
> When more than one patient undergoes EKG testing, report code R0076, but prorate the single allowed transportation cost among all patients. For example, if the single allowed transportation cost is $50 and five patients underwent EKG testing, the prorated cost for each patient is $10.

Temporary National Codes (Non-Medicare) (S0000–S9999)

The Temporary National Codes (Non-Medicare) section of HCPCS level II includes codes reported to non-Medicare third-party payers (e.g., Blue Cross/Blue Shield, commercial payers, and Medicaid) for drugs, services, and supplies that are not classified in CPT or another section of HCPCS level II.

> **EXAMPLE:** The patient was administered butorphanol tartrate (trade name Stadol NS), nasal spray, 25 mg. Report code S0012.

National T Codes Established for State Medicaid Agencies (T1000–T9999)

The National T Codes Established for State Medicaid Agencies section of HCPCS level II includes codes that are reported to Medicaid state agencies for behavioral health, home health, hospice, long-term care, nursing, and other services; substance abuse treatment; supplies; and certain training-related procedures that are not classified in CPT or another section of HCPCS level II.

> **EXAMPLE:** The Medicaid patient required sign language services for 30 minutes. Report codes T1013 and T1013 (because the description of code T1013 states "per 15 minutes").

Vision Services (V0000–V2999)

The Vision Services section of HCPCS level II includes codes for vision-related supplies (e.g., contact lenses, intraocular lenses, lenses, and spectacles).

> **EXAMPLE:** The patient was supplied with a custom plastic prosthetic eye. Report code V2623.

Hearing Services (V5000–V5999)

The Hearing Services section of HCPCS level II includes codes that describe hearing tests and related supplies and equipment, speech-language pathology screenings, and repair of augmentative communicative systems.

> **EXAMPLE:** The audiologist dispenses a monaural, in-the-ear (ITE) hearing aid for a patient diagnosed with sensorineural hearing loss, combined types. Report codes V5050 and V5241.

Exercise 7.3 – Assigning HCPCS Level II Codes

Instructions: Complete each statement.

1. Some services must be reported by assigning both a CPT and a HCPCS code; the most common scenario uses a CPT code for administration of a(n) _____ and the HCPCS code to identify the _____.

2. If a drug is administered in a 100-mg dose and the HCPCS level II code description states "per 50 mg," the quantity billed is _____.

3. If just 10 mg of a drug were administered and the HCPCS level II code description stated "up to 15 mg," the quantity billed is _____.

4. The charge for office visit or procedure usually includes _____ used to perform the procedure or service.

5. Although CMS developed this system, some HCPCS levels I and II services are not payable by _____.

6. Some HCPCS level II coding manuals include a table of drugs that lists J codes assigned to _____.

7. If you have difficulty locating the service or procedure in the HCPCS level II index, review the _____ to locate the code section and read the code descriptions very carefully before selecting a code.

8. Codes sections in HCPCS level II are identified by a(n) _____.

9. CMS developed the level II codes for Medicare, but _____ also adopted them.

10. If no code exists for a procedure or service, report the proper "unlisted procedure" code from _____ and submit documentation explaining the procedure or service.

Determining Payer Responsibility

The specific HCPCS level II code determines whether the claim is sent to the primary MAC that processes provider claims or the DME MAC that processes DMEPOS dealer claims. Providers and DMEPOS dealers obtain annual lists of valid HCPCS level II national codes, which include billing instructions for services.

Note:

At one time, LMCs (now called MACs) processed all claims for DME. The emphasis on keeping seniors in their own homes led to a rapid expansion in DME services and dealers. Also, many of the larger companies operated in several states and sent their claims to multiple Medicare carriers. Unfortunately, a few dealers formed for the sole purpose of collecting as much money as possible from the Medicare program and then closed down. When CMS began to investigate and pursue fraudulent claims, it became apparent that DME billings were out of control. CMS decided to have all DME claims processed by only four DME MACs. This allowed the primary MAC to concentrate on the familiar, traditional claims of providers billing for services, not equipment.

When the doctor treats a Medicare patient for a broken ankle and supplies the patient with crutches, two claims are generated. The claim for the fracture care, or professional service, is sent to the primary MAC; the claim for the crutches is sent to the DME MAC. The physician must register with both, review billing rules, comply with claims instructions, and forward claims correctly to secure payment for both services. If the physician is not registered with the DME MAC to provide medical equipment and supplies, the patient is given a prescription for crutches to take to a local DMEPOS dealer.

Some services, such as cosmetic procedures, are excluded as Medicare benefits by law and will not be covered by either MAC. Splints and casts for traumatic injuries have CPT numbers that are used to report these supplies or services to the primary MAC. Because the review procedure for adding new codes to level II is a much shorter process, new medical and surgical services may first be assigned a level II code and then incorporated into CPT at a later date.

Patient Record Documentation

The patient record includes documentation that justifies the medical necessity of procedures, services, and supplies coded and reported on an insurance claim. This means that the diagnoses reported on the claim must justify diagnostic and therapeutic procedures or services provided. The patient's record should include documentation of the following:

- Patient history, including review of systems

- Physical examination, including impression

- Diagnostic test results, including analysis of findings

- Diagnoses, including duration (e.g., acute or chronic) and comorbidities that impact care

- Patient's prognosis, including potential for rehabilitation

When DMEPOS items are reported on a claim, the DMEPOS dealer must keep the following documents on file:

- Provider order for DMEPOS item, signed and dated

- Signed advance beneficiary notice if medical necessity for an item cannot be established

When the provider reports DMEPOS items on a claim, the provider must keep the following documents on file:

- Diagnosis establishing medical necessity for the item

- Clinical notes that justify the DMEPOS item ordered

- Provider order for DMEPOS item, signed and dated

- Signed advance beneficiary notice if medical necessity for an item cannot be established

 Note:

An **advance beneficiary notice (ABN)** is a waiver signed by the patient acknowledging that because medical necessity for a procedure, service, or supply cannot be established (e.g., due to nature of patient's condition, injury, or illness), the patient accepts responsibility for reimbursing the provider or DMEPOS dealer for costs associated with the procedure, service, or supply.

DMEPOS Claims

For certain items or services reported on a claim submitted to the DME MAC, the DMEPOS dealer must receive a signed certificate of medical necessity (CMN) (Figure 7-6) from the treating physician before submitting a claim to Medicare. A copied, electronic, faxed, or original certificate of medical necessity (CMN) must be maintained by the DMEPOS dealer and must be available to the DME MAC on request. The **certificate of medical necessity (CMN)** is a prescription for DME, services, and supplies.

DME MAC medical review policies include **local coverage determinations (LCDs)** (formerly called local medical review policies, or LMRPs) and **national coverage determinations (NCDs)**, both of which define coverage criteria, payment rules, and documentation required as applied to DMEPOS claims processed by DME MACs for frequently ordered DMEPOS equipment, services, and supplies. (National policies are included in the *Medicare Benefit Policy Manual, Medicare Program Integrity Manual,* and *Medicare National*

U.S. DEPARTMENT OF HEALTH & HUMAN SERVICES
CENTERS FOR MEDICARE & MEDICAID SERVICES

FORM APPROVED
OMB NO. 0938-0679

CERTIFICATE OF MEDICAL NECESSITY   **DMERC 01.02A**

HOSPITAL BEDS

SECTION A   Certification Type/Date: INITIAL ___/___/___   REVISED ___/___/___

PATIENT NAME, ADDRESS, TELEPHONE and HIC NUMBER

(___ ___ ___) ___ ___ ___ - ___ ___ ___ ___ HICN _____

SUPPLIER NAME, ADDRESS, TELEPHONE and NSC NUMBER

(___ ___ ___) ___ ___ ___ - ___ ___ ___ ___ NSC # _____

PLACE OF SERVICE _____
NAME and ADDRESS of FACILITY if applicable (See reverse)

HCPCS CODE

_____

_____

_____

PT DOB ___/___/___ ; Sex ___ (M/F) ; HT.____(in.) ; WT.____(lbs.)

PHYSICIAN NAME, ADDRESS (Printed or Typed)

PHYSICIAN'S UPIN: _____

PHYSICIAN'S TELEPHONE #: (___ ___ ___) ___ ___ ___ - ___ ___ ___ ___

SECTION B   Information in this Section May Not Be Completed by the Supplier of the Items/Supplies.

EST. LENGTH OF NEED (# OF MONTHS): _____ 1-99 (99=LIFETIME)   DIAGNOSIS CODES (ICD-9): _____ _____ _____ _____

ANSWERS	ANSWER QUESTIONS 1, AND 3-7 FOR HOSPITAL BEDS
	(Circle **Y** for Yes, **N** for No, or **D** for Does Not Apply)
	QUESTION 2 RESERVED FOR OTHER OR FUTURE USE.
Y N D	1. Does the patient require positioning of the body in ways not feasible with an ordinary bed due to a medical condition which is expected to last at least one month?
Y N D	3. Does the patient require, for the alleviation of pain, positioning of the body in ways not feasible with an ordinary bed?
Y N D	4. Does the patient require the head of the bed to be elevated more than 30 degrees most of the time due to congestive heart failure, chronic pulmonary disease, or aspiration?
Y N D	5. Does the patient require traction which can only be attached to a hospital bed?
Y N D	6. Does the patient require a bed height different than a fixed height hospital bed to permit transfers to chair, wheelchair, or standing position?
Y N D	7. Does the patient require frequent changes in body position and/or have an immediate need for a change in body position?

NAME OF PERSON ANSWERING SECTION B QUESTIONS, IF OTHER THAN PHYSICIAN (Please Print):
NAME: _____   TITLE: _____   EMPLOYER: _____

SECTION C   Narrative Description Of Equipment And Cost

(1) Narrative description of all items, accessories and options ordered; **(2)** Supplier's charge; and **(3)** Medicare Fee Schedule Allowance for each item, accessory, and option. *(See Instructions On Back)*

SECTION D   Physician Attestation and Signature/Date

I certify that I am the physician identified in Section A of this form. I have received Sections A, B and C of the Certificate of Medical Necessity (including charges for items ordered). Any statement on my letterhead attached hereto, has been reviewed and signed by me. I certify that the medical necessity information in Section B is true, accurate and complete, to the best of my knowledge, and I understand that any falsification, omission, or concealment of material fact in that section may subject me to civil or criminal liability.

PHYSICIAN'S SIGNATURE _____   DATE ____/____/____   (SIGNATURE AND DATE STAMPS ARE NOT ACCEPTABLE)

CMS-841 (04/96)

Courtesy of the Centers for Medicare & Medicaid Services, www.cms.gov.

Figure 7-6 Sample certificate of medical necessity required of DMEPOS dealer

Coverage Determinations Manual.) If DMEPOS equipment, services, or supplies do not have medical review policies established for coverage, the general coverage criteria applies. The DMEPOS equipment, services, or supplies must

- Fall within a benefit category
- Not be excluded by statute or by national CMS policy
- Be reasonable and necessary to diagnose and/or treat an illness or injury or to improve the functioning of a malformed body

The DME MACs are required to follow national policy when it exists; when there is no national policy on a subject, DME MACs have the authority and responsibility to establish local policies. Because many DMEPOS dealers operate nationally, the CMS requires that the medical review policies published by the DME MACs be identical in all four regions.

Exercise 7.4 – Determining Payer Responsibility

Instructions: Complete each statement below.

1. The specific _____ code determines whether the claim is sent to the primary MAC that processes provider claims or the DME MAC that processes DMEPOS dealer claims.

2. Providers and DMEPOS dealers obtain annual lists of valid level II national codes, which include _____ instructions for services.

3. CMS decided to have all DME claims processed by only four DME MACs to reduce _____ claims.

4. When a physician treats a Medicare patient for a fractured femur and supplies the patient with crutches, two claims are generated. The physician's claim for the fracture care is sent to the _____, and the claim for the crutches is sent to the _____.

5. For certain items or services reported on a claim submitted to the DME MAC, the DMEPOS dealer must receive a signed _____.

Summary

Three levels of codes are associated with HCPCS, commonly referred to as HCPCS level I, II, and III codes. HCPCS level I includes the five-digit Current Procedural Terminology (CPT) codes developed and published by the American Medical Association (AMA). HCPCS level II codes (or HCPCS national codes) were created in the 1980s to describe common medical services and supplies not classified in CPT. (Effective December 31, 2003, HCPCS level III local codes were no longer required; however, some third-party payers continue to use them.)

The HCPCS level II national coding system classifies similar medical products and services for the purpose of efficient claims processing. Each code contains a description, and the codes are used primarily for billing purposes. The codes describe DME devices, accessories, supplies, and repairs; prosthetics; orthotics; medical and surgical supplies; medications; provider services; temporary Medicare codes (e.g., Q codes); and other items and services (e.g., ambulance services). Some services must be reported by assigning both a CPT and an HCPCS level II national code. The most common scenario uses the CPT code for the administration of an injection and the HCPCS code to identify the medication.

The specific HCPCS level II code determines whether the claim is sent to the primary Medicare administrative contractor (MAC) that processes provider claims or the DME MAC that processes DMEPOS dealer claims. Providers and DMEPOS dealers obtain annual lists of valid level II national codes, which include billing instructions for services.

Internet Links

CMS Online Manual System: Go to *www.cms.gov* and click on the Regulations & Guidance link, then click on the Manuals link below the Guidance heading.

HCPCS at eICD.com (free registration required): Go to *www.eicd.com* and click on the EHCPCS Online link.

HCPCS coding system: Go to *www.cms.gov* and click on the Medicare link, then scroll down to the Coding heading, and click on the HCPCS – General Information link.

Online drug reimbursement coding and pricing database (free trial): *www.reimbursementcodes.com*

Noridian Medicare Durable Medical Equipment: Go to *www.noridianmedicare.com* and click on the Durable Medical Equipment, Orthotics and Supplies link below the Jurisdiction D heading.

Study Checklist

- ❑ Read this chapter and highlight key concepts.
- ❑ Create an index card for each key term.
- ❑ Access the chapter Internet links to learn more about concepts.
- ❑ Complete the chapter exercises and review, verifying answers with your instructor.
- ❑ Complete Workbook chapter, verifying answers with your instructor.
- ❑ Go to www.cengagebrain.com to access the Student Companion Web Site. Login instructions are located in the Preface.
- ❑ Form a study group with classmates to discuss chapter concepts in preparation for an exam.

Review

Multiple Choice

Instructions: Circle the most appropriate response.

1. Which would be assigned to report DMEPOS on insurance claims?
   - a. CPT codes
   - b. HCPCS level I codes
   - c. HCPCS level II codes
   - d. HCPCS level III codes

2. Which provides suppliers and manufacturers with assistance in determining HCPCS codes to be reported?
   - a. CMS
   - b. DME MAC
   - c. DMEPOS dealers
   - d. PDAC

3. Which temporary codes are reported to all payers?
   - a. G codes
   - b. G codes and Q codes
   - c. H codes and K codes
   - d. H codes, S codes, and T codes

4. When both a CPT code and a HCPCS level II code are available for a procedure, service, or supply, the coder should assign the:
   - a. code according to payer instructions.
   - b. CPT code.
   - c. HCPCS level II code.
   - d. more specific code.

5. Which are reported to generate transitional pass-through payments under the Outpatient Prospective Payment System?
   - a. C codes
   - b. G codes
   - c. Q codes
   - d. S codes

6. HCPCS level II "addition" codes are included in subsections of _____ codes.
   - a. alcohol and drug abuse treatment services
   - b. cellular therapy and chelation therapy
   - c. enteral and parenteral therapy
   - d. orthotics and prosthetics procedures

7. HCPCS level II modifiers:
   - a. contain alphanumeric characters only.
   - b. contain numeric characters only.
   - c. may also be added to CPT codes.
   - d. may be attached to HCPCS level II codes only.

8. Which processes claims for providers?
   a. DME MAC
   b. DMEPOS dealer
   c. DMERC
   d. primary MAC

9. Which processes claims for DMEPOS dealers?
   a. DME MAC
   b. LMC
   c. primary MAC
   d. SADMERC

10. Which is an example of a certificate of medical necessity?
    a. Advance beneficiary notice signed by the patient
    b. Local medical review policy
    c. National coverage determination
    d. Prescription for DMEPOS from treating physician

11. A patient was supplied with an air pressure mattress. Report code _____.
    a. E0181
    b. E0184
    c. E0185
    d. E0186

12. Magnetic resonance imaging without contrast followed by with contrast, left breast. Report code _____.
    a. C8903-LT
    b. C8904-LT
    c. C8905-LT
    d. C8908-LT

13. A patient received an injection of hydrocortisone acetate, 15 mg, for contact dermatitis. Report code(s) _____.
    a. J1700
    b. J1700, J1700
    c. J1720
    d. J1720, J1720

14. A patient received a gradient compression stocking, full length/chap style 30–40 mmHg. Report code _____.
    a. A6531
    b. A6534
    c. A6537
    d. A6539

15. A patient required catheterization for the collection of a specimen. Report code _____.
    a. A4300
    b. A4305
    c. P9612
    d. P9615

16. A patient received 2 mg leuprolide acetate for treatment of prostate cancer. Report code(s) _____.
    a. J1950
    b. J9217
    c. J9218, J9218
    d. J9219

17. A patient in a drug and alcohol rehabilitation hospital received an injection of methadone by the treating physician. Report code _____.
    a. H0020
    b. H0029
    c. H0033
    d. J1230

18. An eight-year-old boy is fitted with a long-arm plaster cast. Service is performed in part by a resident under the direction of a teaching physician. Report code _____.
    a. Q4007
    b. Q4007-GC
    c. Q4008-GC
    d. Q4010

19. The patient's family received 30 minutes of family training and counseling, which was provided for the purpose of child development. Report code(s) _____.
    a. T1025
    b. T1026
    c. T1027
    d. T1027, T1027

20. A patient received a hand-held low-vision aid. Report code _____.
    a. V2020
    b. V2510
    c. V2600
    d. V2610

Note:

The main term *Ambulance* requires review of codes A0021–A0999 to locate the appropriate five-character HCPCS level II code and two-character modifier.

Coding Practice I

Instructions: Assign HCPCS level II code(s) to each statement.

_____ 1.   Ambulance transport of patient from physician's office to hospital emergency department, including advanced life support, level 2.

_____ 2.   Ambulance transport of newborn from rural hospital to a children's specialty hospital.

_____ 3.   Patient received basic life support (BLS) during emergency transport from his home to the hospital via ambulance.

_____ 4.   Patient received life-sustaining oxygen in an ambulance during transport to the hospital from a skilled nursing facility.

_____ 5.   Patient transported in wheelchair van from residential assisted living facility to physician's office.

_____ 6.   Patient's primary care physician administered injection using a sterile 3-cc syringe with needle.

_____ 7.   RN swabbed the patient's upper torso with one pint of pHisoHex solution in preparation for an office procedure.

_____ 8.   Physician inserted a cervical cap for contraceptive use.

_____ 9.   Patient purchased a brand-new replacement adapter for her breast pump from a local DMEPOS dealer.

_____ 10. Patient was supplied with a sterile eye pad.

_____ 11. Patient underwent diagnostic radiology procedure, which required injection of one 30-mCi dose of ammonia N-13 as the radiopharmaceutical diagnostic imaging agent.

_____ 12. Patient rented prescribed exercise equipment from a local DMEPOS dealer.

_____ 13. Patient was administered a 2-millicurie I-131 sodium iodide capsule as the radiopharmaceutical diagnostic agent prior to a diagnostic radiology procedure.

_____ 14. Patient was injected with contrast material prior to echocardiography.

_____ 15. Patient was administered one dose of an oral multvitamin.

_____ 16. Patient was provided with parenteral nutrition administration kits for two days of care.

_____ 17. Patient received 1 unit of nutritionally incomplete/modular nutrients enteral formula via enteral feeding tube.

_____ 18. A new enteral infusion pump with alarm was attached to the patient's enteral feeding tube system.

_____ 19. Patient was provided with a new gravity-fed enteral feeding supply kit, one day.

_____ 20. A Levine-type stomach tube was used during the procedure.

_____ 21. One brachytherapy source of high-dose-rate iridium-192 was inserted into the patient by the radiation oncologist.

_____ 22. A cardiac event recorder was implanted in the patient as a medically necessary service/supply.

_____ 23. Implantable breast prosthesis was provided during surgery.

_____ 24. Patient underwent left breast MRI without contrast, followed by left breast MRI with contrast.

_____   25. A short-term hemodialysis catheter was inserted in the patient's right forearm (patient is left-handed).

_____   26. "Patient helper" trapeze bars and a grab bar were attached to the patient's bed.

_____   27. An adult oxygen tent was supplied to the patient.

_____   28. A bilirubin light with photometer was used to treat the patient.

_____   29. Provider reported a dispensing fee for use of a DME nebulizer with compressor (covered drug).

_____   30. Patient purchased a new folding walker, which has adjustable and fixed-height features.

_____   31. A complete CBC, automated, was performed.

_____   32. Trimming of five dystrophic nails.

_____   33. Patient received 20 minutes of individual smoking cessation counseling as part of a demonstration project.

_____   34. Patient underwent colorectal cancer screening via flexible sigmoidoscopy.

_____   35. Patient underwent full positron emission tomography (PET) imaging for initial diagnosis of breast cancer.

_____   36. Patient received 30 minutes of behavioral health counseling and therapy as provided through his employee assistance program.

_____   37. Patient received 18 hours of partial hospitalization care for mental health crisis.

_____   38. One day of psychiatric health care facility services was provided to the patient.

_____   39. Three days of respite care services were provided to the patient in the hospice unit of the hospital.

_____   40. Patient received 30 minutes of activity therapy delivered as part of outpatient physical therapy plan of care.

_____   41. Injection, caffeine citrate, 5 mg.

_____   42. Injection, gamma globulin, intramuscular, 10 cc.

_____   43. Injection, paricalcitol, 1 mcg.

_____   44. Injection, torsemide, 10 mg/mL.

_____   45. Injection, doxorubicin HCl, 10 mg.

_____   46. Repair service of 10-year-old DMEPOS device required supply of complete front caster assembly for wheelchair with two semipneumatic tires.

_____   47. Patient was supplied with one IV hanger.

_____   48. Patient was supplied with two leg straps for use with her wheelchair.

_____   49. Patient rented a prescribed lightweight portable motorized wheelchair.

_____   50. A replacement alkaline battery, 1.5 volt, was provided for the patient-owned external infusion pump.

_____   51. Patient was provided with a cervical wire frame, semirigid, for occipital/mandibular support.

_____   52. Patient purchased a prescribed custom-fabricated thoracic rib belt.

_____ 53. Patient underwent halo procedure (cervical halo incorporated into Milwaukee orthosis).

_____ 54. Patient purchased a prescribed 2-inch neoprene heel and sole elevation lift.

_____ 55. In conjunction with a previously furnished orthotics prosthetic device, patient was supplied with a posterior solid ankle, plastic, custom-fabricated, ankle foot orthosis (AFO).

_____ 56. Patient was fitted with a knee disarticulation prosthesis that contained a molded socket, external knee joint, shin, and solid ankle cushion heel (SACH) foot.

_____ 57. Patient (adult) was fitted with an Otto Bock electric hand, myoelectrically controlled.

_____ 58. Patient was fitted with a partial foot prosthesis that contained a shoe insert with longitudinal arch, toe filler.

_____ 59. Patient was provided with a glove (for terminal device), right-hand prosthesis.

_____ 60. During breast reconstruction surgery, a silicone breast prosthesis was inserted.

_____ 61. Intragastric hypothermia using gastric freezing.

_____ 62. Cellular therapy.

_____ 63. Chemical endarterectomy via intravenous (IV) chelation therapy.

_____ 64. Fabric wrapping of abdominal aneurysm.

_____ 65. Prolotherapy.

_____ 66. Catheterization for collection of specimen was performed for one patient.

_____ 67. Screening Pap smear, cervical, by technician under physician supervision.

_____ 68. Infusion of 250 mL of 5% albumin (human).

_____ 69. Two units of platelets were infused.

_____ 70. Two units of whole blood were used during transfusion.

_____ 71. Patient received chemotherapy administration, push technique.

_____ 72. Patient underwent a collagen skin test.

_____ 73. Patient injected with 1 mL of 50 mg of teniposide.

_____ 74. As part of fracture treatment, 10-year-old patient received short-arm plaster splint.

_____ 75. Potassium hydroxide (KOH) preparation included as part of patient's treatment.

_____ 76. Transportation of portable chest x-ray and radiology technician to nursing home; 20 patients underwent x-ray.

_____ 77. Transportation of portable EKG equipment to nursing facility; five patients underwent EKG.

_____ 78. Transportation of portable x-ray equipment and radiology technician to patient's home; husband and wife underwent x-ray.

_____ 79. Allogenic cord blood-derived stem cell transplantation.

_____ 80. Echosclerotherapy.

_____ 81. Gastrointestinal fat absorption study.

_____ 82. Global fee for extracorporeal shock wave lithotripsy (ESWL) treatment of kidney stone.

_____ 83. Harvesting of multivisceral organs from cadaver donor with preparation and maintenance of allografts.

_____ 84. Patient underwent 15 minutes of family training and counseling for child development.

_____ 85. Human breast milk processing, storage, and distribution.

_____ 86. Intramuscular medication administration by home health licensed practical nurse (LPN).

_____ 87. Patient received 30 minutes of private-duty nursing from a registered nurse (RN).

_____ 88. Waiver of utility services to support medical equipment and assistive technology/devices.

_____ 89. Bifocal lenses, bilateral, 5.25 sphere, 2.12 cylinder, two lenses.

_____ 90. Deluxe frame.

_____ 91. Photochromatic tinting of two lenses.

_____ 92. Processing, preserving, and transporting corneal tissue.

_____ 93. Reduction of ocular prosthesis.

_____ 94. Patient underwent assessment for hearing aid.

_____ 95. Provision of binaural, behind-the-ear hearing aid.

_____ 96. Provision of digitally programmable monaural hearing aid, analog, in the canal (ITC).

_____ 97. Dispensing fee, binaural contralateral routing of signals (BICROS).

_____ 98. Patient purchased prescribed telephone amplifier assistive listening device.

Coding Practice II

Instructions: Review each SOAP note to identify medications administered, procedures performed, and services provided. Assign appropriate HCPCS level II code(s) and modifier(s) to each medication, procedure, and service. (Do _not_ assign CPT codes to procedures or services.).

1. SUBJECTIVE: The patient is an 89-year-old white female resident of the county nursing facility. I was asked to see her today because the nursing staff had noticed the patient was having difficulty breathing and was coughing up purulent material. A chest x-ray was ordered, and the mobile x-ray service arrived and took the x-ray while I was seeing my other patients.

    OBJECTIVE: The patient appears ill. Temperature is 100.7.

    CHEST: Scattered rhonchi throughout all lung fields, with severely diminished breath sounds in the left lower lung. Expiratory and inspiratory wheezes present.

    HEART: Within normal limits.

    ABDOMEN: No tenderness on palpation.

    EXTREMITIES: Mild dependent edema is noted; otherwise within normal limits.

    ASSESSMENT: The chest x-ray revealed a density consistent with left lower lobe pneumonia.

    PLAN: The patient was administered an injection of Zithromax 500 milligrams. The cough does not seem to be bothersome to the patient right now, so the nursing staff will wait and watch. The nursing staff is to monitor her for any signs of increased fever, lethargy, or medication reaction. They are to encourage fluids and keep the patient up in a chair as much as possible when she is not sleeping. The staff is to contact me immediately if the patient's symptoms worsen.

---

2. SUBJECTIVE: This 45-year-old construction worker was seen in the office today on an emergency basis because he stepped on a sharp edge of steel and lacerated his right foot. He states that he cannot recall his last tetanus shot.

OBJECTIVE: Examination of the right foot reveals a laceration of approximately 3.5 cm at the lateral edge of the foot that extends medially across the heel.

PROCEDURE: The right heel was cleansed with pHisoHex and prepped with Betadine. The wound edges were infiltrated with 1% Xylocaine. After adequate anesthesia was obtained, the laceration was repaired with 3-0 nylon sutures. The wound was dressed with gauze and secured with paper tape.

ASSESSMENT: Laceration of right heel, repaired in the office.

PLAN: The patient was given a tetanus shot today. He was given instructions on wound care and signs of infection and was also given reference sheets on the same. He is to be non-weight-bearing for the next three days and was given a pair of wooden crutches. He will return to the office in three days for reevaluation. The patient was also reminded to call immediately if pain increases or if he shows any signs of fever.

PART IV

Current Procedural Terminology (CPT) Coding System

Introduction to CPT Coding

Chapter Outline

History of CPT

Overview of CPT

Organization of CPT

CPT Index

CPT Appendices

CPT Symbols

CPT Sections, Subsections, Categories, and Subcategories

CPT Modifiers

National Correct Coding Initiative (NCCI)

Chapter Objectives

At the conclusion of this chapter, the student should be able to:

- Define key terms.
- Explain the organization, format, and content of CPT.
- Interpret CPT section guidelines, coding notes, and modifiers.
- Assign CPT procedure and service codes for outpatient care.
- Add CPT and/or HCPCS level II modifiers to codes, as appropriate.

Key Terms

add-on code

Appendix A of CPT

Appendix B of CPT

Appendix C of CPT

Appendix D of CPT

Appendix E of CPT

Appendix F of CPT

Appendix H of CPT

Appendix J of CPT

Appendix K of CPT

Appendix L of CPT

Appendix M of CPT

Appendix N of CPT

Appendix O of CPT

Appendix P of CPT

blue reference symbol (⬏)

bullet symbol (•)

Category I code

Category II code

Category III code

column 1/column 2 edit

descriptive qualifiers

flash symbol (✁)

forbidden (or prohibitory) symbol (⊘)

functional modifier

green reference symbol (⬏)

guidelines

hollow circle symbol (○)

horizontal triangle symbols (▶◀)

inferred words

informational modifiers

mutually exclusive edit

National Correct Coding Initiative (NCCI)

notes

Notice of Exclusions from Medicare Benefits (NEMB)

number symbol (#)

plus symbol (✚)

pricing modifier

range of codes

red reference symbol (⬏)

semicolon (;)

single code

special report

star symbol (★)

triangle symbol (▲)

unlisted procedure

unlisted service

Introduction

This chapter introduces the Current Procedural Terminology (CPT) coding system (or HCPCS level I), a proprietary coding system published annually by the American Medical Association (AMA). Current Procedural Terminology (CPT) is a listing of descriptive terms and identifying codes for reporting medical services and procedures. It provides a uniform language that describes medical, surgical, and diagnostic services to facilitate communication among providers, patients, and third-party payers.

Note:

When reviewing examples and completing exercises and review questions in this chapter (and in Chapters 10 through 18), use your CPT coding manual to locate index entries and to verify them in the tabular list.

History of CPT

The AMA first published CPT in 1966, and subsequent editions expanded its descriptive terms and codes for diagnostic and therapeutic procedures. Five-digit codes were introduced in 1970, replacing the four-digit classification. In 1983, CPT was adopted as part of the Healthcare Common Procedure Coding System (HCPCS) (as HCPCS level I) and its use was mandated for reporting Medicare Part B physician services. In 1986, HCPCS was required for reporting to Medicaid agencies, and the Omnibus Budget Reconciliation Act (OBRA) of 1986 mandated that CPT codes be reported for outpatient hospital surgical procedures.

The Health Insurance Portability and Accountability Act of 1996 (HIPAA) named CPT and HCPCS level II as the procedure code sets for physician services, physical and occupational therapy services, radiological procedures, clinical laboratory tests, other medical diagnostic procedures, hearing and vision services, and transportation services including ambulance. (Also included are ICD-10-CM as the code set for all diagnoses and ICD-10-PCS for inpatient procedures, replacing ICD-9-CM, CDT for dental services, and NDC for drugs. It eliminated HCPCS Level III local codes effective December 2003.)

CMS enforced regulations resulting from the Medicare Prescription Drug, Improvement, and Modernization Act (MMA) in October 2004, which required that new, revised, and deleted CPT codes be implemented each January 1. It is important to purchase updated coding manuals to avoid billing delays and claims rejections. If outdated codes are submitted on claims, providers and health care facilities will incur administrative costs associated with resubmitting corrected claims and delayed reimbursement for services provided.

Note:

The AMA's CPT Editorial Board publishes an "early release" of new and revised codes (e.g., vaccination codes) each July and January (for implementation six months later). Early release codes are further discussed later in this chapter.

Exercise 8.1 – History of CPT

Instructions: Match the year with the event.

_____ **1.** Introduction of five-digit CPT codes.

_____ **2.** Elimination of 90-day grace period for new/revised/deleted CPT codes.

_____ **3.** AMA first published CPT.

_____ **4.** Required reporting CPT codes for outpatient surgical procedures.

_____ **5.** Mandated reporting CPT codes for Medicare services.

a. 1966

b. 1970

c. 1983

d. 1986

e. 2004

Overview of CPT

CPT codes are used to report services and procedures performed on patients by the following types of providers:

- Home health care and hospice agencies

- Outpatient hospital departments (e.g., ambulatory surgery, emergency department, and outpatient laboratory or radiographic procedures)

- Physicians who are employees of a health care facility (e.g., Veterans Administration Medical Centers physicians)

- Physicians who see patients in their offices or clinics and in patients' homes

CPT codes and descriptions are based on consistency with contemporary medical practice as performed by clinical providers throughout the country. The assignment of CPT codes simplifies reporting and assists in the accurate identification of procedures and services for third-party payer consideration. As such, procedures and services reported on a claim must be linked to the ICD-10-CM code that justifies the need for the service or procedure. This demonstrates medical necessity for the service or procedure provided so the payer can judge whether the claim should be paid.

When reporting CPT codes, some services are considered integral to the standard of practice, which means that certain medical and surgical services are not assigned CPT codes. Such services include the following:

- Administering local, topical, or regional anesthetic (by physician performing procedure)

- Administering sedatives (by physician performing procedure)

- Applying, managing, and removing postoperative dressings and analgesic devices

- Cleansing, shaving, and prepping of skin

- Documenting preoperative, intraoperative, and postoperative procedures provided

- Draping and positioning of patient

- Inserting and removing drains, suction devices, dressings, and pumps into same site

- Inserting intravenous access for medication

- Irrigating a wound

- Providing surgical approach, closure, cultures, and supplies (unless CMS policy states otherwise)

CPT Categories

CPT is compatible with electronic data interchange (EDI), the electronic health record (EHR), and reference/research databases. CPT is used to track new technology and performance measures.

In 2000, the AMA completed the CPT-5 Project, resulting in the establishment of three categories of CPT codes.

- **Category I codes** (e.g., 99201): Procedures/services identified by a five-digit CPT code and descriptor nomenclature; these are codes traditionally associated with CPT and organized into six sections.

- **Category II codes** (e.g., 0001F): Optional "performance measurements" tracking codes that are assigned an alphanumeric identifier with a letter in the last field (e.g., 1000F); these codes will be located after the Medicine section.

  EXAMPLE: A physician counsels a patient who smokes during an evaluation and management (E/M) service. Report code 4000F (tobacco use cessation intervention, counseling). If the physician also prescribes a smoking cessation medication, report code 4001F (tobacco use cessation intervention, pharmacologic therapy). (CPT Category II codes are reported in addition to the E/M service code.)

- **Category III codes** (e.g., 0058T): Contain "emerging technology" temporary codes assigned for data collection purposes that are assigned an alphanumeric identifier with a letter in the last field (e.g., 0042T); these codes are located after the Category II codes, and they will be archived after five years if they are not accepted for placement within Category I sections of CPT.

  EXAMPLE: Prior to 2005, Category III code 0012T was reported for a surgical arthroscopy of the knee with osteochondral autograft(s). In 2005, code 0012T was deleted and a Category I code 29866 was created with a code description of "arthroscopy, knee, surgical; osteochondral autograft(s) (e.g., mosaicplasty) (including harvesting of the autograft[s])."

 Note:

According to the AMA, CPT Category II codes minimize administrative burdens because they facilitate data collection about quality of care. Services and test results are assigned codes that support performance measures and that contribute to good patient care. CPT Category II codes also relate to compliance with state or federal law.

 Note:

According to the AMA, Category III codes allow for data collection of "emerging technology" services and procedures, which are conducted as part of ongoing or planned research. Effective 2006, modifiers are reported with Category III codes.

The CPT Editorial Panel also approves the "early release" of new CPT codes. All changes provided as an "early release" take effect on the implementation date, which is six months after the "early release" of the codes. This means that codes included in an "early release" in January are implemented for use in July (and codes included in an "early release" in July are implemented the following January). To assist users in reporting the most recently approved codes, the AMA's CPT website will feature updates of the CPT Editorial Panel's actions and early release of the codes in July and January during a given CPT cycle. These dates for early release correspond with the quarterly CPT Editorial Panel's meetings for each CPT cycle (May, August, November, and February).

Exercise 8.2 – Overview of CPT

Instructions: Complete each statement.

1. CPT codes and descriptions are based on consistency with contemporary medical practice as performed by clinical _____ throughout the United States.

2. The assignment of CPT codes simplifies reporting and assists in the accurate identification of procedures and services for third-party _____ consideration.

3. CPT codes for procedures and services that are reported on a claim must be linked to the ICD-10-CM code that justifies the need for the service or procedure, which demonstrates medical _____ for the service or procedure provided.

4. Category _____ codes contain optional "performance measurements" tracking codes that are assigned an alphanumeric identifier with a letter in the last field.

5. Category _____ codes contain "emerging technology" temporary codes, which are assigned for data collection purposes and contain an alphanumeric identifier with a letter in the last field.

Organization of CPT

To assign CPT codes, it is necessary to become familiar with CPT's organizational characteristics.

- CPT sections
- CPT code number format
- Boldfaced type
- Italicized type
- Cross-reference term
- Single codes and code ranges
- Inferred words
- Guidelines
- Unlisted procedures and services
- Notes
- Descriptive qualifiers

CPT Category I Codes

CPT Organizes Category I procedures and services into six sections.

- Evaluation and Management (E/M) (99201–99499) ✐
- Anesthesia (00100–01999, 99100–99140)
- Surgery (10021–69990)
- Radiology (including Nuclear Medicine and Diagnostic Ultrasound) (70010–79999)
- Pathology and Laboratory (80047–89398)
- Medicine (90281–99607) ✐

> **Note:**
> The E/M section is located at the beginning of CPT because these codes are reported by all specialties.

> **Note:**
> Medicine section codes 99100–99140, which classify Qualifying Circumstances for Anesthesia, are explained in the Anesthesia section guidelines. They are reported with Anesthesia section codes.

CPT Category II Codes

CPT Category II codes are supplemental tracking codes used for performance measurement in compliance with the Physician Quality Reporting System (PQRS). Category II codes (as well as certain HCPCS level II G codes defined by CMS) are assigned for certain services or tests results, which support nationally established performance measures that have proven to contribute to quality patient care. CPT Category II codes are alphanumeric and consist of four digits followed by the alpha character F. (HCPCS level II G codes are alphanumeric and consist of the alpha character G followed by four digits.) The reporting of Category II codes (and CMS-defined HCPCS level II G codes) is optional and is not a substitute for the assignment of CPT Category I codes. When reported on the CMS-1500 claim, the submitted charge is zero ($0.00). CPT Category II codes are arranged according to the following categories:

- Modifiers (1P–8P), reported with CPT Category II codes only
- Composite Codes (0001F–0015F)
- Patient Management (0500F–0584F)
- Patient History (1000F–1505F)
- Physical Examination (2000F–2060F)
- Diagnostic/Screening Processes or Results (3006F–3776F)
- Therapeutic, Preventive, or Other Interventions (4000F–4563F)
- Follow-up or Other Outcomes (5005F–5250F)

- Patient Safety (6005F–6150F)
- Structural Measures (7010F–7025F)
- Nonmeasure Code Listing (9001F-9007F)

The purpose of reporting Category II codes is to facilitate the collection of information about the quality of services provided to patients. The use of Category II is expected to decrease the time required for patient record abstracting and review, thus minimizing the administrative burden on health care providers (e.g., physicians, hospitals).

EXAMPLE: Dr. Ryan is a dermatologist who is participating in a nationwide quality management study about malignant melanoma. CPT Category II code 0015F is reported for each patient who receives melanoma follow-up services, which include obtaining a history about new or changing moles (code 1050F), performing a complete physical skin examination (code 2029F), and providing patient counseling to perform a monthly skin self-examination (code 5005F). Thus, codes 0015F, 1050F, 2029F, and 5005F are reported on the CMS-1500 claim, and the charge for each is zero ($0.00). In addition, reason for encounter code(s) and CPT Category I service/procedure code(s) are reported on the same CMS-1500 claim with appropriate charges entered for each CPT Category I code.

CPT Category III Codes

CPT Category III codes are temporary codes that allow for utilization tracking of emerging technology, procedures, and services. The codes facilitate data collection on and assessment of new services and procedures during the FDA approval process or to confirm that a procedure/service is generally provided. According to the CPT coding manual, the "procedure or service is currently or recently performed in humans; and at least one additional criteria (listed in the CPT coding manual) has been met." CPT Category III codes are alphanumeric and consist of four digits followed by the alpha character T, and they range from 0042T–0463T. In 2002, CMS began designating certain CPT Category III codes as covered by Medicare, which means charges are entered when reporting the codes on a CMS-1500 claim.

In the past, researchers were hindered by the length and requirements of the CPT approval process. Thus, CPT Category III (temporary) codes facilitate the reporting of emerging technology, procedures, and services. They are generally retired if the emerging technology, procedure, or service is not assigned a CPT Category I code within five years. When a Category III code is available, it must be reported instead of an unlisted CPT Category I code (because reporting an unlisted code does not offer the opportunity for collection of specific data). Category III codes were initially released in July 2001 and are included as a separate section in CPT (following the Category II codes). (HCPCS level II codes also describe emerging technology, procedures, and services; when a HCPCS level II code exists, it must be reported for Medicare claims.)

EXAMPLE: The patient's physician administered breath test for heart transplant rejection. Report Category III code 0085T and its charge on the CMS-1500 claim.

CPT Code Number Format

A five-digit code number and a narrative description identify each procedure and service listed in Category I of CPT. Most procedures and services contain stand-alone descriptions. To save space, some descriptions are not printed in their entirety next to a code number. Instead, the entry is indented and the coder must refer back to the common portion of the code description that is located before the semicolon.

EXAMPLE 1: STAND-ALONE CODE DESCRIPTION:

27870   Arthrodesis, ankle, open

EXAMPLE 2: INDENTED CODE DESCRIPTION:

27780   Closed treatment of proximal fibula or shaft fracture; without manipulation

27781   with manipulation

The code description for 27781 is *closed treatment of proximal fibula or shaft fracture with manipulation*.

Exercise 8.3 – Organization of CPT

Instructions: Complete each statement.

1. CPT organizes Category I procedures and services into _____ sections.

2. The Evaluation and Management section of CPT is located at the beginning of CPT because these codes are reported by all _____.

3. Medicine section codes 99100–99140, which classify *Qualifying Circumstances for Anesthesia*, are explained in the _____ section guidelines.

4. Refer to CPT code 55605. Its code description is _____.

5. Refer to CPT code 47562 and review all code descriptions through code 47570. The description for code 47562 is "Laparoscopy, surgical; cholecystectomy." The code description for 47562 includes a semicolon, which means the description for code 47563 is _____ _____ _____.

CPT Index

The CPT index (Figure 8-1) is organized by alphabetical main terms printed in boldface. The main terms represent procedures or services, organs, anatomical sites, conditions, eponyms, or abbreviations. The main term may be followed by indented terms that modify the main term; these are called *subterms*.

The CPT index organizes procedures and services according to

- Procedure or service (e.g., arthroscopy)
- Organ or other anatomical site (e.g., ankle)
- Condition (e.g., wound)
- Synonyms (e.g., finger joint or intercarpal joint)
- Eponyms (e.g., Billroth I or II)
- Abbreviations (e.g., EKG)

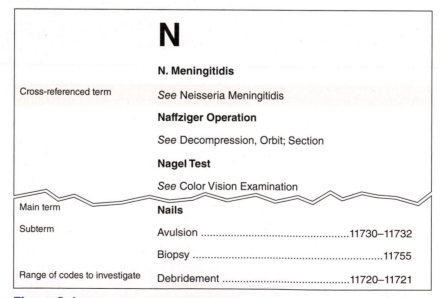

Figure 8-1 Selection from CPT index

To locate a CPT code, review patient record documentation to locate the service and/or procedure performed and locate the main term in the index (located in the back of the coding manual).

EXAMPLE: For the procedure "surgical temporomandibular joint (TMJ) arthroscopy," refer to the index and locate main term *Temporomandibular joint*, subterm *arthroscopy*, and qualifier *surgical*. 29804 is the listed code. Next, verify code 29804 in the tabular portion of the coding manual before reporting it on a claim for submission to a third-party payer. (A diagnosis code must be reported on the claim to justify medical necessity of the procedure. The diagnosis code for articular disc disorder of temporomandibular joint would justify medical necessity.)

> **Coding Tip:**
>
> The descriptions of all codes listed in the index for a specific procedure must be carefully investigated before selecting a final code. CPT coding must never be performed solely from the index.

Boldfaced Type

Main terms in the CPT index are printed in boldfaced type. CPT category and subcategory titles and code numbers are also printed in boldfaced type.

Italicized Type

Italicized type is used for the cross-reference term *See* in the CPT index.

Cross-Reference Term

See is a cross-reference that directs coders to an index entry under which codes are listed. No codes are listed under the original entry.

EXAMPLE: The instructional term *See* directs the coder to index entry "Arteriovenous Shunt" because no codes are listed for the abbreviation *AV Shunt*.

AV Shunt
See Arteriovenous Shunt

Single Codes and Code Ranges

Index code numbers for specific procedures may be represented as a **single code** number, a **range of codes** separated by a dash, a series of codes separated by commas, or a combination of single codes and ranges of codes. All codes should be investigated before assigning a code for the procedure or service.

EXAMPLE: The main term *Acid fast stain* contains just one code. Subterm *esophagus*, which is located below main term *Acid perfusion test*, contains two codes separated by commas. Main term *Acid Reflux Test* contains a range of codes.

Acid-Fast Stain
Analysis 88312
Acid Perfusion Study
Esophagus.. 91013, 91030
Adenoids
Excision 42830–42836

Inferred Words

To save space in the CPT index when referencing subterms, **inferred words** are used.

EXAMPLE: The word *(of)* in parentheses is inferred and does not actually appear in the CPT index.

```
Abdomen
   Exploration (of) ........................................... 49000, 49010
```

Exercise 8.4 – CPT Index

Instructions: Indicate whether each statement is true (T) or false (F).

_____ 1. The cross-reference that directs coders to refer to a different index entry because no codes are found under the original entry is called *See*.

_____ 2. Main terms appear in *italics* in the CPT index.

_____ 3. Inferred words appear in the CPT index to assist coders in assigning appropriate codes.

_____ 4. The main term may be followed by indented terms, known as subterms, which modify the main term.

_____ 5. Cross-reference terms are printed in bold in the CPT index.

CPT Appendices

CPT contains appendices, located between the Medicine section and the index. Insurance specialists should carefully review these appendices to become familiar with coding changes that affect the practice annually.

- **Appendix A** (Modifiers) contains a list of CPT modifiers and detailed descriptions. Place a marker at the beginning of Appendix A because you will refer to it often.

- **Appendix B** (Summary of Additions, Deletions, and Revisions) contains annual CPT coding changes that include added, deleted, and revised CPT codes. Carefully review Appendix B of the current CPT manual because it will serve as the basis for updating interoffice documents and billing tools.

- **Appendix C** (Clinical Examples) contains clinical examples for codes found in the E/M section.

> **! Coding Tip:**
>
> A complete list of code additions, deletions, and revisions is found in Appendix B of CPT. Revisions marked with horizontal triangles (►◄) are not included in Appendix B, and coders need to carefully review all CPT guidelines and notes in the new edition of CPT.

- **Appendix D** (Summary of CPT Add-on Codes) contains a list of add-on codes that are identified throughout CPT with a **+** symbol. An **add-on code** is reported when another procedure is performed in addition to the primary procedure during the same operative session. Modifier -51 (multiple procedures) is *not* added to add-on codes.

- **Appendix E** (Summary of CPT Codes Exempt from Modifier 51) contains a list of codes that are exempt from modifier -51 reporting rules and that are identified throughout CPT with a forbidden (⊘) symbol.

- **Appendix F** (Summary of CPT Codes Exempt from Modifier 63) contains a list of codes that are exempt from modifier -63.

- *Appendix G* (Summary of CPT Codes That Include Moderate (Conscious) Sedation) was removed from the CPT coding manual.

- **Appendix H** (Alphabetic Clinical Topics Listing) was removed from the CPT coding manual and relocated to the AMA website: www.ama-assn.org/go/cpt. The document is a source of information that links CPT Category II codes, clinical conditions, and performance measures.

- *Appendix I* (Genetic Testing Code Modifiers) was removed from the CPT coding manual.

- **Appendix J** (Electrodiagnostic Medicine Listing of Sensory, Motor, and Mixed Nerves) contains an electrodiagnostic medicine listing of sensory, motor, and mixed nerves that are reported for motor and nerve studies codes. There is also a table that indicates the "type of study and maximum number of studies" generally performed for needle electromyogram (EMG), nerve conduction studies, and other EMG studies. The AMA's *CPT Changes 2006: An Insider's View* calls this table a ". . . tool to detect outliers."

- **Appendix K** (Product Pending FDA Approval) contains a list of products that are pending FDA approval but that have been assigned CPT codes. In the CPT manual, these codes are preceded by the flash symbol (✗).

- **Appendix L** (Vascular Families) contains a list of vascular families that is intended to assist in the selection of first-, second-, third-, and beyond third-order branch arteries.

Exercise 8.5 – CPT Appendices

Instructions: Match the appendix with its description. Answers may be assigned more than once.

_____	**1.** Contains a list of add-on codes identified throughout CPT with a **+** symbol	**a.** Appendix A
_____	**2.** Contains a list of CPT modifiers and detailed descriptions	**b.** Appendix B
_____	**3.** Contains a list of codes that are exempt from modifier -63	**c.** Appendix C
_____	**4.** Contains a list of vascular families to assist in the determination of first-, second-, third-, and beyond third-order branches of arteries	**d.** Appendix D
_____	**5.** Contains CPT codes that may be used for synchronous telemedicine services	**e.** Appendix E
_____	**6.** Contains added, deleted, and revised CPT codes	**f.** Appendix F
_____	**7.** Contains codes for MAAA procedures	**g.** Appendix H
_____	**8.** Contains an alphabetic clinical topics listing at the AMA website, which includes performance measures	**h.** Appendix I
_____	**9.** Contains an electrodiagnostic medicine listing of sensory, motor, and mixed nerves	**i.** Appendix J
_____	**10.** Contains clinical examples for codes in the E/M section	**j.** Appendix K
_____	**11.** Contains codes for vaccine products that are pending FDA approval	**k.** Appendix L
_____	**12.** Contains codes that are exempt from modifier -51 reporting rules and that are identified in CPT with a ⊘ symbol	**l.** Appendix M
_____	**13.** Formerly contained genetic testing modifiers	**m.** Appendix N
_____	**14.** Contains a crosswalk of resequenced codes that are identified with a **#** symbol	**n.** Appendix O
_____	**15.** Contains a crosswalk of deleted and renumbered CPT codes	**o.** Appendix P

- **Appendix M** (Renumbered CPT Codes–Citations Crosswalk) contains a summary of crosswalked deleted and renumbered codes from 2007 to 2009.

- **Appendix N** (Summary of Resequenced CPT Codes) contains a list of CPT codes that do not appear in numeric order. CPT codes are resequenced (instead of deleted and renumbered) so that existing codes can be relocated to a more appropriate location. In the CPT manual, out-of-sequence codes are preceded by the number symbol (#).

- **Appendix O** (Multianalyte Assays with Algorithmic Analyses, MAAA) includes administrative codes for procedures that by their nature are typically unique to a single clinical laboratory or manufacturer.

- **Appendix P** (CPT codes that may be used for synchronous telemedicine services) includes codes for electronic communication using interactive telecommunications equipment (e.g., audio, video). In the CPT manual, these codes are preceded by the star (★) symbol. Modifier -95 is reported with Appendix P codes.

CPT Symbols

Symbols (Figure 8-2 contains a partial selection) are located throughout the CPT coding manual.

- A **bullet symbol** located to the left of a code number identifies new procedures and services added to CPT.

▲ A **triangle symbol** located to the left of a code number identifies a code description that has been revised.

▶◀ **Horizontal triangle symbols** surround revised guidelines and notes. These symbols are *not* used for revised code descriptions.

; To save space in CPT, some code descriptions are not printed in their entirety next to a code number. Instead, the entry is indented, and the coder must refer back to the common portion of the code description that is located before the **semicolon**. The common portion begins with a capital letter, and the abbreviated (or subordinate) descriptions are indented and begin with lowercase letters.

> **Note:**
>
> Review your CPT coding manual to locate codes preceded by the bullet, triangle, and horizontal triangle symbols.

EXAMPLE:

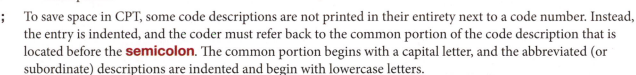
```
20910   Cartilage graft; costochondral
20912        nasal septum ▲
```

- For a patient who undergoes costochondral cartilage graft procedure, report code 20910.

- For a patient who undergoes a nasal septum cartilage graft procedure, report code 20912.

For a patient who undergoes costochondral and nasal septum cartilage graft procedures during the same operative session, report codes 20910 and 20912-51. (Modifier -51 indicates that a multiple procedure was performed. The payer will discount reimbursement for the procedure assigned code 20912.)

> ⚠ **Coding Tip:**
>
> CPT is printed using proportional spacing, and careful review of code descriptions to locate the semicolon may be necessary.

Symbol:	CPT Entry:	
Use of semicolon	**11000**	Debridement of extensive eczematous or infected skin; up to 10% of body surface
Use of plus symbol	**+ 11001**	each additional 10% of the body surface, or part thereof (List separately in addition to code to primary procedure)
Use of -51 modifier exemption symbol	**⊘ 17004**	Destruction (eg, laser surgery, electrosurgery, cryosurgery, chemosurgery, surgical curette- ment), premalignant lesions (eg, actinic keratoses), 15 or more lesions
Use of bull's-eye symbol	**⊙ 33010**	Pericardiocentesis; initial

Figure 8-2 Selection from CPT illustrating symbols

+ The **plus symbol** identifies add-on codes (Appendix D of CPT) for procedures that are commonly, but not always, performed at the same time and by the same surgeon as the primary procedure. Parenthetical notes, located below add-on codes, often identify the primary procedure to which add-on codes apply.

EXAMPLE: For a patient who undergoes posterior osteotomy of the spine, two cervical vertebral segments, report codes 22210 and 22216.

22210	Osteotomy of spine, posterior or posterolateral approach, 1 vertebral segment; cervical
22212	thoracic
22214	lumbar
+ 22216	each additional vertebral segment (List separately in addition to primary procedure)

(Use 22216 in conjunction with codes 22210, 22212, 22214)

 Coding Tip:

- Do not report codes identified with **+** (add-on codes) as stand-alone codes; they must be reported with a primary code.

- Do not add modifier -51 to codes identified with the **+** symbol because payers discount reimbursement for such add-on codes; adding modifier -51 to codes that have the **+** symbol incorrectly reduces reimbursement even more.

⊘ This **forbidden** (or **prohibitory**) **symbol** identifies codes that are exempt from modifier -51. These codes are reported in addition to other codes, but they are not classified as add-on codes.

EXAMPLE: The patient underwent emergency endotracheal intubation.

    ⊘ 31500   Intubation, endotracheal, emergency procedure

When code 31500 is reported with other procedures performed during the same encounter, do not add modifier -51.

★ The **star symbol** indicates that a code may be reported for synchronous telemedicine services. (CPT Appendix P contains a list of CPT codes that may be used for synchronous telemedicine services.)

EXAMPLE: Patient underwent psychiatric diagnostic evaluation using synchronous telemedicine services. Report code 90791-95.

```
★ 90791   Psychiatric diagnostic evaluation
```

⚡ The **flash symbol** indicates codes that classify products pending FDA approval but that have been assigned a CPT code.

EXAMPLE: Patient was administered an influenza virus vaccine, pandemic formulation

```
⚡ 90668   Influenza virus vaccine, pandemic formulation, split virus, for
          intramuscular use
```

○ The **hollow circle symbol** indicates a reinstated or recycled code in Category III of CPT. (It is unknown whether the *hollow circle symbol* will also appear in front of CPT's Category I and II codes in the future.)

EXAMPLE: A performance measurement study was conducted on a patient, and it was determined that a new episode for his condition was documented in the patient record. In CPT 2010, Category II code 1127F was deleted. In CPT 2012, the code was reinstated; thus, a hollow circle symbol appears before code 1127F. As of 2014, the hollow circle was removed from in front of code 1127F.

```
○ 1127F   New episode for condition (NMA-No Measure Associated)
```

\# The **number symbol** indicates out-of-numerical sequence codes.

EXAMPLE: Patient underwent excision of 4-cm subcutaneous soft tissue tumor of the neck.

```
  21555    Excision, tumor, soft tissue of neck or anterior thorax,
           subcutaneous; less than 3 cm
# 21552       3 cm or greater
```

Note:

Prior to 2010, when a new code was added and there was no available code in a "code range," a new range of codes was added to accommodate the new code(s). This meant that all codes in a range were deleted (and added as new codes) for certain procedures even though the procedure text and meaning or applicability of the procedure had not changed.

The new policy of creating out-of-numerical sequence codes facilitates historical data analysis, reduces the number of codes that providers must revise (e.g., superbill, encounter form), and eliminates the need for payers to modify related reimbursement policies. (Payers typically interpreted a new range of codes as "new codes" to CPT, resulting in payment denials.)

Resequenced codes will appear "out of sequence" in the print version of CPT, but that means the codes will be located with concepts to which they are related. CPT code description content will determine placement of out-of-sequence codes. (Codes in the electronic version of CPT will be in numeric order.)

➲ The **green reference symbol** located below a code description in some CPT coding manuals indicates that the coder should refer to the *CPT Assistant* monthly newsletter.

⊃ The **blue reference symbol** located below a code description in some CPT coding manuals indicates that the coder should refer to the *CPT Changes: An Insider's View* annual publication that contains all coding changes for the current year.

EXAMPLE:

43882   Revision or removal of gastric neurostimulator electrodes, antrum, open
⊃ *CPT Assistant Mar 07:4*
⊃ *CPT Changes: An Insider's View 2007*

⊃ The **red reference symbol** located below a code description in some CPT coding manuals indicates that the coder should refer to the *Clinical Examples in Radiology* quarterly newsletter.

EXAMPLE:

73525   Radiologic examination, hip, arthrography, radiological supervision and interpretation
⊃ *Clinical Examples in Radiology Spring 05:6*

Exercise 8.6 – CPT Symbols

Instructions: Match the symbol with its description

_____ 1. Identifies a code that may be used for synchronous telemedicine services

_____ 2. Identifies add-on codes

_____ 3. Identifies codes that are exempt from modifier -51

_____ 4. Identifies codes that classify products pending FDA approval

_____ 5. Identifies new procedures and services added to CPT

_____ 6. Identifies revised code descriptions

_____ 7. Refers coders to *Clinical Examples in Radiology* newsletter

_____ 8. Indicates an out-of-numeric sequence code

_____ 9. Refers coders to *CPT Assistant* newsletter and/or *CPT Changes: An Insider's View* annual publication of coding changes for current year

_____ 10. Indicates a reinstated or recycled code in Category III of CPT

a. ★
b. ▲
c. •
d. +
e. ⊘
f. ⊿
g. ○
h. #
i. ⊃
j. ⊃

CPT Sections, Subsections, Categories, and Subcategories

CPT Category I codes are organized according to six sections that are subdivided into subsections, categories, and subcategories (Figure 8-3). Guidelines are located at the beginning of each CPT section, and the following are located in CPT subsections, headings or categories, subheadings or subcategories, and codes:

- Notes

- Descriptive qualifiers

Section	**Surgery**	
Subsection	**Integumentary System**	
Heading	**Skin, Subcutaneous and Accessory Structures**	
Subheading	**Incision and Drainage**	
Note	(For excision, see 11400, et seq)	
Descriptive qualifier (underlined phrase)	10060	Incision and drainage of abscess (eg, carbuncle, suppurative hidradenitis, cutaneous or subcutaneous abscess, cyst, furuncle, or paronychia); <u>simple or single</u>

Figure 8-3 Selection from CPT illustrating sections, subsections, categories, subcategories, notes, and descriptive qualifiers

 Note:

CPT is inconsistent in its use of subsection, category, and subcategory terminology. For example, the CPT E/M section guideline *Classification of Evaluation and Management (E/M) Services* refers to categories and subcategories (instead of the more logical subsections and categories). (Many years ago, the E/M section was a subsection of the Medicine section. When the codes were relocated to the beginning of the CPT coding manual for easy reference, the E/M section was created. The category and subcategory terminology associated with the E/M codes was retained.)

Remaining CPT section guidelines include lists of subsections except for the Radiology section, which includes some subcategories in the list of subsections. To make matters even more complicated, CPT refers to headings and subheadings in some section guidelines and categories and subcategories in other section guidelines. In addition, the Surgery guidelines include "Subsection Information," which refers to "subheadings or subsections." It would be more logical if the latter phrase had been written as "subheadings or subcategories."

 ICD-10 Alert!

HIPAA has designated CPT as a national code set for reporting outpatient (including physician's office) procedures and services. It further designated *CPT Assistant* as an official source of coding guidelines. CPT guidelines and notes and *CPT Assistant* coding guidelines take precedence over payer-specific rules for reporting codes. However, payers (e.g., CMS and commercial insurance companies) are selective about the guidelines and notes they implement for reimbursement purposes. Thus, payer-specific reimbursement rules often contradict CPT guidelines and notes and *CPT Assistant* coding guidelines. This means that coders must review and follow payer-specific reimbursement rules for reporting codes to obtain appropriate reimbursement.

EXAMPLE: Cautery was used to correct everted lacrimal puncta (small openings in the inner canthus of eyelids that channel tears), right and left eye. (There are two puncta in each eye, an upper and a lower punctum.) Code 68705 is assigned. According to *CPT Assistant*, the puncta code is reported four times. However, Medicare reimbursement rules require the code to be reported twice with modifier -50 (Bilateral Procedure) added to each code.

PROCEDURES, SERVICES, OR SUPPLIES	
(Explain Unusual Circumstances)	
CPT/HCPCS	MODIFIER
68705	
68705	
68705	
68705	

PROCEDURES, SERVICES, OR SUPPLIES	
(Explain Unusual Circumstances)	
CPT/HCPCS	MODIFIER
68705	50
68705	50

Courtesy of the Centers for Medicare & Medicaid Services, www.cms.gov; Copyright © 2018 Cengage Learning®.

This is just one of many cases where official CPT coding guidelines differ from payer reimbursement rules. To obtain appropriate reimbursement, make sure you determine payer reimbursement rules for submitting codes.

CPT Guidelines

Guidelines located at the beginning of each CPT section should be carefully reviewed before assigning a code. **Guidelines** define terms and explain the assignment of codes for procedures and services located in a particular section (Figure 8-4). This means that guidelines in one section do not apply to another section in CPT.

Unlisted Procedures and Services

An **unlisted procedure** or **unlisted service** code is assigned when the provider performs a procedure or service for which there is no CPT code. When an unlisted procedure or service code is reported, a **special report** (e.g., copy of the procedure report) must accompany the claim to describe the nature, extent, and need for the procedure or service.

> **Note:**
>
> Medicare and third-party payers often require providers to report HCPCS level II national codes instead of unlisted procedure or service CPT codes.

Notes

Instructional **notes** appear throughout CPT sections to clarify the assignment of codes. They are typeset in two patterns (Figure 8-5).

Surgery Guidelines

Guidelines to direct general reporting of services are presented in the **Introduction**. Some of the commonalities are repeated here for the convenience of those referring to this section on **Surgery**. Other definitions and items unique to Surgery are also listed.

Services

Services rendered in the office, home, or hospital, consultations, and other medical services are listed in the **Evaluation and Management Services section** (99201–99499), beginning on page 11. "Special Services and Reports" (99000–99091) are listed in the **Medicine** section.

Follow-Up Care for Therapeutic Surgical Procedures

Follow-up care for therapeutic surgical procedures includes only that care which is usually a part of the surgical services. Complications, exacerbations, recurrence, or the presence of other diseases or injuries requiring additional services should be separately reported.

Supplied Materials

Supplies and materials (eg, sterile trays/drugs), over and above those usually included with the procedure(s) rendered are reported separately. List drugs, trays, supplies, and materials provided. Identify as 99070 or specific supply code.

Figure 8-4 Portion of CPT Surgery Guidelines

Cardiovascular System

Blocked unindented note

Selective vascular catheterizations should be coded to include introduction and all lesser order selective catheterizations used in the approach (eg, the description for a selective right middle cerebral artery catheterization includes the introduction and placement catheterization of the right common and internal carotid arteries).

Additional second and/or third order arterial catheterizations within the same family of arteries supplied by a single first order artery should be expressed by 36218 or 36248. Additional first order or higher catheterizations in vascular families supplied by a first order vessel different from a previously selected and coded family should be separately coded using the conventions described above.

Indented parenthetical note located below subsection title

(For monitoring, operation of pump and other nonsurgical services, see 99190–99192, 99291, 99292, 99354–99360)

(For other medical or laboratory related services, see appropriate section)

(For radiological supervision and interpretation, see 75600–75970)

Heart and Pericardium

Pericardium

◉ 33010   Pericardiocentesis; initial

Parenthetical note located below code description

(For radiological supervision and interpretation, use 76930)

Figure 8-5 Selection from CPT illustrating different types of instructional notes

- A *blocked unindented note* is located below the title of a subsection, heading (or category), or subheading (or subcategory). It contains instructions that apply to all codes in the subsection, heading/category, or subheading/subcategory.

- An *indented parenthetical* note is located below the

  o Title of a subsection, heading (or category), and subheading (or subcategory)

  o Code description (and the note applies to that code only unless the note indicates otherwise)

- ⚠ A *parenthetical note* is located in the code description to provide an example. Such notes contain the abbreviation eg, and terminology in the example is *not* required to appear in the procedural statement documented by the provider.

Coding Tip:

Within a code series, parenthetical notes provide information about deleted codes.

Descriptive Qualifiers

Descriptive qualifiers are terms that clarify the assignment of a CPT code. They can occur in the middle of a main clause or after the semicolon and may or may not be enclosed in parentheses. Make sure you read all code descriptions very carefully to properly assign CPT codes that require descriptive qualifiers.

EXAMPLE: The underlining in code descriptions for 17000 and 17003 identify descriptive qualifiers for each.

```
17000     Destruction (eg, laser surgery, electrosurgery, cryosurgery,
          chemosurgery, surgical curettement), premalignant lesions (eg,
          actinic keratoses); first lesion

+ 17003     second through 14 lesions, each (List separately in addition to
            code for first lesion)
```

Coding Tip:

Coders working in a provider's office should highlight descriptive qualifiers in CPT that pertain to the office's specialty. This will help ensure that qualifiers are not overlooked when codes are assigned.

Exercise 8.7 – CPT Sections, Subsections, Categories, and Subcategories

Instructions: Indicate whether the statement is true (T) or false (F).

_____ **1.** The major sections of CPT are nuclear medicine, surgery, medicine, pathology, and radiology.

_____ **2.** When a parenthetical statement within a code description begins with e.g., one of the terms that follows must be included in the provider's description of the surgery for the code number to apply.

_____ **3.** When an unlisted procedure or service code is reported, a special report (e.g., copy of the procedure report) must accompany the claim.

_____ **4.** A blocked unindented note is located below a subsection, category, or subcategory, and contains instructions that apply to all codes in the subsection, category, or subcategory.

_____ **5.** All descriptive qualifiers for a particular code are found in an indented code description.

CPT Modifiers

CPT modifiers clarify services and procedures performed by providers. Although the CPT code and description remain unchanged, modifiers indicate that the description of the service or procedure performed has been altered.

- CPT modifiers are reported as two-digit numeric codes added to the five-digit CPT code (e.g., 99213-25).

- HCPCS level II national modifiers are reported as two-character alphabetic and alphanumeric codes added to the five-digit CPT code (e.g., 11760-TA and 11760-T1).

   EXAMPLE: A patient undergoes repair of nasal septal perforations (30630), which was unsuccessful. Three months later, the patient undergoes repeat repair of nasal septal perforations by a different surgeon (30630-77). The same CPT code is assigned, and a modifier is added to indicate the repeat procedure.

When reporting codes with more than one modifier, enter the **functional modifier** (or **pricing modifier**), which assists in reimbursement decision making (e.g., assistant surgeon). Next, enter **informational modifiers**, which clarify aspects of the procedure or service provided for the payer (e.g., procedure performed on right or left side only). (Medicare carriers originally created the terms *functional modifier, pricing modifier*, and *informational modifier*, which means some payers do not use the terms.)

EXAMPLE: A patient fractured his left femur. An assistant surgeon participated in the open treatment and internal fixation of the femoral fracture, proximal end, neck. Report code 27236-80-LT. (Modifier -80, Assistant Surgeon, is a functional modifier that impacts the reimbursement rate paid by the third-party payer. Modifier -LT is an informational modifier, which indicates that the surgery was performed on the patient's left side. It does not impact the reimbursement amount paid to the physician.)

When multiple modifiers are added to a CPT (or HCPCS level II) code and an informational modifier is listed first, third-party payers manually review the claim. Manual review slows claims processing and results in reimbursement delays to physicians.

Not all CPT modifiers apply to each section of CPT. Table 8-1 summarizes CPT modifiers in numeric order and identifies applicable CPT sections that are recommended for each. (Coders should contact third-party payers to obtain a list of modifiers and applicable CPT sections because each payer has different reporting requirements.)

Coding Tip:

As a general rule, list HCPCS level II modifiers after CPT modifiers (except for HCPCS level II modifier -TC, which is listed before other HCPCS level II modifiers).

Note:

HCPCS level II national modifiers were explained in Chapter 7.

Coding Tip:

Some CPT coding manuals include modifiers with brief descriptions inside the front cover, including CPT and HCPCS level II national modifiers approved for hospital outpatient reporting purposes. Appendix A of the CPT coding manual contains a comprehensive list of modifiers with descriptions.

The AMA and CMS develop new modifiers on a continuous basis, and next available numbers are assigned. This means that there is no relationship among groups of modifier numbers. Reviewing modifiers in strict numeric order does not allow for comparison of those that are related to one another in terms of content; therefore, Table 8-2 organizes modifiers according to reporting similarity.

The following example illustrates how and why modifiers are used.

EXAMPLE: Mrs. T has a history of gallbladder disease. After several hours of acute pain, she was referred to Dr. S for an evaluation of her condition. Dr. S performed a complete history and physical examination and decided to admit the patient to the hospital for an immediate workup for cholecystitis. When the results of laboratory tests and sonogram were received, the patient was scheduled for an emergency laparoscopic cholecystectomy.

Note:

In an attempt to simplify the explanation of modifiers, the wording does not correspond word for word with descriptions found in CPT.

PROCEDURES, SERVICES, OR SUPPLIES
(Explain Unusual Circumstances)
CPT/HCPCS | MODIFIER

99223 | 57

47562 |

99213 | 24

Courtesy of the Centers for Medicare & Medicaid Services, www.cms.gov; Copyright © 2018 Cengage Learning®.

Figure 8-6 Completed Block 24D of CMS-1500 claim

PROCEDURES, SERVICES, OR SUPPLIES
(Explain Unusual Circumstances)
CPT/HCPCS | MODIFIER

47562 | 80

Courtesy of the Centers for Medicare & Medicaid Services, www.cms.gov; Copyright © 2018 Cengage Learning®.

Figure 8-7 Completed Block 24D of CMS-1500 claim

The surgeon was Dr. S, and the assistant surgeon was Dr. A. The surgery was successful, and the patient was discharged the next day and told to return to the office in seven days. Four days later, Mrs. T returned to Dr. S's office complaining of chest pains. Dr. S performed another examination and ordered the necessary tests. After reviewing the test results and confirming with the patient's primary care physician, it was determined that the patient was suffering from mild angina.

Dr. S reports the following services (Figure 8-6):

- Initial hospital visit, comprehensive, with medical decision making of high complexity (99223-57) (Modifier -57 indicates that the decision to perform surgery was made during the hospital evaluation.)

- Laparoscopic cholecystectomy (47562)

- Office visit, established patient, expanded problem focused, with medical decision making of low complexity (99213-24) (Modifier -24 indicates that the reexamination of the patient revealed the problem to be unrelated to the normal postoperative care provided to a cholecystectomy patient. The diagnosis linked to this visit is angina.)

Dr. A reports (Figure 8-7) the following service:

- Laparoscopic cholecystectomy 47562-80 (Modifier -80 indicates that Dr. A is the assistant surgeon.)

Table 8-1 CPT Modifiers in a Quick View Format

Modifier	Title of Modifier	E/M	Anesthesia	Surgery	Radiolology	Laboratory	Medicine	Approved for Hospital Outpateint Use
-22	Increased Procedural Services			X	X	X	X	
-23	Unusual Anesthesia		X					
-24	Unrelated Evaluation and Management Service by the Same Physician or Other Qualified Health Care Professional During a Postoperative Period	X						
-25	Significant, Separately Identifiable Evaluation and Management Service by the Same Physician or Other Qualified Health Care Professional on the Same Day of the Procedure or Other Service	X						X
-26	Professional Component				X			
-27	Multiple Outpatient Hospital E/M Encounters on the Same Date	X						X
-32	Mandated Services	X						

(continues)

Table 8-1 (*continued*)

Modifier	Title of Modifier	E/M	Anesthesia	Surgery	Radiololgy	Laboratory	Medicine	Approved for Hospital Outpateint Use
-33	Preventive Services	X						
-47	Anesthesia by Surgeon			X				
-50	Bilateral Procedure			X				X
-51	Multiple Procedures			X				
-52	Reduced Services			X	X	X	X	X
-53	Discontinued Procedure		X	X	X	X	X	
-54	Surgical Care Only			X				
-55	Postoperative Management Only			X				
-56	Preoperative Management Only	X		X				
-57	Decision for Surgery	X						
-58	Staged or Related Procedure or Service by the Same Physician or Other Qualified Health Care Professional During the Postoperative Period			X			X	X
-59	Distinct Procedural Service		X	X				X
-62	Two Surgeons			X				
-63	Procedure Performed on Infants Less Than 4 kg			X				
-66	Surgical Team			X				
-73	Discontinued Outpatient Hospital/Ambulatory Surgery Center (ASC) Procedure Prior to the Administration of Anesthesia			X				X
-74	Discontinued Outpatient Hospital/Ambulatory Surgery Center (ASC) Procedure After Administration of Anesthesia		X	X				X
-76	Repeat Procedure or Service by Same Physician or Other Qualified Health Care Professional			X				X
-77	Repeat Procedure by Another Physician or Other Qualified Health Care Professional			X				X
-78	Unplanned Return to the Operating/Procedure Room by the Same Physician or Other Qualified Health Care Professional Following Initial Procedure for a Related Procedure During the Postoperative Period			X				X
-79	Unrelated Procedure or Service by the Same Physician or Other Qualified Health Care Professional During the Postoperative Period			X				X
-80	Assistant Surgeon			X				
-81	Minimum Assistant Surgeon			X				
-82	Assistant Surgeon (when qualified resident surgeon not available)			X				
-90	Reference (Outside) Laboratory					X		
-91	Repeat Clinical Diagnostic Laboratory Test					X		X
-92	Alternative Laboratory Platform Testing					X		
-95	Synchronous Telemedicine Service Rendered Via a Real-Time Interactive Audio and Video Telecommunication System						X	
-99	Multiple Modifiers		X	X	X	X	X	

Table 8-2 Organization of CPT Modifiers According to Reporting Similarity

Modifier	Description	Interpretation	Coding Tips and Examples
Special Evaluation and Management (E/M) Cases			
-24	Unrelated Evaluation and Management Service by the Same Physician or Other Qualified Health Care Professional During a Postoperative Period	Assign to indicate that an E/M service was performed during the standard postoperative period for a condition unrelated to the surgery. The *service* to which the modifier is attached *must be* linked to a diagnosis that is *unrelated* to the surgical diagnosis previously submitted. Make sure you submit a copy of documentation with the claim to explain the circumstances.	**EXAMPLE:** One week after surgical treatment to release a frozen shoulder, patient received level 3 evaluation and management services for treatment of the flu. Report code 99213-24.
-25	Significant, Separately Identifiable Evaluation and Management Service by the Same Physician or Other Qualified Health Care Professional on the Same Day of the Procedure or Other Service	Assign when a documented E/M service was performed on the same day as another procedure because the patient's condition required the assignment of a significant, separately identifiable, additional E/M service that was provided "above and beyond the other service provided or beyond the usual preoperative and postoperative care associated with the procedure performed." The documented history, examination, and medical decision making must "stand on its own" to justify reporting modifier -25 with the E/M code. The E/M service provided must be "above and beyond" what is normally performed during a procedure.	**EXAMPLE:** During a routine annual examination, it was discovered that the 65-year-old established patient had an enlarged liver expanding the scope of level 4 evaluation and management services. Report codes 99397 and 99214-25. (Make sure you submit supporting documentation to the payer.)
-57	Decision for Surgery	Assign when the reported E/M service resulted in the *initial* decision to perform surgery on the day before *or* the day of surgery, to exempt it from the global surgery package.	**EXAMPLE:** The patient received level 4 evaluation and management services for chest pain in the emergency department, and a decision was made to insert a coronary artery stent. Report code 99284-57.
Greater, Reduced, or Discontinued Services			
-22	Increased Procedural Services	Assign when a procedure *requires greater than usual service(s)*. Documentation that would support using this modifier includes difficult, complicated, extensive, unusual, or rare procedure(s).	**EXAMPLE:** The patient experienced blood loss of 600 cc, which required intraoperative transfusions. Report the CPT surgery code with modifier -22.
-52	Reduced Services	Report when a service has been partially reduced or eliminated at the provider's discretion and does not completely match the CPT code description. (Attach a copy of documentation to the claim.)	**EXAMPLE:** A surgeon removed a coccygeal pressure ulcer and performed a coccygectomy. However, the surgeon did not use a primary suture or perform a skin flap closure because the wound had to be cleansed for a continued period of time postoperatively. Report code 15920-52. (When the surgeon eventually performs the wound closure procedure, an appropriate code would be reported.)
-53	Discontinued Procedure	Report when a provider has elected to terminate a procedure because of extenuating circumstances that threaten the well-being of the patient. **NOTE:** This modifier applies only to provider office settings and is not reported for elective cancellation (e.g., by the patient) prior to anesthesia induction and/or surgical preparation in the operating suite.	**EXAMPLE:** The surgeon inserted the colonoscope and removed it right away because the patient had not been properly prepared for the procedure. Report code 45378-53. (The patient received instruction about properly preparing for the colonoscopy procedure, and the procedure was rescheduled.)

(continues)

Table 8-2 (*continued*)

Greater, Reduced, or Discontinued Services			
Modifier	**Description**	**Interpretation**	**Coding Tips and Examples**
-73	Discontinued Outpatient Procedure Prior to the Administration of Anesthesia	Report to describe discontinued procedures *prior to the administration of any anesthesia* because of extenuating circumstances threatening the well-being of the patient. (Also report an ICD code to document the reason the procedure was halted.) **NOTE:** This modifier applies only to ASC settings and is *not* reported for elective cancellation (e.g., by the patient) prior to anesthesia induction or surgical preparation in the operating suite.	**EXAMPLE:** Patient developed a heart arrhythmia prior to anesthesia administration, and the laparoscopic cholecystectomy procedure was canceled. Report code 47562-73.
-74	Discontinued Outpatient Procedure After the Administration of Anesthesia	Report to describe discontinued procedures *after the administration of anesthesia* due to extenuating circumstances. (Also report an ICD code to document the reason the procedure was halted.) **NOTE:** This modifier applies only to ASC settings.	**EXAMPLE:** The patient was prepped and draped, and general anesthesia was administered. The anesthesiologist noted a sudden increase in blood pressure, and the laparoscopic cholecystectomy procedure was terminated. Report code 47562-74.

Global Surgery

- These modifiers apply to the four areas related to the CPT *surgical package* (Figure 8-8), which includes local infiltration; metacarpal/digital block or topical anesthesia when used; the procedure; and normal, uncomplicated follow-up care.
- These modifiers do *not* apply to obstetrical coding, where the CPT description of specific codes clearly describes separate antepartum, postpartum, and delivery services for both vaginal and cesarean deliveries.

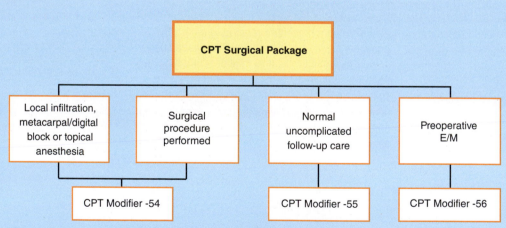

Figure 8-8 Modifiers that apply to components of the CPT surgical package

-54	Surgical Care Only	Report when a provider performed only the surgical portion of surgical package and personally administered required local anesthesia. Different provider(s) will have performed preoperative evaluation and/or provided postoperative care.	**EXAMPLE:** While on vacation, John Jones sustained a tibial shaft fracture and underwent closed treatment by Dr. Charles. Upon return to his hometown, John received follow-up care from Dr. Smith, a local orthopedist. Dr. Charles reports code 27750-54.

Table 8-2 (*continued*)

Global Surgery

Modifier	Description	Interpretation	Coding Tips and Examples
-55	Postoperative Management Only	Report when a provider other than the surgeon is responsible for postoperative management only of a surgery performed by another provider. Documentation in the patient's chart should detail the date of transfer of care to calculate the percentage of the fee to be billed for postoperative care. (The modifier is added to the surgical procedure code. Modifier -55 does *not* apply when a second provider occasionally covers for the surgeon and where no transfer of care occurs.)	**EXAMPLE:** While on vacation, John Jones sustained a tibial shaft fracture and underwent closed treatment by Dr. Charles. Upon return to his hometown, John received follow-up care from Dr. Smith, a local orthopedist. Dr. Smith reports code 27750-55.
-56	Preoperative Management Only	Report when a provider *other than* the operating surgeon performs preoperative care and evaluation of the patient for surgery (e.g., preoperative clearance).	**EXAMPLE:** Dr. Berger preoperatively cleared his patient during a level 4 E/M service for scheduled surgery by Dr. Charles. Dr. Berger reports code 99214-56.

Special Surgical and Procedural Events

Modifier	Description	Interpretation	Coding Tips and Examples
-58	Staged or Related Procedure or Service by the Same Physician or Other Qualified Health Care Professional During the Postoperative Period	Report to indicate that additional related surgery was required during the postoperative period of a previously completed surgery and was performed by the same provider. Documentation should include one of the following: • Original plan for surgery included additional stages to be performed within postoperative period of first stage of procedure. • Underlying disease required a second related, but unplanned, procedure to be performed. • Additional related therapy is required after the performance of a procedure. However, when another modifier is appropriate, it should be reported instead of modifier -59. Modifier -59 is never added to E/M codes.	**CODING TIP:** Do not report modifier -58 if the CPT code description describes multiple sessions of an event. **EXAMPLE:** A surgical wound is not healing properly because of the patient's underlying diabetes. Patient was told prior to the original surgery that if this happened, additional surgery would be required for subcutaneous tissue debridement of the wound. Report code 11042-58 for debridement surgery.
-59	Distinct Procedural Service	Report when same provider performs one or more *distinctly independent procedures* on the same day as other procedures or services, according to the following criteria: • Procedures are performed at different sessions or during different patient encounters. • Procedures are performed on different sites or organs and require a different surgical prep. • Procedures are performed for multiple or extensive injuries, using separate incisions/excisions; for separate lesions; or for procedures not ordinarily encountered/performed on the same day.	**EXAMPLE:** Patient has two basal cell carcinomas removed, one from the forehead with a simple closure (11640) and the other from the nose requiring adjacent tissue transfer (14060). Report codes 14060, 11640-51 (forehead), and 11640-59-51 (nose).

NOTE: CMS has defined HCPCS level II modifiers to selectively identify subsets of modifier -59 (Distinct Procedural Services) for Medicare claims, as follows:
• -XE Separate Encounter, a Service that is Distinct Because it Occurred During a Separate Encounter
• -XS Separate Structure, a Service that is Distinct Because it was Performed on a Separate Organ/Structure
• -XP Separate Practitioner, a Service that is Distinct Because it was Performed by a Different Practitioner
• -XU Unusual Non-Overlapping Service, the Use of a Service that is Distinct Because it Does Not Overlap Usual Components of the Main Service

EXAMPLE: A patient receives an antibiotic infusion as an outpatient and is discharged. She returns later that same day and receives another separate antibiotic infusion. Modifier -XE is reported with each CPT medication administration (infusion) code and each HCPCS level II drug (e.g., clindamycin).

(continues)

Table 8-2 (*continued*)

Special Surgical and Procedural Events			
Modifier	**Description**	**Interpretation**	**Coding Tips and Examples**
-63	Procedure Performed on Infants Less Than 4 kg	Report when infant weighs less than 4 kilograms (kg) because procedures performed may require increased complexity and provider work.	**EXAMPLE:** Baby Girl Markel's weight was 3.5 kg at the time she underwent diagnostic thoracoscopy. Report 32601-63.
-78	Unplanned Return to the Operating/Procedure Room by the Same Physician or Other Qualified Health Care Professional Following Initial Procedure for a Related Procedure During the Postoperative Period	Report for unplanned circumstances that require return to operating room for complications of initial operation. (Also report an ICD code to document the surgical complication that necessitated a return to operating room.) **NOTE:** This modifier applies only to ASC settings.	**EXAMPLE:** Surgical sutures did not hold, and a 12-cm layer closure of axillary wound was performed. Report code 12034-78.
-79	Unrelated Procedure or Service by the Same Physician or Other Qualified Health Care Professional During the Postoperative Period	Report when a new procedure or service is performed by a provider during the normal postoperative period of a previously performed but unrelated surgery. **NOTE:** This modifier applies only to ASC settings.	**EXAMPLE:** Six weeks following cataract surgery performed on the left eye, the patient underwent diathermic repair of retinal detachment, right eye. Report code 67101-79.
Bilateral and Multiple Procedures			
-27	Multiple Outpatient Hospital E/M Encounters on the Same Date	Report for patients who receive multiple E/M services performed by *different providers* on the same day.	**EXAMPLE:** A patient was seen in the hospital's emergency department and received level 4 evaluation and management services due to a fractured ankle. The patient was seen later the same day in the urgent care center and provided with level 3 evaluation and management services due to a migraine that did not respond to prescribed medication taken at home. Report codes 99284-27 and 99213-27.
-50	Bilateral Procedure	Report this directional modifier when a procedure was performed bilaterally *during the same session and when the code description does not specify that the procedure is bilateral.*	**EXAMPLE:** Patient underwent bilateral arthrodesis of the knees. Report code 27580-50 (or report HCPCS level II national modifiers as codes 27580-LT and 27580-RT).

NOTE: Directional modifiers (e.g., -50, -LT, -RT) are reported with CPT and HCPCS level II codes when the code description includes anatomic structures that are found bilaterally (e.g., kidneys, breasts, eyes). When code descriptions include anatomic structures that are found bilaterally along with those not found bilaterally, do not report directional modifiers with the CPT or HCPCS level II code.

EXAMPLE 1: Laparoscopic retroperitoneal lymph node biopsy. Report code 38570. Retroperitoneal lymph nodes are located in the abdomen, which is not a paired anatomic structure; thus, a directional modifier is not reported.

EXAMPLE 2: Percutaneous arterial line inserted into left radial artery. Report code 36620. Although the anatomic structure described in the physician's procedure statement is bilateral, the code description of 36620 is "arterial catheterization or cannulation for sampling, monitoring or transfusion (separate procedure); percutaneous." Because this code is reported for *any* artery, including those that are not bilateral anatomic structures (e.g., brachiocephalic artery), a directional modifier is *not* reported.

| -51 | Multiple Procedures | Report when multiple procedures *other than E/M services* are performed during a single patient encounter by the same provider. The procedures performed are characterized as

 • Multiple related surgical procedures performed at the same session
 • Surgical procedures that are performed in combination, whether through the same or another incision, or that involve the same or different anatomy
 • Combination medical and surgical procedures performed at the same session | **EXAMPLE:** Patient underwent right tibial shaft fracture repair and arthrodesis of left knee. Report codes 27750 and 27580-51. |

Table 8-2 (*continued*)

Repeat Services

Modifier	Description	Interpretation	Coding Tips and Examples
-76	Repeat Procedure or Service by Same Physician or Other Qualified Health Care Professional	Report when a procedure was repeated because of special circumstances involving the original service and the same physician performed the repeat procedure.	**EXAMPLE:** A repeat EKG is performed due to changes in the patient's condition or the need to assess the effect of therapeutic procedures. Report code 93041-76.
-77	Repeat Procedure by Another Physician or Other Qualified Health Care Professional	Report when a physician *other than the original physician* performs a repeat procedure because of special circumstances involving the original study or procedure.	**EXAMPLE:** Patient underwent sterilization procedure (e.g., tubal ligation), but became pregnant. After C-section delivery, she underwent a second sterilization procedure. Report code 58611-77 for the second sterilization procedure.

Multiple Surgeons

Modifier	Description	Interpretation	Coding Tips and Examples
-62	Two Surgeons	Report when two primary surgeons are required during an operative session, each performing distinct parts of a reportable procedure. Ideally, the surgeons represent different specialties.	**EXAMPLE:** A spinal surgeon and a general surgeon work together as primary surgeons to perform an anterior spinal fusion of L5-S1. The spinal surgeon also inserts an intervertebral synthetic cage and performs iliac bone grafting. Each surgeon reports code 22558-62. The spinal surgeon also reports codes 22853 and 20937.
-66	Surgical Team	Report when surgery performed is highly complex and requires the services of a skilled team of three or more surgeons. The procedure reported on the claim for each participating surgeon must include this modifier. The operative reports must document the complexity of the surgery and refer to the actions of each team member.	**EXAMPLE:** Reattachment of severed forearm. Each surgeon reports code 20802-66.
-80	Assistant Surgeon	Report when one physician assists another during an operative session. The assistant surgeon reports the same CPT code as the operating physician.	**EXAMPLE:** Dr. Landry assisted Dr. Bartron during single coronary artery bypass surgery. Dr. Landry reports code 33510-80. (Dr. Bartron reports code 33510 without the modifier.)
-81	Minimum Assistant Surgeon	Report when primary operating physician has planned to perform a surgical procedure alone, but circumstances arise that require the services of an assistant surgeon for a short time. The second surgeon reports the same CPT code as the operating physician.	**EXAMPLE:** Dr. Kelly begins an invasive cholecystectomy procedure and discovers that the gallbladder is the size of a hot dog bun, which necessitates calling Dr. Pietro to assist for a short time. Dr. Pietro reports code 47600-81. (A gallbladder is supposed to be the size of your little finger.)
-82	Assistant Surgeon (when qualified resident surgeon not available)	Report when a qualified resident surgeon is unavailable to assist with a procedure. In teaching hospitals, the physician acting as the assistant surgeon is usually a qualified resident surgeon. If circumstances arise (e.g., rotational changes) and a qualified resident surgeon is not available, another surgeon may assist with a procedure. The nonresident-assistant surgeon reports the same CPT code as the operating physician.	**EXAMPLE:** Resident surgeon Dr. Smith was to assist surgeon Dr. Manlin with a routine laparoscopic appendectomy. Dr. Smith was temporarily reassigned to the emergency department, and Dr. Manlin's partner assisted with the procedure. Code 44970-82 is reported.

(continues)

Table 8-2 (*continued*)

Preventive Services			
Modifier	**Description**	**Interpretation**	**Coding Tips and Examples**
-33	Preventive Service	Alerts third-party payers that the procedure or service was preventive under applicable laws and that patient cost sharing (e.g., coinsurance, copayment, deductible) does not apply when furnished by in-network providers.	**EXAMPLE:** The patient's primary care provider provided 20 minutes of smoking and tobacco use cessation counseling. Report code 99407-33.

Professional and Technical Components			
-26	Professional Component	Report when the provider either interprets test results or operates equipment for a procedure. *Do not report this modifier when a specific separately identifiable code describes the professional component of a procedure (e.g., 93010).*	**EXAMPLE:** Independent radiologist Dr. Minion interprets a stereo frontal chest x-ray that was performed by another provider. Dr. Minion reports code 71021-26.

Mandated Services			
-32	Mandated Services	Report when services (e.g., second or third opinion for a surgical procedure) provided were mandated by a third party (e.g., attorney or payer).	**EXAMPLE:** A patient's primary care provider recommends respiratory therapy. The payer requires the patient to undergo a level 3 evaluation and management service by a respiratory specialist. Code 99243-32 is reported.

Unusual Anesthesia			
-23	Unusual Anesthesia	Report when circumstances (e.g., extent of service or patient's physical condition) require anesthesia for procedures that usually require either no anesthesia or local anesthesia.	**EXAMPLE:** The 30-year-old patient has an intllectual disability and is extremely apprehensive and requires the administration of general anesthesia for ventral hernia repair (instead of regional anesthesia). Code 00832-23 is reported.
-47	Anesthesia by Surgeon	Report when the surgeon provides regional or general anesthesia in addition to performing the surgical procedure.	**CODING TIP:** Modifier -47 is added to the CPT surgery code. It is not reported with Anesthesia codes 00100–01999. **EXAMPLE:** The surgeon administers the regional anesthesia and performs the spigelian hernia repair. Code 49590-47 is reported.

Laboratory Services			
-90	Reference (Outside) Laboratory	Report when a laboratory test is performed by an outside or reference laboratory.	**EXAMPLE:** The provider orders a complete blood count (CBC). Because the office does not perform lab testing, arrangements are made with an outside laboratory to perform the CBC and bill the physician. The physician reports code 85025-90. (Code 36415 is also reported for routine venipuncture.)
-91	Repeat Clinical Diagnostic Laboratory Test	Report when a clinical diagnostic laboratory test is repeated on the same day to obtain subsequent (multiple) test results. *This modifier is not reported when lab tests are repeated to confirm initial results (e.g., due to equipment problems).*	**EXAMPLE:** The patient was in the emergency department for 18 hours for observation of chest pain. He underwent serial (repeated) lab tests for cardiac enzyme testing every six hours. Report codes 82657, 82657-91, and 82657-91.
-92	Alternative Laboratory Platform Testing	Report when laboratory testing is performed using a kit or transportable instrument that wholly or in part consists of a single-use, disposable analytical chamber. Such testing does not require permanent dedicated space because the testing materials can be carried or transported to the patient care area.	**EXAMPLE:** The hospital laboratory technician brought all of the HIV-1 testing materials to emergency department examination room #1 and performed an HIV-1 test on Mary Jones. Report code 86701-92.

Table 8-2 (*continued*)

Multiple Modifiers

Modifier	Description	Interpretation	Coding Tips and Examples
-99	Multiple Modifiers	Report to alert third-party payers that more than four modifiers are added to a procedure or service code. The CMS-1500 claim allows up to four modifiers to be listed after a CPT or HCPCS level II code (Figure 8-9).	**EXAMPLE:** An assistant surgeon (-80) reports an unusual service (-22), bilateral (-50), surgeon-provided general anesthesia services (-47) for lumbar hernia repair procedure (49540). • On the CMS-1500 claim, report as 49540 22 47 50 99 and 49540 80.

1			49540 22 47 50 99		NPI	
2			49540 80		NPI	

Permission to reuse in accordance with http://www.cms.gov Web site Content Reuse Policy.

Figure 8-9 Block 24D of CMS-1500 claim, with multiple modifiers entered

	• The UB-04 claim allows up to three modifiers to be listed after a CPT or HCPCS level II code in Form Locator 44 (Figure 8-10).	• On the UB-04, report as 49540 22 47 99, 49540 and 49540 50 80.

42 REV. CO.	43 DESCRIPTION	44 HCPCS/RATES	45 SERV. DATE	46 SERV. UNITS	47 TOTAL CHARGES	48 NON-COVERED CHARGES	49
		49540 22 47 99					
		49540 50 80					

Permission to reuse in accordance with http://www.cms.gov Web site Content Reuse Policy.

Figure 8-10 Form Locators 44 of UB-04 claim, with multiple modifiers reported

Telemedicine

Modifier	Description	Interpretation	Coding Tips and Examples
-95	Synchronous Telemedicine Service Rendered Via a Real-Time Interactive Audio and Video Telecommunication System	Synchronous telemedicine service is real-time interaction between a provider and a patient who is located at a distant site from the provider.	EXAMPLE: Patient underwent psychiatric diagnostic evaluation with medical services. Report code 90792-95.

Exercise 8.8 – CPT Modifiers

Instructions: Assign appropriate modifier(s) to each statement. Do *not* assign CPT codes.

_____   1. Assistant surgeon reporting patient's cesarean section, delivery only

_____   2. Cholecystectomy reported during postoperative period for treatment of leg fracture

_____   3. Treatment for chronic conditions at same time preventive medicine is provided

_____   4. Inpatient visit performed by surgeon, with decision to perform surgery tomorrow

_____   5. Office consultation as preoperative clearance for surgery

_____   6. Postoperative management of vaginal hysterectomy

_____   7. Repeat gallbladder x-ray series, same physician

_____   8. Arthroscopy of right elbow and closed fracture reduction of left wrist

_____   9. Needle core biopsy of right and left breasts

_____   10. Consultation required by payer

National Correct Coding Initiative (NCCI)

To promote national correct coding methodologies and control the improper assignment of codes that results in inappropriate reimbursement of Medicare Part B claims, the Centers for Medicare & Medicaid Services (CMS) implemented the **National Correct Coding Initiative (NCCI)**. NCCI edits (Table 8-3) are used to process Medicare Part B claims for hospital outpatient and physician services, and NCCI coding policies are based on the following:

- Analysis of standard medical and surgical practice

- Coding conventions included in CPT

- Coding guidelines developed by national medical specialty societies (e.g., CPT advisory committee, which contains representatives of major medical societies)

- Local and national coverage determinations

- Review of current coding practices

☞ The NCCI was initially developed for use by Medicare administrative contractors (MACs) that process Medicare Part B claims for physician office services. NCCI edits were added to the Outpatient Code Editor (OCE) in August 2000, and they are used by MACs to process Medicare Part B claims for outpatient hospital procedures and services. (Some OCE edits that apply to outpatient hospital services claims differ from comparable edits in the NCCI used to process physician office services claims.)

Note:

Locate Medlearn articles that contain OCE updates by going to http://www.cms.gov and clicking on the Outreach & Education link, then clicking on the Medicare link, followed by the MLN Matters Articles link.

Note:

In 2010, 23 Medicare administrative contractors (MACs) replaced the 23 fiscal intermediaries (FIs) that processed hospital inpatient and outpatient claims for Medicare Part A and Part B services and 17 Medicare carriers that processed physician claims for Medicare Part B services. MACs process both hospital inpatient/outpatient and physician Medicare Part A and Part B claims, and are abbreviated as A/B MACs. In addition, MACs also process durable medical equipment claims and home health/hospice claims, abbreviated as DME MACs and HH&H MACs, respectively. (Although FIs and carriers continue to be referenced on government and private websites and newsletters, MACs replaced both entities in 2010.)

Table 8-3 Partial Listing of National Correct Coding Initiative (NCCI) Edits

NCCI Edit	Description	Disposition of Claim
1	Invalid diagnosis code	Return to Provider
2	Diagnosis and age conflict	Return to Provider
3	Diagnosis and sex conflict	Return to Provider
4	Medicare secondary payer alert	Suspend
19	Mutually exclusive procedure that is not allowed by CCI even if appropriate modifier is present	Line Item Rejection
20	Component of a comprehensive procedure that is not allowed by CCI even if appropriate modifier is present	Line Item Rejection
39	Mutually exclusive procedure that would be allowed by CCI if appropriate modifier were present	Line Item Rejection
40	Component of a comprehensive procedure that would be allowed by CCI if appropriate modifier were present	Line Item Rejection

Carefully review parenthetical notes below CPT code descriptions to locate procedures that are separately reported (in addition to the major procedure performed). When reporting codes for outpatient hospital services and physician office services, use OCE software or NCCI software, respectively, to identify bundled codes for procedures and services considered necessary to accomplish the major procedure. Bundled procedure codes are *not* separately coded and reported with the major procedure code. Reporting bundled procedure codes in addition to the major procedure code is *unbundling*, which is characterized as abuse or fraud depending upon intent. The OCE edits are packaged with commercial software, such as Optum360's Encoder Pro Expert. The NCCI edits are available at http://cms.gov. Click on the Medicare link, scroll down to the Coding heading, and click on the National Correct Coding Initiative Edits. (The OCE and NCCI edits are available for purchase from the National Technical Information Service [NTIS] at www.ntis.gov)

CMS Posts Correct Coding Initiative (CCI) Edits on Internet

The Centers for Medicare & Medicaid Services (CMS) has made it easier for physicians and other providers to bill properly and be paid promptly for their services to people with Medicare coverage. CMS has posted on its website (http://www.cms.gov/Medicare/Medicare.html, and click on National Correct Coding Initiative Edits link) the automated edits used to identify questionable claims and adjust payments to reflect what would have been paid if the claim had been filed correctly. The edits, known as the National Correct Coding Initiative (NCCI), identify pairs of services that normally should not be billed by the same physician for the same patient on the same day. The NCCI also promotes uniformity among the contractors that process Medicare claims in interpreting Medicare payment policies.

The posting of NCCI edits is the most recent in a series of steps CMS has taken to use the Internet creatively to reduce the regulatory burden on physicians and make it easier for them to work with Medicare to improve services to beneficiaries. CMS has also added a feature to its website (http://www.cms.gov/Medicare/Medicare.html, and click on the Physician Fee Schedule Look-Up Tool link) that makes it possible for physicians to determine in advance what they will be paid for a particular service or range of services. The Medicare Physician Fee Schedule Look-Up provides the unadjusted payment rates as well as the payment rates by geographic location.

While the NCCI is a cornerstone of efforts to ensure that Medicare and beneficiaries do not pay twice for the same service or for duplicative services, CMS believes physicians should have easy access to the edits used to identify incorrect claims. The NCCI includes two types of edits:

- **Column 1/column 2 edits**: Code pairs that should not be billed together because one service inherently includes the other; previously called comprehensive/component edits

- **Mutually exclusive edits**: Code pairs that, for clinical reasons, are unlikely to be performed on the same patient on the same day (e.g., two different types of testing that yield equivalent results)

CPT codes representing services denied based on NCCI edits may not be billed to Medicare beneficiaries. Since these denials are based on incorrect coding rather than medical necessity, the provider cannot submit an *Advance Beneficiary Notice (ABN)* to seek payment from a Medicare beneficiary. An ABN is a form completed and signed by a Medicare beneficiary each time a provider believes a normally covered service will not be covered *and* the provider wants to bill the beneficiary directly for the service. In addition, because the denials are based on incorrect coding (rather than a legislated Medicare benefit exclusion), the provider *cannot* seek payment from the beneficiary even if a Notice of Exclusions from Medicare Benefits (NEMB) was obtained.

A **Notice of Exclusions from Medicare Benefits (NEMB)** is a form completed and signed by a Medicare beneficiary before items, procedures, and services excluded from Medicare benefits are provided; it alerts Medicare beneficiaries in advance that Medicare does not cover certain items and services because they do not meet the definition of a Medicare benefit or because they are specifically excluded by law. NEMB is completed when an ABN is not appropriate.

The NCCI edits, which are updated quarterly, were previously available to physicians and other providers on a paid subscription basis; but they are now available to anyone with a computer. The NCCI edits are posted as a

(continues)

CMS Posts Correct Coding Initiative (CCI) Edits on Internet (*continued*)

spreadsheet that allows users to sort by procedural code and effective date. A *Find* feature allows users to look for a specific code. The NCCI edit files are also indexed by procedural code ranges to allow for easy navigation.

The website also includes links to documents that explain the edits, including the following:

- Medicare Claims Processing Manual
- NCCI Edits Program Transmittals
- NCCI FAQs (frequently asked questions)
- NCCI Policy Manual for Part B MACs

Courtesy of the Centers for Medicare & Medicaid Services, www.cms.gov

---

EXAMPLE: Code 67911 describes the "Correction of lid retraction." A parenthetical note below the code description advises that if autogenous graft materials are used during the same operative session, tissue graft code 20920, 20922, or 20926 is reported in addition to code 67911.

According to the Medicare Code Editor (MCE), *other procedures necessary to accomplish* the "correction of lid retraction" are included in code 67911, such as full-thickness graft placement (15260). Other such procedures are not separately coded and reported when performed during the same operative session as the "correction of lid retraction."

Unbundling CPT Codes

Providers are responsible for reporting the CPT (and HCPCS level II) code that most comprehensively describes the services provided. NCCI edits determine the appropriateness of CPT code combinations for claims submitted to MACs. NCCI edits are designed to detect *unbundling*, which involves reporting multiple codes for a service when a single comprehensive code should be assigned. The practice of unbundling occurs because

 Note:

Additional content about the NCCI is located in Chapter 19.

- Provider's coding staff unintentionally reports multiple codes based on misinterpreted coding guidelines.
- The reporting of multiple codes is intentional and is done to maximize reimbursement.

Unbundling occurs when one service is divided into its component parts and a code for each component part is reported as if they were separate services.

EXAMPLE: A 64-year-old female patient undergoes total abdominal hysterectomy with bilateral salpingectomy and oophorectomy. Review CPT Surgery code descriptions for 58150, 58700, and 58720. Reporting codes 58700 and 58720 in addition to 58150 is considered unbundling. If all three codes were submitted on a claim, reimbursement for codes 58700 and 58720 would be disallowed (and the provider might be subject to allegations of fraud and abuse, depending upon intent).

Unbundling occurs when a code for the separate surgical approach (e.g., laparotomy) is reported in addition to a code for the surgical procedure. Procedures performed to gain access to an area or organ system are not separately reported.

EXAMPLE: A 54-year-old female patient underwent excision of ileoanal reservoir with ileostomy, which required lysis of adhesions to gain access to the site of surgery. Review CPT Surgery code descriptions for 45136 and 44005. Report CPT code 45136 only because code 44005 is considered a component part of the total procedure (45136). Reporting both codes would be considered unbundling.

Exercise 8.9 – National Correct Coding Initiative

Instructions: Complete each statement.

1. To promote national correct coding methodologies and control the improper assignment of codes that result in inappropriate reimbursement of Medicare Part_____ claims, CMS implemented the NCCI.

2. The NCCI was initially developed for use by Medicare administrative contractors (MACs) that process Medicare Part B claims for physician office services; in August 2000, NCCI edits were added to the Outpatient Code_____ for use by MACs to process Medicare Part B claims for outpatient hospital services.

3. The NCCI code pairs that should not be billed together because one service inherently includes the other are called column 1/column 2 edits, while the NCCI code pairs that, for clinical reasons, are unlikely to be performed on the same patient on the same day are called _____ edits.

4. When a submitted claim for reimbursement is denied because of incorrect coding rather than medical necessity, the provider cannot submit an Advance Beneficiary Notice (ABN) or a Notice of Exclusions from Medicare _____ to seek payment from a Medicare beneficiary.

5. A 34-year-old male underwent upper gastrointestinal endoscopy, which included visualization of the esophagus, stomach, and duodenum. During endoscopy, brushings collected esophageal specimens and esophageal biopsy was performed. Upon review of CPT Surgery code descriptions for 43235 and 43239, the coder assigned 43239 only (because 43235 is considered a component of the total procedure, 43239). Reporting both codes would be considered _____.

Summary

CPT codes are reported for services and procedures provided by home health care and hospice agencies, outpatient hospital departments, physicians who are employees of a health care facility, and physicians who see patients in their offices or clinics and in patients' homes. To promote national correct coding methodologies and to control the improper assignment of codes that result in inappropriate reimbursement of Medicare Part B claims, the Centers for Medicare & Medicaid Services (CMS) implemented the National Correct Coding Initiative (NCCI).

CPT organizes Category I procedures and services into six sections: Evaluation and Management (E/M), Anesthesia, Surgery, Radiology (including Nuclear Medicine and Diagnostic Ultrasound), Pathology and Laboratory, and Medicine. The CPT index is organized by alphabetical main terms printed in boldface, and appendices are located between the Medicine section and the index.

CPT sections are subdivided into subsections, categories, and subcategories. Guidelines, notes, and descriptive qualifiers are also found in CPT sections, subsections, categories, and subcategories. Two-digit modifiers are added to five-digit CPT codes to clarify services and procedures performed by providers.

Symbols are located throughout the CPT coding book. A bullet (•) located to the left of a code number identifies new procedures and services added to CPT. A triangle (▲) located to the left of a code number identifies a code description that has been revised. Horizontal triangles (►◄) surround revised guidelines and notes. This symbol is *not* used for revised code descriptions. A semicolon (;) is used in CPT to save space. The plus symbol (+) identifies add-on codes. The forbidden symbol (⊘) symbol identifies codes that are exempt from modifier -51. The star symbol (★) indicates codes that may be used for synchronous telemedicine services. The flash symbol (⚡) indicates codes that classify products pending FDA approval but that have been assigned a CPT code. The hollow circle symbol (○) indicates reinstated or recycled code. The number symbol (#) indicates out-of-sequence codes.

Internet Links

JustCoding.com: Go to *www.justcoding.com*, and sign up for the free e-newsletter by clicking on the "eNewsletter Signup" link.

Medicare PFS look-up: Go to *www.cms.gov*, and click on the Medicare link. Scroll down to the Medicare Fee-for-Service Payment heading, and click on the Physician Fee Schedule Look-Up Tool link.

MedlinePlus: *www.medlineplus.gov*

National Correct Coding Initiative (NCCI) Edits: Go to *www.cms.gov*, and click on the Medicare link. Scroll down to the Coding heading, and click on the National Correct Coding Initiative Edits link.

RiteCode.com: Go to *www.ritecode.com*, hover over the FREE STUFF link, and then click on the Free Coding Quizzes link.

Study Checklist

- ❑ Read this chapter and highlight key concepts.
- ❑ Create an index card for each key term.
- ❑ Access the chapter Internet links to learn more about concepts.
- ❑ Complete the chapter exercises and review, verifying answers with your instructor.
- ❑ Complete Workbook chapter, verifying answers with your instructor.
- ❑ Go to *www.cengagebrain.com* to access the Student Companion Web Site Login instructions are located in the Preface.
- ❑ Form a study group with classmates to discuss chapter concepts in preparation for an exam.

Review

Multiple Choice

Instructions: Circle the most appropriate response.

1. Which mandated that CPT codes be reported for outpatient hospital surgical procedures?
   a. Health Insurance, Portability, and Accountability Act of 1996 (HIPAA)
   b. Healthcare Common Procedure Coding System (HCPCS)
   c. Medicare Prescription Drug, Improvement, and Modernization Act (MMA)
   d. Omnibus Budget Reconciliation Act (OBRA) of 1986

2. New, revised, and deleted CPT codes that are provided as an "early release" in July by the CPT Editorial Panel are intended to take effect:
   a. after the FDA approves the product.
   b. immediately upon "early release."
   c. 6 months later.
   d. within a 90-day grace period.

3. The E/M section is located at the beginning of CPT because these codes are:
   a. reported by all specialties.
   b. sequenced first on all claims.
   c. the most frequently reported.
   d. used to establish medical necessity.

4. *Arthroscopy, ankle*, and *wound* are examples of _____ in the CPT index.
   - a. cross-references
   - b. main terms
   - c. qualifiers
   - d. subterms

5. Which is the best example of a CPT index cross-reference term?
   - a. Also
   - b. And
   - c. See
   - d. See also

6. When a range *or* series of single codes is listed in the CPT index for a procedure or service:
   - a. a cross-reference will direct the coder to another index entry.
   - b. each code must be verified in the CPT manual before a code is assigned.
   - c. the range of codes is separated by a comma.
   - d. the series of single codes is separated by a dash.

7. Codes identified throughout CPT with a forbidden (⊘) symbol are summarized in Appendix _____.
   - a. C
   - b. D
   - c. E
   - d. F

8. Horizontal triangles (►◄):
   - a. identify a code description that has been revised.
   - b. mark revisions that are included in Appendix B.
   - c. surround new procedures and services that have been added to CPT.
   - d. surround new or revised text.

9. Codes identified with a plus symbol (+):
   - a. are exempt from modifier -51.
   - b. are reported as stand-alone codes.
   - c. contain parenthetical notes.
   - d. identify add-on codes.

10. A code identified by a star symbol (★) indicates that:
   - a. anesthesia is considered medically necessary and payable.
   - b. a code may be used for synchronous telemedicine services.
   - c. general anesthesia was administered by an anesthesiologist.
   - d. no other anesthesia procedures or services may be reported.

11. Which are located at the beginning of each CPT section, define terms, and explain the assignment of codes for procedures and services located in a particular section?
   - a. Descriptive qualifiers
   - b. Guidelines
   - c. Notes
   - d. Unlisted procedures or services

12. Which are typeset as a blocked unindented or a blocked indented parenthetical pattern?
   - a. Descriptive qualifiers
   - b. Guidelines
   - c. Notes
   - d. Unlisted procedures or services

13. Which requires the submission of a special report that describes the nature, extent, and need for the procedure or service?
   - a. Descriptive qualifier
   - b. Guideline
   - c. Note
   - d. Unlisted procedure or service

14. Which code is assigned for "unattended sleep study, interpretation only?"
   - a. 95805
   - b. 95805-90
   - c. 95806
   - d. 95806-26

15. A patient was seeking loss-of-wages benefits due to injuries sustained in a motor vehicle accident. The insurance company requested a second opinion regarding injuries and sent the patient for an Independent Medical Exam (IME), where a level 3 outpatient consultation service was provided. The IME

physician reviewed medical records from the emergency department, the primary care physician, and pain management center. The IME report was sent to the insurance company. Which code is assigned?

    a. 99243-26   b. 99243-32   c. 99243-77   d. 99243-90

16. A patient presented to the physician's office for removal of ten skin tags on his torso. During the procedure, the patient became anxious and the procedure was discontinued. No skin tags were removed. Which code is reported?

    a. 11200-52   b. 11200-53   c. 11200-73   d. 11200-74

17. The patient underwent osteotomy of cervical spine, anterior approach, single segment, by two surgeons. Which code is reported?

    a. 22220-62   b. 22220-66   c. 22220-80   d. 22220-81

18. The patient underwent a T7 index (total thyroxine) lab test, which was sent to an outside laboratory. Which code is reported?

    a. 84436-90   b. 84436-91   c. 84439-90   d. 84437-91

19. If payment of a service or procedure is denied based on National Correct Coding Initiative (NCCI) edits, the provider:

    a. can seek payment from a Medicare beneficiary if an Advance Beneficiary Notice (ABN) or a Notice of Exclusions from Medicare Benefits (NEMB) is obtained.

    b. can seek payment from the beneficiary if a Notice of Exclusions from Medicare Benefits (NEMB) is obtained.

    c. can submit an Advance Beneficiary Notice (ABN) to seek payment from a Medicare beneficiary.

    d. cannot seek payment from a Medicare beneficiary even if an Advance Beneficiary Notice (ABN) or a Notice of Exclusions from Medicare Benefits (NEMB) is obtained.

20. National Correct Coding Initiative (NCCI) edits were developed to promote national correct coding methodologies and control the improper assignment of codes that results in inappropriate reimbursement of Medicare Part _____ claims.

    a. A   b. B   c. C   d. D

CPT Index

Instructions: Refer to the CPT index to respond to each case.

1. Patient underwent debridement of infected subcutaneous tissue, lower left leg. Use the CPT index to identify the following:

    a. Main term _____

    b. Subterm _____

    c. 2nd qualifier _____

    d. 3rd qualifier _____

    e. Code range _____

2. Patient underwent arthrodesis of the elbow. Use the CPT index to identify the following:

    a. Main term _____

    b. Subterm _____

    c. Code range _____

3. Patient underwent Kocher pylorectomy. Use the CPT index to locate the cross-reference for the procedure. Then identify the main term, subterm, and code range.

    a. Main term _____

    b. Cross-reference _____

    c. Main term _____

    d. Subterm _____

    e. Code range _____

4. Patient underwent abdominal hysterectomy with resection of both ovaries due to malignancy. Use the CPT index to locate the following:

    a. Main term _____

    b. Subterm _____

    c. 2nd qualifier _____

    d. Code range _____

5. Patient underwent PET scan, brain. Use the CPT index to locate the cross-reference for the procedure. Then identify the main term, subterm, and code range.

    a. Main term _____

    b. Cross-reference _____

    c. Main term _____

    d. Subterm _____

    e. Code range _____

CPT Symbols

Instructions: Interpret the use of CPT symbols to respond to each case.

1. A 60-year-old patient presents to the physician's office for a vaccination, and the coder notices the flash (✔) precedes the code to be assigned. The flash (✔) symbol that precedes the code means it is pending FDA _____.

2. A 37-year-old female presents to a local hospital for the birth of her second child. After a difficult labor, the patient undergoes a cesarean section. The patient also undergoes a subtotal hysterectomy due to endometriosis. Codes 59510 and 59525 are reported. The plus (+) symbol that precedes code 59525 means it is a(n) _____ code and modifier -51 is not added to the code.

3. A patient undergoes a genetics counseling for a period of 30 minutes. Code 96040 is reported. The star (★) symbol precedes code 96040, which means that _____ services were provided.

4. A patient presents to the emergency department (ED) following an accident in his garage. The patient was working under his car when the jack failed, and the car fell on the patient's chest. The patient requires 65 minutes of critical care time during which he is evaluated and undergoes emergency endotracheal intubation. The patient is admitted as an inpatient and scheduled for an exploratory laparotomy with possible splenectomy. Codes 99291 and 31500 are reported for the ED visit. The forbidden (⊘) symbol precedes code 31500, which means that modifier _____ is not added to the code.

5. Patient underwent initial closed treatment of a temporomandibular dislocation. Code 21480 is reported. The semicolon (;) symbol in the code description is used to save space; thus, the description of code 21480 is closed treatment of temporomandibular dislocation; initial or _____.

CPT Modifiers

Instructions: Assign CPT modifiers to each case.

1. A patient undergoes simple repair of multiple skin lacerations, left foot and toes. The patient also undergoes intermediate repair of left heel laceration. The patient is discharged home after suturing, bandaging, and placing in a soft cast. Codes assigned include 12041 and 12002. Modifier _____ is added to code 12002.

2. An 80-year-old male patient undergoes bilateral mastotomy with deep exploration. Code 19020 is assigned. Modifier _____ is added to code 19020.

3. A patient undergoes magnetic resonance imaging (MRI), lower left leg. Dr. Miller interprets the MRI and documents a report. Modifier _____ is added to the CPT code reported for the MRI.

4. Patient underwent incision and drainage (I&D) of a Bartholin's gland abscess done on April 5. The global period is 30 days. The abscess recurred; on April 28, the patient underwent repeat I&D by the same surgeon. Code 56420 was reported for the procedure performed on April 5. Modifier _____ is added to code 56420 for the procedure performed on April 28.

5. A male patient underwent biopsy of the prostate gland on October 11, performed by Dr. Smith. The global period is zero days. The pathology results were of uncertain behavior; per the pathologist's recommendations, the patient underwent repeat biopsy on November 15, by Dr. Jones, to obtain a larger sample. Code 55700 was reported for the procedure performed on October 11. Modifier _____ is added to code 55700 for the procedure performed on November 15.

CPT Evaluation and Management

Chapter Outline

Overview of Evaluation and Management
   Section
Evaluation and Management Section Guidelines

Levels of Evaluation and Management Services
Evaluation and Management Categories and
   Subcategories

Chapter Objectives

At the conclusion of this chapter, the student should be able to:

- Define key terms.
- Explain the organization, format, and content of the CPT Evaluation and Management section.
- Interpret CPT Evaluation and Management section guidelines, coding notes, and modifiers.
- Select CPT Evaluation and Management levels of service for documented patient care.
- Assign CPT Evaluation and Management service codes for patient care.
- Add CPT and/or HCPCS level II modifiers to codes as appropriate.

Key Terms

advance care planning

care plan oversight
   services

chief complaint (CC)

clinical examples

comprehensive
   examination

comprehensive history

concurrent care

consultation

contributory components

coordination of care

counseling

critical care

critical illness or injury

delivery/birthing room
   attendance and
   resuscitation
   services

detailed examination

detailed history

*Documentation
Guidelines for
Evaluation and
Management Services*

emergency department
   service

established patient

expanded problem
   focused examination

expanded problem
   focused history

extent of examination

extent of history

face-to-face time

family history

history

history of present illness
   (HPI)

home services

hospital discharge
   service

hospital inpatient
   service

infant

inpatient neonatal and
   pediatric critical care
   and intensive service

intensivist

interfacility transport

intraservice time

key components

low birth weight

medical decision making (MDM)

nature of the presenting problem

neonate

newborn care services

new patient

observation service

office or other outpatient services

partial hospitalization

past medical history

pediatric critical care patient transport

physical examination

physician case management

place of service (POS)

preoperative clearance

preventive medicine services

problem focused examination

problem focused history

professional services

prolonged services

referral

review of systems (ROS)

social history

special evaluation and management services

standby service

system review

transfer of care

type of service (TOS)

unit/floor time

very low birth weight

Introduction ⚠

The Evaluation and Management (E/M) section (codes 99201–99499) is located at the beginning of the CPT coding manual because these codes describe services most frequently provided by physicians and other qualified health care professionals. This makes it easier to locate these frequently reported codes. Accurate assignment of E/M codes is essential to the success of a provider's practice because most of the revenue generated by the office is based on provision of these services. Before assigning E/M codes, make sure you review the guidelines (located at the beginning of the E/M section) and apply any notes (located below category and subcategory titles).

Most E/M services are cognitive services. This means that the provider must acquire information from the patient, use reasoning skills to process the information, interact with the patient to provide feedback, and respond by creating an appropriate plan of care. E/M services do *not* include significant procedural services (e.g., diagnostic tests or surgical procedures), which are coded separately. However, some services that arise directly from the E/M service provided are included (e.g., cleansing traumatic lesions, closing lacerations with adhesive strips, applying dressings, and providing counseling and educational services).

Coding Tip:

Notes located beneath categories and/or subcategories in the CPT coding manual apply to all codes in the categories or subcategories. Parenthetical notes that are located below a specific code apply to that code only unless the note indicates otherwise.

Overview of Evaluation and Management Section

CPT 1992 introduced the E/M level of service codes, replacing the office visit codes that were included in the Medicine section of past editions of CPT. The E/M section is organized according to *place of service (POS)* (e.g., office, hospital, home, nursing facility, emergency department, critical care), *type of service (TOS)* (e.g., office or other outpatient service, hospital observation service, preventive medicine service), *content of service* (e.g., detailed history and examination), and miscellaneous services (e.g., prolonged provider service, care plan oversight service). The E/M *level of service* reflects the amount of work involved in providing health care to a patient, and selecting the appropriate level of service requires determining the extent of history and examination performed as well as the complexity of medical decision making.

Documentation in the patient record must support the E/M level of service reported. The Centers for Medicare & Medicaid Services (CMS) often refers to E/M codes by level numbers, and the level often corresponds to the last digit of the CPT code (e.g., 99204 is a level 4 E/M service).

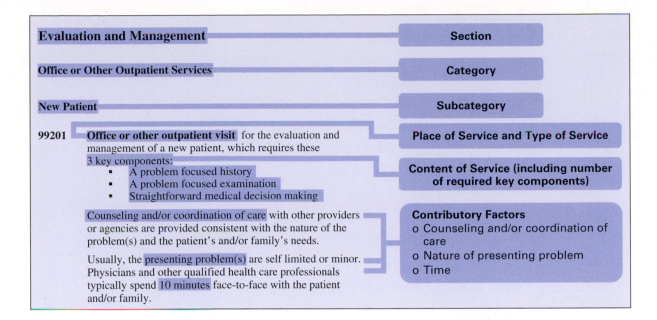

Evaluation and Management	Section
Office or Other Outpatient Services	Category
New Patient	Subcategory
99201 **Office or other outpatient visit** for the evaluation and management of a new patient, which requires these 3 key components:	Place of Service and Type of Service
▪ A problem focused history ▪ A problem focused examination ▪ Straightforward medical decision making	Content of Service (including number of required key components)
Counseling and/or coordination of care with other providers or agencies are provided consistent with the nature of the problem(s) and the patient's and/or family's needs. Usually, the presenting problem(s) are self limited or minor. Physicians and other qualified health care professionals typically spend 10 minutes face-to-face with the patient and/or family.	**Contributory Factors** o Counseling and/or coordination of care o Nature of presenting problem o Time

Accurate assignment of E/M codes depends on: (1) identifying the place of service (POS) and/or type of service (TOS) provided to the patient, (2) determining whether the patient is new or established to the practice, (3) reviewing the patient's record for documentation of level of service components, and (4) applying CMS's Documentation Guidelines for Evaluation and Management Services.

Place of Service (POS)

Place of service (POS) refers to the physical location where health care is provided to patients (e.g., office or other outpatient settings, hospitals, nursing facilities [NFs], home health care, or emergency departments [EDs]).

EXAMPLE 1: The provider treated the patient in her office.

Place of Service: Office

E/M Category: Office or Other Outpatient Services

EXAMPLE 2: The patient received care in the hospital's ED.

Place of Service: Hospital ED

E/M Category: Emergency Department Services

📝 Note:

Refer to the Office or Outpatient Services category of E/M and notice that it contains two subcategories (New Patient and Established Patient). The New Patient subcategory contains five codes, and the Established Patient subcategory also contains five codes. Each code represents a level of E/M service ranked from lowest to highest level. CMS would consider E/M code 99201 a level 1 code.

Type of Service (TOS)

Type of service (TOS) refers to the kind of health care services provided to patients (e.g., consultations, critical care, inpatient care, nursing facility care, observation care, preventive care, and so on).

EXAMPLE 1: The patient underwent an annual physical examination in the provider's office.

Type of Service: Preventive care

E/M Category: Preventive Medicine Services

EXAMPLE 2: The hospital inpatient was transferred to the regular medical-surgical unit where he was recovering from surgery. He suddenly stopped breathing and required respirator management by his provider.

> *Type of Service*: Critical care
>
> *E/M Category*: Critical Care Services

Sometimes *both the TOS and POS* must be identified before the proper code can be assigned.

EXAMPLE 1: Dr. Smith completed Josie Black's history and physical examination on the first day of her inpatient admission.

> *Place of Service*: Hospital
>
> *Type of Service*: Initial inpatient care
>
> *E/M Category*: Hospital Inpatient Services
>
> *E/M Subcategory*: Initial Hospital Care

EXAMPLE 2: Dr. Charles saw Josie Black (age 38) in her office to perform an annual physical examination.

> *Place of Service*: Office
>
> *Type of Service*: Preventive medicine
>
> *E/M Category*: Preventive Medicine Services

 Coding Tip:

The CPT Medicine section includes codes describing specialty services (e.g., ophthalmology, psychiatry) that require E/M. When codes for specialty services are reported, a separate E/M service from the CPT E/M section is *not* reported on the same date *unless a significant, separately identifiable E/M service was provided (and modifier –25 is attached).*

Exercise 9.1 – Overview of Evaluation and Management Section

Instructions: Use your CPT coding manual to complete each statement.

1. When a 49-year-old female patient is seen in the provider's office for an annual physical examination, the coder should refer to the E/M category entitled _____ Medicine Services.

2. For a 24-year-old male patient who received immediate care in the hospital emergency room, the coder should refer to the E/M category entitled _____ Department Services.

3. Codes for E/M levels of service reflect the amount of work involved in providing health care to a patient, and correct coding primarily involves determining the extent of history and _____ performed and the complexity of medical decision making.

4. CMS often refers to E/M codes by level numbers, and the level often corresponds to the last digit of the CPT code. Therefore, code 99215 is a level _____ service.

5. The physical location where health care is provided to patients is called the _____ of service.

6. The kind of health care services provided to patients is called the _____ of service.

Exercise 9.1 (*continued*)

7–10. Mary Smith was seen in her primary care provider's office two months ago when she underwent a routine physical examination. She returns today with complaints of severe abdominal pain and discomfort. Diagnostic testing revealed Crohn's disease, and a treatment plan was discussed. Identify each of the following for services provided to Mary Smith today.

   7. Type of Service: _____ visit

   8. Place of Service: physician's _____

   9. E/M Category: _____ or Other Outpatient Services

  10. E/M Subcategory: _____ patient

Evaluation and Management Section Guidelines

The E/M section guidelines are located at the beginning of the section and include the following contents:

- Classification of Evaluation and Management (E/M) services
- Definitions of commonly used terms
- Unlisted service
- Special report
- Clinical examples
- Instructions for selecting a level of E/M service

Classification of E/M Services

The E/M section of CPT is organized into categories, including office and other outpatient visits, hospital observation and inpatient services, consultations, and emergency department services. Many categories contain subcategories (e.g., new and established patients and team conferences and telephone calls). Each category of E/M contains five-digit numeric codes ranging from 99201 to 99499; most code descriptions include the place and/or type of service, content of service (e.g., detailed history and detailed examination), nature of presenting problem, and time typically required to provide the service. E/M codes classify provider services according to the extent of work (e.g., counseling, history, or physical) and the intensity of the medical encounter (e.g., complexity of medical decision making). This means that a provider who performs and documents extensive work in the diagnosis and treatment of a patient (e.g., comprehensive history and examination, and medical decision making of high complexity) can assign a higher-level E/M code than a provider who performs and documents less extensive work.

Assigning E/M codes can be difficult and confusing; although guidelines and notes include definitions and instructions for selecting codes, they were perceived as insufficient to guarantee consistent coding by providers and reliable medical review by payers. In response, CMS developed **Documentation Guidelines for Evaluation and Management Services**, which explain how E/M codes are assigned according to elements associated with comprehensive multisystem and single-system examinations. The first set of documentation guidelines created by CMS in 1995 was criticized by providers as containing unclear criteria for single-system examinations. CMS then created an alternative set of documentation guidelines in 1997, which was also criticized as being confusing and requiring extensive counting of services and other elements. CMS, therefore, instructed Medicare administrative contractors to use both sets of guidelines when reviewing records, and providers were instructed to use whichever set of guidelines was most advantageous to their practice reimbursement. (The American Medical Association [AMA] continues to work with CMS to develop an acceptable approach for classifying E/M services.)

Definitions of Commonly Used Terms

The E/M guidelines organize definitions of commonly used terms in alphabetical order (except for new and established patient terms). The following terms are discussed below:

- New and established patient
- Concurrent care

The following terms are discussed under the "Levels of Evaluation and Management Services" heading in this chapter:

- Key components
  - History
    - Chief complaint
    - History of present illness
    - Family history
    - Past history
    - Social history
    - System review (review of systems)
  - Examination
  - Medical decision making
- Contributory components
  - Counseling
  - Coordination of care
  - Nature of presenting problem
  - Time

New and Established Patient

A **new patient** is one who has *not* received any professional services from the provider or from another provider of the exact same specialty and subspecialty who belongs to the same group practice, within the past three years. (A provider includes physicians and other qualified health care professionals who report E/M service codes.)

An **established patient** is one who *has* received professional services from the provider or from another provider of the same exact specialty and subspecialty who belongs to the same group practice, within the past three years.

Coding Tip:

- **Professional services** are face-to-face services provided by physicians and other qualified health care professionals (e.g., nurse practitioner, physician assistant), and the services are reported by assigning an E/M code.
- Definitions of new and established patients include professional services rendered by other physicians and other qualified health care professionals of the exact same specialty and subspecialty in the same group practice.
- CPT Evaluation and Management section guidelines contain a decision tree that can be used to determine new versus established patients.

EXAMPLE 1: Sally Dunlop had a prescription renewed by Dr. Smith's office on January 1, 2015, but she did not see the physician. She has been Dr. Smith's patient since her initial office visit on March 15, 2012. On December 1, 2015, Dr. Smith treated Sally during an office visit.

  New Patient: March 15, 2012

  New Patient: December 1, 2015

  Although the patient had the prescription renewed on January 1, 2015, because there was no face-to-face service provided Sally Dunlop is considered a new patient for the December 1, 2015, visit.

EXAMPLE 2: Dr. Charles and Dr. Black share a practice. Dr. Charles is a general surgeon who treated Mary Smith in the office on July 1, 2015. Mary was first seen by the practice on February 15, 2012, when Dr. Black, also a general surgeon, provided preventive care services to her. Mary returned to the practice on November 1, 2015, for her annual physical examination conducted by Dr. Black.

  New Patient: February 15, 2012, and July 1, 2015.

  Established Patient: November 1, 2015

EXAMPLE 3: Dr. Corey left Alfred Medical Group to join Buffalo Physician Group as a family practitioner. At Buffalo Physician Group, when Dr. Corey provides professional services to patients, are those patients considered new or established?

  Answer: Patients who have not received professional services from Dr. Corey and other qualified health care professionals or other physicians of the exact same specialty and subspecialty at Buffalo Physician Group are considered new. Patients who have been treated by such a provider at Buffalo Physician Group within the past three years are considered established. If any of Dr. Corey's patients from the Alfred Medical Group choose to seek care from him at the Buffalo Physician Group, they will be considered established patients.

Concurrent Care and Transfer of Care

Concurrent care is the provision of similar services, such as hospital inpatient visits, to the same patient by more than one provider on the same day. CMS permits the provision of concurrent care by two or more providers on the same day even if the providers are of the same specialty. To avoid reimbursement denials by third-party payers and Medicare administrative contracts, the attending physician is to add modifier -AI (Principal Physician of Record) to the E/M code reported. When possible, each provider should also report different ICD-10-CM diagnosis codes from those reported by other providers who provide E/M services to the patient on the same day.

EXAMPLE: Laurie Birch was admitted to the hospital on October 5 for an acute myocardial infarction. On October 7, her attending physician (a cardiologist) wrote a physician's order requesting a psychiatrist to consult with the patient regarding her anxiety and depression. The cardiologist's insurance specialist should report the ICD code for "acute myocardial infarction" to justify inpatient E/M services provided to the patient (and add modifier -AI, Principal Physician of Record, to the CPT code reported). The psychiatrist's insurance specialist should report the ICD codes for "anxiety and depression" to justify inpatient consultation E/M services provided to the patient. If each provider reported the ICD code for "acute myocardial infarction," the provider who submitted the claim first would be reimbursed (and the other provider's claim would be denied).

Transfer of care occurs when a provider who is managing some or all of a patient's problems relinquishes that responsibility to another provider who explicitly agrees to accept this responsibility and who, from the initial encounter, is *not* providing consultative services. The provider transferring care no longer manages these problems but may continue to manage other conditions.

EXAMPLE: Sally Southern was admitted to the hospital on March 1 by her surgeon for total thyroidectomy that was performed on March 2. During admission, the patient's severe anxiety and depression was initially co-managed with a psychiatrist. Late evening on March 2, the attending physician transferred management of the patient's anxiety and depression to the psychiatrist. At discharge on March 5, the attending physician reported CPT surgery codes for the total thyroidectomy surgery and CPT E/M codes for management of the thyroid condition. The psychiatrist reported CPT E/M codes for management of the patient's anxiety and depression.

Unlisted Service ⚠

An unlisted service code is assigned when the provider furnishes an E/M service for which there is no CPT code. When an unlisted procedure or service code is reported, a special report (e.g., copy of documented encounter note record) must accompany the claim to describe the nature of, extent of, and need for the procedure or service.

Coding Tip:

Payers often require providers to report HCPCS level II national codes (if available) instead of unlisted procedure or service CPT codes.

Special Report

When an unlisted service code is reported, a special report must be submitted with the insurance claim to demonstrate medical appropriateness. The provider should document the following elements in the special report:

- Complexity of patient's symptoms
- Description of nature of, extent of, and need for service
- Diagnostic and therapeutic procedures performed
- Follow-up care
- Patient's final diagnosis and concurrent problems
- Pertinent physical findings
- Time, effort, and equipment required to provide the service

Clinical Examples

Appendix C of the CPT coding manual contains **clinical examples** of E/M service codes. Along with a careful review of the E/M code descriptions, they assist providers in selecting the appropriate code for documented E/M services. The AMA cautions providers that the clinical examples "do not encompass the entire scope of medical practice." They can be used in addition to documented key components (history, examination, and/or medical decision making) that are required to determine a particular level of service.

Exercise 9.2 – Evaluation and Management Section Guidelines

Instructions: Complete each statement.

1. Tim Turner was seen by Dr. Chambers on February 5 of this year for follow-up of his type 2 diabetes mellitus. Tim has been Dr. Chambers' patient since 1984, when he was seen for an initial visit. Tim returned to the office each year since 1984 for an annual physical examination until last year, when he was diagnosed with type 2 diabetes mellitus. Since then, Tim has returned for a recheck office visit with Dr. Chambers every three months. Tim is considered a(n) _____ (new or established) patient for Dr. Chambers' practice.

2. Kristin Broome was seen by Dr. Marlot on March 8 six years ago for treatment of influenza. She returned on January 5 one year later for her annual physical examination, which included a prescription for birth control pills. Kristin called the office on April 10 of that same year to request that the local pharmacy be called so she could receive a refill of her birth control pills. Dr. Marlot called in the prescription that afternoon. Kristin next returned to the office on April 15 of this year for an annual physical examination. Kristin is considered a(n) _____ (new or established) patient for Dr. Marlot's practice.

3. Dr. Peterson, Dr. Slatterly, and Dr. Vaughan are members of the Medex Pediatric Group Practice. Eric Webb is a 15-year-old boy who was initially seen by Dr. Vaughan on August 5 of

Exercise 9.2 *(continued)*

last year for a sports physical. Eric returned to the office on September 10 of this year and was seen by Dr. Peterson for treatment of an ear infection. Eric is considered a(n) _____ (new or established) patient for Dr. Peterson's practice.

4–5. Sandy Tyler was admitted to the hospital on July 4 for treatment of a fractured pelvis, which he sustained while parasailing earlier in the day. On July 5, his attending physician (an orthopedic surgeon) wrote a physician's order requesting a neurologist to consult with the patient regarding numbness of his left foot.

  4. The orthopedic surgeon reports the diagnosis of _____ pelvis to justify inpatient E/M services.

  5. The neurologist reports the diagnosis of _____, left foot, to justify inpatient E/M consultation services.

Levels of Evaluation and Management Services

E/M categories and subcategories contain codes that are classified according to level of services for reporting to third-party payers. Although the last number of some E/M codes represents the level of service (e.g., code 99213 is a level 3 E/M service), the levels within categories and subcategories are not interchangeable. Levels of E/M services include conferences with or about patients, evaluations, examinations, preventive adult and pediatric health supervision, treatments, and other medical services (e.g., determining the need for and location of appropriate care, such as hospice care for a terminally ill patient).

With implementation of the outpatient prospective payment system (OPPS) in 2000, CMS recognized that the majority of CPT code descriptors are applicable to both physician and facility resources associated with specific services. However, CMS also acknowledged from the beginning of the OPPS that they believe CPT E/M codes were defined to reflect the activities of physicians and *do not necessarily fully describe the range and mix of services provided by hospitals during visits of clinic or emergency department patients or critical care encounters.* CMS advised *hospitals to develop internal billing and coding guidelines* that determine the levels of clinic and emergency department visits to be reported. Guidelines created by hospitals follow the intent of CPT code descriptors and are designed to reasonably relate the intensity and volume of hospital resources and services to the different levels of effort represented by the codes. As part of hospital-specific billing and coding guidelines, some facilities create and use *acuity level worksheets*, especially for emergency department services.

CMS originally planned to develop a national set of facility-specific codes and guidelines; however, CMS soon recognized the challenge in developing such guidelines. Thus, in lieu of national guidelines, CMS regularly re-evaluates hospital outpatient visit patterns of reporting through annual analysis of claims data to ensure that

Note:

CPT defines an established patient as *one who has received professional services from the physician or another physician of the same specialty who belongs to the same group practice, within the past three years.* However, CMS modified the definition of an established patient for hospital clinics or emergency departments as *one who has been registered as an inpatient or outpatient of the hospital within the past three years.*

(continues)

hospitals continue to bill appropriately according to their own internally developed guidelines. CMS also recognizes the AHA/AHIMA guidelines as the most appropriate and well-developed guidelines for use in the OPPS.

Go to the Student Companion Web Site to review a sample acuity worksheet as well as the *CMS Draft Visit Guidelines for Hospital Outpatient Care*, which can be used to create acuity level worksheets custom to a hospital's clinic or emergency department intensity of services (intensity and volume of resources required by patients) and severity of illnesses (how sick patients are).

Coding Tip:

- CPT code 99201 classifies a level 1 office or other outpatient service reported for new patients, and it includes a problem focused history and examination and straightforward medical decision making.
- CPT code 99211 classifies a level 1 office or other outpatient service reported for established patients, but it is reported when the physician's and other qualified health care professional's presence may not be required (e.g., office nurse takes patient's blood pressure and documents it in the record).
- The CPT code that classifies a problem focused history and examination and straightforward medical decision making is 99212, a level 2 office or other outpatient service.

Typically, just one E/M code is reported each day by a provider who provides outpatient services. When a separately identifiable E/M service is provided *in addition to a surgical procedure*, the E/M code is reported with modifier -25.

EXAMPLE 1: A physician sutured a patient's 2.5-cm scalp wound in the ED and performed a comprehensive neurological history and exam of the patient. The patient had sustained head trauma as the result of a car accident, and EMT personnel documented that he had been unconscious at the scene. Medical decision making was of high complexity. Report code 12001 for the simple repair of the scalp wound, and report code 99285-25 for the E/M service provided.

EXAMPLE 2: A physician sutured a 5-cm laceration of a patient's left hand and confirmed that the patient was up-to-date regarding tetanus toxoids immunization status. Report code 12002 for the simple repair of the skin laceration, hand. Do *not* report an E/M code because the patient was not evaluated other than for confirmation of her tetanus immunization status.

Coding Tip:

- When more than one provider furnishes E/M services to the same patient on the same day, CPT classifies that as concurrent care.
- Medicare no longer processes claims that include Consultation subsection codes. Thus, when *inpatient* E/M services are performed by more than one provider on the same date of service, to ensure payment, the attending physician adds modifier -AI (Principal Physician of Record) to the E/M code reported.

The levels of E/M services code descriptions include seven components, six of which determine the level of E/M service code to be assigned.

- History
- Examination
- Medical decision making
- Counseling
- Coordination of care
- Nature of presenting problem
- Time

The **key components** of history, examination, and medical decision making are required when selecting an E/M level of service code. **Contributory components** include counseling, coordination of care, nature of presenting problem, and time; they are used to select the appropriate E/M service code when patient record documentation indicates that they were the focus of the visit.

Key Components

E/M code selection is based on three key components.

- Extent of history
- Extent of examination
- Complexity of medical decision making

All three key components must be considered when assigning codes for new patients. For established patients, two of the three key components must be considered. This means that documentation in the patient's chart must support the key components used to determine the E/M code selected.

The E/M code reported to a payer must be supported by documentation in the patient's record (e.g., SOAP or clinic note, diagnostic test results, or operative findings). Although providers are responsible for selecting the E/M code at the time patient care is rendered, insurance specialists audit records to make sure that the appropriate level of E/M code was reported to the third-party payer.

Extent of History

A **history** is an interview of the patient that includes the following elements: history of present illness (HPI) (including the patient's chief complaint, CC), a **review of systems (ROS)**, and a past/family/social history (PFSH) (Table 9-1). The **extent of history** (Figure 9-1A) is categorized according to four types.

- **Problem focused history**: Chief complaint, brief history of present illness or problem
- **Expanded problem focused history**: Chief complaint, brief history of present illness, problem pertinent system review

Table 9-1 History Elements, Definitions, and Examples

History Element	Definition	Example
Chief complaint (CC)	Patient's description of medical condition stated in the patient's own words.	**EXAMPLE:** Patient states, "My knee gives out, and it really hurts when I walk."
History of present illness (HPI)	Chronological description of patient's present condition from time of onset to present. HPI should include location, quality, severity, duration of the condition, and associated signs and symptoms.	**EXAMPLE:** Patient states that for the past several months, his left knee has caused discomfort, especially when walking. Previous evaluation resulted in a diagnosis of probable torn cartilage. Today the knee is very bruised, and the patient complains of severe pain that started one week ago and is constant. The knee is painful when the patient is either resting or walking. Nothing helps reduce the pain. The patient has taken prescription Motrin and has tried using a heating pad as well as an ice pack. He states that nothing helps. Patient denies current injury.

Item	Documentation
location	left knee
quality	bruised, painful
severity	extremely severe
duration	one week
timing	constant
context	resting or walking
modifying factors	nothing makes it better

(continues)

Table 9-1 (*continued*)

History Element	Definition	Example
Past medical history	Summary of past illnesses, operations, injuries, treatments, and known allergies.	**EXAMPLE:** Reveals a healthy individual who has been hospitalized in the past x3 for childbirth; the patient has no known allergies, has no history of diseases, and is not currently on any medications.
Family history	A review of the medical events in the patient's family, including diseases that may be hereditary or that may present a risk to the patient.	**EXAMPLE:** Patient states that father died at age 51 of heart disease and that mother is living and well.
Social history	An age-appropriate review of past and current activities such as daily routine, dietary habits, exercise routine, marital status, occupation, sleeping patterns, smoking, use of alcohol and other drugs, and sexual activities.	**EXAMPLE:** Patient has history of marijuana use as a teenager and currently drinks alcohol socially; previous history of smoking cigarettes (quit three years ago).
System review [ROS]	Inventory by systems to document subjective symptoms stated by the patient. Provides an opportunity to gather information that the patient may have forgotten to mention or that may have seemed unimportant. The ROS includes: • constitutional • cardiovascular • skin • gastrointestinal • head • genitourinary • eyes • musculoskeletal • ears • neurological • nose • endocrine • mouth • psychological • throat • hematologic/lymphatic • breasts • allergic/immunologic • respiratory	**EXAMPLE:** Respiratory: The patient denies shortness of breath. **NOTE:** Providers should not document *negative* or *normal* in response to ROS items. Instead, they should document a statement relative to the item. **NOTE:** The *constitutional* as performed during a system review includes nonspecific symptoms that indicate a person is unwell, such as general aches. During a physical examination, the *constitutional* includes the patient's vital signs (e.g., blood pressure, pulse, and respirations).

- **Detailed history**: Chief complaint, extended history of present illness, problem pertinent system review extended to include a limited number of additional systems, pertinent past/family/social history directly related to patient's problem

- **Comprehensive history**: Chief complaint, extended history of present illness, review of systems directly related to the problem(s) identified in the history of the present illness in addition to a review of all additional body systems, complete past/family/social history

Extent of Examination

A **physical examination** (Table 9-2) is an assessment of the patient's organ (e.g., lungs) and body systems (e.g., cardiovascular). The **extent of examination** (Figure 9-1B) is categorized according to four types.

- **Problem focused examination**: A limited examination of the affected body area or organ system

- **Expanded problem focused examination**: A limited examination of the affected body area or organ system and other symptomatic or related organ system(s)

- **Detailed examination**: An extended examination of the affected body area(s) and other symptomatic or related organ system(s)

- **Comprehensive examination**: A general multisystem examination or a complete examination of a single organ system

SELECTING EXTENT OF HISTORY: To select extent of history, review the following elements documented in the patient record. If an element is not documented, it cannot be considered when selecting the level of E/M service code.

- History of Present Illness (HPI)
- Review of Systems (ROS)
- Past, Family, and Social History (PFSH)

HISTORY OF PRESENT ILLNESS (HPI): Review the patient's record, and for each documented HPI element listed below, enter an **x** in the box located in front of the element on this form.

- ☐ **Duration:** of pain/discomfort or illness; length of time condition has persisted (e.g., pain began 3 days ago)
- ☐ **Location:** of pain/discomfort (e.g., is pain diffuse/localized, unilateral/bilateral, does it radiate or refer?)
- ☐ **Quality:** a description of the quality of the symptom (e.g., is pain described as sharp, dull, throbbing, stabbing, constant, intermittent, acute or chronic, stable, improving or worsening)
- ☐ **Severity:** use of self-assessment scale to measure subjective levels (e.g., "on a scale of 1–10, how severe is the pain?"), or comparison of pain quantitatively with previously experienced pain
- ☐ **Timing:** establishing onset of pain and chronology of pain development (e.g., migraine in the a.m.)
- ☐ **Context:** where was the patient and what was he doing when pain began (e.g., was patient at rest or involved in an activity; was pain aggravated or relieved, or does it recur, with a specific activity; did situational stress or some other factor precede or accompany the pain)
- ☐ **Modifying factors:** what has patient attempted to do to relieve pain (e.g., heat vs. cold; does it relieve or exacerbate pain; what makes the pain worse; have over-the-counter drugs been attempted - with what results)
- ☐ **Associated signs/symptoms:** clinician's impressions formulated during the interview may lead to questioning about additional sensations or feelings (e.g., diaphoresis associated with indigestion or chest pain, blurred vision accompanying a headache, etc.)

_____ **Total Score:** Enter the number of **x**'s entered above. Place an **x** in front of the HPI type below.
- ☐ BRIEF HPI (1–3 elements)
- ☐ EXTENDED HPI (4 or more elements)

REVIEW OF SYSTEMS (ROS): Review the clinic or SOAP note in the patient's record, and for each documented ROS element listed below, enter an **x** in the box located in front of the element on this form.

☐ Constitutional symptoms	☐ Eyes	☐ Musculoskeletal
☐ Allergic or immunologic	☐ Gastrointestinal	☐ Neurological
☐ Cardiovascular	☐ Genitourinary	☐ Psychiatric
☐ Ears, nose, throat, mouth	☐ Hematologic/Lymphatic	☐ Respiratory
☐ Endocrine	☐ Integumentary	

_____ **Total Score:** Enter the number of **x**'s entered above. Place an **x** in front of the ROS type below.
- ☐ NONE
- ☐ PROBLEM PERTINENT ROS (1 body system documented)
- ☐ EXTENDED ROS (2–9 body systems documented)
- ☐ COMPLETE ROS (all body systems documented)

PAST, FAMILY, AND/OR SOCIAL HISTORY (PFSH): Review the clinic or SOAP note in the patient's record, and for each documented PFSH element (below), enter an **x** in the box located in front of the element on this form.
- ☐ Past history (current medications, drug allergies, immunizations, and prior illnesses/ injuries, hospitalizations, surgeries)
- ☐ Family history (health status/cause of death of relatives, specific disease related to CC, HPI, ROS, hereditary diseases for which patient is at risk)
- ☐ Social history (alcohol use, current employment, illicit drug use, level of education, nutritional status, occupational history, sexual history, tobacco use)

_____ **Total Score:** Enter the number of **x**'s entered above. Place an **x** in front of the PFSH type below.
- ☐ NONE
- ☐ PERTINENT PFSH (1 history area documented)
- ☐ COMPLETE PFSH (2 or 3 history areas documented)

Circle the type of HPI, ROS, and PFSH. Select the Extent of History. (Note: 3 of 3 elements must be met or exceeded.)

HPI	Brief	Brief	Extended	Extended
ROS	None	Problem Pertinent	Extended	Complete
PFSH	None	None	Pertinent	Complete
EXTENT OF HISTORY	PROBLEM FOCUSED	EXPANDED PROBLEM FOCUSED	DETAILED	COMPREHENSIVE

Courtesy of the Centers for Medicare & Medicaid Services, www.cms.gov

Figure 9-1A Extent of history

Table 9-2 Physical Examination Elements and Examples

Element	Example
General Survey	Reveals well-developed, somewhat obese, elderly, white male in severe distress with severe substernal discomfort and pain in upper arms. Conscious. Alert. Appears to be stated age. No deformity. Patient cannot sit or stand still because he is in such agony. Gait affected only by pain; otherwise it is normal. Carriage normal. Age 67. Sex male. Height 5'11". Weight 188 lbs. Temperature 98.0°F orally. Pulse 56 and regular. Blood pressure 150/104.
Skin	Reveals pale, cool, moist surface with no cyanosis or jaundice. No eruption. No tumors.
Head	Hair, scalp, skull within normal limits. Facies anxious.
Eyes	Pupils round, regular, equal. Pupils react normally to light and accommodation. Extraocular muscles intact. Corneae, sclerae, conjunctivae clear. Fields intact. Ophthalmoscopic examination reveals fundi discs to be well outlined.
Ears	Examination reveals grossly intact hearing. No lateralization. External canals and ears, and left membrana tympanica clear. No tumor.
Nose and Sinuses	Inspection reveals grossly intact sense of smell. No deformity. No tenderness. Septum benign. Only residual mucus in both nostrils. No tumor. Sinuses within normal limits.
Mouth	Mouth edentulous. Lips, gums, buccal mucosa, and tongue within normal limits.
Throat	Examination reveals posterior oropharynx and tonsils to be very red and inflamed. Palate and uvula benign. Larynx not visualized.
Neck	Reveals cervical structures to be supple with no masses, scars, or abnormal glands or pulsations.
Chest	Chest inspection reveals it to have normal expansion. Thorax observation reveals it to be somewhat obese but with normal shape and symmetry without swellings or tumors or significant lymphadenopathy. Respiratory motions normal. Palpable tactile fremitus physiologically normal.
Breasts	Felt to be symmetrical and without masses or tenderness. Nipples normal. No axillary lymphadenopathy.
Lungs	Investigation reveals lungs clear on inspection, palpation, percussion, and auscultation.
Heart	Examination reveals heart to be indicated as normal since the area of cardiac dullness is normal in size, shape, and location. Heart rate slow. Rhythm regular. No accentuation of A2 and P2.
Abdomen	Appearance is slightly obese with no striae. Has a well-healed herniorrhaphy scar on the right inguinal area. No tenderness, guarding, rigidity, or rebound phenomena. No abnormal abdominal masses palpable. No organomegaly. No distention. No herniae. Bowel sounds are normal.
Genitalia	Reveals male type and circumcised penis. Scrotum, testes, and epididymes appear to be normal in size, shape, and color without skin lesions or tumors.
Rectal	Inspection proves sphincter tone good. Lumen clear. Hemorrhoids, internal and external, found on examination.
Extremities	Examination reveals no loss of motor function of the extremities or back. Patient can sit, stand, squat, and walk, although it causes excruciating pain, and this is in the substernal chest area. Patient advised to avoid doing these things. No evidence of injury. No paralysis. Patient squirms and moves constantly in his agony. He cannot sit long nor can he stand in one position. Extremities exam reveals them to be intact. Shoulder girdle inspection reveals no tenderness, muscle spasms, or abnormality or motion. No crepitation. Examination of the back reveals a slight infected and tender pilonidal cyst over the sacrum. No deformity or limitation of motion of the back noted. No other tenderness. Arms, hands, legs, and feet investigation reveals no deformity, fracture, dislocations, injury, tremors, atrophic muscles, swelling, tenderness, muscle spasms, or abnormality of motion.
Lymphatics	System check reveals lymph glands to be normal throughout.
Blood Vessels	Investigation reveals veins to be normal. Arteries are arteriosclerotic and all peripheral pulses are palpable and undiminished.
Neurological	Examination reveals the patient generally conscious, cooperative, mentally alert, and reasonably intelligent, although he seems to be somewhat confused. Cranial nerves intact. Superficial and deep tendon reflexes intact and equal bilaterally. No pathological reflexes. No abnormality of the sensory perception or of the associated movements, or of the autonomic or endocrine systems felt to be due to neurological disorder. IMPRESSION: Acute myocardial infarction. Essentials hypertension. Arteriosclerosis. Pilonidal cyst with mild infection. Internal and external hemorrhoids. NOTE: Impression is documented at the end of a history and physical examination report. It is not an element of the physical examination

SELECTING EXTENT OF EXAMINATION: To select the level of examination, first determine whether a *single organ examination* (e.g., specialist exam, such as ophthalmologist) or a *general multisystem examination* (e.g., family practitioner) was completed.

SINGLE ORGAN SYSTEM EXAMINATION: Refer to single organ system examination requirements in CMS's *Documentation Guidelines for Evaluation and Management Services.* Place an **x** in front of the appropriate exam type below.
- ☐ PROBLEM FOCUSED EXAMINATION (1–5 elements identified by a bullet)
- ☐ EXPANDED PROBLEM FOCUSED EXAMINATION (at least 6 elements identified by a bullet)
- ☐ DETAILED EXAMINATION (at least 12 elements identified by a bullet)
- ☐ COMPREHENSIVE EXAMINATION (all elements identified by a bullet; document every element in each box with a shaded border and at least 1 element in each box with an unshaded border)

NOTE: for eye and psychiatric examinations, at least 9 elements in each box with a shaded border and at least 1 element in each box with a shaded or unshaded border is documented

GENERAL MULTISYSTEM EXAM: Refer to the general multisystem examination requirements in CMS's *Documentation Guidelines for Evaluation and Management Services.* Place an **x** in front of the organ system or body area for up to the total number of allowed elements (e.g., up to 2 marks can be made for the Neck exam).

☐ Constitutional (2)	☐ Gastrointestinal (5)	☐ Psychiatric (4)
☐ Cardiovascular (7)	☐ Genitourinary (M–3; F–6)	☐ Respiratory (4)
☐ Chest (Breasts) (2)	☐ Musculoskeletal (6)	☐ Skin (2)
☐ Eyes (3)	☐ Neck (2)	
☐ Ears, nose, mouth, throat (6)	☐ Neurological (3)	

_____ **Total Score:** Enter the number of **x**'s entered above. Place an **x** in front of the Examination type below.
- ☐ PROBLEM FOCUSED EXAMINATION (1–5 elements identified by a bullet on CMS's *E/M Documentation Guidelines*)
- ☐ EXPANDED PROBLEM FOCUSED EXAMINATION (at least 6 elements identified by a bullet on CMS's *E/M Documentation Guidelines*)
- ☐ DETAILED EXAMINATION (at least 2 elements identified by a bullet from each of 6 organ systems or body areas or at least 12 elements identified by a bullet in 2 or more systems or areas, on CMS's *E/M Documentation Guidelines*)
- ☐ COMPREHENSIVE EXAMINATION (documentation of all elements identified by a bullet in at least 9 organ systems or body areas, and documentation of at least 2 elements identified by a bullet from each of 9 organ systems or body areas, on CMS's *E/M Documentation Guidelines*)

Courtesy of the Centers for Medicare & Medicaid Services, www.cms.gov

Figure 9-1B Extent of examination

Complexity of Medical Decision Making

Medical decision making (MDM) refers to the complexity of establishing a diagnosis and selecting a management option as measured by the

- Number of diagnoses or management options
- Amount and complexity of data to be reviewed
- Risk of complications and/or morbidity or mortality

Complexity of medical decision-making criteria (Figure 9-1C) reflects the provider's level of uncertainty, volume of data to review, and risk to the patient. Documentation in the patient's record includes:

- Laboratory, imaging, and other test results that are significant to the management of the patient care
- List of known diagnoses as well as those that are suspected
- Opinions of other providers who have been consulted
- Planned course of action for the patient's treatment (plan of treatment)
- Review of patient records obtained from other facilities

The provider is responsible for determining the complexity of medical decision making, and that decision must be supported by documentation in the patient's chart. CPT includes a table in the E/M guidelines that can assist in

Criteria to Determine Minimal, Low, Moderate, and High Levels of Medical Decision Making

	Minimal	Low	Moderate	High
Number of Diagnoses	• One self-limited or minor problem (e.g., cold, insect bite)	• Two or more self-limited minor problems • One stable chronic illness (e.g., controlled hypertension) • Acute, uncomplicated illness or injury (e.g., allergic rhinitis, simple sprain)	• One or more chronic illnesses with mild exacerbation, progression, or side effects of treatment • Two or more stable chronic illnesses • Undiagnosed new problem with uncertain prognosis (e.g., breast lump) • Acute illness with systemic symptoms (e.g., pyelonephritis) • Acute complicated injury (e.g., head injury with unconsciousness)	• One or more chronic illnesses with severe exacerbation, progression, or side effects of treatment • Acute or chronic illnesses or injuries that pose a threat to life or bodily function (e.g., acute myocardial infarction) • An abrupt change in neurological status (e.g., seizure)
Amount/ Complexity of Data to Be Reviewed	• Lab tests requiring venipuncture • Chest x-ray • ECG/EEG • Urinalysis • Ultrasound • KOH prep	• Physiologic tests not under stress (e.g., pulmonary function tests) • Noncardiovascular imaging studies with contrast (e.g., barium enema) • Superficial needle biopsies • Clinical lab tests requiring arterial puncture • Skin biopsies	• Physiologic tests under stress (e.g., cardiac stress test) • Diagnostic endoscopies with no identified risk factors • Deep needle or incisional biopsies • Cardiovascular imaging studies with contrast and no identified risk factors • Obtain fluid from body cavity (e.g., thoracentesis)	• Cardiovascular imaging studies with contrast with identified risk factors • Cardiac electrophysiologic tests • Diagnostic endoscopies with identified risk factors • Discography
Management Options	• Rest • Gargles • Elastic bandages • Superficial dressings	• Over-the-counter drugs • Minor surgery with no identified risk factors • Physical therapy • Occupational therapy • IV fluids without additives	• Minor surgery with identified risk factors • Elective major surgery (open, percutaneous, or endoscopic) with no identified risk factors • Prescription drug management • Therapeutic nuclear medicine • IV fluids with additives • Closed treatment of fracture or dislocation without manipulation	• Elective major surgery (open, percutaneous, or endoscopic) with identified risk factors • Emergency major surgery (open, percutaneous, or endoscopic) • Parenteral controlled substances • Drug therapy requiring intensive monitoring for toxicity • Decision not to resuscitate or to de-escalate care because of poor prognosis

Courtesy of the Centers for Medicare & Medicaid Services, www.cms.gov

Figure 9-1C Complexity of medical decision making

Table 9-3 Complexity of Medical Decision Making

Two of Three Elements Must Be Met or Exceeded			
Number of Diagnoses or Management Options	Amount/Complexity of Data to Be Reviewed	Risk of Complications and/or Morbidity/Mortality	Medical Decision Making
Minimal	Minimal or none	Minimal	Straightforward
Limited	Limited	Low	Low complexity
Multiple	Moderate	Moderate	Moderate complexity
Extensive	Extensive	High	High complexity

determining complexity of medical decision making (Table 9-3). Once the key components for extent of history and examination are determined, the type of medical decision making can be selected, as follows:

- Straightforward
- Low complexity
- Moderate complexity
- High complexity

Assigning the E/M Code

Once the extent of history, extent of examination, and complexity of medical decision making are determined, select the appropriate E/M code (Figure 9-1D).

EXAMPLE: Use Figures 9-1A, 9-1B, 9-1C, and 9-1D and Table 9-3 to determine extent of history and examination and complexity of medical decision making for a patient who is seen by his general practitioner.

SUBJECTIVE: The patient is a 35-year-old established male patient seen today with a CC of severe snoring. He says that this has gone on for years and that he's finally ready to do something about it because he awakens during the night from it and his wife is also losing sleep from his snoring. He says that he wakes up in the morning feeling very tired and notices that he gets very tired during the day. ROS reveals allergies. He denies smoking or alcohol use. He is on no medications.

EXAMPLE OF MEDICAL DECISION MAKING DOCUMENTATION

Review the progress note to identify:

- diagnoses documented.
- whether data were reviewed.
- management options available to treat the patient.
- any risk of complications, morbidity, or mortality.

PROGRESS NOTE

SUBJECTIVE: The patient states that she has had an upset stomach for the past five days, and that it just won't go away. The patient denies recent changes in dietary habits or activities. She states that she was recently notified by her son that he is getting a divorce, and she admits that she is very upset about this news.

OBJECTIVE: GI: Normal bowel sounds. No rigidity. Some pain upon deep organ palpation. No organomegaly. Upon review of the record, it was noted that the patient has not complained about this problem in the past.

ASSESSMENT: Dyspepsia due to anxiety.

PLAN: (1) Gaviscon Extra Strength Relief Formula Liquid, 2 to 4 teaspoonfuls 4 times a day after meals and at bedtime. Follow with half a glass of water or other liquid. (2) Referral to James Kaplan, PhD, Clinical Psychologist. (3) Follow-up appointment in one month.

Notice that documentation included a review of data and a diagnosis. However management options and risk of complications, morbidity, or mortality were not documented.

OBJECTIVE: Blood pressure is 126/86. Pulse is 82. Weight is 185. EYES: Pupils equal, round, and reactive to light and accommodation; extraocular muscles intact. EARS & NOSE: Tympanic membranes normal; oropharynx benign. NECK: Supple without jugular venous distention,

Select the E/M code based on extent of history and examination and complexity of medical decision making:					
History	Problem focused	Expanded problem focused	Expanded problem focused	Detailed	Comprehensive
Examination	Problem focused	Expanded problem focused	Expanded problem focused	Detailed	Comprehensive
Medical Decision Making	Straightforward	Low complexity	Moderate complexity	Moderate complexity	High complexity

Go to the appropriate E/M category/subcategory, and select the code based upon the information above

Courtesy of the Centers for Medicare & Medicaid Services, www.cms.gov

Figure 9-1D E/M code selection based on extent of history, extent of examination, and complexity of medical decision making

bruits, or thyromegaly. RESPIRATORY: Breath sounds are clear to percussion and auscultation. EXTREMITIES: Without edema; pulses intact.

ASSESSMENT: Possible sleep apnea.

PLAN: Patient to undergo sleep study in two weeks. Results to be evaluated by Dr. Jones, ENT specialist, to determine whether patient is candidate for laser-assisted uvuloplasty (LAUP) surgery.

To assign the E/M code, the following is determined:

- **NEW OR ESTABLISHED PATIENT:** This is an established patient.

- **EXTENT OF HISTORY:** HPI elements include quality, severity, timing, and context; extended HPI (four elements) is documented. ROS elements include allergic; problem pertinent ROS (one body system) is documented. PFSH elements include documentation of social history; pertinent PFSH (one history area) is documented for a score of 1. Because three of three HPI/ROS/PFSH types must be selected to determine the higher-level extent of history, expanded problem focused history is assigned.

- **EXTENT OF EXAMINATION:** Constitutional (1), Eyes (1), ENT (2), Neck (1), Respiratory (1), Cardiovascular (1); expanded problem focused examination (six elements) is documented.

- **COMPLEXITY OF MEDICAL DECISION MAKING:** Undiagnosed new problem with uncertain prognosis is documented (possible sleep apnea). Although "physiologic test not under stress" (sleep study) is documented as being ordered, results are not reviewed by this provider. In addition, this provider will not follow through on management options because the patient is referred to an ENT specialist. Therefore, complexity of medical decision making is straightforward because two of three elements are required and just one element is documented.

- **E/M CODE ASSIGNED:** 99213 (Two of three key components are required.)

Contributory Components

The contributory components of counseling, coordination of care, nature of presenting problem, and time play an important role in selecting the E/M code when documentation in the patient record indicates that they were the focus of the visit. Counseling and/or coordination of care components drive CPT code selection only when they dominate the encounter (e.g., office visit), requiring that more than 50 percent of the provider's time be spent on such components. In such circumstances, the provider must be sure to carefully document these elements so as to support the higher-level code selected. (Some E/M code descriptions include notes about time and nature of the presenting problem to assist in determining the appropriate code number to report.)

Note:

The E/M CodeBuilder located in Appendix I will help you to select the correct E/M code.

Counseling ⚠

CPT defines **counseling** as it relates to E/M coding as a discussion with a patient and/or family concerning one or more of the following areas:

- Diagnostic results, impressions, and recommended diagnostic studies
- Prognosis
- Risks and benefits of management (treatment) options
- Instructions for management (treatment) and follow-up
- Importance of compliance with chosen management (treatment) options
- Risk factor reduction
- Patient and family education

Providers typically select the level of E/M code based on extent of history and examination and complexity of medical decision making. However, some patients require counseling services (e.g., nutrition instruction, smoking cessation, and weight management) during an E/M visit. If provided, such counseling should be properly documented and the appropriate level of E/M code selected.

EXAMPLE: Sherry Salins is a 52-year-old established female patient who was diagnosed with type 2 diabetes mellitus five years ago. She has never been able to control her diabetes with diet and exercise alone and was prescribed oral insulin upon onset. During today's expanded problem focused history and examination E/M office visit, Sherry informed me that she is determined to reduce the amount of oral insulin she takes daily, and she requested nutrition instruction and weight counseling. I subsequently spent 45 minutes (of the 70-minute office visit) discussing the fundamentals of nutrition and weight as related to diabetes mellitus. Sherry is scheduled to return in one month for recheck, and she was provided with a referral to a nutritionist as well as a weight counselor.

The patient received 45 minutes of counseling services *in addition to the expanded problem focused E/M service (code 99213), which was 25 minutes in length.* The 45 minutes of additional time represents more than 50 percent of the time associated with the total 70-minute office visit. Thus, code 99215 is reported because its description states *40 minutes face-to-face time with patient.*

Coordination of Care

When the provider makes arrangements with other providers or agencies for services to be provided to a patient, this is called **coordination of care**.

EXAMPLE: Dr. Smith writes a discharge order for inpatient Carol Clark to be discharged home and to receive home health care. Dr. Smith spends 30 minutes contacting the home health agency to make the appropriate arrangements for the patient and instructing the hospital to send copies of the patient's record to the home health care agency.

Nature of the Presenting Problem

CPT defines **nature of the presenting problem** as "a disease, condition, illness, injury, symptom, sign, finding, complaint, or other reason for the encounter, with or without a diagnosis being established at the time of the encounter." The *nature of the presenting problem* is considered when determining the number

Note:

Time spent with the patient (and/or persons responsible for the patient) is the key factor to selecting a level of E/M services *when counseling and/or coordination of care consists of more than 50% of face-to-face time.* The extent of counseling and/or coordination of care must be documented in the patient record.

of diagnoses or management options for medical decision making complexity (Table 9-3). Five types of presenting problems are recognized.

- *Minimal*: A problem may not require the presence of the provider, but service is provided under the provider's supervision (e.g., patient who comes to the office once a week to have blood pressure taken and recorded).

- *Self-limited or minor*: A problem that runs a definite and prescribed course, is transient in nature, and is not likely to permanently alter health status or that has a good prognosis with management/compliance (e.g., patient diagnosed with adult-onset diabetes mellitus controlled by diet and exercise).

- *Low severity*: A problem where the risk of morbidity without treatment is low, there is little to no risk of mortality without treatment, and full recovery without functional impairment is expected (e.g., patient diagnosed with eczema that does not respond to over-the-counter medications).

- *Moderate severity*: A problem where the risk of morbidity without treatment is moderate, there is moderate risk of mortality without treatment, uncertain prognosis, and increased probability of prolonged functional impairment (e.g., 35-year-old male patient diagnosed with chest pain on exertion).

- *High severity*: A problem where the risk of morbidity without treatment is high to extreme, there is a moderate to high risk of mortality without treatment, and high probability of severe, prolonged functional impairment (e.g., infant hospitalized with a diagnosis of respiratory syncytial virus).

Time (Face-to-Face versus Unit/Floor)

Intraservice time is a variable that includes *face-to-face time and unit/floor time*. **Face-to-face time** is the amount of time the office or outpatient care provider spends with the patient and/or family. **Unit/floor time** is the amount of time the provider spends at the patient's bedside rendering services and managing the patient's care on the unit or floor (e.g., reviewing test results). Unit/floor time applies to inpatient hospital care, hospital observation care, initial and follow-up inpatient hospital consultations, and nursing facility services.

As mentioned above, although the key components of history, examination, and medical decision making usually determine the E/M code, visits consisting predominantly of counseling and/or coordination of care are the exception. When counseling and/or coordination of care dominates (more than 50 percent) the provider patient and/or family encounter, it can be considered a key factor in selecting a particular E/M code. The extent of counseling must be documented in the patient's chart to support the E/M code selected.

EXAMPLE: Anne Sider is seen by Dr. Cyrix in the office for her three-month check-up. (She has chronic hypertension controlled by diet and exercise.) During the visit, Dr. Cyrix notes that the patient seems distracted and stressed, and he asks her about these symptoms. Anne starts to cry and spends 10 minutes telling Dr. Cyrix that her "life is falling apart," and that she wakes up in the middle of the night with a pounding heart, feeling as though she's going to die. Dr. Cyrix spends the next 45 minutes (of the 70-minute visit) counseling Anne about these symptoms. He determines that Anne is suffering from panic attacks, so he prescribes a medication and contacts ABC Counseling Associates to arrange an appointment for mental health counseling.

In this example, a routine three-month check-up (for which code 99212 or 99213 would be selected) evolves into a higher-level service (for which code 99215 can be reported). The provider must carefully document all aspects of this visit, which includes the recheck for hypertension, provision of counseling, coordination of care provided, and length of time spent face-to-face with the patient. (The coder should report an ICD-10-CM disease code from category Z70, in addition to the hypertension disease code, when counseling and/or coordination of care dominates the patient encounter *and is documented by the provider*.)

To properly bill an E/M level of service for an encounter based on time, the provider must provide counseling and/or coordination of care *in the presence of the patient* and document the following:

- Total length of time for the encounter

- Length of time spent coordinating care and/or counseling patient

- Issues discussed

- Relevant history, exam, and medical decision making (if performed)

EXAMPLE: Lucy Moreno is a 45-year-old established female patient who was seen in the office on April 22 for problem focused history and examination as follow-up for her diagnosis of lower back pain. Patient states that she is having great difficulty managing her pain, and she says that she realizes part of the problem is that she needs to lose 50 pounds. I discussed a variety of weight loss management options with the patient, including an appropriate exercise program, and she is scheduled to return in one month for recheck. Today's visit was 30 minutes in length, more than half of which was spent discussing weight loss management. Report code 99214.

Exercise 9.3 – Levels of Evaluation and Management Services

Instructions: Complete each of the following.

1. Refer to the Evaluation and Management section of CPT and identify a code for each level of service listed.

   a. Office or other outpatient visit, new patient, level 4 _____

   b. Office or other outpatient visit, established patient, level 1 _____

   c. Hospital inpatient services, initial hospital care, level 2 _____

   d. Home visit, new patient, level 5 _____

   e. Emergency department services, level 3 _____

2. An 89-year-old diabetic female presented to the hospital emergency room for evaluation of a very painful lower left arm. An x-ray revealed a left ulnar fracture. After taking a detailed history and performing a detailed exam, the physician reduced the fracture and applied a short-arm cast. Medical decision making was of moderate complexity. A CPT Surgery code was reported on the claim.

   a. Should an E/M code also be reported for this case? (Yes or No) _____

   b. If so, which code? _____

3. A 14-year-old male presented to his primary care provider's office for treatment of 3-cm laceration, which the physician sutured. The physician also administered a tetanus toxoid after confirming that the patient's tetanus immunization status was not up-to-date. Codes for treatment of the laceration and administration of the tetanus toxoid were assigned from the CPT Surgery and Medicine sections, respectively.

   a. Should an E/M code also be reported for this case? (Yes or No) _____

   b. If so, which code? _____

4. The three key components that determine an E/M code include extent of history, extent of examination, and complexity of medical decision _____.

5. When assigning an E/M code for a new patient, the number of key components that must be considered is two out of _____.

6. When an E/M code is assigned for an established patient, the number of key components that must be considered is _____.

7. Name the contributory components that are considered when determining an E/M code; they are not considered key components: counseling, coordination of care, nature of presenting problem, and _____.

8. Dr. Kuhl performed a level 3 E/M service to treat an 18-year-old established female patient in the office for a urinary tract infection. Urine culture revealed *Escherichia coli* bacteria. The patient was prescribed antibiotics and instructed to return for recheck in 10 days.

   a. The CPT E/M category and subcategory is Office or Other Outpatient Services, _____ Patient.

   b. The appropriate CPT code is _____.

(continues)

Exercise 9.3 (continued)

9. Review the case below and answer the questions to assign the E/M office or other outpatient code. (You will have to identify the elements documented in the case to determine the level of history, level of examination, and complexity of medical decision making.)

SUBJECTIVE: A 54-year-old female patient is seen in the office for routine three-month follow-up for evaluation and management of type 2 diabetes mellitus and hypertension. The patient has no new complaints today; she denies chest pain, headache, numbness of the extremities, shortness of breath, or visual changes. The patient states that she has remained on the diet recommended during the last E/M visit and that she is regularly exercising. Home monitoring of blood pressure and glucose levels are within normal limits.

OBJECTIVE: Blood pressure 130/78. Weight 145. Pulse 78, regular. HEAD, EYES, EARS, NOSE, THROAT: Pupils equal, round, and reactive to light and accommodation. External auditory canals and tympanic membranes negative. Oropharynx benign. NECK: Supple. No bruits, jugular venous distention, or thyromegaly. CHEST: Breath sounds clear to auscultation and percussion. No rubs, rales, rhonchi, or wheezing. HEART: No click, gallop, irregularity, murmur, or rub. EXTREMITIES: Distal pulses intact. No cyanosis, clubbing, or edema. NEUROLOGICAL: Deep tendon reflexes within normal limits and symmetrical. No decreased lower extremity sensation noted. LAB RESULTS: Fasting blood sugar 132. Urinalysis within normal limits.

ASSESSMENT: Type 2 diabetes mellitus, controlled. Benign hypertension.

PLAN: Glucotrol 5 milligrams daily, every morning. Procardia XL 30 milligrams daily. Relafen 1,000 milligrams daily. Continue home glucose monitoring. SMA-7 and glycosylated hemoglobin today. Return for routine follow-up in three months.

a. Is this patient new or established? _____

b. What is the extent of history? _____

c. What is the extent of examination? _____

d. What is the complexity of medical decision making? _____

e. Which E/M code is assigned? _____

10. A home care physician provided E/M home care services to a new 54-year-old male patient who complained of dyspnea due to cirrhosis of the liver and ascites. The home care physician spent 60 minutes reviewing the patient's record, taking a comprehensive history, and performing a comprehensive examination. Medical decision making was of moderate complexity. The home care physician then spent an additional 20 minutes documenting the home visit report and coordinating care with the patient's primary care physician. Assign the appropriate CPT code.

_____

Evaluation and Management Categories and Subcategories

The E/M section (99201–99499) contains notes unique to each category and subcategory. *Remember to review notes before assigning an E/M code.* (As discussed in Chapter 8, CPT refers to E/M subsections and categories as categories and subcategories, respectively.)

CMS No Longer Recognizes CPT Consultation Codes for Medicare Part B Payment

According to CMS, effective January 1, 2010, CPT's consultation codes were no longer recognized for Medicare Part B payment. Instead, providers who perform initial evaluation services for Medicare patients assign CPT's Evaluation and Management (E/M).

- Outpatient or Other Visits (99201–99215) codes for office/outpatient consultations
- Inpatient Hospital Visits: Initial and Subsequent (99221–99223) for hospital inpatient consultations
- Nursing Facility Visits (99304–99318) for nursing facility inpatient consultations

This new rule means that when codes from the Consultations subsection of CPT (99241–99255) are reported on a CMS-1500 claim (or on a UB-04 claim or via electronic data interchange) payment will be denied. All of the codes in the CPT Consultations subsection do not map exactly to codes in the Outpatient or Other Visits, Inpatient Hospital Visits: Initial and Subsequent, or Nursing Facility Visits subsections. (CMS has stated that they will not create a crosswalk of Consultation codes to the CPT codes that are to be reported for each type of service. The mapping tables below are provided for illustrative purposes only.)

Outpatient Consultations: Instead of using criteria for CPT's Consultation subsection codes 99241–99245, providers will use coding guidelines for CPT's Office or Other Outpatient Visit *new patient* codes 99201–99205 and *established patient* codes 99211–99215 to determine (1) whether the patient is new or established and (2) level of history, examination, and medical decision making provided.

CPT's outpatient consultation codes 99241–99245 actually do map to the outpatient or other visit codes (after it is determined whether the service was provided to a new or established patient).

Inpatient Hospital Visits: Instead of using criteria for CPT's Consultation subsection codes 99241–99255, when providers perform an initial consultation on a hospital inpatient, they will use coding guidelines for CPT's Inpatient Hospital Visits *initial* hospital care codes 99221–99223.

Nursing Facility Services: Instead of using criteria for CPT's Consultation subsection codes 99241–99255, when providers perform an initial consultation on a nursing facility patient, they will use coding guidelines for CPT's Nursing Facility Visits initial nursing facility care codes 99304–99306.

 Note:

Multiple reporting of initial hospital care and nursing facility care codes can occur for a single date of service.

- The principal physician of record will add modifier -AI (Principal Physician of Record) to reported initial hospital care codes 99221–99226 and initial nursing facility care codes 99304–99306.

- Any other provider who provides initial hospital care or initial nursing facility care for the same patient will report the appropriate E/M code without modifier -AI.

- Follow-up inpatient visits will be billed as subsequent hospital care visits or subsequent nursing facility care visits *without* modifier -AI.

CPT's inpatient consultation codes do not map exactly to initial inpatient hospital visits or initial nursing facility visits. Thus, providers should report the appropriate E/M code (other than a CPT consultation code) that describes the service provided. The general guideline is that the provider reports the most appropriate available code to bill Medicare for services that were previously billed using the CPT consultation codes. For services that

(continues)

CMS No Longer Recognizes CPT Consultation Codes for Medicare Part B Payment (*continued*)

can be described by previously used inpatient consultation CPT codes, CMS has stated that providers may bill the corresponding initial hospital care service codes or initial nursing facility care codes (where those codes appropriately describe the level of service provided). When the previously used inpatient consultation codes do not apply, providers should report the E/M code that most closely describes the service provided.

 Note:

Low level inpatient consultation codes 99251–99252 do not match any of the initial hospital care codes 99221–99223. For example, inpatient consultation codes 99251 and 99252 require "a problem focused history" and "an expanded problem focused history," respectively. In contrast, initial hospital care code 99221 requires "a detailed or comprehensive history."

CMS has stated that providers can report code 99221 for an E/M service if the requirements for billing that code, which are greater than CPT consultation codes 99251 and 99252, are met by the service furnished to the patient. CMS has also stated that because subsequent hospital care codes 99231 and 99232, respectively, require "a problem focused interval history" and "an expanded problem focused interval history," they could potentially meet the component work and medical necessity requirements to be reported for an E/M service that could be described by CPT consultation code 99251 or 99252. However, nothing official has been released by CMS that states reporting codes 99231 and 99232 is permitted.

 Note:

To review CMS's Q&A regarding the changes in reporting consultation codes, go to http://www.cms.gov, click on the Outreach & Education link, click on the find resources link, click on the MLN Matters Articles link, click on the 2010 MLN Matters Articles link, enter SE1010 in the "Filter On:" box, click on the SE1010 link, and then scroll down and click on the SE1010.pdf file.

Office or Other Outpatient Services

The Office or Other Outpatient Services category of E/M includes the following subcategories:

- New Patient
- Established Patient

Office or other outpatient services are provided in a physician or other provider's office, a hospital outpatient department, or another ambulatory care facility (e.g., stand-alone ambulatory care center). Before assigning an E/M level of service code from this category, make sure you apply the definition of *new* and *established* *patient* and consider the following:

- When a patient receives two E/M services from the same provider on the same day and the patient's problem is the same for each encounter, report just one E/M service.

 Note:

Medicare does not allow providers to report codes from the Consultations category. Thus, providers (e.g., specialists) who provide office consultation services to new and established Medicare patients are to report codes from the Office or Other Outpatient Services category. (It is unknown whether other third-party payers will adopt Medicare's ruling.)

(Providers in the same group practice who are in the same exact specialty and same subspecialty submit claims as though they are a single provider.) This means that when E/M office or other outpatient services are provided to the same patient multiple times on the same day for the same problem by the same provider, the highest-level E/M service is reported. *(An exception to this rule is reporting of critical service codes with an E/M service code.)*

- When multiple E/M office or other outpatient services are provided to the same patient on the same day by the same provider and the patient's problems are different for each E/M service, report multiple E/M codes. To justify medical necessity, make sure you link the appropriate diagnosis or condition code to its respective E/M code. Add modifier -25 to the second and subsequent E/M codes.

- When the patient receives office or other outpatient E/M services *on the same day that the patient is admitted to the hospital as an inpatient by the same provider*, report an E/M code for the initial hospital care only. Do not report an office or other outpatient E/M service code.

- When the provider performs a comprehensive exam in the office and the patient is later admitted to the hospital *on another day as a planned admission*, report a lower-level-of-service initial hospital care E/M code for the hospital admission (because the provider already performed and reported the predominant portion of the E/M during the office encounter). (When the patient is admitted on another day but the admission is unplanned, report the appropriate E/M code for the office visit and an appropriate-level-of-service E/M code for the initial hospital care.)

Coding Tip:

The provider does not have to redocument the history, review of symptoms, and past/family/social history documented during a previous encounter if the provider documents that the previous information was reviewed and then updates the information. The period of time since the previous encounter should generally be no more than one or two years. In addition, the provider should indicate in the current note where the previous documentation can be found (e.g., Refer to office records dated April 14, YYYY.).

EXAMPLE 1: Dr. Smith provides a level 3 E/M service to a new patient in the office for treatment of anxiety. The patient is prescribed medication and referred to a psychologist for therapy. The same patient returns four hours later because she is having difficulty dealing with her anxiety, and Dr. Smith provides a level 2 E/M service and 30 minutes of counseling. The insurance specialist should report code 99203 on the insurance claim. (An E/M code for the return visit four hours later is not reported because the patient's problem was the same as for the first visit.)

EXAMPLE 2: An 89-year-old established patient receives level 3 E/M services from Dr. James to evaluate her blood pressure medication. The same patient returns five hours later and receives level 4 E/M services from Dr. James to evaluate hip pain due to falling at home. The insurance specialist should report 99213 and 99214-25 because this patient received E/M services for two different problems. (The payer may request copies of the patient record to verify the claim.)

EXAMPLE 3: An established patient receives level 4 E/M services in the office from Dr. Peterson and is later admitted to the hospital, where Dr. Peterson provides level 3 initial hospital care E/M services. The insurance specialist should report code 99223 on the insurance claim. (An office or other outpatient services E/M code is not reported.)

Teaching Physicians and Resident Physicians

A teaching physician is a physician (other than another resident) who involves and supervises resident physicians in the care of his or her patients. A resident physician (or resident) is an individual who participates in an approved graduate medical education (GME) program.

Teaching physicians are no longer required to rewrite in its entirety the key elements of a resident physician's E/M documentation. However, a teaching physician cannot bill for a resident physician's history or physical exam *unless present for a significant portion of the exam*. The teaching physician can select an E/M level of service based on time spent later reviewing the resident's documented history and exam (as part of the medical decision-making process), adding it to the history and examination performed by the provider. (These conditions also apply when *any* provider reviews a history and examination performed, for example, six months previously.)

Teaching physicians are also required to substantiate any services reported on a claim by documenting a summary note of services provided personally or directly observed. The summary note can confirm or revise the HPI, physical examination, and medical decision-making activities. (For services such as a single surgical procedure and/or diagnostic test, the teaching physician can indicate his or her physical presence during the key portion of the procedure or test.)

EXAMPLE 1: When all required elements are obtained personally by a teaching physician without a resident present, the teaching physician documents the E/M service as if in a nonteaching setting. The teaching physician's documentation should also include a statement such as, "I performed a history and physical examination of the patient and discussed his management with the resident. I reviewed the resident's note and agree with the documented findings and plan of care."

EXAMPLE 2: When all required elements are obtained by the resident in the presence of or jointly with the teaching physician and documented by the resident, the teaching physician documents that he or she was present during performance of critical or key portion(s) of the service and that he or she was directly involved in the management of the patient's care. The teaching physician's note should also reference the resident's note. The combination of entries must be adequate to substantiate the level of service billed and the medical necessity of the service. The teaching physician's documentation should also include a statement such as, "I was present with resident during the history and exam. I discussed the case with the resident and agree with the findings and plan as documented in the resident's note."

EXAMPLE 3: When selected required elements of the service (e.g., history and physical examination) are obtained by the resident *in the absence of the teaching physician*, the resident documents the services provided. The teaching physician must independently perform the critical or key portion(s) of the service with or without the resident present and discuss the case with the resident. In this situation, the teaching physician must document that he or she personally saw the patient, personally performed critical or key portions of the service, and participated in the management of the patient. The teaching physician's note should also reference the resident's note. For payment consideration by the third-party payer, the combined entries of the teaching physician and resident must be adequate to substantiate the level of service billed and the medical necessity of the service. The teaching physician's documentation should also include a statement such as, "I saw and evaluated the patient. Discussed with resident and agree with resident's findings and plan as documented in the resident's note."

Code 99211

Code 99211 is commonly thought of as a "nurse visit" because it is typically reported when ancillary personnel provide E/M services. However, the code can be reported when the E/M service is rendered by any other provider (e.g., nurse practitioner, physician assistant, or physician). CMS "incident to" guidelines apply when the 99211 E/M level of service is provided by ancillary personnel in the office. The guidelines state that the physician and other qualified health care professional must be physically present in the suite of offices when the service is provided. Documentation of a 99211 level of service includes a CC and a description of the service provided. Because the presenting problem is considered of minimal severity, documentation of a history and examination is not required.

EXAMPLE 1: The office nurse administers a patient's monthly injection of vitamin B12 cyanocobalamin (1,000 µg) based on standing orders. Before administering the injection, the nurse takes and documents the patient's vital signs (blood pressure, height, weight, and body temperature). Report CPT code 99211 and HCPCS level II national code J3420.

EXAMPLE 2: The patient comes to the physician's office, and the office nurse administers the monthly injection of testosterone enanthate (1 mg). The patient had received E/M level 3 services from the physician last week. Report HCPCS level II national code J3121 only. Do not report CPT code 99211 because the only service provided was the injection and the patient did not require or receive other E/M services (e.g., taking vital signs).

Hospital Observation Services

The Hospital Observation Services category includes the following subcategories:

- Observation Care Discharge Services
- Initial Observation Care
- Subsequent Observation Care

Observation services are provided in a hospital outpatient setting, and the patient is considered an outpatient. Observation status is "an outpatient in a bed" because services include use of a bed (including overnight use of a bed) and hourly monitoring by a hospital's nursing or other staff that is reasonable and necessary to evaluate an outpatient's condition or determine the need for possible admission to the hospital as an inpatient. An observation patient may improve and be released *or* be admitted as an inpatient, which requires documentation of a proper admission order that serves as a rationale for an inpatient stay; the word "Admit" as an admission order for inpatient hospitalization is insufficient. Observation services are reimbursed only when ordered by a physician (or another individual authorized by state licensure law and hospital staff bylaws to admit patients to the hospital or to order outpatient tests). Medicare says that "the decision whether to discharge a patient from the hospital following resolution of the reason for the observation care or to admit the patient as an inpatient can be made in less than 48 hours, usually less than 24 hours," after which the provider must order an inpatient admission.

> **Note:**
>
> Observation care is a service that is provided to a patient (e.g., initial observation care). It is *not* a patient status (e.g., inpatient, outpatient). For example, both outpatients and emergency department patients receive observation services.

 Coding Tip:

When observation care is initiated during an encounter for another service (e.g., outpatient surgery), Evaluation and Management services provided by the provider initiating observation care are considered part of the initial observation care *when performed on the same date*. For example, a patient is treated in the emergency department (ED) and then placed under observation in the hospital. The observation service code only is reported to the payer because the ED service is included in the observation service. This rule applies to the supervising provider (who places the patient under observation); other providers who render services to patients under observation will report such services separately. For example, a thoracic surgeon who provides consultative services to a patient under observation reports codes for those services to the payer.

EXAMPLE: A patient underwent open reduction internal fixation (ORIF) in the hospital's outpatient surgery department. The surgeon ordered observation care due to unusual postoperative pain, and the patient is discharged home the next day. CPT codes reported for this encounter include the ORIF procedure, initial observation care, and observation care discharge services. (ICD codes reported include the reason for surgery and the reason for observation care, which was postoperative pain.)

Coding Tip:

A patient who is referred by a provider for hospital observation services, bypassing the outpatient or emergency department, is considered a "direct admission to observation." This can occur when the patient receives E/M services in the provider's office and the provider determines that the patient's status requires observation services. Instead of reporting an office or other outpatient service E/M code, the provider reports an observation service code.

The following services are *not* reported as observation services, and claims submitted for such services will be denied as being not reasonable or necessary:

Coding Tip:

No differentiation is made as to patient status (new versus established) when assigning hospital observation services codes.

- Services *not* reasonable or necessary for the diagnosis or treatment of the patient but provided for the convenience of the patient, patient's family, or provider (e.g., patient is waiting for transfer to nursing facility [NF] or physician is busy when patient is physically ready for discharge).

- Services covered by Medicare Part A (e.g., medically appropriate inpatient admission).

- Services that are bundled with another Medicare Part B service (e.g., postoperative monitoring during standard recovery period of four to six hours). (Such services are billed as recovery room services.)

- Services provided to patients who undergo diagnostic testing in a hospital outpatient department (e.g., routine preparation services furnished prior to the testing and recovery afterward).

- Therapeutic services associated with other treatments (e.g., chemotherapy).

- Standing orders for observation following outpatient surgery. (Such services are provided as part of outpatient surgery services.)

Observation Care Discharge Services

Observation care discharge services include documentation of the following:

- Final examination of the patient
- Discussion of the hospital stay
- Instructions for continuing care

Services also include preparation of discharge records. The *observation care discharge* code is reported when patient discharge is on a date other than for initial observation care.

Initial Observation Care

Initial observation care codes are reported for patients who are admitted for observation services on one date and discharged from observation status on a different date. Reference times are included in descriptions of initial observation care codes, which

Coding Tip:

For patients who are admitted and discharged from observation care on the same date, report codes from the Observation or Inpatient Care Services (including Admission and Discharge Services) subcategory of the Hospital Inpatient Services category.

means the service can be based on time (instead of key components of history, examination, and medical decision making) *when counseling and/or coordination of care dominates (more than 50 percent of) the physician/ patient encounter.* This means that the insurance specialist assigns a code from range 99218–99220 along with code 99217.

Subsequent Observation Care

Subsequent observation care codes 99224–99226 are reported when a patient receives observation services for a second calendar day and is *not* admitted as a hospital inpatient or discharged from observation services.

> **EXAMPLE:** A patient was treated in the hospital's ED for acute asthmatic bronchitis at 9:30 PM on May 14. The ED physician determined that the patient needed to be observed for a period of six to eight hours after provision of emergency treatment. The patient received a detailed level of observation services and was discharged from observation services at 5 AM on May 15. Report codes 99218 and 99217.

CMS's Quick Guide to Coding Observation Care Services		
For Patients Admission/Discharged on the:	Whose Length of Observation Time Is:	Report Codes:
Same date	<8 hours	99218–99220
Same date	>8 hours	99234–99236
Different dates	Any length of time	99218–99220 and 99224–99226 and 99217

Hospital Inpatient Services

Hospital inpatient services codes are reported by acute care hospitals, inpatient psychiatric facilities, comprehensive inpatient rehabilitation facilities, and partial hospitalization settings. The Hospital Inpatient Services category of E/M includes the following subcategories:

- Initial Hospital Care
- Subsequent Hospital Care
- Observation or Inpatient Care Services (Including Admissions and Discharge Services)
- Hospital Discharge Services

 Note:

> Medicare does not allow providers to report codes from the Consultations category. Thus, providers (e.g., specialists) who provide inpatient consultation services to Medicare patients are to report codes from the Initial Hospital Care subcategory. (It is unknown whether other third-party payers will adopt Medicare's ruling.)
>
> When more than one provider (e.g., attending physician and a consultant) delivers inpatient services on the same date of service, the attending physician adds modifier -AI (Principal Physician of Record) to the reported E/M code.

▲ **Hospital inpatient services** are provided to hospital inpatients, including partial hospitalization services; they are indicated when the patient's condition requires services and/or procedures that cannot be performed in any other POS without putting the patient at risk. **Partial hospitalization** is a short-term, intensive treatment program where individuals who are experiencing an acute episode of an illness (e.g., geriatric,

 Coding Tip:

No differentiation is made as to patient status (new versus established) when assigning hospital inpatient services codes.

psychiatric, or rehabilitative) can receive medically supervised treatment during a significant number of daytime or nighttime hours. This type of program is an alternative to 24-hour inpatient hospitalization and allows the patients to maintain their everyday life without the disruption associated with an inpatient hospital stay.

Reporting Codes for Hospitalist Services

The Society of Hospital Medicine defines hospitalists as physicians whose primary focus is the general medical care of hospitalized patients; their activities include patient care, teaching research, and leadership related to hospital medicine. Hospitalists may be employed directly by the hospital, serve as independent contractors, or be part of a group practice of hospitalists.

EXAMPLE: An orthopedic surgeon admits a 40-year-old patient from the emergency department on May 1 and schedules surgery on May 2 to repair a hip fracture. She requests that Dr. Jones, an internal medicine hospitalist, evaluate the patient on May 1 for chronic bronchitis and to provide preoperative clearance.

The orthopedic surgeon reports a code for the initial hospital care (99221–99223), and the hospitalist reports a code for the inpatient consultation (99251–99255). [If the hospitalist had provided E/M services to a Medicare patient, he would report a code from the Initial Hospital Care (99221–99239) subcategory instead of the Inpatient Consultations subcategory.]

Initial Hospital Care

Initial hospital care services cover the first inpatient encounter the provider has with the patient for each admission. An initial hospital care code is reported once per hospitalization by the provider. In addition, providers may not bill for both an admission visit and a discharge visit on the same day; for a patient who is admitted and discharged on the same date, report a code from the Observation or Inpatient Care Services (including Admission and Discharge Services) subcategory (99234–99236). When a patient placed under observation is admitted as an inpatient by the same provider on the same day he or she is placed under observation, report an initial hospital care code (99221–99223) only for that day.

A hospital inpatient is someone who is admitted and discharged and has a length of stay (LOS) of one or more days.

- Initial hospital care codes cover all E/M services provided to a patient by the same provider for a *planned admission*, regardless of where other E/M services were performed (e.g., preoperative history and examination performed in the office just days prior to an elective surgical admission). Report an initial hospital care E/M code only. (An exception is when a surgeon is the primary care provider during an inpatient admission, for which a CPT Surgery code is reported *only*, and inpatient E/M codes are not reported by the surgeon.)

- When a patient receives office or other outpatient E/M services *on the same day as an inpatient admission to the hospital by the same provider*, report an E/M code for the initial hospital care only. *Do not report an office or other outpatient E/M service code.*

- When the provider performs a comprehensive exam in the office and the patient is later admitted to the hospital on another day as a *planned* admission, report a lower-level-of-service initial hospital care E/M code for the hospital admission (because the provider already performed and reported the predominant portion of the E/M during the office encounter).

- When the provider provides E/M services in the office and the patient is later admitted to the hospital on another day as an *unplanned* admission, report the appropriate E/M code for the office visit and an appropriate level-of service E/M code for the initial hospital care.

Providers involved in care of the patient but not designated as the attending physician report services from a different category of E/M depending on where services were rendered (e.g., ED services or consultations).

EXAMPLE: On the day of inpatient admission, Dr. Thompson provided initial hospital care E/M level 3 services to a 42-year-old male patient who was admitted for antibiotic therapy to treat pneumonia due to *Klebsiella pneumoniae* bacteria. Report code 99223.

If Dr. Thompson had provided level 4 or 5 E/M services to the patient in the office, which resulted in admission the next day, the reported code would be 99214 or 99215 for the office or other outpatient services encounter and code 99221 for the initial hospital care service.

Subsequent Hospital Care

Subsequent hospital care includes the review of the patient's record for changes in the patient's condition, the results of diagnostic studies, and/or the reassessment of the patient's condition since the last assessment performed by the provider.

- Code 99231 is reported for a stable, recovering, or improving patient.

- Code 99232 is reported for a patient who did not readily respond to inpatient therapy or who developed a minor complication during the inpatient stay.

- Code 99233 is reported for a patient who is considered unstable because he or she developed a significant complication or a new problem. (Such patients are transferred to NFs or discharged home to receive home health care services.)

EXAMPLE: Dr. Thompson provided subsequent hospital care level 2 services to the 42-year-old male patient who was admitted for antibiotic therapy to treat pneumonia due to *Klebsiella pneumoniae* bacteria. Report code 99232.

If the physician had identified an additional condition (e.g., neurological disorder) that required the participation of another physician in this patient's care, both physicians would report an E/M level of service code and link the appropriate ICD condition code to the E/M code. The other physician would provide consultation services initially; if that physician continued to participate in the patient's inpatient care, report E/M codes from the Subsequent Hospital Care subcategory.

Observation or Inpatient Care Services (Including Admission and Discharge Services)

When observation *or* inpatient care services are provided to patients who are admitted and discharged on the same date, report a code from 99234–99236.

- When a patient is admitted as a hospital inpatient after receiving observation services on the same date, report only an initial hospital care code. (That code should reflect the services provided by the provider during the patient's observation status.)

- When a patient receives observation services on the same date as the result of services provided at another site of service (e.g., physician's office, hospital ED, or NF), report only an observation or an inpatient care services code. (That code should reflect the services provided by the provider at the other site.)

EXAMPLE 1: A patient receives treatment in the hospital ED for an acute asthma attack. The ED physician orders a blood gas analysis laboratory test and an injection of medication to help the patient breathe more easily. The ED physician then orders the patient to be placed in the hospital outpatient observation unit to monitor the patient's breathing and to ensure that the treatment resolves the patient's problem. Five hours later, the ED physician examines the patient, who has normal vital signs and has resumed normal breathing. The patient is discharged to follow-up with his primary care provider (PCP). The patient's record reveals documentation of a comprehensive history, comprehensive examination, and medical decision making that is of moderate complexity. Report code 99235 only. (*Do not report ED services code 99283 for this encounter.*)

EXAMPLE 2: A 38-year-old female patient undergoes a scheduled hospital ambulatory surgical procedure and is taken to the recovery room, where she has difficulty awakening from anesthesia and an elevated blood pressure. Both conditions persist during the usual recovery period, and the surgeon orders the ED physician to evaluate the patient. The patient is placed in the hospital's outpatient observation unit, and the ED physician orders the nursing staff to monitor the patient's condition and note any continued abnormalities that could indicate a drug reaction or other postsurgical complications. After four hours in the observation unit, the patient is no longer lethargic, has a normal blood pressure, and shows no signs of postsurgical complications. The ED physician discharges the patient from the observation unit to home. The patient record documents a comprehensive history, comprehensive examination, and medical decision making of high complexity. Report code 99236. (The coverage of outpatient observation services began when the patient was placed in the observation unit. Services provided to the patient in the hospital's outpatient surgical suite and recovery room are not considered observation status services.)

EXAMPLE 3: A patient is scheduled to undergo outpatient cataract extraction surgery. The patient expresses a preference for spending the night following the procedure at the hospital despite the fact that the procedure does not require an overnight stay. The hospital registered and treated the patient on an outpatient basis to perform the surgery and then permitted the patient to remain at the hospital overnight. Do not report a code for the overnight stay because it is not covered as medically necessary observation status services. (When a patient is accommodated in this manner, make sure that you notify the patient in advance that the overnight stay is not medically necessary and that the patient will be charged for the additional services. If the patient experiences complications postsurgically that necessitate an inpatient admission, the patient is admitted and a Medicare Part A claim is submitted.)

Hospital Discharge Services

Hospital discharge services include the final examination of the patient, discussion of the hospital stay with the patient and/or caregiver, instructions for continuing care provided to the patient and/or caregiver, and preparation of discharge records, prescriptions, and referral forms. Hospital discharge day management codes are reported for services provided by the provider as part of the final hospital discharge of a patient. ⚠

 Coding Tip:

Do not report a hospital E/M visit and a hospital discharge day management code for the same date of service.

EXAMPLE 1: Dr. Taylor provided 30 minutes of hospital discharge day management services to a 44-year-old female patient who was admitted for management of newly diagnosed type 2 diabetes mellitus. The patient responded well to inpatient insulin treatment and, upon examination, is discharged in improved condition. The patient was provided with discharge instructions for diabetes care, including the administration of insulin injections at home. Follow-up appointment in 10 days was scheduled. Report code 99238.

EXAMPLE 2: Dr. Collins provided 70 minutes of hospital discharge day management services to a 94-year-old female patient who was admitted for surgical treatment of a fractured pelvis. During inpatient hospitalization, the patient developed pneumonia, which was successfully treated. Arrangements were made to transfer the patient to an NF for follow-up care. Orders for pain management were provided to the NF. The patient was informed that Dr. Collins would visit her tomorrow to perform a comprehensive nursing facility assessment. Report code 99239.

Consultations

The Consultations category of E/M includes the following subcategories:

- Office or Other Outpatient Consultations

- Inpatient Consultations

Note:

CMS no longer allows providers to report codes from the Consultations category of CPT. Providers (e.g., specialists) who deliver consultation services to Medicare patients in a(n)

- Office or hospital outpatient setting are to report codes from the Office or Other Outpatient Services category

- Inpatient setting are to report codes from the Hospital Inpatient Services category

- Nursing facility setting are to report codes from the Nursing Facility Services category

   - The attending physician reports modifier -AI (Principal Physician of Record) with the initial hospital care code or initial nursing facility care code to distinguish the admitting or attending physician's service from those who provide consultation services.

The OIG reported that most consultation services reported to Medicare in 2001 were inappropriate, and subsequent education efforts to improve reporting failed to produce desired results. Other third-party payers will likely adopt the elimination of CPT's consultation codes. It is unknown whether the AMA will eliminate the "Consultations" category from a future revision of CPT.

EXAMPLE: On May 1, Mary Smith was seen in the hospital's emergency department (ED) and received level 4 Evaluation and Management services from Dr. Axel (ED physician). The patient complained of severe shortness of breath, chest pain radiating down the left arm, back pain, and extreme anxiety. The patient was admitted to the hospital on May 1, and Dr. Rodney (attending physician) provided level 3 initial hospital care. Dr. Axel reported code 99284, and Dr. Rodney reported code 99222-AI.

A **consultation** is an examination of a patient by a health care provider, usually a specialist, for the purpose of advising the referring or attending physician in the evaluation and/or management of a specific problem with a known diagnosis. Consultants may initiate diagnostic and/or therapeutic services as necessary during the consultative encounter. The following criteria are used to define a consultation:

- The consultation is requested by another provider or source such as a third-party payer. (If the consultation is mandated by a payer or other source, attach modifier -32 to the consultation code.)

- The consultant renders an opinion or advice.

- The consultant initiates diagnostic or therapeutic services.

- The requesting provider has documented in the patient's record the request and the need for the consultation.

- The consultant's opinion, advice, and any services rendered are documented in the patient's record and communicated to the requesting provider or source, generally in the form of a written report.

Coding Tip:

- Do not confuse a consultation with a referral. A **referral** is a recommendation to transfer a patient's care from one provider to another. A referring provider does not schedule the appointment or document a request for referral. A referral is not a consultation. To ensure proper coding of the encounter, call the referring provider to inquire whether a consultation was intended instead of a referral.

- No differentiation is made as to patient status (new versus established) when assigning consultation codes.

(continues)

Coding Tip (*continued*)

- When a confirmatory consultation is required by a third-party payer or another party, add modifier -32 to the appropriate code from the Consultations category (non-Medicare patient), Office or Other Outpatient Services category (Medicare office or hospital outpatient), Inpatient Hospital Care subcategory (Medicare inpatient), or Initial Nursing Facility Care subcategory (Medicare nursing facility patient).

Office or Other Outpatient Consultations

The Office or Other Outpatient Consultation category includes services provided in the following health care settings:

- Physician's office
- Outpatient or other ambulatory care facility
- Hospital observation services
- Home services
- Domiciliary, rest home, or custodial care
- Emergency department

Coding Tip:

- When a consultant provides follow-up office or other outpatient consultation services, report codes from Office or Other Outpatient Services, Established Patient (99211–99215).
- When office or other outpatient consultation services are provided to Medicare patients, report codes from the Office or Other Outpatient Services category.
- Guidelines about consultation requests and documentation also apply to consulting providers who report codes from the Office or Other Outpatient Services category.

For a code from the Office or Other Outpatient Consultations category to be reported, the consultation request must be initiated by the attending physician or another health care provider and the attending physician must document all consultation requests in the patient's record. The consultant must document a written report that includes the name of the person requesting the consultation, the reason for the consultation, and the way the findings were communicated to the referring health care provider. Any specifically identifiable diagnostic or therapeutic service performed on the same day as the examination may be billed separately. These separate services must be linked to the appropriate diagnosis to ensure that medical necessity criteria are met. (Some Medicare administrative contractors and third-party payers may disallow payment when surgical procedures and E/M services are performed during the encounter.)

Coding Tip:

- When a consultant provides consultation services in the hospital's emergency department (ED) (at the request of the ED physician), report a code from the Office or Other Outpatient Consultations category of the Consultations subsection.
- When a consultant assumes responsibility for a portion or all management of the case, subsequent care provided by the consultant is reported with the appropriate office or other outpatient services or subsequent hospital care code.

- A **preoperative clearance** occurs when a surgeon requests that a specialist or another provider (e.g., general practitioner) examine a patient and indicate whether the patient can withstand the expected risks of a specific surgery. This is considered a consultation even if the physician performing the preoperative clearance is the patient's primary care provider. (A written request must be documented in the patient's record.)

 Note:

A history and physical examination is performed by the patient's surgeon (in the office or at the hospital).

EXAMPLE: On March 15, a 42-year-old female patient was seen by Dr. Verde, her general practitioner, due to symptoms of chest pain and heart palpitations. Dr. Verde determined that the patient needed to be evaluated by a specialist and arranged for the patient to be seen in consultation by Dr. Falco, a cardiologist. Dr. Falco provided a level 4 office or other outpatient consultation service to the patient on March 20 and ordered diagnostic testing to establish a definitive diagnosis. Code 99244 is reported for the visit to Dr. Falco's office. (If, upon review of diagnostic testing results, Dr. Falco establishes a definitive diagnosis that requires the provision of further E/M services to the patient, report codes from the Office or Other Outpatient Services category of E/M.)

Inpatient Consultations

Inpatient consultation codes are reported when consultation services are provided to non-Medicare inpatients, nursing facility residents, or partial hospitalization patients. Just one inpatient consultation code is reported by a consulting provider per non-Medicare admission. When consulting providers participate in the patient's inpatient care, report codes from the Subsequent Hospital Care or Subsequent Nursing Facility subcategory of E/M, depending on health care setting. When follow-up care is provided in the consultant's office, report a code from the Office or Other Outpatient Services category of E/M.

 Coding Tip:

- When an inpatient consultation is provided to Medicare patients, consultants report a code from the Initial Hospital Care category or the Initial Nursing Facility Care category.
- Guidelines about consultation requests and documentation also apply to consulting physicians who report codes from the Initial Hospital Care or Initial Nursing Facility Care category.

EXAMPLE: A 52-year-old female patient was admitted to the hospital by her PCP to control her type 2 diabetes mellitus and to evaluate possible gangrene of her left foot. The provider ordered inpatient consultation services from an orthopedic surgeon, who provided level 4 E/M initial inpatient consultation services during evaluation of the patient. The orthopedic surgeon told the patient and her PCP that immediate surgical debridement was necessary. (Surgical debridement was performed.) Report code 99254-57 for the consultation services, along with a code from the CPT Surgery section for surgical debridement. (Modifier -57 is attached to code 99254 because the E/M services resulted in a decision to perform surgery. When the orthopedic surgeon provides inpatient and office E/M services to the patient postoperatively, do not report E/M codes. Such follow-up care is part of the global period of surgery; the orthopedic surgeon is paid a fee for having performed the surgery and providing routine follow-up care.)

Coding Tip:

- When consultation services are provided to a nursing facility resident, just one non-Medicare inpatient consultation code (or Medicare patient Initial Nursing Facility Care code) may be reported per nursing facility admission, regardless of the length of time the resident remains in the facility (e.g., years). For additional consultation services, report subsequent nursing care visit codes (even when months or years have passed since the initial consultation service).
- For follow-up inpatient consultation services, report codes from the Subsequent Hospital Care subcategory of E/M.

Emergency Department Services

Emergency department services are provided in a hospital, which is open 24 hours for the purpose of providing unscheduled episodic services to patients who require immediate medical attention. A *medical emergency* is the sudden and unexpected onset of a medical condition or the acute exacerbation of a chronic condition that is threatening to life, limb, or sight and that requires immediate medical treatment or that manifests painful symptomatology requiring immediate palliative effort to relieve suffering. A *maternity emergency* is a sudden unexpected medical complication that puts the mother or fetus at risk. A *psychiatric inpatient admission* is an emergency when, based on a psychiatric evaluation performed by a provider (or another qualified mental health care professional with hospital admission authority), the patient is at immediate risk of serious harm to self or others as a result of a mental disorder, and requires immediate continuous skilled observation at the acute level of care.

While ED physicians employed by the facility usually provide ED services, any physician who provides services to a patient registered in the ED may report the ED services codes. This means that the physician does not have to be assigned to the hospital's ED. When services provided in the ED are determined not to be an actual emergency, ED services codes (99281–99288) are still reportable if ED services were provided. Typically, the hospital reports a lower-level ED services code for nonemergency conditions.

If a physician provides emergency services to a patient in the office, it is not appropriate to assign codes from the Emergency Department Services category of E/M. If the patient's primary care provider (PCP) asks the patient to meet him in the hospital's ED as an alternative to the physician's office and the patient is not registered as a patient in the ED, the physician should report a code from the Office or Other Outpatient Services category of E/M. ED services codes are reported only if the patient receives services in the hospital's ED.

When the same physician provides ED services on the same day as a comprehensive nursing facility assessment, do not report an ED services code. Any E/M services provided at a site other than the NF are included in reimbursement for initial nursing facility care when performed on the same date as the nursing facility admission. (When a different physician provides ED services in addition to services provided by a physician at the NF, each physician reports an appropriate E/M code.)

When a patient's PCP directs the patient to go to the hospital's ED to receive care and that physician is subsequently asked by the ED physician to evaluate the patient and advise the ED physician as to whether the patient should be admitted to the hospital or be sent home, assign codes as follows:

- If the patient is admitted to the hospital by the patient's PCP, the PCP should report a code for the appropriate level of the initial hospital care (99221–99223) only. All E/M services provided by the PCP in conjunction with an inpatient admission are considered part of initial hospital care when performed on the same date as the admission. The ED physician who treated the patient in the ED should report the appropriate ED services code.

- If the ED physician, based on the advice of the patient's PCP who came to the ED to evaluate the patient, sends the patient home, the ED physician should report the appropriate ED services code. The patient's

PCP should also report an ED services code that describes the services provided in the ED. The PCP should not report a consultation services code because no information was provided to the ED physician for use in the patient's treatment. If the PCP does not come to the hospital to evaluate the patient but provides advice to the ED physician via telephone, the PCP should not report any E/M code.

When an ED physician requests that another provider evaluate an emergency patient, the other provider should report a consultation services code if criteria for providing a consultation have been met. If those criteria are not met and the patient is discharged from the ED or admitted to the hospital by another provider, the provider contacted by the ED physician should report an ED services code. If the consulted provider admits the patient to the hospital and the criteria for a consultation have not been met, the provider should report an initial hospital care code.

EXAMPLE: A 54-year-old female patient presented to the hospital ED with the symptoms of abdominal discomfort, severe shortness of breath, and numbness in both hands. The ED physician provided level 5 E/M services, which included diagnostic workup. Report code 99285.

Other Emergency Services

Code 99288 is reported when the provider is in two-way communication contact with ambulance or rescue crew personnel located outside the hospital. The provider directs performance of the following procedures:

- Administration of intramuscular, intratracheal, or subcutaneous drugs
- Administration of intravenous fluids
- Cardiac and/or pulmonary resuscitation
- Electrical conversion of arrhythmia
- Endotracheal or esophageal obturator airway intubation
- Telemetry of cardiac rhythm

Coding Tip:

- No differentiation is made as to patient status (new versus established) when assigning ED services codes.
- Usually Medicare administrative contractors and third-party payers do not provide a separate payment for services reported as code 99288 because they are considered included in the payment for services (e.g., emergency department services reported with CPT codes or ambulance services reported with HCPCS level II codes).

Critical Care Services

Critical care is the direct delivery of medical care by a provider to a patient who is critically ill or injured and who requires the full, exclusive attention of the provider. A **critical illness or injury** is one that acutely impairs one or more vital organ systems, jeopardizing the patient's survival. Critical care involves high-complexity medical decision making to assess and manage life-threatening conditions (e.g., central nervous system failure, circulatory failure, shock, renal failure, hepatic failure, metabolic failure, respiratory failure, postoperative complications, overwhelming infection, and other vital system functions), to treat single or multiple vital organ system failure, or to prevent further deterioration of vital functions. Critical care is usually, but not always, provided in a critical care area (e.g., coronary care unit, intensive care unit [ICU], pediatric intensive care unit [PICU], respiratory care unit, or emergency care facility). Payers will reimburse critical care services provided in any location as long as the care provided meets the definition of critical care and supporting documentation is in the patient's record.

Critical care services are reported when a provider directly delivers medical care for a critically ill or critically injured patient. Critical care services can be provided on multiple days even if no changes are made to the treatment rendered to the patient, as long as the patient's condition requires the direct delivery of critical care services by the provider. Time spent away from the patient's bedside that is documented in the patient's record qualifies as critical care services (e.g., time spent with family members or surrogate decision makers to obtain the patient's history or to discuss treatment options). The documented progress note must include any family discussion to a specific treatment issue and *explain why the discussion was necessary on that day.*

 Note:

Critical care services require personal management by the provider. They are life- and organ-supporting interventions that require personal assessment and manipulation by the provider. Withdrawal of or failure to initiate these interventions on an urgent basis would likely result in sudden and clinically significant or life-threatening deterioration in the patient's condition. The service is of such intensity that the provider must devote his or her full attention to the patient and, therefore, cannot render services to any other patient during that same period of time.

Critical care time may be continuous or interrupted; the time spent engaged in critical care services is directly related to the patient's care, whether that time was spent at the immediate bedside or elsewhere on the floor or unit. The following services performed elsewhere by the provider represent critical care:

- Spending time at the nursing station reviewing test results

- Discussing the patient's care with other medical staff

- Documenting critical care services in the patient's record

- Obtaining the patient's medical history and discussing treatment options with family members if the discussion is absolutely necessary for the treatment decision under consideration that day

Critical care services include the following procedures, which are not coded or reported separately:

- Blood gases

- Chest x-rays

- Gastric intubation

- Information data stored in computers (e.g., EKGs, blood pressures, and hematological data)

- Interpretation of cardiac output measurements

- Pulse oximetry

- Temporary transcutaneous pacing

- Vascular access procedures

- Ventilatory management

 Coding Tip:

- Just because a patient is located in a critical care unit does not mean that he or she is receiving critical care; if the patient is stable, report the appropriate subsequent hospital care service code.
- Report services, such as Swan-Ganz catheterization (93503) and intubation (31500), when provided in addition to critical care services codes.

Table 9-4 Critical Care Services: Total Duration of Critical Care and Codes

Total Duration of Critical Care	Codes
Less than 30 minutes	Assign appropriate E/M code(s)
30–74 minutes	99291
75–104 minutes	99291, 99292
105–134 minutes	99291, 99292, 99292
135–164 minutes	99291, 99292, 99292, 99292
165–194 minutes	99291, 99292, 99292, 99292, 99292
194 minutes or longer	99291 and 99292 as appropriate based on total duration of time

When a patient receives critical care services while located in a critical care unit, on a medical or surgical unit, or in the hospital ED, the critical care services codes are reported *in addition to initial hospital care, subsequent hospital care, and/or initial inpatient consultations service codes.* (Add modifier -25 to the E/M level of service code to report it as a separately identified service provided to the patient.) Comprehensive documentation of critical care services provided is crucial, including the length of time the provider spent providing services. Critical care services codes are selected according to the total duration of time the provider spent delivering services to the patient, even if the time spent was not continuous (Table 9-4). To calculate duration of time, the provider must devote his or her full attention to the patient and cannot provide services to any other patient during that same period of time.

 Coding Tip:

- Critical care code 99292 is reported for up to 30 minutes each beyond the first 74 minutes. Throughout CPT, interpret length of time, burn percentage, number of lesions, and so on, as "up to" the number in the code description.

- If critical care services are provided on the same date as a surgical procedure that has a global period and the services are related to the reason for surgery, critical care services are bundled (included) in the reimbursement for the surgical procedure. In this situation, do not report codes for critical care services.

- If critical care services provided are unrelated to the reason for surgery, report codes for services provided (in addition to the surgery code). Attach modifier -24 or -25 to the critical care services code(s). (The surgeon must document that the critical care was unrelated to the surgical procedure performed or was beyond the typical work of pre- or postoperative care associated with the procedure.)

- If the surgeon is also an intensivist, the surgeon should not report codes for critical care services provided to his or her patient during the pre- or postoperative period. Such critical care services are included in the global surgical fee.

- If a surgeon requires the assistance of another intensivist, the intensivist should report codes for critical care services provided. An **intensivist** is a provider who has received extensive training and experience in critical care and who specializes in the care of critically ill patients, usually in an intensive care unit (ICU). Usually an intensivist has completed a fellowship in critical care following completion of a residency in internal medicine, pulmonary medicine, anesthesia, or surgery. Most intensivists are board-certified or board-eligible in critical care medicine.

- Critical care services (99291–99292) are reported for services provided to patients whose age is over 24 months.

- To report critical care services for patients 24 months and younger, refer to codes 99289–99290 for pediatric critical care patient transport or codes 99471–99746 for inpatient neonatal and pediatric critical care services.

EXAMPLE 1: Mary Jones is seen in the hospital ED for trauma as the result of an automobile accident. Level 4 emergency department E/M services are provided, and the ED physician also provides 60 continuous minutes of critical care services. Report the appropriate ED level of service code along with codes 99284-25 and 99291.

EXAMPLE 2: Dr. Smith delivers critical care services to his patient on June 15 from 8–9 AM, 10:30–10:45 AM, and 3:00–3:45 PM. To assign a critical care services code to this case, total the minutes of critical care services directly delivered by the provider. Codes 99291, 99292, and 99292 are reported.

Nursing Facility Services

Nursing facility services are provided at a nursing facility (NF), skilled nursing facility (SNF), intermediate care facility/mentally retarded (ICF/MR), long-term care facility (LTCF), or psychiatric residential treatment facility. NFs provide convalescent, rehabilitative, or long-term care for patients, and a comprehensive assessment must be completed on each patient that meets the resident's medical, nursing, mental, and psychological needs. The patient's functional capacity, identification of potential problems, and nursing plan to enhance (or at least maintain) the patient's physical and psychosocial functions are assessed and documented. The assessments are written when the patient is admitted or readmitted to the facility or when a reassessment is necessary because of a substantial change in the patient's status.

> **Coding Tip:**
>
> No differentiation is made as to patient status (new versus established) when assigning nursing facility services codes.

 Coding Tip:

- Report a code for hospital discharge services (99238–99239), observation care discharge (99217), or observation or inpatient hospital care (same day admission/discharge) (99234–99236) and initial nursing facility care (99304–99306) *if a patient is discharged and admitted to an NF, an SNF, an ICF, or an LTCF on the same date.*

- Do not report codes for ED or office or other outpatient services with initial nursing facility care when provided on the same day for the same patient by the same provider. E/M services provided at sites other than the NF are bundled into initial nursing facility care when performed on the same date as the nursing facility admission by the same provider.

- Do not report codes for initial or subsequent nursing facility care and initial hospital care on the same date for the same patient by the same provider. Payment for initial hospital care services includes all work performed by the provider in all sites of service on that date.

- Report a code for subsequent nursing facility care when the evaluation of the patient's assessment plan is not required and/or when the patient has not had a major or permanent change of health status.

- For discharge from a nursing facility, report code 99315 or 99316. If the patient has expired, report code 99315 or 99316 if the primary service provided by the provider is pronouncement of death, completion of the death summary, and discussion with the deceased patient's family. The provider must personally visit the patient and document pronouncement of death before midnight on the date the patient expired.

 Note:

> Medicare does not allow providers to report codes from the Consultations category. Thus, providers (e.g., specialists) who provide inpatient consultation services to Medicare residents are to report codes from the Initial Nursing Facility Care subcategories. (It is unknown whether other third-party payers will adopt Medicare's ruling.)
>
> When more than one provider (e.g., attending physician and a consultant) delivers inpatient services on the same date of service, the attending physician adds modifier -AI (Principal Physician of Record) to the reported E/M code.

EXAMPLE: The nursing facility assessment code (99318) is reported when the nursing facility patient's attending physician conducts an annual assessment. The attending physician is responsible for reviewing and affirming the patient's plan of care.

Third-party payers usually reimburse E/M services provided in a nursing facility when the purpose of the visit is to fulfill the minimum federal requirement of at least one provider visit every 30 days for the first three months and at least once every 60 days thereafter and/or the service is reasonable and necessary for the diagnosis or treatment of illness or injury or to improve the functioning of a malformed body member and all of the following conditions are fulfilled:

- The service requires the skill of a physician.

- The service is sufficiently well-documented to satisfy the criteria of the CMS 1995 or 1997 *Evaluation and Management Documentation Guidelines* for the level of service and code reported.

- The service is performed by the attending physician, a consulting physician requested by the attending physician, or a named physician requested by the patient or the patient's interested family member or legal guardian.

For an E/M service in an NF to be considered reasonable and necessary, it must be furnished in accordance with accepted standards of medical practice for the diagnosis or treatment of the patient's condition or with the goal of improving the function of a malformed body member, be ordered and furnished by qualified personnel, and meet, but not exceed, the patient's medical need.

EXAMPLE: On October 14, a 97-year-old female patient was transferred from the hospital to the NF in stable condition. The patient's attending physician provided hospital discharge day management services and provided a level 2 initial nursing facility care service. On November 14, the attending physician provided level 1 subsequent nursing facility care. The patient expired on November 30, and the attending physician was not in attendance. Report codes 99305 (10/14) and 99307 (11/14). (A discharge service code is not reported.)

Domiciliary, Rest Home (e.g., Boarding Home), or Custodial Care Services ⚠

Domiciliary, rest home (e.g., boarding home), or custodial care services are provided to residents of a facility that provides room, board, and other personal assistance services, usually on a long-term basis. Medical services (e.g., 24-hour nursing care) are *not* provided to residents.

Domiciliary, rest home (e.g., boarding home), or custodial care services are also provided to residents of adult living facilities, assisted living facilities, custodial care facilities, group homes, and residential substance abuse treatment facilities. *Assisted living facilities* offer nonmedical senior housing that assists residents with tasks such as cooking and laundry and provides reminders to take medications. *Assisted living* is a general term for living arrangements in which some services are available to residents who still live independently within the assisted living complex. In most cases, assisted living residents pay a regular monthly rent and then pay additional fees for the services they require. *Board and care homes* (or *boarding homes*) are group living arrangements designed to meet the needs of people who cannot live independently but who do not require nursing facility services. These homes offer a wider range of services than assisted living facilities, and most provide help with activities of daily living (e.g., eating, walking, bathing,

⚠ Coding Tip:

Make sure you differentiate as to patient status (new versus established) when assigning domiciliary, rest home (e.g., boarding home), or custodial care services codes.

and toileting). In some cases, private long-term care insurance and medical assistance programs help pay for board and care home services.

> **EXAMPLE:** A 92-year-old established female patient who resides in an assisted living facility received E/M level 1 services from her primary care physician on December 4. Report code 99334 for the December 4 E/M service.

Domiciliary, Rest Home (e.g., Assisted Living Facility), or Home Care Plan Oversight Services

Codes 99339–99340 are reported for care plan oversight services provided for patients who reside at home or in a domiciliary, facility, or rest home. These codes are not reported for home health or hospice patients or for nursing facility residents.

Home Services

Home services are provided to individuals and individuals and families in their place of residence to promote, maintain, or restore health and/or to minimize the effects of disability and illness, including terminal illness. Services are provided by nurses, doctors, social workers, therapists, and home health aides. Services are ordered by a provider (instead of treatment in a hospital or SNF) and may result in a shorter acute care hospital or SNF LOS. Home health care programs must be organized, administered, and supervised by a hospital or qualified licensed personnel under the medical direction of a provider. Home services allow patients to recuperate while remaining at home. Since most home health care is temporary and part-time, in addition to providing direct care, the home health staff teaches patients (and their families or others) how to continue needed care (e.g., medication administration, wound care, and therapy).

Coding Tip:

When home services codes are reported (99341–99350), determine the patient status (new versus established).

The home health care provider is responsible for documenting a plan of care and reviewing data. If the written plan of care was not initially prepared by the provider (e.g., prepared by the home health agency), the patient record must include documentation of the provider's contribution to the development of the plan and/or a review of the specific items entered into the plan. It is not sufficient for a home health agency to maintain documentation in its records for the physician. The provider must maintain his or her own records, including periodic summary reports provided by the home health agency. Documentation of all face-to-face E/M home services visits and any telephone communications with the patient or caretakers must be documented in the patient's record. This documentation must indicate an ongoing knowledge of any changes in the patient's condition, drugs, or other needs and the way they are being addressed.

> **EXAMPLE:** A primary care physician provides level 2 home services to a 72-year-old established patient to evaluate the status of the patient's wound healing. The patient has been receiving daily skilled wound care. The physician determines that an additional 10 days of daily skilled wound care is needed, and he documents that order for the home health agency. Report code 99348.

Home Health Agency Face-to-Face Encounters for Medicare Beneficiaries

For Medicare purposes, certifying providers are responsible for documenting all face-to-face encounters with patients in the patient record, and the encounter must occur no more than 90 days prior to the home health start of care date or within 30 days after the start of care. Such face-to-face encounters can be performed using telehealth services at an approved originating site, which is the location of an eligible Medicare beneficiary at the time such services occur. Originating sites must be located in Rural Health Professional Shortage Areas or in counties outside of metropolitan statistical areas, and they can include provider offices, hospitals, critical access hospitals (CAHs), rural health clinics (RHCs), federally qualified health centers (FQHCs), hospital-based or CAH-based renal dialysis centers, skilled nursing facilities (SNFs), and community mental health centers (CMHCs). Nonphysician providers (e.g., certified nurse-midwives, nurse practitioners, physician assistants) can also provide face-to-face E/M home services, but they must inform the certifying physician of any clinical findings exhibited by the patient during the encounter. Then, the provider must document the encounter and countersign the certification. Documentation requirements include:

- Date of face-to-face encounter between the provider and the patient
- Brief narrative describing how the patient's observed clinical condition supports the patient's homebound status and need for skilled services
- Documentation of the encounter (e.g., handwritten, keyboarded, or EHR format) by the certifying provider on the signed/dated certification form or as a signed/dated addendum to the certification

Certifying providers are permitted to verbally communicate the brief narrative describing how the patient's observed clinical condition supports the patient's homebound status and need for skilled services to the home health agency (HHA). The HHA provider documents the encounter on the certification form, and the certifying provider must sign the form.

Prolonged Services

Provider services involving patient contact that are considered beyond the usual service in either an inpatient or outpatient setting may be reported as **prolonged services**. Codes for prolonged services are reported *in addition to* other provider services (e.g., office or other outpatient services and hospital inpatient services). Prolonged services are reported only when the time involved *exceeds* the typical time associated with an E/M service by at least 30 minutes. Prolonged services of less than 30 minutes total duration on a given date are not separately reported because the work involved is included in the total work for the E/M service code. In addition, prolonged services of less than 15 minutes beyond the first hour and less than 15 minutes beyond the final 30 minutes are not reported separately.

Coding Tip:

The patient's record must include documentation that supports the E/M level of service code reported, as well as the duration and content of prolonged services that the physician furnished.

- Time the office staff spends with the patient or time the patient remains unaccompanied in the office is not reported using prolonged services codes.
- Time spent waiting for inpatient test results, changes in the patient's condition, end of therapy, or use of facilities is not reported using prolonged services codes.

Prolonged Service with Direct Patient Contact

Codes 99354–99357 are add-on codes reported for the total duration of time during which the physician or other qualified health care professional (e.g., nurse practitioner, physician assistant) provided services involving direct face-to-face patient contact that is beyond the usual service provided in an inpatient or outpatient setting. The codes are reported in addition to the primary procedure or service code and other procedure and service code(s) (e.g., E/M level 3 service for new patient, psychotherapy). Direct patient contact includes additional non-face-to-face services (e.g., discussing medical management of patient with consulting physician) on the patient's floor or unit in the hospital or nursing facility during the same session. Because the time spent by the provider does not have to be continuous, report code(s) for cumulative time. Codes 99354–99355 are reported when prolonged services are provided in the provider's office or in another outpatient location, and codes 99356–99357 are reported when prolonged services are provided to inpatients.

> **EXAMPLE 1:** A physician provided level 3 office or other outpatient services to an acutely ill established patient who was treated for an asthma attack with intermittent bronchial dilation and subcutaneous epinephrine. The physician provided intermittent direct services over a period of 65 minutes. Report codes 99213 and 99354.

> **EXAMPLE 2:** A physician provided level 3 initial hospital care services to an acutely ill 4-year-old patient who was admitted with respiratory distress, requiring direct contact by the physician. Total duration of time was 115 minutes. Report codes 99223, 99356, and 99357.

Prolonged Service Without Direct Patient Contact

Codes 99358–99359 are add-on codes reported for the total duration of time during which the physician or other qualified health care professional provided services *without direct patient contact* (e.g., extensive record review) on an outpatient or inpatient basis occurring before and/or after direct patient care.

> **EXAMPLE:** A physician provided level 4 office or other outpatient services to an established elderly male patient who was seen for senile dementia, hypertension, diabetes mellitus, and arrhythmia. It becomes clear during the encounter that the patient needs to be placed in an SNF immediately. The patient's wife becomes upset when the physician discusses this recommendation with her, and the physician spends 45 minutes talking with her about what she and the patient can expect regarding SNF care. The physician also calls the local SNF to arrange for patient admission and to coordinate the patient's plan of care; 15 minutes are spent during this phone call. The total duration of time providing non-face-to-face contact was 65 minutes. Report codes 99214 and 99358.

Prolonged Clinical Staff Services with Physician or Other Qualified Health Care Professional Supervision

Codes 99415 and 99416 are used when a prolonged E/M service is provided to a patient in the office or outpatient setting, which involves prolonged clinical staff (e.g., dietician) face-to-face time with the patient beyond the typical face-to-face time for an E/M services.

Code 99415 is reported for up to the first 45 to 60 minutes of prolonged clinical staff service on a given date, even if the time spent by the clinical staff is not continuous on that date. (Code 99416 is *not* reported for 44 minutes or less of clinical staff time.)

Code 99416 is reported for each additional 15 to 30 minutes of prolonged clinical staff service beyond the first hour, and it is an add-on code, which means it must be reported with code 99415. (Code 99416 is *not* reported for 14 minutes or less of clinical staff time.)

 Note:

Codes 99415 and 99416 are *not* reported by physician or other qualified health care professionals, such as nurse practitioners and physician assistants. Instead, codes 99354–99359 are reported by physicians and other qualified health care professionals.

> **EXAMPLE:** An established patient received E/M services for obesity, and code 99213 was reported for the nurse practitioner's provision of services. The patient is participating in a weight loss program, and the dietician provided 80 minutes of face-to-face time counseling services during the same encounter. Code 99415 was reported for the first 60 minutes of the dietician's time, and code 99416 was also reported for the next 20 minutes of the dietician's time. Thus, the CMS-1500 claim reported codes 99213, 99415, and 99416 for this one encounter.

Standby Services

Standby services involve a physician or other qualified health care professional spending a prolonged period of time *without patient contact* waiting for an event to occur that will require the physician's services. Such services must be requested by another provider (e.g., attending physician) and are reported only if the standby time is

30 minutes or longer. However, if a physician who provides standby services performs surgery, the standby services are included in the surgical procedure's global period. Standby services include the following:

- Operative standby: Surgeon is requested to stand by in the event surgery is required, such as for a trauma case.

- Pathology standby: Pathologist is requested to stand by to evaluate a frozen section while the patient is in the operating room.

- Diagnostics standby: Cardiologist is requested to stand by to monitor diagnostics, such as telemetry.

- Obstetrics standby: Surgeon is requested to stand by in the event that a cesarean section is required.

- Pediatrics standby: Pediatrician is requested to stand by in the event that services are needed after the delivery of a high-risk newborn.

Code 99360 is reported in addition to codes 99460 (history and examination of normal newborn) and 99465 (newborn resuscitation), *but not* 99464 (attendance at delivery and initial stabilization of newborn).

EXAMPLE: An obstetric surgeon was called in for consultation by the patient's attending physician (a family practitioner) and provided 30 minutes of standby services due to fetal distress, as noted on the fetal monitor. During standby, the fetal distress resolved, the patient went into active labor, and the patient's attending physician (not the obstetric surgeon) delivered the baby vaginally. The insurance specialist should report 99360 for the obstetric surgeon (because no cesarean section was required).

Case Management Services

According to CPT, "**physician case management** is a process in which a physician or another qualified health care professional is responsible for direct care of a patient, and for coordinating and managing access to, initiating, and/or supervising other health care services needed by the patient." Case management services include anticoagulant management and medical team conferences.

EXAMPLE: The physician participated in a 30-minute interdisciplinary medical team conference of mental health professionals to discuss a 49-year-old patient's plan of care. Report code 99367.

Care Plan Oversight Services

Care plan oversight services cover the provider's time supervising a complex and multidisciplinary care treatment program for a specific patient who is under the care of a home health agency, hospice, or nursing facility. These codes are classified separately from other E/M codes when the provider is involved in direct patient examinations. The billing covers a 30-day period, and only one provider in a group practice may bill for this service in any given 30-day period.

EXAMPLE: The physician reviewed and revised the hospice agency care plan for a 64-year-old female patient with terminal breast cancer. Care plan oversight services required 25 minutes of the physician's time. Report code 99377.

Preventive Medicine Services

Preventive medicine services include routine examinations or risk management counseling for children and adults who exhibit no overt signs or symptoms of a disorder while presenting to the medical office for a preventive medical physical. Such services are also called *wellness visits*. Discussion of risk factors such as diet and exercise counseling, family problems, substance abuse counseling, and injury prevention are an integral part of preventive medicine. Care must be taken to select the proper code according to the age of the patient and the patient's status (new versus established).

Coding Tip:

- Determine the patient's status (new versus established) when assigning preventive medicine services codes.
- Preventive medicine services are not reported when a patient who is receiving treatment for a specific disorder returns to the office for a "recheck of a known problem."

When a significant abnormality or pre-existing condition is treated during the same encounter as a preventive medicine service (e.g., annual physical exam), it is appropriate to report an office or other outpatient services code (99201–99215) in addition to the preventive medicine services code. To report both codes, the preventive medicine services portion of the visit must be complete and comprehensive and the workup for the significant problem must meet the required key components for assignment of codes 99201–99215. Attach modifier -25 to the code reported from 99201–99215, and link the appropriate diagnosis code to justify medical necessity.

EXAMPLE 1: A 24-year-old new patient receives preventive medicine services from a family practitioner. Report code 99385.

EXAMPLE 2: A 45-year-old established patient receives preventive medicine services as part of an annual physical exam; during examination, the physician notices a breast lump. The physician provides level 3 E/M office or other outpatient services to evaluate the breast lump, which include additional examination and discussion of diagnostic testing plans with the patient. Report codes 99396 and 99213-25.

Counseling Risk Factor Reduction and Behavior Change Intervention

Counseling risk factor reduction and behavior change intervention services are reported by physicians or other qualified health care professionals who provide face-to-face services to promote patients' health and prevent illness or injury. They are distinct from other E/M services (e.g., level 3 new patient E/M service), which can be reported separately by adding modifier -25.

- Risk factor reduction services are reported for patients who do not have a specific illness, but for whom such counseling might otherwise be used as part of treatment. Patient issues include family problems, substance use, sexual practices, and so on.

- Behavior change interventions are provided to patients who exhibit a behavior that is often considered an illness (e.g., obesity, substance abuse or misuse, tobacco use or addiction).

EXAMPLE 1: A patient who has been identified as being the adult child of an alcoholic receives preventive medicine individual counseling lasting 60 minutes. Report code 99404.

EXAMPLE 2: A patient who has a two-pack per day history of smoking cigarettes receives individual behavior change intervention counseling as part of his level 3 E/M service for treatment of type 2 diabetes mellitus. Report codes 99213 and 99406-25.

Non-Face-to-Face Services

Non-face-to-face services include telephone services, online medical evaluations, and interprofessional telephone/Internet consultations. Telephone services are provided by a provider to an established patient using the telephone. Online medical evaluations are provided by a provider to an established patient using Internet resources to respond to a patient's online inquiry. Interprofessional telephone/Internet consultations occur when a patient's treating physician requests the opinion and/or treatment advice of a physician with specific specialty expertise (e.g., consultant) to assist in the diagnosis and/or management of the patient's problem without the need for the patient's face-to-face contact with the consultant.

EXAMPLE 1: A physician called an established patient to discuss the results of laboratory testing and to revise the instructions for taking a prescribed medication. The call was 12 minutes in duration. The patient had previously been seen in the office 10 days ago, and is scheduled to return to the office for follow-up in 2 months. Report code 99442.

EXAMPLE 2: A patient emailed her physician to ask whether her prescribed Effexor could be increased from 75 to 150 mg per day, per the recommendation of her marriage counselor. The counselor suggested that 75 mg per day was not a therapeutic dosage for the patient, and her physician agreed and instructed the patient to take two 75-mg capsules daily. The patient had previously been seen by the physician in the office 30 days ago, and she is scheduled to receive office E/M services in 60 days as part of her routine care. Report code 99444.

EXAMPLE 3: A patient received an Internet assessment and management service that was provided by an ENT specialist during 60 minutes of medical consultative discussion and review with the patient's treating physician, including a verbal and written report. Report code 99449.

Special Evaluation and Management Services

According to CPT, **special evaluation and management services** are provided for establishment of baseline information prior to life or disability insurance certificates being issued and for examination of a patient with a work-related or medical disability problem. During special evaluation and management services, the examining provider does *not* assume active management of the patient's health problems.

EXAMPLE 1: A life insurance company's representative examines a 27-year-old male patient in his home to determine whether a base life insurance policy will be issued. Report code 99450.

EXAMPLE 2: A 42-year-old male who had sustained an on-the-job injury about 10 years ago is evaluated by a court-appointed workers' compensation physician to determine whether the patient's current condition is considered work related. Report code 99456.

Newborn Care Services

Newborn care services are provided to newborns in a variety of health care settings (e.g., hospital, birthing center, and home birth).

EXAMPLE 1: A 34-year-old female patient was admitted to the hospital on May 19 for vaginal delivery, which resulted in a healthy 10-pound newborn boy. The pediatrician provided newborn care services on May 19 to complete a history and examination of the infant, and on the morning of May 20, the patient and her infant boy were discharged home. Report codes 99460 and 99462 for the newborn case.

EXAMPLE 2: A 34-year-old female patient delivered a healthy 8-pound newborn girl at home, and the physician in attendance performed a physical examination of the neonate and provided instruction to the parents about initial care. The patient and her daughter are scheduled to follow-up in the office in three days. Report code 99461 for the newborn case.

Delivery/Birthing Room Attendance and Resuscitation Services

Delivery/birthing room attendance and resuscitation services include attendance at delivery, initial stabilization of the newborn, and delivery/birthing room resuscitation. When delivery room attendance services (99464) or delivery room resuscitation services (99465) are required, they are reported in addition to newborn care services codes.

EXAMPLE: Per the request of the patient's delivering physician, a pediatrician was in attendance at the delivery to provide initial stabilization of the newborn. The pediatrician reports code 99464.

Inpatient Neonatal Intensive Care Services and Pediatric and Neonatal Critical Care Services

Inpatient neonatal and pediatric critical care and intensive services are delivered to critically ill neonates and infants by a provider. A **neonate** is a newborn, up to 28 days old. An **infant** is a very young child, up to one year old. The definitions for critical care services codes provided to neonates are the same as those provided to adults. (Refer to the previous section of this chapter for discussion of critical care services definitions and coding guidelines.) Inpatient neonatal and pediatric critical care and intensive services begin on the date of admission, and codes are reported once per day per patient. These codes are reported for each 24-hour period, not according to total duration of critical care; the appropriate code is reported once per day per patient.

Coding Tip:

- When a neonate or an infant is no longer considered critically ill (e.g., attains a body weight that exceeds 5,000 grams), report subsequent hospital care codes (99231–99233) for inpatient services provided.
- For infants with less than 5,000 grams body weight, who are no longer considered critically ill, report continuing intensive care services codes (99478–99480).

Pediatric Critical Care Patient Transport

Pediatric critical care patient transport (99466, 99467) includes the physical attendance and direct face-to-face care delivered by a provider during the interfacility transport of a critically ill or critically injured patient, aged 24 months or younger. **Interfacility transport** is the transfer of a patient from one health care facility to another (e.g., community hospital to children's hospital), and it usually involves use of an ambulance or a helicopter.

> **EXAMPLE:** A 4-month-old infant requires pediatric critical care patient transport services due to respiratory failure. The infant's pediatrician provided critical care services during a 95-minute interfacility transfer from a rural community hospital, where the patient was initially treated to stabilize him, to a specialty children's hospital in a city located 70 miles away. Report codes 99466 and 99467.

Inpatient Neonatal and Pediatric Critical Care

Inpatient neonatal critical care services provided to patients 28 days of age or less are reported with codes 99468 and 99469. Inpatient pediatric critical care services provided to patients 29 days of age through less than six years of age are reported with codes 99471–99476.

Initial and Continuing Intensive Care Services

Continuing intensive care services codes are reported for services provided subsequent to the day of admission to **very low birth weight** (less than 1500 grams) or **low birth weight** (1500–2500 grams) infants who are no longer considered critically ill.

> **EXAMPLE:** A 25-day-old infant weighing 1400 grams received subsequent intensive care services from her pediatrician on days two and three of her inpatient admission. Report 99478, 99478.

Care Management Services

Care management services are provided by providers, other qualified health care professionals, and clinical staff. Services include patient-centered management and support services that are provided to patients who reside at home or in a domiciliary, rest home, or assisted living facility. Chronic care management services and complex chronic care management services are provided to patients. *Chronic care management services* are provided when the patient's medical and/or psychological needs require establishment, implementation, revision, or monitoring of the care plan. Such patients receive services for two or more chronic conditions or episodic health conditions, which are expected to be managed for a period of at least 12 months or until the death of the patient and that place the patient at significant risk of acute exacerbation or decompensation, death, or functional decline. Code 99490 is reported when at least 20 minutes of clinical staff time is spent providing chronic care management activities. *Complex chronic care management services* are provided to patients who require the establishment or substantial revision of a comprehensive care plan and for which medical decision making of moderate or high complexity was provided. Codes 99487-99489 are reported when a minimum of 60 minutes of clinical staff care management services were provided under the direction of a physician or other qualified health care professional.

> **EXAMPLE:** Established patient received level 3 physician office services for treatment of acute bronchitis. During the same encounter, the provider medically managed the patient's brittle type 1 diabetes mellitus and chronic asthma. Patient's comprehensive care plan was revised to provide education to explain that over-the-counter (OTC) medications cannot be combined with prescribed medications for her acute bronchitis because of the risk to stability of her chronic conditions. The patient had numerous questions about not using OTC medications and how they might impact her chronic conditions; the physician provided education and counseling for 30 minutes to ensure that all of the patient's questions were answered and that the patient understood her treatment plan. Report codes 99213 and 99490.

Transitional Care Management Services

Transitional care management services are provided to patients in their community setting (e.g., home, assisted living facility). Services are provided for medical and/or psychosocial problems that require moderate or high complexity medical decision making during transitions in care from an inpatient hospital setting, partial hospital, observation status in a hospital, or skilled nursing facility.

> **EXAMPLE:** A patient was discharged from a nursing facility to her home. The provider coordinated home health care services, educated the primary caregiver about follow-up care, and communicated with the patient via telephone on the day after discharge. Medical decision making was of moderate complexity. Report code 99495 (in addition to an appropriate code for nursing facility E/M services).

Advance Care Planning

Advance care planning includes face-to-face services between a physician or other qualified health care professional and a patient, family member, or surrogate for counseling and discussing advance directives, with or without completing relevant legal forms (e.g., health care proxy).

> **EXAMPLE:** The patient and her daughter met with the patient's primary care physician for 30 minutes of advance care planning, which included an explanation and discussion of the patient's health care proxy. Report code 99497.

Other Evaluation and Management Services

Code 99499 is assigned when the E/M service provided is not described in any other listed E/M codes.

Exercise 9.4 – Evaluation and Management Categories and Subcategories

Instructions: Indicate whether each statemaent is true (T) or false (F).

_____ 1. When a physician provides more than one Evaluation and Management (E/M) service for the same patient on the same day and the patient's problem is the same for each encounter, report an E/M service code for each encounter.

_____ 2. When a physician provides two E/M office or other outpatient services to the same patient on the same day and the patient's problems are different for each E/M service, report multiple E/M codes and attach modifier -51 to the second code.

(continues)

Exercise 9.4 (*continued*)

_____ **3.** When the patient receives office or other outpatient E/M services *and is admitted to the hospital as an inpatient by the same physician*, report an E/M code for the initial hospital care only.

_____ **4.** When the provider performs a comprehensive exam in the office and the patient is later admitted to the hospital *on another day*, void the previously submitted claim on which the office E/M code was reported and report a higher level of service initial hospital care E/M code for the hospital admission.

_____ **5.** The provider does not have to redocument the history, review of symptoms, and past/family/social history documented during a previous encounter *if the provider documents that the previous information was reviewed and then updates the information*.

_____ **6.** Teaching physicians are required to rewrite in entirety the key elements of a resident physician's E/M documentation.

_____ **7.** Code 99211 is commonly thought of as a "nurse visit" because it can be reported only when a nurse provides office E/M services for an established patient.

_____ **8.** Observation services are provided in a hospital outpatient setting, and the patient is considered an outpatient.

_____ **9.** A patient who is referred by a physician for hospital observation services, bypassing the outpatient or emergency department, is considered a "direct admission to observation."

_____ **10.** Initial observation care codes are reported for patients who are admitted and discharged from observation services on the same date.

_____ **11.** Subsequent hospital care includes the review of the patient's record for changes in the patient's condition, the results of diagnostic studies, and/or the reassessment of the patient's condition since the last assessment performed by the physician.

_____ **12.** When a patient is admitted as a hospital inpatient after receiving observation services on the same date, report only an initial hospital care code.

_____ **13.** A hospital discharge day management code is reported with a subsequent hospital care services code on the same date.

_____ **14.** For a code from the Office or Other Outpatient Consultations category to be reported, the consultation request must be initiated by the attending physician or another health care provider and the attending physician must document all consultation requests in the patient's record.

_____ **15.** Initial inpatient consultation codes are reported when consultation services are provided to acute care hospital inpatients only.

_____ **16.** Reporting emergency department (ED) services codes is not restricted to ED physicians employed by the hospital.

_____ **17.** When a physician provides emergency services to a patient in the office, a code from the Emergency Department Services category of E/M should be reported.

_____ **18.** Critical care services require personal management by the physician.

_____ **19.** A neonate is a newborn, up to one year old.

_____ **20.** Do not report a subsequent nursing facility service code and an initial hospital care service code on the same date for the same patient.

_____ **21.** Medical services are usually provided to residents of an assisted living facility by the facility's staff.

_____ **22.** Documentation of all face-to-face E/M home services visits and any telephone communications with the patient or caretakers must be documented in the patient's record.

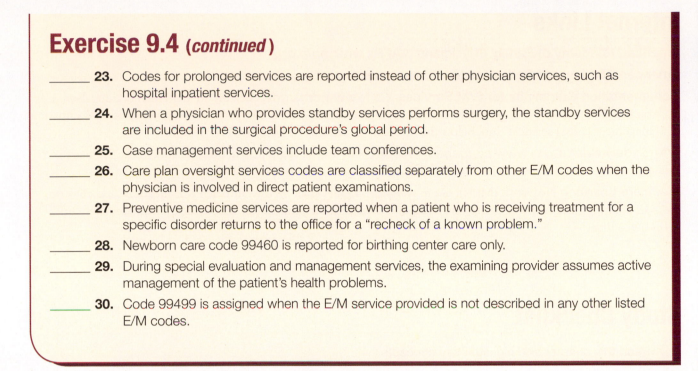

Exercise 9.4 *(continued)*

_____ **23.** Codes for prolonged services are reported instead of other physician services, such as hospital inpatient services.

_____ **24.** When a physician who provides standby services performs surgery, the standby services are included in the surgical procedure's global period.

_____ **25.** Case management services include team conferences.

_____ **26.** Care plan oversight services codes are classified separately from other E/M codes when the physician is involved in direct patient examinations.

_____ **27.** Preventive medicine services are reported when a patient who is receiving treatment for a specific disorder returns to the office for a "recheck of a known problem."

_____ **28.** Newborn care code 99460 is reported for birthing center care only.

_____ **29.** During special evaluation and management services, the examining provider assumes active management of the patient's health problems.

_____ **30.** Code 99499 is assigned when the E/M service provided is not described in any other listed E/M codes.

Summary

The E/M section is organized according to place of service (e.g., office, hospital, home, nursing facility, emergency department, or critical care), type of service (e.g., new or initial encounter, follow-up or subsequent encounter, or consultation), and miscellaneous services (e.g., prolonged physician service or care plan oversight service). The Evaluation and Management (E/M) section guidelines are located at the beginning of the section and include the following contents: classification of E/M services, definitions of commonly used terms, unlisted service, special report, clinical examples, and instructions for selecting a level of E/M service.

E/M categories and subcategories contain codes that are classified according to level of services for reporting to third-party payers. Although the last number of some E/M codes represents the level of service (e.g., code 99213 is a level 3 E/M service), the levels within categories and subcategories are not interchangeable. Levels of E/M services include conferences with or about patients, evaluations, examinations, preventive adult and pediatric health supervision, treatments, and other medical services (e.g., determining the need for and/or location of appropriate care, such as hospice care for a terminally ill patient). The E/M section (99201–99499) contains notes unique to each category and subcategory. *Remember to review notes before assigning an E/M code.*

 Note:

Medicare no longer allows providers to report codes from the Consultations category. Thus, providers (e.g., specialists) who deliver consultation services to office patients, hospital outpatients, hospital inpatients, or nursing facility residents are to report codes from the Office or Other Outpatient Services category, Initial Hospital Care subcategory, or Initial Nursing Facility Care subcategory of CPT. (It is unknown whether other third-party payers will adopt Medicare's ruling.) When more than one provider (e.g., attending physician and a consultant) delivers services to a Medicare inpatient or nursing facility resident on the same date of service, the attending physician adds modifier -AI (Principal Physician of Record) to the reported E/M code.

Internet Links

American Academy of Family Physicians (AAFP): *www.aafp.org*

American Academy of Pediatrics (AAP): *www.aap.org*

Documentation Guidelines for E/M Services: Go to *www.cms.gov*, click on the Outreach & Education link, click on the "Get training" link below the Learn heading, and click on the "Documentation guidelines for Evaluation & Management (E/M) services" link below the Medicare Learning Network® (MLN) heading.

E/M CodeBuilder: Go to *www.cengagebrain.com*, and use the login instructions located in the Preface to locate an online version of the E/M CodeBuilder on the Student Companion Web Site.

Medicare Learning Network (MLN): Go to *www.cms.gov*, click on the Outreach & Education link, click on the "Get training" link below the Learn heading, and then click on a link below the Medicare Learning Network® (MLN) heading.

Study Checklist

- ❏ Read this chapter and highlight key concepts.
- ❏ Create an index card for each key term.
- ❏ Access the chapter Internet links to learn more about concepts.
- ❏ Complete the chapter exercises and review, verifying answers with your instructor.
- ❏ Complete Workbook chapter, verifying answers with your instructor.
- ❏ Go to *www.cengagebrain.com* to access the Student Companion Web Site. Login instructions are located in the Preface.
- ❏ Form a study group with classmates to discuss chapter concepts in preparation for an exam.

Review

Multiple Choice

Instructions: Circle the most appropriate response.

1. The E/M level of service reflects the:
   a. amount of work involved in providing health care to a patient.
   b. kind of health care services provided to a patient.
   c. physical location where health care is provided to a patient.
   d. type of condition for which the patient is being treated.

2. Concurrent care is the provision of similar services to:
   a. different patients by the same provider on the same day.
   b. the same patient by more than one provider on the same day.
   c. the same patient by the same provider on different days.
   d. the same patient by the same provider on the same day.

3. Dr. Benjamin practiced at Hopewell Medical Center until 2002, when he began to practice with Dr. Evans at the Lakewood Clinic. Which would be considered a new patient at Lakewood Clinic?

   a. Debra injured her back two years ago and has been under continuous treatment at another facility. She had her records transferred to Lakewood Clinic and is going to be seen by Dr. Evans for continuing treatment of her chronic condition.

   b. Henrique, who had last seen Dr. Benjamin at Hopewell Medical Center in April 2001, is treated by Dr. Benjamin at the Lakewood Clinic in March 2004.

   c. Martha had a physical performed on June 1, 2003, by Dr. Benjamin and is seen by Dr. Evans on September 30, 2005, for a sinus condition.

   d. Sheryl was treated last month by Dr. Evans. This week she needs to be seen again, but Lakewood Clinic is closed for the holiday. She is seen by an on-call physician who is covering for Dr. Evans.

4. *Problem focused*, *expanded problem focused*, *detailed*, and *comprehensive* are terms used to describe which components of an E/M level of service code?

   a. Extent of exam
   b. Extent of history
   c. Extent of history and extent of exam
   d. Review of systems

5. Which contributory component would be considered when determining the number of diagnoses or management options for medical decision-making complexity?

   a. Coordination of care
   b. Counseling
   c. Nature of the presenting problem
   d. Time

6. There are seven components to a level of E/M service code description. Which are considered key components when selecting the E/M code?

   a. Counseling, coordination of care, and nature of presenting problem
   b. History, exam, and medical decision making
   c. History, exam, and time
   d. Medical decision making, time, and nature of presenting problem

7. Time is a contributing factor in E/M code selection for which scenario?

   a. A patient had an encounter solely for the purpose of discussing treatment options for a recently diagnosed condition.

   b. After Dr. Harris diagnosed Ellen with an ear infection, he explained the prognosis and wrote a prescription for an antibiotic.

   c. Dr. Bender showed frightened little Jimmy the x-ray of his broken arm and explained why a cast would help him get better.

   d. Dr. Knolles spent 10 minutes reviewing information on drugs to find one that the patient could tolerate.

8. Documentation of the review of systems is used to establish:

   a. complexity of medical decision making.
   b. extent of examination performed.
   c. extent of history obtained.
   d. presence of contributing factors.

9. A physician discussed the results of diagnostic testing with his patient. This portion of the encounter is considered:

   a. coordination of care.
   b. counseling.
   c. examination.
   d. history of present illness.

10. Which is reported using a non-face-to-face service code?

    a. A patient came into the emergency department with severe pain in the lower back. She told the physician that she had recently had an MRI at that facility but hadn't received the results yet. The physician looked up the test results and verified that a displaced disc was causing the pain.

b.   A patient involved in a motor vehicle accident came to the emergency department with complaints of a sore neck and blurry vision. The patient was diagnosed with whiplash. The attending physician requested an ophthalmology consultation during the encounter, but no physicians were available so he scheduled the consultation for the following day. He instructed the patient to follow up with her primary care physician if symptoms persisted.

c.   A physician called the patient at home to discuss the results of her lab tests. After reviewing the reports, he believed that further testing was necessary and advised her to make an appointment as soon as possible.

d.   During an encounter, a physician recommended physical therapy to a patient with rheumatoid arthritis. She expressed concern over which facility she should contact and how she would get there. Before she left, the physician provided her with names and numbers of facilities she could contact for treatment, as well as agencies that would assist in her transportation needs.

11. A patient is admitted with head injury. On the initial visit, the physician observes that the patient is unconscious and is bleeding from the right ear. The physician spends 70 minutes treating the patient and coordinating care, during which time a comprehensive history and exam are obtained. Which E/M code is reported?

    a. 99221   b. 99222   c. 99223   d. 99285

12. A six-year-old child is seen by her family physician for her annual check-up and immunizations. Her last encounter was one year ago. Which E/M code is reported?

    a. 99211   b. 99251   c. 99383   d. 99393

13. A patient with severe chest pain is admitted for observation. A comprehensive history and examination are performed. Medical decision making is moderate. The patient is released the same day. Which E/M code is reported?

    a. 99202   b. 99219   c. 99222   d. 99235

14. A 38-year-old patient with neck stiffness and pain radiating down the right arm presents to the neurosurgeon for an office consultation. A detailed history and exam are obtained during the 40-minute encounter. Which E/M code is reported?

    a. 99204   b. 99221   c. 99243   d. 99244

15. A patient was seen in the emergency department after she burned her hand with scalding water. An expanded problem focused history and exam were performed. Medical decision making was of low complexity. Which E/M code is reported?

    a. 99213   b. 99232   c. 99282   d. 99283

16. A physician performs a scheduled follow-up visit to a 65-year-old patient in a nursing facility who is recovering from pneumonia. The patient has responded well to the treatment, and no complications are noted. Which E/M code is reported?

    a. 99307   b. 99308   c. 99324   d. 99341

17. A new patient presents to the physician's office with complaints of severe earache, jaw pain, and facial swelling. The physician obtains a detailed history of the chief complaint, an extended review of systems, and a problem pertinent past/family/social history and performs a detailed exam. Medical decision making is of low complexity. Which E/M code is reported?

    a. 99203   b. 99204   c. 99205   d. 99214

18. An established patient has a four-month office check-up for medical management of high triglyceride levels. A brief history of present illness and a problem pertinent review of systems are obtained. The

physician counsels the patient on diet and exercise and advises the patient to return again in four months. Which E/M code is reported?

    a. 99202   b. 99213   c. 99214   d. 99232

19. A subsequent hospital visit is required for a 58-year-old patient admitted with an esophageal neoplasm who has begun to spit up blood. Metastasis is suspected. Which E/M code is reported?

    a. 99233   b. 99236   c. 99255   d. 99285

20. An inpatient follow-up consultation is performed for a 70-year-old Medicare patient who is experiencing foot drop after leg surgery. The foot has regained normal positioning. Which E/M code is reported?

    a. 99221   b. 99231   c. 99241   d. 99251

Coding Practice

Instructions: Review each case and assign CPT code(s) and appropriate modifier(s).

1. A 4-year-old female established patient received Evaluation and Management services, which included a problem focused history, an expanded problem focused exam, and medical decision making (MDM) of a low level. The patient is diagnosed with influenza.

_____

2. A 16-year-old outpatient who is a new patient to the office complains of severe facial acne. The history and physical examination are expanded problem focused. The physician must consider related organ systems in addition to the integumentary system in order to treat the condition. With minimal number of diagnoses to consider and the minimal amount of data to review, the physician's decision making is straightforward with regard to the treatment of this patient.

_____

3. A patient was in an automobile accident and is complaining of a minor headache and no other apparent injuries. History gathered from bystanders states that the patient was not wearing a seat belt and hit his head on the windshield. A 15-minute loss of consciousness was noted. The patient was then admitted for 24-hour observation to rule out head injury. A comprehensive history and exam are performed by the physician. The MDM is of moderate complexity.

_____

4. A 55-year-old female came in with the complaint of severe abdominal pain. The patient was admitted on 05/07 to observation due to the severity and location of her pain. The admitting physician performed a comprehensive history and a detailed examination and documented medical decision making of a moderate complexity given the amount of possible diagnoses, including appendicitis, gastric ulcer, cholelithiasis, and pyelonephritis. Various diagnostic tests were ordered and done, including barium enema, upper gastrointestinal endoscopy, and KUB (kidneys, ureters, bladder) x-ray. No disease or disorder was found, and the patient was discharged from observation on 05/08. The patient reported a decrease in her pain after 30 hours of IV analgesics and antispasmodics. The physician documented that the patient should follow up with her primary care physician in two days or return to the hospital if the pain worsens. The physician also documented a final detailed examination of the patient and dictated a discharge summary report.

_____

5. A 50-year-old female patient was admitted to the hospital on 10/10 with a diagnosis of pneumonia due to _Staphylococcus aureus_, at which time she received level 2 E/M services from her attending physician. On 10/11 and 10/12, the patient received level 2 E/M services. On 10/13, the patient was discharged from the hospital in improved condition to follow up with the physician at home; the physician spent 30 minutes performing discharge day management functions.

_____

6. An established patient is seen in the hospital on day two of his hospital stay. The patient had been admitted through the emergency department with status asthmaticus and had been undergoing extensive respiratory therapy over the past 24 to 30 hours. The physician performs a detailed interval history and a detailed physical exam. The possibility of pneumonia complicating the asthma must be considered. The patient's respiratory condition is still unstable. The MDM complexity was high.

_____

7. A 52-year-old patient was sent to a surgeon for an office consultation concerning hemorrhoids. An expanded problem focused history and examination were performed. The consultant recommended treating with medication after a straightforward MDM.

_____

8. A 13-year-old male was admitted yesterday for a tympanotomy. Postsurgically, the child developed fever and seizures of unknown origin. A pediatric consultation was requested. This was done on the second hospital admission day and 24 hours after surgery. The history of present illness (HPI) was extended with a complete review of systems (ROS). A complete past/family/social history (PFSH) was elicited from the mother as part of a comprehensive history. A comprehensive examination was conducted on all body areas and organ systems. The MDM complexity was high.

_____

9. A patient in the emergency department (ED) has a temperature of 103°F and is in acute respiratory distress. Symptoms include shortness of breath, chest pain, and gasping. The physician is unable to obtain a history or perform a comprehensive physical examination because the patient's condition is critical. The MDM complexity is high.

_____

10. With two-way communication, the physician directs the emergency medical technicians (EMTs) in an ambulance en route to the emergency department with a patient in apparent cardiac arrest.

_____

11. A patient presents with the complaint of hematemesis. The patient also has a rapid pulse rate and low blood pressure. In the ED, critical care is provided by the ED attending to raise the patient's blood pressure and decrease blood loss. This is done for 70 minutes before the patient is transferred to the surgical suite for an endoscopic procedure to evaluate his esophagus. The ED physician also documents a detailed examination and MDM of high complexity. Due to the patient's medical condition, he is unable to provide any history; no family is present to provide information.

_____

12. A physician is called to the intensive care unit to provide care for a patient who received second- and third-degree burns over 50 percent of his body due to a chemical fire. The patient is in respiratory distress and is suffering from severe dehydration. The physician provides support for two hours. Later that day, the physician returns and provides an additional hour of critical care support to the patient.

_____

13. A 72-year-old patient suffered a cerebral vascular accident (CVA). Today the patient is admitted to a skilled nursing facility (SNF) for rehab and medical care. The patient was just discharged from an acute care facility. The SNF medical director documents a comprehensive history, including the patient's chief complaint of paralysis and weakness, an extended HPI, and a complete ROS. A detailed exam of the patient's cardiovascular, respiratory, musculoskeletal, neurological, and genitourinary systems is documented. The physician orders a multidisciplinary rehabilitation care plan for the patient and the continued treatment of the patient's other medical conditions, including hypertension and diabetes. The MDM complexity is high.

_____

14. Subsequent follow-up care is provided for a comatose patient transferred to a long-term care center from the hospital two days ago. The resident shows no signs of consciousness on examination but appears to have developed a minor upper respiratory tract infection with a fever and rales heard on auscultation. The physician performs an expanded problem focused history and a problem focused interval examination with respiratory status and status of related organ systems such as cardiovascular. The physician is concerned that the respiratory infection could progress to pneumonia and orders the appropriate treatment. The MDM complexity is moderate.

_____

15. A new patient diagnosed with mild intellectual disabilities and self-abuse is sent to a custodial care facility for admission. The patient's family is no longer able to care for the patient at home. The care facility physician documents a problem focused history with a problem focused exam. The medical decision making documented was straightforward.

_____

16. A 21-year-old patient with a recent history of drug abuse is admitted to a rehab center for treatment. In the patient's second week of treatment, she complains of back pain and is seen by the same physician who evaluated her medically upon admission. At this time, the physician documents a problem focused interval history, an expanded problem focused examination, and MDM of moderate complexity.

_____

17. A 64-year-old female patient has diabetes and has been having problems adjusting her insulin doses. She has had an onset of dizziness and sensitivity to light. Her primary care physician, who has treated her for this condition during the past four years, makes a home visit today. At this visit, the physician gathers a brief HPI and a problem pertinent ROS during the problem focused history. The physical exam focuses on the body systems currently affected by the diabetes. The patient's condition is moderately severe and the MDM complexity is of a moderate level.

_____

18. A 15-year-old new patient has cystic fibrosis and is having problems with her Pulmozyme dosage. This medication is used to thin the mucus that clogs her lungs. The patient is having moderate throat pain and slight tightness in her chest. The physician makes a home visit to gather HPI and ROS and pertinent past personal medical information for a detailed history. The detailed exam focuses on the body systems currently affected by the cystic fibrosis and related organ systems: ears, nose, throat, mouth, respiratory, gastrointestinal, and cardiovascular. The MDM complexity is of a moderate level.

_____

19. An established patient with a history of asthma presents in an office visit with acute bronchospasm and moderate respiratory distress. The physician conducts a problem focused history followed by a detailed examination, which shows a respiratory rate of 30. Office treatment is initiated: intermittent bronchial dilation and subcutaneous epinephrine. This service requires the physician to have intermittent direct contact with the patient over a two-hour period. The MDM complexity is moderate.

_____

20. A patient was in the delivery room ready to give birth. When the physician had the patient start pushing, possible complications for the infant were noted and the hospital pediatric neonatal specialist was notified of a possible need for her evaluation of this newborn. The pediatric specialist was notified at 9:20 AM. At 10 AM, she was informed via phone call from the OB/GYN that the infant had normal Apgar scores of 9 and 9.

_____

21. A 72-year-old patient with a history of breast cancer has a suspicious mass in her uterus. A biopsy was done. The determination was that the patient had a carcinoma *in situ* of the uterus. The physician who conducted the surgery called a face-to-face meeting with his fellow surgeons and discussed the case and the patient's outcome for 30 minutes.

   _____

22. A 14-year-old boy twisted his ankle while playing soccer. He received level 3 E/M services from his physician the next morning for which code 99213 was reported on the CMS-1500 claim generated immediately after the visit. The physician ordered an x-ray of the ankle, and the child left the office after the x-ray but did not see the physician. Later that afternoon the patient and his mother came into the office and met with the physician, an orthopedic surgeon, and a rehabilitation therapist. Medical discussion was 45 minutes in duration.

   _____

23. A 75-year-old patient was just diagnosed with type 1 diabetes. This means that the patient will have to give himself insulin shots. The physician supervised the coordination of home health care, which required 30 minutes of his time.

   _____

24. A 50-year-old female has brain cancer, and the physician supervised the coordination of hospice services, which required 45 minutes of his time.

   _____

25. A 13-year-old new patient presents for a well-check examination. The patient does not report any medical complaints.

   _____

26. A 75-year-old established patient presents for his annual physical examination. The patient's chronic conditions are well controlled with diet and exercise.

   _____

27. A physician called an established patient to inform her that the results of a chest x-ray were negative. The call was 5 minutes in duration. The patient had previously been seen in the office 10 days ago.

   _____

28. A patient emailed his physician to ask whether taking 500 mg of cinnamon tablets daily would be acceptable, given the prescribed medications he takes. The physician replied, approving his taking 500 mg of cinnamon tablets daily. The patient had previously been seen by the physician in the office 15 days ago, and he is scheduled to receive office E/M services in 60 days as part of his routine care.

   _____

29. A 58-year-old man was seen by his private physician for an examination as part of his claim for long-term medical disability. The patient has chronic obstructive lung disease with severe emphysema and has been unable to work during the past year. The physician documents a comprehensive medical history and a detailed examination. The physician reviews the patient's current medical treatment plan and recommends that it continue. All of the necessary documentation required by the insurance company is completed, including the physician's opinion that the patient would be unable to work in the future, as his pulmonary function is markedly impaired in spite of continual respiratory and pharmacologic therapy.

   _____

30. A full-term healthy newborn girl received initial and subsequent hospital care services on July 7 and July 8, respectively.

   _____

CPT Anesthesia

Chapter Outline

Anesthesia Terminology

Overview of Anesthesia Section

Anesthesia Section Guidelines

Anesthesia Subsections

Chapter Objectives

At the conclusion of this chapter, the student should be able to:

- Define key terms.
- Explain the organization, format, and content of the CPT Anesthesia section.
- Interpret CPT Anesthesia section guidelines, coding notes, and modifiers.
- Assign CPT evaluation and management service codes.
- Add CPT and/or HCPCS level II modifiers to codes, as appropriate.
- Calculate anesthesia fees.

Key Terms

airway management

A-line

analgesia

analgesic

anesthesia

anesthesia conversion factor

anesthesia time unit

anesthesiologist

anesthetic

arteriography

base unit value

Bier block

cannula

capnography

caudal anesthesia

central nervous system (CNS)

central venous access device (CVAD)

central venous pressure catheter

central venous pressure (CVP) line

certified registered nurse anesthetist (CRNA)

cleft lip

concurrent medically directed anesthesia procedure

contrast medium

dura mater

electroconvulsive therapy (ECT)

electromyogram (EMG)

emergency condition

endotracheal tube (ET)

epidural anesthesia

external catheter

extracorporeal shock wave lithotripsy (ESWL)

extradural procedure

field block

fluid management

general anesthesia

heparin

hypovolemia

implanted port

infiltration anesthesia

internal catheter

interventional therapeutic radiological procedure

intra-arterial cannula

intra-arterial catheter

intra-arterial line	monitored anesthesia care (MAC)	plexus anesthesia	radiopaque
intracranial	nerve plexus	postanesthesia evaluation	regional anesthesia
intravenous regional anesthesia	nontunneled catheter	postoperative pain management	saddle block anesthesia
lesion	one lung ventilation (OLV)	preanesthesia evaluation	sedation
lithotripter	organ harvest	pulmonary wedge pressure	shock therapy
local anesthesia	panniculectomy	pulse oximetry	spinal anesthesia
lumbar puncture (LP)	panniculus adiposus	pump oxygenator	spinal tap
lumen	pannus	qualifying circumstance	surface anesthesia
mass spectrometry	peripheral nerve block		Swan-Ganz catheter
modifying unit	physical status modifier		tunneled catheter
			urethrocystoscopy

Introduction

The Anesthesia section is located after the Evaluation and Management section in the CPT coding manual, and the codes range from 00100 to 01999. Anesthesia codes are reported for services related to the administration of anesthesia (including general and regional), the supplementation of local anesthesia, and other supportive anesthesia services. Anesthesia subsections are organized according to anatomical site, except the last four subsections, which are listed as types of procedure. Any qualified health care provider who administers analgesic or anesthetic agents is permitted to report codes from the Anesthesia section of CPT. Providers include anesthesiologists, certified registered nurse anesthetists (CRNAs), surgeons, and other physicians. However, when the same physician (e.g., surgeon) performs the procedure and administers anesthesia, add modifier -47 to the CPT Surgery section code (and do not report a separate code from the Anesthesia section).

An **anesthesiologist** is a physician who, after medical school, completes a one-year internship and three-year residency in anesthesia. A **certified registered nurse anesthetist (CRNA)** is a licensed registered nurse (RN) who has earned a bachelor's degree in science or nursing, has at least one year of acute care nursing experience (e.g., intensive care, coronary care, or emergency/trauma), has completed a 24- to 36-month nurse anesthesia program leading to a master's degree, and has passed the national certification exam. (Doctorate programs are also available.)

Anesthesia Terminology

Patients who undergo surgical or other invasive procedures (e.g., radiological procedure) require anesthesia services so the procedure can be performed. **Anesthesia** is the process of inducing a loss of sensitivity to pain in all or part of the body, resulting from the administration of an **anesthetic** (drug or agent that causes a loss of feeling, awareness, and/or consciousness). An **analgesic** is a drug that reduces pain, such as aspirin, acetaminophen, and ibuprofen; for surgery, other substances (e.g., morphine) are used to cause **analgesia** (loss of pain sensation without loss of consciousness).

Types of Anesthesia

The following types of anesthesia are used in surgical practice:

- General anesthesia
- Local anesthesia
- Regional anesthesia

General anesthesia is used for extensive surgeries and involves the administration of anesthetic agents that are inhaled (e.g., sevoflurane combined with nitrous oxide) or administered intravenously (e.g., propofol). They act as hypnotics, muscle relaxants, and painkillers and serve to block any memory of the surgery. General anesthesia renders a patient unconscious, which means the brain doesn't perceive pain signals. To determine the general anesthetic agents to administer, the patient's age and health must be considered, along with the type of surgery to be performed.

Local anesthesia is appropriate for minor surgeries (e.g., dental work, skin biopsy, and suture of a laceration) and involves applying a topical agent (e.g., lidocaine) on the body's surface or injecting a local anesthetic agent (e.g., procaine) for the purpose of numbing a small part of the body. As a result, pain signals are blocked and the patient remains alert. Local anesthesia administration techniques include:

- **Surface anesthesia**: Topical application of local anesthetic cream, solution, or spray to skin or mucous membranes

- **Infiltration anesthesia**: Topical injection of local anesthetic into tissue

- **Field block**: Subcutaneous injection of local anesthetic in area bordering the field to be anesthetized

- **Peripheral nerve blocks**: Injection of local anesthetic in the vicinity of a peripheral nerve to anesthetize that nerve's area of innervation

- **Plexus anesthesia**: Injection of local anesthetic in the vicinity of a **nerve plexus**, which is a network of intersecting nerves (Figure 10-1)

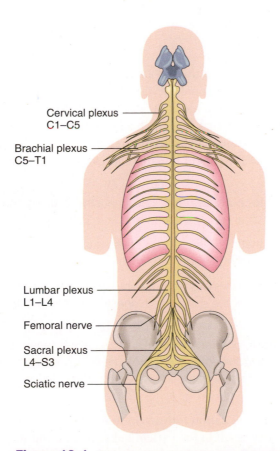

Cervical plexus
C1–C5

Brachial plexus
C5–T1

Lumbar plexus
L1–L4

Femoral nerve

Sacral plexus
L4–S3

Sciatic nerve

Figure 10-1 Spinal cord and nerves. (Most spinal nerves are named for the corresponding vertebrae)

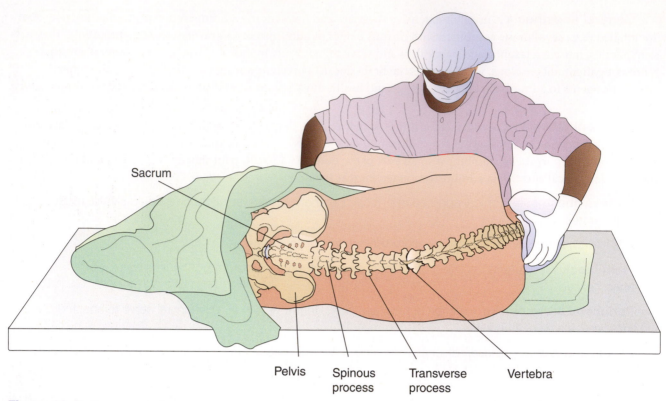

Figure 10-2 Correct position for performing a spinal block or inserting an epidural catheter in the lumbar region

Regional anesthesia is appropriate when there is a need to block pain from a large part of the body (e.g., lower extremity and pelvic surgeries). Regional anesthetic agents are injected into or near the spinal fluid and around a nerve or network of nerves to block the nerve supply to a specific part of the body (Figure 10-2). The patient cannot feel pain in that area when a procedure is performed, and the patient remains awake (or sedated). Intravenous (IV) sedation may be administered prior to regional anesthesia to relax the patient and make him or her drowsy, but the patient remains conscious. Regional anesthesia includes the following:

- **Caudal anesthesia**, or **saddle block anesthesia**: Local anesthetic is injected into the caudal canal, which is the sacral portion of the spinal canal; anesthetized area is the umbilicus, below the navel.

- **Epidural anesthesia**: Local anesthetic is injected into the epidural space where it acts primarily on spinal nerve roots; anesthetized area includes the abdomen, chest, and large regions of the body.

- **Spinal anesthesia**: Local anesthetic is injected into cerebrospinal fluid (CSF) at the lumbar spine, where it acts on spinal nerve roots and part of the spinal cord; anesthetized area extends from the legs to the abdomen or chest.

- **Intravenous regional anesthesia**, or **Bier block**: An IV cannula is inserted into the extremity on which the procedure is to be performed and a tourniquet is applied to interrupt blood circulation; then a large volume of local anesthetic is injected into a peripheral vein, anesthetizing the extremity.

Sedation is the administration of medication into a vein to relieve pain and anxiety; it makes the patient feel calm. Such medications may result in the patient not remembering surgical events (even though the patient remains awake). Sedation medications are often administered in addition to other forms of anesthesia.

Exercise 10.1 – Anesthesia Terminology

Instructions: Match the term with its definition.

_____ 1. Administration of anesthetic agents that are inhaled

_____ 2. Administration of medication to relieve pain/anxiety

_____ 3. Application of a topical agent on the body's surface

_____ 4. Injected into or near the spinal fluid to block the nerve supply to a specific part of the body

_____ 5. Intravenous regional anesthesia

a. Bier block
b. General anesthesia
c. Local anesthesia
d. Regional anesthesia
e. Sedation

Instructions: Match the term with its definition.

_____ 6. Injection of local anesthetic in the vicinity of a network of intersecting nerves

_____ 7. Injection of local anesthetic in the vicinity of a peripheral nerve to anesthetize area of innervation

_____ 8. Subcutaneous injection of local anesthetic in area bordering the field to be anesthetized

_____ 9. Topical application of local anesthetic cream to skin

_____ 10. Topical injection of local anesthetic into tissue

a. Field block
b. Infiltration anesthesia
c. Peripheral nerve block
d. Plexus anesthesia
e. Surface anesthesia

Overview of Anesthesia Section ⚠

The Anesthesia section includes 15 anatomical sites, followed by four additional subsections for radiological procedures, burn excisions or debridement, obstetrics, and other procedures. Codes are organized according to type of procedure (open, closed, endoscopic, and so on), and each anesthesia code relates to corresponding surgical procedures. Because a one-to-one correspondence for anesthesia to surgery codes does not exist, one anesthesia code is often reported for many different surgical procedures that share similar anesthesia requirements. The Anesthesia section guidelines also include four codes (99100–99140) that are located in the Medicine section, which are used to report qualifying circumstances for anesthesia.

⚠ **Coding Tip:**

Notes located beneath headings and/or subheadings apply to all codes in the headings or subheadings. Parenthetical notes that are located below a specific code apply to that code only unless the note indicates otherwise.

Anesthesia services include the preparation and monitoring of the patient, and the services included (bundled) in the anesthesia code reported include the following:

- Draping, positioning, prepping, and transporting the patient
- Inserting nasogastric or orogastric tubes
- Inserting peripheral IV lines for fluid and medication administration
- Interpreting laboratory results (e.g., arterial blood gases, hematology, and blood chemistries)

- Interpreting monitored functions (e.g., blood pressure, brain stem evoked response (BSER), capnography, central nervous system (CNS) pressure, Doppler flow, electroencephalogram, heart rate, oximetry, respirations, and temperature)

- Placing airway tubes (e.g., endotracheal tube [ET] and orotracheal tube), including laryngoscopy (direct or endoscopic) for airway management

- Positioning external devices for capnography, cardiac monitoring, CNS evoked responses, Doppler flow, pulse oximetry, and temperature

- Stimulating nerves to determine level of paralysis or localization of nerve(s)

When the above services are provided to surgical patients, they are included as part of the anesthesia service. They are not coded and reported or reimbursed in addition to the anesthesia code. The previously listed services are typically provided on the same date as the surgery performed.

> **EXAMPLE:** A patient with sepsis underwent a sternal debridement surgical procedure for which the CRNA provided general anesthesia services. The procedure ended at 2 PM, and by noon the next day, anesthesia services were concluded. Later that night at 10 PM, the CRNA inserted an ET to establish an airway for the patient. Report codes 00550-P3-QZ and 31500. 🖉
>
> - Go to the CPT index and locate main term *Anesthesia* and subterm *Sternum* to locate code 00550. Refer to the Anesthesia section guidelines to assign physical status modifier -P3. (Sepsis is considered a severe systemic disease.)
>
> - Go to the CPT index and locate main term *Endotracheal Tube* and subterm *Intubation* to locate code 31500.

Note:

Modifier -59 is added to code 31500 if allowed as a bundled service under the NCCI. This alerts the third-party payer that insertion of the ET was a distinct procedural service.

⚠️ **Coding Tip:**

When an electromyogram (EMG) is performed to assess level of paralysis or localization of nerve(s), and results are documented in the patient's record, report the EMG code separately. An **electromyogram (EMG)** is a graphic tracing of a muscle's electrical activity at rest or during contraction, and it is used to diagnose nerve dysfunction and muscle disorders.

Monitored Anesthesia Care (MAC)

Monitored anesthesia care (MAC) is the administration of varying amounts of local, regional, and certain mind-altering drugs by an anesthesiologist or a CRNA during a patient's diagnostic or therapeutic procedure. CMS defines MAC as "the intraoperative monitoring of the surgical patient's vital physiological signs, in anticipation of the patient's need for general anesthesia or development of adverse physiological patient reaction to the surgery."

During MAC, the anesthesiologist or CRNA administers anesthetic medication through an IV line, monitors the patient's comfort level, and increases or decreases medication as needed (hence the name *monitored anesthesia care*). MAC includes a preoperative visit, intraoperative care, and postoperative anesthesia management. The anesthesiologist or CRNA provides the following services:

- Monitors vital signs and maintains patient's airway and continual evaluation of vital functions

- Diagnoses and treats clinical problems that occur during the procedure

- Administers analgesics, anesthetic agents, hypnotics, sedatives, or other medications as necessary to ensure patient safety and comfort

- Provides other medical services as needed for the safe completion of the procedure

Coding Tip:

Because monitored anesthesia care is a physician service provided to an individual patient and is based on medical necessity, reimbursement may be the same amount as for full general anesthesia services if all required services are properly documented. Report the appropriate anesthesia code and add an appropriate physical status modifier along with modifier -QS (monitored anesthesia care). In addition, report a qualifying circumstances code (from the Medicine section) when indicated. When appropriate, add one or more of the HCPCS level II anesthesia modifiers (discussed in the next section of this chapter) to the anesthesia code. Make sure you report the appropriate ICD-10-CM code(s) that support(s) medical necessity for MAC and identify the reason for the surgical procedure.

Note:

Monitored anesthesia care is not the same as moderate (conscious) sedation, which is reported with codes from the CPT Medicine section. Refer to Chapters 11 and 18 for information about moderate (conscious) sedation.

Exercise 10.2 – Overview of Anesthesia Section

Instructions: Enter a response for each item.

1. Anesthesia services include the preparation and _____ of the patient, along with other services.

2. When services are provided to surgical patients that are not included as part of the anesthesia service code, they are reported separately. Modifier _____ is added to each code to indicate that the service provided was independent of the anesthesia service.

3. When an electromyogram (EMG) is performed to determine nerve dysfunction and report results are documented in the patient's record, the service is included in the reported anesthesia code. True or False?

4. With _____ anesthesia care (MAC), an anesthesiologist participates in care provided to a patient during a diagnostic or therapeutic procedure.

5. When reporting an anesthesia services code for which *monitored anesthesia care* was provided, add modifier _____ to the code along with appropriate CPT and HCPCS level II anesthesia modifiers.

Anesthesia Section Guidelines

Anesthesia services are reported by assigning a five-digit procedure code and adding appropriate modifiers. A physician (e.g., anesthesiologist) is responsible for supervising anesthesia services (which include general and regional), supplementation of local anesthesia, and other supportive services so the patient receives appropriate and optimal anesthesia care. The administration of local infiltration, metacarpal/metatarsal/ digital block, or topical anesthesia by the operating surgeon or obstetrician is included (bundled) in the surgery code; separate codes are not reported. Such anesthesia is not coded or reported separately because it is included in the surgery code (e.g., surgical procedure fee in physician's office, facility charge at an ambulatory surgical center or hospital outpatient department, and accommodation revenue code for a hospital inpatient).

An anesthesiologist's responsibilities include the following services, which are included (bundled) in the anesthesia code:

- Providing **airway management**: Ensuring an open airway to the patient's lungs

- Administering analgesics and general anesthetic drugs and agents

- Providing **fluid management**: Administering IV fluids to avoid dehydration, maintain an effective circulating volume, and prevent inadequate tissue perfusion

- Performing and documenting preanesthesia and postanesthesia evaluations (Figure 10-3) and an anesthesia record (Figure 10-4)

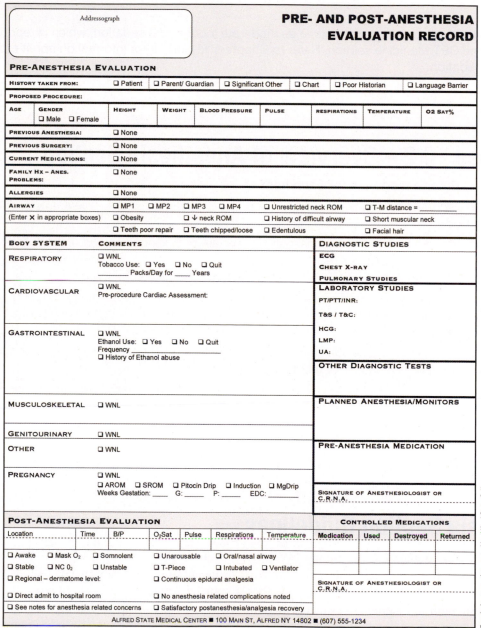

Figure 10-3 Sample pre- and postanesthesia evaluation record

Figure 10-4 Sample anesthesia record

- Monitoring the patient's cardiorespiratory status during surgery to include:

  ○ Blood pressure and temperature

  ○ **Capnography** (monitoring carbon dioxide levels)

  ○ Continuous electrocardiogram

  ○ Continuous **pulse oximetry** (arterial oxyhemoglobin saturation)

  ○ Low oxygen and circuit disconnect alarms

  ○ **Mass spectrometry** (monitors proper levels of the anesthetic)

The anesthesiologist or CRNA is responsible for conducting a **preanesthesia evaluation** of the patient prior to surgery, which includes assessing information from the patient's record, interviewing the patient (e.g., history), conducting a physical examination, evaluating preoperative test results, and ensuring that informed anesthetic consent has been obtained. The preanesthesia evaluation is included (bundled) in the anesthesia services code. If the surgery for which a preanesthesia evaluation was performed is canceled, the anesthesiologist should report an evaluation and management service code (e.g., office or other outpatient consultation or inpatient consultation).

A **postanesthesia evaluation** is also included (bundled) in the anesthesia services code and includes an evaluation of the patient during recovery from anesthesia, as well as evaluation, treatment, and follow-up of possible anesthesia-related complications. When an anesthesiologist or a CRNA provides significant, separately identifiable services (e.g., critical care services, postoperative pain management services, or unrelated ventilator management), the appropriate code(s) are reported for each service.

When a physician (e.g., anesthesiologist) *other than the physician performing the procedure* (e.g., surgeon) provides anesthesia services, report the code(s) from the CPT Anesthesia section. (This means that a surgeon is performing the surgical procedure and the anesthesiologist or CRNA is providing anesthesia services. The surgeon reports the code(s) from the Surgery section, and the anesthesiologist or CRNA reports the code(s) from the Anesthesia section.)

> **EXAMPLE:** An anesthesiologist provides general anesthesia services for a patient who undergoes carpal tunnel surgery. Report code 01810 (with appropriate modifiers, discussed later in this chapter). (In the CPT index, locate main term *Anesthesia* and subterm *Wrist* to locate code 01810.)

When the surgeon (or another physician) provides general or regional anesthesia *in addition to performing the procedure for which anesthesia is administered*, report the code(s) from the CPT Surgery section and attach modifier -47 to each code. *Do not attach modifier -47 to an anesthesia code.* (This means that the surgeon is performing the surgical procedure and providing general or regional anesthesia services to the same patient during the same operative session. No anesthesiologist or CRNA is in the operating room providing anesthesia services.)

> **EXAMPLE:** The surgeon provides regional anesthesia services for a 38-year-old female patient who undergoes a needle biopsy of the thyroid. Report code 60100-47.
>
> - In the CPT index, locate main term *Thyroid Gland* and subterm *Needle Biopsy* to locate code 60100.
>
> - Add modifier -47 to code 60100 to indicate that the physician who performed the surgical procedure also provided anesthesia services.
>
> - Do *not* report code 00322 from the Anesthesia section of CPT.

Reporting Codes for Monitoring or Providing Other Services

When an anesthesiologist or a CRNA (or the surgeon if he or she is providing anesthesia services) performs unusual forms of monitoring or other services, report codes for each procedure or service separately. Add modifier -59 to each code reported in addition to the anesthesia code. Modifier -59 is added to codes that describe distinct procedural services performed during the same encounter, operative session, or patient's stay as the provision of anesthesia services (e.g., endotracheal intubation by anesthesiologist or CRNA after completion of anesthesia services).

 Note:

Peripheral venous access is the IV line that is inserted in a small peripheral vein in the hand or forearm. It is temporary and has to be routinely changed. A midline peripheral catheter (e.g., Landmark) is inserted in the patient's arm near the inside of the elbow and threaded up inside the arm about 6 inches. The catheter can remain inserted for about six weeks (e.g., short-term course of antibiotics) but is not practical for long-term IV therapy. Peripheral venous access and midline peripheral catheters are flushed with saline (to clean the catheter) and heparin (to prevent blood from clotting in the catheter). Neither type can be used to draw blood lab tests. (A peripheral venous access IV line uses a shorter catheter than that used for central venous pressure lines, described later in the chapter.)

EXAMPLE: An anesthesiologist inserts a percutaneous arterial line (catheter) to monitor the patient while providing the anesthesia services during an intracranial surgical procedure. At the conclusion of surgery, the anesthesiologist inserts a Swan-Ganz (flow-directed) cardiac catheter. The anesthesiologist reports codes 00210, 36620-59, and 93503-59.

- In the CPT index, locate main term *Anesthesia* and subterm *Intracranial* to locate code 00210.

- In the CPT index, locate main term *Catheterization*, subterm *Arterial*, and 2nd qualifier *Percutaneous* to locate code 36620.

- In the CPT index, locate main term *Insertion*, subterm *Catheter*, 2nd qualifier *Cardiac*, and 3rd qualifier *Flow Directed* to locate code 93503.

- Modifier -59 indicates that the anesthesiologist provided distinct procedures in addition to anesthesia services on the same date.

Emergency Endotracheal Tube Intubation

An **endotracheal tube (ET)** is an artificial airway used for short-term airway management or mechanical ventilation due to potential or actual respiratory system insufficiency. The indications for endotracheal intubation include administration of medications during cardiopulmonary arrest, airway maintenance, oxygenation and ventilation, and secretion control.

Central Venous Access Devices (CVADs)

A **central venous access device (CVAD)** is a thin plastic tube (or catheter) that is inserted (or placed) into a vein and connected to a monitor. After insertion, a chest x-ray is done to verify that the catheter's tip is in the proper location above the heart. It measures a patient's central venous pressure (CVP) as an indicator of circulating blood volume, the heart's effectiveness as a pump, and the patient's vascular tone and response to treatment. CVADs are inserted due to the absence of a suitable peripheral access for fluid administration (e.g., rapid infusion of a high volume of fluid in a patient with **hypovolemia**, which is abnormally decreased blood volume). CVADs are also used for the administration of medications (e.g., potassium chloride and dopamine) that may be harmful to smaller **lumen** (opening) peripheral veins and/or for the insertion of a pacing wire.

✏ A **central venous pressure (CVP) line** (or **central venous pressure catheter**) is inserted through a vein in the neck (e.g., external or internal jugular vein) or a vein in the upper chest under the collar bone (e.g., subclavian vein) and then into a large central vein in the chest (e.g., superior vena cava). A CVP line can also be inserted through a vein in the leg (e.g., femoral) and then into a large central vein below the chest (e.g., inferior vena cava).

 Note:

A CVP line (or CVP catheter) is also called a central venous catheter (CVC) or central venous line (CVL).

CVP lines are inserted as internal or external catheters depending on the patient's condition as well as the frequency and duration of infusions. An **external catheter** or **nontunneled catheter** is not implanted under the patient's skin, and it does not require a needle to be inserted into the skin to deliver medications. It is used when the patient requires frequent infusions that last several hours, and it requires a sterile dressing that must be changed once or twice daily. In addition, external catheters may require periodic injections of **heparin** (anticoagulant that prevents blood clots from developing in the catheter). The Cook (cystotomy catheter) is an example of an external catheter. Some nontunneled catheters require just a saline flush, and others require both a saline and a heparin flush. Blood can be drawn from a nontunneled catheter.

An **internal catheter** (or **tunneled catheter**) is implanted completely under the skin. (The catheter's tip is inserted in the superior vena cava, and the other end is "tunneled" about 6 inches away under the chest's skin and sealed with a Dacron cuff to prevent infection.) An internal catheter requires no special care when it is not being used since it is located completely under the skin. The AshSplit Cath (hemodialysis catheter), Groshong, and Hickman are examples of internal catheters. Some tunneled catheters require just a saline flush, and others require both a saline and heparin flush. Blood can be drawn from a tunneled catheter.

An **implanted port** is a small reservoir that has a rubber plug attached to the catheter that enters the patient's vein below the collar bone and is threaded into the superior vena cava. The port is implanted underneath the skin (local anesthesia and IV sedation). To access the catheter, the site must be located and cleaned and a special needle is inserted through the skin and into the rubber plug. Blood can be drawn from an implanted port.

Intra-Arterial Lines

An **intra-arterial line** (also called **intra-arterial cannula**, or **intra-arterial catheter**, or **A-line**) is a thin plastic tube, cannula, or catheter that is inserted into an artery and connected to a monitor. Its purpose is to measure immediate changes in intra-arterial blood pressure and concentrations of oxygen and carbon dioxide; it also is used to collect frequent blood samples for lab tests. An A-line is inserted when cardiopulmonary status is unstable or when serial (repeat) blood sampling is necessary.

Swan-Ganz Catheterization

A **Swan-Ganz catheter** is a thin, flexible, flow-directed multilumen plastic tube (or catheter) that is advanced from a peripheral vein into the right atrium and then positioned in a branch of the pulmonary artery. The catheter's balloon tip travels through the pulmonary artery, and pulmonary wedge pressure is measured in front of the temporarily inflated and wedged balloon. **Pulmonary wedge pressure** is the indirect measurement of left atrial pressure that is useful in the diagnosis of left ventricular failure and mitral valve disease. The Swan-Ganz catheter serves to obtain diagnostic information about the heart and to provide continuous monitoring of heart function in critically ill patients. The result is that the physician can evaluate circulatory volume due to acute valvular regurgitation, burns, congenital heart disease, heart failure, kidney disease, or shock. It is also used to monitor complications of myocardial infarction and the effects of certain heart medications.

Postoperative Pain Management

Postoperative pain management includes the administration of epidural or subarachnoid medications on the date(s) of service after the date of surgery. It is provided by the surgeon as part of the surgical procedure's global package, which means reimbursement is included in the CPT surgery code reported. When postoperative pain management is performed by the anesthesiologist, the surgeon must document the reason such care was transferred to the anesthesiologist. The anesthesiologist reports code 01996 just once each day that services are provided. Add modifier -59 to code 01996 on the day of *surgery* to indicate that a distinct procedural service was provided (in addition to administration of anesthesia during surgery that day).

Drug Administration Codes

Anesthesiologists and CRNAs do not report drug administration CPT Medicine section or HCPCS level II codes for anesthetic agents or other drugs administered from the time of the patient's arrival in the operating room through discharge from postanesthesia care.

Anesthesia Modifiers

All anesthesia services require the following types of modifiers to be reviewed for assignment with reported anesthesia codes:

- HCPCS level II modifiers

- Physical status modifiers

- CPT modifiers

HCPCS Level II Anesthesia Modifiers

When applicable, the following HCPCS level II modifiers are added to reported anesthesia codes:

- -AA: Anesthesia services performed personally by anesthesiologist
- -AD: Medically supervised by a physician for more than four concurrent procedures
- -G8: Monitored anesthesia care for a deep, complex, complicated, or markedly invasive surgical procedure

 Note:

Report modifier -G8 with CPT codes 00100, 00400, 00160, 00300, 00532, and 00920 only. Do not report modifier -G8 modifier with modifier -QS.

- -G9: Monitored anesthesia care for patient who has history of severe cardiopulmonary condition
- -QK: Medical direction of two, three, or four concurrent procedures involving qualified individuals
- -QS: Monitored anesthesia care

 Note:

Add -QS to the anesthesia code if monitored anesthesia care (MAC) is provided. MAC involves the intraoperative monitoring of the patient's vital physiologic signs in anticipation of the need for administration of general anesthesia or of the development of adverse physiologic patient reaction to the surgical procedures.

- -QX: CRNA service with medical direction by physician

 Note:

Assign modifier -QX when the CRNA alone provides anesthesia service to the patient and the anesthesiologist is not in the operating room with the CRNA but provides medical direction for the CRNA (e.g., from another operating room).

- -QY: Medical direction of one CRNA by an anesthesiologist

 Note:

Assign modifier -QY when the CRNA and the anesthesiologist both provide anesthesia services to the same patient in the same operating room and the anesthesiologist provides medical direction for the CRNA.

- -QZ: CRNA service without medical direction by physician

EXAMPLE: A CRNA provided general anesthesia services to an otherwise healthy patient who underwent a vaginal hysterectomy due to uterine fibroids. The CRNA received medical direction from an anesthesiologist. Report code 00944-P1-QX. (Modifier -P1 is a physical status modifier added to the anesthesia code, indicating a "normal healthy patient." Physical status modifiers are discussed in the next section of this chapter.)

Physical Status Modifiers

A **physical status modifier** is added to each reported anesthesia code to indicate the patient's condition at the time anesthesia was administered. The modifier also serves to identify the complexity of services provided. (The physical status modifier is determined by the anesthesiologist or CRNA and is documented as such in the patient record.) Physical status modifiers are represented by the letter *P* followed by a single digit from 1 to 6 as follows:

- -P1: Normal healthy patient (e.g., no biochemical, organic, physiologic, or psychiatric disturbance)
- -P2: Patient with mild systemic disease (e.g., anemia, chronic asthma, chronic bronchitis, diabetes mellitus, essential hypertension, heart disease that only slightly limits physical activity, or obesity)
- -P3: Patient with severe systemic disease (e.g., angina pectoris, chronic pulmonary disease that limits activity, history of prior myocardial infarction, heart disease that limits activity, poorly controlled essential hypertension, morbid obesity, or diabetes mellitus, type 1)
- -P4: Patient with severe systemic disease that is a constant threat to life (e.g., advanced pulmonary/renal/hepatic dysfunction; congestive heart failure; persistent angina pectoris; or unstable/rest angina)
- -P5: Moribund patient who is not expected to survive without the operation (e.g., abdominal aortic aneurysm)
- -P6: Patient declared brain dead whose organs are being removed for donor purposes

    EXAMPLE: An anesthesiologist provided general anesthesia services to a 65-year-old male with mild systemic disease who underwent total knee replacement. Report code 01402-P2.

CPT Modifiers

The following CPT modifiers should be reviewed to determine whether they need to be added to the reported anesthesia codes:

- -23: Unusual anesthesia

Coding Tip:

- When a patient's circumstances warrant the administration of general or regional anesthesia (instead of the usual local anesthesia), add modifier -23 to the anesthesia code. The following may require general or regional anesthesia services (when local anesthesia services are usually provided):

    o Extremely apprehensive patients

    o Individuals with an intellectual disability

    o Patients who have a physical condition (e.g., spasticity or tremors)

EXAMPLE: An anesthesiologist provided general anesthesia services to a 49-year-old male patient with chronic obstructive pulmonary disease who underwent extracorporeal shock wave lithotripsy with water bath. The patient was extremely anxious about the procedure, which normally does not require general anesthesia. Report code 00872-P3-23-AA.

- -59: Distinct procedural service

Coding Tip:

- An anesthesiologist or a CRNA reports the anesthesia code with the highest base unit value first. Modifier -59 is added to each separately reported anesthesia code.

- -74: Discontinued outpatient hospital/ambulatory surgery center procedure after anesthesia administration
- -99: Multiple modifiers

Time Reporting

Anesthesia services are reported based on time, which begins when the anesthesiologist or CRNA starts preparing the patient to receive anesthesia and ends when the anesthesiologist or CRNA is no longer in personal attendance. Anesthesia time units are reported for the amount of time the anesthesiologist or CRNA is in personal attendance, providing anesthesia services and reimbursement for anesthesia services varies according to increments of time. (Nonmonitored time is *not* considered when calculating time units.)

 Note:

Teaching anesthesiologists must be present with the resident physician during all critical or key portions of the anesthesia service, and they must be immediately available to furnish anesthesia services during the entire procedure. Teaching CRNAs who are involved with two concurrent cases must be present with the student nurse anesthetist during pre- and postanesthesia care for each case. They are prohibited from being involved in any other activities (e.g., preanesthesia evaluation of the patient for a third case) when two concurrent cases are ongoing.

EXAMPLE: A patient undergoes a cataract extraction and requires 90 minutes of MAC by the anesthesiologist, which includes the administration of a sedative along with a retrobulbar injection for regional block anesthesia. Subsequently, an interval of 30 minutes transpires, during which time the patient does not require monitoring by the anesthesiologist. After this period, monitoring commences for 30 additional minutes until the patient is released to the recovery room. The anesthesiologist reports 120 minutes of time on the claim.

Payment for anesthesia services is based on the sum of an anesthesia code-specific base unit value plus anesthesia time units and modifying units multiplied by the locality-specific anesthesia conversion factor. The formula for calculating the anesthesia fee is as follows: [code-specific base unit value + anesthesia time unit(s) + modifying unit(s)] × locality-specific anesthesia conversion factor (e.g., [5 + 3 + 0] × \$17.04 = anesthesia fee).

- The code-specific **base unit value** for anesthesia codes (00100–01999) represents the degree of difficulty associated with providing anesthesia for a surgical procedure (Table 10-1).

- ✐ **Anesthesia time units** are based on the total anesthesia time, and they are reported as one unit for each 15 minutes (or fraction thereof) of anesthesia time. (Anesthesia time begins when the anesthesiologist or CRNA begins to prepare the patient for anesthesia care and ends when the anesthesiologist is no longer in personal attendance.)

 Note:

Anesthesia time reported includes monitoring during administration of regional block anesthesia and during the procedure. Interval and recovery room times are not included when calculating time, although the anesthesiologist or CRNA is required to document the patient's condition on the recovery room record (Figure 10-5).

Table 10-1 Sample Portion of Anesthesia Base Unit Values

CPT Code	Description Base Unit Value
00100	5
00102	6
00103	5
00104	4
00120	5

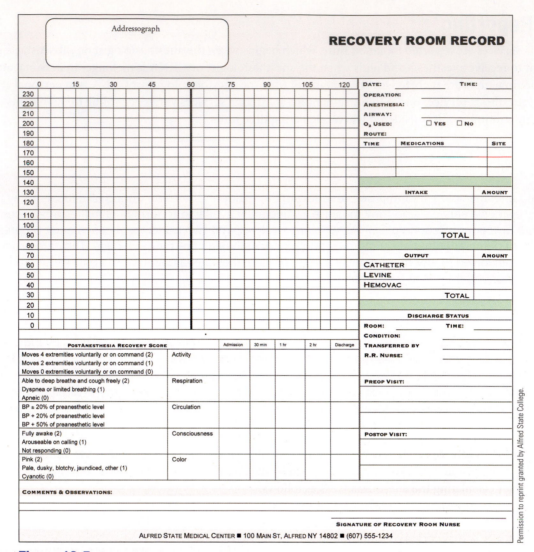

Figure 10-5 Sample recovery room record

- **Modifying units** recognize added complexities associated with the administration of anesthesia, including physical factors and difficult circumstances. Physical factors indicating the patient's condition at the time anesthesia was administered are reported by adding the appropriate physical status modifier (P1 to P6) to the anesthesia code. Difficult circumstances are reported with qualifying circumstances codes, located in the CPT Medicine section. The relative values for physical status modifiers and qualifying circumstances codes are located in the current year's American Society of Anesthesiologists (ASA) *Relative Value Guide* publication (Table 10-2).

- The locality-specific **anesthesia conversion factor** is the dollar amount assigned to a geographic location (Table 10-3).

☞ When the patient undergoes more than one procedure during the same operative episode and the anesthesiologist or CRNA provides multiple anesthesia services for the same patient during the same operative session, the anesthesia fee is based on the *highest* code base unit value when multiple stand-alone

Note:

Base unit values and modifying unit relative values are available as downloadable files at http://www.cms.gov. Click on Medicare, scroll to the Provider Type heading (located toward the bottom of the page), and click on the Anesthesiologists link to locate the Anesthesia Base Units file.

Table 10-2 Sample Portion of Modifying Units and Relative Values

CPT Physical Status Modifier	Relative Value
-P1	0
-P2	0
-P3	1
-P4	2
-P5	3
-P6	0
CPT Qualifying Circumstances Code	**Relative Value**
99100	1
99116	5
99135	5
99140	2

Table 10-3 Sample Portion of Locality-Specific Anesthesia Conversion Factors

Payer Number	Locality Number	Locality Name	Conversion Factor
00500	00	Alabama	$17.04
00830	01	Alaska	$29.66
00832	00	Arizona	$17.83
00520	13	Arkansas	$16.52

Courtesy of the Centers for Medicare & Medicaid Services, www.cms.gov

anesthesia codes are reported (which is added to the total anesthesia time for all services provided). (The anesthesia code with the highest code base unit is reported. The exception is when an anesthesia code has add-on codes, which are also reported, and reimbursement for multiple anesthesia services is based on the sum of the base unit values.)

EXAMPLE 1: A 22-year-old female patient who has chronic asthma underwent a planned vaginal delivery on May 14, during which neuraxial labor anesthesia was administered by an anesthesiologist. Report code 01967-P2. (Anesthesia code 01967 has a base unit value of 5, and physical status modifier -P2 has a relative value of 0.) A review of the patient record indicates 45 minutes of anesthesia time, which is calculated as 3 anesthesia time units (45 ÷ 15 = 3). If a conversion factor of $17.45 is assigned to New York State, payment for anesthesia services is calculated as $139.60. The formula for calculating anesthesia services reimbursement is as follows:

```
STEP 1:  (5 + 3 + 0) × $17.45
STEP 2:  8 × $17.45
AMOUNT:  $139.60
```

EXAMPLE 2: A 22-year-old female patient who has chronic asthma was prepared for a planned vaginal delivery on May 14, during which neuraxial labor anesthesia was administered by an anesthesiologist. Complications required that an emergency cesarean delivery be performed instead of the planned vaginal delivery. Report codes 01968-P2 and 99140 in addition to code 01967-P2. (Reimbursement for multiple anesthesia services is based on the sum of each base unit value because code 01968 is an add-on code.) Anesthesia code 01967 has a base unit value of 5, and code 01968 has a base unit value of 2. The total length of anesthesia time for both procedures was 75 minutes, which is calculated as 5 anesthesia time units (75 ÷ 15 = 5). The patient is assigned physical status modifier -P2, which has a relative value of 0, and code 99140 has a relative value of 2. If the conversion factor is $17.45, payment for anesthesia services is calculated as $244.30. The formula for calculating anesthesia services reimbursement is as follows:

```
STEP 1: (5 + 2 + 5 + 2) × $17.45
STEP 2: 14 × $17.45
AMOUNT: $244.30
```

EXAMPLE 3: A 39-year-old male patient who has otherwise been healthy sustained multiple trauma and was administered general anesthesia by an anesthesiologist during cranial surgery and upper abdominal surgery. Both surgical procedures were performed during the same operative session. (Reimbursement for multiple anesthesia services is based on the highest ASA base unit value when anesthesia for two separate procedures is provided.) Assign codes 00210-P5 and 99140. (Do not report code 00790 for the administration of anesthesia for the upper abdominal surgery because it was provided during the same operative episode as anesthesia administered for the cranial surgery.) If anesthesia code 00210 has a base unit value of 11 and code 00790 has a base unit value of 7, use value 11 when determining anesthesia reimbursement (because code 00790 is not reported). The total length of anesthesia time for both procedures was 120 minutes, which is calculated as 8 anesthesia time units (120 ÷ 15 = 8). Physical status modifier -P5 is assigned a relative value of 3, and code 99140 is assigned a relative value of 2. If the conversion factor is $17.45, payment for anesthesia services is calculated as $418.80. The formula for calculating anesthesia services reimbursement is as follows:

```
STEP 1: (11 + 8 + [3 + 2]) × $17.45
STEP 2: (19 + 5) × $17.45
STEP 3: 24 × $17.45
AMOUNT: $418.80
```

Medicare defines **concurrent medically directed anesthesia procedures** as "the maximum number of procedures an anesthesiologist or CRNA medically directs within the context of a single procedure and when the procedures overlap each other." The ASA base unit value is reduced for subsequent anesthesia services when the definition of *concurrent medically directed anesthesia procedures* applies to the submission of multiple anesthesia codes. (Base unit value reduction of services is determined by the third-party payer.)

EXAMPLE: Procedures A through E are concurrent medically directed anesthesia procedures provided by an anesthesiologist on May 20. The start and end times for each procedure represent the periods during which anesthesia time is counted.

Procedure	Start Time	End Time	Number of Concurrent Procedures	Base Unit Value Reduction
A	8:00 AM	8:20 AM	2	10%
B	8:10 AM	8:45 AM	2	10%
C	8:30 AM	9:15 AM	2	10%

- During procedure A, the anesthesiologist medically directed two concurrent procedures A and B (from 8:10 AM to 8:20 AM).

- During procedure B, the anesthesiologist medically directed two concurrent procedures A and B from 8:10 AM to 8:20 AM and then procedures B and C from 8:30 AM to 8:45 AM.

- Thus, during each procedure A and B, the anesthesiologist medically directed, at most, two concurrent procedures.

Anesthesia Services

Assign the appropriate CPT evaluation and management (E/M) code when anesthesia services are provided in an office, home, or hospital, which includes consultation services and other medical services. *Special Services and Reporting* (99000-99091) are included in the CPT Medicine section.

Supplied Materials

When an anesthesiologist or a CRNA provides materials and supplies (e.g., sterile trays and drugs) over and above those usually included with the office visit or other services rendered, report the materials and supplies separately with CPT code 99070.

Separate or Multiple Procedures

When multiple surgical procedures are performed during the provision of anesthesia services, report the anesthesia code that represents the most complex procedure performed. However, if the additional anesthesia code for multiple surgical procedures performed is an add-on code, report all codes. The time reported for the provision of anesthesia services is the combined total for all procedures performed.

Special Report

When a service is provided that is new, variable, rare, or unusual, a *special report* may be submitted with the claim. The special report should include information that defines or describes the nature, event, and need for the procedure as well as the time, effort, and equipment necessary to provide the service.

Qualifying Circumstances

When anesthesia services are provided during situations or circumstances that make anesthesia administration more difficult, report a **qualifying circumstances** code from the CPT Medicine section (in addition to the anesthesia code). Difficult circumstances depend on factors such as extraordinary condition of patient, notable operative conditions, or unusual risk factors. These codes are reported in addition to the anesthesia codes. Qualifying circumstances codes include the following:

- 99100: Anesthesia for patient of extreme age, under 1 year and over 70

- 99116: Anesthesia complicated by utilization of total body hypothermia

- 99135: Anesthesia complicated by utilization of controlled hypotension

- 99140: Anesthesia complicated by emergency conditions (specify)

> **Note:**
>
> For hernia repair procedures performed on infants younger than one year of age at the time of surgery, assign code 00834 or 00836, depending on the infant's age.

> **Note:**
>
> An **emergency condition** results when a delay in treatment of the patient would lead to a significant increase in threat to life or body part.

EXAMPLE: A 92-year-old female patient received general anesthesia services from a CRNA and was monitored by an anesthesiologist during total left hip arthroplasty. Report codes 01214-P2-QX and 99100.

Exercise 10.3 – Anesthesia Section Guidelines

Instructions: Match the term with its definition.

_____   1. Administering intravenous fluids to avoid dehydration

_____   2. Arterial oxyhemoglobin saturation

_____   3. Ensuring an open airway to the patient's lungs

_____   4. Monitoring proper levels of the anesthetic

_____   5. Monitoring carbon dioxide levels

a. Airway management

b. Capnography

c. Fluid management

d. Mass spectrometry

e. Pulse oximetry

Instructions: Match the type of evaluation with its description. Answers may be assigned more than once.

_____   6. Conducting a physical examination

_____   7. Evaluating the patient during anesthesia recovery

_____   8. Interviewing the patient

_____   9. Obtaining informed anesthetic consent

_____ 10. Treatment of anesthesia-related complications

a. Preanesthesia evaluation

b. Postanesthesia evaluation

Instructions: Indicate whether each statement is true (T) or false (F).

_____ 11. When an anesthesiologist or a CRNA performs unusual forms of monitoring or other services, the codes are reported separately and modifier -59 is added to each code reported in addition to the anesthesia code.

_____ 12. When local infiltration, metacarpal/metatarsal/digital block, or topical anesthesia is administered by the operating surgeon or obstetrician, it is included in the surgery code.

_____ 13. When a physician (e.g., anesthesiologist) other than the physician performing the procedure provides anesthesia services, report the code(s) from the CPT Anesthesia section.

_____ 14. When the surgeon (or other physician) provides general or regional anesthesia in addition to performing the procedure for which anesthesia is administered, report the anesthesia code for the procedure performed and attach modifier -47 to that code.

_____ 15. Anesthesia services are reported based on time, which begins when the anesthesiologist or CRNA is in personal attendance providing anesthesia services, which includes preparing the patient to receive anesthesia and ends when the patient is discharged from the recovery room.

_____ 16. Anesthesia time units are reported for the amount of time the anesthesiologist or CRNA spends administering anesthesia, and reimbursement for anesthesia services varies according to increments of time.

_____ 17. When calculating anesthesia time units, do not include nonmonitored time.

_____ 18. A patient undergoes a surgical procedure that requires 30 minutes of monitored anesthesia care by the anesthesiologist. Then 15 minutes transpires when the patient does not require monitoring by the anesthesiologist. After this interval, the anesthesiologist commences monitoring for 15 additional minutes until the patient is released to the recovery room. The number of anesthesia time units is 3.

_____ 19. Payment for anesthesia services is based on the following formula: [code-specific base unit value + anesthesia time unit(s) + modifying unit(s)] × locality-specific anesthesia conversion factor = anesthesia fee.

_____ 20. A 38-year-old female patient who has diabetes mellitus underwent a planned vaginal delivery on November 14, during which neuraxial labor anesthesia was administered by an

Exercise 10.3 (*continued*)

anesthesiologist. Code 01967-P2 is reported (base unit value of 5 and relative value of 0). A review of the patient record indicates 60 minutes of anesthesia time. The conversion factor is $17.45. The payment for anesthesia services is calculated as $139.60.

Instructions: Match the physical status modifier with its example.

_____ **21.** A patient who is on medication for petit mal seizures undergoes inguinal herniorrhaphy.

_____ **22.** A patient with late-stage adenocarcinoma of the left breast undergoes left mastectomy.

_____ **23.** A healthy patient undergoes colonoscopy.

_____ **24.** A patient with end-stage renal disease undergoes laparoscopic cholecystectomy.

_____ **25.** A patient with cardiomyopathy undergoes heart transplant.

a. P1 (normal healthy patient)

b. P2 (patient with mild systemic disease)

c. P3 (patient with severe systemic disease)

d. P4 (patient with severe systemic disease that is a constant threat to life)

e. P5 (moribund patient who is not expected to survive without the operation)

f. P6 (patient declared brain dead whose organs are being removed for donor purposes)

Anesthesia Subsections

The Anesthesia section is organized according to general anatomical areas or services that relate to a number of surgical procedures. For Medicare purposes, just one anesthesia code is usually reported unless the second and subsequent anesthesia codes are add-on codes. When unusual procedures and services are provided by the anesthesiologist, report separate anesthesia codes. The code that describes the anesthesia service for the procedure that has the *highest* base unit value is reported first.

The Anesthesia section includes add-on codes for anesthesia services provided to patients undergoing burn excisions or debridement and obstetrics procedures. The add-on code is reported in addition to the code for the primary anesthesia service.

Head

Anesthesia services for the Head subsection include procedures on the following anatomical sites: accessory sinuses, ears, eyelids, eyes, facial bones, lips, nose, salivary glands, and skull. Codes for anesthesia services provided for electroconvulsive therapy (ECT) and intraoral and intracranial procedures are also included. Refer to Table 10-4 for coding rules associated with Head subsection anesthesia codes.

 Coding Tip:

- When an anesthesiologist or a CRNA provides distinct procedural services (e.g., insertion of the Swan-Ganz catheter) in addition to anesthesia services, codes for those services are reported separately and modifier -59 is added to each code.

- Surgical endoscopy/arthroscopy always includes diagnostic endoscopy/arthroscopy. This means that if an anesthesiologist or a CRNA provides anesthesia services for a diagnostic and a surgical endoscopy/arthroscopy that are performed during the same operative session, report just one anesthesia services code with appropriate modifiers. This coding tip applies to the following subsections: knee and popliteal area, lower leg (below knee, includes ankle and foot), shoulder and axilla, and upper arm and elbow.

Table 10-4 Sample Coding Rules Associated with Head Subsection Anesthesia Codes

Code	Coding Rule
00102	Code 00102 is reported when anesthesia services are provided for plastic repair of a cleft lip, and code 00172 is reported when a cleft lip repair is performed. To report non-cleft lip repairs, assign code 00300. A **cleft lip** is a congenital deformity of the upper lip that failed to close during development; types include unilateral, bilateral, and median (harelip) and may be accompanied by defects of the maxilla and hard palate. NOTE: Bilateral cleft lip describes the type of defect, not the surgery performed.
00104	When a procedure code for electroconvulsive therapy is reported on a claim that is submitted to a Medicare administrative contractor, it is denied as a noncovered service. This means that code 00104, anesthesia for electroconvulsive therapy, will also be denied by Medicare. **Electroconvulsive therapy (ECT)** (or **shock therapy**) involves briefly applying an electric current to the brain to produce a seizure; its purpose is to relieve depression, schizophrenia, and severe affective disorders.
00170	To justify medical necessity for code 00170, make sure you report an appropriate ICD diagnosis code. Medicare does not cover anesthesia services for the care, filling, removal, replacement, or treatment of teeth or structures directly supporting the teeth.
00190	Code 00190 is reported when anesthesia services are provided during extradural procedures on bone(s) of the skull. An **extradural procedure** is performed on the outer side of the **dura mater**, which is the membrane that forms the outer covering of the **central nervous system (CNS)** (brain and spinal cord).
00218	Code 00218 is reported for anesthesia services provided during any **intracranial** (introduced into or within the skull) procedure performed while the patient is in a seated position.

EXAMPLE: A healthy patient underwent soft tissue biopsy of the accessory sinuses, for which a CRNA provided anesthesia services. The CRNA was supervised by an anesthesiologist. Report code 00164-P1-QX.

Neck

Anesthesia services for the Neck subsection include procedures on the following anatomical sites: integumentary system; muscles and nerves of the head, neck, and posterior trunk; esophagus, thyroid, larynx, trachea, and lymphatic system of the neck; and major vessels of the neck. Refer to Table 10-5 for coding rules associated with Neck subsection anesthesia codes.

EXAMPLE: An anesthesiologist provided anesthesia services to a terminally ill 1-year-old patient who underwent laryngoscopy. Report code 00320-P4-AA.

Table 10-5 Sample Coding Rules Associated with Neck Subsection Anesthesia Codes

Code(s)	Coding Rule
00300	When a patient who undergoes removal of a **lesion** (abnormal tissue resulting from autoimmune or metabolic disorders, infection, neoplasm, or trauma) that requires an anesthesiologist or a CRNA to provide anesthesia services, report code 00300. When such services are provided, make sure you report an appropriate ICD diagnosis code to justify medical necessity (e.g., patient with intellectual disability who exhibits severe anxiety about undergoing the procedure). (And make sure you are prepared to send the payer a copy of the patient record.) The surgeon who removes a lesion usually provides anesthesia services, which involve administration of local anesthesia. If general or regional anesthesia is administered by the surgeon, add modifier -47 to the surgery code. NOTE: Modifier -47 is never added to an anesthesia code.
00326	When procedures on the larynx and trachea are performed on a patient who is younger than 1 year of age, report 00326. *Do not report code 99100 on the same claim as code 00326.*
00350–00352	Codes 00350–00352 are not reported when anesthesia services are provided during arteriography. Instead, report code 01916.

Table 10-6 Sample Coding Rules Associated with Thorax (Chest Wall and Shoulder Girdle) Subsection Anesthesia Codes

Code	Coding Rule
00400	Surgical procedures of the skin are often performed under local anesthesia. When monitored anesthesia care (MAC) is provided by an anesthesiologist or a CRNA due to the patient's age, mental status, or size of the skin lesion, report the appropriate anesthesia code, physical status modifier, and HCPCS level II modifier -QS. Also report a qualifying circumstances code if indicated.
00402	Reconstructive breast procedures are reported with code 00402.
00404	Radical or modified radical breast procedures that do not include internal mammary node dissection are reported with code 00404.
00406	When an internal mammary node dissection is performed *in addition to a radical or modified radical breast procedure*, report code 00406. (If internal mammary node dissection is *not* performed, report code 00404.)

Thorax (Chest Wall and Shoulder Girdle)

Anesthesia services for the Thorax (Chest Wall and Shoulder Girdle) subsection include procedures on the following anatomical sites: integumentary system on the extremities, anterior trunk, and perineum; breast; clavicle; scapula; and ribs. Anesthesia services for an electrical conversion of arrhythmias procedure are also included. Refer to Table 10-6 for coding rules associated with Thorax (Chest Wall and Shoulder Girdle) subsection anesthesia codes.

EXAMPLE: A 79-year-old female patient underwent bilateral radical mastectomy with internal mammary node dissection (12 lymph nodes). She was recently diagnosed with metastatic adenocarcinoma of the breast to the lung. The anesthesiologist provided general anesthesia services. Report codes 00406-P5-AA and 99100.

The surgeon who removes a skin lesion usually provides local anesthesia or MAC. If general or regional anesthesia services are provided by the surgeon, add modifier -47 to the surgery code. (*Do not add modifier -47 to an anesthesia code.*) If general anesthesia, regional anesthesia, or MAC is provided by an anesthesiologist or a CRNA, report the appropriate code, physical status modifier, and qualifying circumstances codes. (Add modifier -QS to the anesthesia code if MAC is provided.) Make sure you report an appropriate ICD diagnosis code to justify medical necessity (e.g., patient with intellectual disability who exhibits severe anxiety about undergoing the procedure).

EXAMPLE: An anesthesiologist provided MAC for a 5-year-old patient who underwent a biopsy of the perineum. Report 00400-P1-QS-AA.

- If the surgeon had provided MAC, you would have reported code 56605. (*Do not report modifier -QS or modifier -47.*)

- If the surgeon had provided general or regional anesthesia services, you would have reported code 56605-47.

Intrathoracic

Anesthesia services for the Intrathoracic subsection include procedures on the following anatomical sites: bronchus, coronary arteries, diaphragm, esophagus, great vessels of chest, heart, lungs, mediastinum, pericardial sac, pleura, sternum, and thorax. Refer to Table 10-7 for coding rules associated with Intrathoracic subsection anesthesia codes.

EXAMPLE: A 39-year-old female patient with severe systemic disease underwent sternal debridement for which the anesthesiologist provided general anesthesia services. Report code 00550-P3-AA.

Spine and Spinal Cord

Anesthesia services for the Spine and Spinal Cord subsection include procedures on the following anatomical sites: cervical, thoracic, and lumbar spine and spinal cord. Refer to Table 10-8 for coding rules associated with Spine and Spinal Cord subsection anesthesia codes.

Table 10-7 Sample Coding Rules Associated with Intrathoracic Subsection Anesthesia Codes

Code(s)	Coding Rule
00500	The "procedures on esophagus" described in code 00500 require (intrathoracic) chest incision. For "procedures on esophagus" that do *not* require (intrathoracic) chest incision, report 00320.
00528, 00529	Anesthesia services for endoscopic procedures (e.g., esophagoscopy, bronchoscopy, mediastinoscopy, and thoracoscopy) are usually provided by the surgeon who performs the procedure. If an anesthesiologist or a CRNA provides general or regional anesthesia services, report 00528 or 00529 and the appropriate physical status and HCPCS level II modifiers. (When MAC is provided by the anesthesiologist or CRNA, also add HCPCS level II modifier -QS.)
00530–00534	General anesthesia or monitored anesthesia care may be reimbursed by Medicare if it is determined to be reasonable and necessary. Adequate documentation of medical necessity is reviewed on a case-by-case basis. When pacemaker surgery involves the use of the transthoracic method of implantation (code 00560), which requires open surgery, it is accepted practice that general anesthesia services will be provided. Medicare will reimburse such services, and it is unnecessary to submit special medical documentation to Medicare for consideration. According to Ingenix's *Coding and Payment Guide for Anesthesia Services*, Medicare will reimburse general anesthesia or MAC when the patient's record documents • Diagnoses of other hyperalimentation, intermediate coronary syndrome, pulmonary valve disorders, and/or congestive heart failure • The fact that the patient is uncontrollable under local anesthesia (e.g., small child), is disoriented, or has mental confusion
00528–00529 00540–00541	**One lung ventilation (OLV)** is the isolation of the right or left lung so that one lung is ventilated and the other is allowed to collapse. OLV is performed to (1) improve surgical access so the surgeon can perform lung surgery, (2) prevent the other lung from being contaminated by blood or pus from the diseased lung during surgery (because an anesthetized patient loses the ability to cough and, thus, the ability to prevent infected material or blood from entering the normal lung), or (3) provide intensive care ventilation to prevent the normal lung from being subjected to the high pressure required to ventilate an abnormal lung (e.g., after a single lung transplant). When OLV is provided, assign code 00529 or 00541. When OLV is not provided (because bilateral lung ventilation is provided), assign code 00528 or 00540.
00561	Do not report qualifying circumstances codes 99100 with code 00561, which includes in its description "under one year of age." Also do not report qualifying circumstances code 99116 or 99135 with code 00561 because "total body hypothermia" and "controlled hypotension" are included in general anesthesia services for procedures on the heart, pericardial sac, and great vessels of the chest.
00560–00566	A **pump oxygenator** is a device that substitutes for the heart (pump) and lungs (oxygenator) during open heart surgery. A pump oxygenator is not typically used for coronary artery bypass grafting (CABG) or laser myocardial revascularization surgery, and the patient's beating heart provides circulatory support.

Table 10-8 Sample Coding Rules Associated with Spine and Spinal Cord Subsection Anesthesia Codes

Code	Coding Rule
00600	When anesthesia services for diagnostic and therapeutic percutaneous image-guided spine and spinal cord procedures are provided, report codes 01935–01936 instead of 00600.
00604	When anesthesia services are provided for a patient who undergoes cervical spine and cord surgery in a sitting position, report code 00604.
00635	A **lumbar puncture (LP)**, or **spinal tap**, involves inserting a **cannula** (hollow needle) at the L3–L4 or L4–L5 (lumbar vertebrae) to remove cerebrospinal fluid (CSF) for diagnostic or therapeutic purposes (e.g., measure CSF pressure or analyze CSF fluid).
00640	Report code 00640 when anesthesia is provided for closed procedures on the cervical, lumbar, or thoracic spine. Third-party payers do not usually reimburse 00640 when reported for spinal manipulation under anesthesia (SMUA) to treat low back pain or other neuromusculoskeletal disorders by improving range of motion and reducing spinal pain.

EXAMPLE: General anesthesia services were provided by an anesthesiologist during an otherwise healthy patient's thoracic spine surgery. Report code 00620-P1-AA.

Note:

When a physician performs spinal manipulation under anesthesia, report code 22505. Other manipulation under anesthesia codes include 23700, 24300, 25259, 26340, 27275, 27570, and 27860. For these codes, *manipulation* refers to "reduction" of a fracture, which is typically reimbursed by payers. When spinal manipulation is performed without anesthesia, report code 97140, which is located in the Physical Medicine and Rehabilitation subsection of the CPT Medicine section.

Upper Abdomen

Anesthesia services for the Upper Abdomen subsection include procedures on the following anatomical sites: upper abdominal wall, liver, major abdominal blood vessels, pancreas, and stomach. This subsection also includes anesthesia codes for upper gastrointestinal (GI) endoscopic procedures and hernia repairs and laparoscopy. Refer to Table 10-9 for coding rules associated with Upper Abdomen subsection anesthesia codes.

> **EXAMPLE:** An anesthesiologist provides general anesthesia services for a patient who undergoes a liver transplant. Report 00796-P5-AA.

Lower Abdomen

Anesthesia services for the Lower Abdomen subsection include procedures on the following anatomical sites: lower abdominal wall, **panniculus adiposus**, or **pannus** (layer of subcutaneous adipose tissue, or fat, below the dermis that contains fat deposits, blood vessels, and nerves). The following anatomical sites are accessed via transabdominal incision: uterus; fallopian tubes; urinary tract, including kidneys and urinary bladder; prostate gland; adrenal glands; lower abdominal vessels; and inferior vena cava. This subsection also includes anesthesia codes for lower intestinal endoscopic procedures and hernia repairs and lower abdomen intraperitoneal procedures including laparoscopy. Refer to Table 10-10 for coding rules associated with Lower Abdomen subsection anesthesia codes.

> **EXAMPLE:** An anesthesiologist provided regional anesthesia services to a diabetic patient who underwent total cystectomy. Report code 00864-P2-AA.

Perineum

Anesthesia services for the Perineum subsection include procedures on the following anatomical sites: anus, rectum, perineum, vulva, vas deferens, seminal vesicles, testes, penis, vagina, labia, cervix, endometrium, uterus, prostate, urethra, urinary bladder, and ureters. Refer to Table 10-11 for coding rules associated with Perineum subsection anesthesia codes.

> **EXAMPLE:** An anesthesiologist provided general anesthesia services to a hypertensive patient who underwent vulvectomy. Report code 00906-P2-AA.

Table 10-9 Sample Coding Rules Associated with Upper Abdomen Subsection Anesthesia Codes

Code	Coding Rule
00740	Anesthesia services (e.g., sedation) for endoscopic procedures (e.g., upper GI endoscopy) are usually provided by the surgeon who performs the procedure. If an anesthesiologist or a CRNA provides general or regional anesthesia services, report 00740 and the appropriate physical status and HCPCS level II modifiers. (When MAC is provided by the anesthesiologist or CRNA, also add HCPCS level II modifier -QS.)
00796	Code 00796 is reported for anesthesia services provided to the recipient of a liver transplant. Assign code 01990 for anesthesia services provided to a brain-dead patient who undergoes liver **organ harvest** (removal of an organ for transplantation).

Table 10-10 Sample Coding Rules Associated with Lower Abdomen Subsection Anesthesia Codes

Code(s)	Coding Rule
00802	**Panniculectomy** is the surgical removal of excess abdominal panniculus (or pannus), which is a redundant layer of fat tissue (or apron) located at the lowest portion of the abdominal wall. (Patients who have lost significant weight after undergoing a previous gastric restrictive procedure for morbid obesity often develop excess pannus.)
00810, 00840	Anesthesia services (e.g., sedation) for endoscopic procedures (e.g., lower intestinal endoscopy and laparoscopy) are usually provided by the surgeon who performs the procedure. If an anesthesiologist or a CRNA provides general or regional anesthesia services, report 00810 or 00840 and the appropriate physical status and HCPCS level II modifiers. (When MAC is provided by the anesthesiologist or CRNA, also add HCPCS level II modifier -QS.)
00834–00836	When a hernia repair is performed on an infant less than 1 year of age, report code 00834 or 00836 (depending on age). *Do not report qualifying circumstances code 99100 with code 00834 or 00836.* For patients 1 year of age or older who undergo hernia repair surgery, report code 00830 or 00832 (depending on type of hernia).
00868	Code 00868 is reported for anesthesia services provided to the recipient of a kidney transplant. Assign code 00862 for anesthesia services provided to a living kidney donor. Assign code 01990 for anesthesia service provided to a brain-dead patient who undergoes a kidney organ harvest.
00872	**Extracorporeal shock wave lithotripsy (ESWL)** uses ultrasound shock waves to crush calculi (stones) located in the bladder, renal pelvis, or ureter. A **lithotripter** is the device that administers a high-voltage electrical discharge through a spark gap under water, which produces a compressive force and breaks apart the stones so they can pass in urine. Typically, the surgeon provides monitored anesthesia care (MAC) to the patient. However, if an anesthesiologist or a CRNA provides general or regional anesthesia services, report 00872 and the appropriate physical status and HCPCS level II modifiers. If MAC is provided by the anesthesiologist, add HCPCS level II modifier -QS.

Table 10-11 Sample Coding Rules Associated with Perineum Subsection Anesthesia Codes

Code(s)	Coding Rule
00902	For anesthesia services provided during lower intestinal endoscopic procedures, report code 00810.
00910–00918	When anesthesia services are provided for **urethrocystoscopy** (visualization of urethra and urinary bladder) and the surgeon completes other procedures through the urethrocystocope (e.g., biopsy of urinary bladder), report the appropriate code from range 00910–00918.
00920–00938	When anesthesia services are provided for procedures performed on male genitalia and an open urethral procedure (incision into urethra) is done to access anatomical sites, report the appropriate code from range 00920–00938.

For anesthesia services provided during perineal muscle and nerve procedures, report code 00300. For anesthesia services provided during perineal skin procedures, report code 00400.

EXAMPLE 1: An anesthesiologist provided general anesthesia services to 4-year-old female healthy patient who underwent perineal skin biopsy. Report code 00400-P1-AA.

EXAMPLE 2: An anesthesiologist provided regional anesthesia services to an anxious diabetic patient who underwent left gluteus maximus muscle biopsy. Report code 00300-P2-AA.

Pelvis (Except Hip)

Anesthesia services for the Pelvis (Except Hip) subsection include procedures on the following anatomical sites: anterior or posterior iliac crest, bony pelvis, interpelviabdominal (hindquarter), pelvis, symphysis pubis, sacroiliac joint, acetabulum, and extrapelvic and intrapelvic obturator nerves. (There are no coding rules for the Pelvis [Except Hip] subsection.)

EXAMPLE: An anesthesiologist provided general anesthesia services to a chronic asthmatic patient who underwent an open procedure involving the sacroiliac joint. Report code 01170-P2-AA.

Upper Leg (Except Knee)

Anesthesia services for the Upper Leg (Except Knee) subsection include procedures on the following anatomical sites: hip joint; upper two-thirds of femur; and arteries, veins, nerves, muscles, tendons, fascia, and bursae of upper leg. (There are no coding rules for the Upper Leg [Except Knee] subsection.)

> **EXAMPLE:** An anesthesiologist provided general anesthesia services to an intellectually disabled patient with mild systemic disease who underwent nerve biopsy of the upper leg. Report code 01250-P2-AA.

Knee and Popliteal Area

Anesthesia services for the Knee and Popliteal Area subsection include procedures on the following anatomical sites: arteries, veins, nerves, muscles, tendons, fascia, and bursae of knee and/or popliteal area; lower one-third of femur; knee joint; upper ends of the tibia and fibula; and patella. (There are no coding rules for the Knee and Popliteal Area subsection.)

> **EXAMPLE:** An anesthesiologist provided general anesthesia services to a normal healthy patient who underwent diagnostic arthroscopy, left knee. Report code 01382-P1-AA.

Lower Leg (Below Knee, Includes Ankle and Foot)

Anesthesia services for the Lower Leg (Below Knee, Includes Ankle and Foot) subsection include procedures on the following anatomical sites: lower leg; ankle; foot; and arteries, veins, bones, nerves, muscles, tendons, and fascia of leg, ankle, and foot. (There are no coding rules for the Lower Leg [Below Knee, Includes Ankle and Foot] subsection.)

> **EXAMPLE:** An anesthesiologist provided general anesthesia services to a normal healthy patient who underwent arthroscopic procedure, right ankle. Report code 01464-P1-AA.

Shoulder and Axilla

Anesthesia services for the Shoulder and Axilla subsection include procedures on the following anatomical sites: arteries, veins, nerves, muscles, tendons, fascia, and bursae of shoulder and axillae; humeral head and neck; sternoclavicular joint; acromioclavicular joint; and shoulder joint. (There are no coding rules for the Shoulder and Axilla subsection.)

> **EXAMPLE:** An anesthesiologist provided general anesthesia services to a normal healthy patient who underwent muscle biopsy, left shoulder. Report code 01610-P1-AA.

Upper Arm and Elbow

Anesthesia services for the Upper Arm and Elbow subsection include procedures on the following anatomical sites: arteries, veins, nerves, muscle, tendons, fascia, and bursae of upper arm and elbow; humerus; and elbow. (There are no coding rules for the Upper Arm and Elbow subsection.)

> **EXAMPLE:** An anesthesiologist provided general anesthesia services to a patient with mild systemic disease who underwent excision of tumor of the right humerus. Report code 01758-P2-AA.

Forearm, Wrist, and Hand

Anesthesia services for the Forearm, Wrist, and Hand subsection include procedures on the following anatomical sites: arteries, veins, nerves, muscles, tendons, fascia, and bursae of forearm, wrist, and hand; radius; ulna; wrist; hand bones; distal radius; distal ulna; and hand joints. (There are no coding rules for the Forearm, Wrist, and Hand subsection.)

> **EXAMPLE:** An anesthesiologist provided general anesthesia services to a normal healthy but very anxious patient who underwent diagnostic and surgical arthroscopy with bone biopsy, right wrist. Report code 01830-P1-AA-23. (Modifier -23 indicates general anesthesia services were provided for a procedure that usually is performed under local anesthesia.)

Radiological Procedures

Anesthesia services for radiological procedures include the following: myelography, discography, and vertebroplasty; diagnostic arteriography/venography; cardiac catheterization, including coronary angiography and ventriculography; noninvasive imaging or radiation therapy; and therapeutic interventional radiology involving the arterial/venous/lymphatic systems. (Refer to Table 10-12 for Radiological Procedures subsection coding rules.)

EXAMPLE: An anesthesiologist provided MAC to a patient with severe systemic disease who underwent cardiac catheterization, including coronary angiography and ventriculography. Report code 01920-P3-AA-QS.

 Note:

Refer to Chapter 16, CPT Radiology, for coding rules about radiological procedures and services.

⚠ Coding Tip:

- Medicare anesthesia billing guidelines require that just one code be reported for anesthesia services provided in conjunction with radiological procedures.

- Radiological supervision and interpretation codes applicable to radiological procedures being performed are reported by the appropriate provider (e.g., radiologist, cardiologist, neurosurgeon, or radiation oncologist). Such codes are not included (bundled) in anesthesia services codes for radiological procedures, and the appropriate provider must report the radiology procedure or service code.

Table 10-12 Sample Coding Rules Associated with Radiological Procedures Subsection Anesthesia Codes

Code(s)	Coding Rule
01916	An **arteriography** is the visualization of an artery via x-ray after injection of a **radiopaque** (cannot be penetrated by electromagnetic radiation) substance. A **contrast medium** is a radiopaque substance (e.g., Renografin dye used for intravenous pyelogram) that obstructs the passage of x-rays so structures containing it appear white on radiographic film. This allows the radiologist to visualize abnormalities and define body structure contours.
01920	CPT code 01920 (Anesthesia for cardiac catheterization including coronary angiography and ventriculography [not to include Swan-Ganz catheter]) is reported for monitored anesthesia care (MAC) in patients who are critically ill or critically unstable. If the physician performing the radiological service inserts a catheter (other than a Swan-Ganz catheter) as part of the anesthesia services provided and a catheter is left in place and used for monitoring purposes, do not report a code for placement of the monitoring catheter (e.g., CPT codes 36500, 36555–36556, 36568–36569, 36580, 36584, and 36597).
01922	When anesthesia is required for a CT scan or MRI due to medical necessity (e.g., patient with intellectual disability), report code 01922 (Anesthesia for noninvasive imaging or radiation therapy) with appropriate modifiers.
01924–01933	**Interventional therapeutic radiological procedures** are the therapeutic application of radiation that includes the following aspects: - Analysis and interpretation of radiation equipment performance measurements - Calibration of equipment associated with production and use of radiation - Analysis and interpretation of measurements associated with patient dosages - Radiation safety aspects associated with production and use of radiation
01935–01936	Percutaneous image guided procedures on the spine and spinal cord involve inserting a peripheral intravenous catheter, administering an anxiolytic (antianxiety) medication, and accompanying the patient to the radiology suite. Once in the radiology suite, sedation and analgesic agents (e.g., diagnostic procedures) or general anesthesia (e.g., therapeutic procedures) are administered.

Burn Excisions or Debridement

Anesthesia services for burn excisions or debridement procedures include the following: second- and third-degree burn excision or debridement with or without skin grafting according to total body surface area. (Refer to Chapter 11, CPT Surgery I, for discussion of total body surface area calculations.) (Refer to Table 10-13 for Burn Excisions or Debridement subsection coding rules.)

EXAMPLE: An anesthesiologist provided general anesthesia services to a 2-year-old type 1 diabetic patient who underwent second-degree burn debridement of the chest, 5 percent of total body surface area. Report code 01952-P2-AA.

Obstetric

Anesthesia services for obstetric procedures include the following: external cephalic version procedure, vaginal delivery, cesarean delivery, urgent hysterectomy following delivery, cesarean hysterectomy without labor analgesia/anesthesia care, abortion procedures, neuraxial labor analgesia/anesthesia for planned vaginal delivery, neuraxial labor analgesia/anesthesia for cesarean delivery following planned vaginal delivery, and cesarean hysterectomy following neuraxial labor analgesia/anesthesia. (Refer to Chapter 15, CPT Surgery V, for detailed discussion of obstetric procedures and services.) (Refer to Table 10-14 for Obstetric subsection coding rules.)

EXAMPLE: An anesthesiologist provided general anesthesia services to a normal healthy patient who suffered a miscarriage and underwent surgery to remove the remaining products of conception. Report code 01965-P1-AA.

Other Procedures

Anesthesia services for other procedures include the following: physiologic support for harvesting organ(s) from brain-dead patients, anesthesia for diagnostic/therapeutic nerve blocks and injections, daily hospital management of epidural or subarachnoid continuous drug administration, and unlisted anesthesia procedure(s). (Refer to Table 10-15 for Other Procedures subsection coding rules.)

Table 10-13 Sample Coding Rule Associated with Burn Excisions or Debridement Subsection Anesthesia Codes

Code(s)	Coding Rule
01952–01953	Code 01953 is reported with code 01952 when the percent of total body surface area or part thereof treated is greater than 9 percent. Do not add modifier -51 (Multiple Procedures) to code 01953 because the word "each" is included in its code description. Be sure to interpret percent of total body surface in code 01952 as up to 4 percent and in code 01953 as up to 9 percent.

Table 10-14 Sample Coding Rule Associated with Obstetric Subsection Anesthesia Codes

Code(s)	Coding Rule
01967–01969	If documentation supports procedures or services provided, code 01968 is reported with 01967, or code 01969 is reported with 01967 and 01968.

Table 10-15 Sample Coding Rules Associated with Other Procedures Subsection Anesthesia Codes

Code	Coding Rule
01996	Report code 01996 when the anesthesiologist or CRNA provides daily hospital management of continuous epidural or subarachnoid drug administration. This management is provided because the anesthesiologist or CRNA inserted an epidural or subarachnoid catheter during a surgical procedure as part of anesthesia services provided.
01999	When reporting code 01999, make sure you submit a copy of the operative report and other pertinent documents to the third-party payer for review.

 Note:

- To report regional intravenous administration of local anesthetic agents or other medication in the upper or lower extremity, assign an Anesthesia code from the appropriate Anesthesia subsection.

- To report a Bier block for pain management, assign code 64999. A *Bier block* is an intravenous regional block, which involves using a tourniquet to restrict the effects of anesthesia to a region of the body (e.g., leg).

- To report intra-arterial or intravenous injections, including that for pain management, assign a code from 96373–96379.

EXAMPLE: An anesthesiologist managed the continuous drug administration of an epidural for a 50-year-old patient who has COPD. Report code 01996-P2-AA.

Exercise 10.4 – Anesthesia Subsections

Instructions: Complete each statement below.

1. For Medicare purposes, just one anesthesia code is usually reported unless the second and subsequent anesthesia codes are _____ codes.

2. When an anesthesiologist or a CRNA provides distinct procedural services such as the insertion of a Swan-Ganz catheter in addition to anesthesia services, codes are reported separately and modifier _____ is added to the procedure (e.g., Swan-Ganz catheter) code.

3. When procedures on the larynx and trachea are performed on a patient who is younger than 1 year of age, report qualifying circumstances code 99100 in addition to 00326. True or False?

4. When an internal mammary node dissection is performed *in addition to a radical or modified radical breast procedure*, report anesthesia code _____.

5. Anesthesia services for endoscopic procedures are usually provided by the surgeon who performs the procedure. When monitored anesthesia care (MAC) is provided by the anesthesiologist or CRNA, add HCPCS level II modifier _____ for MAC.

6. When anesthesia services for therapeutic percutaneous image-guided procedure on the spine and spinal cord are provided, report a code from range _____.

7. When anesthesia services are provided to the recipient of a liver transplant, report code _____.

8. When anesthesia services are provided to a brain-dead patient who undergoes a kidney organ harvest, report code _____.

9. When anesthesia is required for a CT scan or MRI due to medical necessity (e.g., patient with intellectual disability), report code _____.

10. When the percentage of total body surface area or part thereof treated for second- and third-degree burns is greater than 9 percent, report code _____ in addition to 01952.

Summary

The Anesthesia section is located after the Evaluation and Management section in the CPT coding manual, and codes (00100 to 01999) with appropriate modifiers are reported for services related to the administration of anesthesia (including general and regional), supplementation of local anesthesia, and other supportive anesthesia services. The Anesthesia section is organized according to general anatomical areas or services that relate to a number of surgical procedures. For Medicare purposes, just one anesthesia code is reported unless the second and subsequent anesthesia codes are add-on codes. When separate anesthesia codes are reported, the code that describes the anesthesia service for the procedure that has the *highest* base unit value is reported first.

A physician (e.g., anesthesiologist) is responsible for supervising anesthesia services (which include general and regional), supplementation of local anesthesia, and other supportive services so the patient receives appropriate optimal anesthesia care. The administration of local infiltration, metacarpal/metatarsal/digital block, or topical anesthesia by the operating surgeon or obstetrician is included (bundled) in the surgery code; separate codes are not reported. Anesthesia services include the preparation and monitoring of the patient, as well as the following services: draping, positioning, prepping, and transporting the patient; inserting nasogastric or orogastric tubes; inserting peripheral IV lines for fluid and medication administration; interpreting laboratory results; interpreting monitored functions; placing airway tubes, including laryngoscopy for airway management; positioning external devices for capnography, cardiac monitoring, CNS evoked responses, Doppler flow, pulse oximetry, and temperature; and stimulating nerves to determine level of paralysis or localization of nerve(s).

Internet Links

American Society of Anesthesiologists (ASA): Go to **www.asahq.org**, scroll over the Education heading, and click on the Practice Management link to access reimbursement information.

Medicare Information for Anesthesiologists: Go to **www.cms.gov**, click on the Medicare link, and then click on the Anesthesiologists link, located toward the bottom of the page under Provider Type.

Vascular Access Doc: Go to **www.vascularaccessdoc.com**, and click on the Teaching Files link to view presentations that include images of vascular access catheterization.

Study Checklist

❏ Read this chapter and highlight key concepts.

❏ Create an index card for each key term.

❏ Access the chapter Internet links to learn more about concepts.

❏ Complete the chapter exercises and review, verifying answers with your instructor.

❏ Complete Workbook chapter, verifying answers with your instructor.

❏ Go to **www.cengagebrain.com** to access the Student Companion Web Site. Login instructions are located in the Preface.

❏ Form a study group with classmates to discuss chapter concepts in preparation for an exam.

Review

Multiple Choice

Instructions: Circle the most appropriate response.

1. Local anesthesia administration techniques include:
    a. caudal anesthesia, saddle block anesthesia, and epidural anesthesia.
    b. general anesthesia, local anesthesia, and regional anesthesia.
    c. spinal anesthesia, intravenous regional anesthesia, and Bier block.
    d. surface anesthesia, infiltration anesthesia, field block, peripheral nerve block, and plexus anesthesia.

2. The CPT Anesthesia section includes:
    a. subsections for anatomical sites followed by subsections for procedures.
    b. subsections for procedures followed by subsections for anatomical sites.
    c. subsections for anatomical sites only.
    d. subsections for procedures only.

3. Prior to surgery, a professional assesses information from the patient's record, performs a physical examination, evaluates preoperative test results, and ensures that informed anesthetic consent has been obtained. This service is called:
    a. monitored anesthesia care.
    b. postanesthesia evaluation.
    c. postoperative pain management.
    d. preanesthesia evaluation.

4. The professional who assesses information from the patient's record, performs a physical examination, evaluates preoperative test results, and ensures that informed anesthetic consent has been obtained is called a(n):
    a. anesthesiologist or CRNA.
    b. primary care physician.
    c. registration technician.
    d. surgeon.

5. The information assessed from the patient's record, physical examination performed on the patient, evaluation of preoperative test results, and verification that informed anesthetic consent has been obtained is:
    a. documented in the operative report.
    b. included in the anesthesia code.
    c. part of postanesthesia services.
    d. reported as a separate service.

6. If the surgery for which preanesthesia services are performed is canceled, the anesthesiologist should:
    a. not report any codes.
    b. report an evaluation and management service code instead of an anesthesia code.
    c. report the anesthesia code for the procedure that was canceled.
    d. report the anesthesia code for the procedure that was canceled and add modifier -53 for discontinued procedure.

7. When an anesthesiologist provides anesthesia services for a 5-month-old healthy patient who undergoes a procedure on the larynx and trachea, report code(s):
    a. 00326-P1-AA.
    b. 00326-P1-AA and 99100.
    c. 99100.
    d. 99100 and 00326-P1-AA.

8. Code 00218 is reported for anesthesia services provided during an _____ procedure, which is performed on the skull while the patient is in a seated position.
    a. endocranial
    b. innercranial
    c. intercranial
    d. intracranial

9. Which is considered a diagnostic radiological procedure?
    a. Analysis and interpretation of measurements associated with patient dosages
    b. Analysis and interpretation of radiation equipment performance measurements
    c. Calibration of equipment associated with production and use of radiation
    d. Visualization of abnormalities and definition of body structure contours

10. Code 00802 is reported for anesthesia services administered during a procedure in which a redundant layer of fat tissue located at the lowest portion of the abdominal wall is surgically removed. This procedure is called a:
    a. panniculectomy.   b. panniculotomy.   c. panniculus.   d. pannus.

11. An anesthesiologist provided anesthesia services on an otherwise healthy patient who underwent left corneal transplant. Which CPT code is assigned?
    a. 00144-P1-AA   c. 65410-P1-AA
    b. 00580-P1-AA   d. 65710-P1-AA

12. An anesthesiologist provided anesthesia services on a 30-year-old male patient who underwent thyroidectomy for rare thyroid cancer. Which CPT code is assigned?
    a. 00320-P3-AA   c. 01442-P3-AA
    b. 00322-P3-AA   d. 60210-P3-AA

13. An anesthesiologist provided monitored anesthesia care to a patient with history of severe cardiopulmonary condition who underwent a procedure to access central venous circulation. Which CPT code is assigned?
    a. 00530-P3-AA-G9   c. 00560-P3-AA-G9
    b. 00532-P3-AA-G9   d. 01916-P3-AA-G9

14. An anesthesiologist provided anesthesia services on a patient with mild systemic disease who underwent upper abdomen vascular surgery. Which CPT code is assigned?
    a. 00700-P2-AA   b. 00770-P2-AA   c. 00880-P2-AA   d. 00882-P2-AA

15. An anesthesiologist provided anesthesia services on an otherwise healthy patient who underwent intrapelvic obturator neurectomy. Which CPT code is assigned?
    a. 01140-P1-AA   b. 01180-P1-AA   c. 01190-P1-AA   d. 27326-P1-AA

16. An anesthesiologist provided anesthesia services on a patient with mild systemic disease who underwent popliteal thromboendarterectomy. Which CPT code is assigned?
    a. 01440-P2-AA   b. 01442-P2-AA   c. 01400-P2-AA   d. 35303-P2-AA

17. An anesthesiologist provided anesthesia services on an otherwise healthy patient who underwent repair of the Achilles tendon. Which CPT code is assigned?
    a. 01462-P1-AA   b. 01472-P1-AA   c. 27650-P1-AA   d. 28200-P1-AA

18. An anesthesiologist provided anesthesia services on a patient with severe systemic disease who underwent an interthoracoscapular amputation. Which CPT code is assigned?
    a. 01630-P3-AA   b. 01636-P3-AA   c. 01710-P3-AA   d. 23900-P3-AA

19. An anesthesiologist provided anesthesia services to a five-year-old otherwise healthy patient who underwent bilateral orchiopexy. Which CPT code is assigned?
    a. 00926-P1-AA   b. 00928-P1-AA   c. 00930-P1-AA   d. 54650-P1-AA

20. An anesthesiologist provided anesthesia services on an otherwise healthy patient who underwent phleborrhaphy, right wrist. Which CPT code is assigned?
    a. 01782-P1-AA   b. 01852-P1-AA   c. 15850-P1-AA   d. 37650-P1-AA

Coding Practice I—Modifiers

Instructions: Review each case and assign CPT anesthesia code(s) and appropriate modifier(s). (Enter the physical status modifier first, such as 00000-P1-AA.) Some cases require assignment of CPT surgery codes and appropriate modifier(s), per chapter content about anesthesia coding guidelines.

1. While providing regional anesthesia services for a healthy patient who underwent an emergency cesarean section, the anesthesiologist inserted a lumbar catheter to provide continuous epidural analgesia pain management (morphine bolus).

    _____

2. A CRNA (with medical direction by the surgeon) provided general anesthesia services for a controlled diabetic patient who underwent total wrist replacement. At the conclusion of the surgical procedure, the CRNA inserted an epidural catheter to provide continuous postoperative analgesia for pain management. The CRNA monitored the patient's pain management on the day after surgery.

    _____

3. A healthy patient underwent total knee replacement surgery; regional anesthesia services were provided by an anesthesiologist.

    _____

4. An anesthesiologist provided regional pain block for an arthroscopic anterior cruciate ligament repair of the left knee of a healthy 40-year-old male patient. The anesthesiologist also performed a femoral nerve block for postoperative pain management.

    _____

5. A patient with chronic asthma underwent a thoracotomy. The CRNA (without medical direction by a physician) provided general anesthesia services and, at the conclusion of the procedure, inserted an epidural catheter for continuous infusion of morphine for postoperative pain control.

    _____

Coding Practice II—Anesthesia

Instructions: Review each case and assign the appropriate anesthesia code(s) and physical status modifier(s). Make sure you assign qualifying circumstance code(s) where appropriate. All anesthesia services were provided by the anesthesiologist, which means that modifier -AA is added to each anesthesia code. Some cases require assignment of CPT surgery codes and appropriate modifier(s), per chapter content about anesthesia coding guidelines.

1. A 77-year-old healthy male patient with controlled diabetes mellitus underwent intraocular lens transplant surgery for which general anesthesia was administered.

    _____

2. A 5-year-old healthy boy was admitted to the pediatrics floor of an acute care hospital and underwent tympanostomy for which general anesthesia was administered.

    _____

3. A 9-month-old female patient underwent tracheostomy under general anesthesia after having sustained injuries in a motor vehicle accident. The child lost consciousness for 60 minutes after the accident and required cardiopulmonary resuscitation.

    _____

4. A 47-year-old male patient with a history of hypertension underwent a partial thyroid lobectomy due to a thyroid tumor. General anesthesia was administered.

_____

5. A 33-year-old healthy male construction worker fell from a ladder onto a wooden platform. He was brought into the emergency room and diagnosed with a concussion; there was no loss of consciousness. The patient went to the operating room for the complicated removal of wood from the skin of his shoulder. He received general anesthesia.

_____

6. A 14-year-old male is admitted to the pediatrics ward with chest pain, shortness of breath, and possible lordosis. After examination, the diagnosis of pectus excavatum was made. The boy had the condition corrected with an open procedure under general anesthesia.

_____

7. A 78-year-old female smoker was admitted for shortness of breath, hypertension, and bloody sputum. She was diagnosed with pneumonia and underwent pneumocentesis performed under general anesthesia.

_____

8. A 45-year-old male with a history of coronary disease and mild hypertension underwent insertion of a permanent pacemaker with epicardial electrodes by thoracotomy. General anesthesia was administered.

_____

9. A 57-year-old female with a history of osteoporosis underwent posterior arthrodesis in the craniocervical (occipital C2) region. General anesthesia was administered.

_____

10. A 25-year-old male heroin addict complaining of severe headaches was admitted to the psychiatric floor of an acute care hospital. After detoxification, the patient still had headaches; increased spinal fluid pressure was noted. He underwent diagnostic lumbar spinal puncture performed under regional anesthesia.

_____

11. An obese 56-year-old male with benign hypertension complained of recurring heartburn. After examination, he was admitted for surgery and underwent a transabdominal repair of a diaphragmatic hernia. General anesthesia was administered.

_____

12. An otherwise healthy 5-year-old female underwent percutaneous liver biopsy under general anesthesia.

_____

13. A 54-year-old female who lost 100 pounds two years ago underwent panniculectomy under general anesthesia. The patient has no significant medical history or chronic conditions.

_____

14. A healthy 36-year-old female underwent tubal ligation under general anesthesia for voluntary sterilization.

_____

15. A 45-year-old female presented with moderate vaginal bleeding. After being admitted and tested, she underwent hysteroscopy with endometrium biopsy under general anesthesia.

_____

16. A healthy 38-year-old male requested voluntary sterilization and underwent vasectomy. Regional anesthesia was administered.

_____

17. A volunteer offered bone marrow to a needy recipient. He underwent bone marrow aspiration of the posterior iliac crest with general anesthesia to provide a sample to test for a match. The donor has no chronic or current medical conditions.

_____

18. An otherwise healthy 14-year-old-male fell while skateboarding and landed on his back. After radiological exam, he was diagnosed with fractured sacroiliac joint. Open treatment of the anterior ring fracture was performed under general anesthesia.

_____

19. A 46-year-old female fell while in-line skating and fractured her femur at the proximal end. She underwent open treatment of the femoral fracture with internal fixation under general anesthesia. The patient has type 2 diabetes mellitus, controlled.

_____

20. A 76-year-old female with Parkinson's disease fell while getting out of bed. She was unable to walk and was found two days later by her son. She was dehydrated and disoriented. She was seen and evaluated in the emergency department. She was admitted with the diagnosis of a hip fracture. The patient's hip was repaired with total hip arthroplasty under general anesthesia on the day of admission.

_____

21. A 17-year-old male high school football player's knee was injured during a game. Examination revealed fractured patella. He underwent open treatment of the fractured patella under general anesthesia.

_____

22. A 15-year-old female high school gymnast's knee was injured during a meet. Radiological examination revealed torn meniscus. She underwent a surgical arthroscopic procedure of her knee to repair the meniscus, with general anesthesia.

_____

23. A 14-year-old Down syndrome male was stepped on by a horse. Upon radiological exam, it was noted that the boy had a trimalleolar fracture. He underwent closed treatment of the fracture without manipulation under general anesthesia.

_____

24. A 23-year-old female smoker was seen in the emergency room with pain, swelling, and disfigurement in her right lower leg. Radiological exam revealed a fractured tibia. She underwent closed reduction and casting under general anesthesia.

_____

25. An otherwise healthy 27-year-old male fell while riding his motorcycle. He complained of right shoulder pain and swelling. Upon radiological exam, it was noted that he had a fractured humerus. He underwent closed treatment of the humeral head under general anesthesia.

_____

26. A healthy 37-year-old female iron worker had an I beam fall on her shoulder. The joint was crushed. She went to the emergency room and was brought to the operating room for interthoracoscapular amputation under general anesthesia.

_____

27. A healthy 21-year-old female college tennis player complained about pain in her left elbow. The joint was swollen and tender. After orthopedic and radiological exam, reconstruction of the lateral collateral ligament was performed under general anesthesia.

_____

28. A 50-year-old bodybuilder heard a pop and felt severe pain in his right upper arm while lifting heavy weights. Radiological exam revealed a ruptured bicep tendon. He underwent reinsertion of the ruptured tendon under general anesthesia.

_____

29. An otherwise healthy 68-year-old male noticed a lump on his left forearm. Examination determined that he was in need of incision and drainage of a bursa. The procedure was performed under general anesthesia.

_____

30. A 47-year-old healthy male factory worker caught his lower left arm in a commercial washing machine. The patient sustained a fracture and dislocated distal radius. The patient underwent open reduction of the fracture and dislocation under general anesthesia.

_____

31. A 57-year-old obese female with hypertension showed coronary problems during a stress test. A cardiac catherization under general anesthesia was performed.

_____

32. A 63-year-old male was diagnosed with a glioblastoma multiforme. He underwent radiation therapy under regional anesthesia.

_____

33. A firefighter sustained second-degree burns over 35 percent of his body while on duty. He received general anesthesia during the burn debridement.

_____

34. A 59-year-old female chemical factory worker sustained second-degree burns due to a caustic chemical spill to her left arm. Nine percent of her body was burned. She received general anesthesia during burn excision.

_____

35. A healthy 24-year-old female had a normal vaginal delivery under regional anesthesia.

_____

36. A controlled non-insulin-dependent diabetic 29-year-old female underwent cesarean delivery with general anesthesia.

_____

37. A 37-year-old male has recurring back pain. He underwent spinal disc surgery and continued to need daily epidural continuous drug anesthesia while in the hospital.

_____

38. An anesthesiologist provided physiologic support for harvesting organs (for organ donation) from a brain-dead patient.

_____

39. A healthy 30-year-old patient underwent insertion of an epidural catheter on the first day of admission. On the second day of admission, the anesthesiologist was responsible for hospital management of continuous epidural drug administration. (Report the Anesthesia code for the second day of admission only.)

_____

40. General anesthesia was administered to a 6-month-old male child with mild systemic disease who underwent anesthesia for a brand new procedure not yet classified in CPT. The patient was observed in recovery by the nursing staff and evaluated by the anesthesiologist before being transferred to the pediatric unit of the hospital. The nursing staff placed an IV line for saline and postoperative pain medication.

_____

CPT Surgery I

Chapter Outline

Overview of Surgery Section

Surgery Guidelines

General Subsection

Integumentary System Subsection

Chapter Objectives

At the conclusion of this chapter, the student should be able to:

- Define key terms.
- Explain the organization, format, and content of the CPT Surgery section.
- Interpret CPT Surgery section guidelines.
- Interpret CPT Surgery coding notes for the General and Integumentary System subsections.
- Assign CPT Surgery codes from the General and Integumentary System subsections.
- Add CPT and/or HCPCS level II modifiers to codes, as appropriate.

Key Terms

ablation

acellular dermal
 replacement

actinic keratosis (AK)

adjacent tissue transfer/
 rearrangement

advancement flap

allograft

autograft

bedsore

biopsy

blepharoplasty

chemical peel

chemosurgery

cryosurgery

decubitus ulcer

defect

dermabrasion

destruction

diagnostic procedure

donor site

double pedicle flap

electrosurgery

endoscopy

excision

excisional biopsy

extensive cellulitis

fine-needle aspiration
 (FNA)

flap

free flap

free skin graft

full-thickness skin graft

glabellar frown lines

global period

global surgical package

graft

incision

incision and drainage
 (I&D)

incisional biopsy

introduction

island flap

island pedicle flap

LASER (light
 amplification by
 stimulated emission
 of radiation)

Limberg flap

lumpectomy

microdermabrasion

moderate (conscious)
 sedation

modified radical
 mastectomy

Mohs microsurgery	random pattern flap	separate procedure	therapeutic surgical procedure
mycocutaneous flap	recipient site	shaving	tissue approximation
needle core biopsy	reconstruction	simple closure	tissue-cultured autograft
open biopsy	removal	simple repair	tissue rearrangement
paring and curettement	repair	skin substitute graft	total mastectomy
partial mastectomy	revision	split-thickness skin graft	undermining
pedicle skin graft	rhomboid flap	stereotactic localization	V-Y plasty
pilonidal cyst	rhytidectomy	stroma	W-plasty
pressure ulcer	rotation flap	surgical curettement	xenograft
primary defect	rule of nines	surgical package	Z-plasty
radical mastectomy	secondary defect	suture	

Introduction

The Surgery section of CPT contains codes and code descriptions for surgical procedures performed by physicians. Because procedures can be performed using a variety of methods and different combinations, the Surgery section contains multiple codes that describe similar procedures. The intention is to allow for coding specificity and to accurately reflect the actual procedure performed. The patient's diagnosis and physical status (e.g., normal, healthy patient versus patient with severe systemic disease) guides the physician, who determines whether just one procedure or multiple procedures will be performed during an encounter (e.g., office visit) or operative session (e.g., ambulatory surgery). The documented operative report and other patient record documentation guide the selection of appropriate codes for reporting to third-party payers.

Overview of Surgery Section

The CPT Surgery section and its subsections are organized anatomically according to major body area and/or organ system. Categories and subcategories are organized within subsections according to type of procedure. Selecting the appropriate surgery code requires a careful review of the patient record to determine the procedures and services provided. Before referring to the CPT index to begin the process of locating a surgery code, review the documented operative report (Figure 11-1) to determine the following:

- Body system (e.g., digestive)

- Anatomical site (e.g., stomach)

- Surgical approach (e.g., laparotomy)

- Type of procedure performed (e.g., partial gastrectomy)

- Fact that multiple procedures were performed during the same operative session (e.g., gastroscopy followed by exploratory laparotomy and removal of a portion of the stomach)

EXAMPLE 1: When reporting the CPT code for "excision of cervical stump," if an abdominal approach was documented in the operative report, assign code 57540. If a vaginal approach was documented, assign code 57550.

```
57540    Excision of cervical stump, abdominal approach;
57545        with pelvic floor repair
```

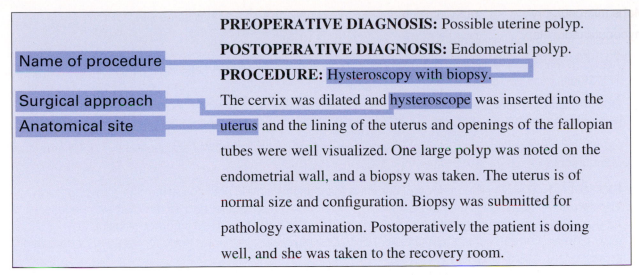

PREOPERATIVE DIAGNOSIS: Possible uterine polyp.

POSTOPERATIVE DIAGNOSIS: Endometrial polyp.

Name of procedure

PROCEDURE: Hysteroscopy with biopsy.

Surgical approach

The cervix was dilated and hysteroscope was inserted into the

Anatomical site

uterus and the lining of the uterus and openings of the fallopian tubes were well visualized. One large polyp was noted on the endometrial wall, and a biopsy was taken. The uterus is of normal size and configuration. Biopsy was submitted for pathology examination. Postoperatively the patient is doing well, and she was taken to the recovery room.

Figure 11-1 Sample operative report with name of procedure, surgical approach, and anatomical site highlighted to illustrate how to locate information needed to assign CPT code

EXAMPLE 2: When reporting the CPT code for "removal of a 0.5-cm malignant lesion of the arm," if a surgical excision was documented in the operative report, assign code 11600. If a destruction procedure (e.g., laser ablation) was documented, assign code 17260.

```
11600    Excision, malignant lesion including margins, trunk, arms, or legs;
         excised diameter 0.5 cm or less

17260    Destruction, malignant lesion (eg, laser surgery, electrosurgery,
         cryosurgery, chemosurgery, surgical curettement), trunk, arms or
         legs; lesion diameter 0.5 cm or less
```

CPT code descriptions include the procedure performed, but they do not include the numerous activities integral to the procedure. It would be impractical to list every event common to all procedures of a similar nature in the code's narrative description. Many common activities reflect the principles of medical and surgical care, and while considered acceptable medical/surgical practice, they are not coded separately. In addition, although many activities are common to all procedures, some are integral only to certain groups of procedures.

The services integral to the standard practice of medical/surgical services, for which no separate code is assigned, include:

- Cleansing, shaving, and prepping the patient's skin

- Draping and positioning the patient

- Inserting intravenous access for medication

- Administering sedatives (by physician performing procedure)

- Administering local, topical, and/or regional anesthetic (by physician performing procedure)

- Establishing the surgical approach (identifying anatomical landmarks, making the incision, evaluating the surgical field, and performing simple debridement of traumatized tissue)

- Performing lysis of simple adhesions

- Isolating neurovascular, muscular (including stimulation for identification), bony, or other structures that limits access to surgical field

- Taking surgical cultures

- Irrigating wounds

- Inserting and removing drains, suction devices, dressings, and pumps into same site

- Closing the surgical incision

- Applying, managing, and removing postoperative dressings, including analgesic devices (e.g., peri-incisional TENS unit, institution of patient-controlled analgesia)

- Documenting preoperative, intraoperative, and postoperative reports, which includes providing photographs, drawings, dictation, and transcription necessary to document services provided

- Identifying surgical supplies (unless third-party payer policy states that they are separately coded and reimbursable)

  EXAMPLE 1: The physician removed cerumen (earwax) impaction prior to performing a myringotomy. The cerumen impaction prevented access to the tympanic membrane, and its removal was necessary for the successful completion of the myringotomy. Report code 69420 (Myringotomy including aspiration and/or eustachian tube inflation) only. *Do not report a separate code for removal of cerumen impaction.*

  EXAMPLE 2: The physician performed a bronchoscopy to assess the patient's lung anatomy prior to performing a lobectomy (single lobe). Report code 32480, which has a CPT code description of "removal of lung, other than total pneumonectomy; single lobe (lobectomy)." *Do not report a code for the bronchoscopy*, which was performed as a scout endoscopy to assess the surgical field and to establish anatomical landmarks, extent of disease, and so on. When an endoscopic procedure is done as part of an open procedure, such as a lobectomy, it is not separately coded and reported.

  If an endoscopy is performed initially to diagnose the patient on the same day as the open procedure, the endoscopy is separately coded and reported. Modifier -58 is added to the endoscopy code to indicate that the procedures are staged or planned services. Also, if endoscopic procedures are performed on distinct, separate areas during the same operative session, separately code and report each procedure (e.g., thoracoscopy and mediastinoscopy). However, if a cursory (brief) evaluation of the upper airway is done as part of a bronchoscopy, do not separately code and report procedures (e.g., laryngoscopy or sinus endoscopy).

Organization of Surgery Section

The guidelines located at the beginning of the Surgery section apply to all codes in the section. The basic organization of the Surgery section is by major body system, with headings and subheadings based on anatomical site and/or type of procedure (Table 11-1). The Surgery section contains the following subsections, which represent organ systems, anatomical sites, or other designations:

- General (10021–10022)

- Integumentary System (10030–19499)

- Musculoskeletal System (20005–29999)

- Respiratory System (30000–32999)

- Cardiovascular System (33010–37799)

- Hemic and Lymphatic Systems (38100–38999)

- Mediastinum and Diaphragm (39000–39599)

- Digestive System (40490–49999)

- Urinary System (50010–53899)

- Male Genital System (54000–55899)

- Reproductive System Procedures (55920)

Table 11-1 Subheadings Typically Organized Below CPT Surgery Subsections

Subheading	Description
Incision	Cut made into body tissue during surgery using a knife, electrosurgical unit, or laser (e.g., 66500)
Incision and Drainage (I&D)	Cutting open a lesion (e.g., abscess) and draining its contents (e.g., 10060)
Excision	Removing a portion or all of an organ or another tissue (e.g., skin), using a scalpel or another surgical instrument (e.g., 11402)
Introduction	Injecting, inserting, or puncturing body tissue (e.g., 11900) or scoping an organ (e.g., 47531)
Removal	Eliminating tissue (e.g., amputating a body part) or taking something out (e.g., removing implants, such as buried wire, pins, or screws) (e.g., 20694)
Endoscopy	Visualizing a body cavity using an instrument that can be inserted into the body through a small incision or a natural opening (e.g., nose) (e.g., 31231) NOTE: An endoscope is also used as a surgical approach for performing other procedures (e.g., laparoscopic cholecystectomy, sigmoidoscopy with removal of polyps)
Repair	Improving improperly functioning body parts (e.g., 49520); types of repair include: • **Grafts**: Moving healthy tissue from one site to another to replace diseased or defective tissue • **Suture**: Closing a wound using catgut, glue, silk thread, wire, or other materials (Figure 11-2)
Revision	Modifying a previous procedure (e.g., gastric restrictive procedure) or a device (e.g., shunt) (e.g., 49426)
Reconstruction	Rebuilding a body part, such as the breast (e.g., 19357)
Destruction	**Ablation** (or removal) of benign, premalignant, or malignant tissue (e.g., 17000); types of destruction include: • **Chemosurgery**: Using chemicals to destroy diseased tissue, such as for skin cancer • **Cryosurgery**: Applying extreme cold, such as liquid nitrogen, to destroy abnormal tissue cells, such as warts or small skin lesions • **Electrosurgery**: Using an electrical device, such as electrocautery, to destroy abnormal tissue • **LASER (light amplification by stimulated emission of radiation)**: Using a device that is filled with a gas, liquid, or solid substance that is stimulated to emit light to a specific wavelength to burn, cut, or dissolve tissue • **Surgical curettment**: Scraping abnormal tissue
Other Procedures	Unrelated procedures, which include arthrodesis, Mohs micrographic surgery, manipulation (of fractures/dislocations), splinting, or casting

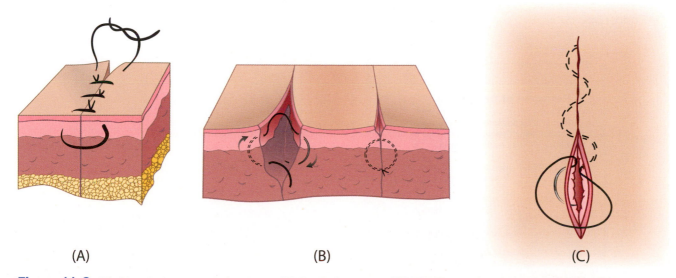

(A)   (B)   (C)

Figure 11-2 (A) Simple interrupted sutures (B) Buried sutures (C) Running subcuticular sutures

- Intersex Surgery (55970–55980)

- Female Genital System (56405–58999)

- Maternity Care and Delivery (59000–59899)

- Endocrine System (60000–60699)

- Nervous System (61000–64999)

- Eye and Ocular Adnexa (65091–68899)

- Auditory System (69000–69979)

- Operating Microscope (69990)

Many of the Surgery subsections contain unique instructions called *notes,* which are located just below the title of the subsection (Figure 11-3), heading, or subheading. Parenthetical notes are located below codes, and they apply to just that code.

> **EXAMPLE:** The note located above code 11200 in the CPT coding manual provides instruction that removal includes "scissoring or any sharp method" and applies to all codes under the heading "Removal of Skin Tags."
>
> The parenthetical note located below code 11201 in the coding manual indicates that code 11201 is reported with 11200, which means that it is never reported as a stand-alone code. This note applies to code 11201 only.

In the Surgery section, procedures are categorized as diagnostic procedures or therapeutic surgical procedures. **Diagnostic procedures** (e.g., arthroscopy, biopsy, and endoscopy) are performed to evaluate the patient's complaints or symptoms and to establish the diagnosis. **Therapeutic surgical procedures** (e.g., removal and repair) are performed to treat specific conditions or injuries; they include the procedure itself and normal, uncomplicated follow-up care.

Surgery section procedures are typically organized according to the following subheadings (below the heading of a subsection). (Some subheadings are not located below each heading, while some headings include additional subheadings, such as fracture and/or dislocation in the Musculoskeletal System subsection.)

- Incision *or* incision and drainage (I&D)

- Excision

- Introduction or removal

- Endoscopy

- Repair, revision, and/or reconstruction

- Destruction

- Other procedures

Removal of Skin Tags

Removal by scissoring or any sharp method, ligature, strangulation, electrosurgical destruction or combination of treatment modalities including chemical destruction or electrocauterization of wound, with or without local anesthesia.

   11200   Removal of skin tags, multiple fibrocutaneous tags, any area; up to and including 15 lesions

+ 11201   each additional 10 lesions, or part thereof (List separately in addition to code for primary procedure)

         (Use 11201 in conjunction with 11200)

Figure 11-3 Sample note in CPT

Exercise 11.1 – Overview of Surgery Section

Instructions: Complete each statement.

1. The organization of the CPT Surgery section is according to _____.

2. Endoscopy, arthroscopy, and biopsy are considered _____ procedures.

3. Gastric resection and knee replacement surgeries are considered _____ procedures.

4. The patient underwent cystourethroscopy with biopsy of urinary bladder wall. Identify the following:

   a. Body system: _____

   b. Anatomical site: _____

   c. Surgical approach: _____

   d. Type of procedure performed: _____

   e. Name of the procedure: _____

   f. Code number assigned: _____

5. The physician performed lysis of adhesions, exploratory laparotomy, and partial colon resection with end-to-end anastomosis. Identify the following:

   a. Body system: _____

   b. Anatomical site: _____

   c. Surgical approach: _____

   d. Type of procedure performed: _____

   e. Name of the procedure: _____

   f. Code number assigned: _____

Surgery Guidelines

Guidelines located at the beginning of the CPT Surgery section clarify the assignment of codes and explain terms. Surgery guidelines include the following:

- Services
- CPT surgical package definition
- Follow-up care for diagnostic procedures
- Follow-up care for therapeutic surgical procedures
- Supplied materials
- Reporting more than one procedure/service
- Separate procedure
- Unlisted service or procedure
- Special report
- Imaging guidance
- Surgical destruction

Services

Codes for services that are provided in the office, patient's home, hospital, and other health care facilities are located in the Evaluation and Management (E/M) section of the CPT. This section also includes codes for consultations and other medical services. Codes for special services and reports are located in the CPT Medicine section.

CPT Surgical Package Definition

Many services performed are integral to the standard of medical/surgical services, such as the cleansing, shaving, and prepping of skin and the insertion of intravenous access for medication. The CPT **surgical package** usually includes the following services, in addition to the surgical procedure:

- Local infiltration, metacarpal/metatarsal/digital block, or topical anesthesia

- One related E/M service following the decision for surgery, which includes the history and physical, on the date of procedure or immediately prior to performance of the procedure

- Immediate postoperative care, which includes dictating the operative report and talking with the family and other physicians or qualified health care professionals

- Documentation of postoperative physician orders

- Evaluation of the patient in the postanesthesia recovery area

- Typical postoperative follow-up care (e.g., removal of sutures)

> **Note:**
>
> When reporting a CPT surgery code, surgical package services are included in that code. They are not separately coded and reported.

In 1992, the Centers for Medicare & Medicaid Services (CMS) established a national definition for a **global surgical package** (that differs from the definition of the CPT *surgical package*) to ensure that payments are made consistently for the same services across all Medicare administrative contractor jurisdictions. The *global surgical package* definition prevents Medicare payments for services that are more or less comprehensive than intended. The CMS global surgical package includes the surgical procedure and a standard package of preoperative, intraoperative, and postoperative services. In addition, CMS categorizes surgeries as major or minor, and it establishes a postoperative **global period** (0, 10, or 90 days) (Figure 11-4) for each surgical procedure, which includes the following policies:

- The global period for major surgery is 90 days.

- The global period begins the day following surgery.

- The global period includes a one-day preoperative period.

    EXAMPLE: To determine the global period for major surgeries, count the day before the day of surgery, the day of surgery, and the 90 days immediately following the day of surgery. For a date of surgery on January 1, the

    - Preoperative day is December 31

    - Last day of the 90-day postoperative period is April 1

CPT Code	Brief Description	Global Period
59050	Fetal monitoring with report	XXX
59160	Dilatation and curettage after delivery	010
59200	Insertion of cervical dilator	000
59400	Obstetrical care	MMM
59525	Removal of uterus after cesarean section	ZZZ
59812	Treatment of miscarriage	090
59899	Maternity care procedure	YYY

Figure 11-4 Sample of CMS global periods

To arrive at April 1, count January 2–31 as 30 days, February 1–28 as 28 days, March 1–31 as 31 days, and April 1 as 1 day, for a total of 90 days *after the day of surgery*.

- The global period for minor surgery (e.g., endoscopies) is zero or 10 days, and physician visits on the day of a minor surgical procedure or endoscopy are included in reimbursement for the procedure.

- The zero-day global period includes the day of surgery only.

   EXAMPLE: To determine the zero-day global period for a minor surgical procedure, count the day of surgery only. For a date of surgery on March 5, the last day of the postoperative period is also March 5.

- The 10-day global period includes the day of surgery and the 10 days that immediately follow the day of surgery.

   EXAMPLE: To determine the 10-day global period for a minor surgical procedure, count the day of surgery and the appropriate number of days immediately following the date of surgery. For a date of surgery on March 5, the last day of the postoperative period is March 15.

CMS publishes a list of the global periods (Figure 11-4) for each CPT code in the *Federal Register*. That list also includes the following alphabetical codes in the global period column:

- MMM: Global period policy does not apply; describes services furnished in uncomplicated maternity cases, including antepartum care, delivery, and postpartum care.

- XXX: Global period policy does not apply.

- YYY: Global period is established by each Medicare administrative contract (e.g., unlisted surgery codes).

- ZZZ: CPT code is related to another service provided, which is always included in the global period of the other service.

Instructions for the CMS's global surgical package describe the components of a global surgical package and payment rules for minor surgeries, endoscopies, and global surgical packages that are split between physicians. In addition to the global surgical package policy, other payment policies and claims processing requirements were established for other surgical issues, including bilateral and multiple surgeries. The CMS global surgical package includes the following:

- Preoperative services (visits after the decision is made to operate)

- The day before the day of surgery for major procedures

- The day of surgery for minor procedures

- Intraoperative services (includes the operation and all usual and necessary parts of a surgical procedure, such as wound irrigation, insertion and removal of drains, surgical closure, and application and/or removal of postoperative dressings)

- Treatment of complications following surgery (additional services provided by the surgeon during the postoperative period because of the development of complications that do not require additional trips to the operating room)

- Postoperative visits (follow-up visits during the postoperative period that are related to recovery from surgery)

- Postsurgical pain management (provided by the surgeon)

- Miscellaneous services (e.g., dressing changes; local incisional care; removal of operative packing; removal of sutures and staples, tubes, drains, and casts; insertion or removal of urinary catheters and/or nasogastric tubes)

 Note:

When a patient receives treatment for an unrelated condition during the global period, add modifier -24 to the CPT code for an E/M service or add modifier -79 to the CPT code for a surgical procedure/service.

The CMS global surgical package does *not* include the following:

- Initial consultation or evaluation services by the surgeon to determine need for major surgery

- Visits unrelated to the diagnosis for which a surgical procedure is performed

- Services provided by other physicians, except when the physicians agree on transfer of care

- Diagnostic tests and procedures, including diagnostic radiological procedures

- Clearly distinct surgical procedures during the postoperative period that are *not* for treatment of complications or procedures done in "stages" (e.g., two or more parts of a procedure planned at the time of the first procedure to occur at a time after the initial surgery, such as a mastectomy, and insertion of a prosthesis during the postoperative global period)

- Treatment for postoperative complications that require a return trip to the operating room

- A required, more extensive procedure when a less extensive procedure fails; in this case, the second procedure is payable separately

> **Note:**
>
> The initial consultation or evaluation services by the surgeon *is included* to determine the need for minor surgery.

It is important to understand that the procedure being performed determines the global follow-up care; the condition being treated does not. The global surgical packages deal with the procedure(s) performed during the global period by the operating surgeon; only the operating surgeon is associated with that particular global period of follow-up care.

EXAMPLE: A patient underwent ventral hernia repair performed by a general surgeon and one week later fractured her ankle. An orthopedic surgeon inserted a pin to repair the fractured ankle. A global follow-up period for the specific surgery performed is associated with the CPT code assigned by each physician. Thus, each physician receives appropriate reimbursement for services provided.

When the patient is seen by the general surgeon for follow-up care related to the ventral hernia repair and such care is provided within the global period, an E/M code for services provided is *not* reported. Payment for such follow-up care is bundled in the CPT code reported for the ventral hernia repair surgery. Likewise, when the patient is seen by the orthopedic surgeon for follow-up care related to the ankle surgery, E/M services are bundled in the CPT code reported for that surgery.

If the patient develops complications subsequent to surgery and receives E/M services within the global period, the respective surgeon should report a CPT code for services provided to receive reimbursement from the third-party payer.

E/M services provided as follow-up to a surgical procedure are included in the reimbursement amount for the surgery, and codes for follow-up E/M services are not reported separately. However, when the patient receives E/M services for an unrelated condition, make sure you report an E/M code to receive reimbursement for services provided.

EXAMPLE: An excision of a malignant lesion on the left arm is performed in the office on May 10. The postoperative global period for code 11606 is 10 days. The patient returns to the office on May 15 and is treated for conjunctivitis. The physician should report an appropriate E/M code and add modifier 24 (Unrelated Evaluation and Management Service by the Same Physician During a Postoperative Period) (e.g., 99213-24).

When an E/M service provided is for the purpose of deciding to perform a major surgical procedure, the E/M service is considered a significant, separately identifiable service. Report an appropriate E/M code and add modifier 57 (decision for surgery) (e.g., 99214-57).

EXAMPLE: A surgeon provided level 5 consultation services to a patient in the office to determine whether surgery was necessary due to complaints of severe abdominal pain. After evaluation, the ambulance is called and the patient is transported to the hospital, where the surgeon performs an emergency gastrotomy with suture repair of a bleeding ulcer. Report code 43501 (Gastrotomy; with suture repair of bleeding ulcer) and 99245-57 (Office consultation for new or established patient, level 5).

Note:

Medicare administrative contractors use software that contains prepayment edits to detect the separate billing of services included in the global package. When E/M codes are reported for services provided during a global period and a modifier is not added to the code to indicate special circumstances, the claims are denied.

Local Infiltration, Metacarpal/Metatarsal/Digital Block, or Topical Anesthesia

Local infiltration, metacarpal/metatarsal/digital block, or topical anesthesia, when provided by the physician performing the procedure, is considered part of the procedure. When the surgeon provides general anesthesia, regional anesthesia, or monitored anesthesia care, add modifier -47 to the surgery code.

Note:

When a physician other than the surgeon (e.g., anesthesiologist) provides general anesthesia, regional anesthesia, or monitored anesthesia care, the other physician reports an anesthesia code for services provided. (Refer to Chapter 10 for anesthesia coding rules.)

EXAMPLE: A surgeon injected a local anesthetic in preparation for performing an inguinal hernia repair on a 42-year-old patient. The local anesthetic procedure performed by the surgeon is included in the surgical procedure and is not separately coded and reported.

Moderate (conscious) sedation is moderate sedation or analgesia that results in a drug-induced depression of consciousness.

EXAMPLE: A surgeon placed radiotherapy afterloading brachytherapy catheters into the breast for interstitial radioelement following a partial mastectomy. The 67-year-old patient required the administration of 30 minutes of moderate (conscious) sedation during the procedure. An independent trained observer monitored the patient's sedation. Report codes 19208, 99156, and 99157.

The management of postoperative pain by the surgeon, including epidural drug administration, is included in the global package with the operative procedure.

Follow-up Care for Diagnostic Procedures

Diagnostic procedures are performed to evaluate a patient's condition, to determine the nature of a condition, and to distinguish between one disease and another. According to CPT, follow-up care for diagnostic procedures includes only that care related to recovery from the diagnostic procedure itself. Codes for services provided should be reported when a physician treats

- The patient's condition for which the diagnostic procedure was performed
- Other conditions that are not related to the reason for performing the diagnostic procedure

When a patient receives services from the physician who performed the diagnostic procedure and those services are in follow-up to the procedure performed (e.g., suture removal or dressing change), do not report a code for services provided.

Follow-up Care for Therapeutic Surgical Procedures

Therapeutic surgical procedures are performed for the definitive treatment of a disease or condition rather than for diagnostic or investigative purposes. Follow-up care for therapeutic surgical procedures includes only the care that is typically considered part of the surgical service. The physician generally sees the patient several times as part of normal, uncomplicated follow-up care (e.g., remove sutures, evaluate the results of the surgery, or check for complications). These postoperative visits are included as part of surgery's global period because normal follow-up care services are a necessary component of the surgical process.

Codes for services provided should be reported when a physician treats the following during the postoperative global period:

- Complications (e.g., postoperative wound infection)

- Exacerbations (e.g., macular degeneration that was treated, but worsens, requiring another treatment)

- Recurrence (e.g., return of cancer)

- Presence of other diseases (e.g., appendicitis during global period for gastric resection)

- Injuries (e.g., fracture resulting from car accident)

Supplied Materials

Supplies commonly included in surgical packages (e.g., dressings, tubing, and Steri-Strips) are not coded separately. *Only those supplies and materials provided by the physician over and above the supplies usually included with the procedure rendered are reported separately.* Assign code 99070 to report these supplies or assign specific HCPCS level II national codes for such supplies or drugs.

The CPT Surgery section guidelines do not identify procedures codes for which it is appropriate to report supply items (e.g., surgical trays) separately. Reimbursement of supplies and materials required to perform the procedure is a specific reimbursement issue, which varies from one third-party payer to another. CMS created specific instructions regarding the separate reporting of "supply" items. With the full implementation of the practice expense component of the Medicare Fee Schedule, all supplies, such as surgical trays, are included (e.g., bundled) in the payment for the procedure; Medicare does *not* reimburse the physician for this code. Some non-Medicare payers may still use it; others may alternatively allow CPT code 99070, Supplies and materials (except spectacles), provided by the physician over and above those usually included with the office visit or other services rendered (list drugs, trays, supplies, or materials provided) instead.

> **EXAMPLE:** A patient underwent a repair of recurrent strangulated abdominal incisional hernia with implantation of mesh. Report code 49566 (Repair recurrent incisional or ventral hernia; incarcerated or strangulated) and HCPCS level II code C1781 (mesh) *or* CPT code 49568 (Implantation of mesh or other prosthesis for incisional or ventral hernia repair). (Do not add modifier -51 to code C1781 or 49568 because they are exempt from that modifier.)

Reporting More Than One Procedure/Service

When a physician performs more than one procedure or service on the same date, during the same operative session, or during a postoperative period and the surgical package concept applies, report one or more CPT modifiers to receive reimbursement consideration from third-party payers.

Note:

Refer to Table 8-2 in Chapter 8 for a comprehensive list of modifiers, descriptions, and examples (including modifiers used for reporting more than one procedure/service).

Add-on Codes

CPT includes a ✚ (plus) symbol next to add-on codes that describe a service that can be reported only in addition to a primary procedure. Add-on codes can also be identified by specific language in the code descriptor, such as *each additional* or *(List separately in addition to primary procedure)*. Add-on codes are never reported as stand-alone codes because they are considered an integral part of another procedure. They are never reported alone because the procedures they describe would not be performed unless another primary procedure was performed.

Add-on codes allow physicians to separately report procedures and services performed in addition to the primary procedure. The key to identifying add-on codes is determining whether the code always has to be reported with another code. If that is the case, the code is considered an add-on code. Also, add-on codes are exempt from the multiple procedure concept, which means -51 is not added.

> **EXAMPLE:** A patient underwent open treatment of three lumbar vertebral fractures. Report codes 22325, 22328, and 22328.
>
> The description for code 22325 includes "one fractured vertebra," and the description for code 22328 states "each additional fractured vertebrae . . . (List separately in addition to code for primary procedure)." This patient underwent treatment for three vertebral fractures, which requires the reporting of three codes. (Do not add modifier -51 to the 22328 codes because they are exempt from that modifier.)

Separate Procedure

CPT code descriptions that contain the term **separate procedure** in parentheses are commonly performed as an integral component of a total service or procedure. When the total procedure or service is performed, do not report as an additional procedure the code that contains the term *(separate procedure)* in its code description. When a separate procedure (e.g., 53020, Meatotomy) is performed during the same operative session as a more comprehensive procedure (e.g., 52285, Cystourethroscopy for treatment of the female urethral syndrome), do *not* code the separate procedure in addition to the more comprehensive procedure.

> **EXAMPLE:** The patient underwent sesamoidectomy and excision of a bone cyst of the middle phalanx of the right hand. Report code 26210.
>
> Do not mistakenly report code 26185 in addition to code 26210. Code 26185 contains the term *(separate procedure)* in its code description. The procedure described in code 26185 is a component part of the more comprehensive "excision of bone cyst" procedure.

When a procedure or service that contains *(separate procedure)* in its code description *is performed independently of or is considered unrelated to or distinct from other procedures performed during the same operative session, report the separate procedure code in addition to codes for other procedures (or services)*.

Reporting separate procedure codes may be necessary to classify the following:

- Procedure performed during a different session or patient encounter, procedure or surgery, site, or organ system
- Procedure performed through a separate incision or excision
- Separate lesion excised during the same operative session as removal of another lesion
- Treatment of a separate injury (or area of injury for extensive injuries)

Add modifier -59 to the separate procedure code to indicate that the procedure is not considered a component of another procedure, but is a distinct, independent procedure.

> **EXAMPLE:** A patient underwent a complete salpingo-oophorectomy, bilateral, during the same operative session as a total abdominal hysterectomy. Report code 58150, Total abdominal hysterectomy (corpus and cervix), with or without removal of tube(s), with or without removal of ovary(s). Do not report code 58720, Salpingo-oophorectomy, complete or partial, unilateral or bilateral (separate procedure), because it is considered an integral component of the procedures described for code 58150.

Unlisted Service or Procedure

CPT unlisted service or procedure codes are assigned when no specific code accurately describes the procedure performed. When reporting an unlisted procedure code on an insurance claim, make sure you include a written report (e.g., copy of operative report) that describes the procedure(s) performed. (During the first year that laparoscopic appendectomies and cholecystectomies were performed, no procedure codes were included in CPT. Unlisted procedure codes were reported.)

> **EXAMPLE:** A physician performs a pressure ulcer excision, using a technique that is not described by any existing pressure ulcer codes. Report code 15999 and include a copy of the operative report with the claim.

Special Report

When an unlisted procedure code is reported to a third-party payer, attach a special report that describes the procedure performed. Special reports may also be required for procedures and services that are rarely provided, unusual, or new to establish medical necessity. As a minimum, to document a special report, include the following:

- Adequate description of the nature, extent, and need for the procedure
- Time, effort, and equipment necessary to provide the procedure or service

The following additional items may also be documented in a special report:

- Complexity of symptoms
- Concurrent problems
- Diagnostic and therapeutic procedures
- Final diagnosis
- Follow-up care
- Pertinent physical findings (e.g., location, number, and size of lesions)

> **EXAMPLE:** An ear, nose, and throat specialist performed an experimental procedure on the pharynx of a 14-year-old prodigy opera singer to treat persistent pharyngitis that has not resolved with traditional medical treatment. Conventional procedures to treat the unusual condition are not an option for this patient because they pose too great a risk of damage to the patient's vocal cords. The procedure was approved by the patient's parents, the health care facility at which it was performed, and the third-party payer that will reimburse its costs. Because the procedure is experimental, no CPT code is available. Report 42999, and attach a copy of the transcribed operative report to the claim. The operative report is the "special report" required by the payer to process the claim for reimbursement.

Imaging Guidance

When imaging guidance or imaging supervision and interpretation is performed with a surgical procedure and included in the Surgery code description, the Radiology guidelines apply.

> **EXAMPLE:** Percutaneous breast biopsy, left, with placement of breast clip and imaging of biopsy specimen, including stereotactic guidance. Report code 19081. (Stereotactic guidance is included in code 19081, and a separate Radiology code is *not* reported.)

Surgical Destruction

Surgical destruction is considered part of a surgical procedure, and different methods of destruction are not reported separately unless the technique substantially differs from the standard management of a problem or condition. (CPT codes are available for exceptions due to special circumstances.) Surgical destruction includes the ablation (or removal) of tissues by any method, including chemical treatment, cryosurgery, electrosurgery, or laser.

> **EXAMPLE:** A physician performed argon laser treatments on a patient with a congenital port wine stain. Report code 17106.

Exercise 11.2 – Surgery Guidelines

Instructions: Indicate whether each statement is true (T) or false (F).

_____ 1. When services performed are integral to the standard of medical/surgical services, they are coded and reported separately.

_____ 2. The CPT surgical package includes typical postoperative follow-up care in addition to the surgical procedure.

_____ 3. CMS categorizes surgeries as major or minor, and it establishes a postoperative global period of 0, 10, or 90 days.

_____ 4. The CMS global surgical package includes preoperative visits before the decision is made to operate.

_____ 5. Visits unrelated to postoperative follow-up for a surgical procedure are included in CMS's global surgical package.

_____ 6. It is inappropriate for a physician to report a code for conscious sedation with the surgical service-described CPT code 19298.

_____ 7. A diagnostic esophagogastroduodenoscopy was performed to rule out gastric ulcer disease. The findings confirmed the diagnosis, and the physician prescribed medication. The patient was seen in the physician's office one week later for a follow-up visit to determine whether the patient's symptoms had been alleviated by medication. The patient was still experiencing acute pain, and the physician increased the medication dosage. The patient was scheduled for a two-week follow-up visit. The evaluation and management code for the follow-up visit during which the physician increased the dosage of the patient's medication is reported separately.

_____ 8. Health care services that are provided above and beyond the original surgical procedure are included in follow-up care for therapeutic procedures.

_____ 9. A physician applied sterile dressings after repairing a laceration. The sterile dressings are not separately coded and reported.

_____ 10. The patient underwent esophageal dilation for esophageal stricture (43450); next, during the same operative session, the patient also underwent esophagoscopy (43200) to investigate the cause of the esophageal stricture. Upon review of both codes, the physician should report 43450 and 43200-59.

Instructions: Complete each statement.

11. The global period for a minor surgical procedure performed on March 15 is zero days. The last day of the postoperative period is _____.

12. The global period for a minor surgical procedure performed on October 4 is 10 days. The last day of the postoperative period is _____.

13. A surgeon performed an incision and drainage of an abscess in the office. The patient developed an infection of the surgical site that required a return visit within 3 days to the surgeon's office. Which CPT modifier is reported with the E/M visit? _____

14. A physician repairs bilateral inguinal hernias on a 2-year-old. The physician reports the code for the inguinal hernia repair and adds modifier _____.

15. A physician performed surgery on a patient to destroy 25 lesions. Review the description for code 17004. How many times should code 17004 be reported? _____

General Subsection

The General subsection contains just two codes.

- 10021 (fine-needle aspiration; without imaging guidance)

- 10022 (fine-needle aspiration; with imaging guidance)

Fine-needle aspiration (FNA) involves the removal of fluid from a cyst or cells from a solid mass. Then the cells are examined cytologically. FNA is a percutaneous procedure; if the cyst or mass is *not* palpable on physical exam, the procedure is typically performed under imaging guidance using fluoroscopy, ultrasound, or computed tomography (CT). Report code 10021 if FNA is performed without imaging guidance. Report code 10022 if imaging guidance is used to assist in locating the lump.

EXAMPLE 1: A physician aspirates a cyst, using FNA technique. Report code 10021.

EXAMPLE 2: A patient presents with a thyroid nodule. Using CT guidance, a FNA is performed on the thyroid nodule; the material is sent for cytologic review. In addition to code 10022, report 77012 (Computed tomography guidance for needle placement [e.g., biopsy, aspiration, injection, localization device], radiological supervision and interpretation). (Directional modifiers, such as -LT and -RT, are not added to codes in CPT's General subsection.)

The parenthetical notes located below the General subsection applies to both codes (10021–10022). CPT notes specify that when percutaneous needle aspiration requires imaging guidance, the appropriate radiological supervision and interpretation code is also reported (e.g., 77002, Fluoroscopic guidance for needle placement). Additional notes specify that codes 10021–10022 are *not* reported for

- Percutaneous needle biopsy other than FNA, which is reported with appropriate codes from the Surgery section (e.g., 20206, percutaneous needle biopsy of muscle)

- Evaluation of fine-needle aspirate, which is reported with code(s) from the Pathology and Laboratory section (e.g., 88172, Cytopathology, evaluation of fine-needle aspirate; immediate cytohistologic study to determine adequacy of specimen[s])

Exercise 11.3 – General Subsection

Instructions: Assign the CPT code(s) and appropriate modifier(s) to each statement.

1. A patient presents with a palpable left breast mass for which fine-needle aspiration biopsy is performed.

   _____

2. A patient has a nonpalpable right breast mass that was identified on a previous screening mammogram. Ultrasound exam at that time revealed that the mass is not a simple cyst. Fine-needle aspiration biopsy of the right breast mass is performed under ultrasonic guidance during today's encounter.

   _____

Integumentary System Subsection

The Integumentary System subsection includes dermatological procedures, plastic surgery, and components of multiple surgical procedures (e.g., closure, flaps, grafts, and tissue transfer). Integumentary procedures (Table 11-2) are often performed as staged procedures (e.g., flaps and grafts) due to the complexity of services rendered. Integumentary procedures include incision, biopsy, removal, paring/curettement, shaving, destruction, excision, repair, adjacent tissue rearrangement, grafts, flaps, and specialized services (e.g., burn management, Mohs micrographic surgery). (Refer to the definitions of surgical terms earlier in this chapter. Additional terms are defined in Table 11-2.)

Table 11-2 Integumentary Procedures and Definitions

Integumentary Procedure	Definition
Adjacent tissue transfer/ rearrangement	Closure of defects by relocating a flap of adjacent normal, healthy tissue from a donor site to a nearby (adjacent) defect, such as a traumatic skin wound or the site of excised lesion; a portion of the flap remains intact to provide a blood supply to the grafted site
Biopsy	Removal and examination of tissue to establish a diagnosis, confirm a diagnosis, or determine the extent of a disease
Flap	Relocation of a mass of tissue (usually skin) that has been partially removed from one part of the body so that it retains its own blood supply
Graft	Any tissue or organ used for implantation or transplant
Mohs microsurgery	Technique of excising skin tumors by removing tumor tissue layer by layer, examining the removed portion microscopically for malignant cells, and repeating the procedure until the entire tumor is removed
Paring and curettement	Removal of growths or other material from the wall of a cavity or another surface, as with a curette; paring of lesions (e.g., corns and calluses) seldom, if ever, require local anesthesia
Shaving	Horizontal slicing to remove epidermal and dermal lesions (e.g., without a full-thickness dermal excision); removal includes scissoring or any sharp method

The CPT Surgery Integumentary subsection contains the following headings:

- Skin, Subcutaneous and Accessory Structures
- Nails
- Pilonidal Cyst
- Introduction
- Repair (Closure)
- Destruction
- Breast

Coding Tip:

- Do not add HCPCS level II modifiers LT and RT to codes in the Skin, Subcutaneous and Accessory Structures; Nails; Pilonidal Cyst; Introduction; Repair (Closure); or Destruction headings—the skin is not a paired organ.

- Add modifiers LT and RT to codes in the Breast heading.

- Add HCPCS level II modifiers FA through F9 or TA through T9 to codes for procedures performed on the fingernails and toenails.

Skin, Subcutaneous and Accessory Structures

The Skin, Subcutaneous and Accessory Structures heading includes the following subheadings: Introduction and Removal, Incision and Drainage (I&D), Debridement, Paring or Cutting, Biopsy, Removal of Skin Tags, Shaving of Epidermal or Dermal Lesions, Excision—Benign Lesions, and Excision—Malignant Lesions.

Introduction and Removal

The *Introduction and Removal* heading includes a code for percutaneous image-guided fluid collection drainage via catheter of soft tissue abscesses, hematomas, seromas, lymphoceles, and cysts.

Incision and Drainage (I&D)

The I&D subheading contains procedures that establish a drainage pathway for fluid that forms at sites of infection. CPT I&D procedures include cutaneous and subcutaneous drainage of cysts, fluid collections, infections, hematomas (Figure 11-5), pustules, and seromas. When a procedure to excise a lesion results in drainage of an

Figure 11-5 Hematoma

area, either as a part of the procedure or as a way to gain access to the lesion, do not report a code for I&D if the excision or another procedure is performed during the same operative session. It is also inappropriate to report a separate code for an I&D of a hematoma (10140) if it is performed during the same operative session as excision, repair, destruction, removal, and so on.

> **EXAMPLE:** A patient undergoes a scheduled procedure to treat a **pilonidal cyst** (entrapped epithelial tissue and hair located in the sacral area at the top of the crease between the buttocks, which can become infected). Treatment options include simple I&D (10080–10081), excision (11770–11772), or a combination of both *if extensive cellulitis is present*.

 Note:

CPT does not define type of excision terms: simple, extensive, or complicated. The provider is responsible for establishing the type of excision.

- When a patient undergoes simple I&D of a pilonidal cyst and there is no mention of infection, report CPT code 10080. During a simple I&D of a pilonidal cyst, if the provider also performs an excision of the pilonidal cyst, report just code 11770 (for simple excision).

- Report 11771 instead of 11770 when a cyst measures 2 cm or larger in size, is recurrent, or requires layered closure.

- If plastic repair (e.g., local flap) will be required in the future, report 11772 instead of 11770 or 11771.

- During simple I&D of a pilonidal cyst, if the provider encounters **extensive cellulitis** (acute inflammation of skin's connective tissue that is caused by infection with bacteria) and the excision of the pilonidal cyst cannot be performed, the provider will prescribe an antibiotic. Report CPT code 10081 for complicated I&D of the pilonidal cyst (due to presence of an infection). If after one week of antibiotic therapy, the patient returns and the provider performs an excision of the pilonidal cyst, report code 11770-78 (or 11771-78 or 11772-78 depending on complexity).

CPT codes describe procedures necessary to address complications, such as code 10180 (Incision and drainage, complex, postoperative wound infection). Such codes are *not* reported with codes for the original surgery that resulted in the complication. If the original surgery code is reported with the procedure to treat the complication, National Correct Coding Initiative (NCCI) edits will deny reimbursement for the procedure performed to treat the complication.

EXAMPLE: A patient who underwent a thoracotomy developed a surgical wound infection, which required I&D. Report code 10180-78 for I&D of the (skin) wound infection.

Exercise 11.4 – Incision and Drainage

Instructions: Assign the CPT code(s) and any appropriate modifier(s) to each statement.

1. Complex incision and drainage, postoperative wound infection.

   _____

2. Incision and drainage of hematoma, skin.

   _____

3. Incision and removal of foreign body, subcutaneous tissue.

   _____

4. Marsupialization acne surgery.

   _____

5. Simple incision and drainage of five infected cysts.

   _____

Lesion Removal

Lesion removal is coded in CPT by referencing the following subheadings:

- Excision—Debridement
- Paring or Cutting
- Biopsy
- Removal of Skin Tags
- Shaving of Epidermal or Dermal Lesions
- Excision—Benign Lesions
- Excision—Malignant Lesions

A skin lesion (Figure 11-6) is a pathologic change in tissue (e.g., benign or malignant). To accurately code the removal of lesions, review the patient record to locate the following information:

- Method of removing the lesion (e.g., paring, shaving, or debridement)
- Malignant or benign status of lesion if excision method is performed
- Site or body part where lesion is located
- Size of the lesion in centimeters (Figure 11-7)
- Type of wound closure/repair (e.g., simple, intermediate, or complex)

Bulla: (Large blister)
Same as a vesicle only greater than 10 mm
Example:
Contact dermatitis, large second-degree burns, bulbous impetigo, pemphigus

Macule:
Localized changes in skin color of less than 1 cm in diameter
Example:
Freckle

Nodule:
Solid and elevated; however, they extend deeper than papules into the dermis or subcutaneous tissues, greater than 10 mm
Example:
Lipoma, erythema, cyst, wart

Papule:
Solid, elevated lesion less than 1 cm in diameter
Example:
Elevated nevi

Pustule:
Vesicles or bullae that become filled with pus, usually described as less than 0.5 cm in diameter
Example:
Acne, impetigo, furuncles, carbuncles

Ulcer:
A depressed lesion of the epidermis and upper papillary layer of the dermis
Example:
Stage 2 pressure ulcer

Tumor:
The same as a nodule only greater than 2 cm
Example:
Benign epidermal tumor, basal cell carcinoma

Vesicle: (Small blister)
Accumulation of fluid between the upper layers of the skin; elevated mass containing serous fluid; less than 10 mm
Example:
Herpes simplex, herpes zoster, chickenpox

Urticaria, Hives:
Localized edema in the epidermis causing irregular elevation that may be red or pale, may be itchy
Example:
Insect bite, wheal

Figure 11-6 Skin lesions

Figure 11-7 Lesions are measured in centimeters.
(Note: 2.5 centimeters equals 1 inch.)

Note:

- To calculate the size of a lesion, refer to "excised diameter" notes located in CPT Surgery (above the Excision—Benign Lesions heading in the Integumentary System subsection). The "excised diameter" includes the size of the lesion plus its margins.

- Documentation of the "excised diameter" should include dimensions for the greatest size (diameter) of the lesion as well as for the margin around the lesion. *When multiple lesions are removed, do not add together the greatest size (or diameter) of each separate lesion even when excised in one ellipse.*

- The margin is the amount of surrounding tissue that must be removed to adequately excise the lesion, and it is calculated as the shortest distance from the lesion to the edge of the skin ellipse.

  - An ellipse is a shape resembling an oval.

  - The narrowest amount of tissue removed from each end of the ellipse is measured and used to calculate the "excised diameter" of the lesion.

  - When multiple lesions are excised using one ellipse, the narrowest margin between lesions is measured and used *in addition to measurements of each end of the ellipse* to calculate the "excised diameter" of the lesion.

EXAMPLE 1: A 2-cm × 1-cm benign lesion of the cheek was excised in an elliptical fashion with 2-mm margins in all directions. Simple closure was performed. The "excised diameter" is calculated as 2.4 cm because

- The greatest size (or diameter) of the lesion is 2 cm.

- The narrowest margin of each end of the ellipse is 2 mm (or 0.2 cm), calculated as 0.2 cm × 2 = 0.4 cm.

- 2 cm + 0.4 cm = 2.4-cm "excised diameter."

Report CPT code 11443. (Do not report a separate code for the simple closure procedure.)

EXAMPLE 2: One elliptical excision was made to remove two nevi from the patient's left arm. Lesion A was 3 cm in diameter, and lesion B was 2 cm in diameter. Skin margins were 4 mm at each end of the ellipse, and 2 mm between the two lesions. Simple closure was performed. The "excised diameter" of lesion A is 3.5 cm and lesion B is 2.5 cm because

- The greatest size (or diameter) of each lesion is 3 cm and 2 cm, respectively. Do not add together the greatest size (or diameter) of separate lesions even when excised in one ellipse.

- The narrowest margin of each end of the ellipse is 4 mm (or 0.4 cm). Thus, associate 0.4 cm with each lesion.

- The narrowest margin between the lesions is 2 mm (or 0.2 cm). Thus, associate 0.1 cm (half of 0.2 cm) with each lesion.

- 3 cm + 0.4 cm + 0.1 cm = 3.5-cm "excised diameter" of lesion A.

- 2 cm + 0.4 cm + 0.1 cm = 2.5-cm "excised diameter" of lesion B.

Report CPT code 11404 for lesion A and 11403-51 for lesion B. (Do not report a separate code for the simple closure procedure.)

From a coding perspective, benign lesions include neoplasms, fibrous cysts, or other inflammatory cystic lesions. Malignant lesions are typically described as melanoma, basal cell carcinoma, or squamous cell carcinoma. When surgery is performed on a lesion, select the appropriate code according to the lesion's "excised diameter," which includes the lesion plus its margins. (Do not refer to the pathology report for the diameter because placing a lesion in formalin, the formaldehyde solution used to preserve organic specimens, can result in shrinkage.)

EXAMPLE: A malignant lesion of the nose measuring 1.0 cm in diameter is excised, and the operative report states that skin margins are 1.1 cm. The "excised diameter" of the lesion is 2.1 cm (1.0 + 1.1 = 2.1). Therefore, report code 11643 (Excision, malignant lesion including margins, face, ears, eyelids, nose, lips; excised diameter 2.1 to 3.0 cm).

 Note:

If an operative report describes the diameter of a lesion as having multiple sides, select the largest size as the diameter (e.g., a lesion described as 2 cm × 3 cm × 5 cm is 5 cm in diameter).

Just one type of removal is reported for each lesion, whether it is destruction (e.g., laser or freezing), debridement, paring, curettement, shaving, or excision. CPT notes describe the nature of each of these forms of removal.

When multiple methods are used to remove one lesion, report a code for just one destruction method. *When multiple distinct lesions are removed using different methods*, report a code for each lesion removal and attach modifier 59 to each code. Modifier 59 indicates different site, different method, or different type of lesion (e.g., benign versus malignant). Make sure the provider has documented the distinct locations of each lesion in the patient's record.

The biopsy of a lesion involves the partial removal of a lesion, and it is frequently performed at the same time as the removal of the entire lesion to obtain a pathologic specimen. The lesion biopsy is performed first, the tissue is submitted to pathology for evaluation and pathologic diagnosis, and then the lesion is completely removed. When a lesion biopsy is performed as part of a lesion removal, it is considered part of the total procedure and is not assigned a separate code. Report only the CPT code for removal of the lesion.

Lesion removal by any method may require simple, intermediate, or complex closure; it is also possible that a tissue transfer procedure will have to be performed. When the lesion removal requires bandaging, strip closure, or simple closure, the closure is included in the lesion excision and is not coded and reported separately. A **simple repair**, or **simple closure** (also called one-layer closure, nonlayered closure, and single-layer closure), involves the use of staples, sutures, and/or tissue adhesives to repair superficial wounds involving epidermis, dermis, and/or subcutaneous tissues.

Simple repair procedures are considered integral to lesion removal. Intermediate and complex repair (closure), when medically necessary, is coded separately. (For Mohs micrographic surgery, all necessary repairs are coded and reported separately.)

 Coding Tip:

- When a benign or malignant lesion is excised and complex closure is performed during the same operative session, two codes are reported.

  - Excision of benign or malignant lesion (11400–11446 or 11600–11646)

  - Complex closure (13100–13153)

- However, when a scar is excised followed by complex closure, report the complex repair code only.

- When multiple lesions are excised during the same operative session, report a code for the excision of each lesion.

- When a malignant lesion is excised and the patient returns for further excision to ensure that the malignancy has been completely resected, report a code for excision of a malignant lesion (even if the pathology report documents no residual malignancy).

Refer to the following table when assigning codes for excision of benign or malignant lesions that require wound repair (closure). When using the table to assign codes, it is important to note that

- When multiple lesions are excised during the same operative session, the number of excision codes must be increased accordingly.

- When intermediate or complex repair (closure) is performed to repair defects resulting from excision of multiple lesions, codes are grouped according to the same anatomical sites.

Type of Procedure	# of Codes	Types of Codes
Simple repair	1	Excision (11400–11471 or 11600–11646)
Intermediate repair	2	Excision (11400–11471 or 11600–11646)
		Intermediate repair (12031–12057)
Complex repair	2	Excision (11400–11471 or 11600–11646)
		Complex repair (13100–13160)

Exercise 11.5 – Lesion Removal

Instructions: Assign the CPT code(s) and any appropriate modifier(s) to each statement.

1. A physician excises a 1-cm benign lesion, left forearm; the defect is closed with a simple repair.

   _____

2. Punch biopsy of a benign skin lesion on the back and another one on the arm.

   _____

3. Excision of a 2.1-cm malignant lesion of the nose and two malignant lesions, including margins, of the chest, each 1.5-cm in diameter, including margins.

   _____

4. Four warts were removed by paring.

   _____

5. A physician excised a 2-cm benign lesion from the face.

   _____

Nails ⚠

The Nails heading classifies procedures that are performed to treat a variety of nail conditions, such as infections, trauma, nail dystrophy, and neoplasms. Most nail surgery is performed using local or digital block anesthetic. These procedures are typically performed on toenails but can be done on fingernails as well.

Nondystrophic nails are normal nails with no abnormal development or changes due to aging, injury, or disease. Nail debridement is generally done to treat hypertrophic dystrophic nails and mycotic (fungal) infections. It is performed mechanically by using instruments such as a nail splitter, a nail elevator, and an electrical burr (sander). For lacerations to the nail bed, where the wound extends under the proximal nail fold, a portion or all of the nail plate must be removed in order to visualize the laceration.

 Coding Tip:

Report HCPCS level II modifiers (-FA through -F9 and -TA through -T9) with codes for procedures performed on a patient's fingernails and toenails.

Pilonidal Cyst

The Pilonidal Cyst heading contains codes for procedures to report excision. A pilonidal cyst contains a tuft of hair that developed as the result of repeated friction, which caused hairs to penetrate the skin; it occurs primarily in the sacrococcygeal area. (For incision of a pilonidal cyst, report the appropriate code from the Incision and Drainage heading.)

Exercise 11.6 – Nails

Instructions: Assign the CPT code(s) and any appropriate modifier(s) to each statement.

1. A diabetic patient was seen by a podiatrist for trimming of nondystrophic nails, which are unaffected by abnormal development or changes in structure or appearance. Following cleansing and drying of all toenails of both feet, clippers are used to cut each nail straight across so that it is in line with the edge of the end of the toe.

   _____

2. Reconstruction of nail bed, second toe on left foot, with graft.

   _____

3. Avulsion of nail plate, simple, 5 nails, right foot.

   _____

4. The physician evacuated blood from a hematoma located beneath a patient's fingernail, second digit, left hand. The physician used an electrocautery needle to pierce the nail plate so the hematoma can drain. Pressure was applied to the nail bed to force the blood from beneath the nail plate. A loose dressing was applied so the area can continue to drain.

   _____

5. Wedge excision of skin of nail fold for ingrown toenail, third digit, right foot.

   _____

Exercise 11.7 – Pilonidal Cyst

Instructions: Assign the CPT code(s) and any appropriate modifier(s) to each statement.

1. Excision of complicated pilonidal cyst.

   _____

2. Pilonidal sinus excision, simple.

   _____

3. Excision of extensive pilonidal cyst.

   _____

4. The physician shaved hair adjacent to a pilonidal cyst and made an incision to allow drainage of cystic fluid.

   _____

5. The patient presented with an infected pilonidal cyst (complicated). The cyst was incised and drained.

   _____

Introduction

Codes located in the Introduction heading include the following procedures: injection of lesion(s); tattooing; subcutaneous injection of filling material (e.g., collagen); insertion, removal, and replacement of tissue expanders; insertion and removal of implantable contraceptive capsules; subcutaneous hormone pellet implantation; and insertion, removal, and removal with insertion of nonbiodegradable drug delivery implants.

CPT codes 11900–11901 describe intralesional injection(s) into one or more lesions, and they are reported for the treatment of lesions such as keloids, psoriasis, and acne (cystic or nodular). Drugs are injected directly into the lesion, and it is appropriate to report HCPCS level II national code(s) for medication(s) administered. CPT codes (11900–11901) reported are determined by the number of lesions treated (not by the number of injections).

Coding Tip:

- Codes 11900–11901 are not reported for local anesthetic injection in anticipation of chemotherapy or any other definitive service performed on a lesion or group of lesions (e.g., lesion destruction or removal).

- The administration (injection) of local anesthesia is included in the surgical procedure performed, and it is not coded separately.

Note:

CPT Medicine section codes that describe intralesional chemotherapy involve the injection of chemotherapeutic agents into one or multiple lesions. Do not report lesion injection codes (11900–11901) with intralesional chemotherapy codes (96405–96406) unless separate lesions are injected with different agents. Make sure you attach modifier -59 to the intralesional injection code(s) if the procedure is performed during the same encounter as lesion injection(s).

EXAMPLE: A physician performed intralesional injection of eight lesions. Report code 11901. (Code 11901 is a stand-alone code; it does not contain the plus symbol next to the code, which would indicate an add-on code. Do not report 11900 with 11901. Report either 11900 or 11901 based on the number of lesions injected.)

Exercise 11.8 – Introduction

Instructions: Assign the CPT code(s) and any appropriate modifier(s) to each statement.

1. Patient presented for subcutaneous implantation of estradiol and testosterone compressed crystalline pellets.

_____

2. A patient presented with acne (cystic), and the physician injected drugs directly into six lesions.

_____

3. Subcutaneous injection of 15.0 cc of collagen was performed.

_____

4. Five implantable contraceptive capsules were removed.

_____

5. Intralesional injection, 12 lesions.

_____

Table 11-3 Medical Terms for Adjacent Tissue Transfer/Rearrangement, Flap, and Graft Procedures

Defect	Wound that is the result of surgical intervention or trauma
Donor site	Anatomical site from which healthy skin is removed
Primary defect	Wound resulting from initial surgical intervention (e.g., excision of lesion) or trauma (e.g., deep abrasions)
Recipient site	Anatomical site to which healthy skin is attached
Secondary defect	Wound resulting from removal of tissue to create flap(s) or graft(s)
Stroma	Supporting tissue (matrix) of an organ
Tissue approximation	Method of replacing sutures with material or substance (e.g., surgical glue), which facilitates enhanced cosmetic results and faster healing of defects
Undermining	Process of using a surgical instrument to separate skin and mucosa from its underlying stroma so that the tissue can be stretched and moved to overlay a defect

Repair (Closure)

The Repair (Closure) heading includes the following subheadings, which require knowledge of additional medical terms associated with repair (closure) procedures (Table 11-3):

- Repair—Simple
- Repair—Intermediate
- Repair—Complex
- Adjacent Tissue Transfer or Rearrangement
- Skin Replacement Surgery

- Flaps (Skin and/or Deep Tissues)
- Other Flaps and Grafts
- Other Procedures
- Pressure Ulcers (Decubitus Ulcers)
- Burns, Local Treatment

Simple, Intermediate, Complex Repairs

Coding wound repairs is sometimes confusing because codes for repairs can be stand-alone procedures, separately reportable services when performed with certain other procedures (e.g., excisions requiring complex repair), or they can be an integral part of a more complex procedure and not separately reportable (e.g., surgical wound closure).

To add to the confusion, repairs are also divided into three categories.

- Simple: Superficial, only simple, one layer, primary suturing is required
- Intermediate: One of the deeper layers of subcutaneous tissue and fascia are involved
- Complex: Requiring more than layered closure; e.g., revision, debridement, creation of a defect, or preparation of the site

 Note:

- Single-layer closure is coded as an intermediate repair if the wound is heavily contaminated and requires extensive cleaning.

- When a physician documents layered closure, do not assume an intermediate repair code is to be reported. Locate documentation of

  - Closure of subcutaneous tissue or more than one layer of tissue beneath the dermis. Such closure of tissue layers under the skin uses dissolvable sutures before suturing the dermis and epidermis.

    or

  - Extensive cleaning or removal of foreign matter from a heavily contaminated wound that is closed with a single layer.

Assign codes in this section to report wound closures utilizing sutures, staples, or tissue adhesives (e.g., 2-cyanoacrylate tissue glue) either alone or in combination with one another or with adhesive strips.

To report wound repairs, review the patient record to locate the length of the repaired wound(s) in centimeters. Then group the wounds by type of repair (e.g., simple, intermediate, or complex) and anatomical site. Finally, add the lengths of multiple wounds in the same category and report the repair code for the total. Make sure you separately code and report wound repairs that are located in more than one anatomical site; report the most complicated service as the first-listed procedure. ▲

Coding Tip:

Wound closures utilizing adhesive strips as the only repair material are reported with an appropriate E/M code.

EXAMPLE 1: A complex repair of two scalp lacerations measuring a total of 4 cm is located in the same anatomical site and is the same type of repair. Report code 13121.

EXAMPLE 2: A complex repair of a 6-cm forehead laceration, 3-cm cheek laceration, and 3-cm chin laceration and an intermediate repair of 3.5-cm lacerations to both hands represent two different sites and types of repair. Report codes 13132, 13133, and 12042-59. (Report codes 13132 and 13133 for complex repair of the total 12-cm laceration [forehead, cheek, and chin]. Report code 12042-59 for the intermediate repair of the 3.5-cm lacerations of both hands.)

Note:

Modifier -51 is not reported with code 13133 because the plus symbol indicates that the code has *modifier -51 exempt* status. However, modifier -59 is reported with code 12042 because notes below the Repair (Closure) heading state, *When more than one classification of wounds is repaired, list the more complicated as the primary procedure and the less complicated as the secondary procedure, using modifier -59.*

Coding Tip:

HCPCS level II national code G0168, Wound closure utilizing tissue adhesive(s) only (e.g., Dermabond), is considered a supply code. Therefore, code G0168 is reported in addition to the appropriate wound repair CPT code.

EXAMPLE: Patient sustained a 2.5-centimeter superficial laceration, right leg, which was repaired using Dermabond tissue adhesive. Report codes 12001 and G0168.

Coding Wound Repair (Closure) Procedures

When reporting wound repair (closure) codes, make sure that you do the following:

- Calculate the size of the wound in centimeters, whether angular, curved, or star-shaped.

- Add together the lengths of all wounds for the multiple repair of wounds in the same anatomical site (e.g., 12001–12007), and report just one code.

- Report the code for the most complicated repair first, followed by less complicated repair codes (with modifier -59).

- Report codes 11042–11047 for skin debridement when

  o Gross contamination requires prolonged cleansing.

  o Large amounts of devitalized or contaminated tissue are removed.

  o Debridement is performed without immediate primary wound closure.

- Report codes 11010–11012 for extensive debridement of subcutaneous tissue, muscle fascia, muscle, and/or bone (including removal of foreign material) at the site of open fracture(s) and/or dislocation(s). To report these codes, debridement must include removal of foreign material *and* be performed to the level of skin and/or subcutaneous tissue (11010), but may extend to muscle (11011) or bone (11012), and documentation must specify precisely the depth of debridement.

- For debridement of skin only (or for active wound care management), without removal of foreign material, report codes 97597 or 97598 from the CPT Medicine section.

- Report codes for the repair of nerves, blood vessels, and tendons (from the specific body system involved, such as nervous, cardiovascular, or musculoskeletal). (However, codes for simple exploration of nerves, blood vessels, and tendons exposed in an open wound are not reported separately.)

- When the physician locates a foreign body and removes it, report a code for its removal only.

EXAMPLE 1: A diabetic male is diagnosed with with a 2.0-cm × 2.0-cm posterior left heel ulceration that involves skin, subcutaneous tissues, and the soleus muscle. Debridement at all levels was performed. Report code 11043 for the 4.0-cm treatment area (2.0 cm × 2.0 cm = 4.0 sq cm).

EXAMPLE 2: A motorcyclist lost control on a 2-lane country road that was covered with loose stone. She suffered an open fracture of her right tibia and extensive abrasions directly over the fracture site, which required debridement down to muscle. The debridement procedure is reported with code 11011. (The open fracture repair is reported separately, according to documentation in the patient record.)

In addition, it is important to remember that

- The simple ligation of vessels in an open wound is included in the wound repair code.

- The simple exploration of nerves, blood vessels, or tendons exposed in an open wound is included in the wound repair code.

- The reported wound repair codes are based on length of the wound (in centimeters), wound site, and complexity of repair.

- Code 13160 describes a secondary or complicated closure of a surgical wound because the initial closure reopened or failed.

- Wound repairs usually require local anesthesia, and the physician usually performs a neurovascular exam prior to administering the anesthetic. The administration of the local anesthesia is included in the wound repair code.

When the closure of a lesion excision cannot be accomplished by simple, intermediate, or complex closure, the following methods are used:

- Adjacent tissue transfer or rearrangement (Table 11-4)

- Skin replacement surgery

Adjacent Tissue Transfer or Rearrangement

Adjacent tissue transfer or rearrangement codes include skin excision and are assigned according to anatomical site. To determine the correct code, calculate the combined area (as square centimeters) of the defect to be repaired *and the defect created by the tissue transfer.* Do not report a separate code for excision of a lesion or another defect when an adjacent tissue transfer or a rearrangement procedure is performed.

When a procedure is performed to repair a secondary defect (e.g., site of donor advancement flap), report an additional procedure code for the repair (e.g., full-thickness skin graft).

EXAMPLE 1: Patient previously underwent excision of lesion, chest. Today, the patient undergoes adjacent tissue transfer repair of resulting 1 sq cm skin defect via advancement flap, created from 2 sq cm of adjacent chest tissue. Dressings were applied to both wounds. Report code 14000 (because 1 sq cm + 2 sq cm = 3 sq cm, and the chest is part of the body's trunk).

Table 11-4 Adjacent Tissue Transfer or Tissue Rearrangement Methods and Definitions

Adjacent Tissue Transfer Method	Definition
Advancement flap	Movement of tissue in a straight line from donor to defect site using a sliding process; once movement is achieved, the flap is sutured in place; advancement flaps are not rotated or moved sideways.
Double pedicle flap	Maintains blood supply from both ends of the flap incision made to create a curvilinear flap contiguous with the defect; flap is pivoted and sutured in place over the defect.
Free flap	Island flap that is detached from donor site and reattached at recipient site via microvascular anastomosis.
Island flap	Flap consisting of skin and subcutaneous tissue with a pedicle comprised only of nutrient vessels; also called **island pedicle flap**.
Mycocutaneous flap	Autologous graft consisting of both skin and muscle tissue from the donor site.
Random pattern flap	Mycocutaneous flap with a random pattern of arteries.
Rhomboid flap	Random pattern flap that can be raised on any or all corners of a parallelogram configuration, typically 120 and 60 degrees; also called **Limberg flap**.
Rotation flap	Incision made to create a curvilinear flap contiguous with the defect; flap is dissected, freed, pivoted, and sutured in place over the defect.
Tissue rearrangement	Defined by anatomical site and size of defect; includes excision of the defect or lesion; terms used to describe transfer or rearrangement include *Z-plasty, W-plasty, V-Y plasty, rotation flap, advancement flap,* and *double pedicle flap.*
V-Y-plasty	After creation of a V-shaped incision, the edges of the incision are drawn together and sutured, converting the incision to a Y shape.
W-plasty	Both edges of the wound or defect are trimmed into the shape of a W or multiple Ws.
Z-plasty	Involves making an incision along with two additional incisions, one above and another below, creating a Z formation.

EXAMPLE 2: Patient previously underwent excision of nasal scar, which resulted in a skin defect. Today, the patient undergoes adjacent tissue transfer repair of the 2 sq cm nasal skin defect using an advancement flap (using 4 sq cm of skin from the left cheek). A full-thickness skin graft (using 6 sq cm of skin from right inner thigh) was required to close the 4 sq cm flap left cheek donor site defect. The right inner thigh was repaired using direct closure. Report codes 14060 (because 2 sq cm + 4 sq cm = 6 sq cm) and 15240-51 (which includes direct closure to repair the right inner thigh).

Skin Replacement Surgery Flaps (Skin and/or Deep Tissues), and Other Flaps and Grafts

CPT graft codes are organized as follows:

- Autograft/tissue cultured autograft
- Acellular dermal replacement
- Allograft/tissue cultured allogeneic skin substitute
- Allograft, skin
- Xenograft, skin

Skin replacement surgery includes surgical preparation and topical placement of an autograft or a skin substitute graft. *Surgical preparation* codes describe initial services performed to prepare a clean and viable wound surface for placement of an autograft, flap, skin substitute graft, or for negative pressure wound therapy. An **autograft** is the transplantation of tissue from the same individual (e.g., harvesting skin from the patient's thigh to graft a defect of the upper arm). **Tissue-cultured autografts** are supplied by laboratories. (Modifier -58 is added to tissue-cultured autograft codes because labs can grow a limited amount of tissue and such grafts are often performed as staged procedures.) **Skin substitute grafts** include nonautologous human skin (e.g., acellular dermal), non-human skin substitute grafts (e.g., xenograft), and biological products that form a sheet scaffolding for skin growth.

Acellular dermal replacement is a bioengineered artificial skin (e.g., Alloderm). An **allograft** is the transplantation of tissue from someone of the same species (e.g., harvesting skin from another person's thigh to graft a defect on the patient's upper arm). A **xenograft** is the transplantation of tissue from a different species (e.g., harvesting skin from a baboon or a pig to graft a defect on the patient's upper arm).

Types of skin grafts include the following:

- Free skin graft
  - Full-thickness skin graft
  - Split-thickness skin graft
- Pedicle skin graft

Free skin grafts are completely separated from the donor site before being transferred to the recipient site. They are classified as **full-thickness skin grafts** (graft of epidermis and dermis) or **split-thickness skin grafts** (graft of entire epidermis and a portion of the dermis). Full-thickness skin grafts are often harvested from the inguinal folds, supraclavicular region, abdomen, thigh, and postauricular skin (because of the availability of excess skin, which eases primary closure of the donor site). Split-thickness grafts are typically used to repair edematous, infected, or large wounds (e.g., result of burns).

Coding Tip:

- Before reporting codes 15002–15278 for free skin grafts, determine whether the graft is full-thickness or split-thickness, what the size of the recipient area is, and where the location of the recipient area is.

- When reporting codes 15100–15278, the area over which a skin graft is placed must be free of infection or other disease; if it is necessary to cleanse the recipient site of a skin graft, also report a code from 15002–15005 for the surgical preparation.

- Although codes 15002–15278 include simple debridement of the recipient area, they do not include repair of the donor site with skin grafts or local flaps. Report additional code(s) when the donor site is repaired in this manner.

Pedicle skin grafts are not immediately completely separated from their donor site. A portion of the graft is transferred to the recipient area, and a remaining portion (the base) is attached to the donor site so that there is a vasculature and nerve supply for the recipient area. Once blood flow to the recipient site is sufficient, the base is grafted to the recipient site.

Coding Tip:

Codes 15600–15630 are reported when the "delay technique" is used to improve the blood supply to the base of a flap. This is accomplished by temporarily obstructing the blood supply to the flap to allow a relatively long flap to be transferred onto a narrow pedicle.

When assigning codes for skin grafts, identify the following:

- Type of graft
  - Permanent or temporary
  - Natural or manufactured graft material
  - Use of skin components (e.g., epidermal, dermal, split-thickness, or full-thickness grafts) (Refer to Figure 11-8 to view full-thickness and split-thickness skin grafts.)
- Recipient site (anatomical location)
- Surface area of the recipient site calculated as square centimeters

Figure 11-8 Depth of full-thickness and split-thickness skin cross-sections

Just one type of skin graft is usually applied to an anatomical location. Thus, primary free skin graft codes are mutually exclusive of one another. When multiple anatomical locations require different grafts, add modifier -59 to the reported code(s) to indicate that different sites underwent grafting.

When a benign or malignant lesion is excised and surgical preparation and free skin grafting are performed, two codes are reported.

- Excision lesion code (11400–11446 or 11600–11646)

- Skin graft code

However, when a benign or malignant lesion is excised with flap closure, just the flap closure code is reported.

Generally, debridement of nonintact skin in anticipation of a skin graft is necessary prior to application of the skin graft and is included in the skin graft. When skin is intact, however, and the graft is being performed after excisional preparation of intact skin, codes 15002–15005 (Excisional preparation) are separately reported. CPT codes 15002–15005 do not describe debridement of nonintact, necrotic, or infected skin, nor is their use indicated with other lesion removal codes.

EXAMPLE: A patient with full-thickness burns of the left arm underwent surgical preparation of the burned tissue. After excision and hemostasis, 100 sq cm full thickness free graft with direct closure was performed. Report codes 15002, 15220, 15221, 15221, and 15221.

Refer to Table 11-5 when assigning codes for tissue rearrangement, free skin grafts, flaps (skin and/or deep tissues), and/or other flaps and grafts. When multiple tissue rearrangement and free skin graft procedures are required during the same operative session, make sure you report each separately. (The total square centimeters for repair of different defects are not added together.)

Other Procedures

"Other procedures" codes classify the following integumentary system procedures:

- Dermabrasion
- Abrasion
- Chemical peel
- Cervicoplasty
- Blepharoplasty
- Rhytidectomy
- Excision, excessive skin and subcutaneous tissue (including lipectomy)

- Graft for facial nerve paralysis
- Removal of sutures under anesthesia
- Dressing change under anesthesia
- Intravenous injection of agent
- Suction-assisted lipectomy

Table 11-5 Types of Codes for Tissue Rearrangement, Free Skin Grafts, and Flaps

Type of Procedure	# of Codes	Types of Codes
Adjacent tissue transfer or rearrangement	1	• Adjacent tissue transfer or rearrangement (14000–14350)
Free skin graft	2 or more	• Free skin graft (15050–15278) • Surgical preparation or creation of recipient site *(15002–15005) for burn and wound preparation and management procedures only* • Repair of donor site if local flap or skin graft is required (14000–14350)
Flap (skin and/or deep tissue)	1 or more	• Flap (skin and/or deep tissue) (15570–15738) • Repair of donor site if local flap or skin graft is required (14000–14350 or 15050)
Other flap and graft	1 or more	• Flap or graft (15740–15777) • Repair of donor site if local flap or skin graft is required (14000–14350)

Dermabrasion (Figure 11-9) is performed for conditions such as acne scarring and wrinkles (facial) and rhytids and general keratosis (facial and other than face). The physician uses a rotary device to sand down raised lesions or thickened tissue, regenerating smoother skin.

EXAMPLE: Patient underwent total face dermabrasion by use of a rotary instrument that penetrates into the dermis layer of skin. Report code 15780.

 Coding Tip:

- The code description for code 15783 includes "tattoo removal" as an example. However, dermabrasion to remove a tattoo usually involves the dermis. According to the AMA's *CPT Assistant,* because code 15783 is reported for superficial abrasion, it should not be reported for tattoo removal. Report a code from 15780–15782 for tattoo removal.

- Microdermabrasion is not classified in CPT, which means that unlisted code 17999 is assigned. **Microdermabrasion** is a skin-freshening technique used to repair facial skin that is damaged by the sun and the effects of aging. A sandblaster device is used to spray tiny crystals across the face, mixing gentle abrasion with suction to remove the outer layer of skin.

Figure 11-9 Dermabrasion

A **chemical peel** involves the use of chemical agents (e.g., glycolic acid or phenol) to remove wrinkles and abnormal pigmentation. Be sure to determine if treatment is localized to surface layers of the facial skin or the deeper dermal layer.

 Note:

Actinic keratosis (AK) is a common sun-induced skin lesion of the epidermis that has the potential to become skin cancer. The most commonly performed treatments for AK includes cryosurgery with liquid nitrogen, topical drug therapy, and curettage. However, AK treatments also include dermabrasion, excision, chemical peels, laser therapy, and photodynamic therapy (PDT).

A **blepharoplasty** is any surgical repair of an eyelid. From a coding perspective, blepharoplasty describes the removal of the orbicularis muscle, orbital fat, and excess eyelid skin around the orbit. Make sure you review the operative report to identify the procedure performed and assign appropriate codes. A blepharoptosis repair is performed on the levator muscle of the eyelid. The code selected is based on the surgical approach used to perform the blepharoptosis repair.

EXAMPLE: Patient underwent blepharoplasty of the left lower eyelid, which required the physician to dissect lower eyelid skin to the subcutaneous and muscle fascial layers and excise excess skin. Report code 15820-E2. (HCPCS level II modifier -E2 is reported to indicate that the procedure was performed on the "lower left, eyelid.")

 Note:

Medicare reimburses services that are reasonable and necessary to diagnose and treat or to improve the functioning of a malformed body member. When blepharoplasty procedures (15822–15823) are performed for cosmetic purposes, they are not covered by Medicare. When the function of the eye is impaired by overlying skin or fatty tissue, the repair is deemed medically necessary and is covered by Medicare.

A **rhytidectomy** involves excising a section of skin to eliminate wrinkles and can be done to reduce **glabellar frown lines**, which are vertical furrows in the forehead area between the eyebrows.

Graft procedures for facial nerve paralysis involve the removal of connective tissue (e.g., fascia) from the body. The graft is transplanted to the face to reanimate previously paralyzed areas.

The removal of sutures by the surgeon is included in the global period associated with that procedure. (The removal of sutures by a physician other than the surgeon who initially placed the sutures is usually reported with an E/M code.)

Abdominal panniculectomy (abdominoplasty) is performed to remove fatty tissue and excess skin from the lower to middle portions of the abdomen. This procedure is typically performed on individuals who have lost considerable weight, resulting in loose-hanging folds of skin in the abdominal area. A lipectomy is the removal of localized subcutaneous fat deposits by suction curettage or blunt cannulization to cosmetically correct obesity and other contour defects.

EXAMPLE: Report 15832 for removal of excess skin and subcutaneous tissue on the thigh, 15833 for the leg, 15834 for the hip, 15835 for the buttock, 15836 for the arm, 15837 for the forearm or hand, 15838 for the submental fat pad, and 15839 for any other area.

When a physician performs a suction-assisted lipectomy, a liposuction cannula is inserted through the fat deposits, removing excess deposits. From a CPT coding perspective, it would be appropriate to report code 15877 for *each* area of liposuction on the trunk.

EXAMPLE: Report 15877 for a suction-assisted lipectomy of the trunk, 15878 if liposuction is done on an upper extremity, and 15879 for a lower extremity. Modifier -51 should be appended to the subsequent procedures performed.

Pressure Ulcers (Decubitus Ulcers)

A **pressure ulcer**, or **decubitus ulcer**, or **bedsore**, is an ulceration of the skin and underlying tissue that occurs over a bony prominence (e.g., sacral decubitus). A decubitus ulcer appears in patients confined to bed or immobilized when blood supply is decreased in pressure areas by pressure on the skin, resulting in inflammation and swelling and ultimately necrosis, ulceration, and infection.

The primary excisional procedure of a staged process does not include the flap/graft procedures, which are reported separately. CPT includes notes that provide instruction to report appropriate repair and skin graft codes.

EXAMPLE: Patient underwent excision of ischial pressure ulcer with ostectomy. Report code 15946.

When a muscle or myocutaneous flap is planned for a subsequent session prospectively (e.g., at the time of the original procedure), report the appropriate flap code and add modifier -58 (Staged Procedure).

Burns, Local Treatment

The introduction to the Burns, Local Treatment heading states that the application of materials (e.g., Biobrane) is included. To assign appropriate codes for the treatment of burns, review the medical record to identify the following:

- Percentage of body surface

- Severity (depth) of the burn

  o Partial-thickness burns (e.g., first-degree or second-degree)

  o Full-thickness burns (e.g., third-degree)

To determine the extent of body surface involved, use the **rule of nines**, which divides total body surface area (BSA) into nine segments by percentage (Figure 11-10). When estimating the percentage of the body affected by burns, review the medical record to locate the patient's age. (The surface area for children is estimated differently than that for adults.)

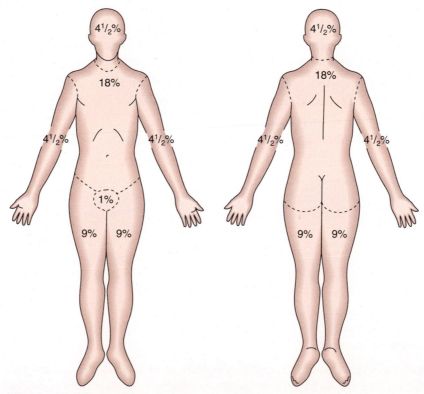

Figure 11-10 The rule of nines

EXAMPLE: The physician surgically debrided blisters and devitalized tissue that involved less than 5 percent of the total BSA. Report code 16020.

Exercise 11.9 – Repair (Closure)

Instructions: Assign the CPT code(s) and any appropriate modifier(s) to each statement.

1. Simple repair of 3.0-cm scalp laceration.

   _____

2. A physician performed a 4-cm wound closure on an established patient using adhesive strips during a level 2 E/M established patient office encounter.

   _____

3. Debridement of partial-thickness burn of the right hand involving 1 percent of total body surface.

   _____

4. Full-thickness skin graft, free, including direct closure of donor site, trunk (20 sq cm). Surgical preparation of recipient site (20 sq cm) was also performed during the same operative session.

   _____

5. Dermabrasion, total face.

   _____

Destruction

Destruction is the ablation of tissue by any method (e.g., electrosurgery, cryosurgery, or laser or chemical treatments). During destruction, excision, incision, removal, repair, or closure procedures, the debridement of nonviable tissue that surrounds a lesion, an injury, or an incision may be necessary to perform the intended procedure. Do not report the debridement codes when the intended procedure (e.g., destruction of lesion) is performed during the same operative session as the debridement procedure; the debridement procedure is considered a necessary part of the total procedure.

Destruction of Benign or Premalignant Lesions and Destruction of Malignant Lesions, Any Method

Each lesion treated is reported as a separate code for the destruction of benign, premalignant, and malignant lesions.

EXAMPLE: The physician uses a small applicator to apply liquid nitrogen directly to the patient's skin to remove a hypertrophic AK lesion. Report code 17000.

During destruction, excision, incision, removal, repair, or closure procedures, the debridement of nonviable tissue that surrounds a lesion, an injury, or an incision may be necessary to perform the intended procedure. Do *not* report a debridement code when the intended procedure (e.g., destruction of lesion) is performed during the same operative session as the debridement procedure. The debridement procedure is considered a necessary part of the total procedure.

EXAMPLE: A physician performed laser surgery to destroy a 0.5-cm malignant facial skin lesion. He also destroyed a premalignant lesion on the skin of the left shoulder. Report codes 17280 and 17000-51.

Mohs Micrographic Surgery

Mohs micrographic surgery is an advanced treatment procedure used to treat basal cell carcinoma and squamous cell carcinoma skin cancers. Dermatologists trained in this technique serve as surgeon, pathologist, and reconstructive surgeon. They use a microscope to trace and ensure the removal of skin cancer to its roots. Mohs micrographic surgery codes (17311–17315) are reported instead of excision codes and surgical pathology codes. Reporting Mohs micrographic surgery and surgical pathology codes on the same claim is inappropriate. A Mohs surgeon who obtains a diagnostic biopsy to make the decision to perform surgery reports the diagnostic biopsy code separately. When Mohs surgery is performed in addition to a skin biopsy (codes 11100, 11101) on the same day, add modifier -59 to the biopsy code, such as 17311 and 11100-59. (Modifier -59 is also added to the reported Pathology code, such as 88331-59.)

> **EXAMPLE:** A patient undergoes Mohs micrographic surgery for basal cell carcinoma of the head (behind the left ear). In Stage I, a layer of tissue is removed and the specimen is subdivided into two smaller specimens for pathologic review. In Stage II, the second layer is excised and subdivided into three smaller specimens for pathologic processing. Report codes 17311 and 17312.

Other Procedures

Other Procedures codes classify cryotherapy, chemical exfoliation for acne, electrolysis epilation, and unlisted procedures. When reporting an unlisted procedure code, include documentation about the procedure performed with the submitted claim.

> **EXAMPLE:** Patient underwent experimental destruction procedure on the skin, which is not currently classified in CPT. Report code 17999.

Exercise 11.10 – Destruction

Instructions: Assign the CPT code(s) and any appropriate modifier(s) to each statement.

1. Destruction of three premalignant facial lesions.

   _____

2. Destruction of 17 skin tags.

   _____

3. Patient underwent removal of five flat warts, using photothermolysis laser.

   _____

4. Laser surgery destruction of two actinic keratosis lesions, chest.

   _____

5. Electrosurgical destruction of 10 skin tags.

   _____

6. Chemosurgery, 3.8 centimeter malignant lesion, scalp.

   _____

7. Surgical curettement of 1.5 centimeter malignant lesion, trunk.

   _____

8. Cryosurgery, 10.0 centimeter malignant lesion, neck.

   _____

9. Electrosurgery, 0.5 centimeter malignant lesion, nose.

   _____

10. Laser surgery, 2.3 centimeter malignant lesion, left shoulder.

    _____

Breast

Diagnostic testing used to detect breast cancer may include a mammogram, ultrasonography, magnetic resonance imaging (MRI), FNA, core biopsy, or surgical biopsy. Treatment plans can include a local therapy approach such as breast-conserving surgery or mastectomy, radiation therapy (e.g., internal or implant radiation or external radiation), and breast reconstruction (e.g., implant or tissue transfer).

Because of the unique nature of procedures developed to address breast disease, codes in CPT are established for services (e.g., incision, excision, introduction, repair, and reconstruction). FNA biopsies, core biopsies, open incisional or excisional biopsies, and related procedures performed to procure tissue from a lesion for which an established diagnosis exists are not to be reported separately at the time of a lesion excision unless performed on a different lesion or on the contralateral breast. However, if a diagnosis is not established *and the decision to perform the excision or mastectomy is dependent on the results of the biopsy*, the biopsy is separately reported. Modifier -58 is used to indicate that the biopsy and the excision or mastectomy are staged or planned procedures.

Breast Biopsies

Breast biopsies are performed according to the following methods:

- Fine-needle aspiration (FNA) (Figure 11-11A)

- Needle core biopsy

  ○ Hand-operated needle

  ○ Stereotactic localization

- Open biopsy

  ○ Excisional biopsy

  ○ Incisional biopsy (Figure 11-11B)

Fine-Needle Aspiration (FNA)

FNA of the breast is reported, depending on whether imaging guidance was used during the procedure. A FNA uses a thin needle (e.g., 20- or 22-gauge needle), which is inserted through the mass several times. Suction is applied as the needle is withdrawn to obtain strands of single cells for cytologic diagnosis.

 Coding Tip:

Do not report code 19100 (needle core breast biopsy) for fine-needle aspiration (FNA) of breast tissue. FNA procedures are reported with codes 10021–10022, which include single and multiple lesions.

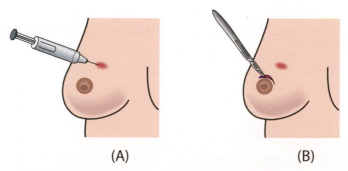

(A)   (B)

Figure 11-11 (A) Fine-needle aspiration. (B) Incisional biopsy

Needle Core Biopsy

A **needle core biopsy** is obtained using a hand-operated needle (e.g., Trucut or Vim-Silverman) or stereotactic localization. Once the tissue is obtained, it is fixed for routine pathologic section. **Stereotactic localization** is indicated for nonpalpable lesions because it uses specialized three-dimensional imaging to target the lesion. The breast is placed in a fixed position, and a biopsy gun (e.g., 14- or 18-gauge needle) is used to obtain needle core biopsies from the lesion.

 Coding Tip:

- A biopsy code (19100–19101) is assigned for each biopsied site (e.g., three needle core biopsy sites are reported as codes 19100, 19100, and 19100).

- Differentiating a puncture aspiration of a breast cyst, a needle core biopsy of the breast, and fine-needle aspiration of breast tissue can be determined by reviewing the operative report (or documented procedure statement).

  - Codes 10021–10022 are assigned for fine-needle aspirations of the breast, depending on whether imaging guidance was used during the procedure.

  - Codes 19000–19001 are assigned for puncture aspirations of breast cysts.

  - Codes 19100–19101 are assigned for needle core breast biopsies. (Code 19101 describes a breast biopsy obtained through an incision.)

However, if the entire lesion is subsequently removed during the same operative session as an excisional biopsy, code 19120 is reported instead of 19101.

Open Biopsy

An **open biopsy** can be incisional or excisional, depending on the amount of lesion removed. An **excisional biopsy** removes the lump or suspicious area in its entirety. An **incisional biopsy** removes a portion of the lesion by slicing into it or incising it; it is usually performed on large tumors (and the patient undergoes mastectomy later).

Excisional breast surgery includes certain biopsy procedures, the removal of cysts or other benign or malignant tumors or lesions, and the surgical treatment of breast and chest wall malignancies. Biopsy procedures may be percutaneous or open. Open excision of breast lesions without attention to surgical margins, with or without the preoperative placement of radiological markers, is reported with codes 19120–19126.

 Note:

An excisional biopsy (19120) is not a **lumpectomy**, which is a partial mastectomy (19301–19302).

 Coding Tip:

- Review the entire operative report and pathology report to determine whether the biopsy was excisional or incisional.

- For an excisional biopsy, report code 19120. (However, if the lesion was identified with preoperative placement of a radiological marker, report codes 19081–19086 and 19125–19126.

- For an open incisional biopsy, report code 19101. (However, if the operative report indicates that the biopsy was "incisional" and the pathology report indicates that the entire lesion was removed, report code 19120 for an excisional biopsy.)

EXAMPLE: The patient was registered for outpatient surgery on August 1. The patient received an explanation from the surgeon that she would undergo excisional left breast biopsy in the morning and that if pathology results were positive for cancer, the patient would undergo left breast lumpectomy during the late afternoon. The excisional left breast biopsy was performed at 9 AM, and tissue was positive for adenocarcinoma. The patient returned to the operating room at 2 PM and underwent left breast lumpectomy. Report codes 19120-LT (Excisional breast biopsy) and 19301-58-LT (Breast lumpectomy, staged or related procedure performed by the same physician during the postoperative period). (Modifier -58 is added to just one CPT code. The pathologist reports an appropriate code from the Pathology and Laboratory section of CPT.)

Coding Tip:

Do not report code 19120 for a breast lumpectomy. Code 19120 (excisional biopsy) is reported when the physician makes an incision in the skin of the breast overlying the site of the mass and dissects skin and tissue (from the site of the aberrant tissue, areola, cyst, fibroadenoma, lesion of the duct, nipple, or tumor). This procedure involves excising the lesion and a rim of surrounding normal tissue. When the excision of more than one lesion is performed in different areas of the breast (through separate incision sites), report code 19120 for each excision site.

A breast lumpectomy is a type of partial mastectomy, and it is reported with code 19301. When more than one lumpectomy is performed in different areas of the breast (through separate incision sites), report code 19301 for each excision site. (Modifier -51 is added to the second and subsequent reporting of code 19301 when multiple lumpectomies are performed during the same operative episode.)

EXAMPLE: A breast mass biopsy was sent to the pathologist during the operative procedure for immediate diagnosis. The pathologist examined the specimen and diagnosed a malignancy. Immediate full-thickness (through the dermis) removal of the lesion, including margins, was performed. The procedure included simple (nonlayered) closure of the mass. Report code 19120. (The pathologist reports an appropriate code from the Pathology and Laboratory section of CPT.)

Mastectomy

Mastectomy (Figure 11-12) procedures are classified in CPT as follows:

- Partial mastectomy (including lumpectomy)
- Radical mastectomy
- Simple or total mastectomy
- Modified radical mastectomy

Lumpectomy   Simple or total mastectomy   Modified radical mastectomy   Radical mastectomy

Figure 11-12 Types of mastectomy

Partial mastectomy procedures describe open excisions of breast tissue with specific attention to adequate surgical margins. A **partial mastectomy** involves making an incision through skin and fascia over the breast tumor and clamping lymphatic and blood vessels; the physician then excises the tumor mass along with a section of breast tissue. A partial mastectomy is also called a lumpectomy, quadrantectomy, segmental mastectomy, and tylectomy.

EXAMPLE: A sentinel node biopsy is performed as part of an axillary lymphadenectomy during a partial mastectomy procedure. Report code 19302, which includes removal of the sentinel node and other axillary lymph nodes.

Total mastectomy procedures include complete mastectomy, modified radical mastectomy, simple mastectomy, and subcutaneous mastectomy. A **total mastectomy** is the surgical removal of the entire breast, including the pectoral fascia and a sampling of axillary lymph nodes. Radical mastectomy procedures include the removal of pectoral muscles, axillary lymph nodes, and/or internal mammary lymph nodes. A **radical mastectomy** is a total mastectomy that includes removal of the breast and nipple, pectoralis muscles (major and/or minor), axillary lymph nodes, and internal mammary lymph nodes. A **modified radical mastectomy** is a total mastectomy that includes removal of the breast and nipple, axillary lymph nodes, and pectoralis minor muscle. ⚠

Coding Tip:

Codes 19260–19272 are not restricted to reporting just the removal of breast tumors. They are used to report resections of chest wall tumors originating from any chest wall component. (Patients diagnosed with breast cancer who undergo mastectomy may be diagnosed with chest wall cancer at a later date, requiring surgical excision.)

Breast Repair and Reconstruction

CPT breast reconstruction codes include the following elements:

- Elevation and transfer of the flap
- Closure of the donor site
- Breast contouring
- Insertion of breast implant or prosthesis, when performed

Breast reconstruction with transverse rectus abdominis myocutaneous flap (TRAM), single pedicle includes closure of donor site. In addition, TRAM flap codes include the following:

- Creation of the breast pocket
- Elevation of the abdominal flap
- Muscle dissection
- Flap transfer
- Fascial closure (donor site) with or without mesh
- Abdominal closure including umbilicoplasty
- Breast contouring

Because excision of lesions is often done during the same operative session as a mastectomy, breast excisions are not separately reported in addition to the mastectomy code *unless performed to establish the malignant diagnosis before proceeding to the mastectomy.* Thus, CPT breast excision codes are not reported in addition to CPT mastectomy codes when performed on the same side. If the breast excision is performed to obtain tissue to determine pathologic diagnosis of malignancy prior to proceeding to a mastectomy, the excision is separately coded and reported with the mastectomy code and modifier -58 is added to the codes.

Use of other integumentary codes for incision and closure are included in the codes that describe various breast excision or mastectomy codes. Because of the frequent need to biopsy lymph nodes or remove muscle tissue in conjunction with mastectomies, these procedures are included in CPT coding for mastectomy. It is inappropriate to separately report ipsilateral lymph node dissection with mastectomy codes. When a breast lesion is identified and treated and medical necessity indicates that biopsy of contralateral nodes should be done, report the biopsy or lymph node dissection codes (and add an appropriate anatomical modifier, such as -LT or -RT for left or right). Breast reconstruction codes also include the insertion of a prosthetic implant, and they are not reported with CPT codes that describe the insertion of breast prosthesis only.

CPT coding for breast procedures generally refers to unilateral procedures; when performed bilaterally, add modifier -50 to the code. (The Repair and/or Reconstruction subheading includes a parenthetical note as a reminder to report modifier -50 when appropriate.) When breast reconstruction is performed unilaterally, add the applicable HCPCS level II modifier -LT (left) or RT (right) to the procedure code.

Other Procedures

The Other Procedures code classifies an unlisted procedure performed on breast. When reporting an unlisted procedure code, include documentation about the procedure performed with the submitted claim.

> **EXAMPLE:** Patient underwent experimental procedure on the breast, which is not currently classified in CPT. Report code 19499.

Exercise 11.11 – Breast

Instructions: Assign the CPT code(s) and any appropriate modifier(s) to each statement.

1. Excision of two lesions, right breast, identified by the placement of radiological markers for each.

   _____

2. A transverse rectus abdominis myocutaneous flap procedure for right breast reconstruction is performed using a single rectus abdominis muscle to transfer the necessary tissue to form a breast mound.

   _____

3. Lumpectomy, left breast.

   _____

4. Physician performed a partial mastectomy of the right breast with right axillary lymphadenectomy and biopsy of the right sentinel node.

   _____

5. Patient underwent percutaneous left breast biopsy with placement of a breast localization clip under stereotactic guidance.

   _____

Summary

The CPT Surgery section and its subsections are organized anatomically according to major body area or organ system. Guidelines located at the beginning of the CPT Surgery section clarify the assignment of codes and explain terms. The General subsection contains just two codes. The Integumentary System subsection includes dermatological procedures, plastic surgery, and components of multiple surgical procedures (e.g., closure, flaps, grafts, and tissue transfer). Integumentary procedures are often performed as staged procedures (e.g., flaps and grafts) due to the complexity of services rendered.

Internet Links

American Academy of Dermatology (AAD): *www.aad.org*

Medicare Learning Network (MLN): Go to *www.cms.gov*, click on the Outreach & Education link, click on the "Find resources" link below the Learn heading, and then click on a link below the Medicare Learning Network® (MLN) heading.

Medscape: Go to *www.medscape.com*, and register for free access to Medscape's medical resource databases.

National Correct Coding Initiative (NCCI) Edits: Go to *www.cms.gov*, and click on the Medicare link, then click on the National Correct Coding Initiative Edits link below the Coding heading.

National Institutes of Health Videos of Surgical Procedures: Go to *www.nlm.nih.gov*, and click on the MedlinePlus link, click on the Videos & Tools link, and then click on the Surgery Videos link.

ORlive (TM) Broadcasts: Go to *www.or-live.com* to view live webcasts in selected health specialties.

Study Checklist

- [ ] Read this chapter and highlight key concepts.
- [ ] Create an index card for each key term.
- [ ] Access the chapter Internet links to learn more about concepts.
- [ ] Complete the chapter exercises and review, verifying answers with your instructor.
- [ ] Complete Workbook chapter, verifying answers with your instructor.
- [ ] Go to *www.cengagebrain.com* to access the Student Companion Web Site. Login instructions are located in the Preface.
- [ ] Form a study group with classmates to discuss chapter concepts in preparation for an exam.

Review

Multiple Choice

Instructions: Circle the most appropriate response.

1. Which is a therapeutic surgical procedure?
   a. Arthroscopy b. Biopsy c. Endoscopy d. Repair

2. A patient undergoing a surgical procedure was draped and positioned. The surgical area was cleansed and shaved, an IV was started, and a sedative was administered. The surgical approach was identified, and an incision was made. The wound was irrigated, and cultures were taken. The incision was closed, and dressings were applied. The procedure was then dictated and transcribed. A CPT code was assigned to the surgical procedure. Which service is assigned a separate code, in addition to the reported CPT Surgery code?
   a. Administration of a sedative
   b. None of the services are reported separately.
   c. Taking cultures and wound irrigation
   d. Transcription of the dictated report

3. Which modifier indicates a staged procedure or service?
   a. -58 b. -59 c. -66 d. -76

4. When a patient receives treatment for an unrelated condition during the global period, which modifier is added to the CPT code?
   a. -51   b. -57   c. -59   d. -79

5. The CMS global surgical package includes:
   a. diagnostic tests and procedures, including diagnostic radiological procedures.
   b. initial consultation or evaluation of the problem by the surgeon to determine the need for surgery.
   c. the day before the day of surgery for major procedures.
   d. treatment for postoperative complications that require a return trip to the operating room.

6. When an evaluation and management (E/M) service provided is for the purpose of deciding to perform a major surgical procedure, which is reported?
   a. E/M code
   b. E/M code with modifier -57
   c. E/M code with modifier -59
   d. No E/M code is reported because the service is bundled in the surgery code.

7. The code reported for fine-needle aspiration is determined based on whether:
   a. fluid is aspirated from a cyst or cells are aspirated from a solid mass.
   b. imaging guidance is used during the procedure.
   c. the cyst or mass is visible.
   d. the procedure is performed percutaneously.

8. If the operative report describes a lesion as 3.5 cm × 4 cm × 5 cm, which is reported as the diameter?
   a. 3.5 cm   b. 4 cm   c. 5 cm   d. 17.5 cm

9. When Mohs micrographic surgery is performed, Mohs micrographic surgery codes are reported instead of:
   a. a diagnostic biopsy code.
   b. excision codes and a diagnostic biopsy code.
   c. excision codes and surgical pathology codes.
   d. surgical pathology codes.

10. Wound repair is coded with an appropriate evaluation and management code when the sole repair material used is:
    a. adhesive strips.   c. sutures.
    b. staples.   d. tissue adhesives.

11. Evacuation of subungual hematoma. Which CPT code is assigned?
    a. 10140   b. 10160   c. 11740   d. 11750

12. Collagen injection, face, 5.1 cc. Which CPT code is assigned?
    a. 11950   b. 11951   c. 11952   d. 11954

13. Puncture aspiration of abscess on lower left eyelid. Which CPT code is assigned?
    a. 10120-E2   b. 10140-E2   c. 10160-E2   d. 10180-E2

14. Open excision of fibroadenomas, right breast. Which CPT code is assigned?
    a. 19100-RT   b. 19120-RT   c. 19301-RT   d. 19260-RT

15. Suction-assisted abdominal lipectomy. Which CPT code is assigned?
    a. 15876   b. 15877   c. 15878   d. 15879

16. Adjacent tissue transfer of 12 sq cm defect of forehead. Which CPT code is assigned?
    a. 14020   b. 14021   c. 14040   d. 14041

17. Mohs micrographic surgery of upper left arm (first stage) with excision of five specimens. Diagnostic skin biopsy performed the same day. Which CPT code(s) are assigned?

    a. 11100, 17313-51   c. 17313

    b. 17313, 11100-59   d. 17313, 11406

18. Modified radical mastectomy, including axillary lymph nodes, excluding pectoral muscles. Which CPT code is assigned?

    a. 19301   b. 19305   c. 19306   d. 19307

19. Epidermal facial chemical peel. Which CPT code is assigned?

    a. 15788   b. 15789   c. 15792   d. 15793

20. Cryosurgery of two plantar warts. Which CPT code(s) are assigned?

    a. 17000, 17000   c. 17000, 17003-51

    b. 17000, 17003   d. 17110

Coding Practice

Instructions: Assign the CPT code(s) and appropriate modifier(s) to each case.

1. Patient underwent fine-needle aspiration to remove fluid sample from a cyst, anterior neck. Physician palpated the cyst, cleansed the site with Betadine solution, and inserted a 25-gauge needle into the cyst. Approximately 2 cc of fluid were removed. The needle was withdrawn, and a small bandage was placed over the insertion area.

_____

2. Patient underwent fine-needle aspiration to remove a cluster of cells from a solid mass, subcutaneous layer of the left upper quadrant, abdomen. Computed tomography imaging guidance for needle placement was performed. Physician palpated the mass, cleansed the area with Betadine solution, and inserted a 22-gauge needle into the solid mass. Approximately 1 cc of tissue was removed. The needle was withdrawn, and a small bandage was placed over the insertion area.

_____

3. A large mass, soft and movable, located on the patient's back between the lower scapular area and midline on the left, was palpated. An elliptical incision was made, a section of the tissue was removed, and the 4.0-cm cyst was resected completely. Bleeding vessels were clamped and coagulated. Penrose drain was left in the wound, and skin edges were closed along with subcutaneous tissue, using interrupted silk sutures.

_____

4. Patient was prepped and draped; after adequate general endotracheal anesthesia, the body was somewhat flexed at the waist to provide adequate exposure after taping in preparation to separate the buttocks at the sacral crease. A probe was inserted into the inferior sinus, and only 3 to 4 cm of fluid were obtained. The area was prepped for excision, and an oval-shaped piece of skin was excised in total, including the 5.0-cm subcutaneous pilonidal cyst sinus end. Bleeding was controlled with electrocautery, the area was copiously irrigated with Betadine saline solution and suctioned and sponged off, and vertical mattress sutures of Prolene were placed in layers to obliterate the dead space.

_____

5. Local anesthesia was injected using 1 percent lidocaine with epinephrine 1.5 cc. Incision was made along the postauricular sulcus through the drainage point with retraction applied. A 3.0-cm

sebaceous cyst was evident, and it was drained. A small bandage was placed over the incision and drainage site.

---

6. Split-thickness skin graft of about 7 sq cm was removed from the left thigh, and sterile dressings were applied. A 6-cm malignant lesion was removed from the left calf by a wide excision, including at least 1 cm of normal skin all around, taking it all the way down to include fascia and overlying muscle. Bleeding points were carefully ligated, wound was treated with Hibiclens, and skin graft was applied and sutured in place with 4-0 Mersilene sutures.

---

7. Patient was using a chain saw, which slipped, and the patient sustained a 5.0-cm laceration to the dorsum of the proximal portion of the left index finger, extending through the extensor tendon and capsule. Debridement of tissue was done to facilitate a better repair of this deep laceration. Tendon and capsule were sutured with five 6-0 silk sutures. Bleeders were ligated with plain catgut. Skin was debrided extensively and approximated with seven sutures of 4-0 Dermal.

---

8. Patient sustained second-degree burn of the right thigh that was less than 5 percent of the total body surface. The skin was completely necrotic. The right thigh was prepared with pHisoHex, and the wound was debrided using a dermatome. Partial thickness, superficial layer of dead skin tissue was removed. Wound was treated with pHisoHex and cleaned, and a sterile outside dressing was applied.

---

9. Digital nerve block was applied to numb the top of the right great toe and the left great toe. Blunt dissection of the nail plate from the nail bed, right great toe, was performed. Bleeding was cauterized. Right great toe was bandaged. Next, the left great toenail plate was removed from the nail bed, bleeding was cauterized, and left great toe was bandaged.

---

10. Patient sustained a 3.0-cm scalp laceration and a 2.0-cm neck laceration after being cut with a knife during a bar fight. Local anesthetic was injected around the scalp and neck laceration sites. Wounds were thoroughly cleansed, explored, and irrigated with a saline solution. One-layer suture repair of scalp and neck wounds was performed.

---

11. An island pedicle flap was formed on the left thigh, and the defect was covered by elevating a flap of skin and subcutaneous tissue. The flap was then rotated into the defect, with transfer being accomplished through a tunnel underneath the skin. The flap was sutured into its new position, and the donor site was closed.

---

12. Bell's palsy patient underwent harvesting of a graft for residual facial nerve paralysis. Connective tissue fascia was removed from the fascia lata, right leg. Fascia graft was transplanted to the face and sutured into place underneath skin to reanimate paralyzed area of the face.

---

13. Using surgical curettement, 3.0-cm malignant lesion of the neck was removed.

---

14. Procedure: Lumpectomy, left breast. Incision was made through skin and fascia over a left breast mass, and lymphatic and blood vessels were clamped. Tumor mass was excised in its entirety along with normal breast tissue. Drainage tube was placed through a separate stab incision. Layered closure was performed, and a sterile dressing was applied.

_____

15. Right breast cyst was palpated, and needle was inserted into skin of the breast overlying the cyst. Needle was inserted into the cyst, and fluid was evacuated into the syringe. Needle was withdrawn, and pressure was applied to the puncture wound.

_____

CPT Surgery II

Chapter Outline

Musculoskeletal System Subsection
Respiratory System Subsection

Chapter Objectives

At the conclusion of this chapter, the student should be able to:

- Define key terms.
- Explain the organization, format, and content of the CPT Surgery Musculoskeletal System and Respiratory System subsections.
- Interpret CPT surgery coding notes for the Musculoskeletal System and Respiratory System subsections.
- Assign CPT surgery codes from the Musculoskeletal System and Respiratory System subsections.
- Add CPT and/or HCPCS level II modifiers to codes, as appropriate.

Key Terms

allogenous	brushing	femur	LeFort III
arthrocentesis	bunion	flexor tendons	ligament
arthrodesis	cadaver donor pneumonectomy	harvesting	luxation
arthroscopy	cell washing	immobilize	manipulation
artificial ankylosis	closed fracture treatment	indirect laryngoscopy	nasal vestibule
arytenoidectomy	concha	internal fixation device	obturator
arytenoidopexy	direct laryngoscopy	knee	open fracture treatment
augmentation	dislocation	laryngoscopy	osteogenesis
autogenous	extensor tendons	larynx	osteotomy
backbench work	external fixation device	LeFort I	percutaneous needle biopsy
bronchoscopy		LeFort II	

percutaneous skeletal fixation	pneumonectomy	skeletal traction	tibial plateau
percutaneous vertebroplasty	pyramidal fracture	stabilize	trachea
pleura	recipient lung allotransplantation	subglottic stenosis	tracheobronchoscopy
pleural effusion	reduction	subluxation	turbinates
pneumocentesis	replantation	thoracentesis	vertebral augmentation
	rhytides	thoracoscopy	
		tibia	

Introduction

The Musculoskeletal System subsection classifies procedures performed on bones, cartilage, joints, ligaments, muscles, and tendons (including casting and strapping). The Respiratory System subsection classifies procedures performed on the nose, accessory sinuses, larynx, trachea and bronchi, lungs, and pleura. CPT guidelines that apply to the subsections are located at the beginning of the Surgery section. Unique coding instructions for Musculoskeletal System or Respiratory System subsections are located in notes below headings or codes.

 Note:

The content in Chapter 12 (and Chapters 13 through 15) is organized exactly as it appears in the CPT Surgery section. This organization facilitates learning by allowing students to move from one CPT Surgery subsection to the next, in order.

The Other Procedures code below each subheading classifies an unlisted procedure performed on the anatomical site. When reporting an unlisted procedure code, include documentation about the procedure performed with the submitted claim. (Other Procedures subheadings are not included throughout Chapter 13 of this textbook except when codes that describe additional procedures are included.)

 Coding Tip:

Notes located beneath headings and/or subheadings apply to all codes under the heading or subheading. Parenthetical notes located below a specific code apply to that code only, unless the note indicates otherwise.

Musculoskeletal System Subsection

The CPT Musculoskeletal System subsection is arranged from head to toe according to body area and includes the following headings:

- General
- Head
- Neck (Soft Tissues) and Thorax
- Back and Flank
- Spine (Vertebral Column)
- Abdomen
- Shoulder

- Humerus (Upper Arm) and Elbow
- Forearm and Wrist
- Hand and Fingers
- Pelvis and Hip Joint
- Femur (Thigh Region) and Knee Joint
- Leg (Tibia and Fibula) and Ankle Joint
- Foot and Toes
- Application of Casts and Strapping
- Endoscopy/Arthroscopy

Each heading includes one or more of the following subheadings:

- Incision
- Excision
- Introduction or Removal
- Repair, Revision, and/or Reconstruction
- Fracture and/or Dislocation (Table 12-1)
- Manipulation
- Arthrodesis
- Amputation
- Other Procedures

Coding Tip:

The Other Procedures code below each subheading classifies an unlisted procedure performed on the anatomical site. When reporting an unlisted procedure code, include documentation about the procedure performed with the submitted claim. (Other Procedures subheadings are not included throughout Chapter 12 of this textbook except when codes that describe additional procedures are included.)

EXAMPLE: Patient underwent experimental procedure on the spine, which is not currently classified in CPT. Report code 22899.

Musculoskeletal System Notes

Musculoskeletal System subsection notes include definitions of fractures (e.g., closed and open) and clarify that the type of fracture does not necessarily correspond to the type of treatment (e.g., closed, open, or percutaneous) provided. In addition, types of injury codes include open or closed fractures and joint injuries. Musculoskeletal system notes also clarify the excision of subcutaneous soft connective tissue tumors, excision of fascial or subfascial soft tissue tumors, and radical resection of bone tumors.

Coding Tip:

Open and closed fractures may not receive the same type of treatment. Closed fractures can receive open treatment, and open fractures can receive closed treatment. Either type of fracture can receive **percutaneous skeletal fixation** treatment.

Table 12-1 Types of Fractures, Joint Injuries, and Fracture Treatment

Term	Definition
Types of Fractures	
Closed fracture (or simple fracture) (Figure 12-1)	• Broken bone(s) do not protrude through skin • No open wounds • Described clinically as "closed"
Dislocation or **luxation** (Figure 12-1)	• Total displacement of bone from its joint • **Subluxation** is the partial displacement of a bone from its joint
Open fracture (or compound fracture) (Figure 12-1)	• Broken bone(s) that can be seen through an open wound or that protrudes through skin • Clinically requires an injury with sufficient force to penetrate skin, subcutaneous tissue, muscle fascia/muscle, and/or bone or joint
Closed and Open Fracture Treatment	

Closed fracture treatment	• Fracture site is not surgically opened or exposed
	• Three methods of treatment
	  ○ With **manipulation**, or **reduction** (Figure 12-2), which means that the bones are realigned
	  ○ Without manipulation, which means that the bones are not realigned and a cast or strapping device is placed around the limb to **stabilize**, or **immobilize**, it, which secures the bone(s) in fixed position
	  ○ With or without **skeletal traction** (Figure 12-3), which exerts a pulling force on the affected limb to realign bone or joint

Open fracture treatment	• Fracture site is surgically opened or exposed • With or without *manipulation* (reduction) • With or without *skeletal traction*
Percutaneous Skeletal Fixation Fracture Treatment	
External fixation device (Figure 12-4)	• Hardware is inserted through bone and skin and held rigid with cross braces outside of the body • Always removed after the fracture has healed • Removal procedure is included in the global service, which means it is *not* separately coded and reported
Internal fixation device (Figure 12-5)	• Pins, screws, and/or plates are inserted through or within the fracture area to stabilize and immobilize the injury • Often called open reduction with internal fixation, or ORIF

Coding Tip:

Fracture management codes are found throughout the Musculoskeletal System subsection. The codes include the following:

- Pinning
- Open or closed treatment of the fracture
- Application and removal of the initial cast or splint
- Normal, uncomplicated follow-up care

    Do not report separate codes for each of the above services when provided during the same encounter, because they are included in the fracture treatment code. Codes for treatment of fractures and joint injuries (dislocations) are classified according to type of manipulation (reduction) and stabilization (fixation or immobilization).

Pathologic
Caused by weakness
from disease

Open (compound)   Closed (simple)

Classification based on skin condition

Colles
Fracture named for physician

Femoral neck
Fracture based on location

Greenstick   Comminuted   Compression   Impacted

Classification based on bone condition

Subluxation

Dislocation

Longitudinal   Transverse   Oblique   Spiral   Stellate

Classification based on position of fracture line

Figure 12-1 Fractures and dislocations

Figure 12-2 Closed manipulation (reduction) of fractured left humerus

Figure 12-3 Traction

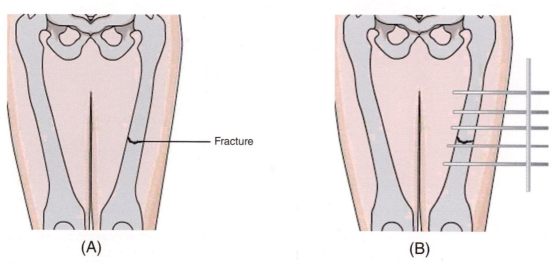

(A)   (B)

Figure 12-4 External fixation (A) Fracture of femur epiphysis (B) External fixation device stabilizes the bone and is removed after the bone has healed

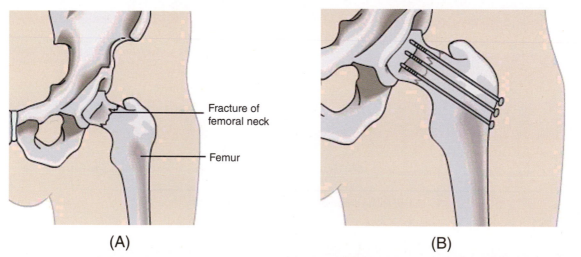

(A)   (B)

Figure 12-5 Internal fixation (A) Fracture of femoral neck (B) Internal fixation device (e.g., pins) is placed to stabilize the bone and is not removed after the bone has healed

Exercise 12.1 – Musculoskeletal System Notes

Instructions: Complete each statement.

1. The Musculoskeletal subsection is arranged from head to toe according to _____.

2. Types of injury codes include _____.

3. Open and closed fractures may not receive the same type of _____.

4. Fracture management codes include pinning, open or closed treatment of the fracture, application and removal of the initial cast or splint, and _____.

5. Codes for treatment of fractures and joint injuries are classified according to type of _____ and stabilization.

General

The General heading contains the following subheadings, several of which are unique to the heading:

- Incision

- Wound Exploration—Trauma (e.g., Penetrating Gunshot, Stab Wound)

- Excision

- Introduction or Removal

- Replantation

- Grafts (or Implants)

- Other Procedures

Incision

When an incision of a soft tissue abscess is performed and it is located in deeper tissues than those associated with the integumentary system, report code 20005. Code 20005 is reported for the incision and drainage of a soft tissue abscess, subfascia, which involves the soft tissue below the deep fascia; the physician thoroughly debrides and irrigates the affected area, examines underlying tissue and bone for signs of infection, removes dead bone or tissue, and closes the site.

Wound Exploration—Trauma

Wound exploration—trauma codes are reported for the treatment of wound(s) resulting from penetrating trauma (e.g., gunshot or stab wound), and they include the following:

- Surgical exploration and enlargement of the wound

- Extension of dissection (to determine penetration)

- Debridement

- Removal of foreign body(s)

- Ligation or coagulation of minor subcutaneous and/or muscular blood vessel(s) of the subcutaneous tissue, muscle fascia, and/or muscle, not requiring thoracotomy or laparotomy

When major structures or major blood vessels require repair via thoracotomy or laparotomy, do not report the -otomy code. Report the repair code. When a simple, intermediate, or complex repair of wound(s) is performed *only* (without enlargement of wound area, extension of dissection to determine penetration, debridement, removal of foreign body, ligation/coagulation of minor blood subcutaneous/muscular blood vessels), report the appropriate repair code(s) from the Integumentary System section.

> **EXAMPLE:** A patient was treated for a 2.5-cm stab wound located above the base of the neck. The physician extended the wound to explore and assess damage; it was determined that the injury extended to the muscle. Muscle fascia and subcutaneous tissue were closed in layers, and the skin was closed. Report code 20100.

Excision

Report excision codes for epiphyseal bar procedures (performed on bone) and biopsies performed on muscle or bone.

> **EXAMPLE:** Patient underwent open bone biopsy of the right femur. Report code 20245-RT.

Introduction or Removal

Introduction and removal procedure codes are reported for injection procedures, removal of a foreign body, insertion and application of surgical hardware, arthrocentesis, and aspirations. Surgical injections are performed by inserting a needle directly into a joint or tendon sheath, trigger point, or ganglion cyst (Figure 12-6) to aspirate fluid or inject medications. Codes for injections are based on anatomical site. **Arthrocentesis** is a procedure done to puncture a joint for fluid removal or medication injection.

> **EXAMPLE 1:** A patient underwent aspiration of ganglion cyst, left wrist. Report code 20612-LT.

> **EXAMPLE 2:** Using ultrasound guidance for needle placement, the physician injected patient's left knee joint with 30 mg of Kenalog for therapeutic relief of knee pain. Report codes 20611-LT and HCPCS level II codes J3301, J3301, and J3301.

Code 20692 is reported in addition to the code for treatment of the fracture or joint injury (unless application of an external fixation system is included in the fracture or joint injury code description).

> **EXAMPLE:** A patient underwent closed treatment of a femoral shaft fracture with manipulation and application of an uniplane external fixation system. Report codes 27502 and 20692-51. Code 27502 does not specify the use of an external fixation device in its code description; therefore, also report code 20692 with modifier -51.

When a traumatic injury with an open wound requires surgical debridement but the type of fracture requires manipulation and casting (instead of an external or internal fixation device), report the appropriate code for closed fracture treatment *in addition to the appropriate debridement code.*

> **EXAMPLE:** A patient underwent closed treatment of tibial fracture with manipulation, application of a cast, and open wound debridement of 15 sq cm of skin using a scalpel around the fracture site. Report codes 27752 and 97597. There is mention of manipulation; therefore, report code 27752. Report code 97597 for the debridement procedure.

Figure 12-6 Ganglion cyst

Replantation

Replantation is the surgical reattachment of a finger, a hand, a toe, a foot, a leg, or an arm that has been completely severed from a person's body. (A severed body part is also called an amputation.) Replantation codes include arthrodesis, cleansing, debridement, internal fixation, and repair of tendons (as well as the surgical reattachment procedure).

EXAMPLE 1: A patient who severed his left arm at the humeral diaphysis in a machine accident underwent replantation of the arm. Wound debridement and shortening were performed on the stump and the amputated part of the arm, along with primary repair of muscles and microsurgical repair of arteries, veins, and nerves and internal fixation. A splint was also applied. Report code 20802-LT.

EXAMPLE 2: A patient who suffered a partially severed right leg in an automobile accident underwent repair of the cruciate and collateral ligaments of the right knee; suture of tendon, right knee; repair of one arterial blood vessel, right knee; and 7.5-cm complex closure of wound. Report codes 27409-RT, 35226-51-RT, 27380-51-RT, and 13121-51-RT. (Modifier -51 is reported to indicate that multiple procedures were performed *in addition* to the first-listed procedure.)

Grafts (or Implants)

Grafts (or implants) codes are reported when **autogenous** (originating in the patient's body) tissue is obtained through separate skin or fascial incisions, *except when the graft procedure code includes* **harvesting** (removing tissue for transplantation) *the graft (or implant) for which a combination code is reported.* Codes with the ✚ (add-on code) symbol mean that modifier -51 is not added. (**Allogenous** grafts involve tissue organ transplanted from one person to another; for example, bone tissue can be obtained from a bone bank. Xenografts are obtained from another species, such as pigs.)

Graft material is harvested (obtained) from bone, cartilage, fascia, or tendon. Harvested bone tissue is transplanted to another site to promote **osteogenesis** (bone growth) or to provide structural stability (e.g., spinal fusion). Harvested cartilage tissue is often used for reconstruction purposes (e.g., facial reconstruction to relieve temporomandibular joint [TMJ] pain). Fascia lata tissue is harvested from gastrocnemius fascia (from the calf) or tensor fascia lata (from the thigh) for soft tissue augmentation (e.g., repair skin defects, such as multiple depressed acne scars or **rhytides**, or wrinkles). (**Augmentation** is the process of enlarging or increasing.) Tendon tissue is harvested for the purpose of repairing another tendon (e.g., reconstruct anterior cruciate ligament).

EXAMPLE: Costochondral cartilage graft was harvested from the left rib of a 4-year-old child for laryngotracheal reconstruction to treat **subglottic stenosis** (narrowing of the airway below the vocal cords, adjacent to the cricoid cartilage). Report codes 31551 and 20910-51.

For bone grafts obtained for spine surgery, just one bone graft code is reported for each operative session (in addition to codes for the definitive procedure, such as spinal fusion) even if graft material is obtained from more than one spinal level (e.g., C1 and C2). ◻

EXAMPLE: A patient diagnosed with spinal stenosis undergoes laminectomy with cervical spine fusion, which requires harvesting a large structural bone graft from the iliac crest (through a separate incision). Report codes 22800, 20902-51, and 20931 in addition to the spinal fusion procedure code. (Do not add modifier -51 to code 20931 because it is an add-on code.)

 Note:

> When a bone marrow biopsy is performed using a needle or trocar, report code 38221 (Bone marrow; biopsy, needle or trocar), which describes the procedure for obtaining the bone marrow tissue for biopsy.

Other Procedures

Other Procedures codes classify monitoring of interstitial fluid pressure in detection of muscle compartment syndrome, bone graft with microvascular anastomosis, free osteocutaneous flap with microvascular anastomosis, electrical simulation to aid bone healing, low-intensity ultrasound stimulation to aid bone healing, bone tumor ablation, computer-assisted surgical navigation, and an unlisted procedure. When reporting an unlisted procedure code, include documentation about the procedure performed with the submitted claim.

EXAMPLE 1: Patient underwent monitoring of interstitial fluid in detection of muscle compartment syndrome. Report code 20950.

EXAMPLE 2: The patient undergoes bone graft of the left fibula, with microvascular anastomosis. This means that the bone tissue is harvested along with its blood supply (but without overlying skin). (The grafted tissue will be used to reconstruct the patient's right tibial bone, which has a filling defect as the result of trauma; surgery will involve microsurgical anastomosis of blood vessels.) Report code 20955-LT for the "bone graft of left fibula, with microvascular anastomosis."

Exercise 12.2 – General

Instructions: Assign the CPT code(s) and appropriate modifier(s) to each statement.

1. The physician treated a soft tissue abscess that was due to osteomyelitis by making an incision and examining, debriding, and draining the subfascia; the physician also irrigated the affected area, examined underlying tissue and bone for signs of infection, and closed the site.

   _____

2. Patient underwent exploration of a penetrating wound of the chest, which involved surgical exploration and enlargement of the wound, debridement, removal of a foreign body, and ligation of subcutaneous tissue.

   _____

3. Open bone biopsy, superficial, left femur.

   _____

4. Patient underwent aspiration of ganglion cyst, right wrist.

   _____

5. Patient received a cortisone injection to a single trigger point, which consisted of the trapezius, deltoid, and latissimus dorsi muscles.

   _____

6. A patient diagnosed with joint contracture of the right ankle underwent application of a multiplane external fixation device.

   _____

7. A patient severed his right index finger while using a chain saw. He underwent successful replantation of the index finger, which included metacarpophalangeal (MCP) joint to insertion of flexor sublimis tendon.

   _____

8. Fascia lata graft was harvested using a stripper.

   _____

9. Patient underwent structural allograft as part of an arthrodesis, posterior technique, craniocervical (occiput-C2).

   _____

10. Electrical stimulation procedure was performed to aid bone healing, invasive type.

    _____

Head

Head codes classify procedures performed on the skull, facial bones, and temporomandibular joint (TMJ).

Incision

The Incision subheading contains just one code for Arthrotomy, temporomandibular joint. When performed on both sides of the joint, add modifier -50 to the code.

> **EXAMPLE:** A patient underwent TMJ arthrotomy, left, to release scar tissue. Report code 21010-LT.

Excision

Report excision codes for surgery performed on bone and soft tissue of the face and/or scalp.

> **EXAMPLE:** Patient underwent TMJ condylectomy, left. Report code 21050-LT.

Manipulation

The Manipulation subheading contains a code for reporting TMJ manipulation, which requires anesthesia services.

> **EXAMPLE:** Patient underwent therapeutic TMJ manipulation for which general anesthesia was administered. Report code 21073. (Do not report modifier -50, -LT, or -RT with code 21073.)

Head Prosthesis

Head prosthesis codes describe professional services that involve designing and preparing a prosthesis for a patient. Prostheses are created for rehabilitation patients who have facial, oral, or other anatomical deficiencies that require an artificial ear, eye, or nose or an intraoral **obturator**, which is used to close a gap (e.g., cleft).

> **EXAMPLE:** A patient was fitted for a mandibular resection prosthesis, which was custom prepared by the physician. Report code 21081.

> **Coding Tip:**
>
> When an outside laboratory prepares the prosthetic device, do not report codes 21076–21089 for physician professional services. (The physician who fits a device made by an outside laboratory should report an appropriate evaluation and management code.)

Introduction or Removal

Introduction or removal codes are reported for other introduction or removal procedures, such as application of halo-type appliance for maxillofacial fixation (including removal), interdental fixation device (e.g., arch bar) for conditions other than fracture or dislocation (including removal), or injection procedure for TMJ arthrography.

> **EXAMPLE:** A physician applied a halo-type appliance for maxillofacial fixation, and he removed it 30 days later. Report 21100. (Do not report a separate code for removal of the halo-type appliance because that procedure is included in the global period for code 21100.)

Repair, Revision, and/or Reconstruction

Codes 21141–21160 that describe reconstruction of the face are called LeFort I, II, or III procedures. **LeFort I** brings the lower midface forward (from the level of the upper teeth) to just above the nostrils. **LeFort II**, or **pyramidal fracture**, is a surgical fracture of the midfacial skeleton at an apex near the superior aspect of the nasal bones. **LeFort III** brings the entire midface forward, from the upper teeth to just above the cheekbones.

> **EXAMPLE:** A patient underwent a LeFort I reconstruction procedure of the midface, which required reconstruction of two pieces without bone graft. Report code 21142.

Note:

- Colpocleisis, also known as a LeFort procedure, involves the surgical repair of a uterine prolapse or a vaginal vault prolapse.

- LeFort I, II, and III fractures are complex bilateral fractures of facial bones that contain large, unstable fragments.

- A Wagstaff-LeFort fracture is an avulsion of the fibula.

Other repair, revision, and/or reconstruction codes are reported for genioplasty, augmentation, and reduction procedures performed on the face, mandible, or forehead. Procedures include reconstruction, osteotomy, arthroplasty, repositioning, augmentation, revision, canthopexy, and reduction.

EXAMPLE: Patient underwent TMJ arthroplasty with allograft. Report code 21242.

Fracture and/or Dislocation

Fracture and/or dislocation codes are reported for treatment of fractures and/or dislocations of the skull, facial bones, and TMJ.

EXAMPLE: A physician performs an open reduction and internal fixation of a left mandibular fracture. Report code 21470-LT.

Code 21497 describes interdental wiring for a condition other than fracture, which is a stabilization procedure that involves the insertion of wire between teeth. Compare this code description to code 21110 (Application of interdental fixation device for conditions other than fracture or dislocation, includes removal); an interdental fixation device is less permanent than wire.

Exercise 12.3 – Head

Instructions: Assign CPT code(s) and appropriate modifier(s) to each statement.

1. Arthrotomy of temporomandibular joint, right and left sides.

   _____

2. Excision of two facial bones (due to bone abscesses).

   _____

3. Impression and custom preparation of speech aid prosthesis.

   _____

4. Sliding osteotomy genioplasty, single piece.

   _____

5. Reconstruction midface, Lefort II with anterior intrusion.

   _____

6. Osteotomy of mandible, segmental.

   _____

7. Malar augmentation with prosthetic material.

   _____

Exercise 12.3 *(continued)*

8. Closed treatment of orbit fracture, with manipulation.

_____

9. Closed treatment of maxillary alveolar ridge fracture.

_____

10. Open treatment of mandibular condylar fracture.

_____

Neck (Soft Tissues) and Thorax

The Neck (Soft Tissues) and Thorax heading includes codes for procedures performed on the soft tissues of the neck and thorax (e.g., incision and drainage, excisional biopsies, repairs, revisions, and reconstruction).

Incision

Incision codes are reported for the incision and drainage of abscesses or hematomas, with code 21510 specifically reported for the deep incision with opening of bone cortex of the thorax.

> **EXAMPLE:** Patient underwent incision and drainage of deep abscess, soft tissues of thorax, with partial rib ostectomy. Report code 21502.

Excision

Excision codes are reported for excision of soft tissue of the neck or thorax (e.g., biopsy or excision of tumor), radical resection of a tumor, partial and total excision of ribs, costotransversectomy, ostectomy of sternum, sternal debridement, and radical resection of sternum.

> **EXAMPLE:** Patient underwent costotransversectomy for decompression of paravertebral mass. Report code 21610.

Repair, Revision, and/or Reconstruction

Repair, revision, and/or reconstruction are performed on the soft tissues of the neck (e.g., muscle) and thoracic soft tissues and bones. When procedures are performed to repair superficial wounds, refer to the Integumentary System subsection to assign an appropriate code.

> **EXAMPLE:** Patient underwent open reconstructive repair of pectus excavatum. Report code 21740.

Fracture and/or Dislocation

Fracture and/or dislocation codes are reported for procedures performed to treat rib and sternum fractures or dislocations.

> **EXAMPLE:** Patient underwent open treatment of sternum fracture with skeletal fixation. Report code 21825.

Back and Flank

The Back and Flank heading contains just one subheading.

Excision

Back and Flank excision codes are reported for biopsy, tumor excision, and radical resection of tumor procedures performed on the back and flank. When a drain is inserted and/or the incision is repaired with multiple layers of sutures, staples, or Steri-Strips, do not separately report codes for those procedures; they are bundled in Back and Flank heading codes.

> **EXAMPLE:** Patient underwent soft tissue biopsy of the back, deep. Report code 21925.

Exercise 12.4 – Neck (Soft Tissues) and Thorax and Back and Flank

Instructions: Assign the CPT code(s) and appropriate modifier(s) to each statement.

1. Deep incision with opening of bone cortex, thorax.

_____

2. Hyoid myotomy and suspension.

_____

3. Closed treatment of sternum fracture.

_____

4. Partial excision of rib.

_____

5. Sternal debridement.

_____

6. Needle biopsy, soft tissue, thorax.

_____

7. Excision of tumor, subcutaneous soft tissue of back, 2.5 cm.

_____

8. The physician removed a 4-cm malignant soft tissue tumor, including adjacent tissue, from the patient's flank. Radical resection was performed to remove the tumor and adjacent tissue. The 5-cm surgical wound was repaired with complex closure.

_____

9. Patient underwent biopsy of superficial soft tissues of the back.

_____

10. Biopsy, soft tissue of flank, deep.

_____

Spine (Vertebral Column)

Spine (Vertebral Column) codes classify procedures performed on the cervical, thoracic, and lumbar spine. Vertebral procedures are sometimes followed by arthrodesis, and they may also include bone grafts and instrumentation. When reporting codes for spinal procedures, make sure you differentiate spinal segments (e.g., T1) and interspaces (e.g., T1–T2 interspace).

- T1–T2 represents two spinal segments of the thoracic vertebrae, at levels 1 and 2.

- L1–L4 represents four spinal segments of the lumbar vertebrae, at levels 1, 2, 3, and 4.

- T1–T2 represents one interspace of the thoracic vertebrae, between levels T1 and T2.

- C1–C2 and C2–C3 represent two interspaces of the cervical vertebrae, between levels C1 and C2 as well as between C2 and C3.

Coding Tip:

- Procedures performed on the bones, connective tissue, and muscles of the spinal column are classified in the Musculoskeletal subsection of CPT.
- Procedures performed on the spinal cord and spinal nerves are classified in the Nervous System subsection of CPT.

The notes located just below the Spine (Vertebral Column) heading should be reviewed before assigning codes.

- Bone graft procedure codes (20930–20938) are reported separately, in addition to arthrodesis procedure codes.
- Instrumentation procedure codes (22840–22855) are reported separately, in addition to arthrodesis procedure codes.
- When an arthrodesis procedure is performed in addition to another procedure, report the arthrodesis procedure code in addition to codes for other procedures performed. Make sure you add modifier -51 to the arthrodesis procedure code(s).
- When two surgeons collaborate to perform a spinal procedure during the same operative session on the same patient and each performs a distinct part of the procedure, add modifier -62 to the procedure code reported by each surgeon. (Additional procedure codes reported by each surgeon are also reported with modifier -62 if the surgeons continue to work as primary surgeons.)

EXAMPLE 1: Patient underwent arthrodesis of T1–T3 using local autograft from the ribs. Dual rods were inserted with multiple hooks and sublaminar wires. Report codes 22610, 22614, 22614, 22842, and 20936.

Three thoracic segments were fused; therefore, report codes 22610, 22614, and 22614. (Code 22614 is an add-on code; therefore, do not add modifier -51.) Report code 22842 for insertion of dual rods with multiple hooks and sublaminar wires; it is also exempt from the addition of modifier -51. Code 20936 describes the local autograft from the ribs.

EXAMPLE 2: Surgeon A performed a posterior exposure procedure on Mary Jones by making an incision overlying the lumbar vertebrae, separating the fascia and supraspinous ligaments in line with the incision. He then lifted ligaments and muscles out of the way. Next, Surgeon B performed a posterior discectomy and fusion at L2, and he performed a partial excision of the vertebral body at L3.

- Surgeon A reports code 22612-62.
- Surgeon B reports codes 22612-62 and 22114.

Although Surgeon A performed just the posterior exposure part of the procedure, because it is significant to the entire procedure, Surgeon A reports code 22612 with modifier -62.

Incision

Incision codes are reported for the open incision and drainage of deep abscesses (subfascial) of the following sites:

- Cervical
- Thoracic
- Cervicothoracic

- Lumbar
- Sacral
- Lumbosacral

EXAMPLE: A patient underwent open incision and drainage of a deep subfascial abscess, sacral region. Report code 22015.

Excision

The Excision subheading contains a note stating that when two surgeons work together to perform a spinal procedure during the same operative session on the same patient, when each performs a distinct part of the procedure, modifier -62 is added to the procedure code reported by each surgeon. (Additional procedure codes are also reported with modifier -62 if the surgeons continue to work as primary surgeons.)

EXAMPLE: A patient underwent surgical repair of L1–L2 and L3–L4. Dr. Berry performed a posterior exposure of the spine with mobilization of great vessels. Dr. Thomas performed posterior discectomy and spinal fusion at L2–L3 and L4, using anterior interbody technique.

Dr. Berry reports codes 22612-62 and 22614-62. Dr. Thomas reports 22612-62 and 22614-62. (Do not add modifier -51 to code 22614.)

Osteotomy

An **osteotomy** is an incision into bone. Spinal osteotomy involves making incisions in vertebral bone to remove pieces or wedges of bone to correct a deformity such as kyphosis, lordosis, or scoliosis (Figure 12-7). Because the osteotomy codes include corpectomy, discectomy, and laminectomy, separate codes are not reported for these procedures when they are documented in the operative report. Osteotomy codes differentiate anterior and posterior approach.

When an osteotomy is performed during the same operative session as a(n)

- Arthrodesis, report the appropriate code(s) from 22590–22634.

- Spinal instrumentation procedure, report the appropriate code(s) from 22840–22848 and 22853–22859; do not add modifier -51 to instrumentation procedure codes. (Do not add modifier -62 to 22840–22848 and 22853–22859.) (When two surgeons perform a procedure that also includes spinal instrumentation, just one of the surgeons performs the spinal instrumentation procedure. Therefore, do not add modifier -62 to the spinal instrumentation code.)

- Bone graft procedure, report an appropriate code from 20930–20938 (and do not add modifier -51 or -62 to the bone graft code). (When two surgeons perform a procedure that also includes bone grafting, just one of the surgeons performs the bone graft procedure. Therefore, do not add modifier -62 to the bone graft code.)

The Osteotomy subheading also includes a note indicating that when two surgeons work together to perform an anterior spine osteotomy procedure during the same operative session on the same patient and each performs a distinct part of the procedure, modifier -62 is added to the appropriate procedure codes (reported by each surgeon).

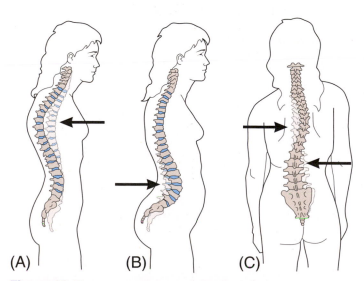

(A)   (B)   (C)

Figure 12-7 Spinal deformities (A) Kyphosis (B) Lordosis (C) Scoliosis

EXAMPLE 1: Patient underwent spinal osteotomy of spine, posterolateral approach, C1. Report code 22210.

EXAMPLE 2: Patient underwent anterior osteotomy of the spine with discectomy, T1. Report code 22222. (Do not report a separate code for the discectomy procedure.)

EXAMPLE 3: Patient underwent anterior spinal osteotomy, L1–L2. Dr. James performed anterior exposure of the spine with mobilization of great vessels. Dr. Smith performed anterior spinal osteotomy of L1–L2 with discectomy. Then Dr. James performed closure procedures. Dr. James reports 22224-62 and 22226-62. Dr. Smith also reports 22224-62 and 22226-62. (Do not add modifier -51 to code 22226 because it is an add-on code.)

Fracture and/or Dislocation

When treatment of fractures and/or dislocations is performed during the same operative session as a(n)

- Bone graft procedure, report an appropriate code from 20930–20938 (and do not add modifier -51 or -62 to the bone graft code).

- Arthrodesis, report the appropriate code(s) from 22590–22634.

- Spinal instrumentation procedure, report the appropriate code(s) from 22840–22855. (Do not add modifier -62 to 22840–22848.)

The Fracture and/or Dislocation subheading also includes a note indicating that when two surgeons work together to treat distinct parts of *open fracture and/or dislocation* procedures during the same operative session and each performs a distinct part of the procedure, modifier -62 is added to procedure codes 22318–22328. Both surgeons must work together as primary surgeons.

EXAMPLE: Patient underwent open treatment and reduction of T3–T4 vertebral fracture with grafting. Dr. Lawson performed posterior exposure of the spine with mobilization of great vessels. Dr. Timber performed open treatment and reduction of T3–T4 vertebral fracture with spinal allograft. Then Dr. Lawson performed closure procedures. Dr. Lawson reports 22327-62 and 22328-62. Dr. Timber also reports 22327-62, 22328-62, and 20931. (Do not add modifier -51 to code 22328.)

Manipulation

"Manipulation of spine" under anesthesia is performed to treat back pain and other disorders. The idea is that the patient is more relaxed while under anesthesia, and better spinal manipulation results. Report code 22505 once for manipulation of any region of the spine, including multiple regions during the same operative session. (For "manipulation of the spine *without* anesthesia," report code 97140 from the Medicine section.)

EXAMPLE: Patient underwent lumbar spinal manipulation under anesthesia. Report code 22505.

Percutaneous Vertebroplasty and Vertebral Augmentation

Percutaneous vertebroplasty is the process of injecting a material (e.g., cement) into the vertebral body to reinforce that structure using image guidance. **Vertebral augmentation** is the process of creating a cavity followed by injecting material (e.g., cement) under image guidance. Both procedures are typically performed to relieve pain due to (1) vertebral compression fractures (e.g., pathologic fractures due to osteoporosis) and (2) benign and malignant infiltrating vertebral lesions (e.g., aneurysmal bone cysts, giant cell tumor, hemangioma, metastatic cancer, or myeloma). Codes for percutaneous vertebroplasty and vertebral augmentation are inclusive of bone biopsy, when performed, moderate sedation, and imaging guidance necessary to perform the procedure.

Percutaneous vertebroplasty is usually performed with the patient under conscious sedation; a bone cement (that hardens in about 10 minutes) is injected under pressure directly into a fractured vertebra. The cement causes fragments of fractured vertebra to congeal, providing stability. Bone cement is also injected to fill minor spaces in cancellous bone.

EXAMPLE: Patient underwent percutaneous vertebroplasty under imaging guidance, L1 and L2, to stabilize pathologic fractures due to osteoporosis. Report codes 22510 and 22512. (Do not add modifier -51 to code 22512 because it is an add-on code.)

Percutaneous Augmentation and Annuloplasty

Percutaneous augmentation and annuloplasty is a minimally invasive technique that is performed under fluoroscopic guidance to treat small tears in the annulus without an associated disc protrusion.

> **EXAMPLE:** Patient underwent percutaneous intradiscal electrothermal annuloplasty, L5, under fluoroscopic guidance. Report code 22526.

Arthrodesis

Arthrodesis, or **artificial ankylosis**, is the surgical fixation (e.g., fusion) of a joint. Arthrodesis may be performed independently of other procedures; when arthrodesis is performed with another procedure, report the arthrodesis code in addition to the definitive procedure and add modifier -51 to the arthrodesis code if applicable. (Some arthrodesis codes are exempt from modifier -51.)

Arthrodesis performed for reasons other than to correct a spinal deformity is classified according to anatomical approach (22548–22634), such as anterior or anterolateral approach, posterior or posterolateral approach, or anterior or posterior interbody technique. Arthrodesis for spinal deformities (e.g., scoliosis and kyphosis) is reported with codes 22800–22812.

- Spinal instrumentation procedures are reported in addition to the arthrodesis code(s), and modifier -51 is added to the instrumentation code(s).

- Bone graft procedures are reported in addition to the arthrodesis code(s).

> **EXAMPLE:** A physician performed posterior arthrodesis of L5–S1 using autogenous iliac bone graft harvested through a separate incision. Report codes 22612 and 20937. (Do not add modifier -51 to code 20937.)

Exploration

Just one code is reported for exploration of spinal fusion.

- When spinal instrumentation is performed during the same operative session as the exploration of spinal fusion, report the appropriate instrumentation code from 22840–22855.

- When exploration of spinal fusion is performed in addition to other definitive procedures (e.g., arthrodesis), add modifier -51 to the "exploration of spinal fusion" code.

Spinal Instrumentation

Report codes 22840–22855 when spinal instrumentation is performed during a surgical procedure. Make sure you add modifier -51 to codes 22849–22850 and 22852–22855 only when spinal instrumentation is performed during the same operative session as other definitive procedure(s).

> **EXAMPLE:** Patient underwent posterior technique arthrodesis of C1–C2. Autogenous iliac bone graft was used, and it was harvested through a separate incision. Anterior instrumentation of the two vertebral segments was also performed. Report codes 22595, 22845, and 20937. (Do not add modifier -51 to code 20937.)

Exercise 12.5 – Spine (Vertebral Column)

Instructions: Assign the CPT code(s) and appropriate modifier(s) to each statement.

1. Patient underwent arthrodesis at L4–L5 interspace. Posterior interbody technique laminectomy was performed. Discectomy was also performed to prepare the vertebral interspace for fusion.

   _____

2. Physician performed "spinal manipulation under anesthesia," cervical, thoracic, and lumbar spine.

   _____

Exercise 12.5 (continued)

3. Patient underwent osteotomy and discectomy of a single cervical spine vertebral segment. Anterior approach was used.

_____

4. Physician performed arthrodesis using posterior technique of atlas-axis (C1–C2) with internal spinal fixation by wiring the spinous processes.

_____

5. Patient underwent posterior arthrodesis of L2–L3 for spinal deformity, with casting. Morselized autogenous iliac bone graft was harvested through a separate skin incision.

_____

Abdomen

The Abdomen subheading contains just two headings.

- Excision
- Other Procedures

The excision procedure code is reported for excision of abdominal wall tumor. The "other procedures" code is reported for unlisted procedures.

> **EXAMPLE:** Patient underwent excision of subfascial abdominal wall tumor. Report code 22900.

Shoulder

The Shoulder heading contains codes for procedures performed on the clavicle, scapula, humerus head and neck, sternoclavicular joint, acromioclavicular joint, and shoulder joint.

> **EXAMPLE:** Physician performed removal of a "total shoulder" implant with replacement of a new implant. Report codes 23335 for removal of the implant and 23472-51 for arthroplasty and insertion of a new total shoulder implant.

 Note:

> To report magnetic resonance imaging (MRI) of the shoulder with intra-articular contrast, report code 23350 (Injection procedure for shoulder arthrography or enhanced CT/MRI shoulder arthrography) in addition to the MRI code (from the Radiology section).

Humerus (Upper Arm) and Elbow

The Humerus (Upper Arm) and Elbow heading includes codes for procedures performed on the humerus, elbow, and head and neck of the radius and olecranon process.

> **EXAMPLE:** Patient underwent closed treatment with manipulation, medial humeral epicondylar fracture. Report code 24565.

Forearm and Wrist

The Forearm and Wrist heading includes codes for procedures performed on the radius, ulna, carpal bones, and joints.

EXAMPLE: A patient was diagnosed with subluxation of extensor carpi ulnaris (ECU) tendon at the wrist. The physician reconstructed the ECU tendon sheath with a retinacular graft harvest from the fourth dorsal compartment. Report code 25275, which includes the procedure for obtaining the graft.

 Coding Tip:

- Open carpal tunnel decompression surgery (for carpal tunnel syndrome) is classified in the Nervous System subsection of surgery.

- Surgical endoscopy to release the transverse carpal ligament to treat carpal tunnel syndrome surgery is assigned code 29848, which is located under the Endoscopy/Arthroscopy heading of the Musculoskeletal System subsection.

Hand and Fingers

The Hand and Fingers heading includes codes for procedures performed on the hands and fingers, which include repairs to tendons, nerves, and blood vessels to provide treatment for injuries or to correct deformities. Tendons include two types.

- **Flexor tendons**: Bend the fingers

- **Extensor tendons**: Straighten the fingers

The following procedures are bundled in the tendon repair codes:

- Application of immobilization

- Extension of the excision

- Repair and closure of tendon sheath

Codes for harvesting and inserting tendon grafts from another site, repairing nerves or arteries, and treating fractures are reported in addition to the tendon repair.

Exercise 12.6 – Abdomen, Shoulder, Humerus (Upper Arm) and Elbow, Forearm and Wrist, and Hand and Fingers

Instructions: Assign the CPT code(s) and appropriate modifier(s) to each statement.

1. The physician performed an excision of a 4-cm subfascial abdominal wall tumor and the surrounding tissue. Incision was repaired in multiple layers with sutures.

   _____

2. The physician removed subdeltoid calcareous deposits, left shoulder joint, by incising the raised area over the calcium deposits and removing the calcareous deposits.

   _____

3. The physician performed a forequarter interthoracoscapular amputation, right shoulder.

   _____

Exercise 12.6 (continued)

4. The physician performed removal of a deep foreign body, left shoulder.

   _____

5. Excision of 2-cm malignant tumor from subcutaneous tissue around right elbow.

   _____

6. Percutaneous medial tenotomy for treatment of tennis elbow, right.

   _____

7. Patient who sustained left elbow trauma developed an elbow contracture that required manipulation under anesthesia.

   _____

8. Percutaneous skeletal fixation of left Colles fracture.

   _____

9. Injection procedure performed to prep patient for right wrist arthrography.

   _____

10. Left palmar fasciectomy with Z-plasty.

   _____

Pelvis and Hip Joint

The Pelvis and Hip Joint heading includes codes for procedures performed on the head and neck of the femur (hip joint). (Codes for procedures performed on the femur and its tibial plateau are located under the Femur [Thigh Region] and Knee Joint heading.)

EXAMPLE: Patient underwent partial hemiarthroplasty of the left hip with insertion of femoral stem prosthesis. Report code 27125-LT. (Insertion of the femoral stem prosthesis is included in code 27125.)

Femur (Thigh Region) and Knee Joint ✎

The Femur (Thigh Region) and Knee Joint heading includes codes for procedures performed on the femur and its tibial plateau and the knee joint. (Codes for procedures performed on the head and neck of the femur are located under the Pelvis and Hip Joint heading.)

The **femur** (Figure 12-8) is the long bone of the thigh, and it articulates with the hip bone, tibia, and patella. The **tibial plateau** is the lower portion of the femur that articulates with the **tibia** (larger of the two lower leg bones). The **knee** is a "hinge" joint comprised of bones, cartilage, ligaments, and tendons. **Ligaments** (e.g., medial collateral ligament) are connective tissue that connects bone to bone (e.g., patella to femur), and they control stability of the knee. Trauma to knee joints can result in ligament tears, which require surgical repair (Figure 12-9).

✎ **Note:**

Arthroscopic knee surgery is a commonly performed procedure, and codes are located under the Endoscopy/Arthroscopy heading of the Musculoskeletal System subsection.

EXAMPLE: Patient was diagnosed with an anterior medial left thigh mass, which was 2 × 2 × 1.5 cm in size. With the patient under local anesthesia, biopsy of the mass above the superficial fascia was performed. Report code 27323-LT (because the mass was removed from "above the superficial fascia").

Figure 12-8 Structure of femur (long bone), including proximal (near) and distal (far) references to the bone's shaft

Figure 12-9 (A) Meniscus and anterior cruciate ligament tears (B) Knee joint

Figure 12-10 Bunion

Leg (Tibia and Fibula) and Ankle Joint

The Leg (Tibia and Fibula) and Ankle Joint heading includes codes for procedures performed on the tibia, fibula, and ankle joint.

> **EXAMPLE:** Patient underwent flexor tenolysis of the right ankle, single tendon. Report code 27680-RT. (When the procedure is performed on multiple tendons that are accessed through separate incisions, report code 27681. When multiple tendons are accessed through the same incision, report code 27680 for each tendon.)

Foot and Toes

The Foot and Toes heading includes codes for procedures performed on the feet and toes. Hallux valgus repair codes (28292–28299) are reported to correct **bunions** (Figure 12-10), which are caused by bone inflammation and swelling and result in medial deviation and axial rotation of the first metatarsophalangeal (MTP) joint. Bunion deformities develop differently, and repair requires different levels of complexity and different techniques, as follows:

- Keller procedure: Simple resection of the base of the proximal phalanx with removal of the medial eminence

- McBride procedure: Distal soft tissue release that corrects soft tissue deformity at the MTP joint

- Mitchell procedure: Complex, double cut osteotomy through the neck of the first metatarsal

> **EXAMPLE:** Patient underwent bilateral hallux valgus correction with sesamoidectomy and resection of proximal phalanx base. Report code 28292-50.

Exercise 12.7 – Pelvis and Hip Joint, Femur (Thigh Region) and Knee Joint, Leg (Tibia and Fibula) and Ankle Joint, and Foot and Toes

Instructions: Assign the CPT code(s) and appropriate modifier(s) to each statement.

1. Proximal hamstring release.

_____

2. Partial hip replacement with bipolar arthroplasty to treat right hip fracture.

_____

(continues)

Exercise 12.7 (*continued*)

3. Removal of a foreign body deep in the left thigh.

_____

4. Complete 1 × 1 × 0.5-cm excision of subcutaneous tumor, posterior left thigh.

_____

5. Excision of 2-cm bone cyst with autograft of harvested femur graft, left, which was performed during the same operative session.

_____

6. Decompression fasciotomy of the lateral and posterior compartments, right knee.

_____

7. Percutaneous repair of ruptured Achilles tendon, right.

_____

8. Incision and drainage of infected bursa, left ankle.

_____

9. Distal Chevron osteotomy, right.

_____

10. Partial ostectomy to surgically correct bunionette involving the right fifth metatarsal head.

_____

Application of Casts and Strapping

The Application of Casts and Strapping heading includes codes that are reported when the cast (or splint) application or strapping is a(n)

- Replacement procedure performed during or after the period of follow-up care

- Initial service performed *without restorative treatment or procedure* to stabilize or protect a fracture, a dislocation, or another injury and/or to provide comfort to a patient

   EXAMPLE 1: A 5-year-old patient was seen in the office to have his left short-arm cast replaced. He was playing a game he invented called "bop it," which involved knocking his cast on top of one of his bedposts. The cast cracked and had to be replaced. The patient was instructed to stop playing "bop it." Report code 29075-LT.

   EXAMPLE 2: A 7-year-old patient injured his left arm while roller-skating. A two-view left forearm x-ray performed at Sylvania Community Hospital's emergency department revealed fractures of the radial and ulnar shafts. A level III emergency department evaluation and management service was provided. The patient's arm was placed in a splint to stabilize the fracture, and the mother was informed that treatment would have to be performed the next day because no orthopedic physician was available in the facility or on call. Report codes 99283, 29125-LT, and 73090-LT. (Do not add modifier -57 to the E/M code or modifier -51 to the surgery and radiology codes.)

   Upon being informed that treatment would not be performed that day, the mother called the facility from which the family normally receives treatment and asked to speak with the orthopedic surgeon on call. That physician called her back within 15 minutes; when the mother explained the circumstances, she was told to bring the x-rays and her child to St. Francis Hospital to meet the surgeon there so he could assess her son and perform treatment. Upon outpatient evaluation and management (level III) of this new patient by the orthopedic surgeon, the mother was informed that same-day treatment was preferred because waiting until the next day would result in swelling, inflammation, and pain, making it more difficult to treat the fractures. Later that day the patient underwent closed manipulation of radial and ulnar shaft fractures under general anesthesia, and a short-arm cast was applied. The patient remained in the hospital until 10 PM, at which time he was released to return home with his parents. Report codes 25565 and 99203-57.

When one physician applies a cast, splint, or strapping device as initial treatment of a fracture or dislocation and a different physician later performs a restorative treatment or procedure, report "treatment of fracture and/or dislocation" code(s) from the appropriate heading in the Musculoskeletal System subsection.

When a physician performs an initial restorative treatment or procedure and an initial cast, splint, or strap is also applied, the physician is responsible for providing all subsequent fracture, dislocation, and/or injury care. Do not report a code for the application of a cast, splint, or strapping device with the initial restorative treatment or procedure; the first cast, splint, or strapping device application is included in the "treatment of fracture and/or dislocation" code.

 Coding Tip:

Do not report modifier -58 (staged or related procedure or service by the same physician during the postoperative period) when a temporary cast, splint, or strapping device is applied and the patient later undergoes a restorative treatment or procedure. In addition, do not report evaluation and management service codes unless significant identifiable further services are provided at the time of the cast application or strapping. (Report only the "treatment of fracture and/or dislocation" code.)

Endoscopy/Arthroscopy

The Endoscopy/Arthroscopy heading includes codes for procedures performed using an endoscope or arthroscope. Endoscopy is the visual examination of the interior of a body cavity or an organ. **Arthroscopy** (Figure 12-11) is the visual examination of the inside of a joint.

Endoscopic and arthroscopic procedures are diagnostic or surgical, and CPT notes indicate that surgical endoscopy/arthroscopy always includes diagnostic endoscopy/arthroscopy. An endoscopy/arthroscopy is considered diagnostic when it is performed to visualize an abnormality or to determine the extent of disease. When anything in addition to visualization is performed, the endoscopy/arthroscopy procedure is considered surgical.

 Coding Tip:

- A surgical endoscopy/arthroscopy always includes a diagnostic endoscopy/arthroscopy. This means that a code for diagnostic endoscopy/arthroscopy is not reported with a code for surgical endoscopy/arthroscopy. A diagnostic endoscopy/arthroscopy code is reported when it is the only endoscopic/arthroscopic procedure performed. (Codes for other procedure codes, other than surgical endoscopy/arthroscopy, can be reported with diagnostic endoscopy/arthroscopy codes.)

- Diagnostic knee arthroscopy is probably the most common type of procedure performed. It is done to examine and diagnose knee joint abnormalities. Diagnostic knee arthroscopy involves inserting an arthroscope through small incisions and using a camera to transmit images onto a monitor so the knee joint's interior can be visualized. During arthroscopic knee surgery, the knee is subdivided into three compartments: medial, lateral, and patellofemoral.

- Surgical knee arthroscopy is often performed to treat diseased or damaged structures of the knee joint (e.g., torn meniscus, meniscal lesions, damaged patella or ligaments, and inflamed or damaged synovium).

(A) Arthroscope in use

(B) Internal view of the knee during arthroscopy

Figure 12-11   Arthroscopic surgery (A) The physician views progress on a monitor
(B) Internal view as diseased tissue is removed during surgery

Exercise 12.8 – Application of Casts and Strapping and Endoscopy/Arthroscopy

Instructions: Assign the CPT code(s) and appropriate modifier(s) to each statement. (Do not assign CPT E/M codes.)

1. Diagnostic arthroscopy, left elbow, with synovial biopsy.

_____

2. Patient's left long-arm cast was removed after getting wet, the site was evaluated, and another long-arm fiberglass cast was reapplied. The same physician who applied the first cast removed the wet cast and applied the new cast.

_____

3. Physician treated flexion contracture of right small finger proximal interphalangeal joint by applying a cast to stabilize the joint.

_____

4. Patient with diabetic neuropathic ulcers had rigid total contact leg cast applied, left.

_____

5. Patient sustained nondisplaced fracture of distal left ulna, and emergency department physician applied a molded splint for immobilization and protection of the fracture. Patient was referred to orthopedic specialist.

_____

6. Patient underwent arthroscopic repair of large osteochondritis dissecans lesion and talar dome fracture with internal fixation, right.

_____

Exercise 12.8 (continued)

7. Surgical arthroscopy of the metacarpophalangeal joint on the right with debridement.

   _____

8. Patient underwent Mumford procedure of distal 1 cm of left clavicle.

   _____

9. Arthroscopic superior labrum anterior/posterior (SLAP) lesion tear repair, right shoulder.

   _____

10. Left knee diagnostic and surgical arthroscopy with partial medial meniscectomy.

   _____

Respiratory System Subsection

The CPT Respiratory System (Figure 12-12) subsection is arranged according to body area from nose to lungs. It includes the following headings:

- Nose
- Accessory Sinuses
- Larynx
- Trachea and Bronchi
- Lungs and Pleura

Figure 12-12 Respiratory system

Respiratory system headings include one or more of the following subheadings:

- Incision
- Excision
- Introduction (and Removal)
- Removal of Foreign Body
- Repair
- Destruction
- Endoscopy
- Other Procedures

The Respiratory System subsection's Lungs and Pleura heading also contains the following subheadings:

- Lung Transplantation
- Surgical Collapse Therapy; Thoracoplasty

Respiratory section guidelines define procedures and provide instruction for the selection of appropriate codes, as follows:

- Approach used for lung procedures
- Amount and type of tissue removed
- Difference between diagnostic and therapeutic procedures
- Ways various removal procedures may be performed

Nose

The Nose heading contains codes for procedures that are performed on the nose, nasal septum, intranasal tissue, nasal turbinates, and skin of the nose. (Refer to Figure 12-13 for structure of the upper respiratory system, including nasal anatomy.) Codes for procedures range from simple control of a nosebleed (30901) to complex surgery (e.g., rhinoplasty, coded as 30400).

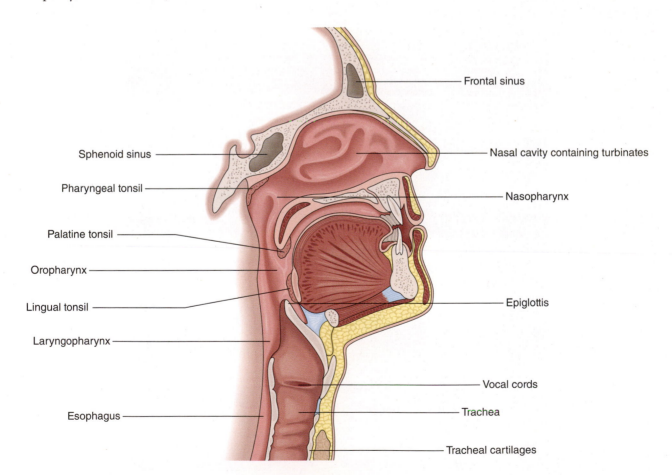

Figure 12-13 Structure of the upper respiratory system

Coding Tip:

When the control of bleeding is performed during a procedure, it is considered an integral part of that procedure and is not separately coded and reported. This means that codes that classify "control of nasal hemorrhage" (30901–30906) are not reported with other procedure codes.

Incision

Incision codes are reported for drainage of abscess of hematoma, nasal (internal approach) or nasal septum. A *hematoma* is a localized collection of blood outside of the blood vessels, usually in liquid form within tissue.

> **EXAMPLE:** Patient underwent drainage of a nasal hematoma via internal approach. Report code 30000.

Excision

Turbinates, or **conchae**, are bony plates covered by spongy mucosa with curved margins. There are three turbinates on each side of the **nasal vestibule** (nose's entrance): inferior, middle, and superior. When surgery is performed on turbinates, it is important to identify the type of turbinate procedure and technique used. Turbinates can be removed by resection or excision with or without endoscopy, cauterization, debridement, laser, cryotherapy, radiofrequency reduction, or ablation. Turbinate excision and submucous resection codes (30130–30140) are typically reported for inferior turbinate surgery. These codes can also be reported separately with other surgical procedures performed on the nose (e.g., sphenoid, maxillary, or frontal sinus procedures; septoplasty). Codes 30130–30140 describe unilateral procedures, which means that if the surgery is performed on both sides, modifier -50 (bilateral procedure) is added to the reported code.

> **EXAMPLE:** Patient underwent anterior intranasal ethmoidectomy for chronic sinusitis. A partial inferior turbinate excision was performed to gain access to the ethmoid bone. Report code 31200. (Code 30130 is not reported for the partial inferior turbinate excision because it was performed only to gain access to the ethmoid bone.)

 Coding Tip:

When a turbinate procedure is performed to gain access to the ethmoid bone, do not report codes 30130–30140. However, if a separate diagnosis justifies medical necessity for excision of turbinate (30130) or submucous resection of turbinate (30140), report the appropriate code and add modifier -59. (NOTE: Even if medical necessity justifies reporting codes 30130–30140, some third-party payers will not reimburse the turbinate excision or submucous resection because the code descriptions do not specify middle or superior turbinates.)

> **EXAMPLE:** Patient underwent a total intranasal ethmoidectomy for chronic sinusitis and a complete excision of the inferior turbinate for sleep apnea. Report codes 31201 and 30130-59.

Introduction

Introduction codes are reported for therapeutic injection into nasal turbinate(s), displacement therapy, and insertion of a nasal septum prosthesis.

> **EXAMPLE:** Patient underwent Proetz type displacement therapy. Report code 30210.

Removal of Foreign Body

Removal of foreign body codes are reported for removal of a foreign body from the intranasal area (office type procedure) and that requiring general anesthesia or by lateral rhinotomy.

> **EXAMPLE:** Patient underwent removal of intranasal foreign body via lateral rhinotomy. Report code 30320.

Repair

When a physician performs surgical nasal/sinus endoscopy with partial ethmoidectomy (anterior) and septoplasty or submucous resection, report codes 31254 *and* 30520 because each is a separate and distinct service.

> **EXAMPLE:** Patient underwent bilateral surgical endoscopic nasal septoplasty with cartilage scoring. Report codes 30520-50 and 31254-50-51.

Destruction

Destruction codes are reported for ablation of soft tissue of inferior turbinates superfically or intramurally.

> **EXAMPLE:** Patient underwent submucosal soft tissue ablation of inferior turbinates, bilateral via electrocautery. Report code 30802.

Other Procedures

Other Procedures codes are reported for the control of nasal hemorrhage, therapeutic fracture of nasal inferior turbinate(s), and unlisted procedures of the nose.

> **EXAMPLE:** Patient underwent therapeutic fracture of the nasal inferior turbinates. Report code 30930.

Exercise 12.9 – Nose

Instructions: Assign the CPT code(s) and appropriate modifier(s) to each statement.

1. Physician made therapeutic injections into the right and left turbinates.

   _____

2. Excision of polyp from inside of nose, left side, via scalpel. Single-layer closure was also performed.

   _____

3. Removal of nasal mucosa from inside left side of nose for biopsy. Some normal tissue adjacent to diseased mucosa is also removed during biopsy.

   _____

4. Excision of intranasal lesion via lateral rhinotomy, left.

   _____

5. Rhinoplasty for nasal deformity secondary to congenital cleft lip and palate, including columellar lengthening of the tip and septum, with osteotomies.

   _____

Accessory Sinuses

The Accessory Sinuses heading contains codes for procedures performed on the maxillary, frontal, ethmoid, and sphenoid sinuses. The Accessory Sinuses heading contains unique coding guidelines for endoscopy procedures. (Refer to Figure 12-13 for location of accessory sinuses.)

Incision

Incision codes classify lavage, sinusotomy, and pterygomaxillary fossa surgery. A *lavage* is the washing out of a body cavity, such as the accessory sinuses, with water or a medicated solution. A *sinusotomy* is a surgical incision of the sinus (e.g., treatment of chronic sinus disease). The *pterygomaxillary fossa* is an opening in the skull, through which arteries and nerves pass.

EXAMPLE: Patient underwent right maxillary sinus lavage by cannulation. Report code 31000-RT.

Excision

Excision codes classify ethmoidectomy and maxillectomy procedures. An *ethmoidectomy* involves removing partitions between the ethmoid sinuses to create larger sinus cavities (e.g., treatment of sinus infections and sinus obstructions). A *maxillectomy* involves removing the upper jaw bone (maxilla) (e.g., treatment of cancer in bones and tissues of roof or hard palate of mouth).

EXAMPLE: Patient underwent total intranasal ethmoidectomy, left. Report code 31201-LT.

Endoscopy

Endoscopy codes classify unilateral procedures unless the code description indicates otherwise. This means that HCPCS level II modifier -LT or -RT is added to the endoscopy code unless the procedure is performed bilaterally and modifier -50 is added to the code.

 Note:

Modifier -50 is not added to code 31231 because "bilateral" is included in its description. However, modifier -LT or -RT can be added to code 31231 if the procedure is performed unilaterally.

Diagnostic endoscopy codes include inspection of the interior of the nasal cavity and its meatus, turbinates, and sphenoethmoid recess. When diagnostic endoscopy is performed, the following procedures are bundled in the reported code: administration of local anesthesia, electrocautery, access to different cavities, and some shaving/debridement. (Extensive shaving/debridement is reported with a separate code and modifier -51.) Report just one code when diagnostic endoscopy is performed on all of these areas on one or both sides. If diagnostic endoscopy of the interior of the nasal cavity is performed on the left and diagnostic endoscopy of the turbinates is performed on the right, report code 31231 just once.

Surgical sinus endoscopy is performed through the nose, using a fiberoptic endoscopy; it includes sinusotomy (when performed) and diagnostic endoscopy. When a physician performs surgical endoscopy of accessory sinuses, evaluation of nasal access regions (diagnostic endoscopy) is also performed as part of the medically necessary service. Do not report a code for diagnostic endoscopy in addition to the surgical endoscopic procedure. This means that when surgical and diagnostic endoscopies are performed during the same operative session, just one code from 31233–31297 is reported to classify both procedures.

EXAMPLE: Patient undergoes surgical endoscopy with anterior ethmoidectomy, left, and the physician uses the endoscope to evaluate other regions of the nasal cavity. Report code 31254-LT. (Do not report code 31231 for the diagnostic nasal endoscopy.)

 Note:

Recognize the difference between endoscopic and open surgical approaches. An endoscopic nasal surgical approach utilizes a fiberoptic endoscope instrument, which is inserted through the nostril(s). An open nasal surgical approach is performed by making an incision into skin or tissues inside the nasal cavity.

Anatomically, the middle turbinate is part of the ethmoid bone. Therefore, if the middle turbinate is removed during endoscopic polypectomy or endoscopic ethmoidectomy, a code for removal of the middle turbinate is *not* reported.

Code 30930, Fracture nasal turbinate(s), therapeutic, usually applies to inferior turbinate surgery. It is considered a distinct and separate procedure from that described in codes 31255 (Nasal/sinus endoscopy, surgical; with ethmoidectomy, total [anterior and posterior]) and 30520 (Septoplasty or submucous resection, with or without cartilage scoring, contouring or replacement with graft). Therefore, when one or more of the previously mentioned procedures is performed during the same operative session, report each code (and add the appropriate HCPCS level II or CPT modifiers). When the surgeon fractures the middle turbinates to facilitate a sinus procedure, that is considered part of the sinus procedure and a separate "fracture nasal turbinate(s)" code is *not* reported.

EXAMPLE: Patient underwent bilateral nasal/sinus surgical endoscopy with total ethmoidectomy and bilateral nasal septoplasty. Report codes 31255-50 and 30520-50-51.

When biopsy of a lesion from the accessory sinuses is obtained as part of an excision, destruction, or other type of removal during the same operative session, do not report a biopsy code in addition to the excision/destruction/removal code. Also, biopsy codes are not separately reported for multiple similar or identical lesions even if the lesions are taken from a different area of the respiratory system.

EXAMPLE: A patient presents with multiple nasal polyps. Patient undergoes surgical endoscopy with polypectomy and total ethmoidectomy. Report code 31255. (Do not report code 31237 for the surgical endoscopy with polypectomy because that procedure is bundled with code 31255.) Even though polypectomy may have been performed prior to total ethmoidectomy, the polypectomy procedure is included in the more invasive ethmoidectomy procedure.

 Coding Tip:

When a sinusotomy (31000–31090) is performed in conjunction with a sinus endoscopy, just one code is reported for both services. If the endoscopy was performed to evaluate the sinus cavity prior to sinusotomy, report just the sinusotomy procedure code. CPT instructions state that a surgical sinus endoscopy always includes sinusotomy and diagnostic endoscopy.

Exercise 12.10 – Accessory Sinuses

Instructions: Assign the CPT code(s) and appropriate modifier(s) to each statement.

1. Anterior ethmoidectomy via intranasal approach.

_____

2. Endoscopic treatment of a nosebleed.

_____

3. Endoscopic anterior and posterior (total) ethmoidectomy, left, with left maxillary antrostomy.

_____

4. Nasal endoscopy with biopsy.

_____

5. Endoscopic frontal nasal exploration with removal of tissue from left frontal sinus and diagnostic endoscopy of left turbinates.

_____

Figure 12-14 View of larynx and vocal cords from above. (A) Vocal cords are open during breathing. (B) Vocal cords vibrate together during speech.

Larynx

The Larynx (Figure 12-14) heading contains codes for procedures performed on the epiglottis and larynx and inside the trachea.

Excision

Excision codes classify laryngotomy, laryngectomy, pharyngolaryngectomy, arytenoidectomy or arytenoidopexy, and epiglottidectomy procedures. A *laryngotomy* involves making a surgical incision into the larynx to provide air passage when breathing is obstructed. A *laryngectomy* involves removal of the larynx (voicebox). A *pharyngolaryngectomy* is the removal of the hypopharynx (laryngeal part of throat) and larynx. An *epiglottidectomy* is the removal of all or part of the epiglottis (e.g., treatment of sleep apnea).

> **EXAMPLE:** Patient underwent total intranasal ethmoidectomy, left. Report code 31201-LT.

According to *CPT Assistant* (October 2001), when a total laryngectomy with bilateral radical neck dissection (31365) is performed, do not add modifier -50 to the code because the larynx is a single midline organ. (A laryngectomy cannot be performed bilaterally.) Instead, report code 31365 for the total laryngectomy and radical neck dissection on one side. Also, report code 38720-59 for the radical neck dissection on the other side. (The description of code 38720 is "Cervical lymphadenectomy [complete].") (Modifier -59 is added to indicate a distinct procedural service.)

An **arytenoidectomy** is the excision of arytenoid cartilage, which is located in the bilateral vocal fold. An **arytenoidopexy** is the surgical fixation of arytenoidal cartilage and/or surrounding muscles. Both procedures are done to treat vocal cord paralysis or to improve patient breathing.

> **EXAMPLE:** Patient underwent endoscopic arytenoidectomy. Report code 31560. (Do *not* report code 31400.)

Introduction

Introduction procedures are performed for emergency endotracheal intubation and to change a tracheotomy tube prior to healing (before an abnormal fistula tract is created by the body).

> **EXAMPLE:** Patient underwent an emergency endotracheal intubation. Report code 31500.

Endoscopy ⚠

Endoscopy codes include the following types of laryngoscopy, and the documented operative report will indicate the instrumentation used:

- Direct
- Indirect

- Use of operating microscope (for magnification)
- Use of fiberoptic scope (that transmits light)

Laryngoscopy is the visualization of the back of the throat, including the **larynx** (voice box) and vocal cords. **Direct laryngoscopy** is the insertion of a flexible or rigid fiberoptic scope or a rigid laryngoscope to visualize throat structures. **Indirect laryngoscopy** is the insertion of a small hand mirror in the patient's mouth at the back of the throat while the physician wears headgear that contains a mirror and light source; the mirror worn by the physician reflects light into the patient's mouth, allowing the physician to visualize the patient's throat.

EXAMPLE: Patient underwent indirect diagnostic laryngoscopy. Report code 31505.

When a laryngoscopy procedure is required for placement of an endotracheal tube to provide air passage in an emergency situation, *do not separately code and report the laryngoscopy*. Report code 31500 (Intubation, endotracheal, emergency procedure) only.

 Coding Tip:

Report code 31500 when emergency endotracheal intubation is performed during the provision of critical care services (99291–99292).

When a laryngoscopy procedure is used to place an endotracheal tube for nonemergent reasons (e.g., general anesthesia or bronchoscopy), *do not separately code and report the laryngoscopy*. (Code 31500, Intubation, endotracheal emergency procedure, is not reported when an elective intubation is performed.) When a laryngoscopy procedure is required for placement of a tracheostomy, report just the tracheostomy code. Do not report a code for the laryngoscopy. When tracheostomy is performed as an essential part of laryngeal surgery (e.g., laryngectomy, laryngoplasty, or laryngotomy), do not separately report code 31600, Tracheostomy, planned (separate procedure).

Repair

Repair codes classify laryngoplasty and laryngeal reinnervation procedures. A *laryngoplasty* involves reconstruction of the larynx (voicebox). A *laryngeal reinnervation* supplies a new, functioning nerve supply to a paralyzed larynx; the purpose is to restore phonation (vocalization).

EXAMPLE: Patient underwent cricoid split laryngoplasty. Report code 31587.

Destruction

Destruction codes classify therapeutic section of recurrent laryngeal nerves, which involves severing the laryngeal nerve, which controls action of the vocal cords.

EXAMPLE: Patient underwent destruction procedure for therapeutic section of recurrent laryngeal nerve, right. Report code 31595.

Exercise 12.11 – Larynx

Instructions: Assign the CPT code(s) and appropriate modifier(s) to each statement. (Do not assign CPT E/M codes.)

1. Emergency department physician places endotracheal tube for a patient in respiratory distress.

   _____

2. Total laryngectomy with radical neck dissection.

   _____

3. Patient with cricoid split (break in the circular cartilage of the larynx) undergoes laryngoplasty.

   _____

4. Complicated tracheotomy tube change (prior to establishment of fistula tract).

   _____

5. Total laryngectomy with bilateral radical neck dissection.

   _____

Figure 12-15 Trachea, bronchi, bronchial trees, and alveoli (air sacs)

Trachea and Bronchi

The Trachea and Bronchi (Figure 12-15) heading contains codes for procedures performed through the trachea and on tracheal cartilage (carinii) and the bronchi.

Incision

Incision codes classify tracheostomy, construction of tracheoesophageal fistula and subsequent insertion of an alaryngeal speech prosthesis, tracheal puncture, and tracheostoma revision procedures. A *tracheostomy* involves creating an opening through the neck into the trachea (windpipe); a tracheostomy tube is usually placed into the opening to provide an airway and/or to remove secretions from the lungs. A tracheoesophageal fistula is constructed with insertion of a one-way valve, which is an alaryngeal speech prosthesis, called a *voice button* or a *Blom-Singer prosthesis*, to allow the patient to phonate (vocalize). A *tracheal puncture* involves piercing the trachea with a hollow point needle to aspirate secretions or inject therapeutic agent(s). A *tracheostoma revision* involves incising the stoma area and resecting redundant scar tissue or a poorly healing wound.

> **EXAMPLE:** Patient underwent emergency transtracheal tracheostomy. Report code 31603.

Endoscopy

A **bronchoscopy** (Figure 12-16) is the visual examination of the interior of the bronchus. A tracheoscopy is the visual examination of the interior of the **trachea** (windpipe). A **tracheobronchoscopy** is the visual examination of the interior of the trachea and bronchus. Endoscopy of the trachea and bronchus is performed with either a flexible fiberoptic scope or a rigid scope, with or without cell washings or brushing. A **brushing** involves combing the mucous lining of the trachea or bronchus with a bronchial brush to collect cells. **Cell washing** involves flushing fluid into an area and removing the fluid, using aspiration technique to collect cells.

Codes 31622–31661 describe procedures that involve use of a bronchoscope, with or without fluoroscopic guidance, to visualize all major lobar and segmental bronchi. These procedures may also include obtaining diagnostic specimens as part of the examination. Fiberoptic bronchoscopy services routinely include inspection of the nasal cavity, pharynx, and larynx. When nasal endoscopy or laryngoscopy is performed, in addition to bronchoscopy, report a code for the bronchoscopy procedure only.

Figure 12-16 (A) Flexible bronchoscopy (B) Rigid bronchoscopy

Diagnostic endoscopy of the trachea and bronchi performed during the same operative session as a surgical endoscopy is included in the surgical endoscopy. Do not report a code for diagnostic endoscopy when it is performed with surgical endoscopy.

Diagnostic endoscopy is often performed during an open surgical procedure to evaluate (or scout or investigate) the surgical field. Do not report a code for diagnostic endoscopy when it is performed with an open surgical procedure.

When a surgical endoscopic procedure fails and is converted to an open procedure, do not report a code for the surgical endoscopic procedure. Report only a code for the open procedure.

EXAMPLE: A patient presents with aspiration of a foreign body. A diagnostic bronchoscopy is performed to locate the foreign body, and a surgical bronchoscopy is performed to remove the foreign body. Report code 31635. (Do not report a code for the diagnostic bronchoscopy.)

Bronchial Thermoplasty

Bronchial thermoplasty codes classify procedures that reduce the amount of smooth muscle in the airway walls in asthmatic patients. *Bronchial thermoplasty* involves introducing a catheter with an electrode array into an area of the lung that is to be treated, and radiofrequency energy is used to heat and reduce the amount of smooth muscle.

EXAMPLE: Patient underwent flexible bronchoscopy with bronchial thermoplasty, one lobe, right lung. Report code 31660-RT.

Introduction

Introduction codes classify catheterization, catheter aspiration with bronchial brush biopsy, and transtracheal introduction of needle wire dilator/stent or indwelling tube for oxygen therapy procedures.

EXAMPLE: Patient underwent nasotracheal catheter aspiration to remove sputum from the lungs. Report code 31720. (Do not report modifier -50 because it does not apply to this code.)

Excision, Repair

Excision, Repair codes classify tracheoplasty, carinal reconstruction, bronchoplasty, excision, suture, and revision procedures.

EXAMPLE: Patient underwent carinal reconstruction. Report code 31766.

Exercise 12.12 – Trachea and Bronchi

Instructions: Assign the CPT code(s) and appropriate modifier(s) to each statement.

1. Emergency transtracheal tracheostomy of 18-month-old child.

_____

2. Bronchial brush biopsy via transglottic catheterization.

_____

3. Flexible bronchoscopy to remove a piece of food inhaled into the left bronchus.

_____

4. Bronchoscopy with bronchial alveolar lavage.

_____

5. Bronchoscopy with brushings, biopsy, and removal of foreign body.

_____

Lungs and Pleura

The Lungs and Pleura (Figure 12-17) heading contains codes for procedures performed on the lungs and **pleura** (membrane that envelops the lungs and lines the walls of the pleural cavity).

Incision

Incision codes classify thoracostomy, pneumonostomy, pleural scarification, and decortication procedures. A _thoracostomy_ is the the construction of an artificial opening through the chest wall, usually for drainage of fluid or release of an abnormal accumulation of air. A _pneumonostomy_ is the surgical formation of an artificial opening into a lung (e.g., drainage of abscess). _Pleural scarification_ is the injection of a chemical solution into the chest cavity (through a chest tube) to create adhesions between the surface of the lung and inside surface of the chest cavity for the treatment of repeat pneumothorax. _Decortication_ is the removal of a a constricting membrane or layer of tissue from the surface of the lung to permit the lung to fully expand.

   EXAMPLE: Patient underwent pleural scarification for repeat pneumothorax. Report code 32215.

Excision/Resection

Excision/Resection codes classify pleurectomy, decortication and parietal pleurectomy, and biopsy procedures. _Pleurectomy_ is the removal of pleura. _Decortication_ is the removal of a constrictive fibrinous covering (to allow the lungs to expand). A _percutaneous pleural biopsy_ involves inserting a long needle through skin into the chest wall to obtain pleural tissue (without direct visualization of the pleura). For **percutaneous needle biopsy**, a long needle is inserted through the skin and into other tissue (e.g., chest wall, lung, or mediastinum) to obtain tissue for diagnostic evaluation. Code 32400 is reported for "biopsy, pleura; percutaneous needle." When fine-needle aspiration is documented, report an appropriate code from the General subsection.

   EXAMPLE: Patient underwent parietal pleurectomy. Report code 32310.

Removal

Removal codes classify lung removal, resection and repair of bronchus, resection of apical lung tumor, thoracotomy, and extrapleural enucleation of empyema (empyemectomy) procedures. **Pneumonectomy** is the removal of the

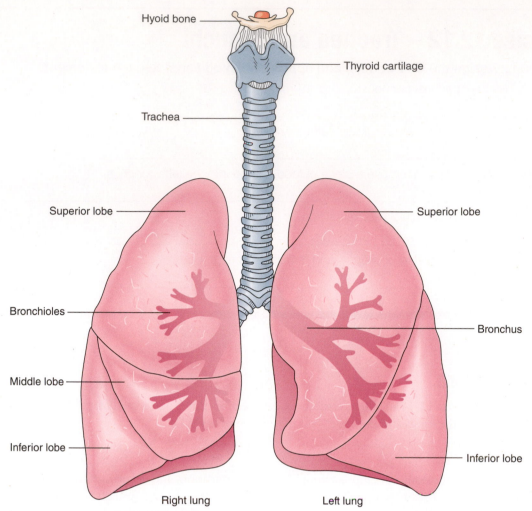

Figure 12-17 External view of lungs. Note three lobes in the right lung and two lobes in the left lung.

entire lung or one or more lobes of the lung. *Thoracotomy* is the surgical incision of the chest wall. *Empyemectomy* is the removal of an *empyema* (abscess in chest cavity between lung and chest wall) in its entirety, including pleural membranes surrounding the abscess.

EXAMPLE: Patient underwent extrapleural pneumonectomy. Report code 32445.

Introduction and Removal

Introduction and Removal codes classify insertion of indwelling tunneled pleural catheter, tube thoracostomy, placement of interstitial device(s) for radiation therapy guidance, thoracentesis, and pleural drainage procedures. **Thoracentesis** (Figure 12-18A) is the surgical puncture of the chest wall with a needle to obtain fluid from the pleural cavity. It is performed to make a diagnostic evaluation or to drain excess fluid from a patient with severe **pleural effusion** (Figure 12-18B) (fluid in the pleural cavity prevents the lung from fully expanding, making it difficult for the patient to breathe).

Pneumocentesis is the puncture of the pleural space with a transthoracic needle to drain *fluid* or to obtain material for diagnostic study.

EXAMPLE: Patient underwent resection of an apical lung tumor with chest wall reconstruction. Report code 32504.

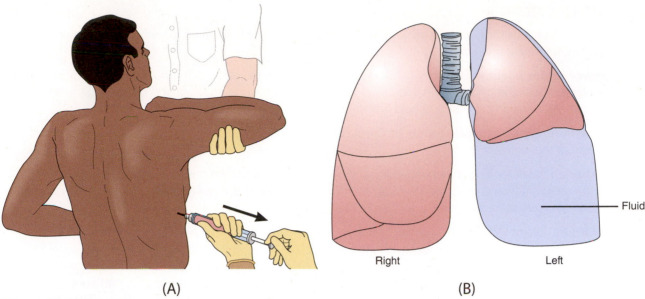

Figure 12-18 (A) Thoracentesis (B) Lung with pleural effusion

Destruction

Destruction codes classify instillation of pleurodesis or fibrinolytic agent procedures. *Pleurodesis agents* (e.g., talc) are instilled to treat recurrent or persistent pneumothorax. *Fibrinolytic agents* (e.g., saline mixture with streptokinase or urokinase) disintegrate or dissolve fibrinous adhesions.

> **EXAMPLE:** Patient underwent instillation of an agent for pleurodesis via chest tube. Report code 32560.

Thoracoscopy (Video-Assisted Thoracic Surgery [VATS])

A **thoracoscopy** is the visual examination of the pleural cavity, and it provides an alternative to open lung or thoracotomy procedures to treat pleural disorders surgically. Surgical thoracoscopy always includes diagnostic thoracoscopy, which means just the surgical thoracoscopy code is reported when both procedures are performed. However, when an open lung procedure, a thoracotomy, or another open chest procedure immediately follows diagnostic thoracoscopy during the same operative episode, report codes for both procedures (and sequence the open procedure first). When a surgical thoracoscopy is converted to an open procedure, report code(s) for the open lung procedure(s) only; do not report a code for the surgical thoracoscopy procedure.

> **EXAMPLE:** Patient presents with lower lateral chest wall pain and shortness of breath. Thoracoscopy with diagnostic biopsy of lobulated lung mass is performed. Biopsy reveals mesothelioma. Report code 32608.

Stereotactic Radiation Therapy

The Stereotactic Radiation Therapy code classifies thoracic target(s) delineation for the purpose of administering stereotactic body radiation therapy. The code is reported just once for an entire course of treatment. *Stereotactic radiation surgery (SRS)* involves identifying and delineating the target(s) for surgery. *Stereotactic body radiation therapy (SBRT)* uses high potent biological radiation to target a malignant tumor (and codes are reported from the Radiology section of CPT). SRS and SBRT procedures usually require the skill of both a surgeon and a radiation oncologist. SRS/SBRT uses a single or up to five fractionated doses of high potent biological radiation, and the high doses of radiation allow a tumor to be precisely localized using four dimensional imaging. Occasionally, separately reportable *fiducial* (fixed) markers are placed during SRS to ensure proper placement of radiation delivery.

> **EXAMPLE:** Patient underwent thoracic target delineation for stereotactic body radiation therapy. Report code 32701.

Lung Transplantation

Lung transplants include the following distinct components, and a code is assigned to each by the physician who performs the component procedure:

- **Cadaver donor pneumonectomy**, which involves harvesting the allograft (graft such as lung tissue that is transplanted between genetically nonidentical individuals of the same species) and preserving the allograft with cold preservation solution and cold maintenance

- **Recipient lung allotransplantation**, which includes transplantation of a single or double lung allograft and care of the recipient

- **Backbench work** for lung transplantation, which involves preparing the cadaver donor lung allograft prior to lung transplantation and dissecting allograft from surrounding soft tissues to prepare the pulmonary venous/atrial cuff, pulmonary artery, and bronchus

  EXAMPLE: Patient with severe respiratory system complications due to cystic fibrosis underwent lung transplant procedure to remove diseased lungs and replace them with healthy lungs from a recently deceased donor. Transplant physician performed donor pneumonectomy including cold preservation from cadaver donor, backbench standard preparation of cadaver donor lung allografts, and double lung transplant with cardiopulmonary bypass. Report codes 32854, 32850, and 32856-51. (The 32854 procedure is performed on the donor, not the recipient. The 32850 and 32856 procedures are performed on the recipient, and modifier -51 is added to code 32856 only.)

Surgical Collapse Therapy; Thoracoplasty

Surgical collapse therapy and thoracoplasty codes classify procedures performed to therapeutically collapse a patient's lung(s).

- *Extrapleural resection of ribs* is the removal of rib(s).

- *Thoracoplasty* is the resection of ribs to allow the chest wall to retract, reducing the size of the pleural space.

- *Pneumonolysis* is the division of tissues that attach the lung to the wall of the chest cavity.

- *Therapeutic pneumothorax* is the injection of air into the pleural space.

  EXAMPLE: A patient underwent extraperiosteal pneumonolysis. Report code 32940.

Other Procedures

Other Procedures codes classify total lung lavage, ablation therapy, and unlisted procedures. When a total lung lavage is performed bilaterally, add modifier -50 to code 32997 (because the code description specifies "unilateral"). When bronchoscopic bronchial alveolar lavage is performed, report code 31624 under the Trachea and Bronchi heading.

  EXAMPLE: Patient underwent total lung lavage, left. Report code 32997-LT.

Exercise 12.13 – Lungs and Pleura

Instructions: Assign the CPT code(s) and appropriate modifier(s) to each statement.

1. Emergency department physician performed a tube thoracostomy for hemothorax, inserting a tube for drainage.

   _____

2. Total lung lavage, right.

   _____

Exercise 12.13 (continued)

3. Percutaneous needle biopsy of lung (right side) and fine-needle aspiration of lung (right side).

_____

4. Diagnostic thoracoscopy with lung biopsy (left side) and surgical thoracoscopy with segmental lobectomy (left side) (both procedures performed during same operative session).

_____

5. Patient with severe respiratory system complications due to chronic obstructive pulmonary disease underwent unilateral lung transplant (right side) procedure to remove one diseased lung, on the right, and replace it with a healthy lung from a recently deceased donor. Donor lung also required repair of intrathoracic blood vessel. Transplant physician performed donor pneumonectomy including cold preservation from cadaver donor, backbench standard preparation of cadaver donor lung allografts, and single lung transplant without cardiopulmonary bypass.

_____

Summary

CPT codes in the Musculoskeletal System subsection are reported for procedures on bones, cartilage, joints, ligaments, muscles, and tendons. The subsection is arranged from head to toe according to body area. The Musculoskeletal System subsection also classifies fracture management, casting and strapping, and endoscopy /arthroscopy. The CPT Respiratory System subsection is arranged from nose to lungs according to body area.

Internet Links

American Academy of Otolaryngology—Head and Neck Surgery (AAO-HNS): Go to **www.entnet.org**, and click on the Patient Health link (located at the top of the website) for information about ENT diseases, disorders, and anatomical structures.

American Lung Association: **www.lungusa.org**

Musculoskeletal Radiology of Fractures: Go to **www.gentili.net**, and scroll down, then click on the Fracture Atlas link below General heading.

National Institute of Arthritis and Musculoskeletal and Skin Diseases (NIAMS): **www.niams.nih.gov**

YourLungHealth.org: **www.yourlunghealth.org**

Study Checklist

❑ Read this chapter and highlight key concepts.

❑ Create an index card for each key term.

❑ Access the chapter Internet links to learn more about concepts.

❑ Complete the chapter exercises and review, verifying answers with your instructor.

❑ Complete Workbook chapter, verifying answers with your instructor.

❑ Go to **www.cengagebrain.com** to access the Student Companion Web Site. Login instructions are located in the Preface.

❑ Form a study group with classmates to discuss chapter concepts in preparation for an exam.

Review

Multiple Choice

Instructions: Circle the most appropriate response.

1. Which is a type of open fracture treatment?
   - a. Closed reduction
   - b. Internal fixation
   - c. Stabilization
   - d. Traction

2. Which is performed to puncture a joint for fluid removal or medication injection?
   - a. Arthrocentesis
   - b. Arthrodesis
   - c. Arthroscopy
   - d. Artificial ankylosis

3. Which are included with osteotomy codes (22210–22226), which means that separate codes are not reported when these procedures are performed during the same operative session as the osteotomy?
   - a. Arthrocentesis, arthroscopy, artificial ankylosis
   - b. Corpectomy, discectomy, laminectomy
   - c. Grafting, reduction, stabilization
   - d. Skeletal fixation, stabilization, traction

4. Open carpal tunnel decompression surgery (for carpal tunnel syndrome) is classified in which CPT Surgery subsection and/or under which heading?
   - a. Integumentary System
   - b. Musculoskeletal System
   - c. Nervous System
   - d. Operating Microscope section

5. The application of casts and strapping are reported when the cast (or splint) or strapping is an initial service performed _____ to stabilize or protect a fracture, a dislocation, or another injury and/or to provide comfort to a patient.
   - a. during restorative treatment/procedure
   - b. instead of placing a cast (or splint) or strap
   - c. when a reduction or manipulation is completed
   - d. without restorative treatment/procedure

6. Calcaneus ostectomy for removal of spurs, left foot. Which CPT code is assigned?
   - a. 28111-LT
   - b. 28116-LT
   - c. 28118-LT
   - d. 28119-LT

7. Unlisted maxillofacial prosthetic procedure. Which CPT code is assigned?
   - a. 21089
   - b. 21299
   - c. 22899
   - d. 23929

8. C3–C4 anterior discectomy performed by two primary surgeons. Which CPT code(s) are reported by Surgeon A?
   - a. 22554, 22585-51
   - b. 22554-62, 22585-51
   - c. 22554-62
   - d. 22554-62, 22585-62

9. Reconstruction of complete shoulder (rotator) cuff avulsion, chronic, right side. Which CPT code(s) are assigned?
   - a. 23130-RT, 23420-RT
   - b. 23130-RT, 23420-51-RT
   - c. 23410-RT
   - d. 23420-RT

10. Incision and drainage of deep abscess, right forearm. Which CPT code is assigned?
    - a. 10060
    - b. 24310-RT
    - c. 25028-RT
    - d. 25031-RT

11. When a physician performs surgical nasal/sinus endoscopy with partial ethmoidectomy (anterior) and septoplasty or submucous resection, report the:
    a. septoplasty code (30520).
    b. endoscopy code (31254).
    c. endoscopy code (31254) and the septoplasty code (30520).
    d. endoscopy code (31254) or the septoplasty code (30520).

12. Which is considered part of the ethmoid bone and, if removed during endoscopic polypectomy or endoscopic ethmoidectomy, is not coded and reported separately?
    a. Frontal sinus
    b. Maxillary sinus
    c. Middle turbinate
    d. Nasal vestibule

13. Which is the surgical fixation of arytenoidal cartilage and/or surrounding muscles?
    a. Arytenoidectomy
    b. Arytenoidopexy
    c. Arytenoidostomy
    d. Arytenoidotomy

14. Which procedure is performed to comb the mucous lining of the trachea or bronchus and uses a bronchial brush to collect cells?
    a. Brushing
    b. Cell washing
    c. Tracheotomy
    d. Bronchoscopy

15. Which component(s) of a lung transplant are reported as distinct code(s) by the physician who performs the component procedure(s)?
    a. Cadaver donor pneumonectomy
    b. Backbench work for lung transplantation
    c. Recipient lung allotransplantation
    d. Each of the above

16. Initial cautery to control posterior nasal hemorrhage. Which CPT code is assigned?
    a. 30901
    b. 30903
    c. 30905
    d. 30906

17. Surgical nasal endoscopy with repair of cerebrospinal fluid leak, sphenoid region, right side. Which CPT code is assigned?
    a. 31287-RT
    b. 31290-RT
    c. 31291-RT
    d. 31292-RT

18. A 3-year-old child undergoes direct laryngoscopy for aspiration of fluid. Which CPT code is assigned?
    a. 31515
    b. 31520
    c. 31520-63
    d. 31525

19. Catheterization with bronchial brush biopsy. Which CPT code is assigned?
    a. 31623
    b. 31717
    c. 31720
    d. 31725

20. Surgical thoracoscopy with excision of a pericardial cyst. Which CPT code is assigned?
    a. 32604
    b. 32658
    c. 32659
    d. 32661

Coding Cases

Instructions: Assign the CPT code(s) and appropriate modifier(s) to each case.

1. Patient sustained a stab wound to the neck during a domestic dispute and underwent wound exploration. The stab wound was extended, and examination of surrounding bones, connective tissue,

muscles, and nerves revealed normal findings. No foreign bodies were found. The area was debrided and irrigated. Coagulation of minor subcutaneous and muscular blood vessels was achieved with electrocautery. The wound was cleaned and closed with 3-0 Vicryl.

2. Patient underwent reconstruction of the entire forehead and supraorbital rims, requiring grafts, to correct a congenital skeletal deformity. After administration of general anesthesia, scalp and upper eyelid incisions were made to access the surgical site. The forehead bones were reshaped and repositioned, and bone allografts were inserted to augment the forehead and supraorbital rims. Incisions were closed after wires were inserted as fixation devices to maintain the proper shape of the facial bones.

3. A 13-year-old male sustained a fractured right femur during a soccer game and underwent open treatment with insertion of two screws and two pins. After administration of general anesthesia, an incision was made over the fracture site and a metal rod was inserted through the bone's shaft to stabilize it. The rod was secured with screws, and the leg was placed in a cast.

4. Patient underwent incision and drainage of bursa, right knee. Needle was inserted into bursa and fluid was drained from the sac, which was located deep within the knee's soft tissue.

5. Patient underwent knee replacement surgery four months ago. Today "manipulation of the left knee under general anesthesia" was performed to flex the knee joint and increase its range of motion.

6. Two-year-old patient underwent reapplication of a long-leg cast to the left femur, which extended from the thigh to the toes. The patient sustained femur fracture four weeks ago when initial reduction was performed and application of long-leg cast was applied. Today that cast was removed and replaced with a long-leg cast due to the patient's age, to ensure optimal bone healing.

7. Patient underwent open reduction of left tibia fracture four weeks ago. Today the orthopedic surgeon cut a hole in the patient's short-leg cast to check for incisional infection due to patient complaints of pain. No infection was noted.

8. Patient underwent diagnostic arthroscopy of the left elbow due to unexplained pain. Surgeon inserted arthroscope into the left elbow joint to determine presence of disease or injury.

9. Patient underwent removal of a metal sliver from the index finger, right hand. The surgeon made an incision between the first and second bones of the right index finger. Joint exploration revealed the presence of a metal sliver, which was removed.

10. Patient underwent closed treatment of fractured tip of the right radius at distal end, which included application of a short-arm cast.

    _____

11. Patient underwent bilateral diagnostic nasal endoscopy. The physician inserted an endoscope into the left nostril to evaluate nasal structures. The right nostril was also examined.

    _____

12. Patient underwent indirect endoscopy of the larynx with biopsy. The physician used a small, round mirror to examine the vocal cords, tongue, and top of the throat for signs of disease or injury. Biopsy of larynx was performed for evaluation and diagnosis.

    _____

13. Patient presents with a six-month history of hoarseness. The physician performs a laryngoscopy. The patient is prepped in the usual fashion. A fiberoptic laryngoscope is passed; the vocal cords are examined under direct visualization. Slight swelling is noted. A biopsy sample is taken to be sent to pathology.

    _____

14. Patient with a history of recurrent spontaneous left pneumothorax was prepped for a thoracoscopy and underwent parietal pleurectomy. An incision was made at the eighth intercostal space, and a thoracoscope was inserted to view patient's lungs. No evidence of disease was found in the lobes. Trocars were then placed, and the pleura was stripped away from the chest wall. A nice surface was accomplished. A chest tube was placed for drainage. The remaining incision was closed with mattress sutures of 4-0 nylon.

    _____

15. A 45-year-old female nonsmoker has had a cough for the last 6 months. With the patient placed under intravenous sedation, a bronchoscope was passed in the patient's oral cavity. Primary structures of upper area visualized and found to be normal. The transbronchial area was examined. A biopsy sample was taken of the lobe. The patient had minimal blood loss. The bronchoscope was then removed, and the patient returned to the outpatient area in satisfactory condition.

    _____

16. A patient with bilateral vocal cord paralysis presents for removal of arytenoid cartilage. This is being done to improve the patient's breathing. With the patient placed under general anesthesia, the laryngoscope with operating microscope is inserted into the oral cavity. The pharynx and larynx are examined under the microscope. After adequate visualization is established, the arytenoid cartilage is exposed by excision of the mucosa overlying it.

    _____

17. A 50-year-old patient has difficulty breathing through the left nostril. The patient has a deformity of the septum and presents for a submucous resection of the septum (SMR). After making an incision, the lining of the septum is detached. The patient's deviated portion of his septum is removed, and the cartilage portion above is scored. Nasal packing is placed.

    _____

18. Patient suffers from anosmia. The patient consents to a diagnostic biopsy of intranasal cavity. This procedure is done under local anesthesia delivered to nasal tissue. A small amount of tissue is removed under direct visualization. Minimal bleeding is noted.

   _____

19. A 2-year-old patient presents to the office with a marble in his nose, per the mother. Using nasal forceps, the marble is removed.

   _____

20. A 5-year-old patient had a cleft lip repair done at 3 months of age. Now the patient has a nasal deformity that requires repair. The physician makes intranasal incisions and pulls back skin from the nasal bone tip. The bone is shaved and lengthened at the tip. The area is irrigated, and nasal packing is placed. The patient has little blood loss.

   _____

CPT Surgery III

Chapter Outline

Cardiovascular System Subsection

Hemic and Lymphatic Systems Subsection

Chapter Objectives

At the conclusion of this chapter, the student should be able to:

- Define key terms.
- Explain the organization, format, and content of the CPT Surgery Cardiovascular System and Hemic and Lymphatic Systems subsections.
- Interpret CPT surgery coding notes for the Cardiovascular System and Hemic and Lymphatic Systems subsections.
- Assign CPT surgery codes from the Cardiovascular System and Hemic and Lymphatic Systems subsections.
- Add CPT and/or HCPCS level II modifiers to codes, as appropriate.

Key Terms

adenoids

adjuvant techniques

aneurysm

angiogenesis

angioscopy

aortic anomaly

aortic sinus

arteriovenous fistula

blood

bone marrow

bone marrow aspiration

bone marrow biopsy

cadaver donor cardiectomy with or without pneumonectomy

cancer staging

cardiac ablation

cardiac tumor

cardiac valve

cardiopulmonary bypass

chyle

commissurotomy

composite graft

coronary artery bypass graft (CABG)

coronary endarterectomy

cross-over vein graft

cutdown

dual chamber

electrophysiology

embolectomy

embolus

en bloc

endocardium

extracorporeal life support (ECLS)

extracorporeal membrane oxygenation (ECMO)

first-order vessels

heart murmur

hemic system

implantable defibrillator

lymph

lymph nodes

lymphatic system

Maze procedure

modified Maze procedure

myocardium

nonselective vascular catheterization

open transluminal angioplasty

pacemaker

patency

percutaneous myocardial revascularization (PMR)

percutaneous transluminal angioplasty (PTA)

percutaneous transmyocardial laser revascularization (PTMR)

pericardial sac

pericardiectomy

pericardiocentesis

pericardiotomy

pericardium

peripherally

recipient heart with or without lung allotransplantation

reconstruction of the vena cava

saphenopopliteal vein anastomosis

second-order vessels

selective vascular catheterization

septal defects

septum

shunting procedure

single chamber

sinus of Valsalva

spleen

splenoportography

stab phlebectomy

stem cells

stented valve

stentless valve

sympathectomy

tetralogy of Fallot

therapeutic apheresis

third-order vessels

thrombectomy

thromboendarterectomy

thymus

tonsils

transluminal angioplasty

transmyocardial revascularization (TMR)

transposition of great vessels

truncus arteriosus

tube pericardiostomy

tunneled

valvular atresia

valvular heart disease

valvular prolapse

valvular regurgitation

valvular stenosis

valvuloplasty

valvulotomy

vascular family

venous anomaly

venous valve transposition

ventricular assist device (VAD)

visceral arteries

Introduction

The Cardiovascular System subsection classifies procedures performed on the heart and pericardium, valves (e.g., mitral and semilunar), and peripheral vascular vessels (e.g., arteries, veins, and capillaries). The Hemic and Lymphatic Systems subsection classifies procedures performed on the spleen, lymph nodes, and lymphatic channels. CPT guidelines that apply to the subsections are located at the beginning of the Surgery section. Unique coding instructions for the cardiovascular system and hemic and lymphatic system are located in notes below headings or codes.

 Coding Tip:

Notes located beneath headings and/or subheadings apply to all codes in the heading or subheading. Parenthetical notes that are located below a specific code apply to that code only unless the note indicates otherwise.

 Note:

The Other Procedures code below each subheading classifies an unlisted procedure performed on the anatomical site. When reporting an unlisted procedure code, include documentation about the procedure performed with the submitted claim. (Other Procedures subheadings are not included throughout Chapter 13 of this textbook except when codes that describe additional procedures are included.)

Cardiovascular System Subsection

Cardiovascular System subsection codes are arranged anatomically and then according to procedure performed. The Cardiovascular System subsection includes the following headings:

- Heart and Pericardium

- Arteries and Veins

Cardiovascular System Notes

Notes located at the beginning of the Cardiovascular System subsection provide instruction about assigning codes for *selective vascular catheterization*. When performed as part of cardiovascular (and radiology) procedures, codes for *selective vascular catheterization* (e.g., 36011) are reported separately.

In addition, parenthetical notes are located just above the Cardiovascular System subsection heading. They serve as reminders to review other codes and sections of CPT to locate additional codes associated with certain cardiovascular system procedures. (Notes are also located throughout the Cardiovascular System subsection as a reminder to report additional surgery codes with some procedures.)

Coding Tip:

During cardiovascular procedures, **cardiopulmonary bypass** is often required to divert blood from the heart to the aorta, using a pump oxygenator. Because some procedures can be performed without cardiopulmonary bypass, make sure you review the operative report to determine whether to assign the cardiopulmonary bypass code for the procedure performed.

EXAMPLE: Patient underwent repair of cardiac wound with cardiopulmonary bypass. Report code 33305.

Selective Vascular Catheterization

When reporting codes for selective vascular catheterization, knowledge of the flow of blood (Figure 13-1) throughout the body's circulatory system is crucial. (In fact, it's a good idea to reference an anatomy and physiology textbook such as Cengage's *Body Structures & Functions* when assigning codes to procedures classified in the

(A) Arterial circulation   (B) Venous circulation

Figure 13-1 Circulatory system (A) Arterial circulation (B) Venous circulation

(A)   (B)   (C)   (D)

Figure 13-2 (A) Insertion of guidewire into and beyond plaque formation in artery (B) Insertion of catheter with attached balloon through plaque formation in artery (C) Expansion of balloon to compress plaque against arterial walls and open the arterial lumen (D) Compressed plaque, creating wider lumen in artery

Cardiovascular System subsection.) Selective vascular catheterization procedures are classified as "vascular injection procedures" and require separate coding of the following:

- Diagnostic procedure (e.g., carotid angiogram) and/or therapeutic procedure (e.g., balloon dilation via catheter)

- Vascular access (e.g., selective vascular catheterization)

Separate codes are not reported for the administration of local anesthesia, introduction of the needle or catheter, or *injection* of contrast material. (The supply of contrast media *is* assigned a HCPCS level II code.) In addition, CPT codes are assigned to the point of catheter placement (not guidewire insertion); catheters (or sheaths) are inserted into blood vessels to serve as conduits for the administration of fluids (or gases), access by surgical instruments (e.g., stent), and other tasks (e.g., balloon angioplasty). A guidewire might be inserted beyond placement of the catheter, and no images are taken or procedures are performed at the insertion point of the guidewire; thus, code to the point of catheter placement (not guidewire insertion) (Figure 13-2).

Selective vascular catheterization is the insertion and manipulation or guidance of a catheter (that is attached to a guidewire) into the branches of the arterial system (other than the aorta or the vessel punctured) for the purpose of performing diagnostic or therapeutic procedures. Selective vascular catheterization is usually performed under fluoroscopic (moving x-ray) guidance. The code reported for selective vascular catheterization includes introduction of the catheter into the punctured vessel and guidance through all lesser- (or first-) order vessels (to get to the intended vessel that undergoes the diagnostic or therapeutic procedure). Thus, codes are *not* reported for **nonselective vascular catheterization**, which involves introducing the catheter directly into a vessel without further advancement past the punctured vessel or introduction of a catheter into any portion of the aorta or vena cava from any approach (e.g., axillary, brachial, femoral, jugular). ⚠

Once the catheter reaches its intended vessel, assign an appropriate code for that selective vascular catheterization. When additional vessels are catheterized for the purpose of performing diagnostic and/or therapeutic procedures, assign codes for selective vascular catheterization of those second- and third- (and beyond) order vessels. First-, second-, and third- (and beyond) order vessel catheterization is discussed next.

 Coding Tip:

When fluoroscopic guidance is provided during selective vascular catheterization, make sure you assign the appropriate supervision and interpretation code from the Radiology section (codes 75600–75989).

(A) Right brachiocephalic artery vascular family

Right lingual artery (fourth order)

Right external carotid artery (third-order)

Right internal carotid artery (third-order)

Right common carotid artery (second-order)

Brachiocephalic artery (first-order)

Note:

The left common carotid artery is a first-order vessel because it branches from the aortic arch. The right common carotid artery is a second-order vessel because it branches from the brachiocephalic artery. (The brachiocephalic artery branches from the aortic arch.)

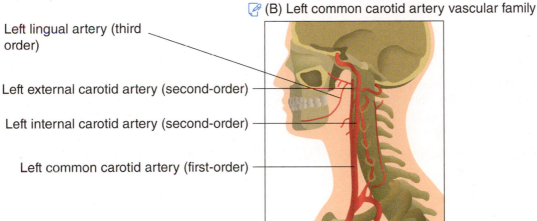

(B) Left common carotid artery vascular family

Left lingual artery (third order)

Left external carotid artery (second-order)

Left internal carotid artery (second-order)

Left common carotid artery (first-order)

Figure 13-3 Artery vascular families (A) First-, second-, third-, and fourth-order vessels in the right brachiocephalic artery vascular family (B) First-, second-, and third-order vessels in the left common carotid artery vascular family

A **vascular family** (Figure 13-3) (CPT Appendix L) is a group of vessels that is accessed by the same first-order vessel, and it is supplied by the same primary branch from the aorta. A vascular family can be compared to a tree with branches. The trunk is the aorta, which contains large and small branches. (Think of the aorta as a zero-order vessel because it is a common starting point for catheterization. The femoral artery, as a starting point for catheterization, is an example of another zero-order vessel.) From the starting point, vessels branch outward (similar to a network of streets from a highway) into the following:

- First-order vessels

- Second-order vessels

- Third-order vessels

First-order vessels extend as primary arterial branches from the aorta (e.g., left common carotid artery in the neck and inferior mesenteric artery or common iliac artery in the abdomen). When an *initial* second- or third-order arterial catheterization is performed within a vascular family, report just one code from 36216–36217 or 36246–36247. **Second-order vessels** branch from first-order vessels, and **third-order vessels** branch from second-order vessels. (Refer to Figure 13-3 for an illustration of first-, second-, and third-order vessels of a vascular family.)

Review the operative report to determine which artery (or arteries) underwent diagnostic or therapeutic procedures after having a catheter inserted. Although multiple arteries might be involved in a catheter being threaded from the insertion point to the intended artery, only one code is reported if just one artery undergoes diagnostic or therapeutic procedures.

EXAMPLE: SELECTIVE VASCULAR CATHETERIZATION INTO FIRST-ORDER VESSELS: After being assaulted, a patient presented to the emergency department, complaining of severe upper left flank pain. Patient underwent left renal angiogram. This required insertion of a catheter into the right femoral artery. The catheter was advanced to the right external iliac and common iliac arteries and aorta and into the left renal artery. Contrast media was injected for visualization of the left renal artery upon x-ray. Report code 36251. The right femoral, right external iliac, and right common iliac arteries underwent nonselective catheterization because they were used to access the left renal artery; no diagnostic or therapeutic procedure was performed on them. (Thus, do not assign catheter placement codes for accessing the right femoral, right external iliac, or right common iliac arteries.)

Selective vascular catheterization was achieved by making a small incision in the skin and performing an arterial puncture into the left femoral artery (groin region). A needle containing a stylet (inner wire) was inserted through the skin into the left femoral artery. The stylet was removed and replaced with a guidewire. Under fluoroscopy, the guidewire was advanced through the external iliac artery and common iliac artery and then into the aorta. From the abdominal aorta, the guidewire was advanced into the left renal artery. The needle was removed, and a catheter was inserted over the length of the guidewire until it reached the renal artery. The guidewire was removed, and the catheter was left in place. Under fluoroscopic guidance, contrast media was injected manually with a syringe or with an automatic injector connected to the catheter. (An automatic injector propels a large volume of dye quickly to the angiogram site.) X-rays were taken, and the catheter was slowly and carefully removed. Pressure was applied to the insertion site (to facilitate clotting and to allow the arterial puncture to reseal), and a pressure bandage was applied.

When procedures are performed on multiple arteries along the path of catheterization from first- through to second-, third-, and/or fourth-order vessels, assign an appropriate code for each.

EXAMPLE: A catheter was introduced into the brachiocephalic artery (first-order) and then inserted into the right common carotid artery (second-order) and the right internal carotid artery (third-order) to the cerebral artery (fourth-order), where contrast media was injected to perform a cerebral angiography. In addition to the cerebral angiography code, report just one selective vascular catheterization code for the cerebral artery. The brachiocephalic, right common carotid, and right internal carotid arteries were used to access the (fourth-order) cerebral artery. No diagnostic or therapeutic procedures were performed on them. Therefore, do not assign selective vascular catheterization codes for catheterization of the brachiocephalic, right common carotid, or right internal carotid arteries.

The note at the beginning of the Cardiovascular System subsection also provides instruction to report add-on code 36218 or 36248 (in addition to the primary code 36215–36217 or 36245–36247) when *additional*

- Selective arterial catheterization of second- and/or third-order vessels is achieved using a single first-order artery.

- First-, second-, or third-order vessels are accessed during selective arterial catheterization, and the vascular families supplied by a first-order vessel are from a *different* family of arteries.

EXAMPLE: A catheter was introduced into the left common carotid artery (first-order) and inserted into the left internal carotid artery (second-order). Contrast media was injected and carotid arteriogram performed. The catheter was further advanced into the left cerebral artery (third-order), additional contrast media was injected, and cerebral angiogram was performed. In addition to radiology codes for the carotid arteriogram and cerebral angiogram, report a selective vascular catheterization code for the (second-order) left internal carotid artery and add-on code 36218 for the selective vascular catheterization of the (third-order) cerebral artery. The left common carotid artery was used to access the other two arteries; therefore, a selective vascular catheterization code is *not* assigned.

Coding Tip:

When multiple selective arterial catheterization procedures of separate and distinct vascular families are performed during the same operative session, report the appropriate number of units in Form Locator 46 of the UB-04.

> **EXAMPLE:** Selective arterial catheterization of the thoracic artery and the brachiocephalic artery: Report code 36215 and the number of units on the UB-04 claim (Figure 13-4).

42 REV. CO.	43 DESCRIPTION	44 HCPCS/RATES	45 SERV. DATE	46 SERV. UNITS	47 TOTAL CHARGES	48 NON-COVERED CHARGES	49
		36215		02			

Figure 13-4 Reporting selective arterial catheterization code by completing form locators 44 and 46 on the UB-04 claim

Heart and Pericardium

Heart and Pericardium codes classify procedures performed on the heart and pericardium.

Pericardium

The **pericardium**, or **pericardial sac**, is the membrane that surrounds the heart. **Pericardiocentesis** is the insertion of a needle to withdraw fluid from the pericardium. Radiological guidance is often performed with pericardiocentesis, so make sure you report a Radiology code if instructed to do so.

A **tube pericardiostomy** is the insertion of a tube for drainage or specimen collection. A **pericardiotomy** requires thoracotomy as incision for pericardial drainage, fluid collection, or foreign body removal.

Pericardiectomy is the removal of part of the pericardium (to treat chronic pericarditis). Also code the cardiopulmonary bypass if documented in the operative report.

> **EXAMPLE:** Patient underwent pericardiotomy for removal of blood clot. Report code 33020.

 Coding Tip:

Report a code from 32658–32661 (instead of a code from the cardiovascular subsection) when surgical thoracoscopy is performed to

- Remove a clot or foreign body from the pericardial sac.
- Create a pericardial window or partial resection of pericardial sac for drainage.
- Carry out a total pericardiectomy.
- Excise a pericardial cyst, tumor, or mass.

Cardiac Tumor

A **cardiac tumor** is a growth that develops in the heart's **endocardium** (inner lining), **myocardium** (muscle layer), or pericardium. The majority of cardiac tumors are benign, although a percentage are malignant. Methods for diagnosing cardiac tumors include complete history and physical examination and diagnostic procedures such as echocardiogram, electrocardiogram, computed tomography (CT scan), magnetic resonance imaging (MRI), chest x-ray, and coronary arteriogram or angiogram.

Benign cardiac tumors include myxoma, rhabdomyoma, and other rare tumors (e.g., fibroma, hemangioma, lipoma, lymphangioma, neurofibroma, and papillary fibroelastoma). Malignant cardiac tumors include cardiac sarcoma, fibrosarcoma, liposarcoma, and rhabdomyosarcoma. Surgical removal of a cardiac tumor is indicated if it causes an arrhythmia or obstructs blood flow through the heart. When a cardiac tumor cannot be removed, a heart transplant may be required.

> **EXAMPLE:** Patient underwent complete resection of cardiac liposarcoma with cardiopulmonary bypass. Report code 33120.

Coding Tip:

When the scheduled resection of an external cardiac tumor requires cardiopulmonary bypass because a significant portion of the heart or a significant number of major vessels must be removed to ensure adequate tumor margins, the procedure becomes an excision of an intra-cardiac tumor and code 33120 is reported.

Transmyocardial Revascularization (TMR)

Transmyocardial revascularization (TMR) uses a high-powered laser to create small channels in the heart muscle to increase blood supply to the myocardium. The procedure also promotes **angiogenesis** (growth of new capillaries) as a blood supply to the heart muscle. TMR is performed to treat severe angina (in patients who are not candidates for coronary artery bypass graft [CABG] or angioplasty surgery), and the procedure may be performed with or without cardiopulmonary bypass. (TMR is usually performed with cardiopulmonary bypass.)

> **EXAMPLE:** Patient underwent TMR, by thoracotomy. Report code 33140.

Coding Tip:

A variation of the TMR procedure is called **percutaneous myocardial revascularization (PMR)**, or **percutaneous transmyocardial laser revascularization (PTMR)**, during which a catheter with the laser inside is inserted through an artery (e.g., from femoral artery to external iliac artery to common iliac artery to aorta) into the left ventricle of the heart. The laser is used to create channels, which do not penetrate the entire heart muscle, as with the TMR. Because there is no specific CPT code, report unlisted code 33999 (and submit a copy of the operative report to the third-party payer).

Pacemaker or Implantable Defibrillator

A **pacemaker** (Figure 13-5) regulates the patient's heartbeat to prevent arrhythmias (e.g., atrial fibrillation and bradycardia) and includes a pulse generator (battery and electronic device) and electrodes (leads). An **implantable defibrillator** (Figure 13-6) is similar to a pacemaker in that it includes a pulse generator and electrodes, but it uses a combination of antitachycardia pacing and low-energy cardioversion or defibrillating shocks to regulate the patient's heartbeat and prevent arrhythmias (e.g., ventricular fibrillation and ventricular tachycardia).

Pulse generators for pacemakers and implantable defibrillators are implanted internally under the skin (permanent), or they are attached externally (temporary). The implantable defibrillator pulse generator is often inserted in a "pocket" below the skin in the infraclavicular region or abdomen. Electrodes are inserted through

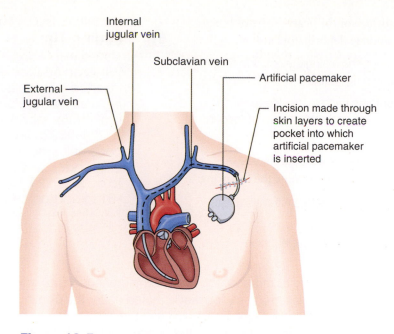

Figure 13-5 An artificial pacemaker is implanted under the skin

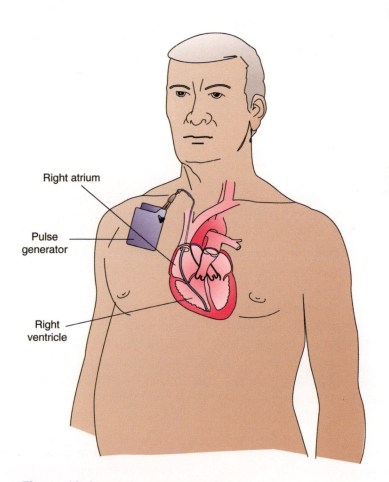

Figure 13-6 Implantable defibrillator

a vein or placed on the surface of the heart. The two types of pacemakers and implantable defibrillators are:

- **Single chamber**: Contains a single electrode that is positioned in the heart's right atrium *or* right ventricle

- **Dual chamber**: Contains two electrodes; one is placed in the right atrium, and the other is placed in the right ventricle

Before assigning the CPT code(s) for pacemaker or implantable defibrillator insertions, determine the following:

- What type of pacemaker device or system is used (e.g., single or dual chamber)

- What surgical approach is used for electrode placement

  o *Epicardial approach*: Sternotomy or thoracotomy is performed or subcostal or xiphoid incision is made and pulse generator is inserted in a "pocket" created under the skin in the upper chest; electrodes are inserted through the incision into a vein and threaded to the heart under fluoroscopic guidance; one end of the electrode is attached to the heart muscle and the other end is attached to the pulse generator.

  o *Endocardial approach (or transvenous approach)*: Cephalic vein cutdown or percutaneous subclavian vein puncture is performed to access the venous system, through which one end of the electrode is attached to the heart muscle; the other end is attached to the pulse generator, which is placed in a "pocket" created under skin in the abdomen.

- Whether insertion is an initial, repair, replacement, or upgrade procedure

- Whether the procedure involves the entire pacemaker system or just a component (e.g., electrode)

- Whether fluoroscopic guidance was used

Coding Tip:

When an additional electrode is inserted into the left ventricle during a single- or dual-chamber procedure, report a code from 33224–33225 (in addition to the pacemaker or implantable defibrillator code). Add modifier -51 to code 33224. Do not add modifier -51 to add-on code 33225.

Coding Tip:

- The CPT *Pacemaker or Implantable Defibrillator* subheading contains a table of transvenous procedures with codes that are reported for pacemakers and implantable cardioverter-defibrillator systems, which helps clarify code assignment.

- When implantable defibrillator electrodes are removed, a transvenous extraction may be attempted; however, if unsuccessful, a thoracotomy may be required to remove the electrodes.

- When a pacemaker or implantable defibrillator "battery" is changed, it is actually the pulse generator that is changed. Replacement of a pulse generator is reported with two codes: a code for removal of the pulse generator and a code for insertion of a new pulse generator.

- When pacemaker or implantable defibrillator electrodes are replaced, report appropriate code(s) from 33206–33208, 33210–33213, 33221, or 33224. Do not report a separate pacemaker removal code in addition to a replacement code, which would be considered overcoding.

EXAMPLE 1: Patient underwent subcutaneous insertion of permanent dual-chamber pacemaker pulse generator with transvenous placement of existing electrodes in the right atrium and right ventricle. Procedure included fluoroscopic guidance. Report code 33213.

EXAMPLE 2: Patient underwent replacement of a single-chamber pacemaker pulse generator. The existing pocket was reopened, and the pulse generator was disconnected from its single lead and removed. The new pulse generator was inserted into the existing pocket and connected to the single existing lead. The incision was closed with sutures. Report code 33227.

EXAMPLE 3: Single-chamber pacemaker system was replaced with dual-chamber system, including insertion of new pulse generator and new electrodes. Report code 33214. (Do not report a code for removal of the existing pacemaker system, because it is included in code 33214.)

EXAMPLE 4: Thirty days after initial insertion of transvenous pacemaker, pacemaker electrode was repositioned. Incision is made into the existing pocket; pulse generator and electrode are removed and tested to ensure that they are not defective. Because the electrode is not defective, the generator is replaced in the pocket. The electrode is reattached to the generator, placed in a new position (repositioned) in the right atrium, and retested. The incision is closed with sutures. Report code 33215.

EXAMPLE 5: Single transvenous electrode was repaired for a single-chamber pacemaker. Incision is made into the existing pocket, and the electrode is disconnected from the pulse generator. After repair, the electrode is reattached to the generator and the incision is closed with sutures. Report code 33218.

EXAMPLE 6: Previously implanted implantable defibrillator was repositioned. Report code 33215.

Note:

When electronic analysis of an internal pacemaker system is performed, report a code from 93279–93299 in the Medicine section. The code is reported for an encounter after the insertion procedure to determine whether the pacemaker or implantable defibrillator is functioning properly and/or has to be reprogrammed.

Electrophysiologic Operative Procedures

Electrophysiology is the study of heart arrhythmias; electrophysiologic (EP) procedures analyze heart rhythm abnormalities and include operative ablation or operative incisions and reconstruction of the atria to correct abnormal pathways. The electrophysiology procedure is invasive, similar to a cardiac catheterization, in that electrode catheters are introduced into the right side of the heart from the femoral, brachial, or jugular vein. The catheters positioned in the heart are used to measure and record cardiac rhythm.

Note:

When the physician performs an "operative" cardiac ablation (also called a Maze procedure), a code is assigned from the CPT Surgery section of CPT (e.g., 33254). Cardiac ablation is sometimes called "cardiac catheter ablation"; however, that procedure is assigned a code from the CPT Medicine section (93650–93657).

- Operative **cardiac ablation** (**modified Maze procedure**) stops atrial or ventricular fibrillation by using radiofrequency waves (modified electrical energy) to create small scars on the heart's surface. Impulses are redirected and follow a normal electrical pathway through the heart.

- The **Maze procedure** stops atrial fibrillation or atrial flutter by using incisions in heart tissue to stop abnormal heart rhythm.

Both types of EP procedures require thoracotomy to access the heart, and cardiopulmonary bypass may or may not be used.

EXAMPLE: Patient underwent operative ablation of ventricular arrhythmogenic focus with cardiopulmonary bypass. Thoracotomy was used to access the heart. Report code 33261.

Patient-Activated Event Recorder

A patient-activated cardiac event recorder (also called an *insertable loop recorder* or a *cardiovascular monitoring system*) is implanted under the skin (of the patient's chest region, under local anesthesia) and is programmed with a looping memory that records electrocardiogram (ECG) tracings. When the patient experiences symptoms (e.g., irregular heart beats, fainting), the patient activates a hand-held telemetry to initiate ECG recording and storage. The physician retrieves the data, which can be displayed, printed, and/or stored. Cardiac event recorders document the heart's rhythms during transient (infrequent or recurrent) cardiac symptoms (e.g., recurrent syncope). The procedure for inserting and removing an event recorder is similar to that for implanting or removing a pacemaker pulse generator.

 Coding Tip:

- Initial implantation of patient-activated event recorders includes programming. When subsequent electronic analysis and/or reprogramming are required, report codes 93279–93299 from the Medicine section.

- Holter monitor and external event recording are reported with codes 93268–93272 from the Medicine section.

EXAMPLE: Patient underwent thoracotomy and implantation of patient-activated cardiac event recorder with programming. Report code 33282.

Heart (Including Valves) and Great Vessels

CPT codes 33300–33335 describe repairs to injuries of the heart and/or great vessels (e.g., stab wounds and gunshot wounds). Cardiopulmonary bypass may or may not be required during the repair procedure; make sure you report the appropriate code.

EXAMPLE: Patient underwent repair of cardiac stab wound, with cardiopulmonary bypass. Separate incision was made to remove atrial thrombus. Report codes 33305 and 33315-59.

Cardiac Valves

Cardiac valves are flaps of tissue that keep blood flowing in one direction to allow for the efficient one-way flow of blood through the heart's chambers. **Valvular heart disease** is the abnormality or dysfunction of one or more of the heart's four valves (aortic, mitral, pulmonary, and tricuspid).

Coding Tip:

To report removal of a thrombus (33310–33315) in addition to codes for other cardiac procedures performed during the same operative session, a separate incision into the heart is required (to remove the atrial or ventricular thrombus). Add modifier -59 to code 33315 when it is reported for "removal of a thrombus with coronary bypass" in addition to codes for other cardiac procedures.

- **Valvular atresia**: Valve fails to develop properly and is completely closed at birth

- **Valvular prolapse**: Two valvular flaps do not close properly

- **Valvular regurgitation**: Backflow of blood due to valvular prolapse

- **Valvular stenosis**: Narrowing of one or more cardiac valves

When coding procedures performed on cardiac valves, first determine the valve involved.

- Aortic
- Mitral
- Tricuspid
- Pulmonary

Then determine the type of procedure performed.

- **Valvuloplasty**: Open-heart surgery during which the surgeon removes the damaged valve and replaces it with a prosthetic, homograft or allograft, stented, or stentless valve (Figure 13-7)

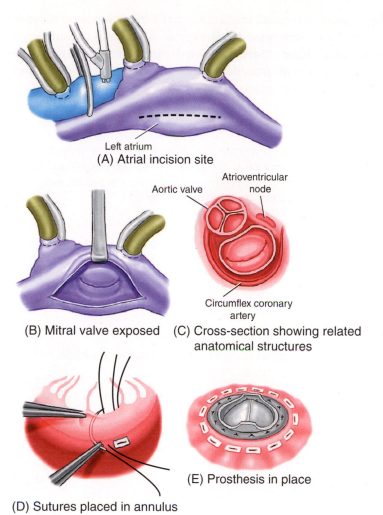

Figure 13-7   Mitral valve replacement: (A) Atrial incision site; (B) Mitral valve exposed; (C) Cross-section showing related anatomical structures; (D) Sutures placed in annulus; (E) Prosthesis in place

 Coding Tip:

When nonsurgical, catheter-based, percutaneous balloon valvuloplasty is performed, report code(s) 92986–92990.

- **Valvulotomy**: Open-heart surgery in which an incision is made into a valve to repair valvular damage; includes **commissurotomy**, in which narrowed valve leaflets are widened by carefully opening the fused leaflets with a scalpel

 Coding Tip:

- When multiple valve procedures are performed during the same operative session, add modifier -51 to the second (and subsequent) valve procedure code(s).
- When a valve requires insertion of a prosthetic ring, report codes 33426–33427.

Code 33405 describes open replacement of the aortic valve with a prosthetic valve, with cardiopulmonary bypass. It is reported for procedures performed on valves *other than* homograft (human donor) or stentless (does not contain any framework) valves. (Code 33410 is reported when a stentless tissue valve is used to replace an aortic valve.) When an allograft (or a homograft) is used in aortic valve replacement, report code 33406.

 Note:

> A **stented valve** includes framework on which the replacement valve is mounted to provide support for the valve's leaflets. A **stentless valve** is often an actual heart valve obtained from either a human donor (homograft) or a pig, and it does not contain framework. Stentless valves are preferred because they are less obstructive and have improved long-term performance.

EXAMPLE 1: Patient underwent aortic valvuloplasty with cardiopulmonary bypass. Report code 33390.

EXAMPLE 2: Patient underwent right ventricular resection for infundibular stenosis, with commissurotomy. Report code 33476.

Other Valvular Procedures

The Other Valvular Procedures code classifies the repair of non-structural prosthetic valve dysfunction with cardiopulmonary bypass as a separate procedure.

EXAMPLE: Patient underwent repair of non-structural prosthetic valve dysfunction with cardiopulmonary bypass. Report code 33496.

Coronary Artery Anomalies

An **arteriovenous fistula** is an abnormal passageway between an artery and a vein that allows blood to flow directly into a vein. It can occur as a congenital defect or as the result of trauma. (A fistula can also be surgically created to provide a site for vascular access.) An arteriovenous fistula can occur anywhere in the body, but it most often occurs in the legs or arms. The fistula might eventually develop into an **aneurysm** (bulge in an artery that can weaken the arterial wall and eventually burst, resulting in hemorrhage). For example, a coronary arteriovenous fistula (or coronary artery fistula) is a congenital fistula that is often located between the right coronary artery and the right heart.

Coding Tip:

- Codes 33500–33507 include endarterectomy or angioplasty when performed during the same operative session.
- Do not add modifier -63 to codes 33502–33503 or 33505–33506.

EXAMPLE: Patient underwent a Takeuchi procedure, which involved constructing an intrapulmonary artery tunnel. Report code 33505.

Endoscopy

CPT code 33508 is an add-on code that is reported when an endoscopic approach is used to harvest veins for coronary artery bypass procedures. Report code 33508 in addition to codes 33510–33523.

Coding Tip:

When an open approach is used to harvest an upper extremity vein, report code 35500 (instead of code 33508).

EXAMPLE: Patient underwent coronary artery bypass graft (CABG) procedure, single coronary venous graft, with endoscopic harvesting of saphenous vein. Report codes 33510 and 33508.

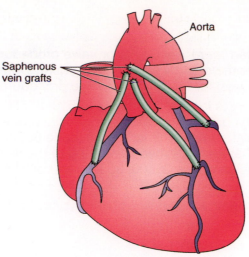

Figure 13-8 Coronary artery bypass graft (CABG) using saphenous vein grafts

Coronary Artery Bypass Graft (CABG) Procedures

The Cardiovasular System subsection contains three headings to classify coronary artery bypass graft (CABG) procedures, which are organized according to type of graft.

- Venous grafting only for coronary artery bypass (33510–33516)
- Combined arterial-venous grafting for coronary bypass (33517–33530) (add-on codes)
- Arterial grafting for coronary artery bypass (33533–33548)

Coronary artery bypass graft (CABG) (pronounced "cabbage") (Figure 13-8) is a procedure performed to improve the flow of blood to the heart. A blood vessel (called a graft) is removed from the arm, leg, or chest and anastomosed to bypass (detour) the blood flow around a narrowed or blocked coronary artery. (The surgery relieves angina symptoms, improves the patient's ability to exercise, and reduces the patient's risk of a heart attack.) Correctly reporting CABG requires careful review of the operative report to determine the number and type of grafts performed.

Venous Grafting Only for Coronary Artery Bypass

Codes 33510–33516 are used to report CABG procedures using venous grafts only, and they are *not* reported when CABG procedures use a combination of arterial and venous grafts during the same procedure.

Combined Arterial-Venous Grafting for Coronary Bypass

Codes 33517–33530 are reported for combined arterial-venous grafts, and they are always reported in addition to codes from the Arterial Grafting for Coronary Artery Bypass subheading.

Arterial Grafting for Coronary Artery Bypass

Codes 33533–33548 are reported for coronary artery bypass procedures using either arterial grafts only or a combination of arterial-venous grafts. The codes include the use of the internal mammary artery, gastroepiploic artery, epigastric artery, radial artery, and arterial conduits procured from other sites.

EXAMPLE: Patient underwent CABG procedure for arteriosclerotic heart disease. A single arterial graft was performed. The sternum was opened, the heart was stopped and cooled, and the patient was connected to cardiopulmonary bypass. A long piece of the saphenous vein was harvested, and one end was attached to the ascending aorta. The other end of the graft was attached to the circumflex coronary artery, just below the blocked area. Report codes 33533-LC and 33517.

Coding Tip:

- CPT code 33530 is reported for repeat CABG or valve procedures that are performed more than one month after the original surgical procedure. Code 33530 is reported in addition to the appropriate code(s) for the CABG or valve procedure.

- Harvesting the vein or artery is included in codes 33510–33536 except when an upper extremity vein (e.g., axillary, brachial, radial, or ulnar vein) (code 35500), upper extremity artery (e.g., axillary, brachial, radial, or ulnar artery) (code 35600), or femoropopliteal vein segment (code 35572) is harvested. When harvesting of the vein or artery is documented in the operative report, assign codes 35500, 35600, and/or 35572 in addition to the CABG procedure code.

- HCPCS level II modifiers identify placement of the bypass grafts and are added to the CABG code.

  ○ -LC (left circumflex coronary artery)

  ○ -LD (left anterior descending coronary artery)

  ○ -RC (right coronary artery)

Coronary Endarterectomy

Coronary endarterectomy is performed to remove the inner layer of coronary arteries that contain cholesterol plaques. When a patient's coronary arteries contain extensive cholesterol plaque, a CABG procedure cannot be performed until the plaque is removed via coronary endarterectomy.

> **EXAMPLE:** Patient underwent coronary endarterectomy of the left anterior descending and left circumflex coronary arteries. During the same operative session, the patient also underwent double CABG. The graft sections were obtained from the internal mammary arteries. Report codes 33534-LC-LD, 33572, and 33572.

Single Ventricle and Other Complex Cardiac Anomalies

Codes 33600–33622 are reported for procedures performed to correct single ventricle and other complex cardiac anomalies. For example, the Norwood procedure is reported with code 33619 (to repair a single ventricle that has an aortic outflow obstruction and aortic arch hypoplasia). During the procedure, the pulmonary artery is connected to the right ventricle, using a shunt, and the underdeveloped aorta is enlarged and reconstructed.

> **EXAMPLE:** Patient diagnosed with tricuspid atresia undergoes repair that involves closure of the atrial septal defect and anastomosis of the aorta to the pulmonary artery. Report code 33615.

Congenital Heart Defects

Congenital heart defects include the following:

- Septal defects
- Sinus of Valsalva defects
- Venous anomalies
- Shunting procedures

- Transposition of great vessels
- Truncus arteriosus
- Aortic anomalies

Septal Defects

The **septum** is tissue that separates the heart's left and right sides. **Septal defects** occur when the tissue doesn't completely close between the heart's chambers (atria or ventricles). This allows oxygen-rich blood from one side of the heart (e.g., left atrium) to mix with oxygen-poor blood on the other side (e.g., right atrium). The extra blood flows through the hole, causing a swishing sound, which is called a **heart murmur** (an extra heart sound).

EXAMPLE: Patient underwent repair of atrial septal defect, secundum, with cardiopulmonary bypass, without patch. The right atrium was opened, and the size and location of the atrial septal defect was assessed. Due to the small size of the atrial septal tissue, it was closed with a suture. Report code 33641.

Codes 33692–33697 describe repair procedures for **tetralogy of Fallot**, which is a congenital heart condition that includes ventral septal defect, stenosis of the infundibulum, hypertrophy of the right ventricle, and an abnormally positioned aorta.

EXAMPLE: Patient underwent complete repair of tetralogy of Fallot without pulmonary atresia using transannular patch. Report code 33694.

Sinus of Valsalva Defects

The **sinus of Valsalva** (or **aortic sinus**) is an anatomical dilation of the ascending aorta that occurs just above the aortic valve (e.g., left anterior aortic sinus that gives rise to the left coronary artery). Defects include aneurysms and fistulas for which repair and closure procedures are performed.

EXAMPLE: Patient underwent surgical repair of a sinus of Valsalva aneurysm. Report code 33720.

Venous Anomalies

Venous anomalies are associated with systemic veins and pulmonary veins and include conditions such as

- *Cor triatriatum* (congenital anomaly in which left atrium or right atrium is divided into two parts by a fold of tissue, membrane, or fibromuscular band; referred to as a heart with three atria)
- *Pulmonary vein stenosis* (abnormal thickening and narrowing of walls of pulmonary veins)
- *Scimitar syndrome* (congenital condition in which aberrant vessel connects pulmonary vein in right lung to inferior vena cava)
- *Supravalvar mitral ring* (rare congenital defect characterized by an abnormal ridge of connective tissue on the atrial side of the mitral valve)
- *Total anomalous pulmonary venous return (TAPVR)* (rare congenital defect in which all four pulmonary veins do not connect normally to left atrium but instead drain to the right atrium by way of an abnormal connection)

EXAMPLE: Patient underwent surgical repair of supravalvular mitral ring via resection of left atrial membrane. Report code 33732.

Shunting Procedures

Shunting procedures are performed to move blood from one area to another, and they are performed for conditions such as

- *Atrial septal defect (ASD)* (opening in atrial septum fails to close after birth)
- *Coarctation of the aorta* (part of the aorta has a very narrow section, similar in appearance to an hourglass timer, reducing blood flow)
- *Patent ductus arteriosus (PDA)* (opening between aorta and pulmonary artery fails to close after birth)
- *Tricuspid atresia* (tricuspid valve is deformed, narrow, or missing)
- *Ventricular septal defect (VSD)* (opening in ventricular septum fails to close after birth)

EXAMPLE: Patient underwent a shunt procedure of the descending aorta to the pulmonary artery to correct patent ductus arteriosus. Report code 33762.

Transposition of Great Vessels

The **transposition of great vessels** is the congenital reversal of the aorta and pulmonary artery. The pulmonary arteries are supplied by the left ventricle, and the aorta is supplied by the right ventricle—the opposite of the normal arrangement. Surgery to correct the transposition of great vessels is reported with codes 33770–33783.

EXAMPLE: Patient underwent repair of transposition of the great arteries with aortic and pulmonary artery reconstruction. Report code 33778.

Truncus Arteriosus

Truncus arteriosus is a congenital malformation in which just one artery arises from the heart to form the aorta and pulmonary artery. Surgery to correct truncus arteriosus is reported with codes 33786–33788.

> **EXAMPLE:** Patient underwent total repair of truncus arteriosus. Report code 33786.

Aortic Anomalies

Aortic Anomalies codes classify repair procedures. **Aortic anomalies** result from unusual patterns of aortic development and include conditions such as

- *Tracheal decompression* (or *tracheomalacia*) (softness of cartridge that supports tracheal walls, which can be due to *vascular ring formation* and results in tracheal collapse and decreased airflow)

- *Aberrant vessels* (or *vascular ring formation*) (abnormal growth of vessels, which encircle trachea and esophagus and result in upper airway obstruction)

- *Aortopulmonary septal defect (APSD)* (deficiency in septum between aorta and pulmonary artery, resulting in abnormal communication between them)

- *Patent ductus arteriosus* (opening between aorta and pulmonary artery fails to close after birth)

- *Coarctation of aorta* (part of the aorta has a very narrow section, similar in appearance to an hourglass timer, reducing blood flow)

- *Hypoplastic aortic arch* (or *interrupted aortic arch*) (absence of a portion of the aortic arch, creating a gap between the ascending and descending aorta)

> **EXAMPLE:** Patient underwent surgical division of aberrant vessels with aortopexy to correct tracheomalacia. Report codes 33802 and 33800-51.

Thoracic Aortic Aneurysm

An aneurysm (Figure 13-9) is a bulge in an artery than can weaken the arterial wall and eventually burst, resulting in hemorrhage. Procedures to repair thoracic aortic aneurysms are reported with codes 33860–33877.

> **EXAMPLE:** Patient underwent transverse arch graft to repair thoracic aortic aneurysm. Cardiopulmonary bypass was provided. Report code 33870.

Endovascular Repair of Descending Thoracic Aorta

Endovascular repair of descending thoracic aorta procedures involve the placement of grafts to repair defects of the thoracic aorta (e.g., aneurysm, intramural hematoma, penetrating ulcer, traumatic disruption). When fluoroscopic guidance is used during endovascular repair procedures, report a code from 75956–75959.

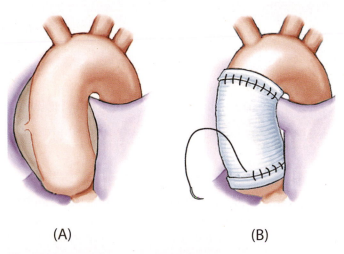

(A)   (B)

Figure 13-9 Aortic aneurysm repair (A) Aortic aneurysm
(B) Graft repair of aneurysm

Note:

Interventional procedures performed with endovascular repair of the descending thoracic aorta are reported separately (e.g., innominate, carotid, subclavian, visceral, or iliac artery transluminal angioplasty or stenting; arterial embolization; and intravascular ultrasound).

EXAMPLE: Patient underwent placement of proximal extension prosthesis for endovascular repair of descending thoracic aorta dissecting aneurysm, initial extension only. Fluoroscopic guidance confirmed appropriate placement. Report codes 33883 and 75958.

Pulmonary Artery

Pulmonary Artery codes classify procedures performed on the pulmonary artery.

EXAMPLE: Patient underwent repair of pulmonary atresia with ventricular septal defect, by construction or replacement of conduit from right or left ventricle to pulmonary artery. Report code 33920.

Heart/Lung Transplantation

Guidelines for heart/lung transplantation include three components.

- **Cadaver donor cardiectomy with or without pneumonectomy**, which involves harvesting the allograft (graft such as lung tissue that is transplanted between genetically nonidentical individuals of the same species) and preserving the allograft with cold preservation solution and cold maintenance (codes 33930 and 33940)

Note:

Cold preservation is a component of the donor organ harvesting procedure, not the backbench preparation. For example, cold preservation of a donor heart allograft is included in code 33940, Donor cardiectomy (including cold preservation).

- Backbench work, which involves preparing the cadaver donor heart and/or lung allograft prior to lung transplantation and dissecting allograft from surrounding soft tissues to prepare the aorta, superior vena cava, inferior vena cava, pulmonary artery, left atrium, and/or trachea for implantation

- **Recipient heart with or without lung allotransplantation**, which includes transplantation of the allograft and care of the recipient

    EXAMPLE: Patient with severe cardiomyopathy underwent heart transplant procedure to remove diseased heart and replace with healthy heart from a recently deceased donor. Transplant physician performed donor cardiectomy including cold preservation from cadaver donor, backbench standard preparation of cadaver donor heart allograft, and heart transplant with cardiopulmonary bypass. Report codes 33940, 33944, and 33945-51. (The 33940 procedure is performed on the donor, not the recipient. The 33944 and 33945 procedures are performed on the recipient, and modifier -51 is added to code 33945 only.)

    When donor cardiectomy and backbench preparation are performed at a facility other than the transplant facility (and the removed organ is transported to the transplant facility), codes 33940 and 33944 are reported by the first facility. Code 33945 is reported by the transplant facility.

Extracorporeal Membrane Oxygenation or Extracorporeal Life Support Services

Extracorporeal membrane oxygenation (ECMO) or **extracorporeal life support (ECLS)** provide cardiac and/or respiratory support to the heart and/or lungs, which allow them to rest and recover when patients are sick or injured. The CPT coding manual contains a table of codes for ECMO/ECLS procedures, which helps provide direction to proper codes.

EXAMPLE: Veno-venous extracorporeal life support was initiated by the patient's physician. Report code 33946.

Cardiac Assist

Cardiac assist procedures include the insertion, implantation, and removal of various devices. A **ventricular assist device (VAD)** provides temporary support for the heart by substituting for left or right heart function (e.g., after myocardial infarction).

EXAMPLE: Patient underwent insertion of intra-aortic balloon assist device into the common femoral artery. Device was to the distal aortic arch. Report code 33967.

Exercise 13.1 – Heart and Pericardium

Instructions: Assign the CPT code(s) and appropriate modifier(s) to each statement.

1. Patient undergoes aortic valve replacement with stentless tissue valve, by division. Cardiopulmonary bypass is provided.

   _____

2. 18-year-old patient underwent repair of ductus arteriosus. Posterolateral thoracotomy was performed to access the heart.

   _____

3. Patient underwent coronary artery bypass, during which a single arterial and single vein graft was performed.

   _____

4. 7-year-old child underwent repair of pulmonary atresia with ventricular septal defect, and a prosthetic conduit was used.

   _____

5. Patient underwent insertion of permanent pacemaker with transvenous electrode(s), ventricular. An additional electrode was inserted in the left ventricle to provide a biventricular (dual chamber) pacing system and attached to the inserted pacemaker.

   _____

6. Patient underwent subtotal pericardiectomy with cardiopulmonary bypass.

   _____

7. Patient-activated cardiac event recorder was implanted in a 54-year-old male patient on May 1. Two weeks later the patient underwent electronic analysis and reprogramming of the recorder on May 16.

   _____

8. Patient underwent sinus of Valsalva fistula repair, with cardiopulmonary bypass.

   _____

9. Operative ablation of ventricular arrhythmogenic focus was performed on a 62-year-old female patient, with cardiopulmonary bypass.

   _____

10. Patient underwent transection of pulmonary artery with cardiopulmonary bypass.

    _____

11. The physician drained fluid from the pericardial space under ultrasonic guidance.

    _____

Exercise 13.1 (*continued*)

12. The physician repositions a previously placed transvenous right ventricular electrode.

_____

13. The physician performed an operative ablation of a supraventricular arrhythmia without cardiopulmonary bypass.

_____

14. The physician performed a surgical vascular endoscopy with video-assisted harvesting of a vein for coronary artery bypass surgery (vein only, single coronary venous graft).

_____

15. Patient underwent banding of pulmonary artery.

_____

16. The physician initiated cardiopulmonary bypass, the right atrium was opened, and a stiff ring was inserted for valvuloplasty of the tricuspid valve.

_____

17. Using cardiopulmonary bypass, the physician repaired an artificial prosthetic valve that was malfunctioning due to leakage.

_____

18. The patient was brought to the operating room, and a triple coronary bypass was performed using only venous conduits.

_____

19. The physician performed a coronary endarterectomy (open), left anterior descending artery, during the same operative session as a coronary artery bypass graft procedure (using an arterial graft).

_____

20. The physician performed a Damus-Kaye-Stansel procedure.

_____

21. Using cardiopulmonary bypass, the right atrium was opened and a patch of Dacron was sutured to the edge of the atrial septal defect (secundum) to close it.

_____

22. The physician repaired a hypoplastic aortic arch using prosthetic material, without cardiopulmonary bypass.

_____

23. The surgeon repaired transposition of the great arteries via Jatene-type aortic pulmonary artery reconstruction, including closure of ventricular septal defect.

_____

24. The physician repaired an atrial septal defect and ventricular septal defect with patch closure.

_____

25. Using hypothermic circulatory arrest methodology, the physician repaired a dissection of the ascending aorta with moderate aortic insufficiency; the ascending aorta was replaced with a prosthetic graft, and the aortic valve was resuspended.

_____

Arteries and Veins

The Arteries and Veins subsection also requires an excellent understanding of the anatomy of vascular structures because it is organized according to artery or vein (and approach). Notes at the beginning of the Arteries and Veins subsection indicate the following:

- Codes for procedures performed on arteries and veins include the establishment of both inflow and outflow by whatever procedures are necessary. This means that separate codes for establishing inflow and outflow are not reported.

- The portion of the operative arteriogram that is performed by the surgeon is included in codes for procedures performed on arteries and veins. (When the radiologist participates by supervising and interpreting an arteriogram, a separate code is reported.)

- When a **sympathectomy** (excision of a segment of the sympathetic nerve) procedure is performed, it is included in the codes for aortic procedures. For example, a lumbar sympathectomy might be performed to improve collateral blood supply to the foot when reconstructive surgery is not possible.

- Unlisted vascular procedures are reported with code 37799.

Embolectomy/Thrombectomy

An **embolectomy** is the surgical removal of an **embolus** (blood clot that circulates throughout the bloodstream), and a **thrombectomy** (fixed blood clot) is the surgical removal of a thrombus. Before reporting a code, make sure you identify the type of blood vessel (artery or vein) and the approach used to remove the embolus or thrombus (e.g., catheter and/or incision).

> **EXAMPLE 1:** Patient underwent carotid embolectomy with catheter, by neck incision. Report code 34001.

> **EXAMPLE 2:** Patient underwent direct subclavian vein thrombectomy, by neck incision. Report code 34471.

Venous Reconstruction

Venous reconstruction procedures are performed to repair venous valves, the vena cava, and venous transposition. Leg veins contain valves, which contain two leaflets to allow blood to flow in one direction toward the heart. When venous valves become damaged and fail to function properly, the backflow of blood occurs, resulting in varicose veins, pain, leg swelling, hyperpigmentation (skin discoloration), and skin ulcers (breakdown of the skin). Valvuloplasty is performed to repair incompetent valves by opening the vein; exposing the leaflets after dissecting the vein from surrounding tissues; and placing very fine sutures to attach the valve edges to the vein wall, which tightens the valve flaps when the vein is closed.

Reconstruction of the vena cava is performed to correct a congenital defect or to repair the vena cava when the patient sustains trauma or the vena cava is damaged due to long-term drug therapy (e.g., chemotherapy). For example, the obstructed or damaged portion of the vena cava is resected and repaired with an autologous (graft from patient's own body) pericardial patch.

Venous valve transposition is performed to treat chronic deep venous insufficiency. An incision is made to expose the venous valve, and the section of the vein that contains the malfunctioning valve is excised. Then a harvested vein that contains functional valves is anastomosed end to end to the remaining vein.

A **cross-over vein graft** procedure involves making an incision to expose the vein's incompetent valve, dividing that section of the vein, and connecting it to a nearby vein that has functioning valves.

A **saphenopopliteal vein anastomosis** involves making an incision to expose the saphenous vein and connecting it to the popliteal vein using end-to-end anastomosis.

> **EXAMPLE:** Patient developed chronic benign superior vena cava syndrome due to long-term use of central venous catheters (CVCs) for administration of chemotherapy. Reconstruction of vena cava was performed by resecting the obstructed segment and placing an autologous pericardial patch. Report code 34502.

Coding Tip:

The list of procedures included and excluded from endovascular repair of an abdominal aortic aneurysm varies slightly from those associated with endovascular repair of an iliac aneurysm. For example, open femoral or iliac artery exposure is included with endovascular repair of an abdominal aortic aneurysm, but it is reported separately when performed with endovascular repair of an iliac aneurysm.

Repair of Aneurysms

The Arteries and Veins heading contains the following subheadings about repair of aneurysms and related procedures:

- Endovascular Repair of Abdominal Aortic Aneurysm

- Fenestrated Endovascular Repair of the Visceral and Infrarenal Aorta

- Endovascular Repair of Iliac Aneurysm

- Direct Repair of Aneurysm or Excision (Partial or Total) and Graft Insertion for Aneurysm, Pseudoaneurysm, Ruptured Aneurysm, and Associated Occlusive Disease

An aneurysm is an abnormal "bulging" of a portion of a vessel, usually due to a weakness or thinning of the vessel wall at that location (Figure 13-10). It can be caused by congenital or acquired weakness of the vessel wall. Minimally invasive procedures are performed to implant endovascular devices (e.g., endovascular graft) for treatment of aortic aneurysms (codes 34800–34834) and iliac aneurysms (code 34900). Direct (open) repair includes partial or total excision of the arterial segment that contains the aneurysm and insertion of a graft, using end-to-end anastomosis (codes 35001–35152) (Figure 13-11).

Because a number of different methods are used to repair abdominal aortic aneurysms, the coder must review the operative report to identify

- Whether an endovascular or direct (open) repair of the abdominal aortic aneurysm was performed

- What the artery and type of exposure were (e.g., open femoral artery exposure for delivery of endovascular prosthesis, by groin incision, unilateral)

- What type of device was used for repair (e.g., modular bifurcated prosthesis)

- What other separately reported procedures or services were provided (e.g., fluoroscopy)

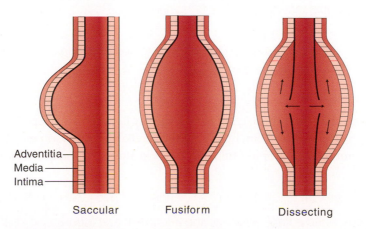

Adventitia
Media
Intima

Saccular   Fusiform   Dissecting

Figure 13-10 Three types of aneurysms

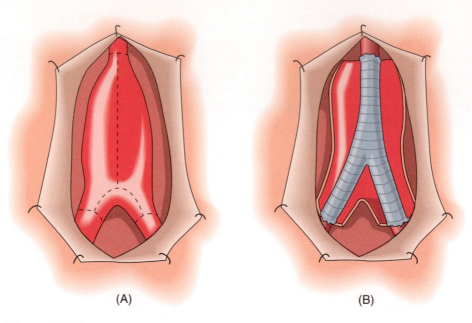

Figure 13-11 (A) Surgical resection of aneurysm (B) Grafting of aneurysm

 Coding Tip:

- Codes for endovascular repair of aneurysms include balloon angioplasty with target treatment zone either before or after graft deployment, distal extensions, manipulation, and positioning.
- When assigning codes for aneurysm repair, review the patient record to determine if the type of repair is direct (open) or endovascular. Direct (open) repairs include procedures performed on the thoracic aorta and all other arteries. Endovascular repairs include procedures performed on the thoracic aorta, abdominal aorta, and the iliac artery.

EXAMPLE 1: Patient underwent open iliac artery exposure for delivery of endovascular prosthesis during endovascular therapy, via abdominal incision (unilateral), with placement of endovascular prosthesis to treat an abdominal aortic aneurysm. Report codes 34820 and 34825-51.

EXAMPLE 2: Abdominal incision was made to expose the right iliac artery, and endovascular graft was placed under fluoroscopic guidance to repair right iliac aneurysm. Report codes 34900-RT, 34820-RT, and 75954-RT.

EXAMPLE 3: Patient underwent direct repair with partial excision of aneurysm and graft insertion to treat a left carotid aneurysm. Report code 35001-LT.

Repair Arteriovenous Fistula

An *arteriovenous fistula* is an abnormal connection or passageway between an artery and a vein, which means blood flows directly from an artery into a vein, bypassing the capillaries. A person may be born with an arteriovenous fistula (congenital fistula), or a fistula may develop after birth (acquired fistula due to trauma or other pathology).

EXAMPLE 1: Patient underwent repair of a congenital arteriovenous fistula, neck. Report code 35180.

EXAMPLE 2: Patient sustained a knife wound to the abdomen, and a traumatic arteriovenous fistula developed. Surgical repair of the abdominal arteriovenous fistula was performed. Report code 35189.

Repair Blood Vessel Other Than for Fistula, With or Without Patch Angioplasty

Generally, the *repair of blood vessels (other than for fistula)* is due to an injured artery or vein, such as a lacerated or torn blood vessel. Repairs include the following types:

- Direct (e.g., a partly divided vessel or one that has been lacerated longitudinally can be sutured, with the cut ends anastomosed)

- Vein graft (e.g., a piece of saphenous vein is harvested from the patient and sutured over lacerated blood vessel to bypass the abnormal section of the vessel)

- Graft other than vein (e.g., synthetic graft material is sutured end-to-end to the vessel, replacing the excised portion)

   EXAMPLE 1: Patient underwent direct repair of superficial basilic vein, left hand. Report code 35207-LT.

   EXAMPLE 2: Patient underwent repair of peroneal artery with synthetic graft, right lower leg. Report code 35286-RT.

Thromboendarterectomy

A **thromboendarterectomy** is the surgical excision of a thrombus and atherosclerotic inner lining from an obstructed artery. It is typically performed to treat calcified plaque or clot formations that don't respond to balloon angioplasty procedures. Coders must carefully review documentation to distinguish between a thrombectomy (e.g., procedure to remove a thrombus or blood clot) and a thromboendarterectomy (e.g., procedure to remove a thrombus and the lining of the artery, including possible placement of a patch graft).

 Coding Tip:

When a carotid thromboendarterectomy procedure is repeated more than one month after the original procedure, report code 35390 in addition to code 35301.

   EXAMPLE: Patient underwent abdominal aortic thromboendarterectomy with patch graft. Report code 35331.

Angioscopy

Angioscopy is the microscopic visualization of substances (e.g., contrast media and radiopaque agents) as they pass through capillaries. The intravenous injection of the substance is performed as part of the procedure.

   EXAMPLE: Patient underwent endovascular repair of infrarenal abdominal aortic aneurysm using aorto-aortic tube prosthesis. Prior to performing the therapeutic portion of the procedure, angioscopy was performed to visualize the interior of the aortic arch. Subsequently, under abdominal aortographic guidance, initial third-order vascular catheterization of left infrarenal artery was performed and atherectomy catheter device was advanced to the aorta. In addition to codes for the endovascular repair (34800, 36247-LT, 75625), report code 35400. (Do not add modifier -51 to code 35400.)

Coding Tip:

Code 35400 (Angioscopy) is reported in addition to the code for the primary procedure performed (e.g., percutaneous transluminal angioplasty, PTA).

Bypass Graft

The Bypass Graft heading includes codes that describe procedures performed on veins and *in situ* veins. Codes also classify the use of "other than vein" material (e.g., synthetic graft) as bypass grafts for arteries. Each code describes the bypass graft anastomosis location. For example, code 35506 describes *carotid-subclavian*, which means that the bypass graft is anastomosed from the carotid artery to the subclavian artery.

EXAMPLE 1: Patient underwent bypass graft, with vein, of the left femoral-popliteal artery. Report code 35556-LT.

EXAMPLE 2: Patient underwent *in situ* vein bypass of the right femoral-popliteal artery. Report code 35583-RT.

EXAMPLE 3: Patient underwent synthetic bypass graft of the right carotid artery. Report code 35601-RT.

Composite Grafts

Add-on codes 35681–35683 describe composite bypass graft harvesting and anastomosis of multiple vein segments as arterial bypass graft conduits. A **composite graft** is comprised of vein and synthetic graft material (code 35681) *or* segments of veins from two or more locations, such as saphenous vein and femoral vein (codes 35682–35683).

EXAMPLE 1: Patient underwent bypass graft procedure of right femoral-popliteal artery with Gore-Tex synthetic graft and a portion of the right saphenous vein. Report 35556-RT and 35681. (Do not add modifier -51 to code 35681.)

⚠ **EXAMPLE 2:** Patient underwent bypass graft procedure of right femoral-popliteal artery. Vein grafts were obtained from the left brachial and left basilic veins. Report codes 35556-RT and 35682-LT. (Do not add modifier -51 to code 35682.)

 Note:

The most common material used for "other than vein" includes synthetic materials such as Gore-Tex.

Adjuvant Techniques

Add-on codes 35685–35686 describe **adjuvant techniques**, which are additional procedures or techniques that may be required during a *lower extremity* bypass graft procedure. They are performed to improve the **patency** (open and unblocked status of a blood vessel or another tube in the body) of *lower extremity* synthetic or autogenous arterial bypass grafts.

Coding Tip:

Report code 35682 or 35683 when more than one vein segment is documented as harvested.

- Add-on code 35685 is reported when a venous patch or cuff is anastomosed between the synthetic bypass and the involved artery.

- Add-on code 35686 is reported when an autogenous vein is used to create a fistula (passageway) during lower extremity bypass graft surgery.

EXAMPLE 1: Patient underwent right popliteal-tibial bypass grafting with Gore-Tex synthetic graft material. Adjuvant distal vein cuff (DVC) of the popliteal-tibial bypass graft was performed during the same operative session. Report codes 35671-RT and 35685-RT. (Do not report modifier -51 with code 35685.)

EXAMPLE 2: Patient underwent left femoral-popliteal bypass grafting with polytetrafluoroethylene synthetic material. Adjuvant distal arteriovenous fistula (DAVF) of the femoral-popliteal graft was performed during the same operative session. Report codes 35656-LT and 35686-LT. (Do not report modifier -51 with code 35686.)

Arterial Transposition

Arterial transposition and/or reimplantation procedures are performed to improve arterial blood flow. ⚠ Codes 35691–35697

 Coding Tip:

Add-on code 35697 is reported in addition to a code for the primary procedure. **Visceral arteries** supply blood to the intestines, liver, and spleen.

describe the pairs of arteries that are anastomosed to each other. For example, code 35691 is reported when the vertebral artery is anastomosed to the carotid artery (to improve arterial blood flow).

EXAMPLE 1: Patient underwent transposition surgery to anastomose the right vertebral artery to the right subclavian artery. Report code 35693.

EXAMPLE 2: Patient underwent bypass graft surgery of splenorenal artery, during which synthetic graft material was used. Replantation of splenic artery to infrarenal aortic prosthesis was performed during the same operative session to ensure adequate blood supply to the spleen. Report codes 35636 and 35697. (Do not add modifier -51 to code 35697.)

Excision, Exploration, Repair, Revision

When assigning CPT codes to excision, exploration, repair, and revision procedures

- Code 35700 is reported when a patient returns to the operating room more than one month after an original procedure on the femoral-popliteal or femoral (popliteal)-anterior tibial, posterior tibial, or peroneal artery or other distal vessels.

- Codes 35701–35761 are reported when a patient undergoes exploration (*not followed by surgical repair*) of the carotid, femoral, or popliteal arteries or other vessels.

- ⚠ Codes 35800–35860 are reported when a patient returns to the operating room for exploration and control of postoperative hemorrhage and/or treatment of thrombosis or infection.

- Code 35870 is reported for repair of graft-enteric fistula. An aortic graft-enteric fistula is a complication of aortic reconstruction surgery; repair includes graft excision with extra-anatomic bypass.

- Codes 35875–35876 are reported when a patient undergoes thrombectomy of arterial or venous graft and/or revision of arterial or venous graft.

- Codes 35879–35884 are reported for revision of bypass grafts.

- Codes 35901–35907 are reported for excision of infected grafts.

Coding Tip:

- Codes 35800–35860 are *not* reported when bleeding occurs during the initial operation.

- Add modifier -78 to codes 35800–35860 when the service provided represents a return to the operating room for a related procedure during the post-operative period.

EXAMPLE: Patient underwent exploration for suspected postoperative hemorrhage, chest. Five days ago patient underwent CABG surgery. Report 35820-78.

Vascular Injection Procedures

Vascular injection procedure codes describe common procedures performed to gain venous access for phlebotomy, prophylactic intravenous access, infusion therapy, chemotherapy, and drug administration. They are reported for

- Diagnostic catheterization (e.g., injecting contrast media into vasculature for radiologic imaging)

- Therapeutic (interventional) catheterization (e.g., balloon dilation or stent placement to open narrowed valves and vessels)

Note:

When you look up "Vascular Injections" in the CPT index, you'll notice that code 36299 for "Unlisted Services and Procedures" is the only entry. There is also no index entry for "Injection, Vascular" in the CPT index. (Some codes are listed for the "Catheter" entry in the CPT index.) Thus, coders must become familiar with codes and descriptions in the Vascular Injection Procedures heading (and subheadings) of CPT.

CPT also classifies cardiovascular procedures in multiple locations. For example, vascular ultrasound procedures for noncoronary vessels are classified in the Cardiovascular Surgery section, but vascular ultrasound procedures for coronary vessels and cardiac catheterizations are located in the Medicine section.

Vascular injection procedures include the following services, which are not coded and reported separately:

- Injection of contrast media, with or without automatic power injection

 Note:

Although the injection procedure is not reported separately, an HCPCS level II code for provision of contrast media is reported separately.

- Introduction of needles or catheters

 Note:

Although the introduction of a needle or catheter is not reported separately, a CPT code for selective vascular catheterization is reported separately.

- Necessary local anesthesia

- Necessary pre- and postinjection care specifically related to the injection procedure

The following supplies are reported with HCPCS level II codes if provided during a vascular injection procedure:

- Catheters

- Drugs

- Contrast media

Notes below the Vascular Injection Procedures subheading provide instruction about coding selective vascular catheterization. (Be sure to review previous content about selective vascular catheterization.)

⚠ Codes for vascular injection procedures include the following routes:

- Intravenous

- Intra-arterial–intra-aortic (including placement of shunts for dialysis)

- Venous

- Central venous access procedures

 Coding Tip:

- When two separate access procedures (e.g., punctures of two different vessels) are performed, report a separate code for each.

- When a nonselective vascular catheterization is converted to a selective vascular catheterization, report a code for the selective vascular catheterization only.

Vascular injection procedures include the introduction of the catheter or needle into a blood vessel and insertion into lesser- (first-) order vessels. ⚠ Then when the catheter is inserted as follows for the purpose of performing diagnostic and/or therapeutic procedures, the code(s) for selective vascular catheterization is reported:

- Second-, third- (and beyond) order vessels (e.g., popliteal angiogram)

- Aorta and first-, second-, third- (and beyond) vessels (e.g., carotid angiogram)

Intravenous vascular injection procedures ⚠ do not include codes for catheterization of third- (or beyond) order vessels. When higher-order vessels undergo venous catheterization procedures, report code 36012 for *each* second-order and third- (and beyond) order vessel.

EXAMPLE: Patient underwent left arm venogram. Catheter was introduced into the superior vena cava and inserted into the brachiocephalic vein and left subclavian vein. Catheter was manipulated into the left axillary vein, and contrast media was injected. Catheter was further advanced into the left brachial and left basilic veins, and contrast media was injected. Good visualization of the left axillary, brachial, and basilic veins was obtained. No deformities were noted. Report code 75820-LT for the left arm venogram. Report code 36011-51-LT for selective vascular catheterization of the left axillary vein. Report 36012-51-LT and 36012-51-LT for selective vascular catheterization of the left brachial and basilic veins, respectively.

CPT code 36200 is reported just once for "introduction of catheter, aorta" regardless of the number of times the catheter is repositioned in the aorta. When multiple vessels are accessed during catheterization, in different vascular families, report the code for the highest level of selectivity in each vascular family (36215–36217 and 36245–36248).

Venous procedures are coded according to the type of procedure, patient's age, and the puncture site (e.g., 2-year-old patient underwent scalp vein venipuncture, 36405). Make sure you carefully review the patient record and code descriptions to determine whether the procedure was a direct puncture or a cutdown and whether a physician's skill was required.

Therapeutic apheresis is the removal of blood components, cells, or plasma solute and the retransfusion of the remaining components into the patient. Procedure codes are based on blood components.

- White blood cells

- Red blood cells

- Platelets

- Plasmapheresis

- Extracorporeal immunoadsorption and plasma reinfusion

- Extracorporeal selective adsorption or selective filtration and plasma reinfusion

Central Venous Access Procedures

Central venous access procedures include insertion, repair, partial replacement, complete replacement, and/or removal of the catheter or device. The CPT coding manual contains the central venous access procedures table, which provides direction for assignment of proper codes. A venous access device is inserted

- Centrally (e.g., femoral, jugular, or subclavian vein or inferior vena cava)

- Peripherally (e.g., basilic or cephalic vein)

Coding Tip:

Codes for cardiac catheterization are assigned from the Medicine section of CPT.

Coding Tip:

When a catheter is removed from a vessel, do not report a separate code for that procedure. However, when implantable venous access devices and/or subcutaneous reservoirs are removed, report an appropriate code (e.g., code 36589).

A CVC or a central venous access device (CVAD) is used to deliver intravenous fluids and medications and to obtain blood samples. These infusions may be administered for short or prolonged periods, using a single-lumen (allows for infusion of one solution) or multiple-lumen catheter (allows for infusion of several solutions simultaneously).

To be considered a central venous access catheter or device, the tip of the CVC or CVAD must terminate in the subclavian, brachiocephalic, or iliac veins; the superior or inferior vena cava; or the right atrium. (Otherwise, the catheter is considered a midline catheter, MLC.) The device is accessed for use (e.g., administration of medications or hyperalimentation) through a(n)

- Exposed catheter (external to the skin)
- Subcutaneous port
- Subcutaneous pump

CVAD codes are reported according to the patient's age and whether the device is nontunneled (not implanted) or tunneled (implanted).

Peripherally inserted CVADs include peripherally inserted central (venous) catheters (PICCs) and MLCs. The type of catheter inserted depends on the technique used, solutions infused, and duration of the intravenous therapy. Any catheter placed with the tip between the antecubital area and the head of the clavicle is called an MLC. Such placement is typically done for infusion therapy, which is expected to last from 1 to 8 weeks (when the catheter tip doesn't need to terminate in the superior vena cava). The PICC can also be shortened if it is needed for midline placement. It is usually inserted below the antecubital fossa and does not require use of a guidewire.

When reporting codes for central venous access procedures (Table 13-1), make sure you determine the following:

- Patient's age
- Whether the catheter was **tunneled** (implanted) or nontunneled
- Whether the procedure was done via

  ○ **Cutdown**: Catheter is inserted directly into a vein through an incision
  ○ **Peripherally**: Catheter is inserted into peripheral vein using a needle or trocar

Note:

Tunneled (implantable) venous access ports are typically used for long-term intravenous therapy, and they contain two parts: catheter and port.

Coding Tip:

When blood is collected from a partially or completely implantable venous access device, report code 36591.

Codes 36575–36590 are reported for procedures performed to repair, replace, and/or remove CVADs and CVCs. These codes do not require selection based on the patient's age or central/peripheral insertion site. However, they do distinguish between nontunneled (with exposed access) and tunneled catheters (require subcutaneous port/pump pocket and connection). They also require knowledge of whether a subcutaneous port or pump was inserted. (Refer to Table 13-1 for a list of centrally inserted and peripherally inserted CVC and CVAD devices.)

Codes 36595–36596 are reported for the mechanical removal of obstructive material (e.g., blood clot) from a central venous device. Code 36597 requires fluoroscopic guidance to reposition a previously placed CVC. (Report code 76000 for fluoroscopic guidance.)

Table 13-1 Coding Central Venous Access Catheters and Devices

Code	Age	Nontunneled	Tunneled (Implanted)	Types of Venous Access Catheters and Devices	Venous Insertion Sites
36555 36556	< 5 ≥ 5	X X		Centrally inserted central venous catheter (CVC), such as • Cook • Leonard • Quinton • Shiley • Triple lumen	• Femoral vein • Inferior vena cava • Jugular vein • Subclavian vein
36557 36558	< 5 ≥ 5		X X	Centrally inserted CVC, without subcutaneous port or pump, such as • Ash Split • Broviac • Double lumen • Groshorg • Hickman • PermCath	• Femoral vein • Inferior vena cava • Jugular vein • Subclavian vein
36560 36561	< 5 ≥ 5		X X	Centrally inserted central venous access device (CVAD), with subcutaneous port, such as • Bard port • Infuse-a-Port • MediPort • Port-a-Cath • Q-Port	• Femoral vein • Inferior vena cava • Jugular vein • Subclavian vein
36563			X	Centrally inserted CVAD, with subcutaneous pump, such as • Chemotherapy pump • Infusion pump • Intravenous pump	• Femoral vein • Inferior vena cava • Jugular vein • Subclavian vein
36565			X	Centrally inserted CVAD requiring two catheters via two separate venous access sites, without subcutaneous port or pump, such as Tesio type catheter	• Femoral vein • Inferior vena cava • Jugular vein • Subclavian vein
36566			X	Centrally inserted CVAD requiring two catheters via two separate venous access sites, with subcutaneous port(s), such as Tesio type catheter, with port	• Femoral vein • Inferior vena cava • Jugular vein • Subclavian vein
36568 36569	< 5 ≥ 5			Peripherally inserted central venous catheter (PICC), without subcutaneous port or pump, such as • Abbott • Angiocath • Jelco • Triple lumen	Superficial veins in the arms, legs, feet, or head, such as • Basilic vein • Cephalic vein • Saphenous vein
36570 36571	< 5 ≥ 5			Peripherally inserted CVAD, with subcutaneous port, such as • Bard port • Infuse-a-Port • Medi-Port • Port-a-Cath • Q-Port	Superficial veins in the arms, legs, feet, or head, such as • Basilic vein • Cephalic vein • Saphenous vein

Arterial

Arterial blood gases (e.g., arterial blood oxygen, carbon dioxide, and bicarbonate levels) are commonly performed to diagnose the patient's effectiveness of respiration. To report an arterial puncture for the purpose of obtaining a sample for arterial blood gas analysis, report code 36600. During an arterial puncture, a needle is inserted into the artery to obtain a sample of blood; a catheter is *not* inserted into the artery.

 Coding Tip:

- When mechanical removal of obstructive material code 36595 or 36596 is reported, report code 75901 or 75902 for radiological supervision and interpretation, respectively. A venous catheterization code (36010–36012) is also reported when performed.

- When a CVC is repositioned, report code 36597 with the appropriate Radiology code.

☞ Code 36620 is reported when a catheter or cannula is inserted into the artery *percutaneously* for blood sampling, monitoring, infusion, or transfusion. Once the procedure is complete, the catheter or cannula is removed. Code 36625 is reported when the physician performs a *cutdown* procedure to access the artery, inserts a catheter or cannula, sutures the artery, and closes the incision in layers.

 Note:

A heparin flush is performed to maintain patency of the catheter/port and to reduce the risk of blood clotting in the catheter. When a heparin flush is performed as a part of an injection or infusion procedure, it is not separately coded.

Intraosseous

Code 36680 is reported when the physician inserts a special needle to puncture the bone marrow cavity (e.g., tibia or femur) to infuse fluids into bone marrow blood vessels.

Hemodialysis Access, Intervascular Cannulation for Extracorporeal Circulation, or Shunt Insertion

Codes 36800–36861 describe the following procedures:

- Arteriovenous anastomosis, direct

- Insertion of cannulas for prolonged extracorporeal circulation of membrane oxygenation (ECMO)

- Arteriovenous fistula

  Arteriovenous hemodialysis access is created by using autogenous venous tissue or inserting a prosthetic graft.

  EXAMPLE 1: Patient underwent forearm vein transposition between the elbow and the wrist. Report code 36820.

  EXAMPLE 2: Patient underwent open arteriovenous anastomosis of the right cephalic vein. (The cephalic vein is located in the upper arm.) Report code 36818-RT.

  EXAMPLE 3: Patient underwent open arteriovenous anastomosis via left basilic vein transposition. (The basilic vein is in the upper arm.) Report code 36819-LT.

Dialysis Circuit

Codes 36901 through 36909 are reported for dialysis circuit procedures and services. Hemodialysis treatment involves circulating arteriovenous (AV) blood outside of the body through the *dialysis circuit*, which is created using an arterial-venous anastomosis (called an AV fistula) or by placing a prosthetic graft between an artery and vein (called an AV graft). The dialysis circuit is designed for easy and repetitive access, and it contains two segments, the peripheral dialysis segment and the central dialysis segment.

> **EXAMPLE:** Patient underwent percutaneous mechanical thrombectomy with infusion for thrombolysis. Report code 36904.

Portal Decompression Procedures

Codes 37140–37183 are reported for the insertion and revision of transvenous intrahepatic portosystemic shunt (TIPS) procedures. A TIPS is inserted to reduce portal pressure associated with portal hypertension. Portal blood flow is diverted into the hepatic vein, which reduces pressure between the portal and systemic circulations.

> **EXAMPLE:** Patient underwent insertion of TIPS. Report code 37182.

Coding Tip:

Codes 37182 and 37183 include radiological supervision and interpretation (e.g., portography and all associated imaging guidance and documentation). Therefore, do not report codes 75885 and 75887 with codes 37182 and 37183.

Transcatheter Procedures

The Transcather Procedures subheading contains notes that provide instruction to report codes separately for catheter placement and radiological supervision and interpretation. When transcatheter therapy services are provided, the introduction of the needle and catheter are included in the code for the primary service.

> **EXAMPLE 1:** Patient underwent open transluminal stent placement of the right femoral artery for revascularization with atherectomy and angioplasty of the same vessel. The catheter was introduced into the right femoral artery (second-order artery), and contrast medium was injected. Femoral magnetic resonance angiogram was performed and revealed blockage of the femoral artery. Repeat femoral magnetic resonance angiogram (Figure 13-12), after stent placement, revealed good arterial circulation in the femoral artery. Report codes 37227-RT, 36246-RT, and 73725-RT.

> **EXAMPLE 2:** Patient underwent cerebral thrombolysis as therapy for acute ischemic stroke. Report code 37195.

Endovascular Revascularization (Open or Percutaneous, Transcatheter)

Endovascular revascularization procedures are performed for lower extremity occlusive disease, and include open, percutaneous, and transcatheter methods. The CPT codes are inclusive of all services provided for the vessel treated, and codes from one vascular family are reported for the purpose of revascularization.

- *Iliac Vascular Territory*, which is subdivided into the common iliac, internal iliac, and external iliac arteries

- *Femoral/Popliteal Vascular Territory*, which includes the femoral and popliteal arteries in one extremity

- *Tibial/Peroneal Vascular Territory*, which includes the anterior tibial, posterior tibial, and peroneal arteries

> **EXAMPLE:** Patient underwent percutaneous transluminal angioplasty (PTCA) (Figure 13-13) for endovascular revascularization of the right common iliac, right internal iliac, and right external iliac arteries. Report codes 37220, 37222, 37222. (Code 37220 is the primary endovascular revascularization code, and code 37222 is reported twice for endovascular revascularization of the two additional arteries. Code 37222 is an add-on code and, thus, exempt from modifier -51.)

Vascular Embolization and Occlusion

Vascular Embolization and Occlusion codes classify vascular embolization and occlusion procedures, including arteries, veins, and lymphatics. (This subheading excludes codes for such procedures performed on the central nervous system and the head and neck.)

Figure 13-12 Femoral angiogram. The use of contrast medium makes arteries visible.

Figure 13-13 Percutaneous transluminal coronary (balloon) angioplasty (PTCA)

EXAMPLE: Patient underwent venous vascular embolization, including radiological supervision and interpretation, intraprocedural roadmapping, and imaging guidance necessary to control venous hemorrhage. Report code 37244.

Intravascular Ultrasound Services

Intravascular ultrasound services (IVUS) of noncoronary vessels are performed during diagnostic evaluation and/or therapeutic intervention. These codes are reported in addition to a code for the primary procedure.

EXAMPLE: Patient undergoes percutaneous thrombectomy of an arteriovenous fistula, autogenous graft, with intravascular ultrasound service. Report codes 36904 and 37252.

Endoscopy

CPT codes 37500–37501 describe vascular endoscopy procedures, and surgical vascular endoscopy always includes diagnostic endoscopy.

EXAMPLE: Patient underwent surgical vascular endoscopy with ligation of subfascial perforator veins. Report code 37500.

Ligation

Ligation of arteries and veins is performed to control bleeding of a ruptured or dissected (torn) artery/vein.

CPT codes 37700–37735 describe ligation, division, and stripping of the saphenous veins. These procedures are different from the stab phlebectomy procedure described in codes 37765 and 37766. For a **stab phlebectomy**, multiple tiny incisions are made over varicose vein sites. At each stab site, the varicosity is extracted and then the varicose segment is removed. (The stab phlebectomy procedure is not typically performed on saphenous veins.)

Code 37760 describes the subfascial ligation of incompetent perforator veins (e.g., connecting superficial veins located below the skin's surface to deep veins in the leg muscle). Perforator vein ligation may also be performed endoscopically, which is reported with code 37500.

Code 37780 describes the ligation and division of the short saphenous vein at the saphenopopliteal junction. An incision is made in the skin overlying the short saphenous vein at its junction with the saphenopopliteal vein at the knee. Vessels are dissected and ties are placed around the short saphenous vein, which is divided between the ties.

Code 37785 describes the ligation, division, and/or excision of varicose vein "clusters." These are large varicose veins that cannot be effectively treated using the stab phlebectomy technique because they require a larger incision. An open surgical dissection of the vein cluster is made using long incisions rather than short stab incisions.

Other Procedures

Other Procedures codes classify penile revascularization, penile venous occlusive procedures, and unlisted procedures involving vascular surgery.

EXAMPLE: Patient underwent penile venous occlusive procedure. Report code 37790.

Exercise 13.2 – Arteries and Veins

Instructions: Assign the CPT code(s) and appropriate modifier(s) to each statement.

1. On the initial treatment day, the physician performed transcatheter therapy, which included arterial infusion for thrombolysis of the inferior vena cava. Radiological supervision and interpretation were included.

   _____

2. A physician performs a right upper extremity arteriogram. Catheter is inserted into the right brachial artery.

Exercise 13.2 (*continued*)

3. Physician uses a transfemoral approach to advance a catheter to the ascending aorta, where nonradioactive contrast media is injected and the descending thoracic aortography and abdominal aortography are performed.

4. Physician punctures the subclavian vein of a 4-year-old, passes a guidewire centrally, and inserts a central venous catheter (nontunneled).

5. Patient underwent left renal venogram, which required introduction of a catheter into the inferior vena cava, insertion into the left renal vein, and manipulation into the left suprarenal vein. Contrast media was injected into both veins, and the structures were well visualized. No obstruction or other deformity was noted.

Hemic and Lymphatic Systems Subsection

The Hemic and Lymphatic Systems subsection headings include the following:

- Spleen
- General
- Transplantation and Post-Transplantation Cellular Infusions
- Lymph Nodes and Lymphatic Channels

The Hemic and Lymphatic Systems subsection contains codes that describe procedures on the spleen, bone marrow transplantation services, the lymph nodes and lymph channels, the mediastinum, and the diaphragm. The **hemic system** is a blood-producing system. **Blood** is tissue that consists of plasma, red blood cells, white blood cells, and platelets (or thrombocytes). The **lymphatic system** (Figure 13-14) consists of the spleen, thymus, tonsils, adenoids, vessels that carry lymph, and lymph nodes. The **spleen** (Figure 13-15) produces mature lymphocytes, destroys worn out red blood cells, and serves as a reservoir for blood. The **thymus** produces T lymphocytes, which are important to the body's immune function. The **tonsils** are located at the back of the throat, and they contain lymphoid tissue that helps fight infections. The **adenoids** are located at the rear of the nose, and they contain lymphoid tissue that helps fight infections. **Lymph** is a clear fluid that contains **chyle** (digestive fluid that contains proteins and fats), some red blood cells, and lymphocytes, which help fight infection and disease. **Lymph nodes** are clusters of bean-shaped nodules that act as the body's filtration system, removing cell waste and excess fluid and helping to fight infection. They are located in the

- Back of the head, just above the hairline (occipital region)
- Neck (cervical region)
- Armpits (axillary region)
- Elbow (cubital region)
- Chest (supraclavicular region)

- Abdomen (retroperitoneal region)
- Groin (inguinal region)
- Knee (popliteal region)

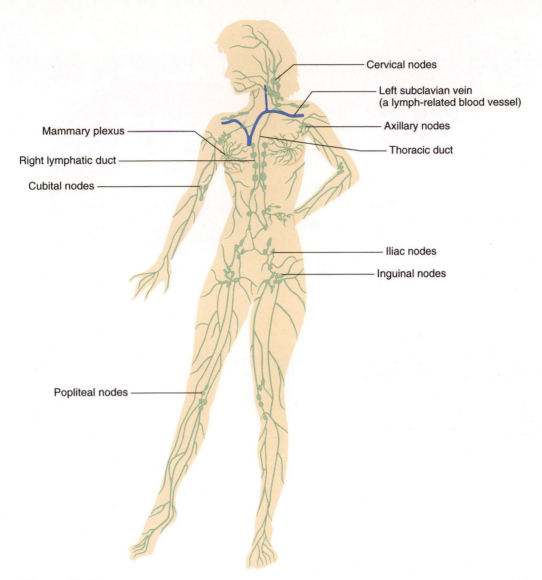

Figure 13-14 Lymphatic circulation and major lymph node locations

Spleen

Codes 38100–38115 are reported for the excision or repair of the spleen. (In code 38102, **_en bloc_** means "as a whole.") Codes 38120–38129 are reported for laparoscopic procedures performed on the spleen. A note below the Laparoscopy subheading provides instruction that "surgical laparoscopy always includes diagnostic laparoscopy." This means that when the physician performs diagnostic and surgical laparoscopies during the same operative session, just the code for surgical laparoscopy is reported. When the physician performs a diagnostic laparoscopy as a separate procedure, report 49320 as an additional code.

> **EXAMPLE:** Patient underwent diagnostic laparoscopy followed by open repair of ruptured spleen with partial splenectomy. Report codes 38115 and 49320.

⚠ Code 38200 is reported when a needle is inserted percutaneously and contrast media is injected into the spleen for direct **splenoportography**, which is the radiographic visualization of the splenic and portal veins.

 Coding Tip:

When reporting code 38200, make sure you report the code for radiological supervision and interpretation (75810).

Figure 13-15 The spleen performs many important functions related to the immune system.

EXAMPLE: Patient underwent splenoportography, with percutaneous injection of contrast medium into the spleen. Report codes 75810 and 38200.

General

The General heading includes the Bone Marrow or Stem Cell Services/Procedures subheading. **Bone marrow** is spongy material that fills large bones' cavities and consists of two types.

- *Red marrow:* Produces red blood cells, white blood cells, and platelets
- *Yellow marrow:* Replaces red marrow with fatty tissue that does not produce blood cells

Bone marrow contains two types of **stem cells**.

- *Hemopoietic:* Produce red blood cells, white blood cells, and platelets
- *Stromal:* Produce fat, cartilage, and bone and have the ability to differentiate into many kinds of tissue, such as nervous tissue

Codes are reported for the harvesting, aspiration, biopsy, and transplantation of bone marrow and/or stem cells. Codes are also reported for the steps involved in the preservation, preparation, and purification of bone marrow and stem cells prior to transplantation or reinfusion. Codes 38205–38206 are reported when stem cells are harvested from a suitable donor (allogeneic) or the patient's bone marrow (autologous).

A **bone marrow aspiration** uses a needle to remove a sample of the liquid bone marrow for examination under a microscope. A **bone marrow biopsy** involves boring a small hole into a long bone (e.g., hip) and using a large, hollow needle to remove bone marrow for examination under a microscope. When bone marrow aspiration and bone marrow biopsy procedures are performed at the same site through the same skin incision (during the same operative session), report just bone marrow biopsy code 38221. When the procedures are performed at separate sites (e.g., different bones or separate skins incisions in the same bone), report codes 38220 and 38221-59.

EXAMPLE: Progenitor cells (stem cells) were harvested from an umbilical cord after delivery, and they were cryopreserved and kept for transplantation to the neonate later in life or to other recipients. This process required transplantation preparation of hematopoietic progenitor cells included cryopreservation and storage. Report code 38207.

Transplantation and Post-Transplantation Cellular Infusions

Hematopoietic cell transplantation (HCT) is the autologous or allogeneic infusion of hematopoietic progenitor cells (HPC) obtained from bone marrow, peripheral blood apheresis, or umbilical cord blood. Codes 38240–38241 are reported for allogeneic, autologous, or HPC boost transplantations to restore bone marrow stem cells. Code 38242 is reported for allogeneic lymphocyte infusions, often used to treat chronic myelogenous leukemia.

> **EXAMPLE:** Hematopoietic cells previously obtained from the patient's bone marrow were implanted because the recipient's immune system had been suppressed using radiation. The autologous harvested cells are injected into the recipient by intravenous drip therapy in a sterile environment. Report code 38241.

Lymph Nodes and Lymphatic Channels

Capillaries surround cells but are not actually connected to cells, which results in the leakage of watery blood plasma (containing oxygen, proteins, glucose, and white blood cells) or lymph (Figure 13-16). This lymph (fluid) is recirculated away from the body's cells in the lymphatic circulatory system, which contains lymphatic channels, called capillaries and lymphatic vessels. The lymph eventually reaches one of about one hundred lymph nodes located throughout the body, which filter the fluid. (Lymph nodes contain white blood cells that filter debris and foreign cells from lymph.) When a patient becomes infected (e.g., bacteria or virus), the number of white blood cells in lymph nodes increases to billions. The lymph nodes work to fight the infection and release the filtered lymph (fluid) back into the bloodstream. Sometimes lymph nodes become infected or abscessed and require surgical treatment.

> **EXAMPLE:** A patient is diagnosed with cervical lymphadenitis and undergoes incision and drainage. The surgeon makes a skin incision overlying the abscessed cervical lymph node, a needle with a syringe attached is inserted into the lymph node, and the abscess is drained. The wound is closed with Steri-Strips. Report code 38300.

Codes 38562–38564 describe the limited excision of lymph nodes for **cancer staging**, which is the determination that cancer has or has not spread anatomically from its point of origin. Codes 38700–38780 describe the complete removal of the lymph nodes, and surgical wound closure is often performed in layers.

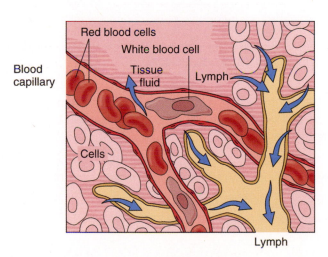

Figure 13-16 Lymph circulation showing interaction with blood vessels and cells

Exercise 13.3 – Hemic and Lymphatic

Instructions: Assign the CPT code(s) and appropriate modifier(s) to each statement.

1. Patient underwent bilateral total pelvic lymphadenectomy via laparoscope with multiple periaortic lymph node samplings.

   _____

2. Physician conducted a donor search to locate a suitable match for a transplant patient and arranged acquisition of cells.

   _____

3. Physician infused a patient with allogeneic lymphocytes.

   _____

4. Previously frozen stem cells were thawed, without washing.

   _____

5. Bone marrow biopsy, sternum, using trocar.

   _____

6. Progenitor cells (allogeneic) were harvested from umbilical and placental blood, cryopreserved, and maintained for transplantation.

   _____

7. Physician made a subcostal incision, dissected tissue surrounding the spleen, doubly ligated the vessels, and removed the spleen.

   _____

8. Physician sutured lacerations in a ruptured spleen and then resected and removed a damaged segment of the spleen.

   _____

9. Physician inserted a catheter into the spleen and injected 20 cubic centimeters of radiopaque dye for splenoportography.

   _____

10. Physician performed a total splenectomy.

    _____

11. A patient with idiopathic thrombocytopenic purpura underwent a laparoscopic splenectomy.

    _____

12. Patient underwent suprahyoid lymphadenectomy.

    _____

13. Patient underwent glossectomy with a composite resection on the left side of the neck with mandibular resection and radical neck dissection (Commando), and a modified radical neck dissection on the right side.

    _____

14. Patient underwent total laryngectomy with bilateral radical neck dissection.

    _____

15. Patient underwent injection of dye to visualize the sentinel node during lymphangiography nuclear imaging test.

    _____

Summary

The Cardiovascular System subsection classifies procedures performed on the heart and pericardium, valves (e.g., mitral and semilunar), and peripheral vascular vessels (e.g., arteries, veins, and capillaries). Cardiovascular System subsection codes are arranged anatomically and then according to procedure performed.

The Hemic and Lymphatic Systems subsection classifies procedures performed on the spleen, lymph nodes, and lymphatic channels.

Internet Links

CTSNet (Cardiothoracic Surgery Network): *www.ctsnet.org*

Medcomp (dialysis and vascular access catheters): *www.medcompnet.com*

Peripheral Vascular Surgery Society: Go to *www.vesurgery.org*, hover over "Patients," and click on the Frequently Asked Questions link.

The Gross Physiology of the Cardiovascular System: *www.cardiac-output.info*

Study Checklist

❑ Read this chapter and highlight key concepts.

❑ Create an index card for each key term.

❑ Access the chapter Internet links to learn more about concepts.

❑ Complete the chapter exercises and review, verifying answers with your instructor.

❑ Complete Workbook chapter, verifying answers with your instructor.

❑ Go to *www.cengagebrain.com* to access the Student Companion Web Site. Login instructions are located in the Preface.

❑ Form a study group with classmates to discuss chapter concepts in preparation for an exam.

Review

Multiple Choice

Instructions: Circle the most appropriate response.

1. When coding cardiovascular system procedures, from which section(s) of CPT are additional procedure codes often reported?
   - **a.** E/M
   - **b.** Anesthesia
   - **c.** Pathology/Laboratory
   - **d.** Radiology, Medicine

2. When reporting codes 33880 and 33881 for endovascular repair of the descending thoracic aorta, which is included?
   - **a.** Placement of all extensions in the distal thoracic aorta
   - **b.** Placement of proximal extensions
   - **c.** Subclavian artery-to-carotid bypass
   - **d.** Subclavian carotid-to-carotid bypass

3. Codes 33500–33507, Coronary Artery Anomalies, include _____ when performed during the same operative session.
   a. arterial embolization
   b. coronary artery bypass grafting
   c. endarterectomy or angioplasty
   d. intravascular ultrasound

4. Review code 33282 (Implantation of a patient-activated cardiac event recorder). The parenthetical note below code 33282 provides instruction to assign codes 93285, 93291, 93298, or 93299 for:
   a. Holter monitor and external event recording.
   b. initial implantation, including programming.
   c. removal and reinsertion of a pacing cardioverter.
   d. subsequent electronic analysis and/or reprogramming.

5. When the "battery" of a pacemaker or implantable defibrillator is changed, it is actually the _____ that is changed.
   a. catheter
   b. electrode
   c. pacemaker
   d. pulse generator

6. An angioscopy (35400) is performed in addition to a transluminal balloon angioplasty of the renal artery during the same operative session. Which code(s) are reported?
   a. Transluminal balloon angioplasty of renal artery only
   b. Transluminal balloon angioplasty of renal artery and angioscopy
   c. Transluminal balloon angioplasty of renal artery, angioscopy, and injection of contrast medium
   d. Transluminal balloon angioplasty of renal artery, angioscopy, injection of contrast medium, and angiography

7. A coder reviews the patient record to determine the patient's age, whether the inserted catheter was tunneled or nontunneled, and whether the procedure was performed peripherally or via cutdown. Which procedure is being coded?
   a. Arteriovenous anastomosis
   b. Central venous access
   c. Portal decompression
   d. Therapeutic apheresis

8. Which is the removal of a fixed blood clot?
   a. Atherectomy
   b. Embolectomy
   c. Sympathectomy
   d. Thrombectomy

9. The two types of aneurysm repair are:
   a. arteriovenous and open.
   b. endocardial and endovascular.
   c. endovascular and direct.
   d. transluminal and direct.

10. *En bloc* means:
    a. closed and blocked status of incision.
    b. implanted.
    c. insertion directly into a vein through a blood vessel.
    d. surgical removal as a whole.

11. Excision of mediastinal cyst. Which CPT code is assigned?
    a. 39000
    b. 39010
    c. 39200
    d. 39220

12. Pericardiectomy with cardiopulmonary bypass. Which CPT code(s) are assigned?
    a. 33030, 33935
    b. 33030, 33935-51
    c. 33030, 33935-59
    d. 33031

13. Suture repair of aorta without shunt or cardiopulmonary bypass. Which CPT code is assigned?
    a. 33300
    b. 33320
    c. 33322
    d. 33330

14. 15-year-old patient admitted for repair of patent ductus arteriosus by division. Which CPT code is assigned?
    a. 33820
    b. 33822
    c. 33824
    d. 33840

15. Patient with cardiopulmonary insufficiency receives 72 hours of daily management of veno-venous extracorporeal life support (ECLS) provided by his physician. Which CPT code(s) are assigned?

    a. 33946

    b. 33946, 33948, 33948

    c. 33948, 33948, 33948

    d. 33949, 33949, 33949

16. Open biopsy of deep cervical nodes. Which CPT code is assigned?

    a. 38500   b. 38510   c. 38520   d. 38525

17. Patient underwent percutaneous thrombectomy of the arteriovenous fistula. Which CPT code is assigned?

    a. 36825   b. 36831   c. 36832   d. 36904

18. Percutaneous venous transluminal balloon angioplasty performed as a distinct procedural service. Which CPT code is assigned?

    a. 37248-59   b. 37248-79   c. 37236   d. 37236-59

19. Percutaneous transcatheter retrieval of intravascular foreign body. Which CPT code is assigned?

    a. 37184   b. 37187   c. 37195   d. 37197

20. Direct repair of a ruptured aneurysm of the abdominal aorta. Which CPT code is assigned?

    a. 33877   b. 34800   c. 35082   d. 35092

Coding Practice

Instructions: Assign the CPT code(s) and appropriate modifier(s) to each case.

1. A patient presents to the ambulatory surgery center for stripping of the long saphenous veins in the right leg and the long and short saphenous veins in the left leg. The long saphenous veins were stripped from the saphenofemoral junction to the knee.

   _____

2. A patient has a 3-year history of mitral regurgitation. The patient presents for mitral valve replacement. The procedure begins with placing the patient on heart-lung bypass machine. After gaining access to the thoracic cavity, the left atrium is identified. The damaged mitral valve is identified and removed. This is replaced with a biprosthetic valve and sewn in. Total time on bypass machine was 2.5 hours.

   _____

3. A patient presents for pacemaker insertion due to diagnosis of bradycardia. After intravenous sedation was obtained, the entire left chest and neck were prepped. A standard incision was made in the left deltopectoral groove. A small venotomy was made, and the ventricular and then the atrial leads were placed into position. These were tested and found to be functioning properly. The leads were anchored at exit sites from the vein attached to the pacemaker. The pacemaker was tested, was functioning, and was placed in the subcutaneous pocket. All connections are checked. The patient will have another check before discharge from the hospital tomorrow.

   _____

4. A 20-year-old male patient presents for surgical treatment of his patent ductus arteriosus (PDA). Under general anesthesia, a thoracotomy is done for access to the PDA. After the pericardium is opened to get to the mediastinum, the ductus is identified and closed via ligation.

   _____

5. A 2-year-old patient presents to the ED after having fallen in a lake, with a near drowning. The patient is in shock. Regular venous access methods have failed, and the emergency department attending physician decides to do a venous cutdown. After a transverse incision over the vein of the patient's ankle is made, a small stab incision is done distal to the first incision. Two sutures are placed around the vein. A cannula is passed though the incision of the vein. The skin is closed in layers with sutures.

_____

6. A 45-year-old patient diagnosed with chronic renal failure underwent surgery to facilitate dialysis access. The surgeon created an arteriovenous fistula by other than direct arteriovenous anastomosis with placement of nonautogenous graft access. The patient was prepped and draped in the usual fashion. Dissection was carried down the brachial artery and basilic vein. Prolene sutures were used to expose the vein. A thermoplastic graft was tunneled subcutaneously. The vein graft was sewn end to side. The graft was flushed with saline and then clamped below the anastomosis. The proximal graft at the 4-mm end was beveled and sewn to the small caliber brachial artery. Anastomosis was secured, and the native artery was flushed up through the graft first. All wounds were closed with Vicryl and nylon sutures.

_____

7. A 57-year-old patient was found to have carotid stenosis after duplex scan and angiogram. The patient presents today for a left carotid thromboendarterectomy with patch angioplasty. The neck area of the patient was prepped. An oblique incision along the sternomastoid muscle was made. Dissection was done through the platysma to the carotid sheath. The hypoglossal and vagus nerves were identified during dissection and preserved with care. The sheath dissection was performed along the anterior border of the left internal jugular vein. The common, external, and internal carotid arteries were dissected. The patient was given heparin, and clamping of the internal carotid did not reveal any changes on EEG monitor. The common and external carotids were clamped. A longitudinal arteriotomy was made. Standard thromboendarterectomy was performed, transecting the proximal end and working distally. The arteriotomy was closed with a patch cut to an ellipse and parachuted into the distal apex. The external and common carotids were opened. There was a good signal in the arteries. No changes were noted on the EEG. The wound was irrigated and closed.

_____

8. The patient had an implantable pacing cardioverter-defibrillator (ICD) placed 6 months ago. The patient now has a malfunction of this device. After adequate anesthesia, an incision was made and the electrodes were removed from the generator. There was a screw problem with the generator that was producing a noise. The leads were tested and found to be working satisfactorily. The original implantable defibrillator pulse generator was removed and then replaced with an implantable defibrillator pulse generator. Both generators were a dual lead system. The ICD was placed back in the pocket, and the wound was closed after irrigation with 3-0 and 4-0 Vicryl.

_____

9. A 35-year-old female patient has been found to have a pericardial cyst via echocardiogram. After adequate anesthesia, a lateral thoracotomy is performed to gain access to the pericardium. The patient's heart is stopped via cardioplegia infused through a heart-lung bypass machine. The pericardial cyst is seen lying next to the diaphragm. It is removed in total. Drainage tubes are placed. The cardioplegia is reversed. The cyst will be sent to pathology for analysis. The wound is closed in layers with Prolene and Vicryl.

_____

10. A patient presents with a history of atherosclerosis. The patient is having surgery to bypass his blocked heart arteries. After anesthesia is administered and the patient is placed on a heart bypass machine, the surgeon makes a thoracic incision. The blockage of the heart is identified. The physician harvests the saphenous vein from the patient's leg to use in the bypass. An opening is made in the aorta. The grafted vein is sutured to the opening in the aorta at one end and below the blockage at the other end.

   _____

11. A patient with a history of pancytopenia presents for a bone marrow biopsy. The physician numbs the skin and inserts a needle into the iliac bone. The core of the needle is discharged, and the sample is placed. The needle is withdrawn. The sample is sent for analysis.

   _____

12. A 14-year-old patient was in a motor vehicle crash and suffered blunt abdominal trauma. Due to internal bleeding and a ruptured spleen, the patient requires a splenectomy. After making the initial abdominal incision, the physician identifies the spleen. Splenic blood vessels are tied off. The spleen is removed in total. The remainder of the abdominal cavity is examined for any injuries or bleeding. No injury or additional bleeding is found. The wound is closed in layers.

   _____

13. A 3-year-old patient with a cystic hygroma of the neck presents for dissection. An incision is made in the neck. The tissue surrounding the hygroma is removed via excision. The hygroma is deep in the neurovascular section of the neck. Extensive and deep dissection is required for complete removal. The cyst is accessed and removed. The skin is closed in multiple layers.

   _____

14. A patient underwent pelvic lymphadenectomy, which included removal of all external iliac, hypogastric, and obturator nodes. The patient has a history of ureteral cancer and now has pelvic pain and swelling. The patient is placed in the supine position. An incision is made over the iliac crest. Blood vessels are identified, and bleeders are cauterized. Enlarged pelvic lymph nodes are identified and removed in total. These are sent to pathology. The wound is closed with sutures.

   _____

15. A patient presents for a cervical node removal. The patient's left neck area is prepped and draped in the usual fashion. An incision is made to access the cervical node. A scalene fat pad is identified and removed to access the deeper node. Both the cervical node and the pad are sent to pathology for analysis. The wound is closed in layers.

   _____

16. A patient suffered a fall from 20 feet. The patient has internal bleeding and has consented for a laparoscopic procedure to identify internal structures that may be causing hemorrhage. The patient is placed in the normal lateral decubitus position. A trocar is placed above the umbilical region through an incision. Gas is introduced into the abdominal cavity. Laparoscopic examination identifies damage to the patient's spleen. An additional two incisions are made to insert trocars for the procedure. The spleen is dissected with hemostasis achieved. The spleen is removed via pouch method through the trocar. The three incision sites are closed with sutures.

   _____

17. The patient presents for lymphangiography of the right pelvic lymph nodes. The radiologist accesses the patient's vein and puts dye in to highlight subcutaneous tissues. A lymph vessel is identified. A small incision is made to allow for the introduction of a needle and catheter. More dye is injected into

this vessel. The needle and catheter are secured with a suture. The first set of films is done. The second set of films is done on the next day. After the second set of films, the radiologist removes the catheter and sutures the incision site closed.

_____

18. A patient with a history of chyle in the pleural cavity presents for suturing of his thoracic duct. Via an abdominal incision, the duct is identified and tied off. The incision is closed in layers with sutures.

_____

19. A patient with leukemia requires a bone marrow donor. The physician contacts the national bone marrow donor registry and provides medical information on the patient. The physician receives two potential matches.

_____

20. A patient has an enlarged lymph node of the axillary region. The physician makes an incision over the lymph node area after adequate local anesthesia. The node is identified and found to be inflamed; drainage of the node yields a pustulant material. The area is thoroughly irrigated, and the incision wound is closed with 4-0 Prolene sutures.

_____

CPT Surgery IV

Chapter Outline

Mediastinum and Diaphragm Subsection
Digestive System Subsection

Urinary System Subsection

Chapter Objectives

At the conclusion of this chapter, the student should be able to:

- Define key terms.
- Explain the organization, format, and content of the CPT Mediastinum and Diaphragm, Digestive System, and Urinary System subsections.
- Interpret CPT surgery coding notes for the Mediastinum and Diaphragm, Digestive System, and the Urinary System subsections.
- Assign CPT surgery codes from the Mediastinum and Diaphragm, Digestive System, and Urinary System subsections.
- Add CPT and/or HCPCS level II modifiers to codes, as appropriate.

Key Terms

anoscopy

biliary system

bipolar cautery

cheiloplasty

cholecystectomy

closed laparoscopy

cold biopsy forceps

colectomy

colonoscopy

colostomy

complex fistulectomy

continent ileostomy

cystometrogram

cystoscopy

cystourethroscopy

diagnostic endoscopy

diaphragm

digestive system

diverticula

diverticulosis

electrocautery snare

endorectal pull-through

endoscopic retrograde cholangiopancreatography (ERCP)

enterectomy

enterolysis

esophageal varices

esophagogastroduodenoscopy (EGD)

esophagogastroscopy

esophagoscopy

gastrectomy

hepatotomy

hernia

hot biopsy forceps

hypopharynx

ileoanal anastomosis

ileostomy

J-pouch

kidney

Kock pouch

laparoscopy

laser technique

laser-assisted uvulopalatoplasty

lithotripsy

Meckel's diverticulum

mediastinum

mucocutaneous margin

nasopharynx

nephrectomy

Nissen fundoplasty

open laparoscopy

oropharynx

ostomy

palatopharyngoplasty

percutaneous lithotomy

peristalsis

peritoneoscopy

proctectomy

proctosigmoidoscopy

pull-through

rhinoplasty

second-stage fistulectomy/ fistulotomy

seton

sigmoidoscopy

stoma

subcutaneous fistulectomy

submuscular fistulectomy

surgical endoscopy

transurethral resection of the prostate (TURP)

transurethral ureteroscopic lithotripsy

upper GI endoscopy

ureter

ureterolithotomy

urethra

urethroplasty

urinary bladder

urinary system

uroflowmetry

volvulus

Whipple procedure

Introduction

The Mediastinum and Diaphragm subsection classifies procedures performed on the mediastinum and diaphragm. The Digestive System subsection classifies procedures performed on gastrointestinal (GI) tract organs as well as the teeth, palate and uvula, adenoids and tonsils, Meckel's diverticulum and mesentery, appendix, biliary tract, pancreas, abdomen, peritoneum, and omentum. The Urinary System subsection classifies procedures performed on the kidneys, ureters, bladder, and urethra.

CPT guidelines that apply to the subsections are located at the beginning of the Surgery section. Unique coding instructions for the Mediastinum and Diaphragm, Digestive System, and Urinary System subsections are located in notes below headings or codes.

Coding Tip:

Notes located beneath headings and/or subheadings apply to all codes in the heading or subheading. Parenthetical notes that are located below a specific code apply to that code only, unless the note indicates otherwise.

 Note:

The Other Procedures code below each subheading classifies an unlisted procedure performed on the anatomical site. When reporting an unlisted procedure code, include documentation about the procedure performed with the submitted claim. (Other Procedures subheadings are not included throughout Chapter 14 of this textbook except when codes that describe additional procedures are included.)

Mediastinum and Diaphragm Subsection

Mediastinum and Diaphragm subsection headings include the following:

- Mediastinum
- Diaphragm

The **mediastinum** is the space in the thoracic cavity between the lungs that contains the aorta, the esophagus, the heart, and other structures. Codes 39000–39499 are reported for procedures performed on the mediastinum.

The **diaphragm** is the thin muscle below the heart and lungs that separates the chest from the abdomen. It functions in respiration by contracting during inspiration, which means that the size of the chest cavity expands when a person is breathing in. Codes 39501–39599 are reported for procedures performed on the diaphragm (e.g., laceration).

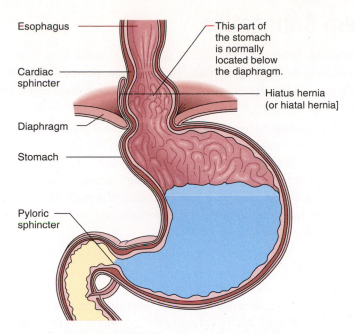

Figure 14-1 In a hiatus hernia (or hiatal hernia), part of the stomach protrudes through the esophageal opening in the diaphragm.

The repair of two types of hernias is coded from the Mediastinum and Diaphragm heading.

- Hiatus hernia (Figure 14-1)

- Diaphragmatic hernia

    EXAMPLE 1: Patient underwent resection of mediastinal cyst. Report code 39200.

    EXAMPLE 2: Patient underwent resection of the diaphragm, with simple repair. Report code 39560.

Exercise 14.1 – Mediastinum and Diaphragm

Instructions: Assign the CPT code(s) and appropriate modifier(s) to each statement.

1. The physician performed a complex repair during resection of the diaphragm and closed the residual defect with synthetic graft material.

    _____

2. Mediastinotomy to remove foreign body using transthoracic approach, including median sternotomy.

    _____

3. Patient underwent repair, laceration of diaphragm.

    _____

4. Physician inserted a medastinoscope through an incision in the sternal notch and performed a mediastinal lymph node biopsy.

    _____

5. Physician repaired an acute traumatic diaphragmatic hernia.

    _____

Digestive System Subsection

The **digestive system** (Figure 14-2) begins at the mouth and extends to the anus. The upper digestive tract consists of the mouth, pharynx, esophagus, and stomach. The esophagus passes through the diaphragm and enters the stomach between its body and fundus. The stomach lies below the diaphragm and is composed of the fundus (upper portion under the diaphragm), body (middle), and antrum (lower).

The liver, gallbladder, and pancreas are digestive accessory organs that produce enzymes and substances that assist with digestion in the small intestine. The absorption of nutrients into the bloodstream occurs in the small intestine (Figure 14-3). The pyloric sphincter controls the passage of digested food from the stomach into the duodenum (first part of the small intestine). The small intestine also contains the jejunum and the ileum, where the ileocecal valve allows for the controlled passage of digested material into the large intestine. The last section of the digestive tract is called the large intestine (Figure 14-4). It includes the cecum, colon, rectum, and anus. The appendix, located off the large intestine, has no known function.

 Note:

When a lesion of the **mucocutaneous margin** (mucous membrane and skin) borders the digestive tract, it may appear that treatment (e.g., biopsy, destruction, or excision) requires the reporting of codes from multiple subsections of CPT to classify procedures performed. In fact, codes from just *one* of the following CPT subsections are reported:

- Integumentary system
- Digestive system

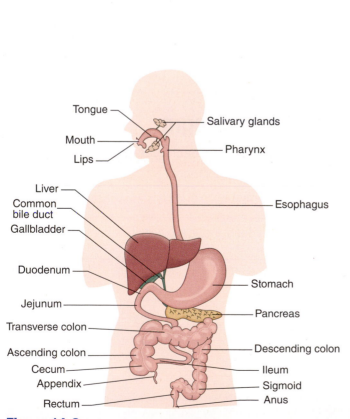

Figure 14-2 Digestive system organs

Figure 14-3 Small intestine

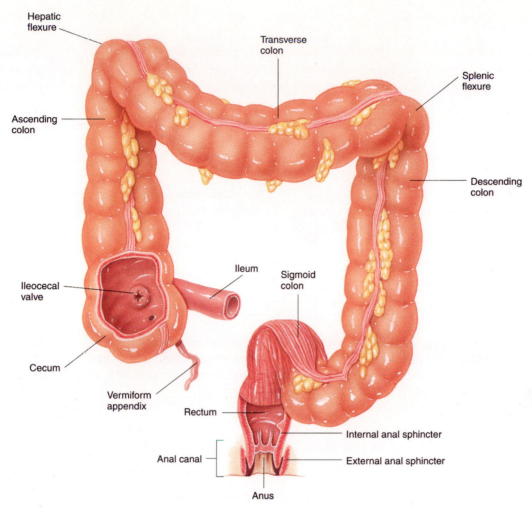

Figure 14-4 Large intestine

The Digestive System subsection includes procedures to diagnose and treat disorders of the digestive system (e.g., GI endoscopy, laparoscopy, and gastric analysis). Similar to other Surgery subsections, procedures are classified first by anatomical area and then by type.

EXAMPLE: Patient underwent upper GI endoscopy of the esophagus, stomach, and duodenum, with specimen collection via brushing technique. Report code 43235.

Digestive System subsection codes are reported for open, endoscopic, and laparoscopic procedures. The operative report must be carefully reviewed to correctly identify the surgical approach.

EXAMPLE: The following codes are reported for gastrostomy procedures (Figure 14-5). A gastrostomy is the surgical creation of an artificial opening into the stomach. Code descriptions differ based on the surgical approach (underlined in each code description below) used to perform the gastrostomy.

- 43246 Upper gastrointestinal endoscopy including esophagus, stomach, and either the duodenum and/or jejunum as appropriate; with directed placement of percutaneous gastrostomy tube

- 43653 Laparoscopy, surgical; gastrostomy, without construction of gastric tube (eg, Stamm procedure) (separate procedure)

- 43830 Gastrostomy, open; without construction of gastric tube (eg, Stamm procedure) (separate procedure)

- 49440 Insertion of gastrostomy tube, percutaneous, under fluoroscopic guidance including contrast injection(s), image documentation and report

Figure 14-5 Gastrostomy

 Note:

The CPT Medicine section also contains codes for digestive system procedures. They are located under the Gastroenterology heading (91010–91299), which classifies diagnostic tests such as electrogastrography. Such tests are generally included in endoscopic procedures, which means that they are not separately coded and reported.

The following headings contain codes that classify procedures performed on the oral cavity (Figure 14-6):

- Lips
- Vestibule of Mouth
- Tongue and Floor of Mouth
- Dentoalveolar Structures

- Palate and Uvula
- Salivary Glands and Ducts
- Pharynx, Adenoids, and Tonsils

Lips

CPT codes for procedures performed on the lips (e.g., biopsy of lip) include the following subheadings:

- Excision
- Repair (cheiloplasty)
- Other procedures

When a procedure is performed on the *skin* of the lip, report an appropriate code from the Integumentary System subsection. Do *not* report codes from both subsections for the same lip procedure.

EXAMPLE 1: Patient underwent a lip biopsy. Report code 40490.

EXAMPLE 2: Patient underwent biopsy of the skin of the lip. The surgeon removed a skin lesion from the lateral side of the bottom lip. Report code 11100 (from the Integumentary System subsection).

Cheiloplasty is the plastic surgery of the lips. To properly assign codes, review the operative report to determine the vertical height associated with the repair (e.g., up to one-half vertical height or over one-half vertical height).

The *full-thickness* repair of a lip laceration is reported with a code from the Repair (Cheiloplasty) heading. Do *not* report a code from the Integumentary System subsection instead of *or* in addition to full-thickness repairs of lip lacerations. (Simple and intermediate repairs of *skin* on the lip are reported with codes from the Integumentary System subsection.)

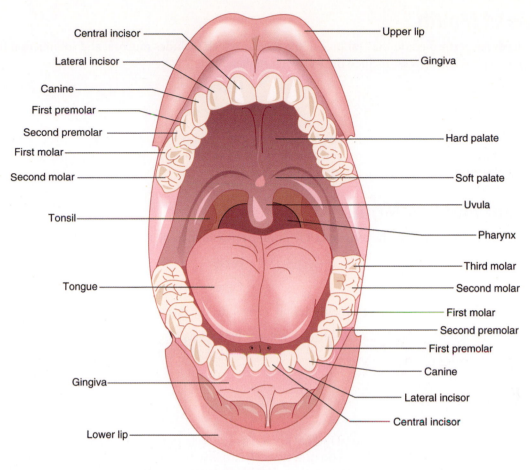

Figure 14-6 Oral cavity

For procedures performed to repair cleft lip and nasal deformities, review the operative report to identify whether the procedure is

- Primary or secondary

- One-stage or two-stage

A primary procedure repairs the cleft lip/nasal deformity without recreating the defect. A secondary procedure re-creates the defect and includes reclosure to repair the cleft lip/nasal deformity.

Codes 40700, 40720, and 40761 are performed unilaterally. For a bilateral procedure, add modifier -50 to the reported code. For a **rhinoplasty** (repair of skin defect of the nose using harvested tissue or plastic surgery to change the nose's shape or size), report a code from the Respiratory subsection (30460–30462). For repair of a cleft lip using a cross-lip pedicle flap (Abbe-Estlander type), report code 40527. For more complicated plastic repair of a cleft lip or nasal deformity using a cross-lip pedicle flap (Abbe-Estlander type) with sectioning/inserting of pedicle (flap), report code 40761.

EXAMPLE 1: Patient underwent full-thickness repair of the vermilion border of the upper lip. Patient sustained a laceration while replacing spark plugs in his classic 1967 Pontiac Bonneville. Report code 40650.

EXAMPLE 2: Patient underwent up to half vertical height full-thickness repair of the lower lip due to laceration acquired during a bar fight. The wound extended through the full thickness of the lip, including the vermilion border. Wound size was up to one-half the vertical height of the lip. Report code 40652.

Vestibule of Mouth

Codes for procedures performed on the vestibule of the mouth, which includes mucosal and submucosal tissue (inner lining) of the lips and cheeks, include the following subheadings:

- Incision
- Excision, destruction
- Repair
- Other procedures

   EXAMPLE: The patient has a habit of sucking on toothpicks; during a recent automobile accident, a toothpick became embedded in submucosal tissue in his mouth. Patient underwent simple removal of embedded foreign body (toothpick). Report code 40804.

Tongue and Floor of Mouth

Codes for procedures performed on the tongue and floor of the mouth include the following subheadings:

- Incision
- Excision
- Repair
- Other procedures

   When reporting codes for excision of a tongue lesion, review the operative report to identify the

- Location of the lesion (e.g., posterior one-third or anterior two-thirds of the tongue)
- Type of excision (partial or complete/total)

 Note:

When a partial glossectomy with bilateral radical neck dissection is performed, report code 41135 for the glossectomy and radical neck dissection on one side. (There is just one tongue, which means modifier -50 cannot be added to code 41135.) Report code 38720-59 for the radical neck dissection on the other side. (Modifier -59 is added to indicate a distinct procedural service.)

   EXAMPLE: Patient underwent partial glossectomy with unilateral radical neck dissection. Report code 41135.

Dentoalveolar Structures

Codes for procedures performed on dentoalveolar structures (e.g., teeth or gums) include the following subheadings:

- Incision
- Excision, destruction
- Other procedures

   (Commonly performed dental procedures are classified in the *Current Dental Terminology* [CDT].)

   EXAMPLE: Patient underwent drainage of gum abscess. Report code 41800.

Palate and Uvula

CPT codes for procedures performed on the hard and soft palates and the uvula include the following subheadings:

- Incision
- Excision, destruction
- Repair
- Other procedures

A **palatopharyngoplasty** is performed to treat oropharyngeal obstructions; it involves surgically resecting excess tissue from the uvula, soft palate, and pharynx to open the airway (e.g., cure extreme cases of snoring with or without sleep apnea).

Note:

Do *not* report code 42145 (Palatopharyngoplasty) for a **laser-assisted uvulopalatoplasty** procedure, which uses a laser technique to remove tissue from the uvula, soft palate, and pharynx. CPT does not list a specific code for laser-assisted uvulopalatoplasty. Therefore, report HCPCS level II code S2080. Because more than one treatment session may be required to achieve optimal results, subsequent visits to repeat the laser-assisted uvulopalatoplasty are included in the global period for the code reported. Therefore, a code for each repeat session is *not* reported separately.

For codes that describe cleft palate repairs (Figure 14-7), the size and location of the cleft determine the type of repair performed (and reported code).

EXAMPLE: The patient underwent primary plastic repair of cleft lip/nasal deformity, complete, unilateral. During the same operative session, the patient also underwent palatoplasty for cleft palate, with closure of alveolar ridge, soft tissue only. Report codes 40700 and 42205-51.

Salivary Gland and Ducts

Codes for procedures performed to treat conditions involving the salivary gland and salivary ducts (e.g., abscess, cyst, and tumor) include the following subheadings:

- Incision
- Excision
- Repair
- Other procedures

The selection of a code for the excision of a parotid tumor or the parotid gland is based on the following:

- What amount of tissue was excised
- Where the location was (e.g., lateral lobe)
- Whether the procedure included nerve dissection
- Whether the procedure included radical neck dissection

Figure 14-7 A child with a cleft palate before and after treatment

EXAMPLE: For the excision of a parotid tumor with bilateral radical neck dissection, report code 42426 for the excision and radical neck dissection on one side. (There is just one parotid gland, which means that modifier -50 *cannot* be added to code 42426.) Also, report code 38720-59 for the radical neck dissection on the other side. (Modifier -59 is added to indicate that a distinct procedural service was provided.)

Pharynx, Adenoids, and Tonsils

Codes reported for procedures performed on the pharynx, adenoids, and tonsils include the following subheadings:

- Incision

- Excision, destruction

- Repair

- Other procedures

  The pharynx contains three segments.

- **Nasopharynx**: Located above the soft palate

- **Oropharynx**: Area between the soft palate and the upper portion of the epiglottis, including the tonsils

- **Hypopharynx**: Extends from the upper edge of the epiglottis to the larynx/esophagus juncture

A variety of techniques and approaches are used when treating conditions of the pharynx (e.g., oral, cervical, thoracic, and horizontal or lateral neck incisions).

EXAMPLE: Patient underwent removal of a lesion of the pharynx via oral approach using curettage. Report code 42808.

Tonsillectomy and Adenoidectomy

Tonsillectomy and adenoidectomy are the most frequently performed procedures coded from this heading. Codes reported for the removal of diseased tonsils or adenoid include the following techniques:

- Cryogenic

- Electrocautery

- Laser

  The selection of a tonsillectomy or adenoidectomy code is based on the following:

- Type of procedure performed (e.g., primary or secondary)

- Age of the patient

A primary procedure code is reported the first time the tonsils or adenoids are removed. A secondary procedure code is reported when there is tissue regrowth requiring subsequent removal. The age of the patient is a factor because age increases the complexity (level of difficulty) of the procedure and lengthens the recovery time.

Separate codes are included to report hemorrhage control following tonsillectomy and adenoidectomy procedures. Make sure you report these procedure codes with modifier -78 to indicate the return to the operating room for a related procedure performed during the postoperative (global) period.

⚠ Codes reported for the radical resection of tonsils include the removal of the tonsils, tonsillar pillars, retromolar trigone, and any infected portions of the maxilla and mandible. Radical resection may also include a hemi- or total glossectomy and/or a full neck dissection.

A limited pharyngectomy is performed to remove a small portion of the pharyngeal wall (e.g., pyriform sinus).

⚠ **Coding Tip:**

Tonsillectomy and adenoidectomy are routinely performed bilaterally, and modifier -50 is not added to the codes.

Exercise 14.2 – Oral Cavity

Instructions: Assign the CPT code(s) and appropriate modifier(s) to each statement.

1. Patient underwent alveoloplasty to remove sharp areas or undercuts of alveolar bone, one quadrant.

   _____

2. Surgeon used a scalpel to slice off a cancerous portion of the vermilion border of the patient's lip; mucosal advancement was performed after excision.

   _____

3. Surgeon made an incision through submucosal tissue and removed a lesion in the vestibule of the mouth. Wound repair was not required.

   _____

4. Patient underwent simple incision of the lingual frenum to free the tongue.

   _____

5. Patient underwent incision in the parotid gland to remove a calcified stone.

   _____

6. Surgeon repaired a tear at the pharyngeal esophageal junction.

   _____

7. Physician drained an abscess near the tonsil.

   _____

8. Surgeon removed an 8-year-old patient's tonsils and adenoids.

   _____

9. Physician controlled secondary oropharyngeal hemorrhaging, status post-tonsillectomy, by using cellulose sponges that expanded when placed in the tonsillar cavity.

   _____

10. Physician performed a tonsillectomy on a 12-year-old male patient.

    _____

Esophagus

Codes reported for procedures performed on the esophagus include the following subheadings:

- Incision
- Excision
- Endoscopy
- Laparoscopy
- Repair
- Manipulation
- Other procedures

When assigning codes to procedures performed on the esophagus, review documentation carefully to identify the approach (e.g., incision or endoscopy).

EXAMPLE 1: Patient underwent esophagotomy via cervical approach, with removal of foreign body. Report code 43020.

EXAMPLE 2: Patient underwent cricopharyngeal myotomy via esophagotomy, thoracic approach, with removal of foreign body. Report code 43045.

Endoscopy

Endoscopic procedures performed to visualize digestive system organs generally use a flexible fiberoptic tube. (Rigid instruments are also used to perform endoscopy.) GI endoscopy is performed to diagnose and treat disorders of the GI tract. Codes are assigned according to the type of instrument used and the anatomical area visualized. The codes are classified in CPT as the following series:

- **Esophagoscopy** is the direct visualization of the esophagus from the cricopharyngeus muscle (upper esophageal sphincter) to and including the gastroesophageal junction (and may include examination of the proximal region of the stomach via retroflexion when performed), using an endoscope.

- **Upper GI endoscopy** (**esophagogastroscopy**) is the direct visualization of the esophagus and the stomach.

- **Esophagogastroduodenoscopy (EGD)** (Figure 14-8) uses a fiberoptic endoscope to visualize the esophagus, stomach, and proximal duodenum.

- **Endoscopic retrograde cholangiopancreatography (ERCP)** involves passing an endoscope through the esophagus, stomach, and duodenum to the ducts of the biliary tree and pancreas. A small plastic tube is passed through the endoscope, through which dye is injected (to allow for visualization of the ducts on x-rays). A radiologist then takes x-rays to diagnose liver, gallbladder, bile duct, and pancreas problems.

Endoscopic procedures are considered diagnostic or surgical, and surgical endoscopy always includes diagnostic endoscopy. This means that when both procedures are performed during the same operative session, report the code for surgical endoscopy only.

- **Diagnostic endoscopy** is performed to visualize an abnormality or determine the extent of disease.

- **Surgical endoscopy** is performed when anything in addition to visualization is performed (e.g., removal of foreign body).

EXAMPLE: Patient underwent diagnostic flexible sigmoidoscopy and biopsy of a lesion during the same operative session. The code for the diagnostic endoscopy (45330) is not reported. Only the code for the surgical procedure (45331) is reported.

Figure 14-8 Esophagogastroduodenoscopy (EGD)

Endoscopic biopsy codes are reported just once regardless of the number of biopsies performed. Likewise, endoscopic polyp or lesion removal codes are reported just once regardless of the number of polyps or lesions treated.

EXAMPLE 1: Patient underwent flexible esophagoscopy with multiple biopsies. Report code 43202.

EXAMPLE 2: Patient underwent flexible esophagoscopy with removal of five polyps by bipolar cautery. Report code 43216 (just once even though five polyps were removed).

EXAMPLE 3: Patient underwent flexible esophagoscopy with removal of three lesions by snare technique. Report code 43217 (just once even though three lesions were removed).

The endoscopic treatment of **esophageal varices** (uneven, enlarged, tortuous veins) (Figure 14-9) includes the following:

- Ligation (similar to the technique used to band hemorrhoids)

- Endoscopic injection of a sclerosing agent (e.g., concentrated saltwater) after passing sclerotherapy needle through scope

EXAMPLE 1: Patient underwent flexible esophagoscopy with band ligation of esophageal varices. Report code 43205.

EXAMPLE 2: Patient underwent direct ligation of esophageal varices. Physician accessed the esophagus through a thoracic incision and ligated the varices with sutures. Report code 43400.

EXAMPLE 3: Patient underwent esophageal transection with repair of esophageal varices. The physician used a stapler that was inserted through an incision in the anterior wall of the stomach to transect and repair the esophagus to remove esophageal varices. Report code 43401.

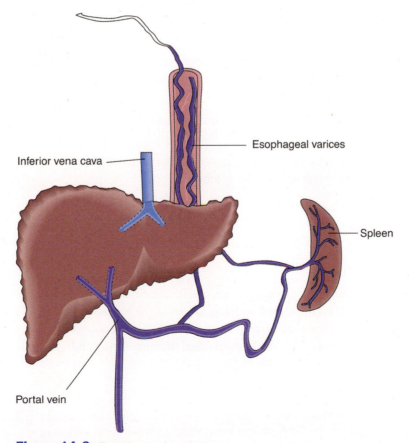

Figure 14-9 Esophageal varices

EXAMPLE 4: Patient underwent ligation at the gastroesophageal junction for preexisting esophageal perforation. The physician ligated the junction of the stomach and esophagus, and a gastrostomy was created for feeding. Report code 43405.

Procedures performed to treat gastroesophageal reflux disease (GERD) typically use moderate (conscious) sedation and radiofrequency energy delivered via endoscopy. The physician performs an EGD with ultrasound examination, and radiofrequency energy is subsequently applied through the endoscope to the muscle of the lower esophageal sphincter and/or the gastric cardia to treat GERD.

> **Note:**
>
> Do not add code 43653 for the gastrostomy because its (separate procedure) note means that part of the procedure is included in code 43405.

EXAMPLE: Patient underwent upper GI endoscopy of the esophagus, stomach, and duodenum with delivery of thermal energy to the lower esophageal sphincter muscle for treatment of GERD. Report code 43257.

Endoscopic retrograde cholangiopancreatography (ERCP) combines upper gastrointestinal (GI) endoscopy and x-rays to detect and treat bile and pancreatic duct problems, such as blockages due to tumors, gallstones that become stuck in ducts, inflammation and infection due to trauma or illness, sclerosis (scarring) of ducts, and pseudocysts (accumulation of fluid and tissue debris). For example, if gallstones are present in the gallbladder (or bile duct), the doctor can remove them through the endoscope. Biopsies may also be taken for evaluation by the pathologist.

EXAMPLE: Patient underwent diagnostic ERCP with single biopsy. Report code 43261.

When a sphincterotomy of the bile duct or pancreatic duct is performed, it includes a diagnostic ERCP. A guidewire is advanced into the biliary tree, and an electrocautery current is applied to make the incision. However, when the patient undergoes gallstone and pancreatic duct stone removal and a sphincterotomy is performed during the same operative session, two codes are reported.

EXAMPLE: A patient undergoes ERCP basket removal of gallstones following a sphincterotomy. Report codes 43262 and 43264–51.

Laparoscopy

A **laparoscopy**, or **peritoneoscopy**, is the examination of the peritoneal contents using a laparoscope that is inserted through the abdominal wall.

> **Note:**
>
> Surgical laparoscopy always includes diagnostic laparoscopy.

- **Closed laparoscopy** is the insufflation of the abdominal cavity and is performed using a percutaneously placed needle.

- **Open laparoscopy** is the insufflation of the abdomen and is performed using a trocar, which is placed under direct vision after making a small celiotomy incision.

EXAMPLE: Patient underwent surgical laparoscopy with Nissen esophagogastric fundoplasty. Report code 43280. (**Nissen fundoplasty** involves mobilizing the lower end of the esophagus by suturing the fundus of the stomach around the circumference of the lower esophagus at the esophagogastric junction.)

Manipulation

When endoscopic esophageal procedures are performed, the advancement of the endoscope through the esophagus expands any stricture. The dilation is considered an integral part of the esophagoscopy procedure. This means that a code for dilation of the esophagus without the use of an endoscope is *not* reported with a code for endoscopy of the esophagus (even if the operative report documents esophageal dilation during endoscopy).

 Note:

Esophageal dilation (without endoscopy) is usually performed under fluoroscopic guidance. Report the appropriate fluoroscopic guidance (x-ray) code in addition to the manipulation code, when performed.

EXAMPLE: The physician uses fluoroscopy to insert a guidewire and to dilate the esophagus by passing dilators over the guidewire. Report 43453. (Code 74360 is also reported for fluoroscopy, which is radiological guidance of "intraluminal dilation of strictures and/or obstructions, such as the esophagus.")

Other Procedures

The free transfer of a short segment of jejunum is usually performed after portions of the pharynx or esophagus have been resected (e.g., cervical esophageal and hypopharyngeal carcinoma).

Stomach

Codes reported for procedures performed on the stomach include the following subheadings:

- Incision
- Excision
- Laparoscopy
- Introduction
- Bariatric surgery
- Other procedures

Stomach procedures include the following:

- **Gastrectomy** (removal of all or a portion of the stomach), which is typically performed to treat ulcers (Figure 14-10) or malignancy.
- Roux-en-Y gastric bypass and small bowel reconstruction procedures that use a Y-shaped anastomosis, which includes the intestines.
- Surgical laparoscopic procedures performed on the stomach. Codes reported for procedures involving the field of bariatric surgery use laparoscopic techniques to perform gastric restrictive procedures for morbid obesity.
- Naso- or orogastric tube placement that requires a physician's skill and fluoroscopic guidance (reported when the nursing staff is unable to successfully insert the tube). Do not report a code when the nursing staff inserts the tube.
- Gastric restrictive procedures involving placement of an adjustable gastric band.

Gastric ulcer

Duodenal ulcer

Figure 14-10 Gastric and duodenal ulcers

- Gastric restrictive procedure, which includes two reconstructive anastomoses (biliopancreatic diversion with duodenal switch).

- Gastric bypass procedure, which includes Roux-en-Y gastroesterostomy.

> **EXAMPLE:** Patient underwent surgical laparoscopic gastric restrictive procedure, which included gastric bypass and Roux-en-Y gastroenterostomy (roux limb 150 cm or less). Report code 43644.

Intestines (Except Rectum)

Codes for procedures performed on the intestines (except rectum) include the following subheadings:

- Incision
- Excision
- Laparoscopy
- Enterostomy–external fistulization of intestines
- Endoscopy, small intestine
- Endoscopy, stomal
- Introduction
- Repair
- Other procedures

Because codes located in the Intestines (Except Rectum) subsection describe similar-sounding procedures (e.g., enterolysis, enterectomy, and enteroenterostomy), coders must carefully review operative report documentation to ensure correct code assignment. (Codes 45000–45999 are reported for procedures performed on the rectum.)

Incision

Enterolysis (freeing of intestinal adhesions) is classified as a separate procedure code, and it is considered an integral component of hernia repair codes. Therefore, do not report the enterolysis code when other surgical procedures include the lysis of intestinal adhesions. However, if documentation indicates that enterolysis was extensive and added significantly to the procedure, add modifier -22 (Increased Procedural Services) to code 44005. There are, however, some instances when it is appropriate to report the enterolysis code with other intestine procedure codes.

Exercise 14.3 – Esophagus and Stomach

Instructions: Assign the CPT code(s) and appropriate modifier(s) to each statement.

1. Physician inserted a flexible esophagoscope into the esophagus and destroyed a lesion, using snare technique.

   _____

2. Surgeon made an incision in the left posterior chest wall into the esophagus to remove a foreign body from the esophagus.

   _____

3. Physician inserted a balloon endoscopically for tamponade of bleeding esophageal varices.

   _____

Exercise 14.3 *(continued)*

4. Dr. Smith performed a partial cervical esophagectomy while Dr. Jones performed a jejunum transfer with microvascular anastomosis.

_____

5. The physician passed an endoscope through the patient's mouth and visualized the entire esophagus, stomach, duodenum, and jejunum. One lesion was removed using biopsy forceps. Another lesion was removed using a snare.

_____

6. Patient underwent incision of the pyloric muscle.

_____

7. The physician performed an open revision of a previously performed gastric restrictive procedure and reversed the previously partitioned stomach to restore normal gastrointestinal continuity.

_____

8. Using fluoroscopic guidance, the physician repositioned a gastric feeding tube through the duodenum.

_____

9. The physician performed a laparoscopic surgical gastric restrictive procedure with gastric bypass and Roux-en-Y gastroenterostomy.

_____

10. The physician percutaneously placed a gastrostomy tube into the stomach under fluoroscopic guidance including contrast injection(s), image documentation, and report.

_____

Codes that describe the surgical treatment of a **volvulus** (twisting or displacement of the intestines, causing obstruction) are located in the Incision subheading.

EXAMPLE: Patient underwent reduction of volvulus (Figure 14-11) via laparotomy. Report code 44050.

Excision

Enterectomy (resection of small bowel segments) procedure codes describe resection of a segment of the intestine, and they require the coder to determine the

- Amount of tissue removed
- Type of repair performed

An *enteroenterostomy* is the creation of an artificial external opening or fistula in the intestines.

EXAMPLE: Patient underwent enterectomy, which involved resection of two segments of the small intestine with anastomosis. Report codes 44120 and 44121.

Colectomy is the removal of part or all of the large intestine (e.g., colon); however, a partial colectomy is more common. Four types of partial colectomies include removal of

- All/part of the right colon (e.g., right colectomy)
- All/part of the left colon (e.g., left colectomy)

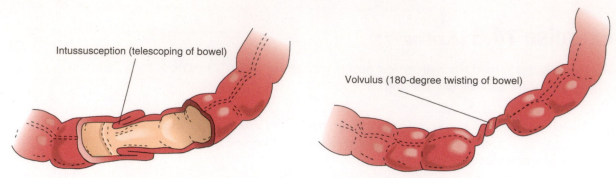

Figure 14-11 Bowel obstructions can be caused by an intussusception or a volvulus.

- All/part of the rectosigmoid colon (e.g., anterior resection)
- The lower rectosigmoid colon, rectum, and anus (e.g., abdominal perineal resection)

EXAMPLE: Patient underwent total colectomy with proctectomy and ileostomy. Report code 44155.

Laparoscopy

Surgical laparoscopy includes diagnostic laparoscopy, which means if both procedures are documented a code for the surgical laparoscopy only is reported. If a diagnostic laparoscopy (peritoneoscopy) only is performed, report code 49320, which contains the (separate procedure) note.

EXAMPLE: Patient underwent laparoscopic jejunostomy for feeding. Report code 44186.

Enterostomy—External Fistulization of Intestines

An **ostomy** refers to surgically creating an opening in the body for the discharge of body wastes. (A **stoma** is a surgically created opening between the ureter, small intestine, or large intestine through to the abdominal wall.) Ostomy procedures are classified according to the portion of the digestive tract that is brought to the surface. (They may be permanent or temporary.) Types of ostomies are the following:

- **Colostomy**: A portion of the colon or rectum is removed, and the remaining colon is brought to the abdominal wall (Figure 14-12).

- **Ileostomy**: The colon and rectum are removed, and the small intestine is brought to the abdominal wall.

A **continent ileostomy**, or **Kock pouch**, is a surgical variation of an ileostomy. A reservoir pouch is created inside the abdomen using a portion of the terminal ileum, a valve is constructed in the pouch, and a stoma is brought through the abdominal wall. A catheter is inserted into the pouch several times each day to empty feces from the reservoir.

EXAMPLE: Patient underwent continent ileostomy. Report code 44316.

Endoscopy, Small Intestine and Endoscopy, Stomal

Jejunal feedings are performed via small intestinal endoscopy. This type of endoscopy is an enteroscopy that is performed beyond the second portion of duodenum. During this procedure, a thin tube is passed through the gastrostomy tube into the stomach and advanced; a direct puncture is *not* made into the jejunum.

Codes 44376–44379 are reported for small intestinal endoscopy, enteroscopy beyond second portion of duodenum (including the ileum), procedures. Codes 44380–44384 are reported for ileoscopy, through a surgically created *stoma* (opening into the ileum). Codes 44385–44386 are reported for the endoscopic evaluation of a small intestinal pouch. Codes 44388–44408 are reported for colonoscopy through stoma procedures.

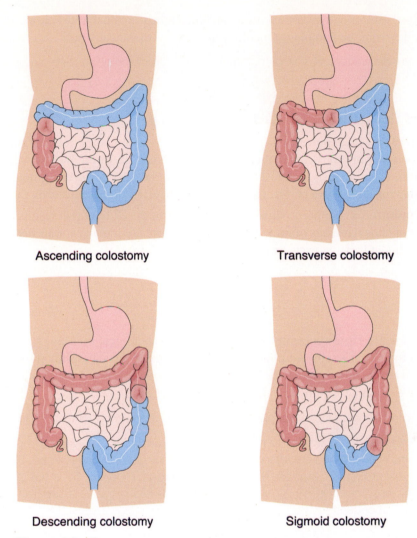

Ascending colostomy

Transverse colostomy

Descending colostomy

Sigmoid colostomy

Figure 14-12 Colostomy locations (Blue section may be surgically removed if colostomy is permanent)

EXAMPLE: Patient underwent small intestinal endoscopy with enteroscopy beyond the second portion of the duodenum and single biopsy. Report code 44361.

Introduction

The introduction of a long gastrointestinal (GI) tube with an inflatable balloon at the end (e.g., Miller-Abbott) is performed to clear GI strictures.

EXAMPLE: Patient underwent introduction of a Miller-Abbott GI tube to clear GI strictures. Report code 44500.

Repair

Codes 44602–44680 are reported for procedures performed to repair the small intestine.

EXAMPLE: Code 44602 is reported for the suturing of a single perforation of the small intestine, while code 44603 is reported for the suturing of multiple perforations.

Other Procedures

Code 44700 describes a procedure performed to exclude the small intestine from the pelvis by implanting mesh or other prosthesis or by using native tissue. When the small intestine is elevated to prevent damage from radiation therapy, mesh, other prosthesis, or native tissue is used (44700). An instructional note below code 44700 provides instruction to report codes from the Radiology Oncology heading for therapeutic radiation treatment.

> **EXAMPLE:** Patient underwent exclusion of the small intestine from the pelvis with placement of mesh. Report code 44700.

Meckel's Diverticulum and the Mesentery

Diverticula (Figure 14-13) are small pouches (herniations) in the colon that bulge outward through weak spots. **Diverticulosis** is the presence of diverticula in the mucosa and submucosa, through or between fibers of the colon's major muscle layer. Diverticulosis is almost always located in the descending or sigmoid colon. Codes 44800–44899 are reported for procedures performed to treat diverticular and mesenteric diseases.

Meckel's diverticulum is a common congenital abnormality of the GI tract that results in a pouch in the wall of the small bowel that contains remnants of fetal GI tissue. The diverticulum may contain gastric, stomach, ectopic, or pancreatic tissue. Treatment includes excision of Meckel's diverticulum.

> **EXAMPLE:** Patient underwent excision of Meckel's diverticulum. Report code 44800.

Appendix

Appendectomies are performed laparoscopically or through an open abdominal incision. An instructional note below code 44950 states that when an appendectomy is performed during intra-abdominal surgery, it is considered incidental; it is not coded and reported separately. When an appendectomy is performed for an indicated purpose during the same operative session as another major procedure, report code 44955.

> **EXAMPLE 1:** Patient underwent laparoscopic appendectomy for acute appendicitis. Report code 44970.

> **EXAMPLE 2:** Patient underwent excision of Meckel's diverticulum. During surgery, the physician noted that the appendix was inflamed and enlarged; an appendectomy was also performed. Report codes 44800 and 44955. (According to Optum360's *Encoder Pro Expert,* modifier -51 is not reported with add-on code 44955. Also, modifier -59 is not added to code 44955 because a separate incision was *not* made to perform the appendectomy.)

Colon and Rectum

Codes reported for procedures performed on the colon and rectum include the following subheadings:

- Incision
- Excision
- Destruction
- Endoscopy

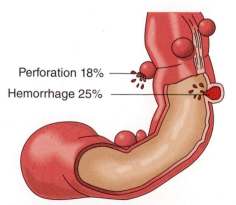

Figure 14-13 Diverticula in the sigmoid colon

Perforation 18%
Hemorrhage 25%

- Laparoscopy
- Repair

- Manipulation
- Other procedures

Endoscopic procedure codes specify the type of instrument used, the purpose of the endoscopy, and the site involved. The CPT coding manual contains a colonoscopy decision tree, which provides direction for assignment of correct codes. When reporting codes for colonoscopies (e.g., colostomy or rectum), the coder must also determine the approach. GI endoscopic procedures involve the small bowel, colon, and rectum and include the following:

- **Proctosigmoidoscopy**: Visual examination of the rectum and sigmoid colon

- **Sigmoidoscopy**: Visual examination of the entire rectum and sigmoid colon and may include a portion of the descending colon (Figure 14-14)

- **Colonoscopy**: Visual examination of the entire colon, from the rectum to the cecum, and may include the terminal ileum (Figure 14-15)

Figure 14-14 Sigmoidoscopy

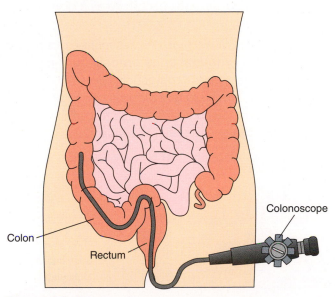

Figure 14-15 Colonoscopy (posterior view)

⚠️ **Coding Tip:**

- When an incomplete colonoscopy is performed and the patient underwent full preparation for a colonoscopy, add modifier -52 (Reduced Services) to the colonoscopy code.

- When multiple endoscopies are performed during the same operative session, report each with a separate code.

- Surgical endoscopy always includes diagnostic endoscopy. This means that when a diagnostic endoscopy is performed during the same operative session as a surgical endoscopy, report just the surgical endoscopy code.

- CMS requires screening sigmoidoscopy procedures to be reported with HCPCS level II code G0104.

Proctosigmoidoscopy and sigmoidoscopy procedures are typically performed without anesthesia. Colonoscopies usually require sedation to avoid severe patient discomfort.

EXAMPLE: Patient underwent sigmoidoscopy and colonoscopy during the same operative session. Report code 45378 for the colonoscopy only. (Do not report a code for the sigmoidoscopy because the endoscope was passed through the sigmoid colon to perform the colonoscopy. Visual examination of the sigmoid colon was performed on the way to visual examination of the rest of the colon.)

When multiple services are provided during an endoscopic procedure, report a code for each. Multiple services are reimbursed according to multiple endoscopic payment rules (e.g., discounted reimbursement for second and subsequent procedures). An exception to this rule is follow-up treatment of bleeding due to the endoscopic procedure.

Different techniques are used to remove lesions or polyps (Figure 14-16) through an endoscope. A **hot biopsy forceps** uses tweezer-like forceps connected to a monopolar electrocautery unit and a grounding pad. **Bipolar cautery** uses an electric current that flows from one tip of the forceps to the other and does not require a grounding pad. An **electrocautery snare** uses a wire loop to encircle, not grasp, the polyp. **Cold biopsy forceps** does not use electrocoagulation; the polyp is simply pulled from the colon wall. **Laser technique** is most suitable for treatment of rectal lesions and uses a waveguide to deliver the laser beam through the endoscope to the lesion (e.g., YAG laser).

EXAMPLE: Patient underwent removal of a polyp by snare technique during a colonoscopy. During the same operative session, another area of the colon was also biopsied. Report a code for the colonoscopy with polypectomy (45385) and a different code for colonoscopy with biopsy (45380-59). (Modifier -59 is added to code 45380 because the colon biopsy was performed as a distinct and separate procedure in addition to the removal of the polyp during the colonoscopy.)

A **proctectomy** is the surgical removal of the rectum. (Do not confuse this procedure with a *prostatectomy*, which is the excision of the prostate gland.) An **ileoanal anastomosis** (or **J-pouch**, **pull-through**, or **endorectal pull-through**) is a common alternative to conventional ileostomy, and it is not considered an ostomy because there is no stoma. The colon and most of the rectum are surgically removed, and an internal pouch is created from the terminal portion of the ileum. An opening at the bottom of the pouch is attached (anastomosed) to the anus so that existing anal sphincter muscles can be used for continence.

EXAMPLE: Patient underwent proctopexy via abdominal approach. Report code 45540.

Figure 14-16 Colon polyp

Anus

Codes reported for procedures performed on the anus include the following subheadings:

- Incision
- Excision
- Introduction
- Endoscopy
- Repair
- Destruction
- Other procedures

Anoscopy is a diagnostic procedure during which anal mucosa and the lower rectum are visualized using an anoscope. Anoscopy is typically performed to detect hemorrhoids (Figure 14-17), polyps, anal fissures, and anal bleeding.

For hemorrhoidectomy procedures, identify what approach was used, where the hemorrhoid(s) were located (e.g., internal or external), and whether a fissurectomy was also performed. The most commonly performed procedure is a hemorrhoidectomy by simple ligature (e.g., rubber band). (Report the appropriate code once regardless of the number of hemorrhoids removed.) Simple hemorrhoidectomy procedures do not include plastic repair; complex and extensive hemorrhoidectomy procedures do require plastic repair. When multiple methods are used to remove multiple hemorrhoids, report a code for each method.

EXAMPLE: Patient underwent hemorrhoidopexy for prolapsing internal hemorrhoids via stapling. Report code 46947.

When reporting codes for the surgical treatment of anal fistulas, apply the following definitions:

- **Subcutaneous fistulectomy**: Removal of an anal fistula, without division of the sphincter muscle

- **Submuscular fistulectomy**: Removal of an anal fistula, including division of the sphincter muscle

- **Complex fistulectomy**: Excision of multiple fistulas

- **Second-stage fistulectomy** or **fistulotomy**: Use of a **seton**, such as a large silk suture or rubber bands, to cut through the fistula; the seton is left in place until later removal

EXAMPLE: Patient underwent subcutaneous fistulectomy. Report code 46270.

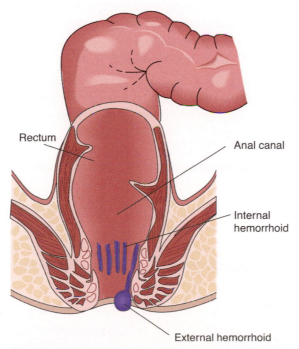

Figure 14-17 Hemorrhoids: internal and external

Exercise 14.4 – Intestines (Except Rectum), Meckel's Diverticulum, Mesentery, Appendix, Rectum, and Anus

Instructions: Assign the CPT code(s) and appropriate modifier(s) to each statement.

1. After performing an emergency cesarean section, the physician noticed that the appendix was distended, resulting in medical necessity for an appendectomy performed during the same operative session.

   _____

2. The physician freed intestinal adhesions.

   _____

3. The physician resected two segments of small intestine and performed an anastomosis between the remaining intestinal ends. An open approach was used for this surgery.

   _____

4. The physician repaired a defect in the mesentery with sutures.

   _____

5. The physician performed a laparoscopic partial colectomy with end colostomy and closure of the distal segment.

   _____

6. The physician drained a pelvic abscess through the rectum.

   _____

7. The physician removed a portion of the rectum through combined abdominal and transsacral approaches.

   _____

8. The physician performed rigid proctosigmoidoscopy and obtained brushings.

   _____

9. The physician performed a flexible sigmoidoscopy and removed a polyp. The physician inserted the sigmoidoscope through the anus and advanced the scope into the sigmoid colon. The lumen of the sigmoid colon and rectum were well visualized, and the polyp was identified and removed with hot biopsy forceps. The sigmoidoscope was withdrawn upon completion of the procedure.

   _____

10. The physician inserted a colonoscope through the anus and advanced the scope past the splenic flexure. Two polyps were identified and removed by hot biopsy forceps.

    _____

Liver

Codes reported for procedures performed to treat liver injuries and diseases, including liver transplantation, include the following subheadings:

- Incision
- Excision
- Liver transplantation

- Repair
- Laparoscopy
- Other procedures

Liver injuries include gunshot wounds, stab wounds, and blunt trauma; treatment includes various methods of hemorrhage control. The management of liver hemorrhage may require a simple suture of the liver wound, or it may require complex suturing of the liver wound or injury, with or without hepatic artery ligation.

Other codes are reported to classify the exploration of a hepatic wound, extensive debridement, coagulation, and/or packing of the liver. For example, code 47362 is reported when reexploration of a hepatic wound is performed for removal of packing.

A **hepatotomy** (open drainage of abscess or cyst) is performed in one or two stages, but when it is performed as a two-stage procedure, the code is not reported a second time.

EXAMPLE 1: Patient underwent wedge biopsy of the liver. Report code 47100.

EXAMPLE 2: Patient underwent surgical laparoscopy with ablation of one liver tumor, using cryosurgery under fluoroscopic guidance. Report codes 47371 and 76940.

Biliary Tract

Codes reported for procedures performed on the organs and duct system that create, transport, store, and release bile into the duodenum (as part of the digestive process) include the following subheadings:

- Incision
- Introduction
- Endoscopy
- Laparoscopy

- Excision
- Repair
- Other procedures

The **biliary system** includes the following digestive accessory organs and structures (Figure 14-18):

- Gallbladder
- Bile ducts inside the liver
- Bile ducts outside the liver

- Hepatic ducts
- Common bile duct
- Cystic duct

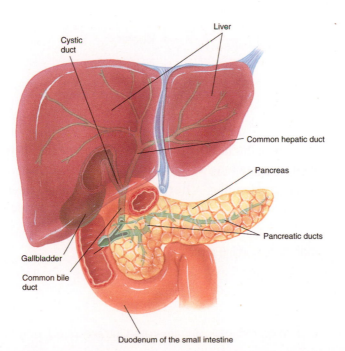

Figure 14-18 Digestive accessory organs (liver, gallbladder, and pancreas)

⚠ A **cholecystectomy** (surgical removal of the gallbladder) (Figure 14-19) can be performed laparoscopically or as an open procedure. During a cholecystectomy, common duct exploration and dilation procedures are often performed through the same incision. An operative cholangiography may also be performed during the same operative session.

> **EXAMPLE:** Patient underwent percutaneous extraction of a stone with a basket. Report code 47544.

Coding Tip:

When a cholecystectomy is attempted laparoscopically and converted to an open procedure, report a code for the open cholecystectomy procedure only.

Pancreas

Codes reported for procedures performed on the pancreas, including pancreas transplantation, include the following subheadings:

- Incision
- Excision
- Introduction

- Repair
- Pancreas transplantation
- Other procedures

The **Whipple procedure** is the excision of the pancreas, duodenum, bile duct, and stomach with reconstruction; code assignment is based on the extent of the excision. The code reported for an internal anastomosis of the pancreatic duct is based on the approach.

> **EXAMPLE:** Patient underwent placement of a peripancreatic drain for pancreatitis. Report code 48000.

Abdomen, Peritoneum, and Omentum

Codes reported for procedures performed on the abdomen, peritoneum, and omentum include the following subheadings:

- Incision
- Excision, destruction
- Laparoscopy
- Introduction, revision, removal

- Repair
- Suture
- Other procedures

When reporting codes for procedures in this heading, make sure you review the operative report to determine whether the procedure was performed via laparotomy or laparoscopy.

Hernia repair codes are classified in this heading. A **hernia** is the protrusion of internal organs (e.g., intestines) through a weakening in the musculature. To report codes correctly for hernia repair procedures, determine the

- Hernia site (e.g., inguinal, lumbar, or femoral) (Figure 14-20)
- Patient's age
- Type of hernia (initial or recurrent)
- Clinical presentation of the hernia (e.g., reducible, incarcerated, strangulated, or recurrent)
- Use of mesh

Dissecting forceps incision

Grasping forceps

Dissecting forceps

To video monitor

Camera

Pneumoperitoneum

Laparoscope

Laparoscope incision

CO_2

Grasping forceps incision

Intestine

Lung

Spine

Liver

Kidney

Cystic duct of gallbladder

Figure 14-19 Laparoscopic cholecystectomy (lateral view)

Umbilical hernia

Inguinal hernia

Figure 14-20 Inguinal and umbilical hernias

Hernia repairs (herniorrhaphies) include

- Traditional/conventional (physician pushes bulging tissue back into the abdominal cavity and sutures surrounding muscle in place)

- Mesh repairs (uses mesh, such as Marlex or Prolene, instead of sutures to repair incisional or ventral hernias)

- Laparoscopic (typically performed to repair bilateral and recurrent hernias)

 Coding Tip:

- Neonatal diaphragmatic and traumatic hiatal hernia repairs are not classified in the Digestive System subsection. To report codes for these repairs, refer to 39503–39541 in the Mediastinum and Diaphragm subsection.

- Implantation of mesh or other prosthesis (49568) is reported for incisional or ventral hernia repairs (49560–49566). When mesh or other prosthesis is used to repair other types of hernias, do not separately report a code. Code 49568 (Mesh) is also reported with Integumentary System codes 11004–11006.

- When strangulated organs are repaired in addition to a strangulated hernia, report a code for each procedure performed.

- When a hernia repair is performed during another open abdominal procedure, a code for the hernia repair is reported only if it was performed through a different incisional site. (Add modifier -59, Distinct Procedural Service, to the hernia repair code.) An incidental hernia repair during the course of an abdominal procedure is not coded and reported.

Exercise 14.5 – Liver, Biliary Tract, Pancreas, Abdomen, Peritoneum, and Omentum

Instructions: Assign the CPT code(s) and appropriate modifier(s) to each statement.

1. Hepatotomy for open drainage of abscess or cyst, 1 stage.

   _____

2. Surgeon removed segments II, III, and IV (the whole left lobe) of the liver from a living donor.

   _____

3. The physician performed radiofrequency ablation of a liver tumor via an open laparotomy.

   _____

4. The physician removed the gallbladder and performed a common bile duct exploration through the laparoscope.

   _____

5. The physician performed a cholecystostomy with removal of calculus.

   _____

6. Subsequent to a previous peritoneocentesis (performed at a different operative session), the physician withdrew fluid and performed infusion and drainage of fluid from the abdominal cavity (peritoneal lavage).

   _____

Exercise 14.5 (*continued*)

7. The physician reopened a recent laparotomy incision, before the incision had fully healed, to drain a postoperative infection.

_____

8. The physician performed laparoscopic repair of an initial inguinal hernia, using mesh.

_____

9. The physician performed a reducible ventral hernia (initial) repair and inserted mesh implantation.

_____

10. The physician repaired an initial, reducible, inguinal hernia with hydrocelectomy in a 5-month-old infant.

_____

Urinary System Subsection

The **urinary system** consists of the kidneys, ureters, urinary bladder, and urethra (Figure 14-21). Blood flows through the renal arteries to the kidneys, where waste materials are filtered and urine is formed. Urine is transported from the kidneys to the bladder by the ureters, and the urine ultimately passes out of the body through the urethra.

A urinary tract infection is a common disorder of the urinary system and may involve different areas of the urinary tract (e.g., urethritis, prostatitis, cystitis, and pyelonephritis). Other urinary system disorders affect the pressure within the urinary system, affect stagnation of flow (stasis), and cause the formation of stones (calculi).

> **Note:**
>
> The *ureter* is the tube that conveys urine from each kidney to the urinary bladder; there are two ureters. The *urethra* is the tube that conveys urine from the urinary bladder to the outside of the body.

Urinary system function can also be affected by disorders such as obstruction (e.g., benign prostatic hypertrophy or strictures), which typically form in three places within the ureter.

- Ureteropelvic junction (between ureter and renal pelvis)
- Ureterovesical junction (between ureter and bladder)
- Ureter/iliac arteries

Various methods are used to treat urinary disorders, including open procedures and endoscopy or laparoscopy. Diagnostic urodynamic procedures (study of urine storage and voiding functions) include tests such as the following:

- Cystometrogram
- Uroflowmetry
- Urethral pressure profile (UPP)
- Neuromuscular studies
- Voiding pressure (VP) studies

(A) Male urinary system

(B) Female urinary system

Figure 14-21 Urinary system (A) Male (B) Female

Urinary System subsection procedures are classified according to anatomical site and surgical approach (e.g., open, incision, percutaneous, endoscopic, or laparoscopic). The subsection also separates endoscopy procedures from open procedures.

Many procedures include the phrase *exclusive of radiologic service*, which means that an additional code from the Radiology section is assigned to report the radiologic service performed.

EXAMPLE: Codes 50551–50580 are reported for renal endoscopy through an established nephrostomy or pyelostomy. The code description states exclusive of radiologic service. If the same physician provides both services, a code from 74400–74485 or 78700–78725 is also reported.

The Urinary System subsection includes the following headings:

- Kidney
- Ureter
- Bladder
- Urethra

Kidney

Codes for procedures performed on the kidney include the following subheadings:

- Incision
- Excision
- Renal transplantation
- Introduction
- Repair
- Laparoscopy
- Endoscopy
- Other procedures

The **kidneys** filter and clean the blood, producing urine that carries waste. In renal (kidney) failure, filtration of blood is slowed or stopped (due to obstruction, bacterial infection, or injury). This causes waste products and other toxic substances to build up in the blood. These problems can lead to renal failure, resulting in the need for treatment such as surgery or dialysis.

In the Kidney heading, the removal of urinary calculi (stones) (Figure 14-22) is coded according to the anatomical site (e.g., renal pelvis, bladder, or urethra) and approach (e.g., open incision, percutaneous, or endoscopic).

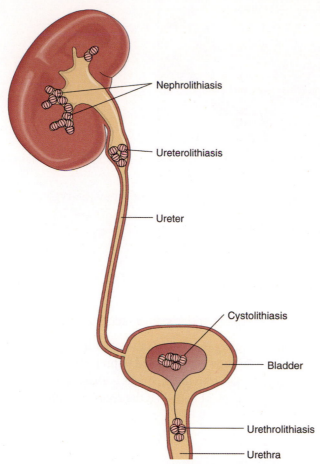

Figure 14-22 Common locations of urinary calculi (stone) formation: nephrolithiasis (kidney stone), ureterolithiasis (ureter stone), cystolithiasis (urinary bladder stone), and urethrolithiasis (urethral stone)

EXAMPLE: Patient underwent nephrolithotomy to remove urinary stones. Report code 50060.

Nephrectomy (surgical removal of a kidney) requires review of the operative report to identify the

- Type of procedure (e.g., partial or total)

- Surgical approach (e.g., laparoscopic or open)

- Other structures removed

EXAMPLE: Patient underwent partial nephrectomy. The physician made a very small periumbilical incision and inserted a fiberoptic laparoscope through a trocar. The kidney and surrounding structures were removed through an enlarged port site. Report code 50543.

When a surgeon performs a retrograde pyelography (or retrograde ureteropyelography), one or both of the ureters are catheterized and contrast is injected slowly through the catheter.

EXAMPLE: Patient underwent injection procedure for ureterogram through existing left nephrostomy tube. Pyelography results were negative. Report code 50431-LT.

Extracorporeal shock wave lithotripsy (ESWL) is a nonoperative procedure that uses ultrasonic shock waves to break up stones in the renal pelvis or ureter (Figure 14-23). The patient then passes the stones in urine, with minimal discomfort. **Percutaneous lithotomy** and **lithotripsy** is a two-stage procedure that requires a percutaneous nephrostomy and dilation of the nephrostomy tract. Instruments (e.g., a basket or lithotripter) are inserted via nephrostomy, and the stones are removed.

Figure 14-23 Extracorporeal shock wave lithotripsy (ESWL)

Renal transplantation codes include three distinct components.

- Harvest of the kidney from a cadaver or living donor

- Physician backbench work, which includes standard preparation of a cadaver or living donor allograft prior to transplantation

- Allotransplantation (e.g., organ removal, if required, and transplantation of the allograft)

The procurement of kidneys involves harvesting organs from a cadaver or living donor. Once the kidney is received by the hospital, backbench standard preparation is performed to prepare the kidneys for transplantation. The actual transplantation of the kidney (Figure 14-24) into the recipient is also reported. (When a bilateral kidney transplant is performed, add modifier -50 to the transplant code.) (If the recipient's nonfunctioning kidney is

Figure 14-24 Renal (kidney) transplantation

resected, code 50340 is also reported. If both nonfunctioning kidneys are resected, modifier -50 is added to code 50340. Nonfunctioning kidneys are not always resected during a transplant procedure.)

Ureter

Codes for procedures performed on the ureter include the following subheadings:

- Incision/Biopsy
- Excision
- Introduction
- Repair
- Laparoscopy
- Endoscopy

The **ureters** convey urine from the kidneys to the urinary bladder. The walls of the ureters contain muscle that propels urine using wavelike motions called **peristalsis**. Procedures performed on the ureters are based on two approaches.

- Open endoscopic
- Laparoscopic

To facilitate the passage of urine through the ureter(s), a physician may insert a ureteral stent. Stents used to relieve or prevent ureteral obstruction can be placed during the course of another diagnostic or therapeutic intervention. Stents may be temporary, and the physician may remove a temporary stent and insert another type of stent (e.g., indwelling).

A **ureterolithotomy** is the surgical removal of stones from the ureter. The procedure should identify the ureteral location from which the stone was removed.

- Upper one-third of ureter
- Middle one-third of ureter
- Lower one-third of ureter

(When stones are removed using the stone basket extraction technique, report code 51065 from the Bladder heading.)

Ureteral anastomosis procedures (50740–50810 and 50860) are mutually exclusive procedures, and codes for these procedures are not usually reported for the same operative session. However, if an anastomosis is performed on one ureter and a different anastomosis is performed on the other ureter, add modifier -LT and -RT to each code (to describe the service performed on the respective ureter).

Ureterostomy, transplantation of ureter to skin (50860), is mutually exclusive of codes 50800–50830 (e.g., ureterostomy, ureterocolon conduit, and urinary undiversion) unless performed on different locations. When reporting code 50860 with a code from 50800–50830, add modifier -59 (distinct procedural service) and -LT or -RT (left side or right side) to code 50860.

Ureteral endoscopy (50951–50980) is the visualization of the ureter(s) using an endoscope. Review the operative report to locate the procedure performed through the endoscope (e.g., biopsy).

EXAMPLE: Patient underwent ureterolysis, with repositioning of ureter for retroperitoneal fibrosis. Report code 50715.

Bladder

Codes for procedures performed on the bladder include the following subheadings:

- Incision
- Removal
- Excision

- Introduction
- Urodynamics
- Repair
- Laparoscopy
- Endoscopy–cystoscopy, urethroscopy, cystourethroscopy
- Transurethral surgery
- Vesical neck and prostate

The **urinary bladder** is a hollow organ that serves as a reservoir for urine until it passes from the body (via urination). Urine enters the urinary bladder from the ureters and exits through the urethra.

 Coding Tip:

> Urethral catheterization codes (51701–51702) are reported only when performed independently.
>
> - When urethral catheterization is performed preceding surgery, a code is not separately reported. Urethral catheterization is considered integral to preoperative services provided and represents the standard of medical practice.
>
> - When urethral catheterization or urethral dilation is necessary to accomplish a more extensive procedure, a code for the urethral catheterization or urethral dilation is not separately reported.

Open excisional procedures of the bladder include the following:

- Excision of urachal cysts and sinuses
- Cystostomy (Figure 14-25)
- Cystectomy
- Pelvic exenteration

Diagnostic urodynamic procedures are performed to study urine storage and voiding functions, and the codes may be reported separately or in combination when more than one procedure is performed. (Report as many codes as necessary to completely describe procedures performed.) Urodynamics includes the following tests:

- Cystometrogram (CMG)
- Uroflowmetry (UFR)
- Urethral pressure profile studies
- Neuromuscular studies
- Voiding pressure studies

A **cystometrogram** records urinary bladder pressure at various volumes, which is useful in diagnosing bladder outlet obstruction and other voiding dysfunctions.

- A simple cystometrogram measures the bladder's capacity, sensation, and intravesical pressure.

- A complex cystometrogram is a procedure in which the physician uses a rectal probe to differentiate abdominal pressure from bladder pressure. Components of complex cystometry include the placement of the transurethral catheter and anal probe, measurement of voiding cystometry and intra-abdominal pressure, and other provocative maneuvers (e.g., patient position changes and trials of anticholinergics or muscle depressants).

Uroflowmetry measures the amount of urine that flows from the urinary bladder per second.

- Simple uroflowmetry measures voiding time and peak flow using nonautomated equipment.

- Complex uroflowmetry measures/records mean, peak flow, and time to reach peak flow during continuous urination, and it is performed using automated equipment.

(A)

(B)

(C)

(D)

(E)

(F)

Figure 14-25 Open cystostomy (A) Incision site (B) Fascia incised (C) Muscle split (D) Bladder incised (E) Cystostomy tube inserted (F) Cystostomy tube secured with purse-string suture

UPP studies (urethral closure pressure profile) describe tests for measuring urethral pressure. A UPP records pressures along the urethra using a special catheter. Electromyography studies measure anal or urethral sphincter muscle activity during voiding and urine flow rate. This study is usually performed on patients with voiding dysfunctions.

Voiding pressure studies involve placing a transducer into the urinary bladder to measure the patient's urine flow rate and pressure during emptying of the urinary bladder. Intra-abdominal VP (e.g., rectal, gastric, and intraperitoneal) can also be measured.

EXAMPLE 1: Patient underwent simple uroflowmetry. Report code 51736.

EXAMPLE 2: Patient underwent complex uroflowmetry, which required the use of calibrated electronic equipment. Report code 51741.

Urinary endoscopy procedures are classified according to

- Anatomical area (e.g., urethra, prostate, or ureter)

- Procedure performed (e.g., cystourethroscopy with insertion of indwelling ureteral stent)

Cystoscopy, or **cystourethroscopy** (Figure 14-26), allows for the direct visual examination of the urinary bladder and urethra.

EXAMPLE: A cystourethroscope was passed through the urethra and urinary bladder to examine the urethra, bladder, and ureteral openings. No other procedure was performed. Report code 52000.

Transurethral surgery is performed on the

- Urethra and bladder

- Ureter and pelvis

Figure 14-26 Use of a cystoscope to examine the interior of the bladder in a male

In addition, a separate subheading for vesical neck and prostate procedures is located under the Bladder heading. It is important to review the operative report to identify the anatomical site for the surgery performed. Diagnostic procedures (e.g., bladder biopsy) and therapeutic procedures (e.g., steroid injection into a urethral stricture) are accomplished using a transurethral approach. Transurethral surgeries include diagnostic cystoscopy, which is not reported separately.

When a physician performs a urethral dilation to determine the size of the cystoscope to be inserted, do not code and report the dilation procedure separately. When the physician performs a cystoscopy and later performs a transurethral dilation for a urethral stricture during the same operative session, assign code 52281.

Cystourethroscopy with removal of foreign body, calculus, or ureteral stent from urethra or bladder is classified as either of the following:

- Simple (52310)
- Complicated (52315)

Before a transurethral therapeutic or diagnostic intervention procedure is performed, a direct visual examination is performed using a cystourethroscope. The cystoscope is passed through the male urethra to visualize the urethra, prostate, and bladder.

Notes in the Ureter and Pelvis subheading clarify the reporting of temporary stents and self-retaining indwelling stents. Indwelling ureteral catheters (Figure 14-27) are inserted into the renal pelvis via the ureter to allow drainage (e.g., when a tumor is impinging on the ureters). Gibbons and double-J stents are the most common ureteral stents. The insertion and removal of a temporary ureteral stent is included in codes 52320–52355. An indwelling stent is reported with code 52332.

When a surgeon performs a **transurethral ureteroscopic lithotripsy** (instead of an ESWL), a cystoscope is inserted through the urethra into the bladder and a ureteroscope is passed into the ureters. Instruments passed through the ureteroscope into the ureters are used to manipulate and disintegrate stones (utilizing transcystoscopic electrohydraulic shock waves, ultrasound, or laser) (52353). When the ureteroscopy is not performed, report code 52325 for cystourethroscopic fragmentation of ureteral calculi (stones) (utilizing electrohydraulic or ultrasonic technique).

Transurethral resection of the prostate (TURP) is an initial resection of the prostate gland via transurethral approach using an electrosurgical device. Specific codes classify laser treatment of the prostate gland. TURP codes include vasectomy, meatotomy, cystourethroscopy, urethral calibration, dilation, and/or internal urethrotomy. Codes for these procedures, when performed during the same operative session as a TURP, are not reported separately.

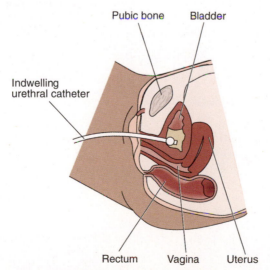

Figure 14-27 Indwelling urethral catheter in a female patient

The physician may perform a prostatectomy using a number of different methods.

- Transurethral two-stage prostatectomy: Physician performs a prostatectomy in two stages, and the operative report specifies the first or second stage. (Code 52601 is reported for the first stage, and code 52601-58 is reported for the second stage.)

- Transurethral destruction of the prostate using microwave therapy: Physician uses microwave thermotherapy. (Code 53850)

- Transurethral destruction of the prostate using radiofrequency: Physician uses radiofrequency thermotherapy to destroy the prostate. (Code 53852)

Urethra

Codes for procedures performed on the urethra include the following subheadings:

- Incision
- Excision
- Repair
- Manipulation
- Other procedures

The **urethra** is a muscular tube that discharges urine from the urinary bladder. In males, the urethra also serves as a passageway for semen. Codes assigned for urethral procedures will vary depending on the sex of the patient.

EXAMPLE 1: Female patient underwent total urethrectomy, including cystostomy. Report code 53210.

EXAMPLE 2: Male patient underwent total urethrectomy, including cystostomy. Report code 53215.

To report codes properly for urethral excision procedures (53200–53275), locate the diagnosis in the patient's record.

EXAMPLE 1: Patient underwent excision of bulbourethral gland. Report code 53250.

EXAMPLE 2: Patient underwent excision of urethral polyp, distal urethra. Report code 53260.

EXAMPLE 3: Patient underwent excision of urethral caruncle. Report code 53265.

For **urethroplasty** (repair of the urethra), identify

- Whether the procedure was staged
- Which stage of the procedure was performed (e.g., stage one or stage two)

EXAMPLE 1: Patient underwent urethroplasty, first stage, to repair stricture. Report code 53400.

EXAMPLE 2: Patient underwent urethroplasty, second stage, to form a urethra. Procedure included urinary diversion. Report code 53405.

EXAMPLE 3: Patient underwent one-stage urethroplasty to reconstruct a male anterior urethra. Report code 53410.

For dilation of urethral stricture, identify

- What surgical approach was used
- What the patient's gender was
- Whether the dilation was initial or subsequent

EXAMPLE 1: Patient underwent initial dilation of urethral stricture by passage of sound or urethral dilator, male. Report code 53600.

EXAMPLE 2: Patient underwent subsequent dilation of urethral stricture by passage of sound or urethral dilator, male. Report code 53601.

EXAMPLE 3: Patient underwent initial dilation of urethral stricture by passage of filiform and follower, male. Report code 53620.

EXAMPLE 4: Patient underwent initial dilation of female urethra including suppository and instillation. Report code 53660.

 Coding Tip:

Urethral repair codes (53502–53515) are performed to treat urethral wounds or injuries (urethrorrhaphy). When urethroplasty is performed, do not report a code for urethrorrhaphy because suture to repair wound or injury is included in the urethroplasty service.

Exercise 14.6 – Urinary

Instructions: Assign the CPT code(s) and appropriate modifier(s) to each statement.

1. Physician made an open incision and inserted multiple drain tubes to drain an infection (abscess) from the kidney.

   _____

2. The physician pulverized a kidney stone (renal calculus) by directing shock waves through a water cushion that was placed against the left side of the patient's body at the location of the kidney stone.

   _____

3. The physician removed a kidney stone (calculus) by making an incision in the right kidney.

   _____

4. The interventional radiologist inserted a percutaneous nephrostomy catheter into the right renal pelvis for drainage. Fluoroscopic guidance was provided.

   _____

5. The physician performed laparoscopic ablation of a solid mass from the posterior hilum of the left kidney.

   _____

6. The physician made an incision in the left ureter through the abdominal wall for examination of the ureter and insertion of a catheter for drainage.

   _____

7. The physician examined the patient's right and left renal and ureteral structures with an endoscope, which passed through an established opening between the skin and the ureter (ureterostomy). He also inserted a catheter into the ureter.

   _____

8. The physician revised a surgical opening between the skin and the right ureter.

   _____

9. The physician injected a contrast agent through an opening between the skin and the left ureter (ureterostomy) for ureterography (study of the renal collecting system).

   _____

10. The physician made an incision in the left ureter (ureterotomy) to insert a catheter (stent) into the ureter.

    _____

(continues)

Exercise 14.6 (*continued*)

11. The physician performed a transurethral resection of a postoperative bladder neck contracture using a resectoscope.

_____

12. The physician inserted a special instrument through the cystourethroscope to fragment a calculus in the ureter using electrohydraulics.

_____

13. The physician inserted a cystourethroscope through the urethra to drain an abscess on the prostate.

_____

14. The physician made an incision through the abdominal wall into the urinary bladder and inserted a suprapubic catheter to withdraw urine.

_____

15. The physician performed a cystourethroscopy with fulguration of the bladder neck and then removed a calculus from the ureter.

_____

16. The physician performed a sling procedure using synthetic material to treat a male patient's urinary incontinence.

_____

17. The physician made an initial attempt to treat a male patient's urethral stricture using a dilator.

_____

18. The physician, in the first of two stages to reconstruct the urethra, identified the area of stricture by urethrography and marked it with ink.

_____

19. The physician performed a transurethral destruction of the prostate using microwave therapy.

_____

20. The physician excised a specimen of tissue from the urethra for biopsy.

_____

Summary

The Mediastinum and Diaphragm subsection classifies procedures performed on the mediastinum and diaphragm (also the titles of subsection headings). The Digestive System subsection includes procedures to diagnose and treat disorders of the digestive system (e.g., gastrointestinal endoscopy, laparoscopy, and gastric analysis). Similar to other Surgery subsections, procedures are classified first by anatomical area and then by type. Digestive System subsection codes are also reported for open, endoscopic, and laparoscopic procedures. The operative report must be carefully reviewed to correctly identify the surgical approach. Urinary System subsection procedures are classified according to anatomical site and surgical approach (e.g., open, incision, percutaneous, endoscopic, or laparoscopic). The subsection also separates endoscopy procedures from open procedures. Many procedures include the phrase "exclusive of radiologic service," which means that an additional code from the Radiology section is assigned to report the radiological service performed.

Internet Links

American College of Gastroenterology (ACG): Go to *www.gi.org*, and click on the Patients link to access information about diseases and treatments.

American Urological Association (AUA): *www.urologyhealth.org*

Society of American Gastrointestinal and Endoscopic Surgeons (SAGES): *www.sages.org*

WebSurg's World Virtual University: *www.websurg.com*

Study Checklist

- ❏ Read this chapter and highlight key concepts.

- ❏ Create an index card for each key term.

- ❏ Access the chapter Internet links to learn more about concepts.

- ❏ Complete the chapter exercises and review, verifying answers with your instructor.

- ❏ Complete Workbook chapter, verifying answers with your instructor.

- ❏ Go to *www.cengagebrain.com* to access the Student Companion Web Site. Login instructions are located in the Preface.

- ❏ Form a study group with classmates to discuss chapter concepts in preparation for an exam.

Review

Multiple Choice

Instructions: Circle the most appropriate response.

1. Which types of hernias are assigned codes from the Mediastinum and Diaphragm subsection of Surgery?
   - a. Abdominal and epigastric
   - b. Hiatus and diaphragmatic
   - c. Incisional and inguinal
   - d. Umbilicus and femoral

2. Procedures performed on the gallbladder, bile ducts, hepatic ducts, and cystic ducts are assigned codes from which heading of the Digestive System subsection of Surgery?
   - a. Abdomen, Peritoneum, and Omentum
   - b. Biliary Tract
   - c. Liver
   - d. Ureter

3. Hernia repair codes (49495–49590) are classified in which heading of the Digestive System subsection of Surgery?
   - a. Abdomen, Peritoneum, and Omentum
   - b. Anus
   - c. Appendix
   - d. Rectum

4. Which procedure(s) has/have age as a factor in determining the correct code?
   - a. Colonoscopy
   - b. Esophagotomy and esophagoscopy
   - c. Palatopharyngoplasty
   - d. Tonsillectomy and adenoidectomy

5. When assigning codes for a ureterolithotomy procedure (50610–50630), which correctly describes the location in the ureter from which the stone was removed?
    a. Right or left side of ureter
    b. Upper-left, lower-left, upper-right, or lower-right quadrant of ureter
    c. Upper, middle, or lower one-third of ureter
    d. Upper or lower half of ureter

6. Diagnostic procedures (e.g., uroflowmetry) that are performed to study urine storage and voiding functions are assigned a code from which subheading of the Bladder heading in the Urinary System subsection of Surgery?
    a. Bladder
    b. Endoscopy
    c. Laparoscopy
    d. Urodynamics

7. Codes for urethral catheterization (51701–51703) are reported when performed _____ another urinary bladder procedure.
    a. in combination with
    b. independently of
    c. preceding surgery for
    d. as a more extensive procedure than

8. Which gastrointestinal (GI) endoscopy procedure involves injecting dye through a tube in the endoscope to allow for visualization of the ducts on x-rays?
    a. Endoscopic retrograde cholangiopancreatography (ERCP) (43260–43273)
    b. Esophagogastroduodenoscopy (EGD) (43235–43259)
    c. Esophagoscopy (43200–43232)
    d. Upper GI endoscopy (esophagogastroscopy) (43235)

9. When an incomplete colonoscopy is performed and the patient underwent full preparation for a colonoscopy, which modifier is added to the colonoscopy code?
    a. -52   b. -53   c. -58   d. -59

10. When a hernia repair is performed through a different incisional site during another open abdominal procedure, which modifier is added to the hernia repair code?
    a. -51   b. -58   c. -59   d. -79

11. Excision of mediastinal tumor. Which CPT code is assigned?
    a. 39200   b. 39220   c. 39401   d. 39402

12. Destruction of dentoalveolar lesion. Which CPT code is assigned?
    a. 41825   b. 41826   c. 41827   d. 41850

13. Simple revision of colostomy. Which CPT code is assigned?
    a. 44320   b. 44322   c. 44340   d. 44345

14. Incision and drainage of ischiorectal abscess. Which CPT code is assigned?
    a. 45020   b. 46040   c. 46045   d. 46060

15. Proximal subtotal pancreatectomy with total duodenectomy, partial gastrectomy, choledochoenterostomy, and gastrojejunostomy with pancreatojejunostomy. Which CPT code is assigned?
    a. 48150   b. 48152   c. 48153   d. 48154

16. Peritoneoscopy with partial laparoscopic colectomy and anastomosis. Which CPT code(s) are assigned?
    a. 44140
    b. 44204
    c. 49320, 44140
    d. 49320, 44204

17. Open drainage of retroperitoneal abscess. Which CPT code is assigned?
    a. 49020   b. 49060   c. 49405   d. 49406

18. Intraoral incision and drainage of hematoma of tongue, submandibular space. Which CPT code is assigned?
    a. 41008   b. 41009   c. 41015   d. 41017

19. Cystourethroscopy with resection of 1.1-cm bladder tumor. Which CPT code is assigned?
    a. 52224   b. 52234   c. 52235   d. 52240

20. Female patient underwent reconstructive urethroplasty. Which CPT code is assigned?
    a. 53410   b. 53420   c. 53430   d. 53431

Coding Practice

Instructions: Assign the CPT code(s) and appropriate modifier(s) to each case.

1. A patient is found to have a cystlike lesion per MRI of the mediastinum. This is to be removed. An incision is made by the physician from the shoulder blade to the spinal column of the thoracic area. Muscles are retracted, and the rib cage is exposed. After gaining access to the thoracic cavity, the physician identified the cyst and removed it. The specimen is sent to pathology. The wound is closed in layers.

   _____

2. A 45-year-old male has an acute diaphragmatic hernia. After adequate general anesthesia, an abdominal incision is made in the epigastric region. A moderate amount of abdominal tissue is protruding through the hernia into the diaphragm. These contents are moved back into proper placement. The opening of the diaphragm is closed with sutures.

   _____

3. Via transabdominal approach, the physician overlaps diaphragm tissue to ensure that the diaphragm is in the correct position and the eventration or partial protrusion is corrected.

   _____

4. A lacerated diaphragm tear measuring 2.5 cm is repaired with sutures.

   _____

5. A patient is being seen to confirm the diagnosis of sarcoidosis. An endoscopic examination of her mediastinum is done under general anesthesia. After making an incision in the area of the sternum, the scope is inserted. The trachea, bronchi, and lymph nodes are examined. A lymph node biopsy is taken. The scope is withdrawn, and the incision is closed with sutures.

   _____

6. A patient had the signs and symptoms consistent with a perforated viscus. After discussion, the patient consented to suture repair of the gastric ulcer. The patient was placed in a supine position. After adequate anesthesia, attention was turned to the anterior abdominal wall. A midline incision was made. Gross contamination was visualized. This was suctioned out. The gastric ulcer was visualized, and copious irrigation with 3 liters of warm saline was performed. All gross evidence of contamination was gone. Checking was done, hemostasis was throughout, and the skin incision was closed.

   _____

7. A patient presented with a lesion of the lip; due to the patient's history of smoking, it was determined to remove the lesion and send it to analysis to rule out carcinoma. After adequate anesthesia,

a wedge incision was done of the lower lip to remove the lesion. The defect was closed with a small flap and sutures.

_____

8. A patient with the diagnosis of carcinoma of the stomach presented for a hemigastrectomy. With the patient in the supine position and after adequate level of general anesthesia, the abdomen was prepped and draped in usual sterile fashion. An upper midline incision was made to access the abdominal cavity. The abdominal ligament was retracted to the right side of the incision. The stoma was mobilized. The duodenum was divided away from the stomach. The tumor was identified. The stomach tumor was transected with cautery, and a specimen was sent for evaluation by pathology. The distal margin of the remaining stomach was cleaned. Staples were used to close the curvature area of the stomach. The abdomen was closed with running Prolene for the fascia. The skin was closed with staples.

_____

9. An 18-year-old patient has a history of chronic tonsillitis. Under general anesthesia, the physician separated the tonsils from the tonsil bed by blunt and sharp dissection followed by the snare. No gross bleeding was found. The adenoids were extracted by the adenotome followed by the sharp curette. Again, no gross bleeding was found. The patient had minimal blood loss.

_____

10. A 72-year-old male patient presented to the emergency department with a 14-hour history of acute right inguinal pain and obstructive symptoms. Examination found a tender nonreducible mass in the right groin. He consented to surgical intervention via exploration and correction of possible hernia. After adequate anesthesia, the patient had an oblique preperitoneal incision through the fascia. The peritoneal cavity was entered. A strangulated loop was found along with the femoral hernia. The lower edge of the inguinal ligament was grasped with clamps, and interrupted Prolenes were used to close the femoral defect using Coopers ligament repair. The defect was closed up to the edge of the external iliac vein. Once the repair was completed, the wound was irrigated with saline. The bowel was inspected and appeared to be totally revascularized, with no evidence of necrosis and no need for resection. The femoral hernia sac was reduced and resected using electrocautery. The abdominal wall was closed with interrupted polypropylene sutures for the anterior wall fascia. A Jackson-Pratt drain was brought out through a separate stab wound. The subcutaneous tissue was closed with interrupted 3-0 Vicryl, and the skin was closed with staples.

_____

11. A patient with chronic cholelithiasis presented for a cholecystectomy. An infraumbilical incision was made, and a trocar was inserted into the abdominal cavity. After insufflation of the cavity, the laparoscope was inserted through the trocar. Two additional incisions were made to place trocars—one on the right side and one on the left. The gallbladder was identified. It was noted to be slightly enlarged and grayish in color. Multiple stones were palpable inside the gallbladder. Tissue surrounding the gallbladder was dissected. The cystic duct and artery were clipped and then cut. The gallbladder was dissected from the liver bed and removed through the umbilical trocar site. Careful irrigation of the cavity was done. The patient had minimal blood loss.

_____

12. A 19-year-old patient presented to the hospital with a history of bloody stools of three weeks' duration. The patient was prepped for a sigmoidoscopy. The sigmoidoscope was passed without difficulty to about 40 cm. The entire mucosal lining was erythematous. There was no friability of the overlying mucosa and no bleeding noted anywhere. No pseudopolyps were noted. Biopsies were taken at about 30 cm; these were thought to be representative of the mucosa in general. The scope was retracted; no other abnormalities were seen.

_____

13. A patient with a history of breast cancer presented for a biopsy of her liver to confirm metastasic disease. The abdomen was exposed by an incision through the skin, fascia, and muscle. A wedge-shaped section of the liver was resected. This specimen was sent to pathology.

_____

14. A patient was found to have a sublingual abscess of the mouth. After consent and normal prep, an incision up through the supramylohyoid muscle was made. The superficial abscess was identified, an extraoral incision made, and clear liquid fluid was drained from the abscess.

_____

15. A 45-year-old patient has been diagnosed with a parotid gland mass via examination and radiograph films. The patient presented for excision of this mass. After adequate anesthesia, the initial incision was made near the midpoint of the mandible. Skin flaps were retracted to expose the parotid gland. The facial nerve was visualized. A mass was identified on the lateral lobe of the gland, and it was carefully dissected free from the space with attention not to damage the facial nerve. The mass was sent in total to pathology for analysis.

_____

16. A patient with the complaint of hematuria presented for an endoscopic examination under conscious sedation. A cystourethroscope was passed through the structures of the urinary system. A lesion was identified on the trigone; this was fulgurated. The cystourethroscope was removed.

_____

17. A patient was diagnosed with a urethral calculus as confirmed by x-ray. Endoscopic treatment was warranted to remove this stone. A cystourethroscope was passed through the urethra, and the stone was extracted through the endoscope. The remaining structures of the system were examined and found to be normal. The cystourethroscope was removed.

_____

18. The patient consented to cystoscopy with possible bladder tumor removal. After the endoscope was inserted through the urethra, the bladder was entered. A lesion approximately 3.0 cm in size was identified in the bladder. This was removed via excision and taken out through the scope. Minimal bleeders were cauterized. The remainder of the bladder was normal in appearance. The cystoscope was removed.

_____

19. Imaging was used to assist in the percutaneous insertion of a guidewire, and a catheter was inserted to drain and collect fluid from the right kidney for analysis. The catheter was removed, and a bandage was applied.

_____

20. The patient was placed on a table. Water-filled bellows using coupling gel to make contact with the skin of the patient's right back were positioned at the area of the kidney stone. Shock waves were administered and directed in short bursts toward the bellows for a total of 35 minutes. The process was overseen by the attending physician, who monitored the fragmentation of the stone. The patient was discharged with instructions to drain urine and collect stone fragments.

_____

21. An endoscope was passed through the urethra. The urethra was normal in appearance, as was the bladder upon examination. The cystourethroscope was then directed to the right ureter. Slight

narrowing was seen in the distal third of this ureter. A double-J stent was placed in the right ureter. The left ureter was then examined and found to be normal. The stent will be removed at a later date.

_____

22. With the patient under general anesthesia, a midline incision was made over the abdominal cavity wall. After the bladder was accessed, a ureterocele was identified. This was removed via an incision made in the bladder. All bleeders were cauterized. Minimal blood loss was noted. The bladder was closed with absorbable sutures. A urethral Foley catheter was placed. The fascia and muscle were closed with staples. The skin was closed with sutures.

_____

23. The patient consented to a renal biopsy. The skin of the back was punctured with the biopsy needle after administration of anesthesia. The needle was advanced to the right kidney. The core of the needle was used to collect the tissue specimen. The needle core was removed to preserve the specimen for pathology. Another core was inserted in the needle, and the same method was used to collect two more specimens. The skin puncture wound was closed with two sutures.

_____

24. The patient received an incision of his back. After access was gained to the left kidney, it was incised. The kidney was examined; a stone was identified and removed. The remainder of the kidney was found to be normal in appearance. The kidney was closed with sutures. A drainage tube was inserted. The tube was allowed to drain outside the body via access through another small incision. The main incision was closed in layers.

_____

25. A patient presented for the first stage of urethroplasty. After an abdominal incision was made, the urethra was identified. The strictures were seen. An incision was made over the first stricture area. The area was opened wide and sutured to the edge of the mucosa. The second stricture area was handled in the same method. The patient will return in eight weeks for stage two of this repair.

_____

CPT Surgery V

Chapter Outline

Male Genital System Subsection
Reproductive System Procedures Subsection
Intersex Surgery Subsection
Female Genital System Subsection
Maternity Care and Delivery Subsection

Endocrine System Subsection
Nervous System Subsection
Eye and Ocular Adnexa Subsection
Auditory System Subsection
Operating Microscope Subsection

Chapter Objectives

At the conclusion of this chapter, the student should be able to:

- Define key terms.
- Explain the organization, format, and content of the CPT Male Genital System, Reproductive System Procedures, Intersex Surgery, Female Genital System, Maternity Care and Delivery, Endocrine System, Nervous System, Eye and Ocular Adnexa, Auditory System, and Operating Microscope subsections.
- Interpret CPT surgery coding notes for the Male Genital System, Reproductive System Procedures, Intersex Surgery, Female Genital System, Maternity Care and Delivery, Endocrine System, Nervous System, Eye and Ocular Adnexa, Auditory System, and Operating Microscope subsections.
- Assign CPT surgery codes from the Male Genital System, Reproductive System Procedures, Intersex Surgery, Female Genital System, Maternity Care and Delivery, Endocrine System, Nervous System, Eye and Ocular Adnexa, Auditory System, and Operating Microscope subsections.
- Add CPT and/or HCPCS level II modifiers to codes, as appropriate.

Key Terms

antepartum care	auditory system	carotid body	choroid
anterior approach	Bell's palsy	carpal tunnel	ciliary body
anterolateral approach	burr hole	carpal tunnel syndrome	ciliary muscle

cochlear implant

conization

conjunctiva

cornea

corpectomy

costovertebral

costovertebral approach

delivery services

discectomy

endocrine system

enucleation of the eye

evisceration of ocular contents

exenteration of the orbit

external ear

extracapsular cataract extraction (ECCE)

eye and ocular adnexa

eyeball

eye socket

female genital system

globe

hysteroscopy

incomplete abortion

induced abortion

inner ear

intersex surgery

intracapsular cataract extraction (ICCE)

iris

lacrimal apparatus

lacrimal puncta

laminectomy

laminotomy

lateral extracavitary approach (LECA)

LEEP electrodissection conization

lens

loop electrodissection conization

male genital system

middle ear

missed abortion

myringotomy

nervous system

neuroplasty

neurorrhaphy

neurostimulator

ocular adnexa

ocular implant

omentectomy

oocyte

oophorectomy

operating microscope

orbit

orbital implant

osteophytectomy

postpartum care

pupil

retina

salpingo-oophorectomy

sclera

septic abortion

somatic nerves

stereotaxis

strabismus

sympathetic nerves

tear apparatus

tenosynovitis

trachoma

transpedicular approach

tympanoplasty

tympanostomy

uvea

vaginal birth after cesarean (VBAC)

varicocele

vas deferens

Introduction ⚠

The Male Genital System subsection classifies procedures performed on the male genitalia and accessory organs. The Reproductive System Procedures subsection classifies the placement of needles into pelvic organs and/or genitalia for subsequent interstitial radioelement application. The Intersex Surgery subsection contains just two codes to classify male-to-female as well as female-to-male sex change procedures. The Female Genital System subsection classifies procedures performed on female genitalia and accessory organs. The Maternity Care and Delivery subsection classifies procedures performed and services provided for obstetrics, including antepartum, delivery, and postpartum care.

 Coding Tip:

Notes located beneath headings and/or subheadings apply to all codes in the heading or subheading. Parenthetical notes that are located below a specific code apply to that code only unless the note indicates otherwise.

The Endocrine System subsection includes codes for procedures performed on endocrine glands. The Nervous System subsection includes codes for procedures performed on the central and peripheral nervous systems. The Eye and Ocular Adnexa subsection classifies procedures performed on the eyeball, anterior segment, posterior segment, ocular adnexa, and conjunctiva. The Auditory System subsection includes codes for procedures performed on the external ear, middle ear, internal ear, and temporal bone (middle fossa approach). The Operating Microscope subsection contains a code that is reported in addition to the primary procedure code when an operating microscope is used during a surgical procedure to perform microsurgery techniques.

CPT guidelines that apply to the subsections are located at the beginning of the Surgery section. Unique coding instructions for the Male Genital System, Intersex Surgery, Female Genital System, Maternity Care and

Delivery, Endocrine System, Nervous System, Eye and Ocular Adnexa, Auditory System, and Operating Microscope subsections are located in notes below headings or codes.

Note:

> The Other Procedures code below each subheading classifies an unlisted procedure performed on the anatomical site. When reporting an unlisted procedure code, include documentation about the procedure performed with the submitted claim. (Other Procedures subheadings are not included throughout Chapter 15 of this textbook except when codes that describe additional procedures are included.)

Male Genital System Subsection

The **male genital system** (Figure 15-1) includes the prostate, seminal vesicles, penis, testicles (testes), epididymis, tunica vaginalis, vas deferens, scrotum, and spermatic cord. Codes are reported for procedures performed on the male genital system. Code assignment is determined according to

- Approach (e.g., incision, destruction, excision, or introduction)

- Reason for surgery

When a circumcision is performed using a clamp or other device with regional dorsal penile or ring block, report code 54150. When the regional dorsal penile or ring block is not used in performing a circumcision, report code 54150 with modifier -52 (Reduced Services). Age of the patient is not at issue when reporting code 54150. When a surgical circumcision is performed on a neonate (28 days or age or less), report code 54160. For a surgical circumcision performed on a male older than 28 days of age (including adults), report code 54161.

When a physician obtains a sample of testicular tissue (Figure 15-2) by needle biopsy, report code 54500. For excision of benign lesions of the male genitalia, report codes 11420–11426. For excision of malignant lesions of male genitalia, report codes 11620–11626.

Figure 15-1 Male genital system

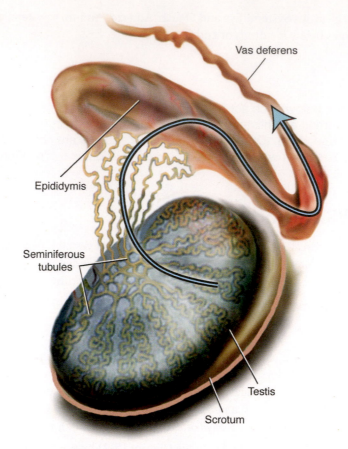

Figure 15-2 Male testicle

When an orchiectomy procedure is performed, identify the following:

- Type of procedure (simple or radical)

- Surgical approach

- Additional procedures performed

EXAMPLE 1: Patient underwent radical orchiectomy (removal of testis) due to testicular tumor, inguinal approach. Report code 54530.

EXAMPLE 2: Patient underwent simple orchiectomy, inguinal approach, which was performed prophylactically to prevent the release of hormones that may promote tumor metastasis. Report code 54520.

When an orchiopexy for intra-abdominal testis is performed laparoscopically, report code 54692. (When performed without laparoscopy, report code 54650 for the repair of a testicle that is located intra-abdominally instead of in its usual anatomical location through the inguinal ring into the scrotum.)

EXAMPLE 1: Patient underwent orchiopexy via abdominal approach for intra-abdominal testis. Report code 54650.

EXAMPLE 2: Patient underwent laparoscopic orchiopexy for intra-abdominal testis. Report code 54692.

The **vas deferens** is the tube that carries spermatozoa from the testis. Report code 55250 for a vasectomy procedure (Figure 15-3). Do not add modifier -50 to the code because its description includes the phrase *unilateral or bilateral*. Code 55250 also includes postoperative semen examination to determine whether the semen contains sperm. Other procedures include vasotomy, vasovasostomy, and ligation.

Figure 15-3 Vasectomy procedure

Figure 15-4 Varicocele affecting the left testicle

A **varicocele** (Figure 15-4) is an abnormal dilation of the veins of the spermatic cord in the scrotum. Treatment typically involves ligation of spermatic veins or excision of the varicocele. For excision or ligation of a varicocele, review the operative report to locate the approach.

- Laparoscopic
- Abdominal

    EXAMPLE: The patient underwent ligation of spermatic veins for varicocele. Report code 55530.

Benign conditions of the prostate gland include infection, inflammation, and benign prostatic hyperplasia (BPH) (also called benign prostatic hypertrophy, BPH). Men with benign prostate disease experience difficulty urinating (voiding). The degree of prostate involvement determines the therapeutic approach. For severe BPH, surgical procedures performed to restore urine flow include the following:

- Transurethral resection of the prostate (TURP) (Figure 15-5)
- Subtotal open prostatectomy (subtotal perineal prostatectomy)
- Subtotal prepubic prostatectomy
- Subtotal retropubic prostatectomy

     EXAMPLE: Patient underwent transurethral electrosurgical resection of the prostate, including control of postoperative bleeding. During the same operative session, complete vasectomy was performed as well as meatotomy, cystourethroscopy, urethral calibration and dilation, and internal urethrotomy. Report code 52601.

Prostate cancer treatment may involve surgery, chemical destruction, electrocautery, or radiation. Surgical procedures that are performed to treat localized prostate cancer include radical prostatectomy, laparoscopic radical prostatectomy, and cryoablation.

Note:

The code for transurethral electrosurgical resection of the prostate is classified in the Urinary System subsection. The procedure requires the use of an electrocautery knife to resect the prostate. (Report code 52601.)

Figure 15-5 A transurethral resection of the prostate (TURP) is performed to treat benign prostatic hypertrophy.

A prostate biopsy is reported with a code from 55700–55706, depending on the type of biopsy. To report the correct CPT code, review the operative report to determine the type of biopsy performed.

- Needle
- Punch
- Incisional

The "transperineal placement of needles or catheters into prostate for interstitial radioelement application, with or without cystoscopy" describes a procedure performed for interstitial radioelement application. Code 55875 is reported for the transperineal placement of needles or catheters only. A parenthetical note provides instruction directing the coder to radioelement application codes (77770-77772 and 77778), which are reported separately.

Exercise 15.1 – Male Genital System Subsection

Instructions: Assign the CPT code(s) and appropriate modifier(s) to each statement.

1. The physician resected diseased scrotal tissue.

   _____

2. The physician removed a lesion from the left spermatic cord by dissection and excision.

   _____

3. The physician made an incision into the scrotum to search for the right testis, which failed to descend into the scrotum.

   _____

4. The physician performed a radical prostatectomy to remove the entire gland along with the seminal vesicles and the vas deferens. The incision was made between the base of the scrotum and the anus. Local lymph nodes were also removed for analysis.

   _____

5. The physician destroyed extensive condyloma of the penis using local application of a chemical.

   _____

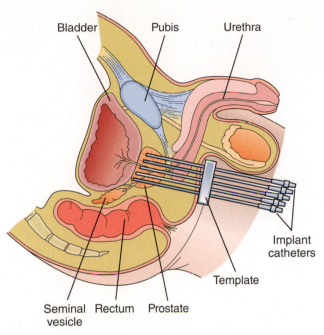

Figure 15-6 Insertion of implant catheters through perineum into prostate and seminal vesicles

Reproductive System Procedures Subsection

The reproductive system procedures subsection contains a code (55920) to report the placement of needles or catheters into pelvic organs and/or genitalia (Figure 15-6) for subsequent interstitial radioelement application. Code 55920 is not reported when needles or catheters are inserted into the prostate gland (for which code 55875 is reported).

> **EXAMPLE:** Patient underwent insertion of catheters into the uterus to facilitate radiation therapy. Report code 55920.

 Note:

> Radioactive isotopes (e.g., iodine-125) contained within tiny seeds remain inside the pelvic organs or genitalia to deliver radiation during an extended period of time (e.g., months). This method targets the prescribed body area, minimizing radiation exposure to normal tissue.

Intersex Surgery Subsection

Intersex surgery (Figure 15-7) is performed as a series of staged procedures to transform the normal adult genitalia of one sex to that of the other sex (genital reconstructive surgery or sex reassignment surgery).

- For male-to-female intersex surgery, portions of the male genitalia are removed and female external genitals are formed.

- For female-to-male intersex surgery, a penis and scrotum are formed using pedicle flap grafts and free skin grafts and a prosthesis is inserted.

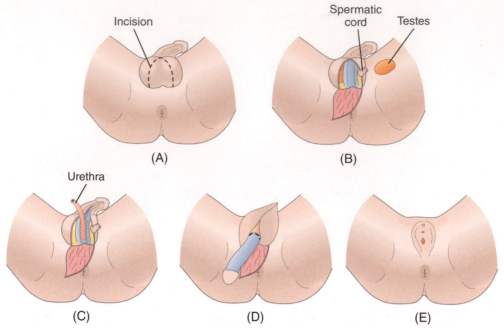

Figure 15-7 Sex reassignment surgery: (A) To change male genitalia to female genitalia, an incision is made into the scrotum. (B) The flap of scrotal skin is retracted, and the testes are removed. (C) Skin is then excised from the penis but remains attached, and a shorter urethra is created. (D) All but a stump of the penis is then removed. (E) Excess skin is used to create labia (external genitalia) and the vagina.

Exercise 15.2 – Reproductive System Procedures and Intersex Surgery Subsection

Instructions: Assign the CPT code(s) and appropriate modifier(s) to each statement.

1. A needle was inserted into the patient's bladder to insert a radiopharmaceutical (HCPCS level II code A9699) for the purpose of radiation therapy.

   _____

2. Surgery was performed to dissect the penis and remove portions of it to fashion a clitoris-like structure. The urethral opening was moved, and a vagina was created by dissecting and opening the perineum. Labia were created using scrotal skin and adjacent tissue.

   _____

3. In the fourth of a series of staged procedures, the physician formed a penis and scrotum using pedicle flap grafts and free skin grafts. Prostheses were placed in the penis and testicles, and the vagina was closed.

   _____

Female Genital System Subsection ✎

Female Genital System subsection codes are reported for procedures performed on the **female genital system** (Figure 15-8), including the following: vulva, perineum, introitus, vagina, cervix uteri, corpus uteri, oviduct/ovary (fallopian tube), ovary, and *in vitro* fertilization (IVF).

Figure 15-8 Female genital system

When reporting codes for procedures performed on the female genital system, review the operative report to identify the following:

- Anatomy on which the procedure was performed (e.g., vulva)
- Surgical approach

 Note:

Codes classified in the Female Genital System heading are reported for procedures performed on women who are *not* pregnant. To report codes for women who are pregnant, refer to the Maternity Care and Delivery heading.

 Coding Tip:

- All laparoscopic procedures and nonobstetrical dilation and curettage procedure codes are classified in the Female Genital System subsection.

- Some female genital procedures are classified in other subsection headings of the CPT coding manual, such as the open destruction of endometriomas, which is located in the Digestive System subsection, Abdomen/Peritoneum/Omentum heading, Excision/Destruction subheading.

For vulvectomy procedure codes, refer to the following definitions when reviewing the operative report (to select the type of procedure performed):

- *Simple procedure*: Removal of skin and superficial subcutaneous tissues
- *Radical procedure*: Removal of skin and deep subcutaneous tissue

- *Partial procedure*: Removal of less than 80 percent of the vulvar area
- *Complete procedure*: Removal of greater than 80 percent of the vulvar area

When an open sling operation is performed for stress incontinence, report code 57288. When a laparoscopic sling operation is performed, report code 51992 from the Urinary System subsection.

Coding Tip:

Make sure you read CPT code descriptions carefully. When the code description states "with or without" another procedure, that other procedure is not reported separately if it is performed (e.g., 57240, anterior colporrhaphy, repair of cystocele with or without repair of urethrocele).

A pelvic exam under anesthesia is a routine evaluation of the surgical field, and it is reported with code 57410 *if performed separately*. This procedure is included in all major and most minor gynecological procedures, and it is *not* reported separately when performed during the same operative session as another female genital system surgical procedure.

Endoscopy codes are reported for examination and magnification, and codes distinguish among anatomical sites (e.g., vulva, vagina, cervix uteri, and oviduct/ovary). Abnormalities of the female genital system (e.g., cancer, tumors, human papilloma virus [HPV], and pruritus) are commonly diagnosed and treated with examination and magnification. For example, laparoscopy/hysteroscopy is performed to visualize the corpus uteri (Figure 15-9).

When dilation of the vagina or cervix is performed during the same operative session as another vaginal approach procedure, do not report the dilation procedure separately. When a pelvic examination under anesthesia is performed during the same operative session as a dilation and curettage (Figure 15-10), report the code for the dilation and curettage only.

In the Cervix Uteri heading, **conization** of the cervix (removal of a cone-shaped piece of tissue) is reported with codes 57520–57522. Conization codes include fulguration, D and C, and repair. Conization procedures can also be performed through use of a cold knife or laser (57520) or through loop electrode excision (57522). Make sure you review the operative report carefully to assign the appropriate code.

Figure 15-9 Laparoscopy/hysteroscopy

Vaginal speculum

Uterus

Uterine dilator
(increases in size
with each insertion)

(A)

Vaginal speculum

Uterus

Enlarged
view of curette

Curette

(B)

Figure 15-10 Dilation and curettage: (A) Dilation is the
expansion of the cervical opening.
(B) Curettage is the removal of material
from the endometrial lining of the uterus.

 Coding Tip:

Physicians use the terms *loop conization* and *LEEP (loop electrosurgical excision procedure)
conization* interchangeably in operative reports. **Loop electrodissection conization** is a deep
dissection of the cervix using a loop wire (instead of the traditional surgical scalpel). **LEEP
electrodissection conization** is a more superficial dissection of the cervix using a loop wire.
Report code 57522 for a loop or LEEP conization of the cervix. Report code 57460 when the
loop or LEEP conization is performed via colposcopy.

Abdominal hysterectomy procedures are reported with codes 58150–58240. Make sure you review the operative
report to identify whether the fallopian tubes and/or ovaries were removed during the same operative session as the
hysterectomy. Then read the code descriptions carefully to select the appropriate code.

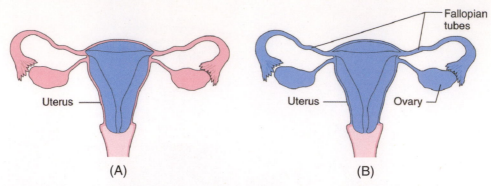

Figure 15-11 Vaginal hysterectomies: (A) For a vaginal hysterectomy, just the uterus and cervix are removed. (B) For a vaginal hysterectomy with bilateral salpingo-oophorectomy, the cervix, uterus, fallopian tubes, and ovaries are removed.

When reporting a code for vaginal hysterectomy (Figure 15-11), determine whether the surgical approach is either of the following:

- Open (58260–58294)
- Laparoscopic (58550–58554)

 Coding Tip:

The code description "with or without removal of tube(s), with or without removal of ovary(s)" indicates that these procedures are bilateral. Therefore, do not report modifier -50 with codes containing such descriptions.

Hysteroscopy is the direct visualization of the cervical canal and uterine cavity using a hysteroscope. It is performed to examine the endometrium and to carry out surgical procedures (e.g., removal of cervical polyp). When a dilation and curettage is performed during the same operative session as a hysteroscopic biopsy or polypectomy (58558), do not report a separate code for the dilation and curettage.

The Oviduct/Ovary heading (58600–58770) includes procedures performed on the fallopian tubes. It also includes codes for endoscopic procedures performed on the ovaries. (The Ovary heading does not contain endoscopic codes.) Make sure you review the operative report to differentiate therapeutic procedures performed using surgical laparoscopy or hysteroscopy from those performed for diagnostic laparoscopy.

Review the operative report to determine the surgical approach before coding a tubal ligation procedure (e.g., ligation, transaction, or other occlusion of the fallopian tubes) (Figure 15-12).

- Abdominal or vaginal approach (58600–58605)
- Vaginal or suprapubic approach (58615)
- Laparoscopic (58670–58671)

Code 58740 is reported for the open lysis of fallopian tube or ovarian adhesions. When the laparoscopic lysis of adhesions is performed as a separate procedure, report code 58660. Do not report code 58660 when the surgeon performs lysis of adhesions during the same operative session as other procedure(s) performed on the ovaries and/or fallopian tubes. However, when lysed adhesions are documented as dense or extensive and involved additional operating room time, increasing the risk to the patient, report code 58660 in addition to code(s) for other procedure(s) performed on the ovaries and/or fallopian tubes.

Fallopian tube

Figure 15-12 Tubal ligation

 Coding Tip:

- When a postpartum tubal ligation is performed during the same hospitalization as a vaginal delivery, report code 58605.

- When a tubal ligation is performed at the time of cesarean delivery or other intra-abdominal surgery, report code 58611 in addition to the primary procedure (e.g., cesarean delivery or appendectomy).

EXAMPLE: Patient underwent a total abdominal hysterectomy during which routine lysis of adhesions was performed to access the abdomen. Report code 58150. (Do *not* report code 58660.)

Codes 58800–58960 are reported for procedures performed on the ovaries. Review the operative report to identify the surgical approach.

- Open (code 58940 is reported for oophorectomy performed via open surgery)

- Laparoscopic (code 58661 is reported for laparoscopic oophorectomy)

Code 58943 is reported for an **oophorectomy** (removal of the ovaries) due to ovarian cancer. When an ovarian malignancy is resected by performing a bilateral **salpingo-oophorectomy** (removal of both fallopian tubes and ovaries) and an **omentectomy** (removal of the omentum), report a code from 58950–58952.

 Codes 58970–58976 are reported for *in vitro* fertilization (IVF) procedures, which are performed during a one- to seven-day period from the time the **oocyte** (immature female reproductive cell, or egg) was aspirated from the ovary until the embryo is transferred to the uterus or is cryopreserved. IVF procedures include both male and female gametes in addition to the subsequent embryos that develop. The physician who performs the oocyte retrieval reports code 58970 (follicle puncture for oocyte retrieval, any method) to describe these services.

Coding Tip:

Any associated laboratory procedures performed during *in vitro* fertilization are reported separately with codes from the Pathology and Laboratory section of CPT.

Exercise 15.3 – Female Genital System Subsection

Instructions: Assign the CPT code(s) and appropriate modifier(s) to each statement.

1. The physician performed a tubal ligation (vaginal approach) immediately following vaginal delivery of a single, live newborn.

_____

2. The physician performed colpocentesis to aspirate fluid from the peritoneum through the vaginal wall.

_____

3. The physician aspirated a mature egg from its follicle for *in vitro* fertilization.

_____

4. The physician inserted an intrauterine device (IUD).

_____

5. The physician performed laparoscopic electrical cautery destruction of an ovarian lesion with the assistance of a fiberoptic laparoscope.

_____

Maternity Care and Delivery Subsection

In clinical terms, pregnancy is subdivided into trimesters.

- First trimester (fetal organ development)

- Second trimester (well-baby visits at the physician's office)

- Third trimester (baby maturity and delivery at 38–40 weeks)

    In coding terms, the three stages of pregnancy care include services provided as part of total obstetrical care.

- Antepartum care

- Delivery of the baby

- Postpartum care

    Total obstetrical care does not include diagnostic procedures (e.g., ultrasound, amniocentesis, or special screening tests), physician office visits for unrelated conditions incidental to pregnancy, and additional visits due to high-risk conditions or medical complications of pregnancy (e.g., cardiac conditions, diabetes mellitus, hyperemesis, hypertension, neurological conditions, premature rupture of membranes, preterm labor, toxemia, or hyperemesis). Codes for these services are separately reported from the Evaluation and Management and Medicine sections of CPT. For treatment of surgical complications associated with pregnancy (e.g., appendectomy, cholecystectomy, hernia repair, or removal of ovarian cyst or Bartholin cyst), codes from the Surgery section are reported separately.

    Most procedures in the Maternity Care and Delivery heading include just what is described in the code description. Additional procedures performed on the same day as a maternity care and delivery service are reported separately, except for the following services, which are included in the code for maternity care and delivery:

- Fetal monitoring during labor

- Episiotomy

- Delivery of the placenta

Services that are reported separately when performed during maternity care and delivery include the following:

- Amniocentesis (Figure 15-13)
- Chorionic villus sampling
- Cordocentesis
- Fetal contraction stress test
- Fetal nonstress test
- Insertion of cervical dilator (e.g., laminaria and prostaglandin)

- External cephalic version with or without tocolysis
- Limited or complete obstetric ultrasound
- Fetal biophysical profile
- Fetal echocardiography
- Administration of Rh immune globulin

Antepartum Services

Antepartum care begins with conception and ends with delivery, and it includes the following:

- Initial prenatal history and examination
- Subsequent prenatal history and examinations
- Documentation of weight, blood pressures, and fetal heart tones
- Routine chemical urinalysis (e.g., glucose)
- Monthly visits up to 28 weeks' gestation
- Biweekly visits to 36 weeks' gestation
- Weekly visits until delivery

Figure 15-13 Amniocentesis and preparation of specimen for amniotic fluid analysis

The previously listed services are included with total obstetrical care, and they are not reported separately. Services that are reported separately with a code from the Evaluation and Management or Surgery section of CPT (in addition to a code for delivery services) include the management of the following:

- Medical problems *unrelated* to pregnancy

- Complications related to pregnancy

    EXAMPLE: Patient develops gestational diabetes, which complicates her pregnancy. She requires additional office visits to monitor her blood sugar and weight. Report an appropriate evaluation and management service code for each office visit during which the patient's gestational diabetes is managed.

When a physician provides *antepartum care only* (e.g., patient's care is transferred to another physician or patient relocates out of the area), report an appropriate evaluation and management code for the first through third antepartum care visit. For the fourth and subsequent visits, report code 59425 (Antepartum care only; 4–6 visits) or 59426 (Antepartum care only; 7 or more visits).

Delivery Services

Delivery services (e.g., vaginal delivery, cesarean delivery, and delivery after previous cesarean delivery) begin with the admission of the patient to the hospital and end with delivery of the placenta (Figure 15-14). Services include the following:

- Admission of the patient to the hospital

- Admission history and physical examination

- Management of uncomplicated labor

- Vaginal delivery (with or without episiotomy and/or with or without forceps) or cesarean delivery

The induction of labor (e.g., Pitocin [oxytocin]) during delivery is included in the code for delivery services. The artificial rupture of membranes (AROM) prior to delivery is also included in the delivery services code.

Services provided during delivery that are reported separately include the following:

- Fetal scalp blood sampling (59030)

- External cephalic version (59412)

- Administration of regional anesthesia (e.g., epidural)

The delivery of the placenta (59414) is included in the delivery service, and it is *not* reported in addition to the delivery service. Code 59414 is reported when the patient delivers vaginally prior to admission to the hospital and subsequent delivery of the placenta is performed by a physician in the hospital.

Services that are reported separately with a code from the Evaluation and Management or Surgery section of CPT (in addition to a code for delivery services) include the following:

- Management of surgical problems that develop during the postpartum period

- Admission to the hospital for observation prior to delivery

- Medical complications of pregnancy, labor, and/or delivery that require additional resources (e.g., diabetes, hypertension, toxemia, preterm labor, or premature rupture of membranes)

- Tubal ligation (58605) performed after delivery

Placenta   Urinary bladder   Pubic bone

Urethra
Vagina
Cervix
Rectum

(A)

Partially dilated cervix

(B)   (C)   Placenta   Uterus   Umbilical cord

(D)

Figure 15-14 Stages of labor (A) Position of the fetus before labor (B) First stage of labor (C) Second stage of labor, fetal delivery (D) Third stage of labor, delivery of the placenta

 Coding Tip:

- Multiple births create the potential for complications during pregnancy, and they present coding challenges.

- When performing diagnostic tests on multiple fetuses (e.g., amniocentesis or biophysical profile), more work is usually required because the procedure must be performed and documented for each fetus. To indicate additional work, report the appropriate code with modifier -22 or report the code for each fetus. (Make sure you report a diagnosis code that indicates multiple gestation.)

- Codes for multiple births are reported as follows:

  o Vaginal delivery of each baby: report code 59400 for Baby A, code 59409-51 for Baby B, code 59409-51 for Baby C, and so on.

  o Vaginal delivery followed by cesarean delivery: report code 59510 for Baby B, code 59409-51 for Baby A (and subsequent vaginal delivery codes if additional babies were delivered vaginally, with modifier -51 added to each code). (Code 59510 for cesarean delivery is reported first because that procedure consumes the most resources. If multiple babies are delivered via cesarean, report code 59510 just once.)

(continues)

Coding Tip *(continued)*

> o Cesarean delivery of each baby: report code 59510 once (because just one cesarean section is performed). When a cesarean delivery is significantly more difficult, add modifier -22 to the code. (Submit a copy of the operative report with the claim.) Report the diagnosis code for multiple gestation.

Postpartum Care

Postpartum care begins after vaginal or cesarean section delivery and includes the recovery room visit; any uncomplicated inpatient hospital and outpatient postpartum visits; follow-up care for episiotomy; and repair of cervical, vaginal, or perineal lacerations, including follow-up care. During delivery, if a vaginal laceration occurs and the repair is minimal, it is included in the delivery services. The repair of the vaginal laceration is not coded separately.

Coding Tip:

> • When a physician provides all or part of the antepartum and/or postpartum care but does not perform the delivery due to termination of pregnancy by abortion or referral to another physician for delivery, report codes from the antepartum and postpartum subheadings (59425–59426 and 59430).
>
> • When a physician performs only the delivery, report a "delivery only" code.

EXAMPLE: The on-call obstetrician performs an emergency cesarean section on a colleague's patient. The on-call obstetrician reports code 59514. The patient's obstetrician reports codes for antepartum and postpartum care.

Delivery After Previous Cesarean Delivery

Codes for delivery after previous cesarean section are reported whether an attempted vaginal birth (after previous cesarean delivery) is successful or a repeat cesarean is performed. A code from 59610–59614 is reported for **vaginal birth after cesarean (VBAC)**, which is a planned vaginal birth after previous cesarean section. When the planned VBAC fails, report a code from 59618–59622.

Abortion

Abortion treatment codes are based on the method used and type of abortion.

- **Incomplete abortion**: Miscarriage in which part, but not all, of the uterine contents are expelled

- **Missed abortion**: Miscarriage in which a dead fetus and other products of conception remain in the uterus for four or more weeks

- **Septic abortion**: Abortion-related pelvic and uterine infection

    EXAMPLE: Patient underwent treatment for a septic abortion, which was completed surgically. Report code 59830.

- **Induced abortion**: Deliberate termination of pregnancy

Exercise 15.4 – Maternity Care and Delivery Subsection

Instructions: Assign the CPT code(s) and appropriate modifier(s) to each statement.

1. The physician treated an ectopic pregnancy by removing the fallopian tube and ovary through an incision in the lower abdomen.

   _____

2. Using ultrasonic guidance, the physician inserted an amniocentesis needle through the abdominal wall into the interior of the pregnant uterus and directly into the amniotic sac to collect amniotic fluid for diagnostic analysis.

   _____

3. Using ultrasonic guidance, the physician inserted an amniocentesis needle through the abdominal wall into the cavity of the pregnant uterus and into the umbilical vessels to obtain fetal blood.

   _____

4. The physician used an external monitor to record fetal heart rate changes during a fetal nonstress test.

   _____

5. A physician provided all antepartum (7 visits) and postpartum care but did not perform the delivery.

   _____

Endocrine System Subsection ⚠

The **endocrine system** (Figure 15-15) includes the following glands:

- Adrenal (2)
- Gonads (ovaries in females, testes in males) (2)
- Pancreas (islets of Langerhans) (1)
- Parathyroid (divided into four lobes) (1)
- Pituitary (divided into two lobes) (1)
- Thymus (1)
- Thyroid (divided into two lobes) (1)

The Endocrine System subsection includes procedures performed on the endocrine glands and the carotid body.

 Coding Tip:

Codes for procedures performed on the pituitary and pineal glands are located in the Nervous System subsection.

Thyroid Gland

Thyroid Gland procedures classify increasingly complex procedures involving excision of the thyroid gland. For example, code 60210 classifies a partial thyroid lobectomy, with or without isthmusectomy, and code 60220 classifies a total thyroid lobectomy with or without isthmusectomy.

Codes 60252 and 60254 describe the total or subtotal resection of the thyroid gland for malignancy, with limited or radical neck dissection, respectively. A "total or subtotal resection" is the removal of both the left and right lobes of the thyroid gland. A "limited neck dissection" is the removal of a limited number of lymph nodes. A "radical neck dissection" is the total removal of lymph nodes from one side (or both sides) of the neck.

Figure 15-15 Endocrine glands

 Note:

You may recall that when a radical neck dissection is performed during the same operative session as the resection of a unilateral organ (e.g., larynx), modifier -50 is not added to the procedure codes. The thyroid gland is a unilateral organ that contains two lobes. Thus, modifiers -50, -LT, and -RT are *never* added to thyroid gland procedure codes.

EXAMPLE: A physician suspects lymphoma in a patient who has signs of diffuse neck swelling. A large-core needle biopsy of the right lobe of the thyroid gland is performed. The tissue is sent for histopathology. Report code 60100.

Parathyroid, Thymus, Adrenal Glands, Pancreas, and Carotid Body

Codes 60500–60699 are reported for procedures performed on the parathyroid, thymus, adrenal glands, and carotid body. The **carotid body** is tissue that contains many capillaries, and it is located at the point where the carotid artery branches in the neck. It contains cells that sense oxygen and carbon dioxide blood levels so that information is sent to the brain's medulla to regulate heart rate.

Surgery performed on the adrenal glands can be performed as open or laparoscopic procedures. Make sure you review the operative report to identify the surgical approach to report the appropriate code.

The exploration of parathyroid glands is often performed using a cervical approach. In cases where further exploration is needed, the physician uses a transthoracic approach.

EXAMPLE 1: Patient underwent laparoscopic exploration with partial removal of the left adrenal gland, performed from a transabdominal approach. Report code 60650-LT.

EXAMPLE 2: Patient underwent surgical laparoscopy with complete right adrenalectomy, performed from a lumbar approach. Report code 60650-RT.

Exercise 15.5 – Endocrine System Subsection

Instructions: Assign the CPT code(s) and appropriate modifier(s) to each statement.

1. The physician determines the location of a thyroid cyst, using palpation, and aspirates it.

   _____

2. The physician performed a total thyroid lobectomy on the right and a contralateral subtotal lobectomy on the left, including isthmusectomy.

   _____

3. The physician removed remaining thyroid tissue on one side, following an earlier partial thyroidectomy.

   _____

4. Patient underwent large-core needle biopsy of the thyroid gland.

   _____

5. Patient underwent incision and drainage of an infected thyroglossal cyst of the neck, which was the result of incomplete closure of the embryonic thyroglossal duct between the thyroid gland and the back of the tongue.

   _____

6. The physician performed a laparoscopic exploration of the adrenal gland through the abdomen.

   _____

7. The physician explored the parathyroid glands. During the same operative session, a parathyroid autotransplantation was also performed.

   _____

8. Patient underwent partial adrenalectomy with biopsy, dorsal approach.

   _____

9. The physician surgically removed the parathyroid glands.

   _____

10. The physician removed a carotid body tumor, which was located just above the bifurcation of the carotid artery.

    _____

Nervous System Subsection

The **nervous system** (Figure 15-16) includes the following:

- Central nervous system (brain and spinal cord)
- Peripheral nervous system (12 pairs of cranial nerves extending from the brain and 31 pairs of spinal nerves extending from the spinal cord).

  Codes for Nervous System subsection procedures are arranged anatomically.

- Skull, meninges, and brain
- Spine and spinal cord
- Extracranial nerves, peripheral nerves, and autonomic nervous system

Nervous system procedures are performed using a variety of approaches (e.g., craniectomy, craniotomy, and laminectomy) and for specific purposes (e.g., decompression and drainage of hematomas).

EXAMPLE: Patient underwent a procedure to create subdural burr holes to drain a hematoma. Report code 61154. (The subdural burr hole is the approach, and drainage of the hematoma is the purpose.)

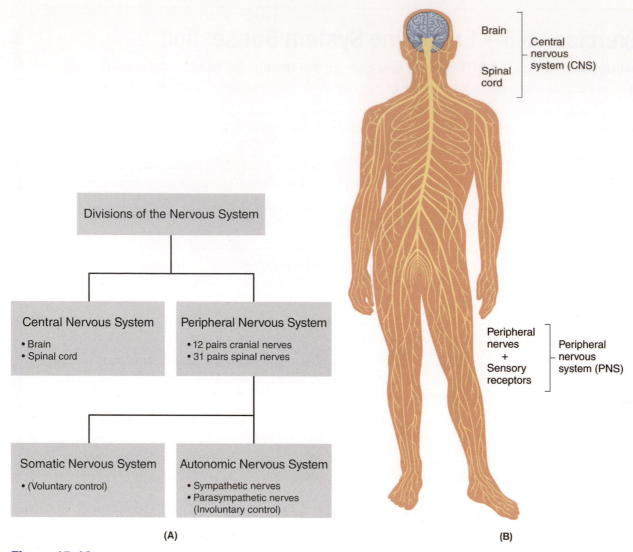

Figure 15-16 Nervous system (A) Divisions of the nervous system (B) Structure of the central nervous system and peripheral nervous system

Skull, Meninges, and Brain

The Skull, Meninges, and Brain (Figure 15-17) heading includes the following subheadings (and for "Surgery of Skull Base," further subdivisions):

- Injection, Drainage, or Aspiration
- Twist Drill, Burr Hole(s), or Trephine
- Craniectomy or Craniotomy
- Surgery of Skull Base
  - Approach Procedures
  - Definitive Procedures
  - Repair and/or Reconstruction of Surgical Defects of Skull Base
- Endovascular Therapy

- Surgery for Aneurysm, Arteriovenous Malformation, or Vascular Disease
- Stereotaxis
- Stereotactic Radiosurgery (Cranial)
- Neurostimulators (Intracranial)
- Repair
- Neuroendoscopy
- Cerebrospinal Fluid (CSF) Shunt

Arachnoid mater

Epidural

Pia mater

Skull

Intracerebral

Bone

Dura mater

Arachnoid mater

Pia mater

Epidural space

Subdural space

Subarachnoid space

Figure 15-17 Skull, meninges, and brain

A **burr hole** is a small opening in the skull made with a surgical drill. This procedure is often necessary when intracranial surgery (e.g., craniotomy or craniectomy) is planned. The burr hole provides access to intracranial contents, it alleviates pressure in preparation of further surgery, and it allows the placement of an intracranial pressure monitoring device. (These services are integral to the performance of subsequent services, and they are not to be separately coded or reported.)

When burr holes, punctures, and/or taps are created for the purpose of performing drainage procedures (e.g., hematoma, abscess, or cyst) and additional procedures are performed, the burr hole and drainage procedure is not separately coded and reported (unless it is performed as a staged procedure). In addition, many intracranial procedures include bone grafting; such grafts are not separately coded and reported.

Injection procedures for imaging of CSF flow are reported with code 61026 in addition to codes from the Radiology section (to report the imaging procedure).

EXAMPLE 1: Patient underwent ventricular puncture through previous burr hole with injection of medication. Report code 61026. (The ventricular puncture through a previous burr hole describes the approach to access a specific area of the brain.)

EXAMPLE 2: A patient with an open head injury and a contrecoup subdural hematoma underwent a craniectomy for the open head injury and creation of a burr hole on the opposite side of the skull to drain the subdural hematoma. Report codes 61304 and 61154. (The creation of the contralateral burr hole and drainage of the subdural hematoma is considered a separate service not integral to the craniectomy. Thus, it is assigned a separate code.)

Surgery of Skull Base

Surgery of skull base codes contain important notes that define anatomical areas included (e.g., skull base includes the base of the anterior, middle, and posterior cranial fossae). Notes further indicate that skull base surgery often requires the skills of several different surgical specialties that work together. Skull base surgery requires review of the operative report to identify the following variables:

- What the size of the lesion or tumor is
- What the anatomy of the individual patient is
- Whether this is an initial procedure to treat the condition or a reoperation

Surgery of skull base codes are arranged anatomically (anterior, middle, and posterior cranial fossae), and they are further subdivided according to the following:

- Approach procedures (provide adequate exposure to the intracranial field so the definitive procedure, such as excision of lesion, can be performed)

- Definitive procedures (e.g., resection, excision, transection, ligation, and obliteration), which include primary closure of dura, mucous membranes, and skin

- Repair and/or reconstruction of skull defects of skull base procedures (reported separately when cranioplasty, extensive dural grafting, extensive skin grafts, or local or regional myocutaneous pedicle flaps are required)

✒ When skull base surgery is performed, a code for each procedure is reported by the surgeon who performed that aspect of the procedure: approach procedure, definitive procedure, and repair and/or reconstructive procedure. Generally, one surgeon performs the approach procedure, which exposes the area (e.g., lesion) to be treated. Another surgeon then performs the treatment (e.g., excision of lesion). A third surgeon repairs the defect created by the treatment (e.g., free tissue graft of dural defect created by excision of lesion). When one surgeon performs both the approach procedure and the definitive procedure, that surgeon reports both codes on the same claim; modifier -51 is added to the secondary procedure.

 Note:

Skull base surgery procedures are not typically considered "staged" because definitive closure of the surgical field (e.g., dura, subcutaneous tissues, or skin) must be performed to avoid serious infections (e.g., osteomyelitis or meningitis).

EXAMPLE: The operative report documents a right maxillectomy with orbital exenteration, bilateral ethmoidectomies, and a sphenoidectomy. The patient underwent resection of a neoplastic lesion at the base of the anterior cranial fossa, extradural.

The approach procedure code is 61581 because a "craniofacial approach to anterior cranial fossa" includes ethmoidectomy, sphenoidectomy, maxillectomy, and orbital exenteration procedures. (Approach procedures for middle cranial fossa and posterior cranial fossa do include such procedures.) The definitive procedure code is 61600. (Do not report a code for repair and/or reconstruction of surgical defects of skull base because such procedures were not documented.)

Codes 61600 and 61601 distinguish between procedures performed extradurally (outside the dura) or intradurally (within the dura). The dura mater is the outermost, fibrous, and toughest of the three meninges (Figure 15-18) that surround the brain and spinal cord.

Some procedure codes in the Surgery of Skull Base heading are add-on procedures. They are not reported alone; they must be reported with another procedure code (e.g., 61605).

Figure 15-18 Meninges (dura mater, arachnoid mater, and pia mater) and other anatomical structures that protect the brain

EXAMPLE: A surgeon performed a resection of an infectious lesion of the parasellar area. During the same operative session, the same surgeon performed a transection of the carotid artery in a cavernous sinus, with repair. (No repair and/or reconstruction of surgical defects of the skull base was required.) Report codes 61607 and 61610. (The approach procedure was performed by a different surgeon; therefore, do not report a code for an approach procedure.)

Neurostimulators (Intracranial)

Codes describing craniotomy procedures are usually bundled with craniectomy codes. Thus, when a craniotomy is performed during the same operative session as a craniectomy, report only the craniectomy code. Do not report the craniotomy code in addition to the craniectomy code.

EXAMPLE: When a patient undergoes "craniectomy or craniotomy for implantation of neurostimulator electrodes" during the same operative session as the creation of "twist drill or burr hole(s) for implantation of neurostimulator electrodes," only code 61860 is reported. Code 61850 is not reported in addition to code 61860.

Cerebrospinal Fluid (CSF) Shunt

A CSF shunt (Figure 15-19) is used to eliminate excess CSF in cases of hydrocephalus.

EXAMPLE: A child underwent creation of a ventriculo peritoneal shunt. Report code 62223.

Spine and Spinal Cord

The Spine and Spinal Cord heading describes percutaneous procedures performed on the spine, as well as spinal injections and extracranial and peripheral nerve injections. To report procedure codes properly, review the operative report to identify the following:

- What the anatomical site is (e.g., epidural or facet joint nerves)
- Whether the procedure is diagnostic or therapeutic
- What type of substance is injected (e.g., contrast media or neurolytic substance)
- Whether the injections are continuous

Figure 15-19 A cerebrospinal shunt allows drainage of cerebrospinal fluid (CSF) from the brain into the peritoneal cavity.

EXAMPLE: Patient underwent percutaneous lysis of epidural adhesions procedure under fluoroscopic guidance on June 14. Hypertonic saline solution 3 × 2 was administered during the procedure. Report code 62264. (Do not report a separate code for fluoroscopic guidance.)

 Coding Tip:

- Report code 01996 from the Anesthesia section for daily hospital management of continuous epidural or subarachnoid drug administration performed with services assigned codes 62324–62327 (injection of diagnostic or therapeutic substances).

- For a spinal puncture procedure, the administration of local anesthesia is included. Reporting a separate code for the administration of local anesthesia (e.g., nerve block or facet block) is inappropriate.

- When an anesthetic block procedure is performed and cerebrospinal fluid is withdrawn during the same operative session (to make room for the anesthetic), do not report a code for diagnostic lumbar puncture. Report a code for the nerve (or other) block only because the removal of CSF is not done for diagnostic purposes.

Catheter Implantation

The *implantation* of an epidural or intrathecal catheter placement involves penetration of the dura. A parenthetical note below the Catheter Implantation subheading provides instruction to see codes 62270–62273, 62280–62284, and 62320–62327 when reporting *percutaneous placement* of an intrathecal or epidural catheter.

EXAMPLE: Patient underwent implantation of tunneled epidural catheter for long-term medication administration via external pump. Report code 62350.

Reservoir/Pump Implantation

Programmable and nonprogrammable infusion pumps provide long-term access to the vascular or nervous system for the administration of medications. When electronic analysis and reprogramming of a programmable implanted pump is performed during the same operative session as refilling and maintenance, report code 62368.

> **EXAMPLE:** Patient underwent implantation of a subcutaneous reservoir for intrathecal drug infusion. Report code 62360.

Endoscopic Decompression of Neural Elements and/or Excision of Herniated Intervertebral Discs

Code 62380 is reported for endoscopic decompression of neural elements and/or excision of herniated intervertebral discs. Surgical approaches include percutaneous, endoscopic, and open. Visualization includes direct and indirect.

> **EXAMPLE:** Patient underwent endoscopic decompression of lumbar spinal cord, which included laminotomy and excision of herniated intervertebral disk. Report code 62380.

Posterior Extradural Laminotomy or Laminectomy for Exploration/Decompression of Neural Elements or Excision of Herniated Intervertebral Discs

A **laminotomy** involves the removal of part of the lamina from one side of the vertebra. A **laminectomy** is the excision of the entire posterior arch or lamina of a vertebra. When reporting codes for a laminectomy or laminotomy (hemilaminectomy) procedure, determine the following:

- Anatomical site
- Surgical approach
- Type of procedure performed

 Coding Tip:

- A laminotomy is also known as a hemilaminectomy. Therefore, review of the operative report to differentiate between laminectomy and laminotomy (or hemilaminectomy) is required.

- When a laminotomy is performed during the same operative session as a laminectomy, the laminotomy code is not reported separately.

When codes are reported for laminotomy procedures, just one vertebral interspace in a specific area of the spine is accessed. When additional interspace(s) are accessed for laminotomy during the same operative session, report appropriate add-on code(s) in addition to the primary procedure code.

When reporting codes for laminectomy procedures, if a facetectomy and foraminotomy were performed, report a code from 63045–63048. Laminectomies without facetectomy and foraminotomy are reported with codes 63001–63011 or 63015–63017.

> **EXAMPLE:** Patient underwent hemilaminectomy with decompression of nerve roots and partial facetectomy and excision of herniated intervertebral disc, C1-C2. Report code 63040. (C1-C2 is one interspace; thus, code 63040 is reported once.)

Transpedicular or Costovertebral Approach for Posterolateral Extradural Exploration/Decompression

Codes 63055–63066 describe extradural exploration/decompression procedures that are performed using a transpedicular or costovertebral approach.

- A **transpedicular approach** is performed through and inside the pedicle (segment between transverse process and vertebral body) of a thoracic vertebra to access a thoracic disc. This approach does not require retraction of the spinal cord, but it may involve removal of the lamina and facet joint.

- A **costovertebral approach** is performed where the ribs articulate (connect) with thoracic vertebrae. (**Costovertebral** refers to that area of the thoracic spine where the rib meets the vertebra.) The physician makes an incision laterally to the spine, cutting through epidermis, dermis, subcutaneous tissue, fascia, muscle tissue, and a section of rib.

  EXAMPLE: Patient underwent decompression of spinal cord at T1 via costovertebral approach. Report code 63064.

Anterior or Anterolateral Approach for Extradural Exploration/Decompression

A **discectomy** is the removal of an intervertebral disc. When reporting codes 63075–63078, make sure you review the operative report to identify the *number of interspaces removed* (e.g., C1-C2 describes one interspace and C1-C2 and C2-C3 describe two interspaces) (Figure 15-20).

A **corpectomy** is the removal of a portion of the vertebra and adjacent intervertebral discs. Its purpose is for the decompression of the spinal cord and spinal nerves. A bone graft is placed to reconstruct the spine and provide stability. When reporting codes 63081–63091, make sure you review the operative report to identify the *number of segments removed* (e.g., C1 describes one segment and C1-C2 describes two segments) (Figure 15-20).

 Coding Tip:

- Codes 63075–63078 include **osteophytectomy**, which is the removal of bone spurs to relieve compression of the spinal cord or nerve roots.

- Codes 63075–63078 include the placement of graft material (obtained from the ilium or the removed rib) into the disc space, when performed. Grafting is performed to allow for proper spacing between vertebrae and to promote spinal fusion.

- When arthrodesis follows procedures coded with 63075–63091, report a code from 22548–22812 (in addition to the extradural exploration/decompression).

- Codes 63081–63091 include discectomy performed above and/or below the vertebral segment involved. Do not report a separate code for discectomy.

- For reconstruction of the spine, report the vertebral corpectomy codes (63081–63091) with bone graft codes (20930–20938), arthrodesis codes (22548–22812), and spinal instrumentation codes (22840–22855).

Figure 15-20 Interspaces and vertebrae (A) One interspace (B) Two segments of vertebrae

Codes 63075–63091 describe exploration/decompression procedures performed using an anterior or anterolateral approach.

- An **anterior approach** involves making an incision overlying the intervertebral disc by cutting through epidermis, dermis, subcutaneous tissue, fascia, and muscle tissue.

- An **anterolateral approach** involves making an incision along (and removing) the rib that corresponds to the vertebra that is located above the compressed intervertebral disc.

EXAMPLE: Patient underwent anterior discectomy with decompression of spinal cord, including osteophytectomy, C2-C3. Report code 63075.

Lateral Extracavitary Approach (LECA) for Extradural Exploration/Decompression

For the **lateral extracavitary approach (LECA)**, a midline incision is made in the area of the affected vertebral segment (e.g., fractured vertebra or vertebral tumor), and the incision is inferiorly curved out to the lateral plane. Paraspinous muscles are mobilized medially (denervating and devascularizing these structures). The muscles are lifted from the spinous process, and they are divided and lifted from the ribs, exposing the vertebral segment.

EXAMPLE: Patient underwent complete vertebral corpectomy with decompression of spinal cord, T1. Report code 63101.

Incision

A laminectomy with cordotomy procedure may be performed as a one-stage or two-stage procedure.

⚠ **EXAMPLE:** Patient underwent one-stage cervical laminectomy procedure with cordotomy and section of one spinothalamic tract. Report code 63194.

On June 10, the patient underwent the first procedure for a two-stage cervical laminectomy procedure with cordotomy and section of both spinothalamic tracts. On June 17, the patient underwent the second of the two-stage procedure. Report code 63198. (Code 63198 is reported just once for this two-stage procedure.)

⚠ **Coding Tip:**

For cervical laminectomy and section of dentate ligaments, with or without dural graft, report a code from 63180–63182. Do not report code 63710.

Excision by Laminectomy of Lesion Other Than Herniated Disc

When reporting codes 63250–63290, review the operative report to identify the following:

- Anatomical site
  - Cervical
  - Thoracic
  - Lumbar
  - Sacral
- Type of procedure performed
  - Excision or occlusion of arteriovenous malformation of spinal cord (63250–63252)
  - Excision or evacuation of intraspinal lesion other than neoplasm, extradural (63265–63268)
  - Excision of intraspinal lesion other than neoplasm, intradural (63270–63273)
  - Biopsy/excision of intraspinal neoplasm, extradural or intradural (63275–63290)

Add-on code 63295 is reported for osteoplastic reconstruction of dorsal spinal elements following a primary intraspinal procedure, such as laminectomy with drainage of intramedullary cyst/syrinx to subarachnoid space (63172). (Do not add modifier -51 to code 63295.)

EXAMPLE: Patient underwent laminectomy for excision of intraspinal neoplasm, extradural, thoracic. Report code 63276.

Excision, Anterior or Anterolateral Approach, Intraspinal Lesion

Code 63300 is reported for "vertebral corpectomy (vertebral body resection), partial or complete, for excision of intraspinal lesion, single segment; each additional segment." Add-on code 63308 is reported for each additional segment in addition to the code for the single segment. (Do *not* add modifier -51 to code 63308.)

EXAMPLE: Patient underwent partial vertebral corpectomy for excision of an intraspinal lesion, extradural, C1 and C2. Report codes 63300 and 63308.

Stereotaxis

Stereotaxis uses a stereotactic guidance system to allow the physician to determine three-dimensional coordinates to

- Create a lesion on the spinal cord (to alleviate chronic pain in a particular part of the body).
- Stimulate the spinal cord percutaneously (to create a lesion that will block pain).
- Facilitate the biopsy, aspiration, or excision of a spinal cord lesion.

EXAMPLE: Patient underwent stereotactic percutaneous electrical stimulation of the spinal cord to create a lesion to block severe pain. Report code 63600.

Stereotactic Radiosurgery (Spinal)

Spinal stereotactic radiosurgery uses externally generated ionizing radiation to inactivate or eradicate spinal targets without the need to make an incision.

Neurostimulators (Spinal)

A spinal **neurostimulator** system includes an electrode and a pulse generator that are implanted along the spine to alleviate pain or control spasms. Neurostimulator codes describe codes for procedures used to implant, revise, and place neurostimulators along the spine. Codes for the implantation or placement and removal or revision of the neurostimulators are reported separately.

EXAMPLE: Patient underwent percutaneous implantation of neurostimulator electrode array, epidural. Report code 63650.

Coding Tip:

Initial and subsequent electronic analysis and programming of neurostimulator pulse generators are reported with Medicine section codes 95970–95982.

Repair

When reporting repair codes, do not add modifier -63 (Procedure Performed on Infants Less Than 4 kg). (Modifier -63 is added to indicate significantly increased complexity and physician work associated with procedures performed on infants who weigh less than 4 kg.) It is not appropriate to add modifier -63 to codes 63700–63706 because the additional complexity and work is included in the procedure codes.

EXAMPLE: Patient underwent repair of meningocele, 10 cm in diameter. Report code 63702.

Shunt, Spinal CSF

The Shunt, Spinal CSF heading classifies procedures performed on the lumbar spine (not the brain).

EXAMPLE: Patient underwent creation of percutaneous shunt, lumbar, subarachnoid-peritoneal. Report code 63741.

Coding Tip:

For CSF shunt procedures performed on the brain, report codes 62190–62192, located under the Skull, Meninges, and Brain heading.

Extracranial Nerves, Peripheral Nerves, and Autonomic Nervous System

The Extracranial Nerves, Peripheral Nerves, and Autonomic Nervous System heading describes procedures performed on these types of nerves. To report procedure codes properly, review the operative report to identify the following:

- Anatomical site (e.g., somatic nerve or sympathetic nerve)
- Type of procedure performed (e.g., injection or neurostimulator implantation)

Introduction/Injection of Anesthetic Agent (Nerve Block), Diagnostic or Therapeutic

Codes 64400–64530 are reported for the introduction or injection of an anesthetic agent (e.g., nerve block). These codes describe injection procedures to somatic and sympathetic nerves for diagnostic and therapeutic reasons (e.g., pain management).

- **Somatic nerves** control voluntary movements (performed by skeletal muscles) and conscious sensation (e.g., hearing, sight, and touch), and they include voluntary motor and sensory nerves.

- **Sympathetic nerves** are part of the involuntary autonomic nervous system and originate in the thoracic and lumbar regions of the spinal cord; they inhibit (or oppose) the physiological effects of the parasympathetic nervous system (e.g., contract blood vessels, increase heart rate, and reduce digestive secretions).

To report codes 64400–64530 properly (e.g., nerve blocks), review the operative report to identify the following:

- Type of substance injected (e.g., anesthetic or neurolytic)
- Nerves involved (e.g., somatic or sympathetic)
- Type of block (e.g., single, multiple, or regional)
- Duration of the infusion

  EXAMPLE: Patient underwent injection of anesthetic agent, facial nerve. Report code 64402.

Neurostimulators (Peripheral Nerve)

A peripheral nerve neurostimulator system includes an electrode and a pulse generator that are implanted along peripheral nerves to alleviate pain or control spasms. Codes (64550–64595) for the implantation or placement and removal or revision of the neurostimulators are reported separately.

  EXAMPLE: Patient underwent percutaneous implantation of neurostimulator electrode array, cranial nerve. Report code 64553.

Destruction by Neurolytic Agent (e.g., Chemical, Thermal, Electrical, or Radiofrequency), Chemodenervation

Codes 64600–64681 are reported for procedures that include destruction by neurolytic agent (e.g., chemical, thermal, electrical, or radiofrequency), somatic or sympathetic nerves. The codes also include the injection of other therapeutic agents, such as corticosteroids.

Coding Tip:

When injections into an area surrounding the spinal cord are performed, report codes 62320–62327 (e.g., pain management). (Codes 64400–64530 are reported when injections into nerves are performed.)

Coding Tip:

Initial and subsequent electronic analysis and programming of neurostimulator pulse generators are reported with Medicine section codes 95970–95982.

EXAMPLE: Patient underwent destruction by neurolytic agent, intercostal nerve. Report code 64620.

Neuroplasty (Exploration, Neurolysis, or Nerve Decompression)

Neuroplasty is the freeing or decompression of an intact nerve from scar tissue. Neuroplasty also includes decompression, exploration, external neurolysis, and/or nerve transposition, which are not coded and reported separately.

> **Coding Tip:**
>
> When internal neurolysis (included in neuroplasty) requires the use of an operating microscope, report add-on code 64727 in addition to the neuroplasty code.

Carpal Tunnel Release

The **carpal tunnel** receives its name from the eight bones in the wrist (carpals) that form a tunnel-like structure. The tunnel is filled with flexor tendons that control finger movement and provide a pathway for the median nerve to reach sensory cells in the hand.

Repetitive flexing and extension of the wrist (e.g., repetitive motion injuries due to a job such as keyboarding or assembly line work) may cause a thickening of the protective sheaths that surround each of the tendons. When the tendon sheaths become swollen (**tenosynovitis**), increased pressure is applied to the median nerve, producing carpal tunnel syndrome.

 Carpal tunnel syndrome (Figure 15-21) is a painful progressive condition caused by compression of the median nerve at the wrist. Symptoms usually begin with numbness, pain, and weakness in the hand and wrist. Then pain radiates up the arm. As symptoms worsen, a tingling sensation may result along with decreased grip strength.

> **Coding Tip:**
>
> When the release of the transverse carpal ligament is performed endoscopically, report Musculoskeletal System subsection code 29848.

Surgical treatment of carpal tunnel syndrome includes surgery to release compression of the median nerve. (Anti-inflammatory drugs and hand/wrist splinting are also used to reduce tendon swelling.)

EXAMPLE: Patient underwent an open procedure that included neuroplasty and transposition of the median nerve at the carpal tunnel. Report code 64721.

Transection or Avulsion

Codes 64732–64772 are reported for transection or avulsion procedures, which involve surgically removing a nerve (e.g., eliminate pain).

EXAMPLE: Patient underwent lingual nerve transection due to continuous pain and burning sensation of the tongue. Report code 64740.

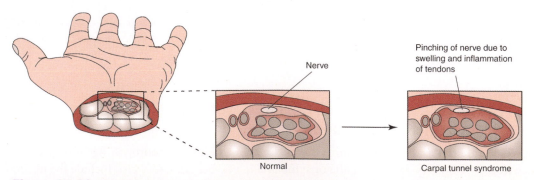

Figure 15-21 Carpal tunnel syndrome

Excision

Codes 64774–64823 are reported for excision of somatic and sympathetic nerve procedures.

 Coding Tip:

- Report code 28080 for a Morton neurectomy procedure.

- When sympathectomy procedures are performed bilaterally (codes 64802–64818), add modifier -50 (Bilateral Procedure) to the reported code.

- When an operating microscope is used to perform sympathectomy procedures (codes 64820–64823), do not report code 69990 (Microsurgical techniques, requiring use of operating microscope) as an additional code. The use of an operating microscope is included in codes 64820–64823.

EXAMPLE: Patient underwent excision of neuroma, digital nerves, left thumb, and left second digit. Report codes 64776-FA and 64778-F1.

Neurorrhaphy and Neurorrhaphy with Nerve Graft, Vein Graft, or Conduit

Codes 64831–64876 are reported for **neurorrhaphy** (repair of nerves) procedures, including the suture and anastomosis of proximal nerves (e.g., facial-spinal and facial-hypoglossal). Codes 64885–64911 are reported for neurorrhaphy with nerve graft, and the operative report should be reviewed to identify the following:

- Anatomical site (e.g., head and neck, hand or foot, or arm or leg)
- Length of the nerve graft (e.g., up to 4 cm in length or more than 4 cm in length)

EXAMPLE: Patient underwent suture of brachial plexus nerve. Report code 64861.

Exercise 15.6 – Nervous System Subsection

Instructions: Assign the CPT code(s) and appropriate modifier(s) to each statement.

1. Burr holes were drilled into the infratentorial area, and an exploratory craniotomy was performed during the same operative session.

   _____

2. Burr holes were created, and a ventricular reservoir was implanted.

   _____

3. The physician inserted a subcutaneous pump for connection to a ventricular (brain) catheter.

   _____

4. The physician reprogrammed a shunt on a patient with an implanted programmable cerebrospinal fluid valve and shunt system to decrease the shunt pressure.

   _____

5. The physician aspirated shunt tubing with a needle to determine functioning.

   _____

6. Gill laminectomy with decompression of lumbar nerve roots.

   _____

7. Diagnostic lumbar puncture.

   _____

(continues)

Exercise 15.6 (continued)

8. Removal of lamina and insertion of lumboperitoneal (LP) shunt for drainage of excess cerebrospinal fluid.
   _____

9. Replacement of a nonprogrammable epidural drug infusion pump.
   _____

10. Decompression of spinal cord with removal of herniated disc via costovertebral approach, T1.
   _____

11. Nerve block, phrenic nerve.
   _____

12. Bilateral lumbar paravertebral facet joint injections, two levels.
   _____

13. Single intercostal nerve block injection.
   _____

14. Excision of sciatic nerve neuroma.
   _____

15. Placement of transcutaneous neurostimulator.
   _____

Eye and Ocular Adnexa Subsection

The **Eye and Ocular Adnexa** subsection describes procedures performed on the eyeball, anterior and posterior segment, ocular adnexa, and conjunctivae (Figure 15-22). When reporting codes, review the operative report to identify the following:

- Anatomical site (e.g., eyeball)

- Type of procedure (e.g., retinal repair)

Eye and Ocular Adnexa subsection codes also include surgery to remove eyelid lesions and the repair or reconstruction of orbits, eyeballs, and eyelids.

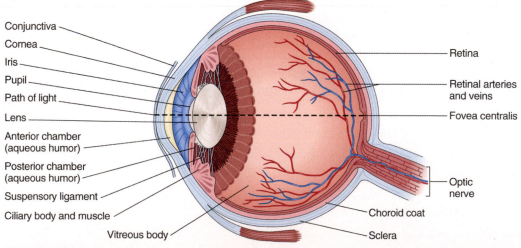

Figure 15-22 Eye and ocular adnexa

Coding Tip:

Ophthalmologic procedures are also located in the

- Integumentary System subsection (CPT Surgery) (e.g., shaving of epidermal lesions from the eyelid, 11310–11313)
- Musculoskeletal System subsection (CPT Surgery) (e.g., orbital wall decompression with nasal/sinus endoscopy, 31292–31293)
- Medicine section (e.g., diagnostic/therapeutic ophthalmologic services, 92002–92499)

 Note:

The following HCPCS level II modifiers are added to Eyelid heading codes when appropriate:

- E1 (upper left eyelid)
- E2 (lower left eyelid)
- E3 (upper right eyelid)
- E4 (lower right eyelid)

Eyeball

The **eyeball**, or **globe**, contains the choroid, retina, and sclera. The **sclera** is the white of the eye that comprises the eye's outer layer; it contains fibrous tissue that maintains the eye's shape and protects the eye's inner layers. The **cornea** is the transparent layer on the eye's surface; it covers the iris and pupil and provides focusing power. The **uvea** is the eye's vascular layer, which includes the choroid, ciliary body (ciliary muscle), and iris. The **choroid** is the opaque layer behind the retina that contains blood vessels. The **iris** is colored tissue that surrounds the pupil. The **pupil** is the black opening in the center of the iris that permits light to enter the eye. The **lens** is a clear, flexible, curved structure that focuses images on the retina. The **ciliary body**, or **ciliary muscle**, adjusts the shape of the lens and focuses light rays onto the retina. The **retina** contains nerve tissue.

An **evisceration of ocular contents** includes removal of the contents of the eyeball (choroid, ciliary muscles, iris, lens, retina, and vitreous); the sclera remains intact. (An implant may or may not be placed into the scleral shell.)

An **enucleation of the eye** includes severing the eyeball from extraorbital muscles and the optic nerve and removing it. (An implant may or may not be placed and attached to extraocular muscles.)

An **exenteration of the orbit** includes the removal of orbital contents and may also include removal of bone, muscle, and/or the myocutaneous flap. When a skin graft is placed, report a code from the Integumentary subsection (in addition to the exenteration of the orbit code). When the eyelid is repaired, report a code from the Reconstruction Area of the Eyelids subheading (in addition to the exenteration of the orbit code).

Codes 65125–65175 are reported for procedures performed to modify an ocular implant (e.g., alter the shape of a prosthesis to create a better fit). An **orbital implant** is inserted outside the muscular cone into the eye socket, and an intraocular lens (IOL) is placed. An **ocular implant** is inserted inside the muscular cone.

EXAMPLE: Patient underwent secondary insertion of ocular implant (after having undergone previous evisceration) into the scleral shell. Report code 65130.

CPT differentiates between the removal of a foreign body located in the eye and removal of implanted material (e.g., ocular implant). When coding the removal of a foreign body from the external eyeball, review the operative report to identify the following:

- Where the location is (e.g., intraocular)
- Whether a foreign body is embedded
- Whether a slit lamp was used

Most foreign bodies of the eye are located in the cornea and conjunctiva. Fluorescein staining with slit lamp inspection is used to visualize a corneal foreign body or abrasion.

Codes 65270–65290 are reported for laceration repairs of ocular structures. An extensive conjunctival laceration may also include a graft or flap. The repair of a laceration includes use of a conjunctival flap and restoration of anterior chamber by air or saline injection. Do *not* separately code and report these procedures.

> **EXAMPLE:** Patient underwent the removal of foreign body, external eye, superficial conjunctiva. Report code 65205.

Anterior Segment

Anterior Segment heading codes are reported for procedures performed on the anterior segment of the eye, which includes the cornea, anterior chamber, anterior sclera, iris, ciliary body (ciliary muscle), and lens.

- Corneal transplant (e.g., keratoplasty) is a common procedure that includes use of fresh or preserved grafts and preparation of donor material.

- Radial keratotomy (Figure 15-23) corrects myopia; the surgeon makes numerous radial incisions (like the pattern of spokes of a wheel) extending from the pupil to the periphery of the cornea. (The procedure was accidentally discovered by Dr. Svyatoslav Fyodorov, who removed pieces of glass from a patient's eye and noted that the patient's eyesight improved after removal of the glass. The lacerations to the cornea resulted in the improved eyesight.)

- Cataract removal codes include the following procedures, which are not separately coded and reported:

  - Anterior and posterior capsulotomy
  - Iridectomy
  - Iridotomy
  - Lateral canthotomy
  - Subconjunctival or subtenon injections

  - Use of viscoelastic agents, enzymatic zonulysis, and other pharmacologic agents
  - Implantation of an IOL prosthesis *when performed during the same operative session*

The following two surgical methods are typically used to remove the lens and cataracts:

- **Intracapsular cataract extraction (ICCE)**: Removal of lens and surrounding capsule

- **Extracapsular cataract extraction (ECCE)**: Removal of lens and anterior portion of capsule

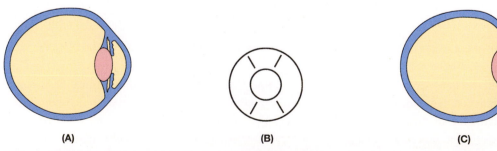

(A)   (B)   (C)

Figure 15-23 Radial keratotomy (A) Cross-section of eye prior to surgery (B) Small incisions are made in the cornea from the middle outward. (C) Radial keratotomy causes the cornea to become flatter, improving vision.

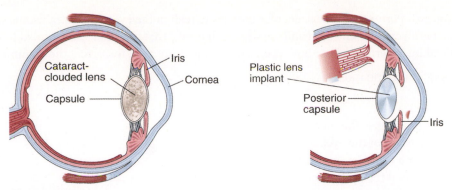

Figure 15-24 Cataract extraction with placement of intraocular lens

 The extracapsular cataract removal with insertion of an IOL (Figure 15-24) is a common procedure. An iridectomy, trabeculectomy, and anterior vitrectomy may also be performed during the same operative session as the cataract removal. Codes for these procedures are *not* reported separately.

EXAMPLE: A patient presents with a cataract and evidence of glaucoma, left eye. Trabeculectomy is performed on August 15 as treatment for the glaucoma. Extracapsular cataract extraction with insertion of IOL prosthesis is performed on August 30 as treatment for the cataract. Report codes 66170-LT (August 15) and 66984-LT (August 30).

Coding Tip:

When an iridectomy is performed to accomplish the cataract extraction, it is considered an integral part of the procedure and is not reported separately.

Posterior Segment

Codes 67005–67299 are reported for procedures performed on the vitreous, retina or choroid, and sclera. Vitreous heading codes include the removal and aspiration of vitreous and other fluids. Retina or Choroid heading codes include subheadings for repair, prophylaxis, and destruction. Some retinal detachment repair procedures also include procedures performed on the vitreous.

EXAMPLE: Code 67108 is reported for the repair of a retinal detachment. The code includes the following procedures: vitrectomy, air or gas tamponade, focal endolaser photocoagulation, cryotherapy, drainage of subretinal fluid, scleral buckling, and/or removal of lens by same technique. This means that separate codes are not reported for the included procedures.

Ocular Adnexa

The **ocular adnexa** includes the orbit, eye muscles, eyelids, eyelashes, conjunctiva, and lacrimal apparatus. The **orbit**, or **eye socket**, is the bony cavity in the skull that contains and protects the eyeball (and its associated blood vessels, muscles, and nerves). The eye muscles work together to enable binocular vision. The eyelids protect the eyeball and keep its surface moist. The eyebrows and eyelashes prevent debris from getting into the eyes. The **conjunctiva** is a mucous membrane that lines the underside of each eyelid and forms a protective covering over the exposed surface of the eyeball. The **lacrimal apparatus**, or **tear apparatus**, contains structures that produce, store, and remove tears.

Codes 67311–67399 are reported for procedures performed on the eyelid that involve more than skin. Many of these codes also include surgery to correct **strabismus**, which is improperly aligned eyes, such as cross-eyes (one eye points inward) and walleye (one eye points outward). Codes 67400–67599 are reported for exploration, excision, and decompression procedures performed on the orbit, in addition to injections and orbital implants.

Strabismus surgery is performed on extraocular muscles to realign the eyes. Each strabismus surgery code reflects a procedure performed on one eye (unilateral), which means that modifier -50 is added to the appropriate code when the procedure is performed on both eyes. Two methods are used to correct the alignment of eye muscles.

- Recession: Lengthening the muscle

- Resection: Shortening the muscle

⚠ For a recession procedure, the muscle is detached from the attachment site on the surface of the eyeball and reattached along the surface of the eye. For a resection procedure, a small portion of the muscle is removed and the eye muscle is reattached to the original insertion site.

When it is medically necessary to inject sclerosing agents during the same operative session as surgery to correct glaucoma, that service is included in the glaucoma surgery. CPT codes 67500, 67515, and 68200 are reported for the injection of sclerosing agents (e.g., fluorouracil, 500 mg, which is reported with HCPCS level II code J9190); they are *not* reported with other pressure-reducing or glaucoma procedure codes.

 Coding Tip:

Codes for the treatment of orbital bone fractures (e.g., frontal, sphenoid, zygomatic, maxilla, ethmoid, and lacrimal) are located in the Musculoskeletal System section.

EXAMPLE: Patient underwent removal of an embedded foreign body, left lower eyelid. Report code 67938-E2.

Conjunctiva

Codes 68020–68899 are reported for procedures performed on the conjunctiva, including the following:

- Incision and drainage
- Excision and/or destruction
- Injection

- Conjunctivoplasty
- Other procedures
- Lacrimal system

EXAMPLE: Patient underwent incision and drainage of a conjunctival cyst of the right upper eyelid. Report code 68020-E3.

The "expression of conjunctival follicles (e.g., for trachoma)" is reported with code 68040. A **trachoma** is a chronic inflammation of the conjunctiva in which granulations form. The physician uses biomicroscopic guidance to remove the conjunctival follicles with a cotton tipped swab or a curette without making an incision. Physicians often use biomicroscopic guidance (e.g., an optical instrument that looks like a microscope with two eyepieces) to treat trachoma. A slit lamp (e.g., a specialized magnifying microscope used to examine the structures of the eye) is also used with the biomicroscope.

 Note:

Per the CPT note below the "Eye and Ocular Adnexa" subsection, do not report code 69990 (microsurgical techniques requiring use of operating microscope) in addition to codes 65091–68850. Use of the operating microscope is not reported separately because it is considered an essential part of eye and ocular adnexa procedures.

When a subconjunctival injection (e.g., CPT code 68200) with a local anesthetic is performed as part of a more extensive anesthetic procedure (e.g., peribulbar or retrobulbar block), do not separately code and report the injection procedure. The injection procedure is considered a routine part of the anesthetic procedure and does not represent a separate service.

Conjunctivoplasty codes (68320–68340) describe plastic surgery procedures performed on the conjunctiva. The following procedures are included in conjunctivoplasty codes, which means that they are *not* coded and reported separately: incision and drainage, excision and/or destruction, and injection of conjunctiva.

The lacrimal system keeps the cornea and conjunctiva moist through tear production. Codes reported for procedures performed on the lacrimal system include incision, excision, repair, and probing and/ or related procedures.

A common procedure is the repair of the **lacrimal puncta**, which are small openings in the inner canthus of the eyelids that channel tears. There are two puncta in each eye, an upper and lower punctum. Thus, when both puncta in one eye are treated, report the appropriate code twice. According to *CPT Assistant* (June 1996), when all puncta in both eyes are treated (four puncta), codes 68705 and 68760–68761 are reported four times.

 Note:

There is no parenthetical note below codes 68705 and 68760–68761, unlike below code 68801, which provides instruction to add modifier -50 (Bilateral Procedure) to each code.

EXAMPLE: Patient underwent closure of the lacrimal puncta via laser surgery, both eyes. Report codes 68760, 68760, 68760, and 68760.

Exercise 15.7 – Eye and Ocular Adnexa Subsection

Instructions: Assign the CPT code(s) and appropriate modifier(s) to each statement.

1. Removal of foreign body from cornea of right eye, using a slit lamp.

2. Repair of corneal laceration with removal of foreign body, left eye.

3. Modification of ocular implant with replacement of pegs.

4. Nonmagnetic extraction of an intraocular foreign body from posterior segment of right eye.

5. A patient complained of sudden onset of tearing and pain in the right eye. After eversion of the upper lid, a small wood fragment was removed.

6. Cryotherapy destruction of corneal lesion, left eye.

7. Endoscopic goniotomy, right eye.

8. Insertion of intraocular lens four weeks after right cataract removal.

9. Removal of corneal lesion using scleral scissors, left eye.

10. Extracapsular cataract removal with insertion of intraocular lens prosthesis, left eye.

11. Aspiration of vitreous fluid, pars plana approach, right eye.

12. Laser photocoagulation of choroidal lesion, right eye, using fluorescein angiogram as a guide.

13. Diathermy for treatment of a patient with progressive diabetic retinopathy, both eyes.

(continues)

Exercise 15.7 *(continued)*

14. Scleral reinforcement with graft, left eye.

_____

15. Prophylactic treatment of retinal detachment, left eye, using cryotherapy, four sessions.

_____

16. Fine-needle aspiration of orbit, right eye.

_____

17. Strabismus surgery that included a recession procedure of two horizontal muscles, both eyes.

_____

18. Removal of chalazions from right upper eyelid and left upper eyelid.

_____

19. Strabismus surgery was performed for the first time on one horizontal muscle of the right eye and on the superior oblique muscle of the left eye.

_____

20. Strabismus surgery performed on two horizontal muscles during which a transposition procedure was also performed to detach and relocate two rectus muscles next to a paralyzed muscle, right eye.

_____

21. Injection of cortical steroid into subconjunctival space, left eye.

_____

22. Closure of a total of four lacrimal puncta using collagen plugs, both eyes.

_____

23. Bilateral nasolacrimal duct probing with irrigation.

_____

24. Cauterization to correct everted upper and lower lacrimal puncta, left eye.

_____

25. Incision and drainage, conjunctival cyst, right eye.

_____

Auditory System Subsection ⚠

The **Auditory System** (Figure 15-25) subsection is organized anatomically according to the following:

- External ear
- Middle ear
- Inner ear
- Temporal bone, middle fossa approach

Subsection notes direct the coder to otorhinolaryngologic service codes in the Medicine section (92502–92700) for diagnostic services performed on the auditory system.

External Ear

The **external ear** includes the auricle (or pinna) and the external auditory meatus (or ear canal). Codes 69000–69399 are reported for the incision, excision, removal of foreign body, repair, and other procedures performed on the external ear.

Coding Tip:

Most procedures classified in the Auditory System subsection are unilateral. Report modifier -LT (Left side), -RT (Right side), or -50 (Bilateral Procedure) as appropriate.

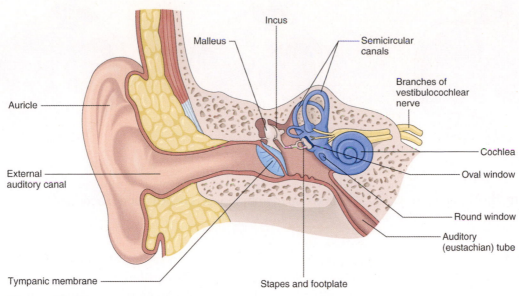

Figure 15-25 The auditory system

Figure 15-26 Removal of impacted cerumen

A frequently performed procedure is the "removal of impacted cerumen (separate procedure), one or both ears," which is reported with codes 69209-69210 (Figure 15-26). Report this code just once when the procedure is performed bilaterally.

EXAMPLE: Patient underwent biopsy, external ear, left. Report code 69100-LT.

Middle Ear

The **middle ear** includes the tympanic membrane, auditory ossicles, muscles, and conduction pathways. A commonly performed procedure is "tympanostomy (requiring insertion of ventilation tube), local or topical anesthesia," which is reported with code 69433. This procedure is typically performed on children who have chronic ear infections.

A **myringotomy**, or **tympanostomy**, is the surgical incision of the tympanic membrane, and it is usually performed to release pressure or fluid. A **tympanoplasty** is the repair or reconstruction of the eardrum (Figure 15-27).

EXAMPLE: Patient underwent complete mastoidectomy, left ear. Report code 69502-LT.

Figure 15-27 Tympanoplasty (A) Tympanic membrane incision (B) Tube placement (C) Tympanoplasty completed

Inner Ear

The **inner ear** includes the cochlea, saccule, acoustic nerve (e.g., auditory portion), semicircular canals, utricle, and superior and inferior vestibular nerves (e.g., vestibular portion). A labyrinthotomy procedure is performed using a transcanal approach (69801). When a transcanal labyrinthotomy is performed, all required infusions performed on initial and subsequent days of treatment are included in the reported code (69801).

A **cochlear implant** is an implanted electronic device for treatment of sensory deafness. A vestibular nerve section using a transcranial approach (69950) includes the removal of the semicircular canals as well as bone over the internal auditory canal.

EXAMPLE: Patient underwent cochlear device implantation with mastoidectomy, right and left ears. Report code 69930-50.

Temporal Bone, Middle Fossa Approach

Codes 69950–69970 are reported for nerve decompression or repair procedures. A common procedure performed to repair facial nerve damage is total nerve decompression, which is used to treat symptoms of **Bell's palsy** (unilateral paralysis of facial muscles resulting from dysfunction of the 7th cranial nerve, probably due to a viral infection).

EXAMPLE: Patient underwent decompression of the internal auditory canal, left ear. Report code 69960-LT.

Exercise 15.8 – Auditory System Subsection

Instructions: Assign the CPT code(s) and appropriate modifier(s) to each statement.

1. Simple incision and drainage, abscess, left external ear.

_____

2. Removal of a button from the left ear canal of a 2-year-old child.

_____

3. Plastic surgeon reduced the size of a protruding right ear.

_____

4. Routine cleaning (simple debridement) of mastoidectomy cavity, right ear.

_____

5. A family physician pierced a 1-year-old girl's ears.

_____

6. With the patient under general anesthesia, the physician removed ventilating tubes from both ears.

_____

Exercise 15.8 *(continued)*

7. With the patient under general anesthesia, tympanostomy with insertion of ventilating tubes was performed.

   _____

8. Transcanal tympanolysis, right.

   _____

9. Replacement of a bone conduction hearing device and removal of old device, left ear.

   _____

10. Mobilization of stapes on the left.

    _____

11. Decompression of intratemporal nerve, lateral to geniculate ganglion.

    _____

12. Physician implanted a cochlear device bilaterally.

    _____

13. A physician repaired a tympanic membrane with patch, right ear.

    _____

14. Mastoidectomy and tympanoplasty with ossicular chain reconstruction, left ear.

    _____

15. Neurectomy of tympanic nerve, left side.

    _____

16. Removal of temporal bone tumor, left side.

    _____

17. A physician treated a patient who was diagnosed with a tumor of the facial nerve by performing total facial nerve repair and grafting the nerve.

    _____

18. Decompression internal auditory canal, right side.

    _____

19. A physician performed an endolymphatic sac operation.

    _____

20. Transcranial vestibular nerve section.

    _____

Operating Microscope Subsection

When an **operating microscope** is used during a surgical procedure to perform microsurgery techniques, report add-on code 69990 in addition to the primary procedure code.

 Coding Tip:

Do *not* report code 69990 for

- Visualization with a magnifying loupe or corrected vision.
- Procedures for which use of an operating microscope is an inclusive component. (Refer to Operating Microscope heading notes for a list of excluded codes.)

EXAMPLE: Patient underwent vestibular nerve section, transcranial approach, with use of an operating microscope. Report codes 69950 and 69990.

Exercise 15.9 – Operating Microscope Subsection

Instructions: Assign the CPT code(s) and appropriate modifier(s) to each statement.

1. An otolaryngologist used a magnifying loupe to perform a tympanic membrane repair.

   _____

2. Diagnostic direct laryngoscopy with use of an operating microscope.

   _____

3. The physician uses an operating microscope while performing a partial mastectomy, right breast.

   _____

4. Microsurgical epididymovasostomy, bilateral.

   _____

5. The physician used an operating microscope to perform a hypophysectomy.

   _____

Summary

For procedures performed on the male genital system, code assignment is determined according to approach (e.g., incision, destruction, excision, or introduction) and reason for surgery. Reproductive System Procedures classify the placement of needles into pelvic organs and/or genitalia for subsequent interstitial radioelement application. Intersex surgery is performed as a series of staged procedures to transform the normal adult genitalia of one sex to that of the other sex (genital reconstructive surgery or sex reassignment surgery).

Codes classified in the Female Genital System heading are reported for procedures performed on women who are *not* pregnant. (Codes for women who are pregnant are reported from the Maternity Care and Delivery heading.) When reporting codes for procedures performed on the female genital system, review the operative report to identify the anatomy on which the procedure was performed (e.g., vulva, perineum, introitus, or vagina) and the surgical approach.

The three stages of pregnancy care include services provided as part of total obstetrical care: antepartum care, delivery of the baby, and postpartum care. Total obstetrical care does *not* include diagnostic procedures, physician office visits for unrelated conditions incidental to pregnancy, and additional visits due to high-risk conditions or medical complications of pregnancy. Codes for these services are separately reported from the Evaluation and Management and Medicine sections of CPT. The treatment of surgical complications associated with pregnancy are separately reported with codes from the Surgery section.

The Endocrine System subsection includes procedures performed on the endocrine glands and the carotid body. Codes for Nervous System subsection procedures are arranged anatomically (skull, meninges, and brain; spine and spinal cord; and extracranial nerves, peripheral nerves, and autonomic nervous system). Nervous system procedures are performed using a variety of approaches for specific purposes.

The Eye and Ocular Adnexa subsection describes procedures performed on the eyeball, anterior and posterior segment, ocular adnexa, and conjunctivae. When reporting codes, review the operative report to identify the anatomical site and type of procedure. The Auditory System subsection is organized anatomically according to the external ear; middle ear; inner ear; and temporal bone, middle fossa approach. When an operating microscope is used during a surgical procedure to perform microsurgery techniques, report add-on code 69990 in addition to the primary procedure code.

Internet Links

American Academy of Family Physicians: Go to *www.aafp.org*, click on the Practice Management link, and then click on the Coding link below the Payment for Physicians heading.

American Academy of Otolaryngology—Head and Neck Surgery: *www.entnet.org*

American Association of Neurological Surgeons: *www.aans.org*

American Congress of Obstetricians and Gynecologists: Go to *www.acog.org*, click on the Practice Management link, and then click on the Coding link.

Center for Male Reproductive Medicine (CMRM): *www.malereproduction.com*

Center for Male Reproductive Medicine and Microsurgery: *www.maleinfertility.org*

The Eye Digest: *http://www.scribd.com/eyeMD*

FamilyDoctor.org: Go to *www.familydoctor.org*, and click on any of the links below the Pregnancy & Newborns heading.

Lacrimedics, Inc.: Go to *www.lacrimedics.com*, and click on the Patient Resources link.

Society for Endocrinology: *www.endocrinology.org*

Women's Health: *www.womenshealth.gov*

Study Checklist

- ❑ Read this chapter and highlight key concepts.
- ❑ Create an index card for each key term.
- ❑ Access the chapter Internet links to learn more about concepts.
- ❑ Complete the chapter exercises and review, verifying answers with your instructor.
- ❑ Complete Workbook chapter, verifying answers with your instructor.
- ❑ Go to *www.cengagebrain.com* to access the Student Companion Web Site. Login instructions are located in the Preface.
- ❑ Form a study group with classmates to discuss chapter concepts in preparation for an exam.

Review

Multiple Choice

Instructions: Circle the most appropriate response.

1. The tube that carries spermatozoa from the testis is the:
    a. prostate gland.
    b. urethra.
    c. varicocele.
    d. vas deferens.

2. Which procedure involves the direct visualization of the cervical canal and the uterine cavity and is performed to examine the endometrium?
    a. Colposcopy
    b. Hysteroscopy
    c. LEEP electrodissection conization
    d. Loop electrodissection conization

3. According to the notes below the Maternity Care and Delivery subsection of Surgery, which service is included in codes reported for maternity care and delivery?
   a. Cordocentesis
   b. Episiotomy
   c. Fetal nonstress test
   d. Insertion of cervical dilator

4. How many glands are included in the endocrine system?
   a. 7
   b. 9
   c. 13
   d. 15

5. When more than one interspace is accessed for laminotomy during the same operative session, report the:
   a. appropriate add-on code(s) in addition to the primary procedure code.
   b. primary code once for each interspace accessed.
   c. primary code only.
   d. primary code with modifier -51.

6. Which surgical approach used in extradural exploration/decompression involves making an incision overlying the intervertebral disc and cutting through epidermis, dermis, subcutaneous, fascia, and muscle tissue?
   a. Anterior approach
   b. Anterolateral approach
   c. Costovertebral approach
   d. Transpedicular approach

7. Which nerves are part of the involuntary autonomic nervous system, originate in the thoracic and lumbar regions of the spinal cord, and inhibit the physiological effects of the parasympathetic nervous system?
   a. Cranial
   b. Median
   c. Somatic
   d. Sympathetic

8. Which is the freeing or decompression of an intact nerve from scar tissue?
   a. Neuroma
   b. Neuroplasty
   c. Neurorrhaphy
   d. Neurostimulator

9. When all puncta in both eyes are treated during the same encounter, the appropriate code is reported:
   a. once.
   b. twice.
   c. three times.
   d. four times.

10. Which includes the tympanic membrane, auditory ossicles, muscles, and conduction pathways?
    a. Cochlea
    b. Inner ear
    c. Middle ear
    d. Outer ear

11. Plastic repair of the penis due to epispadias distal to external sphincter. Patient was diagnosed with incontinence. Which CPT code is assigned?
    a. 54360
    b. 54380
    c. 54385
    d. 54390

12. Patient placed under anesthesia and an impacted foreign body removed from vagina. Which CPT code is assigned?
    a. 57110
    b. 57111
    c. 57135
    d. 57415

13. Surgical treatment of ovarian ectopic pregnancy. Vaginal salpingectomy. Which CPT code is assigned?
    a. 59120
    b. 59130
    c. 59140
    d. 59150

14. Excision of thyroglossal duct cyst. Which CPT code is assigned?
    a. 60200
    b. 60280
    c. 60281
    d. 60600

15. Burr hole with drainage of subdural hematoma. Which CPT code is assigned?
    a. 61150
    b. 61154
    c. 61156
    d. 61253

16. Replacement of cerebrospinal fluid shunt. Which CPT code is assigned?
    a. 62220
    b. 62223
    c. 62225
    d. 62230

17. Cervical laminectomy for extradural excision of intraspinal neoplasm. Which CPT code is assigned?
    a. 63250
    b. 63265
    c. 63270
    d. 63275

18. Laceration repair of conjunctiva by mobilization and rearrangement, with hospitalization. Which CPT code is assigned?
    - a. 65270
    - b. 65272
    - c. 65273
    - d. 65285

19. Patient diagnosed as having dislocated lens in left eye. Physician performed intracapsular removal of lens. Which CPT code is assigned?
    - a. 66920-LT
    - b. 66930-LT
    - c. 66940-LT
    - d. 66982-LT

20. Transcanal labyrinthectomy. Which CPT code is assigned?
    - a. 69801
    - b. 69905
    - c. 69910
    - d. 69915

Coding Practice

Instructions: Assign the CPT code(s) and appropriate modifier(s) to each case.

1. A biopsy needle was passed up the urethra. Using manual guidance, the surgeon identified the prostate gland and performed a punch biopsy. The needle was withdrawn.

   _____

2. The patient had been diagnosed with hydroceles, which are scheduled to be removed via excision. First, an incision was made of the patient's scrotum. The hydrocele on the right was identified and dissected free. The left side of the patient's body was treated in the same manner for the hydrocele there.

   _____

3. The patient has a papilloma of the penis. This is removed via laser surgery.

   _____

4. After being informed of all of the risks, the parents of a newborn male patient consented to a circumcision. Regional dorsal penile block (anesthesia) was administered by the physician performing the circumcision. The foreskin of the penis was clamped, and excess skin was trimmed. The clamp was left in place, and antibiotic ointment was applied.

   _____

5. After adequate general anesthesia, the patient's scrotum was incised. The spermatic cord was identified, dissected, and cross-clamped. The right testis was carefully pushed up from the scrotum and excised. All vessels were clamped, and all bleeders were cauterized. The left testis was removed using a similar method. The spermatic cord was cross-clamped and cut.

   _____

6. Patient underwent bilateral vasectomy including postoperative semen examination. The skin over the spermatic cord was injected with a local anesthetic. The scrotum was exposed via an incision, and the tubular structures of this organ were identified. The vas deferens was identified and cut with a small section of the tube removed. The same method was performed on the opposite side.

   _____

7. A prostatectomy was being performed for prostate cancer. An incision was made at the scrotum. A urethrotomy was used to enlarge the penile urethra. The prostate was dissected via the use of an instrument. The prostate as well as supporting anatomical structures were removed. All bleeding was controlled with cauterization. Attention was then directed to pelvic lymph nodes, which were removed on both sides in total for analysis and staging.

   _____

8. Patient underwent reduction of torsion of the left testis. An incision was made in the patient's scrotum. The twisted left testis was identified. The testis was carefully detangled. Excellent blood flow was seen. Four sutures were used to anchor the testis to the wall of the scrotum to prevent further twisting.

   _____

9. A patient has a spermatocele. After incising the scrotum, the physician identified the testis and the spermatocele. The spermatocele was dissected from the epididymis.

   _____

10. A patient with moderate chordee presents for surgical repair of the penis to straighten the chordee for hypospadias, with mobilization of the urethra.

    _____

11. The patient has a diagnosis of recurrent cervical carcinoma with metastatic disease to the ovaries and bladder. After discussing with the patient and informing her of the risks, the patient consented to an abdominal hysterectomy. An incision was made at the pubic area. The fascia and muscle were retracted. The cervix and uterus were identified and excised. The bladder was found to have numerous lesions; it was also removed. The ureters were transplanted to the skin to allow for urine flow. An ileal urinary conduit, in which the ureters are implanted into a segment of small bowel, was done.

    _____

12. An endoscope was inserted into the vulva and passed into the uterus. After gaining access to the cavity, a biopsy of the endometrium was done. The scope was withdrawn.

    _____

13. An incision was made in the umbilical region for the insertion of laparoscope; a second incision was made on the right side of the abdomen to pass additional trocars. A Falope ring was inserted and advanced through the trocar to the area of the fallopian tubes. This ring was clamped around the fallopian tubes to provide occlusion.

    _____

14. A colposcope was inserted into the patient. This allowed for visualization of the female genital organs. The vagina was found to be normal. The cervix has an area of fibrous tissue, which was biopsied. The endocervical area had an area of inflammation, which was taken away via curettage.

    _____

15. After inserting a speculum into the vagina, the physician was able to visualize a vaginal cyst directly. Forceps were used to clamp the cyst. The cyst was excised and sent to pathology for analysis. The speculum was removed.

    _____

16. After inserting a speculum into the vagina, the physician identified a Bartholin gland; the cyst was directly visualized. An incision was made, and the cyst was dissected free of the surrounding tissue and mucosa. The wound was closed in layers with absorbable sutures.

    _____

17. After insertion of a speculum into the vagina, laser cautery was performed to remove the outer cells of the cervix.

    _____

18. The physician performed a salpingostomy and identified a damaged right fallopian tube.

    _____

19. After insertion of a speculum into the vagina, a catheter was passed that contained several small embryos. With the use of the catheter, the embryos were inserted into the uterus.

    _____

20. After an abdominal incision was made, the left ovary was identified. The ovarian cysts were located and removed in total. The incision was closed with sutures.

    _____

21. Second-stage operation was done with the goal of constructing a penis and scrotum. This was done using multiple grafts from the patient's skin and clitoris. A penile prosthesis was implanted into the constructed organ.

    _____

22. The new construction of a vagina was the goal in this staged procedure. Using tissue from the patient's penis, a clitoris structure was fashioned. The perineum of the patient was opened to form a vagina. The sides of the vagina were lined with skin grafts to add stability.

    _____

23. A neonatologist attached a fetal monitoring electrode to the scalp of the fetus in utero. This was done for seven hours during the labor process. The physician read, interpreted, and made notations on the tracing coming from the electrode data.

    _____

24. A patient at 39 weeks' gestation presented in labor. The patient has requested a VBAC (vaginal birth after cesarean). After 20 hours in labor, fetal distress was noted. The patient required a cesarean delivery. All antepartum and postpartum care was provided by the delivering physician.

    _____

25. A woman with five fetuses presents for fetal reduction due to her severe preeclampsia. Using the potassium chloride method, two fetal sacs are injected. At the conclusion of the procedure, the woman has three fetal sacs intact.

    _____

26. At 11 weeks' gestation, the patient had an incomplete abortion. Due to profuse vaginal bleeding, evacuating the uterus was necessary. Dilation and curettage (D and C) was done with suction of any remaining products of conception.

    _____

27. A woman presents after having delivered her baby vaginally en route to the hospital in a private motor vehicle. The newborn was taken directly to the neonatal intensive care unit (NICU) for evaluation. The placenta had not been delivered on route to the hospital. Using abdominal massage, the placenta was delivered.

    _____

28. An ectopic pregnancy was confirmed by ultrasound. Via a vaginal approach, the pelvic cavity was visualized and examined. All products of conception were removed using curettage. The pelvic cavity was lavaged with saline solution. The patient's right fallopian tube was affected. This tube was excised.

    _____

29. After normal prenatal care, this patient presented in labor at 38 weeks. An episiotomy was done to facilitate delivery. A normal healthy newborn was born via vaginal delivery. The episiotomy was repaired. The patient was discharged with her baby and received postpartum follow-up care in the office.

_____

30. The patient presents for an antepartum visit. This is her fourth scheduled appointment. Her estimated gestational age is 26 weeks. The patient reports heavy vaginal bleeding overnight. After insertion of the speculum, the uterus was examined. Slight bleeding was noted. The patient has had a complete miscarriage. No products of conception are seen. There is no need for surgical intervention.

_____

31. Routine prenatal care was rendered to this patient, who presented at 41 weeks in labor. The patient was examined, and the fetus was found to be in a breech position. The fetus was turned via external abdominal approach into a cephalic position. After the turning of the fetus, an episiotomy was per- formed. A normal healthy 10-pound infant was born via vaginal delivery. The episiotomy was repaired. Postpartum care was delivered.

_____

32. The patient's neck was palpated, and a mass was identified on the left. Local anesthesia was adminis- tered, and the position of the mass was confirmed again by palpation. A percutaneous core needle was inserted through the skin and underlying tissue into the thyroid mass. The needle was withdrawn with the sample inside the core. The sample will be sent for analysis.

_____

33. After adequate general anesthesia, a cervical incision was made. Skin, fascia, and muscle were retracted to expose the thyroid gland. A severely enlarged left lobe of the thyroid was found. The left lobe was removed in total and sent to pathology for analysis. Parathyroid glands were carefully inspected and found to be normal. These were not removed but were left intact. All bleeders were cauterized. The skin and muscle were closed in layers.

_____

34. After adequate general anesthesia, a midline abdominal incision was made. The retroperitoneal area was identified and found to be normal. The adrenal glands were directly visualized. The left adrenal gland was removed in total. A biopsy sample was taken from the right adrenal gland.

_____

35. After adequate general anesthesia, an incision was made along the thyroglossal duct cyst. A portion of the hyoid bone was removed, and recurrent thyroglossal duct cyst was excised. Wound was packed for secondary closure.

_____

36. After adequate general anesthesia, a cervical incision was made to expose the thyroid and parathyroid glands. The parathyroid glands were directly visualized. The right gland was removed.

_____

37. After several small incisions were made in the patient's back, the laparoscope was introduced. The adrenal gland on the right was identified and examined. It was normal in appearance. The left adrenal gland was found to be enlarged at the tip. This section was removed and passed through the trocar. The scope was removed and the skin incision closed with sutures.

_____

38. After a cervical incision was made, the muscles of the neck were separated to expose the thyroid and parathyroid glands. The right lobe was normal in appearance and size. The left upper thyroid gland had a goiter measuring approximately 3.0 cm. This lobe with the goiter was removed.

   _____

39. Based on thyroid biopsy, this patient presented for a total thyroidectomy due to thyroid carcinoma. The neck area was cleaned and draped in the usual fashion. Under general anesthesia, the patient had a cervical incision. A radical neck dissection was performed. After the muscles of the neck were separated, the gland was exposed. Direct visualization showed the gland to be cystic and nodular in nature. The right lobe of the gland was removed first, followed by the left lobe. The parathyroid glands were inspected and appeared to be normal. The thyroid gland in total was removed and sent to pathology for analysis. All bleeders were cauterized. The incision was closed in layers with staples and sutures.

   _____

40. Under general anesthesia, a cervical incision at the previous incision site was done. The neck muscles were divided and retracted. The thyroid area was exposed. The absent left lobe of the thyroid was noted. The right lobe of the thyroid was examined. It was found to be very nodular in appearance. This lobe was removed. The parathyroid glands were examined and appeared normal. The specimen of the right lobe was sent to pathology. The muscles were retracted back and closed with staples. The incision was closed in layers.

   _____

41. After the patient's adrenal area was accessed through a midline abdominal incision, the retroperitoneal space was explored. A mass was identified adjacent to the left adrenal gland. This was removed. The left adrenal gland, which also appeared abnormal, was removed in total. The incision was closed.

   _____

42. After the patient was placed in a prone position, an incision was made over the upper spinal area. The placement of the epidural drug infusion device was in the subcutaneous tissue. The incision was closed with sutures.

   _____

43. The peripheral maxillary facial nerve was identified. A nerve block injection was done.

   _____

44. The patient presented with a laceration of the digital nerve of the left hand. This was repaired with sutures.

   _____

45. A neurostimulator electrode device is placed through the skin to the cranial nerve.

   _____

46. The patient presents with a meningocele approximately 4.0 cm in diameter. This was repaired after placing the patient in a prone position and making an incision. Access was gained to the dura of the thoracic spinal region. The bulging tissue was carefully placed into normal position. The incision was closed.

   _____

47. The patient was placed on his side. After local anesthesia, the biopsy needle was inserted at the lumbar region. The sheath of the needle was pulled back; cloudy fluid was seen. This fluid was collected in the hollow portion of the needle.

   _____

48. This patient presented for drainage of a brain abscess. After a burr hole was drilled, the cranium was accessed to reveal the site of the abscess. The abscess was drained.

_____

49. The patient presented with an arteriovenous (AV) malformation. A craniotomy was performed to gain access to the brain and the site of the malformation. This was done without difficulty. Blood vessels leading to the malformation were identified and ligated. The malformation measured approximately 2.0 cm in size. It was carefully resected supratentorially. The bone portion from the craniotomy was replaced and secured.

_____

50. The patient presented with a nerve compression of the left leg. An incision was made overlying the compressed sciatic nerve midpoint. Scar tissue was identified and dissected free. No adhesions were seen.

_____

51. The patient presented for a replacement of his lumbosubarachnoid shunt, which was performed by first incising at the original incision site. A moderate number of adhesions were seen, which were removed. The old shunt was also removed. A new shunt was placed in the same position.

_____

52. The patient presented with a foreign body sensation of the left eye. Under slit lamp examination, a small metallic foreign body was identified. This object was slightly embedded in the lower corneal area. It was removed via a small incision, using the slit lamp for guidance.

_____

53. The patient presented for correction of cross-eyes. The left eye was immobilized with a speculum. Incisions were made in the conjunctiva. The lateral muscle was identified and incised. The lateral muscle was sutured distally to the sclera. The medial rectus muscle was surgically incised and sutured in the same manner.

_____

54. After injection of a local anesthetic agent, the left upper eyelid was examined closely. A large chalazion was seen. The chalazion was resected in total. A moderate area of infection was noted, and this was drained. The infectious area was flushed with saline solution.

_____

55. After the injection of a local anesthetic agent, an incision was made on the patient's right side at the site of the medial canthal tendon. After careful dissection, the lacrimal sac was identified and removed.

_____

56. The patient presented with a corneal lamellar on the right side. This was excised using scleral scissors. Antibiotic ointment was applied.

_____

57. Using a laser, short bursts were administered to the patient's left eye. This iridotomy was performed to allow for the movement of fluid in the anterior chamber and to treat the patient's glaucoma.

_____

58. Using a xenon arc, spots were made on the patient's retina. This provided a good seal of the retinal tear of the right eye.

_____

59. With the patient under local anesthesia, the right lower eyelid is palpated and a foreign body is found in the upper-right quadrant near the posterior surface. The lid was everted and an incision made under the site. The foreign body was removed.

_____

60. The patient presented with a tumor of the lacrimal gland. An incision was made in the lid crease of the left upper eyelid. This had to be extended down into the lacrimal fossa. An osteotomy was necessary to gain access to the entire mass. The mass was removed in total. The incisional wound was closed.

_____

61. After making an incision in the patient's left eye at the junction of the cornea and sclera, the eye was entered. The nucleus of the eye lens was removed. The operating microscope was brought into the operating field. The soft portion of the lens was removed. This removed the entire cataract, but the capsule of the eye was left intact. An IOL was inserted. The incision was closed, and antibiotic injection was done.

_____

62. Impacted cerumen was removed from the left ear, using lavage and suction. After removal, the ear canal was inspected. No evidence of infection was seen. The same method was done on the right ear.

_____

63. The patient presented with a protruding left ear. The posterior auricle was incised. This allowed for the skin fold to be raised away from the ear cartilage. A new skin fold was created using several sutures. This new fold allowed for the ear to be in a more normal position.

_____

64. The patient reported a buzzing sound from her left ear. Direct examination identified an insect-like foreign object in the canal. Using a cerumen spoon, the object was removed.

_____

65. Using the punch biopsy method, a specimen was taken from the right external auditory canal.

_____

66. With the patient under general anesthesia, an incision was made at the left auricular region and tympanoplasty with mastoidectomy was performed. The outer bone of the mastoid was removed, and the mastoid antrum was entered. The tympanic membrane was identified and perforated. The eardrum was brought forward. The middle ear was examined. A cholesteatoma was found and removed. The ossicular chain was identified and examined and found to be normal.

_____

67. Through the ear canal of the patient's left ear, the aural polyp was identified under direct examination. With an ear snare, the polyp was removed. Antibiotic drops were placed in the canal. Minimal bleeding was noted.

_____

68. After the patient's right auditory canal was examined, an abscess was noted. This required drainage. An incision was made over the location of this external abscess. The abscess was drained, with a puslike material seen. Antibiotic ointment and dressing were applied.

_____

69. The patient underwent bilateral myringotomy including aspiration and eustachian tube inflation.

70. The patient presented with an aural glomus tumor on the left. After an incision of the skin was made posteriorly to the aural, the skin was retracted. The mastoid bone was exposed, and the tegmen was identified. The tumor was also identified. The tumor was removed in total with forceps and sent to pathology for analysis. The incision was closed.

71. The patient presented seven months postmastoidectomy for debridement of the left cavity. This was done under direct visualization using suction. Skin and debris were removed from the left side of the mastoid. No infection was observed. The skin and debris removed appeared normal in appearance.

72. The patient underwent transcanal labyrinthotomy with cryosurgery and multiple perfusion of vestibuloactive drugs. After anesthesia, an incision was made posterior to the ear canal on the right and the external ear was exposed. The operating microscope was brought into the field to facilitate the placement of a temporary stapes plate. The cryolaser was used to debride tissue present in the area.

73. A patient presented with a fistula of the left salivary gland. This area was incised to expose the fistula, and the operating microscope was used to get a better view of the fistula for the purpose of closure.

74. A neonatal patient presented with a diaphragmatic hernia. Under adequate anesthesia, an abdominal incision was made. The operating microscope was used to identify all vessels and small arteries. This was in part due to the size of the infant. The hernia sac was exposed and dissected free, sutures were placed to close the diaphragmatic hernia defect, and the external incision was closed in layers.

75. The patient had a malfunctioning valve of the left femoral vein. After an incision was made over the vein site, the operating microscope was used to isolate the exact site of the valve in the femoral vein. The valve was exposed and repaired with sutures.

76. The patient had an injury to his left pinky finger. The volar plate required repair. The digit was incised at the interphalangeal joint space. The operating microscope was used to identify the area of instability. The plate was sutured to the distal bone. The wound was closed with sutures.

77. An incision was made over the skin at the site of the injured blood vessel, left hand, third finger. The operating microscope was brought into the field to help identify the vessel and used to assist in the dissection. Direct repair of the vessel with sutures was performed. The surgical incision was closed with sutures.

78. The infratemporal facial nerve required repair. First, an incision was made to expose the nerve. The operating microscope was then used to facilitate the repair. The surgical incision wound was closed with sutures.

79. The patient presented with a lesion of the pharynx. The patient's oral cavity was assessed using the operating microscope, and the lesion was identified. After identification, the laser was brought into the field to perform the excision. Minimal bleeding was noted.

_____

80. The patient presented with several small lesions of the epiglottis. Epiglottidectomy was performed using the operating microscope.

_____

81. After an extensor tendon in the patient's left index finger was excised using the operating microscope, a synthetic rod was implanted for delayed tendon graft. The surgical incision was closed with sutures.

_____

82. The patient presented with retained ventilating ear tubes bilaterally. After general anesthesia was administered, the operating microscope was brought into the operating field. The right tympanic membrane was examined under the microscope. The tube was found and removed. The ear canal was irrigated. The left ear was handled in the same method.

_____

83. The patient presented with a cyst of the urachus. This was removed after making an abdominal incision. The urachal portion of the bladder (cord from apex of bladder to the umbilicus) was exposed. The operating microscope was used to identify several small cysts. These were removed under microscopic guidance.

_____

84. Arthrodesis of the carpometacarpal joint was performed on the right hand, second digit. After an incision was made over the joint space, the external bony structures of the carpometacarpal joint space were identified. With both the operating microscope and a small screw, the joint was repaired. The surgical incision was closed with sutures.

_____

85. A decompression fasciotomy of the right forearm was performed using the operating microscope to explore the brachial artery.

_____

Chapter Outline

Radiology Terminology

Overview of Radiology Section

Radiology Section Guidelines

Radiology Subsections

Diagnostic Radiology (Diagnostic Imaging)

Diagnostic Ultrasound

Radiologic Guidance

Breast, Mammography

Bone/Joint Studies

Radiation Oncology

Nuclear Medicine

Chapter Objectives

At the conclusion of this chapter, the student should be able to:

- Define key terms.
- Explain the organization, format, and content of the CPT Radiology section.
- Interpret CPT radiology coding guidelines and notes.
- Assign CPT radiology codes.
- Add CPT and/or HCPCS level II modifiers to codes, as appropriate.

Key Terms

A-mode

amplitude modulation

angiography

anteroposterior
  projection

aortography

arthrography

axial plane

biometric A-scan

biomicroscopy

block

blocking

bone density study

brightness mode

B-scan

cardiac blood pool
  imaging

compensator

component coding

computed axial
  tomography (CT) (CAT)

computed tomography
  angiography (CTA)

contrast agent

contrast material

contrast medium
  injection device

corneal pachymetry

coronal plane

cystography

cytoreduction surgery

debulking

diagnostic
  mammography

Doppler ultrasonography

dosimetry

dual energy x-ray
  absorptiometry (DEXA)

echo

epidurography

equivalent dose

external radiation

fluoroscopy

fraction (in radiation
  treatment
  management)

frontal plane

global service

gray (gy)
gray-scale ultrasound
horizontal plane
hyperthermia
internal radiation
interventional radiologic procedure
intrathecal
lateral projection
magnetic resonance angiography (MRA)
magnetic resonance imaging (MRI)
mammography
megaelectron volt
megavolt
MeV
midsagittal plane

M-mode
motion mode
nuclear imaging
nuclear medicine
oblique projection
parenterally
photons
plane of view
port
positron emission tomography (PET)
posteroanterior (PA) projection
professional component
quantitative A-scan
radiation absorbed dose (rad)
radiation oncology

radiographic projection
radiologic guidance
radiologist
radiology
radionuclide
radiopharmaceutical therapy
real-time scan
roentgen
roentgen-equivalent-man (rem)
sagittal plane
screening mammography
side view
single photon emission computerized tomography (SPECT)

slit lamp exam
supervision and interpretation
systemic radiation therapy
technical component
therapeutic port film
transverse plane
treatment volume determination
ultrasonography
ultrasound
uptake
venography
view
wedge
x-ray
x-ray beam

Introduction

The Radiology section of CPT includes subsections for diagnostic radiology (diagnostic imaging); diagnostic ultrasound; radiologic guidance; breast, mammography; bone/joint studies; radiation oncology; and nuclear medicine. These subsections are further subdivided into anatomical categories. The Diagnostic Radiology (Diagnostic Imaging) subsection includes noninvasive and invasive diagnostic and therapeutic (interventional) procedures, as well as computed (or computerized) tomography and magnetic resonance imaging.

 Note:

Procedures frequently performed by radiologists that are located in other CPT sections include

- Noninvasive vascular diagnostic studies (93880–93998)
- Invasive (or interventional) radiology services (Surgery section), such as
  - Injection procedures
  - Transcatheter procedures

The Other Procedures code below each subheading classifies an unlisted procedure performed on the anatomical site. When reporting an unlisted procedure code, include documentation about the procedure performed with the submitted claim. (Other Procedures subheadings are not included throughout Chapter 16 of this textbook except when codes that describe additional procedures are included.)

Radiology Terminology

Radiology is a branch of medicine that uses imaging techniques to diagnose and treat disease. A **radiologist** is a physician who has undergone specialized training to interpret diagnostic x-rays, perform specialized x-ray procedures, and administer radiation for the treatment of disease (e.g., cancer). Terms unique to the radiographic procedures include the following:

- Planes of view

- Positioning and radiographic projection

EXAMPLE: Axial is a standard plane of reference for most radiology codes. For example, axial images depict the long axis of the body, from the head to foot.

Planes of View

Terminology that describes **planes of view** (Figure 16-1) used when performing radiology procedures includes the following:

- **Coronal plane** (or **frontal plane**): Divides the body into anterior or ventral and posterior or dorsal portions at a right angle to the sagittal plane, separating the body into front and back; also called ventral or dorsal plane

- **Midsagittal plane**: Vertically divides the body through the midline into two equal left and right halves

- **Sagittal plane**: Vertically divides the body into unequal left and right portions

- **Transverse plane** (or **horizontal plane** or **axial plane**): Horizontally divides the body into superior and inferior portions

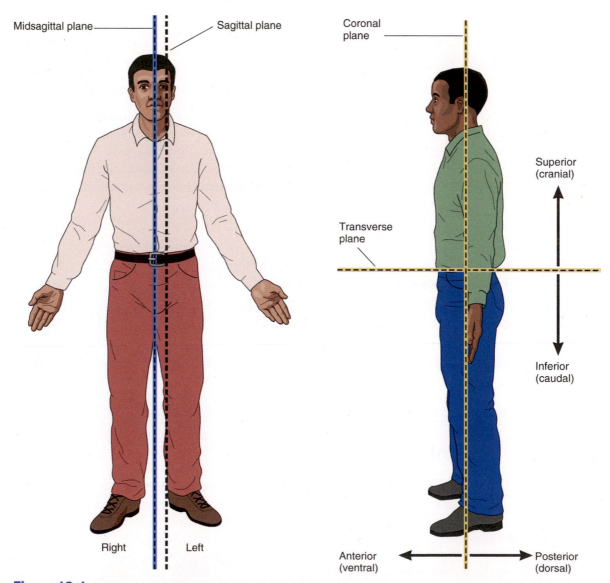

Figure 16-1 Planes that separate body structures

| Posteroanterior (PA) projection | Anteroposterior (AP) projection | Lateral (Lat) position | Left posterior oblique (LPO) position |

Figure 16-2 Radiographic projections

Positioning and Radiographic Projection

Patients are positioned for radiographic procedures so that a certain part of the body is placed closest to the x-ray film. The patient's position in relation to the camera is the **view** (e.g., code 71010 specifies a single frontal view of the chest). **Radiographic projection** (Figure 16-2) describes the path that the x-ray beam travels through the body, from entrance to exit. An **x-ray beam** is made up of invisible electromagnetic energy waves called **photons**, which are emitted from a radiation machine and are used to produce images (x-rays) and treat disease (e.g., cancer). Radiographic projections include the following:

- **Anteroposterior projection**: Patient is positioned with his or her back parallel to the film; the x-ray beam travels from front to back, or anterior to posterior

- **Lateral projection**, or **side view**: Patient is positioned at a right angle to the film; the x-ray beam travels through the side of the body

- **Oblique projection**: Patient is positioned with the body slanted sideways toward the film, halfway between a parallel and right-angle position; the x-ray beam travels through this angle of the body

- **Posteroanterior (PA) projection**: Patient is positioned facing the film and parallel to it; the x-ray beam travels from back to front, or posterior to anterior

Radiology Procedures

Radiology procedures include

- **Angiography**: X-ray of a blood vessel after injection of contrast material (Figure 16-3)

- **Aortography**: X-ray of the aorta after injection of contrast material

- **Arthrography**: X-ray of a joint after injection of contrast material

- **Computed axial tomography (CT) (CAT)**: X-ray of horizontal and vertical cross-sectional views or "slices" of the body that are computer-processed to create three-dimensional, or 3D, images

Figure 16-3 Angiography

- **Computed tomography angiography (CTA)**: X-rays of different angles create cross-sectional images of organs, bones, and tissues to visualize blood flow in arterial and venous vessels throughout the body

- **Cystography**: X-ray of the urinary bladder after injection of contrast material

- **Fluoroscopy**: Continuous x-ray beam generates a movie-like image that is viewed on a monitor; used for invasive procedures such as intravenous/intra-arterial catheterization and extracorporeal shock wave lithotripsy

- **Magnetic resonance imaging (MRI)**: Noninvasive x-ray procedure uses an external magnetic field to produce a two-dimensional view of an internal organ or structure such as the brain or spinal cord

- **Nuclear imaging**: Noninvasive x-ray procedure creates an image by measuring radiation emission, or radiation "uptake," of body areas after the administration of a **radionuclide**, which is a radioactive material, such as an isotope of iodine

- **Positron emission tomography (PET)**: X-ray images of the body are produced after the administration of radioisotopes, which track metabolism or blood flow, not anatomy

- **Single photon emission computerized tomography (SPECT)**: 3D x-ray images of internal organs are produced after administration of a radioactive material, which visualize anatomy *and* function

- **Ultrasound**, or **ultrasonography**: High-frequency sound waves bounce off internal organs and create echoes; the echo pattern is displayed on the ultrasound machine monitor; an **echo** is the effect of a sound that reflects off a distant surface and returns to its source, just like the sound produced when you yell into a well and your voice "bounces back"

- **Venography**: X-ray of a vein is taken after injection of contrast material

- **X-ray**: Radiographic visualization or imaging of internal body structures uses low-dose high-energy radiation (High-dose high-energy radiation is used to treat diseases such as cancer.)

When a radiology procedure is performed, a device called a **block** (e.g., lead apron) made of lead or another heavy metal is placed between the radiation beam and that portion of the patient's body that requires protection from radiation.

The international unit of exposure dose for x-rays or gamma rays is called a **roentgen**, abbreviated as R or r. (Roentgen is named after Professor Wilhelm Konrad Roentgen, who discovered x-rays in 1895.) A unit of **radiation absorbed dose (rad)** is the amount of radiant energy absorbed in a tissue. Newer radiation terminology includes the term **gray**, abbreviated as **gy**, named for British physician L. Harold Gray (1905–1965) (an authority on the use of radiation for cancer treatment). (One gray equals 100 rads.) A **roentgen-equivalent-man (rem)** is the unit of measurement that includes different biological responses to different kinds of radiation. The radiation quantity measured by rem is called an **equivalent dose**. (A millirem is one-thousandth of a rem, the unit for measuring equivalent dose.)

Exercise 16.1 – Radiology Terminology

Instructions: Match each plane of view with its description.

_____ **1.** Divides body horizontally into superior and inferior portions

_____ **2.** Divides body into anterior and posterior portions

_____ **3.** Divides body vertically into unequal left and right portions

_____ **4.** Divides body vertically through midline into equal left and right halves

a. Coronal plane

b. Midsagittal plane

c. Sagittal plane

d. Transverse plane

Exercise 16.1 (*continued*)

Instructions: Match each radiographic projection with its description.

_____ **5.** Patient positioned at right angle to film; x-ray beam travels through side of body.

_____ **6.** Patient positioned facing film and parallel to it; x-ray beam travels back to front.

_____ **7.** Patient positioned with back parallel to film; x-ray beam travels from front to back.

_____ **8.** Patient positioned with body slanted sideways toward the film, halfway between parallel and right-angle position; x-ray beam travels through this angle of the body.

a. Anteroposterior
b. Lateral
c. Oblique
d. Posteroanterior

Instructions: Match each radiology procedure with its description.

_____ **9.** X-ray of a vein after injection of contrast material.

_____ **10.** X-ray of the urinary bladder after injection of contrast material.

_____ **11.** Continuous x-ray beam generates a movie-like image that is viewed on a monitor.

_____ **12.** Use of an external magnetic field to produce a two-dimensional x-ray of an internal organ.

_____ **13.** High-frequency sound waves bounce off internal organs, creating echoes; echo pattern is displayed on the ultrasound machine monitor.

_____ **14.** X-ray of the aorta after injection of contrast material.

_____ **15.** X-ray of a joint after injection of contrast material.

a. Aortography
b. Arthrography
c. Cystography
d. Fluoroscopy
e. MRI
f. Ultrasound
g. Venography

Overview of Radiology Section

The Radiology section includes subsections for diagnostic radiology (diagnostic imaging); diagnostic ultrasound; radiologic guidance; breast, mammography; bone/joint studies; radiation oncology; and nuclear medicine. Procedure descriptions include the

- Type of service (e.g., modality)
- Anatomical site
- Use of contrast material

Professional Versus Technical Components

For radiology coding, the physician responsible for the professional and technical components of an examination must be determined. (Professional and technical components are reimbursement issues, which means that there are no CPT guidelines or notes explaining the three options.) Radiology procedures include the following three components:

- **Technical component:** Use of equipment and supplies and the employment of radiologic technologists to perform diagnostic imaging examinations and administer radiation therapy treatments

- **Professional component**: Services provided by the physician, which include supervising the performance of a diagnostic imaging procedure, interpreting imaging films, and documenting the imaging report

- **Global service**: Combined technical and professional components, as reported with a CPT Radiology code

✐ Most radiology procedures require both professional and technical components, and the following modifiers are added to radiology codes as appropriate:

- -26 (Professional Component)
- -TC (Technical Component)

Modifier -26 is added to the radiology code when a radiologist interprets the radiographic image and documents a report (but does not perform the radiologic procedure). This indicates that only the professional component was provided.

Note:

Some radiology codes include only a professional component, and modifier -26 is *not* added to these codes (e.g., therapeutic radiology treatment planning codes and weekly radiation therapy management codes).

Modifier -TC is added to the radiology code when the provider performs the radiologic procedure. (A radiologist employed by another facility interprets the radiographic image and documents the report. That radiologist adds modifier -26 to the radiology code.)

When a provider owns the equipment and performs both the technical and the professional components, a global CPT code is reported. A modifier is *not* added to the radiology code. (Hospitals own radiology equipment, and they employ radiologic technicians who perform x-rays and employ or contract with radiologists who interpret radiographic images and document reports.)

EXAMPLE 1: Patient undergoes a complete chest x-ray, minimum of four views (71030), which is performed on an outpatient basis at the hospital. (The patient's primary care provider completed a requisition for the chest x-ray after having evaluated the patient in the office for shortness of breath.) The radiologic technician takes the x-ray, and the radiologist interprets the image and documents an x-ray report. A copy of the x-ray report is mailed to the patient's primary care provider. The hospital reports the x-ray code as a global service.

EXAMPLE 2: Patient undergoes a complete wrist x-ray, minimum of three views (73110), which is performed at a freestanding radiology clinic. (The patient's primary care provider had completed a requisition for the wrist x-ray after evaluating the patient in the office for severe wrist pain earlier that day.) The clinic's radiologic technician takes the x-ray, and the clinic's radiologist interprets the image and documents an x-ray report. A copy of the x-ray report is mailed to the patient's primary care provider. The clinic reports the x-ray code as a global service.

EXAMPLE 3: The patient is seen by her primary care provider, who evaluates a lump on her right pinky finger. The office has x-ray equipment and takes a two-view x-ray of the hand (73120). The x-ray is interpreted by a hand specialist who is located in another office. The primary care provider reports the x-ray code with HCPCS level II modifier -TC (technical component). The hand specialist reports the x-ray code with CPT modifier -26 (professional component) added to it.

Note:

Depending on the contract negotiated between radiologists and the health care facility

- Radiologists are considered employees of the health care facility (e.g., hospital) or contractors.
- The facility submits claims to obtain reimbursement for all services provided to patients (including professional services), or the radiologists use a medical billing service to submit claims for professional services.

Use of Modifiers with Radiology Codes

Modifiers commonly added to Radiology codes include

- -52 (Reduced Services), to indicate that a service is partially reduced at the physician's discretion.

EXAMPLE: Patient underwent ultrasound exam of swollen tonsils. Code 76536 is reported for "Ultrasound, soft tissues of head and neck (eg, thyroid, parathyroid, parotid) real time with image documentation." Because just tonsillar tissue was evaluated, code 76536-52 is reported.

- -76 (Repeat Procedure by Same Physician or Other Qualified Health Care Professional) describes a repeat procedure by the same physician on the same date of service. ("Same physician" refers to either the same physician or a physician in the same specialty or group.)

    EXAMPLE: A patient presents to the emergency department (ED) with blunt abdominal trauma. Complete acute abdomen series with supine, erect, and decubitus views and single-view chest x-ray was performed. The patient became unstable several hours later in the ED, and the x-ray was repeated. Code 74022-76 is reported for the repeat x-ray.

 Coding Tip:

> - Modifier -50 (Bilateral Procedure) is not added to each radiology procedure that is performed bilaterally because code descriptions may specify "bilateral." Radiology code descriptions must be carefully reviewed to determine whether modifier -50 should be added.
> - Modifier -51 (Multiple Procedures) is usually not added to radiology codes. However, modifier -51 is added to nuclear medicine codes 78306, 78320, 78802, 78803, 78806, and 78807 when appropriate.
> - HCPCS level II anatomical modifiers -LT (Left) and -RT (Right) are added to radiology codes when appropriate. These modifiers are reported to identify a specific side of the body.

Complete Procedure

The term *complete* as included in radiology code descriptions refers to the number of views required for the study of a designated body part. Code descriptions include language that indicates what constitutes a *complete study* for a specific type of radiologic procedure.

⚠ **EXAMPLE 1:** Code 70120 is reported when a mastoid x-ray of fewer than three views is performed. Code 70130 is reported when a complete mastoid x-ray is performed.

EXAMPLE 2: Code 70332 describes a radiologic diagnostic procedure that contains both radiologic and surgical components. Report code 70332 for the radiologic procedure. Report code 21116 for the injection procedure if it is performed during the same session.

 Coding Tip:

> Do not confuse use of the term *complete* in the code description with its use in a parenthetical note below a code.

Both components comprise a complete procedure when performed by the same physician (e.g., radiologist), and two codes are reported by that physician. However, when two physicians are involved in performing the procedure, each physician submits the code for the respective portion of the procedure performed.

Evaluation and Management (E/M) Services

When the radiologist provides E/M services as part of the radiographic procedure (e.g., invasive or interventional radiology), a CPT code is *not* reported. The services provided by the radiologist include a minimal history and examination to determine the following:

- Reason for the examination
- Presence of allergies
- Acquisition of informed consent
- Discussion of follow-up
- Review of the patient record

The complexity of medical decision making is usually limited to the following:

- Whether the invasive or interventional procedure should be performed
- Whether any comorbidities (coexisting conditions) may impact the procedure
- What discussion and education took place with the patient

However, when a significant, separately identifiable E/M service is provided by the radiologist distinct from the radiographic procedure, an appropriate E/M code is reported (e.g., initial radiation oncology consultation to determine whether to proceed with treatment).

EXAMPLE: The patient's primary care provider requests that a radiologist provide consultation services to render an opinion about the patient's candidacy for a uterine embolization procedure. The radiologist performs a comprehensive history and examination and reviews the patient's record. A pelvic MRI is performed to assist in medical decision making. The radiologist reports a code from the Office or Other Outpatient Consultations category of the CPT E/M section.

Exercise 16.2 – Overview of Radiology Section

Instructions: Complete each statement.

1. Procedure descriptions for codes in the Radiology section include _____, _____, and _____.

2. Services provided by the radiologic technologist include performing diagnostic imaging examinations and administering radiation therapy treatments. This is called the _____ component.

3. Services provided by the physician include supervising the performance of a diagnostic imaging procedure, interpreting imaging films, and documenting the imaging report. This is called the _____ component.

4. The combined technical and professional components, as reported with a CPT radiology code, is called the _____.

5. When a significant, separately identifiable E/M service is provided by the radiologist distinct from the radiographic procedure, the appropriate _____ code is reported.

Radiology Section Guidelines

Guidelines located at the beginning of the Radiology section provide instruction about the following:

- Subject listings
- Separate procedures
- Unlisted service or procedure
- Special report
- Supervision and interpretation
- Administration of contrast material(s)
- Written report(s)

Instructional notes appear throughout the Radiology section to provide coding clarification and direction.

Subject Listings

When radiologic services are performed by or under the responsible supervision of a physician (e.g., radiologist) or other qualified health care professional, radiology codes are reported.

Separate Procedures

Some procedures listed in the Radiology section of CPT are considered an integral component of a total service or procedure and are identified by the descriptor *separate procedure*. These codes are *not* reported in addition to the code for the primary or total x-ray procedure unless the *separate procedure* is unrelated to or distinct from other procedures/services provided at that time.

> **EXAMPLE:** Patient undergoes laparoscopic cholecystectomy with intraoperative cholangiogram and fluoroscopy. Report codes 47563 (surgeon) and 74300.

Unlisted Procedures

As in other CPT sections, unlisted procedure codes are reported for a service or procedure that is not adequately described or listed in CPT (e.g., 76499, Unlisted diagnostic radiographic procedure).

Special Report

The radiology guidelines repeat the special report instructions found in previous sections. As in other CPT sections, when a service is new, unusual, or rarely provided, it requires a special report to validate the medical necessity and appropriateness of the service (e.g., complexity of symptoms). A special report should include all pertinent information (e.g., the time, effort, and equipment needed; diagnostic and therapeutic procedures performed; and description of the nature, extent, and need for the procedure).

Supervision and Interpretation

Imaging procedures may require a surgical procedure to access the imaged area (e.g., injection of contrast material), or a surgical procedure may require image guidance (e.g., lung biopsy with fluoroscopic guidance). In CPT, many radiological services include image guidance in their code descriptions, which means separate *radiological supervision and interpretation* codes for image guidance are *not* reported.

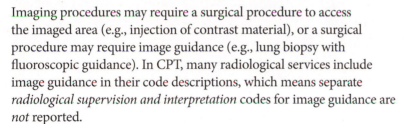

Note:

The radiological supervision and interpretation concept does *not* apply to Radiation Oncology subsection procedures.

Interventional radiologic procedures (e.g., catheterization, injection of contrast media) are used to diagnose and treat conditions using percutaneous or minimally invasive techniques under imaging guidance. Due to the complexity of interventional radiology services, **component coding** allows for reporting a radiology procedure code *and* a surgical procedure code to completely describe the service provided. Component coding provides a mechanism for reporting interventional services whether the services are performed by a single physician or by different physicians (e.g., one physician performs the procedure and the other performs the imaging supervision and interpretation).

- When two different physicians (e.g., surgeon and radiologist) perform the surgical and radiological components, each physician reports the code(s) for his or her component of the procedure performed. The radiological portion of the procedure is designated as "radiological **supervision and interpretation**."

- When one physician performs the procedure and provides radiological supervision and interpretation, that physician reports codes for both components (from the Surgery section *and* the Radiology section).

> **EXAMPLE 1:** In a hospital outpatient setting, a radiologist performed an injection procedure and supervised and interpreted an antegrade pyelography through a previously placed nephrostomy. The hospital reports codes 50431. (Radiologists are salaried hospital employees, and they do not submit insurance claims for reimbursement. The hospital billing department submits the claim.)

> **EXAMPLE 2:** Patient undergoes needle biopsy of the liver under fluoroscopic guidance. Report codes 47000 and 77002.

Administration of Contrast Material(s)

A **contrast agent**, or **contrast material** (or contrast medium), is a radiopaque substance (solid or liquid) that is administered to provide better radiographic visualization of organs studied. The contrast agent is administered orally, rectally, intravenously, percutaneously, or through inhalation or urinary catheterization.

Figure 16-4 Contrast medium injection device

 A **contrast medium injection device** (Figure 16-4) is used to deliver a predetermined amount of contrast, typically for vascular imaging procedures.

Contrast agents are radiopaque (impenetrable by x-rays or other forms of radiation), and they block x-ray beams and provide excellent contrast for body structures. Common contrast agents include

- Barium sulfate (gastrointestinal studies)

- Organic iodine (vascular and renal studies)

- Iodized oils (myelography)

Contrast materials make body structures appear white on x-rays.

 Note:

Radiologic procedures are performed with contrast, without contrast, or with and without contrast. Separate codes are available in the Radiology section to describe all of these combinations.

⚠ **Coding Tip:**

Radiology codes that contain the description "with contrast" include intravascular, intra-articular, or intrathecal administration of contrast material. When contrast material is administered orally or rectally (e.g., barium enema), the administration of the contrast material is not reported separately. It is included in the radiologic procedure performed.

Note:

The supply of contrast material is not included in radiology procedure codes. HCPCS level II codes are reported for the supply of contrast material (e.g., A4641, A4642, A9500, and A9600).

Written Report 🖉

The written report, documented and authenticated by the interpreting individual (e.g., radiologist), is considered an integral part of a radiologic procedure or interpretation. Therefore, before reporting the radiology procedure code on an insurance claim, the documented report must be available in the patient's record.

Radiology guidelines state that the interpreting individual must sign a written report as an integral part of a radiologic procedure. However, the guidelines do *not* specify content or format.

When a teaching physician reviews a radiographic image interpreted by a resident, the teaching physician is responsible for documenting a note indicating that the image was reviewed with the resident, and the teaching physician agreed with the resident's interpretation. (If the teaching physician disagreed with the resident's interpretation, the teaching physician is responsible for documenting a corrected report.) Before a claim is submitted to Medicare for payment, the radiologic report must be authenticated by the teaching physician (and a statement of agreement with the resident's interpretation must be documented by the teaching physician).

 Note:

Code of Federal Regulations, 42 CFR (Conditions of Participation for Hospitals) states, "The radiologist or other practitioner who performs radiology services must sign reports of his or her interpretations. Authentication may include signatures, written initials or computer entry." (Electronic signatures require verification methods to ensure accuracy of the entry, such as encryption.)

Exercise 16.3 – Radiology Section Guidelines

Instructions: Complete each statement.

1. Radiological procedures that are completed as an integral component of a total service or procedure are called _____ procedures.

2. A radiological procedure that is provided to patients but that is not included in the current edition of the CPT coding manual is called a(n) _____ procedure.

3. A #5 French pigtail catheter was placed via femoral puncture in the abdominal aorta. Abdominal aortography, by serialography, with radiological supervision and interpretation was performed. Identify and assign CPT codes to the surgical and radiological components.

    a. Surgical component: _____

    b. Radiological component: _____

4. Radiology codes that contain the description "with contrast" include the _____, _____, and _____ administration of contrast material.

5. When contrast material is administered orally or rectally, its administration is included in the procedure and is separately reported. TRUE or FALSE.

Radiology Subsections

The Radiology section of CPT includes seven subsections.

- Diagnostic radiology (diagnostic imaging) (70010–76499)
- Diagnostic ultrasound (76506–76999)

- Radiologic guidance (77001–77022)

- Breast, mammography (77065-77067)

- Bone/joint studies (77071–77086)

- Radiation oncology (77261–77799)

- Nuclear medicine (78012–79999)

Radiology is the medical specialty that uses x-rays (e.g., radiant energy) to diagnose and treat injuries and disease. Radiology imaging also includes MRI, magnetic resonance angiography (MRA), CT scan, ultrasound, and nuclear scans. Radiology procedure codes are found under the procedural term (e.g., transluminal atherectomy) or the anatomical site (e.g., chest).

Diagnostic Radiology (Diagnostic Imaging)

The Diagnostic Radiology (Diagnostic Imaging) subsection includes the following headings:

- Head and Neck

- Chest (Figure 16-5)

- Spine and Pelvis

- Upper Extremities

- Lower Extremities

- Abdomen

- Gastrointestinal Tract

- Urinary Tract

- Gynecological and Obstetrical

- Heart

- Vascular Procedures

- Other Procedures

The Diagnostic Radiology (Diagnostic Imaging) subsection includes diagnostic and therapeutic procedures, computed tomography (CT) (Figure 16-6), magnetic resonance imaging (MRI), and magnetic resonance angiography (MRA). These diagnostic procedures can be as simple as a routine chest x-ray or as complex as a carotid angiography, which requires selective vascular catheterization.

To code diagnostic radiology procedures accurately, identify the following:

- Anatomical site

- Type of procedure

- Number of views

- Laterality of the procedure (e.g., unilateral or bilateral)

- Use of contrast media

CPT allows for various combinations of codes to address the number and type of radiographic views. For a given radiographic series, the procedure code that most accurately describes what was performed is appropriate.

A variety of combinations of views necessary to obtain medically useful information are classified in the Diagnostic Radiology subsection. A complete review of available codes for radiographic procedures ensures accurate coding so that the most comprehensive code is reported (to describe services performed). Do not report multiple codes to describe a service when a combination code is available.

 Note:

A careful review of the radiology code description is required so that the most comprehensive code is reported. Codes 71010–71035 are reported for chest x-ray procedures. The radiologic report will indicate the view (e.g., single) and type of chest x-ray (e.g., frontal).

- 71010—Radiologic examination, chest, single view, frontal

- 71020—Radiologic examination, chest, two views, frontal and lateral

Figure 16-5 Lateral chest x-ray. Bones of the spine are white, and soft tissues are shades of gray.

Figure 16-6 Abdominal CT scan in which the liver is predominant in the upper left and the stomach is visible in the upper right

When radiographic procedures are repeated during the same encounter due to substandard quality, just one code is reported. However, if after reviewing initial films the radiologist elects to obtain additional views to render further interpretation, determine the third-party payer's policy regarding multiple procedures. Generally, the CPT code that describes the total service provided is reported even if the patient was released from the radiology suite and had to return for additional services.

Descriptions of many radiology codes refer to a "minimum" number of views. When more than the minimum number specified in the code description is performed and a more specific code is not available, report one code for the highest level of service. (When additional x-rays are necessary due to a change in the patient's condition, report separate radiology codes as appropriate.)

EXAMPLE 1: A three-view x-ray of the shoulder was obtained. Report code 73030. (Do *not* report codes 73020 and 73030 even though that combination of codes equals three views.)

EXAMPLE 2: The patient presented to the ED with the complaint of severe shortness of breath. A single-view, frontal, chest x-ray was obtained. A repeat chest x-ray, complete (minimum of four views), was obtained several hours later after it was noted that the patient was experiencing labored breathing unrelieved by medication. Report codes 71010 and 71030-59. (Modifier -59 indicates that the second x-ray was a separate procedure.)

Radiographic procedures are performed without contrast, with contrast, or with and without contrast. (Invasive diagnostic imaging that involves the use of contrast material is discussed later.) Separate codes are available to describe all of these combinations of contrast usage.

Preliminary scout radiographs obtained prior to contrast administration or delayed imaging radiographs are often performed. When a CPT code is available to classify scout radiographs, it is reported. If there is no CPT code, the scout radiograph procedures are included in the reported code for the primary procedure.

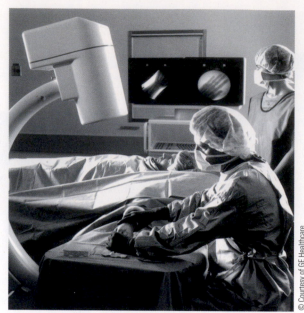

Figure 16-7 Fluoroscopy unit: Fluoroscopy is a dynamic radiographic examination that allows for visualization of flow of barium through the gastrointestinal tract, injection of a contrast agent into the heart, and so on.

Fluoroscopy

According to *CPT Assistant*, when radiologic supervision and interpretation are performed during surgical procedures, fluoroscopy (Figure 16-7) is included in the radiologic procedure. This means that codes for fluoroscopy (76000–76001) are *not* reported in addition to the radiologic procedure code.

> **EXAMPLE:** Patient underwent a laparoscopic cholecystectomy and an intraoperative cholangiogram with fluoroscopy. Report codes 47563 (surgical component) and 74300. Do *not* report code 76000 (fluoroscopy) because it is included in code 74300.

Interventional Radiologic Procedures

Interventional radiologic procedures involve the administration of contrast material orally (by mouth, such as for an upper GI), rectally (by rectum, such as for a barium enema), or **parenterally** (other than by mouth or rectum, such as implantation, infusion, or injection).

When spinal radiologic procedures are performed using CT, MRI, or magnetic resonance angiography (MRA) and the code description includes the phrase *with contrast*, do not report a code for intravenous (IV) injection. The IV injection procedure is included in the radiologic procedure code. However, when an intrathecal injection is performed, report a separate code. (**Intrathecal** refers to the fluid-filled space between layers of tissue that cover the brain and spinal cord.)

Coding Tip:

The administration of oral or rectal contrast material is included as part of the radiologic procedure code. (Do *not* report a separate code for the administration of oral or rectal contrast material.) However, it is acceptable to report an HCPCS level II code for the supply of the contrast material.

EXAMPLE 1: Patient underwent CT of the cervical spine, with IV injection of contrast material. Report code 72126.

EXAMPLE 2: Patient underwent CT of the thoracic spine, with intrathecal injection of contrast material. Report codes 72129 and 62284.

For intra-articular injection of contrast material, report the appropriate joint injection code. When an IV line is placed for administration of contrast material, it is not coded or reported. Placement of the IV line is included in the radiologic procedure code.

EXAMPLE: Patient underwent left femoral venography, which required placement of an IV line and injection of contrast material. Report 75820 and 36005. (Do *not* report code 36000 for placement of the IV line.)

Note:

For urogenital radiography (74400-74775), the insertion of a urethral catheter (51701–51702) is included in the radiographic procedure code and not separately reported. However, a code from the CPT Surgery section for the injection procedure to administer dye or radionuclide material is reported.

EXAMPLE: Patient underwent cystography (three views), which involved insertion of a catheter through the patient's urethra into the bladder and injection of contrast material. X-rays were taken from various angles at various stages of filling to visualize the bladder. Report codes 74430 and 51600. (Do *not* report a code for catheter insertion.) (The supply of dye is reported with a code from HCPCS level II.)

Computed Tomography (CT) and Computed Tomographic Angiography (CTA)

CT (or CAT) is an x-ray of horizontal and vertical cross-sectional views or "slices" of the body (Figure 16-8), which are computer-processed to create 3D images.

CTA (Figure 16-9) (70496–70498, 71275, 72191, 73206, 73706, 74175, and 75635) is a less invasive technique that uses x-ray beams to image blood vessels. (Until the introduction of CTA, vascular evaluation was performed primarily using invasive angiography procedures, which required catheterization.)

Sagittal   Transverse   Coronal (frontal)

Figure 16-8 Computed tomography (CT) sections

(A)   (B)

Figure 16-9 Three-dimensional computed tomography angiography (CTA) reconstructions (A) Carotid arteries (B) Coronary arteries

EXAMPLE 1: Patient underwent CT of the abdomen, with contrast material. Report code 74160.

EXAMPLE 2: Patient underwent CTA of the abdomen, first without contrast material and then followed by the injection of contrast material, and image post processing. Report code 74175.

Do not report a code for the injection of contrast material for a "with contrast" CTA procedure. However, the supply of the contrast material is reported separately with an appropriate HCPCS level II code. (The administration of oral or rectal contrast materials does not qualify as "with contrast." Such contrast materials are not typically used in CTA because they obscure the vasculature.)

EXAMPLE: The patient underwent a CTA of the abdominal aorta with contrast material, including bilateral iliofemoral lower extremity runoff. Post processing of the image was performed. Report code 75635.

Epidurography

Epidurography is performed to assess the structure of the spine's epidural space prior to percutaneous epidural adhesiolysis (to identify nerve construction or inflammation and the degree of fluid flow in the epidural space). Code 72275 (epidurography, radiological supervision and interpretation) is reported for a formally interpreted contrast study that involves multiplanar imaging, generating hard copy images. When epidurography is performed at *multiple* spinal levels, report code 72275 for each spinal region examined (e.g., once for the thoracic region and once for the lumbar region).

EXAMPLE: Using direct fluoroscopy, a catheter is percutaneously placed in the epidural space. Following fluoroscopic confirmation of the needle location, contrast material is injected. Permanent recording of the epidural space is performed. Report code 72275. (Do *not* report code 77003 for fluoroscopic guidance, because fluoroscopy is included as a component of epidurography.)

Figure 16-10 Magnetic resonance imaging (MRI) unit, which includes stationary magnet, radio frequency coil, and gradient coils

Magnetic Resonance Imaging (MRI)

Magnetic resonance imaging (MRI) (Figure 16-10) produces high-quality anatomical images. Code descriptions include studies performed without contrast materials, with contrast materials, and without contrast material followed by injection of contrast materials.

> **EXAMPLE:** A diagnostic MRI of the brain (Figure 16-11) was performed without contrast material. Report code 70551.

Magnetic Resonance Angiography (MRA)

Magnetic resonance angiography (MRA) is a noninvasive diagnostic study that is used to evaluate disorders of arterial and venous structures. MRA is performed to visualize the arteries and vessels without invasive procedures, and it is performed on MRI machines that contain hardware and software enhancements. Post processing procedures to create the images are included in MRA codes.

> **EXAMPLE:** Patient underwent MRA of the abdomen with contrast material. Report code 74185.

Vascular Procedures

Some vascular radiographic procedures performed on the aorta and arteries are designated as selective or

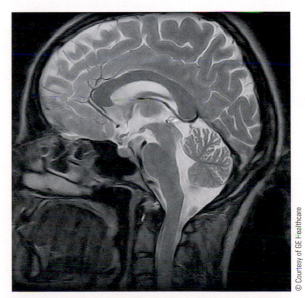

© Courtesy of GE Healthcare

Figure 16-11 Magnetic resonance image (MRI) of the brain nonselective. The radiographic procedure codes are reported in addition to appropriate catheterization codes from the Surgery section. (Chapter 13 contains content about coding of arterial catheterization procedures.)

- *Selective vascular catheterization* is the insertion and manipulation or guidance of a catheter into the branches of the arterial system (other than the aorta or the vessel punctured) for the purpose of performing diagnostic (e.g., angiography) or therapeutic (e.g., endarterectomy) procedures. Selective vascular catheterization includes introduction of the catheter and all lesser-order selective catheterizations used in the approach.

  EXAMPLE: The insertion of the catheter from the aorta into the right common and internal carotid arteries is a selective vascular catheterization procedure. (The catheter was inserted into the aorta from the brachial artery, which is a nonselective vascular catheterization procedure.)

- *Nonselective vascular catheterization* is the introduction of a catheter into a vessel and guidance of the catheter into lesser- (or first-) order vessels (e.g., 75746). (A nonselective catheterization code from the Surgery section is *not* reported with a selective radiological supervision and interpretation code.)

  EXAMPLE: The introduction of a catheter into the femoral artery and threading of the catheter into the aorta is a nonselective vascular catheterization procedure. (If the catheter is further threaded from the aorta into another vessel, such as the brachiocephalic artery, a selective vascular catheterization procedure is performed.)

For diagnostic angiography or venography (radiological supervision and interpretation) (Figure 16-12), the following interventional procedures are included in the procedure code:

- Contrast injections, angiography, roadmapping, and/or fluoroscopic guidance for the intervention

- Vessel measurement

- Post angioplasty/stent angiography

Codes for the above procedures are not coded separately when performed during the same session as an angiography or a venography.

For diagnostic angiography or venography performed during the same session as an interventional procedure, the angiography or venography is separately coded and reported if

- No prior catheter-based angiographic study is available and a full diagnostic study was performed *and the decision to intervene is based on the diagnostic study*

- A prior angiographic study is available, but medical record documentation indicates the following:

  o The patient's clinical condition has changed since the prior study.

  o There was inadequate visualization of anatomy and/or pathology.

  o There was a clinical change during the procedure that requires new evaluation.

  EXAMPLE: Patient underwent selective catheter placement into the left common carotid artery with angiography of ipsilateral (same side) intracranial carotid circulation, extracranial carotid, and cervicocerebral arch. Procedure included associated radiological supervision and interpretation. Report code 36222-LT.

Figure 16-12 Vascular imaging equipment

Vascular Procedures—Transcatheter Procedures

Therapeutic transcatheter radiological supervision and interpretation code(s) include the following services:

- Contrast injections, angiography/venography, roadmapping, and fluoroscopic guidance for the intervention
- Vessel measurement
- Completion angiography/venography (except for those uses permitted by 75898)

Codes for the above procedures are *not* coded separately when performed during the same session as a therapeutic transcatheter procedure.

> **EXAMPLE:** Patient underwent angiography through existing catheter for follow-up study for transcatheter therapy, via infusion. Report code 75898.

Other Procedures

Bone density studies evaluate diseases of the bone and are used to assess the response of bone disease to treatment. The studies assess bone mass (e.g., density) of the wrist, radius, hip, pelvis, spine, or heel. **Dual energy x-ray absorptiometry** (**DEXA** or DXA) is a bone density study that uses two x-ray beams with different levels of energy pulsing alternately (e.g., two-dimensional projection) to create the image. Results are scores, which are reported as standard deviations of bone density of a person the age of peak bone mass (e.g., 30 years of age). To code DEXA studies properly, determine the bone mass being measured.

- Axial skeleton (hips, pelvis, or spine)
- Appendicular skeleton (peripheral bones such as wrist or heel) (vertebra)

To differentiate bone density studies, code 77080 is specific to axial skeleton and code 77081 is reported for a peripheral study. Both codes include the examination of one or more anatomical sites.

 Note:

Both men and women undergo DEXA imaging.

> **EXAMPLE:** Patient underwent DXA bone density study of the hips and pelvis. Report code 77080.

Exercise 16.4 – Diagnostic Radiology (Diagnostic Imaging)

Instructions: Assign the CPT code(s) and appropriate modifier(s) to each statement.

1. Computed tomography guidance for needle placement, radiological supervision, and interpretation.

   _____

2. Orthodontic cephalogram.

   _____

3. Radiologist provided supervision and interpretation of a retrograde angiography, left brachial artery.

   _____

4. Radiological examination, sacrum and coccyx, two views.

   _____

5. Magnetic resonance spectroscopy.

   _____

Diagnostic Ultrasound

Diagnostic ultrasound uses high-frequency sound waves (e.g., mechanical oscillations) to produce an image. Radiologic ultrasound codes are organized according to anatomical site. Radiologic ultrasound procedures are often performed as follow-up studies for inconclusive diagnostic radiology procedures. They are also performed intraoperatively (e.g., during endoscopic procedures). Ultrasound is also used as guidance for the following:

- Biopsies
- Cyst localization
- Invasive procedures (e.g., ablation of renal cysts, coded as 50541)
- Paracentesis
- Pericardiocentesis
- Placement of radiation therapy fields
- Thoracentesis

Ultrasound display modes include

- **A-mode**, or **amplitude modulation**: One-dimensional display that reflects the length of time a sound reaches a structure and is reflected back

- **B-scan**, or **brightness mode**, or **gray-scale ultrasound**: Two-dimensional display that reflects sound waves bouncing off tissues or organs; the diagnostic ultrasound produces a two-dimensional cross-sectional view of tissues that cannot be seen directly (e.g., used to locate a lesion and determine its shape)

- **M-mode**, or **motion mode**: One-dimensional display that reflects the *movement* of structures

- **Real-time scan**: Two-dimensional display of structures and movement that indicates the movement, shape, and size of the tissue or organ

Ophthalmic ultrasound includes the following:

- **Biometric A-scan**: Diagnostic ultrasound that produces a one-dimensional view of normal and abnormal eye tissue and precise measurements of the eye's length (e.g., dimensions of an orbital lesion and exact depth of a foreign body)

- **Biomicroscopy**: Optical instrument that looks like a microscope, with two eyepieces

 Note:

Biomicroscopy is performed with a **slit lamp exam**, which is a high-intensity light source that can be focused to shine as a slit to look at anterior structures, including the eyelid, sclera, conjunctiva, iris, natural crystalline lens, and cornea.

- *B-scan* (see definition noted previously)

  o **Quantitative A-scan**: Diagnostic ultrasound that produces quantitative data about the posterior eye segment and evaluates tissue consistency, mobility, and vascularity (e.g., size of an orbital lesion)

  o **Corneal pachymetry**: Noninvasive ultrasound procedure that determines thickness of the cornea (e.g., prior to performing LASIK surgery)

Complete and Limited Ultrasound Procedures

To report a code for a "complete" ultrasound, the documented report must contain a description of all elements or the reason that an element could not be visualized (e.g., organ is surgically absent). A complete study includes visualization and diagnostic evaluation of all major structures within the anatomical location.

If fewer/less than the required elements for a complete exam are documented (e.g., limited number of organs or limited portion of region evaluated), report the "limited" code for that anatomical region. A limited study could include a follow-up examination, or it might address just a single quadrant or single diagnostic problem. (A "limited" exam of an anatomical region is not reported during the same session as a "complete" exam of the same region.)

 Coding Tip:

The abdomen and retroperitoneum heading include ultrasound codes that are described as one of the following:

- Complete (e.g., entire abdomen)
- Limited (e.g., single organ or single quadrant)

A limited ultrasound of a single organ or a single quadrant is also performed as follow-up to a complete ultrasound procedure. For example, a complete abdominal ultrasound revealed an abnormality of a single organ. Patient was placed on a therapeutic regimen (e.g., medications). A limited abdominal ultrasound of that organ was performed as follow-up to determine whether abnormality still existed.

 Note:

ED physicians perform limited ultrasound procedures to evaluate a specific problem, and diagnostic ultrasound results are used to determine subsequent treatment.

⚠ **EXAMPLE 1:** Patient underwent complete ultrasound of the abdominal region, B-scan and real time with image documentation. Report code 76700. (A complete ultrasound of the abdomen describes all major abdominal structures, and organ-specific findings are reported, such as the liver and spleen.)

EXAMPLE 2: Patient underwent limited ultrasound of the abdomen, B-scan and real time with image documentation. Report code 76705. (A limited ultrasound of the abdomen describes a problem-specific study, such as the presence or absence of intraperitoneal fluid.)

 Coding Tip:

When there is no corresponding limited ultrasound procedure code for a complete procedure and a limited ultrasound was performed, add modifier -52 (Reduced Services) to the complete code.

EXAMPLE 3: Patient underwent a nonobstetrical transvaginal ultrasound to confirm an ectopic pregnancy. Report code 76830-52. (A complete transvaginal ultrasound procedure involves evaluation of the uterus, endometrium, adnexa, and ovaries. Because the transvaginal ultrasound was performed to confirm an ectopic pregnancy only, the procedure is limited and modifier -52 [Reduced Services] is added to the complete study code [76830]).

Doppler Ultrasound ⚠

Doppler ultrasound is effective in the evaluation of major arteries and veins, of the heart, and in obstetrics for fetal monitoring. **Doppler ultrasonography** evaluates movement by measuring changes in the frequency of echoes reflected from moving structures. It uses diagnostic ultrasound to detect moving structures (e.g., blood cells) and measures their direction and speed. Doppler ultrasound allows for real-time viewing of blood flow, which cannot be obtained by other methods.

EXAMPLE: Patient underwent ultrasound of transplanted kidney, real time with image documentation, with duplex Doppler studies. Report code 76776.

 Coding Tip:

Austrian mathematician and physicist (Johann) Christian Doppler is known for a principle called the Doppler effect (frequency of a sound wave appears to change as the source moves toward or away from you).

Coding Tip:

Review Non-Invasive Vascular Diagnostic Studies subsection codes (93880–93990) located in the Medicine section to report venous Doppler studies and duplex scans.

Obstetrical Ultrasound Procedures

An ultrasound of the pregnant uterus includes fetal and maternal evaluation for single and multiple gestations, with limited and follow-up exams.

EXAMPLE: Patient underwent fetal biophysical profile with nonstress testing. Report code 76818. The fetal biophysical profile can include assessment of amniotic fluid, fetal breathing, tone, and movement.

Fetal echocardiography is performed ultrasonically according to specific criteria.

EXAMPLE: Patient underwent fetal echocardiography, cardiovascular system, real time with image documentation (2D), with M-mode recording. Report code 76825.

For female patients known to be pregnant (e.g., established diagnosis of pregnancy), it is appropriate to report an obstetrical ultrasound code from 76801–76817. However, when a female patient does not have an established diagnosis of pregnancy and undergoes an ultrasound evaluation (e.g., dysmenorrhea or pelvic pain), report a nonobstetrical ultrasound code (76856–76857). (Use of code 76856 or 76857 is not dependent upon whether the outcome of the ultrasound procedure is a diagnosis of pregnancy or a complication related to a pregnancy.)

EXAMPLE: A patient with an established diagnosis of pregnancy presents with symptoms that necessitate an ultrasound evaluation of the pelvis. Report a code from obstetrical ultrasound codes 76801–76817 even if the outcome of the procedure is that the patient is not pregnant (e.g., ultrasound confirms that miscarriage occurred).

Ultrasonic Guidance Procedures

Ultrasonic guidance procedures (76930–76965) include the use of ultrasound for the following:

- Pericardiocentesis guidance
- Central venous catheter placement
- Needle placement for other procedures

Report *either* a diagnostic ultrasound *or* a guidance ultrasound code (but not both) for the same patient during the same encounter.

EXAMPLE: Patient underwent ultrasound guidance for pericardiocentesis during the same encounter. Report codes 33010 and 76930.

Other Procedures

CPT code 76970 (Ultrasound study, follow-up) is *not* reported in addition to other echocardiograph procedures or ultrasound guidance procedures because it classifies a follow-up procedure performed on the same day.

Radiologic Guidance

Radiologic guidance is performed during a procedure to visualize access to an anatomical site. The Radiologic Guidance subsection contains four headings: fluoroscopic guidance, computed tomography guidance, magnetic resonance guidance, and other radiologic guidance (Table 16-1).

Table 16-1 Type of Radiologic Guidance and the Purpose of Each

Type	Purpose
Fluoroscopic Guidance	• Guidance for placement, replacement, or removal of: ○ Catheter ○ Central venous access device (CVAD) ○ Needle
Computed Tomography Guidance	• Guidance for stereotactic localization • Guidance for needle placement • Guidance and monitoring of parenchymal tissue ablation • Guidance for placement of radiation therapy fields
Magnetic Resonance Guidance	• Guidance for needle placement • Guidance and monitoring of parenchymal tissue ablation
Other Radiologic Guidance	• Stereotactic localization for breast biopsy or needle placement • Mammographic guidance for needle placement, breast

EXAMPLE: A 75-year-old patient underwent fluoroscopic guidance for visualization of the subclavian vein during placement of a nontunneled central venous catheter. Report codes 36556 and 77001. (Do not report modifier -51 with add-on code 77001.)

Breast, Mammography

Mammography (Figure 16-13) is a radiological examination of the soft tissue and internal structures of the breast.

- **Screening mammography** (Figure 16-14A) is performed when a patient presents without signs and symptoms of breast disease (e.g., routine annual screening for early detection of unsuspected breast cancer) and is reported with code 77067

Figure 16-13 In mammography, the breast is flattened and then radiographed from above

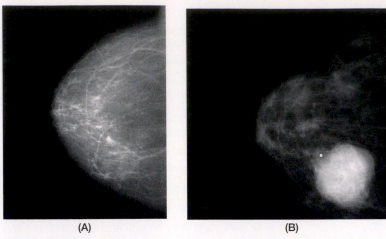

(A)   (B)

Figure 16-14 Mammogram images (A) Normal mammogram
(B) Large breast mass is visible, lower right

- **Diagnostic mammography** (Figure 16-14B) includes an assessment of suspected disease (e.g., suspicious mass is palpated on physical examination) and is reported with codes 77065-77066 when an abnormality is found or suspected

Note:

Mammography code descriptions do not specify male or female, which means that the codes can be reported for either female or male patients.

EXAMPLE: Patient underwent bilateral screening mammography with computer-aided detection, which was reviewed and interpreted by the radiologist. Report codes 77067.

Bone/Joint Studies

CPT codes 77071–77084 classify bone and joint studies.

EXAMPLE: Nine-day-old infant underwent osseous survey. Report code 77076.

Exercise 16.5 – Diagnostic Ultrasound, Radiologic Guidance, Breast Mammography, and Bone/Joint Studies

Instructions: Assign the CPT code(s) and appropriate modifier(s) to each statement.

1. Radiologist performed a complete abdominal ultrasound, real time, with image documentation.

   _____

2. The patient known to have an intrauterine pregnancy based on previous physician evaluation underwent transabdominal real-time ultrasound of pregnant uterus with image documentation, first trimester.

   _____

3. Patient underwent fetal biophysical profile, with nonstress testing, due to suspicion that fetus was in distress.

   _____

4. Abdominal ultrasound with real time and image documentation, stomach.

   _____

Exercise 16.5 *(continued)*

5. Ophthalmic diagnostic ultrasound for bilateral corneal pachymetry.

_____

6. Fluoroscopic guidance for needle placement during liver biopsy.

_____

7. CT guidance for stereotactic localization for treatment during removal of an intracranial lesion.

_____

8. Magnetic resonance guidance and monitoring for parenchymal tissue ablation of osteoid osteoma (bone tumor), left tibia.

_____

9. Stereotactic localization guidance for planned breast biopsy, left, one lesion.

_____

10. Patient underwent limited osseous survey radiologic examination for possible metastases.

_____

Radiation Oncology

Radiation oncology is the specialty of medicine that utilizes high-energy ionizing radiation in the treatment of malignant neoplasms and certain nonmalignant conditions. Distinct therapeutic modalities (methods) are directed at malignant and benign lesions. Modalities include brachytherapy, hyperthermia, stereotactic radiation, and teletherapy.

Radiation oncology codes include professional services and technical procedures that are organized according to the following types of treatment provided:

- Consultation (clinical management)
- Clinical treatment planning (external and internal sources)
- Medical radiation physics, dosimetry, treatment devices, and special services
- Stereotactic radiation treatment delivery
- Other procedures
- Radiation treatment delivery
- Neutron beam treatment delivery
- Radiation treatment management
- Proton beam treatment delivery
- Hyperthermia
- Clinical intracavitary hyperthermia
- Clinical brachytherapy

Consultation (Clinical Management)

Codes from the CPT E/M, Surgery, and/or Medicine sections are reported by the radiation oncologist who does the following:

- Provides preliminary consultation services
- Evaluates a patient prior to the decision to treat
- Delivers full medical care (in addition to treatment management)

Consultation (clinical management) services provided by the radiation oncologist include evaluation of the patient, determination of the need for radiation therapy, identification of site(s) of treatment, assessment of therapy goal(s), and the coordination and sequencing of combined modality therapy with other oncology specialists.

The radiation oncologist subsequently orders and coordinates the technical planning and execution of the treatment with ancillary staff, including radiation therapists, dosimetrists, and physicists. (The treatment is supervised by the radiation oncologist.)

Consultation services provided by radiation oncologists are the same as those provided by other physicians (e.g., a referral is required for initial consultation). The initial consultation is reported with an appropriate CPT code for outpatient consultation services (99241–99245) or inpatient consultation services (99251–99255). (The consultation code is reported just once per course of radiation therapy.)

Once the radiation oncologist has determined the appropriate radiation therapy, the best course of treatment is established. During radiation treatment, patients are monitored closely for adverse reactions that require immediate care. Thus, ongoing patient evaluation is provided as necessary. These services are reported with radiation oncology treatment management codes (77427–77499), *not* E/M service codes.

When a patient completes the course of radiation therapy, the patient continues to see the radiation oncologist during regular follow-up visits. The radiation oncologist monitors the patient's progress and reaction to treatment. This follow-up care is reported with codes from the CPT E/M section (the same as any other established patient follow-up care).

Clinical Treatment Planning (External and Internal Sources)

Clinical treatment planning is performed for each radiation therapy patient, and it includes interpretation of special testing, tumor localization, **treatment volume determination** (region within the body to which radiation therapy is directed), treatment time/dosage determination, choice of treatment modality, determination of number and size of treatment **ports** (sites on the skin where radiation beams enter the body), selection of appropriate treatment devices, and other procedures.

Radiation is administered by a machine outside the body (**external radiation**), is placed inside the body (**internal radiation)** (Figure 16-15), or uses unsealed radioactive materials that travel throughout the body (**systemic radiation therapy**). The internal radiation source is usually sealed in a small container called an *implant* (e.g., thin wire, catheter, ribbon, capsule, or seed) and inserted directly into the body. The type of radiation administered depends on what type of cancer it is, where it is located, how far into the body the radiation has to go, what the patient's general health and medical history are, whether the patient will have other types of cancer treatment, and other factors. Most patients receive external radiation, and some receive both external and internal or systemic radiation therapy.

⚠ Clinical treatment planning and tumor mapping are critical to identifying the location, extent, and volume of tumor(s) to be treated and all critical and sensitive structures surrounding them. The radiation oncologist plans the appropriate course of therapy that will allow for maximum benefit while protecting surrounding tissues and structures. Clinical treatment planning may involve ordering and interpreting special tests such as CT scans, lymphangiography, MRI scans, and radionuclide scans and/or surgical exploration with biopsy. Markers may also be placed for the purpose of treatment planning and tumor localization.

 Coding Tip:

> **Debulking** (surgical removal of part of a malignant tumor; also called **cytoreduction surgery**) may be performed to enhance the effectiveness of radiation oncology treatment.

Therapeutic radiology treatment planning codes are classified according to type of planning, as follows:

- Simple
  - Single treatment area of interest
  - Single port or simple parallel opposed ports
  - Minimal (simple or no) **blocking** (device, such as lead, that shields or protects critical or sensitive organs)
  - No interpretation of special tests for localization of tumor volume

Colpostat

Tandem

(A)

Tandem

Pelvis

Uterus

Cervix

Vagina

Femur

Colpostat

(B)

Figure 16-15 Radium implant devices (A) Colpostat and tandem
(B) Placement of colpostate and tandem within vagina and uterus

- Intermediate
  - Two separate treatment areas
  - Three or more converging ports
  - Multiple blocks to protect critical or sensitive organs
  - Special time/dose constraints
  - Interpretation of special tests for localization of tumor volume
- Complex
  - Three or more separate treatment areas
  - Highly complex blocking to protect critical or sensitive organs

- ○ Custom shielding blocks

- ○ Tangential ports

- ○ Special **wedges** (treatment beam-modifying devices that act to change the beam intensity profile)

- ○ Special **compensators** (irregularly shaped beam-modifying devices used to reconfigure beam intensity so it matches irregular tissue contour)

- ○ Rotational or special beam considerations

- ○ Combination of therapeutic modalities

- ○ Interpretation of complex testing procedures (e.g., CT and MRI localization)

- ○ Possible special laboratory testing

Simulation clinical treatment planning uses a simulator to determine various treatment ports to be used during radiation therapy. The simulator can orient a radiation beam toward a patient according to parameters that imitate the treatment proposed for actual therapy (but it does not deliver radiation therapy). Simulation may be carried out on a dedicated conventional simulator or by use of a CT scanner, radiation therapy treatment unit (e.g., linear accelerator), or other diagnostic imaging equipment (e.g., fluoroscopy, CT, or MRI). Simulation is complex because custom shielding blocks are designed, and the simulation must be coordinated with information from treatment planning CT scans and isodose plan data. Therapeutic radiology simulation-aided field setting codes are classified according to type of setting.

- • Simple

  - ○ Simulation of single treatment area

  - ○ Single port or parallel opposed ports

  - ○ Minimal (simple or no) blocking of critical or sensitive organs

- • Intermediate

  - ○ Simulation of three or more converging ports

  - ○ Two separate treatment areas

  - ○ Multiple blocking of critical or sensitive organs

- • Complex

  - ○ Simulation of tangential (peripheral) portals (or ports)

  - ○ Three or more treatment areas

  - ○ Rotation or arc therapy

  - ○ Three-dimensional (3D)

  - ○ Computer-generated 3D reconstruction of tumor volume and surrounding critical or sensitive normal tissue structures (using CT scans or MRI data in preparation for noncoplanar or coplanar therapy)

  - ○ Simulation uses documented 3D beam's eye view volume-dose displays of multiple or moving beams

  - ○ Documentation with 3D volume reconstruction and dose distribution is required

EXAMPLE: Radiation oncologist provided therapeutic radiology treatment planning services, which required a single treatment area of interest, one port, and no blocking. Report code 77261.

Medical Radiation Physics, Dosimetry, Treatment Devices, and Special Services

"Medical radiation physics, **dosimetry** (measurement and calculation of radiation treatment doses), treatment devices, and special services" codes (77295–77399) are reported by the health care facility (e.g., hospital). There is no professional component for most of these services. (Reimbursement for the radiation oncologist's professional component is included in reimbursement for clinical treatment planning and radiation treatment management codes.)

A basic radiation dosimetry calculation is a photon calculation that includes central axis depth dose, time dose factor (TDF), nominal standard dose (NSD), gap calculation, off-axis and tissue inhomogeneity factors, as well as calculation of nonionizing radiation surface and depth dose. Dosimetry may be repeated during the course of treatment as required. CPT code 77300 is reported as many times as necessary during a course of radiation therapy. However, codes for teletherapy isodose planning services (77306–77307) are reimbursed just once per course of treatment.

Intensity modulated radiation therapy (IMRT) uses high-precision radiotherapy to precisely target cancerous tumors with higher radiation doses by using strategically positioned beams to minimize collateral damage to healthy cells. IMRT varies the intensity of radiation exposure depending on whether tumor is present in the beam pathway. The radiation therapy consists of multiple pencil thin beams (or beamlets) calculated to hit tumors with high-dose radiation beams and sensitive normal tissues with modulated lower-intensity beams, leaving them mostly unaffected. Planning for IMRT involves the use of computer programs that calculate the beam angle configurations and dosage intensities. CPT code 77301 is reported for an IMRT plan, which includes dose-volume histograms for target and critical structure partial tolerance specifications. A CPT code from 77385–77386 is reported for IMRT delivery, and includes guidance and tracking, when performed.

Brachytherapy isodose calculation is also reimbursed just once per course of treatment. The number of units billed for brachytherapy isodose calculation (simple, intermediate, or complex) should equal the number of brachytherapy treatments provided within the billing period. When billing is done for multiple treatment devices, there must be documentation in the clinical record to support the medical necessity of each device or set of devices.

The use of a treatment device (77332–77334) is based on the clinical judgment of the radiation oncologist and is influenced by the patient's anatomy and disease state. The selection and use of any treatment device requires medical necessity, radiation oncologist involvement, and a written and signed order for each device. The radiation oncologist must be directly involved in the design, selection, and placement of any device and must document their involvement with each device.

Treatment devices include the following:

- Beam-shaping devices are called blocks, and they are placed in an external radiation beam to modify its shape to either contour the beam around target structures or to shield normal tissues.

- Immobilization devices (e.g., thermoplastic face and body masks, bite-block head holders, Styrofoam body casts, and breast boards) are used to restrict patient movement during treatment.

- Beam-modifying devices include wedges, compensators, and boluses.

- Shielding devices include bite blocks, eye shields, and testicular shields.

Codes for treatment devices are reported at the onset of the treatment. They may be reported again later during the course of treatment if additional or new devices are required.

Codes 77336 and 77370 are reported for medical radiation physics technical procedures. Although the radiation oncologist orders these procedures, he or she generally has little involvement in the actual procedure. The medical radiation physics measurements are used to evaluate a treatment plan. After these procedures are completed, treatment management and delivery is established. Continuing medical physics consultation (CPT code 77336) is reported "per week of therapy," which means that it may be reported after multiple radiation treatments *if those treatments occurred during one week of treatment. If, however, the multiple radiation treatments occurred over a period of multiple different weeks, code 77336 would be reported once for each week of treatment.* (On the CMS-1500 claim, the start and end dates for multiple treatments in a one-week period are reported with code 77336, and the unit is entered as 1, thus indicating that just one payment is reimbursed to the provider. When multiple treatments are provided during multiple different weeks, code 77336 is reported on five separate lines in Block 24 of the CMS-1500 claim, a date is entered on each line, and the unit entered as 1 for each code; the provider would receive reimbursement for the reporting of each code, and it is likely that a copy of the patient record will be requested to confirm that treatments were spread out over multiple weeks on a single day in each of those weeks, perhaps resulting in reduced reimbursement for each code.) Code 77370 (Special medical radiation physics consultation) is reported just once during a treatment series.

> **EXAMPLE:** Radiation oncologist designed and constructed a simple block treatment device. Report code 77332.

Stereotactic Radiation Treatment Delivery

Stereotactic radiation treatment delivery includes the following types:

- *Stereotactic radiosurgery (SRS)*: Radiation therapy that focuses high-powered x-rays onto a small area, such as a brain, liver, lung, or other lesion; it is a single-session treatment that has such a dramatic effect on its target that the result is considered "surgical"; however, it is not actually considered a surgical procedure; also referred to as *gamma knife* or *cyberknife*

- *Stereotactic body radiation therapy (SBRT)*: Radiation therapy that uses special equipment to position a patient and precisely deliver smaller doses of radiation over several days to bone, liver, and lung tumors in the body; SBRT is not administered to brain tumors; exposure to normal tissue is minimized; also called extracranial *radiotherapy*

> **EXAMPLE:** Patient underwent radiation treatment delivery, which used stereotactic radiosurgery to deliver one large radiation dose to his brain tumor. Report code 77371.

Radiation Treatment Delivery

Radiation treatment delivery codes are reported for the administration of radiation therapy *per treatment*. A nonphysician may deliver radiation treatment; however, the radiation oncologist is responsible for checking and documenting the accuracy of the treatment. The radiation oncologist must also treat any adverse reactions to treatment and monitor the effects of radiation therapy on the tumor and surrounding tissues. (Radiation treatment delivery includes ongoing patient evaluation, and codes for such evaluation are not reported separately.)

- Radiation treatment delivery is measured in units of **MeV** (**megaelectron volts** or **megavolts**), which is 1 million electron volts.

- **Therapeutic port films** are x-rays taken during delivery of radiation treatment that utilize the treatment beam of the machine. Portal films demonstrate the exact shape, size, and area covered by the treatment beam during an actual treatment.

> **EXAMPLE:** Radiation therapy was directed to three separate treatment areas, and 11 MeV was administered. Report code 77412.

Neutron Beam Treatment Delivery

Neutron beam radiation therapy is an external radiation treatment that uses higher linear energy transfer to treat certain tumors (e.g., salivary gland tumors) due to increased susceptibility, as compared with conventional radiation therapy. An interventional radiologist provides this treatment at a facility equipped with a superconducting accelerator (cyclotron). Pretreatment planning usually involves CT to locate and determine the tumor volume prior to radiation therapy.

> **EXAMPLE:** Patient underwent high-energy neutron radiation treatment delivery to a single treatment area with use of a single port. Report code 77422.

Radiation Treatment Management

Radiation treatment management is reported in units of five fractions or treatment sessions even though the service need not be performed on consecutive days. For radiation treatment management purposes, a **fraction** is a single session of radiation treatment delivered to a specific area of interest. The number of calendar days between treatment fractions is not relevant as long as the treatment is directed to the same area and is part of a single course of therapy. Thus, a claim is submitted with the treatment code for every five treatments. *Multiple fractions that represent two or more treatment sessions furnished on the same day are counted separately if there has been a distinct break in therapy sessions.*

> **EXAMPLE:** Patient received 18 daily radiation therapy fractions during a 4-week period. Report codes 77427, 77427, 77427, and 77427.

 Note:

- When a patient who has completed a course of radiation therapy returns with a recurrent tumor and treatment is provided to the same area, report codes for a separate course of radiation therapy.

- HCPCS level II codes for radioactive materials, when supplied by the radiation oncologist, are reported in addition to codes for radiation therapy.

Reimbursement for weekly radiation therapy management includes payment for normal follow-up care during therapy and for three months following its completion.

> **EXAMPLE:** Radiation oncologist provided radiation therapy management for a course of treatment that consisted of two single sessions (fractions). Report code 77431.

Proton Beam Treatment Delivery

Compared to photon beams, proton beams deliver higher radiation doses to tumors, and proton beams do not exceed the radiation tolerance of normal tissue. Proton beam treatment delivery is a modality that consists of delivering smaller doses to intervening normal tissues and organs. Codes are reported according to the following types of treatment:

- *Simple*: Single treatment area utilizing a single nontangential/oblique port, custom block with or without compensation

- *Intermediate*: One or more treatment areas utilizing two or more ports or one or more tangential/oblique ports, with custom blocks and compensators

- *Complex*: One or more treatment areas using two or more ports per treatment area with matching or patching fields and/or multiple isocenters, with custom blocks and compensators

> **EXAMPLE:** Patient underwent proton treatment delivery to two treatment areas using one port per treatment area and custom blocks. Report code 77523.

Hyperthermia and Clinical Intracavitary Hyperthermia

Hyperthermia involves the use of an external heat-generating source (e.g., ultrasound or microwave) to produce localized heating. Hyperthermia is usually performed immediately before or after a session of external beam radiation therapy. Typically, three to six applications of hyperthermia per course of radiation therapy are required. When hyperthermia is generated by intracavitary probe(s), report code 77620.

> **EXAMPLE:** Patient underwent hyperthermia treatment, which was generated by interstitial probe that used 10 interstitial applicators. Report code 77615.

Clinical Brachytherapy

Brachytherapy (Figure 16-16) involves the use of radioactive isotopes for internal radiation, and codes are reported according to the following applications:

- *Simple*: Application has 1 to 4 sources/ribbons

- *Intermediate*: Application has 5 to 10 sources/ribbons

- *Complex*: Application has greater than 10 sources/ribbons

A *source* is an intracavitary placement or permanent interstitial placement. A *ribbon* is a temporary interstitial placement. Intracavitary brachytherapy is performed by placing applicators containing radioactive materials directly into or around a tumor area. A common use of intracavitary brachytherapy is the treatment of carcinoma of the endometrium (uterus) or cervix.

Intracavitary and interstitial applications are seldom used as the sole modality of radiation treatment. Interstitial brachytherapy is performed with needles, ribbons, or wires containing radioactive materials that are inserted directly into and around a cancerous area. The devices remain in place over a period of many days while delivering their relatively low-intensity radiation directly into the tumor. These applications are often used in conjunction with external beam radiation therapy to bring the total dose up to the desired level.

> **EXAMPLE:** Radiation oncologist supervised the handling and loading of a radiation source. Report code 77790.

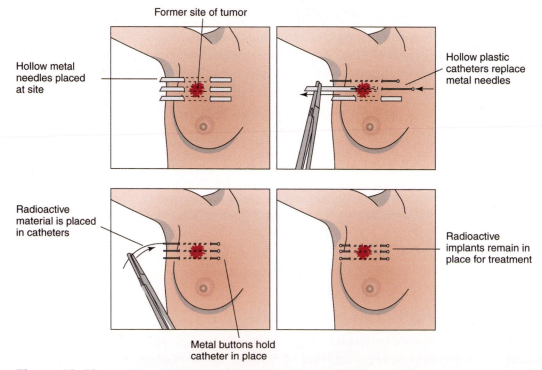

Figure 16-16 Brachytherapy for treatment of breast cancer

Exercise 16.6 – Radiation Oncology

Instructions: Assign the CPT code to each statement.

1. A special teletherapy port plan for the total body.

   _____

2. The patient underwent a hyperthermia treatment that was generated by an intracavitary probe.

   _____

3. A therapeutic radiology simulation-aided field setting of a single treatment area with a single port was performed.

   _____

4. Patient underwent superficial voltage radiation treatment delivery.

   _____

5. The surface application of a radiation source was performed.

   _____

Nuclear Medicine

Nuclear medicine involves the use of radioactive elements (e.g., radionuclides and radioisotopes) for diagnostic imaging (e.g., scan) and **radiopharmaceutical therapy** (destroys diseased tissue, such as a malignant neoplasm). The isotope emits gamma rays as it deteriorates, which enables the radiologist to visualize internal abnormalities (e.g., tumors). The images created by the contrast media (radioactive element) are detected by a gamma camera.

Nuclear medicine codes do not include the provision of radium, which means that the nuclear medicine report must be reviewed to identify the diagnostic or therapeutic radiopharmaceutical provided. Then an appropriate HCPCS level II code is reported for the radiopharmaceutical administered. (The injection of the radionuclide is included as part of the procedure, and a separate injection code is *not* reported.)

Common diagnostic nuclear medicine procedures include bone scans, cardiac scans (e.g., thallium scan and MUGA), renal scans, thyroid scans, and hepatobiliary scans (e.g., HIDA scans). Therapeutic nuclear medicine procedures are used to treat diseases such as chronic leukemia, hyperthyroidism, and thyroid cancer.

The Nuclear Medicine subsection contains two headings.

- Diagnostic
- Therapeutic

The Diagnostic heading contains the following subheadings:

- Endocrine System
- Hematopoietic, Reticuloendothelial, and Lymphatic System
- Gastrointestinal System
- Musculoskeletal System
- Cardiovascular System
- Respiratory System
- Nervous System
- Genitourinary System
- Other Procedures

The Therapeutic heading contains no subheadings.

Endocrine System

Nuclear medicine is commonly used to evaluate thyroid function (e.g., thyroid update). **Uptake** is the absorption by a tissue of a substance, material, or mineral and its permanent or temporary retention.

⚠ A thyroid uptake test measures thyroid function to determine how much iodine the thyroid absorbs (expressed as a percentage of the administered radioiodine present in the thyroid gland at a specific time after administration). Thyroid imaging (scan) is performed to assess anatomical size and physiologic function. A radioactive tracer (e.g., iodide-123 capsule or technetium-99m injection) is administered, which allows blood flow and vascularity of the thyroid to be monitored by imaging at different intervals.

> **EXAMPLE:** Patient underwent thyroid imaging with vascular flow and radioactive tracer. Report code 78013.

Coding Tip:

CPT code 78020 is reported when thyroid carcinoma metastases uptake is calculated. The parenthetical note below code 78020 directs its use only with code 78018 (Thyroid carcinoma metastases imaging; whole body). Since 78020 is an add-on code, it is reported in addition to code 78018 without modifier -51.

Hematopoietic, Reticuloendothelial, and Lymphatic System

Bone marrow scans (78102–78104) evaluate bone marrow functioning and irregular marrow tissue expansion (e.g., malignancy or infection). A radiopharmaceutical radiotracer (e.g., radiolabeled sulphur colloid) is injected, and images are obtained after a two- to three-hour delay using a special camera (e.g., scintillation or gamma camera). The camera takes images by detecting gamma radiation from the radionuclide in bone marrow as it "scintillates" (e.g., emits energy in a flash of light) when coming in contact with the camera's detector.

The radiopharmaceutical volume-dilution technique (78122) evaluates plasma and red cell volume by using radiolabeled protein tracers (e.g., iodinated serum albumin) and autologous radiolabeled red blood cells. The procedure involves collecting blood and recording blood counts to calculate volumes using formulas that compare the dilution factor from a standard sample of each radiotracer.

Code 78195 (Lymphatics and lymph nodes imaging) is reported for lymphoscintigraphy. The injection of a radioactive tracer is included in the lymphoscintigraphy procedure, which means that code 38792 is not reported. Modifier -26 (Professional Component) is added to code 78195 only if the professional component was performed by the physician.

> **EXAMPLE:** Patient underwent a platelet survival study. Report code 78191.

Gastrointestinal System

Tomographic SPECT (78205–78206) is used for evaluation of the anatomy and functionality of the liver. A radiolabeled sulphur colloid is injected, and imaging of the distribution of gamma radiation emitted from the radiopharmaceutical is performed. SPECT imaging is performed by rotating a single- or multiple-head camera around the patient to provide 3D computer-reconstructed views of cross-sectional slices of the liver. For imaging done with a vascular flow test, red blood cells are labeled to enable imaging of the blood flow through the liver.

> **EXAMPLE:** Patient underwent acute gastrointestinal blood loss imaging. Report code 78278.

Musculoskeletal System

Single and dual photon absorptiometry (78350–78351) are noninvasive techniques used to measure the absorption of the photon beam (e.g., mono- or dichromatic) by bone material. The device is placed directly on the patient and uses a small amount of radionuclide to measure the bone mass absorption. This provides a measurement of the bone mineral density of cortical bone and can be used to assess an individual's response to treatment at different intervals.

> **EXAMPLE:** Patient underwent a bone density study with single photon absorptiometry, vertebral column and rib cage. Report code 78350.

Cardiovascular System

Myocardial perfusion and cardiac blood pool imaging may be performed at rest or during stress. When performed during exercise and/or pharmacologic stress, report an appropriate stress test code from the Medicine section (93015–93018). **Cardiac blood pool imaging** uses a gamma camera for sampling, which is performed repetitively over several hundred heartbeats during the transition of the radionuclide (e.g., technetium-99m) through the central circulation.

Nuclear imaging for noncardiac vascular flow studies (78445) is performed to evaluate arterial or venous peripheral vascular diseases or injuries. In radionuclide angiography, red blood cells are tagged with radioactivity and injected intravenously. A scintillation camera takes a series of dynamic images every two to three seconds immediately after injection, followed by static images.

For myocardial perfusion study (78491–78492), PET myocardial imaging is typically performed on patients with coronary artery disease and left ventricular dysfunction. PET scanning is also used in diagnostic and therapeutic procedures for malignant tumors. PET is a noninvasive nuclear medicine technique that produces 3D images of the distribution of radioactivity (e.g., emission of positrons) similar to a CT scan. However, PET uses radiopharmaceuticals instead of dye and x-rays. When the radiopharmaceutical agent is injected into the blood, a positron scanner detects, measures, and displays metabolism of tissues (e.g., heart and brain) and many types of tumors. PET scans are also used to diagnose dementia. (Report appropriate HCPCS level II codes for radiopharmaceutical diagnostic imaging agents or "tracers," in addition to CPT codes for PET scan procedures.)

Coding Tip:

CPT codes 78491 (Myocardial imaging, positron emission tomography (PET), perfusion, single study at rest or stress) and 78492 (Multiple studies at rest and/or stress) are reported with the following tracer codes:

- A9526: Nitrogen N-13 ammonia, diagnostic, per study dose, up to 40 millicuries

- A4641: Radiopharmaceutical, diagnostic, not otherwise classified

EXAMPLE: Patient underwent myocardial imaging, PET, metabolic evaluation. Report code 78459.

Respiratory System

A pulmonary perfusion imaging procedure is used to diagnose pulmonary emboli (Figure 16-17) and pulmonary trauma. The procedure consists of imaging a patient twice.

- Once after inhalation of a radioactive aerosol to determine pulmonary ventilation

- Once again after injection of a radioactive particulate to determine lung perfusion

  Code 78582 represents a combination code that allows accurate reporting of both components of the procedure.

  EXAMPLE: Patient underwent particulate pulmonary perfusion imaging. Report code 78580.

Nervous System

Codes 78600–78699 are reported for brain imaging, cerebral vascular flow, cerebrospinal fluid flow/leakage, and radiopharmaceutical dacryocystography radiographic procedures.

EXAMPLE: Patient underwent radiopharmaceutical dacryocystography. Report code 78660.

Figure 16-17 Pulmonary emboli

Genitourinary System

Codes 78700–78799 are reported for kidney imaging, kidney function study, urinary bladder residual study, ureteral reflux study, and testicular imaging radiographic procedures.

> **EXAMPLE:** Patient underwent multiple kidney imaging studies with vascular flow and function, with and without pharmacological angiotensin intervention as a converting enzyme inhibitor. Report code 78709.

Other Procedures

Tomographic SPECT imaging (78803 and 78807) allows for evaluation of complex anatomy. A radionuclide is introduced, and the distribution of gamma radiation emitted is detected with a camera that rotates around the patient. A 3D computer reconstructs views of cross-sectional slices of the body. When scanning for an inflammatory process, gallium is the radiopharmaceutical used.

> **EXAMPLE:** Patient underwent SPECT radiopharmaceutical localization of a tumor, stomach. Report code 78803.

Therapeutic (Nuclear Medicine)

When radiopharmaceutical therapy is administered orally or intravenously, the reported code includes the mode of administration (e.g., injection or infusion). When intra-arterial, intracavitary, or intra-articular administration is the method used for radiopharmaceutical therapy, an appropriate injection and/or procedure code is reported in addition to the therapy code. When imaging guidance and radiological supervision and interpretation are provided for intra-arterial, intracavitary, or intra-articular administration, appropriate code(s) are reported in addition to the therapy and administration codes.

> **EXAMPLE:** Patient underwent radiopharmaceutical therapy for chronic leukemia, by oral administration. Report code 79005.

Exercise 16.7 – Nuclear Medicine

Instructions: Assign the CPT code to each statement.

1. Therapeutic radiopharmaceutical is injected directly into a vein.

   _____

2. The physician determines the location of the sentinel node(s) using scintigraphy imaging.

   _____

3. The physician administered a radiolabeled monoclonal antibody by intravenous infusion.

   _____

4. Patient underwent aerosol pulmonary ventilation and perfusion imaging.

   _____

5. Patient underwent cardiac shunt detection procedure.

   _____

Summary

Radiology is a branch of medicine that uses imaging techniques to diagnose and treat disease. A radiologist is a physician who has undergone specialized training to interpret diagnostic x-rays, perform specialized x-ray procedures, and administer radiation for the treatment of disease (e.g., cancer). The Radiology section includes subsections for diagnostic radiology (diagnostic imaging); diagnostic ultrasound; radiologic guidance; breast, mammography; bone/joint studies; radiation oncology; and nuclear medicine. Procedure descriptions include the type of service, anatomical site, and use of contrast material. Radiology guidelines are located at the beginning of the section, and they should be carefully reviewed prior to the assigning of codes.

Internet Links

Hospital for Special Surgery: Go to *www.hss.edu*, mouse over Conditions & Treatments, and click on A to Z Listing to view articles and videos.

LearningRadiology: *www.learningradiology.com*

RadiologyInfo.org: *www.radiologyinfo.org*

Study Checklist

❑ Read this chapter and highlight key concepts.

❑ Create an index card for each key term.

❑ Access the chapter Internet links to learn more about concepts.

❑ Complete the chapter exercises and review, and verify answers with your instructor.

❑ Complete Workbook chapter, verifying answers with your instructor.

❏ Go to *www.cengagebrain.com* to access the Student Companion Web Site. Login instructions are located in the Preface.

❏ Form a study group with classmates to discuss chapter concepts in preparation for an exam.

Review

Multiple Choice

Instructions: Circle the most appropriate response.

1. Which are the types of radiographic projection?
   a. Anteroposterior, lateral, oblique, and posteroanterior
   b. Anteroposterior, posteroanterior, midsagittal, and sagittal
   c. Coronal, midsagittal, sagittal, and transverse
   d. Coronal, transverse, lateral, and oblique

2. Which are the three components of a radiologic procedure?
   a. Coronal, transverse, and lateral
   b. Posteroanterior, midsagittal, and sagittal
   c. Simple, intermediate, and complex
   d. Technical, professional, and global

3. Which is a common contrast agent administered to provide better radiographic visualization of organs studied?
   a. Barium sulfate
   b. Betadine
   c. Iodized sodium
   d. Sulfuric acid

4. Which is the rectal administration of contrast material?
   a. Barium enema
   b. Implantation
   c. Infusion
   d. Injection

5. A patient underwent a procedure in which a special catheter tipped with a hollow tube and rotating blades was used to cut away plaque from the arterial wall. The debris was suctioned out of the body through the tube. Which procedure was performed?
   a. Dual energy x-ray absorptiometry
   b. Epidurography
   c. Transluminal atherectomy
   d. Venography

6. Biometric A-scan, quantitative A-scan, B-scan, and corneal pachymetry are considered:
   a. types of ophthalmic ultrasound.
   b. types of x-rays.
   c. radiographic projections.
   d. ultrasound display modes.

7. Brachytherapy, hyperthermia, stereotactic radiation, and teletherapy are considered:
   a. dosimetry techniques.
   b. external heat-generating sources.
   c. therapeutic modalities for radiation oncology.
   d. treatment devices.

8. Radiation treatment management is reported on a _____ basis.
   a. daily
   b. monthly
   c. per session
   d. weekly

9. A pulmonary perfusion imaging procedure is performed to diagnose pulmonary embolism and pulmonary trauma. The code for this procedure allows for imaging a patient:
   a. once.
   b. twice.
   c. three times.
   d. weekly.

10. A patient underwent a nuclear medicine procedure in which radionuclides were administered to destroy a malignant neoplasm. For nuclear medicine purposes, radionuclides are an example of _____ elements and destruction of the malignant neoplasm is considered the _____ procedure.
    - a. radioactive, diagnostic
    - b. radioactive, radiopharmaceutical
    - c. radiopharmaceutical, gamma ray
    - d. therapeutic, gamma ray

11. Complete radiological exam of paranasal sinuses. Which CPT code is assigned?
    - a. 70140
    - b. 70160
    - c. 70210
    - d. 70220

12. Chest x-ray–Bucky studies. Which CPT code is assigned?
    - a. 71021
    - b. 71022
    - c. 71030
    - d. 71035

13. Computed tomography of the cervical spine without contrast on a patient, repeated the same day. Which CPT code(s) are assigned?
    - a. 70450, 70450-76
    - b. 72125, 72125-76
    - c. 72126-76
    - d. 72127-76

14. Hip x-ray, two views, performed on the right side of the patient. Which CPT code is assigned?
    - a. 73501-RT
    - b. 73502-RT
    - c. 73521-RT
    - d. 73525-RT

15. Selective adrenal angiography, left side, with radiological supervision and interpretation. Which CPT code is assigned?
    - a. 75726
    - b. 75731
    - c. 75433
    - d. 75736

16. Screening mammography, bilateral breasts. Which CPT code is assigned?
    - a. 77065-50
    - b. 77066
    - c. 77067
    - d. 77067-50

17. Red cell survival study. Which CPT code is assigned?
    - a. 78110
    - b. 78120
    - c. 78130
    - d. 78140

18. Radiopharmaceutical localization of tumor, tomographic (SPECT), performed twice by the same physician during the same encounter. Which CPT code(s) are assigned?
    - a. 78803
    - b. 78803-51
    - c. 78803-77
    - d. 78803, 78803-76

19. Radiopharmaceutical therapy by intracavitary administration. Which CPT code is assigned?
    - a. 79200
    - b. 79403
    - c. 79440
    - d. 79445

20. Therapeutic radiology treatment planning, simple. Which CPT code is assigned?
    - a. 77261
    - b. 77262
    - c. 77263
    - d. 77280

Coding Practice

Instructions: Assign the CPT code(s) and appropriate modifier(s) to each case.

1. X-RAY OF ABDOMEN: AP view of abdomen reveals no abnormal soft tissue masses, gas shadows, or calcifications. Liver and spleen not enlarged. Visualized bones appear normal.

   _____

2. BARIUM ENEMA: Fluoroscopic and radiographic examination of the colon reveals normal retrograde flow of barium through all segments of the large bowel and into the terminal ileum. No diverticula or other filling defects are demonstrated. Terminal ileum is not unusual. The postevacuation response is normal, and no alteration of the mucosal pattern is demonstrated.

   IMPRESSION: Normal colon and terminal ileum.

   _____

3. GALLBLADDER: Following administration of contrast medium, there is satisfactory concentration within the gallbladder. The outline is normal, and no calculi are detected.

   IMPRESSION: Normal gallbladder series.

---

4. UPPER GASTROINTESTINAL SERIES AND ESOPHAGRAM: Radiographic examination of upper gastrointestinal tract reveals no abnormalities of the swallowing mechanism or of the entire esophagus. The stomach is readily entered, peristalsis traverses this organ in normal fashion, and a very small sliding type of hiatus hernia of the stomach is seen on one of the radiographs. No reflux of gastric contents into the esophagus or radiographic signs of esophagitis can be seen. The mucosal pattern of the stomach is not unusual. There is a suggestion of a small ulcer crater of the lesser curvature aspect of the pyloric canal of the stomach. No additional site of gastric ulceration or other abnormality is seen. The duodenal bulb fills out well, and this structure is noted to be slightly distorted in configuration; however, no ulcer crater of the duodenal bulb is appreciated. Prolapse of gastric mucosa into the base of the bulb is seen. The remainder of the duodenal loop and the upper jejunum mucosal pattern are within normal limits.

---

5. SMALL BOWEL SERIES: Serial films obtained show normal progression of barium through the small intestine. The jejunum and ileum show a normal caliber and position. There is no evidence of filling defect or obstruction. The mucosal pattern is normal.

   IMPRESSION: Normal small bowel series.

---

6. CHEST: Frontal and lateral projections of the chest show increased markings with some honeycomb formations, probably representing bronchiectasis associated with infiltrate. However, as compared with earlier study, there are no significant changes. Linear atelectasis is seen in the lower lung field. Otherwise, the lung fields remain clear. The heart is enlarged in its transverse diameter, and its CT ratio measures 16.0 cm/30.5 cm. Calcification is seen in the thoracic aorta.

   CONCLUSION: Increased markings in both bases with honeycomb formations, most likely representing bronchiectasis probably superimposed with infiltrate. Close follow-up is recommended.

---

7. RIGHT RIB CAGE: AP and oblique views of the right portion of the rib cage show no evidence of fracture or other abnormality of the visualized ribs.

---

8. SKULL: Skull in three views shows calvarium to be intact. There is no evidence of any abnormal calcification or increased intracranial pressure. Sella turcica is normal in size and shape. There are a few teeth in the mandible, and there is poor visualization of the lamina dura.

---

9. LEFT HAND: Left hand in two views shows some osteoporosis of the visualized bones. There is no evidence of fracture or dislocation. Calcification is seen in the arteries around the wrist.

---

10. CHEST: AP upright chest radiograph at 72 inches shows the heart to be transverse in position. Significant enlargement is not apparent on this study. At both bases, there is noted air-bronchogram effect associated with pulmonary infiltration. The thoracic aorta shows atheromatous calcification, and the

right acromioclavicular joint shows degenerative arthrosis, as does the thoracic spine, which also shows a scoliosis with convexity toward the right.

---

11. DRIP TECHNIQUE INFUSION PYELOGRAPHY: Right renal length is approximately 11.3 cm, and the left is approximately 10.8 cm. Right kidney is higher than the left. There is degenerative arthrosis of the lumbar spine. Some large and small bowel gas is present, suggesting a mild ileus. There is no definite sign of bowel obstruction. Following Renografin, there was minimal delay in excretion from the kidneys and rather poor concentration bilaterally throughout the study, particularly on the right. As far as can be seen, the renal collecting structures are grossly normal. Urinary bladder shows floor elevation consistent with a large prostate gland, and there is at least one diverticulum present, which is noted on the right. Questionable one is suggested in the region of the fundus superiorly. Indwelling Foley catheter is present; therefore, a postvoiding film was not obtained.

    CONCLUSION: Drip infusion pyelography shows poorly functioning kidneys. For this reason, one cannot fully assess the kidneys or ureters. As far as can be seen, significant pathology is not apparent. At least one urinary bladder diverticulum is present. Urinary bladder floor shows elevation consistent with a large prostate gland.

---

12. SKULL: Cranial vault is intact. Sella turcica was normal in size and shape. There are no intracranial calcifications.

---

13. CERVICAL SPINE: Two views were done; there is no fracture or dislocation identified. Alignment is normal. There is no disc space narrowing. Neural foramina are patent bilaterally. There are no cervical ribs and no soft tissue calcifications in either side of the neck.

---

14. LEFT ELBOW IN FRONTAL, LATERAL, OBLIQUE, AND AXIAL PROJECTIONS: The elbow is believed to be negative for fracture or dislocation, but because of some irregularity of ossification in the distal metaphysic, conservative management and reexamination is recommended before use is allowed.

---

15. BOTH KNEES IN FRONTAL, OBLIQUE, AND LATERAL PROJECTIONS: There is no fracture or dislocation and no joint effusion.

    IMPRESSION: Negative examination of both knees.

---

16. LEFT WRIST RADIOGRAPHED IN FRONTAL AND LATERAL PROJECTIONS: There has been an anatomical reduction of the distal radial epiphysis.

---

17. ABDOMINAL SERIES: AP, oblique, and cone position abdominal films show gross distention of multiple loops of small bowel in the midabdomen with large air fluid levels. I see very little air in the colon past the hepatic flexure. The fact that this patient is only two days after abdominal surgery more or less points to a paralytic ileus, but I cannot absolutely rule out the possibility of a mechanical obstruction without a small bowel study.

CONCLUSION: Multiple dilated loops of small bowel in the midabdomen. The possibility of a mechanical obstruction cannot be ruled out without a small bowel study. A repeat abdominal series would be advisable before any further studies are done.

---

18. NUCLEAR VENTRICULOGRAM: Following injection of 22 mCi of Tc-99m, ventriculogram was done and ejection fraction was calculated. The study was compared with prior ventricular ejection, which was 42% with a peak ejection velocity of 2.2 EDV/second. This compares with the last reported values of 31%, 33%, and 24%.

---

19. MASTOIDS: The left mastoid shows a surgical defect, apparently due to simple mastoidectomy. There are many small, residual cloudy areas in the periphery of the mastoidectomy defect and in the attic region and anterior to the knee of the sinus and low in the squama extending toward the root of the zygoma. No sequestrum is noted. The tegmen antri appears defective. The left sinus is in good position. The left internal auditory canal is of normal caliber. There are a few small cells along the sinus groove near the tip; these also appear cloudy. The left malleus and incus are partly outlined. The right mastoid is highly pneumatic with cells extending into the zygoma. The right malleus and incus are partly out-lined. The right sinus is in good position. The right internal auditory canal is of normal caliber.

---

20. NUCLEAR LIVER-SPLEEN SCAN: The liver is of normal size with homogeneous uptake. The spleen is enlarged and is almost the same size as the liver. There is also increased activity in the spleen. I do not see any focal areas of diminished activity, and there is no significant bone marrow uptake.

CONCLUSION: Splenomegaly.

---

21. ABDOMINAL ULTRASOUND: The pregnant uterus is examined via a transabdominal view. Estimated gestation is 16 weeks. A single fetus is observed. No abnormalities of the fetus or placenta are seen. Real-time imaging is provided during this ultrasound.

---

22. RADIATION TREATMENT: 4 MeV were delivered to thyroid area.

---

23. DIAGNOSTIC ULTRASOUND: The scrotum is normal in size. All tissue within appears normal. The testes are normal in appearance. The epididymis appears normal in structure.

---

24. CT SCAN: After administration of contrast dye, soft tissue structures of the neck are identified. The thyroid and parathyroid glands are seen. The right parathyroid gland shows a cyst-like structure.

---

25. CT SCAN: The lumbar spine has a right curvature of 3 mm. The vertebra at L4 has a moderate amount of bone spur.

CONCLUSION: Scoliosis.

---

26. X-RAY OF SHOULDER: AP and lateral views of the right shoulder reveal no soft tissue masses or bony abnormalities.

    CONCLUSION: Normal right shoulder.

    _____

27. PET SCAN: The chest region scan reveals no soft tissue masses or bony abnormalities. Ribs, mediastinum, and heart are normal.

    _____

28. X-RAY OF LEFT ANKLE: Lateral, AP, and oblique views reveal fracture of the malleolus bone on the lateral side. Soft tissue swelling is noted at the fracture site. No dislocation is seen.

    CONCLUSION: Fracture of left ankle.

    _____

29. MRI OF HEART: A complete view of the heart and cardiac structures reviewed no abnormalities. Heart valves were normal in appearance. Cardiac function was normal.

    CONCLUSION: Normal imaging of the heart.

    _____

30. NUCLEAR MEDICINE: WHOLE BODY BONE AND JOINT SCAN: Uptake was noted in the nasal area of the sphenoid sinuses. The remainder of the scan is normal. No masses, bony abnormalities, or metastatic disease is seen.

    _____

CHAPTER 7

CPT Pathology and Laboratory

Chapter Outline

Overview of Pathology and Laboratory Section

Pathology and Laboratory Section Guidelines

Pathology and Laboratory Subsections

Chapter Objectives

At the conclusion of this chapter, the student should be able to:

- Define key terms.
- Explain the organization, format, and content of the CPT Pathology and Laboratory section.
- Interpret CPT pathology and laboratory coding guidelines and notes.
- Assign CPT pathology and laboratory codes.
- Add CPT and/or HCPCS level II modifiers to codes, as appropriate.

Key Terms

accession

adjuvant

aliquot

analyte

antibody

antigen

arterial puncture

assay

Bethesda System

block

Chemstrip automated
   urine analyzer

chromatography

chromosomal breakage
   syndrome

Clinical Laboratory
   Improvement Act of
   1988 (CLIA)

cytogenetics

cytopathology

definitive identification

dipstick

evocative

fluorescence *in situ*
   hybridization (FISH)

Gram stain

gross examination

hematology

immunoglobulin

immunology

microbiology

microtechnique

necropsy

phlebotomy

presumptive
   identification

qualitative assay

quantitative assay

reagent strip automated
   urine analyzer

section

specimen

venipuncture

Introduction

The Pathology and Laboratory section of CPT includes subsections for organ or disease-oriented panels, drug testing, therapeutic drug assays, evocative/suppression testing, consultations (clinical pathology), urinalysis, molecular pathology, multianalyte assays with algorithmic analyses, chemistry, hematology and coagulation, immunology, transfusion medicine, microbiology, anatomical pathology, cytopathology, cytogenetic studies, surgical pathology, *in vivo* laboratory procedures, other procedures, and reproductive medicine procedures.

Overview of Pathology and Laboratory Section

CPT pathology and laboratory codes describe services performed on specimens (e.g., body fluids, tissue, or cytological specimens) to evaluate, prevent, diagnose, or treat a disease. A **specimen** (e.g., blood, urine, tissue from an organ) is tissue submitted for laboratory or pathological evaluation. Examinations are the following:

- Biophysical
- Chemical
- Cytological
- Hematological
- Immunohematological
- Microbiological
- Pathological
- Serological

EXAMPLE: A wound culture is obtained from the smear of an infected area. The infective organism is identified as the result of growing the organism on a culture plate and microscopically reviewing the specimen or serologically testing the organism (e.g., antistreptolysin O titer).

Most clinical laboratory service codes include a technical component; however, some include both a technical and a professional component. In addition, because many pathology and laboratory procedures can be performed using different methods, patient record documentation must be reviewed along with code descriptions and instructional notes.

Note:

Hospitals include pathology and laboratory codes on a chargemaster, which is used to report services (and supplies) for inpatients, outpatients, and emergency department patients. Coders do not assign codes to pathology and laboratory procedures that are performed on an inpatient basis because such services do not impact diagnosis-related group (DRG) assignment and facility reimbursement.

Note:

Depending on the contract negotiated between pathologists and the health care facility

- Pathologists are considered employees of the health care facility (e.g., a hospital) or they are considered contractors.

- The facility submits claims to obtain reimbursement for all services provided to patients (including professional services) *or* the pathologists use a medical billing service to submit claims for professional services.

Specimen Collection

Laboratory codes describe the *performance* of lab tests. These codes do not include *collection of the specimen* (e.g., venipuncture, fingerstick, or lumbar puncture) used to perform the test. For safety purposes, after venipuncture, the used needle is placed in an approved *sharps container* made of hard, damage-resistant plastic (Figure 17-1).

Figure 17-1 Sharps containers

For laboratory-testing purposes, a specimen includes tissue (e.g., blood and urine) that is submitted for individual and separate examinations and/or pathological diagnosis. Specimen collection is reported separately, in addition to the laboratory test performed. Collection methods vary from those requiring no patient preparation to invasive-type procedures, and the reason for the test typically determines the appropriate collection method. Special collection methods (e.g., urethral catheterization or suprapubic aspiration) are indicated when a specimen cannot be obtained by more common techniques.

EXAMPLE: With an indwelling urinary catheter in place, a specimen is obtained by inserting the needle into the catheter. The urine is aspirated and placed in a sterile urine container for laboratory testing.

Venipuncture, or **phlebotomy** (36400–36425), is the puncture of a vein using a needle for the purpose of drawing blood, and it is the most common method of collecting blood specimens. **Arterial puncture** (36600) is the puncture of an artery using a needle for the purpose of drawing blood.

A code from range 36400–36410 is reported when a routine venipuncture (which is typically performed by a nurse or a phlebotomist) is unsuccessful and the skill of the physician is required to perform the procedure. It is not appropriate to report a code from range 36400–36410 when a physician performs venipuncture for patient convenience or because the nurse or phlebotomist is unavailable to perform the service. (A routine venipuncture is reported with code 36415.)

 Coding Tip:

The following CPT codes are reported for routine venipuncture under the outpatient prospective payment system (OPPS):

- Collection of venous blood by venipuncture (36415)
- Collection of capillary blood specimen (e.g., finger-, heel-, or ear-stick) (36416)

The venipuncture code is reported just once per encounter for each type of specimen, regardless of the number of specimens drawn. (HCPCS level II code G0001 was deleted effective January 1, 2005.)

Professional and Technical Components

Certain laboratory procedures contain both a professional (e.g., physician) component and a technical component. The technical component of a laboratory procedure or service includes, but is not limited to, the cost of equipment, supplies, and technician salaries. (CPT guidelines do not address reporting the technical component of a pathology and laboratory procedure or service.)

 Coding Tip:

> When a pathology and laboratory procedure or service code description includes both the technical and the professional component, and one of the components was not performed, report the appropriate code with modifier
> - -26, to indicate that only the professional component was performed
> - -TC, to indicate that only the technical component was performed

Pathologists often oversee the clinical laboratory and assume overall responsibility for test results. When reporting codes for professional and technical components of clinical laboratory services, standard practice is for the pathologist to report the professional component of clinical laboratory services. Clinical pathology professional services include the following:

- Directing and evaluating quality assurance and control procedures (e.g., ensuring that tests and procedures are properly performed, recorded, and reported; validating test methodologies)
- Supervising laboratory technicians
- Recommending follow-up diagnostic tests, when appropriate

The hospital reports the technical component, which represents the hospital's costs (e.g., laboratory equipment, supplies, and nonphysician personnel). The hospital's technical component does *not* include the pathologist's professional services.

☞ Pathology and laboratory services can be provided by a physician or by technologists under the supervision of a physician. Although most codes describe clinical laboratory tests, physician laboratory and pathology services are also included. Physician laboratory and pathology services include the following: ⚠

- Surgical pathology services
- Cytopathology, hematology, and blood-banking services that require a physician
- Clinical consultation services
- Clinical laboratory interpretation services

Typically, pathology and laboratory specimens are prepared by laboratory personnel with a pathologist assuming responsibility for the integrity of the results. Certain tests are personally reviewed by the pathologist. Very few CPT pathology and laboratory codes require patient contact; however, occasionally a pathologist provides evaluation and management services. Such services are reported with appropriate CPT evaluation and management codes.

 Note:

Most laboratory services reported with CPT codes are paid by Medicare according to the laboratory fee schedule, which is discussed in Chapter 19.

 Coding Tip:

Modifier -90, Reference (Outside) Laboratory, is reported to indicate that an outside laboratory performed the service. This modifier is often added to pathology and laboratory codes to indicate that the physician did not perform the actual test, but instead sent the specimen to an outside laboratory.

Clinical Laboratory Improvement Act of 1988 (CLIA)

To perform certain pathology and laboratory tests (and to submit claims to Medicare and Medicaid), physician office labs must obtain certification under the **Clinical Laboratory Improvement Act of 1988 (CLIA)**. A waiver is available for small office labs that perform only basic testing (e.g., urine dipsticks and fingerstick glucose testing), and a special CLIA waiver number is assigned to these labs. The list of approved tests is updated periodically, which means that physician office labs must determine if they still qualify for a waiver.

Coding Tip:

When reporting CLIA waived services to Medicare or Medicaid, add HCPCS level II modifier -QW to pathology and laboratory codes.

National Coverage Determinations (NCDs)

The Centers for Medicare & Medicaid Services (CMS) developed National Coverage Determinations (NCDs), which define coverage for services and procedures. Medicare administrative contractors (MACs) apply national coverage determinations nationwide, and local coverage decisions (LCDs) supplement the NCDs. Pathology and laboratory NCDs were developed to

- Simplify administrative requirements for clinical diagnostic services.

- Promote national uniformity in processing Medicare claims.

Pathology and Laboratory Section Tables

The following tables are located prior to Pathology and Laboratory section guidelines in the *CPT coding manual*

- Table of Drugs and the Appropriate Qualitative Screening, Confirmatory, and Quantitative Codes

- Molecular Pathology Table

Exercise 17.1 – Overview of Pathology and Laboratory Section

Instructions: Complete each statement.

1. Although most clinical laboratory service codes include a technical component, some include both a technical and a(n) _____ component.

2. Review of patient record documentation is necessary before assigning pathology and laboratory codes because many procedures can be performed using different _____.

3. Hospital coders usually do not assign pathology and laboratory codes because they are included on a(n) _____, which is used by providers to select services provided to patients.

4. CPT laboratory codes describe the performance of lab tests, and they do not include collection of the _____, which is performed using different methods (e.g., venipuncture, fingerstick, or lumbar puncture) and is reported separately.

5. The puncture of a vein using a needle for the purpose of drawing blood as a common method of collecting blood specimens is called venipuncture, or _____.

6. A routine venipuncture (usually performed by a nurse) is assigned code _____, and it is reported in addition to the laboratory procedure code.

Exercise 17.1 *(continued)*

7. When a physician's skill is required to perform the venipuncture procedure, a code from range _____ is assigned.

8. When a pathology and laboratory procedure code description includes technical and professional components, and both components were not performed, modifier _____ is added to the code to indicate that only the professional component was performed.

9. When an outside laboratory performs pathology and laboratory services, add modifier _____ to the reported code.

10. To perform certain pathology and laboratory tests (and to submit claims to Medicare and Medicaid), physician office labs must obtain certification under the _____.

Pathology and Laboratory Section Guidelines

Guidelines located at the beginning of the Pathology and Laboratory section provide instruction about the following:

- Services in pathology and laboratory
- Separate or multiple procedures
- Unlisted services or procedures
- Special reports

Services in Pathology and Laboratory

Pathology and laboratory services are provided by a physician (e.g., a pathologist) or by technologists under responsible supervision of a physician. The unit of pathology service is a *specimen*, which is tissue that is submitted for individual and separate examination and pathological diagnosis. When multiple specimens are received for pathological examination, each specimen is considered a single unit of service and each is reported with a separate code.

EXAMPLE 1: Two separately identified skin lesions are submitted for individual examination and diagnosis. Report codes 88305 and 88305-59 (Skin, Other Than Cyst/Tag/Debridement/Plastic Repair). (Modifier -59 is added to indicate that the second lesion was evaluated as a "distinct procedural service.")

EXAMPLE 2: The uterus (with or without tubes and ovaries) is considered one specimen and is reported with code 88305 (when the uterus is removed for prolapse and shows no other abnormalities), 88309 (for neoplasia), or 88307 (for other conditions).

EXAMPLE 3: A cell block prepared from cytology fluids, bone marrow aspirates, or fine-needle aspirates is coded as 88305 (Cell block, any source).

(A **block** is a portion of tissue obtained from a specimen that is placed in a support medium, such as paraffin. A **section** is a thin slice of tissue prepared from a block that is examined.)

Separate or Multiple Procedures

It is appropriate to separately code and report multiple pathology and laboratory procedures that are provided on the same date of service. However, it is *not* appropriate to report tests that are repeated simply to confirm initial results (because of an equipment malfunction or technician error) or when a series of tests is performed (e.g., glucose tolerance tests). These services are considered part of the originally ordered test, and codes for repeated tests are not separately coded and reported.

EXAMPLE: A manual platelet count (85032) was performed in addition to an automated hemogram with automated platelet count (85027). Do not report both codes 85032 and 85027 because one serves as a confirmatory test for the other. Report either code 85032 or 85027, depending on the test ordered by the physician.

Unlisted Service or Procedure

A service or procedure that is provided for which there is no CPT code is reported with an "unlisted service or procedure" code. Pathology and laboratory unlisted service and procedure codes include the following:

- Unlisted urinalysis procedure (81099)
- Unlisted chemistry procedure (84999)
- Unlisted hematology and coagulation procedure (85999)
- Unlisted antigen, each (86486)
- Unlisted immunology procedure (86849)
- Unlisted transfusion medicine procedure (86999)
- Unlisted microbiology procedure (87999)
- Unlisted necropsy (autopsy) procedure (88099)
- Unlisted cytopathology procedure (88199)
- Unlisted cytogenetic study (88299)
- Unlisted surgical pathology procedure (88399)
- Unlisted miscellaneous pathology test (89240)
- Unlisted reproductive medical laboratory procedure (89398)

Special Report

When an unlisted procedure or service code is reported on a claim, a "special report" is attached to the submitted claim to clarify the service or procedure performed. A service or procedure that is rarely performed, unusual, variable, or new may require a special report to be submitted so the third-party payer can determine the medical appropriateness of the service or procedure. The special report should include a description of the nature, extent, and need for the procedure. In addition, the following items may be included:

- Complexity of symptoms
- Final diagnosis
- Pertinent physical findings
- Diagnostic and therapeutic procedures
- Concurrent problems
- Follow-up care

Modifier -51 and Modifier -91

- Modifier -51 (Multiple Procedures) is *not* added to pathology and laboratory codes.
- Modifier -91 (Repeat Clinical Diagnostic Laboratory Test) is added to pathology and laboratory codes when procedures or services are repeated on the same date of service to obtain multiple results.

EXAMPLE: A patient undergoes a comprehensive metabolic panel laboratory test (80053). Because of abnormal blood urea nitrogen (BUN) test results, the patient undergoes a repeat BUN test as an individual test (84520). Report codes 80053 and 84520-91.

Exercise 17.2 – Pathology and Laboratory Section Guidelines

Instructions: Complete each statement.

1. The unit of pathology service is a(n) _____, which is tissue submitted for individual and separate examination and pathological diagnosis.

2. During the same operative session, the surgeon submitted "incidental appendix" tissue and a section of fallopian tube (as the result of a sterilization procedure) for pathological evaluation. Refer to the notes located below the Surgical Pathology subsection (codes 88300–88399) to determine whether one or two codes are reported. Code 88302 is reported _____ (once/twice).

3. It is appropriate to separately code and report multiple pathology and laboratory procedures that are provided on the same _____.

4. A service or procedure that is provided for which there is no CPT code is reported with a(n) _____ code, and a(n) _____ is attached to the submitted claim.

5. When procedures or services are repeated on the same date of service to obtain multiple results, add modifier _____ to the reported pathology and laboratory code(s). It is *not* appropriate to add modifier _____ to pathology and laboratory codes.

Pathology and Laboratory Subsections

The Pathology and Laboratory section is organized according to type of procedure performed or service provided. Pathology and laboratory procedures are listed alphabetically within each subsection, which include the following:

- Organ or disease-oriented panels
- Drug assay
- Therapeutic drug assays
- Evocative/suppression testing
- Consultations (clinical pathology)
- Urinalysis
- Molecular pathology
- Genomic sequencing procedures and other molecular multianalyte assays
- Multianalyte assays with algorithmic analyses
- Chemistry
- Hematology and coagulation
- Immunology
- Transfusion medicine
- Microbiology
- Anatomical pathology
- Cytopathology
- Cytogenetic studies
- Surgical pathology
- *In vivo* laboratory procedures
- Other procedures
- Reproductive medicine procedures

Organ or Disease-Oriented Panels

Organ or disease-oriented panels subsection codes are reported for a defined group of tests that are administered for a certain purpose. The panels were developed for coding purposes only and are not considered clinical parameters. The tests listed below each panel identify the components of that panel.

To report an organ or disease-oriented panel code, all tests listed below the panel must be performed. No substitutions can be made.

EXAMPLE: Patient underwent a general health panel (80050). A general health panel must include all of the following procedures:

- Comprehensive metabolic panel (80053)

- Blood count, complete (CBC); automated and automated differential WBC count (85025 or 85027 and 85004) *or* CBC; automated (85027) and appropriate manual differential WBC count (85007 or 85009)

- Thyroid-stimulating hormone (TSH) (84443)

These individual procedure codes are *not* reported in addition to general health panel code 80050.

When only one or several of the tests associated with a panel are performed, do not report the panel code. Instead, report codes for each individual test performed. When additional tests are performed in addition to those listed below the panel, separately code and report the additional tests (in addition to the panel code).

EXAMPLE 1: Patient underwent a glucose test and a sodium test. Report codes 82947 and 84295. (Do *not* report basic metabolic panel code 80048.)

EXAMPLE 2: Patient underwent a basic metabolic panel test and an albumin test. Report codes 80048 and 82040.

The comprehensive metabolic panel (80053) does not include the direct bilirubin test (82248) because code 80053 is reported for an incomplete survey of multiple organ systems. The total bilirubin test (82247) is included in the comprehensive metabolic panel (80053) because it indicates a wider range of pathologic conditions than a direct bilirubin test.

Drug Assay and Therapeutic Drug Assays

CPT codes reported for drug procedures are located in three subsections of pathology and laboratory, and code selection is dependent on the purpose and type of patient results obtained.

- Therapeutic drug assays (80150–80377)
- Chemistry (82009–84999)
- Drug assay (80305–80377)

An **assay** (e.g., lab test) is the measurement of the amount of a constituent in a specimen. Therapeutic drug assay procedures are performed to monitor the patient's clinical response to a known, prescribed medication. The two major categories include the following:

(1) *Presumptive drug class procedures* identify possible use or non-use of a drug or drug class. They may be followed by a definitive test in order to specifically identify drugs or metabolites.

(2) *Definitive drug class procedures* are qualitative or quantitative tests that identify possible use or non-use of a drug. These tests identify specific drugs and associated metabolites, if performed. (A presumptive test is not required prior to a definitive drug test.)

Qualitative assays detect whether a particular substance is present. **Quantitative assays** detect the amount of a substance in a specimen.

The material for drug class procedures may be any specimen type unless otherwise specified in the code descriptor (e.g., urine, blood, oral fluid, meconium, hair). Procedures can be qualitative, semi-quantitative, or quantitative depending on the purpose of the testing. Therapeutic drug assay procedures are typically quantitative tests and the specimen type is whole blood, serum, plasma, or cerebrospinal fluid. When the same procedure(s) is performed on more than one specimen type (e.g., hair and urine), the appropriate code is reported separately for each specimen type using modifier -59.

Drugs or classes of drugs may be commonly assayed first by a presumptive screening method followed by a definitive drug identification method. Presumptive methods include immunoassays, enzymatic methods, chromatographic methods without mass spectrometry, or mass spectrometry without adequate drug resolution by chromatography.

Drugs or classes of drugs may be assayed first using a presumptive screening method followed by a definitive drug identification method. The drug class and methodology must be determined when reporting codes for presumptive procedures. (If a drug class is not listed in Drug Class List A and Drug Class List B, located in the Drug Assay subsection, and if it is not performed by thin layer chromatography, report code 80307 except when the specific analyte is found in the Chemistry subsection, 82009-84999.)

> **EXAMPLE 1:** Patient underwent alcohol drug screen (Drug Class List A) using an instrumented test system. Report code 80305.

> **EXAMPLE 2:** Patient underwent definitive drug testing for three or more types of anabolic steriods on the same encounter date. Report code 80328.

> **EXAMPLE 3:** Patient underwent a total digoxin therapeutic drug assay procedure to monitor his clinical response to treatment. (The patient's blood was drawn for this laboratory procedure.) Report code 80162.

> **EXAMPLE 4:** Patient underwent Breathalyzer testing for presence of alcohol (ethanol). Report code 82075.

Evocative/Suppression Testing

Evocative/suppression test panels (80400–80439) include the administration of evocative or suppressive agents and the baseline and subsequent measurement of their effect on chemical constituents. These codes are reported for the laboratory component of the testing protocol. (**Evocative** means to cause a specific response; this term is used to describe various tests intended to cause production of hormones or other secretions.)

 Coding Tip:

Report a code from the CPT Medicine section for administration (e.g., infusion) of the evocative or suppressive agents. To locate the administration of agent code, refer to the Hydration, Therapeutic, Prophylactic, Diagnostic Injections and Infusions, and Chemotherapy and Other Highly Complex Drug or Highly Complex Biologic Agent Administration subsection of CPT Medicine.

Consultations (Clinical Pathology)

The physician (e.g., the pathologist) review of laboratory test results is typically considered a non-face-to-face service, and the review of laboratory results is not a separately reportable service. However, when a patient's attending physician requests that a pathologist provide consultation services regarding pathology and/or laboratory test results, clinical pathology consultation codes are reported (80500–80502). The clinical pathology consultation requires

- ☞ Additional medical interpretative judgment

- Preparation of a written report

Codes 80500 and 80502 are differentiated according to whether a review of the patient's history and medical records was performed as part of the clinical pathology consultation service.

> **EXAMPLE:** A surgeon orders a clinical pathology consultation to determine a patient's suitability for surgery based on the results of clinical laboratory tests. The pathologist documents a written consultation report that includes a review of patient records, including the patient's history and current laboratory results, and medical judgment about the patient's candidacy for surgery. Report code 80502.

 Note:

A physician (e.g., a pathologist) who reports test results but who does not provide medical interpretive judgment has not provided clinical pathology consultation services.

A pathologist who provides a clinical pathology consultation service (which includes examination of the patient) reports an appropriate evaluation and management code (e.g., outpatient, inpatient, or consultation). The pathologist is responsible for ensuring that the criteria for reporting the evaluation and management code have been met and a report has been appropriately documented in the medical record.

Clinical pathology consultation services are performed

- At the request of another physician when test result(s) require additional medical interpretation

- When material (e.g., tissue slides) is referred by another pathologist or facility

Urinalysis

Most urine tests are performed to diagnose or monitor renal or urinary tract disease. Urine testing is easily performed and does not require an invasive skin puncture. Urine collection containers (Figure 17-2) used for routine urinalysis are made of material that is clear (translucent), and they contain lids that can be secured to prevent spills during transport. For example, protein in the urine may indicate glomerulonephritis, and urine cultures monitor the effectiveness of antibiotic treatment for urinary tract infections.

Figure 17-2 Urine collection container

Codes 81000–81099 are reported for the analysis of one or more components of the urine. The reported code is based on method (e.g., dipstick), purpose (e.g., a pregnancy test), or element evaluated (e.g., bilirubin, bacteriuria screen).

Quantitative urine tests often require a timed collection. Timed urine collection is often performed because substances (e.g., hormones, proteins, and electrolytes) are excreted over a 24-hour period. Because exercise, hydration, and body metabolism affect excretion rates, these time periods may range anywhere from 2 to 24 hours.

A **reagent strip automated urine analyzer** (or **Chemstrip automated urine analyzer**) (Figure 17-3) is used to determine various components in the urine (including glucose, albumin, hemoglobin, and bile concentrations, as well as urinary pH, specific gravity, protein, ketone bodies, nitrites, and leukocyte esterase). A **dipstick** (Figure 17-4) is a small strip of plastic that is infused with a chemical that reacts to products in urine by changing color. It is considered preliminary and may be performed for screening purposes.

⚠ Coding Tip:

Analysis of urine is also classified in other Pathology and Laboratory subsections. For example, a urine chloride test is reported with code 82436 from the Chemistry subsection.

Figure 17-3 Chemstrip automated urine analyzer

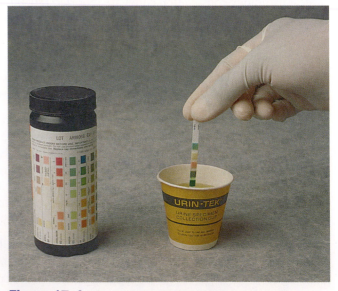

Figure 17-4 Dipstick used for routine urinalysis

The appropriate handling and storage of urine is necessary to prevent changes that adversely impact accurate results. Many **analytes** (substance or chemical compound undergoing analysis) require the use of preservatives so that they remain viable during the collection period. The choice of preservative depends on the type of collection. For example, sodium fluoride is used to preserve glucose in a 24-hour urine collection.

> **EXAMPLE:** Nonautomated urinalysis by dipstick, without microscopy. Report code 81002.

Molecular Pathology

Molecular pathology laboratory procedures involve the analysis of nucleic acid to detect gene variants, which may be indicative of certain conditions (e.g., constitutional disorders, neoplasia, histocompatibility enzymes). Codes are organized as Tier 1 and Tier 2 molecular pathology laboratory procedures. CPT incorporates the Human Genome Organization–approved gene names in code descriptions along with proteins or diseases associated with the genes. ⚠ Molecular pathology notes indicate that any procedures performed prior to cell lysis, such as microdissection, are to be reported separately, and an extensive list of definitions is also included.

Coding Tip:

When tests require that a physician or other qualified health care professional interpret the results, and the provider performs the interpretation only, add modifier -26 (Professional Component) to the code.

- Tier 1 molecular pathology laboratory codes are assigned for gene-specific and genomic procedures according to the *analyte* (substance or chemical compound undergoing analysis) or the *allele* (genetic variants).

- Tier 2 codes are assigned for procedures not listed in Tier 1, and they are classified according to level of technical resources and interpretive professional work required. (Tier 2 procedures are performed less frequently than are Tier 1 procedures.)

- If a tested analyte or allele is not represented by a Tier 1 code or the technical resources/interpretive professional work is not described in a Tier 2 code, report an appropriate methodology code (codes 81200–81479).

> **EXAMPLE:** Patient underwent the *BRCA1* and *BRCA2* gene analysis laboratory procedure to determine her risk for hereditary breast and ovarian cancer. Report code 81211.

Genomic Sequencing Procedures and Other Molecular Multianalyte Assays

Genomic sequencing procedures (GSPs) and *other molecular multianalyte assays GSPs* are DNA or RNA sequence analysis methods that simultaneously assay multiple genes or genetic regions relevant to a clinical situation.

> **EXAMPLE:** Patient underwent genome sequence analysis for Huntington's disease. Report code 81425.

Multianalyte Assays with Algorithmic Analyses

Multianalyte Assays with Algorithmic Analyses (MAAAs) are performed to determine discrete genetic values, properties, or characteristics, and the results are potentially of independent medical significance or useful in the medical management of a patient (e.g., determine patient's risk for certain diseases).

> **EXAMPLE:** Patient underwent oncology (ovarian) biochemical assays of two proteins (CA-125 and HE4), utilizing serum, with menopausal status, with the algorithm reported as a risk score. Report code 81500.

Chemistry

Chemistry codes (82009–84999) are reported for quantitative tests unless the code description indicates otherwise (e.g., chromatography code 82542). Presumptive and/or definitive drug testing procedures are reported with codes 80305–80377. Chemical tests performed on body materials are obtained from any source (e.g., blood or urine) unless the code description specifies otherwise. Codes in the chemistry subsection are listed in alphabetical order.

To properly assign codes from the Chemistry subsection, locate the code that describes the analyte to be tested (the specific substance to be analyzed).

When a chemistry test is performed on multiple specimens from different sources, or on specimens that are obtained at different times, the analyte is reported separately for *each* source and for *each* specimen.

EXAMPLE: Patient underwent two lab tests to determine total bilirubin levels. A specimen was obtained during the morning and afternoon on April 5. Report codes 82247 and 82247-91.

Stool includes waste products of digested food bile, mucus, epithelial cells, and bacteria. Stool studies are performed to evaluate bowel function (e.g., for intestinal bleeding, infections, infestations, inflammation, malabsorption, and diarrhea).

EXAMPLE: Patient underwent occult blood testing by peroxidase activity, qualitative, feces, single specimen. Report code 82272.

Body fluids can be tested for blood urea nitrogen (BUN) and creatinine to determine whether the fluid is urine. For example, code 84560 is reported for uric acid testing, other source, which is helpful in obstetrics to differentiate amniotic fluid from urine.

Hematology and Coagulation

Hematology is the study of the function and disorders of blood (Figure 17-5). *Coagulation* is the process of blood clotting. Hematology and coagulation codes (85002–85999) are reported for laboratory tests performed to evaluate blood and blood clotting, such as CBC, clotting factor tests, clotting inhibitor tests, and prothrombin and thrombin time. Bone marrow, smear interpretation (85097) is also classified in the Hematology and Coagulation subsection. However, bone marrow biopsy and cell block interpretations are reported with code 88305.

Figure 17-5 Blood components

Platelet count codes are integrated into the blood count series of codes (85004–85049).

- Platelet count (platelet estimation) is reported with code 85032 or 85049, depending on whether manual or automated WBC count was performed.

- Code 85041 describes an automated red blood cell count, and it is *not* reported in addition to codes 85025 or 85027 (because those codes include an automated red blood cell count).

- Code 85045 describes an automated reticulocyte count.

- Code 85048 is reported for an automated WBC count.

- Code 85049 describes an automated platelet count, and code 85032 describes a manual platelet count.

Codes 85007–85009 reflect current manual microscopic review of peripheral blood, and code 85007 also describes the microscopic examination of a blood smear with a manual differential leukocyte (WBC) count. Code 85008 describes a microscopic blood smear examination *without* a manual differential WBC count.

Code 85025 (automated CBC and automated differential WBC count) is reported when blood is tested to determine the following levels:

- Hemoglobin (Hgb)
- Hematocrit (Hct)
- Red blood cell (RBC)
- White blood cell (WBC)
- Platelet

The automated differential WBC count determines the number of basophils, eosinophils, monocytes, lymphocytes, and neutrophils. (When a manual cell count of erythrocytes, leukocytes, or platelets is performed, report code 85032 for *each*.)

EXAMPLE: Patient underwent manual CBC to determine Hct, Hgb, RBC, and WBC levels. Report codes 85014, 85018, 85032, and 85032-59. (Code 85032 is reported twice to reflect erythrocyte and leukocyte testing.)

To report an automated CBC with a manual differential WBC count, report code 85027 with either code 85007 or 85009.

EXAMPLE: Patient underwent an automated CBC and an automated differential WBC count. Report code 85025 *or* codes 85027 and 85004, depending on the laboratory's processing of the WBC differential.

Codes 85378–85380 differentiate specific methodologies for measuring D-dimer, based on the sensitivity of the analysis.

- Qualitative or semiquantitative (85378)

- Quantitative (85379)

- Ultrasensitive (85380)

A parenthetical note below code 85379 provides instruction to report that code for ultrasensitive and standard sensitivity *quantitative* D-dimer tests. CPT code 85380 is reported for ultrasensitive qualitative and semiquantitative D-dimer tests.

EXAMPLE: Patient underwent qualitative D-dimer test. Report code 85378.

Immunology

Immunology is the study of the immune system. Immunology codes classify antigen and antibody laboratory studies (86000–86804) and tissue typing (86805–86849). Antigen and antibody studies measure the reaction of

- **Antigens** (Ag): Foreign substances that elicit the formation of antibodies

- **Antibodies** (Ab): Proteins in the body made by the immune system that fight infection and disease

Figure 17-6 Serological centrifuge

(An **adjuvant** is a substance administered with an antigen that enhances the response to the antigen.) Figure 17-6 contains a serological centrifuge, which is used to spin test tubes of blood to test for agglutination reactions (clumping of blood cells). Hemagglutination (agglutination of red blood cells) is a method used to visualize antigen–antibody reactions.

EXAMPLE: Patient underwent HIV-1 antibody test to determine exposure to human immunodeficiency virus and subsequent antibody development. Report code 86701.

Immunoglobulins are proteins produced by plasma cells that help fight infection. Some immunoglobulins (e.g., gamma globulins) are involved in immune responses to bacteria or foreign substances (e.g., allergens or transplanted tissue). Immunoglobulins include IgA, IgD, IgE, IgG, and IgM. Two codes are reported for the quantitative and qualitative measurement of IgE.

- Quantitative or semiquantitative allergen-specific IgE (86003)

- Qualitative allergen-specific multiallergen screen (using a dipstick, paddle, or disk) (86005)

EXAMPLE: Patient underwent quantitative allergen-specific IgE testing, 5 allergens. Report code 86003 five times.

Tumor antigen codes are reported to indicate the presence of a tumor marker in the patient's blood.

EXAMPLE: Patient with previously treated stage II and stage III breast cancer underwent immunoassay for tumor antigen 125 to test for recurrence of breast cancer. Report code 86304.

Codes 86602–86804 are reported for laboratory tests performed to identify specific antibodies. Such tests are performed using a multistep method. Codes for tissue typing (86805–86849) describe procedures performed to determine compatibility between a recipient and donors for organ or bone marrow transplants.

EXAMPLE: Patient underwent HLA typing of a single antigen (A). Report code 86812. (HLA is the abbreviation for human leukocyte antigen, which determines graft acceptance.)

Transfusion Medicine

Transfusion medicine codes (86850–86999) are often reported by blood banks, and they describe blood preparation services for transfusion. For transfusion services, report the appropriate CPT code as well as a HCPCS level II code for the blood product transfused. (The service code is reported with the date of service for the transfusion, not the date the blood was collected.) When autologous blood is collected but not transfused, report code 86890 or code 86891 with the number of units collected but not transfused.

 Coding Tip:

Codes 86850–86870 are classified according to

- Technique

- Elution

- Panel

Coding Tip:

- Do not assign a CPT code for freezing and/or thawing if a HCPCS level II code is available that specifies whether the type of blood product is frozen and/or thawed (e.g., P9054).

- When a HCPCS level II code is unavailable for specified types of frozen/thawed products (e.g., P9035), report a HCPCS level II code for the blood product and a CPT code for the freezing and/or thawing services (e.g., 86932). In addition, assign a CPT code for the transfusion service.

To report the collection, modification, treatment, and processing of autologous blood specimens for transplantation, report code 86890 or code 86891. When processing and storage costs are incurred for unused blood or blood products, the provider may submit charges when patient-specific preparation was done (e.g., blood typing and cross-matching).

EXAMPLE: Patient underwent transfusion of one unit of frozen blood, which included freezing (and preparation) as well as thawing. Report code 86932. (If the type of blood product had been stated in the example, such as plasma, report more specific HCPCS level II code P9017 instead of unspecified CPT code 86932.)

 Note:

A transfusion APC (ambulatory payment classification) payment is paid just once per day regardless of the number of units or different types of products transfused when reporting codes for a health care facility (e.g., acute care hospital).

Microbiology

Microbiology is the study of microbes (e.g., bacteria, parasites, and viruses). Microbiology codes (87003–87999) include bacteriology, mycology, parasitology, and virology, and the codes are intended to describe primary definitive (or final) bacterial cultures. To properly assign microbiology codes, determine the following:

- Source
- Handling method
- Stains performed
- Identification technique used

It is appropriate to separately report multiple procedures when various microbiology testing procedures are performed.

Microscopic examinations evaluate cytologic specimens to identify bacteria and other infecting organisms (e.g., determining hormone receptor assay results, chromatin identification, culture and sensitivity testing). Microbiology subsection notes provide instruction about the presumptive identification of microorganisms and definitive identification.

- **Presumptive identification** is the identification by colony morphology, growth on selective media, Gram stains, or up to three tests (e.g., catalase, oxidase, indole, or urease).

- **Definitive identification** of microorganisms is the identification to the genus or species level that requires additional tests (e.g., biochemical panels or slide cultures). The word "definitive" refers to the final culture that identifies the organism. Reporting these codes indicates that a specific organism genus or group (e.g., *Staphylococcus, Salmonella,* or *Streptococcus*) has been identified.

When additional studies involve molecular probes, chromatography, or immunologic techniques, report the codes separately in addition to definitive identification codes (87140–87158). For multiple specimens/sites, add modifier -59 to the microbiology code. For repeat laboratory tests performed on the same day, add modifier -91 to the microbiology code.

A **Gram stain** is a method of classifying all bacteria as gram positive or gram negative. The shape of the organism (e.g., spherical or rod-shaped) may also be helpful in the identification of the infecting organism. When the Gram stain indicates Gram negative rods, the infection may be caused by *Escherichia coli*. With knowledge of Gram stain results, the physician can initiate antibiotic treatment based on the organism's identity.

> **EXAMPLE:** A fluorescent stain for bacteria, primary source smear with interpretation, was performed. Report code 87206.

Anatomic Pathology

Anatomical pathology codes are reported for physician (pathologist) services only. Physician services involved in performing **necropsy** (autopsy) are reported with codes 88000–88099 (e.g., a postmortem examination). The codes are specific to the following:

- Portions of the body
- Gross examination
- Regional examination
- Forensic examination
- Infant/stillborn

> **EXAMPLE:** The pathologist performed a gross and microscopic autopsy that included the brain of a stillborn infant. Report code 88029. (**Gross examination** involves visually evaluating a specimen with the naked eye.)

Cytopathology

Cytopathology is the study of diseased cells. Specimen cells are typically obtained using brushing, washing, needle biopsy, or fine-needle aspiration. Thus, the patient record must be reviewed to determine the collection method to correctly report cytopathology codes.

- Cervical and vaginal screening codes 88174 and 88175 describe cells collected in preservative fluid using an automated thin manual layer preparation.
- Code 88106 (Cytopathology, fluids, washings or brushings, except cervical or vaginal; filter method only with interpretation) is reported when the filter method only is used.
- CPT code 88108 (Cytopathology, concentration technique, smears and interpretation; e.g., Saccomanno technique) is reported when a concentration technique is used.

Cytopathology subsection codes are reported for various cytopathology procedures, as follows:

- Cervical or vaginal cytopathology physician interpretation (88141–88155, 88164–88167, 88174–88175)
- Cytopathological smears and cytopathology of fluids, washings or brushing from sources other than cervical or vaginal (88160–88162)
- Cytohistologic studies of fine-needle aspirate (88172–88173)
- Flow cytometry tests (88182–88189)

 Coding Tip:

> HCPCS level II codes are also reported for cytopathology services such as
>
> - Screening Papanicolaou smear, cervical or vaginal, up to three smears, by technician under physician supervision [P3000]
> - Screening Papanicolaou smear, cervical or vaginal, up to three smears, requiring interpretation by physician [P3001]

Pap smear (Figure 17-7) screening and physician interpretation using different methods for preparation, screening, and reporting are reported with cytopathology codes.

- Bethesda System of reporting (88164–88167)
- Non-Bethesda reporting (88150–88154)
- Thin-layer preparations (88142–88143)
- Automated screening with any system of reporting (88147–88148)

The **Bethesda System** is a format for reporting cervical/vaginal cytology that includes a state of specimen adequacy, the general category (e.g., if the specimen is within normal limits), and a descriptive diagnosis (e.g., benign cellular changes).

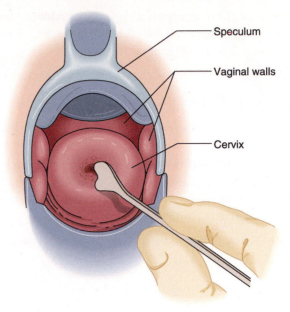

Speculum

Vaginal walls

Cervix

Figure 17-7 Performing a Pap smear

 Coding Tip:

Cytopathology notes provide instruction that codes 88141 and 88155 are reported in addition to the screening code when these additional services are provided.

- Cytopathology, cervical or vaginal (any reporting system), requiring interpretation by physician (88141)
- Cytopathology, slides, cervical or vaginal, definitive hormonal evaluation (e.g., maturation index, karyopyknotic index, estrogenic index) (list separately in addition to code(s) for other technical and interpretation services) (88155)

Fine-needle aspiration cytopathology services are reported with codes 88172–88173. A parenthetical note above code 88172 provides instruction to see codes 10021 and 10022 for fine-needle *aspiration* procedures.

EXAMPLE: Cytopathology evaluation of fine-needle aspirate, interpretation, and report. Report code 88173.

Cytogenetic Studies

Cytogenetics is the study of the cell and its heredity-related components, including chromosomes. Cytogenetic studies codes (88230–88299) are reported for tests performed to study cellular ("cyto") structure and function related to heredity ("genetics").

Cytogenetic tests are performed based on the nature of the disorder for which the patient is being tested because the cell culture and analytical standards are disease dependent, not tissue dependent.

EXAMPLE 1: Tissue culture for non-neoplastic disorders, lymphocyte. Report code 88230.

EXAMPLE 2: Tissue culture for neoplastic disorders, solid tumor. Report code 88239.

Cryopreservation services codes are reported for the freezing, storage, and subsequent thawing of cells, as well as the expansion of established cell lines for subsequent laboratory testing. For some testing procedures (e.g., tests for genetic disorders), the cell line is frozen to preserve the culture, and subsequent thawing must be done before an analysis can be completed. As indicated in the code descriptor, code 88240 is reported for each cell line. Code 88241 is reported separately for each aliquot because these procedures may be performed multiple times. (An **aliquot** is a portion of a specimen used for testing.)

> **EXAMPLE 1:** Cryopreservation, freezing and storage of cells, each cell line. Report code 88240.

> **EXAMPLE 2:** Thawing and expansion of frozen cells, each aliquot. Report code 88241.

White blood cells (e.g., T lymphocytes) are typically used as the specimen for chromosome analysis (88245–88289).

Chromosomal breakage syndromes include genetic disorders that are usually transmitted in agenetic autosomal recessive mode. The syndromes are characterized by a defect in DNA repair mechanismsand a predisposition to cancer. Codes for chromosome analysis for breakage syndromes are classified according to the

- Name of the specific syndrome being investigated (e.g., Fanconi anemia) (88245–88248)
- Specific technique for analysis (88249)

Codes for cytogenetic studies include a combination of codes used to describe the

- Type of tissue cultured
- Special culture techniques or treatments of the culture
- Numbers of cells studied and analyzed
- Special analysis techniques used

Thus, submitting a claim for a single cytogenetic study typically requires reporting three or more codes.

> **EXAMPLE:** Cytogenetic study of a standard karyotype on peripheral blood lymphocytes is reported with a code for lymphocyte culture (88230), a code for chromosome analysis counting 15 to 20 cells, 2 karyotypes with banding (88262), and a code to describe the physician work of interpretation and report of the cytogenetic testing performed (88291).

Molecular cytogenetics includes the **fluorescence *in situ* hybridization (FISH)** method (88271), which is performed to detect submicroscopic changes in chromosomes (e.g., genetic disorders, such as Williams syndrome) or for identification of unknown chromosomal material. Chromosomal aberrations can also be identified using FISH analyses in patients with other constitutional or acquired (e.g., neoplastic) disorders.

> **EXAMPLE:** Molecular cytogenetics test, DNA probe (one test). Report code 88271.

Surgical Pathology ⚠

Surgical pathology codes are reported for the gross and microscopic examination of specimens submitted for pathologic evaluation (Figure 17-8). (A *specimen* is tissue submitted to the pathology department for evaluation; it is also the unit of service used to report surgical pathology codes.) Surgical pathology levels of service are determined by the following:

- Type of exam
- Type of tissue

When multiple individual tissue specimens are submitted from the same patient, a separate code is reported for each specimen.

 Coding Tip:

> Code 88291 is reported for the interpretation and report of cytogenetic and molecular cytogenetic tests. It is reported in addition to the appropriate cytogenetic testing code(s) to describe the physician work of interpretation and report of the cytogenetics and molecular cytogenetics testing performed.

Figure 17-8 Tissue biopsy (A) A small piece of tissue is surgically removed (B) Pathologist views tissue under microscope, looking for presence of disease

⚠️ **EXAMPLE:** Two separate frozen sections of breast tissue were evaluated by the pathologist during surgery. Report codes 88331 and 88332.

Surgical pathology notes provide instruction that surgical pathology services include accession, examination, and reporting. **Accession** is the assignment of a number to record the order of tissue acquisition; an *accession number* is assigned to each pathology case (e.g., 05-00101).

Coding Tip:

Code 88300 is reported for specimens that require gross examination only.

Codes 88311–88365 and 88399 are reported in addition to surgical pathology codes when such services are provided.

- Codes 88311–88319 include decalcification procedures, special stains, and techniques to identify chemical components. These codes are reported in addition to codes 88300–88309.

- Code 88399 is reported for an unlisted surgical pathology procedure.

Notes also identify and define the *specimen* as the unit of service for reporting codes 88300–88309. These codes are reported according to the extent and complexity of the evaluation.

- Level I surgical pathology code 88300 is reported for any specimen the examining pathologist believes can be accurately diagnosed without microscopic examination.

- Level II surgical pathology code 88302 is reported when gross *and* microscopic examination is performed to confirm identification of a specimen or the absence of disease.

- Level III through level VI codes 88304–88309 are reported when gross and microscopic examinations are performed, and these codes represent ascending levels of physician (pathologist) work. The codes are classified according to assigned specimens.

  ○ Uncomplicated specimen (e.g., hemorrhoids)

  ○ Single complicated specimen (e.g., kidney biopsy)

  ○ Multiple complicated specimens (e.g., breast with regional lymph nodes)

EXAMPLE: Cervical carcinoma was diagnosed upon cervical biopsy. Patient subsequently underwent a hysterectomy. Pathologist examined the entire cervix and uterus. Codes 88305 and 88309 are reported whether or not residual cancer is found.

Codes 88321–88325 are reported for consultations and reports on referred slides and materials. Referred slides and materials are forwarded from an outside service (such as another facility) to the pathologist for evaluation.

Pathology consultations performed during surgery are reported with codes 88329–88334. When a section from the first block of tissue from a specimen is examined, code 88331 is reported. When sections from subsequent blocks of the same specimen are examined, report code 88332 for each section examined. When pathology consultation during surgery does not involve microscopic examination of tissue, report code 88329.

EXAMPLE: A sigmoid colon biopsy is sent to the pathologist during surgery for immediate diagnosis. The pathologist examines the specimen and provides a pathological diagnosis without microscopic examination of any of the tissue. Report code 88329.

In Vivo (e.g., Transcutaneous) Laboratory Procedures

The *in vivo* (e.g., transcutaneous) procedures subsection contains codes that classify bilirubin and hemoglobin tests.

EXAMPLE: Patient underwent total transcutaneous bilirubin test. Report code 88720.

 Note:

A total transcutaneous bilirubin test is usually performed on newborns to diagnose jaundice, and testing is done four times a day or more to monitor the condition and determine the efficiency of therapy.

Other Procedures

The other procedures (89049–89240) subsection includes laboratory and pathology procedures that are not classified in other Pathology and Laboratory subsections.

EXAMPLE: Patient underwent sweat collection via iontophoresis. Report code 89230.

Reproductive Medicine Procedures

Reproductive medicine procedures codes (89250–89398) classify new technology and evolving reproductive medical practices such as the following:

- Oocyte/embryo culture and fertilization techniques

- Oocyte/embryo biopsy techniques

- Freezing, thawing, and storage techniques

(These procedures are performed in highly specialized clinical laboratories.)

When reporting the culture and fertilization of oocytes, report the appropriate code (89250 or 89251) one time for the culture and fertilization, regardless of the number of eggs fertilized.

EXAMPLE: Patient underwent culture and fertilization of six embryos in less than four days. Report code 89250. (Code 89250 is reported just once.)

Co-culture techniques performed on tissue cultures of human embryos, oviductal, uterine, granulosa, or other cells involve the isolation of the cells, culture, plating, and the co-culture of these cells with human embryos. This procedure may involve microscopic and cytochemical examination of the culture cells to determine their viability or functionality. Code 89251 describes the work involved in culturing oocytes/embryos along with the additional work of co-culturing the embryos with feeder cells (e.g., granulosa, endometrial, and tubal). Code 89251 does *not* include the following procedures, which are reported separately when performed at the same time as culturing oocytes/embryos along with the additional work of co-culturing the embryos with feeder cells:

- Assisted embryo hatching by any method of microtechniques (89253)

- Oocyte identification from follicular fluid (89254)

- Preparation of embryo for transfer under any method (89255)

- Embryo cryopreservation (89258)

- Oocyte/embryo biopsy (89290, 89291)

The preparation of embryo for transfer, using any method (89255), includes removing the embryo(s) from culture, preparing the embryo(s) for transfer, loading the embryo(s) into a catheter, transporting the embryo(s) to the transfer room for transfer to the patient, and examining the catheter after transfer to ensure that no embryo(s) are retained. ⚠ Code 89255 does *not* include the following procedures, which are reported separately when performed at the same time as preparation of embryo for transfer, using any method:

Coding Tip:

Microtechnique is one of three types of micromanipulation technique that may be used for the preparation of an embryo for transfer. Code 89255 is reported for assisted oocyte fertilization regardless of the micromanipulation type used; there is no specific code for micromanipulation only.

- Intrauterine embryo transfer (58974)

- Gamete, zygote, or embryo intrafallopian transfer (58976)

- Culture of oocyte(s)/embryo(s) (89250)

- Co-culture of oocyte(s)/embryo(s) (89251)

- Extended culture (89272)

- Thawing of cryopreserved embryo(s) (89352)

- Assisted embryo hatching (89253)

However, code 89255 is reported for the preparation of either a fresh or cryopreserved embryo.

The preparation and examination of the oocyte prior to fertilization (e.g., stripping of the granulosa, cumulus oophorous, and corona radiation and verifying extrusion of the first polar body) are included in codes 89280–89281. Preparation and examination procedures are not separately coded and reported.

☞ Sperm identification and preparation prior to injection into the cytoplasm of the oocyte are coded and reported separately with sperm isolation and preparation codes 89260–89261, as appropriate.

Sperm identification from aspiration other than seminal fluid (89257) (e.g., from the vas deferens or epididymis) excludes identification of sperm from seminal fluid, which is described by other codes.

Code 89257 includes the work of identifying sperm and does *not* include the work of assisted oocyte fertilization by any method of microtechnique (89280–89281).

Note:

Methods of assisted oocyte fertilization include the following:

- Intracytoplasmic sperm injection (ICSI)

- Subzonal insertion (SZI)

- Partial zona dissection (PZD)

Exercise 17.3 – Pathology and Laboratory Subsections

Instructions: Assign CPT code(s) and appropriate modifier(s) to each statement.

1. Physician office lab performs a nonautomated dipstick urinalysis with microscopy.

   _____

2. Routine venipuncture. Quantitative therapeutic drugs assay to determine digoxin level.

   _____

3. Laboratory panel that includes carbon dioxide, chloride, potassium, and sodium.

   _____

4. Two separately identified basal cell carcinomas are submitted for diagnosis and evaluation
   of adequacy of the surgical margins. The first basal cell carcinoma specimen required
   frozen section from one block to confirm the adequacy of excision. The second basal
   cell carcinoma specimen required two frozen sections on two blocks to assure adequate
   excision. Surgical pathology evaluation of the two separately identified basal cell carcinomas
   is also performed.

   _____

5. The physician's office staff performed a urine pregnancy test using dipstick reagents that
   chemically react with urine. A change in color indicated positive findings and the presence of
   hormones found in the urine of women in early pregnancy.

   _____

6. Specimen collection via arterial puncture and blood gas determination (pH only).

   _____

7. Laboratory panel included the following tests: total calcium, carbon dioxide, chloride (blood),
   creatinine (blood), serum sodium, and quantitative urea nitrogen.

   _____

8. A segment of sigmoid colon with tumor was sent to the pathologist for frozen section during
   surgery so that immediate diagnosis could be made. The pathologist created the frozen section,
   examined the specimen, and rendered an intraoperative pathological diagnosis.

   _____

9. Partial thromboplastin time to measure the efficiency of plasma in forming thromboplastin.
   Patient has had blood clots, and this test is needed to monitor the effectiveness of anticoagulant
   heparin therapy. The method used was automated coagulation instrumentation.

   _____

10. Glucose screening using Dextrostix reagent strip method, capillary blood, 49-year-old patient.

    _____

11. Breast biopsy was sent to the pathologist during the operative procedure for immediate diagnosis.
    The pathologist examined the specimen and selected a portion to prepare as a block for frozen
    section, which was microscopically examined. Surgical pathology evaluation of the breast biopsy
    tissue was also performed, and it did not require microscopic evaluation of surgical margins.

    _____

12. Lipid panel using automated equipment was performed and included testing of HDL, total
    serum cholesterol, tryglycerides, and quantitative glucose.

    _____

13. General health panel.

    _____

Exercise 17.3 *(continued)*

14. Metabolic panel using automated equipment, which included carbon dioxide, chloride, creatinine, glucose, potassium, sodium, and BUN.

_____

15. Antibody identification test for leukocyte antibodies.

_____

16. Pinworm exam using cellophane tape prep.

_____

17. As the result of an appendectomy due to acute appendicitis, the appendix was sent to surgical pathology for gross and microscopic examination by the pathologist.

_____

18. Sensitivity study using agar diffusion methodology was performed to assess whether antibiotic treatment with methicillin would be effective for a patient diagnosed with a staphylococcal B infection.

_____

19. Collection of sweat from a patient via iontophoresis to rule out cystic fibrosis.

_____

20. Right and left obturator lymph nodes were removed during radical prostatectomy and were submitted as separate specimens for immediate diagnosis to assess metastatic disease involvement. The pathologist examined the specimens and selected two blocks from the right specimen and three blocks from the left specimen to create frozen sections. Each frozen section was examined microscopically. Pathologist also evaluated right and left obturator lymph nodes and prostate tissue for surgical pathology.

_____

Summary

CPT pathology and laboratory codes describe services performed on specimens (e.g., body fluids, tissue, or cytological specimens) to evaluate, prevent, diagnose, or treat a disease. Most clinical laboratory service codes include a technical component, and some include both a technical and a professional component. The Pathology and Laboratory section is organized according to type of procedure performed, and procedures are listed alphabetically within each subsection. Because many laboratory and pathology tests can be performed using different methods, patient record documentation must be reviewed along with code descriptions and instructional notes. Guidelines located at the beginning of the Pathology and Laboratory section provide instruction about services in pathology and laboratory, separate or multiple procedures, subsection information, unlisted services or procedures, and special reports.

Internet Links

Clinical Laboratory Improvement Amendments (CLIA): Go to *www.cdc.gov*, click on "C" in the CDC A–Z Index (at the top), and scroll down and click on the CLIA (Clinical Laboratory Improvement Amendments) link.

National Coverage Determinations for Laboratory Services: Go to *www.cms.gov*, click on the Medicare link, then scroll down to the Coverage heading and click on the Medicare Coverage-General Information link, and click on the Lab NCDs – ICD-10 link, and scroll down and click on the Index of Lab NCDs link to view all of them.

Study Checklist

❏ Read this chapter and highlight key concepts.

❏ Create an index card for each key term.

❏ Access the chapter Internet links to learn more about concepts.

❏ Complete the chapter exercises and review, verifying answers with your instructor.

❏ Complete Workbook chapter, verifying answers with your instructor.

❏ Go to **www.cengagebrain.com** to access the Student Companion Web Site. Login instructions are located in the Preface.

❏ Form a study group with classmates to discuss chapter concepts in preparation for an exam.

Review

Multiple Choice

Instructions: Circle the most appropriate response.

1. Coders do not assign codes to pathology and laboratory procedures performed on an _____ basis because such services do not impact _____ assignment and facility reimbursement.
   - a. inpatient, diagnosis-related group (DRG)
   - b. inpatient, prospective payment system (PPS)
   - c. outpatient, diagnosis-related group (DRG)
   - d. outpatient, prospective payment system (PPS)

2. Laboratory codes (80047–87999) describe which component of lab tests?
   - a. Collection
   - b. Performance
   - c. Performance and collection
   - d. Performance, collection, and clinical consultation

3. Which modifier is added to pathology and laboratory codes when procedures or services are repeated on the same date of service to obtain multiple results?
   - a. -59
   - b. -90
   - c. -91
   - d. -QW

4. When an unlisted procedure or service code is reported on a claim, what is attached to the submitted claim to clarify the service or procedure performed?
   - a. Accession code
   - b. Entire patient record
   - c. Special report
   - d. Waiver number

5. Code(s) from the _____ subsection of Pathology and Laboratory are often reported by blood banks.
   - a. drug testing and therapeutic drug assays
   - b. hematology and coagulation
   - c. other procedures
   - d. transfusion medicine

6. Which is a substance administered with an antigen to enhance the response to the antigen?
   - a. Adjuvant
   - b. Aliquot
   - c. Assay
   - d. Specimen

7. IgA, IgD, IgE, IgG, and IgM are considered:
   - a. analytes.
   - b. antigens.
   - c. immunoglobulins.
   - d. specimens.

8. Physician attendance and monitoring during evocative or suppressive agents testing is reported with codes from the:
   - a. clinical pathology consultation subsection of Pathology and Laboratory.
   - b. Evaluation and Management section of CPT.
   - c. Medicine section of CPT.
   - d. Surgery section of CPT.

9. Which is the study of diseased cells?
   - a. Cytology
   - b. Cytopathology
   - c. Immunology
   - d. Pathology

10. Codes from the _____ subsection of Pathology and Laboratory are reported for tests performed to study cellular structure and function related to heredity.
    - a. anatomical pathology
    - b. cytogenetic studies
    - c. cytopathology
    - d. organ or disease-oriented panels

11. A patient presents with symptoms of dehydration. The physician ordered an electrolyte panel, which included carbon dioxide, chloride, potassium, and sodium. Which CPT code(s) are assigned?
    - a. 80051
    - b. 80051, 82374, 82435, 84132, 84295
    - c. 82374, 82435, 84132, 84295
    - d. 82374, 82435, 84133, 84300

12. Urinalysis. Which CPT code is assigned?
    - a. 81000
    - b. 81001
    - c. 81002
    - d. 81003

13. Qualitative fetal hemoglobin. Which CPT code is assigned?
    - a. 83030
    - b. 83033
    - c. 83036
    - d. 83045

14. Qualitative analysis of organic acids, three specimens. Which CPT code(s) are assigned?
    - a. 83918, 83918, 83918
    - b. 83918, 83918-91, 83918-91
    - c. 83919, 83919, 83919
    - d. 83919, 83919-91, 83919-91

15. Alkaline phosphatase isoenzymes. Which CPT code is assigned?
    - a. 84060
    - b. 84075
    - c. 84078
    - d. 84080

16. CBC, automated, including Hgb, Hct, RBC, WBC, and platelet count. Which CPT code(s) are assigned?
    - a. 85004, 85014
    - b. 85025
    - c. 85027
    - d. 85032

17. ABO, Rh, and MN blood typing for paternity testing. Which CPT code is assigned?
    - a. 86900
    - b. 86901
    - c. 86905
    - d. 86910

18. Thromboplastin time, partial (PTT) in plasma. Which CPT code is assigned?
    - a. 85260
    - b. 85347
    - c. 85705
    - d. 85730

19. RBC antibody screen, two different techniques. Which CPT code(s) are assigned?
    - a. 86850
    - b. 86850, 86850
    - c. 86850, 86850-51
    - d. 86850, 86850-91

20. *Chlamydia* culture. Which CPT code is assigned?
    - a. 87110
    - b. 87270
    - c. 87487
    - d. 87810

Coding Practice

Instructions: Assign CPT code(s) and appropriate modifier(s) to each case.

1. A patient's blood is sent for the following tests: rubella antibody, Rh(D) and ABO blood typing, automated CBC and WBC, qualitative syphilis test, RBC antibody screen, and a hepatitis B surface antigen.

   _____

2. A patient's blood is sent for the following tests: albumin, carbon dioxide, calcium, sodium, glucose, chloride, creatinine, urea nitrogen, potassium, phosphorus inorganic, and complete CBC (automated).

   _____

3. Urinalysis, automated with identification of sediments via microscope.

   _____

4. Sperm isolation procedure including sperm wash and complete semen analysis.

   _____

5. ACTH, prolactin, HGH, cortisol, TSH, LH, and FSH done after intramuscular injection of suppressive agents.

   _____

6. Microorganism analysis of primary source for _Bordetella pertussis_.

   _____

7. _Helicobacter pylori_ blood test.

   _____

8. Blood analysis for hematocrit (Hct) level.

   _____

9. Direct measurement of blood O_2 saturation level.

   _____

10. Intraoperative consultation of breast tissue, single specimen; gross examination and frozen section.

    _____

11. Examination of nail for the presence of fungi using KOH method.

    _____

12. Testing of blood for level of TSH and T3 uptake.

    _____

13. Urine sample used to perform drug screening using a chromatographic method.

    _____

14. Blood test for ANA antibodies to rule out SLE.

    _____

15. Gross and microscopic pathology examination of tissue taken from a patient during a radical TURP procedure.

    _____

16. *Shigella* antibody titer testing of blood sample.

_____

17. Testing for triglyceride level.

_____

18. Blood analysis for presence of *Chlamydia* antibody.

_____

19. Gross and microscopic pathology examination of paranasal tissue taken during a biopsy.

_____

20. Prick test of skin for *Candida albicans*.

_____

21. Testing of blood to determine Rh negative or Rh positive.

_____

22. Radioimmunoassay of blood for total PSA.

_____

23. T-cell count, total.

_____

24. Gross and microscopic examination of Morton's neuroma.

_____

25. CCP antibody test to rule out rheumatoid arthritis.

_____

26. Total postmortem examination of a male stillborn infant.

_____

27. Analysis of thin prep of cervical scraping specimen performed under pathologist supervision (manual screening).

_____

28. Specimen of knee synovial fluid for cell count.

_____

29. Gene analysis, FXN (frataxin) analyte. (Patient is being genetically tested for presence of Freidreich ataxia.)

_____

30. Autopsy of a 45-year-old male patient's heart.

_____

Chapter Outline

Overview of Medicine Section

Medicine Section Guidelines

Medicine Subsections

Chapter Objectives

At the conclusion of this chapter, the student should be able to:

- Define key terms.
- Explain the organization, format, and content of the CPT Medicine section.
- Interpret CPT Medicine coding guidelines and notes.
- Assign CPT Medicine codes.
- Add CPT and/or HCPCS level II modifiers to codes, as appropriate.

Key Terms

adjuvant chemotherapy

allergen

allergen immunotherapy

allergy sensitivity test

autonomic function test

biofeedback

capitated payment
method

cardiac catheterization

cardiography

central motor evoked
potential study

chemotherapy

chiropractic manipulative
treatment (CMT)

determination of
refractive state

dose

duplex scan

echocardiography

electrocardiography

electromyography

gamma globulin

hemodialysis

hyperventilation

immune globulin (Ig)

immune serum globulin

intradermal test
(intracutaneous)

intravenous push

manometry

minimally invasive
procedure

multiple sleep latency

narcosynthesis

needle electromyography

noninvasive procedure

orbicularis oculi

oscilloscope

osteopathic manipulative
treatment (OMT)

patch test (epicutaneous)

peritoneal dialysis

pharmacologic
management

photic stimulation

physiatrist

physical medicine and
rehabilitation

polysomnography

psychotherapy

puncture, prick,
or scratch test
(percutaneous)

renal dialysis

short-latency
somatosensory
evoked potential
study

sleep laboratory

sleep staging

sleep study

Tensilon test

visual evoked potential
(VEP) test

Introduction

The CPT Medicine section classifies *noninvasive* or *minimally invasive* diagnostic and therapeutic procedures and services. **Noninvasive procedures** require no surgical incision or excision, and they are not open procedures. **Minimally invasive procedures** include percutaneous access. Medicine is the last section of CPT, and its codes can be reported along with those from all other sections.

 Note:

> The Other Procedures code below each subheading classifies an unlisted procedure performed on the anatomical site. When reporting an unlisted procedure code, include documentation about the procedure performed with the submitted claim. (Other Procedures subheadings are not included throughout Chapter 18 of this textbook except when codes that describe additional procedures are included.)

Overview of Medicine Section

The Medicine section classifies procedures and services that are procedure oriented (e.g., immunizations), that apply to various medical specialties (e.g., gastroenterology, ophthalmology, otorhinolaryngology, and psychiatry), and that apply to different types of health care providers (e.g., physical therapists and occupational therapists).

Exercise 18.1 – Overview of Medicine Section

Instructions: Complete each statement.

1. When no surgical incision or excision is required to perform a procedure, it is considered
   _____.
2. Percutaneous access procedures are considered _____.
3. Codes from the Medicine section _____ (can/cannot) be reported with codes from other CPT sections.
4. The Medicine section contains codes for _____ procedures and services.
5. The Medicine section classifies procedures and services that are _____, that apply to various medical specialties, and that apply to different types of health care providers.

Medicine Section Guidelines

Guidelines located at the beginning of the Medicine section provide instruction about the following:

- Add-on codes
- Separate procedures
- Unlisted service or procedure
- Special report
- Imaging guidance
- Supplied materials

Instructional notes appear throughout the Medicine section to provide coding clarification and direction. Almost every Medicine subsection contains notes unique to that subsection.

Add-on Codes

Add-on codes are reported for procedures and services performed in *addition* to a *primary procedure*. They are identified in the CPT with a plus symbol (**+**). A parenthetical note located below an add-on code identifies the primary procedure to which an add-on code applies.

> **EXAMPLE:** A 6-year-old male patient underwent Hib booster immunization administration, which required a three-dose schedule of intramuscular injections. Report codes 90460 and 90647.

Separate Procedures

Some procedures and services classified in the Medicine section are considered an integral component of a complete procedure or service, and they are identified by the description "separate procedure." Do not report a "separate procedure" code in addition to a code for the comprehensive (or complete) procedure *unless the "separate procedure" is performed independently or is distinct from other services provided at the same time.*

When a "separate procedure" is performed independently or is distinct from other services provided at the same time, add modifier -59 (Distinct Procedural Service) to the "separate procedure" code. Modifier -59 indicates that the procedure was performed as a distinct, independent procedure.

> **EXAMPLE:** Patient underwent orthoptic training and gonioscopy. Report codes 92065 and 92020-59.

Bundled Medicine Codes

When reporting codes for outpatient hospital services and physician office services, use outpatient code editor (OCE) software or national correct coding initiative (NCCI) software to identify bundled codes for procedures and services considered necessary to accomplish the major procedure. Bundled procedure and services codes are *not* separately coded and reported with the major procedure code. Reporting the component codes in addition to the major procedure code is considered *unbundling*, which is fraud.

> **EXAMPLE:** Patient underwent a stress test. Report code 93015. (Do *not* report codes 93016, 93017, and/or 93018 with code 93015. Doing so is considered unbundling.)

Multiple Medicine Codes

When multiple procedures and/or services are performed on the same date, report a separate code for each procedure and/or service.

> **EXAMPLE:** An established patient received 60 minutes of outpatient individual psychotherapy, and after psychotherapy the psychologist prepared a mandatory progress report and submitted it to the third-party payer. Report codes 90837 and 90889.

Unlisted Service or Procedure

CPT unlisted procedure and service codes are assigned when there is no specific code that accurately describes the procedure or service performed. When reporting an unlisted procedure code to a third-party payer, submit a written report (e.g., a copy of an operative report) that describes the procedure or service performed.

Special Report

When an unlisted procedure or service code is reported to a third-party payer, a special report is submitted that describes the procedure or service performed. Special reports may also be required for procedures and services that are rarely provided or are new in order to establish that the procedure is necessary. As a minimum, documentation in a special report includes the following:

- Adequate definition or description of the nature, extent, and need for the procedure or service

- Time, effort, and equipment necessary to provide the procedure or service

The following additional items may also be documented in a special report:

- Complexity of symptoms
- Concurrent problems
- Diagnostic and therapeutic procedures
- Final diagnosis
- Follow-up care
- Pertinent physical findings

Imaging Guidance

When imaging guidance or imaging supervision and interpretation is performed as part of a Medicine procedure, the Radiology guidelines apply.

Supplied Materials

Supplies and materials provided by the physician (e.g., drugs or sterile trays) other than those typically included with a procedure or service are reported separately. Report CPT code 99070 or a specific HCPCS level II code for materials and supplies provided.

> **EXAMPLE:** Patient underwent chemotherapy administration (intramuscular) of vincristine sulfate, 1 mg. Report CPT code 96401 and HCPCS level II code J9370. (HCPCS level II code J9370 is more specific than CPT code 99070, which is a nonspecific supplies and materials code.)

Exercise 18.2 – Medicine Section Guidelines

Instructions: Complete each statement.

1. Instructional _____ appear throughout the Medicine section to provide coding clarification and direction.
2. When multiple procedures and/or services are performed on the same date, report a(n) _____ code for each procedure and/or service.
3. Add-on codes are reported for procedures and services performed in addition to a primary procedure, and they are identified in CPT with a(n) _____ symbol.
4. Some procedures and services classified in the Medicine section are considered an integral component of a complete procedure or service, and they are identified by the description _____.
5. Supplies and materials provided by the physician, other than those typically included with a procedure or service, are reported with CPT code 99070 or a specific _____ code for materials and supplies provided.

Medicine Subsections

Medicine subsections include the following:

- Immune globulins, serum or recombinant products
- Immunization administration for vaccines/toxoids
- Vaccines, toxoids
- Psychiatry
- Biofeedback
- Dialysis

- Gastroenterology
- Ophthalmology
- Special otorhinolaryngologic services
- Cardiovascular
- Noninvasive vascular diagnostic studies
- Pulmonary
- Allergy and clinical immunology
- Endocrinology
- Neurology and neuromuscular procedures
- Medical genetics and genetic counseling services
- Central nervous system assessments/tests (e.g., neurocognitive, mental status, speech testing)
- Health and behavior assessment/intervention
- Hydration, therapeutic, prophylactic, diagnostic injections and infusions, and chemotherapy and other highly complex drug or highly complex biologic agent administration

- Photodynamic therapy
- Special dermatological procedures
- Physical medicine and rehabilitation
- Medical nutrition therapy
- Acupuncture
- Osteopathic manipulative treatment
- Chiropractic manipulative treatment
- Education and training for patient self-management
- Non-face-to-face nonphysician services
- Special services, procedures, and reports
- Qualifying circumstances for anesthesia
- Moderate (conscious) sedation
- Other services and procedures
- Home health procedures/services
- Medication therapy management services

Immune Globulins, Serum or Recombinant Products

An **immune globulin (Ig)** (**gamma globulin** or **immune serum globulin**) is a sterilized solution obtained from pooled human blood plasma, which contains immunoglobulins (or antibodies) that protect against infectious agents that cause various diseases. (Antibodies are substances in blood plasma that fight infection.) Immune globulins are administered to patients who need to use someone else's antibodies to help fight off or prevent illnesses from occurring. Ig formulations produced from donors include high levels of antibodies against hepatitis B (hepatitis B immune globulin-HBIG), rabies (rabies immune globulin-RIG), tetanus (tetanus immune globulin-TIG), and varicella (chicken pox; varicella zoster immune globulin-VZIG).

⚠ Immune globulin codes are reported for the *supply of the immune globulin product*, which includes broad-spectrum and anti-infective immune globulins, antitoxins, and other isoantibodies. The *administration* of an immune globulin is reported separately with a code from the Therapeutic, Prophylactic, and Diagnostic Injections and Infusions subsection of the Medicine section.

- Intravenous infusion
- Subcutaneous infusion
- Intramuscular or subcutaneous injection
- Intravenous push

 Note:

The administration of an Ig provides temporary protection and is *not* considered an immunization, which provides longer-term protection.

⚠ **Coding Tip:**

Do not add modifier -51 (Multiple Procedures) to immune globulin codes (90281–90399).

EXAMPLE: Intramuscular injection of 250 units of human tetanus immune globulin (TIg) was administered to a patient. Report codes 90389 and 96372.

Immunization Administration for Vaccines/Toxoids

Immunization administration for vaccines/toxoids codes are reported in addition to codes from the Medicine subsection entitled *Vaccines, Toxoids*. The immunization administration for vaccines/toxoids include the following:

- Administrative staff services (e.g., appointment scheduling, preparing a patient's record, and submitting an insurance claim to a payer)
- Clinical staff services (e.g., taking vital signs, assessing past reactions and contraindications, preparing and administering the vaccine/toxoid, monitoring reactions, and documenting in the record)

The following types of immunization administration for vaccines/toxoids are reported:

- Intradermal, intramuscular, percutaneous, and subcutaneous injections
- Intranasal and oral administration

The immunization administration of *pediatric* vaccines/toxoids is reported with codes 90460–90461 to accurately describe the work involved, which includes patient/family counseling provided by the physician during the administration of a vaccine/toxoid. (Codes 90460–90461 are reported when the physician provides face-to-face counseling for the patient/family during the immunization administration of a vaccine/toxoid. Per the CPT, when face-to-face counseling is not provided, report codes 90471–90474.)

EXAMPLE: A 6-year-old female patient received immunization administration (intramuscular injection) of the rabies vaccine. Physician discussed the vaccine composition with the patient's mother, including risks and benefits. Report codes 90460 and 90675.

Coding Tip:

- Report immunization administration for vaccines/toxoids codes (90460–90474) in addition to vaccine/toxoid codes (90476–90749).
- Do not report codes 90460–90474 for the administration of allergy injections or testing, chemotherapy, placement of catheters, transfusions, or venipuncture. Refer to the appropriate Surgery or Medicine subsection for reporting such codes.

Vaccines, Toxoids

Vaccines/toxoids codes (90476–90749) identify the vaccine/toxoid product only. They are reported in addition to immunization administration for vaccines/toxoids codes (90460–90474).

EXAMPLE: An 18-year-old female patient received immunization administration (subcutaneous injection) of an MMR booster. Report codes 90471 and 90707.

Coding Tip:

Do not add modifier -51 (Multiple Procedures) to vaccines/toxoids codes (90476–90749).

- When vaccines/toxoids codes are reported during a preventive medicine encounter, add modifier -25 to the evaluation and management code (e.g., 99392-25).
- New vaccines have been approved for use by the Food and Drug Administration (FDA) over recent years. CPT created a new symbol (⁄⁄) to indicate that FDA approval is pending, which means it is anticipated that the vaccines will receive FDA approval, but that approval was pending at the time of publication. Once the vaccine is approved by the FDA, the symbol will be removed.

Reporting Evaluation and Management Service Codes with Vaccines/Toxoids Codes

There is considerable confusion regarding whether a provider should report an evaluation and management (E/M) service for an encounter for immunization administration of vaccines/toxoids. Correct coding depends on whether the provider performed a medically necessary E/M service *in addition to the immunization administration*. To assign an E/M code in addition to the immunization administration code, the E/M service must exceed services included with immunization administration codes.

EXAMPLE: Physician provided a level 3 E/M service to a 48-year-old male patient to medically manage his hypertension. During the same encounter, the physician administered a flu shot (intramuscular injection). Report codes 99213-25, 90471, and 90658.

 Note:

Reporting E/M service code 99211 does not require the presence of the physician or the documentation of key components.

Psychiatry

Psychiatrists, psychologists, and licensed clinical social workers report psychiatry codes for psychotherapy services, which include the following headings and subheadings:

- Interactive complexity

- Psychiatric diagnostic procedures

  o Psychotherapy

  o Other psychotherapy

  o Other psychiatric services or procedures

 Coding Tip:

- Psychiatric evaluation and management (E/M) services are reported by physicians, nurse practitioners, and physician assistants. Psychologists and licensed clinical social workers do not report codes from the CPT E/M section.

- Psychiatric consultation includes examination of the patient, exchange of information with the primary care physician or other pertinent individuals (e.g., family members and caretakers), and preparation of reports. Because no psychiatric treatment is provided during a psychiatric consultation, report the appropriate evaluation and management consultation code.

Interactive Complexity

Interactive complexity refers to specific communication factors that complicate the delivery of a psychiatric procedure, such as difficult communication with verbally undeveloped patients. The interactive complexity code is reported as an add-on code in addition to codes for diagnostic psychiatric evaluation, psychotherapy, psychotherapy performed with evaluation and management, and group psychology.

Psychiatric Diagnostic Procedures

Psychiatric diagnostic evaluation services include the following:

- History

- Mental status

- Recommendations

EXAMPLE: Patient received interactive psychiatric diagnostic interview examination services as the result of her parents finding out that she was being routinely bullied at elementary school. Report code 90791.

Psychotherapy

Psychotherapy is the treatment of mental illness and behavioral disturbances in which the provider uses definitive therapeutic communication an in attempt to alleviate emotional disturbances, reverse or change maladaptive patterns of behavior, and encourage personality growth and development.

EXAMPLE: Patient underwent 30 minutes of psychotherapy. Report code 90832.

Other Psychotherapy

Psychotherapy for crisis involves an urgent assessment and history of a patient's crisis state, which is typically life threatening or complex, requiring immediate attention to a patient in high distress. A mental status exam and disposition is included, and treatment consists of psychotherapy, mobilization of resources to defuse the crisis and restore safety, and implementation of psychotherapeutic interventions to minimize the potential for psychological trauma.

Psychoanalysis attempts to gain insight into a patient's motivations and conflicts to change maladaptive behavior (e.g., an inability to cope with the challenges of everyday living). The psychoanalysis code is reported on a per-day basis. Do not confuse psychoanalysis and psychotherapy codes. The psychoanalysis code refers to the practice of psychoanalysis (e.g., patient is treated by a physician who is credentialed to practice analytic therapy, and psychoanalysis is the treatment being used).

Family psychotherapy involves the patient's family in the treatment process, and the dynamics within the family are the focus of the psychotherapeutic sessions. Family psychotherapy may be performed with or without the patient present. Codes reported are based on whether the patient is present or not and whether multiple family groups are being treated.

EXAMPLE: Psychotherapy was provided on May 5 to the families of three different patients who reside in a drug treatment center. Report code 90849 on the insurance claim for *each* patient.

Other Psychiatric Services or Procedures

Other psychiatric services or procedures include the following:

- Pharmacologic management
- Narcosynthesis
- Electroconvulsive therapy
- Individual psychophysiological therapy incorporating biofeedback training
- Hypnotherapy
- Environmental intervention for medical management
- Psychiatric evaluation of hospital records
- Interpretation or explanation of psychiatric examination/procedure results
- Preparation of report of patient's psychiatric status, history, treatment, or progress for the benefit of other physicians, agencies, or third-party payers

Pharmacologic management is the evaluation of a patient's medications for affect (such as a patient's reaction to medication), proper dosage (e.g., a therapeutic dose), and renewal of prescribed medications. Pharmacologic management is provided by a physician (such as a psychiatrist) to a patient who undergoes psychotherapy from a nonphysician colleague (e.g., a psychologist or a licensed clinical social worker) or when a patient's condition is being effectively treated by psychotropic drugs alone. Generally, the patient does not receive other services from the physician during the encounter. When an evaluation and management (E/M) service is provided by the physician, the pharmacologic management is included in the E/M service. It is not coded and reported separately. (The psychotherapy provided during pharmacologic management is minimal and is also not coded or reported separately.)

Narcosynthesis is a form of psychotherapy that is provided when the patient is under the influence of a drug, such as a sedative or narcotic (e.g., a barbiturate, benzodiazepine-type drug that is administered intravenously). The administration of a medication to release inhibitions allows a patient to discuss issues that are too difficult to verbalize otherwise.

Electroconvulsive therapy is used to treat depression or life-threatening psychosis (e.g., severe affective disorders or schizophrenia) and involves the application of electric current to the brain through scalp electrodes. The term *electroconvulsive* refers to a convulsive response to an electrical stimulus. In electroconvulsive therapy, it is necessary to monitor the patient (e.g., management of the seizure, observation, and decisions regarding further treatment). If the psychiatrist also administers anesthesia for the electroconvulsive therapy, report the appropriate anesthesia code (00104), which includes cardiac and oxygen saturation monitoring.

EXAMPLE: Patient underwent narcosynthesis for psychiatric diagnostic and therapeutic purposes. Amytal (sodium amobarbital), 125 miligrams was injected prior to therapy. Report codes 90865, 96372, and J0300.

Biofeedback

Biofeedback is a technique that trains the patient to gain some control over autonomic body functions. Biofeedback services include the following:

- Reviewing the patient's history
- Preparing the biofeedback equipment
- Placing electrodes on the patient
- Reading and interpreting responses
- Monitoring the patient
- Controlling muscle responses

Coding Tip:

- Two series of biofeedback codes (90901–90911 and 90875–90876) distinguish between biofeedback training without psychophysiologic therapy and biofeedback training with psychophysiologic therapy.

- Do *not* report code 90901 or 90911 with code 90875 or 90876.

Code 90901 classifies the provision of biofeedback without psychophysiological therapy. Although biofeedback services may include different types of administration (e.g., electromyogram application), code 90901 is intended to identify all methods of biofeedback provided, even when more than one modality is performed during the same session. Electromyogram is a nerve-conduction study that plots the electrical activity produced by muscle contractions. **Manometry** is a diagnostic test that measures muscle function using a pressure-sensitive tube.

EXAMPLE: Patient underwent biofeedback of perineal muscles for bladder training to prevent urinary incontinence. Treatment included use of manometry. Report code 90911.

Dialysis

The Dialysis subsection includes the following headings:

- Hemodialysis
- Miscellaneous dialysis procedures
- End-stage renal disease services
- Other dialysis procedures

Renal dialysis artificially removes toxic waste products from the body when the patient's kidneys are unable to perform this function because of disease or deterioration. Dialysis is used for acute, temporary kidney failure (e.g., acute renal failure) or chronic renal failure (e.g., end-stage renal disease). The following types of dialysis are used, depending on the patient's condition and whether the patient is experiencing acute or chronic renal failure:

- **Hemodialysis**: Process of removing waste products, toxins, and excess fluids from the blood; patient's blood is diverted into a dialyzer, where it is treated and returned into the patient's circulation by another tube inserted into a different blood vessel (Figure 18-1)

- **Peritoneal dialysis**: Soft catheter is inserted into abdominal cavity and dialysate fluid is infused at intermittent times

Figure 18-1 Hemodialysis filters waste from the patient's blood. Blood leaves the body via an artery, is filtered, and then is returned into a vein.

 Coding Tip:

> All evaluation and management (E/M) services related to end-stage renal disease (ESRD) and rendered during dialysis are included in the dialysis procedure code. An E/M service related to ESRD performed on the day of dialysis is not separately coded and reported. When the patient receives E/M services for a completely different condition that is not related to ESRD, report an appropriate E/M service code and add modifier -25 (significant, separately identifiable E/M service by the same physician on the same day as the procedure or other service).

Hemodialysis

Hemodialysis service codes include all E/M services related to the patient's renal disease *on the day of the hemodialysis procedure.* These codes are reported when hemodialysis services are provided to ESRD and non-ESRD patients in an inpatient setting and to non-ESRD patients in an outpatient setting.

EXAMPLE: A 54-year-old patient was admitted as a hospital inpatient for treatment of ESRD. Admission date was August 5, and discharge date was August 10. The patient underwent hemodialysis procedures on August 5, 7, and 9, which included evaluation by his attending physician. Report codes 90935 × 3. (Attending physician should report appropriate inpatient evaluation and management service codes with modifier -25 for provision of services unrelated to ESRD and the hemodialysis procedure on those dates. For other dates, such as August 6, 8, and 10, the attending physician should report appropriate inpatient E/M service codes for daily care and discharge services.)

Miscellaneous Dialysis Procedures

Miscellaneous dialysis procedures codes include peritoneal dialysis, hemofiltration, and other continuous renal replacement therapies (90945–90947) (for single physician evaluation or repeated physician evaluations).

EXAMPLE: Patient underwent peritoneal dialysis, which required repeated physician evaluations on the same date of treatment. Report code 90947.

End-Stage Renal Disease (ESRD) Services

ESRD services are typically performed as outpatient procedures, and reimbursement is usually made according to a monthly capitated payment method.

Note:

A **capitated payment method** is the result of an agreement between a third-party payer and a health care provider in which the provider agrees to provide services to a patient in return for a fixed monthly payment.

- ESRD services codes are reported *once per month per patient* (every 30 days). The appropriate code is reported just once, at the conclusion of a full month of ESRD services.

  EXAMPLE: A 48-year-old patient received ESRD-related services two times each week during the entire month of June. Report code 90960.

- ESRD service codes can also be reported when less than a *full month of services* are provided to a patient. The appropriate code is reported for each day of service (e.g., when a patient requires less than a month's ESRD services after inpatient hospitalization).

  EXAMPLE: A 54-year-old patient was hospitalized for ESRD from July 5 to July 20, and upon discharge received outpatient ESRD services on July 22, 24, 26, 28, and 30. Report codes 90970 × 5 for outpatient ESRD services.

⚠ **Coding Tip:**

- For patients under 20 years of age, ESRD codes include monitoring of nutrition, assessment of growth and development, and parental counseling.

- ESRD codes include physician services related to establishing a dialyzing cycle, evaluation and management of the dialysis visits, and patient management during the dialysis, provided during a full month.

Other Dialysis Procedures

Other dialysis procedures include dialysis training (e.g., completed course of training, an individual training session), hemoperfusion (e.g., using activated charcoal or resin), and unlisted dialysis procedures (inpatient or outpatient).

EXAMPLE: Patient completed an entire course of outpatient dialysis training during the month of June. Report code 90989.

Gastroenterology ⚠

The Gastroenterology subsection classifies gastroenterology tests (e.g., motility, acid perfusion) and also includes the following headings:

- Gastric physiology

- Other procedures

  Gastroenterology procedures (Table 18-1) are found in the Surgery section. Related diagnostic services are found in the Pathology and Laboratory and Radiology sections.

  EXAMPLE: Patient underwent gastric motility (manometric) studies. Report code 91020.

 Coding Tip:

Gastroenterology tests reported with codes 91010–91299 are frequently performed in conjunction with gastrointestinal (GI) endoscopic procedures. Do *not* report codes separately from the Gastroenterology subsection of the Medicine section with GI endoscopic procedures.

Table 18-1 Gastroenterology Procedures and Services

Procedure	Description
Esophageal or gastric intubation and collection of washings	• Tube is inserted through nose or mouth into esophagus or stomach. • One or more washings are obtained for *cytology* (study of cells).
Esophageal, gastric, or duodenal motility	• Tube is inserted through patient's nose or mouth into the esophagus, stomach, or duodenum. • Tube is slowly withdrawn to test muscles for weakness or abnormality (manometry).
Acid perfusion test of esophagus (or Bernstein test)	• Nasogastric tube is inserted into the esophagus. • Mild hydrochloric acid is poured through the tube in an attempt to recreate and evaluate gastric reflux symptoms. • Test is done to determine whether chest pain is due to acid reflux and not a cardiac condition.
Gastroesophageal reflux test	• Electrode is inserted through nasal catheter into esophagus to determine pH levels. • Electrode remains in esophagus over a period of time to obtain multiple levels (to determine acid reflux or non-acid reflux).
Esophageal balloon distention provocation study	• Local anesthetic is administered to numb the throat. • Balloon is inserted into esophagus and is expanded in multiple sites to increasing degrees to provoke chest pain. • This is done to rule out a cardiac source of existing chest pain.
Gastric analysis test (or Hollander test)	• Nasogastric tube is inserted through patient's nose or mouth into the stomach. • Stimulant is injected into the stomach (e.g., histamine, insulin, pentagastrin, calcium, or secretin). • Gastric contents are suctioned through the tube and are analyzed.
Gastric saline load test	• Nasogastric tube is inserted through patient's nose or mouth into the stomach. • Gastric contents are suctioned, and stomach is filled with saline. • After 30 minutes, gastric contents are resuctioned and measured to determine presence of impaired gastric emptying.
Breath hydrogen test	• Patient's exhalations are tested for hydrogen to determine whether undigested food is entering the duodenum. • Test is administered over a period of 3 to 5 hours, after patient has fasted for 12 hours and has swallowed test sugars (e.g., fructose, lactose, or lactulose).
Placement of intestinal bleeding tube	• Intestinal bleeding tube is inserted through mouth into duodenum. • Tube is monitored and used to suppress bleeding, if present.
Gastric intubation for aspiration or lavage	• Nasogastric tube is inserted through patient's nose or mouth into the stomach. • Gastric contents are suctioned to remove ingested poisons or to decompress intestinal blockage.
Gastrointestinal (GI) tract imaging	• Patient swallows a capsule that provides color imaging as it passes through the GI system. • Data are transmitted from the capsule to a data recorder.
Rectal sensation, tone, and compliance test	• Balloon is inserted into the patient's rectum and gradually inflated. • Reactions to various levels of inflation are studied.
Anorectal manometry	• This measures pressure of anal sphincter to diagnose constipation or incontinence.
Pulsed irrigation of fecal impaction (or pulsed irrigation evaluation, PCE)	• Automated enema is inserted for cases of chronic constipation when the patient has no voluntary bowel control (e.g., a paraplegic patient).
Electrogastrography (EGG)	• Electrodes are attached to the patient's abdomen. • Myoelectrical activity is detected and recorded.

Ophthalmology

Ophthalmology services include the following headings:

- General ophthalmological services
- Special ophthalmological services
- Contact lens services
- Spectacle services (including prosthesis for aphakia)

General Ophthalmological Services

General ophthalmological services codes are reported for new or established patient examinations. A physician (such as an ophthalmologist) can report an appropriate evaluation and management (E/M) service code instead of a general ophthalmological service code. *Do not report a general ophthalmological services code (92002–92014) in addition to an E/M service code.*

Ophthalmologists have a choice when assigning codes for E/M services because they provide unique and specialized services that do not match criteria associated with E/M codes. Instead of reporting codes from the E/M section, an ophthalmologist may report codes from the Medicine section. Codes 92002–92014 describe intermediate and comprehensive levels of service, which are defined by CPT.

When services provided are less than those described by codes 92002–92014, the ophthalmologist should report the appropriate E/M codes (99201–99215).

- Intermediate ophthalmological services include history, general medical observation, external ocular and adnexal examination, and other diagnostic procedures as indicated. This may include the use of mydriasis for ophthalmoscopy.

  EXAMPLE: Established patient was seen in the office by her ophthalmologist for evaluation of glaucoma. Interval history, external examination, ophthalmoscopy, biomicroscopy, and tonometry were performed to evaluate the patient's response to glaucoma treatment. Report code 92012.

- Comprehensive ophthalmological services include a general evaluation of the complete visual system (e.g., history, general medical observation, external and ophthalmoscopic examinations, gross visual fields and basic sensorimotor examination, biomicroscopy, examination with cycloplegia or mydriasis, and tonometry). In addition, diagnostic and treatment procedures are included. Comprehensive services may be performed during multiple sessions or visits.

  EXAMPLE: An established patient previously diagnosed with glaucoma was seen in her ophthalmologist's office. The ophthalmic technician tested the patient's visual acuity, gross visual field by confrontation, ocular motility including primary gaze alignment, and intraocular pressures. The ophthalmologist examined the patient's ocular adnexae, including lids, lacrimal glands, lacrimal drainage, orbits, and preauricular lymph nodes. The pupils and irises were also examined. The ophthalmologist performed a slit lamp examination of the corneas, anterior chambers, and lenses. He also inspected the patient's bulbar and palpebral conjunctivae. The ophthalmologist prescribed medication and ordered lab work. Report code 92014.

Special Ophthalmological Services ⚠

Special ophthalmological services codes classify services that are not considered part of a general ophthalmological examination. They are considered significant, separately identifiable services, which means that their codes are reported in addition to codes for general ophthalmological examination services, when performed.

Determination of refractive state establishes whether a prescription is required for vision correction. It is performed using an eye chart and refractor (a device that contains a

Coding Tip:

Routine ophthalmoscopy is included in general ophthalmological services. However, other special ophthalmological services are not included, and they should be coded and reported separately when performed (e.g., a determination of refractive state).

wide range of lens strengths that can be easily and quickly changed). The fitting of glasses or contact lenses is *not* included with determination of refractive state services.

EXAMPLE: Patient underwent determination of refractive state. Report code 92015.

Code 92025 is reported for computerized corneal topography (also called computer-assisted keratography or videokeratography), during which a digital camera is used to capture an image of the patient's cornea for computer analysis.

Contact Lens Services and Spectacle Services (Including Prosthesis for Aphakia)

When contact lens or spectacle services are provided, supply of the contact lenses or spectacles (glasses) is not included. Report an appropriate HCPCS level II code for the supply of materials.

EXAMPLE: Patient underwent fitting of bifocal spectacles. Ophthalmologist provided "sphere, bifocal, plano to plus or minus 4.00d, per lens" glasses to the patient. Report codes 92341 and V2200.

Special Otorhinolaryngologic Services

Special Otorhinolaryngologic services include the following headings:

- Vestibular function tests, without electrical recording
- Vestibular function tests, with recording (e.g., ENG)

- Audiologic function tests
- Evaluative and therapeutic services
- Special diagnostic procedures
- Other procedures

When otorhinolaryngologic services are performed during an evaluation and management (E/M) service, do not code and report the component procedures separately (e.g., otoscopy, tuning fork test, whispered voice test). Special otorhinolaryngologic services that are *not* typically included in a comprehensive otorhinolaryngologic evaluation are reported separately.

EXAMPLE: An otorhinolaryngologist performed a level 4 E/M service in the office, during which he reviewed the established patient's history, performed an external inspection of the ears, and conducted a rhinoscopic examination of the nose. Otoscopic examination of the external auditory canals and tympanic membranes revealed negative findings. Hearing assessment was performed with tuning forks, whispered voice, and finger-rub techniques. Report code 99214 from the E/M section. Do *not* report separate codes for the hearing assessments performed.

 Note:

During a level 4 E/M service, such as presented in the previous example, when the physician also performs a positional nystagmus test and nasal function studies, codes 92532 and 92512 are reported in addition to E/M code 99214.

Audiologic function tests with medical diagnostic evaluation codes include testing of both ears. Do not add modifier -50 (Bilateral Procedure) to these codes. When a service is performed on one ear, add modifier -52 (Reduced Services) to the appropriate code.

EXAMPLE: Patient underwent a pure-tone screening test, air only, both ears. Report code 92551.

Codes for audiometric tests are reported separately only when calibrated electronic equipment is used. For pure-tone audiometry, earphones are used. The patient responds to different tone pitches (frequencies). Air and bone thresholds are similar to pure-tone audiometry procedures, except a bone oscillator is used instead of earphones.

EXAMPLE: Patient underwent pure-tone audiometry, air and bone, left ear. Report code 92553-52.

Cardiovascular

Cardiovascular services include the following headings:

- Therapeutic services and procedures
- Cardiography
- Cardiovascular monitoring services
- Implantable and wearable cardiac device evaluations
- Echocardiography

- Cardiac catheterization
- Intracardiac electrophysiological procedures/ studies
- Peripheral arterial disease rehabilitation
- Noninvasive physiologic studies and procedures
- Other procedures

 Coding Tip:

- Many therapeutic and diagnostic cardiovascular procedure codes (93451–93461, 93600–93624, 93640–93657) include intravenous or intra-arterial access, electrocardiographic monitoring, and agents administered by injection or infusion. Therefore, do not separately report these codes for routine access, monitoring, injection, or infusion services.

- Cardiovascular code descriptions often state "with interpretation," or "tracing only," whereas others describe the total (global, technical, and professional) service. Be sure to carefully review code descriptions before reporting a code.

Therapeutic Services and Procedures

Therapeutic services performed during a heart catheterization, after the diagnostic images are obtained, are reported in addition to the heart catheterization codes (e.g., balloon angioplasty). Therapeutic procedures include the following:

- Cardiopulmonary resuscitation
- Transcutaneous pacing
- Cardioversion
- Circulatory assist procedures

- Thrombolysis
- Transcatheter placement of stents
- Percutaneous transluminal coronary balloon angioplasty
- Atherectomy

Percutaneous coronary artery interventions include stent placement (Figure 18-2), atherectomy, and balloon angioplasty (Figure 18-3). For a given coronary artery and its branches, report only the most complex intervention, regardless of the number of stent placements, atherectomies, or balloon angioplasties performed in that coronary artery and its branches. (Stent placement is considered more complex than an atherectomy. An atherectomy is considered more complex than a balloon angioplasty.) Do not add modifier -59 to codes reported for percutaneous coronary artery stent placement, atherectomy, or balloon angioplasty. These interventions are reported with an appropriate modifier to indicate in which coronary artery the procedure was performed. These modifiers are the following:

- -LC (left circumflex coronary artery)
- -RC (right coronary artery)
- -LD (left anterior descending coronary artery)

Coding Tip:

Medicare recognizes the following three coronary arteries for reimbursement purposes when considering first and additional vessel interventions:

- Left anterior descending
- Left circumflex
- Right coronary

Therefore, it is possible to report up to three percutaneous interventions if an intervention is performed in each of the three coronary arteries or their branches.

- The first procedure is reported with a primary code (e.g., 92920) that describes the most complex procedure performed.
- Procedures performed in other coronary arteries are reported with the add-on codes (e.g., 92921).

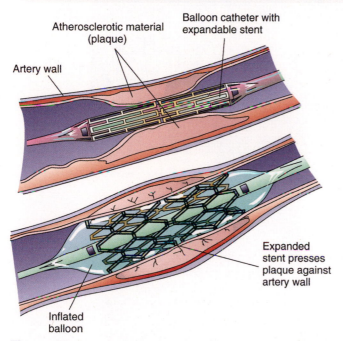

Figure 18-2 A stent is inserted after balloon angioplasty to prevent restenosis of the treated artery.

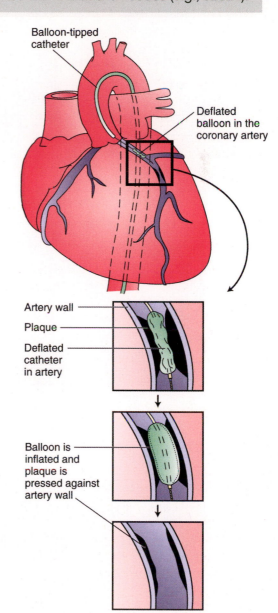

Figure 18-3 Balloon angioplasty is performed to open a blocked coronary artery.

When cardiopulmonary resuscitation (CPR) is performed *without* other evaluation and management services, report code 92950. Because critical care services and prolonged management services are determined by time, when code 92950 is reported separately, the time required to perform CPR is not included in determining the critical care or other time-based evaluation and management services.

EXAMPLE: A "code blue" is called on a hospital inpatient. The responding physician directs cardiopulmonary resuscitation. After the patient is resuscitated, the patient's attending physician resumes patient care. Report code 92950 for CPR.

Cardiography

Cardiography, or **electrocardiography**, is a diagnostic procedure that records the heart's electronic activity with a cardiograph and produces a cardiogram (or electrocardiogram, ECG, or EKG) (Figure 18-4). Cardiography codes are reported for routine electrocardiograms and other procedures (e.g., vector cardiogram, 24-hour monitoring, and patient demand recordings when ordered by the provider). Be sure to identify the total, professional, and technical components (and appropriate modifiers) before reporting cardiography codes.

The routine monitoring of EKG rhythm and hemodynamics, including cardiac outputs, is included as part of critical care evaluation and management services. Therefore, do not separately report EKG rhythm strip and cardiac output measurement review codes with critical care services.

EXAMPLE: Patient underwent routine ECG (tracing only) in the physician's office. Report code 93005.

Figure 18-4 Electrocardiogram showing disruptions of heart rhythms (A) Paroxysmal atrial tachycardia (PAT) (B) Atrial fibrillation (C) Ventricular fibrillation

Cardiovascular Monitoring Services

Cardiovascular monitoring services (e.g., pacemaker programming) use in-person and remote technology to assess cardiovascular rhythm data.

> **EXAMPLE:** Patient underwent transtelephonic rhythm strip pacemaker evaluation of her multiple lead pacemaker system for a period of 60 days, which included physician analysis, review, and documented report. Report code 93293 just once.

Implantable and Wearable Cardiac Device Evaluations

Cardiac device evaluation services are diagnostic medical procedures using in-person and remote technology to assess cardiac device therapy and cardiovascular physiologic data.

> **EXAMPLE:** Patient underwent a 30-day remote interrogation device evaluation that required an implantable loop recorder system. Analysis of recorded heart rhythm data, and physician analysis, review and report were included. Report code 93298.

Echocardiography

Echocardiography (Figure 18-5) is a diagnostic procedure that uses ultrasound to obtain two-dimensional images of the heart and great arteries (aorta, vena cavae). Echocardiography codes include the total procedure. When just the professional component is performed, add modifier -26 to the code.

> **EXAMPLE:** Patient underwent transesophageal echocardiography for congenital cardiac anomalies, which included placement of the probe, image acquisition, and interpretation and report. Report code 93315.

Cardiac Catheterization

Cardiac catheterization (Figure 18-6) is an invasive diagnostic medical procedure that includes several components. The procedure begins when the physician introduces one or more catheters into peripheral arteries and/or veins. Cardiac catheterizations include introduction, positioning (and repositioning) of catheter(s), recording of intracardiac and/or intravascular pressure(s), and final evaluation and preparation of a report.

Cardiac output measurement (93561–93562) is routinely performed during cardiac catheterization procedures. These codes are not reported in addition to cardiac catheterization codes.

Figure 18-5 Echocardiography: The large area of red shows the flow of blood through an abnormal opening between the aorta and right atrium.

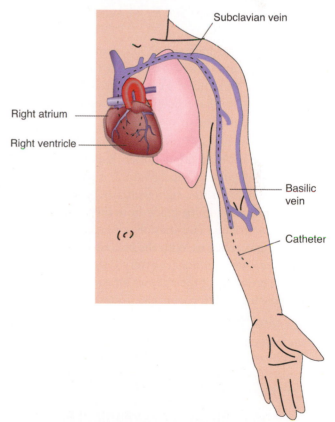

Figure 18-6 Cardiac catheterization: Once the catheter is inserted in the heart, a contrast medium is injected and an angiogram is performed to detect coronary vessel patency (openness).

Fluoroscopic guidance procedures are integral to invasive intravascular procedures, and codes for such procedures are not reported separately. ⚠

When reporting codes for cardiac catheterization procedures, review patient-record documentation to determine the following:

- Catheter placement

- Injection procedure

- Supervision and interpretation of fluoroscopic guidance

Coding Tip:

Do not add modifier -51 (Multiple Procedures) because of the component nature of cardiac catheterization procedures. Procedure codes are assigned once per session. Modifier -26 is added, as applicable, to cardiac catheterization procedures.

The femoral artery is the most common access point for cardiac catheterization (such as left heart catheterization, aortography, coronary angiography, internal mammary artery injection, vein bypass graft injection, and for other left heart procedures and coronary artery interventions). Right heart catheterization and pulmonary arteriography are most often performed via the right femoral vein. Each catheter is then positioned in a branch vessel or a cardiac chamber. During the catheterization procedure, recordings are made for measurement of intracardiac and intravascular pressure, oxygen saturation or blood gases, and cardiac output.

Angiography, frequently performed during a diagnostic catheterization, may require the assignment of a separate code. Angiography involves injecting a contrast medium and imaging the vessel (e.g., in order to determine the location or severity of obstructive lesions or abnormalities). Repositioning the catheter may be necessary during the procedure to perform injection of contrast for angiography. A final evaluation of all data and a report are required.

EXAMPLE: Patient underwent combined right and left heart catheterization, which included intraprocedural injection for left ventriculography with imaging supervision and interpretation. Report code 93453.

Endomyocardial biopsy (93505) provides tissue for direct pathologic evaluation of cardiac muscle using a special biopsy catheter with a bioptome tip (an open tip that closes to obtain tissue sample) to obtain myocardial tissue samples. To monitor a cardiac transplant patient for signs of rejection, the physician inserts a bioptome-tip catheter and, under fluoroscopy, advances it to the right ventricle. The instrument obtains myocardial tissue that is submitted for pathologic examination.

Insertion of a Swan-Ganz catheter (93503) is included in the cardiac catheterization codes. ⚠ A Swan-Ganz catheter is a flexible, multiple-lumen, balloon-tipped flotation catheter that is introduced through a major peripheral vein (e.g., the jugular or subclavian). It is passed under pressure waveform guidance, with or without fluoroscopy, through the right atrium, right ventricle, and pulmonary artery. Then the balloon is inflated and the tip measures pressure-transmitted retrograde from the left side of the heart (left ventricular end-diastolic pressure), as well as central venous pressure. With the balloon deflated, the catheter measures pulmonary artery systolic, diastolic, and mean pressures; it then allows infusion (and some patients are fitted with pacing electrodes).

Coding Tip:

Do not separately report code 93503 for Swan-Ganz catheter insertion unless it is performed as a separate and distinct procedure from the heart catheterization.

EXAMPLE: During postoperative recovery after a heart catheterization, the patient's condition became unstable, and the physician inserted a Swan-Ganz flow-directed catheter for evaluation and monitoring. Report code 93503.

Intracardiac Electrophysiological Procedures/Studies

Intracardiac electrophysiological procedures and studies describe services that record, map, or change heart conduction (e.g., recording bundle of His, mapping tachycardia during repair surgery). Many of these codes contain instructional notes that indicate their use with other codes. Intracardiac electrophysiological procedures (EP) may be diagnostic or therapeutic, and these procedures include the insertion and repositioning of catheters.

Peripheral Arterial Disease Rehabilitation

Peripheral arterial disease (PAD) is a disease in which plaque builds up in arteries that carry blood to the head, organs, and limbs; plaque consists of cholesterol, calcium, fat, fibrous tissue, and other substances in the blood. PAD rehabilitation includes physical exercise that consists of a series of sessions, each session lasting 45-60 minutes, and involves use of either a motorized treadmill or a track.

> **EXAMPLE:** During a series of three sessions, as part of PAD rehabilitation with supervision by an exercise physiologist, the patient exercised on a motorized treadmill for 45 minutes. Report codes 93668, 93668, and 93668.

Noninvasive Physiologic Studies and Procedures

Noninvasive physiologic studies and procedures include bioimpedance-derived physiologic cardiovascular analysis, electronic analysis of antitachycardia pacemaker system, temperature gradient studies, and so on.

> **EXAMPLE:** Patient underwent a procedure for determination of venous pressure. Report code 93770.

Other Procedures

Cardiac rehabilitation is a customized program of exercise and education. Cardiac rehabilitation programs typically last about three to six months, during which the patient works with cardiologists, nurse educators, dietitians, exercise rehabilitation specialists, occupational therapists, physical therapists, psychologists, and psychiatrists. CPT codes 93797 and 93798 describe comprehensive services provided by a physician for cardiac rehabilitation. This includes all services related to cardiac rehabilitation, so it would not be appropriate to report a separate evaluation and management service code unless it is an unrelated, separately identifiable service.

Coding Tip:

All intracardiac electrophysiological procedures/studies codes are exempt from modifier -51.

> **EXAMPLE:** On November 15, 20, and 25, a patient received physician services for outpatient cardiac rehabilitation without continuous ECG monitoring. Report codes 93797, 93797, and 93797 for each date of service.

Noninvasive Vascular Diagnostic Studies

Noninvasive vascular diagnostic studies (e.g., a duplex scan) include ultrasound scanning to display two-dimensional structure and motion, and the codes classify arterial and venous studies. They also identify anatomical structures or areas to be evaluated. (A **duplex scan** is a noninvasive test that is performed to evaluate a vessel's blood flow.) Headings include the following:

- Cerebrovascular arterial studies
- Extremity arterial studies (including digits)
- Extremity venous studies (including digits)
- Visceral and penile vascular studies
- Extremity arterial-venous studies
- Other noninvasive vascular diagnostic studies

> **EXAMPLE:** Patient underwent a duplex scan of lower extremity arteries, bilaterally. Report code 93925.

Pulmonary

Pulmonary codes are reported for therapeutic and diagnostic pulmonary services. When pulmonary services are provided during an evaluation and management (E/M) encounter (e.g., hospital inpatient visit, emergency department service, office visit), report a code from the Pulmonary subsection of the Medicine section in addition to the appropriate E/M code.

Pulmonary headings include

- *Ventilator management* provided to patients in hospital inpatient and observation care settings, nursing facilities, and for whom home care is provided

EXAMPLE: A hospital inpatient was treated with a mechanical ventilator that was applied with a mask over his nose and mouth to assist with breathing due to emphysema. Initial ventilator management services were provided on April 5, and subsequent ventilator management services were provided on April 6 and 7. Report codes 94002, 94003, and 94003. (Do not report modifier -51, multiple services, with code 94003.)

- *Pulmonary diagnostic testing and therapies* that include laboratory procedures and interpretation of test results (e.g., spirometry, vital capacity, thoracic gas volume, and so on)

EXAMPLE: During a level 3 outpatient E/M service to evaluate cystic fibrosis, the patient underwent outpatient pulmonary function testing to assess maximum breathing capacity and maximal voluntary ventilation. The physician interpreted the results of testing and adjusted the patient's medications. Report codes 99213 and 94200.

Allergy and Clinical Immunology

The Allergy and Clinical Immunology subsection includes the following headings:

- Allergy testing
- Ingestion challenge testing
- Allergen immunotherapy

Allergy Testing

Allergy sensitivity tests are performed on skin (cutaneous) and mucous membranes to identify the source of a patient's allergies (e.g., pollen as a source). Allergy skin tests include

- **Puncture, prick, or scratch test (percutaneous):** Tiny drops of purified allergen extracts are pricked or scratched into the skin's surface. The test is performed to identify allergies to pollen, mold, pet dander, dust mites, foods, insect venom, and penicillin (Figure 18-7).

- **Intradermal test (intracutaneous):** Purified allergen extracts are injected into the skin of patient's arm (Figure 18-8). The test is performed when an allergy to insect venom or penicillin is suspected.

- **Patch test (epicutaneous):** An allergen is applied to a patch, which is placed on skin. The test is performed to identify substances that cause contact dermatitis, such as latex, medications, fragrances, preservatives, hair dyes, metals, and resins.

EXAMPLE: Patient underwent two patch tests. Report codes 95044 and 95044.

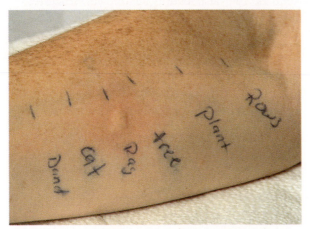

Figure 18-7 In scratch (percutaneous) tests, allergens are placed on the skin, the skin is scratched, and the allergen is labeled. Reactions usually occur within 20 minutes. Pictured is a reaction to ragweed.

Figure 18-8 Intradermal skin test

Ingestion Challenge Testing

Ingestion challenge testing includes the sequential and incremental ingestion of test items. Examples of test items include drugs, foods, and other substances. Patient assessment and monitoring activities (e.g., blood pressure) that are performed during ingestion challenge testing are *not* separately reported. However, intervention therapy (e.g., injection of epinephrine), when performed, is reported separately along with appropriate evaluation and management service code(s).

> **EXAMPLE:** Patient underwent 120 minutes of ingestion challenge testing (strawberries). Report code 95076.

Allergen Immunotherapy

Allergen immunotherapy (also known as allergy shots, allergy vaccines, desensitization shots, or hypo-sensitization shots) contains small amounts of **allergens** (allergy-causing substances to which a patient reacts) to increase the patient's tolerance to allergens. Codes 95115–95117 include the administration of allergenic extract, but they do not include the supply of the allergenic extract. Codes 95120–95134 are reported for complete service, which includes provision of the allergenic extract.

> **EXAMPLE:** A primary care provider administers a single allergy injection using allergenic extract that was previously prepared by an allergist and brought to the office by the patient. Report code 95115.

Allergen immunotherapy is administered on a schedule; patients typically receive treatment once or twice a week for about three to six months, and then once a month for three to five years. There are usually two phases of treatment.

- The buildup phase, during which patients receive shots one or two times per week for about three to six months

- The maintenance phase, during which patients receive shots every two to four weeks for five months or longer

Code 95144 is reported for the preparation and provision of single-dose antigens to be administered by another physician. The number of single-dose vials prepared and provided should be specified when reporting this code. Codes 95145–95170 describe the antigen, its preparation, and the concentration/volume required for the injections. These codes are reported for the supply of antigen for prospectively planned administration. The number of doses prepared and provided must be specified when reporting these codes. Administration of injections is not included in these codes.

Note:

A **dose** is the amount of antigen administered in a single injection from a multiple-dose vial.

 Coding Tip:

Evaluation and management services performed during the same encounter as allergy testing or allergy immunotherapy are reported only if a significant, separately identifiable service was administered.

- Code 95165 describes professional services for the supervision and provision of antigens (e.g., single or multiple) for allergy immunotherapy.

- Code 95165 does not include the injection procedure. Therefore, when a physician prepares the allergenic extract (same or different antigens) and administers the extract using single or multiple injections, report code 95165 in addition to either 95115 or 95117.

Endocrinology

Continual glucose (blood sugar) monitoring for up to 72 hours involves the subcutaneous placement of a sensor from which data are sent to a monitor. The patient calibrates the monitor on a daily basis.

> **EXAMPLE:** Dr. Jones was provided with a printout of recorded data from a subcutaneous sensor inserted into patient Mary Smith. Dr. Jones interpreted the data and prepared a report. Report code 95251.

Neurology and Neuromuscular Procedures

Neurology and neuromuscular codes classify diagnostic and therapeutic services that do not require surgical procedures. The Neurology and Neuromuscular subsection includes the following headings:

- Sleep medicine testing
- Routine electroencephalography (EEG)
- Muscle and range-of-motion testing
- Electromyography
- Ischemic muscle testing and guidance for chemodenervation
- Nerve conduction tests
- Intraoperative neurophysiology

- Autonomic function tests
- Evoked potentials and reflex tests
- Special EEG tests
- Neurostimulators, analysis-programming
- Other procedures
- Motion analysis
- Functional brain mapping

Sleep Medicine Testing

Sleep testing includes sleep studies and polysomnography, which are performed for the continuous monitoring and recording of various physiological parameters of sleep for six or more hours. Sleep testing is usually done in a health care facility's **sleep laboratory**, which is managed by a sleep technologist who explains and performs the sleep studies. (Sleep studies and polysomnographies are ordered, reviewed, and interpreted by physicians.) Sleeping rooms typically contain regular (not hospital) beds, an attached bathroom, and a television.

Sleep medicine testing codes include physician review and interpretation of data, and the preparation of a report.

- **Multiple sleep latency** is the observation of a patient during at least a six-hour period of sleep and includes assessment of sleep latency (dormancy) and/or wakefulness after the sleep period.

- **Sleep studies** evaluate adult and pediatric patients during sleep by monitoring brainwaves, heart rate, and eye movements. They are performed to diagnose sleep disorders, which include breathing, movement, and neurologic disorders that occur at night. Electrodes are applied to the patient's scalp, sides of the head, below the chin, chest, and legs. A sensor is placed next to the nose and mouth to measure airflow. A pulse oximetry clip is placed on the patient's finger to measure blood oxygen levels. Patients are also videotaped while asleep.

- **Polysomnography** is a sleep study that includes sleep staging with additional parameters of sleep (e.g., belts can be placed around the rib cage and abdomen to measure breathing movements). **Sleep staging** includes a 1-4 lead EEG, electro-oculogram (EOG), and submental electromyogram (EMG). Parameters that determine the polysomnography code to report include the following:

- Airflow
- Body positions
- Continuous blood pressure monitoring
- Electrocardiogram
- End tidal gas analysis
- Extended EEG monitoring
- Extremity muscle activity

- Gas exchange by oximetry
- Gastroesophageal reflux
- Motor activity movement
- Penile tumescence
- Snoring
- Transcutaneous monitoring
- Ventilation and respiratory effort

EXAMPLE: A patient with a history of sleep apnea undergoes a sleep study, during which he is monitored for 6 hours. Polysomnography includes the measurement of respiration, airflow, muscle activity, continuous monitoring of blood pressure, and sleep staging with EEG, electro-oculogram, and submental electromyogram. Report code 95808.

Routine Electroencephalography (EEG)

EEG procedures include the use of the following, when appropriate:

- **Hyperventilation**: Deep or rapid breathing
- **Photic stimulation**: Reaction to light

Extended EEG codes (95812–95813) are reported to test various stages of activity and sleep. Codes 95829–95830 are reported when an electrocorticogram is performed during surgery (95829) or the physician inserts sphenoidal electrodes for EEG recording (95830).

EXAMPLE: Patient underwent a 60-minute EEG test, which included photic (pertaining to light) stimulation. Report code 95812.

Muscle and Range-of-Motion Testing

Muscle and range-of-motion testing codes are reported for muscle testing, range-of-motion measurements and reports, and Tensilon testing for myasthenia gravis. The **Tensilon test** involves injecting the drug Tensilon (or its generic, edrophonium chloride) into a vein to block the action of the enzyme that breaks down the neurotransmitter acetylcholinesterase. The patient is then observed for rapid improvement in strength (e.g., use of eye muscles).

EXAMPLE: Patient underwent manual muscle testing, left leg, which included physician interpretation and report. Report code 95831.

Electromyography

Electromyography (EMG) is a test that is used to detect nerve function by measuring the electrical activity generated by muscles. **Needle electromyography** testing involves inserting needle electrodes into skeletal muscles and observing electrical activity of those muscles using an **oscilloscope** (a device that displays electrical waveforms on a monitor) and a loudspeaker.

EXAMPLE: Patient underwent limited needle EMG study of the left bicep muscle. Report code 95870.

Ischemic Muscle Testing and Guidance for Chemodenervation

Ischemic muscle testing and guidance for chemodenervation services are performed to treat nerve various neurological conditions.

EXAMPLE: Patient underwent ischemic limb exercise test with collection of several specimens to determine the presence of muscle metabolites. Report code 95875.

Nerve Conduction Tests

Nerve conduction tests are performed for sensory conduction, motor conduction, or Hoffman's reflex (H-reflex) (knee jerk reflex). For sensory conduction and H-reflex testing, electrodes are placed directly over the nerve; for motor conduction testing, electrodes are placed over the motor point of a specific muscle; then, electrical stimulation is applied. Amplitude, conduction velocity, and latency of the stimulation are measured.

EXAMPLE: Patient underwent three nerve conduction studies due to left leg numbness. Report code 95908.

Intraoperative Neurophysiology

Intraoperative neurophysiology testing codes are reported when performed during a surgical procedure. (The primary procedure code is reported as the first-listed procedure.)

EXAMPLE: Patient underwent EEG needle electromyography of one extremity, during which 15 minutes of intraoperative neurophysiology testing was also performed. Report codes 95860 and 95940.

Autonomic Function Tests

Autonomic function tests evaluate autonomic nervous system functioning (e.g., heart or lungs).

> **EXAMPLE:** Patient underwent autonomic function testing, during which he was instructed to perform the Valsalva maneuver and then lie on a tilt table. The patient's blood pressure was monitored both during the maneuver and while on the tilt table. Report code 95922.

Evoked Potentials and Reflex Tests

A **short-latency somatosensory evoked potential study** involves electrically stimulating nerves to evaluate their responsiveness to the body's superficial surface and internal structures (e.g., the organs). (The appropriate code is reported according to testing site.) A **central motor evoked potential study** uses low-voltage electrodes, which are placed on the scalp and target sites to test the nervous system's pathway. A **visual evoked potential (VEP) test** of the central nervous system (CNS) involves stimulating the eye using the checkerboard or flash technique to monitor the patient's response. An **orbicularis oculi** (blink) test is monitored with sensors.

> **EXAMPLE 1:** Patient underwent a short-latency somatosensory evoked potential study, stimulation of any/all peripheral nerves or skin sites, recording from the central nervous system; in upper limbs. Report code 95925.

> **EXAMPLE 2:** Patient underwent VEP testing of the CNS using the flash technique. Report code 95930.

Special EEG Tests

Continuous electroencephalographic monitoring services codes are reported when a separately identifiable service is performed.

> **EXAMPLE:** Patient underwent 24-hour EEG monitoring and video recording; interpretation to determine localization of cerebral seizure focus by a 16-channel telemetry cable was performed. Report code 95951.

Neurostimulators, Analysis-Programming

Neurostimulators and analysis-programming codes are reported when a previously implanted neurostimulator pulse generator system is electronically analyzed to determine battery status, pulse amplitude and duration, rate, and so on.

> **EXAMPLE:** Patient underwent electronic analysis of implanted neurostimulator pulse generator system without reprogramming. Report code 95970.

Other Procedures

Other procedures codes are reported for the refill and maintenance of implantable infusion pumps or reservoirs. Code 95992 is reported for canalith repositioning, per day. Code 95999 is reported for an unlisted neurological or neuromuscular diagnostic procedure.

> **EXAMPLE:** Medicare patient with terminal cancer undergoes a procedure to have implantable pump located in his spine refilled and maintained to ensure delivery of 100 mg of morphine sulfate, which is the loading dose prescribed for palliative care. Report codes 95990 and J2270 ×10. (Do *not* report S0093 for the morphine because that is a non-Medicare temporary code.)

Note:

> Code 96004 is reported in addition to codes 96000–96003 when a physician reviews and interprets the results of motion analysis and documents a written report. Modifier -51 is added to code 96004 when the service is provided during the same encounter as motion analysis testing.

Motion Analysis

Motion analysis codes are reported for services performed during major diagnostic or therapeutic decision making. During human motion analysis, patient movements are recorded, digitized, copied onto a computer, and processed.

> **EXAMPLE:** In the motion analysis lab, a patient is instructed to walk along a special walkway that includes a pressure sensor platform, which is positioned on the walkway. As the

patient walks, pressure data are recorded and later analyzed for areas of the foot (e.g., hallux, heel, and metatarsal heads). The peak pressure is calculated for all areas, and the highest pressure is measured. Report code 96001. (Do not report bilateral -50 or directional -LT/-RT modifiers.)

Functional Brain Mapping

Functional brain mapping is a process by which a series of tests is administered by a physician or a psychologist to assess cognition, language, memory, movement, and sensation. The results of testing are documented in a report to identify expected versus observed locations of brain activity documented as the patient performs assigned tasks.

> **Note:**
>
> When a functional MRI (fMRI) is performed by a provider other than a physician or a psychologist, such as a psychiatric nurse, report code 70554 only. Do not report code 96020.

During functional brain mapping, the patient undergoes functional neuroimaging of the brain, which is also called functional magnetic resonance imaging (fMRI) of the brain. Report code 70555 in addition to code 96020 when a physician or psychologist entirely administers the functional brain mapping.

> **EXAMPLE:** Dr. Sanders performs a functional brain mapping with fMRI on a 49-year-old patient who has been experiencing memory losses and motor problems, to assess cognition, language, memory, movement, and sensation. Report codes 96020 and 70555.

Medical Genetics and Genetic Counseling Services

Medical genetics and genetic counseling services are reported when a trained genetic counselor meets with an individual, couple, or family to investigate the family's genetic history and to assess risks associated with genetic defects in offspring.

> **EXAMPLE:** A married couple, who was referred to a trained genetic counselor by their fertility doctor, received 60 minutes of medical genetic counseling. Report codes 96040, 96040. (Code 96040 is reported for *each* 30-minute session of counseling.)

Central Nervous System Assessments/Tests (e.g., Neuro-Cognitive, Mental Status, Speech Testing)

Central nervous system assessments/tests codes are reported when tests are performed to measure cognitive function of the central nervous system (e.g., cognitive processes, visual motor responses, and abstractive abilities). Several testing procedures are included, such as psychological testing (code 96101), which includes psychodiagnostic assessment of personality, psychopathology, emotionality, and intellectual abilities (e.g., WAIS-R, Rorschach, and MMPI tests). (Code 96101 is reported for each hour that the provider provided testing, interpreted test results, and prepared the report.)

> **EXAMPLE:** Patient underwent limited developmental testing, and the physician interpreted the results and prepared a report. Report code 96110.

Health and Behavior Assessment/Intervention

Health and behavior assessment/intervention codes are reported for tests that identify the psychological, behavioral, emotional, cognitive, and social elements involved in the prevention, treatment, or management of physical health problems. The focus of the assessment is not on mental health, but on biopsychosocial factors that are considered important to physical health problems and treatments. Health and behavior intervention procedures are used to modify factors affecting the patient. The focus of the intervention is to improve the patient's health and well-being by using cognitive, behavioral, social, and/or psychophysiological procedures.

Health and behavior assessment/intervention codes describe services associated with an acute or chronic illness that does not meet the criteria for psychiatric diagnosis, prevention of a physical disability, and maintenance of health. If the patient requires psychiatric services (90832–90899) and/or health and behavior assessment/intervention (96150–96155), report the primary service performed. Do not report codes 96150–96155 in addition to codes 90832–90899 on the same date of service.

EXAMPLE: A psychiatrist performed a 45-minute face-to-face health and behavior assessment of a child who was diagnosed with leukemia and who was suffering from severe distress and combativeness to chemotherapy administration. Report codes 96150, 96150, and 96150.

Hydration, Therapeutic, Prophylactic, Diagnostic Injections and Infusions, and Chemotherapy and Other Highly Complex Drug or Highly Complex Biologic Agent Administration

The hydration, therapeutic, prophylactic, diagnostic injections and infusions, and chemotherapy and other highly complex drug or highly complex biologic agent administration codes include the following headings:

- Hydration

- Therapeutic, prophylactic, and diagnostic injections and infusions (excludes chemotherapy and other highly complex drug or highly complex biologic agent administration)

- Chemotherapy and other highly complex drug or highly complex biologic agent administration

> **Note:**
>
> Patient record documentation should include physician verification of the patient's treatment plan and direction of staff who provide injection and infusion services.

The following services are included, which means they are not separately coded and reported:

- Administration of local anesthesia

- Intravenous (IV) insertion

- Access to indwelling IV, subcutaneous catheter, or port

- Flushing performed upon completion of infusion

- Routine syringes, tubing, and other supplies

 Coding Tip:

- Report code 36593 for declotting a catheter or port using a fibrinolytic agent (e.g., recombinant tissue plasminogen activator, also known as tPA or alteplase).

- Code 36593 is not reported for the routine flushing of vascular access devices with saline or heparin. For example, this type of flushing is considered integral to chemotherapy administration and is not separately coded and reported.

When multiple injections or infusions or combination services are provided, report the initial code only once except *when two separate intravenous (IV) sites are required.* When the length of infusion time is included in the code description, report the code based on actual infusion time.

Hydration

Hydration codes are reported for the intravenous infusion of prepackaged fluids and electrolytes (e.g., normal saline and normal saline with potassium chloride). When reporting these codes, review the patient record for documentation that the physician supervised

- Patient assessment (e.g., history and examination)

- Patient consent (e.g., discussion of risks and benefits)

- Patient safety (e.g., proper dose was administered; patient's response to infusion, including adverse reaction)

- Staff members who provided infusion services (e.g., the nursing staff)

EXAMPLE: Patient received initial intravenous infusion hydration of 1,000 cubic centimeters lactated Ringer's (pH–balanced electrolyte solution) for 60 minutes. Report codes 96360 and J7120.

 Coding Tip:

- Do not report hydration codes for the infusion of drugs or other substances, which are reported with codes 96365–96379.

- Report HCPCS level II codes for supply of prepackaged fluids and electrolytes (e.g., J7030, normal saline solution).

Therapeutic, Prophylactic, and Diagnostic Injections and Infusions

Therapeutic, prophylactic, and diagnostic injections and infusions codes are reported for the administration of substances (other than hydration) and drugs. When reporting these codes, review the patient record for documentation that the physician supervised

- Patient assessment
- Patient safety

- Patient consent
- Staff members who provided injection and/or infusion services

EXAMPLE 1: Patient underwent therapeutic injection (intramuscular) of kanamycin sulfate, 500 mg. Report codes 96372 and J1840.

EXAMPLE 2: Patient underwent routine insertion of an IV catheter for one-hour IV infusion of 1,000 milliliters of potassium chloride and magnesium sulfate. Report codes 96365 and S5013. Do not report 36000 or 36410.

EXAMPLE 3: Male patient required a nontunneled CVAC procedure prior to one-hour intravenous infusion of 1,000 milliliters of potassium chloride and magnesium sulfate drug therapy. Report codes 36556, 96365, and S5013.

Staff members who administer therapeutic, prophylactic, and diagnostic injections (Figure 18-9) and infusions undergo special training to learn how to assess patients, provide informed consent, monitor patient safety, and administer injections and infusions. **Intravenous push** is an:

- Injection administered by a health care professional who is in constant attendance to administer the injection and observe the patient

- Infusion of 15 minutes or less

Figure 18-9 Angles of injection for administration of therapeutic, prophylactic, and diagnostic medications

Coding Tip:

- Any fluid used to administer a drug (e.g., flushing of IV with saline solution between drug therapies) is considered incidental hydration, and a separate hydration code is not reported.

- Report codes 90281–90399 for provision of immune globulin products.

- Report HCPCS level II codes for the supply of drugs (e.g., J0280, aminophylline).

- The administration of IV fluids to maintain line patency (unblocked condition) is not separately coded and reported.

Chemotherapy and Other Highly Complex Drug or Highly Complex Biologic Agent Administration

Chemotherapy is the treatment of cancer with drugs that serve to destroy cancer cells or slow the growth of cancer cells, keep cancer from spreading to other parts of the body, and prevent recurrence of the cancer. Chemotherapy administered in addition to other cancer treatments, such as surgery and/or radiation therapy, is called **adjuvant chemotherapy**.

Codes in this subheading classify the parenteral administration of chemotherapeutic agents, which means that the chemotherapy is administered by a route *other than by mouth*, such as implantation (of a catheter or port), infusion, or injection.

 Coding Tip:

Do not report chemotherapy infusion with a code from range 96360–96379. To report chemotherapy infusion, select the appropriate code(s) from the chemotherapy administration series (96401–96549). These codes can be separately billed when an E/M service is rendered on the same day as the chemotherapy administration.

- The flushing of a vascular access port (e.g., saline solution) prior to the administration of chemotherapeutic agents is integral to the chemotherapy administration. It is not coded and reported separately.

- When infusion of hydrating solutions (e.g., saline solution) or drugs (e.g., heparin) other than antineoplastic drugs is a necessary and integral part of a procedure, a code from range 96360–96379 is *not* reported separately.

EXAMPLE: The infusion of a hydrating solution is started prior to the administration of chemotherapy. The infusion of the hydrating solution is included in the chemotherapy code, and it is not reported separately.

There are many chemotherapy drugs currently available to treat cancer, and chemotherapy is administered in a variety of ways, depending on the drugs used and the type of cancer.

Oral chemotherapy is administered by mouth in the form of a pill, capsule, or liquid, while parenteral methods of chemotherapy administration include the following:

- Implantation of a catheter or port into a central vein or body cavity

- Infusion or injection of intravenous (IV) chemotherapy into a vein

- Injection of intramuscular (IM) chemotherapy is injected into the muscle

- Injection of subcutaneous (SQ) chemotherapy under the skin

It is the parenteral methods of chemotherapy administration that are reported with codes from 96401–96549. When different techniques are used to parenterally administer chemotherapy (e.g., injection, infusion, implantation) *during the same encounter*, report a separate code for each parenteral method.

EXAMPLE 1: A patient diagnosed with malignant melanoma, skin of scalp, undergoes one hour of intravenous infusion of chemotherapy and intralesional chemotherapy administration to the scalp lesion. Report codes 96405 and 96413.

EXAMPLE 2: A patient was administered three injections of antineoplastic drugs and an infusion of antineoplastic drugs for two hours during one encounter. Report codes 96401, 96401, 96401, 96413, and 96415.

When an intravenous infusion of saline (an antiemetic) or other nonchemotherapy drug is administered at the same time as the chemotherapeutic agent(s), these infusions are not coded and reported separately. However, the supply of the drugs is reported separately with HCPCS level II codes. If the hydration or intravenous infusion is administered on the same day, but sequentially rather than at the same time as the chemotherapeutic agents, the infusions are reported with codes 96360–96368. Modifier -59 (Distinct Procedural Service) is added to these codes to indicate that the infusions were administered at different times.

EXAMPLE: Patient receives nonchemotherapy infusions for 75 minutes. Report code 96365. (A code for the remaining 15 minutes is not reported.) (Also, report level II code[s] for the drugs administered.)

> **Coding Tip:**
>
> Report code 96365 (IV infusion, for therapy, prophylaxis, or diagnosis, initial; up to 1 hour) to indicate an infusion of drugs (e.g., antihypertensive medication) *other than antineoplastic drugs*. Code 96366 is reported for each additional hour of infusion, up to eight hours.

Codes 96401–96549 are independent of the patient's evaluation and management (E/M) services and may occur sequentially on the same day. If performed, the appropriate E/M code should be reported as an additional code. Preparation of chemotherapy agent(s) is included in the service for administration of the agent, and it is not coded and reported separately.

Medications (e.g., antibiotics, steroidal agents, antiemetics, narcotics, analgesics, and biological agents) administered independently or sequentially as supportive management of chemotherapy administration are separately coded and reported, as appropriate. It is appropriate to report separately the appropriate HCPCS level II code(s) for the supply of chemotherapy drugs in addition to the code(s) for chemotherapy administration.

Photodynamic Therapy

Photodynamic therapy is administered by

- External application of light to destroy malignancies

- Endoscopic application of light that activates photosensitive drugs to destroy abnormal tissue

Photodynamic therapy (PDT) is the application of a photosensitizing agent (e.g., 20 percent topical aminolevulinic acid HCl) directly onto a patient's lesions to treat premalignant cells (e.g., nonhyperkeratotic actinic keratosis) or malignant cells. The patient returns for a scheduled encounter during which a photodynamic therapy illuminator (light) is directed on the treated lesions. A cytotoxic reaction results when the topical agent applied to the lesions is irradiated, killing premalignant or malignant cells, preventing their spread.

> **Coding Tip:**
>
> A photodynamic therapy code is reported for each exposure session, *not* for each lesion treated.

 Note:

Ocular photodynamic therapy consultation is reported with code 67221.

Special Dermatological Procedures

Special dermatological procedures codes describe dermatology procedures that are usually (but not always) performed in addition to an appropriate evaluation and management (E/M) service code.

> **EXAMPLE:** During a level 3 outpatient consultation encounter, the dermatologist performed a detailed history and examination; medical decision making was of low complexity. The dermatologist used ultraviolet light (actinotherapy) to treat the two areas of acne frontalis. Report codes 99243 and 96900-51.

Physical Medicine and Rehabilitation

Physical medicine and rehabilitation is a branch of medicine that focuses on the prevention, diagnosis, and treatment of disorders of the musculoskeletal, cardiovascular, and pulmonary systems that may produce temporary or permanent impairment. A **physiatrist** is a physician who specializes in physical medicine and rehabilitation and treats acute/chronic pain and musculoskeletal disorders. Physiatrists also treat disorders of the musculoskeletal system that result in severe functional limitations (e.g., a baby with a birth defect, the victim of a bad car accident, an elderly person with a broken hip). Physiatrists coordinate the long-term rehabilitation process for patients with spinal-cord injuries, cancer, stroke, brain injuries, amputations, and multiple sclerosis or other neurological disorders. The specialty focuses on the restoration of function to people with problems ranging from simple physical mobility issues to those with complex cognitive involvement.

Physiatrists offer a broad spectrum of medical services (e.g., the prescription of drugs or assistive devices such as a brace or artificial limb). However, they do not perform surgery. Physiatrists use diverse modalities (any physical agent applied to produce therapeutic changes) that include therapies such as heat and cold, electrotherapies, massage, biofeedback, traction, and therapeutic exercise.

> **EXAMPLE 1:** Patient underwent diathermy. Report code 97024.

> **EXAMPLE 2:** A diabetic patient presents for treatment of a chronic open wound on the left foot. The wound measures 4 cm × 3 cm (or 12 sq cm), and the physician treats it by using surgical scissors to perform sharp selective debridement. Report code 97597.

Medical Nutrition Therapy

Medical nutrition therapy is classified according to

- Type of assessment
- Individual or group therapy
- Length of time

> **EXAMPLE:** Patient underwent medical nutrition therapy reevaluation and assessment. The provider spent 30 minutes face-to-face with the patient. Report codes 97803 and 97803.

Acupuncture

Acupuncture treatment is classified as face-to-face patient contact for 15-minute increments of time and according to whether electrical stimulation was provided.

> **EXAMPLE:** Patient underwent acupuncture, which included five needles. The provider spent 30 minutes of one-on-one contact with the patient. Report codes 97810 and 97811.

Osteopathic Manipulative Treatment

Manipulative and body-based practices focus primarily on the structures and systems of the body, including the bones and joints, the soft tissues, and the circulatory and lymphatic systems. **Osteopathic manipulative treatment (OMT)** is a manual treatment performed by a physician, during which emphasis is placed on normal body mechanics and manipulative methods to detect and correct structure. Osteopathic practice includes diagnostic and therapeutic techniques (e.g., musculoskeletal manipulations as well as prescriptions and other therapies) and preventive measures. Combining available medical procedures with OMT provides patients the most comprehensive care. The osteopathic codes are reported according to the number of body regions treated. It is also appropriate to report codes for other restorative modalities and procedures performed on the same day when medically necessary.

Coding Tip:

- A provider who performs OMT cannot report anesthesia services separately (e.g., nerve blocks and epidural injections) for OMT.

- According to Medicare, postoperative pain management after OMT (e.g., a nerve block or an epidural injection) is not reported separately. However, epidural or nerve block injections unrelated to the OMT may be reported with an OMT code by adding modifier -59.

EXAMPLE: The osteopathic physician provided osteopathic manipulative treatment to four body regions. Report code 98926.

Chiropractic Manipulative Treatment

Chiropractic manipulative treatment (CMT) is a form of manual treatment to influence joint and neurophysiological function. This treatment may be accomplished using a variety of techniques.

CMT codes include a premanipulation patient assessment. However, additional E/M services may be reported separately by adding modifier -25 if the patient's condition requires a separate E/M service beyond the usual preservice and postservice work associated with the CMT procedure.

For purposes of CMT, the five spinal regions include the following:

- Cervical region (e.g., atlanto-occipital joint)

- Thoracic region (e.g., costovertebral and costotransverse joints)

- Lumbar region

- Sacral region

- Pelvic region (e.g., sacroiliac joint)

The five extraspinal regions include the head (including temporomandibular joint, excluding atlanto-occipital), lower extremities, upper extremities, rib cage (excluding costotransverse and costovertebral joints), and abdomen.

EXAMPLE: A chiropractor provided chiropractic manipulative treatment to four regions of the spine. Report code 98941.

Coding Tip:

Medicare covers CMT for five spinal regions. Physical therapy services reported with codes 97112, 97124, and 97140 are not separately reportable when performed in a spinal region undergoing CMT. If physical therapy services are performed in a different region than CMT, the physical therapy codes are reported with modifier -59.

Confusion about Medicare's chiropractic coverage resulted in publication of the CMS article entitled "Addressing Misinformation Regarding Chiropractic Services and Medicare: Information for Medicare Fee-for-Service Health Care Professionals." (Go to www.cms .hhs.gov, enter "SE0749" in the "Search CMS.gov" box, click the Search button, and locate the PDF file. Or, go to www.Google.com and enter SE0749.pdf to locate the document.)

Education and Training for Patient Self-Management

Education and training for patient self-management is performed by a qualified, nonphysician health care professional who uses a standardized curriculum. The codes are classified according to the length of time spent face-to-face with one or more patients.

> **EXAMPLE:** Patient underwent education and training for self-management of her recently diagnosed diabetes mellitus. The nonphysician health care professional spent 30 minutes providing face-to-face instruction. Report code 98960.

Non-Face-to-Face Nonphysician Services

Non-face-to-face nonphysician services that are provided by a qualified health care professional (nonphysician) include the following:

- Telephone services

 Note:

- Codes for telephone services are not reported when they result in a patient encounter within 24 hours or at the next available urgent visit appointment. Such telephone services are considered part of the preservice work for the subsequent face-to-face encounter.

- Telephone service codes are also not reported when the call is related to a service performed and reported by the provider within the past seven days or within the postoperative period of a previously completed procedure.

- Online medical evaluation in response to a patient's online inquiry using Internet resources

 Note:

To report codes for online medical evaluation services, the health care professional must provide a personal, timely response to the inquiry and the encounter must be permanently stored via electronic means or hard copy.

- Online medical evaluation codes are not reported when related to a service performed and reported by the same provider within the past seven days or within the postoperative period of a previously completed procedure. The online service is considered part of the previous service or procedure.

- Code 98969 is reported just once for the same episode of care during a seven-day period.

Special Services, Procedures, and Reports

Special services, procedures, and reports codes classify the completion of special reports and performance of adjunctive services. These codes describe special circumstances under which a basic procedure is performed.

> **EXAMPLE 1:** The physician office handled and conveyed a specimen for transfer to a laboratory. Report code 99000. (If provided, report a service code for obtaining the specimen, such as venipuncture.)

> **EXAMPLE 2:** A patient was referred to physical therapy after orthopedic surgery. The patient required a 30-day interim visit to the surgeon. Report code 99024 for the surgeon visit. (The code is not reported on a claim, and the payer does not reimburse for the service provided. However, code 99024 allows for internal tracking of postoperative care services provided by the surgeon during the global surgical period.)

Qualifying Circumstances for Anesthesia

Qualifying circumstances for anesthesia codes describe situations that complicate the administration of anesthesia services (e.g., emergencies, extreme age, hypotension, and hypothermia). Codes 99100–99140 are add-on codes, which means that they are reported in addition to the anesthesia service code reported from the Anesthesia section.

> **EXAMPLE:** An otherwise unusually healthy 84-year-old patient underwent left hip replacement surgery, which required the administration of general anesthesia by the anesthesiologist. Report codes 01214-P1-AA (general anesthesia service) and 99100.

Moderate (Conscious) Sedation

Moderate (conscious) sedation codes classify a drug-induced depression of consciousness that requires no interventions to maintain airway patency or ventilation. CPT specifies that moderate (conscious) sedation does not include pain control, minimal sedation (e.g., anxiolysis), deep sedation, or monitored anesthesia care (MAC). Subsection notes specify services that are included in moderate (conscious) sedation codes (e.g., IV access, administration of agent, and monitoring oxygen saturation). The surgeon who performs the surgical procedure provides moderate (conscious) sedation services. An *independent trained observer* is present during surgery to monitor the patient's sedation. When another physician (e.g., an anesthesiologist) provides general anesthesia, regional anesthesia, or monitored anesthesia care, that other physician reports an appropriate anesthesia code and its modifiers.

> **EXAMPLE 1:** A 68-year-old patient received 15 minutes of moderate (conscious) sedation services, which were provided by the same physician who removed a superficial orthopedic wire. An independent trained observer was present to monitor the patient's sedation. Report codes 20670 (removal of superficial implant) and 99156.

> **EXAMPLE 2:** A 19-year-old male patient was prepped and draped for brain surgery, and he received moderate (conscious) sedation in the form of a narcotic called remifentanil (brand name Ultiva) administered in combination with propofol. An independent trained observer was present to monitor the patient's sedation. It was determined that the patient could feel no pain but would be able to communicate with the operating room staff and surgeon during the procedure. Trephination craniectomy and bone flap craniotomy were performed after intraoperative brain magnetic resonance imaging (MRI) confirmed the exact location of the supratentorial tumor. It was noted that the tumor was pressing on the area of the cerebrum that controls the ability to read and speak.
>
> During the procedure, the patient remained heavily sedated but conscious so the surgeon could talk with him while mapping the brain's sensors. The patient read a book aloud during the procedure; when the surgeon pressed on a sensitive region of the brain, the patient's reading was affected, letting the surgeon know which areas to avoid. Upon completion of brain mapping, the risky areas were marked by placing lettered pieces of paper directly onto the brain to identify the areas of risk. The surgeon then opened the brain's outer membrane and, layer by layer, removed the tumor. The patient felt no pain (because the brain has no pain receptors), and the tumor was submitted to pathology for analysis. The patient tolerated the 5-hour procedure well and was transported to the recovery room in stable condition. The patient will undergo repeat MRI in 30 days to verify total resection of the tumor. Report codes 61510, 70551, 99156 (first 15 minutes), and 99157 × 19 (subsequent 4.75 hours). (Code 99156 is reported once for the first 15 minutes of anesthesia. Then, code 99157 is assigned 19 times for the subsequent 4.75 hours of anesthesia; 4.75 hours × 60 minutes = 285 minutes divided by 15-minute increments = 19.)

Other Services and Procedures

Other services and procedures codes are reported for services and procedures that cannot be classified in another subsection of the Medicine section (e.g., anogenital examination, vision screening by nonoptical professionals, hypothermia treatment).

> **EXAMPLE:** Patient underwent therapeutic phlebotomy. Report code 99195.

Home Health Procedures/Services

Home health procedures/services codes are reported by nonphysician health care professionals who perform procedures and provide services to the patient in the patient's residence (the patient's home, assisted living facility, or group home). *Home infusion procedures/services* are reported for the provision of home infusion services, and the codes are based on length of infusion time.

> **EXAMPLE 1:** Patient received a home visit from a registered nurse for mechanical ventilation care. Report code 99504.

> **EXAMPLE 2:** Patient underwent three hours of home infusion on May 14. Report codes 99601 and 99602.

Medication Therapy Management Services

Medication therapy management services (MTMS) describe face-to-face patient assessments and interventions performed by a pharmacist to

- Optimize the patient's response to medications.

- Manage treatment-related medication interactions or complications.

Documentation of MTMS includes review of the pertinent patient history and medication profile (prescription and nonprescription) as well as recommendations for improving health outcomes and compliance with treatment.

 Note:

MTMS codes are not reported to describe the provision of product-specific information at the point of dispensing or any other routine dispensing-related activities.

Exercise 18.3 – Medicine Subsections

Instructions: Assign CPT code(s) and appropriate modifier(s) to each statement.

1. Oral immunization administration.

_____

2. A 60-minute individual psychotherapy session rendered during partial hospitalization, which included modifying the patient's obsessive-compulsive behavior.

_____

3. A physician performed a coronary angioplasty and percutaneous transcatheter placement of intracoronary stents in the left anterior descending coronary artery and the right inferior coronary artery.

_____

4. A 10-year-old patient received ESRD dialysis-related services daily from July 1 through July 10.

_____

5. A patient received a Rocephin intravenous (IV) push through an existing IV line. The IV was flushed with normal saline before and after administration of the antibiotic to check for patency and to clear the IV line.

_____

Summary

The Medicine section classifies procedures and services that are procedure-oriented, that apply to various medical specialties, and that apply to different types of health care providers. Guidelines located at the beginning of the Medicine section provide instruction about multiple procedures, add-on codes, separate procedures, subsection information, unlisted service or procedure, special reports, and materials supplied by the physician. Instructional notes appear throughout the Medicine section to provide coding clarification and direction. Almost every Medicine subsection contains notes unique to the subsection.

Internet Links

American Chiropractic Association: *www.acatoday.org*

American Medical Association: Go to *www.ama-assn.org*, scroll over Resources, click on Solutions for Managing Your Practice, click on CPT Coding, Medical Billing and Insurance, click on CPT(R), click on About CPT(R), and click on Category I Vaccine Codes to view "early release" vaccine product codes.

American Physical Therapy Association (APTA): *www.apta.org*

Chemotherapy: Go to *www.cancer.gov*, and scroll over About Cancer. Click on the Treatment link to view types of cancer treatment, include chemotherapy.

National Center for Complementary and Alternative Medicine: *www.nccam.nih.gov*

Study Checklist

- ❑ Read this chapter and highlight key concepts.
- ❑ Create an index card for each key term.
- ❑ Access the chapter Internet links to learn more about concepts.
- ❑ Complete the chapter exercises and review, verifying answers with your instructor.
- ❑ Complete Workbook chapter, verifying answers with your instructor.
- ❑ Go to *www.cengagebrain.com* to access the Student Companion Web Site. Login instructions are located in the Preface.
- ❑ Form a study group with classmates to discuss chapter concepts in preparation for an exam.

Review

Multiple Choice

Instructions: Circle the most appropriate response.

1. Which is a manual treatment performed to influence joint and neurophysiological function?
   a. Bilevel (biphasic) positive airway pressure (BiPAP)
   b. Chiropractic manipulative treatment (CMT)
   c. Intermittent positive pressure breathing (IPPB)
   d. Osteopathic manipulative treatment

2. A physician who specializes in physical medicine and rehabilitation and who treats acute/chronic pain and musculoskeletal disorders is a(n) _____.
   - a. doctor of osteopathy
   - b. internist
   - c. psychologist
   - d. physiatrist

3. Chemotherapy administered in addition to other cancer treatments, such as surgery and/or radiation therapy, is called _____ chemotherapy.
   - a. adjacent
   - b. adjudicate
   - c. adjunct
   - d. adjuvant

4. Which uses low-voltage electrodes that are placed on the scalp and target sites to test the nervous system's pathway?
   - a. Central motor evoked potential study
   - b. Orbicularis oculi (blink) test
   - c. Short-latency somatosensory evoked potential study
   - d. Visual evoked potential (VEP) test

5. Which is a biofeedback diagnostic test that measures muscle function using a pressure-sensitive tube?
   - a. Electrocardiography
   - b. Electromyogram
   - c. Manometry
   - d. Tensilon test

6. Which Medicine subsection classifies drug-induced depression of consciousness that requires no interventions to maintain airway patency or ventilation?
   - a. Moderate (Conscious) Sedation
   - b. Other Services and Procedures
   - c. Photodynamic Therapy
   - d. Noninvasive Vascular Diagnostic Studies

7. Which is considered an epicutaneous allergy sensitivity test?
   - a. Intradermal test
   - b. Patch test
   - c. Puncture test
   - d. Scratch test

8. End-stage renal disease (ESRD) codes include monitoring of nutrition, assessment of growth and development, and parental counseling for patients under the age of _____.
   - a. 14
   - b. 18
   - c. 20
   - d. 25

9. The Medicine section classifies procedures and services that are:
   - a. diagnosis-oriented and that apply to a limited number of medical specialties.
   - b. diagnosis-oriented and that apply to many medical specialties.
   - c. procedure-oriented and that apply to a limited number of medical specialties.
   - d. procedure-oriented and that apply to many medical specialties.

10. Codes for tests that evaluate autonomic nervous system functioning are classified in which heading in the Neurology and Neuromuscular Procedures subsection of Medicine?
    - a. Autonomic Function Tests
    - b. EEG Tests
    - c. Electromyography and Nerve Conduction Tests
    - d. Evoked Potentials and Reflex Tests

11. A 42-year-old patient received a hepatitis A immunization injection. Which CPT code(s) are assigned?
    - a. 90632, 90471
    - b. 90636, 90471
    - c. 90746, 90471
    - d. 90749, 90471

12. Binaural hearing aid check. Which CPT code is assigned?
     a. 92590   b. 92591   c. 92592   d. 92593

13. Cardiovascular stress test, bicycle with continuous electrocardiographic monitoring, interpretation and report only. Which CPT code is assigned?
     a. 93015   b. 93016   c. 93017   d. 93018

14. A 30-day, patient-initiated spirometric recording, including hook-up, reinforced education, data transmission and capture, trend analysis, and periodic recalibration as well as physician review and interpretation. Which CPT code is assigned?
     a. 94010   b. 94014   c. 94015   d. 94016

15. Inhalation bronchial challenge testing with histamine. Which CPT code is assigned?
     a. 95070   b. 95071   c. 95076   d. 95199

16. Comprehensive, computer-based motion analysis by videotaping and 3D kinematics, with dynamic plantar pressure measurements during walking. Which CPT code is assigned?
     a. 96000   b. 96001   c. 96004   d. 96002

17. Physical therapy reevaluation. Which CPT code is assigned?
     a. 97161   b. 97162   c. 97163   d. 97164

18. A patient and his wife received 30 minutes of face-to-face education and training from a qualified nurse practitioner for patient self-management of diabetic testing supplies. Which CPT code(s) are assigned?
     a. 98960   c. 98961
     b. 98960, 98960-59   d. 99078

19. During a therapeutic service, a 15-year-old patient required 15 minutes of moderate (conscious) sedation in addition to the normal anesthesia. The physician administered the sedation, and an independently trained observer monitored the patient's level of consciousness and physiological status for 30 minutes. Which CPT code is assigned?
     a. 99151   b. 99152   c. 99155   d. 99156

20. A psychiatrist used dolls to communicate with a 5-year-old patient during a psychiatric interview. Which CPT code is assigned?
     a. 90791   b. 90792   c. 90845   d. 90847

Coding Practice

Instructions: Assign CPT code(s) and appropriate modifier(s) to each case.

1. The patient's prescription for bifocal lens was recorded, facial measurements were taken, and adjustment of eyeglasses was done.

_____

2. The patient had the Wisconsin Card Sorting test done on November 15. This was done on a computer. A neuropsychologist interpreted the results and documented the report.

_____

3. The patient arrived at the office for an examination. The patient has never been seen in this practice. The patient complains of redness of both eyes and a decrease in visual acuity. After reviewing the patient's medical history, including medications, the patient's eyes are examined with the

ophthalmoscope. Using a slit lamp exam, several small healing ulcers of the right and left cornea are seen. The patient is given instructions for eye irrigation and a prescription for steroidal eye drops. DIAGNOSIS: viral keratitis.

_____

4. Patient presented for a Bernstein test. After insertion of a nasogastric (NG) tube, a solution was passed through the tube to record any complaints of chest pain. The first solution was saline, and the patient did not report any pain. The second solution was hydrochloric acid, and this solution did elicit a pain response in the patient. The Bernstein test was positive for esophagitis.

_____

5. Patient underwent a complete transcranial Doppler study of his intracranial arteries.

_____

6. The patient, a 7-year-old female, presented for visual reinforcement audiometry (VRA) evaluation. After being placed in a sound booth, both voice and lighted toys were used for hearing assessment. An audiogram recorded the findings, which were normal.

_____

7. The patient, a 14-year-old with cystic fibrosis, was seen for chest wall cupping to help clear mucous secretion. This initial demonstration was also observed by the patient's mother as a teaching opportunity for home care by the parent.

_____

8. Patient received outpatient cardiac rehab during the sixth week of his postoperative period. He had previously undergone coronary artery bypass graft surgery of four vessels. This session included exercise and a review of diet restrictions with the patient.

_____

9. Biofeedback for perineum and urethral muscles to assist with the patient's urine incontinence. Electromyogram (EMG) was used to measure contractions and muscle pressure.

_____

10. The patient presented three years' postimplantation of a dual-chamber pacemaker device. Analysis was done while the patient was at rest and while on a treadmill. No pacemaker reprogramming was needed.

_____

11. After placing the patient in the supine position, ultrasound was used to record cardiac function. The patient's ventricular septal defect (VSD), which is a congenital heart condition, was identified. The size of the defect was 2.0 mm. The remainder of the cardiac structures appeared normal in size and function.

_____

12. After placing the patient on the adjustment table, chiropractic manipulation of C7, T4, and L1 were performed to reduce subluxation and increase blood flow. The patient was scheduled for another appointment in one week's time.

_____

13. A 40-year-old male patient presented for a hepatitis A and hepatitis B vaccine. This was administered by the nursing staff, IM in the left arm.

_____

14. A primary care physician provided 30 minutes of training in using adaptive utensils for eating. During the encounter, safety procedures while cooking were also discussed with this patient, who has diagnoses of arthritis and type 2 diabetes mellitus.

_____

15. Patient was awake when electrodes were placed on his head for recording. An extended electro-encephalogram (EEG) was performed during a three-hour period. The patient was awake for the entire EEG.

_____

16. Gastric electrical activity was measured by placing electrodes on the patient's skin over his abdominal cavity. The recording of gastric activity showed that the patient had decreased activity in the large intestine.

_____

17. The patient presented with facial paralysis of the left side of the lower face. An electroneuronography was done to measure nerve conduction. Electrodes were placed over the site of the paralysis. DIAGNOSIS: Bell's palsy.

_____

18. A 25-year-old patient received intramuscular hepatitis B immune globulin (HBIG) (human) injection, which was administered by the nursing staff.

_____

19. Patient participated in a psychotherapy session for a total of 30 minutes. This session was done at a local community hospital in the mental health inpatient unit.

_____

20. After placing electrodes on the patient's chest, the heart's activity was recorded. The 12-lead strip was reviewed and a report was written by the attending physician.

_____

21. Under adequate anesthesia, incisions were made in the left leg of the patient for access of the femoral catheter. A second site allowed for insertion of the balloon-tipped catheter. After threading the balloon catheter to the heart, the blocked coronary artery was identified. The balloon was inflated, which resulted in movement of the arthrosclerosis plaque to the sides of the artery. The balloon catheter was advanced to the second blocked artery. The same inflation method was done, with good result. The balloon catheter was withdrawn. The incision sites were closed with sutures and pressure dressings.

_____

22. While the patient was exercising on a stationary bicycle, continuous electrocardiogram (ECG) monitoring and recording was done. The patient's cardiologist was in attendance for the entire 45-minute stress test. At the conclusion of the test, the physician provided a written report on the findings and the interpreted ECG recordings.

_____

23. Patient underwent gastroesophageal reflux test via esophagus, which included placement of nasal catheter pH electrodes, recording, analysis, and interpretation.

_____

24. A 15-year-old patient was recently diagnosed with asthma. A home health nurse visited on May 6 to provide training in the use of bronchodilators for both the patient and mother.

_____

25. A patient is status post left side cerebrovascular accident (CVA). He presents for physical therapy evaluation to regain strength and mobility on the left side. The patient will require three visits per week, beginning next week, with a reevaluation after 60 days of treatment.

_____

26. Using allergen vials specifically kept in the office for a certain patient, a pollen and grass mix was injected into the upper-right arm. A dust mites, cat dander, and feather mixture was injected into the patient's upper-left arm. The patient was observed in the waiting room for 30 minutes postinjection, with no reaction.

_____

27. Using a laser, approximately 25 pulses were delivered to a patient's psoriasis lesions on the elbows and forearms. Total area of treatment measured approximately 10 sq cm.

_____

28. Rabies immune globulin was administered intramuscularly (IM) to the patient's upper-left arm.

_____

29. ESRD services for a 25-year-old male for the month of September. Number of visits to a physician for the month totaled 4.

_____

30. Intravenous (IV) infusion of chemotherapy drugs, two hours.

_____

Insurance and Reimbursement Overview

Insurance and Reimbursement

Chapter Outline

Third-Party Payers

Provisions of the Affordable Care Act of 2010

Health Care Reimbursement Systems

Impact of HIPAA on Reimbursement

Health Reform

Chapter Objectives

At the conclusion of this chapter, the student should be able to:

- Define key terms.
- Identify and provide examples of third-party payers.
- List and define each health care reimbursement system.
- Describe the impact of HIPAA on health care reimbursement.
- Explain the components of health reform, as delineated in the Affordable Care Act.

Key Terms

abuse

ambulance fee schedule

ambulatory payment classification (APC)

ambulatory surgical center (ASC) payment rate

ANSI ASC X12N 837

Balanced Budget Act of 1997

Balanced Budget Refinement Act of 1999 (BBRA)

BlueCross and BlueShield (BCBS)

breach of confidentiality

cafeteria plan

capitation

case mix

case-mix adjustment

charge description master (CDM)

chargemaster

chargemaster review process

check digit

Civil Monetary Penalties Act

Civilian Health and Medical Program of the Department of Veterans Affairs (CHAMPVA)

clinical laboratory fee schedule

closed-panel HMO

commercial payer

compliance guidance

confidentiality

Consolidated Omnibus Budget Reconciliation Act of 1985

consumer-directed health plan (CDHP)

conversion factor

covered benefit

covered entity

critical pathways

customized sub-capitation plan (CSCP)

decrypt

Deficit Reduction Act of 1984

Designated Standard Maintenance Organization (DSMO)

diagnosis-related groups (DRGs)

digital

direct contract model HMO

disclosed

DRG creep

durable medical equipment,

prosthetics, orthotics, and supplies (DMEPOS) fee schedule

electronic data interchange (EDI)

electronic transaction standard

employer self-insurance plan

encounter form

encrypt

end-stage renal disease (ESRD) composite payment rate system

exclusion

exclusive provider organization (EPO)

explanation of benefits (EOB)

False Claims Act (FCA)

Federal Anti-kickback Statute

Federal Claims Collection Act of 1966

Federal Employee Health Benefits Program (FEHBP or FEP)

fee schedule

fee-for-service

flat file

flexible spending account (FSA)

fraud

government-sponsored programs

group model HMO

group practice without walls (GPWW)

health care reimbursement account (HCRA)

health insurance claim

health insurance policy

health maintenance organization (HMO)

health reimbursement arrangement (HRA)

health savings account (HSA)

health savings security account (HSSA)

HIPAA administrative simplification (AS)

HIPAA standards for privacy of individually identifiable health information

hold harmless clause

Home Assessment Validation and Entry (HAVEN)

home health prospective payment system (HH PPS)

indemnification

Indian Health Service (IHS)

individual practice association (IPA) HMO

inpatient prospective payment system (IPPS)

inpatient psychiatric facility prospective payment system (IPF PPS)

inpatient rehabilitation facility prospective payment system (IRF PPS)

integrated delivery system (IDS)

integrated provider organization (IPO)

intensity of services (IS)

IPPS 3-day payment window

IPPS 72-hour rule

IPPS transfer rule

IRF PPS 1-day payment window

IRF PPS 24-hour rule

IRF PPS transfer rule

long-term (acute) care hospital prospective payment system (LTCH PPS)

LTCH PPS 1-day payment window

LTCH PPS 24-hour rule

major diagnostic category (MDC)

managed care

management service organization (MSO)

Medicaid

medical foundation

Medicare

Medicare administrative contractor (MAC)

Medicare physician fee schedule (MPFS)

Medicare Prescription Drug, Improvement, and Modernization Act of 2003 (MMA)

Medicare severity diagnosis-related groups (MS-DRGs)

Medicare severity long-term (acute) care diagnosis-related groups (MS-LTCH-DRGs)

Medicare Summary Notice (MSN)

Military Health System (MHS)

minimum data set (MDS)

national health plan identifier (HPID)

national individual identifier (patient identifier)

national limitation amount (NLA)

national provider identifier (NPI)

national standard employer identifier number (EIN)

network model HMO

network provider

noncovered benefits

nonparticipating provider (nonPAR)

Omnibus Budget Reconciliation Act of 1980

Omnibus Budget Reconciliation Act of 1987 (OBRA)

Omnibus Budget Reconciliation Act of 1989

Omnibus Consolidated and Emergency Supplemental Appropriations Act (OCESAA) of 1999

open-panel HMO

outlier

outpatient encounter

outpatient prospective payment system (OPPS)

outpatient visit

overpayment

overpayment recovery

participating provider (PAR)

Payment Error and Prevention Program (PEPP)

physician-hospital organization (PHO)

Physicians at Teaching Hospitals (PATH) initiative

physician self-referral law

point-of-service plan (POS)

preauthorization

pre-existing medical condition

preferred provider organization (PPO)

present on admission (POA) indicator

privacy

privacy rule

privileged communication

Programs of All-inclusive Care for the Elderly (PACE)

prospective cost-based rate

prospective payment system (PPS)

prospective price-based rate

protected health information (PHI)

relative value unit (RVU)

remittance advice (remit)

Resident Assessment Validation and Entry (RAVEN)

resource-based relative value scale (RBRVS) system

resource utilization group (RUG)

revenue code

roster billing

safe harbor regulation

security

security rule

self-referral

severity of illness (SI)

skilled nursing facility prospective payment system (SNF PPS)

staff model HMO

Stark I

Stark II

State Children's Health Insurance Program (SCHIP)

status indicator (SI)

superbill

Tax Equity and Fiscal Responsibility Act of 1983 (TEFRA)

TRICARE

triple option plan

value-based purchasing (VBP)

wage index

workers' compensation

Introduction

This chapter includes a discussion of third-party payers, health care reimbursement methodologies, and the impact of HIPAA on health care reimbursement. Third-party payers process health insurance claims to reimburse providers (e.g., physicians, health care facilities) for services provided to patients for covered benefits. Health care reimbursement methodologies were originally developed by the Centers for Medicare & Medicaid Services (CMS) to control health care costs associated with government programs; however, most third-party payers have also adopted them. HIPAA has impacted health care reimbursement as a result of the implementation of federal regulations such as administrative simplification, privacy and security of protected health information, and more.

Third-Party Payers

A third-party payer is an insurance company or other organization (e.g., a Medicare administrative contractor) that processes health care claims for reimbursement of procedures and services. Payers serve as **Medicare administrative contractors (MACs)** by processing claims for physicians (Medicare Part B); health care facilities (Medicare Part A); suppliers of durable medical equipment, prosthetics, orthotics, and supplies (DMEPOS); and home health and hospice agencies. The CMS, an administrative agency in the Department of Health & Human Services (DHHS), selects the MACs through a competitive bidding process.

Title IX of the **Medicare Prescription Drug, Improvement, and Modernization Act of 2003 (MMA)** called for the elimination of carriers, fiscal intermediaries (FIs), and durable medical equipment regional carriers (DMERCs) and the creation of Medicare administrative contractors. The MMA limits **indemnification** (insurance against loss) for adverse judgments against MACs and associated legal costs. Providers no longer nominate carriers or FIs, and they also no longer have a right to choose who will review claims or pay benefits. MACs integrate Medicare Part A and Part B functions into one contract, and providers have a single point of contact for all claims-related activity. MACs have been established in 15 jurisdictions throughout the United States, and eight specialty MACs were also created to process durable medical equipment claims and home health care claims (four MACs for each).

 Note:

> By 2010, Medicare had eliminated the following to create 23 Medicare Administrative Contractors (MACs) that consolidated the administration of Medicare Part A and B benefits so that Medicare beneficiaries have claims processed by one contractor.
>
> - *Carriers* (processed Medicare Part B claims)
>
> - *Fiscal intermediaries (FIs)* (processed Medicare Part A claims)

- *Durable medical equipment carriers (DMERCs)* (processed durable medical equipment, prosthetics, orthotics, and supplies [DMEPOS])

Durable medical equipment, prosthetics, orthotics, and supplies (DMEPOS) claims are processed by DME MACs, and home health and hospice (HH&H) claims are processed by HH&H MACs.

A **health insurance policy** is an agreement between an individual and a third-party payer (or insurance company) that contains a list of reimbursable medical benefits, or **covered benefits** (which might include office visits, inpatient hospitalizations, laboratory, tests, prescription medications, treatment services, and so on). The policy also lists procedures and services that are *not* covered by the third-party payer, called **noncovered benefits**, and when an individual undergoes procedures or receives services that are not covered by the policy, the individual is responsible for reimbursing the health care provider directly (e.g., with cosmetic surgery). A health care provider is a physician or other health care practitioner (e.g., a nurse practitioner) who provides services to patients.

After patient care has been delivered, the provider submits a **health insurance claim** to an insurance plan to request reimbursement for procedures performed or services provided (e.g., CMS-1500, UB-04). The CMS-1500 (Figure 19-1) is a standard claim submitted by physician offices to third-party payers. The UB-04 (or CMS-1450) (Uniform Bill, first implemented as the UB-92 in 1992 and revised to create the UB-04 in 2004, which was implemented in 2007) (Figure 19-2) is a standard claim submitted by health care institutions to payers for inpatient and outpatient services. CMS-1500 and UB-04 claims can also be submitted as electronic data interchange (EDI) transactions using specialized software (Figure 19-3), which is discussed later in this chapter.

Effective March 1, 2007, health plans and health care clearinghouses were required to accept the new UB-04. A health care clearinghouse processes or facilitates the processing of health information (such as a claim) received from another entity (such as a provider or payer) from a nonstandard into a standard format.

Determining which claim (e.g., CMS-1500, UB-04) to submit, as well as which coding system to use to report codes on the claim, depends on the health care setting (Table 19-1). Noninstitutional providers (e.g., physician offices, independent labs, ambulance companies that are not associated with a hospital, ambulatory surgery centers, and independent diagnostic testing facilities) and suppliers (for durable medical equipment, prosthetics, orthotics, and supplies dealers) submit the CMS-1500 claim to third-party payers, and they report ICD-10-CM diagnosis and HCPCS/CPT procedure and service codes (and HCPCS/CPT modifiers). Institutional providers (e.g., hospitals, nursing facilities, comprehensive outpatient rehabilitation facilities, community mental health centers, outpatient physical therapy facilities, rehabilitation agencies, and end-stage renal facilities) submit the UB-04 (or CMS-1450) claim to payers. For inpatient claims, ICD-10-CM diagnosis and ICD-10-PCS procedure codes are reported, and for outpatient claims (e.g., emergency department and outpatient care), ICD-10-CM diagnosis and HCPCS/CPT procedure and service codes (and HCPCS/CPT modifiers) are reported.

Before delivering health care services to patients, some payers require providers to obtain **preauthorization** (prior approval) of treatment (e.g., when specialists are involved) and to submit post-treatment reports. If the provider does not meet the preauthorization requirements, the claim is denied. If the patient's insurance policy contains a **hold harmless clause** (which holds that the patient is not responsible for paying what the insurance plan denies), the health care provider is prohibited from collecting payment from the patient. Claims are also denied if the medical necessity of procedures or services is not established. This means that every procedure or service reported on the claim must be linked to a condition that justifies the necessity for performing that procedure or providing that service. If the procedures or services delivered are determined to be unreasonable or unnecessary, the claim is denied.

Health Insurance Marketplace

The *Patient Protection and Affordable Care Act (PPACA)* was signed into federal law on March 23, 2010, and resulted in the creation of a *Health Insurance Marketplace* (or *health insurance exchange*), abbreviated as the Marketplace, effective October 1, 2013. The PPACA is abbreviated as the *Affordable Care Act (ACA)*, and it has been nicknamed *Obamacare* (because it was signed into federal law by President Obama). *The Health Insurance Marketplace does NOT replace other health insurance programs (e.g., individual and group commercial health insurance, Medicaid, Medicare, TRICARE).*

HEALTH INSURANCE CLAIM FORM

APPROVED BY NATIONAL UNIFORM CLAIM COMMITTEE (NUCC) 02/12

Courtesy of the Centers for Medicare & Medicaid Services, www.cms.gov; Copyright © 2018 Cengage Learning®

CARRIER

| | PICA | | | | | | | | | | | PICA | |

1. MEDICARE ☐ (Medicare#) MEDICAID ☐ (Medicaid#) TRICARE ☐ (ID#/DoD#) CHAMPVA ☐ (Member ID#) GROUP HEALTH PLAN ☐ (ID#) FECA BLK LUNG ☐ (ID#) OTHER ☒ (ID#)

1a. INSURED'S I.D. NUMBER (For Program in Item 1)
225120661W

2. PATIENT'S NAME (Last Name, First Name, Middle Initial)
PUBLIC, JOHN, Q

3. PATIENT'S BIRTH DATE
MM **03** DD **09** YY **1945** SEX M ☒ F ☐

4. INSURED'S NAME (Last Name, First Name, Middle Initial)
PUBLIC, JOHN, Q

5. PATIENT'S ADDRESS (No., Street)
10A SENATE AVENUE

6. PATIENT RELATIONSHIP TO INSURED
Self ☒ Spouse ☐ Child ☐ Other ☐

7. INSURED'S ADDRESS (No., Street)
10A SENATE AVENUE

CITY **ANYWHERE** STATE **NY**

8. RESERVED FOR NUCC USE

CITY **ANYWHERE** STATE **NY**

ZIP CODE **12345-1234** TELEPHONE (Include Area Code) **(101) 2017891**

ZIP CODE **12345-1234** TELEPHONE (Include Area Code) **(101) 2017891**

9. OTHER INSURED'S NAME (Last Name, First Name, Middle Initial)

10. IS PATIENT'S CONDITION RELATED TO:

11. INSURED'S POLICY GROUP OR FECA NUMBER

a. OTHER INSURED'S POLICY OR GROUP NUMBER

a. EMPLOYMENT? (Current or Previous) YES ☐ NO ☒

a. INSURED'S DATE OF BIRTH
MM **03** DD **09** YY **1945** SEX M ☒ F ☐

b. RESERVED FOR NUCC USE

b. AUTO ACCIDENT? YES ☐ NO ☒ PLACE (State)

b. OTHER CLAIM ID (Designated by NUCC)

c. RESERVED FOR NUCC USE

c. OTHER ACCIDENT? YES ☐ NO ☒

c. INSURANCE PLAN NAME OR PROGRAM NAME
METROPOLITAN

d. INSURANCE PLAN NAME OR PROGRAM NAME

10d. CLAIM CODES (Designated by NUCC)

d. IS THERE ANOTHER HEALTH BENEFIT PLAN?
YES ☐ NO ☒ *If yes*, complete items 9, 9a, and 9d.

READ BACK OF FORM BEFORE COMPLETING & SIGNING THIS FORM.
12. PATIENT'S OR AUTHORIZED PERSON'S SIGNATURE I authorize the release of any medical or other information necessary to process this claim. I also request payment of government benefits either to myself or to the party who accepts assignment below.

SIGNED **SIGNATURE ON FILE** DATE

13. INSURED'S OR AUTHORIZED PERSON'S SIGNATURE I authorize payment of medical benefits to the undersigned physician or supplier for services described below.

SIGNED **SIGNATURE ON FILE**

PATIENT AND INSURED INFORMATION

14. DATE OF CURRENT ILLNESS, INJURY, or PREGNANCY (LMP)
MM **01** DD **05** YY **YYYY** QUAL. **431**

15. OTHER DATE QUAL. MM DD YY

16. DATES PATIENT UNABLE TO WORK IN CURRENT OCCUPATION
FROM MM DD YY TO MM DD YY

17. NAME OF REFERRING PROVIDER OR OTHER SOURCE
DN IVAN GOODOC MD

17a.
17b. NPI **3456789012**

18. HOSPITALIZATION DATES RELATED TO CURRENT SERVICES
FROM MM DD YY TO MM DD YY

19. ADDITIONAL CLAIM INFORMATION (Designated by NUCC)

20. OUTSIDE LAB? YES ☐ NO ☒ $ CHARGES

21. DIAGNOSIS OR NATURE OF ILLNESS OR INJURY Relate A-L to service line below (24E) ICD Ind. **0**

A. **J18.0** B. **R35.0** C. D.
E. F. G. H.
I. J. K. L.

22. RESUBMISSION CODE ORIGINAL REF. NO.

23. PRIOR AUTHORIZATION NUMBER

24. A. DATE(S) OF SERVICE From MM DD YY	To MM DD YY	B. PLACE OF SERVICE	C. EMG	D. PROCEDURES, SERVICES, OR SUPPLIES (Explain Unusual Circumstances) CPT/HCPCS	MODIFIER	E. DIAGNOSIS POINTER	F. $ CHARGES	G. DAYS OR UNITS	H. EPSDT Family Plan	I. ID. QUAL.	J. RENDERING PROVIDER ID. #
1 01 09 YY		11		99213		A	75 00	1		NPI	
2 01 09 YY		11		81001		B	10 00	1		NPI	
3 01 09 YY		11		71020		A	50 00	1		NPI	
4										NPI	
5										NPI	
6										NPI	

25. FEDERAL TAX I.D. NUMBER **111234523** SSN ☐ EIN ☒

26. PATIENT'S ACCOUNT NO. **12-1**

27. ACCEPT ASSIGNMENT? (For govt. claims, see back) YES ☒ NO ☐

28. TOTAL CHARGE $ **135 00**

29. AMOUNT PAID $ **10 00**

30. Rsvd for NUCC Use

31. SIGNATURE OF PHYSICIAN OR SUPPLIER INCLUDING DEGREES OR CREDENTIALS (I certify that the statements on the reverse apply to this bill and are made a part thereof.)

SIGNED **ERIN A HELPER MD** DATE **MMDDYYYY**

32. SERVICE FACILITY LOCATION INFORMATION
a. NPI b.

33. BILLING PROVIDER INFO & PH # **(101) 1111234**
ERIN A HELPER MD
101 MEDIC DRIVE
ANYWHERE NY 12345
a. **1234567890** b.

NUCC Instruction Manual available at: www.nucc.org PLEASE PRINT OR TYPE

PHYSICIAN OR SUPPLIER INFORMATION

Figure 19-1 Completed CMS-1500 claim

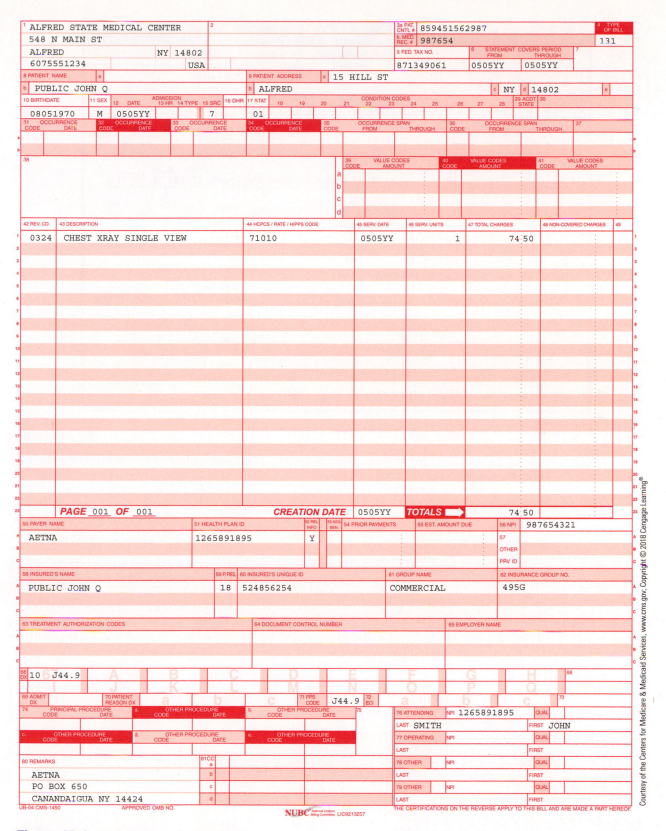

Figure 19-2 Completed UB-04 claim

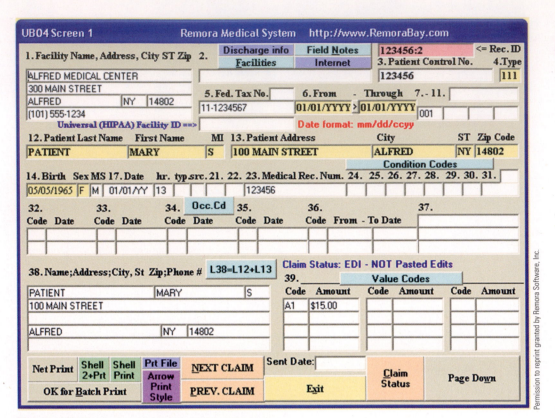

Figure 19-3 Sample UB-04 software screen

The Marketplace allows Americans to purchase health coverage that fits their budget and meets their needs. It is a resource where individuals, families, and small businesses can:

- Learn about their health coverage options
- Compare health insurance plans based on costs, benefits, and other important features
- Choose a plan
- Enroll in coverage

The Marketplace includes information about programs to help people with low to moderate income and resources pay for health coverage. Information includes ways to save on the monthly premiums and out-of-pocket costs of coverage available through the Marketplace and information about other programs, including Medicaid and the State Children's Health Insurance Program (SCHIP). The Marketplace encourages competition among private health plans, and it is accessible through websites, call centers, and in-person assistance. In some states it is run by the state, and in others it is run by the federal government.

Most individuals who do not currently have health insurance through their place of work or otherwise are eligible to use the Health Insurance Marketplace (www.healthcare.gov) to compare and choose a plan. To be eligible for health coverage through the marketplace, individuals must:

- Be a U.S. citizen or national (or be lawfully present)
- Live in the United States
- Not be incarcerated

Types of Third-Party Payers

Third-party payers include the following:

- BlueCross and BlueShield (BCBS)
- Commercial insurance companies

Table 19-1 Claims and Coding Systems According to Type of Health Care Setting

Claim	Codes Reported	Health Care Setting
CMS-1491	ICD-10-CM diagnosis codes and HCPCS level II	Ambulance services
CMS-1500	ICD-10-CM diagnosis codes, CPT, and HCPCS level II	Noninstitutional providers and suppliers • Ambulatory surgery centers[1] • Anesthesiologists who administer hospital-based inpatient and outpatient anesthesia • Certified portable x-ray services • Home health agencies and hospices[2] • Independent clinical laboratories located at physician offices, group practices, hospitals, nursing facilities, end-stage renal disease facilities, pharmacies, home health agencies, rural health clinics, health fairs, anatomical testing laboratories, and nuclear medicine providers • Independent diagnostic testing facilities (e.g., a certified mammography center) • Physician, chiropractor, optometrist, and podiatrist offices • Privately practicing occupational therapists and physical therapists • Roster billing[3] for flu and pneumonia vaccinations
UB-04	ICD-10-CM diagnosis and ICD-10-PCS procedure codes	Institutional providers (inpatient) • Acute care hospitals • Long-term care facilities • Psychiatric hospitals • Rehabilitation facilities • Short-term hospitals • Hospices (inpatient respite care)[4]
UB-04	ICD-10-CM diagnosis codes, CPT, and HCPCS level II	Institutional providers (outpatient) • Hospital emergency departments • Hospital outpatient departments
UB-04	ICD-10-CM diagnosis codes, CPT, HCPCS level II, and HIPPS codes	Noninstitutional providers (outpatient) • Home health agencies[5] • Hospices (home care)[5]

[1]Some ambulatory surgery centers submit the UB-04 claim instead of the CMS-1500 claim.

[2]Some home health agencies and hospices submit the UB-04 claim instead of the CMS-1500 claim.

[3]**Roster billing** is a simplified process available to public health clinics and other noninstitutional entities that offer mass immunization programs. Hospices also submit claims for the administration of pneumococcal pneumonia, influenza virus, and hepatitis B vaccines.

[4]Respite care includes services that provide primary caregivers (e.g., the spouse of a terminally ill person) with temporary relief from tasks associated with caregiving (e.g., in-home assistance, short hospital or nursing facility stays, adult day care).

[5]Physicians who are not employees of the HHA and/or hospice and who provide professional home care services for home health agencies and hospices submit claims with ICD-10-CM diagnosis codes and CPT and HCPCS level II procedure/service codes.

• Employer self-insurance plans

• Government-sponsored programs (e.g., Medicare)

• Managed care plans (e.g., HMO)

• Workers' compensation

Note:

Patient data and ICD-10-CM/PCS, CPT, and/or HCPCS level II codes that are entered in the hospital's computer system populate the UB-04 claim, and the hospital's billing department reviews the completed UB-04 claim for accuracy and submits it to third-party payers.

When third-party payers deny a claim, the billing department collaborates with the health information department to re-review the submitted claim to fix data entry and coding errors. If codes submitted were correct, the billing department and health information department also collaborate when writing an appeal to the third-party payer, which may include supporting patient record documentation.

BlueCross and BlueShield (BCBS)

BlueCross and BlueShield (BCBS) payers cover the costs of hospital care and physicians' services. BlueCross initially covered just hospital care, and BlueShield covered just physicians' services; today, both offer a full range of health care coverage. While each independent BCBS plan serves its local community, its membership in the BCBS Association allows it to link with other local plans so that regional and national employers can be served (e.g., an employee can receive health care services while traveling).

Note:

In some states (e.g., California, Idaho, and Washington), BCBS payers are organized as two separate insurance companies. In other states (e.g., Missouri, New York, and Pennsylvania), BCBS payers are organized as multiple insurance companies according to region.

Commercial Payers

Commercial payers include private health insurance and employer-based group health insurance. Private health insurance usually consists of an indemnity plan, which covers individuals for certain health care expenses. The insurance company reimburses the patient or the provider, depending on the contract language. Individuals pay annual premiums (with predetermined rates).

Employer-based group health insurance is often provided as an employee benefit. The employer typically pays 80 percent of insurance premiums, and the employee pays the remaining 20 percent. The employer generally contracts with a commercial health insurance plan (e.g., Aetna).

Employer Self-Insurance Plans

For **employer self-insurance plans**, an employer accepts direct responsibility (or the risk) for paying employees' health care without purchasing health insurance and creates an employer self-insurance plan. Usually, the plan contracts with a third-party administrator (TPA), which is an organization that provides the following services to employers (and insurance companies):

- *Benefit design*: Medical services covered by the plan

- *Claims administration*: Processing claims to reimburse services

- *Utilization review or utilization management*: Reviewing medical care for appropriateness, necessity, and quality (e.g., preadmission authorization)

Government-Sponsored Programs

 Note:

The Recovery Audit Contractor (RAC) program was implemented nationwide in 2009 as part of the Medicare Prescription Drug, Improvement, and Modernization Act of 2003 (MMA), and four regional RACs were named. Its purpose is to safeguard the Medicare Trust Fund by having RACs evaluate individual provider compliance to (1) identify overpayments (and underpayments) made by Medicare and Medicaid and (2) recover overpayments made to durable medical equipment (DME) providers, health care facilities, and physician practices. For example, RACs use proprietary software to detect errors in codes reported on CMS-1500 claims. (Go to www.cms.gov/rac to review results of RAC activity.) RACs also monitor Medicare's post-acute care transfer (PACT) policy that can result in reduced payments for transferring hospitals, depending on the discharge status code reported (e.g., 03-Medicare SNF with Medicare certification in anticipation of skilled care).

RACs are not the same as Medicare's Comprehensive Error Rate Testing (CERT) program, which was implemented in 2003 (and currently operates parallel to the RAC program) to evaluate Medicare administrative contractors' (MAC) program performance. For example, CERT assesses the ability of an MAC to detect errors that are considered fraudulent.

The MMA also imposed Medicare fee-for-service contracting reform, directing CMS to use competitive measures to replace the Medicare fiscal intermediaries and carriers with MACs. CMS also established Zone Program Integrity Contractors (ZPICs) to perform program integrity functions in the newly established MAC jurisdictions (or zones). ZPICs are expected to perform program integrity functions for Medicare Parts A through D, DME, home health, hospice, and Medi-Medi programs.

Government-sponsored programs include:

- CHAMPVA
- Federal Employee Health Benefits Program (FEHBP or FEP)
- Indian Health Service (IHS)
- Medicaid and SCHIP
- Medicare
- Military Health System (MHS)
- Programs of All-inclusive Care for the Elderly (PACE)
- TRICARE

The **Civilian Health and Medical Program of the Department of Veterans Affairs (CHAMPVA)** program provides health care benefits to dependents of veterans who

- Are rated as 100 percent permanently and totally disabled as a result of service-connected conditions
- Died as a result of service-connected conditions
- Died on duty with fewer than 30 days of active service

The **Federal Employee Health Benefits Program (FEHBP or FEP)** is a voluntary health care program that covers federal employees, retirees, and their dependents and survivors. The **Indian Health Service (IHS)** is a DHHS agency that provides federal health care services to American Indians and Alaska natives.

Medicaid (Title XIX of the Social Security Act Amendments of 1965) is a joint federal and state program that provides health care coverage to low-income populations and certain aged and disabled individuals. It is an entitlement program that is jointly financed by state and federal governments, with federal spending levels determined by the number of participants and services provided. The **State Children's Health Insurance Program (SCHIP)** was established to provide health assistance to uninsured, low-income children either through separate programs or through expanded eligibility under state Medicaid programs.

Medicare (Title XVIII of the Social Security Act Amendments of 1965) provides health care coverage to elderly and disabled persons; federal spending is funded by the Medicare Trust Fund (payroll tax). Medicare administrative contractors review local coverage determinations (LCDs) and national coverage determinations (NCDs) to specify under what clinical circumstances a service is covered, considered to be reasonable and necessary, and correctly coded. The **Programs of All-inclusive Care for the Elderly (PACE)** are community-based Medicare and Medicaid programs that provide integrated health care and long-term care services to elderly persons who require a nursing-facility level of care.

The **Military Health System (MHS)** provides and maintains readiness to provide health care services and support to members of the Uniformed Services during military operations. It also provides health care services and support to members of the Uniformed Services, their family members, and others entitled to Department of Defense health care.

TRICARE is the military health plan that covers active duty and retired members of the Uniformed Services and their dependents. It combines military health care resources (e.g., military treatment facilities) and networks of civilian health care professionals. TRICARE was formerly called CHAMPUS (Civilian Health and Medical Program of the United States).

Managed Care

Managed care combines the financing and delivery of health care services to replace conventional fee-for-service health insurance plans with more affordable care for consumers and providers who agree to certain restrictions (e.g., patients receive care from participating providers). (Managed care plans range from structured closed-panel staff model health maintenance organizations to less structured preferred provider organizations.)

A **participating provider (PAR)** is a member of a managed care plan, while a **nonparticipating provider (nonPAR)** is not a member of the plan. (PAR and nonPAR providers are also associated with traditional health insurance plans. Patients may incur higher out-of-pocket costs when receiving care from nonPARs.)

Fee-for-service plans reimburse providers for individual health care services rendered, while managed care is financed according to a method called **capitation**. *Capitation* is the term used when providers accept preestablished payments for providing health care services to enrollees over a period of time, usually one year. If the managed care physician provides services that cost less than the capitation amount, the physician keeps any profits. If services provided cost more than the capitation amount, the physician loses money. Patients who subscribe to managed care plans receive care from *their primary care provider (PCP)*, the physician responsible for supervising and coordinating health care services, for preauthorizing referrals to specialists, and for inpatient hospital admissions, except in emergencies.

Types of managed care plans include the following:

- Exclusive provider organization (EPO)
- Health maintenance organization (HMO)
- Point-of-service plan (POS)
- Preferred provider organization (PPO)
- Triple option plan (TPO) (also called cafeteria plan)

Exclusive Provider Organization

An **exclusive provider organization (EPO)** is a managed care plan that provides benefits to subscribers if they receive services from network providers. (EPOs are regulated by state insurance departments.) A **network provider** is a physician or health care facility under contract to the managed care plan. Network providers usually sign exclusive contracts with the EPO, which means they cannot contract with other managed care plans. Subscribers are generally required to coordinate health care services through their PCP.

An **integrated delivery system (IDS)** is an organization of affiliated provider sites (e.g., hospitals, ambulatory surgical centers, or physician groups) that offer joint health care services to subscribers. Integrated delivery systems are also known as

- Accountable health plans
- Delivery systems
- Health delivery networks
- Horizontally integrated systems

- Vertically integrated systems
- Vertically integrated plans (VIPs)
- Integrated service networks (ISNs)

Integrated delivery system models include the following:

- **Physician-hospital organization (PHO)**: Owned by hospital(s) and physician groups that obtain managed care plan contracts; physicians maintain their own practices and provide health care services to plan members

- **Management service organization (MSO)**: Usually owned by physicians or a hospital; provides practice management and administrative and support services to individual physician practices

- **Group practice without walls (GPWW)**: Establishes a contract that allows physicians to maintain their own offices and share services such as appointment scheduling and billing

- **Integrated provider organization (IPO)**: Manages the delivery of health care services offered by hospitals, physicians who are employees of the IPO, and other health care organizations such as ambulatory surgery clinics and nursing facilities

- **Medical foundation**: Nonprofit organization that contracts with and acquires the clinical and business assets of physician practices; the foundation is assigned a provider number and manages the practice's business

Health Maintenance Organization

A **health maintenance organization (HMO)** is an alternative to traditional group health insurance coverage that provides comprehensive health care services to voluntarily enrolled members on a prepaid basis. It provides preventive care services to promote "wellness" or good health, thus reducing the overall cost of medical care. An HMO often requires patients to pay a *copayment* (or *copay*), which is a fee paid by the patient to the provider at the time health care services are rendered.

HMOs must meet requirements of the HMO Act of 1973 as well as rules and regulations of individual states. They are organized in the following way:

- **Closed-panel HMO**: Health care is provided in an HMO-owned center or satellite clinic, or by physicians who belong to a specially formed medical group that serves the HMO.

- **Open-panel HMO**: Health care is provided by individuals who are not employees of the HMO or who do not belong to a specially formed medical group that serves the HMO.

Closed-panel HMOs include the following models:

- **Group model HMO**: Contracted health care services are delivered to subscribers by participating physicians *who are members of an independent multispecialty group practice*.

- **Staff model HMO**: Health care services are provided to subscribers by *physicians employed by the HMO*.

Open-panel HMOs include the following models:

- **Direct contract model HMO**: Contracted health care services are delivered to subscribers by *individual physicians in the community*.

- **Individual practice association (IPA) HMO**: Contracted health care services are delivered to subscribers by *physicians who remain in their independent office settings*.

- **Network model HMO**: Contracted health care services are provided to subscribers by *two or more physician multispecialty group practices*.

Point-of-Service Plan

A **point-of-service plan (POS)** offers patients the freedom to use an HMO panel of providers or to self-refer to non-HMO providers. If the enrollee chooses to receive all medical care from the HMO network of health care providers or obtains an authorization from the POS primary care physician for specialty care outside the

HMO network, the enrollee pays only the regular copayment or a small charge for the visit, and no deductible or coinsurance responsibility applies. If the enrollee sees a non-HMO panel specialist without a referral from the PCP, this is called a **self-referral**, and the enrollee will have greater out-of-pocket expenses (e.g., a large deductible of about $250 plus 20 percent of coinsurance charges).

Preferred Provider Organization

A **preferred provider organization (PPO)** is a network of physicians and hospitals that join together to contract with insurance companies, employers, or other organizations. PPOs provide health care to subscribers for a discounted fee.

Triple Option Plan (or Cafeteria Plan)

A **triple option plan**, or **cafeteria plan**, is offered by either a single insurance plan or as a joint venture among two or more third-party payers. They provide a choice of HMO, PPO, or traditional health insurance plans.

Consumer-Directed Health Plan

Managed care is currently challenged by the growth of consumer-directed health plans, which define employer contributions and ask employees to be more responsible for health care decisions and cost-sharing. A **consumer-directed health plan (CDHP)** is a sort of "401(k) plan" for health care. It includes many choices that provide individuals with an incentive to control the costs of health benefits and health care. Individuals have greater freedom in spending health care dollars up to a designated amount and can receive full coverage for in-network preventive care. In return, individuals assume significantly higher cost-sharing expenses after the designated amount has been expended. (The catastrophic limit is usually higher than those common in other plans.)

The CDHP has become a popular alternative to the increased costs of traditional health insurance premiums and the limitations associated with managed care plans. They include the following tiers:

- *Tax-exempt account*, which is used to pay for health care expenses and provides more flexibility than traditional managed care plans in terms of access to providers and services

- *Out-of-pocket payments for health care expenses*, which are made after the tax-exempt account is expended and before the deductible for high-deductible insurance has been met; this tier actually represents a gap in coverage

- *High-deductible insurance policy*, which reimburses allowable health care expenses after the high deductible has been paid

The CDHPs usually provides Internet-based support so individuals can track health care expenses, improve their health by viewing useful information and learning about preventive services, obtain information about provider quality, and receive notification about provider group-rate pricing. A variety of types of consumer-directed health plans are available to individuals, all of which are subject to modification as legislation is passed and payers alter program requirements.

CDHPs include the following types:

- Customized sub-capitation plan (CSCP)
- Flexible spending account (FSA)
- Health reimbursement arrangement (HRA)
- Health care reimbursement account (HCRA)

Customized Sub-Capitation Plan

A **customized sub-capitation plan (CSCP)** funds health care expenses with insurance coverage, and the individual selects one of each type of provider to create a customized network and pays the resulting customized insurance premium. Each provider is paid a fixed amount per month to provide only the care that an individual needs from that provider (*a sub-capitation payment*).

Flexible Spending Account

A **flexible spending account (FSA)** is a tax-exempt account offered by employers to any number of employees, which individuals use to pay health care bills. Employees contribute funds to the FSA through a salary reduction agreement and withdraw funds to pay medical bills. Funds in an FSA are exempt from both income tax and Social Security tax. (Employers may also contribute to FSAs.) By law, employees forfeit unspent funds remaining in the FSA at the end of the year.

Health Savings Account or Health Savings Security Account

A **health savings account (HSA)** or **health savings security account (HSSA)** allows participants to enroll in a relatively inexpensive, high-deductible insurance plan, and a tax-deductible savings account is opened to cover current and future medical expenses. Money deposited (and earnings) is tax-deferred, and money is withdrawn to cover qualified medical expenses tax-free. Money can be withdrawn for purposes other than health care expenses after payment of income tax, plus a 15 percent penalty. Unused balances "roll over" from year to year, and if an employee changes jobs, the HSA or HSSA can continue to be used to pay for qualified health care expenses.

Health Care Reimbursement Account

A **health care reimbursement account (HCRA)** is a tax-exempt account that is used to pay for health care expenses. The individual decides, in advance, how much money to deposit in an HCRA (and unused funds are lost).

Health Reimbursement Arrangement

A **health reimbursement arrangement (HRA)** is a tax-exempt account offered by employers with more than 50 employees, which individuals use to pay health care bills. The Internal Revenue Service (IRS) issued a tax guidance for HRAs in 2002 that stated the HRA must be used for qualified health care expenses, requires enrollment in a high-deductible insurance policy, and a provision must be in place to allow individuals to accumulate unspent money for future years. If an employee changes jobs, the HRA can continue to be used to pay for qualified health care expenses.

Workers' Compensation

Workers' compensation is a state-mandated insurance program that reimburses health care costs and lost wages if an employee suffers a work-related disease or injury. Qualified employees and their dependents are eligible for reimbursement.

Note:

> In managed care, the primary care provider receives a *capitation payment* and is responsible for managing all of an individual's health care, which includes reimbursing health care expenses provided by other caregivers (e.g., labs and specialists).

Exercise 19.1 – Third-Party Payers

Instructions: Complete each statement.

1. Third-party payers that process health care claims for reimbursement of Medicare Part A, Part B, and DME procedures, services, and supplies are called MACs, which is the abbreviation for_____.

2. The administrative agency in the Department of Health & Human Services (DHHS) that selects payers to process Medicare health care claims through a competitive bidding process is called CMS, which is the abbreviation for _____.

3. The standard claim submitted by physician offices to third-party payers is called the CMS-1500, and the claim submitted by health care institutions is called the _____.

4. An organization that processes or facilitates the processing of health information received from another entity from a nonstandard into a standard format is called a(n) _____.

(continues)

Exercise 19.1 (*continued*)

5. If the patient's insurance policy contains a statement that the patient is not responsible for paying what the insurance plan denies, the health care provider is prohibited from collecting payment from the patient. This statement is called a(n) _____ harmless clause.

6. The government-sponsored health program that provides health care benefits to active military and their dependents is called _____.

7. The joint federal and state program that provides health care coverage to low-income populations and certain aged and disabled individuals is called _____.

8. The government-sponsored health program that provides health care coverage to elderly and disabled persons is called _____.

9. The combined financing and delivery of health care services to replace conventional fee-for-service health insurance plans with more affordable care for consumers and providers who agree to certain restrictions is called _____ care.

10. The type of plan that reimburses providers for individual health care services rendered is called _____.

Health Care Reimbursement Systems

Prior to implementation of major government-sponsored health programs (e.g., Medicare and Medicaid) in 1965, health care services were reimbursed by the following payers:

- BlueCross and BlueShield (private and group health plans)

- Commercial health insurance (private)

- Employer-based group health insurance and self-insurance plans

- Government-sponsored programs, limited to the following:

  o Indian Health Service (limited eligibility)

  o Dependents' medical care program (health care for dependents of active military personnel)

- Prepaid health plans (forerunner of managed care)

- Self-pay (patients paid cash)

- Workers' compensation (limited eligibility)

Payers (except prepaid or managed care plans) typically reimbursed physicians on a fee-for-service basis, which is a retrospective payment system that billed payers after health care services were provided to the patient. Hospital reimbursement was generated on a *per diem* basis (Latin meaning "by the day"), which meant payers used a retrospective payment system to issue payment that was based on actual daily charges.

EXAMPLE: Payers typically reimbursed providers for 80 percent of charges submitted, and patients paid the remaining 20 percent (coinsurance). Thus, a provider who submitted a charge of $120 was paid $96 by the payer and $24 by the patient. (Government programs, such as Medicare, establish a physician fee schedule for services provided. The physician is reimbursed 80 percent of the fee schedule.)

Prospective Payment Systems, Fee Schedules, and Exclusions

Health care costs increased dramatically with implementation of government-sponsored health programs in 1965. This led to the creation and implementation of prospective payment systems and fee schedules (Table 19-2)

Table 19-2 Prospective Payment Systems and Fee Schedules, Year Implemented, and Prospective Rate Type

Prospective Payment System (PPS)	Year	Type
Ambulance Fee Schedule	2002	Cost-based
Ambulatory Surgical Center (ASC) Payment Rates[1]	1994	Cost-based
Clinical Laboratory Fee Schedule	1985	Cost-based
Durable Medical Equipment, Prosthetics, Orthotics, and Supplies (DMEPOS) Fee Schedule	1989	Cost-based
End-Stage Renal Disease (ESRD) Composite Payment Rate System	2005	Price-based
Home Health Prospective Payment System (HH PPS) (Home Health Resource Groups, HHRGs)	2000	Price-based
Hospital Inpatient Prospective Patient System (IPPS)	1983	Price-based
Hospital Outpatient Prospective Payment System (OPPS)	2000	Price-based
Inpatient Psychiatric Facility Prospective Payment System (IPF PPS)	2004	Cost-based
Inpatient Rehabilitation Facility Prospective Payment System (IRF PPS)	2002	Price-based
Long-Term (Acute) Care Hospital Prospective Payment System (LTC PPS)	2001	Price-based
Resource Based Relative Value Scale (RBRVS) System	1992	Cost-based
Skilled Nursing Facility Prospective Payment System (SNF PPS)	1998	Cost-based

[1]Effective January 1, 2008, the OPPS payment amount was substituted for the ASC standard overhead amount for surgical procedures performed at an ASC.

NOTE: Hospice services are not paid according to a prospective payment system or fee schedule. They are reimbursed by Medicare according to four different payment rates, which are based on the site where the patient resides at the time of service and/or number of hours of service.

for government health programs. The purpose was to control costs by reimbursing facilities with preestablished rates for inpatient care provided. Shortly after passage of Medicare and Medicaid legislation in 1965, Congress began investigating prospective payment systems. A **prospective payment system (PPS)** is a reimbursement methodology that establishes predetermined rates based on patient category or type of facility (with annual increases based on an inflation index and a geographic wage index). The CMS manages implementation of Medicare PPS, fee schedules, and exclusions according to

- Prospective cost-based rates
- Prospective price-based rates

Prospective cost-based rates are based on reported health care costs (e.g., charges) from which a prospective *per diem* rate is determined. Annual rates are usually adjusted using actual costs from the prior year. This method may be based on the facility's case mix (patient acuity of types and categories of patients). Prospective payment systems based on this reimbursement methodology include resource utilization groups (RUGs) for skilled nursing care.

Prospective price-based rates are associated with a particular category of patient (e.g., inpatients), and rates are established by the payer (e.g., Medicare) prior to the provision of health care services. PPSs based on this reimbursement methodology include diagnosis-related groups (DRGs) for inpatient care.

Typically, third-party payers adopt PPSs, fee schedules, and exclusions after Medicare has implemented them; payers modify them to suit their needs. A **fee schedule** is cost-based, fee-for-service reimbursement methodology that includes a list of maximum fees and corresponding procedures/services, which payers use to compensate providers for health care services delivered to patients. **Exclusions** are "Medicare PPS Excluded Cancer Hospitals" (e.g., Roswell Park Memorial Institute in Buffalo, New York) that applied for and were granted waivers from mandatory participation in the hospital inpatient PPS.

EXAMPLE: Prior to 1983, acute care hospitals generated invoices based on total charges for an inpatient stay. In 1982, an eight-day inpatient hospitalization at $225 per day (including ancillary service charges) would be billed $1,800. This *per diem* reimbursement rate actually discouraged hospitals from limiting inpatient lengths of stay. In 1983, a PPS rate of $950 would be reimbursed for the same inpatient hospitalization, regardless of length of stay (unless the case qualified for additional reimbursement as an outlier). The PPS rate encourages hospitals to limit inpatient lengths of stay because any reimbursement received in excess of the actual cost of providing care can be retained by the facility. (In this example, if the $950 PPS rate had been paid in 1980, the hospital would have absorbed the $850 loss.)

Inpatient Prospective Payment System (1983)

The **Tax Equity and Fiscal Responsibility Act of 1983 (TEFRA)** legislated implementation of the hospital **inpatient prospective payment system (IPPS)**, which uses diagnosis-related groups (DRGs) to reimburse short-term hospitals a predetermined rate for Medicare inpatient services. (Other payers have adopted the IPPS.)

 Note:

Certain cancer hospitals that applied and received waivers from CMS are considered excluded hospitals, which means that they do not participate in the IPPS.

Diagnosis-related groups (DRGs) (Figure 19-4) classify inpatient hospital cases into groups that are expected to consume similar hospital resources.

- Each DRG has a payment weight assigned to it that is based on the average resources used to treat Medicare patients in that DRG.

- DRGs are organized into **major diagnostic categories (MDCs)**, which are mutually exclusive categories that are loosely based on body systems (e.g., nervous system).

- Inpatient cases that are unusually costly are called **outliers**, and the IPPS payment is increased to protect the hospital from large financial losses due to unusually expensive cases.

To determine an IPPS (DRG or MS-DRG) payment, hospitals submit a UB-04 claim for each inpatient to a *Medicare administrative contractor (MAC)*, which is a third-party payer that contracts with Medicare to carry out the operational functions of the Medicare program.

- Based on the information provided on the UB-04, the case is categorized into a DRG, which determines the reimbursement provided to the hospital.

- DRG payments are then adjusted to accommodate the wage index applicable to the area where the hospital is located, a cost-of-living adjustment factor for hospitals located in Alaska and Hawaii, a percentage add-on payment for hospitals that serve a disproportionate share of low-income patients, and/or a percentage add-on payment if the hospital is an approved teaching hospital.

- In addition, if a case is categorized as an outlier, additional payments are added to the DRG-adjusted base payment rate.

Costs not considered when calculating the Medicare DRG-adjusted base payment rates are as follows:

- *Direct costs* of medical education for interns and residents, which are based on a per resident payment amount

- *Reasonable costs* for (1) hospital bad debts attributable to nonpayment of the Medicare deductible and coinsurance, and (2) heart, liver, lung, and kidney acquisition costs incurred by an approved transplant facility

The **IPPS 3-day payment window** (or **IPPS 72-hour rule**) requires outpatient preadmission services provided by a hospital on the day of or during the three days prior to a patient's inpatient admission

Medicare Severity Diagnosis-Related Groups (MS-DRGs)
MDC 02 – Diseases and Disorders of the Eye

CC = complication(s) and/or comorbidity(ies)
MCC = major complication(s) and/or cormorbidity(ies)

MS-DRG	Description
113	Orbital procedures w CC/MCC

> **MS-DRG:** 113
> **Title:** Orbital procedures w CC/MCC
> **Type:** SURG
> **Major Diagnostic Category (MDC):** 02 DISEASES & DISORDERS OF THE EYE
> **Relative Weight:** 1.4141
> **Geometric Mean Length of Stay (days):** 3.8
> **Arithmetic Mean Length of Stay (days):** 5.5
>
> **Related Codes**
>
> | MS-DRG | Title | Relative Weight | Length of Stay |
> |--------|-------|-----------------|----------------|
> | 113 | Orbital procedures w CC/MCC | 1.4141 | 3.8 |
> | 114 | Orbital procedures w/o CC/MCC | 1.0292 | 2.0 |
> | 115 | Extraocular procedures except orbit | 1.1185 | 3.3 |
> | 116 | Intraocular procedures w CC/MCC | 0.8891 | 2.2 |
> | 117 | Intraocular procedures w/o CC/MCC | 0.7094 | 1.5 |
>
> **Crosswalk of CMS-DRG to MS-DRG**
>
> | CMS-DRG | MDC | MS-DRG |
> |---------|-----|--------|
> | 037 - ORBITAL PROCEDURES | 02 | 113 - Orbital procedures w CC/MCC |

MS-DRG	Description
114	Orbital procedures w/o CC/MCC
115	Extraocular procedures except orbit
116	Intraocular procedures w CC/MCC
117	Intraocular procedures w/o CC/MCC
121	Acute major eye infections w CC/MCC
122	Acute major eye infections w/o CC/MCC
123	Neurological eye disorders
124	Other disorders of the eye w MCC
125	Other disorders of the eye w/o MCC

Courtesy of the Centers for Medicare & Medicaid Services, www.cms.gov

Figure 19-4 Medicare severity diagnosis-related groups (MS-DRGs), major diagnostic category 02

to be covered by the IPPS DRG payment and reported on the UB-04 with ICD-10-CM and ICD-10-PCS codes for

- Diagnostic services (e.g., lab testing)

- Therapeutic (or nondiagnostic) services

Medicare also requires that physicians' services clinically related to an inpatient admission and provided within 72 hours of the admission be paid at the lower facility rate (instead of the usually greater office or nonfacility rate). CMS requires that HCPCS level II modifier -PD (diagnostic or related nondiagnostic item or service provided in a wholly owned or wholly operated entity to a patient who is admitted as an inpatient within three days) to identify claims for related services provided within 72 hours of an inpatient admission. As a result of this new requirement

- Physician office claims must be held for at least three days prior to submission, and CMS requires hospitals to notify physician offices about related inpatient admissions.

- Modifier -PD must be added to CPT and HCPCS level II codes that are reported on CMS-1500 claims for any inpatients who received physician office services within 72 hours prior to admission.

In practice, physician offices need to implement a process to ensure that claims submission is delayed by three days. Also, an office staff member needs to review daily list(s) of inpatient admissions received from local hospital(s) to identify patients whose claims need to be modified by adding -PD to CPT codes.

EXAMPLE: A 79-year-old established female Medicare patient receives physician office evaluation and management (E/M) services (99214) for complaints of chest pain and shortness of breath. Her general practitioner (GP) performs a 12-lead ECG (93000), which indicates the patient is currently experiencing a myocardial infarction (MI). The patient is immediately transported by ambulance to the local hospital and admitted to the intensive care unit. Because the patient is admitted within 72 hours of the office visit, the E/M services (99214-PD) are paid to the physician at the lesser facility rate (instead of the physician office rate), and only the professional component rate of the ECG (93010-PD) is paid to the physician (instead of the higher global procedure rate). (CPT code 93010 is reported for the professional component of the ECG, not 93000 which is reported for the global service.)

According to CMS, all nondiagnostic services (other than ambulance and maintenance renal dialysis services) furnished by a hospital on the date of admission or during the three-day payment window are deemed to be related to the admission and, therefore, must be bundled with the inpatient stay if the services were provided on the day of or during the three days prior to a patient's inpatient admission. The exception to the rule is when a hospital determines, attests, and documents that the service furnished during the three-day payment window is *clinically distinct or independent from the reason for the patient's admission.* Hospitals are required to report condition code 51 with the nondiagnostic service CPT or HCPCS level II code on the outpatient UB-04.

 Note:

Medicare implemented **Medicare severity diagnosis-related groups (MS-DRGs)** in 2007 to classify inpatient hospital cases into groups according to similar resource utilization. Hospitals receive a predetermined payment according to MS-DRG for treating Medicare patients. Like the original DRGs, the MS-DRGs are based on diagnoses, procedures, other demographic information, and the presence of complications or comorbidities (CCs). However, hospital inpatients are distinguished according to those with no CCs, CCs, or major CCs (MCCs). This allows Medicare to distinguish "sick patients" from "very sick patients" and to reimburse hospitals accordingly. As such, the number of MS-DRGs expands to 745 (as compared to 538 original DRGs). MS-DRGs also emphasize the importance of proper documentation of patient care, relating it to reimbursement optimization (e.g., increased diagnosis specificity to justify more severe illnesses resulting in increased reimbursement). Facilities implement clinical documentation improvement (CDI) programs to ensure thorough and accurate documentation in patient records. (*To optimize reimbursement* means to legally enhance reimbursement from payers to providers, such as assigning specific codes based on documentation in the patient record.)

Other systems developed for payment purposes (based on CMS's DRG system) include the following:

- *All Patient Refined DRGs (APR-DRGs),* which classify the non-Medicare population, such as HIV patients, neonates, and pediatric patients

- *International Refined DRGs (IR-DRGs),* which were created by other countries that adapted DRGs for their own use, comparing resource usage across health care facilities and regions and incorporating the concept of severity of illness adjustments using multiple levels of comorbid and complication (CC) conditions

- *New York All Patient DRGs (AP-DRGs),* which classify the nonelderly population in New York State

- *Yale Refined Diagnosis-Related Groups (RDRGs),* which refined the original DRGs to incorporate a measure of severity, expanding the number of DRGs to 1,263 RDRGs

An **IPPS transfer rule** states that any patient with a diagnosis associated with one to 10 CMS-determined DRGs who is discharged to a post-acute provider is treated as a transfer case. ✒ This means that hospitals are paid a graduated *per diem* rate for each day of the patient's stay, not to exceed the prospective payment DRG rate. (Outliers are also recognized for extraordinarily high-cost cases.) CMS identified 10 high-volume DRGs that contain a disproportionate percentage of discharges to post-acute care settings (e.g., DRG 14—Specific Cerebrovascular Disorders Except Transient Ischemic Attack). CMS defines the following as post-acute care settings:

Note:

Services that are distinct from and unrelated to the inpatient admission are separately billed by the hospital *if documentation supports that the service is unrelated to the inpatient admission.*

- Hospitals or distinct units excluded from the prospective payment system

- Skilled nursing facilities

- Patient's home under a written plan of care for the provision of home health services from a home health agency if the services begin within three days of discharge

The Department of Health & Human Services, Office of Inspector General (OIG) monitors hospital readmissions that seem to focus on revenue generation rather than medical necessity when determining DRGs. When a patient is readmitted to a hospital on the day of discharge, the hospital should treat the readmission as a continuous episode of care. This means that the new admission is combined with the previous admission and that the hospital receives reimbursement for just one episode of care (according to the DRG generated). If the patient is transferred to another hospital, that admission is considered a transfer (not a new admission) and the two hospitals cost-split the DRG reimbursement rate. To convince the OIG that the hospital is properly classifying readmissions and transfers, consider implementing software that flags same-day readmissions for review, ensure that hospital discharge planners accurately assess the patient's condition upon discharge, and remind providers to document the fact that patients were discharged in a timely manner.

Hospital-Acquired Conditions and Present on Admission Reporting Guidelines

The Deficit Reduction Act of 2005 resulted in implementation of a quality adjustment in Medicare diagnosis-related group (DRG) payments for certain hospital-acquired conditions. CMS calls the program *Hospital-Acquired Conditions and Present on Admission Indicator Reporting (HAC & POA).*

All claims submitted for inpatient admissions to general acute care hospitals or other health care facilities are required to report the **present on admission (POA) indicator**, which is assigned by the coder to the principal and secondary diagnoses and external cause of injury code reported on the UB-04 or 837 Institutional (837I) electronic claim.

- The coder reviews the patient record to determine whether a condition was present on admission or not.

- Issues related to inconsistent, missing, conflicting, or unclear documentation are resolved by the provider as a result of the "physical query" process.

In this context, "present on admission" is defined as "present at the time the order for inpatient admission occurs." Thus, conditions that develop during an outpatient encounter, including emergency department, observation, or outpatient surgery, are considered as present on admission upon admission of the patient as a hospital inpatient. CMS reporting options and definitions include the following, and payment is made for "Y" and "W" indicators:

- Y = Yes (diagnosis was present at the time of inpatient admission)

- N = No (diagnosis was not present at the time of inpatient admission)

- U = Unknown (documentation is insufficient to determine if the condition was present at the time of inpatient admission)

- W = Clinically undetermined (provider is unable to clinically determine whether the condition was present at the time of inpatient admission)

- Blank = Unreported/not used (exempt from POA reporting) (the field is blank for factors that do not represent a current disease or for a condition that is always present on admission)

Coding for Diagnosis-Related Groups (DRGS)

Diagnoses and procedures are assigned ICD-10-CM/PCS codes, and they are sequenced according to CMS official coding guidelines and the Uniform Hospital Discharge Data Set (UHDDS). This means that hospitals are not required to assign codes to every diagnosis and procedure documented in the patient record. However, hospitals must evaluate their institutional data needs to develop coding policies, which will determine the assignment of ICD-10-CM/PCS codes to diagnoses and procedures. When assigning codes to *comorbidities* (coexisting conditions) and *complications* (conditions that develop during inpatient admission), be sure to carefully review patient record documentation to assign the most specific code possible. Revisions to the MS-DRGs comorbidities and complications (CC) list eliminated many diagnoses that were considered CCs in the past. As a result, physicians must be educated about the importance of proper documentation practices.

EXAMPLE: Under MS-DRGs

- Chronic obstructive pulmonary disease (COPD) is not a CC. However, acute exacerbation of COPD is a CC.

- Congestive heart failure (CHF) is not a CC. However, chronic systolic heart failure is a CC and acute systolic heart failure is a major CC (MCC).

ICD-10-PCS codes are assigned for documented OR (operating room) and non-OR procedures. (Non-OR procedures are performed in the patient's room, emergency department, radiology department, and so on.) Whether ICD-10-PCS codes are assigned to other procedures, such as ancillary tests (e.g., EKG, laboratory tests, and so on), is dependent on the hospital's coding policy.

The *present on admission (POA)* indicator differentiates between patient conditions present upon inpatient admission and those that develop during the inpatient admission. Claims that do not report the POA indicator are returned to the facility for correction. *Hospital-acquired conditions* that are reported as not present at the time of admission are not considered when calculating the MS-DRG payment. This means that such conditions, even if included on the CC and MCC lists, are not considered a CC or MCC if diagnosed during the inpatient stay and the facility will not receive additional payment for such conditions.

Value-Based Purchasing

Hospital **value-based purchasing (VBP)** is part of a long-standing CMS effort to link Medicare's inpatient prospective payment system (IPPS) to a value-based system for the purpose of improving health care quality, including the quality of care provided in the inpatient hospital setting, which affects payment for inpatient stays to over 3,500 hospitals. Participating hospitals are paid for inpatient acute care services based on quality of care, not just quantity of services provided. The inpatient hospital VBP was authorized by the Patient Protection and Affordable Care Act (PPACA). A hospital quality data reporting infrastructure was developed as part of the Hospital Inpatient Quality Reporting (IQR) Program, as authorized by the Medicare Prescription Drug, Improvement, and Modernization Act of 2003 (MMA).

The *Hospital Inpatient Quality Reporting (Hospital IQR) program* was developed to equip consumers with quality of care information so they can make more informed decisions about health care options. The Hospital IQR program requires hospitals to submit specific quality measures data about health conditions common among Medicare beneficiaries and that typically result in hospitalization. Eligible hospitals that do not participate in the Hospital IQR program will receive an annual market basket update with a 2.0 percentage point reduction.

Skilled Nursing Facility Prospective Payment System (1998)

The **Balanced Budget Act of 1997** legislated implementation of the **skilled nursing facility prospective payment system (SNF PPS)**, which classifies residents into **resource utilization groups (RUGs)**, version III (RUG-III), to reimburse Medicare SNF services according to a per diem prospective rate adjusted for case mix. A resident assessment instrument (RAI) completed on each SNF patient captures the **minimum data set (MDS)** according to the following schedule: 5, 14, 30, 60, and 90 days after admission. Patients are assigned to one of the RUGs categories (Table 19-3), for which a *per diem* prospective rate is established. **Resident Assessment Validation and Entry (RAVEN)** software, developed by CMS, is a data entry system that allows SNFs to capture and transmit the MDS.

Note:

Medicare introduced the first prospective payment system (PPS) to pay for inpatient hospital care, with other payers adopting their own PPS in subsequent years (e.g., SNF PPS). Under the inpatient prospective payment system (IPPS), inpatients are discharged once the acute phase of illness has passed and hospitals are reimbursed according to diagnosis-related groups. The patients are often transferred to other types of health care, such as outpatient care, skilled care facilities, rehabilitation hospitals, and home health care. The transfer facilities provide an appropriate level of health care in a safe and cost-effective manner after the patient's attending physician (with the assistance of discharge planners, case managers, social workers, nurses, and others) has determined which facility is best by evaluating the patient's medical condition, special needs, and treatment goals.

CMS has also adopted a *SNF all-cause all-condition hospital readmission measure* and a *SNF Value-Based Purchasing (VBP) Program* to promote higher quality and more efficient health care for Medicare beneficiaries as well as value-based incentive payments for qualified SNFs.

Table 19-3 Resource Utilization Groups (RUGs) Categories

Rehabilitation Plus Extensive Services	Residents have a minimum activity of daily living (ADL) dependency score of 2 or more; receive physical, occupational, and/or speech-language pathology services while a resident; and receive complex clinical care and have needs involving tracheostomy care, ventilator/respirator, or infection isolation while a resident.
Rehabilitation	Residents receive physical, occupational, and/or speech-language pathology services while a resident.
Extensive Services	Residents have a minimum activity of daily living (ADL) dependency score of 2 or more; receive complex clinical care or have needs involving tracheostomy care, ventilator/respirator, or infection isolation.
Special Care High	Residents have a minimum activity of daily living (ADL) dependency score of 2 or more; receive complex clinical care or have serious medical conditions involving any one of the following: comatose, septicemia, diabetes with insulin injections and insulin order changes, quadriplegia with a higher minimum ADL dependence criterion (ADL score of 5 or more), chronic obstructive pulmonary disease (COPD) with shortness of breath when lying flat, fever with pneumonia, vomiting, weight loss, or tube feeding meeting intake requirement, parenteral/IV feeding, or respiratory therapy.
Special Care Low	Residents have a minimum activity of daily living (ADL) dependency score of 2 or more; receive complex clinical care or have serious medical conditions involving any of the following: cerebral palsy with ADL dependency score of 5 or more, multiple sclerosis with ADL dependency score of 5 or more, Parkinson's disease with ADL dependency score of 5 or more, respiratory failure and oxygen therapy while a resident, tube feeding meeting intake requirement, ulcer treatment with two or more ulcers including venous ulcers, arterial ulcers or Stage II pressure ulcers, ulcer treatment with any Stage III or IV pressure ulcer, foot infections or wounds with application of dressing, radiation therapy while a resident, or dialysis while a resident.
Clinically Complex	Residents receive complex clinical care or have conditions requiring skilled nursing management, interventions, or treatments involving any of the following: pneumonia, hemiplegia with ADL dependency score of 5 or more, surgical wounds or open lesions with treatment, burns, chemotherapy while a resident, oxygen therapy while a resident, IV medications while a resident, or transfusions while a resident.
Behavioral Symptoms and Cognitive Performance	Residents have a maximum ADL dependency score of 5 or less and behavioral or cognitive performance symptoms involving any of the following: difficulty in repeating words, temporal orientation, or recall (score on the *Brief Interview for Mental Status* <=9), difficulty in making self understood, short term memory, or decision making (score on the *Cognitive Performance Scale* >=3), hallucinations, delusions, physical behavioral symptoms toward others, verbal behavioral symptoms toward others, other behavioral symptoms, rejection of care, or wandering.
Reduced Physical Functions	Residents' needs are primarily for support with activities of daily living and general supervision.

Home Health Prospective Payment System (2000)

The **Omnibus Consolidated and Emergency Supplemental Appropriations Act (OCESAA) of 1999** legislated implementation of the **home health prospective payment system (HH PPS)** for Medicare home health services, which uses home health resource groups (HHRGs) to reimburse Medicare home health care services according to prospectively determined rates and requires recertification every 60 days (or more frequently when there is a beneficiary elected transfer, a

Note:

Medicare does not reimburse durable medical equipment (DME) during the initial 60 days that a patient receives home care services. DME is reimbursed according to a fee schedule during this period.

significant change in condition resulting in a change in the case-mix assignment, or a discharge and return to the same home health agency during the 60-day episode) by the physician who reviews the plan of care.

Home health agencies (HHAs) were reimbursed under a fee-for-service system until Medicare transitioned to the HH PPS for 60-day periods of home health care. Rates for each 60-day episode of HHA care are adjusted by case-mix methodology based on entry of data elements from the outcome and assessment information set (OASIS) into **Home Assessment Validation and Entry (HAVEN)** data entry software. The HHA clinician (such as a registered nurse) conducts a comprehensive assessment and collects OASIS data elements to capture clinical severity factors, functional severity factors, and service utilization factors that influence case mix. Each data element is assigned a score value, and the scores are totaled (by HAVEN software) to determine the patient's case-mix group (and the reimbursement rate).

Outpatient Prospective Payment System (2001)

The Balanced Budget Act of 1997 legislated implementation of the hospital **outpatient prospective payment system (OPPS)**, which uses **ambulatory payment classifications (APCs)** to reimburse hospital outpatient services. Outpatient health care services are organized clinically and according to resources required.

A reimbursement rate is established for each APC (Figure 19-5) and, depending on services provided, hospitals can be paid for more than one APC per encounter, with second and subsequent APCs discounted at 50 percent (if they are designated with status indicator "T").

Each CPT and HCPCS level II code is assigned a **status indicator (SI)** as a payment indicator to identify how each code is paid (or not paid) under the OPPS. For example, status indicator "S" refers to "significant procedures for which the multiple procedure reduction does not apply." This means that the CPT and/or HCPCS level II code is paid the full APC reimbursement rate. OPPS status indicator "T"

Note:

The OPPS does not cover payment of professional services, which are reported on the CMS-1500 claim and reimbursed according to a fee schedule, such as the Medicare Physician Fee Schedule (MPFS). Hospitals report outpatient encounters on the UB-04 (or CMS-1450) claim using ICD-10-CM for diagnoses and CPT and HCPCS level II for procedures and services.

refers to "services to which the multiple procedure payment reduction applies." (CPT modifier -51 is not added to codes reported for OPPS payment consideration.) This means that the reported CPT and/or HCPCS level II code will be paid a discounted APC reimbursement rate when reported with other procedures on the same claim.

The unit of payment for the OPPS is an outpatient visit or encounter. An **outpatient encounter** (or **outpatient visit**) includes all outpatient procedures and services (e.g., same-day surgery, x-rays, laboratory tests, and so on) provided during one day to the same patient. Thus, a patient who undergoes multiple outpatient procedures and receives multiple services on the same day will be assigned to one or more outpatient groups (called APCs). Each APC is weighted and has a prospective payment amount associated with it; if a patient is assigned multiple APCs, the payments are totaled to provide reimbursement to the hospital for the encounter. (APC payments may be discounted when certain procedures or services are provided, such as bilateral procedures.) A **wage index** adjusts payments to account for geographic variations in hospitals' labor costs.

Outpatient Prospective Payment System (OPPS) Formula

(APC Weight × Conversion Factor × Wage Index) + Add-On Payments = Payment

NOTE: When a patient undergoes multiple procedures and services on the same day, multiple APCs are generated and payments are added together. APC software automatically discounts multiple APC payments when appropriate (e.g., bilateral procedure).

EXAMPLE: Using the sample data below, the OPPS payment for a patient who underwent cataract procedure with intraocular lens implant, chest x-ray, and ureteral reflux study in Buffalo, New York is calculated as 437.02. (NOTE: Add-on payments do not apply to this example and APC payments were not discounted.)

$$(22.98 \times \$54.561 \times 0.8192) + (0.78 \times \$54.561 \times 0.8192) + (4.29 \times \$54.561 \times 0.8192)$$

$$\$1,027.12 + \$34.86 + \$191.75 = \$1,253.73$$

Conversion Factor = $54.561
Wage Index = 0.8192

HCPCS Code	Description	APC	APC Weight
66984	Cataract procedure with intraocular lens implant	246	22.98
71020	Chest x-ray	260	0.78
78740	Ureteral reflux study	292	4.29

Figure 19-5 Formula for determining OPPS payments

APC grouper software is used to assign an APC to each CPT and/or HCPCS level II code reported on an outpatient claim, as well as to ICD-10-CM codes as appropriate. Outpatient code editor (OCE) software is used in conjunction with the APC grouper to identify Medicare claims edits and assign APC groups to reported codes.

Note:

Add-ons that can increase OPPS payments include pass-through payments that provide additional reimbursement to hospitals that use innovative (new and improved) biologicals, drugs, and technical devices. During committee meetings, health care personnel routinely discuss "pass-through payments" due to new technology, such as innovative medical devices (e.g., using surgical glue instead of stitches) and new drugs and vaccines (e.g., human papillomavirus [HPV] vaccine). Other add-ons include outlier payments for high-cost services, hold harmless payments for certain hospitals, and transitional payments to limit losses under the OPPS. The hospital profits if the payment rate is higher than the cost of care provided, and the hospital loses money if the payment rate is lower than the cost of care provided.

EXAMPLE: OCE software reviews "to/from" dates of service to identify and reject claims that are submitted for reimbursement as hospital-based outpatient care when, in fact, the claim should be processed as inpatient care.

Note:

A Medicare patient's coinsurance amount is initially calculated for each APC based on 20 percent of the national median charge for services in the APC. The coinsurance amount for an APC does not change until the amount becomes 20 percent of the total APC payment, and no coinsurance amount can be greater than the hospital inpatient deductible in a given year.

Note:

New York State is phasing in ambulatory patient groups (APGs) as a new payment methodology for most Medicaid outpatient services (e.g., outpatient clinic, ambulatory surgery, and emergency department services). Implementation of APGs will result in

- Higher payments for higher intensity services and lower payments for lower intensity services
- The transition of funds from inpatient to outpatient services to support quality outpatient care and to address the problem of avoidable hospitalizations

Inpatient Psychiatric Facility Prospective Payment System

The **inpatient psychiatric facility prospective payment system (IPF PPS)** was implemented as a result of Medicare, Medicaid, and SCHIP Balanced Budget Refinement Act of 1999 (BBRA) provisions that required implementation of a *per diem* patient classification system that reflects differences in patient resource use and costs. The IPF PPS replaced a reasonable cost-based payment system and affected approximately 2,000 facilities; its purpose is to promote long-term cost control and utilization management. Licensed psychiatric facilities and hospital-based psychiatric units were reimbursed according to the new PPS, which was phased in over a three-year period beginning in 2004.

Health information department coders use ICD-10-CM to assign codes to inpatient behavioral health diagnoses and ICD10-PCS to assign codes procedures. Coders then enter data into DRG software to calculate the IPF PPS DRG. Inpatient psychiatric facilities are reimbursed according to a *per diem* payment that is calculated using DRG data, wage-adjusted rates, and facility-level adjusters. (IPPS MS-DRGs reimburse acute care hospitals a flat payment based on ICD-10-CM/PCS codes and other data.) Providers use the *Diagnostic and Statistical Manual of Mental Disorders (DSM)*, which is published by the American Psychiatric Association. Although *DSM* codes do not affect IPF PPS rates, the manual contains diagnostic assessment criteria that are used as tools to identify psychiatric disorders. The *DSM* includes psychiatric disorders and codes, provides a mechanism for communicating and recording diagnostic information, and is used in the areas of research and statistics. (Currently, *DSM-5* is in use.)

Inpatient Rehabilitation Facility Prospective Payment System (2002)

The Balanced Budget Act (BBA) of 1997 authorized implementation of the **inpatient rehabilitation facility prospective payment system (IRF PPS)**, which utilizes information from a patient assessment instrument (IRF PAI) to classify patients into distinct groups based on clinical characteristics and expected resource needs. Separate payments are calculated for each group, including the application of case- and facility-level adjustments. Each facility must demonstrate that during its most recent 12-month cost-reporting period, it served an inpatient population of whom at least 75 percent required intensive rehabilitative services for the treatment of one or more of the following conditions:

- Amputation
- Brain injury
- Burns
- Congenital deformity
- Hip fracture

- Major multiple trauma
- Neurological disorders
- Polyarthritis
- Stroke
- Spinal cord injury

The **IRF PPS 1-day payment window** (or **IRF PPS 24-hour rule**) requires that outpatient preadmission services provided by an IRF up to one day prior to a patient's inpatient admission be covered by the IRF PPS payment.

The **IRF PPS transfer rule** is similar to the IPPS transfer rule, except that for the IRF, the rule covers all patient diagnoses. If a patient is transferred from an IRF to another rehabilitation facility, an acute inpatient hospital, a long-term care hospital, or a nursing home that accepts payment under Medicare or Medicaid, the patient's length of stay must be reviewed. A patient who is discharged to home, outpatient therapy, home health, or a day rehabilitation program is not considered a transfer. If a patient remains in the IRF for more than three days—which is the defining length of stay for a short stay carrying its own payment classification, but fewer days than defined by the case-mix group (CMG)—the transfer payment methodology is triggered. The transfer payment methodology reimburses a *per diem*–based payment for the number of days of care in the facility prior to a transfer.

Long-Term (Acute) Care Hospital Prospective Payment System (2001)

The **Balanced Budget Refinement Act of 1999 (BBRA)** mandated implementation of the **long-term (acute) care hospital prospective payment system (LTCH PPS)**, which uses information from long-term acute care hospital patient records to classify patients into distinct **Medicare severity long-term (acute) care diagnosis-related groups (MS-LTC-DRGs)** based on clinical characteristics and expected resource needs. The LTCH PPS replaced the reasonable cost-based payment system authorized by TEFRA, which mandated DRGs (and exempted long-term acute care hospitals from participation).

The **LTCH PPS 1-day payment window** (or **LTCH PPS 24-hour rule**) requires that outpatient preadmission services provided by a long-term acute care hospital up to one day prior to a patient's inpatient admission be covered by the MS-LTCH-DRG payment.

 Note:

Do not confuse the LTCH PPS with the SNF PPS, discussed previously in this chapter. Long-term acute care hospitals are categorized as short-term hospitals, while skilled nursing facilities (SNFs) are considered long-term care facilities (LTCFs) (e.g., nursing facilities). Medicare even certifies long-term acute care hospitals as "short-term acute care hospitals."

Clinical Laboratory Fee Schedule (1985)

The **Deficit Reduction Act of 1984** established the **clinical laboratory fee schedule** as a methodology for determining fees for existing tests, and one year later the **Consolidated Omnibus Budget Reconciliation Act of 1985** established a **national limitation amount (NLA)**, which serves as a payment ceiling or "cap" on the amount Medicare could pay for each test, originally set at 115 percent of the median of all carrier-set rates. It eventually dropped to 74 percent.

Durable Medical Equipment, Prosthetics, Orthotics, and Supplies Fee Schedule (1989)

The **durable medical equipment, prosthetics, orthotics, and supplies (DMEPOS) fee schedule** is a payment methodology mandated by the **Omnibus Budget Reconciliation Act of 1987 (OBRA)**. The fee schedule was implemented in 1989 (except for the surgical dressing fee schedule, which was implemented in 1994; and the parenteral and enteral nutrition (PEN) fee schedule, which was implemented in 2002). The fee schedule is released annually and updated quarterly to implement fee schedule amounts for new codes and to revise any amounts for existing codes that were calculated in error.

Resource-Based Relative Value Scale System (1992)

The **Omnibus Budget Reconciliation Act of 1989** implemented the **resource-based relative value scale (RBRVS) system**, which is used to reimburse physician services covered by Medicare Part B. The RBRVS system replaced the Medicare physician payment system of "customary, prevailing, and reasonable" (CPR) charges under which physicians were reimbursed according to the historical record of the charge for the provision of each service. This system, now called the **Medicare physician fee schedule (MPFS)**, reimburses providers according to predetermined rates assigned to services, and it is revised by CMS each year. All services are standardized to measure the value of

Note:

Most third-party payers, including state Medicaid programs, have adopted aspects of the MPFS. Thus, the MPFS contains fees for services not commonly provided to Medicare patients (e.g., obstetrical services).

a service as compared with other services provided. These standards, called **relative value units (RVUs)**, are payment components consisting of the following:

- *Physician work*, which reflects the physician's time and intensity in providing the service (e.g., judgment, technical skill, and physical effort)

- *Practice expense*, which reflects overhead costs involved in providing a service (e.g., rent, utilities, equipment, and staff salaries)

- *Malpractice expense*, which reflects malpractice expenses (e.g., costs of liability insurance)

Payment limits were also established by adjusting the RVUs for each locality by geographic adjustment factors (GAF), called *geographic cost practice indices (GPCIs)*, so that Medicare providers are paid differently in each state and also within each state (e.g., New York State has five separate payment localities). An annual **conversion factor** (dollar multiplier) converts RVUs into payments using a formula (Figure 19-6).

Figure 19-6 Formula for determining Medicare physician fee schedule payments

Ambulatory Surgical Centers Payments (1994)

The **Omnibus Budget Reconciliation Act of 1980** mandated that an ambulatory surgery center (ASC) could participate in Medicare if certain conditions were met (e.g., if the ASC was state-licensed) and stated that the **ambulatory surgical centers (ASCs) payment rates** are "expected to be calculated on a prospective basis … utilizing sample survey and similar techniques to establish reasonable estimated overhead allowances for each of the listed procedures which take account of volume (within reasonable limits)." Prior to 2008, procedures included on the ASC list were assigned to one of nine payment groups based on an estimate of the costs incurred by the facility to perform the procedure.

The Medicare Prescription Drug, Improvement, and Modernization Act of 2003 (MMA) mandated implementation of a revised payment system for ASC surgical services by no later than January 1, 2008. Under the revised payment system, implemented January 1, 2008, Medicare will use the ambulatory payment classification (APC) groups and relative payment weights to reimburse ASCs for surgical procedures performed. (The payment weights are multiplied by an ASC conversion factor to calculate ASC payment rates.)

ASC relative payment weights will be updated each year using the national OPPS relative payment weights for that calendar year and, for office-based procedures, the practice expense payments under the physician fee schedule will also be updated for that calendar year. Medicare plans to make the relative payment weights budget neutral to ensure that changes in the relative payment weights from year to year do not cause the estimated amount of expenditures to ASCs to increase or decrease as a function of those changes. Medicare will also maintain and update an "exclusionary list of procedures" for which an ASC facility fee is not paid (because those procedures are included on the OPPS inpatient list).

Ambulance Fee Schedule (2002)

The Balanced Budget Act of 1997 legislated implementation of an **ambulance fee schedule**, which reimburses ambulance service providers a preestablished fee for each service provided. Characteristics of the fee schedule consist of the following:

- Seven categories of ground ambulance services, ranging from basic life support to specialty care transport, and two categories of air ambulance services are established.

- Payment for each category is based on the relative value assigned to the service, adjusted to reflect wage differences in different parts of the country (mileage also will affect payment levels).

- Ambulance providers will not be allowed to charge beneficiaries more than their deductible and 20 percent of Medicare's fee for the service. (Under the old payment system, providers could charge beneficiaries higher rates.)

- The fee schedule allows for increased payments when an ambulance service is provided in rural areas.

End-Stage Renal Disease Composite Payment Rate System (2005)

The **end-stage renal disease (ESRD) composite payment rate system** for dialysis services is based on a case-mix adjusted composite rate. It is a single-payment fixed rate that does not vary according to the characteristics of the beneficiary treated (and includes the cost of some drugs, laboratory tests, and other items and services provided to Medicare beneficiaries receiving dialysis). The Medicare Prescription Drug, Improvement, and Modernization Act (MMA) of 2003 established the ESRD composite payment rate system.

ESRD facilities determine the best payment rate for rendered services. They can maintain their current exception rate or be paid according to the ESRD composite payment rate system, which provides greater payments to facilities that treat more complicated and resource-intensive ESRD patients.

Case-Mix Analysis, Intensity of Services (IS), and Severity of Illness Systems

Implementation of Medicare PPS resulted in health care facilities analyzing their **case mix** (patient acuity) to

- Forecast health care trends unique to their individual settings.

- Ensure that they continue to provide appropriate services to their patient populations.

- Recognize that different patients require different resources for care.

EXAMPLE: Upon review of Sunnyvale Hospital's case mix, the greatest number of patients receive cardiovascular services. Wheaton Hospital's case mix indicates that the majority of its patients receive labor and delivery services. Knowing the case mix allows the hospitals to customize services required of their respective patient populations.

In addition, Medicare and other payers are interested in reviewing case-mix data because they recognize that some facilities may serve caseloads that include disproportionate shares of patients with above-average (or below-average) care needs.

Multiple possible payment rates (e.g., RUG categories) based on patients' anticipated care needs allow payment systems to decrease the average difference between the preestablished payment and each patient's actual cost to the facility (called a **case-mix adjustment**). This also results in a reduced risk to facilities and to payers, and facilities are also willing to admit high-resource cases because higher payments can be anticipated. It creates a disincentive for facilities to admit large volumes of low-need, low-cost patients, which will result in lower payments.

Health care facilities use case-mix and severity of illness software to analyze and measure standards of patient care to assess quality, including the following:

- Acute Physiological and Chronic Health Evaluation (APACHE)

- Atlas Outcomes/MediQual Systems (formerly Medical Illness Severity Grouping System, or MEDISGRPS)

- Comprehensive Severity Index (CSI)

- Patient Management Categories (PMCs)

- Severity of Illness Index (SOII)

A health care facility's utilization management (UM) team determines whether a patient's illness is severe enough to require the current or proposed level of care by evaluating the documentation of objective clinical indicators of illness (e.g., sign, symptoms, laboratory findings). In addition, the UM team also determines **intensity of services (IS)**, which involves determining whether provided services are appropriate for the patient's current or proposed level of care (e.g., intravenous medications, heart monitoring, surgical interventions). The ultimate goal is to ensure that patients receive the appropriate level of care. If the patient's severity of illness and/or intensity of services does not meet criteria for the level of care provided, the patient is transferred to the appropriate level of care.

Severity of illness (SI) is the physiologic complexity that comprises the extent and interaction of a patient's disease(s) as presented to medical personnel. Severity of illness scores are based on physiologic measures (not just ICD-10-CM codes) of the degree of abnormality of individual signs and symptoms of a patient's disease(s). The more abnormal the signs and symptoms, the higher the score.

Note:

Intensity of services and severity of illness is commonly abbreviated as ISSI.

EXAMPLE: A patient is admitted as a hospital inpatient from the facility's emergency department after work up for severe chest pain. Upon initial review of patient record documentation, the patient's laboratory results revealed positive cardiac enzymes, positive electrocardiogram (EKG) suggestive of ischemia, and continued chest pain. Thus, *severity of illness* for inpatient hospitalization was met. Upon further review of the patient record, documentation indicated the patient received intravenous nitroglycerin for chest pain and underwent cardiac catheterization, which revealed two blocked coronary arteries. Patient underwent surgical placement of stents in the blocked arteries. Thus, *intensity of services* for inpatient hospitalization was also met.

Risk management tools that identify the risk of dying include the following:

- Acute Physiological and Chronic Health Evaluation (APACHE)

- Medicare Mortality Predictor System (MMPS)

EXAMPLE: The Health Data Institute created MMPS software to capture data on Medicare patients admitted with stroke, pneumonia, myocardial infarction, and congestive heart failure. The purpose was to predict death within 30 days of hospital admission because these conditions accounted for 13 percent of discharges and 31 percent of 30-day mortality for Medicare patients over age 64 prior to 1988. The MMPS system was "calibrated on a stratified, random sample of 5,888 discharges (about 1,470 for each condition) from seven states, with stratification by hospital type to make the sample nationally representative," and predictors were abstracted from the patient record. The organization determined that "risk-adjusted predicted group mortality rates may be useful in interpreting information on unadjusted mortality rates, and patient-specific predictions may be useful in identifying unexpected deaths for clinical review."

SOURCE: "Predicting hospital-associated mortality for Medicare patients: A method for patients with stroke, pneumonia, acute myocardial infarction, and congestive heart failure," by J. Daley, S. Jencks, D. Draper, G. Lenhart, N. Thomas, and J. Walker, Baxter Healthcare Corp., Health Data Institute, Lexington, Mass. *Journal of the American Medical Association* 260, no. 24 (December 23, 1988).

Physician Documentation for Medical Necessity of Medicare Part A Hospital Inpatient Admissions

In 2014, CMS issued a final rule (CMS-1599-F) called the *2-Midnight Rule*, which modified and clarified the policy about Medicare Administrative Contractor (MAC) review of inpatient hospital and critical access hospital (CAH) admissions for payment purposes. Under the final rule, surgical procedures, diagnostic tests, and other treatments (in addition to services designated as inpatient-only) are generally appropriate for inpatient hospital admission and payment under Medicare Part A when the physician expects the beneficiary to require a stay that crosses at least two midnights and admits the beneficiary to the hospital based upon that expectation. The rule was published as a response to facilities' and beneficiaries' concerns about increasingly long stays as outpatients (e.g., observation care) due to hospital uncertainties about payment.

Physicians are responsible for documenting the medical necessity of an inpatient admission, which CMS calls *physician certification*. Physician documentation includes authentication of the admission order, reason for inpatient services (including the data points physicians use to reach their conclusion that the patient requires inpatient admission), estimated or actual length of time the beneficiary requires inpatient status in the hospital, and plans for posthospital care. In addition, physicians must clearly document any unexpected change in patient status (e.g., improvement) specific to the clinical issues in the case. CMS recommends that such documentation be included in the discharge order.

According to CMS, the regulation specifies that the decision to admit should generally be based on the physician's reasonable expectation of a length of stay spanning two or more midnights, taking into account complex medical factors that must be documented in the medical record. Because this is based upon the physician's expectation, as opposed to a retroactive determination based on actual length of stay, unforeseen circumstances that result in a shorter stay than the physician's reasonable expectation may still result in a hospitalization that is appropriately considered inpatient. As enumerated in the final rule, CMS anticipates that most of these situations will arise in the context of beneficiary death, transfer, or departure against medical advice. However, CMS does recognize that on occasion there may be situations in which the beneficiary improves much more rapidly than the physician's reasonable expectation. Such instances must be clearly documented and the initial expectation of a hospital stay spanning two or more midnights must have been reasonable in order for this circumstance to be an acceptable inpatient admission payable under Part A.

CMS further clarifies that the more usual situation would be the one in which the physician's initial expectation of the beneficiary's length of stay is uncertain. If the physician is uncertain whether the beneficiary will be able to be discharged after one midnight in the hospital or whether the beneficiary will require a second midnight of care, the initial day should be spent in observation until it is clearly expected that a second midnight would be required, at which time the physician may order inpatient admission. If the physician believes that a rare and unusual circumstance exists in which an inpatient admission is warranted, but does not expect the beneficiary to require two or more midnights in the hospital, the physician may admit the beneficiary to inpatient status but should thoroughly document why inpatient admission and Medicare Part A payment is appropriate.

Critical Pathways

Critical pathways are interdisciplinary guidelines developed by hospitals to facilitate management and delivery of quality clinical care in a time of constrained resources. They allow for the planning of provision of clinical services that have expected time frames and resources targeted to specific diagnoses and/or procedures. The targeted clinical services are frequently those that are high in volume and resource use and, therefore, are costly. Critical pathways are usually interdisciplinary in focus, merging medical and nursing plans of care with other disciplines (e.g., physical therapy, nutrition, and mental health). Critical pathways essentially can be viewed as interdisciplinary practice guidelines with predetermined standards of care. They provide opportunities for collaborative practice and team approaches that can maximize the expertise of multiple disciplines.

Note:

Originally, critical pathways began with admission and ended with discharge from the hospital. Now that they are being implemented in other health care settings, there is potential for pathways to be focused more on the full range of an episode of care.

Chargemaster and Encounter Form

Hospitals use a chargemaster to record encounter data about ambulatory care provided to patients. The **chargemaster**, or **charge description master (CDM)** (Figure 19-7), is a document that contains a computer-generated list of procedures, services, and supplies, as well as corresponding revenue codes along with charges for each. A **revenue code** is a four-digit UB-04 code that is assigned to each procedure, service, or supply to indicate the location or type of service provided to an institutional patient, such as radiology or laboratory. Physician offices and clinics use an **encounter form**, or **superbill** (Figure 19-8), to record encounter data about office procedures and services provided to patients.

Chargemaster and encounter form data are entered in a patient accounting system, and charges are automatically posted to the insurance claim (UB-04 or CMS-1500, depending on the health care setting). The claim is submitted to the third-party payer to generate payment for services provided (e.g., emergency department, laboratory, physician office, or radiology). Chargemasters and encounter forms allow for accurate and efficient billing of services rendered.

Chargemaster

A chargemaster usually contains the following:

- *Department code*: Refers to the specific ancillary department where the service is performed

- *Service code*: Internal identification of specific service rendered

- *Service description*: Narrative description of the service, procedure, or supply

- *Revenue code*: Four-digit UB-04 code assigned to each procedure, service, or supply that indicates the location or type of service provided to a patient

- *Charge amount*: Dollar amount the facility charges for each procedure, service, or supply

- *Relative value units (RVUs)*: Numeric value assigned to a procedure that is based on difficulty and time consumed

A **chargemaster review process** is routinely conducted by designated hospital personnel (e.g., coding specialists) to ensure accurate reimbursement by updating CPT and HCPCS level II codes and linking each to appropriate UB-04 revenue codes. These designated individuals must have knowledge of proper revenue and expense

(A)

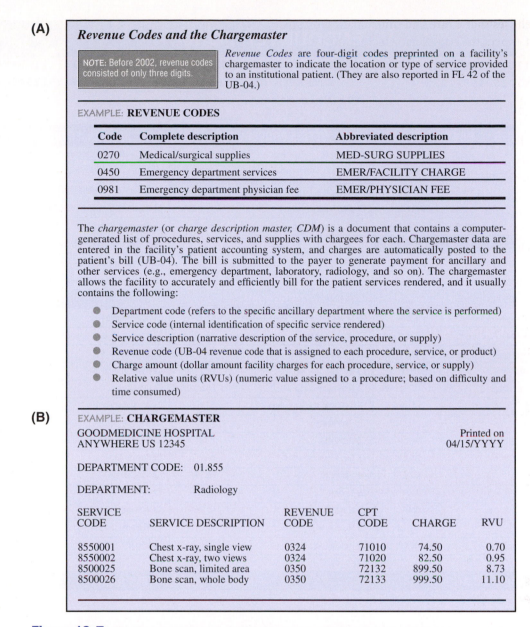

(B)

Figure 19-7 Revenue codes and chargemaster (A) Explanation of revenue codes (B) Sample portion of hospital chargemaster

matching to the Medicare cost center report (e.g., revenue codes) and must be willing to spend the time necessary on an extremely detailed and time-consuming task. Because it results in generation of gross revenue for the health care facility, all who use the chargemaster must be educated about its proper use and its impact on the facility's financial status.

 Note:

Chargemasters (and encounter forms) are usually developed using database software that allows for the entry of thousands of items and potential charges. Each item includes an accounting code number, a CPT/HCPCS code number, and a brief narrative description.

Commercial software (e.g., Optum360's www.ChargemasterExpert.com online product) helps health care facilities maintain an accurate and complete chargemaster for billing and compliance purposes. The result is fewer claims denials and more accurate outpatient reimbursement.

ENCOUNTER FORM

Tel: (101) 555-1111	Kim Donaldson, M.D.	EIN: 11-9876543
Fax: (101) 555-2222	INTERNAL MEDICINE	NPI: 1234567890
	101 Main Street, Suite A	
	Alfred, NY 14802	

OFFICE VISITS	NEW	EST	OFFICE PROCEDURES		INJECTIONS	
❏ Level I	99201	99211	❏ EKG with interpretation	93000	❏ Influenza virus vaccine	___
❏ Level II	99202	99212	❏ Oximetry with interpretation	94760	❏ Admin of Influenza vaccine	G0008
❏ Level III	99203	99213	**LABORATORY TESTS**		❏ Pneumococcal vaccine	90732
❏ Level IV	99204	99214	❏ Blood, occult (feces)	82270	❏ Admin of pneumococcal vaccine	G0009
❏ Level V	99205	99215	❏ Skin test, Tb, intradermal (PPD)	86580	❏ Hepatitis B vaccine	90746
					❏ Admin of Hepatitis B vaccine	G0010
					❏ Tetanus and diptheria toxoids vaccine	90714
					❏ Immunization administration	90471

DIAGNOSIS

❏ Abnormal heart sounds	R00.9	❏ Chronic ischemic heart disease	I25.9	❏ Hypertension	I10
❏ Abdominal pain	R10.8__	❏ Chronic obstructive lung disease	J44.9	❏ Hormone replacement	Z79.890
❏ Abnormal feces	R19.5	❏ Congestive heart failure	I50.9	❏ Hyperlipidemia	E78.5
❏ Allergic rhinitis	J30.9	❏ Cough	R05	❏ Hyperthyroidism	E05.9__
❏ Anemia, pernicious	D51.0	❏ Depressive disorder	F32.9	❏ Influenza	J11.1
❏ Anxiety	F41.9	❏ Diabetes mellitus, type 2	E11.____	❏ Loss of weight	R63.4
❏ Asthma	J45.909	❏ Diarrhea	R19.7	❏ Nausea	R11.0
❏ Atrophy, cerebral	G31.9	❏ Dizziness	R42	❏ Nausea with vomiting	R11.2
❏ B-12 deficiency	D51.9	❏ Emphysema	J43.__	❏ Pneumonia	J18.__
❏ Back pain	M54.9	❏ Fatigue	R53.83	❏ Sore throat	J02.9
❏ Bronchitis	J40	❏ Fever	R50.9	❏ Vaccine, hepatitis B	Z23
❏ Cardiovascular disease	I25.1__	❏ Gastritis	K29.50	❏ Vaccine, influenza	Z23
❏ Cervicalgia	M54.2	❏ Heartburn	R12	❏ Vaccine, pneumococcus	Z23
❏ Chest pain	R07.9	❏ Hematuria	R31.9	❏ Vaccine, tetanus toxoid	Z23
❏	___	❏	___	❏	___

PATIENT IDENTIFICATION		FINANCIAL TRANSACTION DATA	
PATIENT NAME:		INVOICE NO.	
PATIENT NUMBER:		ACCOUNT NO.	
DATE OF BIRTH:		TOTAL FOR SERVICE:	$
ENCOUNTER DATE		AMOUNT RECEIVED:	$
DATE OF SERVICE:	/ /	PAID BY:	❏ Cash ❏ Check ❏ Credit Card
RETURN VISIT DATE			
DATE OF RETURN VISIT:	/ /	CASHIER'S INITIALS:	

Figure 19-8 Sample encounter form (superbill)

Encounter Form

Encounter form data are entered in the office's practice management software to generate the CMS-1500 claim that is submitted to the payer. (Many physician offices still complete paper-based CMS-1500 claims, which are submitted to health care clearinghouses to be converted to a standardized format. The health care clearinghouse submits the standardized claims data to the payer, where they are processed to generate physician reimbursement.) Similar to the chargemaster review process, the encounter form should be assigned to one individual in the physician's office who will take responsibility for reviewing and updating it twice a year when codes (e.g., ICD-10-CM, ICD-10-PCS, CPT, and HCPCS level II codes) are added, deleted, and revised. (This process used to be conducted just once each year until 2004, when federal regulations required that code changes be issued twice each year.)

 Note:

Hospitals submit UB-04 claims to payers for inpatient and ambulatory care encounters, and physicians submit CMS-1500 claims for office encounters. Most health care settings participate in electronic data interchange (EDI) with third-party payers and health care clearinghouses.

Revenue Cycle Management

Revenue cycle management is the process by which health care facilities and providers ensure their financial viability by increasing revenue, improving cash flow, and enhancing the patient's experience. In a physician practice, revenue cycle management is also called *accounts receivable management*. Revenue cycle management includes the following features, typically in this order:

- *Physician order* for inpatient admission or outpatient services is documented by responsible physician.

- *Patient registration*: Patient is admitted as an inpatient or scheduled for outpatient services.

  - Appropriate consents for treatment and release of information are obtained.

  - Patient demographic and insurance information is collected.

  - Patient's insurance coverage is validated and utilization management is performed (e.g., clinical reviews) to determine medical necessity.

  - Preadmission clearance (e.g., precertification, preauthorization, screening for medical necessity).

- *Charge capture (or data capture)*: Providers use chargemasters or encounter forms to select procedures or services provided

(ancillary departments, such as the laboratory, use automated systems that link to the chargemaster).

- *Diagnosis and procedure coding*: Assignment of appropriate ICD-10-CM, ICD-10-PCS, and/or CPT/HCPCS codes, typically performed by health information management personnel, to assign APCs, DRGs, and so on.

- *Patient discharge processing*: Patient information is verified, discharge instructions are provided, patient follow-up visit is scheduled, consent forms are reviewed for signatures, and patient policies are explained to the patient.

- *Billing and claims processing*: All patient information and codes are input into the billing system, and CMS-1500 or UB-04 claims are generated and submitted to third-party payers.

- *Resubmitting claims*: Before reimbursement is received from third-party payers, late charges, lost charges, or corrections to previously processed CMS-1500 or UB-04 claims are entered, and claims are resubmitted to payers—this may result in payment delays and claims denials.

- *Third-party payer reimbursement posting*: Payment from third-party payers is posted to

(continues)

Revenue Cycle Management (*continued*)

appropriate accounts, and rejected claims are resubmitted with appropriate documentation; this process includes electronic remittance, which involves receiving reimbursement from third-party payers electronically.

- *Appeals process*: Analysis of reimbursement received from third-party payers identifies variations in expected payments or contracted rates and may result in submission of appeal letters to payers.

- *Patient billing*: Self-pay balances are billed to the patient; these include deductibles, copayments, and non-covered charges.

- *Self-pay reimbursement posting*: Self-pay balances received from patients are posted to appropriate accounts.

- *Collections*: Payments not received from patients in a timely manner result in collections letters being mailed to patients until payment is received; if payment is still not received, the account is turned over to an outside collections agency.

- *Collections reimbursement posting*: Payments received from patients are posted to appropriate accounts.

- *Auditing process*:

  - *Compliance monitoring*: Level of compliance with established managed care contracts is monitored; provider performance per managed care contractual requirements is monitored; compliance risk is monitored.

  - *Denials management*: Claims denials are analyzed to prevent future denials; rejected claims are resubmitted with appropriate documentation.

  - *Tracking of resubmitted claims and appeals for denied claims*: Resubmitted claims and appealed claims are tracked to ensure payment by payers.

  - *Posting lost charges and late charges*: Late claims are submitted.

Permission to reprint granted by MedAssets.

Exercise 19.2 – Health Care Reimbursement Systems

Completion: Complete each statement.

1. A payer reimburses a provider 80 percent of charges submitted, and the patient is responsible for paying the remaining 20 percent coinsurance amount. Mary Allen underwent an office procedure, for which the physician billed her payer $1,500. The payer reimburses the provider the amount of $1200, and the patient reimburses the provider the amount of $ _____.

2. Two patients each undergo a four-day inpatient stay at an acute care hospital for treatment of a myocardial infarction (heart attack). The patient who has Aetna commercial insurance company can expect the hospital to be reimbursed at 80 percent of the *per diem* basis. The Medicare patient can expect the Medicare administrative contractor (MAC) to reimburse the hospital on a prospective payment basis. Daily charges incurred for the four-day stay were $1,400 per day; the DRG prospective payment rate for a myocardial infarction is $4,500. Aetna will reimburse the hospital $4480. The MAC will reimburse the hospital $ _____.

3. Designated hospital personnel routinely conduct the _____ review process to ensure accurate reimbursement by updating CPT and HCPCS codes and linking each to appropriate UB-04 revenue codes.

4. The federal legislation that resulted in the implementation of the _____ hospital PPS is called TEFRA.

5. The outpatient hospital PPS establishes a payment rate for outpatient care by using APCs, which is the abbreviation for _____, to organize similar health care services clinically and according to resources required.

Matching: Match the payment system with the type of prospective rate. Answers may be used more than once.

_____ 1. Ambulance fee schedule

_____ 2. Ambulatory surgical center rates

_____ 3. Home health prospective payment system

_____ 4. Long-term (acute) care hospital prospective payment system

_____ 5. Resource-based relative value scale system

a. Cost-based

b. Price-based

Matching: Match the present on admission (POA) indicator with each case scenario. Answers may be used more than once.

a. Y = Yes (diagnosis present at the time of inpatient admission)

b. N = No (diagnosis was not present at the time of inpatient admission)

c. U = Unknown (documentation is insufficient to determine if the condition was present at the time of inpatient admission)

d. W = Clinically undetermined (provider is unable to clinically determine whether the condition was present at the time of inpatient admission)

e. Blank = Unreported/not used (exempt from POA reporting) (the field is blank for factors that do not represent a current disease or for a condition that is always present on admission)

_____ 1. A patient is admitted to the hospital for open cholecystectomy due to acute cholecystitis with cholelithiasis. After 24 hours of intravenous antibiotic therapy, the surgery is successfully performed. What is the POA indicator for the acute cholecystitis with cholelithiasis?

(continues)

Exercise 19.2 *(continued)*

_____ **2.** A patient was admitted for inpatient hospitalization due to weakness and unsteady gait, and a diagnosis of cerebrovascular accident was established. What is the POA indicator for the cerebrovascular accident?

_____ **3.** A hospital inpatient falls out of bed on day 2 of his stay and fractures his left hip. What is the POA indicator for the left hip fracture?

_____ **4.** An 84-year-old patient is admitted for inpatient hospitalization due to fever with a temperature of 104 degrees, severe weakness, dehydration, and productive cough. The diagnosis is established as viral pneumonia. During admission, her condition rapidly deteriorates and she is admitted to the intensive care unit. The physician documents severe sepsis as a secondary diagnosis. When queried as to whether the sepsis was present on admission, the physician replies by stating that the patient went downhill so fast that he does not know if the sepsis was present on admission. What is the POA indicator for the severe sepsis?

_____ **5.** Twin liveborn infants are delivered via cesarean section in the hospital. The physician documents that Twin A has neonatal bradycardia. What is the POA indicator for Twin A's neonatal bradycardia?

Impact of HIPAA on Reimbursement

The Health Insurance Portability and Accountability Act of 1996 (HIPAA) amended the Internal Revenue Code of 1986 to improve portability and continuity of health insurance coverage in the group and individual markets; to combat waste, fraud, and abuse in health insurance and health care delivery; to promote the use of medical savings accounts; to improve access to long-term care services and coverage; to simplify the administration of health insurance by creating unique identifiers for providers, health plans, employers, and individuals; to create standards for electronic health information transactions; and to create privacy and security standards for health information.

HIPAA legislation is organized according to five titles.

- Title I—Health Care Access, Portability, and Renewability
- Title II—Preventing Health Care Fraud and Abuse, Administrative Simplification, and Medical Liability Reform
- Title III—Tax-Related Health Provisions
- Title IV—Application and Enforcement of Group Health Plan Requirements
- Title V—Revenue Offsets

 Note:

The Federal False Claims Act provides CMS with regulatory authority to enforce fraud and abuse statutes for the Medicare program, and HIPAA extends that authority to all federal and state health care programs.

Health Care Access, Portability, and Renewability

HIPAA provisions were designed to improve the portability and continuity of health coverage by limiting exclusions for **pre-existing medical conditions**, which are illnesses or injuries that required treatment during a prescribed period of time (e.g., six months) prior to the insured's effective date of coverage under a new insurance policy.

 Note:

This section will cover health care access, portability and renewability, prevention of health care fraud and abuse, administrative simplification, and medical liability reform issues.

HIPAA provisions require that individuals be granted credit for prior health coverage and that a process be implemented to transmit certificates and other information concerning prior coverage to a new group health plan or issuer. Individuals will also be allowed to enroll in health coverage when they lose other health coverage, change from group to individual coverage, or gain a new dependent. HIPAA prohibits discrimination practices associated with health coverage enrollment eligibility and the establishment of premiums (for employees and their dependents) based on health status. The availability of health insurance coverage is also guaranteed to employees of small companies, and both small and large group markets are guaranteed renewability of health insurance coverage. HIPAA preserves the traditional role of individual states in regulating health insurance, and states are provided with flexibility to require greater protection.

Preventing Health Care Fraud and Abuse

HIPAA defines **fraud** as "an intentional deception or misrepresentation that someone makes, knowing it is false, that could result in an unauthorized payment." The attempt itself is considered fraud, regardless of whether it is successful. Fraud is an act that represents a crime against payers or other health care programs (e.g., Medicare), or attempts or conspires to commit those crimes. **Abuse** "involves actions that are inconsistent with accepted, sound, medical, business, or fiscal practices." Abuse includes actions that result in unnecessary costs to payers and government programs (e.g., Medicare), reimbursement for services not medically necessary, or that fails to meet professionally recognized standards for health care services. The difference between fraud and abuse is the individual's intent; however, both have the same impact in that they steal valuable resources from the health care industry.

Examples of fraud include the following:

- Billing Medicare for services or supplies not provided

- Entering another person's Medicare number on a claim to obtain reimbursement for a patient not eligible for Medicare

- Unbundling codes reported on claims (reporting multiple codes to increase reimbursement, when a single combination code should be reported)

- Upcoding claims submitted to payers (reporting codes not supported by documentation in the patient record to increase reimbursement)

- Misrepresenting the diagnosis to justify payment

- Soliciting, offering, or receiving a kickback

- Falsifying certificates of medical necessity, plans of treatment, and medical records to justify payment.

 Note:

According to the Department of Health & Human Services, Office of Inspector General, providers are not subject to criminal, civil, or administrative penalties for innocent or negligent errors. The False Claims Act covers offenses committed with actual knowledge of the falsity of the claim, reckless disregard, or deliberate ignorance of the falsity of the claim. The False Claims Act does not cover mistakes, errors, or negligence. The Civil Monetary Penalties Law is an administrative remedy that is similar in scope and effect to the False Claims Act, and it also has exactly the same standard of proof.

EXAMPLE: The medical review of claims submitted to Medicare by a physician group practice that contains mental health providers identified a pattern of psychiatric services billed on behalf of nursing facility patients with a medical history of dementia. Review of patient record documentation at the nursing facility revealed no mental health care physician orders or plans of treatment. This is considered billing for services not furnished, and it is an example of fraud.

Examples of abuse include the following:

- Billing a Medicare patient using a higher fee schedule rate than used for non-Medicare patients

- Submitting claims to Medicare when Medicare is not the beneficiary's primary payer

- Submitting excessive charges for services or supplies
- Submitting claims for services that are not medically necessary
- Violating Medicare's participating provider agreements with payers
- Improper billing practices that result in payment by a government program when the claim is the legal responsibility of another payer.

 Note:

Medical necessity requires the documentation of services or supplies that are proper and are needed for the diagnosis or treatment of a medical condition; are provided for the diagnosis, direct care, and treatment of a medical condition; meet the standards of good medical practice in the local area; and are not mainly for the convenience of the physician.

EXAMPLE: During her first 30 days on the job, Sally Adams mistakenly submitted CMS-1500 claims to Medicare instead of the patients' workers' compensation payers. When she noticed the error, she informed her supervisor, who immediately contacted the Medicare administrative contractors to cancel processing of the submitted claims. Sally then correctly submitted the CMS-1500 claims to the workers' compensation payers. This is considered submitting claims to Medicare when Medicare is not the beneficiary's primary payer, and it is an example of abuse if not corrected.

DRG Creep

Health Care Fraud and Abuse: Diagnosis Related Group (DRG) Creep, by W. McKay Henderson, Partner, Price Waterhouse Coopers, Health Care Fraud and Abuse Practice. (Permission to reuse granted by W. McKay Henderson, Price Waterhouse, Inc.)

What is it? **DRG creep** is an initiative by the Department of Justice (DOJ) that focuses on the medical necessity and billing patterns of DRG coding to determine whether the claims that hospitals submit accurately reflect the care required or given to the patient. The government believes that hospitals are maximizing their Medicare reimbursements by choosing diagnosis codes that result in higher payments.

In 1993, the Agency for Health Care Policy and Research examined more than 17,000 documented cases of pneumonia to determine the incidences of low-risk versus high-risk pneumonia. The survey found that the diagnosis code for low-risk pneumonia was used in only 3.3 percent of the cases in the study group. While this is significantly lower than you would expect to find in the general population, it is not surprising since the Medicare reimbursement for a diagnosis of low-risk pneumonia is $2,000 less than a diagnosis of high-risk pneumonia. But what separates a simple miscoding error from a false claim? The Office of Inspector General (OIG) contends that upcoding had become a game hospitals play to maximize their revenue, often hiring consultants or investing in sophisticated computer packages to help them to increase their reimbursements. And the DOJ and OIG put a stop to it. (*To maximize revenue* means to fraudulently increase reimbursement from payers to providers, such as reporting codes not supported by documentation that increase the DRG payment rate.)

How does upcoding happen? It is speculated that the government believes the upcoding trend is due to either computer software packages that assign the link between ICD-10-CM/PCS codes and DRGs, and/or to consultants who have trained the hospital staff who assign DRG codes. As part of its investigation, the DOJ requested hospitals to provide not only medical records and hospital documentation but also audit results, analyses of computer programs, and all consultants' reports. Those hospitals and medical centers that voluntarily disclose overpayments related to DRG miscoding may receive a reduction in fines and penalties levied against them.

Deterring Fraud and Abuse

CMS employs a four-part strategy to deter fraud and abuse, which focuses on prevention, early detection, coordination, and enforcement.

- Prevention involves paying the claim correctly the first time, and it is the most desirable approach. It is also the best way to guarantee initial accuracy of claims and payments, and it avoids the requirement to "pay and chase" providers, which is a lengthy, uncertain, and expensive process.

- Early detection identifies patterns of fraudulent activity by using data to monitor unusual billing patterns and other indicators of the integrity and financial status of providers, promptly identifying and collecting overpayments, and making appropriate referrals to law enforcement. If CMS finds errors, repayment is pursued and further action may be warranted depending on the facts and circumstances of each case.

- Coordination with partners is another important way by which CMS maximizes its success in preventing fraud; information and tactics for fighting fraud and abuse are shared with individual states, the DOJ, and the private sector.

- When fraudulent providers are discovered, enforcement action is taken against them (e.g., suspension of payment, referral to OIG for potential exclusion from Medicare program, disenrollment, collection of overpayments, and imposition of civil monetary penalties). Investing in prevention, early detection, and enforcement has a proven record of returns to the Medicare Trust Fund; the Medicare Integrity Program originally saved an estimated $7.5 billion in fiscal year 1997, mostly by preventing inappropriate payments through audits, medical reviews, and ensuring that Medicare does not pay for claims owed by private insurers. The Correct Coding Initiative (CCI) was implemented to reduce Medicare program expenditures by detecting inappropriate coding on claims and denying payment for them.

The Health Insurance Association of America (HIAA) conducts surveys that report statistics about the following health care fraud activities:

- Billing patients for services already paid for and accepting kickbacks for patient referrals

- Committing mail or wire fraud

- Falsifying patient's diagnosis to justify tests, surgeries, or other procedures

- Misrepresenting noncovered treatments as medically necessary covered treatments for the purpose of obtaining higher insurance payments

- Performing medically unnecessary services

- Performing procedures for the sole purpose of producing insurance payments

- Sales of durable medical equipment that is not needed or unnecessary

Regulating Fraudulent Practices

When a Medicare provider commits fraud, an investigation is conducted by the Department of Health & Human Services (DHHS). The Office of Inspector General (OIG) prepares the case for referral to the DOJ for criminal and/or civil prosecution. A person found guilty of Medicare fraud faces criminal, civil, and/or administrative sanction penalties, including the following:

- Civil penalties ranging from $5,000 to $10,000 per false claim *plus* triple damages

- Criminal fines and/or imprisonment for up to 10 years if convicted of health care fraud or, for violations of the Medicare/Medicaid Anti-kickback Statute, imprisonment of up to five years and/or a criminal fine of up to $25,000

- Administrative sanctions, which include up to a $10,000 civil monetary penalty per line item on a false claim, assessments of up to triple the amount falsely claimed, and/or exclusion from participation in Medicare and state health care programs.

In addition to these penalties, those who commit health care fraud can be tried for mail and wire fraud.

Medicare fraudulent practices are regulated by the following:

- Civil Monetary Penalties Act
- Compliance guidelines
- Federal Claims Collection Act of 1966
- Health Insurance Portability and Accountability Act (HIPAA)
- Correct Coding Initiative (CCI)

- False Claims Act (FCA)
- Federal Anti-kickback Statute
- Physician self-referral laws (Stark I and Stark II)
- Physicians at Teaching Hospitals (PATH) initiative
- Payment Error and Prevention Program (PEPP)

The **Civil Monetary Penalties Act** imposes a maximum penalty of up to $10,000 plus a maximum assessment of up to three times the amount claimed by providers who knew that a procedure/service was not rendered as submitted on the claim. Violators can also be excluded from participation in government programs (e.g., Medicaid or Medicare).

EXAMPLE: A provider bills Medicare for services provided to a patient that are not documented in the patient record. The charges submitted on the claim total $95. If found guilty of fraud, the provider would be required to pay a fine in the amount of $10,285.

The DHHS Office of the Inspector General (OIG) developed a series of provider-specific **compliance guidances**, which identify risk areas and offer concrete suggestions to improve and enhance an organization's internal controls so that billing practices and other business arrangements are in compliance with Medicare's rules and regulations. Voluntary compliance guidelines have been established for the following:

> **Note:**
>
> By law, providers are not subject to civil, criminal, or administrative sanction penalties for innocent errors, or even for negligence.

- Ambulance industry
- Ambulance suppliers
- Clinical laboratories
- Durable medical equipment, prosthetics, orthotics, and supply industry
- Home health agencies
- Hospices

- Hospital industry
- Hospitals
- Individual and small-group physician practices
- Nursing facilities
- Medicare Advantage organizations
- Pharmaceutical manufacturers
- Third-party medical billing companies

A voluntary compliance program helps providers avoid generating erroneous and fraudulent claims by ensuring that submitted claims are true and accurate, expediting and optimizing proper payment of claims, minimizing billing mistakes, and preventing conflicts with self-referral and anti-kickback statutes.

EXAMPLE: If a coder determines that a physician's documentation is unclear or conflicting, the coder should ask the physician for clarification. In some facilities, the policy is to have the coder contact the physician directly. In others, the coder completes a preprinted form, entering pertinent information about the need for clarification, and this form is forwarded to the physician.

The National Correct Coding Initiative (NCCI) was developed by CMS to promote national correct coding methodologies, eliminate improper coding, and reduce Medicare program expenditures by detecting inappropriate codes on claims and denying payment for them. The principles for the CCI are to ensure that the service

- Represents the standard of care in accomplishing the overall procedure
- Is necessary to successfully accomplish the comprehensive procedure (and that failure to perform the service may compromise the success of the procedure)
- Does not represent a separately identifiable procedure unrelated to the comprehensive procedure planned

(The HCPCS level II and CPT coding systems are used by physicians and others to describe services rendered.) CCI edits are based on HCPCS level II and CPT coding principles along with current standards of medical and surgical coding practice, input from specialty societies, and analysis of current coding practice. Table 19-4 contains a list of CCI terms, definitions, and examples.

Table 19-4 National Correct Coding Initiative (NCCI) Terms and Definitions

Term	Definition	Example	
CCI Edits	Pairs of HCPCS level II and/or CPT codes, which are not separately payable except under certain circumstances (e.g., reporting appropriate modifier). The edits are applied to services billed by the same provider for the same beneficiary on the same date of service.	A surgeon intends to perform laparoscopic cholecystectomy; upon visualization of the gallbladder, it is determined that an open cholecystectomy is required. If the surgeon reports CPT codes for removal of an organ through an open incision, as well as with laparoscopy, the CCI edit results in claims denial.	**NOTE:** If a laparoscopic procedure becomes an open procedure, report only the open procedure code.
Comprehensive Code	The major procedure or service when reported with another code. The comprehensive code represents greater work, effort, and time as compared to the other code reported (also called *Column 1* codes). Higher payments are associated with comprehensive codes.	A patient undergoes deep biopsy as well as superficial biopsy of the same site. If the surgeon reports CPT codes for the deep and superficial biopsies, the CCI edit results in claims denial.	**NOTE:** Report only the deep biopsy when both deep and superficial biopsies are performed at the same location.
Component Code	The lesser procedure or service when reported with another code. The component code is part of a major procedure or service and is often represented by a lower work relative value unit (RVU) under the Medicare Physician Fee Schedule as compared to the other code reported (also called *Column 2* codes). Lower payments are associated with component codes.	If the surgeon determines that the superficial biopsy code should be reported in addition to the deep biopsy code, supporting documentation in the patient's record must be evident.	**NOTE:** To have component code(s) considered for possible reimbursement, attach a modifier to the code(s). A modifier is a two-digit code added to a code to indicate a procedure or service has been altered (e.g., bilateral procedure).
Column1/ Column 2 Edit Table	Code combinations (or edit pairs), where comprehensive code and only the comprehensive code is paid. (If clinical circumstances justify appending a CCI-associated modifier to either code of a code pair edit, payment of both codes may be allowed.)	Figure 19-9 contains a partial listing of the table of Column 1/Column 2 codes. Refer to Column 1, code 10121. If code 10121 is reported on a CMS-1500 claim, none of the codes from Column 2 can be reported on the same claim (unless a modifier is attached and supporting documentation is found in the patient's record).	NOTE: Column 2 codes are components of Column 1 codes, which means a Column 1 code includes all procedures/services described by Column 2 codes. Thus, Column 2 codes cannot be reported with Column 1 codes because overpayments would result.
Mutually Exclusive Codes	Procedures or services that could not reasonably be performed at the same session by the same provider on the same beneficiary.	A claim that contains codes for cystourethroscopy, with internal urethrotomy of a female (CPT code 52270) with that of a male (CPT code 52275) will result in denial as a result of this CCI edit.	**NOTE:** To have mutually exclusive code(s) considered for possible reimbursement, attach a modifier to the code(s).
Mutually Exclusive Edit Table	Code combinations (or edit pairs), where one of the procedures/ services would not reasonably be performed with the other. (If clinical circumstances justify adding a CCI modifier to either code of a code pair edit, payment of both codes may be allowed.)	Figure 19-10 contains a partial listing of the table of mutually exclusive codes. Refer to Column 1, code 10060. If code 10060 is reported on a CMS-1500 claim, none of the codes from Column 2 can be reported on the same claim (unless a modifier is attached and supporting documentation is found in the patient's record).	**NOTE:** When mutually exclusive codes are reported on the same claim (for the same date of service), reimbursement is based on the lower-paying code.

NATIONAL CORRECT CODING INITIATIVE COLUMN 1/COLUMN 2 EDITS					
Column 1	Column 2	* = In existence prior to 1996	Effective Date	Deletion Date * = no data	Modifier 0 = not allowed 1 = allowed 9 = not applicable
10021	J2001		20040701	*	1
10021	36000		20021001	*	1
10021	64415		20021001	*	1
10021	64416		20030101	*	1
10021	64417		20021001	*	1

Figure 19-9 Sample of NCCI Column 1/Column 2 edits

NATIONAL CORRECT CODING INITIATIVE MUTUALLY EXCLUSIVE EDITS					
Column 1	Column 2	* = In existence prior to 1996	Effective Date	Deletion Date * = no data	Modifier 0 = not allowed 1 = allowed 9 = not applicable
10060	11401		19960101	*	1
10060	11402		19960101	*	1
10060	11403		19960101	*	1
10060	11404		19960101	*	1
10060	11406		19960101	*	1

Figure 19-10 Sample of NCCI mutually exclusive edits

The federal **False Claims Act (FCA)** was enacted in 1863 in response to widespread abuses by government contractors during the Civil War, and it was amended in 1986 to strengthen the law and increase monetary awards (e.g., up to $10,000 per false claim, plus three times the amount of damages that the government sustains). It imposes civil liability on those who submit false/fraudulent claims to the government for payment and can exclude violators from participation in government programs (e.g., Medicaid and Medicare).

Note:

Qui tam provisions of the FCA encourage and reward private individuals (sometimes called *whistle-blowers*) who are aware of fraud being committed against the government to report that information. In addition, the FCA only covers offenses that are committed with actual knowledge of the falsity of the claim, or reckless disregard or deliberate ignorance of the truth or falsity of a claim. The FSA does not penalize mistakes, errors, or negligence. The OIG has stated that it is mindful of the difference between innocent errors (e.g., erroneous claims) and reckless or intentional conduct (e.g., fraudulent claims).

The **Federal Anti-kickback Statute** prohibits the offer, payment, receipt, or solicitation of compensation for referring Medicaid/Medicare patients and imposes a $25,000 fine per violation, plus imprisonment for up to 10 years. Civil penalties may also be imposed, and violators can be excluded from participation in government programs (e.g., Medicaid and Medicare). **Safe harbor regulations** were also implemented, which specify various payment and business practices that, although potentially capable of inducing referrals of business reimbursable under federal health care programs, would not be treated as criminal offenses under the Anti-kickback Statute.

EXAMPLE: The DHHS implemented a safe harbor for the waiver or reduction of coinsurance or deductible amounts (cost-sharing amounts) for inpatient hospital services reimbursed under the PPS. For full or partial waivers to be protected, three standards had to be met: (1) the hospital could not claim waived amounts as bad debt or otherwise shift the cost of the waivers; (2) the hospital could not discriminate in offering waivers or reductions based on the patient's reason for admission; and (3) the waivers or reductions could not result from an agreement between the hospital and a third-party payer. The DHHS concluded that waivers of cost-sharing amounts for inpatient hospital services that complied with these standards would not increase costs to the Medicare program, shift costs to other payers, or increase patient demand for inpatient hospital services.

Subtitle A of the Health Insurance Portability and Accountability Act of 1997 (HIPAA) authorized implementation of a fraud and abuse control program, which coordinates federal, state, and local law enforcement programs to control fraud and abuse with respect to health plans; conducts investigations, audits, evaluations, and inspections relating to delivery of and payment for health care in the United States; facilitates enforcement of health care fraud and abuse provisions; provides for modification and establishment of safe harbors; and issues advisory opinions and special fraud alerts to provide for reporting and disclosure of certain final adverse actions against health care providers, suppliers, or practitioners.

The **Federal Claims Collection Act of 1966** established uniform procedures for government agencies to follow in the collection, compromise, suspension, termination, or referral for litigation of debts owed to the government. This means that MACs (as agents of the federal government) are responsible for attempting to collect **overpayments**, which are funds that a provider or beneficiary receives in excess of amounts due and payable under Medicare and Medicare statutes and regulations. Any review conducted by the MAC for overpayment recovery must be done within three calendar years after the year in which the overpayment was made. Once a determination of overpayment has been made, the amount so determined is a debt owed to the U.S. government.

 Note:

The Act does not apply where there is an indication of fraud, for which such cases are submitted to the OIG for review and referral to the DOJ.

Examples of overpayments include the following:

- Payment based on a charge that exceeds the reasonable charge

- Duplicate processing of charges and/or claims

- Payment made to the wrong payee (e.g., payment made to a provider on a nonassigned claim, or payment made to a beneficiary on an assigned claim)

- Payment for noncovered items and services, including medically unnecessary services

- Incorrect application of the deductible, coinsurance, or copayment

- Payment for items or services rendered during a period of nonentitlement

- Primary payment for items or services for which another entity is the primary payer

- Payment for items or services rendered after the beneficiary's date of death (postpayment reviews are conducted to identify and recover payments with a billed date of service that is after the beneficiary's date of death)

Once a Medicare administrative contractor determines that an overpayment was made, it proceeds with recovery by issuing an overpayment demand letter (Figure 19-11) to the provider. The letter contains information about the review and statistical sampling methodology used, as well as corrective actions to be taken. Corrective actions include payment suspension, imposition of civil monetary penalties, institution of prepayment or postpayment review, and additional edits.

EMPIRE MEDICARE ADMINISTRATIVE CONTRACTOR

P.O. Box 1000 • Albany, NY 12246 • (800) 555-1234

June 15, YYYY

Patient Billing Department
Alfred State Medical Center
100 Main Street
Alfred NY 14802

RE: PATIENT: Mary Sue Patient
       SSN: 123-45-6789
       CLAIM #:   987654321
       DATE OF SERVICE: April 5, YYYY

Dear Provider,

Please be advised that an overpayment of benefits has been made for the above named patient. In order to resolve this matter, we are asking you to make repayment. Please make your check payable to:

EMPIRE MEDICARE ADMINISTRATIVE CONTRACTOR

in the amount of:

$995.00

and forward it to:

EMPIRE MAC
P.O. Box 1000
Albany, NY 12246

We are requesting this refund due to the following reason:

CLAIM WAS PROCESSED IN DUPLICATE.

If you have any questions, please feel free to contact us.

Sincerely,

Mary Louse Smith
Claims Analysis (39-392)

Figure 19-11 Sample overpayment recovery letter

 Note:

A provider is not liable for overpayments received if found to be without fault as determined by the MAC, such as when reasonable care was exercised in billing and accepting payment and the provider had a reasonable basis for assuming that payment was correct. In addition, if the provider had a reason to question the payment and promptly brought the question to the attention of the MAC, the provider may be found without liability.

The **Payment Error and Prevention Program (PEPP)** identifies and reduces improper Medicare payments, resulting in a reduction in the Medicare payment error rate. It also participates in **overpayment recovery** by collecting overpayments made by Medicare, Medicaid, and other payers.

A **physician self-referral law**, **Stark I**, enacted as part of the Omnibus Budget Reconciliation Act of 1989, prohibits a physician from referring Medicare patients to clinical laboratory services where they or a member of their family have a financial interest. (The financial interest includes both ownership/investment interests and compensation arrangements.) By 1994, because some providers routinely waived coinsurance and copayments, the DHHSOIG issued the following fraud alert:

Routine waiver of deductibles and copayments by charge-based providers, practitioners or suppliers is unlawful because it results in (1) false claims, (2) violations of the anti-kickback statute, and (3) excessive utilization of items and services paid for by Medicare.

(The only exception to the alert is waiving deductibles and copayments for financial hardship cases, but this *cannot be done on a routine* basis.)

In 1995, the **Stark II** physician self-referral law expanded the Stark I law by including referrals of Medicare *and* Medicaid patients for the following designated health care services (DHCS):

- Clinical laboratory services
- Durable medical equipment and supplies
- Home health services
- Inpatient and outpatient hospitalization services
- Occupational therapy services
- Outpatient prescription drugs
- Parenteral and enteral nutrients, equipment, and supplies
- Physical therapy services
- Prosthetics, orthotics, and prosthetic devices and supplies
- Radiation therapy services and supplies
- Radiology services, including MRIs, CT scans, and ultrasound services

Medicare Part A reimburses health care facilities for costs associated with training residents. The **Physicians at Teaching Hospitals (PATH) initiative** resulted from the discovery that some health care organizations were billing Medicare Part B for services that were already paid under Part A. The PATH initiative requires a national review of teaching hospitals' compliance with reimbursement rules and training of physicians who provide services at teaching facilities.

Administrative Simplification

The purpose of **HIPAA administrative simplification (AS)** provisions is to develop standards for the maintenance and transmission of health information required to identify individual patients. These standards are designed to improve efficiency and effectiveness of the health care system by standardizing the interchange of electronic data for specified administrative and financial transactions. In addition, the intent is to protect the security and confidentiality of electronic health information. HIPAA provisions require compliance by all health care organizations that maintain or transmit electronic health information. The law also establishes significant penalties for violations (e.g., $100 for each violation, a $25,000 maximum penalty for violations of an identical requirement, a $50,000 wrongful disclosure penalty and/or imprisonment of not more than one year, a $100,000 penalty for offenses under false pretenses and/or imprisonment of not more than 5 years, and a $250,000 penalty for offense with intent to sell information and/or imprisonment of not more than 10 years).

 Note:

> HIPAA established the **Designated Standard Maintenance Organization (DSMO)**, which is made up of organizations that agree to maintain the electronic transactions standards adopted by the Secretary of DHHS and to develop or modify adopted standards. Approved DSMOs include the Accredited Standards Committee X12, Dental Content Committee of the American Dental Association, Health Level Seven (HL7), National Council for Prescription Drug Programs, National Uniform Billing Committee, and National Uniform Claim Committee.

Unique Identifiers

HIPAA administrative simplification provisions require the following national identifiers to be established:

- **National standard employer identifier number (EIN).** The IRS's federal tax identification number was adopted as the national employer identifier, retaining the hyphen after the first two numbers (e.g.,

12-3456789). The EIN is assigned to employers who, as sponsors of health insurance for their employers, must be identified in health care transactions.

- **National provider identifier (NPI)**. HIPAA provisions require hospitals, doctors, nursing homes, and other health care providers to obtain a unique identifier consisting of 10 numeric digits (e.g., 1234567890) for filing electronic claims with public and private insurance programs. Providers apply for the NPI once and keep it if they relocate or change specialties. Currently, health care providers are assigned different ID numbers by each health plan, which results in slower payments, increased costs, and a lack of coordination.

> **Note:**
>
> A **check digit** is a one-digit character, alphabetic or numeric, that is used to verify the validity of a unique identifier.

- **National health plan identifier (HPID)**. The HPID is assigned to third-party payers, and it contains 10 numeric positions including a check digit in the tenth position (e.g., 1234567890). (The HPID was formerly called the PlanID and the PAYERID.)

- **National individual identifier (patient identifier)**. The HIPAA provision for a national individual identifier (or patient identifier) has been withdrawn. Although HIPAA included a requirement for the assignment of a unique personal health care identifier to each person in the United States, Congress is proposing legislation that would eliminate the requirement to establish a national individual identifier.

Electronic Health Care Transactions

HIPAA requires payers to implement **electronic transaction standards**, a uniform language for electronic data interchange. **Electronic data interchange (EDI)** is the computer-to-computer transfer of data between provider and third-party payer (or provider and health care clearinghouse) in a data format agreed upon by the sending and receiving parties. HIPAA's administrative simplification provisions directed the federal government to adopt national electronic standards for the automated transfer of certain health care data among health care payers (e.g., Medicare administrative contractors), payers (e.g., BCBS), and providers (e.g., hospitals and physicians). The provisions enable the entire health care industry to communicate electronic data using a single set of standards, eliminating all nonstandard formats currently in use. The standards allow a health care provider to submit a standard transaction for eligibility, authorization, referrals, claims, or attachments containing the same standard data content to any payer. This "simplifies" clinical, billing, and other financial applications, and it reduces costs.

Computer-generated paper claims are not considered EDI. Providers that generate paper-based claims submit them to health care clearinghouses, which convert them to a standardized electronic format for submission to payers. A health care clearinghouse performs centralized claims processing for providers and health care plans; it receives claims from providers, transmits claims to payers, receives remittance advice and payment instructions from payers, and transmits that information to providers (all in a HIPAA-compliant format). A health care clearinghouse also conducts eligibility and claim status queries in the format prescribed by HIPAA.

A **remittance advice (remit)** (Figure 19-12) is a statement sent by the payer to the provider, which details how submitted claims were processed and contains reimbursement amounts. If a claim is denied, an explanation of denial is included on the remittance advice. Providers may receive an electronic remittance advice (ERA) or a paper-based statement, called a standard paper remittance (SPR). The remittance advice includes the following information: patient name, health insurance claim number (HICN), provider's name, date(s) of service, type of service, procedure codes and modifiers, charges (both submitted and allowed), reimbursement amount including any deductions (e.g., copayments), reason and/or remark codes (e.g., explanation of denial), and an indication that the claim has been forwarded to a supplemental carrier for processing, if applicable.

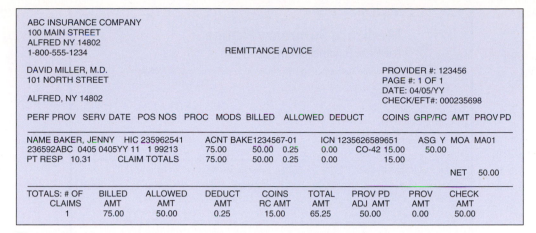

Figure 19-12 Sample remittance advice (single claim)

EXAMPLE: Health care providers submit electronic claims data to payers on computer tape, diskette, or by computer modem or fax. The payer receives the claim, processes the data, and sends the provider the results of processing electronic claims (an electronic remittance advice).

An **explanation of benefits (EOB)** (Figure 19-13A) is sent to the patient by the payer, and it contains the same information as the remittance advice but it is in an easy-to-read format. ☞ Medicare patients receive a **Medicare Summary Notice (MSN)** (Figure 19-13B) (instead of an EOB), which is an easy-to-read monthly statement that clearly lists health insurance claims information.

 Note:

The MSN replaced the Explanation of Medicare Benefits (EOMB), the Medicare Benefits Notice (Part A), and benefit denial letter.

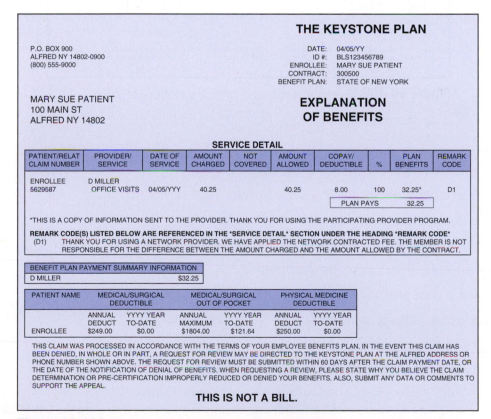

Figure 19-13A Sample explanation of benefits (EOB)

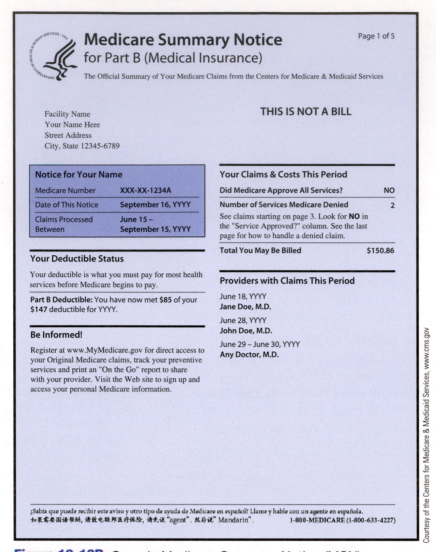

Figure 19-13B Sample Medicare Summary Notice (MSN)

Effective 2003, electronic claims will not be processed by Medicare administrative contractors if they are not in an electronic format. Advantages of EDI include the following:

- Claim status and eligibility information in 24 hours or less

- Cost effectiveness and reduction in opportunity for error

- Electronic funds transfer of accounts receivable into the provider's bank

- Electronic remittances sent to a provider-preferred location

- Faster payment of electronic claims

- Lower administrative, postage, and handling costs

- Online receipt or acknowledgement

- Standardized electronic claims submission, coordination of benefits exchange, and remittance receipts reduce system costs.

Three electronic formats are supported for health care claims transactions, including the UB-04 flat-file format (Figure 19-14), the National Standard Format (NSF) (Figure 19-15), and the **ANSI ASC X12N 837** format

```
MSG_HDR BCBS ECM_Y06 SndApp SndFac RcApp RcFac 200601052369 56941
INS_CLM 562697 20060105 20060110 ADL05691125.00
PRV_DT1M_P Smith DKSL23659
PRV_DT1M_H Jones DLEP65915
PAT_IDF DCB5432 Green 19941205
CRD_STS YYN
SRV_CMN GM 20060105 50.00
SRV_FEE CP 45.00
SRV_FEE CK 12.00
SRV_CMN GM 20060106 55.00
SRV_FEE CO 10.00
SRV_FEE RK
```

Figure 19-14 Sample UB-04 electronic flat-file format

```
ELECTRONIC MEDIA CLAIMS NATIONAL STANDARD FORMAT
RECORD NAME: CLAIM HEADER RECORD "PATIENT DATA"              RECORD TYPE: CA0
```

FIELD NUMBER	FIELD NAME	FIELD LENGTH	FIELD TYPE	FIELD POSITIONS FROM	TO
01.0	RECORD ID "CA0"	3	X	01	03
02.0	RESERVED (CA0-02.0)	2	X	04	05
03.0	PATIENT CONTROL NUMBER	17	X	06	22
04.0	PATIENT LAST NAME	20	X	23	42
05.0	PATIENT FIRST NAME	12	X	43	54
06.0	PATIENT MIDDLE INITIAL	1	X	55	55
07.0	PATIENT GENERATION	3	X	56	58
08.0	PATIENT DATE OF BIRTH	8	X	59	66
09.0	PATIENT GENDER	1	X	67	67
10.0	PATIENT TYPE OF RESIDENCE	1	X	68	68

Figure 19-15 Portion of electronic medical claims National Standard
Format (NSF)

(American National Standards Institute, Accredited Standards Committee, Insurance Subcommittee X12N, claims validation table 837) (Figure 19-16).

 Note:

A **flat file** consists of a series of fixed-length records (e.g., eight spaces for the patient's date of birth). The UB-04 flat file is used to bill institutional services (e.g., hospitals), and the National Standard Format (NSF) flat file is used to bill physician and noninstitutional services (e.g., the physician's office). ANSI ASC X12N 837 is a variable-length file format that is used to bill institutional, professional, dental, and drug claims. The flat-file formats were developed for use in claims processing software application programs because the ANSI ASC X12N 837 format is not suitable for use in an application program, and it must be translated into a flat-file format prior to claims processing.

Medicare administrative contractors do not accept flat-file format transactions for claims submission. Medicare administrative contractors also do not send electronic remittance advices in the flat-file format or exchange electronic eligibility queries/responses in any version not adopted as a national standard in the final rules for the HIPAA Administrative Simplification transaction standards. However, providers can use health care clearinghouses to translate outgoing and/or incoming electronic transactions, which will convert flat-file formats to the ANSI ASC X12N 837 format. Providers who do not use a health care clearinghouse must install software that can send and receive files in the ANSI ASC X12N 837 format.

UB-04 data elements in ANSI ASC X12N 837 format	Description of data elements
ST*837*123456~ BHT*0019*00*A98765*YYYY0504*0830~	Header
NM1*41*2*GOODMEDICINE HOSPITAL*****54*888229999~	Submitter name
NM1*40*2*CAPITAL BLUE CROSS*****54*16000~	Receiver name
HL*1**20*1~	Service provider hierarchical level for submitter
NM1*85*2*GOODMEDICINE HOSPITAL*****54*888229999~ REF*1J*898989~	Service provider name
HL*2*1*22*1~ SBR*P********BL~	Subscriber (patient) hierarchical level
NM1*IL*1*PUBLIC*JOHN*Q**MI*GRNESSC1234~ N3*1247 HILL STREET~ N4*ANYWHERE*US*12345~ DMG*D8*19820805*M**::RET:3::RET:2~ REF*SY*150259874~	Subscriber (patient) name
NM1*PR*2*CAPITAL BLUE CROSS*****PI*00303~	Payer name
CLM*ABH123456*5015***11:A:1~ DTP*096*TM*1200~ DTP*434*RD8*YYYY0504-YYYY0510~ DTP*435*DT*YYYY05101100~ CL1*2*1*01~ HI*BK:66411*BJ:66411~ HI*BF:66331:::::::Y*BF:66111:::::::N*BF:V270:::::::N~ HI*BR:7569:D8:YYYY0510~	Claim information
SE*91*123456~	Trailer

Figure 19-16 Portion of UB-04 data submitted in ANSI ASC X12N 837 electronic format

HIPAA administrative simplification provisions also require the following code sets to be used:

- *Current Dental Terminology (CDT)*: Dental services

- *International Classification of Diseases, 9th Revision, Clinical Modification (ICD-9-CM)*: All diagnoses and inpatient hospital procedures and services ⚠

- *Current Procedural Terminology (CPT)*: Outpatient hospital and physician procedures and services

- *Health Care Common Procedure Coding System, Level II (National)*: Outpatient hospital and physician procedures and services, and institutional/professional pharmacy transactions ✎

- *National Drug Code (NDC)*: Retail pharmacy transactions

In 2009, the Department of Health & Human Services published a final rule entitled *HIPAA Administrative Simplification: Modifications to Medical Data Code Set Standards to Adopt ICD-10-CM and ICD-10-PCS*, which replaced ICD-9-CM with the following:

- *International Classification of Diseases, 10th Revision, Clinical Modification (ICD-10-CM)*: All diagnoses

- *International Classification of Diseases, 10th Revision, Procedure Coding System (ICD-10-PCS)*: Hospital inpatient procedures

 ICD-10 Alert!

ICD-10-CM and ICD-10-PCS were implemented on October 1, 2015.

 Note:

No standard code set was adopted for nonretail pharmacy drug claims.

Privacy and Security Rules

Any information communicated by a patient to a health care provider is considered **privileged communication**, which means that it is private. Patients have the right to **confidentiality**, which is the process of keeping privileged communication secret and means that information cannot be disclosed without the patient's authorization. (Exceptions include information released via *subpoena duces tecum*, court order, and according to statutory reporting requirements.) A **breach of confidentiality** occurs when patient information is **disclosed** (or released) to other(s) who do not have a right to access the information. In this situation, the disclosing provider failed to obtain patient authorization to release privileged communication; this results in violation of federal law (HIPAA). According to HIPAA privacy and security provisions, patients have the right to an expectation of **privacy** regarding their privileged communication, which means information cannot be disclosed without their authorization. **Security** safeguards also must be implemented to ensure that facilities, equipment, and patient information are safe from damage, loss, tampering, theft, or unauthorized access.

The **HIPAA standards for privacy of individually identifiable health information**, or **privacy rule**, include provisions that protect the security and confidentiality of health information. ✒ Because the use and disclosure of health information is inconsistently protected by state laws, patients' privacy and confidentiality is also inconsistently protected. The HIPAA privacy rule establishes standards to protect the confidentiality of individually identifiable health information maintained or transmitted electronically in connection with certain administrative and financial transactions (e.g., electronic transfer of health insurance claims). The rule provides new rights for individuals with respect to protected health information (PHI) and mandates compliance by **covered entities**, which are private and public sector organizations that must follow HIPAA provisions. For the privacy rule, covered entities include health care providers that conduct certain transactions in electronic forms, health plans, and health care clearinghouses.

Note:

HIPAA is the first federal law that governs the privacy of health information nationwide. If security policies and procedures are not established and enforced, concerns might be raised about the security of patient information during legal proceedings. This could result in questioning the integrity of the medical record.

Protected health information (PHI) is information that is identifiable to an individual (or individual identifiers) such as name, address, telephone number, date of birth, Medicaid ID number and other medical record numbers, Social Security number (SSN), and name of employer. In most instances, covered entities are required to obtain an individual's authorization prior to disclosing the individual's health information, and HIPAA has established specific requirements for an authorization form. All medical records and other individually identifiable health information used or disclosed by a covered entity in any form, whether electronically, paper-based, or verbally, are covered by the privacy rule.

The HIPAA **security rule** contains standards and safeguards for PHI that is collected, maintained, used, or transmitted electronically. Covered entities impacted by this rule include health plans, health care clearinghouses, and certain health care providers. CMS is responsible for overseeing compliance with and complaints about security rules.

The standard for electronic signature is **digital**, which applies a mathematical function to the electronic document resulting in a unique bit string (computer code) called a message digest, which is encrypted and appended to the electronic document. (**Encrypt** means to encode a computer file, making it safe for electronic transmission so unauthorized parties cannot read it.) The recipient of the transmitted electronic document **decrypts** (decodes) the message digest and compares the decoded digest to the transmitted version. If they are identical, the message is unaltered and the identity of the signer is proven.

The DHHS Medicare Program, other federal agencies operating health plans or providing health care, state Medicaid agencies, private health plans, health care providers, and health care clearinghouses must assure their customers (e.g., patients, insured individuals, providers, and health plans) that the integrity, confidentiality, and availability of electronic PHI they collect, maintain, use, or transmit is protected. The confidentiality of health information is threatened not only by the risk of improper access to stored information, but also by the risk of interception during electronic transmission of the information. The purpose of the *security rule* is to adopt national standards for safeguards to protect the confidentiality, integrity, and availability of electronic PHI. Prior to publication of the *security rule*, no standard measures existed in the health care industry to address all aspects of the security of electronic health information while being stored or during the exchange of that information between entities. In general, security provisions should include the following procedures:

- Define authorized users of patient information to control access.

- Implement a tracking procedure to sign out records to authorized personnel.

- Limit record storage access to authorized users.

- Lock record storage areas at all times.

- Require the original medical record to remain in the facility at all times (except when a court order requires the original medical record to be submitted to the court clerk).

Although security and privacy are linked, be sure you do not confuse the purpose of each rule. The *security rule* defines administrative, physical, and technical safeguards to protect the availability, confidentiality, and integrity of PHI. The standards require covered entities to implement basic safeguards to protect electronic PHI from unauthorized access, alteration, deletion, and transmission. In contrast, the *privacy rule* establishes standards for how PHI should be controlled; it also establishes what uses (e.g., continuity of care) and disclosures (e.g., third-party reimbursement) are authorized or required, as well as what rights patients have with respect to their health information (e.g., patient access).

Medical Liability Reform

The threat of excessive awards in medical liability cases has increased providers' liability insurance premiums, which has resulted in increases in health care costs. Because of this, some providers have stopped practicing medicine in areas of the country where liability insurance costs are highest, and the direct impact on individuals and communities across the country has been reduced access to quality medical care. Although medical liability reform was included in HIPAA legislation, no final rule was published. Although individual states, such as Ohio, have passed medical liability reform, the U.S. Congress is also formulating separate federal medical liability reform legislation. The Senate introduced legislation that will implement reasonable, comprehensive, and effective health care liability reforms designed to improve the availability of health care services in cases in which health care liability actions have been shown to be a factor in the decreased availability of services; reduce the incidence of "defensive medicine" and lower the cost of health care liability insurance, all of which contribute to the escalation of health care costs; ensure that persons with meritorious health care injury claims receive fair and adequate compensation, including reasonable noneconomic damages; improve the fairness and cost-effectiveness of our current health care liability system to resolve disputes over, and provide compensation for, health care liability by reducing uncertainty in the amount of compensation provided to injured individuals; and provide increased sharing of information in the health care system, which will reduce unintended injury and improve patient care. (Go to http://thomas.loc.gov, and enter medical liability reform in the "Search Bill Text" box to view the list of proposed legislation.)

Health Reform

In 2010, two significant federal laws were implemented that resulted in health reform.

- The Patient Protection and Affordable Care Act (PPACA)

  ○ Allows young adults to remain on a parent's plan until the age of 26

  ○ Assists employers that provide retiree health benefits

  ○ Creates health insurance exchanges

  ○ Ends insurance company abuses

  ○ Establishes a competitive health insurance market

  ○ Expands Medicaid eligibility

  ○ Immediately establishes a plan for the uninsured

- Maintains employer-sponsored coverage for most Americans who currently have it

- Prohibits the denial of coverage/claims based on pre-existing conditions

- Provides 32 million uninsured children and families with access to coverage

- Provides incentives for businesses to provide health care benefits

- Reduces the maximum time period for submitting Medicare fee-for-service claims to one calendar year after the date of service

- Subsidizes insurance premiums

- Supports medical research

• The Health Care and Education Reconciliation Act (HCERA) amended the PPACA to

- Close the Medicare Part D "donut hole" by 2011, and give seniors a rebate of $250.

- Delay implementation on taxing "Cadillac health care plans" until 2018.

- Eliminate several special deals given to senators.

- Establish a Medicare tax on unearned incomes of families who earn more than $250,000 annually.

- Extend the ban on lifetime limits and rescission of coverage to all existing health plans within six months.

- Increase Medicaid payment rates to primary care physicians to match Medicare payment rates, and provide states that already insure childless adults under Medicaid with more federal money for covering that group through 2018.

- Increase tax credits to buy insurance.

- Lower the penalty for not buying insurance from $750 to $695.

- Offer more generous subsidies to lower income groups.

- Provide a 50 percent discount to Medicare patients on brand-name drugs effective 2011 (and by 2020, provide up to a 75 percent discount on brand-name and generic drugs, eventually closing the coverage gap).

- Require doctors who treat Medicare patients to be reimbursed at the full rate.

The costs of the above provisions are offset by a variety of taxes, fees, and cost-saving measures, such as new Medicare taxes for high-income brackets, taxes on indoor tanning, cuts to the Medicare Advantage program in favor of traditional Medicare, and fees on medical devices and pharmaceutical companies. Also included is a tax penalty for citizens who do not obtain health insurance (unless they are exempt due to low income or other reasons).

Exercise 19.3 – Impact of HIPAA on Reimbursement

Matching: Match the term in Column 2 with the example in Column 1. Answers may be used more than once.

_____ 1. Submitting excessive charges for services or supplies	**a.** Abuse
_____ 2. Unbundling codes reported on claims	**b.** Fraud
_____ 3. Billing Medicare for services or supplies not provided	
_____ 4. Submitting claims for services that aren't medically necessary	
_____ 5. Violating Medicare participating provider agreements with payers	

(continues)

Exercise 19.3 (continued)

Completion: Complete each statement.

1. Formerly called the PlanID, the identifier assigned to third-party payers that contains 10 numeric positions including a check digit in the tenth position is called the HPID, which is the abbreviation for _____.

2. The IRS's federal tax identification number is assigned to employers who, as sponsors of health insurance for their employers, must be identified in health care transactions; it was adopted as the national standard EIN, which is the abbreviation for _____.

3. Health care providers must obtain an NPI, which is the abbreviation for _____, which consists of nine alphanumeric characters plus a check digit, and is used for filing electronic claims with public and private insurance programs.

4. The computerized exchange of health information between provider and payer in a format agreed upon by the sending and receiving parties is called EDI, which is the abbreviation for_____.

5. HIPAA requires the implementation of standards and safeguards to protect health information that is collected, maintained, used, or transmitted electronically, which is called the _____ rule.

Summary

A third-party payer is an insurance company or other organization (e.g., a Medicare administrative contractor) that processes health care claims for reimbursement of procedures and services. Third-party payers include BlueCross and BlueShield (BCBS), commercial insurance companies, employer self-insurance plans, government-sponsored programs (e.g., Medicaid, Medicare, and TRICARE), managed care plans (e.g., a health maintenance organization), and workers' compensation. A health insurance policy is an agreement between an individual and a third-party payer (or insurance company) that contains a list of reimbursable medical benefits (or covered benefits) (e.g., office visits, inpatient hospitalizations, laboratory, tests, prescription medications, and treatment services).

Government programs reimburse providers according to prospective cost-based rates and prospective payment systems. Typically, third-party payers adopt prospective payment systems, fee schedules, and exclusions after Medicare has implemented them; payers modify them to suit their needs.

The Health Insurance Portability and Accountability Act of 1996 (HIPAA) amended the Internal Revenue Code of 1986 to improve portability and continuity of health insurance coverage in the group and individual markets; combat waste, fraud, and abuse in health insurance and health care delivery; promote the use of medical savings accounts; improve access to long-term care services and coverage; simplify the administration of health insurance by creating unique identifiers for providers, health plans, employers, and individuals; create standards for electronic health information transactions; and create privacy and security standards for health information.

Internet Links

Accredited Standards Committee X12N (ASC X12N): *www.x12.org*

Centers for Medicare & Medicaid Services: *www.cms.gov*

CMS Quarterly Provider Update: Go to *www.cms.gov*, click on the Regulations & Guidance link, and then click on the Quarterly Provider Updates link below the Regulations & Policies heading.

Health Care Claims Clearinghouse: *www.softcare.com*

Health Care Compliance Association (HCCA): Go to *www.hcca-info.org*, mouse over the Resources heading and HCCA Publications, and click on Compliance Weekly News to subscribe for free.

Health Level Seven (HL7): *www.hl7.org*

Health Reform: Go to *www.healthcare.gov* to learn more about the *Health Insurance Marketplace*.

MedAssets: Go to *www.MedAssets.com* to learn more about revenue cycle management services and solutions.

Medicare Conditions for Coverage and Conditions of Participation: Go to *www.cms.gov*, click on the Regulations & Guidance link, then click on the Conditions for Coverage (CfCs) & Conditions of Participation (CoPs) link below the Legislation heading.

Medicare Payment Systems: Go to *www.cms.gov*, click on the Medicare link, and then click on one or more of the topics below the Medicare Fee-for-Service Payment heading.

Medicare Preventive Services (coverage issues): Go to *www.cms.gov*, click on the Medicare link, then click on one or more of the topics below the Prevention heading.

MEDPAR: Go to *www.cms.gov*, click on the Research, Statistics, Data & Systems link, then click on the Medicare Fee-for-Service for Parts A & B link below the Statistics, Trends & Reports heading, and click on the MEDPAR link.

National Uniform Billing Committee: *www.nubc.org*

National Uniform Claim Committee: *www.nucc.org*

Office of Inspector General of the U.S. Department of Health & Human Services: *www.oig.hhs.gov*

Quality Improvement Organizations: Go to *www.cms.gov*, click on the Medicare link and then scroll down and click on the Quality Improvement Organizations link below the Quality Initiatives/Patient Assessment Instruments heading.

Workgroup for Electronic Data Interchange (WEDI): *www.wedi.org*

Study Checklist

- ❏ Read this chapter and highlight key concepts.
- ❏ Create an index card for each key term.
- ❏ Access the chapter Internet links to learn more about concepts.
- ❏ Complete the chapter exercises and review, verifying your answers with your instructor.
- ❏ Complete Workbook chapter, verifying answers with your instructor.
- ❏ Go to *www.cengagebrain.com* to access the Student Companion Web Site. Login instructions are located in the Preface.
- ❏ Form a study group with classmates to discuss chapter concepts in preparation for an exam.

Review

Multiple Choice

Instructions: Circle the most appropriate response.

1. An insurance policy is an agreement between a third-party payer and a(n):
    a. health care facility.
    b. health care provider.
    c. individual.
    d. insurance company.

2. Which of the following prohibits the health care provider from collecting payment from the patient for claims that the insurance plan has denied?
   - a. Hold harmless clause
   - b. Indemnification
   - c. Medical necessity
   - d. Preauthorization

3. Under an employer self-insurance plan, who would be responsible for payment of the employees' health care?
   - a. Employee
   - b. Employer
   - c. Third-party payer
   - d. Workers' compensation

4. Which third-party payer is state-mandated rather than government-sponsored?
   - a. Indian Health Service (IHS)
   - b. Programs of All-inclusive Care for the Elderly (PACE)
   - c. State Children's Health Insurance Program (SCHIP)
   - d. Workers' compensation

5. A patient who has the option to be seen by a non-HMO provider without obtaining a referral from the primary care physician (PCP), thus incurring a greater out-of-pocket expense, would be using which type of managed care plan?
   - a. Exclusive provider organization (EPO)
   - b. Health maintenance organization (HMO)
   - c. Point-of-service plan (POS)
   - d. Referred provider organization (PPO)

6. In the customized sub-capitation type of consumer-directed health plan, each provider is paid:
   - a. a fixed amount per month to manage all of an individual's health care, which includes reimbursing for services provided by labs and specialists.
   - b. a fixed amount per month to provide only the care that an individual needs from that provider.
   - c. a variable amount per month to manage all of an individual's health care from a tax-exempt account established by an employee.
   - d. both a fixed and a variable amount each month to manage an individual's health care when the employee uses the provider's services.

7. A cancer hospital that has been granted a waiver from mandatory participation in the hospital inpatient prospective payment system is called a(n) _____ by CMS.
   - a. exception
   - b. exclusion
   - c. pardon
   - d. release

8. Which prospective payment system uses information from the patient assessment instrument to classify patients into groups based on clinical characteristics and expected resource needs?
   - a. HH PPS
   - b. IRF PPS
   - c. LTC PPS
   - d. OPPS

9. The IPPS payment window for outpatient preadmission services provided by a long-term (acute) care hospital is _____ hours.
   - a. 24
   - b. 36
   - c. 48
   - d. 72

10. The resource-based relative value scale (RBRVS) system is now commonly called the

    _____.
    - a. Ambulance Fee Schedule
    - b. Clinical Laboratory Fee Schedule
    - c. Diagnosis Related Group (DRG)
    - d. Medicare Physician Fee Schedule (MPFS)

11. Case-mix adjustments:
    - a. allow payment systems to increase preestablished payments.
    - b. create an incentive for facilities to admit large volumes of low-cost patients.
    - c. result in fewer possible payment rates based on anticipated care needs.
    - d. result in higher anticipated payments for high-resource cases.

12. Severity of illness scores are based on _____.
    a. DRG assignment
    b. ICD-10-CM codes
    c. physiologic measures, signs, and symptoms
    d. the admission diagnosis

13. Monitoring unusual billing patterns and other indicators is an example of which of the strategies used by CMS to deter fraud and abuse?
    a. Coordination   b. Early detection   c. Enforcement   d. Prevention

14. A person found guilty of Medicare fraud faces _____.
    a. administrative sanction penalties
    b. civil penalties
    c. criminal, civil, and administrative sanction penalties
    d. criminal penalties

15. When a modifier is added to a code to indicate that the procedure or service is part of a major procedure or service, the code is known as a _____.
    a. code combination   c. comprehensive code
    b. component code   d. mutually exclusive code

16. Under the Federal Claims Collection Act of 1966, any review conducted by a Medicare administrative contractor for recovery of overpaid funds must be done within how many calendar years after the year in which the overpayment was made?
    a. Two   b. Three   c. Five   d. Seven

17. HIPAA administrative simplification provisions require that national identifiers be established. Which identifier has been withdrawn and is awaiting legislation by Congress to eliminate the requirement?
    a. National health plan identifier (HPID)
    b. National individual identifier (patient identifier)
    c. National provider identifier (NPI)
    d. National standard employer identifier number (EIN)

18. Which was published by HIPAA to adopt standards and safeguards to protect health information that is collected, maintained, used, or transmitted electronically?
    a. Confidentiality rule   c. Privacy rule
    b. Disclosure rule   d. Security rule

19. Which is a statement sent by the payer to the provider that contains reimbursement amounts and details how submitted claims were processed?
    a. Electronic data interchange (EDI)   c. Remittance advice
    b. Explanation of benefits (EOB)   d. Transaction for eligibility

20. The threat of excessive awards in medical liability cases has resulted in:
    a. decreased health care costs.
    b. increased access to quality medical care.
    c. increased liability insurance premiums for providers.
    d. increased numbers of practicing providers.

21. The Recovery Audit Contract (RAC) program was implemented as part of _____ legislation.
    a. HIPAA   b. MMA   c. SSA amendments   d. TEFRA

22. Medicare's Comprehensive Error Rate Testing (CERT) program was implemented to evaluate:
    a. individual provider compliance with Medicare regulations.
    b. Medicare administrative contractor (MAC) program performance.
    c. reimbursement made to hospitals serving more acutely ill patients.
    d. the transition from CMS-DRGs to MS-DRGs throughout the country.

23. Under the MS-DRG PPS, the abbreviation MCC refers to _____ comorbid and complication conditions.
    a. major
    b. Medicare
    c. MedPAC
    d. major diagnostic categories

24. All claims submitted for inpatient admissions to general acute care hospitals or other health care facilities are required to report the _____ indicator, which is assigned by the coder to the principal and secondary diagnoses and external cause of injury code reported on the UB-04 or 837 Institutional (electronic) claim.
    a. CMS   b. DRG   c. MDC   d. POA

25. Which did Medicare implement October 1, 2007, to classify inpatient hospital cases into groups according to similar resource utilization?
    a. AP-DRGs   b. APR-DRGs   c. MS-DRGs   d. RDRGs

Appendix I: *E/M CodeBuilder*

For use with CMS *1997 Documentation Guidelines for Evaluation & Management Coding*, which is located on the Student Companion Web Site at www.cengagebrain.com.

CMS also published the *1995 Documentation Guidelines for Evaluation & Management Coding*, which providers can opt to use. It is your author's opinion that because the 1997 guidelines are more specific and require documentation of specific elements, they are easier for students to use when learning how to select CPT E/M codes. (Providers must select one set of guidelines to be consistently used for CPT E/M code selection.)

 Note:

> Make copies of this *E/M CodeBuilder* (or print the document at the Student Companion Web Site at www.cengagebrain.com) to use when assigning E/M codes. Use of this document will reinforce the process required to assign E/M codes, and eventually selecting criteria will make using the form unnecessary.

Introduction

The evaluation and management (E/M) code reported to a third-party payer must be supported by documentation in the patient's record (e.g., SOAP or clinic note, diagnostic test results, operative findings). Although providers are responsible for selecting the E/M code from the encounter form, superbill, or chargemaster at the time patient care is rendered, insurance specialists audit records to make sure that the appropriate level of E/M code was reported to the third-party payer.

This *E/M CodeBuilder* form can be used for that purpose, and it can also be used as a tool to teach appropriate assignment of E/M level codes. To assign a code, just review the documentation in the patient's record, record your findings (based on the directions provided), and refer to the CPT coding manual to select the E/M code to be reported.

E/M code selection is based on three key components: *history, examination,* and *medical decision making.* This *E/M CodeBuilder* form emphasizes those components. It is important to be aware that contributory components (*counseling* and *coordination of care*) also play an important role in selecting the E/M code when documentation in the patient record indicates that counseling or coordination of care dominated the visit. In this situation, the contributory component of *time* can be considered a key or controlling factor in selecting a level of E/M service (code).

 Note:

> *Time* and *nature of presenting problem* are listed in some E/M code descriptions to assist in determining which code number to report.

Selecting the Level of History

To select the level of history, review the following elements in the patient record. If an element is not documented, it cannot be considered when selecting the level of E/M service code.

- History of present illness (HPI)
- Review of systems (ROS)
- Past, family, and/or social history (PFSH)

History of Present Illness (HPI)

Review the clinic or SOAP note in the patient's record, and for each documented HPI element (below), enter an X in the box in front of the element on this form. Then, total the Xs and enter that number on the line in front of the Total Score (below). Finally, select the level of HPI based on the total number of elements documented, and enter an X in the appropriate box.

- ☐ **Location:** Of pain/discomfort (e.g., is pain diffused/localized or unilateral/bilateral; does it radiate or refer?).

- ☐ **Duration:** Of pain/discomfort; length of time condition has persisted (e.g., pain began three days ago).

- ☐ **Quality:** A description of the quality of the symptom (e.g., is pain described as sharp, dull, throbbing, stabbing, constant, intermittent, acute or chronic, stable, improving, or worsening?).

- ☐ **Severity:** Use of self-assessment scale to measure subjective levels (e.g., on a scale of 1–10, how severe is the pain?), or comparison of pain quantitatively with previously experienced pain.

- ☐ **Timing:** Establishing onset of pain and chronology of pain development (e.g., migraine in the morning).

- ☐ **Context:** Where was the patient and what was he or she doing when pain began (e.g., was patient at rest or involved in an activity; was pain aggravated or relieved, or does it recur, with a specific activity; did situational stress or some other factor precede or accompany the pain)?

- ☐ **Modifying factors:** What has patient attempted to do to relieve pain (e.g., heat vs. cold; does it relieve or exacerbate pain; what makes the pain worse; have over-the-counter drugs been attempted—with what results)?

- ☐ **Associated signs/symptoms:** Clinician's impressions formulated during the interview may lead to questioning about additional sensations or feelings (e.g., diaphoresis associated with indigestion or chest pain, blurred vision accompanying a headache, etc.).

- _____ **Total Score:** Enter the score for number of Xs entered above (representing number of HPI elements), and enter an X in front of the HPI type below.

- ☐ Brief HPI (1–3 elements)

- ☐ Extended HPI (4 or more elements)

Review of Systems (ROS)

Review the clinic or SOAP note in the patient's record, and for each documented ROS element, enter an X in the box in front of the element on this form. Then, total the Xs and enter that number on the line in front of the Total Score. Finally, select the level of ROS based on the total number of elements documented, and enter an X in the appropriate box.

Note:

To properly assess review of systems documentation, have *CMS Documentation Guidelines for Evaluation & Management Coding* available as you review the patient's record. (Go to www.cms.gov and click on Outreach & Education, then on "Get training" below the Learn heading, and Documentation guidelines for E & M services to print the guidelines and use with this section of the *E/M CodeBuilder*.)

☐ Constitutional symptoms

  ☐ Allergic/Immunologic

  ☐ Cardiovascular

  ☐ Ears, nose, mouth, throat

  ☐ Endocrine

  ☐ Eyes

  ☐ Gastrointestinal

  ☐ Genitourinary

  ☐ Hematologic/Lymphatic

  ☐ Integumentary (including skin and breast)

  ☐ Musculoskeletal

  ☐ Neurologic

  ☐ Psychiatric

  ☐ Respiratory

_____ **Total Score:** Enter the score for number of Xs entered above (representing number of ROS elements), and enter an X in front of the ROS type below.

☐ None

☐ Problem pertinent ROS (1 body system documented)

☐ Extended ROS (2–9 body systems documented)

☐ Complete ROS (all body systems documented)

Past, Family, and/or Social History (PFSH)

Review the clinic or SOAP note in the patient's record, and for each documented PFSH element, enter an X in the box in front of the element on this form. Then, total the Xs and enter that number on the line in front of the Total Score. Finally, select the level of PFSH based on the total number of elements documented, and enter an X in the appropriate box.

☐ Past history (patient's past experience with illnesses, operations, injuries, and treatments)

☐ Family history (review of medical events in the patient's family, including diseases that may be hereditary or place the patient at risk)

☐ Social history (an age-appropriate review of past and current activities, such as alcohol use, occupation, and so on)

_____ **Total Score:** Enter the score for number of Xs entered above (representing number of PFSH elements), and enter an X in front of the PFSH type below.

☐ None

☐ Pertinent PFSH (1 history area documented)

☐ Complete PFSH (2 or 3 history areas documented)

Level of History

Circle the type of HPI, ROS, and PFSH in the following table (as determined from the entries selected above); then, circle the appropriate Extent of History determined in the following table.

HPI	Brief	Brief	Extended	Extended
ROS	None	Problem Pertinent	Extended	Complete
PFSH	None	None	Pertinent	Complete
EXTENT OF HISTORY	PROBLEM FOCUSED	EXPANDED PROBLEM FOCUSED	DETAILED	COMPREHENSIVE

Selecting the Level of Examination

To select the level of examination, first determine whether a *single organ examination* (specialist exam such as ophthalmologist) or a *general multisystem examination* (e.g., family practitioner) was completed.

Single Organ System Examination

The single organ system examinations recognized by CPT are described in detail beginning on page 18 of the CMS *1997 Documentation Guidelines for Evaluation & Management Services* (located on the Student Companion Web Site at www.cengagebrain.com). Single organ system examinations are usually performed by specialists (e.g., ophthalmologist, psychiatrist). You will notice variations among types of single organ examinations, which reflect differing emphases among specialties. Enter an X in front of the appropriate exam type below, after determining which content and documentation requirements of a single organ system examination have been met.

☐ PROBLEM FOCUSED EXAMINATION (1–5 elements identified by a bullet)

☐ EXPANDED PROBLEM FOCUSED EXAMINATION (at least 6 elements identified by a bullet)

☐ DETAILED EXAMINATION (at least 12 elements identified by a bullet)

☐ COMPREHENSIVE EXAMINATION (all elements identified by a bullet; document every element in each box

General Multisystem Exam

General multisystem examinations are described in detail beginning on page 13 of the CMS *1997 Documentation Guidelines for Evaluation & Management Services* (located on the Student Companion Web Site at www.cengagebrain. com). General multisystem examinations are performed by both general practitioners and specialists. Enter an X in front of the organ system or body area when the maximum number of allowed elements has been documented. For example, when two or more Neck examinations are documented, you can enter an X in front of that body area. *If less than the number of elements located in parentheses is documented, do not enter an X in front of that organ system or body area.*

☐ Constitutional (2)

☐ Cardiovascular (7)

☐ Chest (breasts) (2)

☐ Ears, nose, mouth, throat (6)

☐ Eyes (3)

☐ Gastrointestinal (abdomen) (5)

☐ Genitourinary (male–3; female–6)

☐ Lymphatic (2)

☐ Musculoskeletal (6)

☐ Neck (2)

☐ Neurologic (3)

☐ Psychiatric (4)

☐ Respiratory (4)

☐ Skin (2)

_____ **Total Score:**   Enter the score for number of Xs entered (representing number of exam elements), and enter an X in front of the exam type below.

☐ PROBLEM FOCUSED EXAMINATION (1–5 elements identified by a bullet on *CMS Documentation Guidelines for Evaluation & Management Services*)

☐ EXPANDED PROBLEM FOCUSED EXAMINATION (at least 6 elements identified by a bullet on *CMS Documentation Guidelines for Evaluation & Management Services*)

☐ DETAILED EXAMINATION (at least 2 elements identified by a bullet from each of 6 organ systems or body areas, or at least 12 elements identified by a bullet in two or more systems or areas, on *CMS Documentation Guidelines for Evaluation & Management Services*)

☐ COMPREHENSIVE EXAMINATION (documentation of all elements identified by a bullet in at least 9 organ systems or body areas, and documentation of at least 2 elements identified by a bullet from each of 9 organ systems or body areas, on *CMS Documentation Guidelines for Evaluation & Management Services*)

Medical Decision Making

Select the appropriate level of medical decision making based upon the following criteria:

Number of Diagnoses or Management Options	Amount/Complexity of Data to Be Reviewed	Risk of Complications and/or Morbidity/Mortality	Medical Decision Making
Minimal	Minimal or none	Minimal	Straightforward
Limited	Limited	Low	Low complexity
Multiple	Moderate	Moderate	Moderate complexity
Extensive	Extensive	High	High complexity

E/M Code Selection

Select the E/M code based on selection of level of history, examination, and medical decision making:

History	Problem focused	Expanded problem focused	Expanded problem focused	Detailed	Comprehensive
Examination	Problem focused	Expanded problem focused	Expanded problem focused	Detailed	Comprehensive
Medical Decision Making	Straightforward	Low complexity	Moderate complexity	Moderate complexity	High complexity

Go to the appropriate E/M category/subcategory, and select the code based upon the previously selected information.

Bibliography

Books and Manuals

Abraham, P. R. (2013). *Documentation for health records*. Chicago, IL: American Health Information Management Association.

American College of Radiology & Society of Interventional Radiology. (2015). *Interventional radiology coding update*. Restin, VA: American College of Radiology.

American Medical Association. (2016). *CPT*. Chicago, IL: Author.

American Medical Association. (2016). *CPT changes: An insider's view*. Chicago, IL: Author.

American Medical Association. (2016). *Medicare RBRVS: The physicians' guide*. Chicago, IL: Author.

American Medical Association. (2015). *Principles of CPT coding*. Chicago, IL: Author.

Carlton, R. R., & Adler, A. M. (2013). *Principles of radiographic imaging: An art and a science*. Clifton Park, NY: Cengage Learning.

Centers for Medicare & Medicaid Services. (2016). *Internet-only manuals*. Washington, DC: Department of Health and Human Services.

Ehrlich, A., Schroeder, C. L., Ehrlich, L., & Schroeder, K. (2017). *Medical terminology for health professionals*. Clifton Park, NY: Cengage Learning.

Frank, Eugene D., B. W. Long, & B. J. Smith. (2012). *Merrill's atlas of radiographic positioning & radiologic procedures*. Philadelphia, PA: Elsevier, Inc.

Green, M. A., & Bowie, M. J. (2016). *Essentials of health information management: Principles and practices*. Clifton Park, NY: Cengage Learning.

Green, M. A., & Rowell, J. (2017). *Understanding health insurance: A guide to billing and reimbursement*. Clifton Park, NY: Cengage Learning.

Jones, B. D. (2016). *Comprehensive medical terminology*. Clifton Park, NY: Cengage Learning.

Lazo, D. L. (2015). *Fundamentals of sectional anatomy: An imaging approach*. Clifton Park, NY: Cengage Learning.

Marrelli, T. M. (2011). *Handbook of home health standards: Quality, documentation and reimbursement*. Philadelphia, PA: Elsevier, Inc.

Merriam-Webster. (2006). *Merriam-Webster's medical desk dictionary*. Clifton Park, NY: Cengage Learning.

Neighbors, M., & Tannehill-Jones, R. (2015). *Human diseases*. Clifton Park, NY: Cengage Learning.

Optum360. (2016). *Coder's desk reference for diagnoses (ICD-10-CM)*. Salt Lake City, UT: Author.

Optum360. (2016). *Coder's desk reference for HCPCS level II*. Salt Lake City, UT: Author.

Optum360. (2016). *Coder's desk reference for procedures*. Salt Lake City, UT: Author.

Optum360. (2016). *Coding and payment guide: Anesthesia services*. Salt Lake City, UT: Author.

Optum360. (2016). *Coding and payment guide: Behavioral health services*. Salt Lake City, UT: Author.

Optum360. (2016). *Coding and payment guide: Laboratory services*. Salt Lake City, UT: Author.

Optum360. (2016). *Coding and payment guide: For the physical therapist*. Salt Lake City, UT: Author.

Optum360. (2016). *Coding guide: Dental services*. Salt Lake City, UT: Author.

Optum360. (2016). *Complete guide for interventional radiology*. Salt Lake City, UT: Author.

Optum360. (2016). *DRG desk reference*. Salt Lake City, UT: Author.

Optum360. (2016). *DRG expert*. Salt Lake City, UT: Author.

Optum360. (2017). *HCPCS level II*. Salt Lake City, UT: Author.

Optum360. (2017). *ICD-10-CM*. Salt Lake City, UT: Author.

Optum360. (2017). *ICD-10-PCS*. Salt Lake City, UT: Author.

Rizzo, D. C. (2016). *Fundamentals of anatomy and physiology*. Clifton Park, NY: Cengage Learning.

Scott, A., & Fong, E. (2017). *Body structures & functions*. Clifton Park, NY: Cengage Learning.

Woodrow, R., Colbert, B., & Smith, D. (2015). *Essentials of pharmacology for health occupations*. Clifton Park, NY: Cengage Learning.

Journals and Newsletters

Advance for health information professionals. King of Prussia, PA: Merion Publications.

Coding clinic for HCPCS. Chicago, IL: American Hospital Association.

Coding clinic for ICD-10-CM and ICD-10-PCS. Chicago, IL: American Hospital Association.

CPT assistant. Chicago, IL: American Medical Association.

Family practice management. Leawood, KS: American Academy of Family Physicians.

For the record. Spring City, PA: Great Valley Publishing Co., Inc.

Healthcare Business Monthly. Salt Lake City, UT: AAPC.

Journal of the American Health Information Management Association. Chicago, IL: American Health Information Management Association.

PIVOT points ezine. Gaithersburg, MD: DecisionHealth.

Internet-Based References and Listservs

AAPC ICD-10 Crosswalks
http://www.aapc.com

CMS Medicare Manuals
http://www.cms.gov

Coding Pro-L listserv
http://www.decisionhealth.com

E&M Coder **software by Spring Management Systems**
http://www.emcoder.com

The Coder's Club
http://www.pmionline.com

ICD-10 Code Lookup **by North Carolina State Center for Health Statistics**
http://www.schs.state.nc.us/SCHS/data/icd10/icd10 lookup.cfm

Medical Newswire
http://medicalnewswire.com

Medline Plus Encyclopedia
http://www.nlm.nih.gov/medlineplus

Optum360's online ICD-10-CM, ICD-10-PCS, CPT, and HCPCS level II encoders with ICD-9-CM and ICD-10 crosswalks
http://www.encoderpro.com

The radiology information resource for patients
http://www.radiologyinfo.org

World Health Organization
http://www.who.int

Software

Optum360. (2017). *Encoder Pro Expert.* Salt Lake City, UT: Author.

Glossary

NOTE: The chapter in which each term appears as a key term is indicated in parentheses.

A

ablation (11)   removal.

abuse (19)   actions that are inconsistent with accepted, sound medical, business, or fiscal practices; includes actions that result in unnecessary costs to payers and government programs, that result in reimbursement for services not medically necessary, or that fail to meet professionally recognized standards for health care services.

accession (17)   assignment of a number to record the order of tissue acquisition.

acellular dermal replacement (11)   bioengineered artificial skin.

actinic keratosis (AK) (11)   common sun-induced skin lesion of the epidermis that has the potential to become skin cancer.

acute care facility (ACF) (5)   hospital that provides health care services to patients who have serious, sudden, or acute illnesses or injuries and/or who need certain surgeries.

acute care hospital (5)   *see* short-term hospital.

add-on code (8)   reported when another procedure is performed in addition to the primary procedure during the same operative session; modifier -51 (multiple procedures) is *not* used with add-on codes.

adenoids (13)   located at the rear of the nose; contain lymphoid tissue that helps fight infections.

adjacent tissue transfer/rearrangement (11)   closure of defects by relocating a flap of adjacent normal, healthy tissue to a defect.

adjuvant (17)   substance administered with an antigen that enhances the response to the antigen.

adjuvant chemotherapy (18)   chemotherapy administered in addition to other cancer treatments, such as surgery and/or radiation therapy.

adjuvant technique (13)   additional procedure or technique that may be required during a lower extremity bypass graft procedure.

admitting diagnosis (5)   provisional or tentative diagnosis entered in a field on the inpatient face sheet by admissions office staff; it is often a sign or symptom.

advance beneficiary notice (ABN) (7)   waiver signed by the patient acknowledging that because medical necessity for a procedure, service, or supply cannot be established, the patient accepts responsibility for reimbursing the provider or DMEPOS dealer for costs associated with the procedure, service, or supply.

advance care planning (9)   face-to-face services between physician or other qualified health care professional and patient, family member, or surrogate for the purpose of counseling and discussing advance directives, with or without completing relevant legal forms (e.g., health care proxy).

advancement flap (11)   movement of tissue in a straight line from donor to defect site using a sliding process; once movement is achieved, the flap is sutured in place.

airway management (10)   ensuring an open airway to the patient's lungs.

A-line (10)   *see* intra-arterial line.

aliquot (17)   portion of a specimen used for testing.

allergen (18)   allergy-causing substances to which a patient reacts.

allergen immunotherapy (18)   small amounts of allergens administered to increase a patient's tolerance to allergens.

allergy sensitivity test (18)   performed on skin (cutaneous) and mucous membranes to identify the source of a patient's allergies.

allogenous (12)   graft that involves tissue organ transplanted from one person to another.

allograft (11)   transplantation of tissue from someone of the same species.

ambulance fee schedule (19)   reimburses ambulance service providers a preestablished fee for each service provided.

ambulatory care (6)   *see* outpatient care.

ambulatory patient (6)   patient who is treated and released the same day and who does not stay overnight in the hospital.

ambulatory surgery patient (6)   patient who undergoes procedures that can be performed on an outpatient basis, with the patient treated and released the same day.

ambulatory surgical center (ASC) payment rate (19)   reimbursement rate calculated on a prospective basis; rate is based on sample survey data and use of similar surgical techniques to establish reasonable estimated overhead allowances for each listed procedure.

A-mode (16)   one-dimensional display that reflects the length of time a sound reaches a structure and is reflected back.

amplitude modulation (16)   *see* A-mode.

analgesia (10)   loss of pain sensation without loss of consciousness.

analgesic (10)   drug that reduces pain, resulting in analgesia.

analyte (17)   substance or chemical compound undergoing analysis.

ancillary service (5)   diagnostic and/or therapeutic service provided to inpatients and outpatients.

anesthesia (10)   process of inducing a loss of sensitivity to pain in all or part of the body, resulting from the administration of an anesthetic.

anesthesia conversion factor (10)   dollar amount assigned to a geographic location.

anesthesia time unit (10)   based on total anesthesia time and reported as one unit for each 15 minutes (or fraction thereof) of anesthesia time.

anesthesiologist (10) physician who, after medical school, completes a one-year internship and three-year residency in anesthesia.

anesthetic (10) drug or agent that causes a loss of feeling, awareness, and/or consciousness.

aneurysm (13) bulge in an artery that can weaken the arterial wall and eventually burst, resulting in hemorrhage.

angiogenesis (13) growth of new capillaries.

angiography (16) x-ray of a blood vessel after injection of contrast material.

angioscopy (13) microscopic visualization of substances as they pass through capillaries.

anoscopy (14) diagnostic procedure during which anal mucosa and the lower rectum are visualized using an anoscope.

ANSI ASC X12N 837 (19) variable-length file format that is used to bill institutional, professional, dental, and drug claims.

antepartum care (15) begins with conception and ends with delivery, including initial and subsequent history; physical examinations; documentation of weight, blood pressures, and fetal heart tones; routine chemical urinalysis (glucose); monthly visits up to 28 weeks' gestation; biweekly visits to 36 weeks' gestation; and weekly visits until delivery.

anterior approach (15) making an incision overlying the intervertebral disc by cutting through epidermis, dermis, subcutaneous, fascia, and muscle tissue.

anterolateral approach (15) making an incision along (and removing) the rib that corresponds to the vertebra that is located above the compressed intervertebral disk.

anteroposterior projection (16) patient is positioned with his or her back parallel to the film; the x-ray beam travels from front to back, or anterior to posterior.

antibody (17) proteins in the body made by the immune system that fight infection and disease.

antigen (17) foreign substances that elicit the formation of antibodies.

aortic anomaly (13) results from unusual patterns of aortic development and includes conditions such as tracheal decompression (or tracheomalacia), aberrant vessels (or vascular ring formation), aortopulmonary septal defect (APSD), patent ductus arteriosus, coarctation of aorta, and hypoplastic aortic arch (or interrupted aortic arch).

aortic sinus (13) *see* sinus of Valsalva.

aortography (16) x-ray of the aorta after injection of contrast material.

Appendix A of CPT (8) contains a list of CPT modifiers and detailed descriptions.

Appendix B of CPT (8) contains annual CPT coding changes that include added, deleted, and revised CPT codes; it serves as the basis for updating interoffice documents and billing tools.

Appendix C of CPT (8) contains clinical examples for codes found in the Evaluation and Management section.

Appendix D of CPT (8) contains a list of add-on codes that are identified throughout CPT with a plus (+) symbol.

Appendix E of CPT (8) contains a list of codes that are exempt from modifier -51 reporting rules and that are identified throughout CPT with a forbidden (⊘) symbol.

Appendix F of CPT (8) contains a list of codes that are exempt from modifier -63.

Appendix H of CPT (8) contains an alphabetical index of performance measures by clinical condition or topic; located on the AMA website.

Appendix I of CPT (8) contains genetic testing modifiers.

Appendix J of CPT (8) contains an electrodiagnostic medicine listing of sensory, motor, and mixed nerves that are reported for motor and nerve studies codes.

Appendix K of CPT (8) contains a list of codes that are pending FDA approval but that have been assigned CPT codes; in the CPT manual, these codes are preceded by the flash (✔) symbol.

Appendix L of CPT (8) contains a list of vascular families that is intended to assist in the selection of first-, second-, third-, and beyond third-order branch arteries.

Appendix M of CPT (8) contains a list of deleted CPT codes and descriptions with a crosswalk to new CPT codes.

Appendix N of CPT (8) contains a list of CPT codes that do not appear in numerical order. CPT codes are resequenced (instead of deleted and renumbered) so that existing codes can be relocated to a more appropriate location; out-of-sequence codes are preceded by the number symbol (#).

Appendix O of CPT (8) includes administrative codes for procedures that by their nature are typically unique to a single clinical laboratory or manufacturer.

Appendix P of CPT (8) includes codes for electronic communication using interactive telecommunications equipment (e.g., audio, video). In the CPT manual, these codes are preceded by the star (★) symbol. Modifier -95 is reported with Appendix P codes.

application service provider (ASP) (1) third-party entity that manages and distributes software-based services and solutions to customers across a wide area network (WAN) from a central data center.

arterial puncture (17) puncture of an artery with a needle for the purpose of drawing blood.

arteriography (10) visualization of an artery via x-ray after injection of a radiopaque substance.

arteriovenous fistula (13) abnormal passageway between an artery and a vein, which allows blood to flow directly into a vein.

arthrocentesis (12) procedure done to puncture a joint for fluid removal or medication injection.

arthrodesis (12) surgical fixation of a joint.

arthrography (16) x-ray of a joint after injection of contrast material.

arthroscopy (12) visual examination of the inside of a joint.

artificial ankylosis (12) *see* arthrodesis.

arytenoidectomy (12) excision of an arytenoid cartilage, which is located in the bilateral vocal fold.

arytenoidopexy (12) surgical fixation of arytenoidal cartilage and/or surrounding muscles.

assay (17) measurement of the amount of a constituent in a specimen, such as via laboratory test.

Assessment (A) (1) judgment, opinion, or evaluation made by the health care provider; considered part of the problem-oriented record (POR) SOAP note.

assumption coding (1) inappropriate assignment of codes based on assuming, from a review of clinical evidence in the patient's record, that the patient has certain diagnoses or received certain procedures/services even though the provider did not specifically document those diagnoses or procedures/services.

auditory system (15) organized anatomically according to the external ear; middle ear; inner ear; and temporal bone, middle fossa approach.

augmentation (12) process of enlarging or increasing.

autogenous (12) originating in the patient's body.

autograft (11) transplantation of tissue from the same individual.

automated case abstracting software (1) software program that is used to collect and report inpatient and outpatient data for statistical analysis and reimbursement purposes.

automated record (1) type of record that is created using computer technology.

autonomic function test (18) evaluates autonomic nervous system functioning.

axial plane (16) *see* transverse plane.

axis of classification (ICD-10-PCS) (5) the sections, body parts, root operations, and so on that comprise the 7-character ICD-10-PCS code; each axis specifies information about the procedure performed, and within a defined code range, a character specifies the same type of information for that axis of classification.

B

backbench work (12) preparing the cadaver donor heart and/or lung allograft prior to lung transplantation and dissecting allograft from surrounding soft tissues to prepare the aorta, superior vena cava, inferior vena cava, pulmonary artery, left atrium, trachea, pulmonary venous/atrial cuff, and/or bronchus for implantation.

Balanced Budget Act of 1997 (19) legislated implementation of the skilled nursing facility prospective payment system, which uses resource utilization groups, version III (RUG-III), to reimburse Medicare SNF services according to a *per diem* prospective rate adjusted for case mix; also legislated implementation of an ambulance fee schedule, which reimburses ambulance service providers a preestablished fee for each service provided.

Balanced Budget Refinement Act of 1999 (BBRA) (19) mandated implementation of the long-term (acute) care hospital prospective payment system, which uses information from long-term acute care hospital patient records to classify patients into distinct long-term (acute) care hospital diagnosis-related groups based on clinical characteristics and expected resource needs.

base unit value (10) represents the degree of difficulty associated with providing anesthesia for a surgical procedure.

bed count (5) *see* bed size.

bed size (5) total number of inpatient beds for which a facility is licensed by the state; facility must be equipped and staffed to care for these patient admissions.

bedsore (11) *see* pressure ulcer.

behavioral health care hospital (5) health care facility that specializes in treating individuals with mental health diagnoses.

Bell's palsy (15) unilateral paralysis of facial muscles resulting from dysfunction of the 7th cranial nerve, probably due to a viral infection.

benign (4) not cancerous.

Bethesda system (17) format for reporting cervical/vaginal cytology that includes a state of specimen adequacy, the general category, and a descriptive diagnosis.

Bier block (10) *see* intravenous regional anesthesia.

biliary system (14) organs and duct system that create, transport, store, and release bile into the duodenum (as part of the digestive process); includes the gallbladder, bile ducts inside the liver, bile ducts outside the liver, hepatic ducts, common bile duct, and cystic duct.

biofeedback (18) technique that trains the patient to gain some control over autonomic body functions.

biometric A-scan (16) diagnostic ultrasound that produces a one-dimensional view of normal and abnormal eye tissue and precise measurements of the eye's length.

biomicroscopy (16) optical instrument that looks like a microscope with two eyepieces.

biopsy (11) removal and examination of tissue to establish a diagnosis, confirm a diagnosis, or determine the extent of a disease.

bipolar cautery (14) technique that uses an electric current that flows from one tip of the forceps to the other and does not require a grounding pad.

blepharoplasty (11) any surgical repair of an eyelid.

block (radiology) (16) device used when a radiology procedure is performed; made of lead or another heavy metal, it is placed between the radiation beam and that portion of the patient's body that requires protection from radiation.

block (tissue) (17) portion of tissue obtained from a specimen that is placed in support medium, such as paraffin.

blocking (16) device, such as lead, that shields or protects critical or sensitive organs during radiology treatment.

blood (13) tissue that consists of plasma, red blood cells, white blood cells, and platelets (or thrombocytes).

blue reference symbol (⊃)(8) located below a code description in some CPT coding manuals to indicate that the coder should refer to the *CPT Assistant* monthly newsletter.

BlueCross and BlueShield (BCBS) (19) a health insurance organization that covers the costs of hospital care and physician services; BlueCross initially covered just hospital care and BlueShield covered just physicians' services; today each offers a full range of health care coverage.

bone density study (16) evaluates diseases of the bone; used to assess the response of bone disease to treatment.

bone marrow (13) spongy material that fills large bones' cavities; consists of red marrow (produces red blood cells, white blood cells, and platelets) and yellow marrow (replaces red marrow with fatty tissue that does not produce blood cells).

bone marrow aspiration (13) use of a needle to remove a sample of the liquid bone marrow for examination under a microscope.

bone marrow biopsy (13)   boring a small hole into a long bone and using a large, hollow needle to remove bone marrow for examination under a microscope.

breach of confidentiality (19)   occurs when patient information is disclosed to other(s) who do not have a right to access the information.

brightness mode (16)   *see* B-scan.

bronchoscopy (12)   visual examination of the interior of the bronchus.

brushing (12)   combing the mucous lining of the trachea or bronchus with a bronchial brush to collect cells.

B-scan (16)   diagnostic ultrasound that produces a two-dimensional cross-sectional view of tissues that cannot be seen directly; it reflects sound waves bouncing off tissues or organs; e.g., used to locate a lesion and determine its shape; also called brightness mode (B-mod).

bullet symbol (8)   symbol (•) located to the left of CPT codes that identifies new procedures and services added to CPT.

bull's-eye symbol (8)   symbol (◉) located to the left of CPT codes that identifies procedures that include conscious sedation.

bunion (12)   caused by bone inflammation and swelling and results in medial deviation and axial rotation of the first metatarsophalangeal (MTP) joint.

burr hole (15)   small opening in the skull made with a surgical drill.

C

cadaver donor cardiectomy with or without pneumonectomy (13)   harvesting the allograft (heart with or without lung tissue) and preserving the allograft with cold preservation solution and cold maintenance.

cadaver donor pneumonectomy (12)   harvesting the allograft (lung tissue) and preserving the allograft with cold preservation solution and cold maintenance.

cafeteria plan (19)   *see* triple option plan.

cancer staging (13)   determination that cancer has or has not spread anatomically from its point of origin.

cannula (10)   hollow needle.

capitated payment method (18)   agreement between a third-party payer and a health care provider in which the provider agrees to provide services to a patient in return for a fixed monthly payment.

capitation (19)   provider accepts preestablished payments for providing health care services to enrollees over a period of time, usually one year.

capnography (10)   monitoring carbon dioxide levels.

carcinoma (Ca) *in situ* (4)   malignant tumor that is localized, circumscribed, encapsulated, and noninvasive, but has not spread to deeper or adjacent tissues or organs.

cardiac ablation (13)   stops atrial or ventricular fibrillation by using radiofrequency waves (modified electrical energy) to create small scars on the heart's surface.

cardiac blood pool imaging (16)   use of a gamma camera for sampling, which is performed repetitively over several hundred heartbeats during the transition of the radionuclide through the central circulation.

cardiac catheterization (18)   invasive diagnostic medical procedure that includes several components, beginning when the physician introduces one or more catheters into peripheral arteries and/or veins.

cardiac tumor (13)   growth that develops in the heart's endocardium, myocardium, or pericardium.

cardiac valve (13)   flap of tissue that keeps blood flowing in one direction to allow for the efficient one-way flow of blood through the heart's chambers.

cardiography (18)   diagnostic procedure that records the heart's electronic activity with a cardiograph and produces a cardiogram (or electrocardiogram, ECG or EKG).

cardiopulmonary bypass (13)   procedure to divert blood from the heart to the aorta, using a pump oxygenator.

care plan oversight services (9)   cover the physician's time supervising a complex and multidisciplinary care treatment program for a specific patient who is under the care of a home health agency, hospice, or nursing facility.

carotid body (15)   tissue that contains many capillaries; located at the point where the carotid artery branches in the neck.

carpal tunnel (15)   eight bones in the wrist (carpals) that form a tunnel-like structure; the tunnel is filled with flexor tendons that control finger movement and provide a pathway for the median nerve to reach sensory cells in the hand.

carpal tunnel syndrome (15)   painful progressive condition caused by compression of the median nerve at the wrist.

case-mix (19)   types and categories of patients cared for by a health care facility.

case-mix adjustment (19)   decrease of average difference between preestablished payment and each patient's actual cost to a facility.

category (2)   three-character ICD-10-CM disease code within a section.

Category I code (8)   procedures/services identified by a five-digit CPT code and descriptor nomenclature; this type of code is traditionally associated with CPT and organized within six sections.

Category II code (8)   optional CPT "performance measurements" tracking code that is assigned an alphanumerical identifier with a letter in the last field; this type of code is located after the CPT Medicine section.

Category III code (8)   "emerging technology" temporary CTP code assigned for data collection purposes that is assigned an alphanumerical identifier with a letter in the last field; this type of code is located after the Medicine section, and it will be archived after five years if it is not accepted for placement within Category I sections of CPT.

caudal anesthesia (10)   local anesthetic injected into the caudal canal, which is the sacral portion of the spinal canal.

cell washing (12)   flushing fluid into an area and removing the fluid, using aspiration technique to collect cells.

Centers for Medicare & Medicaid Services (CMS) (1)   administrative agency in the federal Department of Health & Human Services.

central motor evoked potential study (18)   testing a patient's nervous system's pathway by placing low-voltage electrodes on the scalp and target sites.

central nervous system (CNS) (10) brain and spinal cord.

central venous access device (CVAD) (10) thin plastic tube that is inserted into a vein and connected to a monitor.

central venous pressure (CVP) catheter (10) *see* central venous pressure (CVP) line.

central venous pressure (CVP) line (10) catheter that is inserted through a vein in the neck or a vein in the upper chest under the collar bone and then into a large central vein in the chest.

certificate of medical necessity (CMN) (7) prescription for durable medical equipment, services, and supplies.

certified registered nurse anesthetist (CRNA) (10) licensed registered nurse who has earned a bachelor's degree in science or nursing, has at least one year of acute care nursing experience, has completed a 24- to 36-month nurse anesthesia program leading to a master's degree, and has passed the national certification exam.

charge description master (CDM) (19) *see* chargemaster.

chargemaster (19) document that contains a computer-generated list of procedures, services, and supplies and corresponding revenue codes along with charges for each.

chargemaster review process (19) routinely conducted by designated hospital personnel to ensure accurate reimbursement by updating CPT and HCPCS codes and linking each to appropriate UB-04 revenue codes.

check digit (19) one-digit character, alphabetical or numerical, that is used to verify the validity of a unique identifier.

cheiloplasty (14) plastic surgery of the lips.

chemical peel (11) use of chemical agents to remove wrinkles and abnormal pigmentation.

chemosurgery (11) use of chemicals to destroy diseased tissue, such as for skin cancer.

chemotherapy (18) treatment of cancer with drugs that serve to destroy cancer cells or slow the growth of cancer cells and keep cancer from spreading to other parts of the body, preventing recurrence of the cancer.

Chemstrip automated urine analyzer (17) *see* reagent strip automated urine analyzer.

chief complaint (CC) (9) patient's description of medical condition stated in the patient's own words.

chiropractic manipulative treatment (CMT) (18) manual treatment performed to influence joint and neurophysiological function.

cholecystectomy (14) surgical removal of the gallbladder.

choroid (15) opaque layer behind the retina that contains blood vessels.

chromatography (17) separation of chemical substances by differential absorption into a moving two-phase system; in gas-liquid chromatography, gaseous substances are separated by moving through a liquid.

chromosomal breakage syndrome (17) genetic disorder that is usually transmitted in a genetic autosomal recessive mode.

chyle (13) digestive fluid that contains proteins and fats.

ciliary body (15) adjusts the shape of the lens and focuses light rays onto the retina.

ciliary muscle (15) *see* ciliary body.

Civilian Health and Medical Program of the Department of Veterans Affairs (CHAMPVA) (19) program that provides health care benefits to dependents of veterans rated as 100 percent permanently and totally disabled as a result of service-connected conditions, veterans who died as a result of service-connected conditions, and veterans who died on duty with less than 30 days of active service.

Civil Monetary Penalties Act (19) imposes a maximum penalty of up to $10,000 plus a maximum assessment of up to three times the amount claimed by providers who knew that a procedure/service was not rendered as submitted on the claim.

claims examiner (1) *see* health insurance specialist.

classification system (1) *see* coding system.

clearinghouse (1) public or private entity that processes or facilitates the processing of health information and claims from a nonstandard to a standard format.

cleft lip (10) congenital deformity of the upper lip that failed to close during development; types include unilateral, bilateral, and median (harelip) and may be accompanied by defects of the maxilla and hard palate.

Clinical Laboratory Improvement Act of 1988 (CLIA) (17) certification that is required to perform certain pathology and laboratory tests (and to submit claims to Medicare and Medicaid).

clinic outpatient (6) patient who receives scheduled diagnostic and therapeutic care.

clinical examples (9) contained in Appendix C of the CPT coding manual; assist providers in selecting the appropriate code for documented E/M services.

clinical laboratory fee schedule (19) methodology for determining fees for laboratory tests as a result of enacted legislation called the Deficit Reduction Act of 1984; the Consolidated Omnibus Budget Reconciliation Act of 1985 later established a national limitation amount (NLA) on the clinical laboratory fee schedule.

closed fracture (4) type of fracture that is contained beneath the skin and has intact ligaments and skin.

closed fracture treatment (12) fracture site that is not surgically opened or exposed.

closed laparoscopy (14) insufflation of the abdominal cavity using a percutaneously placed needle; performed to examine peritoneal contents using a laparoscope.

closed-panel HMO (19) HMO-owned center or satellite clinic that provides health care services.

CMS-1450 (1) *see* UB-04.

CMS-1500 (1) standard claim submitted by physicians' offices to third-party payers.

cochlear implant (15) implanted electronic device for treatment of sensory deafness.

code (1) numerical and alphanumerical characters that are reported to health plans for health care reimbursement and to external agencies (e.g., state departments of health) for data collection, in addition to being reported internally (e.g., acute care hospital) for education and research.

coder (1) acquires a working knowledge of coding systems (e.g., CPT, HCPCS level II, ICD-10-CM, and ICD-10-PCS), coding principles and rules, government regulations, and third-party payer requirements to ensure that all diagnoses (conditions), services (e.g., office visit), and procedures (e.g., surgery and x-ray) documented in patient records are coded accurately for reimbursement, research, and statistical purposes.

coding (1) assignment of codes to diagnoses, services, and procedures based on patient record documentation.

coding conventions (ICD-10-CM/PCS) (3) general rules used in the ICD-10-CM classification system that are independent of coding guidelines.

abbreviations (3) use of NEC (not elsewhere classifiable) and NOS (not otherwise specified). (NEC and NOS abbreviations do *not* appear in ICD-10-PCS.)

NEC (not elsewhere classifiable) (3) equivalent of "other specified"; identifies codes that are to be assigned when information needed to assign a more specific code cannot be located in the coding manual.

NOS (not otherwise specified) (3) equivalent of "unspecified"; identifies codes that are to be assigned when information needed to assign a more specific code cannot be obtained from the provider.

and (3) interpreted as meaning "and/or."

boxed note (3) defines terms, provides coding instruction, and lists fifth-digit subclassifications for categories that use the same fifth digits; Index to Procedures boxed notes also provide coding instruction and list fourth-digit subclassifications for categories that use the same fourth digits. (Boxed notes do not appear in ICD-10-CM or ICD-10-PCS.)

code also (3) ICD-10-CM note that provides instruction that two codes may be required to fully describe a condition; this note does *not* provide sequencing direction.

cross-references (3) instruction to refer to another entry in the index (e.g., *see*, *see also*, *see* condition) or tabular list (e.g., *see* category) to assign the correct code.

see (3) instructional term that directs the coder to refer to another term in the indexes.

see also (3) instructional term that is located after a main term or subterm in the index and directs the coder to another main term (or subterm) that may provide additional useful index entries.

see category (3) instructional term that directs the coder to the tabular list, where a code can be selected from the options provided there.

see condition (3) instructional term that directs the coder to the main term in the index for a condition.

default code (3) ICD-10-CM code listed next to a main term in the index; represents that condition that is most commonly associated with the main term, or is the unspecified code for the condition.

due to (3) index subterm (in alphabetical order) that indicates the presence of a cause-and-effect (or causal) relationship between two conditions.

eponym (3) disease, syndrome, or procedure named for a person.

etiology and manifestation rules (3) include the following in the tabular list: code first underlying disease; code, if applicable, any causal condition first; use additional code; and in diseases classified elsewhere.

code first underlying disease (3) tabular list instructional note that assists with proper sequencing of codes.

code, if applicable, any causal condition first (3) tabular list instructional note that requires causal conditions to be sequenced first, if present.

in diseases classified elsewhere (3) indicates that manifestation codes are a component of the etiology/manifestation coding convention.

use additional code (3) instructional note that assists in proper sequencing of the codes.

excludes1 note (3) appears below codes in the ICD-10-CM tabular list to direct the coder to another location in the tabular list to classify conditions that are excluded from the code—code either the original code or the code to which the excludes1 note directs you.

excludes2 note (3) appears below codes in the ICD-10-CM tabular list to direct the coder to another location in the tabular list to classify conditions that are excluded from the code; both the original code and the code to which the excludes2 note directs you can be reported if documentation supports both conditions.

format (3) for ease of reference, index subterms are indented two spaces below a main term; second, third, and fourth qualifiers are indented two, four, and six spaces, respectively, below the subterm.

in (3) index subterm (in alphabetical order) that indicates the presence of a cause-and-effect (or causal) relationship between two conditions.

includes note (3) appears immediately below tabular list codes to further define terms or provide examples.

inclusion term (3) listed below certain codes in the tabular lists; includes conditions or procedures for which that code number is to be assigned; can be synonyms of the code title or, for "other" codes, a list of conditions or procedures assigned to that code.

manifestation (3) condition that occurs as the result of another condition; a manifestation code is always reported as a secondary code.

modifier (3) additional term included after the colon in the ICD-10-CM tabular lists that is to be included in the statement to classify a condition or procedure.

other (3) when this word appears in an ICD-10-CM code description, the code is assigned when patient record documentation provides detail for which a specific code does not exist.

other specified (3) when this phrase appears in an ICD-10-CM code description, the code is assigned when patient record documentation provides detail for which a specific code does not exist.

punctuation (3) brackets, parentheses, and colons.

brackets (3) used in the index to enclose manifestation codes; used in the tabular list to encose synonyms, alternative wording, and explanatory phrases.

colon (3) used after an incomplete term in the tabular list when one or more additional terms (called modifiers) after the colon must be documented in the diagnostic or procedural statement to classify a condition or procedure.

parentheses (3) used in the index and tabular list to enclose nonessential modifiers, which are supplementary words that may be present in or absent from the physician's statement of a disease or procedure without affecting the code number to which it is assigned.

syndrome (3) association of clinically recognizable features such as signs, symptoms, and characteristics that often occur together, so that the presence of one or more features alerts the health care provider as to the possible presence of the others; coders should follow ICD-10-CM index guidance when assigning codes to a syndrome; in the absence of index guidance, assign codes for the documented manifestations of the syndrome.

tables (3) index feature that organizes subterms, second qualifiers, and third qualifiers and their codes in columns and rows to make it easier to select the proper code. (Tables also appear in ICD-10-PCS, which facilitate assignment of values to create the seven-character code.)

trust the index (3) concept that inclusion terms listed in the Tabular List of Diseases are not meant to be exhaustive and that additional terms found only in the Index to Diseases (but not in the Tabular List of Diseases) may also be assigned to a code.

typeface (3) for ease of reference, index main terms are boldfaced and manifestation codes are italicized.

unspecified code (3) assigned when patient record documentation is insufficient to assign a more specific code.

use (3) directs the coder to a body part or a device in the ICD-10-PCS index.

with (3) index term that is located immediately below the main term, *not in alphabetical order*.

coding system (1) organizes a medical nomenclature according to similar conditions, diseases, procedures, and services; it contains codes for each.

cold biopsy forceps (14) technique that does not use electrocoagulation; the polyp is simply pulled from the colon wall.

colectomy (14) removal of part or all of the large intestine.

colonoscopy (14) visual examination of the entire colon, from the rectum to the cecum, and may include the terminal ileum.

colostomy (14) removal of a portion of the colon or rectum; the remaining colon is brought to the abdominal wall.

column 1/column 2 edits (8) code pairs that should not be billed together because one service inherently includes the other; previously called comprehensive/component edits.

combination code (4) single code used to classify two diagnoses (or procedures), a diagnosis with an associated secondary process (manifestation), or a diagnosis with an associated complication.

commercial payer (19) private health insurance company or employer-based group health insurance company.

commissurotomy (13) narrowed valve leaflets are widened by carefully opening the fused leaflets with a scalpel.

comorbidity (5) coexisting condition (e.g., diabetes mellitus) that is treated during the same encounter as or impacts the medical management of another condition (e.g., myocardial infarction).

compensator (16) irregularly shaped beam-modifying device used to reconfigure beam intensity so it matches irregular tissue contour.

complex fistulectomy (14) excision of multiple fistulas.

compliance guidance (19) document that identifies risk areas and offers concrete suggestions to improve and enhance an organization's internal controls so that billing practices and other business arrangements are in compliance with Medicare's rules and regulations.

complication (5) condition that occurs during the course of an inpatient hospital episode.

component coding (16) reporting a radiology procedure code and a surgical procedure code to completely describe the service provided.

composite graft (13) vein and synthetic graft material or segments of veins from two or more locations.

compound fracture (4) *see* open fracture.

comprehensive examination (9) general multisystem examination or complete examination of a single organ system.

comprehensive history (9) chief complaint, extended history of present illness, review of systems directly related to the problem(s) identified in the history of present illness in addition to a review of all additional body systems, and complete past/family/social history.

computed axial tomography (CT) (CAT) (16) x-ray of horizontal and vertical cross-sectional views or "slices" of the body that are computer-processed to create three-dimensional, or 3D, images.

computed tomography angiography (CTA) (16) x-rays of different angles to create cross-sectional images of organs, bones, and tissues that visualize blood flow in arterial and venous vessels throughout the body.

computer-assisted coding (CAC) (1) uses computer software to automatically generate medical codes by "reading" transcribed clinical documentation; uses "natural language processing" theories to generate codes that are reviewed and validated by coders for reporting on third-party payer claims.

concha (12) *see* turbinates.

concurrent care (9) provision of similar services, such as hospital inpatient visits, to the same patient by more than one provider on the same day.

concurrent coding (1) review of records and/or use of encounter forms and chargemasters to assign codes during an inpatient stay or an outpatient encounter; typically performed for outpatient encounters because encounter forms and chargemasters are completed in "real time" by health care providers as part of the charge-capture process.

concurrent medically directed anesthesia procedure (10) maximum number of procedures an anesthesiologist or a CRNA medically directs within the context of a single procedure when the procedures overlap.

confidentiality (19) process of keeping privileged communication secret; means that information cannot be disclosed without the patient's authorization.

conization (15) removal of a cone-shaped piece of tissue.

conjunctiva (15) mucous membrane that lines the underside of each eyelid and forms a protective covering over the exposed surface of the eyeball.

Consolidated Omnibus Budget Reconciliation Act of 1985 (19) federal legislation that established a national limitation amount, which serves as a payment ceiling, or cap, on the amount Medicare could pay for each test.

consultation (9) examination of a patient by a health care provider, usually a specialist, for the purpose of advising the referring or attending physician in the evaluation and/or management of a specific problem with a known diagnosis.

consumer-directed health plan (CDHP) (19) a sort of "401(K) plan for health care"; includes many choices that provide individuals with an incentive to control the costs of health benefits and health care.

contiguous sites (4) adjacent locations as in cancer of multiple sites that overlap or border each other (e.g., nasopharynx and oropharynx cancer).

continent ileostomy (14) surgical variation of an ileostomy in which a reservoir pouch is created inside the abdomen using a portion of the terminal ileum, a valve is constructed in the pouch, and a stoma is brought through the abdominal wall.

continuity of care (1) documenting patient care services so that others who treat the patient have a source of information on which to base additional care and treatment.

contrast agent (16) radiopaque substances (solid or liquid) that obstruct the passage of x-rays, making the structure containing the agent appear white on radiographic film; administered to provide better radiographic visualization of organs studied.

contrast material (16) *see* contrast agent.

contrast medium (10) *see* contrast agent; plural is *contrast media*.

contrast medium injection device (16) instrument used to deliver a predetermined amount of contrast, typically for vascular imaging procedures.

contributory components (9) include counseling, coordination of care, nature of presenting problem, and time; they are used to select the appropriate E/M service code when patient record documentation indicates that they were the focus of the visit.

conversion factor (19) dollar multiplier that converts relative value units into payments using a formula.

cooperating parties for the ICD-10-CM/PCS (2) AHA, AHIMA, CMS, and NCHS.

coordination of care (9) component in which physician makes arrangements with other providers or agencies for services to be provided to a patient.

cornea (15) transparent layer on the eye's surface; covers the iris and pupil; provides focusing power.

corneal pachymetry (16) noninvasive ultrasound procedure that determines thickness of the cornea.

coronal plane (16) divides the body into anterior or ventral and posterior or dorsal portions at a right angle to the sagittal plane, separating the body into front and back; also called ventral or dorsal plane.

coronary artery bypass graft (CABG) (13) procedure performed to improve flow of blood to the heart.

coronary endarterectomy (13) removal of the inner layer of coronary arteries that contain cholesterol plaques.

corpectomy (15) removal of a portion of the vertebra and adjacent intervertebral disks.

costovertebral (15) area of the thoracic spine where the rib meets the vertebra.

costovertebral approach (15) procedure performed where the ribs articulate with thoracic vertebrae.

counseling (9) as related to CPT E/M coding, a discussion with a patient and/or family concerning one or more of the following areas: diagnostic results, impressions, and recommended diagnostic studies; prognosis; risks and benefits of management (treatment) options; instructions for management (treatment) and follow-up; importance of compliance with chosen management (treatment) options; risk factor reduction; and patient and family education.

covered benefit (19) reimbursable medical benefit.

covered entity (19) private or public sector organization that must follow HIPAA provisions.

critical access hospital (CAH) (5) located more than 35 miles from any hospital or another CAH; state certified as being a necessary provider of health care to area residents.

critical care (9) delivery of medical care services to critically ill or injured patients who require the full, exclusive attention of the physician.

critical illness or injury (9) one that acutely impairs one or more vital organ systems, jeopardizing the patient's survival.

critical pathways (19) interdisciplinary guidelines developed by health care facilities to facilitate management and delivery of quality clinical care in a time of constrained resources; allow for the planning of provision of clinical services that have expected time frames and resources targeted to specific diagnoses and/or procedures.

cross-over vein graft (13) making an incision to expose the vein's incompetent valve, dividing that section of the vein, and connecting it to a nearby vein that has functioning valves.

cryosurgery (11) application of extreme cold, such as liquid nitrogen, to destroy abnormal tissue cells, such as warts or small skin tumors.

***Current Procedural Terminology* (CPT) (1)** coding system used by physicians and outpatient health care settings to assign CPT codes for reporting procedures and services on health insurance claims; considered level I of the Healthcare Common Procedure Coding System (HCPCS); published and updated by the American Medical Association (AMA) to classify procedures and services; listing of descriptive terms and identifying codes for reporting medical services and procedures; provides a uniform language that describes medical, surgical, and diagnostic services to facilitate communication among providers, patients, and third-party payers.

customized sub-capitation plan (CSCP) (19) funds health care expenses with insurance coverage; individual selects one of each type of provider to create a customized network and pays the resulting customized insurance premium.

cutdown (13) a procedure whereby a catheter is inserted directly into a vein through an incision.

cystography (16) x-ray of the urinary bladder after injection of contrast material.

cystometrogram (14) records urinary bladder pressure at various volumes; useful in diagnosing bladder outlet obstruction and other voiding dysfunctions.

cystoscopy (14) allows for direct visual examination of urinary bladder and urethra.

cystourethroscopy (14) *see* cystoscopy.

cytogenetics (17) study of the cell and its heredity-related components, including chromosomes.

cytopathology (17) study of diseased cells.

cytoreduction surgery (16) *see* debulking.

D

Data Elements for Emergency Department Systems (DEEDS) (1) collection of data reported by hospital-based emergency departments for the purpose of reducing incompatibility in emergency department records.

database (1)   contains a minimum data set of patient information collected on each patient, including chief complaint; present conditions and diagnoses; social data; past, personal, medical, and social history; review of systems; physical examination; and baseline laboratory data; considered part of the problem-oriented record (POR).

debulking (16)   surgical removal of part of a malignant tumor to enhance the effectiveness of radiation oncology treatment.

decrypt (19)   decode.

decubitus ulcer (11)   *see* pressure ulcer.

defect (11)   wound that is the result of surgical intervention or trauma.

DEEDS (1)   *see* Data Elements for Emergency Department Systems (DEEDS)

Deficit Reduction Act of 1984 (19)   established the clinical laboratory fee schedule as a methodology for determining fees for existing tests.

definitive identification (17)   specialized testing performed for identification at the genus or species level.

delivery/birthing room attendance and reuscitation services (9)   services provided for attendance at delivery, initial stabilization of the newborn, and delivery/birthing room resuscitation.

delivery services (15)   services from patient admission to the hospital through delivery of the placenta.

demographic data (1)   patient identification information that is collected according to facility policy (e.g., patient's name, date of birth, mother's maiden name, and Social Security number).

dermabrasion (11)   use of a rotary device to sand down raised lesions or thickened tissue, regenerating smoother skin; performed for conditions such as acne scarring, wrinkles, rhytids, and general keratosis.

descriptive qualifiers (8)   clarify assignment of a CPT code; occur in the middle of a main clause or after the semicolon; may or may not be enclosed in parentheses.

Designated Standard Maintenance Organization (DSMO) (19)   to maintain electronic transactions standards adopted by the Secretary of DHHS and develops or modifies adopted standards.

destruction (11)   ablation of benign, premalignant, or malignant tissues by any method.

detailed examination (9)   extended examination of the affected body area(s) and other symptomatic or related organ system(s).

detailed history (9)   includes chief complaint, extended history of present illness, problem pertinent system review extended to include a limited number of additional systems, and pertinent past/family/social history directly related to patient's problem.

determination of refractive state (18)   establishes whether a prescription is required for vision correction.

diagnosis-related groups (DRGs) (19)   classify inpatient hospital cases into groups that are expected to consume similar hospital resources; each DRG has a payment weight assigned to it that is based on the average resources used to treat Medicare patients in that DRG.

Diagnostic and Statistical Manual (DSM) (1)   manual published by the American Psychiatric Association that contains diagnostic assessment criteria used as tools to identify psychiatric disorders; DSM includes psychiatric disorders and codes, provides a mechanism for communicating and recording diagnostic information, and is used in the areas of research and statistics.

Diagnostic Coding and Reporting Guidelines for Outpatient Services (6)   developed by the federal government and approved for use by hospitals and providers for coding and reporting hospital-based outpatient services and provider-based office visits.

diagnostic endoscopy (14)   use of instrumentation for surgical visualization to determine extent of disease.

diagnostic mammography (16)   assessment of suspected disease of breasts.

diagnostic/management plan (1)   information about the patient's condition and the planned management of conditions; considered part of the problem-oriented record (POR).

diagnostic procedure (11)   laboratory, radiographic, and other tests performed to evaluate the patient's complaints or symptoms and to establish the diagnosis.

diaphragm (14)   thin muscle below the heart and lungs; separates the chest from the abdomen.

digestive system (14)   bodily system that begins at the mouth and extends to the anus.

digital (19)   applies a mathematical function to an electronic document, resulting in a unique bit string (computer code), called a message digest, that is encrypted and appended to the electronic document.

dipstick (17)   small strip of plastic that is infused with a chemical; reacts to products in urine by changing color.

direct contract model HMO (19)   contracted health care services delivered to subscribers by individual physicians in the community.

direct laryngoscopy (12)   insertion of a flexible (fiberoptic) or rigid laryngoscope to visualize throat structures.

discharge note (1)   documented in the progress note section of the problem-oriented record (POR) to summarize the patient's care, treatment, response to care, and condition on discharge.

discectomy (15)   removal of an intervertebral disc.

disclosed (19)   released.

dislocation (12)   total displacement of bone from its joint.

diverticula (14)   small pouches (herniations) in the colon that bulge outward through weak spots.

diverticulosis (14)   presence of diverticula in the mucosa and submucosal, through or between fibers of the colon's major muscle layer.

DME MAC medical review policies (7)   local coverage determinations and national coverage determinations.

document imaging (1)   *see* optical disk imaging.

documentation (1)   includes dictated and transcribed, typed or handwritten, and computer-generated notes and reports recorded in the patient's records by a health care professional.

Documentation Guidelines for Evaluation and Management Services (9)   explain how E/M codes are assigned according to elements associated with comprehensive multi-system and single-system examinations.

donor site (11) anatomical site from which healthy skin is removed.

Doppler ultrasonography (16) evaluates movement by measuring changes in the frequency of echoes reflected from moving structures.

dose (18) amount of antigen administered in a single injection from a multiple-dose vial.

dosimetry (16) measurement and calculation of radiation treatment doses.

double pedicle flap (11) maintains blood supply from both ends of a flap incision that was made to create a curvilinear flap contiguous with the defect; flap is pivoted and sutured in place over the defect.

downcoding (1) routinely assigning lower-level CPT codes as a convenience instead of reviewing patient record documentation and the coding manual to determine the proper code to be reported.

DRG creep (19) federal Department of Justice (DOJ) initiative that focuses on medical necessity and billing patterns of DRG coding to determine whether claims hospitals submit accurately reflect care required or provided to the patient; DOJ investigates claims for which facilities receive higher reimbursement as a result of reporting higher paying ICD codes.

dual chamber (13) contains two electrodes; one placed in the right atrium and the other is in the right ventricle.

dual energy x-ray absorptiometry (DEXA) (16) bone density study that uses two x-ray beams with different levels of energy pulsing alternately to create the image.

duplex scan (18) noninvasive test that is performed to evaluate a vessel's blood flow.

durable medical equipment, prosthetics, orthotics, and supplies (DMEPOS) (7) includes items such as artificial limbs, braces, medications, surgical dressings, and wheelchairs.

durable medical equipment, prosthetics, orthotics, and supplies (DMEPOS) dealer (7) supply patients with durable medical equipment.

durable medical equipment, prosthetics, orthotics, and supplies (DMEPOS) fee schedule (19) payment methodology mandated by the Omnibus Budget Reconciliation Act of 1987 (OBRA); the fee schedule is released annually and updated on a quarterly basis to implement fee schedule amounts for new codes and to revise any amounts for existing codes that were calculated in error.

dura mater (10) membrane that forms the outer covering of the central nervous system.

E

echo (16) effect of a sound that reflects off a distant surface and returns to its source.

echocardiography (18) diagnostic procedure that uses ultrasound to obtain two-dimensional images of the heart and/or great arteries (aorta and vena cavae).

electrocardiography (18) *see* cardiography.

electrocautery snare (14) technique that uses a wire loop to encircle, not grasp, a polyp.

electroconvulsive therapy (ECT) (10) briefly applying an electric current to the brain to produce a seizure; its purpose is to relieve depression, schizophrenia, and severe affective disorders.

electromyogram (EMG) (10) nerve conduction study that plots the electrical activity produced by muscle contractions; results in a graphic tracing of a muscle's electrical activity at rest or during contraction; used to diagnose nerve and muscle disorders.

electromyography (18) test used to detect nerve function by measuring the electrical activity generated by muscles.

electronic data interchange (EDI) (19) computer-to-computer transfer of data between provider and third-party payer (or provider and health care clearing house) in a data format agreed upon by the sending and receiving parties.

electronic health record (EHR) (1) collection of patient information documented by a number of providers at one or more facilities regarding one patient; multidisciplinary and multienterprise approach to record keeping because it has the ability to link patient information created at different locations according to a unique patient identifier; provides access to complete and accurate health problems, status, and treatment data; contains alerts and reminders for health care providers.

electronic medical record (EMR) (1) created on a computer, using a keyboard, a mouse, an optical pen device, a voice recognition system, a scanner, or a touch screen; records are created using vendor software, which also assists in provider decision making regarding patient care and treatment.

electronic transaction standard (19) uniform language for electronic data interchange.

electrophysiology (13) study of heart arrhythmias.

electrosurgery (11) use of an electrical device to destroy abnormal tissue.

embolectomy (13) surgical removal of an embolus.

embolus (13) blood clot that circulates throughout the bloodstream.

emergency care patient (6) patient treated for urgent problems and either released the same day or admitted to the hospital as an inpatient.

emergency condition (10) results when a delay in treatment of the patient would lead to a significant increase in threat to life or body part.

emergency department service (9) provided in a hospital, and open 24 hours a day for the purpose of providing unscheduled episodic services to patients who require immediate medical attention.

employer self-insurance plan (19) employer accepts direct responsibility for (or the risk of) paying employees' health care without purchasing health insurance.

en bloc (13) as a whole.

encoder (2) software that automates the coding process; software search features facilitate the location and verification of diagnosis and procedure codes.

encoding (1) process of standardizing data by assigning numeric values (codes or numbers) to text or other information.

encounter (2) face-to-face contact between a patient and a health care provider who assesses and treats the patient's condition; Medicare uses the term *encounter* in the guidelines for coding and reporting to indicate all health care settings, including inpatient hospital admissions.

encounter form (19) document used to record encounter data about office procedures and services provided to patients.

encrypt (19) to encode a computer file, making it safe for electronic transmission so that unauthorized parties cannot read it.

endocardium (13) inner lining of the heart.

endocrine system (15) composed of glands including the adrenal, gonads, pancreas, parathyroid, pituitary, thymus, and thyroid.

endorectal pull-through (14) *see* ileoanal anastomosis.

endoscopic retrograde cholangiopancreatography (ERCP) (14) passing an endoscope through the esophagus, stomach, and duodenum to the ducts of the biliary tree and pancreas.

endoscopy (11) procedure performed to visualize a body cavity, using a medical instrument that consists of a long tube that can be inserted into the body, either through a small incision or a natural opening.

endotracheal tube (ET) (10) artificial airway used for short-term airway management or mechanical ventilation due to potential or actual respiratory system insufficiency.

end-stage renal disease (ESRD) composite payment rate system (19) single-payment fixed rate that does not vary according to the characteristics of the beneficiary treated (and includes the cost of some drugs, laboratory tests, and other items and services provided to Medicare beneficiaries receiving dialysis).

enterectomy (14) resection of small bowel segments.

enterolysis (14) freeing of intestinal adhesions.

enucleation of the eye (15) severing of the eyeball from extraorbital muscles and the optic nerve and its removal.

epidural anesthesia (10) local anesthetic injected into the epidural space, where it acts primarily on spinal nerve roots; anesthetized area includes the abdomen or chest to large regions of the body.

epidurography (16) performed to assess the structure of the spine's epidural space prior to percutaneous epidural adhesiolysis (to identify nerve construction or inflammation and the degree of fluid flow in the epidural space).

equivalent dose (16) radiation quantity measured by roentgen-equivalent-man (rem).

esophageal varices (14) uneven, enlarged, tortuous veins of the esophagus.

esophagogastroduodenoscopy (EGD) (14) use of a fiberoptic endoscope to visualize the esophagus, stomach, and proximal duodenum.

esophagogastroscopy (14) *see* upper GI endoscopy.

esophagoscopy (14) visualization of the esophagus, using an endoscope.

essential modifier (2) *see* subterm.

established patient (9) one who *has* received professional services within the past three years from the physician or from another physician of the same exact specialty or subspecialty who belongs to the same group practice.

etiology (2) cause of disease.

evidence-based coding (1) clicking on codes that CAC software generates to review electronic health record documentation (evidence) used to generate the code; when it is determined that documentation supports the CAC-generated code, the coding auditor clicks to accept the code; when documentation does not support the CAC-generated code, the coding auditor replaces it with an accurate code.

evisceration of ocular contents (15) removal of the contents of the eyeball; the sclera remains intact.

evocative (17) causing a specific response; this term is used to describe various tests intended to cause production of hormones or other secretions.

excision (11) removal of a portion or all of an organ or another tissue, using a scalpel or another surgical instrument.

excisional biopsy (11) removal of a lump or suspicious area in its entirety.

exclusion (19) "Medicare PPS Excluded Cancer Hospital" that applies for and is granted a waiver from mandatory participation in the hospital inpatient PPS.

exclusive provider organization (EPO) (19) managed care plan that provides benefits to subscribers if they receive services from network providers.

exenteration of the orbit (15) removal of orbital contents; may also include removal of bone, muscle, and/or the myocutaneous flap.

expanded problem focused examination (9) limited examination of the affected body area or organ system and other symptomatic or related organ system(s).

expanded problem focused history (9) chief complaint, brief history of present illness, and problem pertinent system review.

explanation of benefits (EOB) (19) statement sent by the payer to the patient that contains the same information as a remittance advice but in an easy-to-read format.

extensive cellulitis (11) acute inflammation of skin's connective tissue, caused by infection with bacteria.

extensor tendons (12) tendons that serve to straighten the fingers.

extent of examination (9) categorized according to problem focused examination, expanded problem focused examination, detailed examination, and comprehensive examination.

extent of history (9) categorized according to problem focused history, expanded problem focused history, detailed history, or comprehensive history.

external catheter (10) catheter that is not implanted under the patient's skin and does not require a needle to be inserted into the skin to deliver medications.

external ear (15) auricle and external auditory meatus.

external fixation device (12) hardware inserted through bone and skin that is held rigid with cross-braces outside of the body; external fixation is always removed after the fracture has healed.

external radiation (16) radiation administered by a machine outside the body.

extracapsular cataract extraction (ECCE) (15) removal of lens and anterior portion of capsule.

extracorporeal life support (ECLS) (13) *see* Extracorporeal membrane oxygenation (ECMO).

extracorporeal membrane oxygenation (13) provide cardiac and/or respiratory support to the heart and/or lungs, which allow them to rest and recover when patients are sick or injured.

extracorporeal shock wave lithotripsy (ESWL) (10) use of ultrasound shock waves to crush calculi (stones) located in the bladder, renal pelvis, or ureter.

extradural procedure (10) performed on the outer side of the dura mater.

eye and ocular adnexa (15) describes procedures performed on the eyeball, anterior and posterior segment, ocular adnexa, and conjunctivae.

eyeball (15) consists of the choroid, retina, and sclera.

eye socket (15) *see* orbit.

F

face-to-face time (9) amount of time the office or outpatient care provider spends with the patient and/or family.

False Claims Act (FCA) (19) law enacted in 1863 in response to widespread abuses by government contractors during the Civil War; amended in 1986 to strengthen the law and increase monetary awards.

family history (9) review of medical events in the patient's family, including diseases that may be hereditary or that may present a risk to the patient.

Federal Anti-kickback Statute (19) prohibits the offer, payment, receipt, or solicitation of compensation for referring Medicaid/Medicare patients and imposes a $25,000 fine per violation, plus imprisonment for up to 10 years.

Federal Claims Collection Act of 1966 (19) law that established uniform procedures for government agencies to follow in the collection, compromise, suspension, termination, or referral for litigation of debts owed to the government.

Federal Employee Health Benefits Program (FEHBP or FEP) (19) voluntary health care program that covers federal employees, retirees, and their dependents and survivors.

fee-for-service (19) method of reimbursing providers for individual health care services rendered.

fee schedule (19) cost-based fee-for-service reimbursement methodology that includes a list of maximum fees and corresponding procedures/services; payers use fee schedules to compensate providers for health care services delivered to patients.

female genital system (15) includes the vulva, perineum, and introitus; vagina; cervix uteri; and uterus, oviduct (fallopian tube), and ovary.

femur (12) long bone of the thigh; articulates with the hip bone, tibia, and patella.

field block (10) subcutaneous injection of local anesthetic in area bordering the field to be anesthetized.

fine-needle aspiration (FNA) (11) procedure in which a thin needle is inserted through a mass several times to remove fluid from a cyst or cells from a solid mass; suction is applied as the needle is withdrawn to obtain strands of single cells for cytological diagnosis.

first-listed diagnosis (6) diagnosis, condition, problem, or other reason for encounter/visit documented in the patient record to be chiefly responsible for the services provided.

first-order vessels (13) blood vessels that extend as primary arterial branches from the aorta.

flap (11) relocation of a mass of tissue (usually skin) that has been partially removed from one part of the body so it retains its own blood supply.

flash symbol (8) symbol (⚡) located to the left of CPT codes that identifies products pending FDA approval but that have been assigned a CPT code.

flat file (19) fixed-length file format that was developed for use in claims processing (because the ANSI ASC X12 837 variable-length file format is not suitable for use in an application program and must be translated into a flat file format prior to claims processing).

flexible spending account (FSA) (19) tax-advantaged account that contains automatic deposits of a portion of an employee's pretax paycheck; money in the account is used to pay for qualified medical expenses not covered by insurance (e.g., coinsurance, copayments, certain FSA-approved over-the-counter medications and supplies for chronic conditions).

flexor tendons (12) tendons that serve to bend the fingers.

fluid management (10) administering IV fluids to avoid dehydration, maintain an effective circulating volume, and prevent inadequate tissue perfusion.

fluorescence *in situ* hybridization (FISH) (17) test performed to detect submicroscopic changes in chromosomes (e.g., genetic disorders such as Williams syndrome) or to identify unknown chromosomal material.

fluoroscopy (16) procedure in which a continuous x-ray beam generates a movie-like image that is viewed on a monitor; used for invasive procedures such as intravenous/intra-arterial catheterization and extracorporeal shock wave lithotripsy.

forbidden symbol (8) symbol (⊘) located to the left of CPT codes that identifies codes exempt from modifier -51.

fraction (in radiation treatment management) (16) single session of radiation treatment delivered to a specific area of interest.

fracture (4) break in a bone resulting from injury or a disease process.

fraud (19) intentional deception or misrepresentation that someone makes, knowing it is false, that could result in an unauthorized payment.

free flap (11) flap consisting of skin and subcutaneous tissue with a pedicle composed only of nutrient vessels, which is detached from the donor site and reattached at the recipient site via microvascular anastomosis.

free skin graft (11) complete separation of skin from the donor site before being transferred to the recipient site.

frontal plane (16) *see* coronal plane.

full-thickness skin graft (11) removal (harvesting) of epidermis and dermis for grafting.

functional modifier (8) pricing modifier that a third-party payer considers when determining reimbursement.

G

gamma globulin (18) *see* immune globulin.

gastrectomy (14) removal of all or a portion of the stomach.

general anesthesia (10) administration of anesthetic agents that are inhaled or administered intravenously.

general equivalence mapping (GEM) (2) published crosswalks of codes that facilitate the location of corresponding diagnosis and procedure codes between two code sets, such as ICD-9-CM and ICD-10-CM.

general hospital (5) acute care facility that provides emergency care, general surgery, and inpatient admission services based on licensing by the state.

glabellar frown lines (11) vertical furrows located in the forehead area between the eyebrows.

global period (11) time established (0, 10, or 90 days) for each surgical procedure.

global service (16) combined technical and professional components.

global surgical package (11) ensures that payments are made consistently for the same services across all Medicare administrative contractor jurisdictions and prevents Medicare payments for services that are more or less comprehensive than intended.

globe (15) see eyeball.

government-sponsored programs (19) include CHAMPVA, Federal Employee Health Benefits Program, Indian Health Service, Medicaid, Medicare, Military Health System, Programs of All-inclusive Care for the Elderly, and TRICARE.

graft (11) procedures that involve moving healthy tissue from one site to another to replace diseased or defective tissue.

Gram stain (17) method of classifying all bacteria as gram-positive or gram-negative.

gray (gy) (16) newer radiation terminology for the amount of radiant energy absorbed in a tissue; 1 gray equals 100 rads.

gray-scale ultrasound (16) see B-scan.

green reference symbol (8) symbol (⟳) located below a code description to indicate that the coder should refer to the *CPT Assistant* monthly newsletter and/or the *CPT Changes: An Insider's View* annual publication that contains all coding changes for the current year.

gross examination (17) evaluating a specimen visually, with the naked eye.

group model HMO (19) contracted health care services delivered to subscribers by participating physicians who are members of an independent multispecialty group practice.

group practice without walls (GPWW) (19) contract that allows physicians to maintain their own offices and share services such as appointment scheduling and billing.

guidelines (8) define terms and explain the assignment of codes for procedures and services located in a particular section of the CPT.

H

harvesting (12) removing tissue for transplantation.

HCPCS level I (7) five-digit Current Procedural Terminology (CPT) codes developed and published by the American Medical Association (AMA).

HCPCS level II (1) coding system managed by the Centers for Medicare & Medicaid Services (CMS) that classifies medical equipment, injectable drugs, transportation services, and other services not classified in the CPT.

HCPCS level II miscellaneous codes (7) include *miscellaneous/not otherwise classified* codes that are reported

when a DMEPOS dealer submits a claim for a product or service for which there is no existing HCPCS level II code.

HCPCS level II modifiers (7) two-digit alpha or alphanumeric codes added to any HCPCS level I (CPT) or II (national) code to provide additional information regarding the product or service reported.

HCPCS level II permanent national codes (7) maintained by the HCPCS National Panel, which unanimously makes decisions about additions, revisions, and deletions.

HCPCS level II temporary codes (7) maintained by the CMS and other members of the HCPCS National Panel, independent of permanent level II codes, and allow payers the flexibility to establish codes that are needed before the next January 1 annual update.

HCPCS national codes (1) see HCPCS level II.

health care clearinghouse (1) see clearinghouse.

Healthcare Common Procedure Coding System (HCPCS) (1) includes level I codes (CPT) and level II codes (HCPCS level II national codes).

health care provider (1) see provider.

health care reimbursement account (HCRA) (19) tax-exempt account that is used to pay for health care expenses.

health data collection (1) performed by health care facilities to do administrative planning, to submit statistics to state and federal government agencies (and other organizations), and to report health claim data to third-party payers for reimbursement purposes.

health insurance claim (19) electronic transmission or paper-based document submitted by the provider to an insurance plan to request reimbursement for procedures performed or services provided.

health insurance policy (19) agreement between an individual and a third-party payer (or insurance company) that contains a list of reimbursable medical benefits.

Health Insurance Portability and Accountability Act of 1996 (HIPAA) (1) federal legislation that amended the Internal Revenue Code of 1986 to improve portability and continuity of health insurance coverage in the group and individual markets, combat waste/fraud/abuse in health insurance and health care delivery, promote the use of medical savings accounts, improve access to long-term care services and coverage, simplify the administration of health insurance by creating unique identifiers for providers/health plans/employers, create standards for electronic health information transactions, and create privacy/security standards for health information.

health insurance specialist (1) employed by third-party payers to review health-related claims to determine whether the costs are reasonable and medically necessary based on the patient's diagnosis.

health maintenance organization (HMO) (19) alternative to traditional group health insurance coverage that provides comprehensive health care services to voluntarily enrolled members on a prepaid basis.

health plan (1) contract established by an insurance company to reimburse health care facilities and patients for procedures and services provided.

health reimbursement arrangement (HRA) (19) tax-exempt account offered by employers with more than 50 employees, which individuals use to pay health care bills.

health savings account (HSA) (19) allows participants to enroll in a relatively inexpensive, high-deductible insurance plan, and a tax-deductible savings account is opened to cover current and future medical expenses; money deposited (and earnings) is tax-deferred, and money is withdrawn to cover qualified medical expenses tax-free.

health savings security account (HSSA) (19) *see* health savings account.

heart murmur (13) extra heart sound.

hematology (17) study of the function and disorders of blood.

hemic system (13) blood-producing system.

hemodialysis (18) process of removing waste products, toxins, and excess fluids from the blood; patient's blood is diverted into a dialyzer, where it is treated and returned to the patient's circulation by another tube inserted into a different blood vessel.

heparin (10) anticoagulant that prevents blood clots from developing in a catheter.

hepatotomy (14) open drainage of abscess or cyst.

hernia (14) protrusion of internal organs through a weakening in the musculature.

HIPAA administrative simplification (AS) (19) developed standards for the maintenance and transmission of health information required to identify individual patients; designed to improve efficiency and effectiveness of the health care system by standardizing the interchange of electronic data for specified administrative and financial transactions.

HIPAA standards for privacy of individually identifiable health information (19) provisions that protect the security and confidentiality of health information.

history (9) interview of the patient that includes the following elements: history of the present illness (including the patient's chief complaint), a review of systems, and a past/family/social history.

history of present illness (HPI) (9) chronological description of patient's present condition from time of onset to present.

hold harmless clause (19) statement that the patient is not responsible for paying what the insurance plan denies.

hollow circle symbol (8) symbol (O) located to the left of a Category III code to indicate a reinstated or recycled code.

Home Assessment Validation and Entry (HAVEN) (19) software that allows for entry of data elements from the outcome and assessment information set (OASIS), which is used to determine the reimbursement rate for home health agency care based on a case mix methodology.

home health prospective payment system (HH PPS) (19) uses home health resource groups (HHRGs) to reimburse Medicare home health care services according to prospectively determined rates.

home services (9) provided to individuals and families in their place of residence to promote, maintain, or restore health and/or to minimize the effects of disability and illness, including terminal illness.

horizontal plane (16) *see* transverse plane.

horizontal triangle symbols (8) symbols (▶◀) that surround revised guidelines and notes; these symbols are *not* used for revised code descriptions.

hospital discharge service (9) includes the final examination of the patient; discussion of the hospital stay with the patient and/or caregiver; instructions for continuing care provided to the patient and/or caregiver; and preparation of discharge records, prescriptions, and referral forms.

hospital inpatient service (9) provided to hospital inpatients, including partial hospitalization services, and indicated when the patient's condition requires services and/or procedures that cannot be performed in any other place of service without putting the patient at risk.

hospitalist (1) physician who provides care for hospital inpatients.

hot biopsy forceps (14) technique that uses tweezer-like forceps connected to a monopolar electrocautery unit and a grounding pad to remove lesions or polyps.

hybrid record (1) combined paper-based and computer-generated documents.

hyperthermia (16) use of an external heat-generating source to produce localized heating.

hyperventilation (18) deep or rapid breathing.

hypopharynx (14) organ that extends from the upper edge of the epiglottis to the larynx/esophagus juncture.

hypovolemia (10) abnormally decreased blood volume.

hysteroscopy (15) visualization of the cervical canal and uterine cavity using a hysteroscope.

I

ICD-10 Coordination and Maintenance Committee (2) NCHS and CMS Department of HHS federal agencies that are responsible for overseeing all changes and modifications to ICD-10-CM (NCHS) and ICD-10-PCS (CMS).

ileoanal anastomosis (14) common alternative to conventional ileostomy, and it is not considered an ostomy because there is no stoma.

ileostomy (14) removal of the colon and rectum with the small intestine brought to the abdominal wall.

immobilize (12) *see* stabilize.

immune globulin (Ig) (18) sterilized solution obtained from pooled human blood plasma, which contains immunoglobulins (or antibodies) that protect against infectious agents that cause various diseases.

immune serum globulin (18) *see* immune globulin.

immunoglobulin (17) protein produced by plasma cells that help fight infection; antibody that protects against infectious agents that cause various diseases.

immunology (17) study of the immune system.

implantable defibrillator (13) similar to a pacemaker in that it includes a pulse generator and electrodes, but it uses a combination of antitachycardia pacing and low-energy cardioversion or defibrillating shocks to regulate the patient's heartbeat and prevent arrhythmias.

implanted port (10) small reservoir that has a rubber plug attached to the catheter and is inserted into the patient's vein below the collar bone and threaded into the superior vena cava.

incision (11) a cut made with a knife, electrosurgical unit, or laser especially for surgical purposes (e.g., on body tissue).

incisional biopsy (11) removal of a portion of a lesion by slicing into it or incising it.

incision and drainage (I&D) (11) cutting open a lesion and draining its contents.

incomplete abortion (15) miscarriage in which part, but not all, of the uterine contents are expelled.

inconclusive diagnosis (6) see qualified diagnosis

indemnification (19) insurance against loss.

indexed (1) identified according to a unique identification number.

Index (ICD-10-PCS) (5) organizes ICD-10-PCS main terms in alphabetical order, providing the first 3-4 characters (and sometimes all 7 characters) of a code as well as direction to a specific location in the Tables.

Index to Diseases and Injuries (2) alphabetical listing of ICD-10-CM main terms and their codes; subdivided into Index to Diseases and Injuries (includes a Neoplasm Table and a Table of Drugs and Chemicals) and Index to External Causes of Injury; main terms are boldfaced, and subterms and qualifiers are indented below main terms.

Indian Health Service (IHS) (19) DHHS agency that provides federal health care services to American Indians and Alaska Natives.

indirect laryngoscopy (12) insertion of a small hand mirror in the patient's mouth at the back of the throat while the physician wears headgear that contains a mirror and light source; the mirror worn by the physician reflects light into the patient's mouth, allowing the physician to visualize the patient's throat.

individual practice association (IPA) HMO (19) contracted services enables to be delivered to subscribers by physicians who remain in their independent office settings.

induced abortion (15) deliberate termination of pregnancy.

infant (9) very young child, up to one year old.

inferred words (8) used to save space in the CPT index when referencing subterms.

infiltration anesthesia (10) topical injection of local anesthetic into tissue.

informational modifiers (8) clarify aspects of the procedure or service provided for the payer.

initial plan (1) documentation of the strategy for managing patient care and actions taken to investigate the patient's condition and to treat/educate the patient; the initial plan consists of three categories: diagnostic/management plans, therapeutic plans, and patient education plans; considered part of the problem-oriented record (POR).

inner ear (15) includes the cochlea, saccule, acoustic nerve, semicircular canals, utricle, and superior and inferior vestibular nerves.

inpatient (5) patient who remains overnight in a facility for 24 or more hours and who is provided with room and board and nursing services.

inpatient neonatal and pediatric critical care and intensive service (9) provided to critically ill neonates and infants by a physician.

inpatient prospective payment system (IPPS) (19) implemented as part of the Tax Equity and Fiscal Responsibility Act of 1982 (TEFRA); uses diagnosis-related groups (DRGs) to classify inpatient hospital cases into groups that are expected to consume similar hospital resources.

inpatient psychiatric facility prospective payment system (IPF PPS) (19) *per diem* patient classification system that reflects differences in patient resource use and costs; IPF PPS replaced a reasonable cost-based payment system; promotes long-term cost control and utilization management.

inpatient rehabilitation facility prospective payment system (IRF PPS) (19) use of information from a patient assessment instrument (PAI) to classify patients into distinct groups based on clinical characteristics and expected resource needs.

integrated delivery system (IDS) (19) organization of affiliated provider sites that offer joint health care services to subscribers.

integrated provider organization (IPO) (19) manages the delivery of health care services offered by hospitals, physicians who are employees of the IPO, and other health care organizations such as ambulatory surgery clinics and nursing facilities.

integrated record (1) arranged in strict chronological date order (or in reverse date order), which allows for observation of how the patient is progressing according to test results and how the patient responds to treatment based on test results.

intensity of services (IS) (19) determining whether provided services are appropriate for the patient's current or proposed level of care.

intensivist (9) physician who has received extensive training and experience in critical care and who specializes in the care of critically ill patients, usually in an intensive care unit (ICU).

interfacility transport (9) transfer of a patient from one health care facility to another; usually involves use of an ambulance or a helicopter.

internal catheter (10) catheter implanted completely under the skin.

internal fixation device (12) pins, screws, and/or plates inserted through or within a fracture area to stabilize and immobilize the injury; often called open reduction with internal fixation, or ORIF.

internal radiation (16) radiation placed inside the body.

International Classification of Diseases (ICD) (2) published by the World Health Organization and used to classify mortality data from death certificates.

International Classification of Diseases, Ninth Revision, Clinical Modification (ICD-9-CM) (1) adopted in 1979 to classify diagnoses (Volumes 1 and 2) and procedures (Volume 3); all health care facilities assigned ICD-9-CM codes to report diagnoses, and hospitals reported ICD-9-CM procedure codes for inpatient procedures and services; replaced by ICD-10-CM and ICD-10-PCS in 2015.

International Classification of Diseases for Oncology, Third Edition (ICD-O-3) (1) implemented in 2001 to classify a tumor according to primary site (topography) and morphology (histology, behavior, and aggression of tumor).

International Classification of Diseases, Tenth Revision, Clinical Modification (ICD-10-CM) (1) developed by the Centers for Medicare and Medicaid Services (CMS) to classify all diseases and injuries.

International Classification of Diseases, Tenth Revision, Clinical Modification/Procedure Coding System (ICD-10-CM/PCS) (1) shortened name the Centers for Medicare and Medicaid Services uses to identify the classification systems.

International Classification of Diseases, Tenth Revision, Procedure Coding System (ICD-10-PCS) (1) developed by the National Center for Health Statistics (NCHS) to classify inpatient procedures and services.

International Classification of Functioning, Disability and Health (ICF) (1) classifies health and health-related domains that describe body functions and structures, activities, and participation; complements ICD-10, looking beyond mortality and disease.

internship (1) student placement in a health care facility to provide on-the-job experience prior to graduation.

internship supervisor (1) person to whom a student reports at an internship site.

intersex surgery (15) performed as a series of staged procedures to transform the normal adult genitalia of one sex to that of the other sex; also called genital reconstructive surgery or sex reassignment surgery.

interventional radiologic procedure (16) use of percutaneous or minimally invasive techniques under imaging guidance to diagnose and treat conditions.

intra-arterial cannula (10) see intra-arterial line.

intra-arterial catheter (10) see intra-arterial line.

intra-arterial line (10) thin plastic tube, cannula, or catheter that is inserted into an artery and connected to a monitor to measure immediate changes in intra-arterial blood pressure and concentrations of oxygen and carbon dioxide; also used to collect frequent blood samples for lab tests.

intracapsular cataract extraction (ICCE) (15) removal of lens and surrounding capsule.

intracranial (10) introduced into or within the skull.

intradermal test (intracutaneous) (18) injection of purified allergen extracts into skin to test for allergy to suspected insect venom or penicillin.

intraservice time (9) a variable that is predictive of the "work" of E/M services, which includes face-to-face time for office and other outpatient visits or unit/floor time for hospital and other inpatient visits.

intrathecal (16) fluid-filled space between layers of tissue that cover the brain and spinal cord.

intravenous push (18) injection administered by a health care professional who is in constant attendance to administer the injection and observe the patient.

intravenous regional anesthesia (10) insertion of IV cannula into the extremity on which the procedure is to be performed and a tourniquet applied to interrupt blood circulation; then a large volume of local anesthetic injected into a peripheral vein, anesthetizing the extremity.

introduction (11) procedures that inject, insert, puncture, or scope.

IPPS 3-day payment window (19) requires outpatient preadmission services provided by a hospital up to three days prior to a patient's inpatient admission to be covered by the IPPS DRG payment for diagnostic services or therapeutic services for which the inpatient principal diagnosis code (ICD-10-CM) exactly matches that for preadmission services.

IPPS 72-hour rule (19) see IPPS 3-day payment window.

IPPS transfer rule (19) states that any patient with a diagnosis from one of ten CMS-determined diagnosis-related groups who is discharged to a post acute provider is treated as a transfer case.

IRF PPS 1-day payment window (19) requires that outpatient preadmission services provided by an IRF up to one day prior to a patient's inpatient admission be covered by the IRF PPS payment.

IRF PPS 24-hour rule (19) see IRF PPS 1-day payment window.

IRF PPS transfer rule (19) states that any patient who is discharged to an inpatient rehabilitation facility is treated as a transfer case.

iris (15) colored tissue that surrounds the pupil of the eye.

island flap (11) flap consisting of skin and subcutaneous tissue with a pedicle comprised only of nutrient vessels; also called island pedicle flap.

island pedicle flap (11) see island flap.

J

jamming (1) routinely assigning an unspecified ICD-10-CM disease code instead of reviewing the coding manual to select the appropriate code number.

J-pouch (14) see ileoanal anastomosis.

jukebox (1) equipment that stores large numbers of optical disks, resulting in huge storage capabilities.

K

key components (9) history, examination, and medical decision making; required when selecting an E/M level of service code.

kidney (14) filters and cleans blood, producing urine that carries waste.

knee (12) "hinge" joint composed of bones, cartilage, ligaments, and tendons.

Kock pouch (14) see continent ileostomy.

L

lacrimal apparatus (15) contains structures that produce, store, and remove tears.

lacrimal puncta (15) small openings in the inner canthus of the eyelids that channel tears.

laminectomy (15) excision of the entire posterior arch or lamina of a vertebra.

laminotomy (15) removal of part of the lamina from one side of the vertebra.

laparoscopy (14) examination of the peritoneal contents using a laparoscope that is inserted through the abdominal wall.

laryngoscopy (12) visualization of the back of the throat, including the larynx and vocal cords.

larynx (12) voice box.

laser-assisted uvulopalatoplasty (14) procedure that uses a laser technique to remove tissue from the uvula, soft palate, and pharynx.

LASER (light amplification by stimulated emission of radiation) (11) device filled with a gas, liquid, or solid substance that is stimulated to emit light to a specific wavelength for the purpose of burning, cutting, or dissolving tissue.

laser technique (14) technique that is most suitable for treatment of rectal lesions and uses a waveguide to deliver the laser beam through the endoscope to the lesion.

late effect (4) residual (long-term condition produced, called the sequela) that develops after the acute phase of an illness or injury has ended.

lateral extracavitary approach (LECA) (15) making a midline incision in the area of the affected vertebral segment, which is inferiorly curved out to the lateral plane.

laterality (4) in ICD-10-CM, whether the condition occurs on the left, the right, or is bilateral; in CPT, whether the procedure is performed bilaterally; in CPT, when laterality is not indicated in the procedure description for paired organs or body parts, add HCPCS level II modifier -LT or -RT to indicate the left or right side, respectively.

lateral projection (16) positioning patient at a right angle to the film, so the x-ray beam travels through the side of the body.

LEEP electrodissection conization (15) superficial dissection of the cervix.

LeFort I (12) procedure that brings the lower midface forward (from the level of the upper teeth) to just above the nostrils.

LeFort II (12) surgical fracture of the midfacial skeleton at an apex near the superior aspect of the nasal bones.

LeFort III (12) procedure that brings the entire midface forward, from the upper teeth to just above the cheekbones.

legacy classification system (2) see legacy coding system.

legacy coding system (2) classification system that is used as archive data; it is no longer supported or updated; for example, when ICD-10-CM and ICD-10-PCS were implemented, ICD-9-CM became a legacy coding system.

lens (15) clear, flexible, curved structure that focuses images on the retina of the eye.

lesion (10) abnormal tissue resulting from autoimmune or metabolic disorders, infection, neoplasm, or trauma.

ligament (12) tissue that connects bone to bone.

Limberg flap (11) see rhomboid flap.

listserv (1) see online discussion board.

lithotripsy (14) see percutaneous lithotomy.

lithotripter (10) device that administers a high-voltage electrical discharge through a spark gap under water, which produces a compressive force and breaks apart the stones so they can pass in urine.

local anesthesia (10) applying a topical agent on the body's surface or injecting a local anesthetic agent for the purpose of numbing a small part of the body; appropriate for minor surgeries.

local coverage determinations (LCDs) (7) define coverage criteria, payment rules, and documentation required as applied to DMEPOS claims processed by DME MACs for frequently ordered DMEPOS equipment, services, and supplies; formerly called local medical review policies (LMRPs).

Logical Observation Identifiers Names and Codes (LOINC) (1) electronic database and universal standard used to identify medical laboratory observations and for the purpose of clinical care and management.

LOINC (1) see Logical Observation Identifiers Names and Codes (LOINC)

long-term acute care hospital (LTACH) (5) health care facility designed specifically for patients who need functional restoration and/or rehabilitation and medical management for an average of three to six weeks; LTAC hospitals have an average inpatient length of stay of more than 25 days and provide extended medical and rehabilitative care for patients who are clinically complex and may suffer from multiple acute or chronic conditions.

long-term (acute) care hospital prospective payment system (LTCH PPS) (19) uses information from long-term care hospital patient records to classify patients into distinct long-term (acute) care diagnosis-related groups based on clinical characteristics and expected resource needs.

long-term hospital (5) see long-term acute care (LTAC) hospital.

loop electrodissection conization (15) deep dissection of the cervix.

low birth weight (9) less than 1500 grams.

LTCH PPS 1-day payment window (19) requires that outpatient preadmission services provided by a long-term acute care hospital up to one day prior to a patient's inpatient admission be covered by the LTC PPS diagnosis-related group payment.

LTCH PPS 24-hour rule (19) see LTC PPS 1-day payment window.

lumbar puncture (LP) (10) inserting a cannula at the L3-4 or L4-5 (lumbar vertebrae) to remove cerebrospinal fluid for diagnostic or therapeutic purposes.

lumen (10) opening.

lumpectomy (11) partial mastectomy.

luxation (12) see dislocation.

lymph (13) clear fluid that contains chyle, some red blood cells, and lymphocytes, which help fight infection and disease.

lymphatic system (13) consists of the spleen, thymus, tonsils, adenoids, vessels that carry lymph, and lymph nodes.

lymph nodes (13) clusters of bean-shaped nodules that act as the body's filtration system, removing cell waste and excess fluid and helping to fight infection.

M

magnetic resonance angiography (MRA) (16) noninvasive diagnostic study that is used to evaluate disorders of arterial and venous structures.

magnetic resonance imaging (MRI) (16) noninvasive x-ray procedure that uses an external magnetic field to produce a two-dimensional view of an internal organ or structure such as the brain or spinal cord.

main term (2) printed in boldfaced type and followed by the ICD-10-CM code number.

major diagnostic category (MDC) (19) refers to mutually exclusive categories that are loosely based on body systems (e.g., nervous system); diagnosis-related groups (DRGs) are organized into MDCs.

male genital system (15) includes the prostate, seminal vesicles, penis, testicles (testes), epididymis, tunica vaginalis, vas deferens, scrotum, spermatic cord, seminal vesicles, and prostate.

malignant (2) cancerous.

malunion (4) failure of the ends of a fractured bone to heal (unite).

mammography (16) radiological examination of the soft tissue and internal structures of the breast.

managed care (19) combines financing and delivery of health care services; replaces conventional fee-for-service health insurance plans with more affordable care for consumers and providers who agree to certain restrictions.

management service organization (MSO) (19) physician- or hospital-owned organization that provides practice management, administrative, and support services to individual physician practices.

manipulation (12) realignment of bones.

manometry (18) diagnostic test that measures muscle function using a pressure-sensitive tube.

manual record (1) paper-based record that includes handwritten progress notes and physician orders, graphic charts, and so on.

mass spectrometry (10) monitors proper levels of the anesthetic.

maximizing reimbursement (5) reimbursement that is *not* permitted because it involves selecting and reporting as principal diagnosis the ICD-10-CM code that results in the highest level of reimbursement for the facility whether that diagnosis meets the criteria for selection or not; it also includes assigning a higher-paying ICD-10-CM code to a diagnosis (or ICD-10-CM or CPT/HCPCS code to a procedure) even if patient record documentation does not support that code selection.

Maze procedure (13) stops atrial fibrillation or atrial flutter by using incisions in heart tissue to stop abnormal heart rhythm.

Meckel's diverticulum (14) common congenital abnormality of the gastrointestinal tract that results in a pouch in the wall of the small bowel that contains remnants of fetal gastrointestinal tissue.

mediastinum (14) space in the thoracic cavity between the lungs that contains the aorta, the esophagus, the heart, and other structures.

Medicaid (19) joint federal and state program that provides health care coverage to low-income populations and certain aged and disabled individuals.

medical assistant (1) health care professional employed by a provider to perform administrative and clinical tasks.

medical coding process (1) requires the review of patient record documentation to identify diagnoses, procedures, and services for the purpose of assigning ICD-10-CM/PCS, HCPCS level II, and/or CPT codes.

medical decision making (MDM) (9) refers to the complexity of establishing a diagnosis and/or selecting a management option as measured by the number of diagnoses or management options, the amount and/or complexity of data to be reviewed, and the risk of complications and/or morbidity or mortality.

medical foundation (19) nonprofit organization that contracts with and acquires the clinical and business assets of physician practices; the foundation is assigned a provider number and manages the practice's business.

medical management software (1) combination practice management and medical billing software that automates the daily workflow and procedures of a physician's office or clinic.

medical necessity (1) determination that a service or procedure rendered is reasonable and necessary for the diagnosis or treatment of an illness or injury.

medical nomenclature (1) vocabulary of clinical and medical terms (e.g., arthritis, gastritis, and pneumonia) used by health care providers to document patient care.

medical record (1) *see* patient record.

Medicare (19) provides health care coverage to elderly and disabled persons; federal spending is funded by the Medicare Trust Fund (payroll tax).

Medicare administrative contractor (MAC) (19) processes claims for physicians, health care facilities, and suppliers of durable medical equipment, prosthetics, orthotics, and supplies.

Medicare Carriers Manual (MCM) (7) provides direction about services and procedures to be reimbursed by the Medicare administrative contractor.

Medicare National Coverage Determinations Manual (7) indicates whether a service is covered or excluded under the Medicare program.

Medicare physician fee schedule (MPFS) (19) common name for resource-based relative value scale system, which is used to reimburse physician services covered by Medicare Part B.

Medicare Prescription Drug, Improvement, and Modernization Act (MMA) (2) federal legislation that requires all code sets to be valid at the time services are provided.

Medicare Prescription Drug, Improvement, and Modernization Act of 2003 (MMA) (19) eliminated carriers, fiscal intermediaries, and durable medical equipment regional carriers and created Medicare administrative contractors.

Medicare Pricing, Data Analysis, and Coding (PDAC) contractor (7) assists suppliers and manufacturers in determining HCPCS codes to be used; previously called the Statistical Analysis Durable Medical Equipment Regional Carrier (SADMERC).

Medicare severity diagnosis-related groups (MS-DRGs) (19) classify inpatient hospital cases into groups according to similar resource utilization, which results in hospitals receiving a predetermined payment according to MS-DRG for treating Medicare patients; like the original DRGs, MS-DRGs are based on diagnoses, procedures, other demographic information, and the presence of complications or comorbidities (CCs); however, hospital inpatients are distinguished according to those with no CCs, CCs, or major CCs (MCCs), which allows Medicare to distinguish "sick patients" from "very sick patients" and reimburse hospitals accordingly; the number of MS-DRGs expands to 745 (as compared to 538 original DRGs).

Medicare severity long-term (acute) care diagnosis-related groups (MS-LTCH-DRGs) (19) based on clinical characteristics and expected resource needs; replaced the reasonable cost-based LTCH PPS authorized by TEFRA that had mandated the implementation of DRGs (and originally exempted long-term acute care hospitals from participation).

Medicare Summary Notice (MSN) (19) an easy-to-read monthly statement sent to Medicare beneficiaries, which clearly lists health insurance claims information.

megaelectron volt (16) *see* MeV.

megavolt (16) *see* MeV.

metastatic cancer (4) *see* secondary malignancy.

MeV (16) 1 million electron volts.

microbiology (17) study of microbes.

microdermabrasion (11) skin-freshening technique used to repair facial skin that is damaged by the sun and the effects of aging.

microtechnique (17) one of three types of micromanipulation techniques that may be used for the preparation of an embryo for transfer.

middle ear (15) includes the tympanic membrane, auditory ossicles, muscles, and conduction pathways.

midsagittal plane (16) vertically divides the body through the midline into two equal left and right halves.

Military Health System (MHS) (19) provides and maintains readiness to provide health care services and support to members of the Uniformed Services during military operations; also provides health care services and support to members of the Uniformed Services, their family members, and others entitled to Department of Defense health care.

minimally invasive procedure (18) includes percutaneous access.

minimum data set (MDS) (19) standardized, primary screening and assessment tool of health status that forms the foundation of the comprehensive assessment for all residents in a Medicare or Medicaid-certified long-term care facility; contains items that measure physical, psychological and psychosocial functioning, which provide a multidimensional view of the patient's functional capacities and helps staff to identify health problems.

missed abortion (15) miscarriage in which a dead fetus and other products of conception remain in the uterus for four or more weeks.

M-mode (16) one-dimensional display that reflects the movement of structures.

moderate (conscious) sedation (11) moderate sedation or analgesia that results in a drug-induced depression of consciousness.

modified Maze procedure (13) *see* cardiac ablation.

modified radical mastectomy (11) total mastectomy that includes removal of the breast and nipple, axillary lymph nodes, and pectoralis minor muscle.

modifying unit (10) part of anesthesia formula that recognizes added complexities associated with the administration of anesthesia, including physical factors and difficult circumstances.

Mohs microsurgery (11) technique of excising skin tumors by removing tumor tissue layer by layer, examining the removed portion microscopically for malignant cells, and repeating the procedure until the entire tumor is removed.

monitored anesthesia care (MAC) (10) administration of varying amounts of local, regional, and certain mind-altering drugs by an anesthesiologist or a CRNA during a patient's diagnostic or therapeutic procedure.

morbidity (2) disease.

morphology (2) indicates the tissue type of a neoplasm.

mortality (2) death.

motion mode (16) *see* M-mode.

mucocutaneous margin (14) consists of mucous membrane and skin.

multiaxial structure (ICD-10-PCS) (5) a value from each of seven hierarchies (positions) is assigned to construct an ICD-10-PCS code.

multihospital system (5) two or more hospitals owned, managed, or leased by a single organization; these may include acute, long-term, pediatric, rehabilitation, or psychiatric care facilities.

multiple codes (4) more than one ICD-10-CM code that is assigned to completely classify the elements of a complex diagnosis (or procedure) statement.

multiple sleep latency (18) observation of a patient during at least a six-hour period of sleep and includes assessment of sleep latency (dormancy) and/or wakefulness after the sleep period.

mutually exclusive edit (8) code pairs that, for clinical reasons, are unlikely to be performed on the same patient on the same day.

mycocutaneous flap (11) autologous graft consisting of both skin and muscle tissue from the donor site.

myocardium (13) muscle layer of the heart.

myringotomy (15) surgical incision of the tympanic membrane; usually performed to release pressure or fluid.

N

narcosynthesis (18) form of psychotherapy that is provided when the patient is under the influence of a drug, such as a sedative or narcotic.

nasal vestibule (12) entrance to the nose.

nasopharynx (14) located above the soft palate.

National Correct Coding Initiative (NCCI) (8) implemented by the Centers for Medicare & Medicaid Services (CMS) to promote national correct coding methodologies and to control the improper assignment of codes that results in inappropriate reimbursement of Medicare Part B claims.

national coverage determinations (NCDs) (7) define coverage criteria, payment rules, and documentation required as applied to DMEPOS claims processed by DME MACs for frequently ordered DMEPOS equipment, services, and supplies.

National Drug Codes (NDC) (1) contains prescription drugs and a few selected over-the-counter (OTC) products, which pharmacies use to report transactions and some health care professionals use for reporting on claims.

national health plan identifier (HPID) (19) assigned to third-party payers; contains 10 numerical positions including a check digit in the tenth position (e.g., 1234567890); formerly called the PAYERID.

national individual identifier (patient identifier) (19) HIPAA provision for a national individual identifier (or patient identifier) that has been withdrawn.

national limitation amount (NLA) (19) serves as a payment ceiling, or cap, on the amount Medicare could pay for each test.

national provider identifier (NPI) (19) assigned to hospitals, doctors, nursing homes, and other health care providers; contains 10 numerical digits (e.g., 1234567890).

national standard employer identifier number (EIN) (19) IRS's federal tax identification number (EIN) adopted as the national employer identifier, retaining the hyphen after the first two numbers (e.g., 12-3456789); the EIN is assigned to employers who, as sponsors of health insurance for their employees, must be identified in health care transactions.

nature of the presenting problem (9) disease, condition, illness, injury, symptom, sign, finding, complaint, or other reason for the encounter, with or without a diagnosis being established at the time of the encounter.

necropsy (17) autopsy.

needle core biopsy (11) tissue sample obtained using a hand-operated needle or stereotactic localization.

needle electromyography (18) inserting needle electrodes into skeletal muscles and observing electrical activity of those muscles using an oscilloscope and a loudspeaker.

neonate (9) newborn, up to 28 days old.

neoplasm (2, 4) new growth, or tumor, in which cell reproduction is out of control.

nephrectomy (14) surgical removal of a kidney.

nerve plexus (10) network of intersecting nerves.

nervous system (15) includes the central nervous system and the peripheral nervous system.

network model HMO (19) contracted health care services provided to subscribers by two or more physician multispecialty group practices.

network provider (19) physician or health care facility under contract to the managed care plan.

neuroplasty (15) freeing or decompression of an intact nerve from scar tissue.

neurorrhaphy (15) repair of nerves.

neurostimulator (15) electrode and pulse generator that are implanted along the spine to alleviate pain or control spasms.

newborn care services (9) includes services provided to newborns in a variety of health care settings.

newborn patient (5) patient who receives infant care upon birth and, if necessary, receives neonatal intensive care (either within a hospital or as the result of transfer to another hospital).

new patient (9) one who has *not* received any professional services within the past three years from the physician or from another physician of the same exact specialty or subspecialty who belongs to the same group practice.

Nissen fundoplasty (14) mobilizing the lower end of the esophagus by suturing the fundus of the stomach around the circumference of the lower esophagus at the esophagogastric junction.

noncovered benefits (19) procedures and services that are not covered by the third-party payer.

nonessential modifier (2) qualifying word contained in parentheses after the main term in the ICD-10-CM Index to Diseases and Injuries that does not have to be included in the diagnostic or procedural statement for the code number listed after the parentheses to be assigned.

noninvasive procedure (18) requires no surgical incision or excision; not an open procedure.

nonparticipating provider (nonPAR) (19) health care provider (e.g., physician) who is not a member of a health care plan; nonPAR providers do not receive reimbursement directly from a payer; the reimbursement is sent to the patient, and the nonPAR provider must collect payment for services rendered from the patient.

nonselective vascular catheterization (13) introduction of a catheter into a vessel without further advancement past the punctured vessel *or* introduction of a catheter into any portion of the aorta or vena cava from any approach (e.g., axillary, brachial, femoral, jugular).

nontunneled catheter (10) *see* external catheter.

nonunion (4) *see* malunion.

notes (8) appear throughout CPT sections to clarify the assignment of codes.

Notice of Exclusions from Medicare Benefits (NEMB) (8) form completed and signed by a Medicare beneficiary before items, procedures, and services excluded from Medicare benefits are provided.

nuclear imaging (16) noninvasive x-ray procedure that creates an image by measuring radiation emission, or radiation "uptake," of body areas after the administration of a radionuclide.

nuclear medicine (16) use of radioactive elements for diagnostic imaging and radiopharmaceutical therapy.

number symbol (8) symbol (#) located to the left of CPT codes to indicate out-of-numerical sequence codes.

O

Objective (O) (1) observations about the patient, such as physical findings or lab or x-ray results; considered part of the problem-oriented record (POR) SOAP note.

oblique projection (16) positioning the patient with the body slanted sideways toward the film, halfway between a parallel and right-angle position; the x-ray beam travels through this angle of the body.

observation patient (6) patient who receives services furnished on a hospital's premises that are ordered by a physician (or another authorized individual), including use of a bed and periodic monitoring by nursing or other staff, and that are reasonable and necessary to evaluate the outpatient's condition or determine the need for possible admission as an inpatient.

observation service (9) provided in a hospital outpatient setting; the patient is considered an outpatient.

obturator (12) object used to close a gap.

ocular adnexa (15) includes the orbit, eye muscles, eyelids, eyelashes, conjunctiva, and lacrimal apparatus.

ocular implant (15) inserted inside the muscular cone.

office or other outpatient services (9) provided in a physician's office, a hospital outpatient department, or another ambulatory care facility.

***Official ICD-10-CM Guidelines for Coding and Reporting* (2)** rules developed to accompany and complement official conventions and instructions provided in ICD-10-CM.

***Official ICD-10-PCS Guidelines for Coding and Reporting* (2)** rules developed to accompany and complement official conventions and instructions provided in ICD-10-PCS.

omentectomy (15) surgical removal of the omentum.

Omnibus Budget Reconciliation Act of 1980 (19) federal legislation mandating that an ambulatory surgery center could participate in Medicare if certain conditions were met and stating that the ambulatory surgical center's payments are "expected to be calculated on a prospective basis...utilizing sample survey and similar techniques to establish reasonable estimated overhead allowances for each of the listed procedures which take account of volume (within reasonable limits)."

Omnibus Budget Reconciliation Act of 1987 (OBRA) (19)   federal legislation that mandated the payment methodology for durable medical equipment, prosthetics, orthotics, and supplies fee schedule.

Omnibus Budget Reconciliation Act of 1989 (19)   federal legislation that implemented the resource-based relative value scale (RBRVS) system, which is used to reimburse physician services covered by Medicare Part B.

Omnibus Consolidated and Emergency Supplemental Appropriations Act (OCESAA) of 1999 (19)   federal legislation that implemented the home health prospective payment system for Medicare home health services.

one-lung ventilation (OLV) (10)   isolation of the right or left lung so that one lung is ventilated and the other is allowed to collapse.

online discussion board (1)   Internet-based or e-mail discussion forum that covers a variety of topics and issues.

oocyte (15)   immature female reproductive cell, or egg.

oophorectomy (15)   surgical removal of an ovary or ovaries.

open biopsy (11)   incisional or excisional removal of a lesion.

open fracture (4)   type of fracture that has an associated open wound.

open fracture treatment (12)   surgically opening a fracture site or exposing it so treatment can be provided.

open laparoscopy (14)   insufflation of the abdomen using a trocar, which is placed under direct vision (using a laparoscope) after making a small celiotomy incision.

open-panel HMO (19)   health care provided by individuals who are not employees of the HMO or who do not belong to a specially formed medical group that serves the HMO.

open transluminal angioplasty (13)   making an incision in the skin overlying the artery and carrying it down to free the artery from surrounding structures.

operating microscope (15)   used during a surgical procedure to perform microsurgery techniques.

opportunistic infection (4)   one that takes advantage of the body's weakened defenses, such as in an HIV-positive patient.

optical disk imaging (1)   alternative to traditional microfilm or remote storage systems because patient records are converted to an electronic image and saved on storage media.

optimizing reimbursement (5)   determining which of several diagnoses to report as the principal diagnosis when multiple diagnoses equally meet the criteria for selection as the principal diagnosis.

orbicularis oculi (18)   blink test that is monitored with sensors.

orbit (15)   bony cavity in the skull that contains and protects the eyeball and its associated blood vessels, muscles, and nerves.

orbital implant (15)   inserting an implant outside the muscular cone into the eye socket, and placing an intraocular lens (IOL).

organ harvest (10)   surgical removal of an organ for transplantation.

oropharynx (14)   area between the soft palate and the upper portion of the epiglottis, including the tonsils.

orthotics (7)   branch of medicine that deals with the design and fitting of orthopedic (relating to bone disorders) devices.

oscilloscope (18)   device that displays electrical waveforms on a monitor.

osteogenesis (12)   bone growth.

osteopathic manipulative treatment (OMT) (18)   manual treatment performed by a physician during which emphasis is placed on normal body mechanics and manipulative methods to detect and correct structure.

osteophytectomy (15)   removal of bone spurs to relieve compression of the spinal cord or nerve roots.

osteotomy (12)   surgical incision into bone.

ostomy (14)   surgically creating an opening in the body for the discharge of body wastes.

other (additional) diagnoses (5)   any condition that coexists at the time of admission, that develops subsequently, or that affects the treatment received and/or the length of stay.

other significant procedure (5)   surgical in nature, carries an operative or anesthetic risk, requires highly trained personnel, or requires special facilities or equipment; also called a secondary procedures.

Outcome and Assessment Information Set (OASIS) (6)   core set of comprehensive assessments for adult home care patients used to measure patient outcomes for Outcome-Based Quality Improvement (OBQI); conduct patient assessment, patient care planning, and internal HHA performance improvements; and generate agency-level case mix reports that contain aggregate statistics about various patient characteristics such as demographic, health, or functional status at start of care; HHAs use Home Assessment and Validation and Entry (HAVEN) data entry software to report OASIS data.

outlier (19)   inpatient case that is unusually costly.

outpatient (6)   see ambulatory patient.

outpatient care (6)   any health care service provided to a patient who is not admitted to a facility.

outpatient encounter (19)   all outpatient procedures and services (e.g., same-day surgery, x-rays, laboratory tests, and so on) provided during one day to the same patient; also called outpatient visit.

outpatient prospective payment system (OPPS) (19)   uses ambulatory payment classifications (APCs) to reimburse hospital outpatient services.

outpatient visit (19)   see outpatient encounter.

overcoding (1)   reporting codes for signs and symptoms associated, in addition to an established diagnosis code.

overlapping sites (4)   see contiguous sites.

overpayment (19)   reimbursement a provider or beneficiary receives in excess of amount due.

overpayment recovery (19)   collecting excess payments made by Medicare, Medicaid, and other payers.

P

pacemaker (13)   device that regulates the patient's heartbeat to prevent arrhythmias; includes a pulse generator and electrodes.

palatopharyngoplasty (14)   surgical resection of excess tissue from the uvula, soft palate, and pharynx to open the airway.

panniculectomy (10)   surgical removal of excess abdominal panniculus.

panniculus adiposus (10)   layer of subcutaneous adipose tissue, or fat, below the dermis that contains fat deposits, blood vessels, and nerves.

pannus (10)   see panniculus adiposus.

parenterally (16)   other than by mouth or rectum, such as implantation, infusion, or injection.

paring and curettement (11)   removal of growths or other material from the wall of a cavity or another surface.

partial hospitalization (9)   short-term, intensive treatment program in which individuals who are experiencing an acute episode of an illness can receive medically supervised treatment during a significant number of daytime or nighttime hours.

partial mastectomy (11)   involves making an incision through skin and fascia over the breast tumor and clamping lymphatic and blood vessels; the physician then excises the tumor mass along with a section of breast tissue.

participating provider (PAR) (19)   health care provider (e.g., physician) who is a member of a health care plan; PAR providers receive reimbursement directly from the payer.

past medical history (9)   summary of past illnesses, operations, injuries, treatments, and known allergies.

patch test (epicutaneous) (18)   applying an allergen to a patch, which is placed on skin; the test is performed to identify substances that cause contact dermatitis, such as latex, medications, fragrances, preservatives, hair dyes, metals, and resins.

patency (13)   open and unblocked status of a blood vessel or another tube in the body.

patient education plan (1)   program to educate the patient about conditions for which the patient is being treated; considered part of the problem-oriented record (POR).

patient record (1)   business record for an inpatient or outpatient encounter that documents health care services provided to a patient; stores patient demographic data and documentation that supports diagnoses and justifies treatment; and contains results of treatment provided.

Payment Error and Prevention Program (PEPP) (19) identifies and reduces improper Medicare payments, resulting in a reduction in the Medicare payment error rate.

pediatric critical care patient transport (9)   includes the physical attendance and direct face-to-face care provided by a physician during the interfacility transport of a critically ill or critically injured patient aged 24 months or younger.

pedicle skin graft (11)   transferring a portion of skin graft to the recipient area, and attaching a remaining portion (the base) to the donor site so there is a vasculature and nerve supply for the recipient area.

percutaneous lithotomy (14)   two-stage procedure that requires a percutaneous nephrostomy and dilation of the nephrostomy tract.

percutaneous myocardial revascularization (PMR) (13)   insertion of a catheter with a laser inside through an artery into the left ventricle of the heart.

percutaneous needle biopsy (12)   insertion of a long needle through the skin and into other tissue (e.g., chest wall, lung, or mediastinum) to obtain tissue for diagnostic evaluation.

percutaneous skeletal fixation (12)   use of an external or internal fixation device to stabilize and immobilize a fracture; types include external fixation and internal fixation.

percutaneous transluminal angioplasty (PTA) (13)   puncturing an artery and inserting a sheath, guidewire, and guiding catheter (after removing the guidewire).

percutaneous transmyocardial laser revascularization (PTMR) (13)   see percutaneous myocardial revascularization (PMR).

percutaneous vertebroplasty (12)   process of injecting material (e.g., cement) into vertebral body to reinforce that body using image guidance.

pericardial sac (13)   see pericardium.

pericardiectomy (13)   removal of part of the pericardium (to treat chronic pericarditis).

pericardiocentesis (13)   insertion of a needle to withdraw fluid from the pericardial sac.

pericardiotomy (13)   requires thoracotomy as incision for pericardial drainage, fluid collection, or foreign body removal.

pericardium (13)   membrane that surrounds the heart; also called pericardial sac.

perinatal period (4)   interval of time occurring before, during, and up to 28 days following birth.

peripherally (13)   access via a peripheral vein.

peripheral nerve block (10)   injection of local anesthetic in the vicinity of a peripheral nerve to anesthetize that nerve's area of innervation.

peristalsis (14)   wavelike motions that propel urine.

peritoneal dialysis (18)   insertion of soft catheter into abdominal cavity and infusion of dialysate fluid at intermittent times.

peritoneoscopy (14)   see laparoscopy.

pharmacologic management (18)   evaluation of a patient's medications for effect, proper dosage, and renewal of prescribed medications.

phlebotomy (17)   see venipuncture.

photic stimulation (18)   reaction to light.

photons (16)   invisible electromagnetic energy waves.

physiatrist (18)   physician who specializes in physical medicine and rehabilitation and treats acute/chronic pain and musculoskeletal disorders.

physical examination (9)   assessment of the patient's organ and body systems.

physical medicine and rehabilitation (18)   branch of medicine that focuses on the prevention, diagnosis, and treatment of disorders of the musculoskeletal, cardiovascular, and pulmonary systems that may produce temporary or permanent impairment.

physical status modifier (10)   added to each reported anesthesia code to indicate the patient's condition at the time anesthesia was administered.

physician case management (9)   process in which a physician is responsible for direct care of a patient and for the coordination and control of access to or initiation and/or supervision of other health care services needed by the patient.

physician-hospital organization (PHO) (19)   owned by hospital(s) and physician groups that obtain managed care plan contracts; physicians maintain their own practices and provide health care services to plan members.

physician query process (1)   contacting the responsible physician to request clarification about documentation and codes to be assigned; the process is activated when the coder notices a problem with documentation quality.

Physicians at Teaching Hospitals (PATH) initiative (19) federal program that resulted from the discovery that some health care organizations were billing Medicare Part B for services that were already paid under Part A.

physician self-referral law (19)   prohibits a physician from referring Medicare patients to clinical laboratory services where they or a member of their family have a financial interest; enacted as part of the Omnibus Budget Reconciliation Act of 1989.

pilonidal cyst (11)   entrapped epithelial tissue and hair located in the sacral area at the top of the crease between the buttocks, which can become infected.

placeholder (2)   use of the letter "x" in certain ICD-10-CM codes to allow for future expansion.

place of service (POS) (9)   the physical location where health care is provided to patients.

plan (P) (1)   diagnostic, therapeutic, and education plans to resolve the problems; considered part of the problem-oriented record (POR) SOAP note.

plane of view (16)   terminology used when performing a radiology procedure.

pleura (12)   membrane that envelopes the lungs and lines the walls of the pleural cavity.

pleural effusion (12)   fluid in the pleural cavity preventing the lung from fully expanding, making it difficult for the patient to breathe.

plexus anesthesia (10)   injection of local anesthetic in the vicinity of a nerve plexus.

plus symbol (8)   symbol (+) located to the left of CPT codes that identifies add-on codes (also located in Appendix D of CPT) for procedures that are commonly, but not always, performed at the same time and by the same surgeon as the primary procedure.

pneumocentesis (12)   puncture of the pleural space with a transthoracic needle to drain fluid or to obtain material for diagnostic study.

pneumonectomy (12)   removal of the entire lung or one or more lobes of the lung.

point-of-service plan (POS) (19)   offers patients the freedom to use an HMO panel of providers or to self-refer to non-HMO providers.

polysomnography (18)   sleep study that includes sleep staging with additional parameters of sleep.

port (16)   skin site where radiation beams enter the body.

positron emission tomography (PET) (16)   producing x-ray images of the body after administering radioisotopes, which tracks metabolism or blood flow, not anatomy.

postanesthesia evaluation (10)   evaluation of the patient during recovery from anesthesia, as well as evaluation, treatment, and follow-up of possible anesthesia-related complications.

posteroanterior (PA) projection (16)   positioning the patient as facing the film and parallel to it; the x-ray beam travels from back to front, or posterior to anterior.

postoperative pain management (10)   administration of epidural or subarachnoid medications on the date(s) of service after the date of surgery.

postpartum care (15)   begins after vaginal or cesarean section delivery and includes the recovery room visit; any uncomplicated inpatient hospital and outpatient postpartum visits; episiotomy; and repair of cervical, vaginal, or perineal lacerations.

preadmission testing (PAT) (6)   occurs after a surgical patient registers with a facility's admitting department, when the patient undergoes preoperative nursing assessment and receives preanesthesia evaluation by an anesthesiologist.

preanesthesia evaluation (10)   assessing information from the patient's record, interviewing the patient, conducting a physical examination, evaluating preoperative test results, and ensuring that informed anesthetic consent has been obtained.

preauthorization (19)   prior approval.

pre-existing medical condition (19)   illness or injury that required treatment during a prescribed period of time prior to the insured's effective date of coverage under a new insurance policy.

preferred provider organization (PPO) (19)   network of physicians and hospitals that join together to contract with insurance companies, employers, or other organizations.

preoperative clearance (9)   occurs when a surgeon requests that a specialist or another physician examine a patient and indicate whether the patient can withstand the expected risks of a specific surgery.

present on admission (POA) indicator (19)   assigned to each diagnosis and external cause of injury code that is coded and reported on inpatient UB-04 or 837 Institutional (electronic) claims.

pressure ulcer (11)   ulceration of the skin and underlying tissue that occurs over a bony prominence.

presumptive identification (17)   identification by colony morphology, growth on selective media, or Gram stains.

preventive medicine services (9)   include routine examinations or risk management counseling for children and adults who exhibit no overt signs or symptoms of a disorder while presenting to the medical office for a preventive medical physical.

pricing modifier (8)   see functional modifier.

primary care (6)   acute care and preventive services provided as outpatient care and referred to as the point of first contact.

primary care provider (6)   manages and coordinates the patient's care, including referring the patient to a medical specialist for consultation and a second opinion; physician responsible for supervising and coordinating health care services and preauthorizing referrals to specialists and for overseeing inpatient hospital admissions, except in emergencies.

primary defect (11)   wound resulting from initial surgical intervention (e.g., excision of lesion) or trauma (e.g., deep abrasions).

primary malignancy (4)   original tumor site.

principal diagnosis (5)   condition established after study to be chiefly responsible for occasioning the admission of the patient to the hospital for care.

principal procedure (5)   performed for definitive treatment rather than for diagnostic or exploratory purposes, necessary to treat a complication, or is most closely related to the principal diagnosis.

privacy (19)   patient's right to prohibit disclosure of information without his or her authorization.

privacy rule (19)   see HIPAA standards for privacy of individually identifiable health information.

privileged communication (19)   any information communicated by a patient to a health care provider.

problem focused examination (9)   limited examination of the affected body area or organ system.

problem focused history (9)   consists of chief complaint and brief history of present illness or problem.

problem list (1) serves as a table of contents for the patient record because it is filed at the beginning of the record and contains a numbered list of the patient's problems, which helps to index documentation throughout the record; considered part of the problem-oriented record (POR).

problem-oriented record (POR) (1) systematic method of documentation that consists of four components: database, problem list, initial plan, and progress notes.

proctectomy (14) surgical removal of the rectum.

proctosigmoidoscopy (14) visual examination of the rectum and sigmoid colon.

professional component (16) services provided by the physician, which include supervising the performance of a diagnostic imaging procedure, interpreting imaging films, and documenting the imaging report.

professional services (9) face-to-face services provided by a physician or nonphysician practitioner (e.g., nurse practitioner, physician assistant) and reported by assigning an E/M code.

Programs of All-inclusive Care for the Elderly (PACE) (19) community-based Medicare and Medicaid programs that provide integrated health care and long-term care services to elderly persons who require a nursing-facility level of care.

progress notes (1) narrative notes documented by the provider to demonstrate continuity of care and the patient's response to treatment; when using the SOAP format, a narrative is documented for each problem assigned to the patient according to subjective (S), objective (O), assessment (A), and plan (P).

prohibitory symbol (8) *see* forbidden symbol.

prolonged services (9) physicians' services involving patient contact that are considered beyond the usual service in either an inpatient or an outpatient setting.

prospective cost-based rate (19) based on reported health care costs from which a prospective *per diem* rate is determined; annual rate is usually adjusted using actual costs from the prior year; may be based on the facility's case mix (patient acuity of types and categories of patients).

prospective payment system (PPS) (19) reimbursement methodology that establishes predetermined rates based on patient category or type of facility, with annual increases based on an inflation index and a geographic wage index.

prospective price-based rate (19) associated with a particular category of patient; rate is established by the payer prior to the provision of health care services.

prosthetics (7) branch of medicine that deals with the design, production, and use of artificial body parts.

protected health information (PHI) (19) information that is identifiable to an individual, such as name, address, telephone numbers, date of birth, and Medicaid ID number.

provider (1) physician or other health care professional who performs procedures or provides services to patients.

psychotherapy (18) treatment of mental and emotional disorders by having patients talk about their condition(s) and related issues with a mental health physician or therapist.

pull-through (14) *see* ileoanal anastomosis.

pulmonary wedge pressure (10) indirect measurement of left atrial pressure that is useful in the diagnosis of left ventricular failure and mitral valve disease.

pulse oximetry (10) arterial oxyhemoglobin saturation.

pump oxygenator (10) device that substitutes for the heart (pump) and lungs (oxygenator) during open heart surgery.

puncture, prick, or scratch test (percutaneous) (18) procedure in which tiny drops of purified allergen extracts are pricked or scratched into the skin's surface; performed to identify allergies to pollen, mold, pet dander, dust mites, foods, insect venom, and penicillin.

pupil (15) black opening in the center of the iris that permits light to enter the eye.

pyramidal fracture (12) *see* LeFort II.

Q

qualified diagnosis (6) diagnosis documented as probable, suspected, questionable, rule out, or working diagnosis.

qualifying circumstance (10) coded when anesthesia services are provided during situations or circumstances that make anesthesia administration more difficult.

qualitative assay (17) detects whether a particular substance is present.

quantitative A-scan (16) diagnostic ultrasound that produces quantitative data about the posterior eye segment and evaluates tissue consistency, mobility, and vascularity.

quantitative assay (17) detects the amount of a substance in a specimen.

R

radiation absorbed dose (rad) (16) amount of radiant energy absorbed in a tissue.

radiation oncology (16) specialty of medicine that utilizes high-energy ionizing radiation in the treatment of malignant neoplasms and certain nonmalignant conditions.

radical mastectomy (11) total mastectomy, which includes removal of the breast and nipple, pectoralis muscles (major and/or minor), axillary lymph nodes, and internal mammary lymph nodes.

radiographic projection (16) describes the path that the x-ray beam travels through the body, from entrance to exit.

radiologic guidance (16) performed during a procedure to visualize access to an anatomical site fluoroscopic guidance to guide the placement, replacement, or removal of a catheter, central venous access device (CVAD), or needle.

radiologist (16) physician who has undergone specialized training to interpret diagnostic x-rays, perform specialized x-ray procedures, and administer radiation for the treatment of disease.

radiology (16) branch of medicine that uses imaging techniques to diagnose and treat disease.

radionuclide (16) radioactive material, such as an isotope of iodine.

radiopaque (10) cannot be penetrated by electromagnetic radiation.

radiopharmaceutical therapy (16) destroys diseased tissue, such as a malignant neoplasm.

random pattern flap (11) mycocutaneous flap with a random pattern of arteries.

range of codes (8) code numbers separated by a dash or a series of codes separated by commas in the CPT index.

reagent strip automated urine analyzer (17) instrumentation used to determine various components in the urine.

real-time scan (16)   two-dimensional display of structures and movement that indicates the movement, shape, and size of the tissue or organ.

recipient heart with or without lung allotransplantation (13)   removal (harvesting) of heart with or without lung tissue; includes transplantation of the allograft and care of the recipient.

recipient lung allotransplantation (12)   transplantation of a single or double lung allograft and care of the recipient.

recipient site (11)   anatomical site to which healthy skin is attached.

reconstruction (11)   surgical rebuilding of a body part, such as the breast or the knee joint.

reconstruction of the vena cava (13)   surgical procedure performed to correct a congenital defect or to repair the vena cava when the patient sustains trauma or the vena cava is damaged due to long-term drug therapy.

red reference symbol (8)   symbol (⊃) located below a code description to indicate that the coder should refer to the *Clinical Examples in Radiology* quarterly newsletter.

reduction (12)   *see* manipulation.

referral (9)   recommendation to transfer a patient's care from one provider to another.

referred outpatient (6)   patient who receives diagnostic or therapeutic care because such care is unavailable in the primary care provider's office.

regional anesthesia (10)   anesthesia agents injected into or near the spinal fluid and around a nerve or network of nerves to block the nerve supply to a specific part of the body.

rehabilitation hospital (5)   health care facility that admits patients who are diagnosed with trauma or disease and who need to learn how to function.

relative value unit (RVU) (19)   payment component that consists of physician work, practice expense, and malpractice expense.

remittance advice (remit) (19)   statement sent by the payer to the provider that details how submitted claims were processed and contains reimbursement amounts.

removal (11)   procedures performed to eliminate tissue (e.g., amputations) or take something out (e.g., removal of implants, such as buried wire, pins, or screws).

renal dialysis (18)   artificial removal of toxic waste products from the body when the patient's kidneys are unable to perform this function due to disease or deterioration.

repair (11)   procedure performed to surgically improve improperly functioning parts of the body.

replantation (12)   surgical reattachment of a finger, a hand, a toe, a foot, a leg, or an arm that has been completely severed from a person's body.

Resident Assessment Validation and Entry (RAVEN) (19) data entry system that allows a skilled nursing facility (SNF) to capture and transmit the minimum data set (MDS).

resident physician (1)   individual who participates in an approved graduate medical education (GME) program.

residual condition (4)   long-term condition produced after the acute phase of an illness or injury has terminated, which is called the sequela.

residual effect (4)   condition produced (sequela) after the acute phase of an illness or injury has terminated.

resource-based relative value scale (RBRVS) system (19)   used to reimburse physician services covered by Medicare Part B, and is now now called the Medicare physician fee schedule (MPFS).

resource utilization group (RUG) (19)   prospective payment system implemented by the federal government to control costs in nursing facilities.

retina (15)   part of eye that contains nerve tissue.

revenue code (19)   four-digit UB-04 code that is assigned to each procedure, service, or supply to indicate the location or type of service provided to an institutional patient, such as radiology or laboratory.

review of systems (ROS) (9)   *see* system review.

revision (11)   surgical modification of a previous procedure or a device.

rhinoplasty (14)   repair of a skin defect of the nose using harvested tissue or plastic surgery to change the nose's shape or size.

rhomboid flap (11)   random pattern flap that can be raised on any or all corners of a parallelogram configuration, typically 120 and 60 degrees; also called Limberg flap.

rhytidectomy (11)   excision of a section of skin to eliminate wrinkles.

rhytides (12)   wrinkles.

roentgen (16)   international unit of exposure dose for x-rays or gamma rays.

roentgen-equivalent-man (rem) (16)   unit of measurement that includes different biological responses to different kinds of radiation.

roster billing (19)   simplified claims submission process available to public health clinics and other noninstitutional entities that offer mass immunization programs.

rotation flap (11)   incision made to create a curvilinear flap contiguous with the defect; flap is dissected, freed, and pivoted and sutured in place over the defect.

rule of nines (11)   divides total body surface area (BSA) into nine segments by percentage.

RxNorm (1)   provides normalized names for clinical drugs and links its names to many of the drug vocabularies commonly used in pharmacy management and drug interaction software, including those of First Databank, Micromedex, MediSpan, Gold Standard Drug Database, and Multum; by providing links among these vocabularies, RxNorm can mediate messages among systems that do not use the same software and vocabulary.

S

saddle block anesthesia (10)   *see* caudal anesthesia.

safe harbor regulation (19)   specifies various payment and business practices that, although potentially capable of inducing referrals of business reimbursable under the federal health care programs, would not be treated as criminal offenses under the anti-kickback statute.

sagittal plane (16)   vertically divides the body into unequal left and right portions.

salpingo-oophorectomy (15)   surgical removal of both fallopian tubes and ovaries.

saphenopopliteal vein anastomosis (13) surgical incision to expose the saphenous vein and connect it to the popliteal vein using end-to-end anastomosis.

scanner (1) equipment that captures paper record images onto the storage media.

sclera (15) white of the eye that comprises the eye's outer layer; contains fibrous tissue that maintains the eye's shape and protects the eye's inner layers.

screening mammography (16) radiographic (x-ray) of the breast that is performed when a patient presents without signs and symptoms of breast disease.

secondary defect (11) wound resulting from removal of tissue to create flap(s) or graft(s).

secondary malignancy (4) tumor that has metastasized, or spread, to a secondary site either adjacent to the primary site or to a remote region of the body.

secondary procedure (5) *see* other significant procedure.

second-order vessels (13) branch from first-order vessel.

second-stage fistulectomy/fistulotomy (14) in treatment of anal fistulas, use of a seton to cut through the fistula; the seton is left in place until later removal.

section (2) group of ICD-10-CM three-character disease categories within a chapter.

sectionalized record (1) *see* source-oriented record.

security (19) ensures that facilities, equipment, and patient information are safe from damage, loss, tampering, theft, or unauthorized access.

security rule (19) HIPAA regulation that requires covered entities to adopt standards and safeguards to protect health information that is collected, maintained, used, or transmitted electronically.

sedation (10) administration of medication into a vein to relieve pain and anxiety, making the patient feel calm.

selective vascular catheterization (13) insertion and manipulation or guidance of a catheter into the branches of the arterial system (other than the aorta or the vessel punctured) for the purpose of performing diagnostic or therapeutic procedures.

self-referral (19) an enrollee seeing a non-HMO panel specialist without a referral from the primary care physician.

semicolon (8) symbol (;) used to save space in CPT code descriptions.

separate procedure (11) performed as an integral component of a total service or procedure.

septal defects (13) occurs when the tissue does not completely close between the heart's chambers.

septic abortion (15) abortion-related pelvic and uterine infection.

septum (13) tissue that separates the heart's left and right sides.

sequela (4) residual (long-term condition produced) that develops after the acute phase of an illness or injury has ended. (Historically, ICD-9-CM referred to a sequela as a *late effect* of an illness or injury.)

seton (14) large silk suture or rubber bands.

severity of illness (SI) (19) physiological complexity that comprises the extent and interactions of a patient's disease(s) as presented to medical personnel.

shaving (11) horizontal slicing to remove epidermal and dermal lesions; removal includes scissoring or any sharp method.

shock therapy (10) *see* electroconvulsive therapy.

short-latency somatosensory evoked potential study (18) electrical stimulation of nerves to evaluate their responsiveness to the body's superficial surface and internal structures.

short-term hospital (5) average length of stay (LOS) of 4–5 days and a total LOS of fewer than 25 days.

shunting procedure (13) performed to move blood from one area to another for conditions such as atrial septal defect (ASD), coarctation of the aorta, patent ductus arteriosus (PDA), tricuspid atresia, and ventricular septal defect (VSD).

side view (16) *see* lateral projection.

sigmoidoscopy (14) visual examination of the entire rectum and sigmoid colon and may include a portion of the descending colon.

simple closure (11) *see* simple repair.

simple fracture (4) *see* closed fracture.

simple repair (11) involves the use of staples, sutures, and/or tissue adhesives to repair superficial wounds involving epidermis, dermis, and/or subcutaneous tissues; also called one-layer closure, nonlayered closure, and single-layer closure.

single chamber (13) contains a single electrode that is positioned in the heart's right atrium *or* right ventricle.

single code (8) single code number listed in the CPT index.

single hospital (5) hospital that is self-contained and not part of a larger organization.

single photon emission computerized tomography (SPECT) (16) three-dimensional x-ray images of internal organs produced after administration of a radioactive material, which visualize anatomy and function.

sinus of Valsalva (13) anatomical dilation of ascending aorta that occurs just above aortic valve (e.g., left anterior aortic sinus that gives rise to the left coronary artery); defects include aneurysms and fistulas for which repair and closure procedures are performed.

skeletal traction (12) exerts a pulling force on the affected limb to realign bone or joint.

skilled nursing facility prospective payment system (SNF PPS) (19) classifies residents into resource utilization groups.

skin substitute graft (11) include nonautologous human skin (e.g., acellular dermal), non-human skin substitute grafts (e.g., xenograft), and biological products that form a sheet scaffolding for skin growth.

sleep laboratory (18) area in a hospital facility that is managed by a sleep technologist who explains and performs the sleep studies.

sleep staging (18) during a sleep study (polysomnography), involves the use of a 1-4 lead electroencephalogram (EEG), electro-oculogram (EOG), and submental electromyogram (EMG).

sleep study (18) evaluation of adult and pediatric patients during sleep by monitoring brain waves, heart rate, and eye movements; performed to diagnose sleep disorders, which include breathing, movement, and neurologic disorders that occur at night.

slit lamp exam (16)   high-intensity light source that can be focused to shine as a slit to visualize anterior structures, including the eyelid, sclera, conjunctiva, iris, natural crystalline lens, and cornea.

SNOMED (1)   see SNOMED Clinical Terms

SNOMED CT (1)   see SNOMED Clinical Terms

social history (9)   age-appropriate review of past and current activities such as daily routine, dietary habits, exercise routine, marital status, occupation, sleeping patterns, smoking, use of alcohol and other drugs, and sexual activities.

somatic nerves (15)   control voluntary movements and conscious sensation; include voluntary motor and sensory nerves.

source-oriented record (SOR) (1)   reports organized according to documentation source, each of which is located in a labeled section of the record.

special evaluation and management services (9)   provided for establishment of baseline information prior to life or disability insurance certificates being issued and for examination of a patient with a work-related or medical disability problem.

special report (8)   document that must accompany the claim to describe the nature, extent, and need for the procedure or service when an unlisted procedure or service code is reported.

specialty coders (1)   individuals who have obtained advanced training in medical specialties (e.g., anesthesia, obstetrics) and who are skilled in that medical specialty's compliance and reimbursement areas. In addition to maintaining core credential(s), completes rigorous, in-depth exam, and earns additional continuing education units biannually. Specialty coders typically analyze provider documentation for accuracy, completeness, and timeliness; maintain and update charge-masters and/or encounter forms; meet with coding staff to educate them about revised rules and regulations; review patient charges to accuracy in reported codes and modifiers and enter billing edits; and write letters of appeals to address third-party payer reimbursement denials.

specialty hospital (5)   health care facility that delivers care to a particular population of patients or type of disease.

specimen (17)   tissue submitted for laboratory or pathological evaluation; also the unit of service used to report surgical pathology codes.

spinal anesthesia (10)   local anesthetic injected into cerebrospinal fluid at the lumbar spine, where it acts on spinal nerve roots and part of the spinal cord; anesthetized area extends from the legs to the abdomen or chest.

spinal tap (10)   see lumbar puncture.

spleen (13)   organ that produces mature lymphocytes, destroys worn-out red blood cells, and serves as a reservoir for blood.

splenoportography (13)   radiographic visualization of the splenic and portal veins.

split-thickness skin graft (11)   graft of entire epidermis and a portion of the dermis; typically used to repair edematous, infected, or large wounds (e.g., result of burns).

stabilize (12)   to secure bone in a fixed position.

stab phlebectomy (13)   multiple tiny incisions made over varicose vein sites; at each stab site the varicosity is extracted and then the varicose segment is removed.

staff model HMO (19)   health care services provided to subscribers by physicians employed by an HMO.

standby service (9)   physician, or other qualified health care professional, spending a prolonged period of time *without patient contact* waiting for an event to occur that will require the physician's or professional's service.

Stark I (19)   see physician self-referral law.

Stark II (19)   expanded the Stark I physician self-referral law by including referrals of Medicare and Medicaid patients for designated health care services.

star symbol (★) (8)   indicates that a code may be reported for synchronous telemedicine services. (CPT Appendix P contains a list of CPT codes that may be used for synchronous telemedicine services.)

State Children's Health Insurance Program (SCHIP) (19)   federal health program established to provide health assistance to uninsured, low-income children either through separate programs or through expanded eligibility under state Medicaid programs.

status indicator (SI) (19)   payment indicator that identifies how each code is paid (or not paid) under the Outpatient Prospective Payment System (OPPS).

stem cells (13)   cells contained in bone marrow.

stented valve (13)   includes framework on which the replacement heart valve is mounted to provide support for the valve's leaflets.

stentless valve (13)   an actual heart valve obtained from either a human donor (homograft) or a pig; it does not contain framework.

stereotactic localization (11)   use of specialized three-dimensional imaging to target a nonpalpable lesion.

stereotaxis (15)   use of a stereotactic guidance system to allow the physician to determine three-dimensional coordinates in order to create a lesion on the spinal cord (to alleviate chronic pain in a particular part of the body); to stimulate the spinal cord percutaneously (to create a lesion that will block pain); or to facilitate the biopsy, aspiration, or excision of a spinal cord lesion.

stoma (14)   surgically created opening between ureter, small intestine, or large intestine, through to abdominal wall.

strabismus (15)   improperly aligned eyes.

stroma (11)   supporting tissue (matrix) of an organ.

subacute care patient (5)   receives specialized services such as chemotherapy, injury rehabilitation, ventilator support, wound care, and other types of health care services provided to seriously ill patients.

subcategory (2)   ICD-10-CM codes that contain four, five, six, or seven characters; subcategory codes that require additional characters are invalid if the fifth, sixth, or seventh character(s) is absent.

subcutaneous fistulectomy (14)   removal of an anal fistula, without division of the sphincter muscle.

subglottic stenosis (12)   narrowing of the airway below the vocal cords, adjacent to the cricoid cartilage.

subjective (S) (1)   patient's statement about how he or she feels, including symptomatic information; considered part of the problem-oriented record (POR) SOAP note.

subluxation (12)   partial displacement of a bone from its joint.

submuscular fistulectomy (14)   removal of an anal fistula, including division of the sphincter muscle.

subterm (2)   qualifying word listed below the main term in the ICD-10-CM Index to Diseases and Injuries; list alternate sites, etiology, or clinical status.

superbill (19)   *see* encounter form.

supervision and interpretation (16)   term for the radiological portion of a procedure when two different physicians perform the surgical and radiological components of a procedure.

surface anesthesia (10)   topical application of local anesthetic cream, solution, or spray to skin or mucous membranes.

surgical curettement (11)   scraping tissue to remove abnormal tissue.

surgical endoscopy (14)   performed when anything in addition to visualization is done, such as the removal of a foreign body.

surgical package (11)   services performed that are integral to the standard of medical/surgical services, such as the cleansing, shaving, and prepping of skin and the insertion of intravenous access for medication.

suture (11)   surgical closure of a wound, using catgut, glue, silk thread, wire, or other materials.

Swan-Ganz catheter (10)   thin, flexible, flow-directed multilumen plastic tube (or catheter) that is advanced from a peripheral vein into the right atrium and then positioned in a branch of the pulmonary artery.

swing bed (5)   allows a rural hospital to admit a nonacute care patient.

sympathectomy (13)   excision of a segment of the sympathetic nerve.

sympathetic nerves (15)   part of the involuntary autonomic nervous system; originate in the thoracic and lumbar regions of the spinal cord; inhibit the physiological effects of the parasympathetic nervous system.

system review (9)   inventory by systems to document subjective symptoms stated by the patient; also provides an opportunity to gather information that the patient may have forgotten to mention or that may have seemed unimportant.

systemic radiation therapy (16)   unsealed radioactive materials that travel throughout the body.

***Systematized Nomenclature of Medicine, Clinical Terms* (SNOMED CT) (1)**   includes comprehensive coverage of diseases, clinical findings, therapies, procedures, and outcomes; combines the content and structure of a previous revision of SNOMED with medical nomenclatures titled the United Kingdom's *National Health Service's Clinical Terms Version 3* (formerly called *Read Codes*, developed in the early 1980s by Dr. James Read to record and retrieve primary care data in a computer).

T

Tables (ICD-10-PCS) (5)   used to construct a complete and valid ICD-10-PCS code; contain terms (and definitions) and rows that contain values (characters) needed to construct a valid code.

Tabular List of Diseases and Injuries (2)   chronological list of ICD-10-CM codes, divided into 21 chapters based on body system or condition.

Tax Equity and Fiscal Responsibility Act of 1983 (TEFRA) (19)   federal legislation that resulted in implementation of the inpatient prospective payment system, which uses diagnosis related groups to reimburse short-term hospitals a predetermined rate for Medicare inpatient services.

teaching hospital (1)   hospital engaged in an approved graduate medical education (GME) residency program in medicine, osteopathy, dentistry, or podiatry.

teaching physician (1)   physician (other than another resident physician) who supervises residents during patient care.

tear apparatus (15)   *see* lacrimal apparatus.

technical component (16)   use of equipment and supplies as well as the employment of radiological technologists to perform diagnostic imaging examinations and administer radiation therapy treatments.

tenosynovitis (15)   swollen tendon sheaths.

Tensilon test (18)   involves injecting the drug Tensilon (or its generic form edrophonium chloride) into a vein to block the action of the enzyme that breaks down the neurotransmitter acetylcholinesterase.

tetralogy of Fallot (13)   congenital heart condition that includes a ventral septal defect, stenosis of the infundibulum, hypertrophy of the right ventricle, and an abnormally positioned aorta.

therapeutic apheresis (13)   removal of blood components, cells, or plasma solute and retransfusion of the remaining components into the patient.

therapeutic plan (1)   specific medications, goals, procedures, therapies, and treatments used to treat the patient; considered part of the problem oriented record (POR).

therapeutic port film (16)   x-rays taken during delivery of radiation treatment that utilize the treatment beam of the machine.

therapeutic surgical procedure (11)   performed to treat specific conditions or injuries; includes the procedure itself and normal, uncomplicated follow-up care.

third-order vessels (13)   blood vessels that branch from second-order vessels.

third-party administrator (TPA) (1)   entity that processes health care claims and performs related business functions for a health plan; the TPA might contract with a health care clearinghouse to standardize data for claims processing.

third-party payer (1)   *see* health plan.

thoracentesis (12)   surgical puncture of the chest wall with a needle to obtain fluid from the pleural cavity.

thoracoscopy (12)   visual examination of the pleural cavity; provides an alternative to open lung or thoracotomy procedures to treat pleural disorders surgically.

thrombectomy (13)   surgical removal of a thrombus.

thromboendarterectomy (13)   surgical excision of a thrombus and atherosclerotic inner lining from an obstructed artery.

thymus (13)   produces T lymphocytes, which are important to the body's immune function.

tibia (12)   larger of the two lower leg bones.

tibial plateau (12)   lower portion of the femur, which articulates with the tibia.

tissue approximation (11)   method of replacing sutures with material or substance (e.g., surgical glue), which facilitates enhanced cosmetic results and faster healing of defects.

tissue-cultured autograft (11)   graft material supplied by laboratories; such grafting is often performed as part of a staged procedure.

tissue rearrangement (11)   defined by anatomical site and size of defect; includes excision of the defect or lesion.

tonsils (13)   located at the back of the throat; contain lymphoid tissue that helps fight infections.

total mastectomy (11)   surgical removal of the entire breast, including the pectoral fascia and a sampling of axillary lymph nodes.

total pneumonectomy (12)   removal of the entire lung.

trachea (12)   windpipe.

tracheobronchoscopy (12)   visual examination of the interior of the trachea and bronchus.

trachoma (15)   chronic inflammation of the conjunctiva in which granulations form.

transfer note (1)   documentation when a patient is transferred to another facility; summarizes the reason for admission, current diagnoses and medical information, and reason for transfer.

transfer of care (9)   occurs when a provider who is managing some or all of a patient's problems relinquishes that responsibility to another provider who explicitly agrees to accept this responsibility and who, from the initial encounter, is *not* providing consultative services; the provider transferring care no longer manages these problems but may continue to manage other conditions.

transitional pass-through payment (7)   temporary additional payment (over and above the OPPS payment) made for certain innovative medical devices, drugs, and biologicals provided to Medicare beneficiaries.

transluminal angioplasty (13)   surgical repair of a blood vessel through its lumen (opening).

transmyocardial revascularization (TMR) (13)   procedure that uses a high-powered laser to create small channels in the heart muscle to increase blood supply to the myocardium.

transpedicular approach (15)   performed through and inside the pedicle (segment between transverse process and vertebral body) of a thoracic vertebra to access a thoracic disk.

transposition of great vessels (13)   congenital reversal of the aorta and pulmonary artery.

transurethral resection of the prostate (TURP) (14)   resection of the prostate gland via transurethral approach using an electrosurgical device.

transurethral ureteroscopic lithotripsy (14)   procedure in which a cystoscope is inserted through the urethra into the bladder and a ureteroscope is passed into the ureters.

transverse plane (16)   horizontally divides the body into superior and inferior portions.

treatment volume determination (16)   region within the body to which radiation therapy is directed.

triage (6)   organized method of identifying and treating patients according to urgency of care required.

triangle symbol (8)   symbol (▲) located to the left of CPT codes that identifies revised code descriptions.

TRICARE (19)   military health plan that covers active duty and retired members of the uniformed services and their dependents.

triple option plan (19)   health plan that is offered as a single insurance plan or as a joint venture among two or more third-party payers.

truncus arteriosus (13)   congenital malformation in which just one artery arises from the heart to form the aorta and pulmonary artery.

tube pericardiostomy (13)   insertion of a tube for drainage or specimen collection.

tunneled (13)   implanted.

tunneled catheter (10)   *see* internal catheter.

turbinates (12)   bony plates covered by spongy mucosa with curved margins; there are three turbinates on each side of the nasal vestibule: inferior, middle, and superior.

tympanoplasty (15)   repair or reconstruction of the eardrum.

tympanostomy (15)   *see* myringotomy.

type 1 diabetes mellitus (4)   a condition in which the patient's body is unable to produce insulin.

type 2 diabetes mellitus (4)   a condition in which the patient's body is unable to properly use insulin produced.

type of service (TOS) (9)   refers to the kind of health care services provided to patients, including critical care, consultation, initial hospital care, subsequent hospital care, and confirmatory consultation.

U

UB-04 (1)   standard claim submitted by health care institutions to payers for inpatient and outpatient services.

ultrasonography (16)   *see* ultrasound.

ultrasound (16)   high-frequency sound waves that bounce off internal organs and create echoes; the echo pattern is displayed on the ultrasound machine monitor.

UMLS (1)   *see* Unified Medical Language System (UMLS)

unbundling (1)   reporting multiple codes to increase reimbursement when a single combination code should be reported.

uncertain behavior (4)   subsequent morphology or behavior that cannot be predicted based on the submitted specimen; the tissue appears to be in transition, and the pathologist cannot establish a definitive diagnosis.

undermining (11)   process of using a surgical instrument to separate skin and mucosa from its underlying stroma so that the tissue can be stretched and moved to overlay a defect.

Unified Medical Language System (UMLS) (1)   set of files and software that allows many health and biomedical vocabularies and standards to enable interoperability among computer systems; used to enhance or develop applications, including electronic health records, classification tools, dictionaries and language translators; used to link health information, medical terms, drug names, and billing codes across different computer systems.

Uniform Ambulatory Care Data Set (UACDS) (6)   established by the federal government as a standard data set for ambulatory care facility records.

Uniform Hospital Discharge Data Set (UHDDS) (5)   established by the federal government to define data collected for inpatient hospitalizations.

unit/floor time (9) amount of time the provider spends at the patient's bedside and at management of the patient's care on the unit or floor.

Unified Medical Language System (UMLS) (1) set of files and software that allows many health and biomedical vocabularies and standards to enable interoperability among computer systems; used to enhance or develop applications, including electronic health records, classification tools, dictionaries and language translators; used is used to link health information, medical terms, drug names, and billing codes across different computer systems.

unlisted procedure (8) code assigned when the provider performs a procedure or service for which there is no CPT code.

unlisted service (8) *see* unlisted procedure.

unspecified nature (4) neoplasm is identified, but the results of pathology examination are not available; thus, there is no indication as to histology or nature of the tumor.

upcoding (1) reporting codes that are not supported by documentation in the patient record for the purpose of increasing reimbursement.

upper GI endoscopy (14) direct visualization of the esophagus and the stomach.

uptake (16) absorption by a tissue of a substance, material, or mineral and its permanent or temporary retention.

ureter (14) tube that conveys urine from each kidney to the urinary bladder; there are two ureters.

ureterolithotomy (14) surgical removal of stones from the ureter.

urethra (14) muscular tube that discharges urine from the urinary bladder to the outside of the body.

urethrocystoscopy (10) visualization of urethra and urinary bladder.

urethroplasty (14) surgical repair of the urethra.

urinary bladder (14) hollow organ that serves as a reservoir for urine until it passes from the body (via urination).

urinary system (14) consists of the kidneys, ureters, urinary bladder, and urethra.

uroflowmetry (14) measures the amount of urine that flows from the urinary bladder per second.

uvea (15) eye's vascular layer, which includes the choroid, ciliary body, and iris.

V

vaginal birth after cesarean (VBAC) (15) planned vaginal birth after previous cesarean section.

value (ICD-10-PCS) (5) characters (individual letters and numbers) assigned to each of seven unique hierarchies (positions), which construct a valid ICD-10-PCS code.

value-based purchasing (VBP) (19) part of a long-standing CMS effort to link Medicare's inpatient prospective payment system (IPPS) to a value-based system for the purpose of improving health care quality, including the quality of care provided in the inpatient hospital setting, which affects payment for inpatient stays to over 3,500 hospitals; participating hospitals are paid for inpatient acute care services based on quality of care, not just quantity of services provided.

valvular atresia (13) valve failure to develop properly; completely closed at birth.

valvular heart disease (13) abnormality or dysfunction of one or more of the heart's four valves (aortic, mitral, pulmonary, and tricuspid).

valvular prolapse (13) condition in which two valvular flaps do not close properly, resulting in backflow of blood.

valvular regurgitation (13) backflow of blood because one or more cardiac valves close improperly.

valvular stenosis (13) narrowing of one or more cardiac valves.

valvuloplasty (13) open-heart surgery during which the surgeon removes the damaged valve and replaces it with a prosthetic, homograft or allograft, stented, or stentless valve.

valvulotomy (13) open-heart surgery in which an incision is made into a valve to repair valvular damage.

varicocele (15) abnormal dilation of the veins of the spermatic cord in the scrotum.

vascular family (13) group of vessels that is accessed by the same first-order vessel and is supplied by the same primary branch from the aorta.

vas deferens (15) tube that carries spermatozoa from the testis.

venipuncture (17) puncture of a vein with a needle for the purpose of drawing blood; most common method of collecting blood specimens.

venography (16) x-ray of a vein after injection of contrast material.

venous anomaly (13) associated with systemic veins and pulmonary veins, and includes conditions such as cor triatriatum, pulmonary vein stenosis, Scimitar syndrome, supravalvar mitral ring, and total anomalous pulmonary venous return (TAPVR).

venous valve transposition (13) surgical procedure performed to treat chronic deep venous insufficiency.

ventricular assist device (VAD) (13) provides temporary support for the heart by substituting for left or right heart function.

vertebral augmentation (12) process of creating a cavity in a vertebral body followed by injecting material (e.g., cement) under image guidance.

very low birth weight (9) 1500–2500 grams.

view (16) patient's position in relation to the camera during radiographic procedures.

visceral arteries (13) supply blood to the intestines, liver, and spleen.

visual evoked potential (VEP) test (18) stimulation of the eye using the checkerboard or flash technique to monitor the patient's response.

volvulus (14) twisting or displacement of the intestines, causing obstruction.

V-Y plasty (11) procedure whereby, after surgical creation of a V-shaped incision, the edges of the incision are drawn together and sutured, converting the incision to a Y shape.

W

wage index (19) adjusts payments to account for geographic variations in hospitals' labor costs.

wedge (16) treatment beam-modifying device that acts to change the beam intensity profile.

Whipple procedure (14) surgical removal of the pancreas, duodenum, bile duct, and stomach with reconstruction.

workers' compensation (19) state-mandated insurance program that reimburses health care costs and lost wages if an employee suffers a work-related disease or injury.

W-plasty (11) surgical trimming of both edges of a wound or defect into the shape of a *W* or multiple *W*s.

X

xenograft (11) surgical transplantation of tissue from a different species.

x-ray (16) radiographic visualization or imaging of internal body structures using low-dose high-energy radiation.

x-ray beam (16) consists of invisible electromagnetic energy waves that are emitted from a radiation machine and used to produce images and treat disease.

Z

Z-plasty (11) making a surgical incision along with two additional incisions, one above and another below, creating a *Z* formation.

Index